W9-DAO-142
DISCARDED

Louvre, Paris

Vincent Van Gogh

In art, as in literature, true appreciation depends upon our sharing the experience or feeling of the artist. During his lifetime Van Gogh was able to sell only four pictures. Now, fifty years later, we are just beginning to understand the fierce energy which caused him to splash his canvases with heavy daubs of rich, brilliant color.

In the picture above, the important point is not the bouquet but *the way Van Gogh saw the flowers*. In this picture, as in the literature in this book, can you enter into the thoughts or feelings of the artist, sharing his understanding and vision?

ADVENTURES

in Appreciation

LUELLA B. COOK

CENTRAL HIGH SCHOOL
MINNEAPOLIS, MINNESOTA

H. A. MILLER, JR.

PETERSBURG HIGH SCHOOL
PETERSBURG, VIRGINIA

WALTER LOBAN

SCHOOL OF EDUCATION
NORTHWESTERN UNIVERSITY
EVANSTON, ILLINOIS

STANDARD SECOND EDITION

Harcourt, Brace and Company

NEW YORK · 1943 · CHICAGO

[f · 6 · 43]

This book is complete and unabridged. It is manufactured in conformity with government regulations for saving paper.

PRINTED IN THE UNITED STATES OF AMERICA

Preface

Adventures in Appreciation is the second book of the new *Adventures* series for the last four years of high school. It is intended for the sophomore year and is preceded by *Adventures in Reading;* it is to be followed by the other books in the series — *Adventures in American Literature, Adventures in English Literature, Adventures in Modern Literature* — in a sequence left to the discretion of the individual school.

In the school, as well as in the world at large, an era of change has announced its arrival! Not only has a better understanding of the learning process modified methods of teaching, but also the serious social problems of the twentieth century have influenced the revision of curricula in almost every city and state. Most significant of all, perhaps, is this development: secondary education has become nearly universal; today over six million students are in schools on the secondary level. Lawyer and elevator operator, plant foreman and stenographer, housewife and aviator — all the future citizens in our increasingly interdependent society mingle even now in our classrooms. Despite the diversity of abilities and future occupations of these students, the underlying purposes of their education are the same: (1) the development of critical intelligence in social living, (2) sensitivity to others in human relations, and (3) realization of the individual's best potentialities in personal living. These are the goals of education in a democracy. They are stated in terms of the learner's development rather than in terms of the amount of subject matter he is to cover.

In the teaching of literature such goals imply an emphasis upon human values. Except for a handful of specialists and scholars, the average cultured adult reads literature for a picture of living people, for an understanding of himself and others, for a heightened awareness of himself in relation to this drama of living. Only insofar as form, technique, or a detailed analysis of style contribute to these larger objectives should they receive attention in the classroom.

This does not mean that the appreciation of literary form must be eliminated. On the contrary, the editors of this text feel that an increased sensitivity to the manner of communication in a work of art enables students to understand better the totality of effect, the blending of form and content. However, such an understanding is clearly not an end in itself, but only a means to a sharpened insight concerning people and life, an insight made clearer by the craft of the writer. Consequently the main emphasis in the new *Adventures in Appreciation* is upon the significance of literature as a comment on life.

It is with this greater emphasis upon literature as a record of human experience that the new *Adventures in Appreciation* has been planned. Selections have been retained from the previous edition or newly chosen on two bases: (1) the editors' experience in teaching them to boys and girls and (2) the value of the selections in meeting the needs and interests of high school students.

The introductions to the selections establish a point of contact between the student's own experience and the selection he is about to read. In addition they direct his attention to the kind of pleasure, profit, or satisfaction which he may expect to derive. Biographical facts, technical analysis, and historical development have been eliminated or placed in separate sections at the end of each division where they may be used at the discretion of the teacher. These sections present a fresh point of view, stressing the effect of the selections upon the reader. By such a method, the student's attention is directed to the significance and purpose of form instead of its mechanics.

Organization of the selections by literary types has been retained in this revision, but certain important modifications have been made. Lyric poetry has been grouped by theme or for some special purpose such as choral reading; short stories have been grouped by central purpose for the teacher's convenience; and the old classifications of essay, travel, and biography have been merged into a new section called *Chronicles of Experience* which contains some of the most compelling materials for teaching in the entire text. This last change has resulted from the overwhelming testimony of teachers that the essay as a form has little appeal to the great number of students in the early years of high school. Consequently in this new division of the book the editors have grouped by theme selections which are close to the natural interests of present day youth.

The impact of modern problems and the serious need of young people to understand a world whose insecurity they already share have led the editors to substitute *Julius Caesar* for *As You Like It* in the drama section. No play could be found which more richly delineates the serious questions of our day. The parallel between the death of the Roman Republic and the crisis of democracy in modern Europe is only one strand of a richly-woven drama which offers unlimited possibilities for study in the English classroom. Students have always liked *Julius Caesar*. With new study helps to emphasize the eternal problem of liberty, teachers should find this drama especially helpful for developing in their students a sensitivity to human relations and to today's social problems.

With this edition of *Adventures in Appreciation* a new plan for increasing the student's vocabulary is inaugurated. At the end of each individual selection or group of selections will be found a section under the heading *Increase Your Power Over Words*. In these sections the editors have selected for treatment some 200 words which appeared in the selections and which, on the basis of their judgment and teaching experience, (1) might present a problem of difficulty to students or (2) will enrich their vocabularies. The editors have set as a lower limit for their words any which are commonly known to students below the ninth grade as listed in the *Combined Word List*.[1] The upper limit was set by excluding from the vocabulary studies any words beyond the 20,000 most frequently used words in the language. Only in some

[1] *A Combined Word List* by B. R. Buckingham and Edward W. Dolch, Ginn and Co., 1936.

few cases have the editors, on the basis of classroom experience, decided to retain a word which does not fall within these limits.

Out of this refined list of words, a program for increasing the student's power over words has been established. This is not an artificial listing of words whose definitions a student must memorize in isolation from their context. A word's meaning is invariably determined by its total setting. The words in these exercises are discussed not only in relation to other words but also with reference to experiences which are meaningful to high school students. Insofar as possible, each word study unit is handled as a problem in thinking, and words are treated as ideas, not as items for rote memorization.

Two new features of the second edition, the program to provide for individual differences, and the illustrations, deserve special mention. A heading *For Ambitious Students* follows nearly every selection. The suggestions included under this heading should be challenging and stimulating to those students who finish assignments quickly and should be helpful to teachers who wish to enrich the study of literature for individuals or entire classes.

The illustrations have been chosen to symbolize the spirit or tone of certain groups of selections rather than to typify definite scenes from any story. From some of them, the student will discover feeling, atmosphere, and tempo. Others will provide him, in addition, with a visual background which will deepen his appreciation of such stories as *Silas Marner* and "The Wind Fighters."

Differing tremendously in abilities, interests, and personal goals, the students whom we teach are soon to become citizens of a nation founded on the belief that the good society is possible only when its members are educated to choose between wisdom and folly. Inasmuch as only fifteen percent of these students even enter college, the last and crucial opportunity for realizing the goals of education exists in the secondary school. In this serious task, the teacher of English discovers a challenge, an opportunity which does not end with the students' last day in school. To form in these boys and girls the habit of lifelong association with good books, to extend through reading their understanding and their interests, to develop standards of appreciation which will enable them to choose between books of deep, lasting value and those of flashy, superficial content is a labor to which a teacher may bring all his training, all his ability, all his inspiration.

Adventures in Appreciation: Second Edition has been shaped to meet more directly the needs of such inspiration. The constant aim of the editors has been to provide a text which will improve both the student's attitude toward reading literature and the development of his taste in selecting it. Both are necessary for building a lasting appreciation of quality in literature.

THE EDITORS

CONTENTS

THE SHORT STORY

CHRONICLES OF EXPERIENCE

BALLADS AND TALES

LYRIC POETRY

THE DRAMA

LONG NARRATIVE POEMS

THE NOVEL

THE SHORT STORY

MANKIND has always loved a story, but through the ages the storyteller has varied the manner of telling it. Long ago, when the race was young, he sang epics and ballads to celebrate the marvelous feats of heroes. The play was the popular form of a story in Shakespeare's day. In the middle of the eighteenth century the novel was born. As a literary form the short story is of comparatively recent development. It is, moreover, an American contribution which, since the beginning of the nineteenth century, has undergone a series of important changes. Twisting and turning and deepening its channel through the passing decades to conform to popular taste, it stands finally as a unique form of literary craftsmanship. As a result of its luxuriant growth the modern reader has a varied assortment of story forms to choose from.

The short story a high point in literary development. You have looked through a pair of field glasses out of focus, most likely, and seen the landscape only indistinctly. Objects were lost, you remember, in a blur of light and shadow. But by a turn of a screw you suddenly brought the picture into sharp relief; outlines became clearly defined and edges clean-cut. This is a very rough picture of how our minds improve.

Perhaps you have been vaguely aware of your own development in thinking power. As you gained greater skill of expression, you became less and less rambling and wordy, and more and more brief and accurate. Your thoughts were less sprawling and more shapely. Your sentences became less and less vague and general and more and more ordered and close-knit. Strange as it may sound, it is very difficult to be simple and brief. Cicero once said, "If I had more time, I would write you more briefly." Perhaps you have already discovered that it is not easy to bring random thoughts under control. When we have learned to be simple and clear, we have reached the end of a long trail of development.

By such a route have story writers learned to be concise, to bring the leisurely tale and the rambling narrative into the neat confines of an artistic plan. By this token, then, you might expect the short story, with its sharp focus of attention, to belong to one of the later periods of literary history and to represent, as it does, a high peak of artistic power.

How to appreciate short stories. In olden times reading a story was invariably like the leisurely unfolding of a scroll. Today it is more like turning a powerful searchlight upon one of the dark corners of the earth. Again, it might be like riding in a railway coach — or in an automobile or airplane — and watching the landscape slip by. Or — on rarer occasions — like peering thoughtfully into a glass case in some museum and feeling the past surge over you. As you read the stories chosen for you in this section of the text, think of each one as a relish to be sampled — something to be tasted in adventurous mood and enjoyed for its own distinct flavor. Here you will find humorous stories, stories of adventure, tales of horror, stories of insight, realistic stories, and true stories — each type offering you a somewhat different kind of satisfaction, and each story within each type offering you a still greater variation of interest.

Humorous Stories

ZENOBIA'S INFIDELITY

by Henry Cuyler Bunner
(1855–1896)

The circus is coming to town! What boy or girl hasn't wished he might get up early and watch the circus train come in and unload its precious cargo of lions, tigers, giraffes, 'n' everything! Or envied the roustabouts who helped pitch the tents, or wished he might hang about and watch the attendants feed the animals? Perhaps, even, meet the boss himself and see what a circus showman is really like. Well, here's your chance to meet the most amazing circus elephant you have ever heard about. Later on, in your reading of essays (page 265), you will have occasion to recall your acquaintance with Zenobia. Here's an amusing yarn written by an author who was popular in your grandmother's day. Notice, as you read, his clever use of words. Like those of O. Henry — whom you will meet later on — they fairly sparkle with merriment and provide no end of fun.

DR. TIBBITT stood on the porch of Mrs. Pennypepper's boardinghouse and looked up and down the deserted Main Street of Sagawaug with a contented smile, the while he buttoned his driving gloves. The little doctor had good cause to be content with himself and with everything else — with his growing practice, with his comfortable boardinghouse, with his own good looks, with his neat attire, and with the world in general. He could not but be content with Sagawaug, for there never was a prettier country town. The doctor looked across the street and picked out the very house that he proposed to buy when the one remaining desire of his soul was gratified. It was a house with a hip roof and with a long garden running down to the river.

There was no one in the house today, but there was no one in any of the houses. Not even a pair of round bare arms were visible among the clothes that waved in the August breeze in every back yard. It was circus day in Sagawaug.

The doctor was climbing into his gig when a yell startled him. A freckled boy with saucer eyes dashed around the corner.

"Doctor!" he gasped. "Come quick! The circus got afire an' the trick elephant's most roasted!"

" Don't be silly, Johnny," said the doctor reprovingly.

" Hope to die — honest Injun — cross my breast! " said the boy. The doctor knew the sacredness of this juvenile oath.

" Get in here with me," he said, " and if I find you're trying to be funny, I'll drop you in the river."

As they drove toward the outskirts of the town, Johnny told his tale.

" Now," he began, " the folks was all out of the tent after the show was over, and one of the circus men, he went to the oil barrel in the green wagon with Dan'l in the Lion's Den onto the outside of it, an' he took in a candle an' left it there, and fust thing the barrel busted, an' he wasn't hurted a bit, but the trick elephant she was burned awful, an' the ringtailed baboon, he was so scared he had a fit. Say, did you know baboons had fits? "

When they reached the circus grounds, they found a crowd around a small side-show tent. A strong odor of burnt leather confirmed Johnny's story. Dr. Tibbitt pushed his way through the throng and gazed upon the huge beast, lying on her side on the grass, her broad shoulder charred and quivering. Her bulk expanded and contracted with spasms of agony, and from time to time she uttered a moaning sound. On her head was a structure of red cloth, about the size of a bushel basket, apparently intended to look like a British soldier's forage cap.[1] This was secured by a strap that went under her chin — if an elephant has a chin. This scarlet cheesebox every now and then slipped down over her eye, and the faithful animal patiently, in all her anguish, adjusted it with her prehensile trunk.

By her side stood her keeper and the proprietor of the show, a large man with a dyed mustache, a wrinkled face, and hair oiled and frizzed. These two bewailed their loss alternately.

" The boss elephant in the business! " cried the showman. " Barnum[2] never had no trick elephant like Zenobia. And them lynes and Dan'l was painted in new before I took the road this season. Oh, there's been a hoodoo on me since I showed ag'inst the Sunday-school picnic! "

" That there elephant's been like my own child," groaned the keeper, " or my own wife, I may say."

The doctor had been carefully examining his patient.

" If there is any analogy — " he began.

" Neuralogy! " snorted the indignant showman. " 'Tain't neuralogy, you jay pillbox; she's *cooked!* "

" If there is any analogy," repeated Dr. Tibbitt, flushing a little, " between her case and that of a human being, I think I can save your elephant. Get me a barrel of linseed oil, and drive these people away."

The doctor's orders were obeyed with eager submission. He took off his coat and went to work. He had never doctored an elephant, and the job interested him. At the end of an hour Zenobia's sufferings were somewhat alleviated. She lay on her side, chained tightly to the ground and swaddled in bandages. Her groans had ceased.

" I'll call tomorrow at noon," said the doctor — " good gracious, what's that? " Zenobia's trunk was playing around his waistband.

" She wants to shake hands with you," her keeper explained. " She's a lady, she is, and she knows you done her good."

" I'd rather not have anything of the sort," said the doctor decisively.

When Dr. Tibbitt called at twelve on the morrow, he found Zenobia's tent

[1] **forage cap:** a small, low cap worn by officers when not in full dress.

[2] **Barnum:** a great circus proprietor, whose fame is still green in the minds of boys and girls.

nearly roped in, an amphitheater of circus benches constructed around her, and this amphitheater packed with people.

" Got a quarter apiece from them jays," whispered the showman, " jest to see you dress them wounds." Subsequently the showman relieved his mind to a casual acquaintance. " He's got a heart like a gunflint, that doctor," he said. " Made me turn out every one of them jays and give 'em their money back before he'd lay a hand on Zenobia."

But if the doctor suppressed the clinic, neither he nor the showman suffered. From dawn till dusk people came from miles around to stare a quarter's worth at the burnt elephant. Once in a while, as a rare treat, the keeper lifted a corner of her bandages and revealed the seared flesh. The show went off in a day or two, leaving Zenobia to recover at leisure; and as it wandered westward, it did an increased business simply because it had had a burnt trick elephant. Such, dear friends, is the human mind.

The doctor fared even better. The fame of his new case spread far and wide. People seemed to think that if he could cure an elephant he could cure anything. He was called into consultation in neighboring towns. Women in robust health imagined ailments, so as to send for him and ask him shuddering questions about " that *wretched* animal." The trustees of the orphan asylum made him staff physician — in this case the doctor thought he could trace a connection of ideas, in which children and circus were naturally associated. And the local newspaper called him a savant.[1]

He called every day upon Zenobia, who greeted him with trumpetings of joyful welcome. She also desired to shake hands with him, and her keeper had to sit on her head and hold her trunk to repress the familiarity. In two weeks she was cured, except for extensive and permanent scars, and she waited only for a favorable opportunity to rejoin the circus.

The doctor had got his fee in advance.

Upon a sunny afternoon in the last of August, Dr. Tibbitt jogged slowly toward Sagawaug in his neat little gig. He had been to Pelion, the next town, to call upon Miss Minetta Bunker, the young lady whom he desired to install in the house with the garden running down to the river. He had found her starting out for a drive in Tom Matson's dogcart. Now, the doctor feared no foe in medicine or in love; but when a young woman is inscrutable as to the state of her affections, when the richest young man in the county is devoting himself to her, and when the young lady's mother is backing the rich man, a young country doctor may well feel perplexed and anxious over his chance of the prize.

The doctor was so troubled, indeed, that he paid no heed to a heavy, repeated thud behind him on the macadamized road. His gentle little mare heard it, though, and began to curvet and prance. The doctor was pulling her in, and calming her with a " soo — soo — down, girl, down! " when he interrupted himself to shout:

" Great Caesar! Get off me! "

Something like a yard of rubber hose had come in through the side of the buggy, and was rubbing itself against his face. He looked around, and the cold sweat stood out on him as he saw Zenobia, her chain dragging from her hind foot, her red cap acock on her head, trotting along by the side of his vehicle, snorting with joy, and evidently bent on lavishing her pliant, serpentine, but leathery caresses upon his person.

His fear vanished in a moment. The animal's intentions were certainly pacific,

[1] **savant:** a man of special learning.

to put it mildly. He reflected that if he could keep his horse ahead of her, he could toll her around the block and back toward her tent. He had hardly guessed, as yet, the depth of the impression which he had made upon Zenobia's heart, which must have been a large organ if the size of her ears was any indication — according to the popular theory.

The doctor tolled his elephant around the block without further misadventure, and they started up the road toward Zenobia's tent, Zenobia caressing her benefactor while shudders of antipathy ran over his frame. In a few minutes the keeper hove in sight. Zenobia saw him first, blew a shrill blast on her trumpet close to the doctor's ear, bolted through a snake fence, lumbered across a turnip field, and disappeared in a patch of woods, leaving the doctor to quiet his excited horse and to face the keeper, who advanced with rage in his eye.

"What do you mean, you cuss," he began, "weaning a man's elephant's affections away from him? You ain't got no more morals than a Turk, you ain't. That elephant an' me has been side partners for fourteen years, an' here you come between us."

"I don't want your confounded elephant," roared the doctor. "Why don't you keep it chained up?"

"She busted her chain to git after you," replied the keeper. "Oh, I seen you two lally-gaggin' all along the road. I knowed you wa'n't no good the first time I set eyes on yer, a-sayin' hoodoo words over the poor dumb beast."

The doctor resolved to banish "analogy"[1] from his vocabulary.

The next morning, about four o'clock, Dr. Tibbitt awoke with a troubled mind. He had driven home after midnight from a late call, and he had had an uneasy fancy that he saw a great shadowy bulk ambling along in the mist-hid field by the roadside. He jumped out of bed and went to the window. Below him, completely covering Mrs. Pennypepper's nasturtium bed, her prehensile trunk ravaging the early chrysanthemums, stood Zenobia, swaying to and fro, the dew glistening on her seamed sides beneath the early morning sunlight. The doctor hastily dressed himself and slipped downstairs and out, to meet this Frankenstein monster[2] of affection.

There was but one thing to do. Zenobia would follow him wherever he went — she rushed madly through Mrs. Pennypepper's roses to greet him — and his only course was to lead her out of the town before people began to get up, and to detain her in some remote meadow until he could get her keeper to come for her and secure her by force or stratagem. He set off by the least frequented streets, and he experienced a pang of horror as he remembered that his way led him past the house of his one professional rival in Sagawaug. Suppose Dr. Pettengill should be coming home or going out as he passed!

The doctor found a secluded pasture, near the woods that encircled the town, and there he sat him down, in the corner of a snake fence, to wait until some farmer or market gardener should pass by to carry his message to the keeper. He had another message to send, too. He had several cases that must be attended to at once. Unless he could get away from his pachydermatous[3] familiar, Dr. Pettengill must care for his cases that morning. It was hard — but what was he to do?

[1] The keeper had interpreted **analogy** as a hoodoo word. Guess why.

[2] **Frankenstein monster:** a fictional monster supposed to have turned upon his creator and destroyed him. [3] **pachydermatous:** pertaining to the thick-skinned forebear of the elephant, used humorously here to refer to Zenobia.

Zenobia stood by his side, dividing her attention between the caresses she bestowed on him and the care she was obliged to take of her red cap, which was not tightly strapped on and slipped in various directions at every movement of her gigantic head. She was unmistakably happy. From time to time she trumpeted cheerily. She plucked up tufts of grass, and offered them to the doctor. He refused them, and she ate them herself. Once he took a daisy from her, absent-mindedly, and she was so greatly pleased that she smashed his hat in her endeavors to pet him. The doctor was a kind-hearted man. He had to admit that Zenobia meant well. He patted her trunk, and made matters worse. Her elephantine ecstasy came near being the death of him.

Still the farmer came not, nor the market gardener. Dr. Tibbitt began to believe that he had chosen a meadow that was *too* secluded. At last two boys appeared. After they had stared at him and at Zenobia for half an hour, one of them agreed to produce Dr. Pettengill and Zenobia's keeper for fifty cents. Dr. Pettengill was the first to arrive. He refused to come nearer than the farthest limit of the pasture.

" Hello, doctor," he called out, " hear you've been seeing elephants. Want me to take your cases? Guess I can. Got a half-hour free. Brought some bromide down for you, if you'd like to try it."

To judge from his face, Zenobia was invisible. But his presence alarmed that sensitive animal. She crowded up close to the fence, and every time she flicked her skin to shake off the flies she endangered the equilibrium of the doctor, who was sitting on the top rail for dignity's sake. He shouted his directions to his colleague, who shouted back professional criticisms.

" Salicylate of soda for that old woman? What's the matter with salicylate of cinchonidia? Don't want to kill her before you get out of this swamp, do you? "

Dr. Tibbitt was not a profane man, but at this moment he could not restrain himself. He burst forth with such vigor that the elephant gave a convulsive start. The doctor felt his seat depart from under him — he was going — going into space for a brief moment, and then he scrambled up out of the soft mud of the cow wallow back of the fence on which he had been sitting. Zenobia had backed against the fence.

The keeper arrived soon after. He had only reached the meadow when Zenobia lifted her trunk in the air, emitted a mirthful toot, and struck out for the woods with the picturesque and cumbersome gallop of a mastodon pup.

" Dern *you,*" said the keeper to Dr. Tibbitt, who was trying to fasten his collar, which had broken loose in his fall; " if the boys was here and I hollered ' Hey, Rube! ' there wouldn't be enough left of yer to spread a plaster for a baby's bile! "

The doctor made himself look as decent as the situation allowed, and then he marched toward the town with the light of a firm resolve illuminating his face. The literature of his childhood had come to his aid. He remembered the unkind tailor who pricked the elephant's trunk. It seemed to him that the tailor was a rather good fellow.

" If that elephant's disease is gratitude," thought the doctor, " I'll give her an antidote."

He went to the drugstore, and, as he went, he pulled out a blank pad and wrote down a prescription from mere force of habit.

When the druggist looked at it, he was taken short of breath.

" What's this? " he asked. " A bombshell? "

" Put it up," said the doctor, " and don't talk so much." He lingered nervously on the druggist's steps, looking up and down the street. He had sent a boy to order the stableman to harness his gig. By and by the druggist put his head out of the door.

" I've got some asafetida pills," he said, " that are kind o' tired, and half a pound of whale-oil soap that's higher 'n Haman — "

" Put 'em in! " said the doctor grimly, as he saw Zenobia coming in sight far down the street.

She came up while the doctor was waiting for the bolus.[1] Twenty-three boys were watching them, although it was only seven o'clock in the morning.

" Down, Zenobia! " said the doctor thoughtlessly, as he might have addressed a dog. He was talking with the druggist, and Zenobia was patting his ear with her trunk. Zenobia sank to her knees. The doctor did not notice her. She folded her trunk about him, lifted him to her back, rose with a heave and a sway to her feet, and started up the road. The boys cheered. The doctor got off on the end of an elm branch. His descent was watched from nineteen second-story windows.

His gig came to meet him at last and he entered it and drove rapidly out of town, with Zenobia trotting contentedly behind him. As soon as he had passed Deacon Burgee's house, he drew rein; and Zenobia approached, while his perspiring mare stood on her hind legs.

" Zenobia — pill! " said the doctor.

As she had often done in her late illness, Zenobia opened her mouth at the word of command and swallowed the infernal bolus. Then they started up again, and the doctor headed for Zenobia's tent.

But Zenobia's pace was sluggish. She had been dodging about the woods for two nights, and she was tired. When the doctor whipped up, she seized the buggy by any convenient projection and held it back. This damaged the buggy and frightened the horse, but it accomplished Zenobia's end. It was eleven o'clock before Jake Bumgardner's " Halfway House " loomed up white, afar down the dusty road, and the doctor knew that his roundabout way had at length brought him near to the field where the circus tent had been pitched. He drove on with a lighter heart in his bosom. He had not heard Zenobia behind him for some time. He did not know what had become of her, or what she was doing, but he learned later.

The doctor had compounded a pill well calculated to upset Zenobia's stomach. That it would likewise give her a consuming thirst he had not considered. But chemistry was doing its duty without regard to him. A thirst like a furnace burned within Zenobia. Capsicum and chloride of lime were doing their work. She gasped and groaned. She searched for water. She filled her trunk at a wayside trough and poured the contents into her mouth. Then she sucked up a puddle or two. Then she came to Bumgardner's, where a dozen kegs of lager beer and a keg of what passed at Bumgardner's for gin stood on the sidewalk. Zenobia's circus experience had taught her what a water barrel meant. She applied her knowledge. With her forefoot she deftly staved in the head of one keg after another, and with her trunk she drew up the beer and the gin and delivered them to her stomach. If you think her taste at fault, remember the bolus.

Bumgardner rushed out and assailed her with a bung starter.[2] She turned upon him and squirted lager beer over him until he was covered with an iridescent lather of foam from head to foot. Then

[1] **bolus:** large pill.

[2] **bung starter:** a mallet for removing the stopper in a keg.

she finished the kegs and went on her way to overtake the doctor.

The doctor was speeding his mare merrily along, grateful for even a momentary relief from Zenobia's attentions, when, at one and the same time, he heard a heavy, uncertain thumping on the road behind him and the quick patter of a trotter's hoofs on the road ahead of him. He glanced behind him first, and saw Zenobia. She swayed from side to side more than was her wont. Her red cap was far down over her left eye. Her aspect was rakish, and her gait was unsteady. The doctor did not know it, but Zenobia was drunk.

Zenobia was sick, but intoxication dominated her sickness. Even sulphide of calcium withdrew courteously before the might of beer and gin. Rocking from side to side, reeling across the road and back, trumpeting in imbecile inexpressive tones, Zenobia advanced.

The doctor looked forward. Tom Matson sat in his dogcart, with Miss Bunker by his side. His horse had caught sight of Zenobia, and he was rearing high in air and whinnying in terror. Before Tom could pull him down, he made a sudden break, overturned the dogcart, and flung Tom and Miss Minetta Bunker on a bank by the side of the road. It was a soft bank, well grown with mint and stinging nettles, just above a creek. Tom had scarce landed before he was up and off, running hard across the fields.

Miss Minetta rose and looked at him [1] with fire in her eyes.

"Well!" she said aloud. "I'd like mother to see you *now!*"

The doctor had jumped out of his gig and let his little mare go galloping up the road. He had his arm about Miss Minetta's waist when he turned to face his familiar demon — which may have accounted for the pluck in his face.

[1] **him:** Tom — not the doctor.

But Zenobia was a hundred yards down the road, and she was utterly incapable of getting any farther. She trumpeted once or twice, then she wavered like a reed in the wind; her legs weakened under her, and she sank on her side. Her red cap had slipped down, and she picked it up with her trunk, broke its band in a reckless swing that resembled the wave of jovial farewell, gave one titanic hiccup, and fell asleep by the roadside.

An hour later Dr. Tibbitt was driving toward Pelion, with Miss Bunker by his side. His horse had been stopped at the tollgate. He was driving with one hand. Perhaps he needed the other to show how they could have a summerhouse in the garden that ran down to the river.

But it was evening when Zenobia awoke to find her keeper sitting on her head. He jabbed a cotton hook firmly and decisively into her ear, and led her homeward down the road lit by the golden sunset. That was the end of Zenobia's infidelity.

THINK BACK OVER WHAT YOU HAVE READ

Enjoying the Humor of the Story

1. What sentences describing the personality of the doctor amused you?

2. What sentences can you quote to show the author's amusing trick of stating a fact indirectly? Notice, for example, *how* the author tells you that the doctor is in love.

3. What incidents relating to Zenobia's familiarity with the doctor struck you as particularly funny?

4. How did Zenobia assist the genial doctor in his courtship?

5. What humor was created by Zenobia's red cap?

6. Of all the plights caused by Zenobia, which was the funniest?

7. What effect is created by reprinting the doctor's prescription in the story?

8. Of what amusing experiences of your own does the story remind you? Of what incidents remembered from your reading?

Noticing How Skillfully the Story Is Told

9. Around what single idea does the story revolve?

10. What is the author's purpose in telling the story? How consistently does he hold to that purpose? With what effect?

11. To what degree does Bunner appeal to the reader's senses? What word pictures can you quote to show his vivid descriptive powers?

The kind of power to be found in words. Perhaps you have observed how a dog makes his wants known *without* words. He can't tell you, for example, that there is a rat under the woodpile, and will you please move a piece of lumber so that he may get at it. He can only bark to attract your attention, then hope that you will try to find him and guess from his actions what he means. And if you are slow to interpret his noise or his struggle, he must keep on repeating his signal until you finally do.

Or — to take another simple example — suppose that you yourself did not know the names of familiar objects, and that every time you wished to call someone's attention to a hat or a bicycle you had to produce one and point to it. Can you imagine how clumsy such communication would be?

From such simple illustrations perhaps you can see the kind of power that lies in words, and what a great step forward it was when man first invented language. He found words to stand for things (nouns). He no longer had to point and gesture; he could name the things he saw yesterday as well as those he saw today, and he didn't have to wait for the other fellow to guess what it was he referred to. He learned to name actions (verbs) as well as things, and by putting words together he came to express ideas (sentences). Now he was on the road to discovering what things meant. He could not only name the animal whose tracks he saw; he had a word for what it would *do,* and he could tell his son about what the footprints meant, and his son could learn more quickly and easily than by himself how to become a better hunter.

Language as a tool of thought. Words gave early man a still different kind of power. He had found a way to hold on, in his mind, to what he saw and heard and felt. Now he could talk it over with himself. Language had become a tool of thought; here was the key by which he might eventually explain the mysteries of the universe.

This brief sketch of the origin of language follows roughly your own development in the use of words, and should suggest to you the great advantage to be found in a rich and varied vocabulary. Such an advantage, however, depends not only on the number of words at your tongue's tip, but upon the accuracy with which you use them. Let us examine this idea more closely and see what it means.

It was a great day when man first learned to generalize: when, for example, he was able to see that most deer were *fleet* and that most foxes were *cunning,* and to invent words to stand for these qualities. He had learned by this means to classify his impressions, and so he could get on with the business of understanding his universe. As he continued to explore with his new tool, more and more words like *strength* and *clan* appeared in language — abstract words to denote qualities, and general words to stand for groups of things. Now man could talk about more and more things, using fewer and fewer words. One word sufficed to indicate what he had noticed about all the foxes he had ever seen. Thus communication became easier — perhaps too easy. For the ease of saying *clan* quite possibly deceived him about the actual complexities of clan life. In talk, at least, he could dispose of a whole clan without the difficulties which he must actually face when dealing with many separate members of the clan. And that is where our language troubles began. General words and abstract words are not only a great aid to thinking; they are, indeed, an indispensable tool of thinking; unless intelligently used, however, they are also a great obstacle to clear thinking.

The danger of using words as words. This tendency to lose sight of what words stand for can be illustrated from your own experience. You speak glibly, let us say, of what "all the kids at school" think about the class play, when, as a matter of fact, "all the kids" stands for only Mabel and Tom. With words at your command — picked up easily from others — it is easy to ignore facts. Or you speak confidently about the value of school spirit without any clear idea of what the words stand for. If pressed to explain, you might even grow angry; for the words, not the thing they stand for, have acquired in your mind a particular importance. Sometimes, too, you recite accurately from a book words which have no real meaning for you, and you "get by." Like the rest of us, you have learned that words may be used with very little knowledge of what they mean. They may be used with very little sense of responsibility for making their meaning clear. In other words, language may — if we are not careful — become a kind of false front which, far from revealing what we do think, conceals the fact that we aren't thinking at all.

Reading offers experience with words. All this points to the fact that in order to gain real power *from* language we must learn to exercise power *over* language. We must know specifically what our own words stand for; we must learn to use words accurately. Such power over words comes largely from experience with language in actual use, such experience as reading offers. It comes, too, from an occasional "time out" to sharpen and refine our understanding of a particular word in a particular context such as is to be offered to you periodically in this book under the caption "Increase Your Power over Words." In these brief vocabulary studies you may expect to find, however, not dull memory drills on words as words, but interesting little excursions into thought. The following exercise in the appreciation of humor — the first of the series — should set you off to a good start on the realization that not the least interesting part of your reading is the gaining of a more exact knowledge of words.

Increase Your Power over Words

12. The humor of the following italicized words will be clear to you only if you understand their full meaning. You can probably guess the meaning of some of the words from the way they are used in the story you have just read. For the meaning of other words you will need to consult the Glossary or a dictionary. Come to class prepared to discuss what the words stand for. What is the humorous implication? What actual picture do the words suggest?

a. "bent on *lavishing her pliant, serpentine,* but leathery caresses upon his person" (page 4).
b. "*elephantine* ecstasy" (page 6).
c. "*asafetida pills* that are kind of *tired*" (page 7).
d. "*iridescent* lather of foam" (page 7).
e. "Her aspect was *rakish*" (page 8).
f. "*titanic* hiccup" (page 8).

For Ambitious Students

13. *A minute-movie cartoon strip.* Surely there will be someone in the class who will picturize Zenobia's escapade for the amusement of the class. An Ed Wheelan Minute-Movie will suggest a pattern to work from.

14. *A collection of the droll sayings of H. C. Bunner.* Some budding columnist will welcome

the opportunity of reviewing several Bunner volumes and culling the best sayings to be found in his stories. Perhaps someone with a secret ambition to be a radio-broadcast feature — someone on the order of Alexander Woollcott — will plan a humorous half-hour, drawing upon the wit and wisdom of H. C. Bunner.

15. *A comparison of Bunner and O. Henry.* After you have read "The Princess and the Puma" on page 24 you will appreciate the similarity between the styles of O. Henry and Bunner. Which do you think is the more finished artist? Which one do you like the better? Why?

MR. K*A*P*L*A*N THE MAGNIFICENT

by Leonard Q. Ross (1908–)

In 1936 readers of *The New Yorker,* Manhattan's sophisticated magazine, were first introduced to the character of Hyman Kaplan. Mr. Kaplan, a foreigner, was a student in the American Night Preparatory School for Adults, and his amusing adventures with the English language have won for him a popularity which, according to popular comment from the Bronx to Bermuda, rivals that of Donald Duck.

In appearance Mr. Kaplan is described as a plump, red-faced gentleman with wavy blond hair, two fountain pens in his outer pocket, and a perpetual smile. To his teacher, Mr. Parkhill, however, he was known particularly through his signature — H*Y*M*A*N K*A*P*L*A*N — printed firmly in red crayon, each letter outlined in blue, and the stars between a brilliant green.

The story that follows, like all the other chapters in the book *The Education of Hyman Kaplan,* features the magnificent misuse of the English language for which Mr. Kaplan — and his creator, Leonard Q. Ross — have now become famous. Here is a story which may be read over and over again without loss of flavor, for behind each "Kaplanism" lies an amusing glimpse into human nature that grows funnier the more you think of it.

MR. PARKHILL had decided that perhaps it might be wise for the class to attempt more *practical* exercises. On a happy thought, he had taken up the subject of letter writing. He had lectured the students on the general structure of the personal letter: shown them where to put the address, city, date; explained the salutation; talked about the body of the letter; described the final greeting. And now the fruits of Mr. Parkhill's labors were being demonstrated. Five students had written the assignment, "A Letter to a Friend," on the blackboard.

On the whole Mr. Parkhill was satisfied. Miss Mitnick had a straightforward and accurate letter — as might be expected — inviting her friend Sylvia to a surprise party. Mr. Norman Bloom had written to someone named Fishbein, describing an exciting day at Coney Island. Miss Rochelle Goldberg had told "Molly" about a "bos ride on a bos on 5 av." Mrs. Moskowitz, simple soul, had indulged her fantasies by pretending she was on vacation in "Miame, Floridal," and had written her husband Oscar to be sure "the pussy should get each morning milk." (Apparently Mrs. Moskowitz was deeply attached to "the pussy," for she merely repeated the admonition in several ways all through her epistle, leaving no room for comment on the beauties of "Miame, Floridal.") And Mr. Hyman Kaplan — Mr. Parkhill frowned as he examined the last letter written on the blackboard.

"It's to mine brodder in Varsaw," said Mr. Kaplan, smiling in happy anticipation.

Mr. Parkhill nodded, rather absently; his eyes were fixed on the board.

"Maybe it vould be easier I should readink de ladder alod," suggested Mr. Kaplan delicately.

"'*Letter,*' Mr. Kaplan," said Mr. Parkhill, ever the pedagogue. "Not '*ladder.*'"

"Maybe I should readink de *lat*ter?" repeated Mr. Kaplan.

"Er — no — no," said Mr. Parkhill

hastily. "We — er — we haven't much time left this evening. It *is* getting late." He tried to put it as gently as possible, knowing what this harsh deprivation might mean to Mr. Kaplan's soul.

Mr. Kaplan sighed philosophically, bowing to the tyranny of time.

"The class will study the letter for a few minutes, please," said Mr. Parkhill. "Then I shall call for corrections."

The class fell into that half stupor which indicated concentration. Miss Mitnick studied the blackboard with a determined glint in her eye. Mr. Pinsky stared at Mr. Kaplan's letter with a critical air, saying "Tchk! Tchk!" several times, quite professionally. Mrs. Moskowitz gazed ceilingward with an exhausted expression. Apparently the vicarious excitements of the class session had been too much for poor Mrs. Moskowitz: an invitation to a surprise party, a thrilling day at Coney Island, a Fifth Avenue bus ride, and her own trip to Florida. That was quite a night for Mrs. Moskowitz.

And Mr. Kaplan sat with his joyous smile unmarred, a study in obvious pride and simulated modesty, like a god to whom mortals were paying homage. First he watched the faces of the students as they wrestled with his handiwork, and found them pleasing. Then he concentrated his gaze on Mr. Parkhill. He saw anxious little lines creep around Mr. Parkhill's eyes as he read that letter; then a frown — a strange frown, bewildered and incredulous; then a nervous clearing of the throat. Any other student might have been plunged into melancholy by these dark omens, but they only added a transcendental quality[1] to Mr. Kaplan's smile.

This was the letter Mr. Kaplan had written:

[1] **Transcendental quality:** as used here, a kind of not-of-this-earth quality, superior to such melancholy as that referred to earlier in the sentence.

459 E 3 Str
N.Y.
New York
Octo. 10

HELLO MAX!!!

I should telling about mine progriss. In school I am fine. Making som mistakes, netcheral. Also however doing the hardest xrcises, like the best students the same. Som students is Mitnick, Blum, Moskowitz — no relation Moskowitz in Warsaw. Max! You should absolutel coming to N.Y. and belonging in mine school! . . .

It was at this point, visualizing too vividly *another* Mr. Kaplan in the class, that anxious little lines had crept around Mr. Parkhill's eyes.

Do you feeling fine? I suppose. Is all ok? You should begin right now learning about ok. Here you got to say ok. all the time. ok the wether, ok the potatos, ok the prazident Roosevelt.

At this point the frown — a strange frown, bewildered and incredulous — had marched onto Mr. Parkhill's face.

How is darling Fanny? Long should she leave. So long.

With all kinds entusiasm

Your animated brother

H * Y * M * I * E

Mr. Kaplan simply could not resist the aesthetic impulse to embellish his signature with those stars; they had almost become an integral part of the name itself.

Mr. Parkhill cleared his throat. He felt vaguely distressed.

"Has everyone finished reading?" he asked. Heads nodded in half-hearted assent. "Well, let us begin. Corrections, please."

Mrs. Tomasic's hand went up. "Should be 'N.Y.' after 'New York' and 'New York' should be on top of."

" Correct," said Mr. Parkhill, explaining the difference and making the change on the board.

" In all places is ' mine ' wrong," said Mr. Feigenbaum. " It should be ' my.' "

Mr. Parkhill nodded, happy that someone had caught that most common of Mr. Kaplan's errors.

The onslaught went on: the spelling of words, the abbreviation of " October " and " street," the tenses of the verbs.

" Mr. Kaplan got so many mistakes," began Mr. Bloom with hauteur.[1] Mr. Bloom was still annoyed because Mr. Kaplan had rashly offered to correct the spelling of Coney Island, in Mr. Bloom's letter, to " ' Corney Island,' like is pernonced." " He spelled wrong ' progress,' ' some,' ' natural.' He means ' Long should she *live* ' — not ' Long should she *leave*.' That means going away. He even spelled wrong my name! " It was clear from Mr. Bloom's indignant tone that this was by far the most serious of Mr. Kaplan's many errors. " Is double ' o,' not ' u.' I ain't like *som* Blooms! "

With this jealous defense of the honor of the House of Bloom, Mr. Bloom looked at Mr. Kaplan coolly. If he had thought to see Mr. Kaplan chagrined by the barrage of corrections, he did not know the real mettle of the man. Mr. Kaplan was beaming with delight.

" Honist to Gott, Bloom," said Mr. Kaplan with admiration, " you soitinly improvink in your English to seeink all dese mistakes! "

There was a fine charity in this accolade. It had, however, the subtle purpose of shifting attention from Mr. Kaplan's errors to Mr. Bloom's progress.

Mr. Bloom did not know whether to be pleased or suspicious, whether this was a glowing tribute or the most insidious irony.

[1] **hauteur:** pride or arrogance, from the same root as *haughty*.

" Thenks, Kaplan," he said finally, acknowledging the compliment with a nod, and considered the injuries of " Corney Island " and " Blum " expiated.

" I see more mistakes," said Miss Mitnick, intruding an unwelcome note into the happy Kaplan–Bloom rapport. Mr. Kaplan's eyes gleamed when he heard Miss Mitnick's voice. Here was a foe of a caliber quite different from that of Norman Bloom. " ' Absolutel ' should be ' absolute*ly*.' ' Potatoes ' has an ' e.' ' Prazident ' is wrong; it should be ' e ' and ' s ' and a capital." Miss Mitnick went on and on making corrections. Mr. Parkhill transcribed them to the board as swiftly as he could, until his wrists began to ache. " ' ok ' is wrong, should be ' O.K.' — with *capitals* and *periods* — because it's abbreviation."

All through the Mitnick attack Mr. Kaplan sat quiet, alert but smiling. There was a supreme confidence in that smile, as if he were waiting for some secret opportunity to send the whole structure that Miss Mitnick was rearing so carefully crashing down upon her head. Miss Mitnick rushed on to the abyss.

" Last," she said, slowing up to emphasize the blow, " *three* exclamation points after ' Max ' is wrong. Too many."

" Aha! " cried Mr. Kaplan. It was The Opportunity. " Podden me, Mitnick. De odder corractinks you makink is fine, foist-cless — even Hau Kay, an' I minn Hau Kay mit *capitals* an' *periods*," he added sententiously. " But batter takink back abot de tree haxclimation points! "

Miss Mitnick blushed, looking to Mr. Parkhill for succor.

" Mr. Kaplan," said Mr. Parkhill with caution, sensing some hidden logic in Mr. Kaplan's tone, " a colon is the proper punctuation for the salutation, or a comma. If you *must* use an — er — exclamation point " — he was guarding himself [1] on all fronts — "then, as Miss Mitnick says, *three* are too many."

"For de vay *I'm* fillink abot mine *brodder?*" asked Mr. Kaplan promptly. In that question, sublime in its simplicity, Mr. Kaplan inferentially accused his detractor of (1) familial [2] ingratitude, (2) trying to come between the strong love of two brothers.

"But, Kaplan," broke in Mr. Bloom, jumping into the fray on the side of Miss Mitnick, "*three* exclama — "

"Also he's mine *faworite* brodder!" said Mr. Kaplan. "For mine *faworite* brodder you eskink *vun — leetle — haxclimation point?*" It was an invincible position. "Ha! Dat I give to *strengers!*"

Mr. Bloom retired from the field, annihilated. One could hardly expect a man of Mr. Kaplan's exquisite sensitivity to give equal deference and love to *strangers* and his favorite brother. Mr. Parkhill paused to mobilize his forces.

"How's about 'entusiasm'?" said Miss Mitnick, determined to recover face.[3] "Is spelled wrong — should be 'th.' And 'With all kinds enthusiasm' is bad for ending a letter."

"Aha!" Mr. Kaplan gave his battle call again. "Maybe *is* de spallink wronk. But not de vay I'm *usink* 'antusiasm,' becawss" — he injected a trenchant quality into his voice to let the class get the deepest meaning of his next remark — "becawss *I* write to *mine* brodder in Varsaw *mit real antusiasm!*"

The implication was clear: Miss Mitnick was one of those who, corrupted by the gaudy whirl of the New World, let her brothers starve, indifferently, overseas.

Miss Mitnick bit her lip. Mr. Parkhill, trying to look judicious, avoided her eyes.

"Well," began Miss Mitnick yet a third time, desperately, "'animated' is wrong. 'Your *animated* brother, Hymie.' *That's* wrong."

She looked at Mr. Parkhill with a plea that was poignant. She dared not look at Mr. Kaplan, whose smile had advanced to a new dimension.

"Yes," said Mr. Parkhill. "'Animated' is quite out of place in the final greeting."

Mr. Kaplan sighed. "I looked op de void 'enimated' *spacial.* It's minnink 'full of life,' no? Vell, I falt *planty* full of life ven I vas wridink de ladder."

Miss Mitnick dropped her eyes, the rout complete.

"Mr. Kaplan!" Mr. Parkhill was left to fight the good fight alone. "You may say 'She had an animated expression' or 'The music has an animated refrain.' But one doesn't say 'animated' about one's *self.*"

The appeal to propriety proved successful. Mr. Kaplan confessed that perhaps he had overreached himself with "Your animated brother."

"Suppose we try another word," suggested Mr. Parkhill. "How about 'fond'? 'Your *fond* brother — er — Hyman'?" (He couldn't quite essay "Hymie.")

Mr. Kaplan half-closed his eyes, gazed into space, and meditated on this moot point. "'Fond,' 'fond,'" he whispered to himself. He was like a man who had retreated into a secret world, searching for his Muse. "'Your fond brodder, Hymie.'" He shook his head. "Podden me," he said apologetically. "It don' have de *fillink.*"

"What about 'dear'?" offered Mr. Parkhill quickly. "'Your *dear* brother,' and so on?"

Once more Mr. Kaplan went through the process of testing, judgment, and con-

[1] From what was Mr. Parkhill **guarding himself?** Here is an important clue to the relationship between Mr. Parkhill and his pupil. [2] **familial:** you can probably guess the meaning of this word from its similarity to *family.* Try it! [3] **to recover face:** to save one's dignity.

sultation with his evasive Muse. "' Dear,' ' dear.' ' Your dear brodder, Hymie.' Also no." He sighed. "' Dear,' it's too *common.*"

" What about —"

" Aha! " cried Mr. Kaplan suddenly, as the Muse kissed him. His smile was as the sun. " I got him! Fine! Poifick! Soch a void! "

The class, to whom Mr. Kaplan had communicated some of his own excitement, waited breathlessly. Mr. Parkhill himself, it might be said, was possessed of a queer eagerness.

" Yes, Mr. Kaplan. What word would you suggest? "

"' Megnificent! '" cried Mr. Kaplan.

Admiration and silence fell upon the class like a benediction. " Your magnificent brother, Hymie." It was a *coup de maître,*[1] no less. Mr. K * A * P * L * A * N the Magnificent.

As if in a trance, the beginners' grade waited for Mr. Parkhill's verdict.

And when Mr. Parkhill spoke, it was slowly, sadly, aware that he was breaking a magic spell. " N-no, Mr. Kaplan. I'm afraid not. ' Magnificent ' isn't really — er — appropriate."

The bell rang in the corridors, as if it had withheld its signal until the last possible moment. The class moved into life and toward the door. Mr. Norman Bloom went out with Mr. Kaplan. Mr. Parkhill could hear the last words of their conversation.

" Kaplan," said Mr. Bloom enviously, " *how* you fond soch a beautiful woid? "

"' Megnificent,' ' megnificent,'" Mr. Kaplan murmured to himself wistfully. " Ach! Dat *vas* a beautiful void, ha, Bloom? "

" Believe me! " said Mr. Bloom. " *How* you fond soch a woid? "

" By *dip* tinking," said Mr. Kaplan.

He strode out like a hero.

[1] coup de maître: master stroke.

THINK BACK OVER WHAT YOU HAVE READ

Appreciating the Interplay of Personality in the Story

Come to class prepared to illustrate, from the text of the story itself, the following:

1. Mr. Parkhill's uneasiness in the presence of Mr. Kaplan; his fear that Mr. Kaplan will produce an embarrassing situation
2. Miss Mitnick's seriousness; her blushing retreats before Mr. Kaplan's onslaughts; her silent appeals to Mr. Parkhill for help
3. Mr. Bloom's undisguised annoyance at Mr. Kaplan
4. Mrs. Moskowitz's — simple soul — vicarious excitement
5. Mr. Kaplan's childlike love of attention; his amusing forbearance under fire; his supreme self-confidence; his shrewd seizure of the opportunity for defending himself; his cleverness in getting around his teacher; his amusing observations of life in America

Enjoying the Humor of " Kaplanisms "

6. What amusing misuses of language can you point to?
7. What is your idea of a " Kaplanism "? What is the best illustration of one that you can find?

Increase Your Power over Words

The following italicized words, suggested for study, are interesting because of their *context;* that is, because of the particular way in which they are used in combination with other words. Behind each one lies an amusing or picturesque suggestion implied between the lines.

8. " The *onslaught* went on " (page 13). You can guess what *onslaught* means from the rest of the sentence. Just what did the particular *onslaught* referred to consist of?

9. " chagrined by the *barrage* of corrections " (page 13). If you are not already familiar with the word *barrage,* look up its literal meaning in the dictionary and be prepared to explain to the class the comparison which is implied in the sentence.

10. " There was a fine charity in this *accolade* " (page 13). Here is a word whose meaning reaches far back into history. Look the

word up in the dictionary and find out what picturesque period it is associated with. Perhaps someone in the class, familiar with the period, will be able to describe in detail what an *accolade* originally was. In the story what does the word refer to? What simpler word could you substitute for it? What humorous suggestion lies behind the use of such a big, rare word? Can you see?

11. "intruding an unwelcome note into the happy Kaplan–Bloom *rapport*" (page 13). To explore the meaning of this word is to increase your understanding of life. Look up its origin in the dictionary. Notice that the English idiom is *in rapport* and the French, *en rapport.* Name three situations in which you might be said to be *in rapport* with your environment. Of what did the Kaplan–Bloom *rapport* consist?

12. "Admiration and silence fell upon the class like a *benediction*" (page 15). Where are you accustomed to hearing this word used? Look up its literal meaning in the dictionary. What does the prefix *bene* mean? *diction?* Why is this a well-chosen word in the story?

For Ambitious Students

13. Report on any other Kaplan adventure chosen from the book *The Education of Hyman Kaplan* by Leonard Q. Ross.

14. Perhaps someone in the class will read "Mr. K*a*p*l*a*n the Magnificent" aloud and bring out by means of the voice the full flavor of Mr. Kaplan's personality.

15. Perhaps someone in the class will report on other characters who misuse words humorously: for example, Amos and Andy or Burns and Allen, both of radio fame; Mrs. Malaprop, in *The Rivals* by Richard Brinsley Sheridan.

JEEVES AND THE YULE-TIDE SPIRIT

by P. G. Wodehouse (1881–)

If you aren't already familiar with the name P. G. Wodehouse, here is a chance to make a literary acquaintance who will hereafter help you to while away many an hour pleasantly in the company of his two inimitable characters, Bertie Wooster and his man Jeeves. Bertie Wooster is an English gentleman of the frivolous sort, and Jeeves, to all outward appearances, is the perfect English servant. Over the ridiculous fence that separates them into different social stations, however, these two carry on a most amusing friendship, with Jeeves, behind his correct manners, always managing to "slip a fast one" over on his hilarious employer. It is the relationship between Jeeves and Bertie that provides the story with most of its humor.

If you like Jeeves, you will wish to pursue his acquaintance further in the book from which this story was taken, *Very Good, Jeeves.* Other recent exploits of Bertie and Jeeves you will find under the title *The Code of the Woosters.*

THE LETTER arrived on the morning of the sixteenth. I was pushing a bit of breakfast into the Wooster face at the moment; and, feeling fairly well fortified with coffee and kippers,[1] I decided to break the news to Jeeves without delay. As Shakespeare says, if you're going to do a thing you might just as well pop right at it and get it over. The man would be disappointed, of course, and possibly even chagrined; but, dash it all, a spot of disappointment here and there does a fellow good. Makes him realize that life is stern and life is earnest.

"Oh, Jeeves," I said.

"Sir?"

"We have here a communication from Lady Wickham. She has written inviting me to Skeldings for the festivities. So will you see about bunging the necessaries together? We repair thither on the twenty-third. We shall be there some little time, I expect."

There was a pause. I could feel he was directing a frosty gaze at me, but I dug into the marmalade and refused to meet it.

"I thought I understood you to say, sir, that you proposed to visit Monte Carlo[2] immediately after Christmas."

[1] **kippers:** kippered (that is, cured) fish, a favorite English breakfast dish. [2] **Monte Carlo:** a fashionable gambling resort on the Mediterranean.

"I know. But that's all off. Plans changed."

At this point the telephone bell rang, tiding over nicely what had threatened to be an awkward moment. Jeeves unhooked the receiver.

"Yes? . . . Yes, madam. . . . Very good, madam. Here is Mr. Wooster." He handed me the instrument. "Mrs. Spenser Gregson, sir."

You know, every now and then I can't help feeling that Jeeves is losing his grip. In his prime it would have been with him the work of a moment to have told my Aunt Agatha that I was not at home. I gave him one of those reproachful glances and took the machine.

"Hullo?" I said. "Yes? Yes? Yes? Bertie speaking. Hullo? Hullo? Hullo?"

"Don't keep on saying Hullo," yipped the old relative, in her customary curt manner. "You're not a parrot. Sometimes I wish you were, because then you might have a little sense.

"Bertie, Lady Wickham tells me she has invited you to Skeldings for Christmas. Are you going?"

"Rather!"

"Well, mind you behave yourself. Lady Wickham is an old friend of mine."

"I shall naturally endeavor, Aunt Agatha," I replied stiffly, "to conduct myself in a manner befitting an English gentleman paying a visit —"

"What did you say? Speak up. I can't hear."

"I said, 'Right ho.'"

"Oh? Well, mind you do. And there's another reason why I particularly wish you to be as little of an imbecile as you can manage while at Skeldings. Sir Roderick Glossop will be there. Now, Bertie, I want you to listen to me attentively. Are you there?"

"Yes. Still here."

"Well, then, listen. I have at last succeeded, after incredible difficulty and in face of all the evidence, in almost persuading Sir Roderick that you are not actually insane. He is prepared to suspend judgment until he has seen you once more. On your behavior at Skeldings, therefore —"

But I had hung up the receiver. Shaken. That's what I was. S. to the core.

This Glossop was a formidable old bird with a bald head and outsize eyebrows, by profession a loony-doctor. How it happened, I couldn't tell you to this day, but I once got engaged to his daughter Honoria, a ghastly dynamic exhibit who read Nietzsche[1] and had a laugh like waves breaking on a stern and rockbound coast. The fixture was scratched, owing to events occurring which convinced the old boy that I was off my napper; and since then he has always had my name at the top of his list of Loonies I Have Lunched With.

My hostess, Lady Wickham, was a beaky female built far too closely on the lines of my Aunt Agatha for comfort; but she had seemed matey enough on my arrival. Her daughter Roberta had welcomed me with a warmth which, I'm bound to say, had set the old heartstrings fluttering a bit. And Sir Roderick, in the brief moment we had had together, had said, "Ha, young man!" — not particularly chummily, but he said it; and my view was that it practically amounted to the lion lying down with the lamb.

So, all in all, life at this juncture seemed pretty well all to the mustard, and I decided to tell Jeeves exactly how matters stood.

"Jeeves," I said, as he appeared with the steaming.

"Sir?"

"I'm afraid scratching that Monte Carlo trip has been a bit of a jar for you, Jeeves."

[1] **Nietzsche:** a German philosopher whom only the most sophisticated readers would tackle.

" Not at all, sir."

" Oh, yes, it has. The heart was set on wintering in the world's good old plague spot, I know. I saw your eye light up when I said we were due for a visit there. You snorted a bit and your fingers twitched. I know, I know. And now that there has been a change of program, the iron has entered your soul."

" Not at all, sir."

" Oh, yes, it has. I've seen it. Very well, then. What I wish to impress upon you, Jeeves, is that it was through no light and airy caprice that I accepted this invitation to Lady Wickham's. I have been angling for it for weeks, prompted by many considerations. It was imperative that I should come to Skeldings for Christmas, Jeeves, because I knew that young Tuppy Glossop was going to be here."

" Sir Roderick Glossop, sir ? "

" His nephew. You may have observed hanging about the place a fellow with light hair and a Cheshire-cat grin. That is Tuppy, and I have been anxious for some time to get to grips with him. The Wooster honor is involved."

I took a sip of tea, for the mere memory of my wrongs had shaken me.

" Well, then, as I say, I sought this Tuppy out, Jeeves, and hobnobbed; and what do you think he did ? "

" I could not say, sir."

" I will tell you. One night, after dinner at the Drones' Club, he bet me I wouldn't swing myself across the swimming bath by the ropes and rings. I took him on, and was buzzing along in great style until I came to the last ring. And then I found that this fiend in human shape had looped it back against the rail, thus leaving me hanging in the void with no means of getting ashore to my home and loved ones.

" There was nothing for it but to drop into the water. And what I maintain, Jeeves, is that, if I can't get back at him somehow at Skeldings — with all the vast resources which a country house affords at my disposal — I am not the man I was."

" I see, sir."

" And now, Jeeves, we come to the most important reason why I had to spend Christmas at Skeldings. Jeeves," I said, diving into the old cup once more for a moment and bringing myself out wreathed in blushes, " the fact of the matter is, I'm in love."

" Indeed, sir ? "

" You've seen Miss Roberta Wickham ? "

" Yes, sir."

" Very well, then."

There was a pause while I let it sink in.

" During your stay here, Jeeves," I said, " you will, no doubt, be thrown a good deal together with Miss Wickham's maid. On such occasions pitch it strong."

" Sir ? "

" You know what I mean. Tell her I'm rather a good chap. Mention my hidden depths. These things get round. A boost is never wasted, Jeeves."

" Very good, sir. But — "

" But what ? "

" Well, sir — "

" Carry on, Jeeves. We are always glad to hear from you, always."

" What I was about to remark, if you will excuse me, sir, was that I would scarcely have thought Miss Wickham a suitable — "

" Jeeves," I said coldly, " what is your kick against Miss Wickham ? "

" It merely crossed my mind, sir, that for a gentleman of your description Miss Wickham is not a suitable mate. I would always hesitate to recommend as a life's companion a young lady with such a vivid shade of red hair. Red hair, sir, is dangerous."

I eyed the blighter squarely.

" Jeeves," I said, " you're talking rot."

" Very good, sir."

" Absolute drivel."

" Very good, sir."

" Pure mashed potatoes."

" Very good, sir."

" Very good, sir — I mean very good, Jeeves; that will be all," I said.

And I drank a modicum of tea with a good deal of hauteur.

It isn't often that I find myself able to prove Jeeves in the wrong; but by dinner-time that night I was in a position to do so, and I did it without delay.

" Touching on that matter we were touching on, Jeeves," I said, coming in from the bath and tackling him as he studded the shirt, " I should be glad if you would give me your careful attention for a moment. I warn you that what I am about to say is going to make you look pretty silly."

" Indeed, sir? "

" Yes, Jeeves. Pretty dashed silly it's going to make you look. This morning, if I remember rightly, you stated that Miss Wickham was volatile, frivolous, and lacking in seriousness. Am I correct? "

" Quite correct, sir."

" Then what I have to tell you may cause you to alter that opinion. I went for a walk with Miss Wickham this afternoon; and, as we walked I told her about what young Tuppy Glossop did to me in the swimming bath at the Drones'. She hung upon my words, Jeeves, and was full of sympathy."

" Indeed, sir? "

" Dripping with it. And that's not all. Almost before I had finished she was suggesting the ripest, fruitiest, brainiest scheme for bringing young Tuppy's gray hairs in sorrow to the grave that anyone could possibly imagine."

" That is very gratifying, sir."

" 'Gratifying' is the word. It appears that at the school where Miss Wickham was educated, Jeeves, it used to become necessary from time to time for the right-thinking element to slip it across certain of the baser sort. Do you know what they did, Jeeves? "

" No, sir."

" They took a long stick, Jeeves, and — follow me closely here — they tied a darning needle to the end of it. Then, at dead of night, it appears, they sneaked into the party of the second part's [1] cubicle and shoved the needle through the bedclothes and punctured her hot-water bottle.

" Well, Jeeves, that was the scheme which Miss Wickham suggested I should work on young Tuppy, and that is the girl you call frivolous and lacking in seriousness. Any girl who can think up a wheeze like that is my idea of a helpmate. I shall be glad, Jeeves, if by the time I come to bed tonight you have waiting for me in this room a stout stick with a good sharp darning needle attached."

" Very good, sir."

" Have you any idea where young Tuppy sleeps? "

" I could ascertain, sir."

" Do so, Jeeves."

In a few minutes he was back with the necessary informash.

" Mr. Glossop is established in the Moat Room, sir."

" Where's that? "

" The second door on the floor below, sir."

" Right ho, Jeeves. Are the studs in my shirt? "

" Yes, sir."

" And the links also? "

" Yes, sir."

" Then push me into it."

The task to which I had set myself was one that involved hardship and discom-

[1] **party of the second part:** a term used in legal contracts to refer to the person with whom an agreement is made.

fort, for it meant sitting up till well into the small hours, and then padding down a cold corridor. But I did not shrink from it. After all, there is a lot to be said for family tradition. We Woosters did our bit in the Crusades.

Allowing for everything, it didn't seem that it was going to be safe to start my little expedition till half-past two at the earliest; and I'm bound to say that it was only the utmost resolution that kept me from snuggling into the sheets and calling it a day. I'm not much of a lad now for late hours.

However, by half-past two everything appeared to be quiet. I shook off the mists of sleep, grabbed the good old stick and needle, and was off along the corridor. And presently, pausing outside the Moat Room, I turned the handle and went in.

At first, when I had beetled in, the room had seemed as black as a coal cellar; but after a bit things began to lighten. The curtains weren't quite drawn over the window, and I could see a trifle of the scenery here and there.

The bed was opposite the window, with the head against the wall and the end where the feet were jutting out toward where I stood, thus rendering it possible, after one had sown the seed, so to speak, to make a quick getaway.

There only remained now the rather tricky problem of locating the old hot-water bottle. I was a good deal cheered, at this juncture, to hear a fruity snore from the direction of the pillows. Reason told me that a bloke who could snore like that wasn't going to be awakened by a trifle. I edged forward and ran a hand in a gingerly sort of way over the coverlet. A moment later I had found the bulge. I steered the good old darning needle onto it, gripped the stick, and shoved. Then, pulling out the weapon, I sidled toward the door, and in another moment would have been outside, buzzing for home and the good night's rest, when suddenly there was a crash that sent my spine shooting up through the top of my head, and the contents of the bed sat up like a jack-in-the-box and said:

"Who's that?"

In order to facilitate the orderly retreat according to plan, I had left the door open, and the beastly thing had slammed like a bomb. But I wasn't giving much thought to the causes of the explosion. What was disturbing me was the discovery that, whoever else the bloke in the bed might be, he was not young Tuppy. Tuppy has one of those high, squeaky voices that sound like the tenor of the village choir failing to hit a high note. This one was something in between the last trump and a tiger calling for breakfast after being on a diet for a day or two.

I did not linger. Getting swiftly off the mark, I dived for the door handle, and was off and away, banging the door behind me. I may be a chump in many ways, as my Aunt Agatha will freely attest, but I know when and when not to be among those present.

And I was just about to do the stretch of corridor leading to the stairs in a split second under the record time for the course when something brought me up with a sudden jerk. An irresistible force was holding me straining at leash, as it were.

The night being a trifle chillier than the dickens, I had donned for this expedition a dressing gown. It was the tail of this infernal garment that had caught in the door and pipped me at the eleventh hour.

The next moment the door had opened, light was streaming through it, and the bloke with the voice had grabbed me by the arm.

It was Sir Roderick Glossop.

For about three and a quarter seconds,

or possibly more, we just stood there, drinking each other in, so to speak, the old boy still attached with a limpetlike [1] grip to my elbow.

"You!" said Sir Roderick finally. And in this connection I want to state that it's all rot to say you can't hiss a word that hasn't an *s* in it. The way he pushed out that "You!" sounded like an angry cobra.

By rights, I suppose, at this point I ought to have said something. The best I could manage, however, was a faint, soft, bleating sound.

"Come in here," he said, lugging me into the room. "We don't want to wake the whole house. Now," he said, depositing me on the carpet and closing the door, and doing a bit of eyebrow work, "kindly inform me what is this latest manifestation of insanity?"

I pulled myself together with a strong effort.

"Awfully sorry about all this," I said in a hearty sort of voice. "The fact is, I thought you were Tuppy."

"You thought I was my nephew? Why should I be my nephew?"

"What I'm driving at is, I thought this was his room."

"My nephew and I changed rooms. I have a great dislike for sleeping on an upper floor. I am nervous about fire.

"I should have thought that your manservant would have informed you," said Sir Roderick, "that we contemplated making this change. I met him shortly before luncheon and told him to tell you."

This extraordinary statement staggered me. That Jeeves had been aware all along that this old crumb would occupy the bed which I was proposing to prod with darning needles and had let me rush upon my doom without a word of warning was almost beyond belief. You might say I was aghast. Yes, practically aghast.

"You told Jeeves that you were going to sleep in this room?" I gasped.

"I did. I was aware that you and my nephew were on terms of intimacy, and I wished to spare myself the possibility of a visit from you. I confess that it never occurred to me that such a visit was to be anticipated at three o'clock in the morning. What the devil do you mean," he barked, suddenly hotting up, "by prowling about the house at this hour? And what is that thing in your hand?"

I looked down, and found that I was still grasping the stick.

"This?" I said. "Oh, yes."

"What do you mean, 'Oh, yes'? What is it?"

"Well, it's a long story."

"We have the night before us."

"It's this way: I will ask you to picture me some weeks ago, perfectly peaceful and inoffensive, after dinner at the Drones', smoking a thoughtful cigarette and —"

I broke off. The man wasn't listening. He was goggling in a rapt sort of way at the end of the bed, from which there had now begun to drip on the carpet a series of drops.

"Did you do this?" he said in a low, strangled sort of voice.

"Er — yes. As a matter of fact, yes. I was just going to tell you —"

"And your aunt tried to persuade me that you were not insane!"

"I'm not. Absolutely not. If you'll just let me explain —"

"I will do nothing of the kind."

He did some deep-breathing exercises.

"My bed is drenched!"

"The way it all began —"

"Be quiet!" He heaved somewhat for a while. "You wretched, miserable idiot," he said, "kindly inform me which bedroom you are supposed to be occupying."

[1] **limpetlike:** as though attached, like a limpet, to a rock.

" It's on the floor above. The Clock Room."

" Thank you. I will find it. I propose," he said, " to pass the remainder of the night in your room, where, I presume, there is a bed in a condition to be slept in."

Well, we Woosters are old campaigners. We can take the rough with the smooth. I pinched a couple of pillows off the bed, shoved the hearthrug over my knees, and sat down and started counting sheep.

I was just wondering if I would ever get to sleep again in this world when a voice at my elbow said, " Good morning, sir," and I sat up with a jerk.

I could have sworn I hadn't so much as dozed off for even a minute; but apparently I had. For the curtains were drawn back and daylight was coming in through the window, and there was Jeeves with a cup of tea on a tray.

" Merry Christmas, sir! "

I reached out a feeble hand for the restoring brew.

" You think so, do you? " I said. " Much, let me tell you, depends on what you mean by the adjective 'merry.' If, moreover, you suppose that it is going to be merry for you, correct the impression, Jeeves," I said, taking another half oz. of tea and speaking in a cold, measured voice, " I wish to ask you one question. Did you or did you not know that Sir Roderick Glossop was sleeping in this room last night? "

" Yes, sir."

" You admit it! "

" Yes, sir."

" And you didn't tell me! "

" No, sir. I thought it would be more judicious not to do so. It seemed to me, sir, that whatever might occur was all for the best. I thought that possibly, on reflection, sir, your views being what they are, you would prefer your relations with Sir Roderick Glossop and his family to be distant rather than cordial."

" My views? What do you mean, 'my views'? "

" As regards a matrimonial alliance with Miss Honoria Glossop, sir."

Something like an electric shock seemed to zip through me. The man had opened up a new line of thought. I suddenly saw what he was driving at, and realized all in a flash that I had been wronging this faithful fellow. All the while I supposed he had been landing me in the soup he had really been steering me away from it.

I give you my honest word, it had never struck me till this moment that my Aunt Agatha had been scheming to get me in right with Sir Roderick so that I should eventually be received back into the fold, if you see what I mean, and subsequently pushed off on Honoria.

" Great Scott, Jeeves! " I said, paling.

" Precisely, sir."

" You think there was a risk? "

" I do, sir. A very grave risk."

A disturbing thought struck me.

" But, Jeeves, on calm reflection, won't Sir Roderick have gathered by now that my objective was young Tuppy, and that puncturing his hot-water bottle was just one of those things that occur when the Yuletide spirit is abroad, and all the good work will have been wasted? "

" No, sir. I fancy not. That might possibly have been Sir Roderick's mental reaction had it not been for the second incident."

" The second incident? "

" During the night, sir, while Sir Roderick was occupying your bed, somebody entered the room, pierced his hot-water bottle with some sharp instrument, and vanished in the darkness."

I could make nothing of this.

" What! Do you think I walked in my sleep? "

" No, sir. It was young Mr. Glossop

who did it. I encountered him this morning, sir, shortly before I came here. He was in cheerful spirits, and inquired of me how you were feeling about the incident — not being aware that his victim had been Sir Roderick."

"But, Jeeves, what an amazing coincidence!"

"Sir?"

"Why, young Tuppy getting exactly the same idea as I did. Or, rather, as Miss Wickham did. You can't say that's not a miracle."

"Not altogether, sir. It appears that he received the suggestion from her."

"From Miss Wickham?"

"Yes, sir."

"You mean to say that, after she had put me up to the scheme of puncturing Tuppy's hot-water bottle, she went off and tipped Tuppy off to puncturing mine?"

"Precisely, sir. She is a young lady with a keen sense of humor, sir."

I sat there — you might say, stunned. When I thought how near I had come to offering the Wooster heart and hand to a girl capable of double-crossing a strong man's honest love like that, I shivered.

"The occurrence, if I may take the liberty of saying so, sir, will perhaps lend color to the view which I put forward yesterday that Miss Wickham, though in many respects a charming lady —"

I raised the hand.

"Say no more, Jeeves," I replied. "Love is dead."

I brooded for a while.

"You've seen Sir Roderick this morning?"

"Yes, sir."

"How did he seem?"

"A trifle feverish, sir."

"Feverish?"

"A little emotional, sir. He expressed a strong desire to meet you, sir."

"What would you advise?"

"If you were to slip out by the back entrance, sir, it would be possible for you to make your way across the field without being observed and reach the village, where you could hire an automobile to take you to London. I could bring on your effects later in your own car."

"But London, Jeeves? Is any man safe? My Aunt Agatha is in London."

"Yes, sir."

"Well, then?"

He regarded me for a moment with a fathomless eye.

"I think the best plan, sir, would be for you to leave England, which is not pleasant at this time of the year, for some little while. I would not take the liberty of dictating your movements, sir, but as you already have accommodation engaged on the Blue Train[1] for Monte Carlo for the day after tomorrow —"

"But you canceled the booking?"

"No, sir."

"I told you to."

"Yes, sir. It was remiss of me, but the matter slipped my mind."

"Oh?"

"Yes, sir."

"All right, Jeeves. Monte Carlo, ho, then."

"Very good, sir."

"It's lucky, as things have turned out, that you forgot to cancel that booking."

"Very fortunate indeed, sir. If you will wait here, sir, I will return to your room and procure a suit of clothes."

THINK BACK OVER WHAT YOU HAVE READ

Enjoying the Amusing Relationship between Bertie and Jeeves

1. As illustrated by the story, what are the correct manners of an English gentleman's "man"? With what illustration can you testify to Jeeves's perfect form?

[1] **Blue Train**: the name of a crack French train.

2. At what moments in the story do Jeeves's perfect manners seem highly amusing?

3. Find examples from the story which show that Bertie's manners as gentleman are far less correct than Jeeves's as gentleman's man. What amusing situations does this lead to?

4. Behind his mask of correct form what selfish ends is Jeeves able to carry on in secret? What amusing situations does his plotting lead to? Why is he allowed to get away with his designs after they are discovered?

5. What is the amusing lie in the relationship between Jeeves and Bertie?

Savoring Wodehouse Humor

The fun of reading a Wodehouse story lies in a full appreciation of its humorous detail. Perhaps you missed the full flavor of some of the most amusing observations. For that reason it should prove interesting for each member of the class to call attention to various passages which produced a chuckle.

6. What sentences can you point to that contain an unexpectedly familiar and commonplace detail, such, for example, as the following: "I could feel he was directing a frosty gaze at me, but *I dug into the marmalade* and refused to meet it."

7. What amusing comparisons can you quote?

8. What extravagant epithets do you find? (When you call people names, you are using epithets. An *epithet* is a word or phrase which denotes some quality noticed. For example, when Bertie calls Honoria — the girl he was once engaged to — "a ghastly dynamic exhibit who read Nietzsche," he was using an epithet.) What amusing observation do you see behind Bertie's epithets? Does he usually shoot far wide of the mark? Or does he show real insight into human nature?

9. With what crazy detail are the absurd incidents of the story built up? Such incidents, for example, as the telephone conversation between Bertie and his aunt Agatha, the catching of his bathrobe in the door, and so forth. What incident in the story was presented in the most humorous light?

10. Much of the humor of the Wodehouse story you have just read lies in the ridiculous contrast between the language and the occasion on which it is used. What examples can you find of high-sounding words being used in an absurd situation?

11. What mixed-up allusions (see word study on page 148 if you are not sure what an allusion is) can you cite that are particularly funny?

12. What examples of English slang delighted you? Of what words could you guess the meaning from the context?

THE PRINCESS AND THE PUMA

by O. Henry (1867–1910)

Perhaps you are already familiar with the name of O. Henry, that most mischievous of storytellers, whose sudden twists and turns of plot make the reading of his yarns a hilarious adventure. No matter where life took him he always found experience entertaining. And out of each major period of his career there grew a volume of short stories to stand as a monument to his whimsical observations. *Cabbages and Kings* springs from his months of wandering in Central America. From his years in New York City comes *The Four Million.* Out of his trip to Texas, whence he had gone as a young man in search of health, came *The Heart of the West,* from which the following story is taken. And these tales are but a small beginning of a long list of titles which have delighted readers ever since they first appeared in the popular magazines of your grandmother's day. O. Henry is the pen name of William Sydney Porter.

"The Princess and the Puma" is a typical sample of O. Henry humor. His situations, you will see, are dipped in humorous irony,[1] and the story ends as a kind of practical joke. You will find in his witchery of words no end of fun. And while they are thin of substance, his stories are delicious tidbits on which to whet the reading appetite.

THERE HAD to be a king and queen, of course. The king was a terrible old man who wore six-shooters and spurs, and shouted in such a tremendous voice that the rattlers on the prairie would run into their holes under the prickly pear. Before there was a royal family they called the man "Whispering Ben." When he came to own fifty thousand acres of land

[1] For an explanation of irony, turn to page 59.

and more cattle than he could count, they called him O'Donnell "the Cattle King."

The queen had been a Mexican girl from Laredo. She made a good, mild, Colorado-claro[1] wife, and even succeeded in teaching Ben to modify his voice sufficiently while in the house to keep the dishes from being broken. When Ben got to be king, she would sit on the gallery of Espinosa Ranch and weave rush mats. When wealth became so irresistible and oppressive that upholstered chairs and a center table were brought down from San Antone in the wagons, she bowed her smooth, dark head and shared the fate of the Danaë.[2]

To avoid *lèse-majesté*[3] you have been presented first to the king and queen. They do not enter the story, which might be called "The Chronicle of the Princess, the Happy Thought, and the Lion That Bungled His Job."

Josefa O'Donnell was the surviving daughter, the princess. From her mother she inherited warmth of nature and a dusky, semitropic beauty. From Ben O'Donnell the royal she acquired a store of intrepidity, common sense, and the faculty of ruling. The combination was one worth going miles to see. Josefa while riding her pony at a gallop could put five out of six bullets through a tomato can swinging at the end of a string. She could play for hours with a white kitten she owned, dressing it in all manner of absurd clothes. Scorning a pencil, she could tell you out of her head what 1545 two-year-olds would bring on the hoof at $8.50 per head. Roughly speaking, the Espinosa Ranch is forty miles long and thirty broad — but mostly leased land. Josefa, on her pony, had prospected over every mile of it. Every cowpuncher on the range knew her by sight and was a loyal vassal.[4] Ripley Givens, foreman of one of the Espinosa outfits, saw her one day and made up his mind to form a royal matrimonial alliance. Presumptuous? No. In those days in the Nueces[5] country a man was a man. And, after all, the title of cattle king does not presuppose blood royal. Often it only signifies that its owner wears the crown in token of his magnificent qualities in the art of cattle stealing.

One day Ripley Givens rode over to the Double Elm Ranch to inquire about a bunch of strayed yearlings. He was late in setting out on his return trip, and it was sundown when he struck the White Horse Crossing of the Nueces. From there to his own camp it was sixteen miles. To the Espinosa ranch house it was twelve. Givens was tired. He decided to pass the night at the Crossing.

There was a fine water hole in the river bed. The banks were thickly covered with great trees, undergrown with brush. Back from the water hole fifty yards was a stretch of curly mesquite grass — supper for his horse and bed for himself. Givens staked his horse and spread out his saddle blankets to dry. He sat down with his back against a tree and rolled a cigarette. From somewhere in the dense timber along the river came a sudden, rageful, shivering wail. The pony danced at the end of his rope and blew a whistling snort of comprehending fear. Givens puffed at his cigarette, but he reached leisurely for his pistol belt, which lay on the grass, and twirled the cylinder of his weapon tentatively. A great gar[6] plunged with a loud splash into the water hole. A little brown rabbit skipped around a

[1] **Colorado-claro:** as applied to a cigar, medium in color and strength and somewhat mild. [2] **Danaë:** a mortal, in Greek mythology, with whom the god Jupiter was in love. When her father imprisoned her in a tower in his castle, her lover came to her in the form of a golden shower. [3] **lèse-majesté:** a French expression referring to any offense which violates the dignity of a ruler.

[4] **vassal:** subject, as of a queen. [5] **Nueces:** a river in Texas. [6] **gar:** a fish, belonging to a particularly ferocious family.

bunch of catclaw and sat twitching his whiskers and looking humorously at Givens. The pony went on eating grass.

It is well to be reasonably watchful when a Mexican lion sings soprano along the arroyos [1] at sundown. The burden of his song may be that young calves and fat lambs are scarce, and that he has a carnivorous desire for your acquaintance.

In the grass lay an empty fruit can, cast there by some former sojourner. Givens caught sight of it with a grunt of satisfaction. In his coat pocket tied behind his saddle was a handful or two of ground coffee. Black coffee and cigarettes! What ranchero could desire more?

In two minutes he had a little fire going clearly. He started, with his can, for the water hole. When within fifteen yards of its edge, he saw, between the bushes, a side-saddled pony with down-dropped reins cropping grass a little distance to his left. Just rising from her hands and knees on the brink of the water hole was Josefa O'Donnell. She had been drinking water, and she brushed the sand from the palms of her hands. Ten yards away, to her right, half concealed by a clump of sacuista, Givens saw the crouching form of the Mexican lion. His amber eyeballs glared hungrily; six feet from them was the tip of the tail stretched straight, like a pointer's. His hindquarters rocked with the motion of the cat tribe preliminary to leaping.

Givens did what he could. His six-shooter was thirty-five yards away, lying on the grass. He gave a loud yell, and dashed between the lion and the princess.

The "rucus," [2] as Givens called it afterward, was brief and somewhat confused. When he arrived on the line of attack, he saw a dim streak in the air and heard a couple of faint cracks. Then a hundred pounds of Mexican lion plumped down upon his head and flattened him, with a heavy jar, to the ground. He remembered calling out, "Let up, now — no fair gouging!" and then he crawled from under the lion like a worm, with his mouth full of grass and dirt and a big lump on the back of his head where it had struck the root of a water elm. The lion lay motionless. Givens, feeling aggrieved and suspicious of fouls,[3] shook his fist at the lion and shouted, "I'll rastle you again for twenty —" and then he got back to himself.

Josefa was standing in her tracks, quietly reloading her silver-mounted .38. It had not been a difficult shot. The lion's head made an easier mark than a tomato can swinging at the end of a string. There was a provoking, teasing, maddening smile upon her mouth and in her dark eyes. The would-be rescuing knight felt the fire of his fiasco burn down to his soul. Here had been his chance, the chance that he had dreamed of; and Momus,[4] and not Cupid, had presided over it. The satyrs [5] in the wood were, no doubt, holding their sides in hilarious, silent laughter. There had been something like vaudeville — say, Signor Givens and his funny knockabout act with the stuffed lion.

"Is that you, Mr. Givens?" said Josefa, in her deliberate, saccharine contralto. "You nearly spoiled my shot when you yelled. Did you hurt your head when you fell?"

"Oh, no," said Givens quietly; "that didn't hurt." He stooped ignominiously and dragged his best Stetson hat from under the beast. It was crushed and wrinkled to a fine comedy effect. Then he

[1] **arroyos:** watercourses. [2] **rucus:** a rumpus or quarrelsome uproar. Do you see the humor of calling a fight with a lion a *rucus?*

[3] **fouls:** Givens, still dazed by the blow on his head, thinks he is in a wrestling bout.
[4] **Momus:** in Greek mythology, the God of Ridicule. [5] **satyrs:** creatures of the woods, half god and half man, with the tail and ears of a horse, given to riotous merriment.

knelt down and softly stroked the fierce, open-jawed head of the dead lion.

" Poor old Bill ! " he exclaimed mournfully.

" What's that ? " asked Josefa sharply.

" Of course, you didn't know, Miss Josefa," said Givens, with an air of one allowing magnanimity to triumph over grief. " Nobody can blame you. I tried to save him, but I couldn't let you know in time."

" Save who ? "

" Why, Bill. I've been looking for him all day. You see, he's been our camp pet for two years. Poor old fellow, he wouldn't have hurt a cottontail rabbit. It'll break the boys all up when they hear about it. But you couldn't tell, of course, that Bill was just trying to play with you."

Josefa's black eyes burned steadily upon him. Ripley Givens met the test successfully. He stood rumpling the yellow-brown curls on his head pensively. In his eyes was regret, not unmingled with a gentle reproach. His smooth features were set to a pattern of indisputable sorrow. Josefa wavered.

" What was your pet doing here ? " she asked, making a last stand. " There's no camp near the White Horse Crossing."

" The old rascal ran away from camp yesterday," answered Givens readily. " It's a wonder the coyotes didn't scare him to death. You see, Jim Webster, our horse wrangler,[1] brought a little terrier pup into camp last week. The pup made life miserable for Bill — he used to chase him around and chew his hind legs for hours at a time. Every night when bedtime came, Bill would sneak under one of the boys' blankets and sleep to keep the pup from finding him. I reckon he must have been worried pretty desperate or he wouldn't have run away. He was always afraid to get out of sight of camp."

Josefa looked at the body of the fierce animal. Givens gently patted one of the formidable paws that could have killed a yearling calf with one blow. Slowly a red flush widened upon the dark olive face of the girl. Was it the signal of shame of the true sportsman who has brought down ignoble quarry ? Her eyes grew softer, and the lowered lids drove away all their bright mockery.

" I'm very sorry," she said humbly; " but he looked so big, and jumped so high that — "

" Poor old Bill was hungry," interrupted Givens, in quick defense of the deceased. " We always made him jump for his supper in camp. He would lie down and roll over for a piece of meat. When he saw you, he thought he was going to get something to eat from you."

Suddenly Josefa's eyes opened wide.

" I might have shot you ! " she exclaimed. " You ran right in between. You risked your life to save your pet ! That was fine, Mr. Givens. I like a man who is kind to animals."

Yes ; there was even admiration in her gaze now. After all, there was a hero rising out of the ruins of the anticlimax. The look on Givens's face would have secured him a high position in the S. P. C. A.[2]

" I always loved 'em," said he ; " horses, dogs, Mexican lions, cows, alligators — "

" I hate alligators," instantly demurred Josefa ; " crawly, muddy things ! "

" Did I say alligators ? " said Givens. " I meant antelopes, of course."

Josefa's conscience drove her to make further amends. She held out her hand penitently. There was a bright, unshed drop in each of her eyes.

" Please forgive me, Mr. Givens, won't you ? I'm only a girl, you know, and I was frightened at first. I'm very, very sorry I shot Bill. You don't know how ashamed

[1] **horse wrangler:** a man who herds horses.

[2] **S.P.C.A.:** abbreviation for the Society for the Prevention of Cruelty to Animals.

I feel. I wouldn't have done it for anything."

Givens took the proffered hand. He held it for a time while he allowed the generosity of his nature to overcome his grief at the loss of Bill. At last it was clear that he had forgiven her.

"Please don't speak of it any more, Miss Josefa. 'Twas enough to frighten any young lady the way Bill looked. I'll explain it all right to the boys."

"Are you really sure you don't hate me?" Josefa came closer to him impulsively. Her eyes were sweet — oh, sweet and pleading with gracious penitence. "I would hate anyone who would kill my kitten. And how daring and kind of you to risk being shot when you tried to save him! How very few men would have done that!" Victory wrested from defeat! Vaudeville turned into drama! Bravo, Ripley Givens!

It was now twilight. Of course, Miss Josefa could not be allowed to ride on to the ranch house alone. Givens resaddled his pony in spite of that animal's reproachful glances, and rode with her. Side by side they galloped across the smooth grass, the princess and the man who was kind to animals. The prairie odors of fruitful earth and delicate bloom were thick and sweet around them. Coyotes yelping over there on the hill. No fear. And yet —

Josefa rode closer. A little hand seemed to grope. Givens found it with his own. The ponies kept an even gait. The hands lingered together, and the owner of one explained:

"I never was frightened before, but just think! How terrible it would be to meet a really wild lion! Poor Bill! I'm so glad you came with me!"

O'Donnell was sitting on the ranch gallery.

"Hello, Rip!" he shouted. "That you?"

"He rode in with me," said Josefa. "I lost my way and was late."

"Much obliged," called the cattle king. "Stop over, Rip, and ride to camp in the morning."

But Givens would not. He would push on to camp. There was a bunch of steers to start off on the trail at daybreak. He said good night and trotted away.

An hour later, when the lights were out, Josefa, in her night robe, came to her door and called to the king in his own room across the brick-paved hallway:

"Say, Pop, you know that old Mexican lion they call the 'Gotch-eared Devil' — the one that killed Gonzales, Mr. Martin's sheep-herder, and about fifty calves on the Salado range? Well, I settled his hash this afternoon over at the White Horse Crossing. Put two balls in his head with my .38 while he was on the jump. I knew him by the slice gone from his left ear that old Gonzales cut off with his machete.[1] You couldn't have made a better shot yourself, Daddy."

"Bully for you!" thundered Whispering Ben from the darkness of the royal chamber.

THINK BACK OVER WHAT YOU HAVE READ

Appreciating O. Henry's Style

1. Contrast the following sentences:
   a. "It is well to be reasonably watchful when a Mexican lion sings soprano along the arroyos at sundown."
   b. It is well to look out when you hear a Mexican lion at night.

You will have no difficulty in recognizing the first of the two sentences as O. Henry's. What other sentences can you quote which show humorous exaggeration, picturesque comparison, or amusing under- or overstatement?

2. Compare O. Henry's style with that of H. C. Bunner. (Refer again to assignment 3, page 11.)

[1] **machete**: a large, heavy knife used for clearing paths.

Composition Suggestion

3. Imagine that Mr. Givens, before "pushing on to camp," overhears what Josefa says to her father; then write another episode to the story. Here is a chance to put into practice what you have learned in your study of composition.

Increase Your Power over Words

4. The jest in this story may be summed up in the word *fiasco,* a word which has been selected for special study. Thus your interest in the word will in large measure depend upon your appreciation of the story. The following questions are designed to help you figure out for yourself what the word means from what happens in the story.

a. On page 26 the word *fiasco* is used in the following sentence: "The would-be rescuing knight felt the fire of his *fiasco* burn down to his soul." Of what does this particular *fiasco* consist? What, then, does *fiasco* seem to you at this point to mean?

b. Answer the following questions with the idea of discovering the *fiasco* on which the story is based:

With what words does Givens start his big fib?

What motive lies behind Givens's fib? How can you tell?

Through what amusing phases does Givens's fib pass? What climax does it reach?

In what ways, unbeknown to Givens, does Josefa aid him in building up his fib?

At what point does Givens seem to "get away" with his fib? At what point are you, the reader, aware that he didn't?

What, at this point, does *fiasco* seem to you to mean?

c. Phrase your own definition of *fiasco* on the basis of the way it is illustrated by the story.

d. Look up the word *fiasco* in the dictionary. Notice first its literal meaning and second its derived meaning. Compare your own definition with that of the dictionary.

e. Relate briefly to the class any *fiasco* in which you played a part, making sure that you bring the word itself into the conversation.

Look up the word *ignominiously* in the Glossary, and note the way it is used on page 26. Does the word have any relation to *fiasco?* Can you use the word in describing your own *fiasco?*

5. Notice how O. Henry uses the word *magnanimity* in the following sentence:

"'Of course, you didn't know, Miss Josefa,' said Givens, with an air of one allowing *magnanimity* to triumph over grief."

Can you guess its meaning from the way it is used in the sentence? The word *magnanimity* means a *magnanimous* deed, and *magnanimous* belongs to an interesting family of words, which you can best remember by associating them with one another as follows:

VERB	NOUNS	ADJECTIVES
magnify	magnitude	magnanimous
	magnate	magnificent
	magnanimity	

Look up each word in the dictionary and come to class prepared to discuss (a) their common root and (b) their common use.

THE MILK PITCHER

by Howard Brubaker (1882–)

In Phil Fuller, the hero of this amusing story, you will discover, perhaps, something of yourself. Like many another youth, Phil was extremely self-conscious and sensitive to ridicule. He was far too aware of his faults, and he didn't know how to make the most of himself. He had, furthermore, many a secret complaint to make against nature's endowment. His hair was red; he had freckles; his hands and ears were too large. He couldn't keep a tune and he couldn't make a speech, although he was expected to do both. People laughed at him a lot, and he blushed and went shy.

But he had one saving grace: a natural instinct for fun, so that when he put on a baseball mitt his self-consciousness vanished. Herein lies the bit of wisdom to be extracted from the story. For running through the rollicking humor of the story is a bright thread of truth which you must not overlook — a useful hint of how to turn aside the sly darts of ridicule before their poisoned tip inflicts a real wound. From the start you will like Phil Fuller, a modern boy reared on a farm, and his baseball adventures at school will perhaps convince you that "a new style of play," such as the director of athletics at Sparta Agricultural College decided to build around Phil, is in order in all school sport.

Howard Brubaker, the author of the story, is a popular columnist who appears in *The New Yorker* every week. Like H. C. Bunner and O. Henry, he appreciates the comedy in life. His humor is kindly and understanding, as you will see for yourself when you read what follows.

THE FULLERS named their son Philip after his maternal grandfather. That was an error in judgment because the time came when the name Phil Fuller aroused chuckles and snickers among the pleasure-loving faces of the countryside. At the age of one Phil had practically settled upon red as the best color for hair. Sometime in his third year the truth was established that he was left-handed. When given something he did not want he threw it away with violence.

This act seemed to set up pleasurable emotions in his young soul. His simple face widened into a grin and before long he was heaving things around for the sheer love of heaving.

At four Phil sprouted a genuine freckle on his nose, the forerunner of a bumper crop, and even his prejudiced mother had to admit that his ears were large for their age.

The youth spent his fourth summer in the society of a Jersey calf named Lily, who was tethered in the orchard. Phil had nothing to do except to throw green apples at a tree with his left hand, and Lily's time was also her own. The child learned not to wince when she licked his pink nose with her rough tongue, and the calf put up with some pretty rowdy conduct too. Both infants cried when separated for the night. The tender attachment between Phil and Lil was the subject of neighborhood gossip as far away as the Doug Morton place at the bend of Squaw Creek.

Phil had a misguided sense of humor. It seemed to him that throwing things was the world's funniest joke. As he picked up a stone and let it fly, the freckles on his face arranged themselves into a pleasure pattern, his features widened, and he grinned expansively, showing vacant spots where he was changing teeth.

By this time his love for the cow stable had become a grand passion. Horses, dogs, cats, and pigs meant rather less in his young life than they do to most farm boys, but cows meant more. Phil attended all the milkings with his father, dealt out bran, and threw down hay. He wandered in and out among bovine legs without fear; hoofs, horns, and teeth had no terrors for him. He was soon old enough to drive the cattle to pasture and bring them back.

At the age of eight he was probably the ablest redheaded cowboy and left-handed stone thrower in Clinton Township. At this date in history he had drunk enough milk to float a battleship and thrown enough stones, sticks, bones, horseshoes, apples, corncobs, and baseballs to sink one. He was now the owner in fee simple [1] of Lily's knock-kneed daughter, Dolly. This white-faced blond flapper followed Phil around with adoration and bleated at the barnyard gate until her playmate came home from school.

That fount of knowledge was Clinton Township, District No. 5, known locally as Tamarack School. There he absorbed a reasonable quantity of booklore and learned to pitch a straight ball with speed and control.

Baseball was the great joy of Phil's school years. Every spring when the frost came out of the ground his flaming head sprang up on the soggy field like a tulip. He had never learned to bat well, but he was a thrower of great ability and a

[1] **owner in fee simple:** a legal term which means, here, without any restrictions placed upon him.

laugher and yeller of great audibility. In school when asked to give the boundaries of Baluchistan he could scarcely make the teacher hear, but on the diamond his disorderly conduct was noted and deplored as far away as Grandma Longenecker's cottage.

The game uncorked his inhibitions and released his ego.[1] His habitual shyness vanished and gave place to vociferous glee. He did frolicsome things with his feet; his arms went around like a windmill wheel; sometimes he burst into what he wrongly believed to be song. Miss Willikans, the teacher, testified that Phil had easily the worst singing voice that had attended District No. 5 in her time — which would be nineteen years if she lived through this term, as seemed highly unlikely.

Inevitably there came an afternoon in late May when Phil's career as a Tamaracker had run its course. He twisted a button almost off his new coat, whispered a graduating piece about Daniel Webster, took his books and his well-worn right-hand glove, and went back to the cows.

At five o'clock of the following morning the fourteen-year-old Phil became the vice-president and general manager of the dairy department of the Fuller farm. His father was overworked, help was scarce and expensive, and the graduate of Tamarack was judged strong enough to handle the job. He milked all the cows that summer, cleaned the stalls, helped to get in the hay and fill the silo. He ran the separator; he churned; he carried skim milk to the pigs. The end of the summer found him a stocky lad of rather less than normal height but with a rank growth of feet, arms, and ears. He had the complexion of a boiled beet and hair exactly the shade of a two-cent stamp. His hands were large and fully equipped with freckles, calluses, bumps, cracks, warts, knuckles, and rough, red wrists.

Phil could lift with one hand Dolly's new calf, Molly, he could throw a ten-pound sledge hammer over the hay barn, he could sing like a squeaky pump, and he shattered all known speed records from the stable to the dining room. He was an able performer with the table fork as well as with the pitchfork.

In September he took all these assets and liabilities[2] and his first long pants and went to Branford to live with Aunt Mary and Uncle Phineas and attend high school. As he was winding up his affairs preparatory to this great adventure, it was clear that he had something on his mind. It came out one night at supper in the hiatus[3] between the fifth and sixth ears of Golden Bantam.

"It's too bad they don't keep a cow," he said, apropos of nothing.

"Oh, sakes alive, child!" his mother exclaimed in surprise. "They wouldn't want to be bothered with a cow."

Phil's ears went red. He polished off his corncob and returned to the attack. "They wouldn't need to be bothered much. They have no horse any more and there's room in the barn. I could feed her and milk her and everything. I bet Aunt Mary would be glad to have lots of nice milk and cream. We could tie her behind the buggy and take her in with us."

"Tie who — Aunt Mary?" asked father with ill-timed facetiousness.

"Dolly," said Phil.

A dozen objections were raised and disposed of. Aunt Mary and Uncle Phineas were consulted by telephone and after the first shock they agreed to the outrageous plan. And thus it came about that Phil Fuller was the first case in recorded history of a boy who went to Branford

[1] In other words, he lost all his self-consciousness.

[2] **all these assets and liabilities:** literally, what he owned and what he owed; or, in this case, all the virtues and all the handicaps mentioned in the preceding paragraphs. [3] **hiatus:** gap.

High School accompanied by a private and personal cow.

During those first months of strangeness and homesickness, Dolly was his comfort and his joy, his link with the familiar. He brushed and polished that blond cow until her upholstery was threadbare, pampered her with choice viands and clean bedding, scrubbed and whitewashed the interior of the old barn, put in window sashes to give Dolly more sunlight and a better view. Often when the day was fair he led her around the block to take the air and see a little city life.

Dolly was now in the full flush of her splendid young cowhood and home was never like this. The milk inspector passed her with high honors, and doctors recommended her for ailing babies. Presently she was one of Branford's leading citizens, a self-supporting twenty-quart cow commanding a premium of three cents over the market price. Phil had discovered his lifework.

His second great discovery did not come until spring. On a blustery March day he was out on the diamond, behind the high-school building warming up his left wing and chuckling over his favorite joke when Mr. Huckley, chemistry teacher and baseball coach, came along.

"Southpaw,[1] eh!" he demanded. "Let's see what you've got, Fuller."

Phil gave a brief exhibition of his wares, with Dinky Doolittle holding the catcher's glove.

"Plenty of steam and good control," the teacher said, "and your footwork is terrible. Now show us your curve."

"I haven't got any," Phil answered. "Nobody ever showed me how to pitch a curve."

"Somebody will now," Mr. Huckley said. "Whether you can do it or not is another question."

[1] **Southpaw:** a left-handed pitcher.

That was the beginning of a beautiful friendship and a new era in the life of Philip Fuller.

After a week of such instruction, Mr. Huckley handed down this decision: "You have the makings of a good pitcher, Phil, if you're willing to learn. You have a couple of fine qualities and not over twenty-five or thirty serious faults."

Phil's ears flushed with pleasure and embarrassment.

"Well, maybe I can get shut of some of them — I mean those — faults. I've got four years to do it in."

"Righto. You have good control of your fast one, you have a nice little out, and you have the worst style at windup these eyes have ever seen."

Four years of study, dairying, and baseball, with summers of hard work on the farm made Phil a different boy — different and yet curiously the same. His shoulders were broader, his arms stronger, but he did not add many inches to his stature. He knew more mathematics, science, and history, but Latin was still Greek to him. Although he took on some of the manners and customs of his town contemporaries, he still had the gait of one walking over a plowed field. In time he learned to talk with girls without being distressed, but as a social light he was a flickering flame in a smoky chimney. He was a conspicuous success on the barn floor but a brilliant failure on the dance floor. His voice changed but not for the better. His matin song to Dolly now sounded like a bullfrog.

Though much ridiculed, he was universally liked and genuinely respected. On the ball field he was a source of low comedy to friend and foe because of the eccentric behavior of his face and feet, but in his succeeding seasons on the mound he pitched the Branford High School out of the cellar position into respectable company, into select society, and finally, in his senior year, into the state championship of the small-town division.

At the joy fest in the assembly hall in celebration of this final triumph, Phil was forced to make a speech. He fixed his eyes upon his third vest button and informed it in confidence that it was Mr. Huckley who had made him what he was today — which wasn't so very much.

When his turn came, the chemist and coach arose and told the world a great secret about this Phil Fuller who had now pitched his last game for dear old B. H. S. Phil, he said, owed his success as a pitcher to his having been brought up in a cow barn. Constant milking had developed his forearm muscles to surprising strength, and the knots and knobs on his good left hand had enabled him to get a spin on the ball that produced his deadliest curves.

"I therefore propose," he said, "that Phil's girl friend, Dolly, be elected an honorary member of the team."

This motion was seconded with a will and carried with a whoop, and Dolly became, as far as anyone could learn, the only cow that ever belonged to a ball club.

"Phil has told you," Mr. Huckley went on, "that he got some help from my coaching. If so, he has chosen a rotten way to pay his debt. Instead of going to a high-class and fancy culture factory like Athens, he has decided to enter Sparta Agricultural College. Athens and Sparta are deadly enemies in athletics and someday Phil may use what I have taught him against my own alma mater. There is no use trying to keep Phil from running after the cows, but this is a sad blow to me. I didn't raise my boy to be a Spartan."

It was the county agricultural agent who had first put Sparta into Phil's head. The boy had naturally assumed that his education would cease with high school, but this Mr. Runkleman came into Dolly's palatial quarters one day and spoke a piece in favor of his own Sparta.

"A boy who intends to be an expert dairy farmer," he said in part, "ought to learn all there is on the subject. You have a natural gift for taking care of cows, but what you don't know about scientific dairying would fill a ten-foot shelf."

"That's so," Phil answered, "but I haven't got much money."

"You don't need much money. Lots of the boys are working their way through. I'll guarantee that you get a job in the college dairy barn. The work will pay your board, teach you the practical side, and you'll meet the nicest cows in the world."

This was a weighty inducement, and one crisp day in late September found Phil knocking at the door of the higher education. He was a youth of five feet with fiery hair and complexion, with ears that stuck out like red semaphores; a homely, awkward, likable boy, full of hope, inexperience, diffidence, and whole raw milk. His only regret was that he could not take Dolly with him to college.

Because of Mr. Runkleman's hearty recommendation, he got his job in the dairy barn and he took a room in a house near by. His days sped by in a new kind of eternal triangle [1] — boardinghouse, dairy, and classrooms — and he was happy in all three places.

Sibyl Barnett Samboy, the wife of Kenneth Samboy, director of Sparta athletics, said after Phil had been introduced to her at the freshman reception, "That's the first time I ever shook hands with a Stillson wrench." [2]

Although he honestly intended to keep

[1] **eternal triangle:** when a third person is involved in a love affair, the resulting conflict is often referred to as the "eternal triangle."
[2] **Stillson wrench:** an adjustable wrench, pressure on the handle of which increases the grip.

out of baseball, the first warm afternoon in March brought on an attack of the old spring fever. There was no harm, he thought, in getting out a ball and glove and tossing a few to " Spider " Coppery behind the barn while waiting for milking time. Before long it was a regular practice among the " cowboys " to beguile their idle moments with playing catch and knocking up flies, and presently there was talk of forming a team to play a game with the students of the horticultural department, otherwise the " greenhouse gang."

An insulting challenge was given and taken, and the game took place on a pleasant Saturday. This contest was held upon the old ball grounds. Along about the fifth inning of a ragged ball game an uninvited guest appeared among the handful of spectators in the grandstand. Phil was on the mound at the time.

So Mr. Samboy's eyes were gladdened by the sight of a stocky, freckled, redheaded southpaw who burned them over with power, who laughed from head to foot and uttered unfortunate noises.

Samboy talked with him after the game, poked his nose into his past, and urged him to try for the college team.

Phil protested that he was too busy with his classes and his cows. It was a long argument, but Samboy won.

" Report to Donnigan on Monday," said the director, " and tell him I suggested that he look you over. Every coach has a free hand with his own team, you know; but if he turns you down, let me know and I'll give you a tryout on the freshman team. I'll speak to Professor Wetherby, if you like, and ask him to let you shift hours at the dairy while you're trying your luck on the diamond."

H. B. Donnigan — " Hardboiled Donnigan " — had learned his trade under the great Tim Crowley, of the Eagles. Donnigan's big-league days were over and he was making a living coaching college teams. He used the Crowley method and the Crowley philosophy. All ballplayers were worms and should be treated as such.

One trouble with his policy was that it did not work at all. It was rumored that when his contract expired at the end of the season Samboy would let him go. A sense of his failure did not improve the coach's technic — or his temper. It was to this man-eating tiger that Samboy had cheerfully thrown the redheaded rookie from the cow barn.

" And who let you in? " was Hardboiled Donnigan's address of welcome.

" Mr. Samboy said would you please look me over."

" All right. Tell him I've done it, and if you're Lillian Gish I'm Queen Marie."

" I'm a pitcher — southpaw." Phil's hard-earned grammar fled in this crisis. " I was pretty good in high school."

" Oh, all right, stick around," said the testy coach. " When I get time, I'll see if you've got anything."

He seemed to forget all about Phil — who had not the slightest objection. The boy had a bad case of stage fright, partly from Donnigan's ill-nature, but more from the immensity of the empty stadium. He had almost made up his mind to sneak back to his beloved cows when he realized that he was being addressed.

" Hey, you — Carrots — come out to the box and pitch to the batters." Donnigan took his place behind the plate. " Murder this guy," he muttered to Risler, a senior and the captain of the team.

Risler murdered, instead, the bright April sunshine in three brutal blows. The old miracle had happened again. The moment Phil took hold of the ball and faced the batter, he forgot his fears; he remembered only that throwing a baseball was the greatest fun in the world.

" Hey, wipe that grin off your map,"

yelled the coach. "What do you think this is, a comic opery?"

Phil controlled his features with an effort while two more batters showed their futility. Donnigan handed his catcher's glove to "Swede" Olson.

"Gimme that stick," he growled. "You birds belong in the home for the blind!"

There were two serious mistakes that Phil could make in this crisis, and he made them both without delay. He struck out Hardboiled Donnigan and he laughed. Of course, he knew better than to ridicule the coach; but there was something irresistible about the way Donnigan lunged for that last slow floater.

"All right, now you've had your stuff, get out!" yelled the offended professional. "And stay out. I can't monkey with a guy who won't take his work serious. Laugh that off."

A few snickers were thrown after the defeated candidate, but the players knew that Donnigan had committed a manager's unpardonable sin of turning down a promising recruit on a personal grudge — and he knew that they knew.

As for Phil, he left the stadium with genuine relief. The more he saw of Donnigan, the better he liked cows. He had kept his promise to Samboy; now he would just sink out of sight and stick to business.

But Phil was heartily welcomed into the freshman squad. In the presence of Samboy he performed ably in a practice game. His fast ball, well-controlled curve, and change of pace made the inexperienced batters helpless, and his strange conduct landed him in the public eye with a bang.

The college comic paper, *The Cutup,* had a fine time over Phil. It discovered that the eccentric left-hander was a cow barner and it almost died of laughter at this joke.

"Phil Fuller, the Milk Pitcher," was the title of the piece. He was one of the wide-open faces from the wide-open spaces, the wit said, and sure winner of the standing broad grin. Also he proved the truth of the old saying, "Little pitchers have big ears."

But the result of the publicity was that the crowd at the freshman-sophomore game was the largest of the season. Among those present were old President Whitman, Professor Wetherby, and Mr. and Mrs. Kenneth Samboy.

The assembled underclassmen laughed until they ached at the grinning, gesticulating, noisy southpaw with the red-thatched roof. They greeted his queer, awkward windup with a yell invented by the sophomore cheer leader, a long, rhythmic "So-o-o, boss." But when he had won the game handily for the freshmen, the jeers turned to cheers.

Sibyl Samboy looked at her husband.

"And why," she asked, "is this infant phenomenon not on the varsity?"

"Hank can't see him somehow, and if I butt in it upsets my whole system of government. Personally I'd pitch him in a game or two to season him and then try him on the Athens. But it isn't worth a rumpus, Sib. After all, Fuller will be with us a long time yet and Donnigan won't."

"Poor old Hank! I wonder what he's got against the boy."

"It's incompatibility of temperament,[1] I guess. Hank thinks baseball is cosmic and Phil thinks it's comic."[2]

"And you," said Sibyl, "think you're wisecracking on *The Cutup.*"

In the next issue of that little weekly there was a marked difference in tone. The frosh cowboy, it said, was showing ability as well as risibility. It was time Donnigan tried him out on the team.

[1] **incompatibility of temperament** is one of the stock reasons offered for divorce. [2] **cosmic:** as used here, of tremendous importance (from the Greek word *cosmos,* meaning the universe).

There was something inevitable about the Phil Fuller movement. Donnigan did not want him on the team, Samboy was committed to keep his hands off, and Phil himself had no craving to appear in that big stadium. But the team was limping through a disastrous season and there were signs of disaffection among the players. The crowds dwindled, finances were suffering, and the all-important Athens game, the schedule's climax, was approaching like the day of doom.

Donnigan resisted as long as he could; but, schooled as he was in the professional game, he recognized one power greater than players, managers, or owners — the customer. And when white-haired Doctor Whitman called him into the president's office and intimated ever so gently that it might be just as well to give the public what it wanted, he gave in.

He did not surrender, but he retreated inch by inch. He gave Phil a uniform and let him practice with the team and learn the signals, then put him in at the end of a game that was already hopelessly lost. On the eve of the Athens contest he announced that he would pitch Hagenlaucher with Graybar and Fuller in reserve.

Any contest with the traditional foe always brought out the largest crowd of the season, but this year there was a novelty in the situation. The freshmen were out in full force prepared to make an organized nuisance of themselves on behalf of their favorite character. When he appeared on the field for practice, they gave him a tremendous ovation.

Just before the game started, Phil realized that somebody was calling him from the edge of the stand. To his great delight this proved to be Mr. Huckley, who had traveled all the way from Branford to see the game.

" Phil," he said, " if you get a chance today, I want you to do your darnedest."

" I'd kinda hate to play against Athens after all you did for me."

" I know. That's why I spoke. Forget all that, Phil. If they put you in, pitch as you did last year against Milltown, Three Falls, Oderno, and Jefferson. Good luck! "

" Thank you, Mr. Huckley. I'll meet you right here after it's over. I've got something to tell you."

As he took his seat on the bench, his smile faded and he lapsed into gloom. " He's scared stiff," thought Donnigan. " I won't dare to stick him in if Haggy blows."

The score stood six to five in favor of the visitors in the fifth inning when the umpire made the momentous announcement: " Greenwich batting for Hagenlaucher." At the same moment Graybar and Fuller left for the bull pen to warm up. The next inning would see a new face in the box.

Whose face? That was what all Sparta wanted to know; that was what Samboy wanted to know as he stepped out of the stand and walked up to Donnigan.

" Graybar," said the coach. " Fuller is scared to death. I guess he's got a yellow streak."

Samboy hesitated. The teams were changing sides now and the embattled freshmen were booming in unison, like a bass drum, " Phil! Phil! Phil! "

" All right, you're the doctor, Hank. But I'll go and talk to the boy."

The new pitcher did his best, but he was a broken reed. A base on balls, a single, and a hit batter filled the bags, with nobody out, and the air was full of disaster. Captain Risler stepped out to the box as if to steady the wabbly pitcher; Swede Olson, the catcher, joined this conference, which was further enriched by

Vicentini

HOW DOES YOUR ENVIRONMENT AFFECT YOUR LIFE? People's lives and personalities are influenced by their environments. For instance, the cowboy who escaped the sheriff in Will James' short story, page 38, differs in many ways from the Penn family in "The Revolt of Mother," page 125. If he had been a New Englander, what different traits of behavior would he reveal? On the other hand, what can you say for the persistence and courage of both Sarah Penn and the cowboy?

The land in Millard Sheets' painting "California" (*above*) seems capable of molding the people who dwell on it. The cowboy (*right*) differs from the man whose ice water is served in delicate glassware.

Southern Pacific R.R.

Warner F. Clapp

THE MAJESTY OF AMERICA'S WESTERN COUNTRY. The sense of space and freedom, so characteristic of the West, has interested the photographer in the picture above. Josefa O'Donnell in "The Princess and the Puma," page 24, knew land like that in the background of the round-up camp shown below. Her father's ranch, the Espinosa, was forty miles long and thirty broad, and she had explored every mile of it.

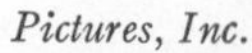

Pictures, Inc.

Rothstein, Resettlement Administration

MEN, MUSTANGS, AND LAND. In "Under the Lion's Paw," page 108, you read about the farm lands of the Middle West. There, men like the farmer in the picture above leave their mark upon the land just as the land marks them. The galloping wild horses in the picture below will remind you of many stories in this section as well as of "Mustangs," page 252, and "The Drive," page 258.

Acme

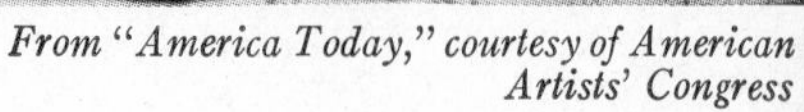

From "America Today," courtesy of American Artists' Congress

FIGHTING TO SAVE THE LAND. "The Wind Fighters," page 118, will remind you of America's fearful dust storms in the early 1930's. Since then we have become conscious of soil erosion and our wasteful use of the land. Movies like *The Plow that Broke the Plains* and the spread of scientific information through our governmental agencies are bringing knowledge and hope to people like Jim and Nora Dara. (*Above*) "Sun and Dust," an aquatint by LeRoy Flint. (*Left*) Potato field planted on contour to prevent erosion.

USDA

the presence of the lanky first baseman, Keeler.

Now Graybar handed the ball to Risler, who made a sign toward the bench. There was an instant of suspense, and then out of the dugout appeared the gaudy head of Phil Fuller.

An avalanche of sound slid down upon the field. From the freshman bloc came the long, rhythmic yell, " So-o-o, boss." In the general confusion Hardboiled Donnigan was scarcely seen emerging from the dugout. He seemed to shrink before the wave of noise, then he disappeared through an opening out of the field and out of the athletics department of Sparta.

Scarcely anyone in the audience knew that Donnigan had not ordered the change of pitchers, nor had Samboy. It was Risler, backed by Olson, Keeler, and the whole team. It was mutiny; it was rebellion.

But this was not the familiar Phil Fuller who had laughed and danced his way into the hearts of the fans. This was a serious Phil, a gloomy Phil. Life was now real; life was earnest. He took his long, queer windup and he threw the ball high — far too high. Olson made a jump for the ball, missed it, and landed in a heap. Before he could recover the ball, two runs had come over and Athens rocked with laughter.

But so, to the amazement of the universe, did Phil Fuller. It suddenly seemed to the misguided youth that it was the funniest thing in the world that he should have thrown away the ball and let in two runs. The infield laughed in imitation.

Now the tension under which the team had been working suddenly relaxed as if a tight band had snapped and brought relief. The nervous, eager, do-or-die spirit suddenly disappeared, leaving the natural instinct of youth to have a good time. With the utmost ease the pitcher and the infield disposed of the next three batters, and in their half of the inning they began their climb toward victory.

It was a strange, exciting, hilarious game. Phil had never played in such fast company before or faced such a murderous array of bats. He was in hot water half a dozen times, but he never lost the healing gift of laughter.

And the team played as if baseball came under the head of pleasure.

Samboy said to Risler, who sat beside him on the bench in the eighth, " Whether we win or lose, this is the answer. We're going to build a new idea and a new style of play around that southpaw. You watch our smoke for the next three years, Rissy."

Samboy now addressed the departing warriors.

" All right boys — last frame and two to the good. All you have to do is hold 'em."

Now it appeared that Phil had been saving the finest joke of all for the end. The season was over and he could take liberties with his arm. He dug his warts and bumps and callouses into the horsehide and proceeded to retire the side with three straight strike-outs, nine rowdy laughs, two informal dances, and an incredible noise that was a hideous parody on song.

But it was an altered and sobered Phil who found his old coach after the game and received his congratulations.

" Were you worried, Phil? " Mr. Huckley asked.

" Yes, but I was glad they let me play. I had so much fun I forgot my trouble."

" What trouble, Phil? "

" Well, I got a letter from father this morning and my Dolly is terribly sick. Seems she got hold of an old paint can someplace. Cows like to lick paint, you know, and it's deadly poison. They don't think Dolly will live. Maybe I left a can of paint somewhere myself. That's what bothers me."

"Listen, Phil, I was supposed to tell you but you got away too quick. Your father telephoned me this morning Dolly's out of danger. She's doing fine."

"Oh, boy!" cried Phil, and his eyes shone with tears.

Down in the field the Sparta students, led by the band, were circling the stadium in that parade of victory which must follow every triumph over Athens.

"There'll be plenty more ball games," cried Phil, "but there'll never be another cow like Dolly."

THINK BACK OVER WHAT YOU HAVE READ

The following topics, which will help you appreciate the leading character, offer possibilities either for class discussion or for special topics. With what illustrations can you develop the topic of your choice?

1. Phil — a most amusing baby
2. his abiding interest in cows
3. his odd appearance
4. his amusing eccentricities
5. the secret of his popularity
6. his genius for laughter
7. his playing baseball just for the fun of it
8. the way he won friends

Stories of Adventure

ON THE DODGE

by Will James (1892–)

There is a bit of the outlaw in everyone. That's why certain legendary figures like Robin Hood are almost universally popular. And that's why legends grow up around such figures as cowboys and pirates. For lurking in human nature is the common desire to be independent, to trust to our own wits, and to make our own decisions without interference of the law. Such a secret, only half-expressed desire is part of our selfhood, part of nature's endowment on us as individuals who are expected to perform not only as followers but now and then as leaders.

In modern times the demands of group life have increased markedly, and it grows more and more difficult for the individual to exercise his own judgment freely. And so in imagination he turns back to the "good old days" when there were fewer rules to follow, back to the days of the open frontier when man relied on his own prowess, back to the role of cowboy or scout or plainsman such as our forefathers played.

In the story that follows you are to play the role of cowboy — or, perhaps, of a brown-eyed rancher's daughter who is partial to cowboys, if they are quick-witted and brave. Their adventure becomes your adventure, and for the time being you will be riding a mountain trail, with a posse hot in pursuit, while your thoughts turn back to the girl who saddled your horse and provided "jerky" and rice, with a "cup throwed in to cook and eat it out of." Herein lies the thrill of the story: the thrill of adventure, the thrill of temporary escape from a humdrum life.

The story is written by a real cowboy who writes as cowboys talk. If you like this story, perhaps you will ask for the book from which it is taken — *Sun Up: Stories of the Cow-camps* — next time you go to the library.

I'D HEARD a few shots the night before, and I had a hunch they was being *exchanged;* but as the deer season was open and the town dudes was out for 'em, I just figgered maybe a couple of bucks had made their last jump, and I let it go at that.

The next morning when I went to run in the ponies for a fresh horse to do the day's riding on, I finds that my big buckskin was missing, my own horse, and one of the best I ever rode. I makes another circle of the pasture and comes to a gate at one corner and stops. On the ground, plain as you wanted to see, was bootmarks where some *hombre* [1] had got off to open the gate and lead my buckskin through.

I sure knowed my horse's tracks when I saw 'em, 'cause in shoeing him I'd always take care to round the shoe aplenty so it'd protect the frog when running through the rocks. I'd recognize that round hoofprint anywheres, and I wasn't apt to forget the spike-heel bootmark either.

I remembers the shots I'd heard, and I wonders if my horse missing that way wasn't on account of somebody being after somebody else and one of 'em, needing a fresh horse right bad, just "borrowed" mine.

Well, I thinks he must of needed him worse than I did, and I sure give him credit for knowing a good horse when he sees one, but I wasn't going to part with my buckskin that easy.

I runs the other horses in the corral and snares me the best one the company had, opens the gate, and straddles him on the jump. Out we go, him a-bucking and a-bawling and tearing down the brush. I didn't get no fun out of his actions that morning — I was in too big a hurry — and when I started to get rough, he lined out like the good horse he was.

I picks up the tracks of the horse thief out of the fence [2] a ways, gets the lay of where he'd headed, and rides on like I was trying to head a bunch of mustangs. About a mile on his trail I comes across a brown saddle horse looking like he'd been sat on fast and steady, and says to my own brown as we ride by like a comet, "Looks like that *hombre* sure did need a fresh horse."

I'm heading down a draw on a high lope, wondering why that feller in the lead never tried to cover his tracks, when I hear somebody holler, and so close that I figgered they must of heard me coming and laid for me. I had no choice when I was told to hold 'em up, and that I done.

My thirty-thirty was took away from me; then the whole bunch, that I reckoned to be a posse, circled around and a couple searched me for a six-gun without luck. "Do you recognize that horse, any of you?" asked the one I took to be the sheriff. "Sure looks like the same one," answers a few, and one goes further to remark that my build and clothes sure tallies up with the description.

"Where do you come from and where was you headed in such a hurry?" asks the sheriff.

"I'm from the cow-camp on Arrow Springs," I says, "and I'm headed on the trail of somebody who stole my horse last night." And riding ahead with half a dozen carbines pointed my way, I shows 'em the trail I was following. "Most likely one of our men," one of 'em says; and the sheriff backs him with, "Yes, we just let a man go a while back."

"The devil you say!" I busts in, getting peeved at being held back that way. "Do you think you house plants can tell me anything about this track or any other tracks? What's more," I goes on, getting red in the face, "I can show you where I started following it, and where whoever stole my horse left his wore-out pony in the place of mine." [3]

"Now, don't get rambunctious, young feller. Tracks is no evidence in court nohow; and if I'm lucky enough to get you there without you decorating a limb [4] on the way, that's all I care. Where was you night before last?" he asks sudden.

"At the camp, cooking a pot of *frijoles*; and bedded there afterward," I answers just as sudden.

"Fine for you so far, but is there any-

[1] **hombre:** the Spanish word for man or fellow.
[2] **fence:** refers here to the corral.

[3] Do you remember the brown saddle horse mentioned five paragraphs back? [4] Guess what **decorating a limb** refers to.

body up at the camp who can prove you *was* there?"

"No, I'm there alone and keeping tab on a herd of dry stuff[1]; but if you'll go to the home ranch, the foreman'll tell you how he hired me some two weeks back, if that'll do any good."

"I'm afraid it won't," he says. "That wouldn't prove anything on your whereabouts the time of the holdup. Your appearance and your horse are against you; you're a stranger in these parts, and the evidence points your way; and till your innocence is proved, I'll have to hold you on the charge of murder along with the robbery of the Torreon County Bank."

That jarred my thoughts a considerable, and it's quite a spell before I can round 'em to behave once more. The whole crowd is watching the effect of what the sheriff just said, and I don't aim to let 'em think I was rattled any. I showed about as much expression as a gambling Chink and finally remarks:

"I reckon you ginks has got to get *somebody* for whatever's been pulled off; and it sure wouldn't look right to go back empty-handed, would it?" I says as I sized up the bunch.

A couple of the men are sent toward my camp to look for evidence, and two others start on the trail I was following, which leaves the sheriff and three men to escort me to town some sixty miles away.

I'm handcuffed; my reins are took away from me, and one of the men is leading my horse. We travel along at a good gait, and I'm glad nobody's saying much; it gives me a chance to think, and right at that time I was making more use out of that think-tank of mine than I thought I'd ever need to. I knowed I couldn't prove that I was at my camp the night of the holdup, and me being just a drifting cowboy happening to drop in the country at the wrong time looked kinda bad for suspicious folks.

After sundown when we strike a fence and finally come to a ranch house, I was noticing a couple of the men was slopping all over their saddles and getting mighty tired; but I only had feelings for the tired horses that had to pack 'em. One of 'em suggests that they'd better call it a day and stop at the ranch for the night, and we rides in, me feeling worse than a trapped coyote.

I'm gawked at by all hands as we ride up; and I'm not at all pleased when I see one *hombre* in the family crowd that I do know, 'cause the last time I seen him I'd caught him blotting the brand on a critter belonging to the company I was riding for and putting his own iron in the place of it.[2] I was always kind of peaceable and kept it to myself, but between him and me I offered to bet him that if he'd like to try it again I could puncture him and stand off five hundred yards while I was doing it. I'd never seen him since till now.

He gives me a kind of a mean look and I sees he's pleased to notice that I'm being took in for something. They hadn't heard of the holdup as yet, but it wasn't long till the news was spread.

Between bites of the bait that was laid before us, the sheriff took it onto hisself to tell all about it. I was interested to hear what was said, 'cause the details of the holdup was news to me too, and what was most serious was that the two masked bandits killed one man, and another wasn't expected to live; they'd got away with about ten thousand dollars. The womenfolks sure kept a long ways from me after that.

The conversation was just about at its

[1] **keeping tab on a herd of dry stuff:** slang for raising crops rather than cowpunching or horse wrangling.

[2] **putting his own iron in the place of it:** changing the brand.

worst, for me, when the door opened and in walked a young lady, the prettiest young lady I remember ever seeing. All hands turned their heads her direction as she walked in, and the talk was checked for a spell.

"One of the family," I figgers as she makes her way to the other ladyfolks. I hears some low talk and feels accusing fingers pointing my way. In the meantime the sheriff and his men had cleared most everything that was fit to eat off the table; one of the ladies inquires if they'd like more, but none seemed to worry if *I* had my fill.

I glances where I figger the young lady to be, and instead of getting a scornful glance, as I'd expected, I finds a look in her eyes that's not at all convinced that I could of done all that was said; and a few minutes later there's more warm spuds and roast beef hazed[1] over *my* shoulder, and I knowed the hand that done the hazing was none other than that same young lady's.

From then on, the rest of the talk that was soaring to the rafters about me being so desperate was just like so much wind whistling through the pines. I could see nothing and feel nothing but two brown eyes, pretty and understanding brown eyes.

Arrangements was made for a room upstairs; and as the sheriff took the lead, me and the deputies following, I glanced at the girl once more, and as I went up the stairs I carried with me visions of a pretty face with a hint of a smile.

The three deputies unrolled a roundup bed that was furnished, and jumped in together; the sheriff and me took possession of a fancier bed with iron bedsteads. My wrist was handcuffed to his and we made ourselves comfortable as much as we could under the circumstances.

[1] **hazed:** cowboy slang for *brought in.* Bringing in stray cattle was called *hazing.*

A lot of trouble was made, before the lamp was blowed out, to show there was no use me trying to get away.

In turning over, my fingers come acrost a little mohair rope I used for belt and emergency "piggin' string" (rope to tie down cattle). It was about six feet long, and soft.

The three deputies, after being in the cold all day and coming in a warm house tired and getting away with all that was on the table, was plumb helpless, and they soon slept and near raised the roof with the snoring they done.

The sheriff, having more responsibility, was kind of restless; but after what seemed a couple of hours he was also breathing like he never was going to wake up, leaving me a-thinking and a-thinking.

The girl's face was in my mind through all what I thought; and the hint of her smile was like a spur a-driving me to prove that she was right in the stand she'd took. There was three reasons why I should get away and try to get the guilty parties: one was to get my good old buckskin back; another was to clear myself; but the main one, even though I didn't realize it sudden, was the girl.

If the guilty parties wasn't found, I knowed I'd most likely take the place of one of 'em. I just had to clear myself somehow, and the only way was to break loose to do it.

I was still fingering the piggin' string at my belt. I couldn't see the window and concludes it must be pitch-dark outside. A coyote howled, and the dogs barked an answer.

"Wonder if I can make it?" And something inside tells me that I'd *better* make it, and now, or I'd never have another chance.

The sheriff acts kinda fidgety as I try to ease my piggin' string under his neck. I lays quiet a while and tries it again, and about that time he turns over just right and lays over that string as though I'd asked him to. His turning over that way scared me, so that I didn't dare move for a spell; but finally I reach over and grab the end of the string that was sticking out on the other side, makes a slipknot, and puts the other end of the string around a steel rod of the bedstead; and still hanging onto that end, I'm ready for action.

From then on, I don't keep things waiting. With my handcuffed arm, I gets a short hold on the string; and with my free arm, I gets a lock on the sheriff's other arm all at once. That sure wakes him up, but he can't holler or budge; and the more he pulls with the arm that's handcuffed to mine, the more that string around his neck is choking him. I whispers in his ear to tell me where I can get the keys for the handcuffs before I hang him to dry, and by listening close I hears, " In my money belt."

I had to let go of his arm to get that key; but before he had time to do anything, my fist connected with the point of his chin in a way that sure left him limp. I takes the handcuffs off my wrist, turns the sheriff over on his stomach, and relocks the handcuffs with his arms back of him, stuffs a piece of blanket in his mouth, and cutting the piggin' string in two, ties the muffler in place and uses the other piece to anchor his feet together.

The three deputies on the floor was still snoring away and plumb innocent of what was going on. I sneaks over to where I'd seen 'em lay my rifle, picks out an extra six-shooter out of the holster of one of the sleeping men, and heads to where I thought the window to be.

It was locked from the inside with a stick, and removing that, I raised it easy; and still easier I starts sliding out of the window and down as far as my arms lets me, and lets go.

I picks myself up in a bunch of dry weeds and heads for the corrals for anything I could find to ride. I'm making record time on the way and pretty near bumps into — somebody.

My borrowed six-shooter is pointed right at that somebody sort of natural, and before I can think —

" Don't shoot, cowboy," says a soft voice. " I knowed you'd come, and I been waiting for you. I got the best horse in the country saddled and ready; and if you can ride him, nothing can catch you."

I recognized the young lady; she came closer as she spoke and touched my arm.

" Follow me," she says, pulling on my shirt sleeve, and the tinkle of her spurs and the swish of her riding skirt sounded like so much mighty fine music as I trotted along.

But there was sounds of a commotion at the house. Either the weeds [1] had give me away or the sheriff come out of it. Anyway, a couple of lights was running through the house, doors was slamming, and pretty soon somebody fires a shot.

" Them folks sure have learnt to miss me quick," I remarks as we push open the corral gate. Then I'm up to the snorting pony in two jumps. I see he's hobbled and tied ready to fork [2]; and sticking my rifle through the rosadero,[3] I takes the hobbles off of him, lets him break away with me a-hanging to his side, and I mounts him flat-footed as he goes through the gate.

I was making a double getaway, one from the sheriff and the other from the girl. I knowed, the way I felt, it would have seemed mighty insulting for me to try and thank her with little words. I wanted to let her know somehow that *if* she ever wished to see me break my neck I'd do it *for her,* and with a smile.

[1] Can you see how the *weeds* could give him away? [2] **to fork:** as used here, to straddle or to mount. [3] **rosadero:** pack or bedroll.

"I sure thank you," I says as I passes her (which goes to prove that there's times when a feller often says things he wants to say least), but I had to say something.

The whole outfit was coming from the house. There was a couple more shots fired; and with the noise of the shots, my old pony forgot to take time to buck and lined out like a scared rabbit, me a-helping him all I could. We hit a barb-wire fence and went through it like them wires was threads, and went down the draw, over washouts and across creeks like it was all level country.

The old pony was stampeding,[1] and it was the first time in my life that I wanted a ride of that kind to last; and being that we was going the direction I wanted to go, I couldn't get there any too fast to suit me.

I'm quite a few miles away from the ranch when I decides I'd better pull up my horse if I wanted to keep him under me after daybreak, and that I did, but I managed to keep him at a stiff trot till a good twenty-five miles was between us and where we'd left.

Daybreak catches up with us a few miles farther on, and I figgers I'd better stop a while to let the pony feed and water. I takes a look over the way I just come, and being that I'm halfways up a mountain, I gets a good view of the valley; and if anybody is on my trail, I'd sure get to see 'em first and at a good ten miles away.

The little old pony buckles up and tries to kick me as I gets off, and not satisfied with that, takes a run on the hackamore rope[2] and tries to jerk away; but his kind of horseflesh was nothing new to me, and in a short while he was behaving and eating as though he knowed it was the best thing for him to do.

A good horse always did interest me, and as I'm off a-ways studying his eleven hundred pounds' worth of good points, I notices a sackful of something tied on the back of the saddle. "Wonder what it can be," I thinks out loud as I eases up to the horse and unties it. I opens the sack, and finds all that's necessary to the staff of life when traveling light and fast the way I was. There was "jerky"[3] and rice, salt and coffee, with a big tin plate and cup throwed in to cook and eat it out of.

"Daggone her little hide!" I says, grinning and a-trying to appreciate the girl's thoughtfulness. "Who'd ever thought it?"

I cooked me a bait in no time, and getting around on the outside of it, am able to appreciate life, freedom, and a good horse once again. And wanting to keep all that, I don't forget that these hills are full of possemen and that the other bunch at the ranch would soon be showing themselves on my trail. There was what I took to be a small whirlwind down on the flat. If it was a dust made by the posse, they'd sure made good time considering the short stretch of daylight they'd had to do any tracking by.

I takes another peek out on the flat before cinching up, and sure enough there was little dark objects bobbing up and down under that dust.

I had the lead on 'em by ten miles, and I knowed if I could get on my horse and was able to stick him that I'd soon lose 'em; but doing that away from the corral sure struck me as a two man's job. What I was afraid of most was him getting away from me; his neck was as hard to bend as a pine tree, and his jaw was like iron,[4]

[1] **stampeding:** usually said of a herd, and means running away in a panic. [2] **hackamore rope:** a special halter used for breaking horses.

[3] **jerky:** beef cut in strips and dried. [4] In other words, the horse was resisting with all his might.

but I had to get action, and mighty quick, 'cause the distance between me and them was getting shorter every minute.

It helped a lot that I'd hobbled him before he was rested up from the ride I'd give him that night, and taking the rope off the saddle, I passes one end of it through the hobble and tied it. About then the old pony lets out a snort and he passes me like a blue streak. I just has time to straighten up, give a flip to the rope that was running through my hands, follow it a couple of jumps, and get set.

My heels was buried out of sight when the stampeding pony hits the end and the rope tightens up; he made a big jump in the air and as his front feet are jerked out from under him he lands in a heap and makes the old saddle pop. I follows the rope up to him, keeping it tight so's he can't get his feet back under him, and before he knows it I've got him tied down solid.

I takes a needed long breath and looks out on the flat once more; there's no time to waste, that I can see; them little dark objects of a while ago had growed a heap bigger and was a-bobbin up and down faster than ever. I straightens up my stirrups, gets as much of the saddle under me as I can, and twists the pony's head so's to hold him down till I'm ready to let him up, and starts to take the rope off his feet.

He knows it the minute he's free, and is up like a shot; he keeps on getting up till I can near see the angels, and when he hit the earth again he lit a-running — and straight toward the posse and the ranch.

I tries to haze and turn him with my hat, but he'd just duck out from under it and go on the same way. So far he didn't act as though he wanted to take the time to buck with me, and I'd been glad of it, but now we just had to come to a turning point and the only way I seen was to scratch it out of him.

Screwing down on my saddle as tight as I could, I brings one of my ten-point "hooks" right up along his neck far as I could reach and drags it back. That sure stirred up the dynamite in him of a sudden, and I had a feeling that the cantle of my saddle was a fast mail train and I was on the track; but he turned, and as luck would have it I was still with him. He kept on a-turning and all mixed in with his sunfishing and side-winding[1] sure made it a puzzle to tell which was heads or tails.

What worried me most was the fear of being set afoot, and I'd been putting up a *safe* ride on that account, but that old pony wasn't giving me a fair deal. He fought his head too much, and I was getting tired of his fooling. I reaches down, gets a shorter holt on the hackamore rope, and lets him have it, both rowels a-working steady — and two wildcats tied by the tail and throwed across the saddle couldn't of done any more harm.

We sure made a dust of our own out there on the side of that mountain, and I'd enjoyed the fight more if things had of been normal; but they wasn't, and I had the most to lose. The little horse finally realized that, the way I went at him, 'cause pretty soon his bucking got down to crowhopping and gradually settled down to a long run up the slope of the mountain. That young lady was sure right when she said that if I could ride him nothing could catch me.

He was pretty well winded when we got to the top, but I could see he was a long ways from tired; and letting him jog along easy, we started down into a deep canyon.

My mind is set on tracking down the feller what stole my buckskin horse, and I figgers the way I'm heading I'll some-

[1] **sunfishing and side-winding:** picturesque terms used in connection with bronchos, meaning bucking and side-stepping.

time come across his trail, but I'd like mighty well to shake loose from that bunch chasing me before I get much farther; and thinking strong on that, I spots a bunch of mustangs [1] a mile or so to my left, and there was my chance to leave a mighty confusing trail for them that was following.

I sneaks up out of sight and above the "fuzztails" [2]; and when I am a few hundred yards off, I shows up sudden over a ridge and heads their way. I let out a full-grown war whoop as I rides down on 'em, and it sure don't take the wild ones long to make distance from that spot.

My horse being barefooted and his hoofs wore smooth, his tracks blend in natural with that of the mustangs, and I keeps him right in the thick of 'em. The wild ones makes a half circle which takes me out of my way some; but I'm satisfied to follow, seeing that it also takes me on the outskirts of where I figgered some of the posse outfit might be.

My horse was ganting up and getting tired, but them wild ponies ahead kept him wanting to catch up; and me holding him down to a steady long lope made him all the more anxious to get there with 'em. I was wishing I could stop to let him feed and rest a while, but I didn't dare to just yet; my trail wasn't covered up well enough.

The sun is still an hour high when the wild ones I was following came out of the junipers and lined out across a little valley. I figgers I'm a good seventy-five miles from where I made my getaway; and even though my horse hates to have the mustangs leave him behind, he's finally willing to slow down to a walk. I rubs his sweaty neck and tells him what a good horse he is, and for the first time I notice his ears are in a slant that don't show meanness.

The wild ones run ahead and plumb out of sight; the sun had gone over the hill, and it was getting dark, and on the back trail I don't see no sign of any posse. Still following the trail the mustangs had left, I begins to look for a place where I can branch off; and coming across a good-sized creek, I turns my horse up it into the mountains.

"Old pony," I says to my horse as we're going along in the middle of the stream, "if that posse is within twenty miles of us, they're sure well mounted; and what's more," I goes on, "if they can tell our tracks from all the fresh tracks we've left scattered through the country behind, in front, and all directions, why, they can do a heap more than any human I know of."

I'm a couple of miles up the mountain and still following the stream, when a good grassy spot decides me to make camp. The little horse only flinches as I get off this time, and he don't offer to jerk away. I pulls the saddle off, washes his back with cool water and hobbles him on the tall grass, where he acts plumb contented to stay and feed.

Clouds are piling up over the mountain; it's getting cold and feels like winter coming on. I builds me a small Injun fire, cooks me up a bait, and rolling a smoke, stretches out.

"Some girl," I caught myself saying as I throwed my dead cigarette away. . . . The little horse rolled out a snort the same as to say, "All is well," and pretty soon I'm not of the world no more.

It's daylight when a daggone magpie hollers out and makes me set up, and I wonders as I stirs up the coffee what's on the program for today. My horse acts real docile as I saddles him up; he remembers when I give his neck a rub that it pays to be good.

[1] **mustangs:** wild horses. Refer to page 252 in this connection. [2] **fuzztails:** the mustangs he had just "spotted."

I crosses on one side of a mountain pass and on over a couple of ridges and down into another valley of white sage and hard-pan. I don't feel it safe to come out in the open and cross that valley, so I keeps to the edge close to the foothills and junipers.

My horse, picking his way on the rocky trail, jars a boulder loose and starts it down to another bigger boulder that's just waiting for that much of an excuse to start rolling down to the bottom of the canyon; a good many more joins in, and a noise echoes up that can be heard a long ways.

As the noise of the slide dies down, I hears a horse nicker, and it sounds not over five hundred yards away. I didn't give my horse a chance to answer, and a hunch makes me spur up out of the canyon and over the ridge. I was afraid of the dust I'd made in getting over the ridge.

I'm splitting the breeze down a draw; and looking back over my shoulder, I'm just in time to get the surprise of my life. A whole string of riders are topping the ridge I'd just went over, and here they come heading down on me hell-bent for election. I know it's them, and I know they seen my dust; and worse yet, I know they're on fresh horses.

"Now," I asks the scenery, "how in Sam Hill do you reckon for them to be in this perticular country, and so quick?" And the only answer I could make out was that when I struck the mustangs and put too many tracks in front of 'em for 'em to follow, they just trusted to luck and cut acrost to where they thought I'd be heading.

My only way out is speed, and my pony is giving me all he can of that; but it's beginning to tell on him, and I don't like the way he hits the other side of the wash-outs we come across.

A bullet creases the bark off a piñon not far to my right; another raises the dust closer, and even though I sure hated to, I had to start using the spurs. The little horse does his final best, and I begins to notice that the bullets are falling short, and it ain't long when I'm out of range of 'em.

"Old-timer," I says to my tired horse as we're drifting along, "if you only had a few hours' rest, we'd sure make them *hombres* back of us wonder how thin air could swallow us so quick."

We tops a rise in the foothills, and ahead of us is a bunch of mustangs. They evaporate quick, leaving a big cloud of dust. They can't do me any good this time; my horse is too far gone; but I thinks of another way and proceeds to act.

I reaches over, takes the hackamore off my horse's head, and begins to loosen the latigo. My pony'd took heart to keep up the speed a while longer, on account of them wild ones ahead and wanted to catch up with 'em.

My saddle cinch is loose and a-flapping to one side; my chance comes as we go through a thick patch of buckbrush, and I takes advantage of it. I slides off my horse and takes my saddle with me; the old pony has nothing on him but the sweat where my saddle'd been. There's mustangs ahead, and with a snort and a shake of his tail he bids me good-by and disappears.

About that time me and my "riggin'"[1] ain't to be seen no more; and when the posse rides by on the trail my horse'd left, there was a big granite boulder and plenty of buckbrush to keep me hid, and looking straight ahead for a dust, the sheriff and his three men kept right on a-going.

But I figgered they'd be back, sometime, and thinks I'd better be a-moving. I hangs my saddle up a piñon tree, leaves

[1] **"riggin'"**: picturesque for saddle.

most of the grub with it, and, tearing up the gunny sack that was around it, proceeds to pad up my feet so they'd leave as little track as possible. Then I picks up my rifle and heads up toward a high point on the mountain where I could get the lay of the country.

I'm on what seems to be a high rocky ledge, and looking around for some shelter in it from the cold wind, and where I can hole up for the night, I comes to the edge of *nothing* — and stops short!

Another step, and I'd went down about three hundred feet; a fire at the bottom of it showed me how deep it was, and by that fire was two men; maybe they're deer hunters, I thinks. I keeps a-sizing up the outfit, and then I spots three hobbled ponies feeding to one side a ways, and there amongst 'em was my good old buckskin. I'd recognize his two white front feet and his bald face anywheres.

I'm doing some tall figgering by then, and I has a hunch that before daybreak I'll be well mounted again and on my own horse. Seeing that my rifle was in good working order, I slides down off my perch to where going down is easier and surer of a foothold. I'm down about halfways, and peeking through a buckbrush, I gets a better look at them two *hombres* by the fire. The more I size 'em up, the surer I gets of my suspicions.

I'm close enough to see that one of the men is about my build; and not only that, but it looks like he had on my clothes. The other man I couldn't make much out of — he was laying down on his face as though he was asleep; but I could see he was some stouter and shorter.

Well, all appearances looked a safe bet to me, and beating my own shadow for being noiseless, I gets to within a hundred feet of 'em.

"Stick 'em up," I says quiet and steady for fear of their nerves being on edge and stampeding with 'em. One of 'em flinches some but finally reaches for the sky, the other that's laying down don't move, and I warns him that playing 'possom don't go with me; but threatening didn't do no good there. I'm told that he's wounded and out of his head — I remember the sheriff saying that one of the men had been wounded, which altogether tallied up fine as these being the men *me* and the sheriff wanted.

"Take his hands away from his belt and stretch 'em out where I can see 'em then," I says, not wanting to take the chance. That done, I walks over toward 'em and stops, keeping the fire between. I notice that the man laying has no gun on or near him; the other feller with his arms still up is packing two of 'em, and I makes him shed them by telling him to unbuckle his cartridge belt.

I backs him off at the point of my rifle and goes to reaching for the dropped belt and six-guns, when from behind and too close for comfort somebody sings out for me to drop my rifle and reach for the clouds. I does that plenty quick, and looking straight ahead like I'm told to, I see a grin spreading all over the face of the man I'd just held up a minute ago.

"Where does this third party come in?" thinks I. My six-shooter is jerked out of my belt as I try to figger a way out, and is throwed out of reach along with my rifle; and then of a sudden the light of the fire in front of me was snuffed out, and with a sinking feeling all went dark. . . .

When I come to again, I hear somebody groaning, and I tries to get my think-tank working; my head feels about the size of a washtub, and sore. Whatever that *hombre* hit me with sure wasn't no feather pillow. I tries to raise a hand and finds they're both tied; so is my feet, and about all I can move is my eyelashes. Things come back to me gradual, and stargazing at the sky I notice it's getting daybreak.

Hearing another groan, I manages to turn my head enough to see the same *hombre* that'd been laying there that night and in the same position. I hears the other two talking, off a ways. It sounds by the squeak of saddle leather that they're getting ready to move, and that sure wakes me up to action.

I know I can't afford to let 'em get away, and I sure won't. Raising up far as I can, I hollers for one of 'em to come over a minute. There's some cussing heard; but soon enough here comes the tallest one, and he don't no more than come near me when I asks him to give me a chance to loosen up my right boot, that my sprained ankle was bothering me terrible.

"You needn't think you can pull anything over on me," he says sarcastic. He sizes my boot up a while and then remarks, "But I'll let you pull 'em both off. I need a new pair."

My arms and feet are free, but awful stiff; he's standing off a few feet, and with rifle ready for action is watching me like a hawk while I'm fidgeting around with my right boot; I gets my right hand inside of it as though to feel my ankle, but what I was feeling for mostly was a gun I'd strapped in there.

(When I started out on the trail of my buckskin I figgered on getting him; I also figgered on running acrost somebody riding him that'd be a gunman, and I'd prepared to compete with all the tricks of the gun-toter. This gun in my boot was what I called *my hole card.*[1])

My foot is up and toward him, and I'm putting on a lot of acting while getting hold of the handle and pulling back the hammer; but I manages that easy enough and, squeezing my finger toward the trigger, I pulls.

That shot paralyzed him, and down he come. He'd no more than hit the ground when I falls on the rifle he'd dropped, and I starts pumping lead the direction of the other feller. His left arm was bandaged and tied up, but he was sure using his right so that our shots was passing one another halfways and regular. . . . Then I felt a pain in my left shoulder. I begins to get groggy — and pretty soon all is quiet once more.

I must of been disconnected from my thoughts for quite a spell, 'cause when I come to this time the sun is way high. I straightens up to look around and recollect things, and it all came back some as I gets a glimpse of my buckskin feeding off a ways.

My shoulder's stiff and sore, but feeling around for the harm the bullet has done, I finds I'd just been creased,[2] and being weak on account of not having anything under my belt either in the line of grub or moisture for the last twenty-four hours, that bullet was enough to knock me out.

I'm hankering for a drink right bad and starts looking for it on all fours, when in my rambling I comes across a shadow, and looking right hard, I can make out horse's hoofs, then his legs, and on up to a party sitting on top of him and looking down at me. The warm sun had made me weak again, and I quits right there.

Somebody's pouring cool water down me; and when I opens my eyes again, I feels better control of 'em. I'm asked when I et last and I can't seem to remember; then I gets a vision of a pot of coffee, and flapjacks, smells frying bacon, and the dream that I'm eating evaporates with the last bite.

"Well, I see you found your buckskin," says a voice right close, and recognizing that voice makes me take notice of things. It was the sheriff's; the posse'd rode in on me.

[1] **hole card:** gambling slang for weapon held in reserve.

[2] **creased:** wounded, slightly, from a shot; a term applied ordinarily to animals.

"And by the signs around here," the same voice goes on, "it looks like you just got here in time and had to do a heap of shooting in order to get him, but I'm sure glad to see you did, 'cause along with that horse you got the two men we wanted for the robbery, which makes you free to go. No mistake this time."

That last remark brought real life to me, and interested again, I takes a look around. The two men was setting against a rock looking mighty weak and shot up. I looks for the third, and I'm told that he was being took in to the nearest ranch for care he was needing mighty bad.

"How does he come to be with these *hombres?*" I asks.

"He's a government serviceman out after these two outlaws," says the sheriff, "and your dropping in when you did is all that saved him — if we hadn't heard your shot, we'd never found this hole, and he'd been left to feed the buzzards."

Not wanting to hog all the credit, I says, "I've sure got to hand it to you too — for camping on a feller's trail the way you do; it wasn't at all comfortable."

"Neither is a piggin' string around a feller's neck," comes back the sheriff, smiling.

It's after sundown as I tops a ridge and stops my buckskin. Out across a big sage and hardpan flat is a dust stirred up by the posse and their prisoners. I watches it a spell, and starting down the other side of the ridge, I remarks, "Buck, old horse, I'm glad you and me are naturally peaceable, 'cause being that way not only saves us from a lot of hard traveling, but it's a heap easier on a feller's think-tank."

The evening star looks near as big as the moon as I glances up to keep my bearings straight; I finds myself gazing at it, and then comes a time when my vision is plumb past it, a vision of two brown eyes and a hint of a smile.

Then the buckskin shook himself and at the same time shook me back to realizing that I was on a horse.

"Someday soon we're going visiting, Buck," I says, coming to; and untangling the knots out of my pony's mane as I rides, I heads him up the trail back to the cow camp on Arrow Springs.

THINK BACK OVER WHAT YOU HAVE READ

Enjoying the Role of Cowboy

1. Come to class prepared to share with your classmates interesting examples of the following appealing traits of the cowboy found in the story you have just read:

a. quick-witted resourcefulness
b. keen observation
c. good sportsmanship
d. bravery and daring
e. gallantry

Appreciating the Story Pattern

How does this story conform to the typical "Western" which you see on the screen? The following questions will help you decide:

2. What is Jim's predicament at the opening of the story? What element has it in common with other stories of its type? What element has it in common with what we would all like to believe about the less spectacular predicaments we ourselves get into?

3. In what way does the sheriff in the story run true to type, as found in Western movies? What common, secret wish do you think he represents? Can you tell? Suppose he had been a wise, understanding sheriff: Would he have "spoiled" the story? Why?

4. How much of a part does luck play in the story? How much does luck play in daydreams? Can you put two and two together and come to any conclusion about why people *like* to believe in luck? In the story what was the hero's greatest piece of luck? In what way does it conform to the kind of luck you always have in daydreams and seldom have in real life?

Recognizing the Kind of Language Used in the Story

Nowadays stories are written in language that is appropriate to the purpose of the story, and characters are allowed to speak as they would in real life. You will have occasion to reckon with this fact in your reading of other stories in this section of the book. This does not mean, however, that the author of a story himself uses that kind of language or intends his readers to believe that he recommends it to them. He offers it, rather, as a kind of faithful sample of the way certain people talk.

In the story you have just read, two qualities may be recognized: (1) grammatical inaccuracy and (2) picturesque slang. Both of these qualities offer an interesting opportunity for class discussion. The following questions will help you identify them:

5. What error in the use of tense runs through the whole story? What other errors in the use of tense can you cite?

6. How would you correct the cowboy's use of adjectives and adverbs? To what errors would you point?

7. Which of your own careless errors in speech does the hero frequently make?

8. What kind of sentences does the cowboy use? Would they be acceptable to your teacher? Why not? Cite examples of sentence building that you regard as faulty from the point of view of educated speech.

9. What words can you identify as cowboy slang?

10. What picturesque phrases testify to keen senses on the part of the cowboy?

THE WHITE TIGER

by Samuel Scoville, Jr. (*1872–*)

This is a story of strange adventure far away among the brown-skinned people of Malay. You will be impressed, as you read, by the beauty of the jungle setting: the rich coloring of birds and reptiles, the haunting sounds of night, and the lithesome grace of man and beast. The hero of the story is a young girl, quick-witted and fearless in a moment of great danger.

The story is taken from a book entitled *Man and Beast,* a book in which its author, Samuel Scoville, Jr., reveals, as in this story, his ardent love of nature.

NOT SINCE the days when Solomon's navy sailed to Tarshish [1] and brought back gold and silver and ivory and apes and peacocks has the Malay Peninsula [2] changed. Still the swift, silent little men of the deep forest snare great, jeweled peacocks and trap the langurs [3] of the high treetops with hollow gourds; still the seladang,[4] the tiger, the rhinoceros, and the python contend for the mastery of the jungle, and still the Semarang, the Little People, rule them all by virtue of that spark of the eternal flame which makes man the lord of the beast.

There in the jungle one night, when the white moonlight filtered through the treetops like melting snow, Teloa was born. Mala, her mother, was a woman of the Semarang, and she named her daughter after that rose-and-gold orchid, Teloa, Star of the Forest.

Fourteen wonderful years the girl lived in the jungle with her tribe, wild and free as the sambur [5] whose belling aroused her at dawn. Her days were full of little, happy adventures. Sometimes it was the finding of a crimson hibiscus flower which she thrust into the great coil of blue-black hair which came down low over her forehead or wore in the sarong [6] of plaited bark which covered a skin like pale-gold satin. Other days she hunted the jungle for "lansat," that white fruit of the deep woods, and mangosteens [7] and custard apples, or caught para, sluggish, fruit-eating fish, out of still pools, and snared mouse deer for pets.

Always, too, there was Nion, the son of the chief of her little band. It was he who taught her to walk up the tallest trees, leaning against a twist of liana [8] about her waist, and to imitate the call of the rainbirds whose notes fall from the

[1] **Tarshish:** an ancient Phoenician maritime province in southwestern Spain. The reference here is to I Kings 10:22 and II Chron. 9:21.

[2] **Malay Peninsula:** the south tip of the Asiatic mainland. [3] **langurs:** a species of long-tailed monkeys. [4] **seladang:** the wild buffalo. [5] **sambur:** the Asiatic deer. [6] **sarong:** the native dress, a kind of petticoat tucked round the waist. [7] **mangosteens:** a tropical fruit, orangelike in appearance, whose flavor suggests both the peach and the pineapple. [8] **liana:** a climbing plant.

treetops like drops of molten silver. Together they caught bird-wing butterflies with velvet-black and emerald wings, and minivets [1] like flames of fire in the forest, and trogons [2] with blue backs and crimson breasts.

Then came the raid of the Pehang Malays, who had their village at the edge of the jungle. They owed allegiance to the Sultan of Parak and every year had to deliver to him as tribute either two slaves or two elephant tusks. As it was safer to hunt men than elephants, slavers annually invaded the jungle of the Semarang.

It all happened at dawn. One moment the forest was velvet-black, starred with the white blossoms of the moonflowers, while the vines hung in dim green webs against the sepia shadows of the trees. Then, like the opening of the door of some vast furnace, the risen sun flamed through the darkness, and the silence was shattered by a thousand voices of bird and beast. Near where the Semarang slept by their banked fires, with only the smoke for a coverlet, sounded the yelling, ringing challenge of an argus pheasant. At once it was answered from all three sides of the camping place. The notes had hardly died away before the grizzled old leader of the band leaped to his feet like a cat, as his trained ears caught something unusual in the call.

" Up, up, brothers! " he hissed. " The hunters of men be upon us."

Even as he spoke, every one of the little company was on his feet, with the swift silence of startled animals, just as the fierce " sorak," that war cry of the Malays, sounded, and from all sides the raiders rushed upon them. Like a covey of quail the forestfolk scattered. Some dived into the thickets; others went up the dangling lianas hand over hand. None stayed to fight. Teloa waited an instant to lend a hand to the wrinkled old grandmother whom she had been helping. Even as she thrust her into safety in the densest part of a thorn thicket, an arm like a steel band wound about her waist; and a second later a rope was twisted tight around her wrists. Nion sprang at the man, but another slaver slashed at him with a barong, that deadly Malay knife. A swinging liana broke the force of the blow; yet the boy's brown skin was suddenly laced with crimson, and Teloa's last memory of him, as he disappeared among the treetops, was of a face distorted with pain and grief.

A moment later everything went black before her straining eyes, and she knew nothing more until she found herself in the house of old Ahmad, one of the elders of the Malay village, where she was to be kept until the Sultan sent for the tribute. There, although not ill-used, she was watched every moment, day and night, and spent most of her time on a tiny platform of bamboos hung from the ceiling in a corner, like a swallow's nest.

Soon after her arrival came the were-tiger. It was old Ahmad himself who first glimpsed the dreadful visitor. He was following a twisting path through the jungle when suddenly a peacock stepped out into a clearing ahead of him, its breast a blaze of emerald and sapphire. Ahmad crouched back of a bush, while the regal bird spread its tail, and with its crested head held high, moved slowly forward. Spread out across the trail before it lay what seemed a strip from an Eastern rug, ringed and blotched with chocolate-brown, yellow, and clove-black. At the end of that carpet of death showed the flat, cruel head and deadly eyes of the fatal " Tic polonga," the Russell's viper, dreaded by man and beast alike throughout all Malaysia.

As the jeweled bird approached, the serpent seemed to become imbued with

[1] **minivets:** tropical birds of brilliant plumage.
[2] **trogons:** another species of tropical birds.

a sudden malignant life, and throwing its mottled five-foot body into a mass of irregular coils, hissed fiercely, while its eyes shone like black diamonds.

There are few creatures who will dare the death which lurks within the grim jaws of a Russell's viper. The peacock, however, is one of those few, and that one strode on without stopping. As it came nearer, the snake's jaws gaped; its movable fangs thrust themselves out like curved spear points, and a second later its flat head struck the peacock's padded breast with a thump. A single coruscating feather floated slowly to the ground, and the next instant the bird had gripped the thick coils tightly in its strong, sharp claws. Again and again the great snake struck, but each time its fangs failed to pierce the thick layer of feathers which sheathed the bird's breast. Then, as the cruel jaws opened for a third time, the peacock seemed suddenly to lose patience and with a single swift movement of its steel-like talons ripped the viper's head from its squat body as a man might tear apart a piece of paper.

A moment later, as the gleaming jungle fowl began to feed upon the serpent's white flesh, Ahmad crept forward, foot by foot; for the peacock is one of the prizes of the jungle, and the range of his old blunderbuss was strictly limited. Then, even as he raised his clumsy weapon, he saw something which struck from his mind everything save an overpowering desire to be elsewhere. Between himself and the unconscious bird was suddenly thrust from the underbrush the sinister head of a great tiger. Old Ahmad had seen tigers before and in his youth had even helped to hunt them, but never a tiger like that one. Once or twice in a century there is born in the jungles of the Malay Peninsula a white tiger, one of those rare albinos which occur among all mammals. Such a one crept out, foot by foot, before the old man's startled eyes. Instead of being orange-yellow with black stripes, the great beast was cream-white from the tip of his muzzle to the end of his tail, and the stripes on his body showed like the watered pattern of moiré silk.

Crouching double, the old hunter crept back along the trail just as the tiger sprang upon the gleaming bird. Although the beast was a good ten feet long and weighed half a thousand pounds, it rose in the air light as thistledown. There was one terrified squawk from the peacock, and the next moment, with its brilliant body in his jaws, the tiger disappeared in a near-by thicket.

As soon as he reached a bend in the trail, Ahmad straightened up and ran like the wind toward the village, where he spread the news that a white tiger was abroad. That evening, as the men of the tribe gossiped beneath the great baobab [1] tree which stood in the center of the market place, the talk was all of the strange beast which had come to their jungle. Most of those present believed the tiger, like the werewolf of the North, was none other than one of those ghastly evil men who have the power to take on at will the form of an animal.

" I remember," said Igi, the best hunter of the tribe, " that when I was a boy and lived far to the south there were two brothers in our village whom we found to be weretigers, when they disgorged feathers, as a tiger does after it has fed upon a jungle fowl."

" My mother told me," ventured Toku, a newcomer, " that a cousin of hers was married to such a man. One night she woke up and missed him, and when she looked out of the window-hole she saw in the moonlight a great tiger coming up the path. At the door it became her husband,

[1] **baobab:** a timber tree, the trunk of which often grows to a diameter of thirty feet. Its gourdlike fruit is called *monkey bread.*

and she had just time to slip back into her bed and pretend to be asleep before he came in. The next day she left him, and he fled from the village and never claimed her dowry — which proved that she was telling the truth," he concluded sagely.

Orgoba, the priest, felt strongly that the direful visitor was a devil tiger sent by Siva the Destroyer[1] because of a lack of reverence on the part of the villagers and their failure to pay their tithes[2] promptly, while on the other hand Ulti, the barber, was positive that the strange animal was a vampire.

Whether demon, vampire, or weretiger, the white beast soon showed that it was at any rate a man-killer. Two days after its arrival, at that hour which the Malays have named "When-the-buffalo-go-down-to-drink," which is about five o'clock in the afternoon, it sprang upon Baruga, the usurer, at the outskirts of the village, killed him with one terrible blow, and with his body in his jaws rushed along the street, while the people scattered before him as if blown away by some great wind of fear.

That night the elders of the village met at Ahmad's house. They would not have ventured even so far had it not been for their blood-bought knowledge of tiger ways. For two days the gorged beast would not kill again.

White men would have spoken openly of the enemy who lurked at their gate. The little brown men who sat that night around a sputtering stone lamp filled with palm oil knew better. No Malay will call a tiger by his real name lest he hear and come. Moreover, they believe that, after a tiger has killed, the ghost of the dead man rides on his head and directs him to his next victim. Wherefore that night there was a long silence broken only by the conventional grunts and groans which a Malay employs in place of conversation. It was the priest who spoke first.

"What is thy counsel, my father?" he said deferentially to Ahmad. "Thou art the oldest and wisest hunter of the village. What thinkest thou of the White One?"

The old man looked at him sardonically.

"Thou hast said," he answered at last, "that he is a demon. Whether that be so I know not. That he is a man-killer, however, we all know. . . . The dead man hated me when he was alive," he went on after a pause. "More than thrice have I plucked poor men from out of his clutches and saved them from jail and the torture. Moreover, this, my house, is the nearest to the jungle. Wherefore it is probable that he who was Baruga will guide the killer to me first of all. It is my counsel that we meet here every night and kill the White One when at last he comes, lest he destroy us and our women and our children separately."

There was another long silence after Ahmad's speech. Then the company began to melt away.

"Who can contend with demons?" murmured Toku, as he slipped unobtrusively out of the door.

"Thou shalt have my prayers," Orgoba assured the old man — and was gone.

One by one the others left, each with some evasive farewell, until of them all only Igi, the hunter, remained.

"Why stayest thou?" old Ahmad inquired of him bitterly. "Follow the others. It may be that the White One will be satisfied with my old carcass and leave the rest of you unharmed."

"Not so, my father," returned the younger man. "I, too, know something of the Striped Folk. When one takes to man-killing he never stops. Moreover, I would rather fight this one with thee alone

[1] **Siva the Destroyer**: a Hindu god. [2] **tithes**: a tenth portion set aside for a contribution.

than with the whole company of those cowards who have fled."

From that night Igi lived at the house of Ahmad. With him he brought his arms, a smoothbore musket which would go off three times out of five, a spear with a yard-long, razor-edged head of gray steel, the inevitable barong shaped like a butcher's cleaver, and his kreese, a long, narrow dagger with a wavy blade.

Three days passed, and there was no sign of the white tiger. Then came the night of the full of the moon. That evening Ahmad and Igi sat long at table, served by the old man's three wives, while Teloa, as always, was above them, hidden in her tiny loft.

Suddenly from far out in the jungle there came a sound like a ghastly laugh with a hideous leer running through it. As it died away the men started to their feet.

"The pheal," whispered old Ahmad, and Igi nodded and looked to the priming of his long gun. Again came the ghoulish cry, this time much nearer. Somewhere in the jungle a jackal was giving the unearthly howl which it only makes when hunting with a tiger. For a third time it sounded from the darkness of the jungle, followed by absolute silence. Even the frogs seemed to have stopped their notes for a moment. Then the stillness was shattered by perhaps the most dreadful sound on earth — the roar of a hunting tiger. It began close to the earth, a long-drawn-out "how-ow-own," and rose and increased in volume until the whole jungle vibrated. As the last echo died away there came screams of uncontrollable fear from the women; Teloa, of them all, made no sound.

"Quiet, foolish ones," hissed Ahmad. "Do you wish to bring the White One to our very door?"

At his voice the wailing cries stopped instantly — but it was too late. Peering through one of the window-holes cut in the bamboo wall, Igi saw a white figure glide like a ghost toward the house and caught the gleam of terrible green-shadowed eyes showing like molten gold in the dark.

Suddenly, not fifty yards from the cabin, came the deep moan which a tiger gives when he is sure of his kill. In the sound was the very essence of cold-blooded cruelty and withal a certain quality of triumph which made it doubly horrible. There was a moment of stillness, and then from the edge of the jungle came a grunting cough.

"Stand fast, my brother," whispered old Ahmad; "now he charges."

Igi nodded, and loosening the barong in his belt, drew back the clumsy hammer of his musket. As he did so, from without came the pad, pad, pad of hurrying feet; and in a moment the light bamboo house shook and creaked under the weight of the great beast. Misjudging his distance, the tiger had sprung short and for an instant clung to the edge of the sloping thatch with bent forepaws as he tried in vain to pull himself up on the roof itself. A second later there was the thud of his body striking the ground within a couple of yards of the two men, crouched back of the thin bamboo wall. Snarling horribly, the tiger rose up on his hind legs and clawed at the door, making deep grooves in the thick pinang[1] planks.

Before Ahmad could stop him, the younger hunter clapped his musket to his shoulder, and aiming hurriedly through one of the window-holes, pulled the trigger. The crashing report was followed instantly by a dreadful screech from without as the bullet cut through one of the great cat's ears, the most sensitive part of a tiger's body.

With a thunderous roar the enraged brute sprang again, landing this time on

[1] **pinang:** a palm tree.

the very peak of the roof, and began to rip off great masses of the loose thatch. With a quick movement old Ahmad put out the smoking lamp and motioned the sobbing women to take refuge in the farthest corner of the room, so as to clear a space for the fight to the death which he knew must now come. As the two men looked to their weapons and the women huddled together, the moonlight shone through the great gap in the roof, white and still, as if there were no such thing in the world as fear or death.

Suddenly the opening in the roof was darkened by such a head of horror as few men, indeed, have had to face. The eyes of the tiger glared down upon them like incandescent emeralds; his terrible mouth snarled open, showing his glittering white teeth and the hot red gullet beyond, while his grim face was wrinkled with a scowl of utter fury. While Igi was frantically trying to load his musket in the dark, Ahmad took careful aim and fired at the tiger's head, shouting the " sorak " as he did so. The handful of stones which the old man used for bullets failed to pierce the thick bones, and the great cat, maddened by the pain, thrust his head and burly shoulders clear through the roof. Grasping his spear, Igi jabbed up at him desperately, but the weapon was suddenly caught out of his hands by the clutch of a great paw and hurled up against the ceiling, to fall across the little loft where Teloa lay. Instinctively she gripped it with her slim, strong hands, as with a rending crash the great beast burst through the flimsy roof and leaped to the floor below. As he landed, Ahmad clubbed his gun and struck a tremendous blow at the beast's head with its flashing eyes and snarling mouth, just as Igi slashed at him with his barong. Neither stroke went home. Springing back out of range of their blows, before either could recover his balance, the fierce brute was upon them. To the girl watching from above, it seemed as though he gave each a soft pat with his great paw; yet both men went spinning back against the opposite wall, bruised and disabled. Through the ripped-out roof the moon shone so brightly that every detail of the life-and-death struggle in that little room showed vividly to the watcher above. In a corner huddled the women, whimpering with terror. Against one wall Igi moved feebly, while Ahmad lay stunned near the door. The great head of the tiger seemed to mask his ten-foot body, while his long tail switched back and forth, and the giant muscles rippled up and down his sleek sides as he moved toward the men.

For a moment he crouched before he sprang, as if choosing his victim. On that moment, that tiny tick of time, hung the lives of every one there. As it was passing, the girl from the jungle gripped the great spear mightily, and leaning far out over the side of the little platform on which she lay, drove it with a sure eye and a steady hand clear through the great body crouched below her. The yard-long, double-edged point, razor-sharp and keen as a rapier, slipped through the white skin and tough muscles just back of the beast's left forepaw, and as the girl threw all her weight and strength upon the thrust, split the tiger's very heart. With a fearful yelling screech, the deadly brute sprang straight up into the air, and turning over, fell back quivering in death, its open mouth not a foot from where Igi lay.

As he slowly came to himself the first thing the young hunter saw was the gaping jaws of the tiger close to his face. With a grunt of horror he executed a most creditable back somersault, came up on his feet, and backed against the wall, his barong gripped in one hand and his naked kreese in the other, to meet the spring which he expected. Only when he saw by the white moonlight that the dreadful eyes which stared up into his were glazed and sightless and that his own spear was buried clear to the crossbar in the vast body, did his tense muscles relax.

For a full minute he stared at the white bulk stretched out stark before him. Then he moved cautiously toward the grim carcass and tried to withdraw the spear, but it was fixed so deep in the bone of the opposite shoulder blade that he was unable to pull it out.

" A brave stroke indeed," the Malay muttered to himself as he tugged at the spear. " Strange that I do not remember making it."

An involuntary giggle came from the women's corner at his words, echoed by a little laugh from above. Looking up, Igi saw for the first time the jungle girl smiling down at him in the moonlight.

" Whose was the hand, O Princess, that killed the White One ? " he asked, gazing up at her admiringly.

" It was I who borrowed thy spear and thrust with it at the Grandfather-of-Stripes," she answered in the slow, clear tones of her tribe. " No princess am I, but a slave girl of the Semarang." And she swung herself to the floor and stood before him, clothed only in the long amber-yellow veil which the maidens intended for the Sultan must always wear.

Before the young hunter could speak again, there sounded the creaking voice of Ahmad, who had recovered his senses just in time to hear Teloa's last words.

" Thou art a slave no longer," he announced. " I will send the Sultan the skin of the white tiger, which he would rather have than a thousand slave girls, and thou shalt be free and become my fourth wife and the ruler of my household."

" Not so, my father," returned the girl hurriedly; " thou hast three such wives as might gladden the heart of any man. Who am I to make a fourth ? "

" I have but one wife," spoke up Igi hopefully.

" That is one too many for me," returned the girl, and again her laugh rang out like a silver bell.

" If in truth thou wouldst make Teloa happy," she went on, turning to Ahmad, " let her go back to the jungle and her own people."

" So be it," said the old man at last, somewhat disappointedly. " Do thou go and rouse the village," he directed Igi. " Bring back those cowards who were here. Let theirs be the task of flaying the tiger which they dared not face."

Igi went about his errand with much enthusiasm. Every house he came to was locked and barred, for all who lived in the village had heard about the pheal, the reports of the guns, and the roars and growls and screams of the fight which came after, and had decided, one and all, that Ahmad and all of his household were dead and devoured.

Igi corrected this mistake by pounding on the door of each house and heaping abuse on those within.

" Come out, cowards, three-toed sloths ! " he bellowed mightily. " The weretiger is dead. Come to the house of Ahmad and help strip off his hide for the Sultan, snails and decayed durians that ye are ! "

Heartened by the good news and much impressed by the magic of Igi's oratory, in a short time all the men of the village were gathered together at the house of the old hunter, and under his direction removed the magnificent pelt of the white tiger. When it was finally stretched out to be dried and tanned, it measured a good eleven feet from muzzle to tail tip, a mass of golden-white with the stripes making a pattern of dull silver across the shimmering silken skin.

With Igi, Ahmad shared the whiskers of the dead beast, solid bristles, each one as large around as a slate pencil and guaranteed to bring long life and good luck to him who owned it.

For his own perquisite the old man kept the two lucky bones, curved, detached bits of floating clavicle peculiar to the tiger and found imbedded in the great muscles at the point of either shoulder. The lucky bone of any tiger was worth a small fortune to him who possessed it, while those of a white tiger were beyond price.

As for Teloa, the other elders of the village all acquiesced in Ahmad's decision, and the skin was sent to the Sultan with a special deputation, who were instructed to tell that great ruler of her bravery and to offer him the white pelt in her place. A week later they returned triumphantly with the news that the Sultan, in consideration of receiving the magic skin, had forever remitted the tribute of the village.

"As for Teloa," announced Orgoba, the priest, "the Great One is willing to receive her, slave though she be, into his harem."

A loud shout went up from the assembled villagers at the news of the great distinction offered to the girl, whom they had learned to regard as one of themselves. Only Teloa herself failed to appreciate the Sultan's condescension. Her small mouth drooped piteously, and the panne velvet [1] of her eyes was dimmed with the tears which ran unheeded down her face.

"Ah, me! Ah, me!" she cried. "What should such a one as I care for courts and harems and honors? The jungle, the glory of the sunrise, the sweet, white moon above the scented trees, the flowers and the birds and the wind from far away, that is what I have chosen. Send not thy Teloa to fret her life away like a rajah bird in a golden cage," and she held fast to Ahmad and sobbed so pitifully that the old man resolved at all costs to comfort her.

"Peace, silly one," he said at last. "'Tis an honor which no other woman in all Malay Land, save thyself, would refuse, but — I would have thee happy. Myself, I will go to the Great One; and thou shalt have thy dawns and sunsets and moonrises again."

Entering the house, the old man fumbled in the hiding place where he kept his few treasures and in a moment came out with one of the lucky bones of the white tiger tightly tied up in his turban and departed down the river to Parak. A week later he returned.

"Thou art to have thy way," he said, shaking his head at the radiant girl. "I have redeemed thy worthless self with such a treasure that the Great One hath commanded that not only art thou to go free, but never again so long as winds blow and waters flow shall any of thy people be harmed or harried in this his kingdom. Forget not old Ahmad when thou art back again in thy jungle."

The next morning the sky was like dark-blue velvet just before the dawn. Suddenly the sun showed through the green of the jungle like some vast ruby set in jade. An "arjuna" butterfly, all gold and crimson, floated over the treetops, and the scented air was full of bird-calls as Teloa moved among the trees, free once more to claim her birthright of beauty and joy. Once again she wore a crimson hibiscus flower in her blue-black hair and a bark sarong in place of the Sultan's veil. Following a hidden trail, she moved through the tangle of trees and vines until in the distance the flash of a cataract showed against the slope of a faraway hill.

As she caught the gleam, the girl stopped, and from her parted lips came

[1] **panne velvet**: a soft fabric with a particularly lustrous finish.

the sweet rippling call of the rainbird. Suddenly it was answered, and flitting through the treetops came one of the birds itself. Black and claret, with a cobalt-blue bill and emerald eyes, it flew around her head and finally disappeared in a near-by thicket.

At the foot of the waterfall Teloa gave the call again, and once more it was answered, this time from the ground instead of the treetops. For the last time she whistled the lovely laughing notes. There was a rustle in the bushes ahead, and suddenly into the trail burst the figure of Nion. A white scar stretched clear across his face, but Teloa saw nothing but the look in his eyes, felt nothing but the clasp of his arms about her, knew nothing but the urge of his lips against hers. Then, hand in hand, the two disappeared down the trail which led to freedom and life and love.

THINK BACK OVER WHAT YOU HAVE READ

Admiring the Simple Virtues of Primitive Folk

In this story you have had a chance to observe — vicariously, through the senses of the author — life lived on a far more simple scale than you yourself are used to. Here you have had a chance to witness those first shining virtues which show man valiantly engaged in his own self-education. What did you notice about the behavior of the "swift, silent little men of the deep forest"? of the elders of the Malay village? How many of the lessons of life which you are set to learn had they, too, mastered? The following questions will help you to decide:

1. What examples can you cite to show that Teloa loved beauty?

2. Notice the picturesque way in which the natives of Malay described events. What names given to animals and persons and events show vivid imagination?

3. What examples of bravery can you cite? Of what did their bravery consist? What were its limitations?

4. What acts of generosity can you cite? With what acts of primitive cruelty can you contrast them?

5. What acts of unselfishness can you cite? How did Ahmad compare with a modern tax collector? Did he seem more or less thoughtful of those in his power?

6. How was justice meted out in the story? Was the Sultan fair, according to his lights? Of what did his fairness consist? Did his justice go far enough, according to your view? Wherein did it fall short? Did it go farther than you might have expected from a Sultan?

7. What examples of faithfulness and loyalty can you cite?

Enjoying the Beauty of the Setting

8. What brief passages can you quote which describe the gorgeous coloring of the peacock? the tiger? the viper?

9. What words and phrases of sound made the jungle seem alive to you? What sounds struck you as particularly terrifying?

10. What sentences can you find that describe beautifully the grace of the tiger?

Increase Your Power over Words

11. The following words give a distinctly Oriental flavor to the story you have just read. Look them up first in the story itself to see with what events they are associated. The footnotes, in some cases, will give you their meaning.

barong (page 51)	jade (page 57)
sarong (page 50)	rajah bird (page 57)
liana (page 50)	pheal (page 54)
pinang (page 54)	kreese (page 54)

12. These words are associated with the superstitions of mankind, which have not yet been wholly outgrown. Look them up in both dictionary and encyclopedia and come to class prepared to discuss their historical background. On what superstitions are they based, or with what superstitions are they connected?

vampire (page 52)	ghoulish (page 54)
werewolf (page 53)	albino (page 52)

For Ambitious Students

13. The following stories offer you still other beautiful glimpses into jungle life and into the hearts of simple people: "The Heart of Little Shikara" by Edison Marshall, *Island Nights Entertainment* by Robert Louis Stevenson, and *Khambu* by Samuel Scoville, Jr.

Tales of Horror

THE MONKEY'S PAW

by W. W. Jacobs (1863-)

Certain stories belong more to the race than to an individual. These are the stories told over and over again through the ages. In such stories lies buried an important lesson which mankind has learned from experience. You are already familiar with stories of this sort in the myths and legends and fables you read as a child. Such stories we call *folklore* because they spring up anonymously among simple people at work or at play together and then are passed on by word of mouth to future generations.

The story that follows is based on an old folk tale, a story which has appeared in many different versions in many different lands. In each version, however, there are three wishes granted to some supposedly lucky person; and always the third wish must be used to offset the mischief wrought by the other two, so that the net result of the three wishes is nothing gained and often something lost.

This story is a modernized version of the old fable. It is a grim tale based on a very old superstition which the author skillfully tricks your senses into believing is true. Therein lies the thrill of the story.

But the thrill of the story is only temporary. On second thought it is some deeper meaning that gives the story its power. What is there about the old tale that bears repetition? Is there some hidden truth to be discovered behind the fantastic elements in the story? As you read the story, keep this question in mind.

The dramatic force of irony. There is another element of interest to be found in the story, an element with which as yet you are probably no more than vaguely familiar. The particular force of this story can be traced to the irony which underlies the incidents related. *Irony* is a very difficult word to define, for it is one of those complicated reactions to life which cannot be summed up simply and briefly. It is, however, a word well worth learning to understand. Of all the ingredients of story interest it is one of the most powerful.

Behind the word *irony* lies the ancient belief in fate — a belief that everything that happens has been planned by some designing power. Thus an accident or a coincidence was a kind of practical joke played upon the human race by some god who sometimes seemed to have a maniac's sense of humor. So it is that when things happen together and suggest a perverse plotting behind the scenes of life we speak of the *irony of circumstance.*

In " Jeeves and the Yuletide Spirit " you have already encountered humorous irony, although you may not have known it by that name. Perhaps you recall the " amazing coincidence " where Tuppy and Wooster both got the idea at the same time of puncturing each other's hot-water bottle and soaking the bed. Only, at the start it wasn't an " amazing coincidence " at all. On the sly, Miss Wickham played the role of Fate in order to land both her suitors — as Wodehouse would say — " in the soup "; which she did. But Fate took a hand in the affair, even so, when she suggested to Sir Roderick that he change rooms with both of the culprits. Herein lies that element of unplanned mischief which we call *irony.*

You encountered it, too, in " On the Dodge," in that perverted twist of circumstances by which a man who sets out to capture those who stole his horse is himself accused of implication in the crime. In both stories, you can see, there is the suggestion of a practical joke played upon unsuspecting people by a designing Fate. Therein lies their irony, from which a reader derives the same sort of quick thrill that he gets from any well-timed jest in life. As you read the story that follows, you will have a chance to test out your appreciation of irony.

WITHOUT, the night was cold and wet; but in the small parlor of Lakesnam Villa the blinds were drawn and the fire burned brightly. Father and son were at chess, the former, who possessed ideas about the game involving radical changes, putting his king into such sharp and unnecessary perils that it even provoked comment from the white-haired old lady knitting placidly by the fire.

"Hark at the wind," said Mr. White, who, having seen a fatal mistake after it was too late, was amiably desirous of preventing his son from seeing it.

"I'm listening," said the latter, grimly surveying the board as he stretched out his hand. "Check."

"I should hardly think that he'd come tonight," said his father, with his hand poised over the board.

"Mate," replied the son.

"That's the worst of living so far out," bawled Mr. White, with sudden and unlooked-for violence; "of all the beastly, slushy, out-of-the-way places to live in, this is the worst. Pathway's a bog, and the road's a torrent. I don't know what people are thinking about. I suppose because only two houses on the road are let they think it doesn't matter."

"Never mind, dear," said his wife soothingly; "perhaps you'll win the next one."

Mr. White looked up sharply, just in time to intercept a knowing glance between mother and son. The words died away on his lips, and he hid a guilty grin in his thin gray beard.

"There he is," said Herbert White as the gate banged to loudly and heavy footsteps came toward the door.

The old man rose with hospitable haste and, opening the door, was heard condoling with the new arrival. The new arrival also condoled with himself, so that Mrs. White said, "Tut, tut!" and coughed gently as her husband entered the room, followed by a tall burly man, beady of eye and rubicund of visage.

"Sergeant Major Morris," he said, introducing him.

The sergeant major shook hands and, taking the proffered seat by the fire, watched contentedly while his host got out whisky and tumblers and stood a small copper kettle on the fire.

At the third glass his eyes got brighter and he began to talk, the little family circle regarding with eager interest this visitor from distant parts as he squared his broad shoulders in the chair and spoke of strange scenes and doughty deeds, of wars and plagues and strange peoples.

"Twenty-one years of it," said Mr. White, nodding at his wife and son. "When he went away, he was a slip of a youth in the warehouse. Now look at him."

"He don't look to have taken much harm," said Mrs. White politely.

"I'd like to go to India myself," said the old man, "just to look round a bit, you know."

"Better where you are," said the sergeant major, shaking his head. He put down the empty glass and, sighing softly, shook it again.

"I should like to see those old temples and fakirs and jugglers," said the old man. "What was that you started telling me the other day about a monkey's paw or something, Morris?"

"Nothing," said the soldier hastily. "Leastways, nothing worth hearing."

"Monkey's paw?" said Mrs. White curiously.

"Well, it's just a bit of what you might call magic, perhaps," said the sergeant major offhandedly.

His three listeners leaned forward eagerly. The visitor absent-mindedly put his empty glass to his lips and then set it down again. His host filled it for him.

"To look at," said the sergeant major, fumbling in his pocket, "it's just an ordinary little paw, dried to a mummy."

He took something out of his pocket and proffered it. Mrs. White drew back with a grimace, but her son, taking it, examined it curiously.

"And what is there special about it?" inquired Mr. White as he took it from his son and, having examined it, placed it upon the table.

"It had a spell put on it by an old fakir," said the sergeant major, "a very holy man. He wanted to show that fate ruled people's lives, and that those who interfered with it did so to their sorrow. He put a spell on it so that three separate men could each have three wishes from it."

His manner was so impressive that his hearers were conscious that their light laughter jarred somewhat.

"Well, why don't you have three, sir?" said Herbert White cleverly.

The soldier regarded him in the way that middle age is wont to regard presumptuous youth. "I have," he said quietly, and his blotchy face whitened.

"And did you really have the three wishes granted?" asked Mrs. White.

"I did," said the sergeant major, and his glass tapped against his strong teeth.

"And has anybody else wished?" inquired the old lady.

"The first man had his three wishes, yes," was the reply. "I don't know what the first two were, but the third was for death. That's how I got the paw."

His tones were so grave that a hush fell upon the group.

"If you've had your three wishes, it's no good to you now, then, Morris," said the old man at last. "What do you keep it for?"

The soldier shook his head. "Fancy, I suppose," he said slowly. "I did have some idea of selling it, but I don't think I will. It has caused enough mischief already. Besides, people won't buy. They think it's a fairy tale, some of them, and those who do think anything of it want to try it first and pay me afterward."

"If you could have another three wishes," said the old man, eying him keenly, "would you have them?"

"I don't know," said the other. "I don't know."

He took the paw and, dangling it between his front finger and thumb, suddenly threw it upon the fire. White, with a slight cry, stooped down and snatched it off.

"Better let it burn," said the soldier solemnly.

"If you don't want it, Morris," said the old man, "give it to me."

"I won't," said his friend doggedly. "I threw it on the fire. If you keep it, don't blame me for what happens. Pitch it on the fire again, like a sensible man."

The other shook his head and examined his new possession closely. "How do you do it?" he inquired.

"Hold it up in your right hand and wish aloud," said the sergeant major, "but I warn you of the consequences."

"Sounds like the *Arabian Nights*," said Mrs. White as she rose and began to set the supper. "Don't you think you might wish for four pairs of hands for me?"

Her husband drew the talisman from his pocket, and then all three burst into laughter as the sergeant major, with a look of alarm on his face, caught him by the arm.

"If you must wish," he said gruffly, "wish for something sensible."

Mr. White dropped it back into his pocket and, placing chairs, motioned his friend to the table. In the business of supper the talisman was partly forgotten, and afterward the three sat listening in an enthralled fashion to a second installment of the soldier's adventures in India.

"If the tale about the monkey paw is not more truthful than those he has been telling us," said Herbert as the door closed behind their guest, just in time for him to catch the last train, "we shan't make much out of it."

"Did you give him anything for it, father?" inquired Mrs. White, regarding her husband closely.

"A trifle," said he, coloring slightly.

" He didn't want it, but I made him take it. And he pressed me again to throw it away."

" Likely," said Herbert, with pretended horror. " Why, we're going to be rich, and famous, and happy. Wish to be an emperor, father, to begin with; then you can't be henpecked."

He darted round the table, pursued by the maligned Mrs. White armed with an antimacassar.

Mr. White took the paw from his pocket and eyed it dubiously. " I don't know what to wish for, and that's a fact," he said slowly. " It seems to me I've got all I want."

" If you only cleared the house, you'd be quite happy, wouldn't you," said Herbert, with his hand on his shoulder. " Well, wish for two hundred pounds, then; that'll just do it."

His father, smiling shamefacedly at his own credulity, held up the talisman as his son, with a solemn face somewhat marred by a wink at his mother, sat down at the piano and struck a few impressive chords.

" I wish for two hundred pounds," said the old man distinctly.

A fine crash from the piano greeted the words, interrupted by a shuddering cry from the old man. His wife and son ran toward him.

" It moved," he cried, with a glance of disgust at the object as it lay on the floor. " As I wished, it twisted in my hands like a snake."

" Well, I don't see the money," said his son as he picked it up and placed it on the table, " and I bet I never shall."

" It must have been your fancy, father," said his wife, regarding him anxiously.

He shook his head. " Never mind, though; there's no harm done, but it gave me a shock all the same."

They sat down by the fire again while the two men finished their pipes. Outside, the wind was higher than ever, and the old man started nervously at the sound of a door banging upstairs. A silence unusual and depressing settled upon all three, which lasted until the old couple rose to retire for the night.

" I expect you'll find the cash tied up in a big bag in the middle of your bed," said Herbert as he bade them good night, " and something horrible squatting up on top of the wardrobe watching you as you pocket your ill-gotten gains."

In the brightness of the wintry sun next morning as it streamed over the breakfast table, Herbert laughed at his fears. There was an air of prosaic wholesomeness about the room which it had lacked on the previous night, and the dirty, shriveled little paw was pitched on the sideboard with a carelessness which betokened no great belief in its virtues.

" I suppose all old soldiers are the same," said Mrs. White. " The idea of our listening to such nonsense! How could wishes be granted in these days? And if they could, how could two hundred pounds hurt you, father? "

" Might drop on his head from the sky," said the frivolous Herbert.

" Morris said the things happened so naturally," said his father, " that you might if you so wished attribute it to coincidence."

" Well, don't break into the money before I come back," said Herbert as he rose from the table. " I'm afraid it'll turn you into a mean, avaricious man, and we shall have to disown you."

His mother laughed and, following him to the door, watched him down the road and, returning to the breakfast table, was very happy at the expense of her husband's credulity. All of which did not prevent her from scurrying to the door at the postman's knock, nor prevent her from referring somewhat shortly to retired sergeant majors of bibulous habits when she found that the post brought a tailor's bill.

"Herbert will have some more of his funny remarks, I expect, when he comes home," she said as they sat at dinner.

"I dare say," said Mr. White, pouring himself out some beer; "but for all that, the thing moved in my hand; that I'll swear to."

"You thought it did," said the old lady soothingly.

"I say it did," replied the other. "There was no thought about it; I had just — What's the matter?"

His wife made no reply. She was watching the mysterious movements of a man outside, who, peering in an undecided fashion at the house, appeared to be trying to make up his mind to enter. In mental connection with the two hundred pounds, she noticed that the stranger was well dressed and wore a silk hat of glossy newness. Three times he paused at the gate, and then walked on again. The fourth time he stood with his hand upon it, and then with sudden resolution flung it open and walked up the path. Mrs. White at the same moment placed her hands behind her and, hurriedly unfastening the strings of her apron, put that useful article of apparel beneath the cushion of her chair.

She brought the stranger, who seemed ill at ease, into the room. He gazed furtively at Mrs. White and listened in a preoccupied fashion as the old lady apologized for the appearance of the room and her husband's coat, a garment which he usually reserved for the garden. She then waited as patiently as her sex would permit for him to broach his business, but he was at first strangely silent.

"I — was asked to call," he said at last, and stooped and picked a piece of cotton from his trousers. "I come from Maw and Meggins."

The old lady started. "Is anything the matter?" she asked breathlessly. "Has anything happened to Herbert? What is it? What is it?"

Her husband interposed. "There, there, mother," he said hastily. "Sit down, and don't jump to conclusions. You've not brought bad news, I'm sure, sir," and he eyed the other wistfully.

"I'm sorry — " began the visitor.

"Is he hurt?" demanded the mother.

The visitor bowed in assent. "Badly hurt," he said quietly, "but he is not in any pain."

"Oh, thank God!" said the old woman, clasping her hands. "Thank God for that! Thank — "

She broke off suddenly as the sinister meaning of the assurance dawned upon her and she saw the awful confirmation of her fears in the other's averted face. She caught her breath and, turning to her slower-witted husband, laid her trembling old hand upon his. There was a long silence.

"He was caught in the machinery," said the visitor at length, in a low voice.

"Caught in the machinery," repeated Mr. White, in a dazed fashion, "yes."

He sat staring blankly out at the window and, taking his wife's hand between his own, pressed it as he had been wont to do in their old courting days nearly forty years before.

"He was the only one left to us," he said, turning gently to the visitor. "It is hard."

The other coughed and, rising, walked slowly to the window. "The firm wished me to convey their sincere sympathy with you in your great loss," he said, without looking round. "I beg that you will understand I am only their servant and merely obeying orders."

There was no reply; the old woman's face was white, her eyes staring, and her breath inaudible; on her husband's face was a look such as his friend the sergeant might have carried into his first action.

" I was to say that Maw and Meggins disclaim all responsibility," continued the other. " They admit no liability at all, but in consideration of your son's services they wish to present you with a certain sum as compensation."

Mr. White dropped his wife's hand and, rising to his feet, gazed with a look of horror at his visitor. His dry lips shaped the words, " How much ? "

" Two hundred pounds," was the answer.

Unconscious of his wife's shriek, the old man smiled faintly, put out his hands like a sightless man, and dropped, a senseless heap, to the floor.

In the huge new cemetery, some two miles distant, the old people buried their dead, and came back to a house steeped in shadow and silence. It was all over so quickly that at first they could hardly realize it, and remained in a state of expectation as though of something else to happen — something else which was to lighten this load, too heavy for old hearts to bear. But the days passed, and expectation gave place to resignation — the hopeless resignation of the old, sometimes miscalled apathy. Sometimes they hardly exchanged a word, for now they had nothing to talk about and their days were long to weariness.

It was about a week after that that the old man, waking suddenly in the night, stretched out his hand and found himself alone. The room was in darkness, and the sound of subdued weeping came from the window. He raised himself in bed and listened.

" Come back," he said tenderly. " You will be cold."

" It is colder for my son," said the old woman, and wept afresh.

The sound of her sobs died away on his ears. The bed was warm, and his eyes heavy with sleep. He dozed fitfully, and then slept until a sudden wild cry from his wife awoke him with a start.

" The monkey's paw ! " she cried wildly. " The monkey's paw ! "

He started up in alarm. " Where ? Where is it ? What's the matter ? "

She came stumbling across the room toward him. " I want it," she said quietly. " You've not destroyed it ? "

" It's in the parlor, on the bracket," he replied, marveling. " Why ? "

She cried and laughed together and, bending over, kissed his cheek.

" I only just thought of it," she said hysterically. " Why didn't I think of it before ? Why didn't you think of it ? "

" Think of what ? " he questioned.

" The other two wishes," she replied rapidly. " We've only had one."

" Was not that enough ? " he demanded fiercely.

" No," she cried triumphantly ; " we'll have one more. Go down and get it quickly, and wish our boy alive again."

The man sat up in bed and flung the bedclothes from his quaking limbs. " Good God, you are mad ! " he cried, aghast.

" Get it," she panted ; " get it quickly, and wish — Oh, my boy, my boy ! "

Her husband struck a match and lit the candle. " Get back to bed," he said unsteadily. " You don't know what you are saying."

" We had the first wish granted," said the old woman feverishly. " Why not the second ? "

" A coincidence," stammered the old man.

" Go and get it and wish," cried the old woman, and dragged him toward the door.

He went down in the darkness, and felt his way to the parlor and then to the mantelpiece. The talisman was in its place, and a horrible fear that the unspoken wish might bring his mutilated son before him ere he could escape from the room seized upon him, and he caught his breath as he found that he had lost the direction of the door. His brow cold with sweat, he felt his way round the table and groped along the wall until he found himself in the small passage with the unwholesome thing in his hand.

Even his wife's face seemed changed as he entered the room. It was white and expectant, and to his fears seemed to have an unnatural look upon it. He was afraid of her.

" Wish! " she cried, in a strong voice.

" It is foolish and wicked," he faltered.

" Wish! " repeated his wife.

He raised his hand. " I wish my son alive again."

The talisman fell to the floor, and he regarded it shudderingly. Then he sank trembling into a chair as the old woman, with burning eyes, walked to the window and raised the blind.

He sat until he was chilled with the cold, glancing occasionally at the figure of the old woman peering through the window. The candle end, which had burnt below the rim of the china candlestick, was throwing pulsating shadows on the ceiling and walls, until, with a flicker larger than the rest, it expired. The old man, with an unspeakable sense of relief at the failure of the talisman, crept back to his bed, and a minute or two afterward the old woman came silently and apathetically beside him.

Neither spoke, but both lay silently listening to the ticking of the clock. A stair creaked, and a squeaky mouse scurried noisily through the wall. The darkness was oppressive and, after lying for some time screwing up his courage, the husband took the box of matches and, striking one, went downstairs for a candle.

At the foot of the stairs the match went out, and he paused to strike another, and at the same moment a knock, so quiet and stealthy as to be scarcely audible, sounded on the front door.

The matches fell from his hand. He stood motionless, his breath suspended until the knock was repeated. Then he turned and fled swiftly back to his room, and closed the door behind him. A third knock sounded through the house.

" *What's that?* " cried the old woman, starting up.

" A rat," said the old man, in shaking tones, " a rat. It passed me on the stairs."

His wife sat up in bed listening. A loud knock resounded through the house.

" It's Herbert! " she screamed. " It's Herbert! "

She ran to the door, but her husband was before her and, catching her by the arm, held her tightly.

" What are you going to do? " he whispered hoarsely.

" It's my boy; it's Herbert! " she cried, struggling mechanically. " I forgot it was two miles away. What are you holding me for? Let go. I must open the door."

" For God's sake don't let it in," cried the old man, trembling.

" You're afraid of your own son! " she cried, struggling. " Let me go. I'm coming, Herbert; I'm coming."

There was another knock, and another. The old woman with a sudden wrench broke free and ran from the room. Her husband followed to the landing, and called after her appealingly as she hurried downstairs. He heard the chain rattle back and the bottom bolt drawn slowly and stiffly from the socket. Then the old woman's voice, strained and panting.

" The bolt! " she cried loudly. " Come down. I can't reach it."

But her husband was on his hands and knees groping wildly on the floor in search of the paw. If he could only find it before the thing outside got in. A perfect fusillade of knocks reverberated through the house, and he heard the scraping of a chair as his wife put it down in the passage against the door. He heard the creaking of the bolt as it came slowly back, and at the same moment he found the monkey's paw and frantically breathed his third and last wish.

The knocking ceased suddenly, although the echoes of it were still in the house. He heard the chair drawn back and the door opened. A cold wind rushed up the staircase, and a long loud wail of disappointment and misery from his wife gave him courage to run down to her side and then to the gate beyond. The street lamp flickering opposite shone on a quiet and deserted road.

THINK BACK OVER WHAT YOU HAVE READ

Recognizing the Irony in the Story

1. With what later events in the story do you couple the following statements?
   a. " If you must wish for something," said the sergeant major, " wish for something *sensible.*" What *sensible* thing did Mr. White wish for?
   b. " Did you give him anything for it? " inquired Mrs. White. In the light of what happens later, why does this question strike you as ironic?
   c. " Why," said Herbert, " we're going to be rich, and famous, and happy." Is there irony in this utterance? Why?
   d. " I don't know what to wish for, and that's a fact," Mr. White said dubiously. " It seems to me I've got all I want." Wherein lies the irony of this statement?
   e. " If you only cleared the house you'd be happy, wouldn't you? " said Herbert. What force do you see in the word *only?*
   f. " How could two hundred pounds hurt you, father? " asked Mrs. White. Ironically enough, how did it?
   g. " Might drop on his head from the sky," said the frivolous Herbert. What ironic force do you see in the word *frivolous?* What has been Herbert's characteristic attitude toward the monkey's paw? What other remarks of Herbert strike you as ironic?
   h. " We have had the first wish granted. Why not the second? " said the old woman feverishly. Looking backward, what irony do you see in the old woman's question?

2. What was the grim " joke " in the first wish? in the second?

3. What was the net result of the three wishes which were granted?

4. Of what statement made early in the story by the sergeant major does this fact remind you? What was the joker in the charm of the monkey's paw?

5. What lesson do you see in the story? What truth do you think it illustrates?

Increase Your Power over Words

6. The word *maligned* (page 62) in this story represents an interesting word family. Look first at the way it is used in the story; then consult the dictionary for information about other words introduced by the prefix *mal,* meaning bad. Come to class prepared to use in a sentence of your own each word which you find.

7. The word *enthralled* (page 61), like the word *accolade* on page 13, has a picturesque past. Look the word up in the dictionary and find, first, its original meaning, dating back to the days of chivalry; second, its modern, derived meaning. In what context would you yourself feel justified in using the word?

THE MASQUE OF THE RED DEATH

by Edgar Allan Poe (1809–1849)

Have you ever stopped to think why you like to read tales of horror? Does it surprise you a little to think that you do? Horror and terror are two strong stimulants to the imagination which have the effect of waking you up and making you feel intensely alive. After such strong reactions as those produced by horror or terror you are inclined to relax with a sense of blessed relief, such as you feel when you awake from a bad dream. " Thank goodness," you say to yourself, " *I'm* all right "; and your own life, which but a moment ago seemed dull and drab, becomes of a sudden very satisfactory. This is one explanation — the psychologist's explanation — of why mystery thrillers are popular.

The writer of the story that follows plays upon an age-old fear — the fear of the unknown. A " nameless awe " is Poe's name for it. Doubtless you have read other stories in which a mysterious enemy or an unseen foe robbed brave men of their courage. And from your own experience you are aware that the worst that can be imagined, once known to be a fact, is easier to bear than uncertainty.

Herein lies a truth upon which the artist capitalizes in such stories as this one which you are about to read. And here is a clue for appreciating Poe's artistry; that is, the amazing skill by which he succeeds in giving maximum power to an idea. Let us see what this means.

The dramatic force of personification. To the medieval man, you can well understand, a plague was a mysterious evil. For at that time little or nothing was understood about germs and the nature of contagion, and disease was therefore a mysterious affliction that seemed to descend upon a city like an evil spirit. Since at that time man's reason could not identify the real enemy, could not point and say, " There, that's the villain; *he's* responsible for all these ghastly deaths," it remained for man's imagination to explain the terrible mystery. This he did by a trick of the mind with which you yourself are quite familiar. He *personified* the evil; that is, he imagined it to be a *person* or a being which bore some horrible likeness to a person. Thus, at least, the horror was named and traced to a " cause."

This, then, is what Poe does in " The Masque [1] of the Red Death ": he takes you back to the Middle Ages and fastens upon you an ancient dread — a kind of dread that mankind still remembers, a kind of dread that seems to be in your very bones. Then gradually he makes that dread take definite shape, so that at the end of the story it becomes something no longer guessed at but something recognized and known. Thus the particular thrill of this story comes from feeling yourself under the spell of a " nameless awe " and drawn irresistibly toward a climax of horror where the worst that can happen does happen.

Poe's place in the history of the short story. The author of the story lived at a time when the horror story was as popular as the mystery thriller of today, and his " tales of effect," as he called them, are one of his significant contributions to literature. He created them after his own philosophy of the short story, producing that " unity of effect " which distinguishes it from the tale that is merely brief. His skill lies in his ability to " hold the soul of the reader at his mercy " while he builds up a powerful impression to haunt the imagination.

Edgar Allan Poe is one of the strangest personalities of American literature. His life is a sordid story of bitter struggle and disappointment without a happy ending. A proud, sensitive nature, uprooted early in life and denied the security he had been taught to take for granted, he kept the wolf from the door chiefly by writing tales of horror for popular magazines. He never lived to know that he would later be regarded as a master of style and technique.

THE " Red Death " had long devastated the country. No pestilence had ever been so fatal, or so hideous. Blood was its avatar [2] and its seal — the redness and the horror of blood. There were sharp pains, and sudden dizziness, and then profuse bleeding at the pores, with dissolution. The scarlet stains upon the body and especially upon the face of the victim were the pest ban [3] which shut him out from the aid and from the sympathy of his fellow men. And the whole seizure, progress, and termination of the disease were the incidents of half an hour.

But the Prince Prospero was happy and dauntless and sagacious. When his dominions were half depopulated, he summoned to his presence a thousand hale and lighthearted friends from among the knights and dames of his court, and with these retired to the deep seclusion of one of his castellated abbeys. This was an extensive and magnificent structure, the creation of the prince's own eccentric yet august taste. A strong and lofty wall girdled it in. This wall had gates of iron. The courtiers, having entered, brought

[1] **Masque:** Masquerade.

[2] **avatar:** a word associated with Hindu religion. As used here, it means symbol. [3] **pest ban:** we would say quarantine.

furnaces and massy hammers and welded the bolts. They resolved to leave means neither of ingress or egress to the sudden impulses of despair or of frenzy from within. The abbey was amply provisioned. With such precautions the courtiers might bid defiance to contagion. The external world could take care of itself. In the meantime it was folly to grieve, or to think. The prince had provided all the appliances of pleasure. There were buffoons; there were improvisatori; there were ballet dancers; there were musicians; there was Beauty; there was wine. All these and security were within. Without was the " Red Death."

It was toward the close of the fifth or sixth month of his seclusion, and while the pestilence raged most furiously abroad, that the Prince Prospero entertained his thousand friends at a masked ball of the most unusual magnificence.

It was a voluptuous scene, that masquerade. But first let me tell of the rooms in which it was held. There were seven — an imperial suite. In many palaces, however, such suites form a long and straight vista, while the folding doors slide back nearly to the walls on either hand, so that the view of the whole extent is scarcely impeded. Here the case was very different; as might have been expected from the duke's love of the bizarre.[1] The apartments were so irregularly disposed that the vision embraced but little more than one at a time. There was a sharp turn at every twenty or thirty yards, and at each turn a novel effect. To the right and left, in the middle of each wall, a tall and narrow Gothic window looked out upon a closed corridor which pursued the windings of the suite. These windows were of stained glass whose color varied in accordance with the prevailing decorations of the chamber into which it opened. That at the eastern extremity was hung, for example, in blue — and vividly blue were its windows. The second chamber was purple in its ornaments and tapestries, and here the panes were purple. The third was green throughout, and so were the casements. The fourth was furnished and lighted with orange, the fifth with white, the sixth with violet. The seventh apartment was closely shrouded in black velvet tapestries that hung all over the ceiling and down the walls, falling in heavy folds upon a carpet of the same material and hue. But in this chamber only, the color of the windows failed to correspond with the decorations. The panes here were scarlet — a deep blood color. Now in no one of the seven apartments was there any lamp or candelabrum, amid the profusion of golden ornaments that lay scattered to and fro or depended from the roof. There was no light of any kind emanating from lamp or candle within the suite of chambers. But in the corridors that followed the suite there stood, opposite to each window, a heavy tripod, bearing a brazier of fire, that projected its rays through the tinted glass and so glaringly illumined the room. And thus were produced a multitude of gaudy and fantastic appearances. But in the western or black chamber the effect of the firelight that streamed upon the dark hangings through the blood-tinted panes was ghastly in the extreme, and produced so wild a look upon the countenances of those who entered that there were few of the company bold enough to set foot within its precincts at all.

It was in this apartment, also, that there stood against the western wall a gigantic clock of ebony. Its pendulum swung to and fro with a dull, heavy monotonous clang; and when the minute hand made the circuit of the face, and the hour was to be stricken, there came from

[1] **bizarre:** a word of French origin meaning strikingly out of the ordinary.

the brazen lungs of the clock a sound which was clear and loud and deep and exceedingly musical, but of so peculiar a note and emphasis that, at each lapse of an hour, the musicians of the orchestra were constrained to pause momentarily in their performance to hearken to the sound; and thus the waltzers perforce ceased their evolutions; and there was a brief disconcert[1] of the whole gay company; and, while the chimes of the clock yet rang, it was observed that the giddiest grew pale and the more aged and sedate passed their hands over their brows as if in confused revery or meditation. But when the echoes had fully ceased, a light laughter at once pervaded the assembly; the musicians looked at each other and smiled as if at their own nervousness and folly, and made whispering vows, each to the other, that the next chiming of the clock should produce in them no similar emotion; and then after the lapse of sixty minutes (which embrace three thousand and six hundred seconds of the Time that flies), there came yet another chiming of the clock, and then were the same disconcert and tremulousness and meditation as before.

But, in spite of these things, it was a gay and magnificent revel. The tastes of the duke were peculiar. He had a fine eye for colors and effects. He disregarded the decora[2] of mere fashion. His plans were bold and fiery, and his conceptions glowed with barbaric luster. There are some who would have thought him mad. His followers felt that he was not. It was necessary to hear and see and touch him to be *sure* that he was not.

He had directed, in great part, the movable embellishments of the seven chambers, upon occasion of this great fete; and it was his own guiding taste which had given character to the masqueraders. Be sure they were grotesque. There were much glare and glitter and piquancy and phantasm — much of what has been since seen in *Hernani*.[3] There were arabesque figures with unsuited limbs and appointments. There were delirious fancies such as the madman fashions. There were much of the beautiful, much of the wanton, much of the bizarre, something of the terrible, and not a little of that which might have excited disgust. To and fro in the seven chambers there stalked, in fact, a multitude of dreams. And these — the dreams — writhed in and about, taking hue from the rooms and causing the wild music of the orchestra to seem as the echo of their steps. And, anon, there strikes the ebony clock which stands in the hall of the velvet. And then, for a moment, all is still, and all is silent save the voice of the clock. The dreams are stiff-frozen as they stand. But the echoes of the chime die away — they have endured but an instant — and a light, half-subdued laughter floats after them as they depart. And now again the music swells; and the dreams live and writhe to and fro more merrily than ever, taking hue from the many-tinted windows through which stream the rays from the tripods. But to the chamber which lies most westwardly of the seven there are now none of the maskers who venture; for the night is waning away; and there flows a ruddier light through the blood-colored panes; and the blackness of the sable drapery appalls; and to him whose foot falls upon the sable carpet, there comes from the near clock of ebony a muffled peal more solemnly emphatic than any which reaches *their* ears who indulge in the more remote gaieties of the other apartments.

But these other apartments were

[1] **disconcert:** breaking-up. [2] **decora:** the plural of the more familiar word *decorum*, meaning that which is befitting.

[3] **Hernani:** the name of a tragedy by Victor Hugo.

densely crowded, and in them beat feverishly the heart of life. And the revel went whirlingly on, until at length there commenced the sounding of midnight upon the clock. And then the music ceased, as I have told; and the evolutions of the waltzers were quieted; and there was an uneasy cessation of all things as before. But now there were twelve strokes to be sounded by the bell of the clock; and thus it happened, perhaps, that more of thought crept, with more of time, into the meditations of the thoughtful among those who reveled. And thus, too, it happened, perhaps, that before the last echoes of the last chime had utterly sunk into silence there were many individuals in the crowd who had found leisure to become aware of the presence of a masked figure which had arrested the attention of no single individual before. And the rumor of this new presence having spread itself whisperingly around, there arose at length from the whole company a buzz, or murmur, expressive of disapprobation and surprise — then, finally, of terror, of horror, and of disgust.

In an assembly of phantasms such as I have painted, it may well be supposed that no ordinary appearance could have excited such sensation. In truth, the masquerade license of the night was nearly unlimited; but the figure in question had out-Heroded Herod [1] and gone beyond the bounds of even the prince's indefinite decorum. There are chords in the hearts of the most reckless which cannot be touched without emotion. Even with the utterly lost, to whom life and death are equally jests, there are matters of which no jest can be made. The whole company, indeed, seemed now deeply to feel that in the costume and bearing of the stranger neither wit nor propriety existed. The figure was tall and gaunt, and shrouded from head to foot in the habiliments of the grave. The mask which concealed the visage was made so nearly to resemble the countenance of a stiffened corpse that the closest scrutiny must have had difficulty in detecting the cheat. And yet all this might have been endured, if not approved, by the mad revelers around. But the mummer had gone so far as to assume the type of the Red Death. His vesture was dabbled in *blood*—and his broad brow, with all the features of the face, was besprinkled with the scarlet horror.

When the eyes of Prince Prospero fell upon this spectral image (which, with a slow and solemn movement, as if more fully to sustain its role, stalked to and fro among the waltzers), he was seen to be convulsed, in the first moment with a strong shudder either of terror or distaste; but, in the next, his brow reddened with rage.

"Who dares" — he demanded hoarsely of the courtiers who stood near him — "who dares insult us with this blasphemous mockery? Seize him and unmask him — that we may know whom we have to hang, at sunrise, from the battlements!"

It was in the eastern or blue chamber in which stood the Prince Prospero as he uttered these words. They rang throughout the seven rooms loudly and clearly, for the prince was a bold and robust man, and the music had become hushed at the waving of his hand.

It was in the blue room where stood the prince, with a group of pale courtiers by his side. At first, as he spoke, there was a slight rushing movement of this group in the direction of the intruder, who at the moment was also near at hand and now, with deliberate and stately step, made closer approach to the speaker. But from a certain nameless awe with which the mad assumptions of the mummer had in-

[1] **had out-Heroded Herod:** had outdone or exceeded. Originally, had outdone in violence Herod, King of the Jews.

spired the whole party, there were found none who put forth hand to seize him; so that, unimpeded, he passed within a yard of the prince's person; and while the vast assembly, as if with one impulse, shrank from the centers of the rooms to the walls, he made his way uninterruptedly, but with the same solemn and measured step which had distinguished him from the first, through the blue chamber to the purple, through the purple to the green, through the green to the orange, through this again to the white, and even thence to the violet, ere a decided movement had been made to arrest him. It was then, however, that the Prince Prospero, maddening with rage and the shame of his own momentary cowardice, rushed hurriedly through the six chambers, while none followed him on account of a deadly terror that had seized upon all. He bore aloft a drawn dagger and had approached, in rapid impetuosity, to within three or four feet of the retreating figure when the latter, having attained the extremity of the velvet apartment, turned suddenly and confronted his pursuer. There was a sharp cry — and the dagger dropped gleaming upon the sable carpet, upon which, instantly afterward, fell prostrate in death the Prince Prospero. Then, summoning the wild courage of despair, a throng of the revelers at once threw themselves into the black apartment and, seizing the mummer, whose tall figure stood erect and motionless within the shadow of the ebony clock, gasped in unutterable horror at finding the grave cerements and corpselike mask, which they handled with so violent a rudeness, untenanted by any tangible form.

And now was acknowledged the presence of the Red Death. He had come like a thief in the night. And one by one dropped the revelers in the blood-bedewed halls of their revel, and died each in the despairing posture of his fall. And the life of the ebony clock went out with that of the last of the gay. And the flames of the tripods expired. And Darkness and Decay and the Red Death held illimitable dominion over all.

THINK BACK OVER WHAT YOU HAVE READ

Responding with Imagination to the Atmosphere of the Story

Look back over the story and find brief passages which communicated to you vividly:

1. the *horror* of the Red Death
2. the *grandeur* of the rooms in which the revelry took place
3. the *delirious fancifulness* of the masquerade
4. the *eerie* sounds that interrupted the gaiety
5. the *strange, dreamlike movement* of the dancers

What words and phrases seem to you particularly well chosen? What particular details gave you a keen sense of the scene?

Applying to the Story the Ideas Gained from the Introduction

6. At what point in the story did you first become aware that a nameless fear clutched at the heart of each guest?

7. What brief passages can you read to the class to show how this fear grows as the evening wears on?

8. At what point in the story did the guests first begin to realize the nature of their fear?

9. At what point in the story did you, the reader, first suspect the presence of the Red Death?

10. With what sensations did you come to the end of the story?

11. As you think back over the story, what seems to you most clever about Poe's method of telling it? With what brief quoted passages can you illustrate your point?

Increase Your Power over Words

Perhaps you noticed in your reading of "The Masque of the Red Death" that Poe uses a great many rare and uncommon words. Instead of the word *wise,* for example, he uses the word *sagacious;* instead of *face,* the word *visage.* In order that you may see for yourself just what effect is created by Poe's choice of words, the following exercises in vocabulary have been planned:

12. Rewrite the fourth paragraph in the story substituting a common word or phrase for each of the following:

voluptuous	candelabrum
imperial suite	profusion
vista	depended from the roof
impeded	
bizarre	emanating
irregularly disposed	corridors
vision embraced	illumined
eastern extremity	multitude
chamber	produced upon the countenances
casements	
shrouded	

Come to class prepared to read the amended paragraph aloud to the class and to discuss the change in effect which the altered vocabulary produces. What quality in the story seems to you to be lost in the amended version? What kind of words would you call those in the list above? Where would you be most likely to hear them? With what kind of scene are they associated in your mind?

13. What words does Poe use in place of the following italicized synonyms? Find the sentence in the story and notice the unusual word which Poe uses in its place:

a. There were sharp pains . . . profuse bleeding . . . with *death.*
b. They resolved to leave means neither of *entrance* nor *exit* to the sudden impulses of despair or of frenzy from within.
c. . . . the *older people* passed their hands over their brows as if in *thought.*
d. . . . it was a gay and magnificent *party.*
e. And, *presently,* there strikes the *black* clock . . . in the hall.

14. In summary what comments can you make about Poe's use of language? What kind of words will you hereafter associate with him? In what particular words has he interested you?

15. *Multus* is a Latin word meaning many. *Multus,* changed to *multi,* still means many when it is used to begin a word. Although *multitude* (page 69) is often used to mean a crowd of many people, it can also mean a great number of things, such as: A *multitude* of tasks awaited Mary when she returned home from the parade.

You know how to *multiply.* Isn't it a fast way of getting many numbers? Have you ever seen a *multigraph* work?

What kind of millionaire is a *multimillionaire?* If *ped* means *foot,* what kind of animals are *multipeds?*

Stories of Insight

THAT'S WHAT HAPPENED TO ME

by Michael Fessier (*1906–*)

The following story you will perhaps recognize as a kind of glorified daydream which Bottles, the fellow who tells the story, first told himself in secret and then *wished* to be true. Here, also, you may recognize something of the way in which you, too, like to think of yourself as a hero in order to salve the wounds of life. Bottles was hurt daily by his nicknames — especially "old Rubbernose," inflicted upon him by a girl whom he wished to please.

This story may be called a psychological story, for its author offers you a glimpse into the workings of a boy's mind. You may imagine that the author, Michael Fessier, who writes in the modern manner, conceived the aim of his story to be something like this: "Here's the story Bottles Barton would like to have told the world; the story, however, that he could really tell only to himself in secret. I'll tell it for him, and let those who read it see what kind of stuff a daydream is made of."

That's the kind of story introduced to you here. From it you may expect to derive two particular benefits: (1) you will be more sympathetic, hereafter, with boys like Bottles whose ambitions are thwarted; (2) you will, in a measure perhaps, grow a bit wiser about yourself.

The story is written as Bottles Barton — not Michael Fessier — actually thinks and talks. Thus the language is in keeping with the psychological aim of the story; it is, in other words, realistic rather than literary.

I HAVE done things and had things happen to me and nobody knows about it. So I am writing about it so that people will know. Although there are a lot of things I could tell about, I will just tell about the jumping because that is the most important. It gave me the biggest thrill. I mean high jumping, standing and running. You probably never heard of a standing high jumper but that's what I was. I was the greatest jumper ever was.

I was going to high school and I wasn't on any team. I couldn't be because I had to work for a drugstore and wash bottles and deliver medicine and sweep the floor. So I couldn't go out for any of the teams because the job started soon's school was over. I used to crab to the fellows about how old man Patch made me wash so many bottles and so they got to calling me Bottles Barton and I didn't like it. They'd call me Bottles in front of the girls and the girls'd giggle.

Once I poked one of the fellows for calling me Bottles. He was a big fellow and he played on the football team and I wouldn't have hit because I was little and couldn't fight very well. But he called me Bottles before Anna Louise Daniels and she laughed and I knew that it was her I should have taken the first poke at. I was more mad at her than the football player although it was him pulling my nose and sitting on me.

The next day I met Anna Louise in the hall going to the ancient-history class and she was with a couple of other girls and I tried to go past without them noticing me. I don't know why but I had a funny feeling like as if somebody was going to throw a rock at me or something. Anna Louise looked at me and giggled.

"Hello, old Rubbernose," she said.

The girls giggled and I hurried down the hall and felt sick and mad and kind of like I was running away from a fight, although nobody'd expect me to fight a girl. And so they called me Bottles sometimes and Rubbernose other times and always whoever was near would laugh. They didn't think it was funny because Jimmy Wilkins was called Scrubby or Jack Harris was called Doodles. But they thought it was funny I was called Rubbernose and Bottles and they never got tired of laughing. It was a new joke every time.

Scrubby pitched for the baseball team and Doodles was quarterback on the football team. I could have pitched no-hit games and I could have made touchdowns from my own ten-yard line. I know I could. I had it all figured out. I went over how I'd throw the ball and how the batter'd miss and it was easy. I figured out how to run and dodge and straight-arm and that was easy too. But I didn't get the chance because I had to go right to Patch's Drugstore after school was out.

Old man Patch was a pretty good guy but his wife she was nothing but a crab. I'd wash bottles and old man Patch he would look at them and not say anything. But Mrs. Patch, old lady Patch, she would look at the bottles and wrinkle her nose and make me wash half of them over again. When I swept up at night she'd always find some corner I'd missed and she'd bawl me out. She was fat and her hair was all straggly and I wondered why in the deuce old man Patch ever married her, although I guess maybe she didn't look so awful when she was a girl. She couldn't have been very pretty though.

They lived in back of the drugstore and when people came in at noon or at six o'clock either old man or old lady Patch'd come out still chewing their food and look at the customer and swallow and then ask him what he wanted.

I studied salesmanship at high school and I figured this wasn't very good for business and I wanted to tell them but I never did.

One of the fellows at school was in

waiting for a prescription and he saw me working at some of the things I did at the drugstore. So when another fellow asked me what I did, this fellow he laughed and said, " Old Bottles! Why, he rates at that store. Yes, he does! He rates like an Armenian's helper."

That's about the way I did rate; but I was planning on how I'd someday own a real, modern drugstore and run the Patches out of business, so I didn't mind so much.

What I did mind was Anna Louise at school. She was the daughter of a doctor and she thought she was big people and maybe she was but she wasn't any better'n me. Maybe my clothes weren't so good but that was only temporary. I planned on having twenty suits some day.

I wanted to go up to her and say, " Look here, Anna Louise, you're not so much. Your father isn't a millionaire and someday I'm going to be one. I'm going to have a million dollars and twenty suits of clothes." But I never did.

After she laughed at me and started calling me Rubbernose, I began planning on doing things to make her realize I wasn't what she thought I was. That's how the jumping came about.

It was the day before the track meet and everybody was talking about whether or not our school could win. They figured we'd have to win the high jump and pole vault to do it.

" Gee, if we only had old Heck Hansen back," said Goobers MacMartin. " He'd outjump those Fairfield birds two inches in the high and a foot in the pole vault."

" Yeah," somebody else said, " but we haven't got Heck Hansen. What we got is pretty good but not good enough. Wish we had a jumper."

" We sure need one," I said.

There was a group of them all talking, boys and girls, and I was sort of on the outside listening.

" Who let you in? " Goobers asked me.

Frank Shay grabbed me by the arm and dragged me into the center of the circle.

" The very man we've been looking for," he said. " Yessir. Old Bottles Rubbernose Barton. He can win the jumping events for us."

" Come on, Bottles," they said. " Save the day for us. Be a good old Rubbernose."

Anna Louise was one who laughed the most and it was the third time I'd wanted to pop her on the nose.

I went away from there and didn't turn back when they laughed and called and whistled at me.

" She'd be surprised if I did," I said.

I kept thinking this over and pretty soon I said, " Well, maybe you could."

Then when I was sweeping the drugstore floor I all of a sudden said, " I can."

" You can what? " Mrs. Patch asked me.

" Nothing," I said.

" You can hurry about sweeping the floor, that's what you can do," she said.

There was a big crowd out for the track meet and we were tied when I went up to our coach. It was just time for the jumping to start.

" What are you doing in a track suit? " he asked me.

" I'm going to save the day for Brinkley," I said. " I'm going to jump."

" No, you aren't," he said. " You run along and start a marble game with some other kid."

I looked him in the eye and I spoke in a cold, level tone of voice. " Mr. Smith," I said, " the track meet depends on the high jump and the pole vault and unless I am entered we will lose those two events and the meet. I can win and I am willing to do it for Brinkley. Do you want to win the meet? "

He looked amazed.

" Where have you been all the time? " he asked. " You talk like you've got something on the ball."

I didn't say anything; I just smiled.

The crowd all rushed over to the jumping pits and I took my time going over. When everybody had jumped but me the coach turned and said, " Come on now, Barton, let's see what you can do."

" Not yet," I said.

" What do you mean? " he asked.

" I'll wait until the last man has been eliminated," I said. " Then I'll jump."

The crowd laughed but I just stared coldly at them. The coach tried to persuade me to jump but I wouldn't change my mind.

" I stake everything on one jump," I said. " Have faith in me."

He looked at me and shook his head and said, " Have it your own way."

They started the bar a little over four feet and pretty soon it was creeping up toward five feet and a half. That's always been a pretty good distance for high-school jumpers. When the bar reached five feet, seven inches all our men except one was eliminated. Two from Fairfield were still in the event. They put the bar at five feet, nine inches and one man from Fairfield made it. Our man tried hard but he scraped the bar and knocked it off.

The crowd started yelling, thinking Fairfield had won the event.

" Wait a minute," I yelled. " I haven't jumped yet."

The judges looked at their list and saw it was so. Maybe you think it was against the rules for them to allow me to skip my turn but anyway that's the way it was.

" You can't make that mark," one of the judges said. " Why try? You're not warmed up."

" Never mind," I said.

I walked up close to the jumping standard and stood there.

" Go ahead and jump," one of the judges said.

" I will," I said.

" Well, don't stand there," he said. " Come on back here so's you can get a run at it."

" I don't want any run at the bar," I said. " I'll jump from here."

The judge yelled at the coach and told him to take me out on account of I was crazy.

I swung my arms in back of me and sprung up and down a second and then I jumped over the bar with inches to spare. When I came down, it was so silent I could hear my footsteps as I walked across the sawdust pit. The judge that'd crabbed at me just stood and looked. His eyes were bugged out and his mouth hung open.

" Jumping Jehoshaphat! " he said.

Our coach came up and he stood beside the judge and they both looked the same, bug-eyed.

" Did you see that? " the coach asked. " Tell me you didn't. Please do. I'd rather lose this track meet than my mind."

The judge turned slowly and looked at him.

All of a sudden everybody started yelling and the fellows near me pounded me on the back and tried to shake my hand. I smiled and brushed them aside and walked over to the judge.

" What's the high-school record for this state? " I asked.

" Five feet, eleven inches," he said.

" Put her at six," I said.

They put the bar at six and I gathered myself together and gave a heave and went over the bar like I was floating. It was easy. Well, that just knocked the wind out of everybody. They'd thought I couldn't do anything and there I'd broken the state record for the high jump without a running start.

The crowd surrounded me and tried to

shake my hand and the coach and judge got off to one side and reached out and pinched each other's cheeks and looked at the bar and shook their heads. Frank Shay grabbed my hand and wrung it and said, "Gosh, Bottles, I was just kidding the other day. I didn't know you were such a ring-tailed wonder. Say, Bottles, we're having a frat dance tonight. Will you come?"

"You know what you can do with your frat," I said. "I don't approve of them. They're undemocratic."

A lot of the fellows that'd made fun of me before crowded around and acted as if I'd been their friend all along.

When Anna Louise crowded through the gang and said, "Oh, you're marvelous," I just smiled at her and said, "Do you think so?" and walked away. She tagged around after me but I talked mostly with two other girls.

They didn't usually have a public-address system at our track meets but they started using one then.

"Ladies and gentlemen," the announcer said, "you have just witnessed a record-breaking performance by Bottles Barton — "

He went on like that telling them what an astonishing thing I'd done and it came to me I didn't mind being called Bottles any more. In fact, I kind of liked it.

Mr. and Mrs. Patch came up and Mrs. Patch tried to kiss me but I wouldn't let her. Old man Patch shook my hand.

"You've made our drugstore famous," he said. "From now on you're a clerk. No more bottle washing."

"We'll make him a partner," old lady Patch said.

"No, you won't," I said. "I think I'll go over to the McManus Pharmacy."

Then they called the pole vault and I did like I'd done before. I wouldn't jump until our men'd been eliminated. The bar was at eleven feet.

"It's your turn," our coach told me. "Ever use a pole before?"

"Oh, sure," I told him.

He gave me a pole and the crowd cleared away and grew silent. Everyone was watching me.

I threw the pole down and smiled at the crowd. The coach yelled for me to pick up the pole and jump. I picked it up and threw it ten feet away from me. Everybody gasped. Then I took a short run and went over the bar at eleven feet. It was simple.

This time the coach and the judge took pins and poked them in one another's cheeks. The coach grabbed me and said, "When I wake up I'm going to be so mad at you I'm going to give you the beating of your life."

Anna Louise came up and held my arm and said, "Oh, Bottles, you're so wonderful. I've always thought so. Please forgive me for calling you Rubbernose. I want you to come to our party tonight."

"All right," I said. "I'll forgive you but don't you call me Rubbernose again."

They moved the bar up again and the fellow from Fairfield couldn't make it. I took a short run and went over. I did it so easy it came to me I could fly if I wanted to but I decided not to try it on account of people wouldn't think it so wonderful if a fellow that could fly jumped eleven feet without a pole. I'd won the track meet for Brinkley High and the students all came down out of the stand and put me on their shoulders and paraded me around the track. A lot of fellows were waving papers at me asking me to sign them and get one thousand dollars a week as a professional jumper. I signed one which threw in an automobile.

That's what I did once and nobody knows about it, so I am writing about it so that people will know.

THINK BACK OVER WHAT YOU HAVE READ

Looking into the Way Bottles's Mind Works

1. Bottles had what is popularly known as an "inferiority complex." Find examples which show that he wasn't sure of himself at school, at the store. To what circumstances in his life do you attribute his sense of defeat? What change in circumstances would, in all probability, have permitted Bottles to develop as a normal, competent boy?

2. How did Bottles excuse himself to himself? Whom or what did he blame for his failures? Did you accept his explanations as true?

3. Look back over the story and notice how often Bottles uses the word *someday: someday* he'd own a real, modern drugstore, and so forth. What explanation can you give of his reliance on *someday?* Does it sound to you like wholesome ambition?

4. At what point in the story do you think Bottles is sticking to facts? At what point do you first recognize that a wish has become father to the thought and that from there on Fancy is telling the story?

5. Into what kind of an emergency does Bottles, the hero, miraculously step? Is this situation in any way similar to those in your own daydreams? in what particulars?

6. By what means does Bottles reinstate himself in his own eyes? What lines can you quote to show how in Bottles's mind his new victory offsets the old defeats?

7. What significance do you attach to Bottles's statement on page 76: ". . . and it came to me I didn't mind being called Bottles any more. In fact, I kind of liked it"?

Interpreting the Story in the Light of Your Own Experience

What common weaknesses in human nature do you recognize in the following of Bottles's statements?

8. "I *could have* pitched" for the baseball team. . . . "I know I could. . . . But I *didn't get the chance*" (page 73).

9. Patch's wife "was nothing but *a crab*" (page 73).

10. "Anna Louise . . . *thought she was big people* . . . but she wasn't any better'n me" (page 74).

11. "I wanted to go up to her and say . . . But *I never did*" (page 74).

12. "I smiled and *brushed them aside*" (page 75).

TONIGHT IN PERSON

by Corey Ford (1903-)

The pleasure to be gained from this story by a modern author lies chiefly in its power to stir thought; and, contrary to popular notion, thinking is often a pleasant pastime. Not always is thinking to be regarded as a task. Much of our pleasure in experience comes from thinking about it afterward — not only reliving it, but taking it apart in our minds and seeing what it's made of. What does this or that situation *mean?* From what strange causes did it arise? And where will it lead? It is this kind of thinking — *reflection,* we call it — that occupies the minds of all persons who really savor life to the full. It is this kind of thinking that follows the reading of stories which are drawn from real life.

It is out of this kind of thinking that we gradually build for ourselves an attitude toward life, or — if you aren't afraid of a big word — a *philosophy* of life. Everyone has a philosophy of life — of a kind — whether he calls it by that name or not; he has, that is, a set of beliefs to steer by. Some people's lives are ruled by their belief in luck — that's their philosophy. Louisa May Alcott, the celebrated author of *Little Women* and *Little Men,* based her life on the homely philosophy of "jolly hard work," as she named it. You must not think of *philosophers* as haunting only the great halls of learning. On the contrary, philosophers — that is, persons who extract wisdom from experience — turn up in the most amazing places. Over the radio comes the voice of a farmer who has turned philosopher and retails his wisdom "Over the Barnyard Fence." In the story that follows, it is the chambermaid who, surprisingly enough, turns out to be a philosopher; and it is her wisdom that helps set a spoiled boy back on his feet.

St. Louis, Mo., June 16:

Cheering crowds jammed the railroad station today to greet young David — "Davey" — Jones, eighteen-year-old film sensation and star of the forthcoming Colossus picture, *Jungle Boy,* who passed through this city bound for his first visit to New York. As a reward for " Davey's " stellar work in the film version of the Kipling classic, he has been given this little pleasure trip to the East, where he will rest and enjoy himself in the big city to his heart's content while making four personal appearances a day at the Colossus Theater.

Accompanying " Davey " on his vacation jaunt are Adolph J. Kessler, president of Colossus Pictures; Dennis Duffey, who directed *Jungle Boy;* and a large delegation of vice-presidents, executives, supervisors, and other officials of the film company, including Lou Ernst, director of public relations, who was constantly at the side of the juvenile star.

" St. Louis is sure a wonderful city," said young Jones, as the train pulled out. " I wish I could stay here longer. I hope you like my picture."

Chicago, Ill., June 17: Yesterday a humble student in a Los Angeles high school — today the DARLING of a million fans!

Like the fable of Cinderella reads the TRUE LIFE story of " Davey " Jones, boy wonder of Colossus Pictures, who was selected from a field of over a THOUSAND applicants to play the coveted role of " Mowgli " in *Jungle Boy,* forthcoming screen version of the never-to-be-forgotten *Jungle Books* by Rudyard Kipling.

Surely such a SUDDEN rise to FAME would turn the head of any ordinary mortal! Yet through it all Davey has managed to remain MODEST and UNSPOILED! Interviewed at the Victoria Hotel here today as he paused between trains, en route to New York to attend the PREMIÈRE of his picture tomorrow, the fair-haired and handsome young screen star — he is barely eighteen — kept his eyes lowered and maintained a bashful silence.

" Davey is just PLAIN BOY," said Lou Ernst, who acted as spokesman for the shrinking youth during the conversation. " He likes to swim and play baseball, and shoot marbles with the ' gang.' He never forgets to write his mother every single day he is away."

" Chicago is sure a WONDERFUL city," added Davey, his eyes sparkling. " I wish I could stay here longer. I hope you like my picture."

New York, N. Y., June 18: " It's all just a great, big, beautiful dream. I keep pinching myself to see if I'll really wake up! "

Such were the words of young " Davey " Jones, Hollywood's latest discovery and overnight sensation of the screen, as he was greeted by eager fans when arriving this morning upon his initial visit to the metropolis. Davey told newspapermen that New York was " sure a wonderful city."

" Davey is going to ' take in ' all the sights while he is here," said Lou Ernst, speaking for the youthful star on his arrival here. " He wants to see Bronx Park, and Coney Island, the biggest buildings, and Grant's Tomb. He worked very hard while he was making *Jungle Boy,* the Colossus classic opening at the Colossus Theater tonight, and now he just wants to ' loaf ' and have a real vacation."

Later Davey was escorted up Broadway to the Merrick Hotel in an open car with a loud-speaker which announced: " All New York is welcoming Davey Jones, the Jungle Boy! " After posing for photographers and newsreel men, Davey left to attend the luncheon of the Advirtising Club at the Houghton, the A.M.P.A. luncheon at Purcella's, and later the Dutch Treat luncheon at the Manning. From there he will proceed to City Hall, where he will shake hands with the mayor, after which he will address a meeting of the Downtown Women's Club, lay the cornerstone of a new Y.M.C.A., and toss out a baseball at the Yankee Stadium in the Bronx. At five o'clock he will speak over the radio on the topic "How It Feels to Be a Star," following which he will hand out free dinners to the newsboys of New York. Tonight he will be guest of honor at a banquet for the motion-picture critics before he departs for the Colossus Theater. . . .

"Ladies and gentlemen [*pause and smile*], thank you very much for your applause. [*Smile*] Gosh — you must know how glad I am and all that. After all, when you're looking for a job one day, and the next day the whole world seems to be patting you on the back [*smile*] — I guess that anyone can see that I'm jumping out of my skin — well — with just plain happiness." . . .

Mr. Lou Ernst rested his fingers on the typewriter keys and let his wrists droop as he looked up wearily. He scowled as his secretary thrust her head through the door.

"What is it?"

"Mr. Kessler on the phone," said the secretary.

"Again?"

"He says it's very important."

"Tell him I'll call him back," said Lou Ernst. "I got to get this speech ready for the boy-wonder to hand out at the Colossus tonight."

"That's who he says it's about," the secretary persisted. "He says Mr. Jones is carrying on kind of funny — like he don't feel good. He says he's a little hysterical. Over the radio just now, he nearly broke down and cried."

Lou Ernst glanced irritably at his watch. "O. K. Call off the free dinners to the newsboys. They can eat some other time. Tell him to take Davey back to the hotel instead and get him to take a nap. He'll be all right by night."

The secretary hesitated dubiously. "Mr. Kessler was worried. He says Mr. Jones really don't act very well — "

"You're telling me?" interrupted Lou Ernst bitterly, returning to his typewriter.

"People say that the age of miracles has passed," he typed again rapidly. "Well, folks, it hasn't [*smile*] — 'cause one of them smacked me right in the eye just now when I got the chance to play the part of Mowgli in *Jungle Boy*." He sighed, ripped out the sheet of yellow paper from his machine, and inserted a second. "Of course," he resumed, blinking smoke stolidly out of his eyes, "most of the credit for this wonderful picture really should go to Mr. Adolf Kessler, the kind and sympathetic president of Colossus Pictures." . . .

"And now, ladies and gentlemen," concluded the master of ceremonies, "it is our privilege and pleasure to present to you tonight the youthful star of this great picture — Mr. Davey Jones!"

He gestured dramatically toward the wings. The lights dimmed, the orchestra swelled to a crescendo, the spotlight sped to the left of the proscenium and picked up a diminutive figure cowering in the flies. The audience rocked with applause, stamped, and yelled. Davey shuffled forward uncertainly.

The spot followed him relentlessly as he moved slowly across the huge stage. He seemed incredibly tiny in the center of that revealing circle of light, like a bug under a reading glass. In contrast with his recent heroic image, leaping tall and naked through the jungle shrubbery, he was disappointingly short and stocky off the screen, a prosaic young man in a blue serge suit, his blond hair a little rumpled and his face pale beneath the tan grease paint. He halted awkwardly before the microphone, and stood for a moment locking and unlocking his hands.

" Ladies and gentlemen," Davey began in a shaky voice. He had commenced unaccountably to rock back and forth on his toes. " Thank you very much." He remembered to force a smile. " Gosh — you must know how glad I am — I mean — and all that — "

His voice was rising unnaturally. He could hear it singing. He was rocking faster and faster, bouncing a little on his heels. The smile hardened on his face.

" After all — when the whole world seems to be patting you on the back one day — "

He paused, confused. Someone tittered. He was bumping up and down, unable to stop himself. His face had begun to twitch uncontrollably.

" I guess anyone can see I'm jumping out of my skin — well — with just plain happiness — " Suddenly his voice broke and he bounded into the air. " Oh, please," he screamed, *" let me alone ! "*

He ran blindly toward the wings.

The master of ceremonies stepped forward with rare presence of mind, raised his hand, and quieted the excited audience. " Ladies and gentlemen," he began, " owing to the sudden illness of Mr. Jones — "

Blue tobacco smoke drifted and prowled in slowly rippling planes across the living room of Mr. Kessler's suite at the Merrick. In gloomy silence the executives and officials of Colossus Pictures sat slumped in their chairs in various despondent positions. Mr. Rickenheimer, manager of the Colossus Theater, puffed glumly at a dead cigar butt; Dennis Duffey sat cleaning his fingernails and glancing occasionally at Lou Ernst, crouching in a corner and blinking like a mandarin through the thin trickle of smoke that rose from his cigarette. They looked up expectantly as Mr. Kessler opened the door.

" I can't do anything with him," Mr. Kessler sighed, in reply to their unspoken question. " He just lies there on his stomach on the bed and kicks his heels and screams."

" Did you talk to him ? " asked Mr. Boomer, the supervisor. " Did you tell him he's got to go on this afternoon ? That it was for old Colossus Pictures."

Mr. Kessler sighed. " He just chewed on the corner of his pillow," he said, " and yelled for me to go away and leave him alone."

" What did the doctor say ? " asked Miss Pinkham, the head of distribution.

" He didn't say anything," said Mr. Kessler. " He said he's all right. He's just a little upset."

" All right, great gosh ! " snorted Mr. Rickenheimer, springing to his feet and pacing up and down. " He bursts out crying all over the stage of the Colossus Theater, he spoils my *première* last night, he makes me the laughingstock of the profession — and he's just a little upset."

" We've got to do something, A. J.," said Mr. Leslie, in charge of advertising and promotion. " We've sunk over twenty grand in this campaign so far, and we got to go through with it now. Think of the money ! "

" Think of our distribution," said Miss Pinkham.

" Think of my professional reputation," added Mr. Duffey.

" Of course," Mr. Rickenheimer groaned, " please don't nobody bother to think of my theater — "

The room lapsed into thoughtful silence.

" Maybe we ought to offer him more money, A. J.," suggested Mr. Boomer.

" Break his contract," interrupted Mr. Rickenheimer. " Cancel his tour, call off his next picture, and put him in the doghouse. Just scare him enough and he'll come around — "

"If it would cheer him up," suggested Mr. Leslie, "I could arrange to have him run down to Washington tomorrow and shake hands with the President — "

Mr. Kessler threw up his hands. "No, no, no," he moaned, gnawing his cigar. "What we lack around here is a dearth of good ideas. Hasn't anybody in all this collection of fabulous brains got even a remotest inkling what's wrong?"

His gaze swept the room and came to rest on the quizzical features of Lou Ernst. Lou lifted his eyes and gazed up obliquely at his chief for a moment.

"I was thinking, A. J.," he murmured, "maybe he's just lonely." . . .

She heard the sound vaguely as she selected a key from the big ring in the pocket of her work dress and opened the door of his suite. She paused and closed the door behind her uncertainly, listening. The sound seemed to come from the bedroom.

"Would you rather I come back later?" she inquired at last.

Davey Jones lifted his head from the pillow in surprise. His sobs died and he rose on his elbows, gazing at her blankly for a moment. She might have been young or middle-aged or old, he could not tell at a glance. Her hair was that indeterminate yellow-gray, faded almost white at her temples. The skin on her face was colorless and gray, and the color seemed to have faded even from her lips and her pale blue eyes. She paused uneasily, clutching the bundle of sheets and towels against her chest.

"I'm just the chambermaid," she said. "I can make your room some other time if you'd rather be alone."

"I beg your pardon," said Davey. He swung his legs off the bed and sat erect on the edge of the bed, still staring at her. "It's all right. Come in."

"I won't be a minute," she called, putting fresh towels on the rack in the bathroom. "Go right ahead and cry your eyes out, if you want to, and get it over with."

"I wasn't," said Davey uneasily.

"It's good for you," she called from the bathroom. "Go ahead. Don't mind me. I know how it is. I got a couple myself at home like you."

"I wasn't crying," Davey insisted.

"I suppose you were doubled up laughing," she smiled, emerging from the bathroom. She began to wipe the top of the dresser rapidly with a used towel. "What's the matter? All alone in the big city?"

Suddenly he began to laugh.

"Maybe I must of said something funny."

He laughed harder, rocking back and forth on the bed and holding his sides weakly. He laughed until the tears rolled down his cheeks. She turned and regarded him, puzzled.

"Make up your mind, now," she murmured uncertainly. "Either laugh or else cry, one or the other, but don't be changing back and forth so sudden."

"All alone," Davey gasped, choking with laughter. "With everybody following me wherever I go — telling me where to appear — what to say — when to smile. Talk over the radio. Lunch. Interview. Pose with a newsboy. Smile. Pose with the mayor. Smile. Pose with this and that big building," he screamed, his laugh rising shrilly. "Smile — smile — "

"All right," she said at last. He still laughed idiotically as she crossed the room toward him. "All right, now, that's enough of that," she repeated. Suddenly she shook him roughly by the shoulder. "All right. Do you hear?"

He stopped laughing suddenly, and stared at her.

"I'm sorry," she said, a little embarrassed. "I guess I shouldn't have done that. I should have minded my own business, I guess."

"That's all right," he said slowly.

"I was only afraid you'd make yourself sick, taking on like that," she explained.

"I hate to see anybody all upset, particularly a youngster. It's none of my business, I guess, but it's like if it was one of my own kids. I know how I'd feel — "

"How many kids have you got?" asked Davey, leaning back against the pillow and watching her curiously.

"Two. They ain't my kids, really," she explained, dusting the window sill rapidly. "They're my sister's. I take care of them."

"Isn't your sister — "

"She went away," she replied shortly. She emptied an ash receiver briskly into the wastebasket, polished it clean with the towel, and set it back on the dresser. "Now, then," she said briskly, "why don't you put some cold water on your face and get out and get a breath of air? You'll feel better for it."

He shook his head slowly. "I can't."

"Won't they let you?"

"They'd follow me wherever I went," he said. "They wouldn't let me alone. There'd be police around in no time, and reporters, and people trying to get me to sign things — "

She was backing away from him, a little frightened. "What have you done, then?"

"I'm Davey Jones," he said in surprise.

"I mean, why would they follow you on the street?"

"I'm in the movies," he explained rather stiffly.

She looked puzzled. "What's wrong with that?"

Davey flushed. "I'm in *Jungle Boy,* that just opened last night," he mentioned casually. "You may have read about me in the papers."

"I don't read the papers," she said, still eying him suspiciously.

"I'm the star," he said.

"You a movie star!" she grinned skeptically.

"I have a three years' contract in Hollywood," he replied, goaded, "and I get five hundred a week to start in with — "

She laughed. "Well, and I'm glad to meet you, I'm sure," she said gaily. "I'm the Queen of Roumania, myself. It's a small world."

"You don't have to believe me if you don't want to," Davey sulked.

"If what you're saying was true, for instance," she demanded triumphantly, "then why would you be crying just now, and taking on? Five hundred dollars all in one week, and crying about it? Go 'long."

"It's true, though," he insisted weakly.

"In that case," she interrupted, "you'd ought to be ashamed of yourself."

He hesitated. "You don't understand" — sheepishly. "It's what I've got to do to earn it — "

"For five hundred dollars," she said grimly, "I'd take off my clothes and ride down Broadway on a white horse." [1]

"Luncheons," he recalled miserably, "and speeches, and shaking hands here, and smiling there, and always being in the spotlight — it makes you feel so cheap — "

"Listen, sonny!" Her eyes flashed. "Don't talk to *me* about feeling cheap. I used to think that way, too, until I figured it all out for myself. Let me give you a tip. There's no reason why you, or me, or anybody should be ashamed of what he's doing for a living, so long as he does his job. Let the rest of the world

[1] The chambermaid is thinking, probably, of Godiva, a Saxon lady of legendary fame, who did just that — not down Broadway but through the streets of Coventry, England, in about the year 1040.

be ashamed of you, if it wants to, but *you* don't need to be. I am the captain of my soul.[1] Do you read poetry?"

He shook his head.

"My oldest is learning it in school," she explained.

He sighed unhappily. "But it's this business of never being alone — never being able to do what I want to do —"

"Look here to me, young man." She faced him. "I don't know who you are or what you do, or whether you're telling me the truth, and of course it's none of my business, for the matter of that, but there's something you ought to know for your own good. You're being sorry for yourself. That's all is the matter with you. You're crying over yourself and pitying yourself, and feeling how hard a time you're having, just as if you were the only one in all the world that ever had a hard time. There's others. You'd ought to be ashamed."

He was staring at her.

"You may be a star in the movies," she said disbelievingly, "but to me you're just a selfish, spoiled brat, and I wish you was mine for about two minutes."

He grinned slowly. "I wish I was."

"Yes, well, if you was, you'd get out and hustle," she retorted, relaxing a little. "And there'd be no lalligagging around in bed at noon or having breakfast in your room, or being pampered and fussed over, or feeling sorry for yourself; not at all. You'd work for a living. You'd get out and earn your keep like John — that's my oldest. He works from right after school till nearly midnight sometimes delivering for the drugstore; or else my younger one — he's been selling papers to help out ever since my husband left me —" She checked herself abruptly.

[1] William Ernest Henley's poem "Invictus" (which means "Unconquerable") ends with this stirring line.

"I'm sorry," said Davey.

She began to pile the soiled linen in a heap on top of a bath towel. "He went away with my sister," she added casually, as she knotted the ends of the bath towel around the linen. "There, now. Put some cold water on your face, sonny; you'll feel better." She reached over and patted his shoulder clumsily. "Sometimes if you feel sorry for somebody else," she whispered, "there's not so much time to be sorry for yourself."

"I guess I was a little lonely, too," he said thoughtfully.

"Who isn't?" she demanded. "Everybody's lonely. Nobody understands anybody else, and why should they? Just go ahead with whatever you got to do, and do your job, and never mind what they think. But way down inside of you — always be a little lonely. That's your privilege," she said. "That's one thing they can never take away from you."

He nodded.

"Well." She picked up the linen again, and grinned over her shoulder. "I'll be seeing you in the movies!" . . .

Mr. Kessler opened the door of Davey's suite and listened curiously.

Then he stepped to the door of the bedroom and blinked. Davey was marching up and down the room, the typewritten copy of his speech in his hand, reciting it aloud, with gestures, at the mirror. He nodded over his shoulder casually.

"Hello, Mr. Kessler." He glanced down again at the copy of his speech. "I guess anyone can see," he resumed, "that I'm jumping out of my skin — well — with just plain happiness —"

"You feel all right, Davey?" asked Mr. Kessler, unable to believe his eyes.

"Sure," said Davey pleasantly.

Mr. Kessler turned. Behind him Lou Ernst had halted and was gazing through the bedroom door. Mr. Kessler winked at him triumphantly.

"I thought you said he was lonely, Lou," he chided. "I guess you was wrong for once."

Lou Ernst shrugged.

"Because there ain't been a soul he could of talked to since I left," Mr. Kessler pointed out serenely. "The door's even been locked the whole time."

The chambermaid came out of the bedroom and shuffled past them apologetically, carrying a wastebasket into the hall to empty.

"Except the chambermaid," said Lou Ernst.

"Yeah, except the chambermaid, of course," Mr. Kessler chuckled casually, "and nobody ever pays any attention to the chambermaid."

He beamed again through the bedroom door. Davey was watching himself critically in the mirror as he spread his arms in a dramatic gesture.

"People say the age of miracles is past," he recited. "Well, folks, it hasn't." He smiled at the mirror. "'Cause one of them smacked me right between the eyes just now." . . .

THINK BACK OVER WHAT YOU HAVE READ

Reading "between the Lines" of the Story

What thoughts occurred to you as you came to the following sentences in the story? Glance back over the story and see whether you can recognize the hidden force behind each sentence.

1. ". . . maybe he's just lonely" (page 81). In the light of what has occurred so far in the story, why does this statement sound odd? What strange truth, discernible to Mr. Ernst, lies behind this statement?

2. "I'm just the chambermaid" (page 81). In the light of what follows, what is the force of the word *just?* What pathos lies behind the word? What irony?

3. "Five hundred dollars all in one week, and crying about it" (page 82)? These words must have startled Davey into realizing — what?

4. "Because there ain't been a soul he could of talked to since I left" (page 84). What irony lies behind these words of Mr. Kessler? What lines that follow add force to the irony?

5. "People say the age of miracles is past. . . . Well, folks, it hasn't. . . . 'Cause one of them smacked me right between the eyes just now" (page 84). What is Davey thinking to himself as he comes to this part of his memorized speech? What *miracle* is he thinking about?

Understanding the Characters

6. Which of the following characters seemed to you most understanding of Davey: Mr. Kessler, president of Colossus Pictures? Mr. Rickenheimer, manager of the Colossus Theater? Mr. Leslie, in charge of advertising and promotion? Mr. Lou Ernst, ghost writer for the boy wonder? or Miss Pinkham, head of distribution? What evidence can you cite from the story itself to support your decision?

7. What truths about life has the chambermaid learned from experience? Which of her sentences to Davey seem to you most worth quoting? What did she teach him?

8. What kind of boy is Davey? In the first part of the story what is the matter with him? What change comes over him at the end of the story? How do you account for the change? What proof of character does this change reveal?

Thinking about What You Have Read

9. What ideas did you gain from the story about loneliness? the loneliness of fame? everybody's loneliness? How does the chambermaid solve the problem of loneliness? What is the best cure for feeling sorry for oneself?

10. What impressed you most about the life of a film star? Did your glimpse behind the scenes change any idea previously held? What facts did you learn about the *business* of building up a star? In what way were you impressed? Have you any criticism to make of the methods used to promote and advertise a motion-picture star?

11. What do *you* mean by the word *spoiled* when applied to a boy? Does it square with the chambermaid's use of the word? Was Davey

spoiled? What factors contribute to the *spoiling* of a boy or a girl? How would you recognize an adult who had been spoiled as a child?

For Ambitious Students

12. Come to class prepared to read aloud Henley's poem " Invictus," which, you remember, the chambermaid's " oldest " was learning in school. In the light of what the story reveals about the character of the chambermaid, be prepared to discuss the influence of the poem on her thoughts about life.

THE UNFAMILIAR

by Richard Connell (1893–)

It isn't always a serious story that succeeds in making us think about life. Sometimes our minds are prodded into reflection when we least expect them to be by an amusing or exciting adventure. Such is the case in the story that follows. Behind the unpretentious title lies an important social idea, closely related to your own experience, presented to you with such lightness of touch and appealing grace that you will find thinking about it afterward a pleasure.

Prejudice! It's an ugly word that stands for an ugly trait in human nature. Literally the word means judging beforehand or making up our minds about people or places or situations *before* we have any right to. We call people cowards, perhaps, before we know anything about the dangers which they have had to face. We call a book dull before we have so much as looked at it. We make up our minds constantly on this basis and call " the unfamiliar " (notice that that's the title of the story) by all sorts of names — names which tell how we feel about things we know nothing about.

In the story that follows it is Velvet Pants — as the " small, scared man " who came to Crosby Corners was called — who carries this truth about human behavior through the line to a most spectacular touchdown.

WHO HE was and what he was and where he came from no one knew. How he came to be in Crosby Corners was a mystery, and at harvest time Connecticut farmers are too busy to peer into mysteries. He could not speak much English beyond " Yes," " No," and " Hungry," but he could gesture — with his hands, his elbows, his eyes, his feet. He appeared to be trying by pantomime to convey the idea that he had been forcibly seized in his native land, which was remote; had been pressed into service aboard a ship; had been very ill at sea; had escaped at a port; had fled on a train; and had dropped, or been dropped, at Crosby Corners. The farmers, however, had no time to interpret pantomime. Farm hands were scarce, and, if a man had two hands and at least one good eye, they did not delve into his past or his pedigree: they put him to work.

It was thus that the small, scared man in the velvet trousers entered the employ of Ben Crosby, richest farmer in that region.

" I found the little rascal," Ben Crosby told his wife, " squealing like a pig in a hornet's nest, and frightened almost out of his wits, with Constable Pettit marching him along by the ear. 'Constable,' I says, 'what is that and where did you get it?' He says to me, 'I dunno what it is, Ben, but it looks foreign. I found it down by the railroad tracks trying to eat a raw potato. When I asked it what its name was, it said, " See." ' I says to the constable, 'He may be a Gypsy, or he may be a Hindu, and he looks as if he suspected you of being a cannibal. But,' I says, 'he seems wiry and he didn't get that lovely tobacco-brown finish of his at a pink tea or from working in an office. Now I need hands worse than ducks need ponds. So turn him over to me 'stead of sticking him in the calaboose, and I'll give him a job.' Pettit didn't want to be bothered with him, so he turned him over to me; and there he is out at the pump, washing the dirtiest pair of hands I ever saw and now and then rubbing his stomach to show how hungry he is. I'll send him to the back door, Hannah; you give him a lining of ham and eggs and pie, and then send him down to me. I'll be in the twenty-acre lot."

Presently there came a knock on the back door of the Crosby house. It was not at all a robust knock; it was a tap as faint and timid as a butterfly's kick.

Mrs. Crosby opened the door and saw a small man standing there; his face was a rich brown; his eyes were black and apprehensive; he appeared to be ready to flee if the occasion demanded it. When he saw Mrs. Crosby, however, he bowed deeply. Such a bow had never before been executed at Crosby Corners except in the moving pictures. It was a sweeping, courtly thing, that bow, in which the small man swept off his wide felt hat and dusted the steps with it.

Then he smiled; it was a humble, ingratiating smile. He looked toward the stove, where the sizzling ham was sending its aroma heavenward, and sighed. Mrs. Crosby pointed to a chair at the kitchen table, and he, with another bow, took it and presently was eating hungrily and freely. Mrs. Crosby now and then lifted an eye from her canning to regard the exotic stranger; she had a doubt or two at first whether it was safe for her to stay there. She glanced into the dining room where, above the mantel, hung Grandpa Crosby's Civil War sword, a long, heavy weapon; its presence reassured her. As she studied the man, she decided that any fear of him was groundless; if anything, he was afraid of her. His hair, she observed, was blue-black and long, but arranged in a way that suggested that he was a bit of a dandy. The stranger's trousers surprised her greatly; they were of black velvet, really painfully tight, except at the bottom of each leg, where they flared out like bells. He had no belt but, instead, a scarlet sash. His shirt, when new and clean, must have been a remarkable garment; it had been plaid silk, but it was now neither new nor clean. His boots were of patent leather and excessively pointed.

When he had eaten a very great deal, he arose, bowed, smiled beatifically, and made gestures of gratitude. Mrs. Crosby pointed in the direction of the twenty-acre lot, and he understood. She saw him picking his way down the path; he was the first man she had ever seen whose gait at one and the same time included a mince and a swagger.

When Ben Crosby came in to his late supper that evening he announced, "I was wrong about that new little fellow. He doesn't seem to have done farm work. He's willing enough, but he handles a hayfork as dainty as if it was a toothpick. And say, he certainly is the most scary human being I ever set eyes on. You should have seen him when the tractor came into the field with the mowing machine. He gave a yelp and jumped on the stone wall, and, if there'd been a tree handy, I guess he'd have climbed it. He looked as if he was afraid the machine would eat him. Pete High, who was driving it, said, 'I guess it ain't only his skin that's yellow.' I hope Pete is wrong. I hate a coward."

"Don't you let Pete High pick on him," admonished Mrs. Crosby. "Perhaps the man never saw a mowing machine before. I remember how scared I was when I saw the first automobile come roaring and snorting along the road. And so were you, Ben Crosby."

"Well, I didn't let on I was," replied her husband, harpooning a potato.

"No, you old hypocrite, maybe you didn't; but I saw you looking around for a tree."

He laughed, and was on the point of sending the potato to its final resting place when they both heard a cry — a high, terrified cry that came through the dusk. He started up.

"That's not Janey?" he asked.

"No; she's still in town taking her music lesson."

"Who is it, then?" he asked quickly.

They heard the patter of running feet on the path outside; they heard the sound of feet landing after a leap to the porch; they heard someone banging frantically on the front door. Ben Crosby called out:

"What's the matter?"

A flood of words in a strange tongue answered him.

"It's Velvet Pants," he exclaimed, and flung open the door. The small man, breathless, tumbled in.

"What in the name of thunderation!" demanded Ben Crosby. The small man pointed through the open door with quivering fingers.

"I don't see anything out there but the evening," said Ben Crosby.

"Ice!" cried the man, very agitated. "Ice!"

"What do you want ice for?" asked Ben Crosby.

The man made eloquent gestures; first he pointed at his own face, then he pointed outside; his index finger stabbed at the gloom once, twice, a dozen times.

"Ice! Ice! Ice! Ice! Ice! Ice!" he said.

"Why, Ben, he means 'eyes'!" exclaimed Mrs. Crosby.

"Eyes? What eyes, Hannah? I don't see any eyes. There's nothing out there but lightning bugs."

One of the circling fireflies flew quite near the open door. The small man saw it coming, and made an earnest, but only partly successful, attempt to climb into the grandfather's clock that stood in the corner of the hall.

Ben Crosby threw back his head and laughed.

"Why, dog my cats! If the little cuss ain't afraid of lightning bugs!" he said. "Hey, Velvet Pants, look here."

He plucked the man out of the clock with one big hand, and with the other captured the firefly and held it near the stranger's wide eyes.

"Look!" said Ben Crosby in the loud tone that is supposed to make the American language intelligible to those who do not understand it when it is spoken in an ordinary tone of voice. "Bug! Bug! No hurt! Lightning bug! *Lightning bug!*"

The small man pulled away from the insect.

"Not know lightnong boogs," he said.

Ben released his hold on the small man and pointed upstairs; then he gave a highly realistic imitation of a snore. The man comprehended, and his velvet-clad legs twinkled upstairs toward his bedroom. Ben Crosby returned to his supper, shaking his head.

"It beats me," he remarked to his wife. "He's afraid of mowing machines and he's afraid of lightning bugs. I wonder if he's afraid of the dark. I need farm hands, but may I be fried like a smelt if I'll tell 'em bedtime stories or sing 'em to sleep. What's the world coming to, anyhow? Can you imagine a real, honest-to-goodness farm hand like Pete High being afraid of lightning bugs?"

"Boneheads are seldom afraid of anything," remarked Mrs. Crosby, pouring buttermilk.

They heard the front door open.

"There's Janey," said Mrs. Crosby. "Hello, dear. Come right to the table. I've made ice cream — coffee, the kind you like."

Janey, daughter of the household, came in, bearing her guitar. She kissed both her parents. Janey was nearly eighteen, a pretty, elflike girl. All the masculine hearts in Crosby Corners beat a little faster when she went down the village street; her blue eyes had been the cause of many black eyes. Her father told her of the new man, of his extraordinary velvet trousers, and of his still more extraordinary fears.

"Poor little fellow!" she said.

As the harvest days hurried along, Velvet Pants atoned somewhat for his lack of expertness as a farmer by his unfailing good nature. He even learned to speak a little English of a certain hesitant species, but he had little opportunity to talk with his fellow workers. Mostly they ignored him, or, if they addressed him at all, did so loftily and with contempt; a man who paled at the sight of mowing machines and lightning bugs was not of their stout-hearted kind.

The incident at the swimming hole added little to Velvet Pant's reputation for bravery. The swimming hole was Sandy Bottom, where all the workers, hot from their day in the fields, went for a cool plunge after work. They noticed that Velvet Pants never went with them.

"How does he keep so neat and clean?" they asked. It was Pete High who solved this mystery.

"Yesterday morning," said Pete, "I woke up earlier than usual, and what do you suppose I see? Well, I hear a tap, tap, tap, like somebody was stealing downstairs on his tiptoes. I peek out o' the door, and it's Velvet Pants. Just for fun, I follow him. He goes down the creek — not to Sandy Bottom, but a couple of rods downstream where the water ain't more than ankle-deep. He takes a stick and goes like this, 'Ah, ah, ah, ah, ah, ah,' and pokes at the bushes each time he says 'ah.' Then he gives one big loud 'Ahhhhhhh,' and lunges with his stick at the bushes; then he bows low, like he was an actor in a show. He takes a bath then, dabbling a little water on himself like a cat does; but he doesn't go in above his ankles. I guess he's afraid of the water."

"Mebbe he ain't much on swimming," said one of the other hands, "but he sure can twang a mean guitar. He's giving Janey Crosby lessons."

Pete High scowled.

"He is, is he? First I heard about it. Well, the first thing he knows he won't know nothing."

"She likes him," teased the other man. "Says he got such lovely manners; just like what you ain't, Pete."

"She don't know how yella he is," Pete High growled, "but she will."

On Saturday afternoons most of Crosby Corners — men, women, and children — come to Sandy Bottom, bringing bathing suits. It is not a very big pool; at its deepest part it is not much over six feet deep.

How it happened that the small man with the velvet trousers should be passing Sandy Bottom that Saturday noon at the precise moment when the freckled Johnny Nelson was floundering in the water and calling loudly for help does not matter. Why Johnny Nelson should be drowning at all is something of a puzzle, for he was the best swimmer in the county. It also happened that just as Johnny was going down for the ninth or tenth time, and was calling piteously for Velvet Pants to dive in and save him, Janey Crosby and a party of girl friends came down to the pool.

They saw Velvet Pants, his dark face ivory-colored, trying to reach Johnny with a young tree wrenched from the bank. The small man was a picture of frantic helplessness.

"Save me, Velvet Pants! Save me!" bawled Johnny, submerging and coming up for the fourteenth time.

"Not know how," screamed Velvet Pants in agony. "Not know how."

Janey Crosby and her companions grew mildly hysterical; Johnny Nelson went down for the seventeenth time. Velvet Pants, finding that he could not reach Johnny with the tree, had fallen on his knees and with clasped hands was praying aloud in his own tongue. Then it also happened that Pete High came racing through the bushes.

"I'll save you, Johnny!" he cried dramatically. Overalls and all, he plunged in and brought the dripping Johnny to the bank. The prayers of Velvet Pants became prayers of thanksgiving. Pete High stood regarding him with disgust.

"Oh, Velvet Pants," said Janey Crosby, "why didn't you jump in and save him?"

Slowly, sadly, the small man shrugged his shoulders.

"Not know water," he said; "not know sweem."

He did not seem nearly so abashed as he said this as he might very well have been under the circumstances; he said it very much as if he were stating a fact — a lamentable fact the truth of which he regretted, but a fact nevertheless. He looked dismayed and surprised when Janey Crosby and the others turned away from him.

After that Velvet Pants was an outcast. The men spoke to him only when it was necessary to do so, and then briefly and even harshly. He did not seem to understand; he would try to tell them things, making many gestures; but he had not the words to make himself clear, nor had they the inclination to listen to him.

In the evening, when the men were sitting about the porch competing for Janey Crosby's smiles, there was no place for him there. He had tried to join in their talk and play, to be friendly, to be one of them; they froze him out, and still he did not seem to understand that they did it because he was so flagrant a coward. At last he seemed to accept his status as a pariah without really understanding it, for he would take his guitar, which he had constructed from the ruin of an old one, and go alone into the woods. It was said that he sang there to himself sad songs in his native tongue.

Janey Crosby's birthday came toward the end of the harvest season, and it was the most important social event of the year in Crosby Corners. All the village was invited, and all the village came — the girls in their fresh dimities; the men soaped and collared and uncomfortable, but happy. They brought presents as if they were bringing tribute to a queen, and Janey, as graciously as a reigning sovereign, took them all and smiled.

The party was held in the Masonic hall, it was an affair of considerable tone, with dancing, two helpings of ice cream all round, and a three-piece orchestra.

The dancing was half over. Janey and Pete High, her current partner, had gone out on the porch; a harvest moon silvered the village streets.

"Look!" exclaimed Pete. "What's that sitting down there on the horse block?"

"It's a man," said Janey, her eyes following his pointing finger. "But who can it be?"

The girl looked again, and made out a small, bent figure sitting there, chin on hands, eyes turned toward the lighted hall, ears toward the music and the buzz and laughter of the guests.

"Why, it's Velvet Pants!" she exclaimed.

"Shall I chase him away?" asked Pete, swelling out his chest and looking belligerent. Janey laid a restraining hand on his arm.

"No; don't chase him, Pete. Let him stay. The poor fellow's probably lonesome. Everybody is here but him."

"He deserves to be lonesome," said Pete; "he's yella."

"Would you jump in to save a person from drowning if you didn't know how to swim?" asked Janey.

"Of course I would," replied Pete promptly. "Now, see here, Janey Crosby, don't you go sticking up for that chap.

He's not fit to associate with white men."

She sat gazing at the small, miserable figure; then she made a sudden resolution.

"I'm going to ask him to come up to the party," she said.

"No, you ain't."

"Whose birthday is this, Pete High? I guess it won't do any harm to give him a dish of ice cream. You don't have to associate with him. Run down and tell him I'd like to see him, Pete."

Pete mumbled protests, but he went. Very diffidently, as if he momentarily expected to be kicked, Velvet Pants approached the porch. Janey Crosby saw that he was wearing a new, clean shirt, that his black locks had been parted and buttered, and that his shoes had been rigorously shined. Over his shoulder was slung his wreck of a guitar.

"This is my birthday, Velvet Pants," said the girl. "I want you to help me celebrate it. Pete, will you get another plate of ice cream?"

The small man seemed overcome; he bowed twice very low. Then he spoke. He spoke mechanically, as if the words had been often rehearsed.

"I had no gif' for you on your birthday, Mees Crosby, but I haf learn a song American to seeng for you. I hear heem on funnygraf. I hope you like."

He said it humbly, but not without a certain pride that attends the accomplishment of a difficult feat.

Janey laughed delightedly.

"So you learned an American song just for my birthday? Well, now, wasn't that a sweet idea! Wait! I'll call the others; no, better still, you come into the hall and sing, so they can all hear."

Velvet Pants looked horrified at this suggestion.

"But, no," he protested. "I do not seeng good."

"That's all right. They won't know the difference," said Janey laughingly. "Come along."

She pushed him through the open doorway. The guests looked up. What would Janey Crosby do next?

"Folks," announced Janey Crosby, "Mr. Velvet Pants is going to sing for us. He learned a little American song just for my birthday. Wasn't that nice of him?"

It was evident from the face of Pete High, who stood in the doorway, that he did not think it was particularly nice.

The small brown man glanced uncertainly about the hall; then he began to play chords upon his guitar. Some of the girls tittered. In a round, clear tenor Velvet Pants began to sing:

"Kees me hagain, kees me hagain,
Kees me hagain, and hagain."

His memory seemed to go back on him at this point; he groped for a moment for the words. There was a slight, dubious ripple of applause that was checked suddenly. Pete High had stridden up to Velvet Pants and was facing him.

"Just a minute there," said Pete. "You and me has got a little bone to pick. What do you mean by singing a song like that to Miss Crosby?"

The small man looked puzzled.

"It ees only song American I know," he said.

"Yeah? Well, I'm going to teach you to sing it out of the other side of your mouth. Come outside with me."

"Pete High," broke in Janey, "don't you go fighting with him. He didn't mean any harm; he probably doesn't know what the words mean."

"I told him never to say anything to you whether he understood it or not," stormed Pete. "Come on, you."

Velvet Pants made an attempt to steal away, but Pete blocked his path.

"You're going out on the lawn with me," said Pete.

"And seeng?" asked the little man, who seemed somewhat dazed by what was happening.

"No; fight."

"Fight?"

"Yes; fight."

"But I do no hate you, Meester Pete."

"Well, I hate you. Come on."

"But how we fight?" inquired the small man; he was pale beneath his tan, and trembling. For answer Pete thrust a clenched fist under the man's nose. The man drew his head back and shivered.

"No!" he said, shaking his head. "No! No! No! No!"

"You won't fight?"

"No."

"You're a coward," declared Pete.

Velvet Pants shrugged his shoulders.

"Not know hand fights," he said.

Pete slapped him across the face with his open hand.

"Now will you fight?"

"Not know hand fights," said the man, drawing away. Pete, contempt on his face, gave him a push into the night. They heard the sound of feet on the path; Velvet Pants was running.

"Not know hand fights," Pete mimicked. "Did you ever in your life see such a rat?"

Next day excitement swept Crosby Corners. Defender Monarch had gone crazy; and when that news spread, they forgot all about the conduct of Velvet Pants on the night before. As for him, he went about his work with a puzzled and hurt look on his brown face; he seemed still uncertain why the others did not respond to his smiles and attempts at friendliness.

Defender Monarch was the pride, and the terror, of the county. His owner, Ben Crosby, had raised him from a gawky calf, wobbly on his legs, into a massive ton-and-a-half bull, with a chest like a haystack, a voice like thunder, and the temper of a gouty demon. Ben Crosby had not dehorned him, because in cattle shows a good pair of horns is considered a point of merit in judging bulls, and the giant bull had won many blue ribbons. On this day Ben Crosby wished most earnestly that he had forgone the blue ribbons and taken off those horns. A savage bull without horns is bad enough, but a savage bull with a pair of sharp, wicked horns is just about the most dangerous animal that walks.

Perhaps on that morning Defender Monarch had realized that he had reached the end of his usefulness and that before very long he was doomed to end a proud career ingloriously, as steak, roast, and stew. He stood in his pasture, roaring a challenge to the world that he would die fighting. By blind luck Ben Crosby was able to trick him into entering the big pen, but in the process Defender Monarch had given a sample of his viciousness by ripping Johnny Nelson's arm from elbow to shoulder and had failed by a hair's breadth in a sincere attempt to crush the life out of Ben Crosby himself. Once confined in the pen, Defender Monarch's rage knew no bounds. He hurled himself against the thick board sides so furiously that they creaked and trembled, and the crowd that had gathered to see him darted back to places of greater safety.

Luckily the pen was a stoutly built affair; it was not really a pen at all, but a small corral perhaps fifty feet square. About it moved Defender Monarch, his small eyes blazing, alert. And, perched on boxes and ladders, Crosby Corners, fascinated as all men are by dangerous things, watched the mad king of the herd.

"Isn't he just too terrible?" said Janey Crosby to Pete High.

"Oh, I don't know," answered Pete airily. "I've worked round him often."

"But not since he went crazy, Pete."

"No," admitted Pete, "mebbe not. I'm used to cattle of all kinds, but I never saw one that acted this way. Just plain bulls I'm none too fond of fooling with, but a crazy one! Excuse me!"

"See how he's looking right at us with those mean little eyes of his," said Janey. "It's just as if he were saying, 'If I only had you down here for a minute!' I'm scared, Pete."

"I'm here," said Pete High reassuringly. "Look, Janey, he's getting another fit; he's going to try to buck that other opposite wall."

Janey Crosby, to get a better view, climbed to the very top of the stepladder that leaned against the wall of the corral. There was a sharp crack as the top rail gave way, then horrified cries. She had fallen into the pen and lay unconscious almost at the feet of the mad bull.

The women screamed; the men ran about aimlessly, wildly, shouting orders at one another.

"Help! Janey's fallen into the pen!"

"Oh, he'll kill her! He'll kill her! He'll kill her!"

"Get pitchforks!"

"Get a gun!"

"No use; we've only got bird shot. It would just make him madder to hit him with that."

"Someone will have to jump in."

"Where are you running to, Pete High?"

"To get a rope or something."

"You'll be too late."

Defender Monarch looked down at the girl, and his eyes were evil. Then he looked at the ring of white faces that lined the top of the corral. He seemed to understand the situation; he seemed to know that he had plenty of time, and he gloated. He turned away from Janey, trotted to the farther end of the corral, wheeled about, and surveyed the distance between himself and the girl's body; then he lowered his head, with its gleaming prongs, and gathered his body for a charge.

The aghast onlookers became aware that something was in the corral besides the girl and the bull. A figure had come through the gate of the inclosure silently and swiftly. It was a small man in velvet trousers, and he was strolling toward Defender Monarch as casually and placidly as if the bull were a rosebush. On the brown face of Velvet Pants there was not the slightest trace of fear; indeed, he was smiling a slight, amused smile. Otherwise he was as matter-of-fact as if he were about to sit down to his breakfast. A brown-paper cigarette hung limp from one corner of his lips; with the mincing strut they had noticed and made fun of, he walked slowly toward Defender Monarch. The animal, distracted, stood blinking at the little man. Within a few feet of the bull Velvet Pants halted; there was a flash of something red. It was Ben Crosby's red-flannel shirt that a few moments before had been drying on the line. The small man had flicked it across the bull's face. Defender Monarch forgot for the moment his plan for smashing Janey Crosby; he saw the red, and he plunged toward it. The women turned their heads away; the men clenched their teeth. They saw Velvet Pants slip aside with the quickness of a jungle cat and the bull, unable to check himself, jolt his head against one of the sides of the corral. Velvet Pants turned round, smiled pleasantly, and bowed very low to the spectators. They saw that he had in his right hand something long and bright that caught the rays of the sun; they realized that it was Grandpa Crosby's old Civil War sword that had hung in the dining room.

He was holding it as lightly and as easily as if it were a butter-knife.

Defender Monarch, recovering from his fruitless charge against the wall, spun about; once more the red shirt was deftly flapped before his bright, mad eyes. Once more, with a roar of wrath, he launched his bulk straight at Velvet Pants. Then something happened to Defender Monarch. It happened with such speed that all the onlookers saw was a flash; then the huge frame of the bull tottered, crumpled, and sank down. Sticking from his left shoulder was the hilt of Grandpa Crosby's sword; the spectators saw the hilt only, for Velvet Pants had driven the point into Defender Monarch's heart.

The people of Crosby Corners allege that Ben Crosby kissed the little tanned man on both cheeks, but this he denies; he admits, however, that he hugged him and patted him, and said many husky words of gratitude and admiration to Velvet Pants, who seemed abashed and quite unable to understand why everyone was making so much of a fuss about him.

"And I called you a coward," Ben Crosby kept saying. "I called you a coward, and you went in and faced a mad bull without batting an eyelash."

"It was nuzzing," murmured the small brown man.

"Nothing to face a mad bull?"

Velvet Pants shrugged his shoulders.

"But I am toreador,"[1] he said. "In my country, Andalusia, I keel one, two, t'ree bull every Sunday for fun. Why should I fear bulls? I know bulls."

THINK BACK OVER WHAT YOU HAVE READ

Finding the Thought behind the Title

1. With how many American ways that you can recount was Velvet Pants unfamiliar?
2. What false conclusion did Pete High draw from Velvet Pants's *unfamiliarity* with life at Crosby Corners?
3. What did Velvet Pants mean when he said "it was nuzzing" to face a mad bull?
4. What lesson did Velvet Pants teach Pete High?
5. At the very end of the story Velvet Pants says, "I *know* bulls." Earlier in the story Janey asked Pete, "Would you jump in to save a person from drowning if you didn't know how to swim?" and Pete replied, "Of course I would." What thought occurs to you as you weigh these remarks one against the other? What event in the story makes you doubt Pete's boast? What event proves the wisdom behind Janey's question?

Interpreting the Story in the Light of Your Own Experience

6. Why was Mrs. Crosby apprehensive when Velvet Pants first appeared at her door? Would you have been fearful, too? Why?
7. In your opinion was the constable prejudiced against the stranger in town because he was a foreigner? Was Ben Crosby less given to prejudice than the constable? or more so? What instances of prejudice against foreigners have you yourself witnessed? In what details do they remind you of the constable's behavior? Mrs. Crosby's? Pete High's?
8. Have you ever heard a person called "yellow"? What were the circumstances? Did you think the person really deserved the name? What do you think of the person who did the calling? Did he have any characteristics in common with Pete High? On second thought which person deserves your scorn, the person who was called yellow or the person who did the calling? Why? In what way has the story you have just read reduced your respect for the word, as used to denote cowards?
9. With what illustrations from your own experience can you match Velvet Pants's fear of the unfamiliar? Was his fear of fireflies as silly as it seemed? What reply would you give to Ben Crosby's question, "Can you imagine a real, honest-to-goodness farm hand like Pete High being afraid of lightning bugs?"
10. To what extent have you yourself observed that prejudice is based on mere surface acquaintance? What examples can you cite of persons deceived about the real worth of others by differences in dress? by differences in language? What is the lesson to be derived from the misunderstanding of Velvet Pants in the story?

[1] **toreador:** a bullfighter.

Increase Your Power over Words

11. The word *pariah* on page 89 is rich in suggestive power, for it is a word with a historical background. Look up the word first in the dictionary, then trace its association with the *caste system* by consulting an encyclopedia. Basing your judgment on the use of the word in the story, what is its modern meaning?

Composition Suggestion

12. Write a formal composition based on your understanding of the word *pariah* as illustrated by the experience of Velvet Pants in the story. The following questions will help you organize your thoughts on the subject:

a. Why was Velvet Pants referred to as a "pariah"?
b. What instances of excluding people can you cite from your own observation?
c. In your opinion is it a selfish or unselfish impulse that usually causes people to snub others? Is it just and right? or unjust and wrong? For example, consider Pete High's snubbing of Velvet Pants: Can it be justified on the grounds of right conduct? Are Pete High's motives the common motives that lie behind snubbing?
d. From what primitive impulses did the caste system arise? To what extent do the same human impulses operate within the range of your own observation? What is the best way to combat these impulses?

NOW THERE IS PEACE[1]

by Richard Sherman (1906–)

You have been reading stories that make you laugh, stories that make you think, and stories that make you wonder. Here is a story that will make you *feel*. From the moment that you enter "the long, book-lined room" to the moment that you leave it to walk out "into a world of white," its atmosphere will seem to you charged with emotion. Here is one of those stories in which very little seems to happen. A boy pays a brief visit to a grief-stricken mother and father; that's all the "action" there is. Nonetheless, the story is exciting, and a strange tumult will linger for some time after you come to the end of the sorrowful interview which is recorded.

This story touches upon life as you know it. You will feel at home in the setting of the story and sympathetically drawn to the characters to whom you are introduced. The situation, too, is one which you probably know something about, not in exact detail but in essence. It will be your feeling about these familiar elements that will seem new. Never before, perhaps, have you stopped to think — or only vaguely — about what lies behind the more or less familiar scene. Herein, then, lies the special appeal of this modern story.

[1] From *Vanity Fair*, copyright, 1933, by the Condé Nast Publications, Inc.

THE LONG, book-lined room was overheated, and the air above the radiators shimmered in upward waves. Outside in the gray December street, whose traffic sounded faintly muffled through the magenta-draped windows, snow had begun to fall; but of the three people seated near the fire only the boy noticed the flakes, which seemed to be coming not from the sky but from the pavement below. The woman's gaze was on the portrait over the mantel, and the man looked into the coals.

Then the man shifted and traced a thin, dry finger over the leather of his chair.

"It was very kind of you to come," he said. "I know how precious your holiday time at home must be, and Mrs. Bentham and I appreciate your courtesy."

"Yes, sir," the boy answered, and blushed. "I mean — I mean I was glad to come."

The woman's eyes left the portrait, to rest on her folded hands.

"Perhaps, Edward, if you would explain to . . ." She turned. "Your first name is Martin, isn't it?" The boy nodded, and she again regarded her hands. "Perhaps if you would explain to Martin why we have asked him here . . ."

Martin spoke quickly. "I know. You

wanted me to tell you about — " And then he stopped, confused.

" About Arthur," Mr. Bentham said, and at the name his wife's hands unclenched slowly.

" But I can't tell you anything." The words came even more rapidly now, as if this was all he had to say and as if after he had said it he would leave them there alone. " You see, this is my first year at the school. Your — Arthur was my senior counselor, but I didn't really know him. He was older than I am, and — "

" Yes, yes." Mr. Bentham nodded. " Dr. Abbott told us all that. Indeed, it was the fact that you were only slightly acquainted with him that caused us to send for you."

" Tell him what you want, Edward."

" What we want. Yes, my dear." He rose and began to pace the room, retreating into a shadowy corner and then reappearing. " We are planning," he said, " a small memoir to Arthur, a little book or pamphlet which we hope will be a tribute to his memory. A tribute to the sort of boy he was, and an inspiration to others."

" Oh," said Martin.

" I have talked with various friends of his, his chums, and each has volunteered to write a short paragraph or two about him. Dr. Abbott and several of the instructors have also signified their willingness, even their desire, to contribute too. We want to have as many different points of view as possible. Dr. Abbott gave me your name as one who might picture Arthur as he seemed to a new boy."

There was a silence in the room, a silence broken only by the dull murmur of the street outside and the sound of Mrs. Bentham's nervous breathing. Martin himself said nothing, had no opportunity to say anything, for almost at once Mr. Bentham continued.

" I believe that I am not overstating the case," he announced, " when I say that Arthur was an unusual boy. Since his death we have received many letters, some even from strangers, testifying to his all-round physical and mental brilliance. Though of slight build, he was a splendid athlete — "

For the first time Mrs. Bentham lifted her head and met her husband's gaze.

" So splendid they killed him," she said.

" My dear, we have discussed that so often. Simply because one boy is killed in one football game — "

" Killed for sport. Like a bull. . . . It wasn't as if he enjoyed playing." Martin thought that she was going to cry, but she did not. Instead, she returned to her former attitude of lowered eyes and folded hands.

" A splendid athlete," Mr. Bentham went on, his face serene. " A distinguished student, a leader in church and social service work — yet not a prig — and extremely popular with his classmates."

" He was." The boy's voice was earnest, and it held a note of relief. " Everybody liked him. He was a big man at the school."

Mr. Bentham smiled. " He was indeed. ' Always be a leader,' I often told him. And he remained a leader to the end."

" Yes. The end," Mrs. Bentham said, and then her eyes found Martin's. " You say they liked him. Did you like him too? "

He replied without hesitation. " Of course; though I didn't see much of him. You see, he was always so busy."

At the mantel Mr. Bentham had paused, and was looking upward.

" Here," he said. " This is a painting of him, done last summer when he was just eighteen."

The boy did not move.

" Come over this way," Mr. Bentham commanded. " The light is better here."

Rising slowly from his chair, Martin went toward him.

" It's a very good likeness, isn't it? " he said. " He was — he was always smiling."

" It's more than a likeness," the man answered. " It is symbolic of Arthur — just as Arthur was symbolic of the best in boyhood, in young manhood. And that is what we want this memoir to be too. We shall call it *Arthur Bentham: The Record of a Happy Boyhood.*"

Looking about the room now, Martin saw that everywhere there were relics of the son who had been killed. On the mahogany desk stood two large photographs of him; a catcher's mitt hung incongruously near a family shield; and on a table lay several copies of the school paper of which he had been the editor.

" It is a source of great comfort to us," Mr. Bentham resumed, not as if he were speaking to Martin but as if he were addressing a larger audience, " that Arthur's short life was a completely joyous one. Fortunately we were able to surround him with all the material advantages that any boy could wish; and also we tried — and I believe succeeded — to mold his moral and mental character to a point nearing — " he fumbled — " to a point nearing perfection. He lived in the sunlight always. Never did he give us cause for grief or worry."

There was a pause.

" Edward," Mrs. Bentham said. " Perhaps Martin is not interested in all that."

" Oh, but I am," Martin put in, embarrassed. " I — I . . ."

" Of course he is." Mr. Bentham's tone to his wife was sullen, almost cold. " And so will other boys be, and their parents. In a way, you see," he continued, turning to Martin, " this book will be a guide to adolescence. Not, of course, that it will be a moral preachment — we want it to be gay and high-spirited, as Arthur was, and vigorous and manly too. But by recreating his happy life, year by year, and by giving the testimonies of his friends and his teachers as to his character — by doing that we will be helping other parents and their sons."

" Martin." Mrs. Bentham stood and waited for him to come to her.

" Martin, why is it that you don't want to write for Arthur's book? "

Involuntarily he caught his breath in a sharp little gasp.

" But I haven't said — "

" Phyllis, my dear — " Mr. Bentham turned from the portrait to face them — " of course Martin wants to do it."

" No, he doesn't. . . . Do you? "

For a moment the three of them were silent. Then the boy looked at the rug.

" No," he said.

Mr. Bentham started slightly, and a flush began to creep up his cheeks. Then he said, with quiet dignity, " I am very sorry. I had thought that anyone would welcome the privilege of — "

" Don't, Edward."

The room had grown darker now, and outside the snow was falling thicker, whiter. Martin looked not at the man but at his wife. Her face, obscure in the gloom, gave no sign of what was in her mind.

" I — I'd better go," he said, and headed toward the door. Mr. Bentham had already turned away and was fingering a sheaf of papers. His back was stony, outraged.

" Good-by," said Martin.

Mr. Bentham did not even look up.

Hurrying down the wide, dim hall, he heard light footsteps behind him and, turning, saw Mrs. Bentham.

" Wait," she called.

He stopped, in a sort of alcove. Immediately she was near him, very near.

"Tell me," she said, in a low, pleading voice — a voice different from that which she had used in her husband's presence.

"It's nothing," he answered. "I'd like to do what he asks, but — "

It was as if she had not heard him at all.

"Tell me about Arthur."

She was almost touching him now — a slight, frail woman, only a little taller than he was, with great eyes. And then she placed a hand on his lapel, lightly.

"Don't think that you will hurt me. Nothing can hurt me now. But I want to know everything about him. You have no right to keep anything from me, bad or good. Don't you understand?"

"It isn't bad. I never knew of him to do or say anything that was bad."

"What is it then? Why don't you wish to write about him? Is it that you think the idea is sentimental? It *is* sentimental, but — but his father wants it."

"No. No, it isn't that."

Her hand fell away from his coat. "Then you won't tell me. You will go now and leave me knowing that there was something in Arthur's life that was a secret. Something that you, who saw him only a few times, were aware of but won't share with me."

Their eyes met in a long glance. And then Martin began to speak, uneasily.

"It isn't important. I told you it wasn't important. . . . I liked him a lot, even the first time I saw him. He was nice to me, not conceited the way most senior counselors are. He talked to me about my studies, and about what activities I should go out for. 'If ever you get in trouble,' he said, 'or if you're homesick, come and see me.' He was that way with everybody."

"Yes." She knew.

"One afternoon, the day before he was — the day before the game, I went to him. I didn't have anything on my mind except maybe that I was a little homesick, as he said I might be. I knocked at his door, and no one answered. Then I knocked again, and waited. Somehow I felt that he was there, and I thought maybe he hadn't heard me. So I opened the door. I shouldn't have done it, but I did."

He stopped, but the pressure of her hand made him go on.

"He was crying. That's all. He was sitting in a chair with his head down and he was crying. You see, it's really nothing at all. But I can't forget it."

He waited for her to speak.

"Why should he cry?" he asked. "He was always laughing when people were around. Why should he cry up there alone?"

Mrs. Bentham's voice was hardly a whisper.

"I found him that way once too," she said. "A year ago."

"And don't you know why either?" He was insistent now, demanding. "Didn't he tell you?"

She had turned away from him, and was looking at the closed door at the end of the hall.

"He didn't have to tell me," she said. "I knew."

"But I can't understand." . . .

Now she was facing him again, and she placed her hands on his shoulders.

"I don't know who your mother and father are," she said. "But tell them to let you be what you are, not what they want you to be."

For a moment he waited for her to continue; and when he saw that she only wanted to be left alone, he turned away and began to walk down the hall. At the head of the stairs she called, "Thank you, Martin."

He walked down the stairs and out of the house and into a world of white.

THINK BACK OVER WHAT YOU HAVE READ

Interpreting the Feeling behind Important Lines in the Story

The following brief passages in the story are charged with emotion, and suggest a great deal more than they say. Find the place in the story where the following lines occur and with the aid of the questions see whether you can interpret their full meaning:

1. " My dear, we have discussed that so often " (page 95). What is the dispute which has been racking the feelings of husband and wife? What barrier has it created between them?

2. " Yes. The end " (page 95). What special meaning does Mrs. Bentham give to these words which is different from her husband's?

3. " He was — he was always smiling " (page 96). When you read these lines, perhaps you noticed Martin's hesitation. How do you interpret the dash between *was* and *he?* What does it signify?

4. " We shall call it *Arthur Bentham: The Record of a Happy Boyhood* " (page 96). What irony do you see in this title?

5. " Mr. Bentham resumed, not as if he were speaking to Martin but as if he were *addressing a larger audience* " (page 96). What clue to Mr. Bentham's character is implied by the italicized words?

6. " There was a pause " (page 96). How do you interpret this pause? What does it mean? Why doesn't Mr. Bentham go on? Has he finished his speech? Is Mrs. Bentham responsible for the pause? Is Martin? Has some unwelcome thought come to Mr. Bentham?

7. " ' Of course he is.' Mr. Bentham's tone to his wife was sullen, almost cold " (page 96). What clue to Mr. Bentham's character is given by the words " Of course he is "? Are you surprised at Mr. Bentham's tone? Why is he " sullen, almost cold "?

8. " Involuntarily he caught his breath in a sharp little gasp " (page 96). What has surprised Martin? Was his surprise natural? Why?

9. " Don't, Edward " (page 96). *Don't* — what? What was Mr. Bentham about to say before Mrs. Bentham interrupted him? Why does his wife stop him? With what effect on Mr. Bentham?

10. " He was crying. That's all " (page 97). With what effect do these last two words strike upon your ears? Why does Martin keep repeating that " it's really nothing at all "? Was it " nothing at all "?

For Ambitious Students

11. The story which you have just read ends with: " ' I don't know who your mother and father are,' she said. ' But tell them to let you be what you are, not what they want you to be.' " As you know, Mrs. Bentham is thinking of Arthur, who was not allowed to be himself but must be what his father wanted him to be. Can you think of other Arthurs sacrificed to the secret, unfulfilled ambitions of their parents? Perhaps a recent book or movie is an illustration of the same theme. Or you may be able to think of an illustration from real life which you can relate without personal reference. Some students in the class should try their hand at imitating the easily recognized pattern of " Now There Is Peace."

Realistic Stories

SLEET STORM

by Louise Lambertson (1901–)

Our own experience cannot possibly be broad enough, and deep enough, and long enough to teach us all we need to know about life in order to get on happily through the years allotted us. That's why reading is so important — as an extension of our own experience, so that we may learn from others what there isn't time to learn for ourselves.

In the story that follows, a young bus driver extracts a fine bit of wisdom from his dangerous experience on the road during a sleet storm. Since he was a thoughtful young fellow, and bothered to think about what was happening, he learned his lesson quickly, during the course of one long and very uncomfortable evening. That is relatively quick learning. But it need not take you even that long. Without any of the danger and discomfort which he experienced, you may learn the same lesson in one-tenth of the time it took him.

You may do so by imagining yourself to be the bus driver, feeling the sensations he feels, and thinking his thoughts. This is just what you do, anyway, whenever you lose yourself in a story or a moving picture; only you probably do not always make the most of such vicarious experience — that is, experience through others — any more than all bus drivers make the most of their firsthand experience. Thus reading gives you practice, not only in vicarious experiencing, but in learning to interpret experience as well. And it is the ability to profit from experience that counts more than the experience itself.

THE RAIN, a fine drizzle, froze instantly as it touched the windshield of the black bus. The warmth within had beaded the windows with drops of cold moisture, which blended into distorted rainbows the myriad changing lights of night traffic, white and green and red. The floor was wet with tramped-in mud and the leather seats clammy to the touch; one of the windows, insecurely fastened, rattled in the wind. Already the air was stale.

Just as the City Hall clock boomed six, the bus driver collected the tickets, closed the door, then slid behind the wheel. He was a young man, slim and dark, with competent-looking hands and a worried frown. The shoulders of his trim brown uniform were spotted from the rain which beat in the partly opened window at his side, and the visor of his cap glistened with moisture. A license card, dangling from the windshield in a woven-straw holder, gave his name and age: "Scott Colton, 23."

The five passengers, vaguely apprehensive, drawn together by a community of fear and the intimacy of light and oily warmth amid all the blackness outside, began to chat with each other even before the city lights and clamor had given place to the dark emptiness of country. Listening to them, the driver smiled faintly.

"A terrible night," the stout woman in the wet seal coat murmured to the flippant girl who had slid low in her seat in order to prop thin-soled patent leather pumps against the floor heater.

"Gee, yes!" the girl exclaimed, with a little self-conscious laugh. She was very pretty, and she knew it. "I was afraid to come, sort of, but I'd promised and Tommy would have been so disappointed." The dim light bulb directly above her red-hatted head cast an odd shadow on her face, making it seem foreshortened and the powdered skin unnaturally soft and pink. "I'm going to a fraternity dance at the university," she confided proudly.

The matron, not usually sympathetic to pert youth, nodded with understanding and leaned forward, with an involuntary gasp at the effort required, to unbuckle her galoshes.

"Well, I hope you get there," the anxious-eyed fellow in the shabby brown coat which smelled of popcorn interposed. "Me, I've got a sick wife. Nothing less than that would bring me out on a night like this." He rubbed a stubby forefinger against the frosted window and peered out at the blackness. Seeing nothing, he sighed deeply.

The fat traveling salesman, chewing an unlighted cigar, stared at the girl with thoughts of flirtation scarcely veiled beneath his heavy eyelids. He decided against it. Too short a trip.

"The road is just a glare of ice," the middle-aged individual who looked like a school teacher said in sonorous tones. He was looking over the driver's shoulder at the road ahead. "You couldn't hire *me* to drive a car tonight."

One corner of the driver's mouth twitched spasmodically. At the foot of a hill he changed gears with care. The hum of the motor changed to a labored roar.

" A bus is about as bad as a car," the worried man said, fluttering his hands. He was young and gaunt; and his hair was too long, as if the price of a haircut mattered.

" No, no! A bus is much heavier! Even a small bus like this is *so* much heavier. They never skid," said the teacher with the calm voice of authority.

" Even an army tank could skid tonight," the shabby one stated stubbornly.

The traveling salesman laughed with the ease of one to whom a laugh is part of stock in trade. " These big buses don't skid often," he said with the patronizing manner of a habitual traveler enlightening the unsophisticated. " And we have a very experienced driver with us tonight. The best of the lot, chosen for his ability, they told me at the station."

The driver's ears grew faintly pink. His eyes flickered momentarily to the mirror above the windshield which reflected the interior. They were dark eyes, moody tonight with bitter thoughts. Anna, the ticket girl, had told the salesman that. She always said it, a reassuring formula, to any timid traveler who questioned her. Still, it was praise of a sort.

Through the six inches of windshield cleaned by the automatic wiper, the pavement shone deceptively clear. It seemed safe enough. But it was ice, wet ice, than which there is nothing more dangerous.

What fools these people were to travel in weather like this! That girl, and her dance; and the salesman, with his array of sample cases about which he had fussed like an old woman. For such as these, good men had to take their lives in their hands. And what did it matter? The girl would dance in whatever town she was in, and the salesman peddle his samples. Why, then, was it necessary to cater to their silly impulse to go from place to place?

It was the fault of the company! They ought not to have sent out a bus on a night like this. It wasn't safe! But what did they care? They had insurance . . . if anything happened, let the insurance companies pay!

All they thought about was keeping the schedule. Always urging the drivers not to be late. Proud of the record of never having missed a day during the last five years. They liked to advertise that the buses went, come what might. . . .

He ought to have refused to come!

They couldn't know what it meant, those office men! They couldn't realize what it was like to be driving a machine of almost human malevolence on a pavement as smooth as a mirror and as slippery as oil.

It would be better — or worse — when they got on the gravel road.

Perhaps if he had refused to drive tonight, they would have realized what he was up against; how impossible it was. Too much responsibility for one man, and the cards stacked against him.

But no! He knew what would have happened. They would have sent someone else; and in a few days, on another pretext, he would have been discharged. There would have been vague whisperings among the other drivers. But it wasn't yellow to be reasonably cautious! He was as brave as the next man. It wasn't just himself he was afraid for, either; it was these others, his passengers — the silly fools who hadn't sense enough to stay at home but must go gadding about on trivial errands, trusting him to get them to their futile destinations safely. That thin, pretty girl going to her dance, and the man with the sick wife; they must not be disappointed, delayed.

No, he could not have refused to come.

And he had to keep this job of his, now that he had met Gwen. So sweet, Gwen was; like an independent kitten.

Courtesy of Los Angeles City Schools

WHAT PROBLEMS OF YOUR OWN DO THESE STORY-PICTURES REMIND YOU OF? Behind each picture in this group lies the germ of a story still to be told. (*Above*) Have these students solved a problem which "Bottles" in "That's What Happened to Me," page 72, failed to solve except in his daydreams? Is it possible for a boy who works after school to make friends? (*Below*) What conflicts arise out of the overcrowded home? Is the boy in this picture facing a kind of problem familiar to you?

Life Magazine

Eisenstaedt-Pix

IN CLASS. It isn't easy to pay attention in class. What hints of unusual success do you see in the faces of these students? Do they by comparison or contrast remind you of students in your own classroom?

Eisenstaedt-Pix

AT GAMES. Learning to accept defeat gracefully is one of the first lessons we all have to learn. What hints of minor tragedy do you see in the faces of this football crowd? You'll find an interesting treatment of the problem of overcoming defeat in "The Milk Pitcher," page 29.

HENRY ALDRICH IN TROUBLE. In these pictures the same boy is in trouble. Perhaps you know the boy as a radio character, Henry Aldrich, hero of the popular stage hit, *What a Life!* (*Above*) Henry has just been caught in a gigantic fib by the principal of Central High School. (*Below*) He had a fight in the principal's office while his girl looked on. You probably have run across Henry Aldriches in your own experience. How would you handle such problems? How are the even more serious problems of youth handled in the stories in this book?

Photos, Jerome Robinson

Courtesy of Los Angeles City Schools

WHAT PROBLEMS OF YOUR OWN DO THESE STORY-PICTURES REMIND YOU OF? Behind each picture in this group lies the germ of a story still to be told. (*Above*) Have these students solved a problem which "Bottles" in "That's What Happened to Me," page 72, failed to solve except in his daydreams? Is it possible for a boy who works after school to make friends? (*Below*) What conflicts arise out of the overcrowded home? Is the boy in this picture facing a kind of problem familiar to you?

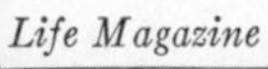

Life Magazine

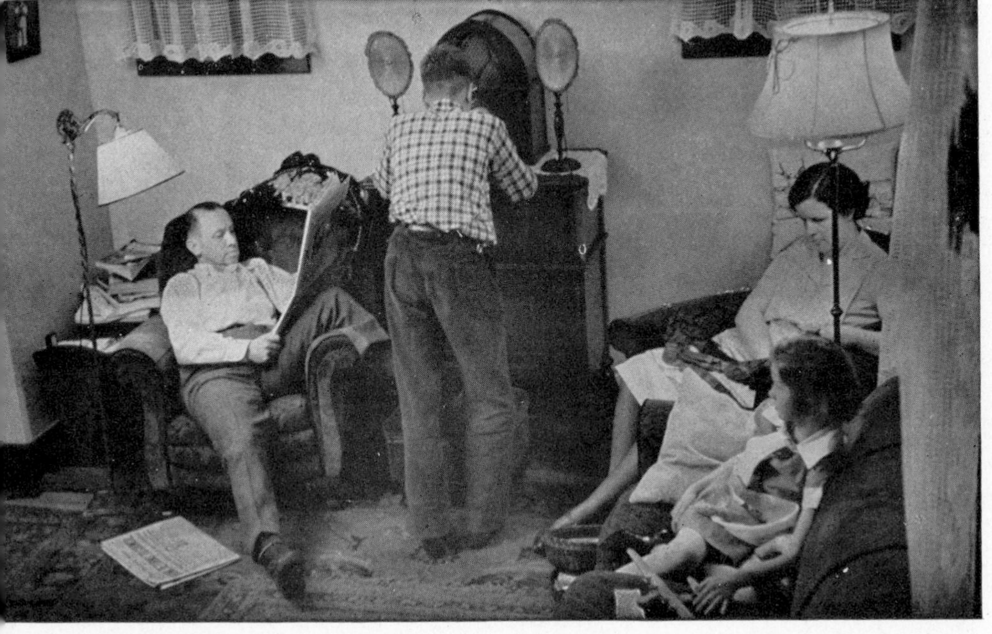

Eisenstaedt-Pix

IN CLASS. It isn't easy to pay attention in class. What hints of unusual success do you see in the faces of these students? Do they by comparison or contrast remind you of students in your own classroom?

Eisenstaedt-Pix

AT GAMES. Learning to accept defeat gracefully is one of the first lessons we all have to learn. What hints of minor tragedy do you see in the faces of this football crowd? You'll find an interesting treatment of the problem of overcoming defeat in "The Milk Pitcher," page 29.

HENRY ALDRICH IN TROUBLE. In these pictures the same boy is in trouble. Perhaps you know the boy as a radio character, Henry Aldrich, hero of the popular stage hit, *What a Life!* (*Above*) Henry has just been caught in a gigantic fib by the principal of Central High School. (*Below*) He had a fight in the principal's office while his girl looked on. You probably have run across Henry Aldriches in your own experience. How would you handle such problems? How are the even more serious problems of youth handled in the stories in this book?

Photos, Jerome Robinson

He knew that she would be thinking about him, worrying about him skating along on treacherous wheels on greasy, black marble.

They were on the gravel now. It was no better; not so smoothly dangerous, but the ruts gave added momentum to any chance slide. The rain was slanting in long needles against the windows and dancing in big drops upon the hot engine. They were nearing the river. It was warmer in the lowlands, and a faint fog was rising. It was harder to see the road now that it was no longer a ribbon of blackness. On the curves there were white guard posts, but the straight road had no guards. The hills were long, easy grades, with many curves. To the danger of skidding was added the danger of running off the bank . . . and the river was twenty feet below.

"Well, we haven't skidded yet," said the salesman with easy jocularity, leaning toward the flippant young thing.

There was a sickening lurch, a breathtaking spin. Slipping, sliding, turning! A crash into a white guard post, which snapped as if it were the nearest twig. The invisible wire supports of the post sang in an overtone of emergency as they cracked. The bus, weaving crazily, ricocheted from one side of the road to the other, like a pebble skipping over water, and came to a stop, after a circling slide, with the right back wheel resting in the jagged hole where the guard post had been.

Young Colton, saying nothing, his mouth set in a grim line, shut off the engine and kicked the lever which swung open the door.

"Oh," gasped the girl in the sudden silence, puckering her red mouth into a bud. "That was kind of exciting, wasn't it?"

The salesman managed to laugh. "Well, we're still here," he said.

The girl's slanting eyes met his for a brief second. Then, like a cloud of scented, ocher powder, sophistication settled on her again. "For a minute," she qualified. "I mean it was kind of exciting for a minute!"

Cold with fury, the driver stepped out into the sleet. What fools these people were! What utter fools! Death and the rushing river had been mocked by the slender strength of a white post, and yet they could laugh and joke and call it "kind of exciting, for a minute."

Flashlight in hand, he went around to the back of the bus and found, as he had suspected, that a spike from the broken post had penetrated the right tire. In the icy hole the rubber lay spread out as flatly awkward as the webbed feet of a duck on land. Hazel bushes, ice-laden, brushed close to the fender; the wind whistled, and the rain beat down the back of his neck as he leaned over the tire. He began to get out his tools, then put them back again. He was careful not to look.

The shabby young man had clambered out of the bus and come to stand beside Colton. "Gee!" he marveled. "That tire going flat was what saved us, I'll bet! It didn't spin so easy as the others, and so that wheel got caught in the hole." The low, red light on the back of the bus and the three green lights above etched his sharp-featured face into shiny relief against the charcoal of the night. A curiously tense expression came creeping into his eyes. He listened, head cocked on one side, to the rushing whisper of the rain and that other more distant whisper, which was the river. "Must be a river down there," he said, surprised. Unconsciously, he edged closer to his companion. "Say! I guess that was a pretty close call!" he muttered.

A pretty close call! And that was all it meant to this blind simpleton. He didn't have the responsibility of it: it wasn't up to him, somehow, someway, to inch that clumsy monster of a bus away from the edge of the unguarded bank to a place where it was possible to change a tire. It wasn't up to him to do that, and then change the tire, and go on the way again expecting any moment that worse might follow.

He said to the nervous man in a voice which was quite expressionless, " I've got to get the bus to the top of the grade before I can change the tire. Can't do it here. Couldn't get the jack under, in that hole; and, anyway, it's too dangerous to leave the bus here. It might start to slip off the bank any minute."

" Yes, yes," agreed the brown-coated one. He blew his nose on a wrinkled, yellow-bordered handkerchief. " Yes, yes," he repeated.

The teacher, dignity forgotten, was trying to stare through the ice-incrusted back window. Looking up at him, the driver felt again that strange wave of fury.

He strode to the door of the bus and spoke sharply. " Everybody get out! "

They hastened to obey, the elderly woman with the remnants of her stately bearing, the girl laughing shrilly; they gathered around the rear of the bus, chattering their futile comments. The driver set about the business at hand.

In back of the wheel he propped the splintered post and half a dozen stones, feeble semblance of protection. Then he gave curt orders. " I've got to get this bus to the top of the grade before I dare try to change the tire. It will be hard to start up, on the ice, with a flat tire. I want you to stand out of the way, on the other side of the road; but the men have got to push."

" Sure! " said the men, all together.

" But listen! " continued Colton. " At the first sign of a skid, you get out. Run! If it gets to skidding, you can't stop it. Only thing to do is to let it go. And keep on the left side when you're pushing — because if she does go, it will be . . . to the right! " He didn't say " over the bank "; let them figure that out for themselves.

" Sure! " said the fat salesman. " But I guess the old girl will make the grade all right when she feels my heft behind her."

The elderly woman had wrapped her coat high about her throat. From its snugness she spoke. " But what about you? " she asked Colton. " If it starts to skid, what will you do? "

The driver's face was a mask. What did she care what happened? She was all right, wasn't she? She'd thought that she had to travel tonight; and it was on account of her and these other fools that he had to take that chance. " I'll jump if I can," he said quietly, knowing well that he could not jump. Not with the single door opening to the side which overhung the river.

He stepped in, lowered the windows so that he might shout directions, and started the engine. The motor purred in low gear a full minute before he dared to slip the clutch. There was a rocking movement as the engine strained; but he did not dare to let it rock much, not with that rear wheel in the hole where the post had been on the very edge of the embankment.

The salesman came running, panting, his face plastered with mud. " The wheels keep spinning round and round! " he shouted.

The fat buffoon! How else would a wheel spin but round and round!

He got out and went back to the group. The wheel had churned deeper and deeper into the gravel; closer and closer to the edge. Gravel lay spattered over the ice, like nut frosting on a white cake. " The trouble is not so much with this wheel, as with the others," he decided. " They can't get started, on the ice." He took a shovel from the bus and began to dig down through the snow and ice at the side of the road to the gravel. The others stood about watching him with eyes that gleamed in the darkness like those of hungry animals. He spread the gravel in front of the other three wheels, pounding it down into the ice as well as he was able.

"Now!" he said, finally. "When I shout, you are all to push as hard as you can. Every bit of added effort helps! But remember to stay on the left side, so you can jump out of the way if it starts to skid. If we don't get out this time . . ." He did not finish the sentence. Let them imagine what would happen if they didn't get out this time, he thought savagely. Let them imagine themselves walking down that lonely road for miles and miles, thinking of him, dead, in the river. . . . Perhaps on another such night they might not be so eager to set out on their futile trips! Perhaps they would be willing to stay at home, where a sensible human being should be.

He crawled into his seat, noting that the list toward the river had increased. The motor roared for a moment while he smiled to himself, deriving a sort of sardonic amusement at the thought of the exhaust gases which must be pouring forth. Then he put the machine in gear and shouted.

Again the wheels spun. There was a faint smell of rubber. He saw that it was no good, unless he worked the car into a rhythmic rocking. If he did that, on top of the forward push, sometime, the front wheels might catch on the solid gravel and pull out.

But there was a terrible alternative. On the back sway there was nothing between him and the river but six inches of loose gravel.

He made the decision. The bus should rock! Again he shouted, and fed the gas. It swayed backward and forward a matter of inches, like a giant cradle pushed by careless children to the very limits of its rockers, where it teetered momentarily before swaying sickeningly backward.

The gaunt, long-haired man ran forward to the open window. His face was streaked with mud and he gasped for breath, showing a very red tongue. "Keep it up!" he shouted. "We've almost got it. But say! Don't force it quite so much. Take it slow and easy on that back rock!"

Warning him, was he? The poor, blind fool! Did the fellow think he didn't know he was hanging over the brink of eternity? Did he think because he couldn't see it that he couldn't imagine that frozen gravel crumbling under the heavy back pressure?

"Keep to the left and be ready to jump!" he said between his teeth.

The matron, big-eyed, came cautiously picking her way across the slippery road. "I'm going to push, too," she announced. "I weigh one hundred and eighty pounds, and I guess that'll help."

Out of the corner of his eye, he watched them move over to give her room. The red-cheeked girl, not to be outdone, began to push on the fender. The depth of the swing increased perceptibly. His own hands tightened on the wheel; unconsciously he, too, was pushing.

For a wonderful instant, the monster trembled on the forward extremity of its swing; then, with a gathering of power, the wheels caught the gravel. With motor racing, it crawled forward up the grade, slowly, slowly — to the top of the hill.

He shut off the engine and sat there, not moving, not even thinking. Behind him the passengers were climbing the hill, panting, mud-splattered, chattering at each other. Stiffly he got out and stood beside the door.

"It's ruined my coat," complained the matron. Her white hair was hanging in careless locks on the collar of the coat. "Absolutely ruined it. And it's new, too."

"I've lost a rubber," grumbled the teacher, as he clambered into the bus. His voice was deep with irritation, and he kept flapping his coattails to shake off the sleet. "How's a man going to walk on this ice without rubbers?"

The fat salesman was last. He climbed into the bus and sank into a seat, gasping for breath. His face, in the yellow overhead light, was an unhealthy purple, and the veins of his eyes showed in significant tracery. But he managed a smile at the young girl as she sat down across the aisle. "Kind of hard work, that," he said apologetically.

"Gee, yes!" she agreed. "And we're going to be just simply hours late getting in! Isn't it just terrible?"

The driver turned away to conceal the spasm of irritation which had printed itself on his face. He went around to the back again and set about the business of changing the tire. They were alive! They were safe. He had kept them safe. And now they were complaining about their lost rubbers and ruined coats and a delay of half an hour. He'd risked his life for them, and that was all it amounted to: half an hour's delay. If he had gone over that bank in the tomb of a bus, it might have meant several hours' delay, and that, to them, would have been real tragedy! But they weren't in enough of a hurry to help him with the tire. Not they!

He wasn't complaining; it was his job and he was doing it, while they sat safe and snug inside.

He thought how differently he would feel about it if it really amounted to anything. Suppose he had soldiers with him, going into battle! Suppose he had some famous doctor, speeding to save life! A man could feel, then, that it wasn't wasted effort. It would be vital, important, satisfying to know that much depended on getting through on time. But he was carrying a girl to a dance and a shabby man to a sick wife (sick with toothache?) and an old woman to some party where she could show off her new seal coat.

His bitter thoughts were interrupted by the little man in the brown coat, who came plodding up the road with a rubber dangling from his hand. "Found this," he said laconically, handing it in the door to the teacher. But he did not get in the bus with the others. He came back to the driver and squatted beside him on the ice. "Let me help," he volunteered, reaching for the wrench. He grew voluble. "That was a pretty ticklish situation!" he said. "Believe me, I know it was! The river was a good ways down, and there wasn't much between us and it but a couple of inches of post. And a lot of space. And space isn't so good to lean up against!" His arm, tightening bolts, was going round and round like a wheel. He grinned at the driver companionably. "We're getting this job done in short order," he rambled on. "I'm in kind of a hurry tonight. Anxious to get there." The grin slowly faded from his wide mouth. Staring straight ahead into the sleet, he heaved a deep sigh. "I'm sure in a hurry to get there," he muttered again.

"Thanks for helping," Colton said gruffly, beginning to put away his tools. "I guess maybe it saved a couple of minutes for us." If there was sarcasm in his tone, the other did not notice it.

"Yeah," he agreed absently. "We ready to go now?"

They got back in the bus, and the driver slammed the door. The salesman was saying to the girl, "Say! If that bus had gone over the bank, I'll bet I'd have lost my samples!" The joy of a born salesman shone in his face. "I've got the slickest new kind of dress goods you ever saw! Something brand-new! Just invented. I tell you the women are going wild over it.

It's a long, loose weave that looks just like straw and kind of crackles when you rub it."

"Like hula-hula skirts?" giggled the girl.

"Yeah! That'd be a good name for it, huh?"

The matron had stopped scrubbing her coat with a muddy handkerchief and was listening intently. "But it isn't really straw, is it?" she asked mildly.

"No," said the salesman quickly, with the faintest hint of contempt. "Course it's silk."

The teacher leaned forward, watch in hand, to speak to the driver. "How much farther is it?"

"Five miles."

The slim thing made a great show of consulting her wrist watch. "We're going to be just dreadfully late," she wailed. "And Tommy will be furious. And it will make me hurry so, to get ready for the dance!"

A derisive smile pulled down a corner of the driver's mouth. How vastly important! He'd risked his life to get her to a dance on time. . . .

"It's most annoying," said the teacher's voice. "I'm to make a speech tonight at the schoolmasters' meeting. I'll just be able to get there, but I won't have time to glance over my notes first. I always like to have time to get acclimated before making a speech."

The matron was leaning forward eagerly. "You're Dr. Lee, aren't you?" she asked. "I've been wondering . . ."

"Yes," said the man. "I'm Dr. Lee."

"I'd like so much to hear your talk tonight," she murmured. "I've admired your work for a long time, Dr. Lee."

"One does what one can," said the teacher, smiling. "They aren't really bad boys, most of them. What they need is a good home and discipline, and that is what we try to give them."

"I know," she agreed. Her voice was soft. "You're doing a wonderful work."

In the distance, through the slanting sleet, the lights of the city became dimly visible, like jewels frozen in ice. The road, made softer by recent traffic, was no longer dangerous. The driver rubbed his hand across his left cheek, wet with rain. Unconsciously he sighed. He had got them in, safe and sound; the girl to her dance and the teacher to his convention. He had done his job. Tomorrow was payday. A man risked his life and was paid thirty dollars that fools might go to dances and conventions.

"Let me out at the Elwood," said the teacher. "It's only two blocks from there to the auditorium. Maybe I'll have time to glance over my notes, after all."

"Me, too," said the salesman. He was cleaning the mud from under his fingernails. "The Elwood is the best hotel in this town. Magnificent oyster stews. Hope the dining room isn't closed."

The white-haired woman was fumbling in her handbag for a clean handkerchief. Her face was contorted with some sudden emotion. She began to mop her eyes, subduing little sobs. "Hearing you talk about where you're going . . . it sort of got me. The schoolmasters' meeting and everything!" She blew her nose. "*I'm* going to a funeral. My only sister. She was a teacher. She died today."

In an embarrassed silence they drew up in front of the brightly lighted hotel. The salesman, no longer jovial, cuddled the elderly woman's arm in his hand while he hailed her a taxi. Gallantly he seated her in it and stood, bald head recklessly exposed to the storm, until she was on her way. Then, and only then, he came back to the bus to superintend the unloading of his precious sample cases.

The schoolmaster had already disappeared around the corner. The salesman, surrounded by his cases, waved a hand at the two remaining passengers. " Good-by," he said. " Don't get in the ditch again."

As they started on, the girl and the shabby man moved ahead to the seats just back of the driver. " It was kind of too bad about that woman, wasn't it? " said the girl. " I don't wonder she cried. Seeing all of us so happy, and everything! " She was peering ahead eagerly. " I want to stop at the university," she said, taking out a vanity case and powdering her nose. " The light here is so dim I can't see a thing! " She turned to the little man. " He'll surely be waiting for me, don't you think? " she asked ingenuously. " He wouldn't go away and leave me? "

" Sure, he'll be there."

The girl patted the soft locks of hair against her cheek. " I know he will," she said confidently. " But wouldn't it be terrible if he wasn't! "

At the University Drugstore corner, where the bus halted, a young man was waiting, staring out into the night over a window display of toothbrushes. " Tommy! " said the pretty girl ecstatically, stepping down in her thin pumps to the slushy sidewalk. He rushed to meet her, and they stood looking at each other. " Oh, Tommy! " she said again. The wild rose color in her cheeks had deepened; she was dancing on tiptoe, thrilling to life and love. The pertness had gone from her manner; she was all sweetness.

The young man bundled her tenderly into a battered car. " I was worried about you," he said softly. She puckered her lips at him in a pretty grimace. " I know," she said. " It's a bad night. But I couldn't let a bad night keep me away from you, Tommy! "

The bus driver slammed the door shut. There was an ache in his throat. When that girl had looked up at the young man, it had made him think of Gwen. He had wished he were seeing Gwen tonight. . . .

" A pretty girl, that," said the brown-coated man. " I like to see them bright and happy like her."

" Yes," Colton agreed.

" You'll be turning right at Anne Street, won't you? "

" No. We turn left."

" Oh! Then I'll have to walk all the way back from downtown." There was no protest in the voice, only a quiet acceptance.

The driver's shoulders twitched. " Supposed to keep to our regular route," he said gruffly. There was a silence. Colton felt uncomfortable. After all, the fellow had helped him with the tire. " But I guess it won't make any difference tonight if we go down Anne," he said abruptly. " As long as there aren't any other passengers to kick about it."

" Oh, thanks! "

At the corner the bus turned right. " It's three blocks down," said the shabby man. His voice had again an anxious pitch; he coughed twice, nervously. His blunt fingers kept fumbling with the handle of the small bag on the floor at his feet; and he was leaning forward, half-crouching as if to spring — as if, in the immediate necessity of reaching his destination, inches and seconds of time were important.

A moment later he gave a happy laugh, and the tension of his position noticeably relaxed. " There's a light there! " he exclaimed. " Oh, that's fine! "

He turned to grin at the driver in a sort of embarrassed goodfellowship; his elation was so great that he could not keep it to himself. Words bubbled from his mouth. " That light means everything is all right," he explained. " If anything had happened, she'd be at the hospital. I've been so worried! "

The bus stopped in front of a modest white house. " You know how it is," said the passenger, clambering out backward. " We've only been married a year. It will be our first child."

" Good night," said the driver, and smiled at the shabby young man — a smile no longer politely trained, but warm and friendly.

On the curb the man lingered, fumbling with his bag, for a last word. " I feel that I ought to thank you for getting me through tonight," he said. " This terrible storm! But we can always depend on you fellows, can't we? " He turned to run up the steps. " Good night," he called back over his shoulder, " Good night! "

As Colton waited, hands limp on the wheel, tired eyes staring at the red traffic light on the corner, a curious thought came to him. He saw himself in a new light, not as a slave to gadabout humanity but as a modern messenger of Destiny, carrying his ill-assorted passengers through an interlude of storm to life itself: to birth, and death, and love. Men such as he were the very warp in the pattern of civilization. Their creed was one of service and dependability against whatever odds.

Pride came to him, and the pleasant sense of accomplishment which follows a necessary job well done. He laughed aloud, thinking: he had wished to have soldiers and doctors for passengers, to justify the risks he had taken; and all the time there had been riding with him the hopes and fears, the joys and sorrows, of all mankind. " They can always depend on us fellows! " he said soberly. " We'll get them through! "

THINK BACK OVER WHAT YOU HAVE READ

Entering into the Thoughts and Feelings of the Leading Character

1. During the trip what were Colton's " bitter thoughts " about the following?

a. the people who " travel in weather like this "
b. the company he worked for
c. his job, including his salary and the schedule he was supposed to maintain
d. the comments made by the passengers

What sentences in the story strike you as most revealing of the bus driver's mood?

2. At what point in the story did Colton's mood begin to change? What happened in the story to pull the bus driver's thoughts away from himself? What line can you quote to show that he has forgotten all about himself and is thinking of others?

3. Summarize in your own words the " curious thought " that came to Colton after the last passenger had left the bus. How does this final thought erase each of the " bitter thoughts " listed above? How, for example, has Colton at the end of the story changed his mind about the people who " travel in weather like this "? about the company he works for? about his job?

4. How do you account for this change in attitude?

Responding to the Setting with Alert Imagination

5. The story you have just read derives much of its power from the use of concrete detail and from picturesque comparison. What brief passages can you quote that gave you a keen realization of the following?

a. the " terrible night "
b. the difficulties of driving
c. the " close call " when the bus skidded
d. the difficulties of getting the bus out of the icy hole
e. the discomfort of changing a tire on such a night
f. the approaching city in the distance

Increase Your Power over Words

6. Doubtless you have sat through a moving picture a second time and enjoyed picking up various threads of interest which you lost in the first swift flow of action. In similar fashion may the second reading of a story offer you a second kind of satisfaction.

In the first reading of a story there is ordinarily no time to linger over particular words and phrases and extract their full flavor, no time in which to pursue the little bypaths of meaning suggested by a picturesque comparison.

It is in this second mood — in no sense to be regarded as an enemy of the first mood mentioned — that you are invited to consider the following phrases. What, exactly, does the whole phrase mean within the sentence in which you find it? What is the particular force of each italicized word? If you are not familiar with the word, look up its meaning in the dictionary; then consider its modified meaning within the phrase. What new light does each phrase, when more fully grasped, throw upon the story? upon the mood of the characters, for example, or upon the beauty of the scene?

a. " which blended into *distorted rainbows* the *myriad* changing lights of night traffic " (page 99).
b. " drawn together by a *community of fear* and the *intimacy of light* and oily warmth " (page 99).
c. " The . . . supports of the post sang in an *overtone of emergency* as they cracked " (page 101)
d. " a machine of almost *human malevolence* " (page 100).
e. " The fat *buffoon!* " (page 102).
f. ". . . he was hanging over the *brink of eternity* " (page 103).
g. " A *derisive* smile pulled down a corner of the driver's mouth " (page 105).
h. " I always like to get *acclimated* before making a speech " (page 105).
i. ". . . carrying his *ill-assorted* passengers through an *interlude* of storm to life itself " (page 107).

7. Nothing adds more distinction to speech than the use of concrete words; that is, words that appeal to the senses. Familiarity with the following words offers a kind of test of your observing powers. Look up each word in its context, then come to class prepared to illustrate or demonstrate the action expressed in these words.

clambered (page 101)	grimace (page 106)
etched (page 101)	ricocheted (page 101)
teetered (page 103)	spasmodically (page 99)
momentum (page 101)	

UNDER THE LION'S PAW

by Hamlin Garland (1860–1940)

The author of this story knew the life of a farmer because he was once a farmer himself. Picturesque homesteads, old oaken buckets, and pretty girls in gingham down by the old millstream do not appear in his stories. He wrote, instead, about back yards littered with scraps thrown out to the chickens; of monotonous, backbreaking work in the fields. The automobile, the radio, the tractor have helped to brighten the picture since Garland wrote; yet his stories remain faithful pictures of life on the farm in his time.

" Under the Lion's Paw " is taken from a book of short stories entitled *Main-Traveled Roads,* which Hamlin Garland dedicated to his father and mother " whose half-century pilgrimage on the main-traveled road of life brought them only toil and deprivation." Here is another realistic story for you to read; and here is an opportunity for you to think about what you have read and compare life in the past with life as you know it today.

" Along this main-traveled road trailed an endless line of prairie schooners, coming into sight at the east and passing out of sight over the swell to the west. We children used to wonder where they were going and why they went."

IT WAS the last of autumn and first day of winter coming together. All day long the plowmen on their prairie farms had moved to and fro in their wide level fields through the falling snow, which melted as it fell, wetting them to the skin — all day, notwithstanding the frequent squalls of snow; the dripping, desolate clouds; and the muck of the furrows, black and tenacious as tar.

Under their dripping harness the horses swung to and fro silently, with that marvelous uncomplaining patience which marks the horse. All day the wild geese, honking wildly, as they sprawled sidewise down the wind,[1] seemed to be fleeing from an enemy behind, and with neck outthrust and wings extended, sailed down the wind, soon lost to sight.

Yet the plowman behind his plow, though the snow lay on his ragged greatcoat and the cold, clinging mud rose on his heavy boots, fettering him like gyves,[2]

[1] **down the wind:** in the same course as the wind. [2] **gyves:** a piece of harness which prevents the free motion of a horse's legs.

whistled in the very beard of the gale. As day passed, the snow, ceasing to melt, lay along the plowed land, and lodged in the depth of the stubble, till on each slow round the last furrow stood out black and shining as jet between the plowed land and the gray stubble.

When night began to fall, and the geese, flying low, began to alight invisibly in the near cornfield, Stephen Council was still at work "finishing a land." He rode on his sulky plow when going with the wind, but walked when facing it. Sitting bent and cold but cheery under his slouch hat, he talked encouragingly to his four-in-hand.[1]

"Come round there, boys! Round agin! We got t' finish this land. Come in there, Dan! *Stiddy,* Kate — stiddy! None o' y'r tantrums, Kittie. It's purty tuff, but got a be did. *Tchk! tchk!* Step along, Pete! Don't let Kate git y'r singletree[2] on the wheel. *Once* more!"

They seemed to know what he meant and that this was the last round, for they worked with greater vigor than before.

"Once more, boys, an' then, sez I, oats an' a nice warm stall, an' sleep f'r all."

By the time the last furrow was turned on the land it was too dark to see the house, and the snow was changing to rain again. The tired and hungry man could see the light from the kitchen shining through the leafless hedge, and he lifted a great shout, "Supper f'r a half a dozen!"

It was nearly eight o'clock by the time he had finished his chores and started for supper. He was picking his way carefully through the mud when the tall form of a man loomed up before him with a premonitory cough.

"Waddy ye want?" was the rather startled question of the farmer.

"Well, ye see," began the stranger in a deprecating tone, "we'd like t' git in f'r the night. We've tried every house f'r the last two miles, but they hadn't any room f'r us. My wife's jest about sick, 'n' the children are cold and hungry — "

"Oh, y' want 'o stay all night, eh?"

"Yes, sir; it 'ud be a great accom — "

"Waal, I don't make it a practice t' turn anybuddy 'way hungry, not on sech nights as this. Drive right in. We ain't got much, but sech as it is — "

But the stranger had disappeared. And soon his steaming, weary team, with drooping heads and swinging singletrees, moved past the well to the block beside the path. Council stood at the side of the "schooner"[3] and helped the children out — two little half-sleeping children — and then a small woman with a babe in her arms.

"There ye go!" he shouted jovially to the children. "*Now* we're all right! Run right along to the house there, an' tell Mam' Council you wants sumpthin' t' eat. Right this way, Mis' — keep right off t' the right there. I'll go an' git a lantern. Come," he said to the dazed and silent group at his side.

"Mother," he shouted, as he neared the fragrant and warmly lighted kitchen, "here are some wayfarers an' folks who need sumpthin' t' eat an' a place t' snooze." He ended by pushing them all in.

Mrs. Council, a large, jolly, rather coarse-looking woman, took the children in her arms. "Come right in, you little rabbits. 'Most asleep, hey? Now here's a drink o' milk f'r each o' ye. I'll have s'm tea in a minute. Take off y'r things and set up t' the fire."

While she set the children to drinking milk, Council got out his lantern and went out to the barn to help the stranger about

[1] **four-in-hand:** team of four horses that he was driving. [2] **singletree:** the crossbar to which the tugs of a harness are attached.

[3] **schooner:** short for prairie schooner, the canvas-covered wagon used by immigrants crossing the prairie, with which you are probably familiar.

his team, where his loud, hearty voice could be heard as it came and went between the haymow and the stalls.

The woman came to light as a small, timid, and discouraged-looking woman, but still pretty in a thin and sorrowful way.

"Land sakes! An' you've traveled all the way from Clear Lake t'day in this mud! Waal! waal! No wonder you're all tired out. Don't wait f'r the men, Mis' — " She hesitated, waiting for the name.

"Haskins."

"Mis' Haskins, set right up to the table an' take a good swig o' tea whilst I make y' s'm toast. It's green tea, an' it's good. I tell Council as I git older I don't seem to enjoy Young Hyson n'r Gunpowder.[1] I want the reel green tea, jest as it comes off'n the vines. Seems t' have more heart in it, someway. Don't s'pose it has. Council says it's all in m' eye."

Going on in this easy way, she soon had the children filled with bread and milk and the woman thoroughly at home, eating some toast and sweet-melon pickles, and sipping the tea.

"See the little rats!" she laughed at the children. "They're full as they can stick now, and they want to go to bed. Now, don't git up, Mis' Haskins; set right where you are an' let me look after 'em. I know all about young ones, though I'm all alone now. Jane went an' married last fall. But, as I tell Council, it's lucky we keep our health. Set right there, Mis' Haskins; I won't have you stir a finger."

It was an unmeasured pleasure to sit there in the warm, homely kitchen, the jovial chatter of the housewife driving out and holding at bay the growl of the impotent,[2] cheated wind.

The little woman's eyes filled with tears which fell down upon the sleeping baby in her arms. The world was not so desolate and cold and hopeless, after all.

"Now I hope Council won't stop out there and talk politics all night. He's the greatest man to talk politics an' read the *Tribune* — How old is it?"

She broke off and peered down at the face of the babe.

"Two months 'n' five days," said the mother, with a mother's exactness.

"Ye don't say! I want 'o know! The dear little pudzy-wudzy!" she went on, stirring it up in the neighborhood of the ribs with her fat forefinger.

"Pooty tough on 'oo to go gallivant'n' 'cross lots this way — "

"Yes, that's so; a man can't lift a mountain," said Council, entering the door. "Mother, this is Mr. Haskins, from Kansas. He's been eat up 'n' drove out by grasshoppers."

"Glad t' see yeh! Pa, empty that wash-basin 'n' give him a chance t' wash."

Haskins was a tall man, with a thin, gloomy face. His hair was a reddish brown, like his coat, and seemed equally faded by the wind and sun, and his sallow face, though hard and set, was pathetic somehow. You would have felt that he had suffered much by the line of his mouth showing under his thin, yellow mustache.

"Hain't Ike got home yet, Sairy?"

"Hain't seen 'im."

"W-a-a-l, set right up, Mr. Haskins; wade right into what we've got; 'tain't much, but we manage to live on it — she gits fat on it," laughed Council, pointing his thumb at his wife.

After supper, while the women put the children to bed, Haskins and Council talked on, seated near the huge cooking stove, the steam rising from their wet clothing. In the Western fashion Council told as much of his own life as he drew from his guest. He asked but few ques-

[1] **Young Hyson n'r Gunpowder:** new brands of tea for which Mrs. Council apparently has little relish. [2] **impotent:** powerless. The wind was *powerless* to work harm to those "in the warm, homely kitchen."

tions, but by and by the story of Haskins's struggles and defeat came out. The story was a terrible one; but he told it quietly, seated with his elbows on his knees, gazing most of the time at the hearth.

"I didn't like the looks of the country, anyhow," Haskins said, partly rising and glancing at his wife. "I was ust t' northern Ingyannie,[1] where we have lots o' timber 'n' lots o' rain, 'n' I didn't like the looks o' that dry prairie. What galled me the worst was goin' s' far away acrosst so much fine land layin' all through here vacant."

"And the 'hoppers eat ye four years, hand runnin', did they?"

"Eat! They wiped us out. They chawed everything that was green. They jest set around waitin' f'r us to die t' eat us, too. I ust t' dream of 'em sittin' 'round on the bedpost, six feet long, workin' their jaws. They eet the fork handles. They got worse 'n' worse till they jest rolled on one another, piled up like snow in winter. Well, it ain't no use. If I was t' talk all winter I couldn't tell nawthin'. But all the while I couldn't help thinkin' of all that land back here [2] that nobuddy was usin' that I ought o' had 'stead o' bein' out there in that cussed country."

"Waal, why didn't ye stop an' settle here?" asked Ike, who had come in and was eating his supper.

"Fer the simple reason that you fellers wanted ten 'r fifteen dollars an acre fer the bare land, and I hadn't no money fer that kind o' thing."

"Yes, I do my own work," Mrs. Council was heard to say in the pause which followed. "I'm a-gettin' purty heavy t' be on m' laigs all day, but we can't afford t' hire, so I keep rackin' around somehow, like a foundered horse.[3] S' lame — I tell Council he can't tell how lame I am, f'r I'm jest as lame in one laig as t'other." And the good soul laughed at the joke on herself as she took a handful of flour and dusted the biscuit board to keep the dough from sticking.

"Well, I hain't *never* been very strong," said Mrs. Haskins. "Our folks was Canadians an' small-boned, and then since my last child I hain't got up again fairly. I don't like t' complain. Tim has about all he can bear now — but they was days this week when I jest wanted to lay right down an' die."

"Waal, now, I'll tell ye," said Council, from his side of the stove, silencing everybody with his good-natured roar, "I'd go down and *see* Butler, *anyway,* if I was you. I guess he'd let you have his place purty cheap; the farm's all run down. He's ben anxious t' let t' somebuddy next year. It 'ud be a good chance fer you. Anyhow, you go to bed and sleep like a babe. I've got some plowin' t' do, anyhow, an' we'll see if somethin' can't be done about your case. Ike, you go out an' see if the horses is all right, an' I'll show the folks t' bed."

When the tired husband and wife were lying under the generous quilts of the spare bed, Haskins listened a moment to the wind in the eaves, and then said, with a slow and solemn tone:

"There are people in this world who are good enough t' be angels, an' only haff t' die to *be* angels."

Jim Butler was one of those men called in the West "land poor." Early in the history of Rock River he had come into the town and started in the grocery business in a small way, occupying a small building in a mean part of the town. At this period of his life he earned all he got and was up early and late sorting beans, working over butter, and carting his goods to and from the station. But a change came

[1] **Ingyannie:** a mispronunciation of Indiana. [2] **back here:** refers to Iowa. The Haskinses were returning from Kansas. [3] **foundered horse:** one that suffers from over eating.

over him at the end of the second year, when he sold a lot of land for four times what he paid for it. From that time forward he believed in land speculation as the surest way of getting rich. Every cent he could save or spare from his trade he put into land at forced sale, or mortgages on land, which were " just as good as the wheat," he was accustomed to say.

Farm after farm fell into his hands, until he was recognized as one of the leading landowners of the county. His mortgages were scattered all over Cedar County; and as they slowly but surely fell in, he sought usually to retain the former owner as tenant.

He was not ready to foreclose; indeed, he had the name of being one of the " easiest " men in the town. He let the debtor off again and again, extending the time whenever possible.

" I don't want y'r land," he said. " All I'm after is the int'rest on my money — that's all. Now, if y' want 'o stay on the farm, why, I'll give y' a good chance. I can't have the land layin' vacant." And in many cases the owner remained as tenant.

In the meantime he had sold his store; he couldn't spend time in it; he was mainly occupied now with sitting around town on rainy days smoking and " gassin' with the boys," or in riding to and from his farms. In fishingtime he fished a good deal. Doc Grimes, Ben Ashley, and Cal Cheatham were his cronies on these fishing excursions or hunting trips in the time of chickens or partridges. In winter they went to northern Wisconsin to shoot deer.

In spite of all these signs of easy life Butler persisted in saying he " hadn't enough money to pay taxes on his land," and was careful to convey the impression that he was poor in spite of his twenty farms. At one time he was said to be worth fifty thousand dollars; but land had been a little slow of sale of late, so that he was not worth so much.

A fine farm, known as the Higley place, had fallen into his hands in the usual way the previous year, and he had not been able to find a tenant for it. Poor Higley, after working himself nearly to death on it in the attempt to lift the mortgage, had gone off to Dakota, leaving the farm and his curse to Butler.

This was the farm which Council advised Haskins to apply for; and the next day Council hitched up his team and drove downtown to see Butler.

" You jest let *me* do the talkin'," he said. " We'll find him wearin' out his pants on some salt barrel somew'ers; and if he thought you *wanted* a place he'd sock it to you hot and heavy. You jest keep quiet; I'll fix 'im."

Butler was seated in Ben Ashley's store telling fish yarns when Council sauntered in casually.

" Hello, But. Lyin' agin, hey? "

" Hello, Steve! How goes it? "

" Oh, so-so. Too dang much rain these days. I thought it was goin' t' freeze up f'r good last night. Tight squeak if I get m' plowin' done. How's farmin' with *you* these days? "

" Bad. Plowin' ain't half done."

" It 'ud be a religious idee f'r you t' go out an' take a hand y'rself."

" I don't haff to," said Butler, with a wink.

" Got anybody on the Higley place? "

" No. Know of anybody? "

" Waal, no; not eggsackly. I've got a relation back t' Michigan who's ben hot an' cold on the idee o' comin' West f'r some time. *Might* come if he could get a good layout. What do you talk on the farm? "

" Well, I d' know. I'll rent it on shares or I'll rent it money rent."

" Waal, how much money, say? "

"Well, say ten per cent on the price — two-fifty."

"Waal, that ain't bad. Wait on 'im till 'e thrashes?"[1]

Haskins listened eagerly to this important question, but Council was coolly eating a dried apple which he had speared out of a barrel with his knife. Butler studied him carefully.

"Well, knocks me out of twenty-five dollars' interest."

"My relation'll need all he's got t' git his crops in," said Council in the safe, indifferent way.

"Well, all right; *say* wait," concluded Butler.

"All right; this is the man. Haskins, this is Mr. Butler — no relation to Ben — the hardest-working man in Cedar County."

On the way home Haskins said, "I ain't much better off. I'd like that farm; it's a good farm, but it's all run down, an' so 'm I. I could make a good farm of it if I had half a show. But I can't stock it n'r seed it."

"Waal, now, don't you worry," roared Council in his ear. "We'll pull y' through somehow till next harvest. He's agreed t' hire it plowed, an' you can earn a hundred dollars plowin' an' y' c'n git the seed o' me, an' pay me back when y' can."

Haskins was silent with emotion, but at last he said, "I ain't got nothin' t' live on."

"Now, don't you worry 'bout that. You jest make your headquarters at ol' Steve Council's. Mother'll take a pile o' comfort in havin' y'r wife an' children 'round. Y' see, Jane's married off lately, an' Ike's away a good 'eal, so we'll be darn glad t' have y' stop with us this winter. Nex' spring we'll see if y' can't git a start agin." And he chirruped to the team, which sprang forward with the rumbling, clattering wagon.

"Say, looky here, Council, you can't do this. I never saw —" shouted Haskins in his neighbor's ear.

Council moved about uneasily in his seat and stopped his stammering gratitude by saying, "Hold on, now; don't make such a fuss over a little thing. When I see a man down, an' things all on top of 'm, I jest like t' kick 'em off an' help 'm up. That's the kind of religion I got, an' it's about the *only* kind."

They rode the rest of the way home in silence. And when the red light of the lamp shone out into the darkness of the cold and windy night, and he thought of this refuge for his children and wife, Haskins could have put his arm around the neck of his burly companion and squeezed him like a lover. But he contented himself with saying, "Steve Council, you'll git y'r pay f'r this someday."

"Don't want any pay. My religion ain't run on such business principles."

The wind was growing colder, and the ground was covered with a white frost, as they turned into the gate of the Council farm, and the children came rushing out, shouting, "Papa's come!" They hardly looked like the same children who had sat at the table the night before. Their torpidity, under the influence of sunshine and Mother Council, had given way to a sort of spasmodic cheerfulness, as insects in winter revive when laid on the hearth.

Haskins worked like a fiend, and his wife, like the heroic woman that she was, bore also uncomplainingly the most terrible burdens. They rose early and toiled without intermission till the darkness fell on the plain, then tumbled into bed, every bone and muscle aching with fatigue, to rise with the sun next morning to the same round of the same ferocity of labor.

[1] **Wait on 'im till 'e thrashes:** in other words wait for payment until the crop is sold.

The eldest boy drove a team all through the spring, plowing and seeding, milked the cows, and did chores innumerable, in most ways taking the place of a man.

An infinitely pathetic but common figure — this boy on the American farm, where there is no law against child labor. To see him in his coarse clothing, his huge boots, and his ragged cap as he staggered with a pail of water from the well, or trudged in the cold and cheerless dawn out into the frosty field behind his team, gave the city-bred visitor a sharp pang of sympathetic pain. Yet Haskins loved his boy, and would have saved him from this if he could; but he could not.

By June the first year the result of such Herculean toil [1] began to show on the farm. The yard was cleaned up and sown to grass, the garden plowed and planted, and the house mended.

Council had given them four of his cows.

"Take 'em an' run 'em on shares. I don't want 'o milk s' many. Ike's away s' much now, Sat'd'ys an' Sund'ys, I can't stand the bother anyhow."

Other men, seeing the confidence of Council in the newcomer, had sold him tools on time; and as he was really an able farmer, he soon had round him many evidences of his care and thrift. At the advice of Council he had taken the farm for three years, with the privilege of re-renting or buying at the end of the term.

"It's a good bargain, an' y' want 'o nail it," said Council. "If you have any kind ov a crop, you c'n pay y'r debts, an' keep seed an' bread."

The new hope which now sprang up in the heart of Haskins and his wife grew great almost as a pain by the time the wide field of wheat began to wave and rustle and swirl in the winds of July. Day after day he would snatch a few moments after supper to go and look at it.

"Have ye seen the wheat t'day, Nettie?" he asked one night as he rose from supper.

"No, Tim, I ain't had time."

"Well, take time now. Le's go look at it."

She threw an old hat on her head — Tommy's hat — and, looking almost pretty in her thin, sad way, went out with her husband to the hedge.

"Ain't it grand, Nettie? Just look at it."

It was grand. Level, russet here and there, heavy-headed, wide as a lake, and full of multitudinous whispers and gleams of wealth, it stretched away before the gazers like the fabled field of the cloth of gold.[2]

"Oh, I think — I *hope* we'll have a good crop, Tim; and oh, how good the people have been to us!"

"Yes; I don't know where we'd be t'day if it hadn't been f'r Council and his wife."

"They're the best people in the world," said the little woman, with a great sob of gratitude.

"We'll be in the field on Monday, sure," said Haskins, gripping the rail on the fence as if already at the work of the harvest.

The harvest came, bounteous, glorious; but the winds came and blew it into tangles, and the rain matted it here and there close to the ground, increasing the work of gathering it threefold.

Oh, how they toiled in those glorious days! Clothing dripping with sweat, arms aching, filled with briers, fingers raw and bleeding, backs broken with the weight of heavy bundles, Haskins and his man toiled on. Tommy drove the harvester,

[1] **Herculean toil:** toil which required the strength of Hercules, a hero of Greek mythology famed for achieving twelve very difficult tasks.

[2] **field of the cloth of gold:** a magnificent display on a plain in France where Henry VIII of England and Francis I of France held an interview in 1520.

while his father and a hired man bound on the machine. In this way they cut ten acres every day, and almost every night after supper, when the hand went to bed, Haskins returned to the field shocking the bound grain in the light of the moon. Many a night he worked till his anxious wife came out at ten o'clock to call him in to rest and lunch.

At the same time she cooked for the men, took care of the children, washed and ironed, milked the cows at night, made the butter, and sometimes fed the horses and watered them while her husband kept at the shocking.

No slave in the Roman galleys could have toiled so frightfully and lived, for this man thought himself a free man and that he was working for his wife and babes.

When he sank into his bed with a deep groan of relief, too tired to change his grimy, dripping clothing, he felt that he was getting nearer and nearer to a home of his own and pushing the wolf of want a little farther from his door.

There is no despair so deep as the despair of a homeless man or woman. To roam the roads of the country or the streets of the city, to feel there is no rood of ground [1] on which the feet can rest, to halt weary and hungry outside lighted windows and hear laughter and song within — these are the hungers and rebellions that drive men to crime and women to shame.

It was the memory of this homelessness, and the fear of its coming again, that spurred Timothy Haskins and Nettie, his wife, to such ferocious labor during that first year.

" 'M, yes; 'm, yes; first-rate," said Butler, as his eye took in the neat garden, the pigpen, and the well-filled barnyard. " You're gitt'n' quite a stock around yeh. Done well, eh? "

Haskins was showing Butler around the place. He had not seen it for a year, having spent the year in Washington and Boston with Ashley, his brother-in-law, who had been elected to Congress.

" Yes, I've laid out a good deal of money durin' the last three years. I've paid out three hundred dollars f'r fencin'."

" Um — h'm! I see, I see," said Butler, while Haskins went on:

" The kitchen there cost two hundred; the barn ain't cost much in money, but I've put a lot o' time on it. I've dug a new well, and I — "

" Yes, yes, I see. You've done well. Stock worth a thousand dollars," said Butler, picking his teeth with a straw.

" About that," said Haskins, modestly. " We begin to feel's if we was gitt'n' a home f'r ourselves; but we've worked hard. I tell you we begin to feel it, Mr. Butler, and we're goin' t' begin to ease up purty soon. We've been kind o' plannin' a trip back t' *her* folks after the fall plowin's done."

" *Eggs*-actly! " said Butler, who was evidently thinking of something else. " I suppose you've kind o' calc'lated on stayin' here three years more? "

" Well, yes. Fact is, I think I c'n buy the farm this fall, if you'll give me a reasonable show."

" Um — m! What do you call a reasonable show? "

" Well, say a quarter down and three years' time."

Butler looked at the huge stacks of wheat which filled the yard, over which the chickens were fluttering and crawling, catching grasshoppers, and out of which the crickets were singing innumerably. He smiled in a peculiar way as he said, " Oh, I won't be hard on yeh. But what did you expect to pay f'r the place? "

" Why, about what you offered it for

[1] **rood of ground:** a square measure of land equivalent to one-fourth of an acre.

before, two thousand five hundred, or *possibly* three thousand," he added quickly, as he saw the owner shake his head.

"This farm is worth five thousand and five hundred dollars," said Butler, in a careless and decided voice.

"*What!*" almost shrieked the astounded Haskins. "What's that? Five thousand? Why, that's double what you offered it for three years ago."

"Of course, and it's worth it. It was all run down then; now it's in good shape. You've laid out fifteen hundred dollars in improvements, according to your own story."

"But *you* had nothin' t' do about that. It's my work an' my money."

"You bet it was; but it's my land."

"But what's to pay me for all my — "

"Ain't you had the use of 'em?" replied Butler, smiling calmly into his face.

Haskins was like a man struck on the head with a sandbag; he couldn't think; he stammered as he tried to say, "But — I never'd git the use — You'd rob me! More'n that: you agreed — you promised that I could buy or rent at the end of three years at — "

"That's all right. But I didn't say I'd let you carry off the improvements, nor that I'd go on renting the farm at two-fifty. The land is doubled in value, it don't matter how; it don't enter into the question; an' now you can pay me five hundred dollars a year rent, or take it on your own terms at fifty-five hundred, or — git out."

He was turning away when Haskins, the sweat pouring from his face, fronted him, saying again:

"But *you've* done nothing to make it so. You hain't added a cent. I put it all there myself, expectin' to buy. I worked an' sweat to improve it. I was workin' for myself an' babes — "

"Well, why didn't you buy when I offered to sell? What y' kickin' about?"

"I'm kickin' about payin' you twice f'r my own things — my own fences, my own kitchen, my own garden."

Butler laughed. "You're too green t' eat, young feller. *Your* improvements! The law will sing another tune."

"But I trusted your word."

"Never trust anybody, my friend. Besides, I didn't promise not to do this thing. Why, man, don't look at me like that. Don't take me for a thief. It's the law. The reg'lar thing. Everybody does it."

"I don't care if they do. It's stealin' jest the same. You take three thousand dollars of my money — the work o' my hands and my wife's." He broke down at this point. He was not a strong man mentally. He could face hardship, ceaseless toil, but he could not face the cold and sneering face of Butler.

"But I don't take it," said Butler, coolly. "All you've got to do is to go on jest as you've been a-doin', or give me a thousand dollars down, and a mortgage at ten per cent on the rest."

Haskins sat down blindly on a bundle of oats near by, and with staring eyes and drooping head went over the situation. He was under the lion's paw. He felt a horrible numbness in his heart and limbs. He was hid in a mist, and there was no path out.

Butler walked about, looking at the huge stacks of grain and pulling now and again a few handfuls out, shelling the heads in his hands and blowing the chaff away. He hummed a little tune as he did so. He had an accommodating air of waiting.

Haskins was in the midst of the terrible toil of the last year. He was walking again in the rain and the mud behind his plow; he felt the dust and dirt of the threshing. The ferocious husking time, with its cutting wind and biting, clinging snows, lay hard upon him. Then he thought of his wife, how she had cheerfully cooked and baked without holiday and without rest.

"Well, what do you think of it?" inquired the cool, mocking, insinuating voice of Butler.

"I think you're a thief and a liar!" shouted Haskins, leaping up. "A black-hearted houn'!" Butler's smile maddened him; with a sudden leap he caught a fork in his hands, and whirled it in the air. "You'll never rob another man!" he grated through his teeth, a look of pitiless ferocity in his accusing eyes.

Butler shrank and quivered, expecting the blow; stood, held hypnotized by the eyes of the man he had a moment before despised — a man transformed into an avenging demon. But in the deadly hush between the lift of the weapon and its fall there came a gush of faint, childish laughter and then across the range of his vision, far away and dim, he saw the sun-bright head of his baby girl, as with the pretty, tottering run of a two-year-old she moved across the grass of the dooryard. His hands relaxed; the fork fell to the ground; his head lowered.

"Make out y'r deed an' mor'gage, an' git off'n my land, an' don't ye never cross my line agin; if y' do, I'll kill ye."

Butler backed away from the man in wild haste and, climbing into his buggy with trembling limbs, drove off down the road, leaving Haskins seated dumbly on the sunny pile of sheaves, his head sunk in his hands.

THINK BACK OVER WHAT YOU HAVE READ

Appreciating the Story's Realism

1. The average movie is geared to popular taste; it offers picture fans what they want. How would this story need to be changed in order to make it a box-office hit? What features would need to be changed? What features would need to be added? What features would be stressed in advertising?

2. Do the characters in this story seem to you like real people? What characteristics do Farmer Council and his wife have in common with Western farmers as you know them or have read about them? In what respects do they differ from city people as you know them? Does Jim Butler seem real? Mr. Haskins? In what scenes do they seem to you the most convincing?

3. What pictures did you form of the Council farm? the Council kitchen? the Haskins farm? Ben Ashley's store? What details helped you form the picture? At what points in the story did you feel conscious of the weather?

4. What does the title of the story mean? To whom does the lion refer? Who was the lion's victim? Find the sentence in the story which refers directly to the title. Does the story end as you think it would in real life? Why?

5. Judging from your observation in real life, what do you thing will happen to Haskins and his family after the close of the story? What will become of Jim Butler?

Thinking about Problems Raised by the Story

6. If Butler had the law on his side, how could Haskins say, "It's stealin' jest the same. You take three thousand dollars of my money — the work o' my hands and my wife's"?

7. Does any of the responsibility for what happened to Haskins fall on his own shoulders? If so, what?

8. What undesirable traits are the outcome of tenant farming? on the tenants? on the landowners? What is the common attitude toward tenant farmers? Do the Haskinses support this attitude or contradict it? What is the common attitude toward landowners? Are they held in more or less respect than tenants? How does the character of Jim Butler fit in with popular notion about the virtues of landowners?

Increase Your Power over Words

9. The following words are associated with harvesttime on the farm. With how many of them are you familiar? Distinguish their meanings carefully.

shelling (page 116) husking (page 116)
shocking (page 115) stubble (page 109)

10. Jove was an ancient Latin god of the heavens. As Jove was the father of the gods, so was Jupiter the father of the planets. It used to be believed that when Jupiter was in a

certain position in the sky people were joyful and merry. *Jovial* (page 109) still means merry or jolly.

11. *Tenacious* (page 108) comes from a Latin verb meaning to hold. We use *tenacious* as an adjective. A *tenacious* memory is one which holds on to ideas or facts for a long time; a *tenacious* metal is a tough one — one in which the small chemical particles hold tightly to one another. A *tenant* is a person who holds land or buildings.

12. The Latin people tried to avert evil by prayer. Their word meaning to pray was *precari. Deprecating* (page 109) now means disapproving of something. It is interesting that we should now use the word in this way when before it suggested fear, hatred, and anguish. Should we be afraid of a *deprecating* smile?

THE WIND FIGHTERS

by Keene Abbott (1876–   )

By this time it is becoming increasingly clear that stories of realism offer you a chance to extend your own experience, and through the thoughts and feelings of those you read about to touch life at many more points than would otherwise be possible for you to do. In the story that follows, you are to experience drought and disaster on the prairie. You are to see what it feels like to " watch the things you gave your life to, broken, and stoop and build 'em up with worn-out tools."[1] And just as the young husband and wife wrested a living truth out of their bitter experience, so may you, too, learn an important lesson from life — their life — without actually experiencing the pain and sorrow which accompanied it.

IN ANXIOUS haste the settler had begun chopping down the two bone-dry, scraggy trees in front of the sod house. And his wife, hearing the stroke of the ax, came promptly to see what he was about.

" It's a heartless thing," she protested — " a heartless thing you're doing, Jim Dara! "

In quality and accent and deep modulation her voice was unmistakably Irish, as was also the voice of the man. But he did not reply at once. It was not until the first of the trees, the maple, had crashed upon the ground that he answered quietly:

" It's no heartless thing I'm doing. It would be morbidness only to keep them standing."

The woman said, looking at a white chip she had picked up:

" There would be sap enough, maybe, for new leaves this year."

" I know, dear, what you want of the trees. If they would live and come green again! The one of them, the maple, we planted when the little girl was born, and the elm was for the boy. But they couldn't grow, dear." His toilworn hand gently patted her shoulder. " Last year I knew they couldn't, only I hadn't the heart to be cutting them down."

That evening, with the chores all done and the sun gone down, Dara sat with his wife on the doorstep and would have played a while on his flute, for the tunes of their sweetheart time had come singing back to him as they were wont to do in the spring of the year. But the three parts of the instrument, once they had been taken out of the grooves of purple velvet in the leather case, were too shrunken at the joints for them to fit together.

" Never mind," he said. " I'll have to soak them up before they're any good." As he closed the leather case, he added, " We'll just listen to the flute notes of the meadowlarks calling. They know how so much better, anyhow, than I do."

As they hearkened a while, the woman gazed afar at some upfloating wraiths — thin plumes, gray and violet, that lifted themselves above the horizon, a vast bluish line, sharp-cut as if done by the colossal sweep of a scythe. It was smoke she was looking at, the burning of cornstalks cleared away from fields where the soil was being prepared for yet another seed planting. For, though a great number of

[1] from Kipling's "If."

people had moved back East, deserting their homesteads, many settlers still remained; and now Dara's wife could see that this spring, as in other springs, they were courageously doing their work.

"Do you think, Jim boy," she musefully asked, "it will be a good year, this one?"

He said decisively:

"There were snows aplenty; the rains have come; the soil is black and rich. It will be a good year for crops, this one."

He looked across a field at the plow standing at the end of a furrow. The shovel, scoured bright, was like a mirror stuck in the ground — was like a clear looking glass reflecting the red of the west.

"A good year," Dara repeated. "A fine year for crops."

His wife, reflecting upon winds and drought and hard times, presently observed:

"We've done real well, considering. We're not like them that had to take aid."

"No, and what's owing Martin Byrne" — he was referring to his good friend the storekeeper in the prairie town — "what's owing him," Dara repeated, "we'll wipe it all out, every cent, in one year or two."

"Charity," his wife proudly asserted, "we have not had to take."

Dara sighed a little as he said:

"You never got the lace, dear, to put on the dress of the little girl."

"They were sweet dresses the baby had," she replied. "You said so yourself. You said there was nobody could tell they were made of flour sacks."

"Fine dresses, Nora; they were that — they were, for a fact."

The twilight faded out, and now that the bluish, lukewarm night was come, pale stars began to quiver in the tender sky as if they were fire drops trembling. The woman, as she sat looking at them, heard her name spoken.

"Nora?"

"What is it, Jim boy?"

"I didn't like to cut down the trees."

"They couldn't grow," she told him.

"No, dear, they couldn't."

Before long he was saying with mild self-contempt:

"It was a senseless thing not to plant cottonwoods; for such trees, Nora, do be easy growers."

"Yes, they do be easy growers, the cottonwoods."

"It would be a grand thing to have them, the green trees!"

And his wife said courageously:

"I do have my house plants. There be the two geraniums, dear — both growing fine in tin cans, and the one of them coming into bloom."

By and by she was whispering, as she rested her head against his shoulder:

"We have had two little babies."

Her husband boastfully replied:

"There is Martin Byrne — he never had any babies at all."

"Poor Martin Byrne!" sighed the woman, and her husband went on:

"It's the like of us, Nora, can pity him. He's the same, almost, as a widower; his woman leaving him, and all, and going back to her folks. Fond of him, too, I'm thinking. Only she couldn't stand it out here. She was that lonesome and sorry on account of the winds blowing always."

"He did what he could to make her easy and contented," said the woman. "He even got her the fine piano I told him to get."

"Yes, Nora; and now — he would be selling the piano, to get rid of it, and not have it standing like a tombstone in the house."

"Think of that!" said Nora, as if she did not know what Jim was coming to. In the fear of what he was about to propose she clasped her hands, and the dry palms of them made a raspy sound before they stiffly slunk away into hiding in the sag of her skirt between her knees.

" If we were to take the thing off his hands, as a kindness. . . . What do you say, Nora ? "

" A fine thing to have, Jim boy. Would look too grand in the room."

" We could practice up some of the old tunes," he went on.

" The old tunes," she repeated, and he did not know she was wringing her knuckly hands in the sag of her skirt.

" Sometimes," her husband added, " we could have the neighbors for a bit of music, to cheer them up."

Neighbors! And the nearest of them living five miles away!

" It's a cheerful thing, is music," said Nora.

" A grand thing," Dara called out.

" A grand thing," said Nora, his wife.

Only there was no time, neither this week nor the next, for bringing the piano to the farm. It must wait. There was the spring work to be done: the plowing, the harrowing, the planting. He was in the field when the sun rose; in the evening also, after the sun went down, until darkness came, he held to his labor in the field.

All was going well. On the doorstep, beside his wife, before they went to bed, he played his flute in the starshine, while slumbrous odors out of the darkness, good, grassy odors — " the smell of bigness," Nora called it — came breathing in upon them. Sometimes, in a hushed voice, the woman sang to the playing of the flute, sang those pensive little ballads of Ireland that are not mournful and yet have tears in them.

" It's going to be a fine year, this one," said Dara. And the barking of the little prairie wolves, coming from afar, was like friendly voices out yonder in the night. " We'll pay off everything, the piano included! "

" Yes," said Nora. But by and by she was humbly adding, " Say, Jim boy . . ."

" Well? "

" Don't get it, that piano."

" Don't get! What's that you're saying? "

" I want no piano."

" You want — Look here, Nora, is it plum daft you are? "

" I am not, and won't be, God help us; for I work outdoors, doing a man's work when I'm able. You've been all for shutting me up in the house and protecting me from hard labor. But if them that have gone queer in their heads had done the same as me — had worked in the fields the way they wouldn't hear the winds whining — "

Abruptly she held out to him her stiffened hands, and she said, not bitterly, but with kindness, " Understand, James Dara, you will be getting me no piano."

The husband clasped one of those hands in his. He felt of it wonderingly. How very curious it could have come to this, and he never have noticed!

Now he clung to that hand. He began rocking back and forth; he fondled the knuckly thing against his cheek, against his lips, but there came out of him neither groan nor cry. Quiet words only he spoke.

" It was soft once," he was saying. " It was limber and white. The fingers could touch the notes that lightly I couldn't mind my flute playing for watching them, the curve of them, and they touching the keys that gently."

" Get the piano! " his wife said.

" You couldn't play it, dear."

" I could play it."

" We will not hear the old tunes again," he went on, " never any more, never, never! "

" We *will* play them, Jim boy. I'll learn them again, all of them. Get the piano. The stiffness will come out of my hands. Lard will soften them. We will have the neighbors in for a bit of music to cheer them up. Will you get me the piano, Jim?"

"No," he said.

But in May he brought it home; and, a neighbor helping him, the instrument was set in place, against the wall of the front room, beneath the crayon portraits of two children. Then, as soon as he was in the field, distantly guiding the cultivator up and down the golden green of the corn rows, she began her practicing. And she tried to play softly, that he might not hear how clumsily her fingers stumbled over the keys.

Each day, indefatigably, she toiled at her exercises, the simple ones, the rudimentary and tiresome scales. Then, at the end of a week, he said to her at suppertime:

"We'll have a try at it tonight, Nora — flute and piano together."

"Not tonight, Jim," she replied.

On the doorstep, in the dusk of a June evening, they sat listening to the quiet wash and soothing sibilance of the pale-green lake aripple under the stars.

"It's a fine stand of corn, that one," said Dara.

"Yes," Nora replied.

"Will go sixty bushels to the acre."

"Will it, Jim?"

"Or maybe seventy. Shouldn't wonder a bit if she would come seventy bushels to the acre."

"It's fine growing weather," Nora declared.

"It is, by the grace of God; it is that — fine growing weather."

So June passed, and now July was passing. By day, all day long, there was the amazing sun fire, an enormous white light, quivering. By night no cooling of the earth. Heat rising continuously from the soil—black heat, moist and powerful.

"Good corn weather," people say, and sometimes they say it with the hush of fear in their voices. For there are winds that blow. Winds come up out of the south — dry winds, dust-choked and terrifying. They are a flameless burning of the air. In a day, a half day, an hour's time, they shrivel green fields and meadow grass to parched and brittle mockeries.

In the afternoon, on the fourteenth day of August, something ominous appeared. Now and again, in a swooning cornfield, a gray and vaporous streak lifted itself. It rose like a spinning plume of smoke, and, having trailed skyward, it whirled away and vanished — a scarf of dust abruptly sucked up by a mysterious air current, and as suddenly dissolved. Corn leaves, violently agitated, stirred with a papery rustle for a time, then hung stiffly motionless, weighed down once more by the overpressure of heat.

Throughout the afternoon, intermittently, the phenomenon continued; and again, the following day, the dust whirls were seen. Then, by noon, when the earth was stripped of its purplish shadows, there came something even more sinister.

Dara's wife, standing in the doorway of the sod house, felt an acrid sultriness — felt it as if she were testing the heat of a flatiron by raising it near her cheek. She looked out upon the tasseled cornfield, immense, blue-green, opulent — a field of vast acreage, representing so much toil, so many hopes, so brave a fight!

But what cares nature for courage, or for hopes, or for human aspiration? Wind had begun to blow. Viewless fire, enormously puffing, ran in repeated whiffs across the prairie.

"It's blowing up a rain," said Dara. He spoke cheerfully as he came clumping into the house for his dinner.

A shudder passed through the great field. The woman, still gazing out yonder at the billowing of the glossy leaves, whispered with husky dryness in her voice:

" The corn is firing." [1]

It was true. Unfailingly, each year, ever since this homestead was new to the plow, the same sinister forecast of drought had appeared — the yellow crispening of short leaves, close to the earth, at the base of the cornstalks.

But Dara said to his wife:

" We're going to have rain."

To humor him, she anxiously agreed:

" Yes, Jim, the rain's coming."

" The range cattle sense it," he added. " They sense it. They're restless; they're on the move. A sure sign! "

" A sure sign," said Nora, his wife.

Then she shut the door, shut the windows, sealed up her house against the whining of the wind.

Heat, dry heat, thinned the air with a burning acridity. A smell of dust became more penetrating.

" Look here, Nora! Look! " Dara excitedly called out, peering through the window. " There's a rain cloud bulging up."

" Dust! " said Nora.

Both were wrong. It was the gray swell of a wagon sheet showing above a ridge, beyond the twin cottonwoods. After the first there came a second prairie van, then a third.

" Only look at that, now! " Dara said contemptuously. " Deserting their homesteads! "

" Don't be scornful, Jim boy. Maybe it's the winds they're going from. Maybe they can't get used to the winds grieving always, come summer, come winter, snow winds and dust winds, ice and fire forever! "

" Yes, dear; the winds do be grieving in lean times. But come fat times, and our corn all cribbed, and the gold of it looking through the cracks, then will the winds be changing their tune. They will sing *then,* I'm telling you. They will, so they will! "

Mad rejoicing was in Dara's face. He took down his flute; he fitted its parts together. Nothing could be stranger than his boyish exultation as he hurriedly added:

" We'll hold those people, Nora. We'll stop them; we'll play for them. If they've lost their nerve, it's music will be giving it back to them."

Dumbly hearkening for a time to the slow clack and creak of the three wagons drawing nearer and nearer, the woman huskily whispered:

" Let them not be stopping here, James Dara. If green trees do be calling them, and the gurgle of clear water over mossy stones, and bees humming in the pink clover, let those people not be stopping here."

But stop them he did. Bareheaded, the jointed flute in his hand, he ran out to the barbed-wire fence and hailed the emigrants.

" Better take a nooning," he insisted. " You'll be wanting to feed your teams and rest them a spell, and they dripping sweat from their fetlocks in the hot sun. Come in, neighbors; come right in! "

A bristle-faced man, driver of the first wagon, leaned forward, a wisp of hay caught in his shaggy beard.

Dara added earnestly:

" There's a piano in the house. Nora will play for you, and me with my flute knocking out tunes beside it if you would care for a bit of music."

Con Lewis, the bearded man, laughed raucously.

" Music! There's the hot wind will make music for us! "

But the frail woman on the seat with him, a baby in her arms, nudged him in the side with her elbow.

" It's the piano you got off Martin Byrne," said she to Dara. " We've heard

[1] **The corn is firing:** that is, scorching and withering.

tell your woman can finger it just grand."

From the second wagon, with the curve of the bows showing through the gray canvas like the ribs of a starved elephant, a man's voice called out:

" Better load up your stuff, Jimmy, and throw in with us."

The woman with the baby added:

" We could easy get overhet if we was to dance on a day like this; but it would be nice, all the same, to hear some tunes played on the piano and the flute."

Almost jovially the man in the second wagon called out:

" In three weeks or four we'll land you all hunky-dory in God's country if you throw in with us. Then you won't have to see your corn burning up the same as last year and every year."

Dara said impatiently:

" Fetch in some of the chairs you have roped to the tail of your wagon when you get your horses watered and fed."

The flute player had his way with these people from homesteads newly abandoned. The company assembled in the house for the concert; three men, four women, eight children, including the baby.

When the music began, the little folks grew quiet, the baby stopped fretting, and, mildly interested, the men condescended to listen.

As for the women, they leaned forward, forgetting the suffocation of heat. They drank in the simple melodies — drank of that music as if they were thirst-famished things come upon a rill of clear water.

Flute and piano may have sung together in a poor performance. No matter! Familiar tunes pulsed graciously through the house: first " The Wearing of the Green," next " Swanee River," then " The Minstrel Boy," then " The Harp That Once through Tara's Halls."

In the pauses after each duet a silence of growing sultriness made itself felt in the two crowded rooms. In the garden plot, seen from the window, yellow sunflowers stared into the ominous hush, each bloom and leaf listlessly hanging.

Long the heat torpor held. The flat, sick land lay in a stupefaction, stunned, naked to the enormous glare. Once the whir of a harvest fly half a mile away in the twin cottonwoods wearily rasped the silence, and stopped, and began again. The two ragged tree shapes, far off, crouched together, sulkily waiting for something. For what?

" Rain is coming," said Dara.

Nobody believed him.

" Play something else, please," a frail-voiced woman requested.

He would have called attention to dark blotches flitting along the ground, light, transparent shadows rapidly herding together across the prairie; but the Confederate veteran Con Lewis, the bearded man, said peremptorily:

" Yes, tear loose again. Something lively! "

He frowned. He did not like waiting here so long.

But Dara did not begin at once. He shut his eyes, wiped the mouthpiece of his flute upon his sleeve; then, getting to his feet, he reached across his wife's shoulder and struck a sounding chord upon the piano. She understood. Looking up at her husband, as he took a deep breath with the flute to his mouth, her hands suddenly leaped upon the keys.

Carefree and swift, a rousing melody was evoked. The wind instrument lost its crooning mellowness. Now it was like a fire. Its breath was martial, gay, exultant. It shrilled with a mad, frolicking, rollicking triumph.

" Dixie " was the tune. The shaggy head of Lewis swayed in time to the music. His feet began shuffling. He hummed in an undertone. His fists were beating upon the wooden arms of his chair. And he could not remain seated. Abruptly he stood up; he waved his hat; he stamped and shouted.

"That's it!" Dara called out. "There's a charge and a yell and a big fight in that tune. *Well* you know that, Con Lewis. You were a soldier once for your Dixie Land. You didn't run from bullets, I'm thinking. But will you now be running from the land?"

The enthusiasm of the bearded man was quenched at once.

"Why *not* pull out?" he sullenly questioned. "What's to stay for? Don't you know, you Irish son of a gun, when you're clean licked? You can't fight the winds," he added. "Nobody can."

"They did it in Iowa," said Dara. "They did it in Illinois. They made a corn empire of it, the richest in all the world. Cultivation of the soil brought the rains. Trees grew; climate changed. God's country, you call it."

"Was never the same as this," said Lewis, stubbornly shaking his head. "Could *grow* something, that country could — something besides sage and soapweed and buffalo grass. Me, I won't stay to see my crop burn up."

"There's something grows here better than corn."

"In God's name, what?"

"I'll tell you what!" said Dara. "There's Mrs. Arnold sitting yonder; she who came to us when darkness was in our house and our little children dying. She stayed with us. She gave us comfort. We had no money for her. We had no money for the doctor; but he came, too. He did what he could for us. Coal and groceries and clothes we needed, and there was Martin Byrne, in town, let us have them. And he's done the like of that for the rest of you, I'm thinking. So, will you tell me, Con Lewis, is there any country, anywhere, can produce a bigger crop of kindness?"

Dumbly unwilling to reply, Lewis sat down and looked at the floor between his two dusty boots. And Dara suddenly called out:

"There, see that?"

A bluish light, abrupt and livid, had twitched in the room. It was followed by a low grumble, as if an empty wagon might be rumbling far off. Distantly, against the blue-black storm gloom of the sky, the two cottonwoods, cowering above the horizon, had begun to shudder. Their glossy leaves were all aripple as if a shiver of cool wind had passed through them. And suddenly the cornfield broke into billows, as of green flames dancing.

As swiftly their whispering was hushed. Silence once again, expectancy! Something clicked on the window glass. With a sounding spat a silver needle, a big water blob, had flattened itself against the pane. Then, as scraggy fire slit the sky with a branching quiver, a winking brightness jiggled in, bluishly flaring upon tense faces.

A horse neighed; thunder broke. Prodigiously it exploded, and the quake of it jarred the house, shook the windows, cavernously rumbled and tumbled down the sky, in prolonged reverberations.

Rain began to fall. On came the rush of it — tumultuous rain; panic-whirling films of the silvery, racing rain; the green ocean of corn heaved and streamed. Down plumped the water. It roared on the roof, spouted from the eaves, slapped in great splashes against the window.

A damp, dusty odor penetrated the house, and people drank of it — that wet, good smell! They watched the storm, enormously swishing. Sunflowers bobbed and throbbed. The drenching waste blurred the twin cottonwoods into gray phantoms that seemed trying to skip and leap and dance.

Men whacked each other, laughed, hopped about, yelled like prankish boys. Then they flung wide the doors. They plunged out into the downpour, shot off their guns, chased to and fro, shouted themselves hoarse. Children followed, prancing and skipping, adding their cries to the common din.

Women kissed each other, clung to each other. One laughed, one sobbed. And the rain continuously fell.

It was a good year, that one.

THINK BACK OVER WHAT YOU HAVE READ

Feeling the Impact of Prairie Life upon Pioneers

1. What brief passages can you quote which show Jim's and Nora's keen sensitiveness to wind and heat and drought and rain? Of what smells and sounds were they constantly aware?
2. What effect did the whining wind of the prairies have upon them?
3. What passages can you quote to show the particular horrors of drought? What effect did drought and the fear of drought have upon Jim's and Nora's spirits?
4. What kind of courage did Jim and Nora have? How did they show it?
5. How do you explain Jim's and Nora's tenderness to each other? What incidents from the story can you relate which show husband and wife trying to keep from hurting each other? How do you explain the fact that disappointment and failure seemed to make Nora and Jim kind to each other and to their neighbors? Do disappointment and failure usually have that effect on people?
6. What truths about life did you learn from Jim's and Nora's experience? What was the big lesson that life on the prairie taught them? Where in the story does Dara summarize it?

Comparing "The Wind Fighters" with "Under the Lion's Paw"

7. What qualities does living close to the soil seem to you to produce in men and women? What qualities were revealed to you in "The Wind Fighters"? in "Under the Lion's Paw"? Are they similar? In what respects?
8. In what way do Jim and Nora remind you of Mr. and Mrs. Council?

For Ambitious Students

9. You will find "The Wind Fighters" one of an interesting group of short stories about life on the prairie gathered together under the title *Golden Tales of the Prairie States,* compiled by May Lamberton Becker. Perhaps you will volunteer to review the book for the benefit of the class and point out: (a) the effect of climate and geography on personality and character; (b) the beauty or the terror of the prairie.
10. Perhaps you became especially interested in Nora and Jim because they were Irish. Maybe their speech interested you in Irish idiom and their personalities interested you in Irish temperament. If so, you might like to prepare a special report on either of the following subjects: (a) Irish settlements in America; (b) contributions of the Irish to American life.

THE REVOLT OF MOTHER

by Mary E. Wilkins Freeman (1862–1930)

As you know, mothers don't often rebel at their lot, whatever it may be. When they do, something is wrong somewhere and the family had better take notice. It is so in the following story — a story in which you may pretend that you are Nanny or Sammy Penn looking on, bewildered, at the quiet struggle going on between their parents. What do you make of this clash of interests between husband and wife? The family situation which you are to read about isn't typical of most families; still there are elements in the story which will remind you of your own family or of families you yourself have observed.

The author of the story, Mary E. Wilkins Freeman, in her time was regarded as a bold realist, for she was among the most prominent of a small group of short-story writers who said, "Let us worship the God of things as they are." Thus her pictures of life in New England as it was lived during the last quarter of the nineteenth century ring true, and her people — people on the farm, in this story — talk and act like real people. Notice as you read how simple and direct the style is, how natural seems the author's choice of words.

"FATHER!"

"What is it?"

"What are them men diggin' over there in the field for?" There was a sudden dropping and enlarging of the lower part of the old man's face, as if some heavy weight had settled therein; he shut his mouth tight, and went on harnessing the great bay mare. He hustled the collar onto her neck with a jerk.

"Father!"

The old man slapped the saddle upon the mare's back.

"Look here, father, I want to know what them men are diggin' over in that field for, an' I'm goin' to know."

"I wish you'd go into the house, mother, an' 'tend to your own affairs," the old man said then. He ran his words together, and his speech was almost as inarticulate as a growl.

But the woman understood; it was her most native tongue. "I ain't goin' into the house till you tell me what them men are doin' over there in the field," said she.

Then she stood waiting. She was a small woman, short and straight-waisted like a child in her brown cotton gown. Her forehead was mild and benevolent between the smooth curves of gray hair; there were meek downward lines about her nose and mouth; but her eyes, fixed upon the old man, looked as if the meekness had been the result of her own will, not of another.

They were in the barn, standing before the wide-open doors. The spring air, full of the smell of growing grass and unseen blossoms, came in their faces. The deep yard in front was littered with farm wagons and piles of wood; on the edges, close to the fence and the house, the grass was a vivid green, and there were some dandelions.

The old man glanced doggedly at his wife as he tightened the last buckles on the harness. She looked as immovable to him as one of the rocks in his pasture land, bound to the earth with generations of blackberry vines. He slapped the reins over the horse, and started forth from the barn.

"Father!" said she.

The old man pulled up. "What is it?"

"I want to know what them men are diggin' over there in that field for."

"They're diggin' a cellar, I s'pose, if you've got to know."

"A cellar for what?"

"A barn."

"A barn? You ain't goin' to build a barn over there where we was goin' to have a house, father?"

The old man said not another word. He hurried the horse into the farm wagon, and clattered out of the yard, jouncing as sturdily on his seat as a boy.

The woman stood a moment looking after him; then she went out of the barn across a corner of the yard to the house. The house, standing at right angles with the great barn and a long reach of sheds and outbuildings, was infinitesimal compared with them. It was scarcely as commodious for people as the little boxes under the barn eaves were for doves.

A pretty girl's face, pink and delicate as a flower, was looking out of one of the house windows. She was watching three men who were digging over in the field which bounded the yard near the road line. She turned quietly when the woman entered.

"What are they digging for, mother?" said she. "Did he tell you?"

"They're diggin' for — a cellar for a new barn."

"Oh, mother, he ain't going to build another barn?"

"That's what he says."

A boy stood before the kitchen glass combing his hair. He combed slowly and painstakingly, arranging his brown hair in a smooth hillock over his forehead.

He did not seem to pay any attention to the conversation.

" Sammy, did you know father was going to build a new barn? " asked the girl.

The boy combed assiduously.

" Sammy! "

He turned, and showed a face like his father's under his smooth crest of hair. " Yes, I s'pose I did," he said reluctantly.

" How long have you known it? " asked his mother.

" 'Bout three months, I guess."

" Why didn't you tell of it? "

" Didn't think 'twould do no good."

" I don't see what father wants another barn for," said the girl in her sweet, slow voice. She turned again to the window, and stared out at the men digging in the field. Her tender, sweet face was full of a gentle distress. Her forehead was as bald and innocent as a baby's, with the light hair strained back from it in a row of curl papers. She was quite large, but her soft curves did not look as if they covered muscles.

Her mother looked sternly at the boy. " Is he goin' to buy more cows? " said she.

The boy did not reply; he was tying his shoes.

" Sammy, I want you to tell me if he's goin' to buy more cows."

" I s'pose he is."

" How many? "

" Four, I guess."

His mother said nothing more. She went into the pantry, and there was a clatter of dishes. The boy got his cap from a nail behind the door, took an old arithmetic from the shelf, and started for school. He was lightly built, but clumsy. He went out of the yard with a curious spring in the hips that made his loose homemade jacket tilt up in the rear.

The girl went to the sink, and began to wash the dishes that were piled up there. Her mother came promptly out of the pantry, and shoved her aside. " You wipe 'em," said she; " I'll wash. There's a good many this mornin'."

The mother plunged her hands vigorously into the water, the girl wiped the plates slowly and dreamily. " Mother," said she, " don't you think it's too bad father's going to build that new barn, much as we need a decent house to live in? "

Her mother scrubbed a dish fiercely. " You ain't found out yet we're womenfolks, Nanny Penn," said she. " You ain't seen enough of menfolks yet to. One of these days you'll find it out; an' then you'll know that we know only what menfolks think we do, so far as any use of it goes, an' how we'd ought to reckon menfolks in with providence, an' not complain of what they do any more than we do of the weather."

" I don't care; I don't believe George is anything like that, anyhow," said Nanny. Her delicate face flushed pink, her lips pouted softly, as if she were going to cry.

" You wait an' see. I guess George Eastman ain't no better than other men. You hadn't ought to judge father, though. He can't help it, 'cause he don't look at things jest the way we do. An' we've been pretty comfortable here, after all. The roof don't leak — ain't never but once — That's one thing. Father's kept it shingled right up."

" I do wish we had a parlor."

" I guess it won't hurt George Eastman any to come to see you in a nice, clean kitchen. I guess a good many girls don't have as good a place as this. Nobody's ever heard me complain."

" I ain't complained either, mother."

" Well, I don't think you'd better, a good father an' a good home as you've got. S'pose your father made you go out an' work for your livin'? Lots of girls have to that ain't no stronger an' better able to than you be."

Sarah Penn washed the frying pan with a conclusive air. She scrubbed the outside of it as faithfully as the inside. She was a masterly keeper of her box of a house. Her one living room never seemed to have in it any of the dust which the friction of life with inanimate matter produces. She swept, and there seemed to be no dirt to go before the broom; she cleaned, and one could see no difference. She was like an artist so perfect that he has apparently no art. Today she got out a mixing bowl and a board, and rolled some pies, and there was no more flour upon her than upon her daughter who was doing finer work. Nanny was to be married in the fall, and she was sewing on some white cambric and embroidery. She sewed industriously while her mother cooked; her soft milk-white hands and wrists showed whiter than her delicate work.

"We must have the stove moved out in the shed before long," said Mrs. Penn. "Talk about not havin' things; it's been a real blessin' to be able to put a stove up in that shed in hot weather. Father did one good thing when he fixed that stovepipe out there."

Sarah Penn's face as she rolled her pies had that expression of meek vigor which might have characterized one of the New Testament saints. She was making mince pies. Her husband, Adoniram Penn, liked them better than any other kind. She baked twice a week. Adoniram often liked a piece of pie between meals. She hurried this morning. It had been later than usual when she began, and she wanted to have a pie baked for dinner. However deep a resentment she might be forced to hold against her husband, she would never fail in sedulous attention to his wants.

Nobility of character manifests itself at loopholes when it is not provided with large doors. Sarah Penn's showed itself today in flaky dishes of pastry. So she made the pies faithfully, while across the table she could see, when she glanced up from her work, the sight that rankled in her patient and steadfast soul — the digging of the cellar of the new barn in the place where Adoniram forty years ago had promised her their new house should stand.

The pies were done for dinner. Adoniram and Sammy were home a few minutes after twelve o'clock. The dinner was eaten with serious haste. There was never much conversation at the table in the Penn family. Adoniram asked a blessing, and they ate promptly, then rose up and went about their work.

Sammy went back to school, taking soft, sly lopes out of the yard like a rabbit. He wanted a game of marbles before school, and feared his father would give him some chores to do. Adoniram hastened to the door and called after him, but he was out of sight.

"I don't see what you let him go for, mother," said he. "I wanted him to help me unload that wood."

Adoniram went to work out in the yard unloading wood from the wagon. Sarah put away the dinner dishes, while Nanny took down her curl papers and changed her dress. She was going down to the store to buy some more embroidery and thread.

When Nanny was gone, Mrs. Penn went to the door. "Father!" she called.

"Well, what is it!"

"I want to see you jest a minute, father."

"I can't leave this wood nohow. I've got to git it unloaded an' go for a load of gravel afore two o'clock. Sammy had ought to helped me. You hadn't ought to let him go to school so early."

"I want to see you jest a minute."

"I tell ye I can't, nohow, mother."

"Father, you come here." Sarah Penn stood in the door like a queen; she held her head as if it bore a crown; there was that patience which makes authority royal in her voice. Adoniram came.

Mrs. Penn led the way into the kitchen, and pointed to a chair. "Sit down, father," said she; "I've got somethin' I want to say to you."

He sat down heavily; his face was quite stolid, but he looked at her with restive eyes. "Well, what is it, mother?"

"I want to know what you're buildin' that new barn for, father."

"I ain't got nothin' to say about it."

"It can't be you think you need another barn?"

"I tell ye I ain't got nothin' to say about it, mother; an' I ain't goin' to say nothin'."

"Be you goin' to buy more cows?"

Adoniram did not reply; he shut his mouth tight.

"I know you be, as well as I want to. Now, father, look here"—Sarah Penn had not sat down; she stood before her husband in the humble fashion of a Scripture woman—"I'm goin' to talk real plain to you; I never have sence I married you, but I'm goin' to now. I ain't never complained, an' I ain't goin' to complain now; but I'm goin' to talk plain. You see this room here, father; you look at it well. You see there ain't no carpet on the floor, an' you see the paper is all dirty an' droppin' off the walls. We ain't had no new paper on it for ten year, an' then I put it on myself, an' it didn't cost but ninepence a roll. You see this room, father; it's all the one I've had to work in an' eat in an' sit in sence we was married. There ain't another woman in the whole town whose husband ain't got half the means you have but what's got better. It's all the room Nanny's got to have her company in; an' there ain't one of her mates but what's got better, an' their fathers not so able as hers is. It's all the room she'll have to be married in. What would you have thought, father, if we had had our weddin' in a room no better than this? I was married in my mother's parlor, with a carpet on the floor, an' stuffed furniture, an' a mahogany card table. An' this is all the room my daughter will have to be married in. Look here, father!"

Sarah Penn went across the room as though it were a tragic stage. She flung open a door and disclosed a tiny bedroom, only large enough for a bed and bureau, with a path between. "There, father," said she, "there's all the room I've had to sleep in forty year. All my children were born there—the two that died, an' the two that's livin'. I was sick with a fever there."

She stepped to another door and opened it. It led into the small, ill-lighted pantry. "Here," said she, "is all the buttery I've got—every place I've got for my dishes, to set away my victuals in, an' to keep my milk pans in. Father, I've been takin' care of the milk of six cows in this place, an' now you're goin' to build a new barn, an' give me more to do in it."

She threw open another door. A narrow, crooked flight of stairs wound upward from it. "There, father," said she, "I want you to look at the stairs that go up to them two unfinished chambers that are all the places our son an' daughter have had to sleep in all their lives. There ain't a prettier girl in town nor a more ladylike one than Nanny, an' that's the place she has to sleep in. It ain't so good as your horse's stall; it ain't so warm an' tight."

Sarah Penn went back and stood before her husband. "Now, father," said she, "I want to know if you think you're doin' right an' accordin' to what you profess. Here, when we was married, forty year ago, you promised me faithful that we should have a new house built in that lot over in the field before the year was out. You said you had money enough, an' you wouldn't ask me to live in no such place as this. It is forty year now, an' you've been makin' more money, an I've been savin' of it for you ever sence, an' you ain't built no house yet. You've built sheds an' cowhouses an' one new barn, an' now you're goin' to build another. Father, I want to know if you think it's right. You're lodgin' your dumb beasts better than you are your own flesh an' blood. I want to know if you think it's right."

"I ain't got nothin' to say."

"You can't say nothin' without ownin' it ain't right, father. An' there's another thing — I ain't complained; I've got along forty year, an' I s'pose I should forty more, if it wa'n't for that — if we don't have another house, Nanny, she can't live with us after she's married. She'll have to go somewheres else to live away from us, an' it don't seem as if I could have it so, noways, father. She wa'n't ever strong. She's got considerable color, but there wa'n't never any backbone to her. I've always took the heft of everything off her, an' she ain't fit to keep house an' do everything herself. She'll be all worn out inside of a year. Think of her doin' all the washin' an' ironin' an' bakin' with them soft white hands an' arms, an' sweepin'! I can't have it so, noways, father."

Mrs. Penn's face was burning; her mild eyes gleamed. She had pleaded her little cause like a Webster[1]; she had ranged from severity to pathos; but her opponent employed that obstinate silence which makes eloquence futile with mocking echoes. Adoniram arose clumsily.

"Father, ain't you got nothin' to say?" said Mrs. Penn.

"I've got to go off after that load of gravel. I can't stan' here talkin' all day."

"Father, won't you think it over, an' have a house built there instead of a barn?"

"I ain't got nothin' to say."

Adoniram shuffled out. Mrs. Penn went into her bedroom. When she came out, her eyes were red. She had a roll of unbleached cotton cloth. She spread it out on the kitchen table, and began cutting out some shirts for her husband. The men over in the field had a team to help them this afternoon; she could hear their halloos. She had a scanty pattern for the shirts; she had had to plan and piece the sleeves.

Nanny came home with her embroidery, and sat down with her needlework. She had taken down her curl papers, and there was a soft roll of fair hair like an aureole over her forehead; her face was as delicately fine and clear as porcelain. Suddenly she looked up, and the tender red flamed all over her face and neck. "Mother," said she.

"What say?"

"I've been thinking — I don't see how we're goin' to have any — wedding in this room. I'd be ashamed to have his folks come if we didn't have anybody else."

"Mebbe we can have some new paper before then; I can put it on. I guess you won't have no call to be ashamed of your belongin's."

"We might have the wedding in the new barn," said Nanny, with gentle pettishness. "Why, mother, what makes you look so?"

Mrs. Penn had started, and was staring at her with a curious expression. She turned again to her work, and spread out a pattern carefully on the cloth. "Nothin'," said she.

[1] **Webster:** the great orator, Daniel Webster.

Presently Adoniram clattered out of the yard in his two-wheeled dumpcart, standing as proudly upright as a Roman charioteer. Mrs. Penn opened the door and stood there a minute looking out; the halloos of the men sounded louder.

It seemed to her all through the spring months that she heard nothing but the halloos and the noises of saws and hammers. The new barn grew fast. It was a fine edifice for this little village. Men came on pleasant Sundays, in their meeting suits and clean shirt bosoms, and stood around it admiringly. Mrs. Penn did not speak of it, and Adoniram did not mention it to her, although sometimes, upon a return from inspecting it, he bore himself with injured dignity.

"It's a strange thing how your mother feels about the new barn," he said, confidentially, to Sammy one day.

Sammy only grunted after an odd fashion for a boy; he had learned it from his father.

The barn was all completed ready for use by the third week in July. Adoniram had planned to move his stock in on Wednesday; on Tuesday he received a letter which changed his plans. He came in with it early in the morning. "Sammy's been to the post office," said he, "an' I've got a letter from Hiram." Hiram was Mrs. Penn's brother, who lived in Vermont.

"Well," said Mrs. Penn, "what does he say about the folks?"

"I guess they're all right. He says he thinks if I come up-country right off there's a chance to buy jest the kind of a horse I want." He stared reflectively out of the window at the new barn.

Mrs. Penn was making pies. She went on clapping the rolling pin into the crust, although she was very pale and her heart beat loudly.

"I dun' know but what I'd better go," said Adoniram. "I hate to go off jest now, right in the midst of hayin', but the ten-acre lot's cut, an' I guess Rufus an' the others can git along without me three or four days. I can't get a horse round here to suit me, nohow, an' I've got to have another for all that wood haulin' in the fall. I told Hiram to watch out, an' if he got wind of a good horse to let me know. I guess I'd better go."

"I'll get out your clean shirt an' collar," said Mrs. Penn calmly.

She laid out Adoniram's Sunday suit and his clean clothes on the bed in the little bedroom. She got his shaving water and razor ready. At last she buttoned on his collar and fastened his black cravat.

Adoniram never wore his collar and cravat except on extra occasions. He held his head high, with a rasped dignity. When he was all ready, with his coat and hat brushed, and a lunch of pie and cheese in a paper bag, he hesitated on the threshold of the door. He looked at his wife, and his manner was defiantly apologetic. "If them cows come today, Sammy can drive 'em into the new barn," said he; "an' when they bring the hay up, they can pitch it in there."

"Well," replied Mrs. Penn.

Adoniram set his shaven face ahead and started. When he had cleared the doorstep, he turned and looked back with a kind of nervous solemnity. "I shall be back by Saturday if nothin' happens," said he.

"Do be careful, father," returned his wife.

She stood in the door with Nanny at her elbow and watched him out of sight. Her eyes had a strange, doubtful expression in them; her peaceful forehead was contracted. She went in, and about her baking again. Nanny sat sewing. Her wedding day was drawing nearer, and she was getting pale and thin with her steady sewing. Her mother kept glancing at her.

" Have you got that pain in your side this morning ? " she asked.

" A little."

Mrs. Penn's face, as she worked, changed, her perplexed forehead smoothed, her eyes were steady, her lips firmly set. She formed a maxim for herself, although incoherently with her unlettered thoughts. " Unsolicited opportunities are the guideposts of the Lord to the new roads of life," she repeated in effect, and she made up her mind to her course of action.

" S'posin' I had wrote to Hiram," she muttered once, when she was in the pantry. " S'posin' I had wrote, an' asked him if he knowed of any horse? But I didn't, an' father's goin' wa'n't none of my doin'. It looks like a providence." Her voice rang out quite loud at the last.

" What you talkin' about, mother ? " called Nanny.

" Nothin'."

Mrs. Penn hurried her baking; at eleven o'clock it was all done. The load of hay from the west field came slowly down the cart track, and drew up at the new barn. Mrs. Penn ran out. " Stop ! " she screamed. " Stop ! "

The men stopped and looked; Sammy upreared from the top of the load, and stared at his mother.

" Stop ! " she cried out again. " Don't you put the hay in that barn; put it in the old one."

" Why, he said to put it in here," returned one of the haymakers wonderingly. He was a young man, a neighbor's son, whom Adoniram hired by the year to help on the farm.

" Don't you put the hay in the new barn; there's room enough in the old one, ain't there ? " said Mrs. Penn.

" Room enough," returned the hired man in his thick, rustic tones. " Didn't need the new barn, nohow, far as room's concerned. Well, I s'pose he changed his mind." He took hold of the horses' bridles.

Mrs. Penn went back to the house. Soon the kitchen windows were darkened, and a fragrance like warm honey came into the room.

Nanny laid down her work. " I thought father wanted them to put the hay into the new barn ? " she said wonderingly.

" It's all right," replied her mother.

Sammy slid down from the load of hay, and came in to see if dinner was ready.

" I ain't goin' to get a regular dinner today, as long as father's gone," said his mother. " I've let the fire go out. You can have some bread an' milk an' pie. I thought we could get along." She set out some bowls of milk, some bread, and a pie on the kitchen table.

" You'd better eat your dinner now," said she. " You might jest as well get through with it. I want you to help me afterward."

Nanny and Sammy stared at each other. There was something strange in their mother's manner. Mrs. Penn did not eat anything herself. She went into the pantry, and they heard her moving dishes while they ate. Presently she came out with a pile of plates. She got the clothes-basket out of the shed, and packed them in it. Nanny and Sammy watched. She brought out cups and saucers, and put them in with the plates.

" What you goin' to do, mother ? " inquired Nanny in a timid voice. A sense of something unusual made her tremble, as if it were a ghost. Sammy rolled his eyes over his pie.

" You'll see what I'm goin' to do," replied Mrs. Penn. " If you're through, Nanny, I want you to go upstairs an' pack up your things; an' I want you, Sammy, to help me take down the bed in the bedroom."

" Oh, mother, what for ? " gasped Nanny.

"You'll see."

During the next few hours a feat was performed by this simple, pious New England mother which was equal in its way to Wolfe's storming of the Heights of Abraham.[1] It took no more genius and audacity of bravery for Wolfe to cheer his wondering soldiers up those steep precipices, under the spying eyes of the enemy, than for Sarah Penn, at the head of her children, to move all their little household goods into the new barn while her husband was away.

Nanny and Sammy followed their mother's instructions without a murmur; indeed, they were overawed. There is a certain uncanny and superhuman quality about all such purely original undertakings as their mother's was to them. Nanny went back and forth with her light loads, and Sammy tugged with sober energy.

At five o'clock in the afternoon the little house in which the Penns had lived for forty years had emptied itself into the new barn.

Every builder builds somewhat for unknown purposes, and is in a measure a prophet. The architect of Adoniram Penn's barn, while he designed it for the comfort of four-footed animals, had planned better than he knew for the comfort of humans. Sarah Penn saw at a glance its possibilities. Those great box stalls, with quilts hung before them, would make better bedrooms than the one she had occupied for forty years, and there was a tight carriage room. The harness room, with its chimney and shelves, would make a kitchen of her dreams. The great middle space would make a parlor, by and by, fit for a palace. Upstairs there was as much room as down. With partitions and windows, what a house would there be! Sarah looked at the row of stanchions before the alloted space for cows, and reflected that she would have her front entry there.

At six o'clock the stove was up in the harness room, the kettle was boiling, and the table set for tea. It looked almost as homelike as the abandoned house across the yard had ever done. The young hired man milked, and Sarah directed him calmly to bring the milk to the new barn. He came gaping, dropping little blots of foam from the brimming pails on the grass. Before the next morning he had spread the story of Adoniram Penn's wife moving into the new barn all over the little village. Men assembled in the store and talked it over; women with shawls over their heads scuttled into each other's houses before their work was done. Any deviation from the ordinary course of life in this quiet town was enough to stop all progress in it. Everybody paused to look at the staid, independent figure on the sidetrack.[2] There was a difference of opinion with regard to her. Some held her to be insane; some, of a lawless and rebellious spirit.

Friday the minister went to see her. It was in the forenoon, and she was at the barn door shelling peas for dinner. She looked up and returned his salutation with dignity; then she went on with her work. She did not invite him in. The saintly expression of her face remained fixed, but there was an angry flush over it.

The minister stood awkwardly before her and talked. She handled the peas as if they were bullets. At last she looked up, and her eyes showed the spirit that her meek front had covered for a lifetime.

"There ain't no use talkin', Mr. Hersey," said she. "I've thought it all over

[1] In the French and Indian War the English commander defeated the French general, Montcalm, on the **Heights of Abraham**, a plateau near Quebec.

[2] Sarah Penn is the independent figure standing on the **sidetrack** of the town's **progress**.

an' over, an' I believe I'm doin' what's right. I've made it the subject of prayer, an' it's betwixt me an' the Lord an' Adoniram. There ain't no call for nobody else to worry about it."

"Well, of course, if you have brought it to the Lord in prayer, and feel satisfied that you are doing right, Mrs. Penn," said the minister helplessly. His thin, gray-bearded face was pathetic. He was a sickly man; his youthful confidence had cooled; he had to scourge himself up to some of his pastoral duties.

"I think it's right jest as much as I think it was right for our forefathers to come over from the old country 'cause they didn't have what belonged to 'em," said Mrs. Penn. She arose. The barn threshold might have been Plymouth Rock[1] from her bearing. "I don't doubt you mean well, Mr. Hersey," said she, "but there are things people hadn't ought to interfere with. I've been a member of the church for over forty year. I've got my own mind an' my own feet, an' I'm goin' to think my own thoughts an' go my own ways, an' nobody but the Lord is goin' to dictate to me unless I've a mind to have him. Won't you come in an' set down? How is Mis' Hersey?"

"She is well, I thank you," replied the minister. He added some more perplexed apolegetic remarks; then he retreated.

He could expound the intricacies of every character study in the Scriptures, he was competent to grasp the Pilgrim Fathers and all historical innovators, but Sarah Penn was beyond him. He could deal with primal cases, but parallel ones[2] worsted him. But, after all, although it was aside from his province, he wondered more how Adoniram Penn would deal with his wife than how the Lord would. Everybody shared the wonder. When Adoniram's four new cows arrived, Sarah ordered three to be put in the old barn, the other in the house shed where the cooking stove had stood. That added to the excitement. It was whispered that all four cows were domiciled in the house.

Toward sunset on Saturday, when Adoniram was expected home, there was a knot of men in the road near the new barn. The hired man had milked, but he still hung around the premises. Sarah Penn had supper all ready. There were brown bread and baked beans and a custard pie; it was the supper that Adoniram loved on a Saturday night. She had on a clean calico, and she bore herself imperturbably. Nanny and Sammy kept close at her heels. Their eyes were large, and Nanny was full of nervous tremors. Still there was to them more pleasant excitement than anything else. An inborn confidence in their mother over their father asserted itself.

Sammy looked out of the harness-room window. "There he is," he announced, in an awed whisper. He and Nanny peeped around the casing. Mrs. Penn kept on about her work. The children watched Adoniram leave the new horse standing in the drive while he went to the house door. It was fastened. Then he went around to the shed. That door was seldom locked, even when the family was away. The thought of how her father would be confronted by the cow flashed upon Nanny. There was a hysterical sob in her throat. Adoniram emerged from the shed and stood looking about in a dazed fashion. His lips moved; he was saying something, but they could not hear what it was. The hired man was peeping around a corner of the old barn, but nobody saw him.

Adoniram took the new horse by the bridle and led him across the yard to the new barn. Nanny and Sammy slunk close to their mother. The barn doors rolled

[1] The Pilgrims, you remember, landed at **Plymouth Rock.** [2] **parallel ones:** immediate problems for which there was no law of Scripture to guide him in his judgment.

back, and there stood Adoniram, with the long, mild face of the great Canadian farm horse looking over his shoulder.

Nanny kept behind her mother, but Sammy stepped suddenly forward and stood in front of her.

Adoniram stared at the group. "What on airth you all down here for?" said he. "What's the matter over to the house?"

"We've come here to live, father," said Sammy. His shrill voice quavered out bravely.

"What"—Adoniram sniffed—"what is it smells like cookin'?" said he. He stepped forward and looked in the open door of the harness room. Then he turned to his wife. His old, bristling face was pale and frightened. "What on airth does this mean, mother?" he gasped.

"You come in here, father," said Sarah. She led the way into the harness room and shut the door. "Now, father," said she, "you needn't be scared. I ain't crazy. There ain't nothin' to be upset over. But we've come here to live, an' we're goin' to live here. We've got jest as good a right here as new horses an' cows. The house wa'n't fit for us to live in any longer, an' I made up my mind I wa'n't goin' to stay there. I've done my duty by you forty year, an' I'm goin' to do it now; but I'm goin' to live here. You've got to put in some windows and partitions; an' you'll have to buy some furniture."

"Why, mother!" the old man gasped.

"You'd better take your coat off an' get washed—there's the washbasin—an' then we'll have supper."

"Why, mother!"

Sammy went past the window, leading the new horse to the old barn. The old man saw him, and shook his head speechlessly. He tried to take off his coat, but his arms seemed to lack the power. His wife helped him. She poured some water into the tin basin, and put in a piece of soap. She got the comb and brush, and smoothed his thin, gray hair after he had washed. Then she put the beans, hot bread, and tea on the table. Sammy came in, and the family drew up. Adoniram sat looking dazedly at his plate, and they waited.

"Ain't you goin' to ask a blessin', father?" said Sarah.

And the old man bent his head and mumbled.

All through the meal he stopped eating at intervals, and stared furtively at his wife; but he ate well. The home food tasted good to him, and his old frame was too sturdily healthy to be affected by his mind. But after supper he went out and sat down on the step of the smaller door at the right of the barn, through which he had meant his Jerseys to pass in stately file but which Sarah designed for her front house door, and he leaned his head on his hands.

After the supper dishes were cleared away and the milk pans washed, Sarah went out to him. The twilight was deepening. There was a clear, green glow in the sky. Before them stretched the smooth level of field; in the distance was a cluster of haystacks like the huts of a village; the air was very cool and calm and sweet. The landscape might have been an ideal one of peace.

Sarah bent over and touched her husband on one of his thin, sinewy shoulders. "Father!"

The old man's shoulders heaved; he was weeping.

"Why, don't do so, father," said Sarah.

"I'll—put up the—partitions, an'—everything you—want, mother."

Sarah put her apron up to her face; she was overcome by her own triumph.

Adoniram was like a fortress whose walls had no active resistance and went down the instant the right besieging tools were used. "Why, mother," he said hoarsely, " I hadn't no idee you was so set on't as all this comes to."

THINK BACK OVER WHAT YOU HAVE READ

Understanding the Characters

1. What method did Adoniram use to subdue Sarah?

2. What incident can you quote to show that Sammy had learned from his father the same method of eluding the womenfolks of the family?

3. Why was this method effective? What is your opinion of people who use it? How did Sarah defeat it?

4. By what standards would Adoniram have to admit that Sarah had been a " good wife " to him for forty years? What comment are you led to make about such a standard?

5. How do you explain the fragile quality in Nanny?

6. Of what quality in Sarah did the children stand in awe?

7. What quality held the minister at bay? Do you admire the quality? What kind of environment had produced such a quality? How had Adoniram quite unconsciously fostered such a quality in his wife?

8. What picture of New Englanders does the story give you? What qualities are bred by this section of the country?

9. What insight into Adoniram's nature does the ending of the story suggest to you?

For Ambitious Students

10. *Understanding America through stories of local color.* The reading list below will suggest an interesting reading project by which the class may come to understand something of the picturesque variety in American life during the past fifty years. Different groups of students might agree to explore different periods and sections and share their reactions with the other members of the class.

11. *A comparison between Sarah Orne Jewett and Mary E. Wilkins Freeman.* In order to understand somewhat more in detail the progress made by the short story, it should prove interesting to compare two writers who depicted the New England scene. You will find listed below the short-story volumes of these two authors. Can you see any vital difference in the approach of these two authors? Which one is more romantic? Which is more realistic in her style of writing? Which do you regard as the better interpreter of New England life? Why? Such questions as these might form the basis of class discussion.

Stories of Local Color for Further Reading

Cable, G. W., *Old Creole Days; Strong Hearts; Posson Jone and Père Raphaël*

Freeman, Mary E. Wilkins, *The New England Nun; Best Stories of Mary E. Wilkins*

Harris, J. C., *Uncle Remus, His Songs and His Sayings; Mingo and Other Sketches in Black and White; Free Joe and Other Georgian Sketches; Tales of the Home Folks in Peace and War*

Howells, W. D., *Suburban Sketches*

Jewett, S. O., *Deephaven; A White Heron and Other Stories; The Country of the Pointed Firs*

Matthews, Brander, *Vignettes of Manhattan; Outlines in Local Color*

Page, T. N., *In Ole Virginia; Marse Chan and Other Stories; The Burial of the Guns; Bred in the Bone; Under the Crust*

Thanet, Octave, *Knitters in the Sun; Stories of a Western Town*

TWENTY CIGARETTES

by Philip Wylie (1902–)

This is a grim story about war. You won't enjoy it, in the ordinary sense of the word; but you will feel its power over you — power to lead you where the author wishes you to go — and that is one kind of reading satisfaction.

Don't let the title mislead you. There's a deadly earnestness about the story which in the end gives the title a terrible meaning. " Twenty Cigarettes " — during the smoking of which you will have lived through the horrors of battle! By the time the last cigarette is smoked you will have come to the " terrible meaning " which the author intends you to get from his story.

Although this story first appeared (in *Liberty*) in 1931, its message is even more important today than it was then.

WESLEY GRAHAM PHELPS tried to remember where they came from as he took the first cigarette from the package.

Were they some of the cigarettes his family had sent to him? Had the Y [1] man handed them to him? Or another soldier? He could not be sure. It was not possible to engage in retrospect at that hour.

A shell fell on the parapet, and he felt a clod of earth spatter against his helmet. Men walking behind him pressed him against the trench wall. He cupped his cigarette in his hand so that it would not be accidentally extinguished.

The whistle blew.

In the middle of a stream of men he went up the ladder and into the open. He felt naked. He felt as if it were necessary to struggle to move through the air. Going up was like diving, and walking forward was like swimming under water.

A moment later he thought that nothing was as he had imagined it. The day should have been cold and misty and the hour dawn. The ground should have been ripped and muddy. It was none of those things. Noon in a blistering sun. Where the shells broke, dust mingled with the smoke.

To the left and to the right was a long line of men. From a brush heap far ahead he could see a wavering pencil of smoke. In the distance a line of shells broke in a row, like the first drops of a heavy rain. Nobody threw hands in the air; nobody sat down; nobody lunged face forward. It might have been a bird walk, except for the tumultuous noise.

He became afraid again only when he realized that he had walked a long way and was not yet dead.

The man on his immediate right yelled what he thought was "There's the wire!"

He yelled back, "Yeah."

He discovered that he was now carrying his rifle in both hands. Sunlight hit the bayonet. A piece of wire wrapped around his leg, and he kicked it loose. He jumped over a low post. In front of them was a row of tumbledown sandbags. He stuck his head over the top of them. At least twenty men were there. Out of the corner of his eye he saw the arch of a Mills bomb, and so he threw himself on the ground. The explosion did not make much noise. Afterward, according to the instructions he had been given, he jumped into the trench.

A few men lay there quietly. He could see no one else. With two others he rounded a traverse. There were retreating backs. A soldier at his side knelt and fired, so he also knelt and fired. More men poured in.

Phelps turned. The speaker belonged to his company. His rifle. Not far away was the entrance of a dugout. He was looking at it, and considering the possibility of tossing a bomb into it, when a half dozen men emerged with their hands in the air. They said, "Kamerad!" [2] They looked frightened. They kept staring at their own dead.

"That's that," a voice said in his ear.

Phelps turned. The speaker belonged to his company. His face was familiar. Phelps produced his cigarettes and handed one to him. They stood there together, smoking. The other man had a rip straight across the middle of the back of his tunic, as if he had split it by lifting a weight off the ground.

"Now what do we do?"

"Hold this trench," Phelps said. He would have said "Take the train to Evanston" in the same tone.

There was a man with chevrons organizing an enterprise. It consisted in reversing the defenses of the trench. Everyone began to dig up the dusty earth and fill sandbags. These were lifted to the top of the rear wall.

Presently the air screamed, and for the

[1] **Y:** short for Y.M.C.A.

[2] **Kamerad:** the German word for comrade. Used as an appeal for mercy by German soldiers in the World War.

next twenty minutes they all lay on the floor of the trench among their own and the enemy dead. When the bombardment stopped, Phelps had to drag his legs from a pile of earth several feet deep. The man in his company helped him.

"Hurt?"

"No."

The second lieutenant had a periscope.[1] He arranged himself fussily and looked through it.

He said, "I think —" and then, "No —" and finally, "Here they come!"

They had put up a machine gun — men sweating and panting under heavy loads and trying to control themselves to the accomplishment of delicate operations. The gun began to stutter.

Phelps noticed that he had sweat through his uniform. The whole area of his chest was wet. He put a bucket on a box and stood on that.

The enemy was not far away. Perhaps fifty yards. Each time he fired his rifle, he looked for a new target without waiting to see what had happened to the last one. Once the bucket slid off the box and he fell. He climbed back and continued to shoot. They came close enough so that he could see their faces. But there was nothing either terrible or pitiful in those faces. They looked like men doing hard work.

By and by they turned around and went back. Nobody cheered. The man in his company kept punching Phelps lightly.

"Got another of those butts?"

"Yeah."

"Thanks, buddy."

"All right."

They stood around for an hour or two. A wounded man crawled in from the ground they had crossed. He was helped over the sandbags, and he sat down on Phelps's box and swore. He'd been hit in the leg and he had made a bandage for it himself.

Phelps asked, "Does it hurt?"

The man hesitated, and then a slow, surprised expression came over his face. He said, "No, I'll be dashed if it does."

"Well, what are you talking about?"

"Nothing," the man answered. "Nothing. The bones aren't even broken."

"That's good."

"I ought to know," the man continued. "I used to be a doctor."

"How come —"

The man shrugged. "I was a horse doctor."

The conversation seemed above the plane of sense.[2] Phelps gave the ex-veterinary a cigarette. He didn't smoke one himself. The wounded man sighed and fainted. Two men with brassards carried him into the dugout.

His corporal approached Phelps.

"Well, if you aren't still here! I didn't think you had it in you!"

Phelps looked at the man eye to eye. "Had what in me?"

"You were always such a soft, lazy son of a gun —"

Phelps didn't answer. The firing began again. He clambered up on the pile of earth that had buried his feet. He had arranged it for a stance. This time the enemy came closer. One of them fell into the trench. He was fat; but he dropped his rifle and jumped quickly to his feet, with his hands up and a feeble grin on his face. Phelps stood looking at him, rubbing the spot where the man's shoe had hit his shoulder as he stumbled into the trench. He pointed to the dugout.

"Down there!" he shouted.

The man's grin spread and he said, "Sure!"

Their own shells began to come over.

[1] **periscope:** used in trenches, as well as submarines, to enable observers to obtain a view of the enemy otherwise impossible to get without great danger.

[2] In other words, the conversation seemed not to take into account the suffering of the wounded man.

They dropped on the second enemy line. It was a sincere concentration of fire and it made the lip of the second defenses look something like a volcano, something like the sun in eclipse. There was no color in the bursts, however. Only white, eye-shaking flashes that had at one point a form and outline as if the explosion increased to a certain degree and then stood still, imprinting itself on the retina.

The second lieutenant rounded up a dozen men. " When that stops, we're going after them again," he said. Then he went along the line.

When it stopped, they scrambled into the silence. Phelps walked through a little stretch of dry, undisturbed grass, and he could hear his feet swishing in it. Again, far ahead, was the fire of the enemy. He went toward it. There was no struggle within himself any longer. The nights when he'd dreamed about this with sweaty palms and incurled toes were gone. The days that had made him haggard. Even the efforts to be transferred.

He thought about that, now, for a little while. The distance to the second line was immense. There was a wheat field between the two trenches. It was harvest-time and the wheat had been cut — but not for the rich heads of grain. It had been cut to increase defensive visibility.

The effect became evident. Phelps passed one of their own men who was lying on the ground on his back with his blanket roll under his head. He stared up at the blue sky. He was dead, and on his face no expression of any sort. A machine gun made a little row of periods along the ground to one side of Phelps. He dropped to earth just in time. The bullets ran through the stubble behind him now — a sickle swung by a blind man,[1] without a crop to cut down.

He realized that this was the place where he would probably meet — what he had expected.[2] But he knew simultaneously a great caution. He would dally with death, postponing it until the last possible moment. He felt that the machine-gun crew in front was watching and waiting for him alone. And so it seemed. He would lie down and roll, then rise, crouch, and rush forward. Each time the row of periods would not be distant from him.

Somewhere on the way was a cellar. The house had been blown off it and the cellar was full of broken glass. When he stumbled into it, twenty or thirty men knelt there. Presently, in little groups, they went out. Three or four trickling first from one corner and then the other. Phelps went when he had rested.

In a ditch a man beside him said, " If we could work around past those stumps . . ."

So they did. Phelps lost the man, but he found another and repeated the phrase, " If we could work around past those stumps . . ."

The stumps were large, when they reached them. Each stump could be gained by one complete roll. Finally they came to the end.

" Could you throw that distance? " the man said in his ear.

Phelps peered out. Not very far away was a machine gun. It was behind them now, at an obtuse angle.[3] Its shelter was made of concrete, painted. A half dozen men served it. One of them sat astride like a horse rider. And, like a rider, he jounced with the gun's perpetual recoil.

Phelps said, " No."

" I think I can," the man said.

" Go ahead."

The soldier took two bombs from his pockets. He lay on his back and weighed

[1] Death is sometimes symbolized by a man with a scythe.

[2] You can guess **what he had expected.** Why do you suppose the author does not mention it outright? [3] **obtuse angle:** an angle greater than a right angle.

them in his hands. Then he pulled the pins. After that he stood up very slowly and walked forward. Phelps leaned out to watch. The men saw. One pointed. One shouted. One pounded on the back of the soldier astride the gun. Phelps's companion threw his first bomb with immense deliberation, and his second quickly; and the man on the gun swung it with his feet and put a burst directly into him.

There was a ticked instant of infinite time and then the husky explosion of the bombs. Phelps ran in and did what was necessary, which was very little. He pivoted the gun around then, and sat beneath it. There was a little spur of shallow trench that ran into the second line. An enemy face appeared there. Phelps didn't know how to operate the captured gun, but he was beginning to understand his rifle.

After that he held a bomb in his hand and waited for the recapture of the piece, but it never took place. Men dashed forward on every side of him, and the second trench was taken. Phelps rose to go with them; but he thought of the grenade he held which would explode with any violent contact, so he sat there.

After a while the sergeant crawled through the sap trench.[1]

He said, "Hello, Phelps."

"Hello."

"You do this?"

"No."

"Who did?"

"Some guy. He chucked a couple of bombs. Then I wiped up."

"Yeah?"

"Yeah."

"Ain't hurt?"

"No."

"Got a cigarette?" the sergeant asked.

"Yeah. Here."

Each man smoked. The first lieutenant looked into the sap. His arm was in a bandage. He came up.

"What's this man's name?" he asked.

"Phelps," the sergeant said.

"Phelps. I'll remember that. I'm going back as soon as it's dark enough. The second's dead. Page — you're in command."

The sergeant did not say, "Yes, sir." He said, "O.K."

Together they dragged the gun into the trench. A number of men looked at it; and finally someone came to mount it on the parapet, facing the way they had been going all day. In low tones he commenced to tell several others how it was operated. Phelps was just out of earshot. He could hear the murmur but not the words.

It was growing dark. The sun settled and, while the horizon could not safely be observed, the colors reached far into the sky and cast a lurid light on the men. It was a red-and-purple sunset with long banks of stratified clouds. It would be as hot on the next day and as bright. It became dark little by little. The blues of the sky changed in a manner that just eluded precise detection. It was as if an air brush, blowing constantly deeper shades, were passed back and forth above the clouds.

Phelps looked at it for a long time. At last he thought of himself by an elaborate process which included thinking of other twilights, and thinking that he was thinking of other twilights, and wondering why he thought of them, and making contrasts — rather than comparisons. When he thought of himself, he realized he was thirsty. He reefed the strap on his canteen, but it came up light. The bottom half of the water container had been raggedly removed. He lowered it again to see where the wound would have been if he had been standing six inches to the left. It would have been between hip and navel. He thought about that for a while.

[1] **sap trench**: a trench protected by a parapet.

A man said, "Coffee!" in a voice that was like singing. It was cold, chlorinated,[1] and miserable coffee. He drank it. Then he went over to the sap that had been dug to the machine gun. He felt he had a proprietary interest in it. He lay down there.

He thought, as he might well have thought, of other things. He had a yacht and half a dozen cars. His father's house was on Lake Shore Drive. In Chicago his name meant a great deal. Everything he had done in the first twenty years of his life had been correct. But when the war came and he was a pacifist, that was not correct.

He had always thought of his father as a strong, sane, genial man. His father had been good to everyone — to his family, to his city, to his six thousand employees. Old "G. J." — financier, philanthropist, politician. It was only when America entered the war that his father changed. He seemed to have been seized by the war, his reason enslaved and his immense energies misdirected. He regarded the war as a magnificent *beau geste,*[2] a spectacle, a sort of supergame which was exciting rather than tragic or formidable.

He had pounded his son's back the day war was declared. "Well — you'll be in it now, eh, son?"

At that moment they had their first quarrel. Young Phelps differed from his father — and from most of the people of his time.

"I don't think so, Dad," he had said. "Not if it can be helped."

"Helped? What do you mean?"

Phelps was embarrassed. He couldn't explain what he felt — that war was hideous; that the young should not die; that he wanted to go on living, sailing his yacht on the Great Lakes, driving his roadster to his appointments, running a business, loving a girl someday, marrying, working. He could not make that clear. At first he tried.

"I mean — war is a rotten way to settle things. It's — uncivilized. It's — biologically unsound.[3] I don't want to die. Do you, Dad?"

His father did not speak from the comfortable knowledge that he would not be asked to die. He spoke, rather, from a vehemence that had grown up in him, from tradition, from a great unexamined sentiment.

"Are you trying to tell me that you're yellow?"

"No. I'm trying to tell you that I have the courage of my convictions."

The older man was shaken. "Why — I've seen you on a team in school. I — I remember the day you dove off your boat for that kid in Lake Michigan. I didn't think that, when the country needed you, you'd lie down and snivel. Not you — not a Phelps."

"It isn't that — "

"It is that!"

So he had stayed at home while the other youths went to war. His father did not speak to him. A time came when his mother, too, replied to him only with a look. Then young Phelps went to a recruiting station and enlisted. He did not come home to let them see his uniform. He did not come home at all.

He wrote a letter of restrained farewell, and he went to camp somewhere — hating the drudgery, the dirt, the routine, the machine. He was a stubborn, unpopular soldier. He could not help occasional outbursts of the resentment he felt. He went up to the trenches at last with the conviction that by some overwhelming flame his family would be paid in the common coin for their delusions.[4]

[1] The coffee had been made out of water disinfected by chlorine. [2] **beau geste**: a French expression meaning a gallant gesture.

[3] Biology is the science of life, not of death.
[4] **their delusions** about the glory of war.

Lying in the sap trench, he remembered all that. The tumbrels of war bumped through the sky. His heart was cold. Nobody wanted a wise young man these days; a dead one was preferable.

He went to sleep presently. The sergeant passed him, walking through the dark with the captain.

"There's that man I was telling you about."

The officer bent over. "The one that took the machine gun?"

"Yeah. And held it."

"Phelps, you said?"

"Yeah. Funny — isn't it?"

The captain said that it was funny. He qualified the adjective with a list of epithets.

Phelps continued to sleep. In the morning somebody woke him. He was stiff and sore; but they had let him sleep there undisturbed, so he was rested — which made him poignantly conscious of himself and his multitudinous discomforts.

For his breakfast he had a cigarette.

The new day was enlivened suddenly by a tearing apart of the sky and a helter-skelter attempt on the part of the men to reach cover quickly. Most of them did. The cover found by a few was inadequate. Phelps pressed his face into the earth and flinched a little as each shell struck.

The sergeant elbowed along to where he lay.

"We are going to take the war out of the trenches," he said. "They're sending us on. Replacements came up last night."

"O.K." Phelps said.

"Listen, guy, I want to tell you something. I'm making you my sergeant for today. I'm acting looie.[1] Stick with me."

"Right."

Phelps crawled on after the sergeant. His eyes were ordinarily brown and aloof. They were, on this day, as impersonal as ever, but the brown was recessive and a redness showed in them.

At the new zero hour they went out on the fields again. This movement was ragged and uneven. Technically it was a charge. Actually it had the appearance of mass hide-and-seek. The old men were becoming veterans, and the fresh men were afraid.

They were met by shrapnel. The artillery resistance had been strengthened during the night. Phelps lost Page to the shrapnel in the first hundred yards. He waited until stretcher bearers came, and he helped them back to the trench. Then he returned.

He was at liberty to go where and as he pleased — subject only to the fortunes of trespass in the bursting caldron ahead. He entered it by a series of little foot races with death. The air was full of lethal bees.[2] It occurred to Phelps that at the end of every war there are some men left alive.

He fell into a shell hole that was still stirring from the impetus of its creation. The pandemonium increased; so he remained there, smoking another cigarette. By and by he looked over the rim.

The terrain ahead sloped down, and at the bottom was a valley. In the valley was a village; and through the fog of powder smoke he could see it, full of lights that went on and off.

He crawled forward for an indefinite distance. Finally he fell in with three men.

They had an argument.

One said, "We better wait here."

Another said, "They're going over this place with a fine-tooth comb. We better beat it."

The third said, "I ain't seen nobody since we went out."

So they lay down together and looked up at the sky. Where there was no smoke,

[1] **looie:** short for lieutenant.

[2] **lethal bees:** picturesque for humming, deadly bullets.

the blue showed clearly; but it seemed to be mysteriously disturbed. Phelps passed around his cigarettes. Each man hinted that the other ought to take a look around. No one cared to peer over the casual barricade of earth which sheltered them. At last Phelps raised his head.

There were four of five enemy soldiers on the other side of the mound. They did not see him at once — they lay flat with their faces pressed in the earth. Phelps tossed a grenade over.

A moment later, abruptly, the gunfire swept away — a loud broom moving across the ground.

The men rose to their feet. They looked into the nest on the other side of the barricade.

" It's a good thing they didn't see us first," somebody said.

Phelps had thought of that. He dropped his cigarette on the earth and automatically stepped on it. He considered for a moment the vanity of extinguishing a cigarette when the whole world was on fire.

" We could run down to that first house," he said to the men.

They ran.

The town was as still as death. It seemed that none of their own troops had entered it.

They sat behind a wall, fearful of what might come around the corners.

" We'll wait here," one of the men said. He wiped his face with a bandanna handkerchief.

" We'll take a look around," Phelps replied.

" Like fun we will."

" I will, then."

" Go ahead."

Phelps went. The village was a mess. He made his way through it over back walls. Before and behind him was din; but the village was a vortex of quiet, a place that sucked up stillness and held it. Phelps could see two men in the tower of a church that was still standing. They scrambled around among the big bells. He shot them.

Finally he climbed up on a penthouse and from there onto a thatch roof. He slid off twice, but each time he hoisted himself back.

When he looked over the ridgepole, he found that he was staring directly down on the rear guard of the town. The street behind it was evacuated. Camions moved along the remote road.

Far away, now, he could see diminutive figures rising up on the surface of the earth. Their appearance set the men below him into a fever of activity. There were no shells anywhere. The smoke cleared in a midmorning wind. It was like looking at a painting of a battle. He lay on the roof, empty-stomached, feeling like a man in a dream. He watched the figures advance. They were like bugs. Like fleas. They hopped up, scuttled, and settled again.

Here, perhaps, it would come, he thought. Out of his pockets he took the grenades he had been issued in the morning. He bit out a pin, tossed the sphere, cracked another, tossed it, and then waited.

A dozen men survived. They jumped about, looking up. He gave them the last Mills bomb. Three men ran away. Two stood. One shot at him. The bullet sang past his head. He returned the fire, shooting coldly, accurately. Then he aimed at the men who were hastening toward the last camion.

The hopping insects had identified themselves as human beings. They straggled toward the street. When they reached the place where the rear guard had arranged to make its stand, they became audible. They were shouting. They behaved singularly. They upended the muzzles of the machine guns before they looked over the pile of rubbish that sheltered them. Then they climbed to the top. They leveled their bayonets and leaped down among the dead men.

When they found they were dead, the fury faded from them and they stood there like confused animals. They were numbed by the discovery that all their self-protective enterprise had been unnecessary.

It was still very quiet. Among the men was the captain. He made a careful examination.

" Somebody's beaten us to it," he said.

Another man replied, " It's a good thing. We'd never have made it."

The captain shrugged. " Yeah? Who says we wouldn't! We were supposed to take this place and hold it. Now we only got to hold it."

Phelps realized that the captain was disappointed. He had wanted to rush those guns and get credit for the valor involved. At least he had wanted his company to have the credit. Phelps belonged to that company. He appreciated that his fortunate situation would retrieve the captain's pride. He sat up on the roof. His emotions were nil.

Intellectually [1] he felt that the captain deserved to have had his chance to charge the guns; he would surely have been killed doing it. One of the men in the street below raised his rifle and almost shot at him before he realized that he was a friend.

" Lookit! " that man shouted. " There's the Yank that mopped up this gang."

Everyone looked at his pointed finger, and then at Phelps. Phelps slid down the front of the roof and landed on the cobblestones. The cottage was not very high, but his feet stung nevertheless. He shuffled them to ease the discomfort.

The captain put on a face of official congratulation.

" You're the man who bombed this ambuscade? " he said.

" Yes, sir."

" What company? "

Phelps realized that his insignia was gone. " Yours."

The captain recognized him. " You're Phelps. The man who took that gun yesterday afternoon. The man Page spoke about. The — "

" The slacker," Phelps said.

The captain perceived that all was well. In his next dispatch he could write, " I dispersed our men in a flanking movement to take a heavily manned barricade from which four Maxims [2] were operated to cover enemy retreat. Private Phelps was successful in reaching a vantage point on a roof above them and — "

The captain let his voice quaver. " Private Phelps," he said, " on behalf of the company and the regiment, I wish to thank you. I will see that you are mentioned again in the dispatches."

A runner came up after a while. There was a technical discussion. The rear of the retreating enemy was to be harried.

One man said he couldn't drag himself another fifty feet. One said he hadn't eaten for two days. But there was a light in the eyes of the captain. He sent his command forward after the camions which had gone over a hill. They went forward all afternoon. There was nothing to see.

They were hungry and tired. They kept a random contact with the flanks, so that progress along the line was relatively even. It was a bright, hot, peaceful afternoon, and the conquest of death seemed to have been temporarily arrested.

Toward nightfall Phelps found himself in a small woods. About seven o'clock

[1] In other words, his thoughts were wholly unattended by feeling.

[2] **Maxims:** machine guns, named after their inventor.

it was shelled by the enemy. A splinter of one of the shells hit him squarely in the right shoulder. He fell down, bleeding and groaning.

The stretcher bearers came for him at twilight. They asked him if he was ready to go. He said he was. They helped him get his cigarettes out of his pocket. He lit one and smoked it while they went along over the uneven ground, bumping, swinging, resting. Before the nightmare of the field dressing station he had another smoke. There was one cigarette left. He wrapped it up carefully and put it back.

Lying in a dark hole that was the inside of an ambulance, dreaming through the uncertain misery of wound and drugs, he recalled his family again. They did not know what it was to be merely a piece of damaged war material; to be repaired if possible, regardless of the pain; to be cast aside if repair was out of the question. Perhaps they would send him home now. What would his family say then?

He suddenly thought of a plan — a way of telling them, if he lived to have the opportunity.[1] It ran through his head with a nightmarish insistency and he made half-conscious attempts to organize the details. His father had called him yellow, and his mother would not speak to him. The coldness of many months increased now, and he shut his eyes so he would not see the dark.

A month later he was sent back to America. But before that he stood in line, in a brand-new uniform, to step out when his name was called, to salute, to feel the mustache of a French general on his cheek, to shake the hand of his own general, to gather on his breast a cluster of bright ribbons and flashing metal.

His father met him at the station. His father was thinner than he had remembered him, but he was not much different. He had a badge on his lapel. His eyes shone. Outside there was a band playing for young Phelps, and an impromptu parade ready to wheel proudly along the boulevard.

His father embraced him and then stiffened. "Good Lord, Wes, you're not wearing your uniform!"

"I've been demobilized."

"But," his father protested — "but we're having a big day for you. Chicago's read all about you. A dinner tonight with everyone in the city present. By George, I'm going to get you the Congressional Medal! I knew you could do it! And you've got to tell me all about it. Your mother and sister, too. How you got that machine gun, and how you captured that village. Man!"

"I can change to a uniform later," Phelps said.

At home the confusion obscured the behavior of Phelps. People came and went, shaking his hand and talking in loud voices about "the front" and "our boys." Even his mother.

Sometime after dark they went to their rooms to dress. Mr. Phelps waited in the library for his son. He waited with a feeling of glory; he contemplated the triumphant dinner party. Presently he heard footsteps.

Young Phelps came into the room. He walked past the rows of leather-bound books, beneath the crystal chandelier, to the big center table. He was wearing a uniform, but there were no medals on it.

It was a strange garment. The coat was gone. In the right side of the tunic was a rent. The cloth around it was black and stiff. The edges of the rent were seared. The blackness ran down the trousers and through the puttee on one leg into the shoe.

A canteen hung at Phelps's hip, and half of it had been twisted off. The uniform was heavy with dust and dirt. In

[1] Keep this thought in mind as you read on.

a dozen places it was torn. The shoes were almost unrecognizable.

Phelps stood in his filthy tatters. In his hand was a rifle. The bayonet was stained. In his other hand was a grenade. The helmet on his head was caked with dirt. He was like the hideous survivor of a dreadful catastrophe.

His father said, "What does this mean?"

Phelps ejected an empty cartridge from the magazine of his rifle and reloaded it.

The older man at last comprehended one fact. He knew what had made the rip in the shoulder of the tunic and he knew what the black stain was. He paled and swallowed.

"This is ghastly!" he said. "Take that off!"

His son did not reply. He looked directly into his father's eyes, as if to find a cue for himself in them. Then, abruptly, he commenced the lesson he had planned on a certain night in France. He made it as realistic as he could, and its effect was heightened because his face was not dreadful and not pitiful: it was only the face of a man doing very hard work.

He suddenly threw himself on the floor and commenced to wriggle along frantically.

To the other man the pantomime took on meaning — terrible meaning. Cautiously his son detached the bayonet from his rifle. With a tense, calm face he slid forward and dug it into the back of a chair, ripping out the uphostery. Then he hid behind the chair. After that he reattached the bayonet.

He was at that instant near the door of the den. He raised the rifle to his shoulder. He knelt. There were five loud explosions, and with each a picture shattered or a vase burst into fragments. Finally he tossed the grenade around the corner of the door and into the den. The noise it made was terrific. In the ear-singing silence that followed could be heard the dropping of debris. The room was a shambles.

For one dreadful instant he stood over his father, his rifle raised, the long bayonet pointing downward. His father was beyond speech. Then Phelps grabbed his own right shoulder. He turned halfway around and sat down quietly, his head bent forward.

For a moment he remained in that position; his legs stirred automatically. Then he rose and left the room.

Smoke rolled from the den. It stung the nostrils of the man who sat in the chair with blank eyes. In his heart was no pomp and circumstance now, but only an iciness and a realization of unspeakable things. Frightened voices were raised. Women ran, their heels sharp where the floor was bare. "What happened?" "Anybody hurt?" "Was that one of Wesley's war trophies?" But the father sat still.

People came to the dinner, but the guest of honor did not appear. They waited a long time, and finally a butler told them that Lieutenant Phelps was indisposed and that his father was remaining with him. So the meal was eaten — a silent affair.

In the mansion on Lake Shore Drive the clock hands went slowly round and round. Young Phelps had locked himself in his room, and his father sat in the library without speaking.

At last he rose and went upstairs. He knocked on his son's door and was admitted. The young man had bathed and put on pajamas and a silk dressing gown. He was as he had always been before the war. In a heap in the center of the room was a melee [1] of garments and gear from which protruded a stained bayonet.

Wesley Phelps said nothing. He sat

[1] **melee:** as used here, a confused mass. The French word for skirmish or fray.

down and watched his father, who moved toward the dirty garments and began to stir them. From the pocket of a shattered and blackened tunic there dropped a crumpled package. He picked it up. Inside it, damaged and dirty, was a single cigarette. It needed no second glance to reveal to the older man the events through which that cigarette had passed and the conditions under which the absent nineteen cigarettes had been smoked.

" You didn't use this one," he said in a low voice, " because — "

" Because I didn't get to it," young Phelps said.

" Yes. And the others — " It was a question.

" The others? "

" You carried them — "

The youth looked for the gleam that would have come in his father's eye if the story had been told differently. But there was no gleam.

" Dead men smoked most of them," he answered.

His father nodded and sank in a deep chair. He turned the cigarette reverently in his fingers. It was a symbol. He wanted to make it into an icon.[1] And then he perceived a way. He put the rusty, grimy object between his lips. His eyes met his son's. " May I? " he asked.

" Sure," the young man said softly.

His father lit the cigarette. He breathed the smoke into the air as if it were incense, as if it had a significance at once holy and infinitely poignant.

" Ever since you went upstairs," he said finally, " I've been seeing things I never saw before. It's a long way from Chicago to France. And a gold star is different from that — that crawling along the ground. I — "

Young Phelps looked away from his father's face. He was momentarily ashamed of the savagery with which he had presented his story of the war. He mustered his voice.

" It's O.K., Dad. Forget it."

Then his father demonstrated that he had learned a great deal since the homecoming of the hero. " That," he answered gently, " is what I propose never to do."

[1] **icon:** an image, to be worshiped or revered.

THINK BACK OVER WHAT YOU HAVE READ

Getting the Author's Message

1. What sentences can you quote which bring home to you the truth of Phelps's statement on page 141 that " war is a rotten way to settle things "? What sharp contrasts in detail, set side by side, make war seem the more horrible?

2. Did you find yourself at any point in the story sympathizing with the enemy? Where? By what means does the author enlist your sympathy?

3. At what point in the story did you feel critical of army discipline? What did you find to criticize? What opinion did you form of the captain of Phelps's regiment?

4. Why do you suppose Phelps accepted his heroism so calmly? so indifferently? Did he act the way " heroes " are supposed to act? What thoughts do you think lay behind his indifference? Why was he so unmoved by his successes?

5. How does a soldier in action accept the constant threat of death? What was Phelps's attitude? Did it surprise you? How?

6. What do you consider to be wrong with the elder Phelps's attitude toward war? *Was* his son " yellow "? What do you think about the current use of the word " yellow " in time of war? (Refer, in this connection, to page 93).

7. What was the " terrible meaning " of Phelps's pantomime acted out in his father's library? Was it justified? On page 147 Phelps says he was " momentarily ashamed " of his " savagery "; should he have been? Should Phelps have acted differently on his return home?

8. How do you explain the significance of the smoking of the last cigarette? How, in detail, do you interpret the sentence on page 147 that reads: " He [the elder Phelps] breathed the smoke into the air as if it were incense,

as if it had a significance at once holy and infinitely poignant "?

Appreciating the Peculiar Power of the Story over the Mind of the Reader

9. What kind of sentences predominate in this story: long sentences? short sentences? simple, direct sentences? complex, involved sentences? Does the style of sentence used seem to you particularly appropriate? Why? Reread aloud to yourself any paragraph which struck you as particularly forceful. Does the way in which it is written seem to you just right? What effect does the paragraph leave upon you? How does it make you feel?

10. Can you think of any reason why the author should prefer to present his scenes with such calm? Perhaps you noticed that there is very little excitement in the way he tells the story. Can you find and read to the class an illustration of a horrible happening described in a purely matter-of-fact manner? What is the effect of such restraint on the reader? Does it heighten or lessen the sense of tragedy? Does the lack of excitement increase or decrease your interest?

11. In what does your chief interest in the story lie? in the events of the story? in the outcome? in their effect on Phelps? in their " terrible meaning " for Phelps's father?

12. What part does the smoking of a package of cigarettes play in the story? Glance back over the story and notice each time a fresh cigarette is smoked. What does each of the twenty cigarettes seem to mark?

Increase Your Power over Words

The following words which you have just met offer interesting practice in learning how to discriminate accurately between meanings of words that look or sound somewhat alike.

13. *Delusion, illusion, allusion.* All these words stem from the Latin word *ludere* which means to play in the sense of pretend. Literally the words mean as follows:

delusion — the act of *deluding,* or of leading from the truth, or making sport of (a kind of play)

allusion — the act of *alluding,* or playing *with*

illusion — the act of *illuding,* or of playing upon by trickery

In common usage, delusion and illusion are closely related.

An *illusion* is something which presents a false appearance to the senses. A mirage, for example, is an *illusion.*

A *delusion* is a false belief. The belief that the earth was flat was a common *delusion* in ancient times.

An *allusion* is something quite different, and should never be confused with *illusion.* For example, " Frankenstein," a word you met in " Zenobia's Infidelity," is an *allusion,* or reference, to a character in a famous story who constructed a monster out of materials from a churchyard and dissecting room and then gave it a sort of life.

14. *Circumspect, inspect, respect, retrospect, suspect.* Here is a famous family of words all issuing from the Latin root *spicere,* to look:

a. circumspect — to look *around.* You might say, " John was very *circumspect;* he didn't commit himself to rash promises."
b. inspect — to look *into.* This is a familiar word. Let's say that you *inspected* the skating rink to see whether the ice was hard.
c. retrospect — to look *back.* In *retrospect* the occasion had taken on a special glamour for Tom. (Tom is looking back on the past through rose-colored glasses.)
d. respect — to look back, but in a less literal sense than above. Sam did not *respect* the family tradition. (He did not look back upon it with veneration.)
e. suspect — to look *under.* Here is another familiar word whose derived meaning follows closely its literal meaning. We *suspected* the boy's tale as false. (We looked beneath its surface for the truth.)

For Ambitious Students

One reason why wars continue — according to popular view — is that each new generation must learn for itself about its horrors. There have been signs, however, dim though they are at present, that man is waking up, that he is learning to profit from the experience of others without the terrible waste that comes from having to learn such a lesson by himself. Here is another reason why reading is so important, or rather it is the same reason offered you on pages 98–99 put in another way.

The following stories offer you lessons learned in the past about war. If war seems to you romantic and glorious, then you by all means should read these stories and learn once and for all time the danger of such false belief.

Or read them, anyway, to confirm your belief in the sanity of peace. If you have a Peace Day in your school, you may find these stories useful illustrative material. If you were moved by "Twenty Cigarettes," perhaps you will find a basis for an interesting comparison of story-telling power in the list that follows.

15. "War" by Jack London [1] is a very moving description of a scout on horseback undertaking a lonely and dangerous mission. From this story you gain a vivid sense of what it feels like to be in danger.

16. In "The Secret" by H. M. Tomlinson the pathos of a father and mother each trying to spare the other the news of their son's death on the battlefield is a touching reminder of the daily suffering that goes on behind the lines of battle.

17. Fantastic tales are likely to spring up around some major catastrophe such as war. In "The Call" by Oscar Firkins, a story of unusual power, a dead man's whistle plays an eerie part in the grim business of war.

18. "A Fishing Party" by Guy de Maupassant shows you the grim savagery of war, yet not at all in the way you might expect. The story of two simple fishermen who were mistaken for spies is told quite simply, with very few adjectives and adverbs laid on for effect. The result, however, drives home to you with great force the utter mercilessness of war.

True Stories

THE MAN WHO WON THE WAR

by Robert Buckner (1906–)

The story that follows illustrates the proverb that truth is stranger than fiction. Here is a dramatic bit of history which allows you to look for a moment behind the scenes of a great event, and to see how large a part is played by chance and how sometimes very "unimportant" happenings are turning points in history. The result of this discovery is always to make you feel that life itself is intensely dramatic and that an accidental encounter with a strange man on a train might turn out to be as thrilling for you as for the man who tells the following story. This true story of the World War of 1914–18 appeared in 1936 in the *Atlantic Monthly,* one of our most distinguished literary magazines of today.

Once to every writer there comes the perfect story, straight from life. But the great fault of most true stories is their improbability: it is far simpler to imagine a convincing plot than to borrow one from actual facts. Neither the official records of the Belgian War Office in Brussels nor the British Admiralty Archives in London contain the whole proof of what I am about to tell. The sole legal evidence, I can assure you, is buried in a small stone urn on the coast of Flanders, and in the embittered heart of an exiled Englishman.

LATE ON a winter evening in 1927 I was returning to England after a holiday spent with friends in Cologne. The Brussels Express was running far behind time, and I remember how it sped down the dark Ruhr Valley toward the Belgian border as if frightened by the red flares from the steel furnaces. It was January and bitter cold. The windows sweated in rivulets, between the frost and the overheated train.

At Düren I descended to the platform for a breath of the wet night air. When I returned to my compartment the only other occupant was awake, filling his pipe and glancing absently at the station.

"What place is this, please?" he asked in German.

"Düren, I believe," I replied in English, and smiled.

[1] This and the following stories will be found in the volume *War or Peace,* edited by Alfred Brant and Frederick H. Law.

" I say, are you British? " he exclaimed with mild interest, halting the match midway to his face.

" No, American."

" Oh," he murmured, and turned back to his pipe.

The train pulled slowly through the town, across the Ruhr bridge and the black river jeweled with the lights of barges. Suddenly in the north the sky flamed red again, throwing a weird infernal glow over the dreary plain and the mountainous slag heaps.

" Looks like hell, doesn't it? "

" Hell? " The Englishman laughed shortly. " Aye, they turn out a rather good grade of hell here. One of the best."

" What do you mean? "

" Steel! " he barked, removing the briar and pointing with its stem. " Steel for guns and shells! " And then quietly, as if to himself, " Oh, the fools, the bloody fools! Didn't they get enough of it last time? "

This outburst from one whose countrymen are usually so taciturn and reserved [1] alarmed me at first. But it also awakened my senses, drugged by the stale air and a desire to sleep. I began to study my companion with new interest.

He was perhaps fifty years old, tall, his powerful body contradicted by a face which bore the marks of many illnesses. The effect was that of an oak tree whose death had begun in the topmost branches. But his gray eyes were keen and friendly. He wore a dark flannel suit, brown brogues, and blue shirt, that uniform of the Englishman abroad. His luggage consisted of one battered suitcase and a square, paper-wrapped parcel, lying beside him on the seat. From the bitter tone of his remark about the war, together with his general bearing, I put him down as an ex-officer.

[1] The English have a reputation for holding back their feelings.

" Do you think the Germans are arming again? " I asked in surprise. It was exciting news then, since I had seen only poor people trying desperately to be happy around their Christmas trees.

" They can never forget." He nodded. " Like the Irish, they are a fighting people. Ten years, twenty — they can wait. Only, God help us when they are ready again."

" But the League of Nations would stop them," I protested with all the fierce idealism of youth.

" Ah, yes " — he smiled indulgently — " the League. I forgot. No, make no mistake about it, son; not even that clever Yankee invention will help us then. Nor your dollars and men, I'm afraid."

" That's true enough," I agreed. " We won't be so easily dragged in again. This 'winning the war' has turned out to be a pretty expensive party for us."

" Oh? " he inquired. " So it was America who won the war, eh? That's most interesting. I've often wondered where the credit belonged, really."

It was an old trap [2] into which I had fallen before. Now I stepped cautiously around it, and then decided to grab the bait out of curiosity concerning the man himself.

" We-ll " — I gazed innocently at the rack above his head — " if we didn't win the war, who did? "

When, after a short silence, I lowered my eyes, it was to observe the tall Englishman looking at me puzzledly, as if trying to determine my seriousness. Then his deeply lined face softened with an oddly tragic humor as he turned to the square package at his side.

" Do you really want to know? " he asked quietly, at length.

" Of course," I replied. " I imagine your guess would be better than mine."

[2] The **trap** is being "put on the spot"; that is, forced to defend his statement.

"I'm not guessing at all." He looked up quickly. "*I* did. I won the war."

There followed a rather embarrassing pause. Obviously the fellow was a megalomaniac; I hoped of the harmless variety. "Oh, so *you're* the man?" I smiled. "Well, my congratulations."

He waved my words aside. "You're thinking I'm quite mad, I dare say." He watched me with narrowed eyes, leaning forward slightly in his seat.

"Oh, not at all," I insisted, now definitely alarmed at the serious intensity in his wide gray eyes.

"It doesn't matter." He sat back, observing the distant lights of Aachen slide past us in the dark. "Only one man ever really believed me, anyway. Poor devil, I only wish he might have doubted it, too."

"But you misunderstand," I replied. "I haven't said that I doubted you. I should like very much, indeed, to hear about it."

He turned his head slowly and for a long while looked at me, through me, his eyes drilling down into the years.

"Well, why not?" he asked himself aloud. "It would be rather appropriate just now, and after tomorrow's job, I dare say, I shan't ever feel like telling it again."

At this moment the conductor, a pompous little Prussian with gimlet mustaches, opened the door of our compartment, bowed, and informed us with gruff pride that our baggage would be inspected by the customs office in Brussels, as the Express did not stop at the border. We should arrive in an hour and a quarter, he replied to the Englishman's question, and with another stiff bow he withdrew.

"Time enough," my companion murmured; and then, "My name is Roger Bradman." I introduced myself. We shook hands.

"Of course, you've never heard of me," he began. "Nor of the Bradman Spy Case, back in 1913. All that would be before your time."

It was. But I had read of the famous case in Dr. Spingard's book. "Wasn't that the incident that nearly caused war between Germany and England? Are *you* that Bradman?"

"Yes"—he nodded—"I am. The Naval Intelligence had sent me to Berlin to get the plans of the Heligoland forts. Well, I got them—and then they got me. Stupid error, of course; but there I was, caught red-handed.

"Then the fun began. They didn't care particularly about shooting me. They would have, quickly enough, but we weren't at war. But the Kaiser jumped at the chance to pin a bit of incriminating evidence on Great Britain. They were all fairly certain that I was a British officer, but they couldn't prove it. We had taken care of that.

"All the same, my arrest created a terrific shindy.[1] Every brass hat in the German army must have had a go at me, and all their newspapers were howling for my head. Oh, they put the fear of God into me, right enough; but finally, through some major miracle which I've never been able to figure out, they let me go.

"Naturally England had disowned me from the start. Never heard of me. Refused me permission to return and all that. You see, it was the only way she could save her face—and my neck. It's the usual treatment when a spy is caught.

"So for a year I simply knocked about the Continent, avoiding my fellow countrymen. Once in every two months I received my expenses from one of the Queen's messengers. A cushy[2] job for me, but a trifle wearing on the nerves.

[1] **shindy:** slang for uproar or disturbance.
[2] **cushy job:** We would say a "soft job."

"Then in August of '14,[1] when the lid finally blew off, orders came through for me to return at once to London, and I was given command of the *Firedrake,* a scouting destroyer attached to Admiral Hood's battle force on North Sea patrol."

At this point the Englishman paused and reached across for my newspaper, which he spread flat upon his knees. Then with a pencil he sketched a rough map of the Belgian coast, marking Ostend and Nieuport and the crooked course of the Yser River.

"Have a look at this," he suggested. "It may give you a clearer picture of what happened that night.

"As you remember"—he pointed with his pencil—"Germany attacked France from three directions, southward through the Vosges, in the center along the Marne, and a third army under Von Kluck smashed through Belgium. Their plan was to converge upon Paris in a series of swift flanking movements. This would compel the French army to switch its center of mobilization, and in attempting to re-form its lines the French might conceivably be thrown into such confusion and disorder that a gigantic victory, a Sedan[2] on a colossal scale, might be won by the Germans. Paris could be taken later, at their leisure.

"And they came jolly near to doing it, too! You see, after grabbing Antwerp they pushed along to capture the coast towns, Dunkirk, Calais, and Boulogne. This would have cut off England's best line of communication and also turned the Allied flank. That would have finished the war then and there.

"Meanwhile they had shoved the little Belgian army almost into the Channel. Retreating day after day, hammered to pieces by the heavy guns, unable to care for their dead and wounded, the Belgians were at the frayed end of their rope. They were praying for the British to come to their rescue, but Haig[3] was having his own trouble on their right.

"On the night of the twenty-eighth of October the two armies were within half a mile of each other, with the Belgian left flank ending in the sand dunes of the North Sea at a point a mile below Nieuport. The men were completely done in, standing asleep in their trenches. The Yser, which flowed behind the lines, had swollen with the fall rains until the whole Flanders plain was a waste of bottomless mud.

"As you can readily see, it was a hopeless situation. King Albert knew that the Germans would attack again at daybreak, though they, too, were worn out from the long chase across Belgium and had outdistanced their supply trains. Albert knew with grim certainty that his exhausted forces would never be able to withstand the attack.

"Shortly before midnight on the twenty-eighth, the Belgian king ordered a council of his staff. When the men gathered, they could scarcely bring themselves to look into each other's eyes. None of them believed there was any possible way out. They knew, too, that it would mean the certain end of the war when the Germans broke through, for there would be nothing between them and Paris. If the French dropped back to cover their flank, the Crown Prince and Von Hindenburg would smash through, throwing the Allied forces into a complete rout.

"The Belgian officers discussed this problem from every conceivable angle, but could find no satisfactory solution. Finally a Colonel of Dragoons offered this last desperate suggestion.

"He proposed that they send a small

[1] The first World War started in 1914. [2] In 1870 the French were defeated by the invading German forces and compelled to surrender at **Sedan.**

[3] **Haig:** Field Marshal Douglas Haig, in command of the British forces.

patrol of picked men down to the beach on their extreme left; attempt there to overcome the German sentries and then to signal to sea, in hopes that some part of the British fleet, cruising in the darkness, would spot the signals and come to their rescue, either by landing men or else by drawing within range so that their heavy guns might bombard the German lines.

"This suggestion was immediately accepted as a last resort, but with little real hope of its success.

"Eight men, including two officers, were chosen for the expedition. They traversed the shallow trench until it became lost in the sand dunes; and from there they crept eastward toward the enemy lines, ready with their bayonets for what they hoped would be a short and silent action. The night was pitch-black, with a low storm-sky blotting out the stars. The Belgians were afraid of passing the sentries in the dark, so they spread out to ten-yard intervals and moved slowly up the beach."

Here Bradman paused again, this time to pick up the square box resting beside him on the seat. His large powerful fist closed over it until the veins stood out like earthworms in contrast to the bloodless knuckles.

"They found the sentry?" I prompted eagerly.

"Yes, they found him," Bradman continued grimly, "*asleep!* A boy of twenty or so, haggard with weariness, seated on a driftwood log, his rifle clutched between his knees. He had taken off his boots to bury his aching feet in the cool sand, and his trousers were rolled up above his knees.

"One of the officers slugged him with the butt of a revolver. They tied him up with belts and carried him into the dunes, after leaving his spiked helmet with one of their men who stayed at the post and later captured the relief sentry.

"Then the Belgians searched about until they discovered a spot shielded from sight of the German lines by high sand hills. Here they started a fire with driftwood and oil. After they had it blazing well, they threw handfuls of gunpowder upon it at half-minute intervals, making a sort of recurrent-flare beacon.

"Now this"— Bradman hesitated and smiled —"is where I enter the story.

"That night of the twenty-eighth the *Firedrake* and the *Myrmidon* were passing up the Belgian coast on our way to join the main fleet. Following Beatty's show in the Bight[1] there was the expectation of a general action in the air, and we were bringing up extra shells, torpedoes, and a few cases of Scotch whisky. That is, we *thought* it was Scotch whisky when we loaded the crates at Plymouth. The boxes were labeled "Cameron Highlander," the name of a popular brand. But on our first night out one of my men, in checking the stores, discovered that the cases, in fact, contained uniforms intended for the regiment of First Cameron Highlanders, somewhere in France! There were a hundred and eighty complete uniforms, kilts, Glengarries, and all. Oh, there were hundreds of mistakes more ridiculous than that made in those days, and we considered it lucky that the matter was more humorous than tragic.

"I was on the bridge at about one in the morning of the twenty-ninth when one of our lookouts spotted the fire on shore. I watched the flares for a long while through my night glasses; but as they were not in code, I could make neither head nor tail of them. There were

[1] **Beatty's show in the Bight:** Soon after the outbreak of the World War the English raided Heligoland Bight, an arm of the North Sea, sinking three German cruisers and one destroyer without loss. Beatty was the officer in command.

no lighthouses along this stretch of coast, nor any town. We thought we knew the approximate extent of the German advance, but none of us believed they had pushed this far.

"Now we had orders to offer any possible assistance to the land forces, but this was supposed to mean only that our monitors such as the *Mersey* and the *Severn* might be called upon. Such private investigations as this were, of course, strictly forbidden. Nevertheless, I found myself developing a most persistent curiosity about this light where no light should be. Call it a hunch if you like. At any rate, I ordered the ship dropped to half speed and swung in closer. I watched the flares again, but again could deduce nothing. One thing was obvious, however: *someone* was signaling to sea.

"I ordered the *Myrmidon* to continue at reduced speed along her course, and said that we would pick her up again toward daybreak. Then I dropped anchor, lowered a small launch, and together with a dozen sailors, all of us heavily armed, landed on the coast at a point less than a mile below the light. You see, for all I knew this signal might very well have been a ruse of the Germans; and my suspicions were becoming greater by the minute.

"We advanced cautiously up the beach until we were within a hundred yards of the fire. Here I split our force and we closed in upon them from three sides. At thirty yards or so I was able to make out the Belgian uniforms and challenged them in French.

"*Jove!* You've never seen such amazement on any men's faces in your life! When they saw us walk into the circle of firelight, they rushed forward like so many lost children and threw their arms about us, weeping for joy.

"It must have been fully five minutes before any of them was able to talk coherently, or slowly enough for me to understand. Over and over they kept repeating *men, guns,* and pointed out to sea. Finally I pulled one of the officers aside and learned something of their desperate situation. In the light from my hand torch the fellow knelt upon the sand and sketched the battle lines. He made clear the strategic position of the enemy, waiting for morning to push through the thin Belgian line. Then he drew a small circle below and to the left. 'Paris,' he said simply, and looked up at me.

"I explained to him that British destroyers of the *Firedrake* class carried a crew of only a hundred men, and that our light guns hadn't the range necessary for offshore bombardment.

"At this bad news the Belgian major fell silent. He stared at me almost reproachfully for a second and then spoke quietly to his men. Exactly what he said I do not know, for he spoke in Flemish; but I could fairly well guess.

"I looked away, I dare say to avoid the anguish in the poor chap's eyes, and saw the German sentry lying crumpled on the sand. He had recovered consciousness, but they had gagged him with a muddy puttee and his eyes rolled up at the light as wide with fear and pain as those of a child who has been stuck in a dark closet. In fact, he looked very much like a little boy — with his trousers rolled up and his bare legs stretched out on the sand.

"I stared at his knees for a moment, trying to remember something, and then suddenly I recalled the eight cases of Cameron Highlander uniforms in the hold of the *Firedrake!* Why not turn them over to the Belgians? A company dressed in the bright Scottish kilts, by risking to display themselves in the early morning light, might alarm the battle-weary troops of Von Kluck into thinking that the British had rushed up a picked division in support of the Belgians. It was a long chance, a psychological trick,[1] that might possibly work. Also I could spare them a crate or two of Lewis guns. It was a terrifically long shot at best; but we were in no position to weigh the odds, and we should have to work fast.

"I rushed back to the major and described my plan. He listened dully at first, like a man in whom all hope is dead, but his head lifted slowly as I talked; and before I had finished he leaped to his feet, clutched my arm and cried, 'Yes, yes! It might work. It is at least *something!*'

"'Then bring up several ambulances or ammunition trucks,' I directed, 'as close to the beach as you can get. We can carry the crates to them across the sand.'

"The Belgian major called to the younger officer, described the plan in a staccato sentence, and sent him hurrying back to their lines with four of the men. Then he ran back with us to the launch, wading into the surf with the sailors to shove us off. I left him my torch to guide us in landing.

"Back on the ship, I roused out the entire crew to give a hand with the crates of uniforms. We lowered two lifeboats and roped them in tandem behind the launch. Then we ferried the boxes ashore, the whole lot of them. Meanwhile the Belgians had detailed two companies to meet us at the beach and change uniforms there in order to save time. We broke open the crates with bayonets and assembled the complete uniforms in orderly piles on the sand. It was a sight I shall never forget — a hundred and eighty men changing their clothes around that fire, laughing at the bright red and yellow kilts and putting on the caps backwards so that the ribbons fell over their gray, muddied faces. We assembled the Lewis guns and piled them into a truck.

"The job was finished just about an hour before dawn. We put out the fire, tossed the two German sentries into an ambulance, and waited until the last kilted figure had disappeared into the dunes. Then we hurried back to the *Firedrake,* hauled the boats aboard, and headed out to sea just as the first faint streaks of morning appeared in the east.

"It had been a damned close thing," Bradman mused, rubbing the bowl of his briar against his nose. "*Too* close for comfort. It's a tricky piece of coast there off Nieuport, all sand bars and cross-currents. Besides, the tide had gone out on us; and before we cleared the last shoals, we heard the first German guns beginning their barrage. The final day of the first battle of Flanders had begun — "

"When they stopped them by opening the dikes of the Yser." I recalled after so many years a headline which had once inflamed a boy's mind.

The Englishman nodded. "That's how they have put it into the history books, no doubt. But it was really the kilts that did it — they and a few machine guns.

"The Belgian machine gunners piled the enemy three-deep as they came across the marshes. Thousands were drowned in the rivers and canals. Next to Verdun and Gallipoli, it was probably the ghastliest slaughter of the war. All day it went on like that, with wave after wave of the enemy melting away, the men dropping out of sight beneath the water as they fell. Once or twice the gunners held their fire until the Germans were near enough to see the British uniforms.

"By late afternoon the marshes were literally paved with dead, and still the enemy floundered in their company-front formations. But the heart had gone out of the attack when they saw that they

[1] **psychological trick:** in other words, deception.

were confronted by what they believed to be fresh troops in the uniforms of a crack Scottish regiment. At last, just before dark, the Belgians opened the lower dikes of the Yser, and the battle was over. From that hour until the end of the war the Germans never came a foot farther through Flanders, and the Allies' left flank was saved."

Bradman smiled and spread his hands, palms upward, upon his knees as if the story had ended.

"But great Scott, man," I exclaimed, "go on!"

He shrugged and looked away. "What more is there to tell? I never knew the outcome of it myself until many years later. Then it was too late."

"How do you mean — too late?"

"When I reported to the fleet with the crates missing, there was the devil to pay. The mistake about loading uniforms was put down as a deliberate scheme on my part. The Admiral's staff thought I had turned the stuff over to the Germans. They clapped me in irons and sent me back to England under arrest for treason. Even the sailors who had landed with me on the beach admitted at my court-martial at Hull that the men to whom we had given the Scottish uniforms might possibly have been Germans. A telegram was sent off to the Belgian headquarters, but for some reason in the confusion there was never any answer. This was proof enough for my judges; and while they could actually prove nothing, neither could I. They stripped me of my command and rank and handed me over to a prison camp for the duration of the war."

"You never told anyone about this?" I asked incredulously. "No one ever knew?"

"Yes, there *was* someone else who knew," he replied. "One man, the only man who ever believed me" — and the friendly smile crept back into his eyes — "unless *you* do."

Bradman turned back a cuff to glance at his watch, and then peered out at the fog-dimmed lights of a town. The Express clattered over the points of a siding and passed the station at unchecked speed, the lights soon dropping away in the distance.

"I don't know why I should care whether you believe me or not," he remarked, "but I do, oddly enough. Perhaps you have wondered why I fasten on you, an absolute stranger, to tell this to; but you may find some explanation in the end of my story. I say, how much time have we left?"

"That was Louvain we just passed," I replied. "We've a good quarter hour yet."

"At any rate, I shan't be long," he continued, slipping the cord which bound the square package in his lap.

"After the Armistice I had to get out of England. I changed my name and crossed over to Canada. But my story, or rather *their* story about me, somehow always caught up with me. Ottawa, Vancouver, Melbourne, Freemantle, even far back in the Australian bush country, sooner or later some ex-navy man would turn up who recognized me and I would have to move on.

"Then three years ago, when I was returning to Europe on a freighter from Matadi, it suddenly occurred to me, while we were passing that same bit of coast where I had taken the *Firedrake,* that it had been just ten years ago, almost to the day, since my expensive little party on the beach. I can't explain it, but I had a feeling of overpowering curiosity to go back there and see the place again. 'The criminal returning to the scene of his crime,' [1] I dare say. Whatever it was, I went.

[1] This is a common saying.

" We docked at Antwerp on the morning of the twenty-ninth and by evening I was in Nieuport. I put up at the village hotel, where there was but one other guest, a quiet German, a bit younger than myself. His name was Bechtel — Gunnar Bechtel. We met at dinner, the proprietor of the hotel, his wife, Bechtel, and I sitting all together at the same table.

" We were a long time over the meal, and it must have been close to midnight before the proprietor and his wife left for bed. Bechtel and I sat on for a while to finish the wine. Then he arose, bowed his apologies, and withdrew — also, as I imagined, to bed.

" I finished my pipe, then wandered out into the hall, unlatched the front door, and strolled along the cobbled streets toward the sea. There was enough of a moon to guide me through the dunes, and soon I was on the beach. I faced west, remembering how the village had been above us to the east on that other night, and walked slowly along the hard sand, thinking of all that had happened in the years since.

" Suddenly from the corner of my eye I caught sight of a man seated upon a log. It gave me quite a start. Just as I was about to walk on, my eyes still guardedly upon him, I recognized that it was Bechtel, my fellow lodger at the hotel. I laughed and called out to him in relief.

" We sat there for quite a time, smoking and talking, and finally he asked me in his politely abrupt way what might have brought me to Nieuport in October.

" I told him this story, exactly as I have told it to you. I remember when I had finished I felt a bit embarrassed, as if I had talked too much; so I wound up by saying half-jokingly, ' So you see, Herr Bechtel, I am the original man who won the war,' and then stood up to go.

" The German rose, too, and laid his hand gently on my arm. ' Do you know who I am, my friend? ' he asked me quietly.

" I shook my head.

" ' I am the man who *lost* the war,' he replied, looking me squarely in the eyes. ' *I am the sentry they found asleep.*'

" It was true. Bechtel was the lad they had caught napping that night, whose bare muddy knees had given me the idea of the kilts.

" For ten years his ' sin,' as he called it, had been gnawing at his conscience, driving him nearly mad; and he had hoped in his simple peasant way that by returning to the scene of his disgrace he might conquer the feeling. Since the end of the war he had watched all the horrors of revolution, the starvation of his people, the acres of war dead, the millions of widows and orphans, and he had seen all these things as *his* monstrous crime against the Fatherland. For Bechtel knew clearly, just as I knew, that if only he had been awake that night the battle of Flanders would have been quite another story, and the German army would unquestionably have been in Paris by Christmas.

" We stood there on that strip of sand in the moonlight, looking at each other, ' the man who won the war ' and ' the man who lost it.' There was nothing to say, nothing at all. We turned and walked slowly back along the beach, I suppose the two loneliest men on earth." . . .

The Englishman spoke in a voice scarcely above a whisper, as a man talks to himself. His eyes returned from the window to the square box, and an expression of infinite weariness settled over his features.

In the early morning the Waterloo Road was dark but for the lanterns swinging at the crossings, dim and misty in the rain; and the squat black barges of the Willebroeck Canal were huddled like beetles for comfort from the cold. Far away the lights of Brussels flickered through a leafless grove.

"Where is he now? Have you seen him since?" I asked, moved by curiosity as well as by a desire to say something kind.

"No," replied Bradman. "I never saw him afterward. Once each year we wrote. He worked in an iron foundry near Dortmund. A week ago he wrote to me from a hospital there, saying that there was something he wanted me to do for him. *There'll be a little dirt in a box,* he wrote, and he asked me to bury it for him on the beach near Nieuport.

"That is where I am going now," said Bradman, "and this is the box."

Tenderly he removed the brown paper from the package on his knees, disclosing a small stone urn. He held it so that I might read the simple inscription: GUNNAR BECHTEL.

THINK BACK OVER WHAT YOU HAVE READ

Appreciating the Dramatic Quality of the Story

1. What effect did the following sentences have upon you when you read them?

"I'm not guessing at all." He looked up quickly. "I did. I won the war" (page 151).

"I am the man who *lost* the war. . . . I am the sentry they found asleep" (page 157).

How did the author react to the first statement when it was uttered? Would your response have been similar to his? Why?

What was the effect of the second statement on Mr. Bradman when he first heard it from his fellow lodger, Herr Bechtel?

2. If you were to illustrate the most dramatic scenes in the story, what scenes would you choose? What passages would you mark for an artist and say, "Here, picture these"? What lines or captions or titles would you inscribe below each?

3. On page 150 you will find the sentence: "His luggage consisted of one battered suitcase and a square, paper-wrapped parcel, lying beside him on the seat." The parcel is mentioned four other times in the story. Look back over the story and find each reference. Under what circumstances is the parcel mentioned? At what point in the reading of the story was your curiosity about the contents of the package first awakened? At what point was it satisfied?

4. The man who won the war made three trips, all told, to the beach near Nieuport. Each time his path crossed that of the man who lost the war. What happened the first time? the second? the third? Which of the three scenes strikes you as most dramatic?

Thinking about the Story Afterward

5. After reading the story, what conclusions do you come to about any of the following topics?

a. the treatment of spies
b. the humorous side of war
c. the feeling of enmity
d. the importance of "hunches"
e. the unreliability of circumstantial evidence

6. What incidents in the story helped you to formulate your ideas?

For Ambitious Students

7. Someone in the class, perhaps a special group particularly interested in the military aspects of the great war, should look up and report to the class the historical background of the battle of Flanders. For a full appreciation of the detail in the story the following references need to be explained:

a. "Aye, they turn out a rather good grade of hell here [in the *Ruhr Valley*]" (page 150).
b. ". . . make no mistake about it . . . not even that clever Yankee invention [the *League of Nations*] will help us then" (page 150).
c. "But I had read of the famous case [*The Bradman Spy Case,* back in 1913] in Dr. Spingard's book" (page 151).
d. "The Naval Intelligence had sent me to Berlin to get the plans of the *Heligoland forts*" (page 151).
e. "I was given command of the *Firedrake,* a scouting destroyer attached to *Admiral Hood's battle force on North Sea patrol*" (page 152).

f. "As you remember . . . Germany attacked France from three directions" (page 152).
g. "Meanwhile they had shoved the little Belgian army almost into the channel. . . . They were praying for the British to come to their rescue" (page 152).
h. "[The Belgians] knew, too, that it would mean the certain end of the war when the Germans broke through" (page 152).
i. "Following *Beatty's show in the Bight* there was the expectation of a general action in the air" (page 153).
j. "The final day of the first battle of Flanders had begun —" "When they stopped them by *opening the dikes of the Yser*" (page 155).

R.M.S.[1] TITANIC

by Hanson W. Baldwin (1895–)

Courage in the face of almost certain death is not so rare as is sometimes believed. On the contrary, it is relatively common; and brave men and brave women have existed in all ages. In every language, among all peoples, it occurs over and over again as a theme in song and story. It is thus a deep-lying human trait peculiar to no single time or place, but characteristic of mankind as a whole.

Courage is man's triumph over his instinctive fear of death. It is as if he said to the grim old reaper, "Very well! You win. But mark you. I shall not 'wince nor cry aloud.' My spirit still remains 'unbowed.'" Thus does he cheat Death of complete victory.

Here is a thought to keep in mind as you read the following tragic account of a grim disaster at sea, a thought which will draw you into proud kinship with your fellow man and perhaps rob death of some of its terror for you. Take time as you read to notice the men and women who are named in the story, and whose last words and last deeds have been recorded. What did these people do or say when all hope of rescue was gone? What might you have done? It's a horrible question but one which periodically we ask ourselves, cherishing the hope that if such a test should come, our valor would not be found wanting. And it is out of such questioning, perhaps, that our own courage is born.

[1] **R.M.S.:** Royal Mail Steamer.

THE White Star liner *Titanic,* largest ship the world had ever known, sailed from Southampton [2] on her maiden voyage to New York on April 10, 1912. The paint on her strakes [3] was fair and bright; she was fresh from Harland and Wolff's Belfast [4] yards, strong in the strength of her forty-six thousand tons of steel, bent, hammered, shaped, and riveted through the three years of her slow birth.

There was little fuss and fanfare at her sailing; her sister ship, the *Olympic* — slightly smaller than the *Titanic* — had been in service for some months and to her had gone the thunder of the cheers.

But the *Titanic* needed no whistling steamers or shouting crowds to call attention to her superlative qualities. Her bulk dwarfed the ships near her as longshoremen singled up her mooring lines and cast off the turns of heavy rope from the dock bollards.[5] She was not only the largest ship afloat, but was believed to be the safest. Carlisle, her builder, had given her double bottoms and had divided her hull into sixteen watertight compartments, which made her, men thought, unsinkable. She had been built to be and had been described as a gigantic lifeboat. Her designers' dreams of a triple-screw [6] giant, a luxurious, floating hotel, which could speed to New York at twenty-three knots, had been carefully translated from blueprints and mold-loft [7] lines at the Belfast yards into a living reality.

The *Titanic's* sailing from Southampton, though quiet, was not wholly uneventful. As the liner moved slowly toward the end of her dock that April

[2] **Southampton:** a seaport in the southern part of England.[3] **strakes:** breadths of planks or plates forming continuous strips on the bottom or sides of a ship. [4] **Belfast:** a city in Ireland where the *Titanic* was built. [5] **bollards:** upright wooden or iron posts around which to fasten a rope. [6] **triple-screw:** with three propellers. [7] **mold loft:** a large floor on which the lines of a vessel are laid down and molds made.

day, the surge of her passing sucked away from the quay[1] the steamer *New York,* moored just to seaward of the *Titanic's* berth. There were sharp cracks as the manila mooring lines of the *New York* parted under the strain. The frayed ropes writhed and whistled through the air and snapped down among the waving crowd on the pier; the *New York* swung toward the *Titanic's* bow, was checked and dragged back to the dock barely in time to avert a collision. Seamen muttered, thought it an ominous start.

Past Spithead[2] and the Isle of Wight[3] the *Titanic* steamed. She called at Cherbourg[4] at dusk and then laid her course for Queenstown.[5] At 1:30 P.M. on Thursday, April 11, she stood out of Queenstown harbor, screaming gulls soaring in her wake, with 2,201 persons — men, women, and children — aboard.

Occupying the Empire bedrooms and Georgian suites[6] of the first-class accommodations were many well-known men and women — Colonel John Jacob Astor and his young bride; Major Archibald Butt, military aide to President Taft, and his friend, Frank D. Millet, the painter; John B. Thayer, vice-president of the Pennsylvania Railroad, and Charles M. Hays, president of the Grand Trunk Railway of Canada; W. T. Stead, the English journalist; Jacques Futrelle, French novelist; H. B. Harris, theatrical manager, and Mrs. Harris; Mr. and Mrs. Isidor Straus; and J. Bruce Ismay, chairman and managing director of the White Star line.

[1] **quay:** solid landing place at the side of a navigable body of water. [2] **Spithead:** a strait of the English Channel between the southern coast of England and the Isle of Wight. [3] **Isle of Wight:** an island south of England. [4] **Cherbourg:** a seaport town in France. [5] **Queenstown:** a seaport in southern Ireland. [6] **Empire bedrooms and Georgian suites:** that is, bedrooms furnished in styles that prevailed in the first French Empire (1804–15) and suites furnished in styles that prevailed in the reign of the Georges, kings of England.

Down in the plain wooden cabins of the steerage class were 706 immigrants to the land of promise, and trimly stowed in the great holds was a cargo valued at $420,000: oak beams, sponges, wine, calabashes, and an odd miscellany of the common and the rare.

The *Titanic* took her departure on Fastnet Light and, heading into the night, laid her course for New York. She was due at Quarantine the following Wednesday morning.

Sunday dawned fair and clear. The *Titanic* steamed smoothly toward the west, faint streamers of brownish smoke trailing from her funnels. The purser held services in the salon in the morning; on the steerage deck aft the immigrants were playing games and a Scotsman was puffing "The Campbells Are Coming" on his bagpipes in the midst of the uproar.

At 9:00 A.M. a message from the steamer *Caronia* sputtered into the wireless shack:

> Captain, *Titanic* — Westbound steamers report bergs growlers and field ice in 42 degrees N. from 49 degrees to 51 degrees W. 12th April.
>
> Compliments —
>
> Barr.

It was cold in the afternoon; the sun was brilliant, but the *Titanic,* her screws turning over at seventy-five revolutions per minute, was approaching the Banks.

In the Marconi cabin Second Operator Harold Bride, earphones clamped on his head, was figuring accounts; he did not stop to answer when he heard *MWL,* Continental Morse for the near-by Leyland liner, *Californian,* calling the *Titanic.* The *Californian* had some message about three icebergs; he didn't bother then to take it down. About 1:42 P.M. the rasping spark[7] of those days spoke

[7] **rasping spark:** a reference to the crude radio signals of the time.

again across the water. It was the *Baltic,* calling the *Titanic,* warning her of ice on the steamer track. Bride took the message down and sent it up to the bridge.[1] The officer of the deck glanced at it, sent it to the bearded master of the *Titanic,* Captain E. C. Smith, a veteran of the White Star service. It was lunchtime then; the captain, walking along the promenade deck, saw Mr. Ismay, stopped, and handed him the message without comment. Ismay read it, stuffed it in his pocket, told two ladies about the icebergs, and resumed his walk. Later, about 7:15 P.M., the captain requested the return of the message in order to post it in the chartroom for the information of officers.

Dinner that night in the Jacobean dining room [2] was gay. It was bitter on deck, but the night was calm and fine; the sky was moonless but studded with stars twinkling coldly in the clear air.

After dinner some of the second-class passengers gathered in the saloon, where the Reverend Mr. Carter conducted a "hymn sing-song." It was almost ten o'clock and the stewards were waiting with biscuits and coffee as the group sang:

"O, hear us when we cry to Thee
For those in peril on the sea."

On the bridge Second Officer Lightoller — short, stocky, efficient — was relieved at ten o'clock by First Officer Murdoch. Lightoller had talked with other officers about the proximity of ice; at least five wireless ice warnings had reached the ship; lookouts had been cautioned to be alert; captain and officers expected to reach the field at any time after 9:30 P.M. At twenty-two knots,[3] its speed unslackened, the *Titanic* plowed on through the night.

Lightoller left the darkened bridge to his relief [4] and turned in. Captain Smith went to his cabin. The steerage was long since quiet; in the first and second cabins lights were going out; voices were growing still; people were asleep. Murdoch paced back and forth on the bridge, peering out over the dark water, glancing now and then at the compass in front of Quartermaster Hichens at the wheel.

In the crow's-nest Lookout Frederick Fleet and his partner, Leigh, gazed down at the water, still and unruffled in the dim, starlit darkness. Behind and below them the ship, a white shadow with here and there a last winking light; ahead of them a dark and silent and cold ocean.

There was a sudden clang. "Dong-dong. Dong-dong. Dong-dong. Dong!" The metal clapper of the great ship's bell struck out 11:30. Mindful of the warnings, Fleet strained his eyes, searching the darkness for the dreaded ice. But there were only the stars and the sea.

In the wireless room, where Phillips, first operator, had relieved Bride, the buzz of the *Californian's* set again crackled into the earphones:

Californian: "Say, old man, we are stuck here, surrounded by ice."

Titanic: Shut up, shut up; keep out. I am talking to Cape Race; [5] you are jamming my signals."

Then, a few minutes later — about 11:40 . . .

Out of the dark she came, a vast, dim, white, monstrous shape, directly in the *Titanic's* path. For a moment Fleet doubted his eyes. But she was a deadly reality, this ghastly *thing*. Frantically Fleet struck three bells — *something dead ahead.* He

[1] **bridge:** platform elevated above the rail and extending across the deck. [2] **Jacobean dining room:** a dining room furnished in the style characteristic of the time of James I of England.

[3] **knots:** nautical miles in reference to the speed of a ship. [4] **his relief:** the officer who relieved him. [5] **Cape Race:** in Newfoundland.

snatched the telephone and called the bridge:

"Iceberg! Right ahead!"

The first officer heard but did not stop to acknowledge the message.

"Hard-a-starboard!"[1]

Hichens strained at the wheel; the bow swing slowly to port.[2] The monster was almost upon them now.

Murdoch leaped to the engine-room telegraph. Bells clanged. Far below in the engine room those bells struck the first warning. Danger! The indicators on the dial faces swung round to "Stop!" Then "Full speed astern!" Frantically the engineers turned great valve wheels; answered the bridge bells. . . .

There was a slight shock, a brief scraping, a small list to port. Shell ice — slabs and chunks of it — fell on the foredeck. Slowly the *Titanic* stopped.

Captain Smith hurried out of his cabin. "What has the ship struck?"

Murdoch answered, "An iceberg, sir. I hard-a-starboarded and reversed the engines, and I was going to hard-a-port around it; but she was too close. I could not do any more. I have closed the watertight doors."

Fourth Officer Boxhall, other officers, the carpenter, came to the bridge. The captain sent Boxhall and the carpenter below to ascertain the damage.

A few lights switched on in the first and second cabins; sleepy passengers peered through porthole glass; some casually asked the stewards:

"Why have we stopped?"

"I don't know, sir, but I don't suppose it is anything much."

In the smoking room a quorum of gamblers and their prey were still sitting round a poker table; the usual crowd of kibitzers[3] looked on. They had felt the slight jar of the collision and had seen an eighty-foot ice mountain glide by the smoking-room windows; but the night was calm and clear, the *Titanic* was "unsinkable." They hadn't bothered to go on deck.

But far below, in the warren of passages on the starboard side forward, in the forward holds and boiler rooms, men could see that the *Titanic's* hurt was mortal. In No. 6 boiler room, where the red glow from the furnaces lighted up the naked, sweaty chests of coal-blackened firemen, water was pouring through a great gash about two feet above the floor plates. This was no slow leak; the ship was open to the sea; in ten minutes there were eight feet of water in No. 6. Long before then the stokers had raked the flaming fires out of the furnaces and had scrambled through the watertight doors in No. 5 or had climbed up the long steel ladders to safety. When Boxhall looked at the mailroom in No. 3 hold, twenty-four feet above the keel, the mailbags were already floating about in the slushing water. In No. 5 boiler room a stream of water spurted into an empty bunker. All six compartments forward of No. 4 were open to the sea; in ten seconds the iceberg's jagged claw had ripped a three-hundred-foot slash in the bottom of the great *Titanic*.

Reports came to the bridge; Ismay in dressing gown ran out on deck in the cold, still, starlit night, climbed up the bridge ladder.

"What has happened?"

Captain Smith: "We have struck ice."

"Do you think she is seriously damaged?"

Captain Smith: "I'm afraid she is."

Ismay went below and passed Chief Engineer William Bell fresh from an inspection of the damaged compartments. Bell corroborated the captain's statement, hurried back down the glistening

[1] **starboard:** the right side of a vessel (as one faces from stern to bow). [2] **port:** the left side of a vessel (as one faces from stern to bow). [3] **kibitzers:** onlookers.

steel ladders to his duty. Man after man followed him — Thomas Andrews, one of the ship's designers, Archie Frost, the builder's chief engineer, and his twenty assistants — men who had no posts of duty in the engine room but whose traditions called them there.

On deck, in corridor and stateroom, life flowed again. Men, women, and children awoke and questioned; orders were given to uncover the lifeboats; water rose into the firemen's quarters; half-dressed stokers streamed up on deck. But the passengers — most of them — did not know that the *Titanic* was sinking. The shock of the collision had been so slight that some were not awakened by it; the *Titanic* was so huge that she must be unsinkable; the night was too calm, too beautiful, to think of death at sea.

Captain Smith half ran to the door of the radio shack. Bride, partly dressed, eyes dulled with sleep, was standing behind Phillips, waiting.

"Send the call for assistance."

The blue spark danced: "CQD [1] — CQD — CQD — CQ —" Miles away Marconi men heard. Cape Race heard it, and the steamships *La Provence* and *Mt. Temple*.

The sea was surging into the *Titanic's* hold. At 12:20 the water burst into the seamen's quarters through a collapsed fore and aft wooden bulkhead.[2] Pumps strained in the engine rooms — men and machinery making a futile fight against the sea. Steadily the water rose.

The boats were swung out — slowly; for the deck hands were late in reaching their stations, there had been no boat drill, and many of the crew did not know to what boats they were assigned. Orders were shouted; the safety valves had lifted, and steam was blowing off in a great rushing roar. In the charthouse Fourth Officer Boxhall bent above a chart, working rapidly with pencil and dividers.

12:25 A.M. Boxhall's position is sent out to a fleet of vessels: "Come at once; we have struck a berg."

To the Cunarder [3] *Carpathia* (Arthur Henry Rostron, Master, New York to Liverpool, fifty-eight miles away): "It's a CQD, old man. Position 41–46 N.; 50–14 W." [4]

The blue spark dancing: "Sinking; cannot hear for noise of steam."

12:30 A.M. The word is passed: "Women and children in the boats." Stewards finish waking their passengers below; life preservers are tied on; some men smile at the precaution. "The *Titanic* is unsinkable." The *Mt. Temple* starts for the *Titanic;* the *Carpathia,* with a double watch in her stokeholds,[5] radios: "Coming hard." The CQD changes the course of many ships — but not of one; the operator of the *Californian,* near by, has just put down his earphones and turned in.

The CQD flashes over land and sea from Cape Race to New York; newspaper city rooms leap to life and presses whir.

On the *Titanic* water creeps over the bulkhead between Nos. 5 and 6 firerooms. She is going down by the head [6]; the engineers — fighting a losing battle — are forced back foot by foot by the rising water. Down the promenade deck Happy Jock Hume, the bandsman, runs with his instrument.

[1] **CQD:** the original code letters of the signal of distress, later changed to SOS. [2] **bulkhead:** upright partition separating the compartments of a ship.

[3] **Cunarder:** that is, of the Cunard Line, a well-known British steamship company. [4] **41–46 N.; 50–14 W.:** the position of the ship was 41 degrees, 46 minutes, North; 50 degrees, 14 minutes, West. Find this location on a map of the Atlantic Ocean. [5] **double watch in her stokeholds:** because of the emergency twice as many men as usual were set to work at firing the boilers. [6] **down by the head:** the ship was sinking bow first.

12:45 A.M. Murdoch, in charge on the starboard side, eyes tragic but calm and cool, orders boat No. 7 lowered. The women hang back; they want no boat ride on an ice-strewn sea. "The *Titanic* is unsinkable." The men encourage them, explain that this is just a precautionary measure. "We'll see you again at breakfast." There is little confusion; passengers stream slowly to the boat deck. In the steerage the immigrants chatter excitedly.

A sudden sharp hiss — a streaked flare against the night; Boxhall sends a rocket toward the sky. It explodes, and a parachute of white stars lights up the icy sea. "Rockets!" The band plays ragtime.

No. 8 is lowered, and No. 5. Ismay, still in dressing gown, calls for women and children, handles lines, stumbles in the way of an officer, is told to "get the hell out of here." Third Officer Pitman takes charge of No. 5; as he swings into the boat, Murdoch grasps his hand. "Good-by and good luck, old man."

No. 6 goes over the side. There are only twenty-eight people in a lifeboat with a capacity of sixty-five.

A light stabs from the bridge; Boxhall is calling in Morse flashes, again and again, to a strange ship stopped in the ice jam five to ten miles away. Another rocket drops its shower of sparks above the ice-strewn sea and the dying ship.

1:00 A.M. Slowly the water creeps higher; the foreports of the *Titanic* are dipping into the sea. Rope squeaks through blocks; lifeboats drop jerkily seaward. Through the shouting on the decks comes the sound of the band playing ragtime.

The "Millionaires' Special"[1] leaves the ship — boat No. 1, with a capacity of forty people, carries only Sir Cosmo and Lady Duff Gordon and ten others. Aft, the frightened immigrants mill and jostle and rush for a boat. An officer's fist flies out; three shots are fired in the air, and the panic is quelled. . . . Four Chinese sneak unseen into a boat and hide in its bottom.

1:20 A.M. Water is coming into No. 4 boiler room. Stokers[2] slice and shovel as water laps about their ankles — steam for the dynamos; steam for the dancing spark! As the water rises, great ash hoes rake the flaming coals from the furnaces. Safety valves pop; the stokers retreat aft, and the watertight doors clang shut behind them.

The rockets fling their splendor toward the stars. The boats are more heavily loaded now, for the passengers know the *Titanic* is sinking. Women cling and sob. The great screws aft are rising clear of the sea. Half-filled boats are ordered to come alongside the cargo ports and take on more passengers, but the ports are never opened — and the boats are never filled. Others pull for the steamer's light miles away but never reach it: the lights disappear; the unknown ship steams off.

The water rises and the band plays ragtime.

1:30 A.M. Lightoller is getting the port boats off; Murdoch, the starboard. As one boat is lowered into the sea, a boat officer fires his gun along the ship's side to stop a rush from the lower decks. A woman tries to take her Great Dane into a boat with her; she is refused and steps out of the boat to die with her dog. Millet's "little smile which played on his lips all through the voyage" plays no more; his lips are grim, but he waves good-by and brings wraps for the women.

Benjamin Guggenheim, in evening clothes, smiles and says, "We've dressed

[1] **"Millionaires' Special"**: a sarcastic reference to the lifeboat that left the ship with only a few rich, prominent people on board.

[2] **stokers**: men employed to tend a furnace and supply it with fuel.

up in our best and are prepared to go down like gentlemen."

1:40 A.M. Boat 14 is clear, and then 13, 16, 15, and C. The lights still shine, but the *Baltic* hears the blue spark say, "Engine room getting flooded."

The *Olympic* signals: "Am lighting up all possible boilers as fast as can."

Major Butt helps women into the last boats and waves good-by to them. Mrs. Straus puts her foot on the gunwale of a lifeboat, then she draws back and goes to her husband. "We have been together many years; where you go I will go." Colonel John Jacob Astor puts his young wife in a lifeboat, steps back, taps cigarette on fingernail. "Good-by, dearie; I'll join you later."

1:45 A.M. The foredeck is under water, the fo'c'sle head[1] almost awash; the great stern is lifted high toward the bright stars; and still the band plays. Mr. and Mrs. Harris approach a lifeboat arm in arm.

Officer: "Ladies first, please."

Harris bows, smiles, steps back. "Of course, certainly; ladies first."

Boxhall fires the last rocket, then leaves in charge of boat No. 2.

2:00 A.M. She is dying now; her bow goes deeper, her stern higher. But there must be steam. Below in the stokeholds the sweaty firemen keep steam up for the flaring lights and the dancing spark. The glowing coals slide and tumble over the slanted grate bars; the sea pounds behind that yielding bulkhead. But the spark dances on.

The *Asian* hears Phillips try the new signal — SOS.

Boat No. 4 has left now; boat D leaves ten minutes later. Jacques Futrelle clasps his wife. "For God's sake, go! It's your last chance; go!" Madame Futrelle is half forced into the boat. It clears the side.

There are about 660 people in the boats, and 1,500 still on the sinking *Titanic.*

On top of the officers' quarters men work frantically to get the two collapsibles stowed there over the side. Water is over the forward part of A deck now; it surges up the companionways toward the boat deck. In the radio shack Bride has slipped a coat and life jacket about Phillips as the first operator sits hunched over his key, sending — still sending — "41–46 N.; 50–14 W. CQD — CQD — SOS — SOS —"

The captain's tired white face appears at the radio-room door. "Men, you have done your full duty. You can do no more. Now, it's every man for himself." The captain disappears — back to his sinking bridge, where Painter, his personal steward, stands quietly waiting for orders. The spark dances on. Bride turns his back and goes into the inner cabin. As he does so, a stoker, grimed with coal, mad with fear, steals into the shack and reaches for the life jacket on Phillips's back. Bride wheels about and brains him with a wrench.

2:10 A.M. Below decks the steam is still holding, though the pressure is falling — rapidly. In the gymnasium on the boat deck the athletic instructor watches quietly as two gentlemen ride the bicycles and another swings casually at the punching bag. Mail clerks stagger up the boat-deck stairways, dragging soaked mail sacks. The spark still dances. The band still plays — but not ragtime:

> "Nearer my God to Thee,
> Nearer to Thee . . ."

A few men take up the refrain; others kneel on the slanting decks to pray. Many run and scramble aft, where hundreds are clinging above the silent screws

[1] **fo'c'sle head:** contraction of *forecastle head,* the forward part of the upper deck of a vessel in front of the foremast.

on the great uptilted stern. The spark still dances and the lights still flare; the engineers are on the job. The hymn comes to its close. Bandmaster Hartley, Yorkshireman violinist, taps his bow against a bulkhead, calls for "Autumn" as the water curls about his feet, and the eight musicians brace themselves against the ship's slant. People are leaping from the decks into the near-by water — the icy water. A woman cries, "Oh, save me, save me!" A man answers, "Good lady, save yourself. Only God can save you now." The band plays "Autumn":

"God of Mercy and Compassion!
Look with pity on my pain . . ."

The water creeps over the bridge where the *Titanic's* master stands; heavily he steps out to meet it.

2:17 A.M. "CQ —" The *Virginian* hears a ragged, blurred CQ, then an abrupt stop. The blue spark dances no more. The lights flicker out; the engineers have lost their battle.

2:18 A.M. Men run about blackened decks, leap into the night, are swept into the sea by the curling wave which licks up the *Titanic's* length. Lightoller does not leave the ship; the ship leaves him; there are hundreds like him, but only a few who live to tell of it. The funnels [1] still swim above the water, but the ship is climbing to the perpendicular [2]; the bridge is under and most of the foremast; the great stern rises like a squat leviathan. Men swim away from the sinking ship; others drop from the stern.

The band plays in the darkness, the water lapping upwards:

"Hold me up in mighty waters,
Keep my eyes on things above,
Righteousness, divine atonement,
Peace and everlas . . ."

[1] **funnels:** smokestacks. [2] **climbing to the perpendicular:** the bow was pointing straight down, the stern high in the air.

The forward funnel snaps and crashes into the sea; its steel tons hammer out of existence swimmers struggling in the freezing water. Streams of sparks, of smoke and steam, burst from the after funnels. The ship upends to 50 . . . to 60 degrees.

Down in the black abyss of the stokeholds, of the engine rooms, where the dynamos have whirred at long last to a stop, the stokers and the engineers are reeling against hot metal, the rising water clutching at their knees. The boilers, the engine cylinders, rip from their bedplates; crash through bulkheads; rumble — steel against steel.

The *Titanic* stands on end, poised briefly for the plunge. Slowly she slides to her grave — slowly at first, and then more quickly . . . quickly . . . quickly.

2:20 A.M. The greatest ship in the world has sunk. From the calm, dark waters, where the floating lifeboats move, there goes up, in the white wake of her passing, "one long continuous moan."

The boats that the *Titanic* had launched pulled safely away from the slight suction of the sinking ship, pulled away from the screams that came from the lips of the freezing men and women in the water. The boats were poorly manned and badly equipped, and they had been unevenly loaded. Some carried so few seamen that women bent to the oars. Mrs. Astor tugged at an oar handle; the Countess of Rothes took a tiller. Shivering stokers in sweaty, coal-blackened singlets and light trousers steered in some boats; stewards in white coats rowed in others. Ismay was in the last boat that left the ship from the starboard side; with Mr. Carter of Philadelphia and two seamen he tugged at the oars. In one of the lifeboats an Italian with a broken wrist — disguised in a woman's shawl and hat —

huddled on the floor boards, ashamed now that fear had left him. In another rode the only baggage saved from the *Titanic* — the carryall of Samuel L. Goldenberg, one of the rescued passengers.

There were only a few boats that were heavily loaded; most of those that were half empty made but perfunctory efforts to pick up the moaning swimmers, their officers and crew fearing they would endanger the living if they pulled back into the midst of the dying. Some boats beat off the freezing victims; fear-crazed men and women struck with oars at the heads of swimmers. One woman drove her fist into the face of a half-dead man as he tried feebly to climb over the gunwale. Two other women helped him in and stanched the flow of blood from the ring cuts on his face.

One of the collapsible boats, which had floated off the top of the officers' quarters when the *Titanic* sank, was an icy haven for thirty or forty men. The boat had capsized as the ship sank; men swam to it, clung to it, climbed upon its slippery bottom, stood knee-deep in water in the freezing air. Chunks of ice swirled about their legs; their soaked clothing clutched their bodies in icy folds. Colonel Archibald Gracie was cast up there. Gracie, who had leaped from the stern as the *Titanic* sank; young Thayer, who had seen his father die; Lightoller, who had twice been sucked down with the ship and twice blown to the surface by a belch of air; Bride, the second operator, and Phillips, the first. There were many stokers, half-naked; it was a shivering company. They stood there in the icy sea, under the far stars, and sang and prayed — the Lord's Prayer. After a while a lifeboat came and picked them off, but Phillips was dead then or died soon afterward in the boat.

Only a few of the boats had lights; only one — No. 2 — had a light that was of any use to the *Carpathia,* twisting through the ice field to the rescue. Other ships were "coming hard" too; one, the *Californian,* was still dead to opportunity.

The blue sparks still danced, but not the *Titanic's*. *La Provence* to *Celtic:* "Nobody has heard the *Titanic* for about two hours."

It was 2:40 when the *Carpathia* first sighted the green light from No. 2 boat; it was 4:10 when she picked up the first boat and learned that the *Titanic* had foundered. The last of the moaning cries had just died away then.

Captain Rostron took the survivors aboard, boatload by boatload. He was ready for them, but only a small minority of them required much medical attention. Bride's feet were twisted and frozen; others were suffering from exposure; one died, and seven were dead when taken from the boats, and were buried at sea.

It was then that the fleet of racing ships learned they were too late; the *Parisian* heard the weak signals of *MPA,* the *Carpathia,* report of the death of the *Titanic*. It was then — or soon afterward, when her radio operator put on his earphones — that the *Californian,* the ship that had been within sight as the *Titanic* was sinking, first learned of the disaster.

And it was then, in all its white-green majesty, that the *Titanic's* survivors saw the iceberg, tinted with the sunrise, floating idly, pack ice jammed about its base, other bergs heaving slowly near by on the blue breast of the sea.

But it was not until later that the world knew; for wireless then was not what wireless is today, and garbled messages had nourished a hope that all of the *Titanic's* company were safe. Not until Monday evening, when P. A. S. Franklin, vice-president of the International Mercantile Marine Company, received relayed messages in New York that left little hope, did the full extent of the disaster begin to be known. Partial and garbled lists of the survivors; rumors of heroism and cowardice; stories spun out of newspaper imagination, based on a few bare facts and many false reports, misled the world, terrified and frightened it. It was not until Thursday night, when the *Carpathia* steamed into the North River, that the full truth was pieced together.

Flashlights flared on the black river when the *Carpathia* stood up to her dock. Tugs nosed about her, shunted her toward Pier 54. Thirty thousand people jammed the streets; ambulances and stretchers stood on the pier; coroners and physicians waited.

In midstream the Cunarder dropped over the *Titanic's* lifeboats; then she headed toward the dock. Beneath the customs letters on the pier stood relatives of the 711 survivors, relatives of the missing — hoping against hope. The *Carpathia* cast her lines ashore; stevedores looped them over bollards. The dense throngs stood quiet as the first survivors stepped down the gangway. The woman half staggered — led by customs guards — beneath her letter.[1] A " low wailing " moan came from the crowd, fell, grew in volume, and dropped again.

Thus ended the maiden voyage of the *Titanic*. The lifeboats brought to New York by the *Carpathia*, a few deck chairs and gratings awash in the ice field off the Grand Banks[2] eight hundred miles from shore, were all that was left of the world's greatest ship.

[1] **letter:** when ships dock, each passenger's baggage is assembled and inspected by customs officers at a place designated by the initial of the passenger's name. [2] **Grand Banks:** the famous fishing waters off the coast of Newfoundland.

THINK BACK OVER WHAT YOU HAVE READ

Appreciating the Heroism Displayed in the Story

1. The following persons are mentioned directly in the account of the sinking of the *Titanic*. Of what does their bravery consist? What is the common element to be found in their heroism? Which persons belong, in your opinion, on a special roll of honor? Why?

THE SHIP'S CREW

Captain Smith
First Officer Murdoch
Second Officer Lightoller
Fourth Officer Boxhall
Quartermaster Hichens
Lookout Fleet and his partner, Leigh
First Operator Phillips
Second Operator Bride
Bandmaster Hartley
Bandsman Hume

PASSENGERS

Major Butt, military aide to President Taft
Benjamin Guggenheim
Mrs. Straus
Colonel and Mrs. John Jacob Astor
Frank D. Millet, painter
The Countess of Rothes

2. To what groups of people would you offer special commendation for heroic sacrifice?

3. What examples can you cite to show that courage sometimes appears where you least expect it? Did it always appear just where you did expect it? Where?

Appreciating the Tragic Irony to Be Found in the Story

4. Under what bad omen did the *Titanic* set out from Southampton?

5. What were the " superlative qualities " which made the *Titanic* seem so utterly safe?

6. What was ironic about the Reverend Mr. Carter's choice of hymn for his evening " sing-song "?

7. What irony lies in Phillips's reply to the *Californian:* " Shut up . . . keep out . . . you are jamming my signals "?

8. What brave jests are uttered in farewell?

Appreciating the Style in Which the Story is Told

9. What effect is produced by the periodic mention of time between 11:40 P.M. and 2:20

A.M.? Is something gained by this device? What?

10. How is detail handled in the story? Does the author linger over gruesome detail? Does he hurry over it? omit it entirely? What passage can you quote which to your mind shows just the right amount of restraint — neither too much nor too little detail? What, in this story, is *enough* detail? enough for what?

11. How might an amateur have bungled this story? To what kind of excess does the story lend itself?

DID YOU NOTICE HOW THE SHORT STORIES WERE TOLD?

Almost everything we do, we do in a particular way — a way that makes a difference not only to ourselves but to those who observe us. We walk, perhaps, in an awkward, ungainly manner. We hit a ball in clumsy, blundering fashion. Or we run gracefully, laugh good-naturedly, or smile understandingly.

Everything that is made, furthermore, is made in a special way — a way that furthers a particular end. Houses are designed in relation to climate, location, or the kind of life which is to be lived in them. Dresses and suits are cut to a particular pattern — a pattern appropriate to sportswear, evening wear, or street wear. There is hardly a phase of life that is not composed of a *what* and a *how:* a *what* is made, or done, or said; and a *how* it is made or done or said.

Thus everything that you speak or write is spoken or written in a particular manner, and *how you say it* is at times more eloquent in expressing your true meaning than is *what you say.* For example, you can say *yes* in such a way as to indicate *no;* you can say *please* or *thank you* grudgingly, generously, or irritably. Every idea which you express, furthermore, might have been expressed in a different manner — a manner more or less suitable, a manner more or less effective, than that in which you did express it. You might have expressed your opinion about a book less positively and more open-mindedly. You might have told an anecdote more pointedly, more dramatically.

Similarly every idea which you meet in your reading has been offered to you in a particular form — a form which either increases your satisfaction in what you read or decreases it. Perhaps you do not ordinarily pay much conscious attention to *how* a story has been presented to you; quite probably you are only vaguely aware of the style in which the author has written. Yet had the story been told differently you might not have liked it so well. Indeed, the chief reason you enjoyed it, or failed to enjoy it, might very well have been due to the way in which it was told.

Here, then, is an idea for you to consider as you review this first section of the book: How have the authors told their stories? In just the right way to give maximum power to their ideas?

Before attempting to answer these questions it is well to remember that, although a story is in itself a particular way of communicating an impression, there are many different ways of telling stories and that no single way is the best way. To ask that a story always be told in the old, familiar way — the way that we have learned to follow with ease — is to defeat at the outset a growing interest in form. Thus, instead of looking always for the usual form, we should look for the appropriate form — the form best suited to the author's purpose in telling the story.

By this time you are aware that behind each different type of story lies a different purpose. And you wouldn't expect "That's What Happened to Me" to follow the same pattern as "The Masque of the Red Death."

These two stories, so different in form, have only three elements in common —

elements which they share with all stories. Both have (1) *characters;* both have (2) *setting;* and both *move* toward the accomplishment of the author's purpose (in technical language we call this movement (3) *plot*). Each author, however, puts his own value on these elements: Poe stresses setting, while Fessier stresses character. And each uses *plot* in quite his own way. There is practically no similarity between the way Poe's story moves majestically toward its destined goal and the way Fessier's story meanders along the path of reminiscence. Each story *moves* at a pace determined by the author's purpose.

Sometimes an author's purpose is to express an idea. When such an idea is more or less openly stated, the story is said to have (4) a *theme.* Sometimes, as in " Under the Lion's Paw," the theme is revealed in the title.

The following questions, based on the twenty short stories just completed, are intended to help you think about the form of the short story. Previously in your reading you have been thinking not so much about form as about content. Now that you know *what* each author says, it should prove interesting to discuss with your classmates the manner or style in which the author has communicated his thought to you. The following questions, to be used as a basis for review of the short story, will help you:

1. Of what would you say Wodehouse humor consists? Wherein does the humor of " Jeeves and the Yuletide Spirit " differ from that of " Mr. K*a*p*l*a*n the Magnificent "?

2. Which of the five humorous stories depend for their humor chiefly on amusing incident? In which ones does the humor center in character? Who are the funny people whose oddities you can't help remembering?

3. On what grounds is poor English acceptable in the story " On the Dodge "? What would the story lose were its inaccuracies corrected?

4. What purpose, vital to the story, do the descriptions serve in these stories: " The White Tiger," " The Wind Fighters," " Sleet Storm "? On what basis can you justify the almost complete absence of description in " The Revolt of Mother "?

5. What is the special manner in which " That's What Happened to Me " is told? What is the author's purpose in telling the story? How does the form in which he tells the story serve that purpose?

6. On what basis can you justify the ending of " Now There Is Peace "? Why can't the story end happily? What is its theme? In what sense would you say that " The Masque of the Red Death " ends satisfactorily? What, then, is a " good " ending? Can you formulate for yourself a basis for judging? Try it.

7. Why is it impossible to compare the stories " On the Dodge " and " Under the Lion's Paw " and to say that the first mentioned is a " better " story than the second? What would you say in reply to a junior-high-school student who said that " On the Dodge " is the best short story in this whole book?

8. What device did the author of " Twenty Cigarettes " use to make you feel keenly the fateful passing of time? Within what unit of time is his story made to fit? What device is used for a similar purpose by the author of " R. M. S. *Titanic* "? Into what unit of time does this tragic story fit?

9. What justification do you see for the use of big, rare words in " The Masque of the Red Death "? for the simple, ordinary diction in " The Monkey's Paw "? Suppose Poe were to have written the latter story? In what particulars would it have turned out to be a different story altogether? It might be fun to speculate.

10. On what grounds can you praise the restraint shown in " R. M. S. *Titanic* "? How might a less skillful writer have ruined the story?

11. In which stories does interest center in setting? in characterization? in theme?

12. In which stories were you most interested in what finally happened? Compare the different rates at which these stories *moved.* What story would you rate as a fast-moving story? a slow-moving story? On what basis can you justify such fast or slow movement?

13. In which of the stories did you feel an absence of sharp climax? How can you justify it? In which stories did you feel the most suspense? the least? How would you answer the student who said of any story, " Aw, it wasn't exciting enough "?

CHRONICLES OF EXPERIENCE

ANY PROSE writing that does not tell an imaginary story is a record of some form of human experience. Biography, autobiography, history, essay, oratory, scientific writing, travel, philosophy, magazine and newspaper articles — all are the outgrowth of man's thought, study, or activity. They appeal, through almost endless subject matter, to a wide variety of readers, attempting to satisfy the desire for limitless knowledge and entertainment. In the selections which follow, you will find examples of several of these types, notably the essay, biography, and autobiography.

The essay. You will come to appreciate essays more readily, perhaps, if you will think of them as good conversation. Imagine yourself listening to an entertaining talker. For the essay has much in common with good talk; indeed, some of our greatest essays were originally delivered as lectures. Like conversation, the essay may be long or short; it may be light or serious; it may deal with any kind of subject. Like conversation, its purpose is to inform, to influence, or to amuse. Furthermore, to be effective, it must be well written. A badly written essay can hold our attention no better than a dull conversation. Therefore, the essay must be composed in an effective style if its author wishes our attention. It is like conversation in another respect also: it is always highly personal, reflecting the personal feelings, opinions, experiences of the author. That, perhaps more than any other reason, is why we read essays. We meet so many charming and interesting people. This personal touch is, of course, more evident in the light, informal essays than in the more serious, informative ones — just as informal conversations reveal personality more readily than formal orations. Nevertheless, essays are *always* personal to a degree.

Another interest that we find in essays is their reflection of our own tastes. You are going to like some of the essays in this collection better than others because certain ones speak of things in which you are particularly interested. Perhaps you love adventure. If so, you will thrill to the air exploits of St. Exupéry. Are you interested in science? Then you will read with interest the story of Beebe's exploration of the ocean floor. Do you like the exciting and dramatic? What a treat is in store for you when you help round up the cattle on a Western ranch. Or perhaps you prefer a bit of good-natured fun and humor. Then Clarence Day will give you many a hearty laugh. So you see it will be great fun reading these essays, for you will become acquainted with really interesting people and share their lives and thoughts and feelings.

Biography. From the earliest days, people have been inspired by the lives of famous figures. Almost from the beginning of literature, biography has occupied an important place. The Bible is a storehouse of biography with its lives of Joseph and Moses and Joshua and Daniel and Jesus. All the ancient literatures are rich in biography, and on the very threshold of English history we find a life of Alfred the Great written by a man named Asser.

In spite of its long record, however, biography did not, with a few notable exceptions, reach a very high state of excellence until recent times. The older biographies were too prone to glorify their subjects, recording only the pleasant and favorable aspects of their lives. Writers of biography took the position of "see no evil, hear no evil, speak no evil" about their heroes; only the worthy and good should be mentioned. As a result, those heroes lack human qualities; they are one-sided and unreal. Indeed, it was not until the latter part of the eighteenth century that biography became a vital form of literature. Dr. Samuel Johnson, the compiler of the first English dictionary, had recently died. One of his closest friends had been James Boswell, a Scotch lawyer. Boswell had spent years in daily comradeship with Johnson. He had accompanied him to the theater; he had listened to him converse in his club; he had observed him in the little, everyday events of life. He came to know his virtues and his faults. He took copious notes on his very words. On Johnson's death Boswell, in *The Life of Samuel Johnson*, wrote of the man, not as a glorified hero, but as a living human being with a human being's strength and weakness.

In spite of this great example, however, it was not until the twentieth century that the principle of honest character analysis was applied to biography. The writer who set the pace for what is frequently called the "new biography" was the Englishman Lytton Strachey, whose life of Queen Victoria was the first of a multitude of notable biographies that have subsequently appeared. Today biographers try to find the real character of their subjects — be it good or bad or both — and report it faithfully and entertainingly. For this reason modern biography has torn away much of the false glitter from the imposing figures of history and has shown us the real men and women underneath. George Washington, for example, in the modern treatment, is no longer a saint who "cannot tell a lie." He is a man of flesh and blood with a man's failings as well as virtues. Therefore, he appears as a real man.

Why do we read biography? Largely because most of us like to know as intimately as we can those great people of the earth who have done so much to shape the destiny of the world. We find in the lives and characters of the great much to inspire and encourage our own way of life. We enjoy a certain satisfaction in seeing ourselves — our hopes, our ambitions, our dreams — expressed in those personalities who have achieved the things we dream of and so demonstrate the truth that dreaming is not in vain.

Therefore, you will find much to admire in the people whose acquaintance you are about to make: the rugged frontiersman, Davy Crockett, the greatest hunter of the West and hero of the Alamo; the heroic Byrd, who has flown to both poles and who has done more than any living man to uncover the secrets of the great Antarctic Continent; the scientist Bruce, who, patient and painstaking, found the cause of sleeping sickness and thus gave life and hope to the natives of tropical Africa. These and others you will come to know, and you will find them worth knowing.

Autobiography. Closely akin to biography is autobiography, the story of a person's life told by himself. Though far less critical than biography, autobiography is much more personal, for we are enabled to see life through the actor's eyes. Much of the great adventure literature of the world has been written by those who lived through the adventures and, therefore, are in a position to make them more real to us.

In the selections which follow, you will read examples of the essay, biography, and autobiography. They will interest you because they are the records of many human experiences. By imagining yourself in the place of each actor, you will share vicariously the rich rewards of those experiences.

Interesting People

DAVY CROCKETT

by Constance Rourke (1885–)

I. CRADLED IN A SNAPPING TURTLE'S SHELL

In this first chapter from *Davy Crockett* you will experience the difficult life of the men and women who settled in the wilderness of Tennessee in the eighteenth century. Imagine yourself living in one of the early settlements. Around you are dense forests, peopled by restless savages who seem friendly enough but who may at any time descend upon your home with the evil purpose of killing you and those whom you love. Few schoolhouses offer you an education. You must work hard in the scanty clearing to help raise a few vegetables and a little grain. Most of your food must be supplied by the game with which the woods abound. When you travel, no automobile or train will take you whizzing over the country; instead, you must make slow progress in a lumbering wagon or in a flatboat on the river. Such hardships had a way of developing strong, self-reliant men skilled in the none-too-easy art of mastering life.

From the very beginning of his life Davy Crockett was a son of this wilderness. What that wilderness had to teach him you will discover in the selection that follows.

IN THE early summer of 1673 a small party of white men floated in two canoes down the wide waters of the Mississippi. They had passed the mouth of the Ohio, and soon discovered rising bluffs on the eastern shore of the great river. Presently Indians were seen among the trees, armed and observant. They belonged to a small tribe ruled by the powerful Chickasaws. The travelers spoke to them in the Huron [1] language, which this tribe did not understand, and held aloft a feathered calumet [2] given them by the Illinois Indians to the north for use as a friendly sign on their journey. The white men landed, were welcomed, and joined the tribe in a feast of buffalo meat, bear's oil, and delicious white plums.

The travelers were Father Marquette

[1] **Huron:** an Indian tribe. [2] **calumet:** Indian pipe, used as a symbol of peace.

and Sieur Jolliet,[1] and the country they briefly visited along its western boundary was later to be known as Tennessee.

In the same year, perhaps in the same month, a young man named James Needham entered the Tennessee country from the east, coming from Virginia. Explorers had long believed that somewhere beyond the Appalachian Mountains lay a great body of water which they called the South Sea. With eight Indians and a white servant Needham crossed the mountains, following ancient buffalo paths and trails, and at last from an escarpment of the Blue Ridge he saw, not a great sea, but wide rolling valleys where clear waters coursed down the green lower hills like long sprays of silvery fern.

Descending, Needham crossed many small streams and paused at the Cherokee[2] village, where his party was hospitably received. He was probably the first white man to enter the Tennessee country from the east. On a second journey into this region he was killed by an Indian servant, and it was many years before other white men ventured there again.

For almost another century this rich land remained in the possession of the Indians. On the east, in the valleys bordering Virginia and the Carolinas, were the Cherokees. To the south, in the broad territory that was to become Georgia and Alabama and Mississippi, the Creeks[3] held sway. To the west, where Father Marquette had landed, the Chickasaws still flourished. To the north was that dark and bloody ground called Kentucky, where no Indians dwelt but where many came for hunting.

Slowly white men made their way from the eastern colonies into the Tennessee country, as fur traders and trappers, and for the land — to seize great tracts of it but not to dwell there. Then the American Revolution began. The battle of King's Mountain[4] was fought, and before the Revolution was ended a few settlers had come over the Blue Ridge from the Carolinas and Virginia to build cabins.

Among these was a David Crockett, of sound stock and Irish descent, with his wife and grown sons and daughters, some of them married with children of their own. Either Crockett or his son John — perhaps both — had fought at the battle of King's Mountain. With this David Crockett's gear was "a parsel of books," weighing fifteen pounds. The family settled in the valley of the Nolachucky, not far from the mountains they had crossed, on land from which the Cherokees had receded.

A roving band of Creeks or Cherokees descended swiftly one day and killed the older Crockett, his wife, and some of his children, wounded one son, left him for dead, and carried off another. John Crockett and his family were living only a few miles distant, at the mouth of the Limestone where it pours into the Nolachucky, but the Indians did not attack his cabin. A short time after the raid, on the seventeenth of August, 1786, a son was born in this cabin to John and Rebecca Crockett, their ninth child. He was named for his grandfather, David, and he became the famous Davy Crockett of American history and legend.

John Crockett was unlucky. He built a mill on a small creek to grind corn for his distant neighbors, and in a stormy April the mill was carried away by high water. He moved to a point on the Holston near a ford where a trail from the Blue Ridge

[1] **Father Marquette and Sieur Jolliet:** early French explorers of the Mississippi River. [2] **Cherokee:** an Indian tribe. [3] **Creeks:** members of an Indian tribe.

[4] **King's Mountain:** a decisive battle near the close of the Revolutionary War fought at King's Mountain in South Carolina, October 7, 1780.

crossed the river and wound away through the forest. This was to become the road from Abingdon to Knoxville. Here he established a small tavern, a humble affair of logs with a few rudely partitioned rooms.

The country was still wild. Deep buffalo paths showed, leading to salt licks,[1] though the herds were gone. Deer ranged through glades and thickets. Panthers crouched in tall sycamores. Wildcats were at home there. Black bears crept into hollow trees. Settlers in the new country were buried in corners of the river valleys with cabins far apart, each with a small tract chopped out of the wilderness.

In spite of warring Indians they soon began to raise small surplus crops and to set cattle grazing in the rich silky grass of the meadows. There was a stir, a small bit of trade, as drovers and hunters passed the tavern. Settlers would sometimes gather from a distance of forty miles for a frolic — a dance, with songs, jovial drinking, fighting, and games of marksmanship. Stories were told of encounters with the Indian enemy. Young Davy heard many such tales, and he could decide for himself whether to believe some of them.

A man who stayed one night at the tavern told of a brush with some Indians late one summer's day when he had finished cutting his clover field. He had hung his scythe on a hickory limb and was on his way to the barn for his oxen when one of his dogs growled. He turned and saw some Indians swiftly gathering up his cocks of clover. He knew that if they stole the clover they would probably come back that night and burn his cabin. From the shelter of his barn he took aim and picked off one, then four more as they scattered.

[1] **salt licks:** places to which animals come for salt.

Since a few black and copper heads were still popping up among the clover cocks, he dashed at them with rifle and scythe. The clover field became a small battlefield. The ground was wet with Indian blood.

" And do you know," said the settler slowly, " the next year a double crop of Indian grass came up with my clover? Every tuft of it was stiff and sharp like an Indian scalplock,[2] and all the clover heads were copper red! "

" Haw! " said a man in a corner, and the ring of laughter went up in the tavern.

Together, Tennessee and Kentucky made a land of marvels. Stories were told of a great race who lived there before the Indians, and of strange caves in the mountains to the west. Many tales were told of curious animals. Huge snapping turtles of western Tennessee were talked about, with shells as big as kegs, heads as big as a boy's head, and a swift snap of the jaws when annoyed. This snapping turtle — the alligator terrapin — became a symbol of the touchy hunter of the West, quick and savage in his own defense.

There was always high talk of hunting and marksmanship. " Why, I know a man can nick the edges of a silver shilling at three hundred yards," said a hunter, lounging in front of the tavern.

" I know one that can cut the string of a kite as it flies out of eyesight," said another, " or bring down a wild goose flying."

Overhead in early spring great flocks of gray wild geese might be seen going north, their long necks with heavy black banding outstretched, far out of range. In the thick of the forest a flock of red and green parakeets would rise suddenly

[2] **scalplock:** a long tuft of hair left on the crown of the head by the warriors of certain Indian tribes.

from a tree, startled by Davy's approach, then settle again in a brightly colored shower.

Davy's father let him have a long rifle and a single load and ball and powder when he was eight years old. With this he could go out any day. If he missed, he went without his dinner. Soon he was bringing home a squirrel or possum. Once he slipped away with the rifle and caught sight of a small fat bear cub in a thicket and rashly took aim. A she-bear seemed to rise out of the ground. He knew enough not to prolong the encounter. Holding fast to the heavy rifle, he ran with the angry she-bear after him. The thicket was more favorable to a bear's progress than a boy's, and he would probably have been overtaken had not the little cub raised a sharp whining howl. The bear stopped, listened, turned. Davy had his advantage and, reaching an open space, sped away.

The boy was of small use about the tavern, carrying water or holding strangers' horses. His father called him quirky. Out in the forest, when his single round of ammunition was gone, there were always sounds to be listened to — faint rustles, breathings, the cry of birds and small animals. The danger of Indian raids still lingered; all sounds were important. Gradually the boy came to distinguish between many of them, delicately. Soon he was mimicking many birds and small beasts.

When he was not in the forest hunting he was on the river, paddling a canoe up to the edge of white water where the current might take him over steep falls, then skillfully and suddenly whirling, pushing far upstream, watching for small turtles on the gravelly bottom, sometimes snaring fish. He was hardy and muscular with bold features. His color was high, his eyes and hair dark. In fringed deerskin he looked like a young Indian. He could run like an Indian.

Some hunters were talking as young Davy rode in a canoe, alone on the river.

"That lad could float down all the rivers of Tennessee to the Mississippi, paddling with his hands and an old horn spoon."

"I heard he was cradled in a snapping turtle's shell."

"I heard that cradle had a pair of elk's horns over the top. With an alligator skin over the horns. And a wildcat's skin for a pillow!"

Perhaps this hunter had heard of an infant named Hercules.[1] Or he may have followed his own fancy. In any case, labors lay ahead of young Davy that were not much to his liking.

THINK BACK OVER WHAT YOU HAVE READ

Learning the Lessons of the Forest with Davy

1. In what ways did the scattered settlers find amusement? Which of these amusements, do you think, helped in the education of young Davy?

2. In what practical way did Davy's father teach his son self-dependence? Was his method a good one? Why? Have you ever been taught to do anything by similar methods? What? Tell the class about it.

3. What valuable lessons did Crockett learn in the forests? Why do so few people today gain that kind of information? What is its value?

4. If you are a Boy Scout, tell what the Scout organization is doing to reawaken interest in woodcraft.

Sensing the Pioneer Spirit

5. What motives led white men to go to Tennessee? When did the real settlement of the country begin?

6. What amusing story, told by one of the

[1] **Hercules:** the fabulous strong man of Greek mythology. Many stories were told of his strength even as an infant.

settlers, is typical of the exaggeration that characterized many of the tales told?

7. What animal became a symbol of the pioneer hunters? Why? How was this animal later associated with Crockett?

8. What qualities were most highly valued in the men of the region? Can you explain why? Would they be so highly regarded today?

II. ALONG THE RIVERS

In your study of history surely you have noticed that many of the greatest men were those who were forced to overcome great hardships and handicaps. Hardship is a splendid character builder, and our hardy pioneers developed a strength of character that did much to mold the destiny of America. Perhaps you have found in your own experience that the things hard to do were best worth doing. You may have noticed, too, that those schoolmates for whom life is not easy are often the ones who make the most of opportunities which your school offers.

Davy Crockett was the product of the difficult life of which you have read in the preceding chapter. Reared in the wilderness, he quickly learned the practical lessons that a hard existence taught. But his education was not wholly that of the forests, for at the age of twelve he left his home to accompany a German farmer to the latter's plantation in Virginia. He did not remain there long but wandered about the East on one mission or another, getting as far as Baltimore. At last, however, he made his way homeward over the Blue Ridge Mountains. Once home, he worked on the farm of a kindly Quaker who sent him to school in the winter months, thus providing him with a scanty formal education. As he approached manhood, he began to think of striking out on his own, especially since he had found the girl whom he desired to marry.

Let us now follow him, in his young married life, along the rivers to a new home.

WHEN THE grain was reaped and flax pulled there were frolics in the neighborhood, and this lively stripling was warmly welcomed at such gatherings. "Nobody can dance longer or sing longer or get into more scrapes than that lad of Crockett's," said a neighbor.

The Quaker did not approve of these gaieties. "Thee'd best stay at home," he told Davy. "Thee's bound to be a rolling stone, I fear, for all that thee can bend thy back and work hard. Thee's as mettlesome as my bay mare."

One night Davy let himself down from his attic by a thick strand of grapevine, and borrowed the bay mare, and went to a frolic. All his life he was a dancer; one of the last glimpses we have of him is at a dancing party at a little frontier post in Texas, where he footed it gaily with some charming ladies. The dances of the day were bold and free; but young Crockett's tall figure must have had a sturdy grace, for someone who saw him said that when he bowed before a certain pretty girl he bent like a young sapling swept by the south wind.

The two were partners in the dances, and Davy believed from what the girl said before the evening was over that she would be willing to marry him. A few days later he walked at evening several miles to the cabin where she lived. She was not to be seen in the clearing as he came up. Instead, a knot of men was gathered there, talking. Among them was the girl's father. David did not wish to make his errand known in so many words, so he asked, "Has anybody here seen a bay filly?"

The men guffawed, and someone told him that the fickle young woman had ridden away to Kentucky with a man she had married the day before. Davy walked away speechless, and decided that he was born only for misery.

But he had perfected his skill with the rifle in the few years since he had returned to Tennessee, and it happened that only a few days before he had been lucky at a shooting match. To watch his neat and dexterous movements as he handled his hunting tools was to watch a skilled craftsman. He would quickly blow through the rifle barrel to make sure that it was clear, glance at his flint, and thrust a feather through the touchhole. With a turn of the wrist and fingers he put in a bullet and filled the powder pan. His long, flexible lift of the gun, his easy swift aim, and the accommodating drop of the rifle as he fired seemed a single curving movement. He had already walked away with many small prizes in the neighborhood. This time a prime beef had been offered at a match, and David, shooting from longer and longer distances, had shot against a crowd of older men of the neighborhood. He had ended by winning the whole beef and had sold it for five dollars in gold. He was seldom low-spirited for long; and he still had the money, which seemed a little fortune. As he thought of it and considered the hundred agreeable things for which it might be spent, his spirits rose.

He forgot about the girl who had jilted him, and when another frolic was announced he was earliest on the ground. There was to be a great reaping and flax pulling, and all the young men and women from clearings for miles around were to gather for the work. The frolic was to follow.

The day began with yellow sunlight pouring down and only enough wind to stir the grain in gentle waves. David joined the reapers; the songs of the men and boys could be heard rising above the swish of the reap hooks. In another field the girls were pulling flax, vying with each other to see who would finish soonest. When the grain was cut and stacked, the men strolled over to the flax field. Each chose a girl and helped her end her task. Each pair then became partners for the frolic. David chose a fair-haired, blue-eyed girl named Polly Finley.

Negro slaves made the music at the frolics, thrumming a banjo or playing an old fiddle, shaking the bones, calling the tunes and changes of step. Some of them sat in the corner of the cabin at the reaping party, singing to fiddle tunes. The bones sounded a quick rat-tat-tat that set every foot shaking, and a few of the company led out, with the rest joining in the chorus of the song. But the great swing of the party was not within the cabin. All soon were out of doors where bran of Indian meal had been strewn over the ground to make it smooth, and tall trees formed shadowy walls. Pitch-pine torches cast a thick yellow light.

The figures of the girls were not squeezed in fashion's mold, nor were their feet encased within the light prunella.[1] Most of the company were barefoot. All wore homespun. They danced as though they would never tire. Play-party songs like " Sell the Thimble " and " Grind the Bottle " and " We're on the Way to Baltimore " were sung and danced. Davy knew the way to Baltimore well, but this was a pleasanter journey than the one he had taken. The dance was wild and irregular, with slow and measured steps for the line of the chorus:

We're on our way to Baltimore,
With two behind and two before,
Around, around, around we go,
Where oats, peas, beans, and barley grow,
In waiting for somebody.

'Tis thus the farmer sows his seed,
Folds his arms and takes his ease,
Stamps his feet, and claps his hands,
Wheels around, and thus he stands,
In waiting for somebody.

Some of the boys and girls had picked up steps from the Negroes and could dance the double shuffle and the double trouble. Reels from Scotland and Ireland were played and sung in new keys with new words.

With his young partner Davy was quick at the lively steps. The pair was readiest when the turns were called,

[1] **prunella:** a smooth woolen material used for the uppers of shoes.

loudest in the singing. They danced the night through, and when Davy climbed to the Quaker's attic at dawn he was betrothed to Polly Finley and he was sure this time there was to be no mistake.

He was now past eighteen. Marriages took place early in the new country. His own people were willing to have him marry. To set himself up for farming he bargained with the Quaker's son to purchase a horse, for which he was to work six months.

Toward the end of this time, when the marriage papers had been drawn and the infare for the bride arranged at John Crockett's tavern, Mrs. Finley declared that Davy should not have her daughter. She would give no reason.

Davy turned to the girl. " I'll come to you next Thursday on horseback, leading a horse," he told her squarely, " and you must be ready to go with me."

The following Thursday he set out with two of his brothers and their wives, and two young men who were to be his waiters at the wedding. When they came to the Finleys' cabin, they found Mrs. Finley as unwilling as ever to let her daughter go. But the girl's father — who is said to have been descended from the house of Macbeth — firmly gave his consent. The parson was sent for, the wedding took place. Afterward at John Crockett's there was a great infare or wedding frolic to receive the bride.

Later Mrs. Finley explained that she had only dreaded to lose her daughter. In a fine good humor she gave the pair two cows and two calves. This was a small marriage portion; but Polly's wheel and loom were added, and Polly was a good weaver. The Quaker gave David a substantial order at the store for such things as his wife could use. Davy rented a small farm, and in little or no time Polly Crockett had woven a fine web of cloth and had it ready to make up.

" She's good at that," Davy boasted, " and at pretty near everything else a woman can do."

They lived for some years in a small cabin on a rented farm, but farming was less than ever to young Crockett's taste. He complained that he could never make a fortune that way. He hunted, but now the country round about the Holston was becoming too well settled for wild life. Stone houses had been built, and men often came over the eastern mountains in fine chaises. The road to Knoxville was steadily traveled.

Davy and Polly soon had two little boys. " I want my boys to grow up in new country," said Davy, " and learn to hunt. I want to hunt myself. It's best to be gone."

He resolved to take up wild land in the Duck and Elk River country, over the Cumberland Mountains in southern Tennessee.

" Thee's going to roll," said the Quaker when he heard this news, " as I said. Thee'll never make a farmer, I fear, but perhaps thee'll become the greatest hunter in the West." Davy smiled and said he couldn't change his mind.

In the spring he packed a few pieces of household gear on two well-grown colts. Polly and the two little boys rode the old horse, and with Davy and a pair of dogs on foot the family set out early for a point on the Holston where they would take passage on a flatboat. This was the river country of the West, and most men traveled by the rivers when they could.

Arks, broadhorns, flatboats — each of these names was given them — might now be seen on the smaller streams as well as on the Ohio and the Mississippi. Travel by flatboat was the easiest way of pushing into new country where there were no roads and when trails were what they were often called — traces. The boats, of rough planking, were sometimes a hundred feet in length and could carry several families of settlers, with their horses, cattle, chickens, sheep, and gear. Long beech oars were set in the square bow, each manned by two or more boatmen. A broad cabin was planted in the middle of the deck and a tall crotched pole was fastened against its rear, reaching well above the flat roof. Through this another long oar slanted down over the square stern into the water and was used as a rudder by two or three boatmen standing on the roof, where they could see every turn and riffle of the stream.

On the river Polly and Davy met other young settlers, going like themselves into wild land. The red-shirted river boatmen kept up a running repartee with men ashore or on other boats along the river. Like the wagoners they consorted together, had their own lingo, their own way of bantering, their wit, which was quick, and their songs, which were both rowdy and sentimental. Thousands of them were now afloat on the western rivers, noisy, quarrelsome, full of sport, gathering for short holidays at taverns when a journey was ended, and then away again up or down the rivers.

The waters of the Holston were high in spring, and it was a perilous affair to steer the heavy craft over riffles and chutes and around sharp bends. A collision of flatboats on a rapidly running stream was the danger. On rounding a bend the steersmen would blow great wooden staved horns, whose soft, melancholy notes were loved and remembered by many who traveled along the western rivers.

On open easy water the boatmen would sing out:

> " Hard upon the beech oar!
> She moves too slow! "

The air was full of boatmen's songs and full of talk. Flatboats passed, plying the rivers as shops or " doggeries," drawing alongside the arks to sell food or spirits or fancy notions to travelers.

Small empty boats made their way upstream, " bushwhacking." A boatman in the bow would seize a bush or the branch of a willow tree on the bank and then, holding fast to this, would walk toward the stern. Another boatman quickly followed, seizing a bush, then another and another, making a line that walked to the stern, holding fast to the bushes. Around to the bow they went and again seized bushes or branches one after another, holding fast to them and again walking to the stern and around to the bow. Slowly the heavy craft moved upstream and the steersman kept the boat true. Large boats were broken up for lumber at the end of the long voyages down the Ohio and the Mississippi to New Orleans.

The Holston poured into the broad silver Tennessee, and then there were many winding miles to the southwest through fresh spring weather, past grassy valleys and open glades, past glinting stands of red maple, persimmon, tall sweet gum, and broad chestnut. The ark on which the Crocketts were traveling skirted rocky spurs of the Cumberlands. At last the Tennessee crossed a trail that ran crookedly over the mountains and down into the Elk River country.

Here the Crocketts' gear was packed again on the two colts, and Polly mounted the old horse with the little boys. Davy was on foot, the dogs alongside, and the journey was made over a rough steep trail, wet with spring rains. The vistas were fine and far, the mountainside rosy with laurel. Maypops could be found in the woods, and fresh wild ginger.

Davy bought a little clearing at the

head of the Mulberry Fork of the Elk River. He had come in time for planting, and in putting up his small, windowless cabin he had the help of other settlers who came, sometimes from a distance, to help with logrolling. The cabin had an earthen floor and a clay fireplace across one end. Later Crockett expected to have bearskins for rugs.

Many settlers thereabouts had never seen a carpet. A Virginian had come into this region, built a puncheon floor [1] for his cabin, and laid a carpet over it. He invited the neighbors in for a treat. They looked at his carpet and thought it was a bedquilt spread down to make a show. " It's naught but a piece of pride," they said severely among themselves.

Bears were to be had in this region, though not in great enough numbers to please Crockett. The country had been hunted for years by the Indians, some of whom still lived there, and white men had also raided the forests. But wild turkeys were to be had, and possums and raccoons.

A few coonskins over a hunter's shoulder were like money jingling in his pocket. A pair of them was worth a quarter, and a dozen pairs could be traded for flour and sugar.

Raccoons were fond of turtles' eggs, and in summer they would look for traces made by soft-shelled turtles as the turtles crawled over the sandy bottom of some quiet little creek. Stealthily the wary coons would follow these traces, walking along the banks, until they discovered the eggs. Leaning over the clear water of a little stream or branch, they would swiftly scoop up tadpoles with their paws. Troops of them would swiftly and quietly raid the cornfields, finding the sweet milky young ears.

In autumn when the woodpiles were larger than the cabins and the frost glimmered white, when the corn was still on the stalk though its blades were dry or gone, they prowled out of the woods at night, their eyes shining like emeralds. Neat, wise, swift, they would climb the cornstalks, bending, breaking them, rapidly feasting on the yellow ears, making for the woods at the slightest rustle within the cabin or at the sound of a dog stirring.

On spring mornings that other thief, the possum, haunted the little streams or branches that flowed through deep forests into the Mulberry Creek, looking for delicious morsels, young frogs, or pokeberry, or young nettle, and listening for the morning call of the wild turkey. It was the female's answer he wanted. Slipping toward her and following her to the nest, waiting for hours sometimes until she left it, he would gain a chance to suck the eggs. Sly as a drop of snow, the possum was as great a thief around the clearing as the coon. Eggs in the henhouse were his plunder, and in autumn he topped off a good meal with grapes and ripe persimmons.

It was when the persimmons were in their most delicious state and the frost lay white on the ground that the wily possum, after so many succulent meals, himself became most excellent eating. Roast possum tasted like young suckling pig.

Alone with his dogs or sometimes joining with one or two other hunters, Crockett was more often in the forests than on his little farm. The dogs would pick up a scent and with their bell voices rolling would be gone through the woods, the clear notes of the hunting horn urging them on. Young Crockett could raise his own strong voice in a high call that floated far through the air and roused the dogs as keenly as the horn. Hunters said that he knew how to throw his voice so that it would follow his dogs along the

[1] **puncheon floor:** a floor made of split timber.

ground between ridges of the hills, and that his hunting call could travel even round the shoulder of a steep bluff.

Then would come the deep, full, insistent baying of the dogs. "Treed!" Crockett would cry and be off full-swing through woods and bottom land.

The scent was not always hot. Sometimes there were so many traces of it as to confuse the dogs, for wary raccoons would circle and cut in on their own tracks to throw them off. When dogs were barking up a great oak the coon could slip into the upper branches where leaves hung thick, and it was a puzzle to find him with his rings and stripes as he lay curled round the farther side of a limb. But Crockett was long-sighted, sure of aim, ready to guess what a coon would do.

"Crockett can outsmart most any coon or possum," his neighbors said.

He soon had enough coonskins to barter for provisions at the neighboring doggery [1] and enough sweet possum meat to keep his boys round and fat.

Hunting far into the forests, he shot an occasional black bear; so when winter came, jerked bearmeat [2] hung from the rafters of the little cabin. The corn pone was full of cracklings,[3] with wild honey eaten with it, for a treat, gathered before winter set in. In winter there were plenty of warm fox furs for caps, deerskin for leggings, coonskins for coats and furs to pile on the beds at night.

Quail and wild pigeons Crockett never hunted. "Since I was a little boy," he said, "I never did shoot a bird. Birds are trifling — except wild turkeys."

A fine wild gobbler stood nearly four feet high, with wide velvety black satin breast and small white turban cap, a great breadth and spread of tail — bronze, purple, and gold — the gorgeously colored head lifted erect when alarmed or curious, the small clear hazel eyes showing bright. Hunting wild turkeys meant matching wits with the wariest creatures of the forest. Wild turkeys were so shy that some hunters never saw them and thought that they had been driven from the woods by the arrival of the settlers. Only their light footprints in the dust of a path or in soft soil beside a creek showed that they still belonged to this region. In a hard winter when they were all but starved, they would pass by a wealth of scattered grain over a trap. So cautious were the gobblers that even when their mates called they would listen as if they were trying out every quaver, every half tone to make sure they were not deceived. They might not answer at all, or only with a single small muffled note.

It was with the call of the female bird that hunters tried to lure the great gobblers. Crockett would set out alone with his gun and a turkey call made from a bone of a turkey's wing or a bit of wood with a nail driven through it. Scraping this with a stone or blowing through it, he could imitate the small cry of the fledglings if he liked, or the love notes of the female, or even her soft throaty gurgle as she found a tempting bit of food. He was now a master mimic; he could imitate the sound of any wild creature so that its mates in the forest would stop and listen. He could play so craftily on his turkey bone that even the wary gobbler would at last hesitate, listen and perhaps answer, and finally be drawn toward the bit of brush or wood from which the notes arose.

During a whole long morning he might see no sign of a turkey. Then toward noon he might catch a slight sound from a distance, a sound which even to other hunters might seem like innumerable small sounds of the forest.

[1] **doggery:** shop. [2] **jerked bearmeat:** bear meat that has been cut in long strips and dried in the sun. [3] **cracklings:** the crisp bits left when lard is tried out.

"That might be a woodpecker trying to yawn, or it might — " A good hunter knew it was the faint, very distant cluck of a turkey gobbler. The sound might be repeated, still in the distance. Crockett would find a place behind a fallen tree with a thatch of green leaves before him through which he placed the muzzle of his gun; he waited. At last with his turkey call he would give a single answering soft cluck, so quietly that the sound fell in with all the quiet sounds of the forest.

Half a mile away a gobbler would start, every feather instantly in place, rising in bronze and purple glory to his full height. An intensely curious bird, he would listen. Hearing nothing, he might at last begin to trot over the ground, looking for food. Again that soft tempting cluck would reach him. Starting suddenly forward, he would answer. There would be no reply; a skilled turkey hunter knew the ways of his quarry too well to call again immediately. A slow hour might pass. Finally impatient, the bird might give a positive *cluck,* and ten minutes later hear the low reply. If really aroused he would now press forward at full speed, half running, half flying, yet stopping cautiously from time to time, distracted by half a dozen pleasures. A little branch whose waters were deep and still might bring him to a halt. Wild turkeys were vain as peacocks, and he might parade up and down before the branch as before a mirror, back and forth, back and forth, more and more slowly. Or he might start looking for insects as though nothing were more important. Or he might be flightily upset by the rustle of a cricket or some other small sound. There would be long pauses as he picked his way about in underbrush: then that *cluck.*

The gobbler suddenly opened his beak wide and rolled forth a loud, satisfying answer. He crossed the stream in bold flight. He stopped cautiously from time to time, it is true, with his long neck outstretched, his bright eyes peering, but on he went until he came to an open space. Then another of his pleasures brought him to a pause. The sun rather than the mirroring stream attracted him. A turkey loves the sun, and will stand for hours in bright light. It seemed now that this great gobbler was to preen his fine feathers until sundown.

Several hundred yards away, out of gunshot, was the fallen tree and thicket where Crockett lay flat on the ground, his gun at his shoulder, looking in his worn leather clothes like a dead log. He hardly winked. At last the turkey tired of the sun, and with a long memory returned to his original errand. He gobbled — gobbled loudly. Crockett gave a long soft enticing *cluck.* This was the test of his art, with the turkey so close. The gobbler began proudly to strut. His plumage unfolded; his wattles[1] grew scarlet. His gorgeous bronze and purple tail rose and opened in a great fan; his fine head glittered in rainbow tints. On he came with a hitching gait, glowing in the sunshine. On he came — slowly, still not within gunshot. He paused — looked about with suspicion; then he came forward with a bold sure movement, advancing toward his final goal, as a turkey hunter said, "like a gay horse toward the music of a drum or a fine ship beating against the wind."

In the stillness Crockett could hear the brush of wings over the ground. At the last the turkey moved into range. There was a shot.

Even with the soft perfection of his call and a long patience — which Crockett did not enjoy — the great bird might come within half a dozen yards of his range and a squirrel would suddenly dash

[1] **wattles:** the fleshy flaps that hang from the throats of turkeys.

down a tree with a rattle of twigs. Wheeling quickly, the turkey would be off at a furious speed, tail down, feathers flat, running and flying through brush and trees, over streams, far into some deep thicket from which he was not to be drawn again that day.

THINK BACK OVER WHAT YOU HAVE READ

Learning the Ways of the Pioneers

1. What impression did you get of the dances in pioneer communities? How do they compare with modern dances?

2. Tell what happened at the reaping and flax pulling. What pioneer customs did you learn? Were the pleasures of the pioneers merely frolics, or did they serve some useful purpose? Do you think amusements unpleasant if they have a practical purpose? Can you think of any ways in which the young people of today might mix work and play?

3. Describe the river transportation of the time. What kind of boats were used? How were they propelled? How steered? What were the chief dangers of travel? What is meant by "bushwhacking"? How does this form of travel compare with the travel of today?

4. How did the Crocketts travel on land? Where did they settle? Describe the typical pioneer home. Read aloud a passage that shows how little the pioneers were accustomed to luxury.

Getting Better Acquainted with Crockett

5. What prophecy concerning Crockett was made by the Quaker? Was it a true prophecy? What does it show us about Davy's character?

6. What impressions did you get of the girl whom Davy married? Do you think her a suitable wife for a man like Crockett? What sentences tell you? Name the chief elements of her character.

7. What reasons did Crockett have for moving farther west? Do they seem sensible reasons? Are they consistent with Davy's character? How do you know?

8. What game did Crockett find plentiful at his new home? What tricks did he employ to help him catch game? Select for class reading a description of Crockett's hunting methods. Do you imagine that these methods were learned from other hunters, or did he develop them from experience? What passages support your answer?

III. INTO THE SHAKES

There is a certain type of person who readily becomes the subject of popular legend. Usually he is a remarkably skillful and courageous man living in primitive surroundings. You remember the stories of Samson in the Bible. Surely you know many tales of Robin Hood in England and Paul Bunyan in America. All three became heroes in the eyes of plain folk, who repeated again and again marvelous stories about them, exaggerating in the telling their remarkable feats. Davy Crockett also became a folk hero, and many were the tales told of his accurate marksmanship. Legends sprang up about him until he became "the greatest hunter of the West."

In the preceding chapter you saw Davy establishing a home in the river country of Tennessee. But he never stayed long in one place. In 1812, when the second war with Great Britain began, the Creek Indians in the far South, hopeful of driving the white man from their lands, rose in rebellion. Many frontiersmen volunteered for service against the Creeks, Crockett among them. He fought with distinction until the treaty between the Indians and the United States was signed. Not long after his return home his beloved wife Polly died. Saddened by her death, Crockett with his children moved into wilder country. Before long, however, he married Elizabeth Patton and again moved on to new country, from which a series of misfortunes sent him wandering once more — this time "into the Shakes," a section of Tennessee about which you are to learn in the chapter that follows.

IN THE year 1811 befell one of the great earthquakes in the known history of the world, in western Tennessee near the Mississippi River. Age-old trees were twisted from top to root. Deep cracks opened in the earth and fissures split the river bends. The river became a booming flood whose huge waves pushed far inland to overflow in small streams. The first steamboat to navigate the Mississippi, the *New Orleans,* commanded by

Nicholas Roosevelt, approached this stretch of territory just before the great upheaval. The pilot saw that a storm was approaching and made fast to the riverbank for the night. Before long the great shivering motion began. The riverbank became an island. At dawn the island began to sink and finally disappeared. Through the skill of the pilot the steamer escaped into less turbulent waters, though no landmarks now existed; but flatboats were caught in the vortex, lifted high in the air, and sunk. With a whirl of furious movement the river turned about on its current and flowed upstream for a time. It was only because there was as yet little river travel, because the land there was but sparsely inhabited, that a great human devastation was not wrought.

The country came to be known as the Shakes. Father Marquette had passed its margin nearly a hundred and fifty years before in his canoe and had been welcomed some miles below by Indians. For many decades the Chickasaws had dwelt there undisturbed. Like the Cherokees, they had at last been persuaded to cede their land to the United States, but they still hunted there since few white men had cared to penetrate this strange and tangled land. This was now full of turbulent small rivers and wide lakes.

Among these was a short deep river that emptied into the Mississippi. According to a Chickasaw legend an Indian chief had lived by its banks before the earthquake, whose only son was born with a clubfoot that made him reel as he walked. Though his father tried to please and arouse him, he was always an unhappy lad. When he grew to manhood he wandered to the south among the Choctaws, where he saw a most beautiful Indian maiden whom he loved at once and wished to marry. Her father refused to give his daughter to a man with a clubfoot. When Reelfoot succeeded in stealing the maiden the Choctaw chief put a curse upon him and all his tribe, saying that the Great Spirit would stamp upon their land in anger and destroy it.

When the earthquake came, this was taken by the Indians to be the outcome of the curse and the prophecy. The mouth of the river was dammed by the upheaval and a long, deep, winding lake was created, which was called the Reelfoot. It was wild and strange, with cypresses showing their black-green tops in lines above the water. The earthquake had shaken them many feet below the hillsides where they had grown. Soon the lake was covered by great yellow lilies, so that to come upon it suddenly was to find a yellow light glowing in the midst of the shadowed water. Mink, otter, beaver were to be found there. Wild geese haunted the shore. Here, too, were the great snapping turtles with great heads and armored scales that became famous in Tennessee legend. It was to one of these that a hunter had referred when he said that Davy was cradled in a snapping turtle's shell.

Other smaller lakes had been sunk within the land. The Obion River was a short distance south of the Reelfoot, then the Forked Deer, and the Hatchie, all flowing westward into what the Indians called the Old Big Deep Strong River.

For nearly a year deep quakes continued, stirring the region across the river as well. At their heaviest they were noticed by the Indians in Canada; they were felt in New Orleans, and eastward as far as Boston. For some time light quakes were often felt. When Crockett came into this region in 1822 to take up land and build a cabin, his cap was shaken from his head as he was planting corn.

The land was immensely fertile, so fertile that the settler was hindered rather than helped by the rich soil. Great trees still remained, and others quickly sprang up — gum, walnut, pecan, sassafras, hickory, and the delicious white plum that had been offered Father Marquette. There were deep tangles of large, sweet wild grapes. Here and there canebrakes made a labyrinthine wilderness, with paths trodden by wild creatures on their way to a stream or to the salt licks. The cane grew from twelve to thirty feet in height, on the richest soil, often beneath great trees and along the rivers. Hunters were obliged to cut their way through the dense thickets with their knives or to wedge their way backward through them. Soon after the great earthquake a hurricane had passed over this region, leveling many trees, stacking the cane in dense masses. Perhaps because of this, perhaps because of the crowding, slapping cane and the perils that lurked there, western settlers called a canebrake "a harricane." Black bears and panthers haunted the brakes.

The land was hard to clear, but everywhere there was a great abundance of game — black bear, deer, even elk, panthers, wildcats, coons, possums, squirrels, turkeys in great numbers. For many years this was almost lost territory, known only to a few trappers and hunters. In later times men called it the land of the Chickasaws and Davy Crockett.

Early in the spring of 1822 Crockett set out for this region with John, his oldest boy, on foot. Provisions were packed on one of the horses; and two hunting dogs followed, old Whirlwind and Soundwell. It was a long rough journey. They were obliged to ford the Tennessee at high water where it turned north toward the Ohio. When they reached the Shakes, Crockett chose a tract of land near the Obion a few miles south of Reelfoot Lake. The first settler had come into this country only three years before, and the nearest cabin was seven miles away. There was none other for more than fifteen miles.

Hobbling the horse, Crockett and his son set out to explore the country across the Obion. The river had overflowed its banks and stretched like a wide lake as far as eye could see. They took to the water, sometimes walking on the bottom, swimming when they had to. Far on the other side was a flatboat, bound up the river with provisions. They made for it, and the boatmen gave them shelter for the night.

Elizabeth heard the story later.

"The next day it rained riproariously," Crockett said, "and the river rose considerably, but not enough for the boat to move upstream. So I got the boatmen to go over with me to where I was going to settle, and we slapped up a cabin in little or no time. I bought four barrels of meal, some salt, and a big middling of bacon from the boatmen, and left all in the cabin. For pay I agreed to help move the boat. We got up the river very well, but quite slowly, and we landed on the eleventh day at the place where the load was to be delivered.

"Then I got a skiff and we cut down the river for the cabin. A young man came with me, and we turned in and planted corn. The place has a little open prairie. It was so late I didn't make rails to fence it; but there's nothing to disturb our corn except the wild varmints, and the old serpent himself couldn't keep 'em out with a fence to help him if they want to get in. The cabin is set near a living spring.

"It's all a wilderness," Davy added with satisfaction, "and the woods was full of Indians, hunting. We'll get together our little plunder and go."

The family procession set out, a lively party. There were now eight children in all, the two youngest so small that Crockett carried them much of the way perched on his shoulders or asleep in his arms while the older boys led the horses. No one rode, not even Elizabeth.

Deer, possums, and coons had spared the corn in the new clearing, and the Crocketts were soon settled. Besides corn there was another crop; for Davy had sowed a few gourd seeds, and the long sprawling vines with their great yellow bottles lay far over the little prairie. Dry gourds could be used for dippers or as milkpans when milk was to be had, or to keep sugar in, or wild honey. Negroes in the back country made fiddles out of gourds.

As soon as the crop was in, Davy began to hunt. The wild face of the country lay before him, and he had much to do before winter began — furs to seek; bear-meat and venison to find, and small game. Bear and deer he found at once. Often he took the boys hunting with him, teaching them to discover deer against the brown bushes and to lie quiet and disguise themselves when they heard a rustle or saw the flicker of a white tail. If a deer was grazing near by, Crockett could turn himself into something that appeared to be a gnarled stump, with his fur cap like old tufted moss, his head bent, his hands hidden. When he wanted to find a clear space for aim he sometimes got down on all fours, snorting and rooting along toward the deer like a wild hog. Curled and humped in the grass, his smallest boys looked like big jack rabbits in their fur coats and caps as they watched him.

With the boys Crockett went to a small sunken lake where a water line ran along the trunks of the bordering trees, high up, marking the place where water rose in the spring. Even in autumn many trees were set deep in the water. Black oaks, the graceful pecan, the delicate spreading beech — bronze and red and purple — lifted their tops above the silvery surface and were mirrored there. Squirrels lived in the treetops nearest the shore. A hunter in a canoe could have looked into their nests. In the thickets near by were raccoons, possums, deer. Crockett and his boys came home laden with game.

" See that little dark hummock of weed over there amongst the beech leaves," said William to Robbie, the smallest boy, as they tramped toward the cabin at dusk. " That's a possum and no mistake. If you was to go up to him he'd be stiff as a poker with that grin on his little face."

Some Chickasaws passed in the shadow. " Good hunting, neighbors," said Crockett.

At night every cranny of the cabin would be lighted by a great hickory fire. Elizabeth would be spinning, and young Polly would wind the ball. One of the heavy packs brought by the Crocketts into the Shakes was filled with flax and wool. There were always stories — stories of wild beasts and their ways, among others. It would have been strange if settlers friendly to the Indians, like Crockett, had not picked up some of their many tales about animals. He came to know the Chickasaws and Choctaws well, living in the Shakes. One way or another he had known many Cherokees, in Tennessee and in the Mississippi Territory — known them under friendly circumstances. His own tales often had a touch of animal impersonation. Consider him then, cleaning and oiling his rifle — " my Betsey " — and asking his boys if they ever heard why a possum's tail is bare.

" Seems the possum used to have a long bushy tail same as the coon's or even handsomer, and he was so proud of it that he used to comb it out every morning and every night, and he made a song about it that he used to sing at the frolics.

The rabbit was jealous, for you could hardly notice *his* tail at all. So the rabbit made up his mind to play the possum a trick. There was to be a big frolic and all the animals in the woods was going.

"It was the rabbit's business to send out the news, so as he was passing the possum's house he stopped and asked him if he was coming to the frolic. 'I'll come,' said the possum, 'if I can have a special seat. I have such a handsome tail that I ought to sit where everybody can see it.' And he spoke rather short and nippy. The rabbit said yes, the possum could have a special seat, and he promised to send someone to comb and dress the possum's tail to make it look extra nice.

"Then the rabbit went over to see the cricket, and he told him just what to do. When the morning of the frolic came, the cricket went to the possum's house; and the possum stretched himself out and shut his eyes and took his ease, while the cricket went about his work. He combed that tail and he combed it with those little forelegs of his, with little fine teeth in 'em like a comb. And he wrapped a red string around the possum's tail to keep it smooth till night for the frolic. But all the time he was awinding that red string he was aclipping and acutting off all the hair. You know a cricket can cut most anything with his little sharp scissors, even a web of cloth.

"The possum kept the red string on all day and he had it on at night when he went to the frolic. The best seat was ready for him, the way the rabbit promised. The drummers began to drum, and the fiddlers began to fiddle, and all the animals began to stamp their feet. Then the possum loosened the red string and skipped out into the middle of the floor and began asinging his song. 'See my beautiful tail!' he sang. Everybody shouted, and he danced around in a circle and sang, 'See what a beautiful color it is!' They shouted again, and he danced around and sang, 'See how it sweeps the ground!' Then he sang, 'See how fine the fur is!'

"Then all the animals laughed, and they laughed so long the possum wondered what they were laughing at. He looked around and pretty soon he looked down at his tail, and it was bare as a lizard's tail. He was mighty astonished and ashamed. He couldn't say a word. He just rolled over onto the ground the way a possum will do when he's surprised. And he just stayed there and grinned."

There was a laugh and a pause. Since it was the custom among hunters to match one story with another, William spoke up. "An Indian boy told me a different story. He said the old possum lost his tail because he wanted rings round it like a coon's. Somebody made out to him he could singe 'em on with fire, and he burned all the fur off his tail and most burned himself to a cracklin' besides."

"I heard how he got his grin," said Robbie. "The old possum was hungry when he was walking through the woods, and he saw a nice sweet little plum on the ground. Anyway he thought it was a plum. But it was a bitter-oak ball that puckered his mouth up and made him grin, and he's been agrinnin' ever since."

Just then there was a faint tremor that set the furs hanging from the rafters swinging. "I s'pose that's our old earthquake," said Robbie.

"This cabin's asitting on the earthquake's grave," said William.

They looked outside, but the earth was still except for the snap of a twig and the creak of frost.

When Christmas drew near, wild meat hung in the cabin and beside the doors. Some Chickasaws, passing by on their winter hunt, had left a gift of rabbits and turkey gobblers. Tall and stately, they had paused for only a few moments at this new cabin of the white man. The gift was welcome for Crockett was out of powder. "This meat won't last long with ten in the family," he said to Elizabeth, "and anyway we have to have powder to shoot off for Christmas. I know there's been another of Noah's floods, but I must have my powder."

A friend had settled in the autumn across the Obion near one of its forks and had brought a keg of powder for Crockett on the journey into the Shakes. Crockett had been too busy hunting to go after it and now the Obion had overflowed its banks after the rains.

Elizabeth opposed the trip. "The river's a mile wide anyway from hill to hill, and we might as well all starve as for you to freeze to death or get drowned."

But Crockett tied up some dry clothing and moccasins in a bundle, took his gun and hunting tools, and started. The snow was about four inches deep; the weather had turned cold. He admitted afterward that when he reached the river it looked like an ocean, stretching wide and gray. He had no canoe. He stepped into the water and waded along the flooded ground until he came to the channel. Here was a long log above water. He mounted the log, and balancing with his gun and bundle, he crossed the channel. Then he waded again over flooded ground until he reached a deep slough that he knew well. He had often crossed the slough to a small island raised part way across, using a sunken log as a bridge.

The log, if there, lay three or four feet beneath the surface, and below it was a further depth of eight or ten feet of water. He felt for the log cautiously with his feet, but could not find it. He could swim, but he had to keep his gun and bundle dry.

In times of low water a tall stout sapling stood alongside the log. The sapling was still there, a dozen feet away from where he stood. At his side were other saplings, a clump of them. Laying his gun in the crotch of one and tying his bundle to a branch, he cut another below the crotch. This he lodged against the sapling in the slough, thrusting it firmly within some branches. The end nearest him he fastened in the crotch of another tree.

Then he cut a pole and crawled along his bridge until he reached the sapling in the slough. Here with his pole he felt for the log, and found it. It was as deep as he supposed, and seemed firm, making a bridge to the farther side of the slough, but he dared not risk traveling back along it for his gun and bundle. Slowly he returned along the sapling bridge, took the gun and bundle, crept back again, and finally let himself down upon the sunken log. He felt his way along this with his feet, balancing, in water about waist-deep. "It was ticklish business," he admitted afterward.

The log held firm as he traversed the end of it. He came to a stretch of flooded ground, crossed it, and came to another slough over which a long log had been placed as a bridge. This was now loosened and was floating in the water. Crockett mounted the log, thinking that with care he could walk along it; but when he had reached the middle of deep water the log rolled over and he went down, quickly thrusting his gun and bundle above his head as he went. The water came up to his neck. Keeping his gun and bundle in the air, he walked slowly along the bottom until he reached another wide space of flooded ground where the water was shallow again.

When at last he waded ashore his feet

were numb. He had been in icy water all the way except when he was crossing the high log and when he was crawling back and forth on his sapling bridge. But his gun and his bundle were dry. He changed his clothes and tried to run so as to warm himself a little, but he could only trot. At last he covered the five miles to his friend's cabin. The family could hardly believe that he had crossed the river at such a time.

The next morning was piercing cold, and Crockett was persuaded not to start for home that day. He went hunting instead and brought in two deer. The weather grew colder, and his friend insisted that he would be unable to return home for some time. But Crockett knew that his wife and children would soon be without food, and he set out.

When he reached the river with his keg of powder, his gun, and bundle, a sheet of ice lay before him as far as he could see. He hadn't gone far over it before the ice broke. Shifting his load to one arm, he took out his tomahawk and opened the way before him until he found a place where the ice was thick enough to bear his weight. But it broke again, and he was obliged to wade until he came to the floating log that had rolled him into the water. This was now frozen fast in the ice. He crossed on it without much difficulty and worked along until he reached the log under water in the slough.

The swiftness of the current here had kept the water from freezing. Crockett found the log and managed to balance his load and keep a foothold, moving slowly until he reached his sapling bridge. Then he had to make two trips back and forth, one for the keg of powder, one for his gun and bundle. At last through broken ice and water he reached the high log set on the other side. As he crept over the last stretch of ice toward high ground, he came to an open broken trail. He decided a bear had gone that way and he decided to follow the bear; but the trail led to his cabin, and he found it had been made by a young man, traveling past, who had volunteered to go out and look for him.

Elizabeth and the children thought he had been lost in the icy current. "No, I'm not dead," said Crockett, "but there was times when I felt mighty nigh it. I've got my powder, and that's what I went for, and it's dry too."

The next morning he was out at sunrise with the two older boys. They hunted hard most of the day, finding small game in abundance but nothing more. Toward midafternoon William came galloping through the woods with word that he had seen two elk. He showed the direction they had taken. Crockett had only four balls left, and the boys had none. "I think I'll go after the elk," he said, "and I reckon I'd better go alone." The boys started homeward with the load of small game.

The afternoon was calm and still and frosty. Crockett walked for some distance through the woods, seeing only squirrels or an occasional raccoon or possum. He did not fire, wishing to save powder and bullets, fearing also that gunfire might alarm the elk. He walked until the sun was hardly more than two hours high, and at last he found what he was looking for. The ground was hard. The elk had left no tracks, but Crockett noticed places where the grass was bruised a little and saw a few bushes where either elk or deer had nibbled. As the nibbled leaves were very high he decided that he had found the trail of the elk. After another mile he saw two elk feeding in an open space. He approached so quietly that they did not hear him.

Since there were no trees near by, he got down and rooted his way toward them like a wild hog; but they got wind of something, and turned their heads back and looked at him, then ran off a little way. Rooting along as they moved, he followed them into some woods. When the elk began to feed again he stood up behind a tree, then ran as hard and as lightly as he could to a nearer tree. He peeped out after a moment, saw them feeding, and ran still nearer. The woods were open. As Crockett made ready to fire, he heard a sudden rustle and saw five deer coming toward him. He raised Betsey and dropped the largest, then a second one, then a third, for they hadn't moved.

" I never saw anything like it before in all my hunting," he said afterward. " I don't believe they ever saw a man before, for they wasn't in the least afraid of me."

But the two elk had fled, crashing through the woods. With only one ball left, Crockett decided that he still must have his elk; and following their traces, he walked for more than an hour before he saw them again. At last he came upon the two great beasts feeding in an open space. They appeared restless and shy. He couldn't get a close shot. The sun was down, and it was dim. Dodging among the trees that thickly bordered the little prairie, he at last got one of the elk within range. Quickly, surely, he leveled and fired, and the great creature fell. The other ran among the dusky trees, then stopped and wheeled. Even when Crockett came forward into the clearing, the elk did not run but began to paw the ground and shake his head with its great horns branching six feet high and wide across. He lowered them angrily, pawed the ground again, then with a great crash bounded forward. Crockett could not fire, for his last shot was gone; nor would he run as the animal bore down upon him. He gave a sudden shrill high cry, and the elk wheeled and was lost in the woods.

He dragged the elk he had brought down to the place where the deer lay, left it, and took one of the deer across his shoulders and walked home through the dark, sure of the way, for he had hunted through this country before. The next morning the boys helped him bring the other deer and the elk to the cabin.

" But I can't waste more time without hunting bears," said Crockett that night, " for bears is fat now, and they'll be going into their holes for winter soon. We must have enough bearmeat to last a long while. Tomorrow I'll try the harricane."

In the night a heavy rain fell, turning to sleet before morning. When Crockett rose the bushes were white, bent, and locked together with ice. " The ground looks slippery as a soaped eel," he said, " but I'll go all the same."

Outside the cabin the dogs were snuffing and crying. " My dogs always know when there's going to be a bear hunt." As he went out they bounded up against him — Whirlwind, Old Rattler, Soundwell, Tiger, Growler, Holdfast, Grim, Deathmaul, and Thunderbolt. Years had passed since Crockett brought Whirlwind over the Cumberlands. This dog was too old to hunt now. Crockett took only five of the dogs, with Soundwell as lead, whose deep tones could be heard at far distances.

They were soon off, slipping and sliding over the ice. This was to be no hunt for boys, and Crockett went alone to the big " harricane." He promised to return at night with a bear, but when night came he had not appeared. Nor did he come the next night. In the meantime a heavy snow had fallen.

Toward dusk of the third evening his tall figure was seen striding toward the cabin. He had a heavy pack on his shoulders, and his dogs were limping at his heels with heads down.

That night Crockett told his story. " It

took us quite a while to get to the harricane because of the ice; but once there my dogs began prowling round, and soon they were up. I gave them the word, and they went off in full cry with Soundwell singing out like a bell and the others most as true. The bear was sliding along through the cane, and 'twas such a thick place I was afraid the dogs would lose him. It's a wonder to me they ever got through that part of the brake. I had to go myself for more than a mile after that bear on my hands and knees, creeping through briars. If I hadn't had on deer-leather clothes, the briars would have picked me to pieces.

"The first thing I knew I was up to my neck in a sinkhole of water. It made me so mad I had a good notion not to get out of it; but I began to think that wouldn't spite anybody, so out I scrambled. I could hear the old bear arustling through the canebrake beyond, and the canes crashing. I harked my dogs on and presently I could hear my dogs and the bear fighting. They sang out, but the bear got away in the tangle. On we went till we come to the big creek, and there was the bear swimming across. My dogs plunged in and made a streak across the water following that bear. It was now past noon, and they had been running since sunrise, and we had passed through the harricane, which of itself was a day's work.

"All at once I heard my dogs fighting on the other side. This put me all in a storming humor and I rolled an old log I saw at my feet into the creek, which is pretty wide just there. I straddled the log with my feet in the water and pushed off, paddling with one hand and pushing with my feet and holding up my gun. The log was old and didn't half float, so I was up to my thighs; but I got over safe and pushed the log up the bank to go back on. Way off in the distance I heard my dogs tree, and I ran to 'em as fast as I could. Sure enough when I came up, there was the bear in the crotch. My dogs were all lying down under him, and I don't know which was the most tired, they or the bear. I knew I had him, so I rested a minute; but I had to keep my dogs quiet, so old Betsey thundered. When he fell I was sorry, for he'd fought all day like a man and would have got clear but for me.

"He was pretty big, and it took me four turns on the log to bring him over the creek. When I'd packed the meat in a crotch the sun was most down, and the sky looked red and cold. I built a great fire of hickory and ash in a sheltered place and raised up a snowbank to keep the wind off the dogs. By that time in spite of everything I was most frozen. I recollected there was a mighty big spring not far off, and a notion struck me to go and get into it. When I got there, I took off most of my clothes and put my legs in; and it felt so warm I sat right flat into it, and slid down so as to leave nothing out but my mouth and the upper part of my head. You don't know how good I did feel. When I think of it, I believe the happiest time I ever spent was while I was in that spring. It was harder getting out; but I went back to the fire, and piled up more wood, and dried my clothes, and stamped, and the dogs snuggled up close. By morning I was warm again, and my clothes were almost dry. Why some of my frolics haven't killed me, I don't know.

"The next morning the dogs were feeling lively as wildcats, and began snuffing, and at the word they were off. I thought it was turkeys and, sure enough, two gobblers rose over the harricane. I got 'em, and a very little time afterward I heard the dogs abarking. I found they were up the wrong tree; but they went on, barking again, and stopping, and still there was no bear. I was pretty mad then, and pulled out my horn and harked 'em on. We pushed through the harricane and past it for a long time till we came to an open prairie, and out there beyond my dogs there was about the biggest bear I ever saw. He looked like a big black bull. My dogs was afraid to attack him; and that's why they'd stopped so often, waiting for me to come up.

" I took the gobblers from my back and hung them on a sapling, and went after the bear, for the sight of him put new springs into me. The dogs got up to him and were soon in a roaring thicket. It was pretty close work for me to pick my way along. But the bear climbed up into a big black oak tree, and I crawled on till I got within about eighty yards of him. I put fresh priming in my gun and fired, and loaded again as quick as I could. He snorted at the first shot, but on the second he came tumbling down among the dogs. They piled in on him, and I heard old Grim cry out. I ran up with my tomahawk in one hand and my knife in the other. At that the bear let Grim go and fixed his eyes on me. I got back in all sorts of a hurry, for I knew if that bear got his paws on me he'd hug me too close for comfort. I called the dogs off, and fired again, and that was the end. He weighed no less than six hundred pounds, and I knew I'd have to make another day of it. I got him ready, packed part of the meat in the crotch of a tree, and in order to find him again I blazed [1] saplings back to where the other bear was packed. The next day I got all the meat in the same place, and brought down some more gobblers.

" I guess my dogs know what they're about even when they seem to be barking up the wrong tree. Tomorrow we'll go after all that meat with the horses, and the boys can help."

There was silence, broken only by the snapping of the fire and the whir of Elizabeth's wheel. Robbie spoke. " But tomorrow's Christmas, and you said — "

" Sure enough. I said you might fire one of the Christmas guns."

The next morning at daybreak Robbie shot Betsey straight upward. John and William both fired off guns. Around the cabin there was a thunder of noise in the frosty air with light echoes. Christmas guns were echoing in many a clearing in the Southwest.

As the early sun sparkled yellow over the snow, Crockett was off with John and William — all on horseback. " We must make haste," he said; " there's hardly a week's more bear hunting, and we'll need more meat and bear oil than we've got now, to last, and I must have more skins to trade." It took them the day to bring home all the game.

The Obion was now frozen fast. That night Crockett's friend from across the river was waiting for him at the cabin. He had come for a hunt and the next day they were off with William and John. They made a camp near the " harricane " with walls of snow, and soon the branches of the trees round about were hung with venison, wild turkeys, raccoons, bearmeat, and skins. At the end of a week they had brought down seventeen bears.

Spring wheeled round; and after corn planting Crockett was off on horseback forty miles through cane and forest to the little settlement of Jackson, where he sold his peltry [2] and bought coffee, sugar, powder, lead, and salt enough for several months' supplies. Back again at the Obion, he went ranging through the Shakes, sometimes on horseback, sometimes on foot. The boys were often with him. They skirted the great cracks still left by the earthquake, crossed low streams, and found Reelfoot Lake with its waters aglow with the yellow light of the great lilies. Fish floundered and

[1] **blazed:** marked by cutting off a portion of the bark.

[2] **peltry:** furs.

jumped from the water, great catfish, gar, and others. Crockett was no fisherman, preferring to hunt, but since little time or patience was required for catches in the Reelfoot the boys brought home strings of great yellow catfish.

Once they passed a little hut at the head of the lake, thatched with moss and black with age, and caught a glimpse of the old hermit who lived there. " He's an old trapper," Crockett told the boys, " and there's stories about why he's hid himself in the woods all these years, but we won't bother him since he wants to be by himself. I know that feeling well."

Some days they went hunting bee trees, with clusters of yellow bottle gourds slung over their shoulders, tied with thongs of deerskin. Bee trees abounded in the Shakes. They could collect enough honey in a few days to fill all their gourds. Here and there they would pass a clearing where, as Crockett said, " some man's grubbed out a patch," but neighbors were still few and far between.

Once they all tramped over to the Mississippi and stood on the high bluffs, watching until a small steamer came noisily round a bend.

Hunters now came into the country occasionally, riding down from Kentucky or northern Tennessee. They sought out Crockett. The abundant fine peltry he had carried to Jackson had already given him farther fame. He was now spoken of as the great bear hunter of the Shakes—even as the great bear hunter of the West.

One cool November evening Crockett was sitting before the fire in his cabin, roasting potatoes and playing with his children, when someone hallooed at the fence. Three strangers on horseback were there who said they had come to hunt bear and elk. They wanted Crockett to join them. " Light, strangers, and come in," said Crockett. Soon Elizabeth was cooking game and Crockett was pounding corn in a mortar for corncakes. The strangers spent the night.

The next morning, sounding his horn and harking on his dogs, he led the party through open woods. One of the strangers suddenly cried, " I'd give my horse to see a bear! "

" Well, give me your horse," said Crockett; and he pointed to a bear three or four hundred yards ahead, feeding on acorns.

They all strained off, and the woods echoed as they came up. The bear hardly stirred until the dogs reached him. " He's buckling for it! " shouted Crockett.

When the dogs reached him, the bear turned and reared and boxed them right and left with his great paws. Howling, they came back. Two of them threw themselves upon him. The men were off their horses in an instant. Crockett had all he could do to keep the strangers from shooting; he feared they would shoot the dogs.

The dogs succeeded in getting the bear down. With a single blow of his knife, Crockett killed him. The strangers perceived the skill and strength of the stroke. The dogs leaped upon the bear again and again. The strangers capered about almost as freely. " Blow me, if they didn't cut more capers jumping about than ever the dogs or the old bear did," said Crockett to Elizabeth. " I had fun just looking at 'em."

" Now we're all rested and ripe for the drive," Crockett told his new friends when all had mounted again and were riding toward the " harricane." " The fight with the bear just took the wiry edge off my dogs and they're in a better humor than ever."

Elk had been seen on the far side of the " harricane," and Crockett placed the strangers at stands before some open glades through which the elk might pass. Everything was quiet. Crockett leaned Betsey against a stump and lay down. Nearly an hour passed before Tiger opened. He howled once or twice, and Rattler gave a long howl, and the others joined in. One of the strangers shouted, "He's up, he's up!" Crockett seized his rifle. He could hear nothing but the continued roar of the dogs, coming toward him. A gun went off. The dogs stopped but not for long. They took a little tack toward the glades where the strangers were posted, then circled way round to Crockett's left.

Crockett ran about a quarter of a mile toward them, then heard the dogs making a bend as though they were turning. He heard the bushes breaking lower down and started to run there. Just then two elk burst out of the cane, a buck and a doe, about a hundred and fifty yards below him. He waited until they reached an open space, then leveled and fired. He brought down the buck.

"I don't know that I ever heard my dogs give such music," Crockett told the strangers. "Old hunter as I am, it made my hair stand right on end." Tiger lay against the buck. For a time the dog wouldn't let Crockett touch the great creature.

All at once the whole pack bounded up, growling, their hair stiff. "Perhaps it's the doe," said one of the strangers.

"Maybe," said Crockett doubtfully. "They act more as if 'twas a painter."[1] Off they went at full cry. "Stranger, this will be hunting. Follow on!"

The eight dogs still sang out, clear as a bell. On several hundred yards through a glade in the cane Crockett saw a panther's tracks in the wet slash. Then they all entered the cane, following the dogs, pushing against the dry, thick, crackling stalks. All at once the dogs treed, and Crockett, peering over the brake into a gulley where an old beech stood, cried, "There he is on a limb, with his head pointed downward!" It was the panther, tawny-dark against the gray limbs and trunk of the beech.

"He's more than a hundred yards off!" cried one of the strangers.

For a moment there was silence, then the ring of the rifle, then the sound as Crockett crashed through the cane. The panther, struck, had leaped; and with the leap a dog's cry arose, then another. The dogs had covered him, and he was about to deal out death to them with powerful strokes when Crockett ran up. Furiously the beast turned. Crockett pressed the muzzle of his gun against him as he came on, fired, and killed him.

"That took courage, Colonel!" cried one of the strangers admiringly. But Crockett was looking at his dogs. They were badly mauled.

"I must stop for the painter skin; then we'll shoot only what comes our way as we go back."

On the return the dogs, though tired, started the doe elk, seen earlier, and one of the strangers was lucky enough to bring her down.

At night there was the usual talk after the hunt. "I suppose you've been in many a tight place," said one of the men to Crockett.

"I could tell you a thousand frolics I've had," he replied, "but perhaps this one will amuse you. I like bear hunting best of all. Bears is witty.

"It was evening and I was coming along, my pack horse loaded and my dogs following. All at once Soundwell held up his head and looked about, then rubbed his nose against a bush, and opened. I knew from the way he sung out that it was an old he-bear. The other dogs buckled in, and off they went like a thundergust right up a hollow. I tied my horse and set out after the dogs. The hollow up which the bear had gone made a bend, and I knew he would follow it, so I run across to head him. The sun was down

[1] **painter:** dialect for panther.

now. 'Twas growing dark mighty fast, and 'twas cold: so I buttoned my jacket fast around me and run on. I hadn't gone far when I heard the dogs tack, and then come atearing right down the hollow. Then I heard the old bear rattling through the cane, and the dogs like lightning after him. I dashed on and felt like I had wings, my dogs made such a roaring cry. They rushed by me and I harked them on. They all broke out again in their deep tones, and the woods echoed back and back and back with their voices.

" 'Twasn't long before they overhauled him and I could hear 'em fighting not far from me. Just before I got there the old bear made a break and got loose; but the dogs kept close up, and every once in a while they stopped him and had a fight. I tried for my life to get up but before I'd get there he'd get loose. I followed him this way for three or four miles through briars and cane, and he deviled me mightily.

" Once I thought I had him. 'Twas so dark I couldn't tell him from a dog, and I started to go to him; but I found out there was a creek between us. How deep it was I didn't know; but it was too late to turn back, so I held up my rifle and walked right in. Before I got across, the old bear got loose and shot for it through the cane. Well, I kept on, and once in a while I could hear my dogs fighting and baying just before me. I followed this way about four or five miles as near as I could guess, when the old bear couldn't stand it any longer and took a tree. I went up, but at first it was so dark I could see nothing; but after looking about and getting the tree between me and a star, I could see a very dark-looking place, and I raised old Betsey, and she lightened. Down came the old bear, but he wasn't much hurt.

" Of all the fights you ever see that one beat all. I had six dogs, and for nearly an hour they kept rolling and tumbling right at my feet. I couldn't see anything but an old white dog I had, but every now and then the bear made 'em sing out right under me. After a while bear, dogs, and all rolled down into a crack just before me, and I could hear 'em fighting like they was in a hole. I loaded Betsey and felt around in the hole with her till I got her agin the bear, and I fired, but I didn't kill him. Out of the hole he bounced, and the dogs fought harder than ever. They just formed a lump, rolling about, and presently they all went down into the hole again.

" My dogs began to sing out mighty often now. It had been the hardest fight I ever saw. I found out how the bear was laying, and I looked for old Betsey to shoot him again; but I had laid her down somewheres and I couldn't find her, so I thought I would git down into the crack and kill him with my knife. I knew my bear was in a crack made by the shakes, but how deep it was and whether I could get out if I got in were things I couldn't tell. But my dogs would sing out as if they wanted help, so I let myself down into the crack behind the bear. Where I landed was about as deep as I am high, and I felt mighty ticklish. I couldn't see a thing in the world but I drew my knife and kept feeling about with my hands and feet till I touched the bear; this I did very gently. Then I got on my hands and knees and inched my left hand up his body with the knife in my right, though all the time he was twisting and turning with the dogs. I got pretty far up and then I plunged it into him. He sunk down, and for a minute there was a great struggle, but by the time I scrambled out everything was getting quiet. My dogs come out, one at a time, and laid down at my feet.

" I didn't know the direction of my tent, so I determined to stay the night. I took out my flint and steel and raised a little fire, but the wood was so cold and wet it wouldn't burn much. I had sweated so after the bear that I began to get very thirsty and felt like I would die if I didn't get some water, so I went to look for the creek I had waded; and as good luck would have it, I found the creek and got back to my bear. But from having been in a sweat all night I was now very chilly. I set to work again to build me a fire, but all I could do wouldn't make it burn. The excitement I had been laboring under had all died away and I was so cold I felt very much like dying, but a notion struck me to get my bear up out of the crack; so down into it I went and worked till I got myself into a sweat again, and just as I would get him up so high that if I could turn him over once he'd be out, he'd roll back. It began to hail mighty fine; but I kept on, and in about three hours I got him out.

"I came up almost exhausted. I laid down and soon fell asleep, but 'twasn't long before I waked almost frozen. The wind sounded mighty cold as it passed along, and I called my dogs and made them lie upon me to keep me warm; but it wouldn't do. I got up and began to grope about in the dark, and the first thing I hit agin was a tree. It felt mighty slick and icy as I hugged it, so up I started; and I climbed that tree for thirty feet before I came to any limb, and then slipped down. It was warm work. How often I clomb that tree I never knew, but I was going up and slipping down and when day first began to break I was still going up that tree. As soon as it was clearly light I saw it was a slim sweet gum, so slick that it looked like every varmint in the woods had been sliding down it for a month.

"Then I looked down the crack where I had taken my bear. Where we had all fought together was on a ledge in the crack and, just beyond, it went off so deep that I couldn't see to the bottom though all the morning light began to pour into it. It made me giddy to look at the dangers I'd escaped.

"Then I took old Betsey here, greased her, and laid her away to rest a while. She's a mighty rough old piece but I love her, for she and I have seen hard times together. If I hold her right she always sends the ball where I tell her. She mighty seldom tells me a lie. My dogs and I have had many a high time of it, with old Betsey."

THINK BACK OVER WHAT YOU HAVE READ

Appreciating Crockett's Courage and Skill

1. What does Crockett's choice of a home site near Reelfoot Lake tell you of his character? What words can you think of to describe his character?

2. What steps did he take first to establish a home? What were the first crops raised? Why? Upon what did he rely for his main food supply?

3. Was Crockett's skill as a hunter due wholly to his accurate marksmanship, or were there other means that he used in bagging his game? Quote passages to prove your answer.

4. Read aloud the passage describing Crockett's trip to get powder for his gun. What particular skills did he use to gain his purpose? What examples of intelligent thinking do you find? Explain why a less skillful and courageous man would have failed.

5. What examples of keen eyesight do you find in the account of the trailing of the elk? What skill did Crockett use? What example of quick thinking can you cite?

6. What have you learned about bear hunting from this chapter? After Crockett killed the big bear, how did he make sure that he would find it again?

7. What other sources of food supply did the Shakes offer?

8. What examples of Crockett's courage occurred when he was hunting with the three strangers? How was his courage revealed in the story he told the strangers?

9. List some of the qualities in a pioneer necessary for a successful life. Do you think that people still possess these qualities? Under what conditions do such qualities appear?

Discovering the Origin of Folk Tales

10. What Indian legend was told of the Reelfoot Lake section of the Shakes? How can you account for the origin of legends of this sort? Have you ever heard of other legends similar to this one? If so, be prepared to recount them to the class.

11. What was the probable reason for calling a canebrake a "harricane"? Have you ever seen a canebrake? Try to describe it for the benefit of those who have never seen one.

12. Tell Crockett's story about how the possum lost his bushy tail. What was William's version of the same story? Why, according to Robbie, does a possum have a grin on his face? Do you understand how stories like these grew?

13. Are you familiar with the Uncle Remus stories of Joel Chandler Harris? What similarity do you find between them and the animal stories in this chapter? Do you think they grew up in the same way?

14. Were stories such as these told for amusement or as genuine attempts to explain peculiar animal characteristics? Give reasons for your answer.

Noticing the Customs of Davy Crockett's Time

15. How was Christmas celebrated by the pioneers? Do you happen to know any other interesting ways in which Christmas is celebrated by simple folk? If so, tell the class about them.

16. What examples of folk customs do you find in other chapters of *Davy Crockett?*

IV. THE STORY OF FIVE STRANGE COMPANIONS

Texas in 1835! Imagine it if you can. You must not think of the great, prosperous state about which you have studied in your geography classes. Here were no imposing cities, no well-ordered ranches, no oil derricks pointing skyward. Instead, you must imagine an outlying province of Mexico; a land of boundless, uncultivated, sparsely inhabited prairies, where great herds of buffalo grazed and where roving bands of Comanche Indians boded ill for any luckless whites who crossed their paths. Settlements were few, the best known perhaps being the little town of San Antonio de Bexar, and there was a growing spirit of restlessness among the American settlers. Dissatisfied with Mexican rule, they dreamed of an independent country, a republic of Texas. The mood of rebellion was in the air, and news of it reached the ears of Davy Crockett. By this time you know him well enough to imagine how great must have been the temptation to throw in his lot with the Texans. New adventure, new lands — lands where a man could breathe freely — these were calling him, and he must answer the call.

But before we accompany him on his journey to Texas, let us see what had been happening to him since we left him in the Shakes. You will recall that he had become almost a legendary figure to the people of that section. These people liked him, and it is not surprising that he was thought of as a likely candidate for political office. He did not take kindly to the idea at first; but, after considerable persuasion, he consented to run and was elected, first, to the state legislature and, later, to the Congress of the United States. Here he served with some distinction, but failed to be reelected after he had vigorously opposed a bill renouncing a treaty with the Indians and providing for their removal from their lands. This bill, sponsored by President Jackson, under whom he had served in the Creek War, he regarded as unjust. He never quite forgave Jackson for what he regarded as a stain on his country's honor, a fact which may help to account for his presence at the famous battle of the Alamo. It was on his return home from Washington that Crockett heard that Texas was preparing to secede from Mexico.

Let us now join him on his journey to San Antonio.

BEFORE THIS last adventure is traced, another story about Davy Crockett must be told — a tale that has a gala touch of light opera, yet is singularly lifelike. This appeared in *Colonel Crockett's Exploits and Adventures in Texas,* which was published early in the summer of 1836. The book was said to be based on a diary of his journey, kept by Crockett. A pattern of evidence may yet be woven to prove that it had a basis in fact. In the main story Crockett often speaks as he might have spoken. Passages of his journey are lighted that otherwise remain dim. The principal adventures might have occurred. The tale was — and remains — part of the spreading Crockett legend; it is part of the Texas legend, and so must have a place in this narrative.

In this brightly colored story the shadowy companions who joined Crockett somewhere along the way to Texas take on definite character — a character belonging to the region and the time. They have far less dignity than those mentioned elsewhere as his fellow travelers, but Crockett relished connections with all kinds of people. He would have consorted with any of these. Instead of a dozen companions there were four. Crockett was pictured as meeting the first of them on board the galloping little steamboat by which he traveled down the Red River from Fulton to Natchitoches.

Here is the story. Take it as true for a time.

When Crockett came out on deck, he saw a cluster of men in the bow and heard an occasional burst of laughter. Seated on a chest was a tall, lank blackleg,[1] looking like a sea serpent that had just crawled out of the black den of Natchez-under-the-Hill, down the Mississippi. He was amusing the passengers with his skill at thimblerig [2] and was picking up their shillings as quickly as a hungry gobbler would pick up a pint of corn.

The thimble conjuror looked at Crockett carelessly and said, "Come, stranger, won't you take a chance?"

All this time he was passing the pea from one thimble to another. The game, of course, was to make someone wager a shilling that he could guess under which thimble the pea would be found. It seemed easy enough. The thimbles were arranged a few inches apart, in a triangle, with one in the middle. The audience would see the pea placed under one thimble and would guess that it was there. But as Thimblerig lifted this thimble he would slip out the pea, then with a few passes slip it under another. The spectator would lose his shilling.

Crockett wagered drinks for the company that he could put his finger on the thimble under which the pea was concealed. As Thimblerig stopped shifting the thimbles and the pea, Crockett cried, "The pea is under the middle thimble," and with a swift motion he lifted it before the blackleg could raise a finger. Sure enough, the pea was there; but it would not have been if Thimblerig had moved first.

"Your eye is keen as a lizard's, stranger," a man who had lost a shilling said to Crockett.

"You've won the bet," said Thimblerig. "You've a sharp eye, sure enough, and I don't mind if I give you another chance."

"It would be little better than picking your pocket," said Crockett. "Anyway you've lost the wager."

"What about that ideer?" said a spectator who had lost a shilling. Thimblerig gathered up his thimbles and laughed, but his laugh was not altogether pleasant. He was obliged to stand treat for the entire crowd.

Afterward on deck he set to work with his thimbles again and tried to banter Crockett into another wager, but Crockett would not be drawn. Talk dwindled, and the others moved away. Thimblerig was obliged to break off his conjuring for lack of customers, and with nothing better to do he told Crockett his story.

"I was brought up a gentleman," he said, "but through sad misfortunes I came down in the world and finally became an actor. It was a hard life. I was often hissed, and old oranges and eggs were often my portion as I was speaking

[1] **blackleg:** a professional gambler. [2] **thimblerig:** a sleight-of-hand trick in which a pea is manipulated under three thimble-shaped cups, the spectators gambling on its location.

my finest lines. The manager didn't appreciate my talents any more than the public," said Thimblerig, whimpering. "He put on a fine spectacle play one evening in a little town in Mississippi, called *The Cataract of the Ganges*. Naturally for a play like that he had to have a procession with some Eastern animals, and he could hardly do without an elephant. But where to find an elephant in Mississippi? Alligators were plentiful, but there were no elephants. He made a pasteboard elephant, large as life. Looking around to find means of locomotion for the elephant, he spied *me*, tall and rather gaunt, and he cast me for the rump. If it had been the forequarters," said Thimblerig with a noble air, "I might have had a speaking part or at least I could have snorted. I refused to act, as beneath my dignity, and I was discharged, sir. I went to New Orleans and hired myself as a marker [1] to a gambling table; and from there I moved on to Natchez-under-the-Hill, to bask amid magnolias and wickedness. Oh, I've been a bad man in my time," said Thimblerig boastfully, cocking his tall white hat on the back of his bushy head and shifting from one long leg to another.

In fact, Crockett thought, he had enough brass in his face to make a wash kettle. He decided that Thimblerig could be trusted about as far as a tailor could throw a bull by the tail.

As they stood talking a tall chap came up from below who looked roughhewn, as though he had been cut out of a gum log with a broad ax — one of those chaps, Crockett decided, who are always ready for a fight or a frolic and don't care a toss of a copper which. Quickly another little lean chap came up from below, in a sailor's round jacket and a pigtail. The two looked at each other and evidently did not like what they saw. The tall man neighed like a horse; the little one crowed like a rooster. The two squared off. A fight might have started, but at the sound of crowing and neighing Thimblerig leaped high into the air and, gathering up his thimbles, dashed to the other end of the boat, rocking it until the rail nearly dipped water. The two fighters laughed. Thimblerig was lost to view even when the steamer reached the wharf at Natchitoches.

The one street of the village lay on the right bank of the river on low ground. "That swamp will grow forty bushels of frogs to the acre and alligators enough to fence it," said a traveler as the steamer tied up.

"It grows cotton, sir," shouted a stout red-faced man in a broad white hat. "Cotton! Cotton!" He shook with rage.

Crockett went briskly to the tavern, for dusk had fallen. Thimblerig had made an adroit departure from the steamer and was there before him. In the light of pitch pine and candles — highly favorable to his enterprise — he was seated at a table with a little crowd, playing with his thimbles and picking up shillings.

The next morning at dawn Crockett was strolling through the village when the hush was broken by a voice singing a scrap of song. At the turn of a corner he came upon the stalwart but graceful figure of a young man in a hunting shirt, looking at the sunrise. He was sunburned as dark as mahogany except where his tilted cap showed the line of his forehead. He had a highly finished rifle in one hand, a shot pouch covered with Indian ornaments in the other, and he looked as cool as a morning in spring.

A swaggering fellow came down the street who seemed irritated by this composure. He came up and called the youth a scoundrel. The young man quickly handed his rifle and knife to Crockett and in a moment the swaggerer found himself under the spout of a neighboring

[1] **marker:** one who keeps the score.

pump, deluged by a downpour of icy cold water. The young man came back, claimed his knife and rifle, and asked if this were not Davy Crockett. He had seen pictures of Crockett, knew his story, and had even heard that Crockett was bound for Texas. He declared that he would like to join him.

"I know the country well," said the young man. "I am a bee hunter, and you may find me of use in navigating the prairies."

Bees will move in a straight line on their flight to the hive after gathering a store of honey, and the hunter must be clear of sight to follow them, and swift of foot. On the flower-strewn prairies of Texas the honey had a peculiar sweetness, but the fine wax was coveted even more. This was gathered and sold for candles. The youth, whom Crockett liked at once, would be a welcome companion. The Bee Hunter was to procure a pair of horses.

The next morning as the two stood ready to mount, a whimper was heard. There stood the tall Thimblerig, his high white hat in his hand, begging to go on the journey. The Bee Hunter, who had known him in New Orleans, called him by name and said he wasn't half the blackguard he looked. Another horse was bought with the shillings Thimblerig had collected; and the three set out westward toward the Texas border, on the way to Nacogdoches.

The Bee Hunter was said to belong to a good family in New Orleans. In his youth he had quarreled with his father over a trivial matter and had taken to adventures along the border and on the Texas prairies. Later a reconciliation had been effected, but by that time the Bee Hunter was wedded to wild life and could not be persuaded to return.

As the three traveled, they talked of the coming conflict.[1] They had heard that Bexar[2] was to be held at any cost. When talk ran out the Bee Hunter sang, and the list of his songs was as long as a rainy Sunday. They followed the old King's Highway to Nacogdoches, and at last rode into the gay little town. When Crockett's presence was known, cannon were fired in his honor. Here, too, the Bee Hunter met a sweetheart, Kate of Nacogdoches. But the trio, eager to be off, did not linger. When they set out for Bexar, Kate came up with a pretty curtsy to Crockett and, turning to the Bee Hunter, gave him a large gourd swung by a thong, for carrying water, some biscuits, and a new deerskin sack for his wax. A crowd had gathered, and Crockett made a speech.

The three had exchanged their horses for mustangs. At the start they hardly looked like dangerous warriors. Seated on a little mustang with his feet nearly touching the ground, the tall and hardy Crockett might have been a circus rider, except for his coonskin cap and hunter's garb. Thimblerig's high white Vicksburger[3] was stuck on the side of his bushy head, and he, too, was tall in contrast to the small beast he was riding. The Bee Hunter with his trim costume and new deerskin sack made a fancy picture. Thimblerig swept the ground with his tall hat by way of a last salute, and the three were off with a clatter over the boundless plains of Texas.

Their route lay through a far expanse of canebrake. Twenty or thirty feet overhead the slender canes drooped and mingled, with tops fringing over the narrow trail. Light slanted in brokenly. They rode in a pale greenish twilight.

After many jogging hours they emerged from the dim forest of cane, and the prairie lay broad and brilliant before them. Three black wolves were running along, at too great a distance to shoot. Wild

[1] **coming conflict:** between Texas and Mexico.

[2] **Bexar:** San Antonio, originally known as San Antonio de Bexar. [3] **Vicksburger:** tall hat.

horses were scattered far off on the horizon. Flocks of wild turkey scurried and flew fanwise over the plain.

Sharply the green of the prairie grew denser, the sky black. Crockett and his companions pushed hastily on toward a distant grove of live oaks, but the storm overtook them in great gusts. Bent forward in the white downpour, the three tall figures on their little mustangs looked like skiffs in a tempest at sea, leaning against the wind. When at last they reached the grove the night had thickened. They found a wide dry patch under the bending branches of a live oak; their fire lighted up the leaves and boughs above them, making a great rosy dome. Lightning flashes still broke the blackness outside, revealing the wide prairie. Other groves in the far distance, with rolling verdure and small streams, would come into view for an instant, then vanish again into gloom.

They were away the next morning in bright sunlight and rode for two days, fording small rivers and streams, shooting prairie chickens and jack rabbits for food, camping at night. When they had crossed the Trinidad River they came at nightfall to a hut where an old woman lived alone. They could not be sure whether she was Indian or white, Mexican or American; she had little to say, but she offered them shelter for the night.

Within an hour two other travelers appeared, armed with hunting knives and rifles. One was about sixty years old, tall and rawboned, with fierce black whiskers, coal-black hair, a deep scar across his forehead and another across the back of his right hand. He wore a scarlet handkerchief tied around his head and a sailor's round jacket. " Seems all made up for a pirate," said Crockett to the Bee Hunter as they drew near. After a little conversation the stranger remarked that he was a pirate, and that he had sailed the main with the wicked Lafitte,[1] whose lair had been on an island off the shore of Texas. He did not explain why he was now cruising the prairies, but he talked pleasantly enough and declared that he was on his way to join the American forces at Bexar. He seemed tired. His companion was an old Indian, stumpy in appearance, with little to say. To what tribe he belonged no one ever knew.

The Indian drew a brace of fat rabbits from his bag and some eggs of wild fowl, and a good meal was soon set on the table. But Thimblerig, who had audibly sniffed when the Pirate had announced his profession, was now giving himself lofty airs. He declined to sit down. Plainly he thought these travelers were not his equals. Perhaps he considered himself a more accomplished impostor than the Pirate.

" Stranger, I think you'd better take supper with us," said the Pirate in a mild tone. Thimblerig remained aloof. The Pirate drew his long hunting knife from his belt and laid it on the table. " You'd better take supper with us," he repeated still more mildly. Thimblerig eyed the knife, then the Pirate's fierce whiskers. He sat down. The Pirate instantly picked up his knife and cut up his meat with it.

The next morning the five started out, the Pirate and the Indian trudging along on foot at a distance. They had promised to keep the others in view.

When Crockett and his companions stopped at noon to refresh their horses beneath a cluster of trees, Thimblerig took out his thimbles and began slipping the pea from one thimble to another with as much earnestness as if he had a crowd around him and a dozen shillings at stake. " Have to practice," he muttered.

All at once the Bee Hunter sprang to his feet, looked about for a moment, leaped on his mustang, and without a

[1] **Lafitte**: a famous pirate.

word was off at full speed to the northeast in the general direction from which they had come, riding faster and faster, it seemed, gradually growing diminutive in size until he seemed no larger than a squirrel, and finally disappearing in the distance.

"He's gone back," said Thimblerig mournfully.

"Maybe it's a bee," said Crockett.

The Bee Hunter was hardly lost to sight when a noise arose like the rumbling of far thunder. The sky above was clear, but to the south an immense black cloud showed on the horizon.

"Burn my old shoes if *I* know what it is," said Thimblerig, whimpering and gathering up his thimbles.

The cloud approached and a roaring became distinct. The two mustangs ceased to graze and cocked their ears. Crockett caught them, took off their hobbles, and brought them within the grove. Suddenly a headlong figure emerged from the distant cloud, and in another moment a vast herd of buffalo was visible with a great black bull in front, his tail straight as a javelin in the air, his head low, his stout horns projected straight before him.

As they came close to the little island of trees Crockett drew his rifle and fired. The bull roared, and stopped. The herd behind him stopped likewise, and there was a sound of sharp concussion as the animals pressed suddenly one against another. The bull stood for a few moments pawing the ground, then darted off at an angle round the grove with the herd following, sweeping along like a tornado. Crockett's bullet had had no effect. Only a shot precisely aimed at the heart could bring a buffalo down.

As the last of the herd dashed by with a furious upturning of dust, Crockett jumped on his mustang, clapped his spurs, and followed in their wake. He had never hunted buffalo, and he was piqued by the failure of his shot. He rode on the trail for at least two hours, but the herd gradually became a black cloud again and merged into the horizon. Presently all sign of it vanished.

Crockett might have retraced his path to the grove by following the buffalo trail along a back track, but he believed that he knew his bearings for a quicker route. He had not ridden an hour before he realized that he was completely lost. Around him was country apparently in the highest state of cultivation, spreading as far as the eye could see, melting into purple haze. Extended fields were framed by borderings of trees. They looked like the luxuriant meadows of some thrifty farmer, brilliantly green. There were groves free from underbrush, with trim margins. Here and there was the white and silver glint of running water. But Crockett heard no sound of the ax, saw no sign that man had ever visited this region before. This smooth fair country was a wilderness.

Following the sun, trying to chart a course as best he could, he pushed along. If he had found a trail he would not have dared follow it, for the Bee Hunter had told him that once when he had been lost on the prairies he had accidentally struck into the path his own horse had made earlier in the day and had traveled round and round for hours before he discovered his mistake.

As he emerged from a great grove of trees Crockett passed from the rich meadowland again into the prairie, and saw before him at a short distance a drove of about a hundred horses pasturing quietly. Some were mustangs, and there were a few beautiful coursers, descendants perhaps of those Arabian steeds brought two hundred and more years earlier into the country by the Spanish. They no sooner spied Crockett's mustang than they raised their heads, whinnied, and began moving about Crockett in a circle that gradually grew smaller and smaller until they completely surrounded him.

Crockett's little mustang seemed to enjoy the attention. He playfully bit the neck of one, rubbed noses with another, kicked up his heels at a third. Crockett decided in a few moments that the little animal had had sport enough, and applied the spur. The mustang rose straight in the air on his forefeet. Crockett kept his seat, but the mustang was off in a moment at full speed, his head up, his thin little mane and tail streaming, the whole drove following swiftly in his wake. Occasionally the little horse neighed as if to keep the others near him, and on they came. The prairie lay before them as far as eye could reach, a boundless racetrack. Still the little horse ran at full speed. Crockett had long since lost control of him.

The mustang kept the lead over the drove for more than half an hour, neighing now and then in triumph and derision. But he was obliged to carry Crockett's weight while his competitors were free. A fine bay that had been close behind all the way came up side by side with him; they had it, hip and thigh. At length the bay darted ahead. Presently a second horse shot by. Others began to pass, until at last even the scrubbiest little horse in the drove passed the mustang. They had almost reached the banks of a broad river, and the bay leaped into its waters. The others followed, stemming the current and climbing the opposite bank. Freshened by the plunge, they dashed off over the farther plain. The mustang sank exhausted by the riverbank.

Crockett loosened the saddle and rubbed him down. The little horse, completely exhausted, lay on his side, now and then heaving a deep sigh. At times he seemed hardly to breathe at all. Crockett was convinced he would not live until morning. The predicament was dangerous enough. Where were the Bee Hunter, Thimblerig, the Pirate, the Indian? How would he reach Bexar? Even if the mustang survived, Crockett was many times lost after that headlong ride. A roaming band of Indians from any one of the hostile tribes might bear down upon him at any moment. He had no way of knowing how far he had wandered toward the Indian country.

Near the riverbank was a great oak that had recently been blown down, and he decided to make a place to sleep in its branches for what protection these would afford. He gave some further attention to the little horse, then turned back to the tree, took a swift step and leaped to an upper branch, and looked through an opening in the leaves to see a restless Mexican cougar [1] half curled on a higher limb, surveying him as a nervous epicure surveys a table before taking a good dish. His eyes glittered in the shadow like great topazes, his teeth showed white, his flat head was stretched forward. As a rule the cougar will not attack a man unless hungry or cornered, but because of Crockett's swift movement and position the animal — hungry no doubt — was now at bay. He crouched to spring. Crockett's rifle lay in a crotch of the tree, placed there by habit. He seized it instantly, leveled, and fired.

In the fraction of a second the animal had moved slightly; the ball struck the top of his head and glanced off. The cougar shook his head as though nothing more than a bee had stung him. Crockett slipped down and the cougar sprang. Crockett struck at him with the butt of his rifle, but the cougar wheeled quickly and sprang again. They were now on the ground. The gun was useless. Crockett let it fall and drew his knife as the cougar closed upon his left arm. The big cat let

[1] **cougar:** panther. Also called *puma, catamount, mountain lion.*

go as the knife sank into his side but, freeing himself, came back again with increased fury. Crockett tried to blind him by a blow across the eyes, but the animal turned and the blow struck his nose instead. Stepping backward, Crockett tripped on a vine and fell. The cougar was down on him and seized Crockett's thigh. At that moment, since the cougar was turned about, Crockett grasped his tail and struck at his ribs with his hunting knife. As they scuffled they reached the river and Crockett summoned all his strength to throw the big cat over the bank, but he could not free himself and the cougar dragged him to the very edge. They seemed about to go over together, but Crockett was uppermost in the tight grasp and aimed a blow at the animal's neck. The knife entered the gullet up to the handle. The cougar struggled for a few moments, grew lax, and fell dead.

"Hunting bears is child's play to this," thought Crockett. "That cat was down on me, when I fell, like a nighthawk on a June bug." He was badly scratched and his leggings torn, but that was all. The cougar had probably seen Crockett from a distance as the horses dashed to the river; had prowled swiftly through the long grass and cactus, stealthily slipping into the tree to find a vantage point from which to watch.

Crockett ate one of the few biscuits left in his pouch and looked at the mustang. The gallant little horse had stopped breathing. With no very happy reflections Crockett hung his saddle in the tree, threw his blankets across some branches, and stretched himself along this rough hammock as best he could.

At daybreak he awoke, stiff and sore from the encounter with the cougar and his uncomfortable bed. As he looked about he found not even the bones of the mustang or a piece of his hide in sight. Not so much as a mark showed near the place where he had lain. Crockett had heard nothing during the night. Another prowling cougar could hardly have carried the little horse away without noise, without leaving a trace. Whatever the cause of the mystery, the horse was gone. Lost on the prairie, Crockett knew that his danger was now more than doubled, and the biscuit had been a thin breakfast.

As he sat by the riverbank trying to make a decision, he saw a familiar sign in the sky far in the distance — a dark wedge that came nearer and nearer, widening. He crouched down under the cover of the fallen tree and watched until the flock of wild geese suddenly dipped toward the river, some alighting on each side. He shot a fine gander, and the flock was off, soaring high in sudden flight, honking, flapping, again pointed northward in a long wedge and soon gone. Stripping the gander of his feathers, he quickly had him on a spit roasting.

Crockett made a hearty meal and was preparing to depart with the sun for a guide when he heard the trampling of many horses. Walking out from the shelter of the tree, he saw a large cavalcade of Indians on horseback riding toward him full tilt, their knives and feather headdresses and scarlet paint glittering in the sun. Advancing rapidly, the column divided into two semicircles; and in an instant Crockett was surrounded by a hundred or more Comanches,[1] the dreaded warriors of the plains, half naked and fully armed. The Comanches had learned of the growing strife on the Mexican border and had chosen a touch-and-go alliance with the Americans which might be broken at any time. They showed their sentiment to Crockett by signs and broken words. The little stream of smoke from his fire had caught their attention and they had come to investigate. When they saw the tawny body of the cougar on the

[1] **Comanches:** members of an Indian tribe.

riverbank, they were more than friendly. They saluted Crockett as a great hunter. "Brave hunter, brave man," said the chief.

By talk and signs Crockett made known his predicament and explained that he was bound for Bexar. The chief offered him one of the spare horses and said the band would accompany him as far as the Colorado River.

Crockett rode all day with the Comanches over the prairie, in the midst of the bright glitter of their accouterments and their pleasant signs and talk. No horsemen sat more gracefully than they. Crockett was on his mettle not to disturb the reputation he had made as a hunter by an awkward turn in riding.

They had not ridden many miles before they saw a drove of horses quietly pasturing in the distance. Some of the Indians got lassos ready and darted toward them. The drove let the party approach fairly close, then with one motion started up at a canter, first circling briskly about as if to spy out what was wanted, then abruptly changing their course and running with heads outstretched, so swiftly that all but two or three soon grew small on the horizon. These were swiftly lassoed, and they reared and pawed and tore at the thongs — all but one, that made no attempt to escape but stood planted, alone and quiet, with his head down. This was a little mustang. The Indian bridled him.

When Crockett came up, the rascally, scrawny, rusty little horse cast down his head and looked sheepish as if he knew what a shabby trick he had played in shamming death and stealing away in the night. It was Crockett's own mustang. One of the Comanches explained that he had been captured the more easily because he had been thoroughly broken.

Crockett rode with the Comanches all day. Toward evening they saw a small herd of buffalo in the distance, and moved to a point where they could shoot, and brought down two or three. Crockett, quickly learning the art, killed a young fat heifer, and rich steaks were soon roasting over coals. The humps were sewed in a skin with the tongues and marrow bones, put into a hole in the earth, and covered with fire that would be kept burning until the following noon, when the luscious meat would be ready to eat. The Comanches were preparing a feast for their new white friend.

The sun went down as they sat at supper. The air of evening was pure and transparent. For a little while the rich green of the prairie showed against the sky.

The chief asked Crockett about the white people of his own country, and Crockett told what the Comanches would be most pleased to hear about hunting. The Comanche chief in turn told a tale of coyotes of the prairie. Crockett had learned of the comanche song or wolf song, and asked the chief about this.

When an attack was planned it was the duty of certain warriors to move ahead of the war party at night, discover the moment for falling upon the enemy unawares, and give the signal. These warriors were called wolves, and from ancient days a song about them had come down to the tribe. As the fire died Crockett heard the chanting of the Comanches who sat in the wide circle, their wild and mournful tones rising in the blackness of the night. The tones grew deeper; but this song was not a signal for battle, and soon all was quiet.

At noon the next day the feast of juicy humps and marrow bones was held; and presently the whole band was off, riding by easy stages until they reached the Colorado River. Here Crockett might have proceeded alone, but the Comanches seemed unwilling to leave him and offered to go on until they reached a point where the Colorado crossed the old Spanish road to Bexar.

In the morning they saw a light column of smoke ascending in the clear sky from a small cluster of trees some distance away. Quickly the Indians divided in two wide semicircles, at first moving cautiously, then with a quick plunge bearing down on the little grove, surrounding it, and drawing up with a loud, raucous whoop. In the center stood Thimblerig, his brassy countenance white. He had been playing with the thimbles on the top of his white hat. His Vicksburger had now rolled to the ground, and on a bit of turf lay the thimbles and peas.

Crockett spoke. " Thimblerig is my friend," he said with a handsome gesture. The Indians gazed upon this new paleface and his queer toys with intense curiosity. Thimblerig seemed flattered by this attention and gradually regained some of his color and his swagger.

The grove was near the road to Bexar, and the Comanches pointed to the trail. Thanking the chief for his guidance and friendship, Crockett gave him a bowie knife;[1] and the chief replied that he would always keep it for the sake of a brave hunter. Soon the Comanches were off, vanishing in a thin glittering line into the deep purple haze of the horizon.

When Crockett turned to the fire, there stood the Bee Hunter as though he had sprung out of the ground, staggering under the weight of a huge wild turkey. He had been traveling with Thimblerig, but Thimblerig had been too much occupied by his adventure with the Comanches to mention this.

When the Bee Hunter had departed so abruptly he had, as Crockett thought, spied a solitary bee taking its course toward home, and he had been unable to control his ruling passion. He had traced his tiny game through the labyrinths of the air and had found the bees many miles away in a tall oak set within a little grove. It had taken him a long time to gain his plunder, for he carried only a small ax. At first the tree had barely trembled with the sharp cracking; it was hard to fell. At last it had broken with a thundering sound, its limbs splintering and plunging into the ground, and the sun shone with splendor on the spoils of golden honey. The hollow trunk contained, as the Bee Hunter said, a " big chance of it." At least nine feet of its length was full of honey.

" There was a nation of bees," he went on, " a whole nation of bees, and they came down on me at first like Comanches on the warpath. I got stung a little; but I built a big smoky fire, and that quelled them. It seemed almost a pity to rob them of their hive when I couldn't carry the honey away. But I drained the wax and have it here in my bag. That was what took me so long. See yonder! " he cried. " There's a fine bee! He went into that tree," and the Bee Hunter pointed to a towering oak, blue in the distance. " On a clear day, I can see a bee a mile away — easy."

Thimblerig looked at Crockett. The lid of one of Thimblerig's eyes fell upon his cheek. Crockett stared at him and said nothing.

" It's a curious fact," continued the Bee Hunter meditatively, " that bees are never found in wild country, but they always appear before the white men arrive. When the Indians see a bee, they say there comes the white man."

Then he went on with the story, with flourishes from Thimblerig. When the Bee Hunter had raced away over the prairies after his bee and Crockett had sped in a different direction in pursuit of the buffaloes, Thimblerig, left alone, had decided to retrace his steps to Nacogdoches. He expected to meet the Pirate and the In-

[1] **bowie knife:** a strong hunting knife with a cross guard and a long blade curved at the point.

dian along the trail, but he saw nothing of them. At length, however, since the Bee Hunter was returning along the track they had all first followed, the two met and decided to continue on the way to Bexar. They were almost bound to meet or overtake Crockett on the way since the Comanches were guiding him to the Spanish road.

" Well," said Thimblerig lazily, " what about a meal? " He had been eying the turkey with favorable glances.

" You've plucked many a traveler; you ought to know how to pluck a bird," said Crockett. " Fall to," and he looked so threatening that Thimblerig promptly went to work.

The neighing of their horses startled the trio as they were about to sit down for supper. Out on the prairie they saw two men approaching on horseback, armed with rifles. The three sprang to their feet, seizing their own weapons; for as the Bee Hunter had said, they were now more likely to meet enemies than friends. These might be Mexican scouts. But the pair turned out to be the old Pirate and his Indian companion. The Pirate explained that after they had walked a good many miles they had been fortunate enough to find a pair of mustangs hobbled in some woods.

" Couldn't say just where. They was asking to be taken. Mexican saddles," he added.

The Pirate did not tell what route he had followed with the Indian but said that he had heard somewhere along the way a rumor that Santa Anna, the Mexican general, had come out of hiding and that the Mexican forces were now no great distance from the border.

But nothing could have been less eventful than the journey of the five men for many miles. They rode through open country in which the redbud was coming toward bloom, where the grass lay like a lawn. They passed great live oaks covered with silvery Spanish moss. They rode into an arid region, covered by dwarf live oaks and twisted mesquite, then out again into green country. They saw nothing in motion except the billowing of grass in a light wind or scurrying jack rabbits and prairie chickens.

Then in the afternoon, when they were a few hours' ride from Bexar, a band of fifteen or twenty men on horseback appeared suddenly over a slight rise of ground in the distance and approached at full speed. " Look out for squalls," said the Pirate. " They're Mexicans."

" Spread and dismount and trust to our guns," said Crockett, and the five scattered in a little line, each behind his horse, Thimblerig alert with the rest.

When the Mexicans perceived this movement they checked their speed and spread their own line, then drew nearer. The leader, a tall man with a red feather in his hat, called out in Spanish. The Pirate said that he demanded surrender.

" It'll be a brush," said Crockett. " Each pick out his man for the first shot."

The Mexicans shouted again.

" Fire and be damned," said the Pirate at the top of his voice.

The Mexicans discharged their muskets, but their aim happened to be poor. Crockett and his companions fired at the same moment, and when the smoke rose some of the Mexican horses were seen running riderless; the leader and two others lay quiet on the ground. The remainder of the party swept away in rapid retreat. Crockett and his friends tried to follow them, but the Mexicans had the start. Their horses seemed to be fresh, and they were soon lost to view.

The five companions turned toward Bexar. At last, after dusk, they saw the low outlines of the little town spread along the banks of the San Antonio. Dim lights shone out. With Crockett at their head the small band entered and was received with shouts of welcome.

As the story continues, the Bee Hunter, Thimblerig, the Pirate, the Indian, showed a noble courage at the great siege of the Alamo,[1] and Thimblerig's bravery was touched with his usual bravado. When the Mexicans were scouting in the town of Bexar he sat on the walls and played with the thimbles, and afterward took pot shots at the enemy from this highly exposed position. The old Pirate trudged off on a dangerous mission to Goliad, and the Bee Hunter went out in the dusk in the midst of the hot fire of the enemy to help save him on the return journey. They all died bravely. Thimblerig stayed with Crockett to the last.

These four are figures in a story; they remain as part of a legend. Yet threads of circumstance draw them toward reality. Among the defenders of the Alamo were many such obscure men; some of these had come to Bexar in groups of three or four, as volunteers. An early muster gave the name of Daniel Jackson, a sailor. At Natchitoches the Bee Hunter has been identified in tradition with a man named Johnson; and a young man named Johnson is known to have acted as a courier from Bexar to Goliad during the siege. A famous gambler of the day may perhaps be identified with the figure of Thimblerig — Jonathan Harrington Green, who was well known at Mill's Point, where Crockett left Tennessee, and in Little Rock, in Fulton, the upper Red River country, and on many western river boats. He was traveling in Arkansas when Crockett was; he afterward referred to Crockett as though he had known him, and spoke of events of this time as a participant. A gambler is said to have been one of Crockett's company when he entered Texas.

[1] **the Alamo:** the chapel of the Mission San Antonio de Valero. It was named from the grove of cottonwood — *álamo* — in which it stands.

On this long and fateful journey, in those obscure weeks when he was away from Nacogdoches, Crockett may have engaged in exploits not unlike those related in the story. These exploits, as they are told, were drawn from tales of the time about many men, but none is incredible; any one of them might have belonged to Crockett; they are consistent with his powers and with his character. And those wild beautiful rides over open country in the oncoming spring — on the way to Bexar, Crockett must have known something equally fresh and exhilarating. In the end he must have approached Bexar much as he does in the story, to meet a hearty welcome.

THINK BACK OVER WHAT YOU HAVE READ

Getting Better Acquainted with Crockett

1. What episodes in this chapter show Crockett's friendliness? bravery? self-reliance?
2. How do you account for the readiness of the Indians to make friends with Crockett? How did their friendship help him? What evidence can you find in this and other chapters to support the belief that Crockett was friendly toward the Indians?
3. Judging from the stories told in this chapter, what were some of the outstanding characteristics of Davy Crockett?
4. What stories about Crockett and his companions read more like legend than history? Why do you think so? Can you name other heroes of our country about whom legends have sprung up? What legends?
5. How did Davy react to his five companions? If you had to make a similar journey, which ones would you select to accompany you? Why? Which ones would you try to avoid? Why?

V. THE ALAMO

Like all people, you admire bravery — most of all, the bravery that men show in a losing fight. Perhaps your favorite heroes are those who, with their backs to the wall, fought the good fight to the finish, unflinching and unafraid, though they knew that their struggle was useless. With such heroes we always associate the spirit of romance. Elsewhere in this book you will read poems about Sir Richard Grenville and General Robert E. Lee — fighters whom the world admires, not because they won, but because they lost gloriously.

Perhaps in your own experience you have given unstinted admiration to the teams of your school or those of other schools which put up a spirited fight against superior opposition. You have learned that it is the fight that matters, not the winning.

Here is a story of a great battle — Crockett's last — that will stir your deepest emotions, for it was fought by men who faced their duty in the best American tradition.

THE SMALL town of Bexar was now almost as solitary on the great plains of Texas as the first mission had been a century before, when the Spanish fathers came, bringing their faith to wandering tribes of Indians. A hundred miles or more to the east was the small village of Goliad. Perhaps seventy miles to the southeast was Gonzales. Each was held by small numbers of Texans. There were a few settlements on the Gulf and on the Brazos River. Here and there over the wide spaces farmers' cabins had been built. The rest was open empty country. Now even the small farms and plantations clustering about Bexar were for the most part deserted.

The rumors that Crockett and others had heard on the way to Nacogdoches were true. An army of two thousand men had reached the Rio Grande under the command of Santa Anna, the Mexican dictator. A larger number had been equipped and was moving by forced marches to join them.

After wresting Bexar from the Mexicans in the early winter, the Texan forces had scattered. Only a small number remained in the town, about one hundred and forty-five men. James Bowie, in command, was noted for his strength and agility as well as for his prowess with the famous bowie knife. It was said that he could rope and tie alligators. He had come into Texas searching for great tracts of rich farm land. He had also been looking for fabled silver mines which had drawn many adventurers into the Southwest from the days of the Spanish *conquistadores* [1] onward. A tall, fair, quiet man, with slender supple hands, he hardly looked as though he had engaged in the desperate clashes attributed to him.

William Travis, at Bexar with a company, had played a part in many encounters along the Texas border. He was ambitious, passionate, with a capacity for swift action and a great gift with words.

Many of the men were hunters from Kentucky and Tennessee; Crockett undoubtedly knew some of them, besides those in his company. He was promptly offered a command by Travis; but he refused this, saying that he preferred to remain a private. He had always been a lone hunter and he maintained this position until toward the end, though there seems to have been an understanding that the men from Tennessee should stand together.

From the first there had been small clashes of authority, jealousies, and uncertainties at Bexar. The place had been stripped of supplies; Houston [2] had sent Bowie there from Goliad about the middle of January with orders to have the town abandoned; he was certain that sufficient forces could not be mustered to defend it. But Bowie, on arriving, had decided otherwise, and wrote, "We had rather die in these ditches than give it up to the enemy." Travis, courageous to the point of rash-

[1] **conquistadores:** conquerors (Spanish), those who first conquered Mexico. [2] **Houston:** Sam Houston, commander in chief of the Texan army; elected governor after Texas won its independence from Mexico.

ness, probably wanted the command held by Bowie. There was constant friction between the two men, and this may have been deepened by other forces whose direction cannot be fully traced. Beneath all the exultant movement of the new settlers in Texas were swift political undercurrents. Since the outbreak of the Texas Revolution it had been difficult to maintain a clear policy among men who were widely scattered, whose interests were diverse. Houston, in general command, was not yet secure in that position.

Perhaps the rankling of an old anger [1] and the force of settled conviction had caused Crockett to throw in his lot with Bowie and Travis. Houston was a sworn friend of Jackson's, and partisanship as to the Jacksonian policies had reached into Texas.

The strange circumstance was that these three men, with different purposes, should have clung to their position at Bexar. The magnet that held them there seemed to hold the volunteers as well. For the most part they had come to this new land as Crockett had come: because distances spoke to them, because they liked unpremeditated adventure, for land — a handful out of many in those days who flung themselves against heavy odds and took hardy enterprises easily. In the face of oncoming danger they determined to hold Bexar because it was a last outpost, a key to Texas; enthusiasm for a free Texas was running high. They were governed by another motive, mighty if intangible. Frontiersmen were accustomed to hold what they had taken, then move onward. In the glowing future which Crockett saw so plainly — of which he had written with such warmth to his children — Bexar would become only one of a succession of settlements, stretching farther and farther into the West. A whole people was resistlessly moving, claiming new land, often quickly leaving it, pressing onward, "ahead!" They gave many reasons for their eagerness, but their reasons were not so good as their courage, not so clear as the power that drew them to untouched country.

In spite of differences in authority these obscure days of mid-February at Bexar must have been full of suppressed triumph, glittering purposes, gay talk. Crockett was popular with all the men; he made speeches, told stories. Never a fiddler, he apparently found an old instrument somewhere in the town and amused the company by his efforts to play. Sometimes he joined in rousing competition against a Scotsman's bagpipes, lifting his voice in song against the lusty medley. News from east of the Mississippi was to be traded. Headrights to land were surely discussed. There must have been tales of the warring tribes of Indians to the north, and of trappers who had gone into the Rockies and beyond. There was warm gossip of men and events along the border, much laughter, many jokes, much drinking. If the talk turned to the Mexican advance, there could have been only one shout, "Let 'em come!"

Suddenly, silently, the Mexicans in Bexar fled from the town. Within a few days it was clear that the Mexican army was approaching at last.

The story goes that one evening something that might have been a pile of leaves was seen to move in a distant patch of chaparral [2] where the ground was gray and dry. Presently a figure stood up, ran, and drew near a cluster of men on the edge of the town. It was a hunter who had been

[1] **an old anger:** Although Crockett had served in the Creek War under General Andrew Jackson, he later bitterly opposed the latter's plan to remove the Indians from the states of the far South. Crockett believed such removal dishonorable, since a treaty with the Creeks had promised them security and protection. His opposition to Jackson cost Crockett his seat in Congress.

[2] **chaparral:** a close, low-growing thicket.

absent from Bexar for several days on a scouting expedition. His jacket and leggings were so gray and tattered that he could easily have lain down again against a hillock and have been taken for part of it. Indians to the south had told him that the Mexican army was now nearing Bexar, planning their first great attack there. The shout went up, " Let 'em come! "

" I'm a whole menagerie, Colonel," the hunter told Crockett after delivering his news, " shaggy as a bear, wolfish about the head, stealthy as a cougar on the hunt. I've heard you could grin [1] till the bark'll peel off a gum log. So can I. Let 'em come! "

A more substantial account is that scouts were sent to discover whether the Mexicans were proceeding toward Bexar, as had been reported in the town. A party went out and from a rise of ground could discern the great army drawn up for parade, with the officers moving up and down, gesticulating.

As a signal to the people of Bexar the bells of the church of San Fernando were rung; and the defending forces moved into the fortified mission of the Alamo, about half a mile from the town. A stoutly built granary adjoined it, with a baptistry and other small rooms. From the northwest corner of the church a wall twelve feet high extended for fifty feet to the long barracks, a two-story building. From the southwest corner a strongly built stockade ran for seventy-five feet to the low barracks. The buildings and walled inclosures covered about two acres of ground. Cannon had been mounted on the scaffold of the church and on the barrier walls. The stockades and walls were thick. But at least a thousand men were needed to defend the Alamo.

Santa Anna arrived at the Medina River with his army on the night of February the twentieth. The next morning the dark line of the Mexican forces was seen in advance. Provisions at Bexar were short. Travis hastily sent out a scouting force which brought in eighty or ninety bushels of corn and twenty or thirty beeves.

Bowie suddenly became helplessly ill. The command passed to Travis. Within a few days Travis became sick. According to one story — flying no one knows from where — Travis, realizing his condition, begged Crockett to assume command of the forces in the coming struggle. Crockett declined, but there was no question as to the eagerness of his service. In one of his many letters Travis wrote that " Colonel Crockett was seen at all points, animating the men to do their duty." Crockett offered to go on a dangerous errand to Goliad, but Travis evidently preferred to have him remain at the Alamo.

Within a day or two the great Mexican army was seen approaching Bexar in solid regular formation, their officers on brightly decked horses. They entered the town and took possession. The next morning a messenger was sent by Santa Anna to Travis, demanding unconditional surrender and declaring that he would put every man to the sword in case of refusal. The only answer from the Alamo was a cannon shot. In counter reply the Mexicans ran up a blood-red flag to show that they would give no quarter. They then bombarded the Alamo for twenty-four hours from a distance. So thick were its walls, so securely were its defenders entrenched that not one was lost. The fortress seemed as solid at the end of the bombardment as before. The Mexicans, weary from their long forced marches, did not press the siege. But those within the mission can have had no sense of security; to a man they must have known their peril.

[1] **grin**: Many stories were told about Crockett's grin, most of them having to do with his mastery over animals.

The night of February twenty-fourth Travis dispatched Colonel Bonham to Goliad, bearing a letter that has been called the most heroic document in American history. It was addressed "To the People of Texas & All Americans in the World."

Fellow Citizens and Compatriots, I am besieged by a thousand or more of the Mexicans under Santa Anna. I have sustained a continual Bombardment for 24 hours & have not lost a man. The enemy has demanded a surrender at discretion; otherwise, the garrison are to be put to the sword if the fort is taken. I have answered the demand with a cannon shot & our flag still waves proudly from the walls. *I shall never surrender or retreat*. Then, I call upon you in the name of Liberty, of patriotism & everything dear to the American character, to come to our aid with all dispatch. The enemy is receiving re-enforcements daily & will no doubt increase to three or four thousand in four or five days. If this call is neglected, I am determined to sustain myself as long as possible and die like a soldier who never forgets what is due to his own honor & that of his country.

VICTORY OR DEATH.

W. Barrett Travis
Lt. Col. Comdt.

At the same time Travis sent a volunteer who knew the land to go east to Gonzales for assistance there. At the most fortunate nothing could be expected from any of these expeditions for several days.

The Mexicans rested, awaiting re-enforcements, contenting themselves with intermittent firing. Within the Alamo there was the restless waiting of men who were compelled to remain inactive, who would gladly have faced their fate at once. Fresh Mexican contingents were arriving.

At the end of six days, in the gray dark of the earliest dawn, thirty-two volunteers crept into the Alamo. They had come from Gonzales. They were all cheerful, though they knew well what the outcome would be if the Alamo were lost. There was still no word from Bonham. Another messenger had been sent to follow him. Thinking that both might have been captured by a Mexican contingent, Travis sent another volunteer to carry word to Goliad.

The same evening when dark had fallen Travis sent still another messenger bearing a letter to the village of Washington-on-the-Brazos, where Texans were writing a Declaration of Independence:

The spirits of my men are still high, although they have had much to depress them. We have contended for ten days against an enemy whose number are variously estimated at from fifteen hundred to six thousand men. . . . Col. Fannin is said to be on the march to this place with re-enforcements but I fear it is not true, as I have *repeatedly* sent to him for aid without receiving any. . . . I look to the colonies alone for aid; unless it arrives soon I shall have to fight the enemy on his own terms. I will, however, do the best I can under the circumstances; and I feel confident that the determined valor and desperate courage, heretofore exhibited by my men, will not fail them in the last struggle; and although they may be sacrificed to the vengeance of a Gothic enemy, the victory will cost the enemy so dear that it will be worse for him than defeat. I hope your honorable body will hasten re-enforcements, ammunitions, and provisions to our aid as soon as possible. We have provisions for twenty days for the men we have. Our supply of ammunition is limited. At least five hundred pounds of cannon powder, and two hundred rounds of six-, twelve-, and eighteen-pound balls, ten kegs of rifle powder, and a supply of lead should be sent to the place without delay, under a sufficient guard.

If these things are promptly sent and larger re-enforcements are hastened to this frontier, this neighborhood will be the great and decisive ground. The power of Santa Anna is to be met here or in the colonies; we had better meet it here than to suffer a war of devastation to rage in our settlements. A blood-red banner waves from the church in Bexar and in the camp above us, in token that the war is one of vengeance against rebels; they have declared us as such; demanded that we should surrender at discretion, or that this garrison should be put to the sword. Their threats have no influence on me or my men but to make all fight with desperation and that high-souled courage which characterizes the patriot who is willing to die in defense of his country's liberty and his own honor.

During the night the Mexicans had established two batteries on the farther side of the river and had posted a company there. Cavalry was sent to occupy the eastern boundaries beyond the town and the trail toward Gonzales. Clearly the enemy was attempting to surround the Alamo, but on two sides lay open country cut by ditches that the defenders could easily command.

Provisions in the garrison grew still more meager. Bowie became critically ill. The next morning heavy cannonading began; bombs were thrown into the stockades. These exploded without mischief. Another day passed, of tension, expectancy.

Before dawn on the following morning Bonham returned. There was no hope of assistance from Goliad. Colonel Fannin had assembled three hundred men with cannon, other arms, and ammunition, and had started out with a wagon train for Bexar, on receiving Travis's message. But the expedition had been too hastily improvised. The wagons with their heavy loads had broken down on the rough trail and the scant provisions had given out. It was impossible to cross the swollen rivers and streams with the artillery. Fannin with his men had been obliged to turn back; and as they did so, word came that another contingent of the Mexican army was marching on Goliad. He was compelled to retain his forces for the protection of the people of Goliad. Fannin had urged Bonham to remain in Goliad, since he was certain either to be intercepted by the enemy or to fight against overwhelming forces at Bexar. Bonham had said, " I will report to Travis," and had started back at once on the hazardous journey, making his way by night, stealthily evading the enemy who were now widely posted over the prairie. A few hours later the second messenger who had gone to Goliad slipped in. He, too, had declined to remain there.

There were cheers when Travis said that if the enemy took the Alamo his men could only fight to the last gasp, making conquest mean the heaviest possible loss to the victors. Even as they cheered, shells began to fall about the fort with increasing frequency, now from shorter range. Though not in command Crockett was everywhere at once with the swiftness of the hunter of the forest, taking shot after shot over the parapets, hastening below to re-enforce the doors still further, mustering more men to take positions above and hurrying there again to use his own sure aim.

The defenders remained at their posts all day with shells flying into their midst; not one of them was lost. They picked off Mexican gunners from a distance. They shot warily into the chaparral, catching the enemy as they dodged from low hillock to hillock or crept near the fort from buildings within the town. Toward nightfall the Mexican forces had succeeded in maintaining positions nearer the Alamo, making a partial ring just out of gunshot.

At midnight Travis had his cot carried into the nave of the church and summoned the entire garrison before him. The Mexican bombardment had not begun. Travis's words echoed in the dim stillness.

" We are overwhelmed," he said, " and our fate is sealed. Within a few days, perhaps within a few hours, we must be in eternity. It is no longer a question of how we may save our lives, but how best to prepare for death and serve our country. If we surrender we shall be shot without taking the life of a single one of our enemy. If we try to make our escape we shall be butchered before we can dispatch our adversaries. To either of these courses I am opposed, and I ask you to withstand the advance of the enemy. When they shall storm the fort and scale our walls at last, let us slay them as they come. As they leap over the ramparts, slay we all of them until our arms are powerless to lift our swords in defense of ourselves, our comrades, our country. Yet to every man I give permission to surrender or attempt to escape. My desire and decision is to remain in the fort and fight as long as breath remains in my body. Do as you think best, each of you. Those who consent to remain with me to the end will give me joy unspeakable."

Weak as he was, Travis raised himself from his pallet, stood, and stepped forward. With his sword he drew a line across the floor. He called upon the men to take their position.

" Those who will remain and fight until we die, step across this line to my right."

Crockett was the first to step forward. At the same moment James Bowie, who was still sick, called upon his friends to carry his bed across the line and place it beside Travis. Every man in the garrison walked across the line except one, who covered his face with his hands.

" You seem unwilling to die with us," said Travis.

" I am not prepared to die, and shall not if I can help it," he answered. " I speak the language of the enemy fluently. Perhaps I can get through the lines."

No one interfered with his departure. Nothing further was ever heard of him. It has been denied, with good evidence, that even this one man left.

What Crockett thought during these moments none can guess. Perhaps he remembered rivers and forests he had known well. Perhaps he thought of his children and of his wife. Since he was given to action, he may have thought most of the desperate work that lay ahead.

At least five thousand of the enemy were now assembled. During the night of March the fifth Santa Anna quietly prepared a great assault upon the mission. In silence four storming columns took their places, provided with ladders, crowbars, axes. With the hoofs of their horses muffled, cavalrymen seized strategic points around the town to cut off the possibility of escape or re-enforcement. Sharpshooters ceased their sniping in the chaparral; the artillery was still. The thick ring about the Alamo was now complete. Men were posted at every vantage point in the houses and on the streets.

As the first glitter of light fell upon the river and the town, a bugle was sounded by the Mexicans and the assault began. Afterward Santa Anna insisted that he would have surprised the garrison had not one of the columns raised a shout as the bugle sounded: but the men within the Alamo had been expecting such an attack and were at their posts as the solid masses of the enemy pressed forward with the rat-tat-tat of drums. Guns roared from the streets. Shells rained over the parapets of the fortress, faster, nearer.

On the walls the defenders — Crockett among them — picked off cavalry leaders and those infantrymen who were rolling cannon forward. But the enemy pushed over the dead bodies of their comrades, advancing, narrowing the space between themselves and the fort. Their numbers were overwhelming. Their ranks, now blurred by clouds of smoke, moved still nearer. As many dropped under fire others crowded into their places. The ring of men, horses, cannon, smoke, grew dense. The

Mexicans reached the plaza in front of the Alamo, and its walls were battered with rams and cannon. Soldiers swarmed over the ruins into the monastery court, and from the north side battering rams struck against the thick walls of the church. Ladders were raised.

As the enemy climbed the ramparts, they were met by the swift crack and deadly fire of rifles; but as half a dozen of them fell backward to the earth, others were ready to clamber into their places. The cannon on the roof no longer spoke. Fierce hand-to-hand fighting followed as the Mexicans climbed over the walls. Most of the Texans were quickly cut down by the overwhelming numbers. Some of them fought their way in retreat to the church below, only to find the enemy in full force there. After persistent ramming the monastery wall had given way, and the Mexicans had swept through the breach. The north door was being attacked with rams. Some of the Texans, drawing together in the nave of the church, had thrown together sacks of sand for ramparts and began shooting with nails, scraps of iron, whatever they could find with which to load their guns.

The doors of the church were now shattered by great blasts of powder, and the outer walls of some of the little rooms that opened upon the courtyard were attacked. The Texans still held the nave of the church but they were now approached from three, then four, sides. Fighting inch by inch against the rain of grape and canister, inflicting a terrible carnage, a small party of the defenders reached the baptistry, which had withstood the battering rams from without and was still uninvaded. One of the men tried to blow up a powder magazine there that they might die by their own act rather than at the hand of the enemy. He failed in this, shot through the heart by a Mexican bullet as he was lighting the fuse. The Texans fought in a blaze of powder, in clouds of smoke. Their ammunition gave out and they fought with clubs, with their bare hands.

Travis had manned a gun at the beginning of the attack and was almost instantly killed. The command was said to have passed to John Baugh, and after his death to Crockett. In the wild confusion Crockett seems to have been everywhere at once. A story was told afterward that as he leveled and fired his famous " Betsey " he sang invitingly to the Mexican, " Won't you come into my bower? " This would have been like him; perhaps he was heard singing this song in the earlier days of the siege. But when the final attack began there would have been no time for song, nor could any tune have been heard in the terrific din.

In later years it was said that five men were captured by the Mexicans at the end of the siege and that Crockett was of this number; these men were supposed to have been taken before General Santa Anna, who ordered them put to the sword. But Crockett was not taken prisoner. In the remembrance of a man like Crockett, in telling a story so heroic as that of the Alamo, the imagination of many people was touched. They evoked scenes as sharply as though they had been present, and told of them as though each episode in stories they had heard contained the entire truth. Strangely, a woman, Mrs. Dickinson, a little girl, and a Negro lad were safely concealed in one of the outer rooms; they were spared by the Mexicans, and it is in some of the tales told about them that Crockett was pictured as among the group of captives taken by General Castrillon before Santa Anna. Five Texans were captured, it is true, and slain at Santa Anna's command, but Crockett was not among that number. Mrs. Dickinson herself told the true story.

No quarter was given in battle; none

was intended. Throughout the assault the Mexicans played the diabolical *degüello,* meaning "no mercy," an ancient battle tune played by the Spanish centuries before in their wars against the Moors.[1] Crockett fell in the thickest of the swift and desperate clash. Travis had asked him to defend the wall on the south side toward the barracks; it was here that the fighting was hottest. The men from Tennessee fought with him. He fell with them, fighting bitterly. Mrs. Dickinson spoke afterward of seeing him lying among the slain, with his fur hunting cap at his side.

For twelve days the small garrison of Texans had withstood an army that had increased to numbers thirty times its size. The final assault was over within an hour. All the defenders were gone, none remained to tell the whole history. "Thermopylae[2] had its messenger of defeat; the Alamo had none."

All were lost, but their final end in that lonely place had something of barbaric glory. A huge pyre was built with cords of wood, and the bodies of the defenders were destroyed by great towering flames near the charred, broken walls of the Alamo.

Spring was coming in abundance. The acacia was golden. Blue buffalo clover would flower fresh as rain, lying in sheets of deep azure like water showing the southern sky. Along the creeks and water-courses the redbud and wild plum were feathered white and purple-red.

The harsh struggle was not ended by this great disaster. The wide, empty land was still a prize. Other battles swiftly followed between the Mexican and the Texan forces, at Goliad, at small places farther south along the Gulf. "Remember the Alamo! Remember the Alamo!" became the Texan battle cry. The Republic of Texas was declared, and Sam Houston directed the scattered forces. Triumph came at last under Houston. Santa Anna, with all his great army, was forced to sue for peace. The end of the conflict was ten years distant when the Americans sought both to hold Texas and to gain California, and the issue was fought in the Mexican War.

"Remember the Alamo! Remember the Alamo!" Even in those later years the words became a rallying cry. Songs were made about Crockett. One of these would have pleased him, for it was sung to an old and lively frolic tune called "Gray Goose."

> Remember gallant Crockett's bones
> Have found a glorious bed there.
> Then tell them in your thunder tones
> No tyrants' feet shall tread there.
> Come gather east, come gather west,
> Come round with Yankee thunder,
> Break down the power of Mexico
> And tread her tyrants under.

It was an odd circumstance that the tune "Gray Goose" should have been linked with Crockett's name, for the gray goose had been an emblem in his family.

In the reign of Louis XIV of France a handsome youth was for a time a member of the court, named Antoine Desasure Perronnette de Crocketagne. He became a Huguenot.[3] When the Huguenots were expelled from France he went to England with his young wife, then to Ireland, and changed his name to Crockett. He took for his crest the wild gray goose, noted for the altitude of its flight, its grace of motion, its power of wing, and for the fact that it flies against the wind.

Other Crocketts went from France to England and to Scotland, and the arms of the English family also showed wild birds, three crows, with a motto that Davy himself might have chosen, "Crow not, croak

[1] **Moors:** Mohammedans who invaded Spain in the Middle Ages. [2] **Thermopylae:** a pass between Thessaly and Greece where the Greek hero Leonidas died resisting the Persians (480 B.C.).

[3] **Huguenot:** a French Protestant of the sixteenth or seventeenth century.

not." The arms of the Scottish Crocketts showed words that a frontiersman might have spoken, " Let sleeping dogs lie."

But it was the Irish family that formed the ancestral line of Davy Crockett. The son of the handsome Huguenot married a girl from Donegal.[1] His son in turn married a Huguenot who had come to Ireland, and these two emigrated to Virginia. They were Davy Crockett's great-great-grandparents. The fate was a strange one that could lead a single family in successive generations from the gayest court in the world to the early frontier of the West, then farther and farther into wild land, and finally into one of the great battles of history on a far frontier. In one way or another they had all flown against the wind. The gray goose with its great power of wing was a fitting emblem for Davy Crockett.

THINK BACK OVER WHAT YOU HAVE READ

Admiring the Bravery of the Defenders of the Alamo

1. What political reasons may have influenced Crockett to cast his lot with the defenders of the Alamo? Do you consider these reasons worthy ones? the only ones? What do they tell you about Crockett?

2. How did the amusements engaged in by the men in the Alamo reveal their spirit?

3. What were the demands of Santa Anna? How were they answered? What does the answer show you about the spirit of the defenders?

4. Give reasons why the letter from Travis has been called " the most heroic document in American history " (page 213). What reason have you to believe that it reflected the feelings of all the defenders?

5. Pick out what you consider examples of conspicuous bravery.

6. Explain the statement on page 217: " Thermopylae had its messenger of defeat; the Alamo had none." What does this statement make you feel about the defenders?

[1] **Donegal:** a county in Ireland.

7. What later Texan battle cry was inspired by the defense of the Alamo? How does it reflect the popular opinion of the day?

8. What great examples of leadership do you recall? What effect do you imagine this leadership had on the spirit of the defenders? How important is good leadership?

9. What evidence can you find that Crockett did much to strengthen the morale of the defenders?

Looking Back over Davy Crockett's Life and Profiting from His Experience

10. Under what conditions may reckless bravery be a desirable trait? When may it be undesirable?

11. Do you think that Crockett did right to leave his wife to help the cause of the Texans? Be prepared to discuss this question fully.

12. What traits of Crockett did you find most worthy of imitation? How can those traits help you in your school life? in your life after you leave school?

13. What traits of Crockett would you avoid? Why?

14. What evidences of a lack of co-operation did you notice in the chapter on the Alamo? Do you think that better co-operation would have changed the outcome?

15. Why may we be justified in calling Crockett's companions " wasted lives "? Do you think that a brave death can atone for a worthless life? Were these companions wholly worthless? What elements of character did they need?

16. Was Travis, in your opinion, a good or bad leader? In your opinion what qualities are necessary for good leadership? Would Crockett have made a better or worse leader? Why?

Increase Your Power over Words

17. The word *epicure* (page 204) means one who enjoys luxurious things, especially the delicacies of the table. It is derived from Epicurus — a Greek philosopher who taught that pleasure is a good thing, and whose name came to be associated with the idea of luxury, especially the extravagant love of good food.

18. Another word of interesting derivation is *nave* (page 214), which names the main body of a church. It is derived from the Latin word *navis,* which means ship. Two different explanations have been given for the origin of the word: one points out a resemblance be-

tween the vaulted roof of the church and the inverted keel of a ship; the other, that the ship was an early symbol of the church.

For Ambitious Students

19. There are seven other chapters of *Davy Crockett* besides those reproduced for you in this text. Perhaps several students will volunteer to review the missing chapters for the benefit of the rest of the class.

20. An interesting history of Davy Crockett's time is *Andrew Jackson* by Marquis James. *Sam Houston,* a biography by the same author, also gives an interesting account of the times. Both of these books provide background for a fuller appreciation of *Davy Crockett.*

STRANGE CUSTOMS

by Etsu Inagaki Sugimoto (1874–)

From Richard Connell's story entitled "The Unfamiliar" you learned something of the part which ignorance plays in building up in the minds of unthinking people a prejudice against foreigners. Such prejudice is not confined to Crosby Corners. Sometimes it sweeps a whole nation like an epidemic and is directed against a whole race.

The cure for prejudice, you learned too, is understanding, and an easily available antidote is reading. Books break down the barriers between peoples created by ignorance, for they give the reader glimpses into the lives of foreigners which show that the same heart beats in every human breast.

The selection which you are about to read is taken from *A Daughter of the Samurai,* an appealing autobiography which has done much to dispel American prejudice against the Japanese. Here you will see American ways through the eyes of a foreigner, and come to realize that what seems familiar and natural to you may look strange and incomprehensible to others and that just as you expect foreigners to look upon American customs with understanding and tolerance, so must you — if you are to keep free of prejudice — accord this same understanding to them.

WE HAD a large stone church in our suburb which was not quite paid for, and a society of churchwomen called "The Ladies' Aid" occasionally gave a fair or concert and sometimes a play with local talent in order to obtain money to add to the fund.

One evening Mother,[1] Matsuo,[2] and I attended one of these concerts. On the program was a vocal solo of some classic selection. The singer was the gifted daughter of a wealthy citizen and had received her musical education in Europe. I knew her as a rather quiet young woman with a gentle voice and dignified manner; therefore, I was surprised, when the music began, to see her step forward briskly and informally; bow smilingly to the audience, right and left; and then, with much facial expression, give a vocal exhibition of high, clear trills and echoes that to my untrained ears was a strange and marvelous discord, but the most wonderful thing that I had ever heard in my life.

The effect left on my mind was of brightness, quick motion, and high-pitched sound. In strong contrast is our classic music, which always suggests subdued colors, slow movement, and deep, mellow tones. Also, like most Japanese art, our music requires listening eyes as well as ears. Otherwise its appeal is lost.

Our classic stage is always the same. The entire back is one solid board of natural cedarwood, on which is painted a gigantic dwarf pine. The floor is of camphorwood and is bare. On this the singers, who, of course, are always men, sit as motionless as dolls. Their dress is the old-fashioned, soft-hued garment of ceremony. Each one, before beginning to sing, makes a slow, deep bow and, with studied deliberation, places his fan horizontally before him on the floor. Then, with his hands on his knees, palms down, and sitting very erect and motionless, he tells in

[1] **Mother:** not Mrs. Sugimoto's real mother, but an American lady with whom Mr. and Mrs. Sugimoto lived. Mrs. Sugimoto calls her "my American mother." [2] **Matsuo:** Mr. Sugimoto.

song, and with incredible elocutionary power, some wonderful tale of war and romance; but wholly without movement of body or change of facial expression.

At the close the singer's face is often flushed with feeling; but, with no change of expression, he bows, then gently takes up his fan and resumes his former impassive attitude. The audience sits in profound silence. The listeners may be touched to tears or raised to the highest pitch of excitement, but this can be detected only by the sound of subdued sniffling or the catch of a quick sigh. For centuries repression has been the keynote of everything of a high character, and the greatest tribute that can be paid to a singer or an actor of classic drama is to be received in deep silence.

One thing in America to which I could not grow accustomed was the joking attitude in regard to women and money. From men and women of all classes, from newspapers, novels, lecturers, and once even from the pulpit, I heard allusions to amusing stories of women secreting money in odd places, coaxing it from their husbands, borrowing it from a friend, or saving it secretly for some private purpose. There was never anything dishonorable implied in this. Perhaps the money was saved to get new curtains for the parlor or even a birthday present for the husband. These jokes were a puzzle to me — and a constantly growing one; for as time passed on, I myself saw things which made me realize that probably a foundation of serious truth might lie beneath some of the amusing stories.

Our suburb was small and we were all interested in each other's affairs, so I was acquainted with almost everybody. I knew the ladies to be women of education and culture, yet there seemed to be among them a universal and openly confessed lack of responsibility about money. They all dressed well and seemed to have money for specific purposes, but no open purse to use with free and responsible judgment. Once at a church fair, where I had a table, several ladies, after walking around the hall and examining the various booths, had bought some small, cheap articles but left the expensive ones, saying, "My husband will be here later on and I'll get him to buy it," or "When the gentlemen come, those high-priced things will sell." I had never known a Japanese man to buy anything for his home, or be expected to.

Once when I was shopping with a friend, she stopped at her husband's office to ask him for money. I thought that was strange enough, but a still more curious thing happened when I went with Mother to a meeting of the church ladies where they were raising a certain amount for some unusual purpose. The Ladies' Aid had recently made a great many calls on the husbands' purses, and so this time each member had pledged herself to bring five dollars which she must obtain without asking her husband for it. The meeting I attended was the one where the money was handed in, each lady telling, as she gave it, how she had succeeded in getting her five dollars. Most had saved it in various ways, a little at a time. One said that she had made a real sacrifice and returned to her milliner a new hat — paid for, but not worn — receiving in exchange one that was five dollars less in price. Another had sold two theater tickets which had been given her. Still another told, in very witty rhyme, how she, a poor Ladies' Aid lady, had spent most of her leisure time for a week, and had pledged herself for a week longer, in darning stockings for the children of her neighbor, a rich non-Ladies' Aid lady.

The meeting was intensely interesting. It reminded me of our poem-making parties — only, of course, this was gayer and these stories were on an undignified subject. I enjoyed it all until a pretty, bright, and beautifully dressed woman rose and said that she didn't know how to save money and she didn't know how to earn it. She had promised not to cheat in her charge account at the store, and she had promised not to ask her husband for the five dollars, so she had done the only thing that was left for her to do: she had stolen it from her husband's pocket when he was asleep.

This report caused a great deal of merriment, but I was saddened. All the reports seemed tragic after she said, "That was the only thing left to do." It seemed incredible, here in America, where women are free and commanding, that a woman of dignity and culture, the mistress of a home, the mother of children, should be forced either to ask her husband for money or be placed in a humiliating position.

When I left home, Japan, at large, was still following the old custom of educating a girl to be responsible for the well-being of her entire family — husband included. The husband was the lord of the family; but the wife was mistress of the home and, according to her own judgment, controlled all its expenses — the house, the food, the children's clothing and education, all social and charitable responsibilities, and her own dress — the material and style of which were expected to conform to her husband's position.

Where did she get the money? The husband's income was for his family, and his wife was the banker. When he wanted money for himself he asked her for it, and it was her pride to manage so that she could allow him the amount suitable for a man of his standing. As to what the requirements of his position might be, there was little question; for to know this was part of the wife's education. The husband might shrug his shoulders and say, "It's very inconvenient"; but the entire house and its standing were his pride, and any disarrangement that would mar the whole was his loss. Therefore, the needs of the home came first. A man married, primarily, as a duty to the gods and to his ancestors; secondarily, to obtain a mistress for his home who would guide it in such a manner that it and his family might be a credit to him. If she managed well, he was complimented by his friends. If she failed, he was pitied.

This was true of all classes except lords of large estates or financial kings of business. In these cases there was a home treasurer; but he was at the call of the mistress, and her judgment as to her needs was supreme. The treasurer's only power of protest lay in the right to say, with many apologies, "The Honorable Mistress is about to overdraw her account." The hint was generally sufficient, for a Japanese woman, like everyone in a responsible position, desired to do her duty creditably.

Conventional forms are losing in rigidity year by year, but even yet the people are considerably influenced by rules which in the past were uniform and recognized by all. Any marked deviation from these is still considered bad form.

The standards of my own and my adopted country differed so widely in some ways, and my love for both lands was so sincere, that sometimes I had an odd feeling of standing upon a cloud in space and gazing with measuring eyes upon two separate worlds. At first I was continually trying to explain, by Japanese standards, all the queer things that came every day before my surprised eyes; for no one seemed to know the origin or significance of even the most familiar customs, nor why they existed and were followed. To me, coming from a land where there is an unforgotten reason for every fashion of dress, for every motion in etiquette — indeed, for almost every trivial act of life — this indifference of Americans seemed very singular.

Mother was a wonderful source of information, but I felt a hesitation about asking too many questions, for my curiosity was so frequently about odd, trifling, unimportant things, such as why ladies kept on their hats in church while men took theirs off; what was the use of the china plates which I saw hanging on the walls of some beautiful houses; why guests are taken to the privacy of a bedroom and asked to put their hats and cloaks on the *bed* (a place that suggested sleep or sickness); why people make social calls in the *evening* (the time of leisure in Japan); what originated the merriment and nonsense of Halloween and April Fools' Day; and why such a curious custom exists as the putting of gifts in stockings — *stockings,* the very humblest of all the garments that are worn.

It seemed strange to me that there should never be any hint or allusion to these customs in conversation, in books, or in newspapers. In Japan, tradition, folklore, and symbolism are before one all the time. The dress of the people on the streets, the trademark on the swinging curtains of the shops, the decorations on chinaware, the call of the street vender, the cap of the soldier, the pleated skirt of the schoolgirl — each points back to some well-known tale of how or why. Even the narrow blue and white towel of the jinrikisha [1] man and the layer lunch box of the workman bear designs suggesting an ancient poem or a bit of folklore, as familiar to every Japanese child as are the melodies of Mother Goose to the children of America.

One afternoon, at a small reception, a lady spoke pleasantly to me of the healthfulness to the foot of a shoe like my sandal and then referred with disapproval to the high heels and pointed toes then in vogue.

"Why are these shapes worn?" I asked. "What started them?"

"Oh, for no reason," she replied. "Just a fashion, like — well, like your folding your dress over left-handed."

"But there is a reason for that," I said. "It is only on a corpse that the kimono is folded over from the right."

That interested her; and we had a short talk on the peculiarity of Japanese always honoring the left above the right in everything, from the Imperial throne to the tying of a knot. Then, lightly touching the back of my sash, she asked, "Would you mind telling me what this bundle is for? Is it to carry the babies on?"

"Oh, no," I replied, "it is my sash, and is only an ornament. A baby is carried in a hammocklike scarf swung from the nurse's shoulders."

"This material of your sash is very beautiful," she said. "May I ask why you arrange it in that flat pad instead of spreading it out, so that the design can be seen?"

Since she seemed really interested, I willingly explained the various styles of tying a sash for persons differing in rank, age, and occupation; and for different occasions. Then came the final question, "Why do you have so much goods in it?"

That pleased me, for to a Japanese the material beauty of an article is always secondary to its symbolism. I told her of the original meaning of the twelve-inch width and twelve-foot length, and explained how it represented much of the mythology and astrology of ancient Oriental belief.

"This is very interesting," she said as she turned to go, "especially about the signs of the zodiac [2] and all that; but it's

[1] **jinrikisha:** a small, two-wheeled Japanese carriage drawn by one or more men.

[2] **signs of the zodiac:** the twelve divisions of the zodiac, a belt of constellations about the earth containing the paths of the moon and planets.

a shame to hide so much of that magnificent brocade by folding it in. And don't you think, yourself, little lady" — and she gave me a merry smile — "that it's positively wicked to buy so many yards of lovely goods just to be wasted and useless?"

And she walked away with a long train of expensive velvet trailing behind her on the floor.

Mother's furniture, which was of beautiful wood and some of it carved, at first made me feel as if I were in a museum; but when I went into other homes, I found that none were simple and plain. Many reminded me of godowns,[1] so crowded were they with not only chairs, tables, and pictures but numbers of little things — small statues, empty vases, shells, and framed photographs, as well as really rare and costly ornaments — all scattered about with utter disregard, according to Japanese standards, of order or appropriateness. It was several months before I could overcome the impression that the disarranged profusion of articles was a temporary convenience, and that very soon they would be returned to the godown. Most of these objects were beautiful, but some of them were the shape of a shoe or of the sole of the foot. This seemed to be a favorite design, or else my unwilling eyes always spied it out, for in almost every house I entered I would see it in a paperweight, a vase, or some other small article. Once I even saw a little wooden shoe used as a holder for toothpicks.

Generations of prejudice made this very objectionable to me, for in Japan the feet are the least honored part of the body; and the most beautiful or costly gift would lose all value if it had the shape of footwear.

And Japanese curios! They were everywhere, and in the most astonishingly inappropriate surroundings. Lunch boxes and rice bowls on parlor tables; cheap roll pictures hanging on elegant walls; shrine gongs used for dining-room table bells, sword guards for paperweights, ink boxes for handkerchiefs and letter boxes for gloves, marriage cups for pin trays; and even little bamboo spittoons I have seen used to hold flowers.

In time my stubborn mind learned, to some extent, to separate an article from its surroundings; and then I began to see its artistic worth with the eyes of an American. Also I acquired the habit, whenever I saw absurd things here which evidently arose from little knowledge of Japan, of trying to recall a similar absurdity in Japan regarding foreign things. And I never failed to find more than one to offset each single instance here. One time a recollection was forced upon me by an innocent question from a young lady who told me, in a tone of disbelief, that she had heard in a lecture on Japan that elegantly dressed Japanese ladies sometimes wore ordinary, cheap chenille table covers around their shoulders in place of scarfs. I could only laugh and acknowledge that, a few years before, that had been a popular fashion. Imported articles were rare and expensive; and since we never used table covers ourselves, we had no thought of their being anything but beautiful shawls. I had not the courage to tell her that I had worn one myself, but I did tell her, however, of something that occurred at my home in Nagaoka when I was a child.

On my father's return from one of his visits to the capital he brought Ishi and Kin[2] each a large Turkish towel with a colored border and a deep fringe. The maids, their hearts swelling with pride, went to temple service wearing the towels

[1] **godowns:** Japanese warehouses.

[2] **Ishi and Kin:** Ishi was Mrs. Sugimoto's nurse and Kin was a servant.

around their shoulders. I can see them yet as they walked proudly out of the gateway, the white lengths spread evenly over their best dresses and the fringe dangling in its stiff newness above their long Japanese sleeves. It would be a funny sight to me now, but then I was lost in admiration; and it seemed perfectly natural that they should be, as they were, the envy of all beholders.

Of all my experiences in trying to see Japanese things with American eyes, one particularly inharmonious combination was a foolishly annoying trial to me for many months. The first time I called on Mrs. Hoyt, the hostess of an especially beautiful home, my eyes were drawn to a lovely carved *magonote*—"hand of grandchild," it is called in Japan; but in America it has the practical name, "scratch-my-back"—which was hanging by its silk cord on the cover of an ebony cabinet. Beside it, thrown carelessly over the same cord, was a rosary of crystal and coral beads. The little ivory finger rake was exquisitely carved, and the rosary was of rare pink coral and flawless crystal; but to the eye of an Oriental all beauty was ruined by the strange arrangement. It was like putting the Bible and a toothbrush side by side on a parlor table.

I did not criticize the judgment of the hostess. Her superior taste in all things artistic was beyond question, and in America the *magonote* was an object of art only. From that viewpoint it was properly placed. I realized this, and yet, whenever afterward I entered that room, I persistently kept my eyes turned away from the ebony cabinet. It was only after two years of close friendship with the hostess that I had the courage to tell her of my shocked first visit to her home. She laughs at me even yet, and I laugh too; but there is a warm feeling of satisfaction in my heart this moment as I remember that the rosary and the *magonote* no longer hang side by side.

One day I went into the city with a friend to do some shopping. We were on a streetcar when my attention was attracted by a little girl sitting opposite us who was eating something. Children in Japan do not eat on the street or in a public place, and I did not know then that it is not the custom in America as it is with us never to eat except at a table.

My friend and I were busy talking, so for a while I did not notice the child; but when I chanced to glance at her again, I was surprised to see that she was still eating. Two or three times afterward I looked at her, and finally I turned to my friend.

"I wonder what that child is eating," I said.

"She is not eating anything," my friend replied. "She is chewing gum."

Again I looked at the child. She was sitting, drooped and weary, her loose hands lying in her lap and her feet spread around her bundle in a very awkward and difficult position. As I watched her tired face, suddenly I remembered something that had happened on the train on my trip across the continent.

"Is she sick?" I asked.

"No, I think not. Why do you ask?"

"I think I took that medicine on the train," I replied.

"Oh, no!" my friend said, laughing. "Chewing gum is not medicine. It's a sort of wax, just to chew."

"Why does she do it?" I asked.

"Oh, most children of her class chew gum, more or less. It's not an elegant thing to do. I don't allow my children to touch it."

I said nothing more, but a partial light began to dawn upon my experience on the train. I had been uncomfortably carsick, and Mrs. Holmes had given me a small, flat block of fragrant medicine which she said would cure nausea. I put it in my mouth and chewed a long time, but I could not swallow it. After a while I got tired, but Mrs. Holmes was still eating hers; so, concluding that it must be a medicine possessing wonderful merit, as it would not dissolve, I wrapped it carefully in a piece of white tissue paper and put it in the little mirror case that I wore in my sash.

I never heard what originated this peculiar custom, but I think I never found anything odd in America for which I could not find an equivalent in Japan. Gumchewing reminded me of *hodzuki* blowing, a habit common among some Japanese children; and also much practiced by teahouse girls and women of humble class. The *hodzuki* is made from a little red berry having a smooth, tough peeling. The core is very soft and with proper care can be squeezed out, leaving the unbroken peeling in the shape of a tiny round lantern. This little ball is elastic and, though it has no special taste, children love to hold it in the mouth and by gently blowing the hollow shell make what they call "mouth music." It sounds somewhat like the soft, distant croaking of a pond frog. *Hodzuki* blowing is not beautiful music, nor is it a pretty custom, but it is neither harmful nor unclean. The worst that can be said of it is what many a nurse calls to her charge:

"Take that squeaky thing out of your mouth. It will make your lips pouty and ugly."

THINK BACK OVER WHAT YOU HAVE READ

Appreciating Japanese Customs

1. How does the theater in Japan differ from that in America? How do Japanese audiences show their approval of good acting? What Japanese trait is thus revealed?

2. What illustrations can you give to show that in Japan the wife is mistress of the home?

3. How did Mrs. Sugimoto feel about ornaments in the shape of shoes? Why?

4. What interesting traditions did you learn about the wearing of the kimono? the sash?

5. Have you ever seen a "hand of grandchild" (page 224)? Describe it. For what is it used? How did Mrs. Sugimoto feel when she saw one hanging beside a rosary in an American home? Can you explain her attitude?

Seeing America through Japanese Eyes

6. What trait of American women was most puzzling to Mrs. Sugimoto? Why? Can you explain her bewilderment in the light of Japanese custom?

7. What passages can you quote to show Mrs. Sugimoto's fair-mindedness in her judgment of American peculiarities? With what example of American prejudice can you contrast it?

8. In another chapter of *A Daughter of the Samurai* Mrs. Sugimoto writes, "I think I am a good Christian." What support of this statement do you find in this chapter? What are some of the characteristics of a "good Christian" which she illustrates?

9. What criticisms of American customs does Mrs. Sugimoto make? Which ones in your opinion are justified? In what spirit does she make her criticisms?

10. Of what Japanese habit was Mrs. Sugimoto reminded by the chewing-gum episode? To what extent do you share her attitude toward gum-chewing?

Increase Your Power over Words

11. The following sentence (page 222) offers a clue to an understanding of the Japanese: "In Japan, *tradition, folklore,* and *symbolism* are before one all the time." To understand this sentence, however, you — the reader — must be able to supply your own examples of the three italicized words. You must be able to name particular traditions, particular folk tales or folk customs, and particular symbols which might be referred to. Otherwise the sentence will be no more than a string of words. We call such particular examples *referents.*

If you are not already familiar with the general meaning of these three words, look them up in the dictionary. Then look back over the selection just read and find as many *referents* for each of the three words as the author gives you. With these in mind you are ready to interpret the sentence. Suppose that such things (as you listed as *referents* for each of the three words) were a regular part of *your* life! What difference would it make? How would you be different?

For Ambitious Students

12. If the foregoing selection has aroused your interest in Japanese customs, you should read all of the book *A Daughter of the Samurai.* Other books by the same author are: *A Daughter of the Narikin* and *A Daughter of the Nohfu.* Both of these are stories of upper-class life in Japan.

13. A good novel of Chinese life is *The Good Earth* by Pearl Buck, a story of the poor farming class. If you read this book, you will note the contrast between the life of the Japanese aristocrat and that of the low-class Chinese.

14. For an intimate picture of native life in India read Kipling's *Kim.*

All these suggestions for outside reading offer you an opportunity to learn more about life in the Far East.

THE EDUCATION OF HELEN KELLER

by Helen Keller (*1880–*)

It is a sad truth that we rarely appreciate our greatest blessings until we lose them. Health, freedom, youth — how infrequently do we pause to be grateful for these until we become ill, or lose our freedom, or grow old; then they become priceless. Do you ever think of the wonder of hearing and sight? Can you imagine how blank life would be without them? And do you value the privilege of going to school, which is the door to the treasures of the ages? Do you really regard that as a privilege? Young Abraham Lincoln in his frontier cabin would have given all he possessed for the chance of schooling which you enjoy. In the world of today there are thousands of boys and girls who are hungry for education because, since it is out of their reach, they realize its importance.

In the following selection you will read about the education of Helen Keller. As a little child she had suffered an illness which left her without sight and hearing. You will read how she overcame these dreadful handicaps. Perhaps, as you read, this deaf and blind girl will help you to appreciate the great blessings of education. Perhaps, also, she will help you to look with keener interest upon this great and beautiful world.

THE NEXT important step in my education was learning to read.

As soon as I could spell a few words, my teacher gave me slips of cardboard on which were printed words in raised letters. I quickly learned that each printed word stood for an object, an act, or a quality. I had a frame in which I could arrange the words in little sentences; but before I ever put sentences in the frame I used to make them in objects. I found the slips of paper which represented, for example, "doll," "is," "on," "bed" and placed each name on its object; then I put my doll on the bed with the words *is, on, bed* arranged beside the doll, thus making a sentence of the words and at the same time carrying out the idea of the sentence with the things themselves.

One day, Miss Sullivan[1] tells me, I pinned the word *girl* on my pinafore and stood in the wardrobe. On the shelf I arranged the words *is, in, wardrobe.* Nothing delighted me so much as this game. My teacher and I played it for hours at a time. Often everything in the room was arranged in object sentences.

From the printed slip it was but a step to the printed book. I took my *Reader for Beginners* and hunted for the words I knew; when I found them my joy was like that of a game of hide-and-seek. Thus I began to read. Of the time when I began to read connected stories I shall speak later.

For a long time I had no regular lessons. Even when I studied most earnestly it seemed more like play than work. Everything Miss Sullivan taught me she

[1] **Miss Sullivan:** Miss Anne Sullivan, Miss Keller's teacher.

illustrated by a beautiful story or a poem. Whenever anything delighted or interested me she talked it over with me just as if she were a little girl herself. What many children think of with dread, as a painful plodding through grammar, hard sums and harder definitions, is today one of my most precious memories.

I cannot explain the peculiar sympathy Miss Sullivan had with my pleasures and desires. Perhaps it was the result of long association with the blind. Added to this she had a wonderful faculty for description. She went quickly over uninteresting details, and never nagged me with questions to see if I remembered the day-before-yesterday's lesson. She introduced dry technicalities of science little by little, making every subject so real that I could not help remembering what she taught.

We read and studied out of doors, preferring the sunlit woods to the house. All my early lessons have in them the breath of the woods — the fine, resinous odor of pine needles, blended with the perfume of wild grapes. Seated in the gracious shade of a wild tulip tree, I learned to think that everything has a lesson and a suggestion. "The loveliness of things taught me all their use." Indeed, everything that could hum, or buzz, or sing, or bloom, had a part in my education — noisy-throated frogs, katydids, and crickets held in my hand until, forgetting their embarrassment, they trilled their reedy note; little downy chickens and wild flowers, the dogwood blossoms, meadow violets, and budding fruit trees. I felt the bursting cotton bolls and fingered their soft fiber and fuzzy seeds; I felt the low soughing of the wind through the cornstalks, the silky rustling of the long leaves, and the indignant snort of my pony as we caught him in the pasture and put the bit in his mouth — ah me! how well I remember the spicy, clovery smell of his breath!

Sometimes I rose at dawn and stole into the garden while the heavy dew lay on the grass and flowers. Few know what joy it is to feel the roses pressing softly into the hand, or the beautiful motion of the lilies as they sway in the morning breeze. Sometimes I caught an insect in the flower I was plucking, and I felt the faint noise of a pair of wings rubbed together in a sudden terror as the little creature became aware of a pressure from without.

Another favorite haunt of mine was the orchard, where the fruit ripened early in July. The large, downy peaches would reach themselves into my hand, and as the joyous breezes flew about the trees the apples tumbled at my feet. Oh, the delight with which I gathered up the fruit in my pinafore, pressed my face against the smooth cheeks of the apples, still warm from the sun, and skipped back to the house!

Our favorite walk was to Keller's Landing, an old tumble-down lumber wharf on the Tennessee River, used during the Civil War to land soldiers. There we spent many happy hours and played at learning geography. I built dams of pebbles, made islands and lakes, and dug river beds, all for fun, and never dreamed that I was learning a lesson. I listened with increasing wonder to Miss Sullivan's descriptions of the great round world with its burning mountains, buried cities, moving rivers of ice, and many other things as strange. She made raised maps in clay, so that I could feel the mountain ridges and valleys, and follow with my fingers the devious course of rivers. I liked this, too; but the division of the earth into zones and poles confused and teased my mind. The illustrative strings and the orange stick representing the poles seemed so real that even to this day the mere mention of temperate zone suggests a series of twine circles; and I believe that if anyone should set about it he could convince me that white bears actually climb the North Pole.

Arithmetic seems to have been the only study I did not like. From the first I was not interested in the science of numbers. Miss Sullivan tried to teach me to count by stringing beads in groups, and by arranging kindergarten straws I learned to add and subtract. I never had patience to arrange more than five or six groups at a time. When I had accomplished this my conscience was at rest for the day, and I went out quickly to find my playmates.

In this same leisurely manner I studied zoology and botany.

Once a gentleman, whose name I have forgotten, sent me a collection of fossils — tiny mollusk shells beautifully marked, and bits of sandstone with the print of birds' claws, and a lovely fern in bas-relief. These were the keys which unlocked the treasures of the antediluvian world for me. With trembling fingers I listened to Miss Sullivan's descriptions of the terrible beasts, with uncouth, unpronounceable names, which once went tramping through the primeval forests, tearing down the branches of gigantic trees for food, and died in the dismal swamps of an unknown age. For a long time these strange creatures haunted my dreams and this gloomy period formed a somber background to the joyous Now, filled with sunshine and roses and echoing with the gentle beat of my pony's hoof.

Another time a beautiful shell was given me, and with a child's surprise and delight I learned how a tiny mollusk had built the lustrous coil for his dwelling place and how on still nights, when there is no breeze stirring the waves, the Nautilus[1] sails on the blue waters of the Indian Ocean in his "ship of pearl."[2] After I had learned a great many interesting things about the life and habits of the children of the sea — how in the midst of dashing waves the little polyps[3] build the beautiful coral isles of the Pacific and the Foraminifera[4] have made the chalk hills of many a land — my teacher read me "The Chambered Nautilus" and showed me that the shell-building process of the mollusks is symbolical of the development of the mind. Just as the wonder-working mantle of the Nautilus changes the material it absorbs from the water and makes it a part of itself, so the bits of knowledge one gathers undergo a similar change and become pearls of thought.

Again, it was the growth of a plant that furnished the text for a lesson. We bought a lily and set it in a sunny window. Very soon the green, pointed buds showed signs of opening. The slender, fingerlike leaves on the outside opened slowly, reluctant, I thought, to reveal the loveliness they hid; once having made a start, however, the opening process went on rapidly, but in order and systematically. There was always one bud larger and more beautiful than the rest, which pushed her outer covering back with more pomp, as if the beauty in soft, silky robes knew that she was a lilyqueen by right divine, while her more timid sisters doffed their green hoods shyly, until the whole plant was one nodding bough of loveliness and fragrance.

Once there were eleven tadpoles in a glass globe set in a window full of plants. I remember the eagerness with which I made discoveries about them. It was great fun to plunge my hand into the bowl and feel the tadpoles frisk about, and to let them slip and slide between my fingers. One day a more ambitious fellow leaped

[1] **Nautilus:** a variety of mollusks with spiral shell. [2] **"ship of pearl"**: a quotation from "The Chambered Nautilus," a poem by Oliver Wendell Holmes. This poem might be read aloud in class.

[3] **polyps:** simple, invertebrate animals. [4] **Foraminifera:** an order of tiny animals with shells perforated by minute holes. In many cases the shells are formed of sand grains cemented together. White chalk and limestone consist largely of these shells.

beyond the edge of the bowl and fell on the floor, where I found him to all appearance more dead than alive. The only sign of life was a slight wriggling of his tail. But no sooner had he returned to his element than he darted to the bottom, swimming round and round in joyous activity. He had made his leap, he had seen the great world, and was content to stay in his pretty glass house under the big fuchsia tree until he attained the dignity of froghood.[1] Then he went to live in the leafy pool at the end of the garden, where he made the summer nights musical with his quaint love song.

Thus I learned from life itself. At the beginning I was only a little mass of possibilities. It was my teacher who unfolded and developed them. When she came, everything about me breathed of love and joy and was full of meaning. She has never since let pass an opportunity to point out the beauty that is in everything, nor has she ceased trying in thought and action and example to make my life sweet and useful.

It was my teacher's genius, her quick sympathy, her loving tact which made the first years of my education so beautiful. It was because she seized the right moment to impart knowledge that made it so pleasant and acceptable to me. She realized that a child's mind is like a shallow brook which ripples and dances merrily over the stony course of its education and reflects here a flower, there a bush, yonder a fleecy cloud; and she attempted to guide my mind on its way, knowing that like a brook it should be fed by mountain streams and hidden springs, until it broadened out into a deep river, capable of reflecting on its placid surface billowy hills, the luminous shadows of trees, and the blue heavens, as well as the sweet face of a little flower.

[1] **attained the dignity of froghood:** Tadpoles grow into frogs.

Any teacher can take a child to the classroom, but not every teacher can make him learn. He will not work joyously unless he feels that liberty is his, whether he is busy or at rest; he must feel the flush of victory and the heart-sinking of disappointment before he takes with a will the tasks distasteful to him and resolves to dance his way bravely through a dull routine of textbooks.

My teacher is so near to me that I scarcely think of myself apart from her. How much of my delight in all beautiful things is innate, and how much is due to her influence, I can never tell. I feel that her being is inseparable from my own, and that the footsteps of my life are in hers. All the best of me belongs to her — there is not a talent or an aspiration or a joy in me that has not been awakened by her loving touch.

THINK BACK OVER WHAT YOU HAVE READ

Understanding How the Blind Learn to Read

1. The system of raised letters to enable the blind to read is called Braille. Perhaps some member of the class will volunteer to borrow a page or two of Braille writing so that you may understand the part played by the fingers in reading.

2. Explain, step by step, how Miss Keller was taught to read. How did play help in the process? Why was play important?

3. What qualities specially fitted Miss Sullivan for teaching? Could any of her methods be used to teach normal children?

4. Read the next to the last paragraph. Explain what Miss Keller means by "liberty." Do you agree with the thought of this paragraph?

5. Compare Miss Keller's opportunities for study with those of the ordinary classroom.

Enjoying Nature with Miss Keller

6. Find passages in the selection which show how Helen Keller appreciates sound in spite of the fact that she does not hear.

7. By what method was she taught geography? Are similar methods ever used in the schools?

8. Read aloud a passage that shows how Miss Sullivan related the study of literature to nature study. Why was this method effective?

9. What truths did Miss Keller learn from the lily? from the tadpole? How did she apply these lessons to life?

Appreciating Helen Keller's Style

10. What passages in this chapter particularly stirred your feelings?

11. Read aloud the sentences that strike you as most pleasing to the ear.

12. What beautiful comparisons do you find in this chapter?

13. What words are particularly expressive? What words are descriptive of sound? What words indicate the pleasure which Miss Keller derived from the sense of touch?

14. What adjectives seem most appropriate and expressive?

Increase Your Power over Words

15. The word *sough* (pronounced suf or sou) on page 227 means the whistling of the wind. When our language was forming, many words were coined to suggest sound. Some of these words are *boom, bang, tinkle, clash, whistle, murmur. Sough* is such a word, for it imitates the sound of the wind. Can you think of any others?

16. The prefix *ante* in the word *antediluvian* (page 228) means before. *Diluvian* is derived from the Latin word that means a flood. *Deluge* comes from the same word. *Antediluvian,* therefore, means before the Flood, or pertaining to very ancient times. What does *antecedent* mean? *anteroom? antedate?*

Do not confuse the prefix *ante* with the prefix *anti.* The latter means against or opposed to. Thus *antislavery* means opposed to slavery; *antisocial* means opposed to the principles upon which society is based.

Do you know the prefix which means after? What word means written as an afterthought?

17. Whenever you see the syllables *lumin* in a word, you may know that it means light; for it comes from the Latin word for light, *lumen.* Thus *luminous* (page 229) means giving forth light. *Illuminate* means to light up. Other words from the same root are *luminary, illumine.* Find in the dictionary more words from the same root.

Composition Suggestion

18. You can gain some idea of the strange world which Helen Keller lives in, at the same time that you sharpen your sense of touch and smell, by exploring an unfamiliar room, or garden, with your eyes closed. Describe your impressions under some such title as "Seeing through Your Fingers" or "Following One's Nose."

The Conquest of the Air

BYRD FLIES TO THE NORTH POLE

by Charles J. V. Murphy (1904–)

Of course you know Dick Byrd. All boys and girls do, for he is one of the most romantic of modern heroes and his courage is an inspiration to all who love daring deeds. However, you must not think of him as a dare-devil who performs dangerous exploits merely for the fun of doing them or for the publicity which they gain. Byrd regards himself first of all as a scientist. The airplane to him is a laboratory; in that laboratory he strives to demonstrate the truth or falsity of many of the physical laws which, prior to the airplane, were mere matters of theory. His flights to both poles were made in the interests of geography. His flight across the Atlantic, in the days when such a flight was indeed spectacular, was made to discover the possibilities of commercial aviation. His two winters spent in Little America were designed primarily to collect data in such sciences as geology and meteorology.

As you read the exciting account of his flight to the North Pole, remember that he is an explorer with a purpose, yet one who manages always to get a lot of fun out of his experience.

IT WAS on the snow-terraced slopes of King's Bay [1] that Byrd fought and won his greatest battle. To those who are inclined to measure accomplishment in terms of italics — in terms of the spectacular — the two weeks or so that he and his shipmates spent in the frozen bowl, before the flight to the pole itself, may not have seemed to contain particularly stirring condiments. Five thousand miles from the scene, the action resolved itself into a series of mishaps, delays, and contretemps. In many quarters, for a time, there was frank doubt that Byrd would ever get off and away to the pole successfully.

He was meeting and solving a thousand unanticipated difficulties. He was abandoning preconceived plans and boldly undertaking new ones. Three times he was to poise unwilling over the brink of disaster. And, finally, in utter desperation but with cold calculation, he was to stake everything on a single toss and win as boldly. It was struggle of the most trying kind. But he and Bennett [2] and the stouthearted men about them, recognizing the challenge, responded with a zestfulness that demolished every barrier and provided posterity with one of the most brilliant flights on the record books.

The first challenge lay in the squat, slate-colored body of a Norwegian gunboat, tied up at the only dock in the harbor. Months before, fearful that some such difficulty like this might arise, Byrd had cabled the authorities and learned he would have no difficulty in mooring the *Chantier* [3] at the dock and unloading the *Josephine Ford* [4] there. But there was no smoke curling from the stacks of the man-o'-war; her boilers were cold, and workmen were scurrying about her.

Considerably nettled, Byrd and Bennett ordered a landing crew and went ashore. They politely asked for the use of the dock. Could not the gunboat be moved for a few hours while they unloaded their heavy plane? It was most urgent. How else could they land it? The bay was chock-full of floating ice, with a narrow black ribbon of open water running out to sea. Surely the gunboat could be anchored there a moment?

The Norwegians were most gracious and understanding, but firm. The request could not be granted. Could not the Americans see that the gunboat was laid up for repairs and coal? It would be dangerous to move the ship into the bay when a sudden shift of the wind might swing the full weight of the ice pack against it. Only the other day it barely escaped destruction from the same cause.

Byrd listened in amazement. He thanked them most graciously. He turned on his heel and hastened back to the whaleboat. In his usually mild eyes there was fire; and his orders had a crispness to them. "Row like fury," he told the oarsmen. Scarcely waiting for the small boat to reach the side of the *Chantier,* he vaulted up the ladder, Bennett following at his heels. A council of war was called in his cabin, and the officers gathered about his table.

"We can't obtain use of the dock," Byrd snapped out. "But we can land the plane. It is dangerous, but it can be done. Listen!"

Talking rapidly, he sketched his plan. How many whaleboats (lifeboats) were there? Four. Very well, lash them together into a raft, load the *Josephine Ford* on it, attach the wing, and row it ashore!

It was audacious, and the others fairly gasped. Row a clumsy raft through a mile of floating jagged ice, dangerous enough

[1] **King's Bay:** in Spitzbergen, an island north of Norway, a convenient starting point for Arctic explorers. [2] **Bennett:** Floyd Bennett, Byrd's mechanician and pilot. [3] **Chantier:** the ship which carried Byrd and his plane to King's Bay. [4] **Josephine Ford:** Byrd's plane.

in itself but triply hazardous because of the body-bending winds they had already learned sweep unexpectedly out of the north! And then hoist a three-ton plane over the ten-foot precipice of ice at the shore!

"It can't be done!" answered one of the officers. "You're taking a terrible chance. A bit of wind, a single ice floe — pouf! good-by plane and expedition."

Byrd eyed him smilingly. "It can be done," he answered without a trace of irritation. "We're going to do it right now." Bennett nodded his head and said nothing. He recognized it was the only alternative.

All hands were mustered out in the emergency; the whaleboats were dropped into the water beside the ship and "Chips" Gould, the carpenter, grabbed his saws and hammers and prepared to make his raft. Sometime before dawn it was ready. The *Chantier* was then anchored in the middle of the channel five miles wide between the headlands, and it lay nearly a mile from the shore.

The little Curtiss Oriole, its bright orange fuselage and yellow wing standing out in bright contrast against the whiteness, was at once lowered upon the raft and carefully guided to the shore. It was snowing fiercely; at times the men in the boat could scarcely see the shore. Meanwhile another group of men had laboriously chiseled with ax and shovel a six-hundred-foot runway through the solid precipice of ice on the shore. It ran from the water's edge well up toward the shore.

Byrd, after superintending the landing of the little plane, ordered the raft back to the ship for the Fokker. It took almost two hours to navigate the clumsy composite through the shifting ice. Preparations were made at once to lower the fuselage to the platform on the raft. When this was accomplished, the crane reached down into the hold and plucked forth the seventy-four-foot wing.

And then a sixty-mile-an-hour gale broke like a thunderclap from clear skies, hitting with such vigor that the ship lurched drunkenly. It caught the wing with frightful impact and nearly wrenched it from the derrick. The crew came scrambling from every part of the ship, and by sheer force of muscle pulled the wing to the deck and secured it with ropes. Then they turned their attention to the raft and its precious cargo, which the action of the wind and waves was slamming against the iron sides of the ship and which was in dire danger of being demolished by the suddenly released ice floes.

With great difficulty the raft was towed to the stern, where the bulk of the ship protected it most, and for twelve long hours, while the storm raged with undiminishing intensity, the men held it safely in position, staving off the thrusts of ice and keeping the boats afloat. Time and time again, when a change in the wind would snap the cables so tautly they fairly sung, there was real fear that the raft would break up. But the drenched and shivering men who kept vigil aboard her did not give up; when the storm swept out of the bay as swiftly as it had come, the raft and the fuselage were intact.

There was no rest for exhausted men. At once the raft was towed around, the fuselage attached, and the weary pull to shore begun. Inasmuch as the fierceness of the storm had broken up the solid sheath of ice, there was much loose ice floating in the path. The Norwegian dispatch boat was asked to break open a path for them, but the captain was compelled to decline. He was afraid his craft would ground on the shallow shoals. More, he frankly expressed the belief that Commander Byrd was about to do a very risky thing.

"Go out and break up the ice," Byrd ordered half a dozen men. They did, and as they opened up a narrow crack of clear water the raft bearing the *Josephine Ford* faltered behind them. Once a huge berg, carried before the wind, bore down on them, and Byrd sent out a crew to intercept it. A charge of dynamite blasted it into innocuous fragments. Few of the men knew how to row, and half a dozen times, before the more expert men could back water, the greenhorns, misinterpreting Byrd's nautical commands, brought them perilously close to jagged ice.

There was more than relief in the hearts of Byrd and Bennett when finally the craft struck against the shore. There was something approaching pride. For his mad gesture had succeeded. He had chanced everything, and had won.

From the crew of the gunboat, who lined its decks, came a throaty cheer in appreciation of a task well done; and a moment later its musicians, hastily assembled, played "The Star-Spangled Banner." It was, indeed, a good omen, and Byrd felt within himself a strange confidence.

Difficult as was the marine trip of the plane, the landing of it was scarcely less so. No less than four hours of unmitigated effort were necessary to lift it from the raft and pull it up the slope to the shore. Of course, they had no machinery or tractors to help them; it must be done by brute strength — by "muscle grease," in the words of Tom Mulroy — aided by block and tackle. But at last it was done; and Byrd's chosen plane, the *Josephine Ford,* at last had laid its rubber wheels upon the slopes from which it was to make its spectacular dash.

The citizenry of this desolate spot — in the wintertime, under usual conditions, it numbered less than a dozen — came down from the hillside to see the monster plane. Never before had they seen a three-motored flying machine, and it fascinated them. In the crowd, too, were a dozen members of the Amundsen-Ellsworth expedition,[1] who were engaged in preparing for the arrival of the big dirigible. Amundsen and Ellsworth were in charge, and they joyfully welcomed Byrd, their friend. Byrd introduced his flying officers — Bennett and Noville — and the "competitors" strolled off to a cabin for a pleasant talk.

No stranger conference was ever held in that northern outpost of civilization, which three hundred years before echoed to the shouts of Dutch, British, French, and Scandinavian sailing men. Fate had transported them here with the parallel objectives of demonstrating the feasibility of polar exploration by aircraft. The one group would embark in a dirigible, convinced it was the logical craft; the other in the airplane, for the same reason. Fate, too, had decreed that their departures should almost synchronize. Yet each man — Byrd and Bennett, Amundsen and Ellsworth — affably, but not directly, impugned the idea of competition.

"We have no fixed time of departure," declared Amundsen. "We hope to start soon after the *Norge*[2] arrives."

"Nor have we," answered Byrd. "As soon as the Fokker has been tested, and the weather is good, we shall go."

Amundsen, his bronzed face smiling, lifted his glass. "To your health, Byrd, and the success I know will come to you."

They drank deeply, and Byrd rose.

"And to you, Captain Amundsen, and your splendid colleague, Ellsworth, I wish

[1] **Amundsen-Ellsworth expedition:** an expedition led by Roald Amundsen, the famous Norwegian discoverer of the South Pole, and Lincoln Ellsworth, an American. The object of this expedition was to fly across the North Pole in a dirigible balloon. [2] ***Norge:*** the dirigible in which Amundsen and Ellsworth flew to the pole.

a pleasant voyage and the brilliant accomplishments I know will be yours."

The glasses tinkled again. There were promises of mutual assistance; but not once did the determination in the heart of each man to be the first to fly across the pole find voice. So deeply was it understood that it wasn't necessary. They were essentially sportsmen, each conceding the other fair play but rigidly bound to achievement of their own objectives.

Meanwhile the crew had hauled the *Josephine Ford* to the crest of a gentle slope about a mile from the shore. It was arduous work, and the temperature was at zero. No one thought of sleep. A dugout was cut into the solid ice, and a lean-to was built to protect the workmen while resting. A field kitchen was set up in the ice, and a hundred tons of supplies, gasoline, and oil were ferried from the ship, pulled up the slope, and stored on the ice.

For Byrd, Noville, Bennett, and Doc Kinkade there was little sleep. The midnight sun enabled twenty-two hours of work a day, and the rarefied air filled the men with strange energy. On May 3 Kinkade stepped away from the singing motors, turned to Commander Byrd, and said:

"She's O. K."

Bennett and Byrd hopped in, the pilot gave it the gun, and the *Josephine Ford* shot down the slope. Then the motors faded into silence, and the plane skidded to a halt. A landing strut had broken, a crash averted by the narrowest of margins.

All through the night, the carpenter and Mulroy worked repairing the strut and strengthening the skis.[1] It was clear that the skis, in their present shape, could not withstand the strain. The struts were made stronger.

The next day Byrd and Bennett made another attempt. Halfway down the slope the left ski stubbed against a hummock; the plane pitched abruptly and dug its nose, with a great screaming of motors, into a soft snowbank. The men on the hill watched with sinking hearts.

Byrd was out of the plane first, examining the damage. He worked swiftly, impatiently. Then he turned to Bennett with joy in his face.

"Holy Mose, nothing damaged at all beyond the skis!"

While his crew dug the big plane out of the snowbank, a strapping young man, with the blue eyes and the flaxen hair of a Norwegian, strolled across the plain and humbly introduced himself.

"My name is Balchen,"[2] he said, "and I'm connected with the Amundsen-Ellsworth expedition. I've flown a lot around here and I came over to see if I could help you."

Byrd looked at the shattered runner.

"We've used a mixture of paraffin and resin on the runners," said the Norwegian, "and found it very effective. You see, about this time of the year, when the snow begins to melt, the friction is greater. If you use this mixture, I don't think you'll have so much trouble."

It was Bernt Balchen, twenty-five-year-old Norwegian naval flying officer, a calm, confident young man, who, though he did not realize it then, was to play an important part in Byrd's life. Then he was deferential, eager to be of assistance to this American who had come so far. Even so, the outlook was not encouraging. With no sort of a load at all the Fokker had been unable to get off the snow. What chance did it have with a full load? The extra supplies of skis had been exhausted by the crashes; Gould and Mulroy, lacking other resources, were compelled to recre-

[1] **skis:** Since the ground was covered with snow, skis were used instead of wheels.

[2] **Balchen:** Bernt Balchen, who later flew with Byrd across the Atlantic and to the South Pole.

ate them from the wreckage and a set of oars.

But Byrd had profited by his mishaps. He set the men at work building a runway from the crest of the hill almost to the tongue of the bay, removing the bumps that had caused the terrific shocks before. By six o'clock the next afternoon Bennett was ready for another attempt. There was no denying the seriousness of the situation. Another failure and there might be nothing to reclaim.

Lunging under full throttle,[1] the *Josephine Ford* swung down the new runway, kicked up a flurry of snow, and long before it passed the halfway mark nosed upwards and soared into its natural element. Bennett and Lieutenant Noville, who was with him, put it through a most intensive two-hour test, and then the pilot brought it down gracefully. Bennett met Byrd with radiant eyes. "It's fine," he told him. "Load it up, and let's go."

That night the two men decided to abandon the idea of the intermediate base at Cape Morris Jessup. The ease with which the Fokker had risen indicated it could easily carry enough fuel for a non-stop flight to the pole from King's Bay. There was no need of the precautionary base. Why not do it in one jump?

The next day — the sixth — the Fokker stood on the lip of the precipice, fuel enough for twenty-two hours in its tanks. The weather, while still retaining traces of fogginess and changeability, was unmistakably improving. The cold was diminishing and the thermometer showed ten degrees above zero.

Whatever ideas Byrd might have had for a take-off the next day were dissipated in the morning. Shortly after ten o'clock the silence of the bay was alive with a throbbing, exciting clamor; then across the hills to the south stole a great cigar-shaped vessel, moving with confident majesty. It was the *Norge!* The Americans rushed to the huge hangar on the hill, just behind their runway, to see the giant landed.

That night the two ships were in fretful anchorage not two hundred yards apart; and whatever advantage Byrd might have had by his early arrival had become, through the series of misfortunes, no better than an even break. That night, too, his men worked at high speed, checking the plane and instruments.

Thirty minutes after midnight, on the eighth, Byrd and Bennett boarded the plane. Haines, the meteorologist, had said the weather was good. There was little ceremony, although the Italians, Swedes, and Norwegians on the Amundsen-Ellsworth expedition came out to see them start. The midnight sun cast a rare brilliancy over the valley and there was a touch of spring in the air.

The motors had been heated, and Kinkade stepped back without a word. His was the responsibility. He waved his hand. Bennett nudged the throttles and the Fokker burst down the hill. But it obviously lacked speed. Three hundred feet down, it lifted savagely from the slope and banged down again; at full speed it continued headlong toward the bay, spread flat and uninvitingly before it, its sullen waters filled with dangerous growlers.[2]

Again the plane struggled to rise . . . but no. Emerging for a split second from its self-created blizzard, it lurched drunkenly to the side, fluttered, and then slipped awkwardly into a huge snowbank. The clamor of motor in the hills was sucked into silence; and to the little group of watchers on the runway it seemed no less than a final silence. Not daring to hope, they rushed down the hill — to find Byrd and Bennett already plowing under the plane.

The gods who watch over planes — and

[1] **under full throttle:** at full speed.

[2] **growlers:** small icebergs.

surely this new department must have been created in Olympus — had been judicious. Beyond a straining of the skis, the plane had escaped damage!

But the investigation disclosed an extraordinary thing. Loaded as it was to the last thin rim of safety, the plane was found to contain no less than two hundred pounds or so of stuff that Byrd and Bennett had not calculated upon — flags, pictures, trinkets, hats, coats that the crew had smuggled aboard to reclaim later and present to admiring friends as trophies of the first aerial crossing of the pole. Only a few hundred pounds, but by such a narrow margin did this $150,000 expedition, not to mention the human lives involved, tremble on the last boundary of safety.

The stuff was thrown out on the snow, as were five hundred gallons of gasoline. Bennett, drawn and thin from lack of sleep, would not wait for the men to drag the plane back to the starting position.

" I'll taxi up! " he shouted. He did.

Byrd remained long enough to give a few final orders, and then returned to the ship for as much sleep as he could get. In thirty-six hours he had been to bed but once, and then only for a cat nap. Bennet, whose fighting spirit had been aroused, would not leave the scene of action. He curled up in the fuselage and slept, undisturbed by the racket of the men working about him.

A hundred men toiled inside the half-open hangar — it really was nothing more than two curving walls — that housed the *Norge*. The word crept across the ice that the *Norge* was ready to leave. Excitement reached a high pitch in both camps, even while the leaders, who avoided all impression of competition, remained aloof from it.

Midnight came. Half an hour later Mulroy tapped Bennett on the shoulder. " All ready," he said quietly. Meanwhile another runner was en route to the ship to awaken Byrd. And fifty minutes later Byrd was back, after having risked life and limb in what was probably the fastest rowboat ride ever undertaken through the ice-laden bay.

He was all eagerness when he came up the hill, running as fast as he could.

" Everything ready? " he asked. The crew individually submitted reports. Haines, the weatherman, told that the immediate outlook was splendid. What he would meet over the polar seas, of course, was conjectural.

Mulroy stood waiting behind the plane, an ax in his hand, waiting to cut the rope that lashed it to a stake buried in the ice. Men pressed up to shake hands, while the two flyers tugged at their flying suits; the motors were thrumming sweetly. Bennett jumped in first, and Byrd followed a moment later. From the cabin they waved cheerfully. The motors responded to the throttle, and the propellers washed up a great storm of snow particles behind.

At 1:58 o'clock A.M. Mulroy's ax fell effectively upon the rope, and the Fokker leaped forward.

Twenty seconds later it leaped clear of the runway and headed across the bay in a broad, arching rise that carried it into the brilliant sunlight. The tumult of its going fell away; and a few minutes later, as a little black speck pushed into the northern skies, a great hush fell over the valley. It was awesome, almost like that hush one finds in European cathedrals. And Byrd's men, left inarticulate by the sudden cessation of action and clamor, watched the speck until it disappeared.

Two men in a five-ton flying machine hurtling one hundred miles an hour toward a nondimensional point[1] that had guided navigators before Columbus — a point enfolded by floating seas, pack ice,

[1] **nondimensional point:** that is, the North Pole.

and a drifting, strangling mist that shrouded it through the centuries, had closed mercilessly about the hopes of a thousand men. With wide-opened eyes, Byrd, the idealist and scientist, is speeding into an unknown that opens before him more than six thousand square miles of space every hour. And the thin, angular Bennett, more engrossed in his engines and throttles than anything else, sits beside him with half-shut eyes, listening to the important orchestration of two thousand parts of motor, watching his compasses.

The Fokker is a traveling laboratory, machine shop, and explorational mission. In the fuselage, behind the great fuel tanks, is a long sled, the gift of Amundsen. There is a ten weeks' supply of food, highly concentrated stuff, to be loaded on it if motors should fail, if they should crash for any one of a number of causes. There is, too, a spare tent, rifles, special clothing, everything that would make the walk home humanly possible.

But Byrd, checking over this stuff half-intuitively, rather hopes that it will not be necessary to walk. Through his mind flits a recollection of the awful disappearance of Andrée, the first man to try to reach the pole by air, who quit King's Bay three decades before and vanished. It is not a pleasant thing to contemplate, this idea of spending the Arctic night on a sea of ice drifting across the pole, when slogging feet are to try to carry you in the opposite direction.

Motors . . . motors . . . motors. The steel pistons that give wings to men's imagination must not fail!

Skillfully accumulating altitude, Bennett heads the Fokker due north. The familiar mountainous topography of Spitzbergen sweeps majestically underneath, rugged, wild, torn, and churned as if by the angry wheels of mighty chariots. At two thousand feet Bennett halts the climb and levels off the plane for a straight flight to the pole.

An hour passes, and they cut athwart the last barrier of land and strike across the Arctic pack. Although it is not long after midnight, the sun is bright as day; and a hundred miles ahead, brilliantly clear, the pack ice stretches its flatness toward a misty horizon . . . a vast grayish raft, showing an irregular black lead [1] here and there. And as the Fokker swings on, its motors chortling in unison, Byrd jots in his log:

"I cannot but marvel at the superiority of the airplane. To think that men toiled for years over this ice, a few hard-won miles a day; and we travel luxuriously a hundred miles an hour. How motors have changed the burdens of man!"

But there is little opportunity for philosophical thought. The two men face a terrific problem in navigation. From now on, mathematics will be as important as motors. Byrd checks over his instruments. In the tail of the plane, where it is comparatively free from local magnetism (that is, the magnetic influence from metallic parts of the plane itself), is the earth-inductor compass.[2] At his right hand is the famous sun compass devised for his first polar flight by Alfred Bumstead; and beside these his sextant and master compasses.

A great navigator, Byrd is acutely aware of the navigational difficulties inherent in polar exploration, and particularly so at the high speed required by an airplane. For one thing, he knows that the magnetic compass is inclined to be sluggish in certain parts of the North, where the directive force of the earth's magnetism is lessened, and therefore

[1] **lead:** an open channel in an ice field. [2] **earth-inductor compass:** Since the magnetic pole is far south of the North Pole, the magnetic compass is worthless in Far Northern latitudes. The earth-inductor compass is an electrical compass devised for navigation purposes in the Far North.

susceptible to troublesome deviation. He must calculate the drift from the normal caused by the wind. There are countless technical problems, each of them freighted with tremendous possibilities.

He must know his position to the last fraction of a mile. Otherwise, with engines popping for want of fuel, a forced landing in the ice, hopelessly lost. Indeed, as they slide onward, the angular shadow of the Fokker trailing miles behind them on the ice, rippling over huge, distorted pressure ridges [1] and hummocks, he wonders if they will find the rolling, confusing mist that Peary [2] found at the pole; if so, he has his work cut out for him. Airplane navigation in fog is difficult enough; at the pole it must amount, he realizes, almost to an impossibility.

What an extraordinarily stable platform the airplane gives these modern observers of the Arctic pack. The air is clear and steady. There is little of the pitching they encountered in the rougher air in their own country. The thermometers in the cabin show a reading of zero, and they are comfortably warm in their reindeer and polar-bear suits.

They are steering a straight course between the routes Peary and Nansen [3] followed so laboriously; and the better to view the ice pack Bennett depresses the nose, and the Fokker skims along not three hundred feet from the ice. In the drop they watch with mingled emotions the extraordinary changes in the panorama. How clear and flat the sweep of ice seemed from half a mile above! A perfect landing field for an airplane. But the hurried descent works a bewildering alchemy. The artificial flatness gives way to contorted architecture — great pressure ridges, twenty to thirty feet high, symbols of the travail of the moving ice fields that meet, clash, and crush irresistibly — vast stretches of a mobile frozen sea, decades old, extending in rafter, hummocky formation as far as the eye can see, the chaos of which is visible evidence of the tremendous physical power of the Arctic pack and the eternal conflict born of shifting currents and the crush of new ice against the old.

But they notice that it has not yet yielded to the first softening touches of the spring. Occasionally pools glint in hollow depressions in the middle of the raft; the lanes and channels of open water, black as coal, are filled with floating "growlers" (small bergs) that have been torn free from the pack, perhaps by wind, perhaps by the shock of impact from another field.

After absorbed contemplation Byrd clambers from the cabin into the fuselage, where he has fixed up a navigational compartment. Here is a second set of instruments; a short-wave radio set to be employed in case they should be forced down. Attached to the trap door in the roof is a second sun compass. There, too, is a drift indicator. Every three or four minutes he checks the wind drift, to make certain that Bennett is following the course. At his elbow is an ample chart board, and on this he calculates copiously.

Every now and then, too, he sights the sun with his sextant. It is a most careful system of cross-checking; in this way does he determine where the line of flight actually intersects the fixed lines of position.

From his place under the great wing Byrd can see Bennett bathed in sunlight filtering through the windowed cabin, and over him comes a great feeling of pride for this quiet, imperturbable young man whose slender body houses a singularly

[1] **pressure ridges:** The smooth surface of the ice had been broken into ridges by the terrific pressure of the ice. [2] **Peary:** Robert E. Peary, discoverer of the North Pole. [3] **Nansen:** Fridtjof Nansen, famous Norwegian Arctic explorer.

brave and confident heart. He moves forward and takes a turn at the controls.

When Bennett again relieves him, Byrd notices that he shows a marked inclination to swing to the right. Byrd warns him, and Bennett brings the plane back. But again it slips off to the right. " You must keep on your course," Byrd writes on a slip of paper. Thereafter Byrd watches carefully; each calculation shows that Bennett is ranging obliquely from the course he has set, and always to the right.

When Byrd takes his turn at the controls, he compensates for the deviation by swinging to the left. And he compares closely the increasing error indicated by the magnetic compass, as they progress northward, with the reliable sun compass.

" The error, which amounted to eleven degrees after we reached the polar sea," he records, " is now nearly doubled."

What a possibility that offers for fatal error!

They swing swiftly into vast areas that only once before had echoed the pulsing throb of an airplane engine. Somewhere was the open lead in which Amundsen and Ellsworth had landed their flying boats, and fought for twenty-five days to free them. The pole is only one hundred and thirty-six miles away. In a moment they roared tumultuously into areas that had never before been seen by human eyes.

Will they see land — the yet-to-be-discovered land that beckoned Peary, De Long,[1] Nansen, and the others? Each is scanning the horizon, alert for evidences of life — a polar bear, birds. There is nothing but the dazzling whiteness; the profusion of pressure ridges, analogous — in Byrd's mind — to the edges of a crazy quilt, telling of a free motion of the ice pack that would be impossible if a continent existed there.

Just as Byrd completes another observation, fixing their position at ninety miles from the pole; just when he has permitted himself an inward rejoicing of accomplishment, Bennett plucks his sleeve and points to the starboard window. It is flecked with oil. Something is wrong with the wing motor!

Byrd scrambles to the window and sees that the oil tank has developed a copious leak. The wind wash from the propeller is whipping it against the windows and fuselage, coating them with a heavy film which freezes almost as it strikes. He turns back to Bennett, worry in his eyes. Bennett nods, and cuts the motors to half speed so that he can be heard.

" That motor," he scrawls on a piece of paper, " is going to stop." His hand is steady.

Byrd is doubtful.

" We'd better make a landing," the pilot writes. " Can't go on like this; we'll burn out the motors. If we land, we've got a chance of fixing it."

Byrd glances at the ice. It looks smooth enough. Then he remembers the chaotic condition of the ice fields they passed. He remembers, too, what happened to Amundsen and Ellsworth, who landed their flying boat in open water, where they have only fragile skis. Oh, no, too many expeditions came to grief because they landed.

" Don't forget what happened to the PN-9 and the NC-boats when they landed," Byrd bawled in reply. " We'll keep going."

Quite happily Bennett nods in agreement. Now — on with their mission, with disaster lurking in the drenching leak, or shall they wheel about and race for home? Bennett points his finger toward the pole. Byrd nods, and the plane does not vary from its northward path.

[1] **De Long:** George Washington De Long, one of the earlier American Arctic explorers.

It is a brave decision, carelessly arrived at. Having come this far, they are determined to complete their task. The next hour or two will tell the story. The difference between two or three hundred miles in this desolation is not important — only a trivial distance in an infinity. They exchange smiles, and Bennett turns over the wheel to Byrd.

For the next half-hour or so, Byrd's eyes never falter from the instrument board. If the oil-pressure indicator shows a drop, it can mean only one thing — a burned-out motor, struggling along with terrific gas consumption on the other two and, finally, the forced descent. But the needle holds steadily. Deeply relieved, although not a bit optimistic, he turns over the wheel to Bennett, for the goal for which he has dreamed is actually in sight.

It is not quite nine o'clock as he sights the sun, computes rapidly, and then stares into the whiteness. They are 89° 55.3′. In a few minutes now — the Fokker sweeps into the sunlight at reduced speed, seventy-four miles an hour. Tense, as immobile almost as a statue, Byrd bends over his chronometer, watching the second hands.

Nine o'clock. At 9:03 o'clock he straightens up, taps Bennett's shoulder, and shouts: " The pole! " Yet he cannot permit himself more than a momentary satisfaction. If they are to get back to Spitzbergen, he must confirm his calculations. Here every direction is south; a most minute error means hundreds of miles from their objective. He orders Bennett to maneuver sharply to the right, and then takes quick observations; then he orders him to wheel about, and he takes two more; then, using the pole as a center, he has the Fokker maneuvered in a great circle four miles in diameter.

It is thrilling; it is exhilarating. And during those few minutes, while they pivot on the great wing above the spot that only Peary accomplished, they forget the leaking oil tank — forget everything except the wonderment that comes from having stood face to face with the unknown.

Perhaps it is a desolate spot. Perhaps it does seem almost folly that men should stand ready to sacrifice so much, simply to contemplate the emptiest spot on the globe. From his lofty place Byrd for the first time in his life feels the restless longings within him suddenly extinguished. He was poised over immense solitude, and the infinite wastes stretching into the horizon so easily might engulf the mightiest human urge and leave no trace. Here is a world that never would feel the trampling feet of armies, nor hear the din of factories, nor respond to the ennoblements of architecture. It was nature in a fierce, suspended repose — in a far-flung chaos that must never yield to humanly conceived order.

Down below, Peary planted his flags; but seventeen Arctic nights and the ceaseless flux of currents have erased all vestiges of his coming. Throughout the hundred and twenty miles of vision from three thousand feet of altitude they see nothing but the seemingly fixed and frozen sea, here and there interspersed with open leads. Toward the horizon it loses definiteness and merges into bluish-gray mist.

There is no land at the pole. The vast corrugations and telescopings in the ice sea show that. What Peary found, so Byrd finds. He shall return without the joy of discovering the chimerical continent of the Arctic, but in his heart he has found something greater and as lasting.

For five minutes the Fokker riots in the sky. Halfway around the circle they lost a whole day in time; completing the circle, they almost instantly recovered it.[1]

[1] If you will stop and think how we set our watches back or ahead as we travel from east to west on a larger circle of the earth's circumference, this sentence will become clear.

They make an astonishing flight around the world in three minutes. One second, without visible change in direction, they hurtle north, and the next they hurtle south. "An instant," he writes, "can be an age; an age an instant." While Bennett steadies the plane in a broad sweeping bank, Byrd snaps a motion picture of the pole. It is 9:15 o'clock, and they have been over the pole something like thirteen minutes. Bennett smiles again and shouts, "Let's go back."

Byrd is more than willing. It is already confusing enough to his orderly mind in this chaos of time and space, where the intelligence of an Einstein[1] must be required to fix their kaleidoscopic movements. Now he must get back — must hit the little island of Spitzbergen right on the nose. Then, just as Bennett banks abruptly, Byrd's sextant slides from the chart table and crashes to the floor as he futilely reaches to save it. It is hopelessly injured. His most important navigational guide is gone! He must depend upon dead reckoning.[2]

But Byrd is resourceful. At the moment when he estimates the sun should be crossing the fifteenth meridian, along which he has laid his course, he orders Bennett to steady the plane and head it directly into the sun. He notices that the shadow falls straight athwart the middle of the hand of the compass, proof that he is directly on the meridian.

"We'll hit at Grey Hook," Byrd writes on a note. Grey Hook is a tiny promontory on the northwest coast of Spitzbergen. Bennett does not hear; the continuous roar of the motors has deafened him, but he smiles encouragingly. So they begin the long dash home, with the motor still spurting oil and the vague fear in their hearts that it will stop — and not a little wonderment over the fact that it had not already done so.

Byrd studies the leak idly. He is conscious of no sense of helplessness. To the contrary, it rather fascinates him. Upon such trivial things — in this case probably the loss of a rivet — do the lives of men depend. A skyscraper might crumple in time for an improperly placed rivet. But here, half a mile above the polar ice, it does seem such a futile, inconsequential thing. Then through his musing there suddenly breaks the realization that the leak is stopped. He grabs Bennett by the arm.

The pilot looks out for a moment and grins in agreement. It is almost beyond comprehension. The oil gage shows ample pressure. There must have been an extra quantity of lubrication in the tank. They hurtle toward home with the motor at nearly full throttle, a gentle tail wind nudging them along. The air-speed indicator shows a speed of a hundred and ten miles an hour; and the altitude varies from twelve hundred feet or so to half a mile, depending upon wind currents and the advantages to be gained thereof. And Byrd regrets the destruction of the sextant; these last observations would be technically important.

Both are dead tired. The inevitable reaction has set in; the thrill of achievement has come and gone, and the sleepless nights demand compensation. Every half-hour Byrd relieves Bennett at the controls, and the lanky pilot rubs his eyes and flexes his arms. He smiles wearily. The brilliant sun is soporific.

A steel-gray shoulder of land bulks vaguely seventy miles in the foreground and dead ahead. It is Grey Hook, and Byrd has hit it on the nose. Bennett stares in amazement at this demonstration of "dead reckoning." There can be no doubt of their having reached the pole. Other-

[1] **Einstein**: Albert Einstein, the celebrated mathematician. [2] **dead reckoning**: that is, without the aid of astronomical observations; solely by means of calculations with compass.

wise they never could have reached Grey Hook.[1] He claps Byrd on the shoulder.

Now they bear sharply to the right. King's Bay lies down the coast, behind the gold-flecked mountains that are slowly precipitated out of the mist as they approach. At 4:30 o'clock the Fokker crests the rugged bluffs overhanging the fishing village, spins in a wide turn, and comes to land. The first flight to the North Pole has been made; the second expedition in four hundred years has succeeded; and Byrd and Bennett, thinking only of sleep and rest, tumble out on the snow.

Amundsen dashes across the snow and is among the first to reach Byrd. There are tears in his eyes as he greets the man who beat him — tears that choke off words. He embraces the American, kisses him on both cheeks, and helps him down the slope. Thus closes one of the most glorious days in Byrd's career. A day rich in knowledge of unknown things and of hidden things within himself. He is drowsy before he reaches the *Chantier*. And that brilliant reporter Russell Owen, of the New York *Times,* is flashing the news to the world that Byrd has achieved his goal and fought his struggle in pure, cloudless skies.

That night there was another party aboard the *Chantier,* and it was as merry and gay a one as that before the take-off. The gallant and sporting Amundsen and Ellsworth once more toasted him vivaciously, this time for having succeeded.

But two years later Byrd was to remember it differently; for, two years later, the *Italia,* under command of General Nobile,[2] staggered to the ice on a return flight from the pole and contributed one of the most ghastly tragedies to the history of polar exploration. Nearly a dozen of the men who dined with Byrd that night were to perish. And, above all, he was to remember the prophetic words of Amundsen as they stood at midnight on the deck of the *Chantier* and gazed out upon the waters dancing under the midnight sun.

"Tomorrow the *Norge* starts," he said, "and, I think, it is my last exploration. I am getting old, and I want to spend the rest of my days in my old country home, in the ice and snow I love. Once I felt that I should like to die, when the time came, in the field.[3] But now I seem to want peace and rest. You have done well. In a few hours you have succeeded where my years of effort ended in failure."

He shook hands warmly and clambered down the steps, a broad-shouldered man with the imprint of the Arctic wind deep in his face and illimitable fortitude in his calm eyes. At 10:00 A.M., on May 11, the *Norge* lifted its stubby nose into clear skies, its great sides plump and flat in the morning sun, and surged toward the pole with a great beating of propellers, starting a flight that was to end three days later at Point Barrow, Alaska, on the other side of the world. Before he left, Byrd gave Ellsworth all his polar equipment — his sun compass, gloves, bearskin trousers, shoes, and jacket. When the *Norge* landed in Alaska, the craftsman who had made the shoes for Byrd recognized them on Ellsworth, and his astonishment knew no bounds. Today they are in a New York museum.

As a tribute to Amundsen and Ellsworth, Bennett and Byrd escorted the *Norge* out of Spitzbergen, waggled the wings in a gesture of farewell, and turned back to prepare for their own departure.

[1] In other words, they were back from where they started; and calculations showed they must have hit the North Pole. [2] **Nobile:** General Nobile, representing the Italian government, from which the *Norge* was purchased, was also a member of the *Norge* expedition.

[3] **in the field:** Amundsen, on a flight to effect a rescue of the Nobile party, did not return; therefore, he *did* die "in the field."

There remained only the task of dismantling the camp and starting for home. Congratulatory wires were pouring in from all parts of the world; from presidents, dictators, and governors. Like the man who made a good mousetrap,[1] Byrd found that the world will beat a path, if only by radio, to the door of the explorer who flies to the North Pole.

Bad weather held them up for a few days and, during the lull, Byrd, Bennett, Kinkade, and Mulroy, in response to a request from the local governor, flew fifty miles up the coast in search of three trappers who had been missing all winter and who were believed to be running short of food. The flyers spotted them camped in the lee of a ridge, smoke rising cheerfully from a huge fire. Bennett circled low, and the others parachuted a supply of pemmican and canned food to which was attached a note suggesting that the trappers wave if everything was all right. The trappers recovered the food and signaled they were in no distress, and the *Josephine Ford* returned.

Thursday, May 20, the *Chantier* steamed out of King's Bay while the ground crew of the *Norge,* who were also preparing to follow, and the handful of citizens, who had grown to be quite fond of these Americans, cheered them off.

Byrd was off to London — then to New York.

THINK BACK OVER WHAT YOU HAVE READ

Appreciating the Quality of Byrd's Leadership as Portrayed by His Biographer

1. What qualities do you associate with leadership? What illustrations can you give of Byrd's living up to these qualities?

2. What part does "taking a chance" play in successful exploration? What illustrations of Byrd's taking a chance impressed you? What other qualities went along with his daring?

3. What aspects of Byrd's and Bennett's disposition did you notice? How did they react to delay? to mishap? to danger? to uncertainty? to hardship? How does the ordinary person react to these difficulties? What comment are you led to make about the character traits necessary for exploration?

4. What illustrations of fine sportsmanship can you cite from the narrative? What extension of this idea are you tempted to make after reading about Byrd and Amundsen?

5. What comments are you led to make about Byrd's relations with his men? What was the relationship of Byrd and Bennett? In what spirit did Byrd's men obey orders? What illustrations can you cite to emphasize the points that you make?

6. How great a part does imagination play in scientific discovery? At what points in the story does Byrd's imagination travel ahead? What mishaps are averted by foresight?

7. What part does "learning by experience" play in exploration? At what points in the story did "hindsight" play its part? What comments are you led to make about the relationship between foresight and hindsight?

8. Were you impressed by the organization of effort as revealed in the account? How many different kinds of experts were you aware of? How smoothly did they work together? What illustrations can you cite of fine co-ordination of different kinds of ability? What does this co-ordination suggest to you about social welfare?

Responding with the Senses to the Thrill of Exploration

9. What pictures does your imagination see of the landing of equipment? At what moments were you excited? By what details of adventure?

10. What details gave you a sense of the final take-off? What did you "see"? "hear"? "feel"?

11. What details communicated to you the sense of being off on a thrilling adventure? How did Byrd feel? Bennett? By what words can you tell? What emotion held them?

12. What pictures did you take in your imagination from the plane? Quote brief passages that gave you a sense of desolation, of weird

[1] **mousetrap:** made famous by Ralph Waldo Emerson in a proverb to the effect that if a man made a better mousetrap than his neighbor the world would beat a path to his door.

topography. What would have been *your* reactions to the scene below? What were Byrd's? Bennett's?

13. What impression did you form of the interior of the plane? What details gave you a sense of its size? of its equipment?

14. What details gave you a sense of navigation?

15. What details gave you a dizzy sense of being at the pole? What were Byrd's and Bennett's reactions? What interesting sense of confusion is inevitable at the pole?

16. What details gave you a sense of how Byrd and Bennett felt when their success was assured?

Increase Your Power over Words

17. The Latin word *optimus* means best. From it is derived the word *optimistic* (page 240), which means looking on the best side of things. An *optimist* is one who is always cheerful.

The opposite of *optimistic* is *pessimistic* (from the Latin *pessimus* meaning worst), which means looking on the worst side of things. A *pessimist* is one who is gloomy.

18. The word *chronometer* (page 240) is derived from two Greek words: *chronos,* which means time, and *metron,* measure. A chronometer is, therefore, any instrument for measuring time. Whenever you see words built on the stem *chron,* you can know that they refer to time. *Chronic, chronicle, chronological* are some of these words. The suffix *meter,* found in so many words with which you are familiar, always means measure: thus, *kilometer, pedometer, speedometer.* Can you figure out what these words mean? If not, look them up in the dictionary.

For Ambitious Students

19. *Exploring the poles through biography.* The following books will extend your acquaintance with Arctic and Antarctic exploration:

Amundsen, Roald, *My Life as an Explorer*
Bartlett, R. A., *The Log of Captain Bob Bartlett*
Byrd, Richard, *Little America*
Nansen, Fridtjof, *Farthest North*
Peary, R. E., *The North Pole*
Shackleton, Ernest, *South*
Stefansson, Vilhjalmur, *My Life with the Eskimo*
Wilkins, Hubert, *Flying the Arctic*

THE ELEMENTS

by Antoine de St. Exupéry [1]
(*1900–*)

"Horror or fear is something invented *after* the fact." Perhaps you have already discovered the truth of this statement for yourself. At the moment of great danger you were too absorbed in the possibilities of escape, or too fascinated by the spectacle which you were witnessing, to give way to fear. It was only *after* you were safe that your nerves relaxed enough for you to feel afraid.

So it was with St. Exupéry, the aviator who wrote the following vivid account of what he noticed during the time his plane wrestled with a cyclone in the Andes. As you read of his thrilling flight, keep your mind centered on the strange sights that he saw — that's what he did — and the strange sensations he felt while nature performed her spectacular feats. Herein lies the chief charm of the essay.

St. Exupéry is a Frenchman who has devoted the best years of his life to flying. As a commercial flyer in France and a mail pilot in South America he not only has experienced all the thrills of flying himself but has the ability to describe them so that others may share them.

With him you are about to make an amazing journey. So strap yourself tight in the cockpit of your plane. Ready? Contact. We are off.

EVERY air-line pilot has flown through tornadoes, has returned out of them to the fold — to the little restaurant in Toulouse [2] where we sat in peace under the watchful eye of the waitress — and there, recognizing his powerlessness to convey what he has been through, has given up the idea of describing hell. His descriptions, his gestures, his big words would have made the rest of us smile as if we were listening to a little boy bragging. And necessarily so. The cyclone of which I am about to speak was, physically, much the most brutal and overwhelming experience I ever underwent; and yet beyond a certain point I do not know how

[1] **Antoine de St. Exupéry:** pronounced ăn-twän′ de sän t'ex-ū-pay-ree. [2] **Toulouse:** a city in southern France.

to convey its violence except by piling one adjective on another, so that in the end I should convey no impression at all — unless perhaps that of an embarrassing taste for exaggeration.

It took me some time to grasp the fundamental reason for this powerlessness, which is simply that I should be trying to describe a catastrophe that never took place. The reason why writers fail when they attempt to evoke horror is that horror is something invented after the fact, when one is re-creating the experience over again in the memory. Horror does not manifest itself in the world of reality. And so, in beginning my story of a revolt of the elements which I myself lived through, I have no feeling that I shall write something which you will find dramatic.

I had taken off from the field at Trelew and was flying down to Comodoro-Rivadavia, in the Patagonian Argentine.[1] Here the crust of the earth is as dented as an old boiler. The high-pressure regions over the Pacific send the winds past a gap in the Andes into a corridor fifty miles wide, through which they rush to the Atlantic in a strangled and accelerated buffeting that scrapes the surface of everything in their path. The sole vegetation visible in this barren landscape is a plantation of oil derricks looking like the aftereffects of a forest fire. Towering over the round hills on which the winds have left a residue of stony gravel, there rises a chain of prow-shaped, saw-toothed, razor-edged mountains stripped by the elements down to the bare rock.

For three months of the year the speed of these winds at ground level is up to a hundred miles an hour. We who flew the route knew that, once we had crossed the marshes of Trelew and had reached the threshold of the zone they swept, we should recognize the winds from afar by a gray-blue tint in the atmosphere, at the sight of which we would tighten our belts and shoulder straps in preparation for what was coming. From then on we had an hour of stiff fighting and of stumbling again and again into invisible ditches of air. This was manual labor, and our muscles felt it pretty much as if we had been carrying a longshoreman's load. But it lasted only an hour. Our machines stood up under it. We had no fear of wings suddenly dropping off. Visibility was generally good, and not a problem. This section of the line was a stint, yes; it was certainly not a drama.

But on this particular day I did not like the color of the sky.

The sky was blue. Pure blue. Too pure. A hard blue sky that shone over the scraped and barren world while the fleshless vertebrae of the mountain chain flashed in the sunlight. Not a cloud. The blue sky glittered like a new-honed knife. I felt in advance the vague distaste that accompanies the prospect of physical exertion. The purity of the sky upset me. Give me a good black storm in which the enemy is plainly visible. I can measure its extent and prepare myself for its attack. I can get my hands on my adversary. But when you are flying very high in clear weather, the shock of a blue storm is as disturbing as if something collapsed that had been holding up your ship in the air. It is the only time when a pilot feels that there is a gulf beneath his ship.

Another thing bothered me. I could see on a level with the mountain peaks not a haze, not a mist, not a sandy fog, but a sort of ash-colored streamer in the sky. I did not like the look of that scarf of filings scraped off the surface of the earth and borne out to sea by the wind. I tightened my leather harness as far as it would go, and I steered the ship with one hand

[1] **Patagonian Argentine:** the southern part of Argentina in South America.

while with the other I hung onto the *longéron*[1] that ran alongside my seat. I was still flying in remarkably calm air.

Very soon came a slight tremor. As every pilot knows, there are secret little quiverings that foretell your real storm. No rolling, no pitching. No swing to speak of. The flight continues horizontal and rectilinear. But you have felt a warning drum on the wings of your plane, little intermittent rappings scarcely audible and infinitely brief, little cracklings from time to time as if there were traces of gunpowder in the air.

And then everything round me blew up.

Concerning the next couple of minutes I have nothing to say. All that I can find in my memory is a few rudimentary notions, fragments of thoughts, direct observations. I cannot compose them into a dramatic recital because there was no drama. The best I can do is to line them up in a kind of chronological order.

In the first place, I was standing still. Having banked right in order to correct a sudden drift, I saw the landscape freeze abruptly where it was and remain jiggling on the same spot. I was making no headway. My wings had ceased to nibble into the outline of the earth. I could see the earth buckle, pivot — but it stayed put. The plane was skidding as if on a toothless cogwheel.

Meanwhile I had the absurd feeling that I had exposed myself completely to the enemy. All those peaks, those crests, those teeth that were cutting into the wind and unleashing its gusts in my direction, seemed to me so many guns pointed straight at my defenseless person. I was slow to think; but the thought did come to me that I ought to give up altitude and make for one of the neighboring valleys, where I might take shelter against a mountainside. As a matter of fact, whether I liked it or not I was being helplessly sucked down toward the earth.

[1] **longéron:** one of the chief longitudinal members of the body of an airplane.

Trapped this way in the first breaking waves of a cyclone about which I learned, twenty minutes later, that at sea level it was blowing at the fantastic rate of one hundred and fifty miles an hour, I certainly had no impression of tragedy. Now, as I write, if I shut my eyes, if I forget the plane and the flight and try to express the plain truth about what was happening to me, I find that I felt weighed down; I felt like a porter carrying a slippery load, grabbing one object in a jerky movement that sent another slithering down, so that, overcome by exasperation, the porter is tempted to let the whole load drop. There is a kind of law of the shortest distance to the image, a psychological law by which the event to which one is subjected is visualized in a symbol that represents its swiftest summing up: I was a man who, carrying a pile of plates, had slipped on a waxed floor and let his scaffolding of porcelain crash.

I found myself imprisoned in a valley. My discomfort was not less; it was greater. I grant you that a down current has never killed anybody, that the expression "flattened out by a down current" belongs to journalism and not to the language of flyers. How could air possibly pierce the ground? But here I was in a valley at the wheel of a ship that was three-quarters out of my control. Ahead of me a rocky prow swung to left and right, rose suddenly high in the air for a second like a wave over my head, and then plunged down below my horizon.

Horizon? There was no longer a horizon. I was in the wings of a theater cluttered up with bits of scenery. Vertical, oblique, horizontal, all of plane geometry was awhirl. A hundred transversal valleys were muddled in a jumble of perspectives. Whenever I seemed about to take my bearings, a new eruption would swing me round in a circle or send me tumbling wing over wing and I would have to try all over again to get clear of all this rubbish. Two ideas came into my mind. One was a discovery: for the first time I understood the cause of certain accidents in the mountains when no fog was present to explain them. For a single second, in a waltzing landscape like this, the flyer had been unable to distinguish between vertical mountainsides and horizontal planes. The other idea was a fixation: the sea is flat; I shall not hook anything out at sea.

I banked — or should I use that word to indicate a vague and stubborn jockeying through the east-west valleys? Still nothing pathetic to report. I was wrestling with chaos, was wearing myself out in a battle with chaos, struggling to keep in the air a gigantic house of cards that kept collapsing despite all I could do. Scarcely the faintest twinge of fear went through me when one of the walls of my prison rose suddenly like a tidal wave over my head. My heart hardly skipped a beat when I was tripped up by one of the whirling eddies of air that the sharp ridge darted into my ship. If I felt anything unmistakably in the haze of confused feelings and notions that came over me each time one of these powder magazines blew up, it was a feeling of respect. I respected that sharp-toothed ridge. I respected that peak. I respected that dome. I respected that transversal valley opening out into my valley and about to toss me, God knew how violently, as soon as its torrent of wind flowed into the one on which I was being borne along.

What I was struggling against, I discovered, was not the wind but the ridge itself, the crest, the rocky peak. Despite my distance from it, it was the wall of rock I was fighting with. By some trick of invisible prolongation, by the play of a secret set of muscles, this was what was pummeling me. It was against this that I was butting my head. Before me on the right I recognized the peak of Salamanca, a perfect cone which, I knew, dominated the sea. It cheered me to think I was about to escape out to sea. But first I should have to wrestle with the gale off that peak, try to avoid its down-crushing blow. The peak of Salamanca was a giant. I was filled with respect for the peak of Salamanca.

There had been granted me one second of respite. Two seconds. Something was collecting itself into a knot, coiling itself up, growing taut. I sat amazed. I opened astonished eyes. My whole plane seemed to be shivering, spreading outward, swelling up. Horizontal and stationary it was, yet lifted, before I knew it, fifteen hundred feet straight into the air in a kind of apotheosis.[1] I who for forty minutes had not been able to climb higher than two hundred feet off the ground was suddenly able to look down on the enemy. The plane quivered as if in boiling water. I could see the wide waters of the ocean. The valley opened out into this ocean, this salvation. And at that very moment, without any warning whatever, half a mile from Salamanca, I was suddenly struck straight in the midriff by the gale off that peak and sent hurtling out to sea.

There I was, throttle wide open, facing the coast. At right angles to the coast and facing it. A lot had happened in a single minute. In the first place, I had not flown out to sea. I had been spat out to sea by a monstrous cough, vomited out of my valley as from the mouth of a howitzer.[2] When, what seemed to me instantly, I banked in order to put myself where I wanted to be in respect of the coast line, I saw that the coast line was a mere blur, a characterless strip of blue; and I was five miles out to sea. The mountain range stood up like a crenelated fortress against the pure sky while the cyclone crushed me

[1] **apotheosis:** (pronounced ȧ-pŏth′ē-ō′sĭs) glorification; exaltation. [2] **howitzer:** short cannon.

down to the surface of the waters. How hard that wind was blowing I found out as soon as I tried to climb, as soon as I became conscious of my disastrous mistake: throttle wide open, engines running at my maximum, which was one hundred and fifty miles an hour, my plane hanging sixty feet over the water, I was unable to budge. When a wind like this one attacks a tropical forest, it swirls through the branches like a flame, twists them into corkscrews, and uproots giant trees as if they were radishes. Here, bounding off the mountain range, it was leveling out the sea.

Hanging on with all the power in my engines, face to the coast, face to that wind where each gap in the teeth of the range sent forth a stream of air like a long reptile, I felt as if I were clinging to the tip of a monstrous whip that was cracking over the sea.

In this latitude the South American continent is narrow and the Andes are not far from the Atlantic. I was struggling not merely against the whirling winds that blew off the east-coast range, but more likely also against a whole sky blown down upon me off the peaks of the Andean chain. For the first time in four years of airline flying I began to worry about the strength of my wings. Also, I was fearful of bumping the sea — not because of the down currents, which, at sea level, would necessarily provide me with a horizontal air mattress, but because of the helplessly acrobatic positions in which this wind was buffeting me. Each time that I was tossed I became afraid that I might be unable to straighten out. Besides, there was a chance that I should find myself out of fuel and simply drown. I kept expecting the gasoline pumps to stop priming; and, indeed, the plane was so violently shaken up that in the half-filled tanks as well as in the gas lines the gasoline was sloshing round, not coming through, and the engines, instead of their steady roar, were sputtering in a sort of dot-and-dash series of uncertain growls.

I hung on, meanwhile, to the controls of my heavy transport plane, my attention monopolized by the physical struggle and my mind occupied by the very simplest thoughts. I was feeling practically nothing as I stared down at the imprint made by the wind on the sea. I saw a series of great white puddles, each perhaps eight hundred yards in extent. They were running toward me at a speed of one hundred and fifty miles an hour where the down-surging wind spouts broke against the surface of the sea in a succession of horizontal explosions. The sea was white and it was green — white with the whiteness of crushed sugar and green in puddles the color of emeralds. In this tumult one wave was indistinguishable from another. Torrents of air were pouring down upon the sea. The winds were sweeping past in giant gusts as when, before the autumn harvests, they blow a great flowing change of color over a wheat field. Now and again the water went incongruously transparent between the white pools, and I could see a green and black sea bottom. And then the great glass of the sea would be shattered anew into a thousand glittering fragments.

It seemed hopeless. In twenty minutes of struggle I had not moved forward a hundred yards. What was more, with flying as hard as it was out here five miles from the coast, I wondered how I could possibly buck the winds along the shore, assuming I was able to fight my way in. I was a perfect target for the enemy there on shore. Fear, however, was out of the question. I was incapable of thinking. I was emptied of everything except the vision of a very simple act. I must straighten out. Straighten out. Straighten out.

There were moments of respite, nevertheless. I dare say those moments themselves were equal to the worst storms I had hitherto met, but by comparison with the cyclone they were moments of relaxation. The urgency of fighting off the wind was not quite so great. And I could tell when these intervals were coming. It was not I who moved toward those zones of relative calm, those almost green oases clearly painted on the sea, but they that flowed toward me. I could read clearly in the waters the advertisement of a habitable province. And with each interval of repose the power to feel and to think was restored to me. Then, in those moments, I began to feel I was doomed. Then was the time that little by little I began to tremble for myself. So much so that each time I saw the unfurling of a new wave of the white offensive I was seized by a brief spasm of panic which lasted until the exact instant when, on the edge of that bubbling caldron, I bumped into the invisible wall of wind. That restored me to numbness again.

Up! I wanted to be higher up. The next time I saw one of those green zones of calm it seemed to me deeper than before, and I began to be hopeful of getting out. If I could climb high enough, I thought, I would find other currents in which I could make some headway. I took advantage of the truce to essay a swift climb. It was hard. The enemy had not weakened. Three hundred feet. Six hundred feet. If I could get up to three thousand feet I was safe, I said to myself. But there on the horizon I saw again that white pack unleashed in my direction. I gave it up. I did not want them at my throat again; I did not want to be caught off balance. But it was too late. The first blow sent me rolling over and over, and the sky became a slippery dome on which I could not find a footing.

One has a pair of hands and they obey. How are one's orders transmitted to one's hands?

I had made a discovery that horrified me: my hands were numb. My hands were dead. They sent me no message. Probably they had been numb a long time and I had not noticed it. The pity was that I had noticed it, had raised the question. That was serious.

Lashed by the wind, the wings of the plane had been dragging and jerking at the cables by which they were controlled from the wheel, and the wheel in my hands had not ceased jerking a single second. I had been gripping the wheel with all my might for forty minutes, fearful lest the strain snap the cables. So desperate had been my grip that now I could not feel my hands.

What a discovery! My hands were not my own. I looked at them and decided to lift a finger: it obeyed me. I looked away and issued the same order: now I could not feel whether the finger had obeyed or not. No message had reached me. I thought: "Suppose my hands were to open. How would I know it?" I swung my head round and looked again: my hands were still locked round the wheel. Nevertheless, I was afraid. How can a man tell the difference between the sight of a hand opening and the decision to open that hand, when there is no longer an exchange of sensations between the hand and the brain? How can one tell the difference between an image and an act of the will? Better stop thinking of the picture of open hands. Hands live a life of their own. Better not offer them this monstrous temptation. And I began to chant a silly litany which went on uninterruptedly until this flight was over. A single thought. A single image. A single phrase tirelessly chanted over and over again: "I shut my hands. I shut my hands. I shut my hands." All of me was condensed into that phrase and for me the white sea, the whirling eddies, the saw-toothed range ceased to exist. There was only "I shut my hands." There was no danger, no cyclone, no land unattained. Somewhere there was a pair of rubber hands which, once they let go the wheel, could not possibly come alive in time to recover from the tumbling drop into the sea.

I had no thoughts. I had no feelings except the feeling of being emptied out. My strength was draining out of me and so was my impulse to go on fighting. The engines continued their dot-and-dash sputterings, their little crashing noises that were like the intermittent cracklings of a ripping canvas. Whenever they were silent longer than a second I felt as if a heart had stopped beating. There, that's the end! No, they've started up again.

The thermometer on the wing, I happened to see, stood at twenty below zero, but I was bathed in sweat from head to foot. My face was running with perspiration. What a dance! Later I was to discover that my storage batteries had been jerked out of their steel flanges and hurtled up through the roof of the plane. I did not know then, either, that the ribs on my wings had come unglued and that certain of my steel cables had been sawed down to the last thread. And I continued to feel strength and will oozing out of me. Any minute now I should be overcome by the indifference born of utter weariness and by the mortal yearning to take my rest.

What can I say about this? Nothing. My shoulders ached. Very painfully. As if I had been carrying too many sacks too heavy for me. I leaned forward. Through a green transparency I saw sea bottom so close that I could make out all the details. Then the wind's hand brushed the picture away.

In an hour and twenty minutes I had succeeded in climbing to nine hundred feet. A little to the south — that is, on my left — I could see a long trail on the surface of the sea, a sort of blue stream. I decided to let myself drift as far down as that stream. Here where I was, facing west, I was as good as motionless, unable either to advance or retreat. If I could reach that blue pathway, which must be lying in the shelter of something not the cyclone, I might be able to move in slowly to the coast. So I let myself drift to the left. I had the feeling, meanwhile, that the wind's violence had perhaps slackened.

It took me an hour to cover the five miles to shore. There in the shelter of a long cliff I was able to finish my journey south. Thereafter I succeeded in keeping enough altitude to fly inland to the field that was my destination. I was able to stay up at nine hundred feet. It was very stormy, but nothing like the cyclone I had come out of. That was over.

On the ground I saw a platoon of soldiers. They had been sent down to watch for me. I landed near by and we were a whole hour getting the plane into the hangar. I climbed out of the cockpit and walked off. There was nothing to say. I was very sleepy. I kept moving my fingers, but they stayed numb. I could not collect my thoughts enough to decide whether or not I had been afraid. Had I been afraid? I couldn't say. I had witnessed a strange sight. What strange sight? I couldn't say. The sky was blue and the sea was white. I felt I ought to tell someone about it, since I was back from so far away! But I had no grip on what I had been through. " Imagine a white sea . . . very white . . . whiter still." You cannot convey things to people by piling up adjectives, by stammering.

You cannot convey anything because there is nothing to convey. My shoulders were aching. My insides felt as if they had been crushed in by a terrible weight. You cannot make drama out of that, or out of the cone-shaped peak of Salamanca. That peak was charged like a powder magazine; but if I said so, people would laugh. I would myself. I respected the peak of Salamanca. That is my story. And it is not a story.

There is nothing dramatic in the world, nothing pathetic, except in human relations. The day after I landed I might get emotional, might dress up my adventure by imagining that I who was alive and walking on earth was living through the hell of a cyclone. But that would be cheating, for the man who fought tooth and nail against that cyclone had nothing in common with the fortunate man alive the next day. He was far too busy.

THINK BACK OVER WHAT YOU HAVE READ

Bucking a Cyclone with St. Exupéry

1. What pictures does your imagination see of the land below before the cyclone? after it was over? Out of what phrases did you paint the pictures?

2. What phrases make clear to you the sensations of flying? For example, the author speaks of his wings "nibbling" into the outline of the earth. Of course, they don't. They merely look to a flier as though they did. What other phrases can you find that give you a keen realization of how things look to a flier? How did the approaching storm look?

3. What sounds announced the approach of the storm?

4. The author speaks of feeling "imprisoned," of standing still. What was happening?

5. What tricks did the storm play on the author's senses?

6. With what sensations was he hurtled out to sea? What phrases reveal those sensations? How did the sea look during the storm?

7. On what "simple act" was his mind constantly fastened? With what difficulties did he wrestle?

8. What was the discovery about his hands that horrified him? How do you explain it?

9. At what moments did fear overtake the author? What were his sensations after landing?

Appreciating St. Exupéry's Style

10. Which of the following comparisons do you regard as particularly forceful? Which ones stirred in you a fellow feeling for the author? With what other comparisons from the selection can you compare them?

a. "Here the crust of the earth is as dented as an old boiler" (page 245).
b. "The sole vegetation visible in this barren landscape is a plantation of oil derricks looking like the aftereffects of a forest fire" (page 245).
c. "A hard blue sky that shone over the scraped and barren world while the fleshless vertebrae of the mountain chain flashed in the sunlight. Not a cloud. The blue sky glittered like a new-honed knife" (page 245).
d. "I was a man who, carrying a pile of plates, had slipped on a waxed floor and let his scaffolding of porcelain crash" (page 246).
e. "For a single second, in a waltzing landscape like this, the flyer had been unable to distinguish between vertical mountainsides and horizontal planes" (page 247).
f. "I had been spat out to sea by a monstrous cough, vomited out of my valley as from the mouth of a howitzer" (page 247).
g. "Hanging on with all the power in my engines . . . I felt as if I were clinging to the tip of a monstrous whip that was cracking over the sea" (page 248).

Increase Your Power over Words

11. Look up the meanings of the italicized words in the following sentences. Then explain the sentences in your own way.

a. "*Vertical, oblique, horizontal,* all of plane geometry was awhirl. A hundred *transversal* valleys were muddled in a *jumble of perspectives*" (page 246).
b. "Despite my distance from it, it was the wall of rock I was fighting with. By some trick of *invisible prolongation,* by the play of a secret set of muscles, this was what was *pummeling* me" (page 247).

For Ambitious Students

12. Now that you have read "The Elements," you will want to read other chapters from *Wind, Sand, and Stars*. You will especially like the chapter "Prisoner of the Sand" — an account of St. Exupéry's forced landing in a desert, where he was miraculously saved after a desperate experience.

13. Another book by St. Exupéry is *Night Flight,* a story of the mail pilots and the dangers they encounter.

Strange Adventures

MUSTANGS

by J. Frank Dobie (1888–)

This selection is taken from *A Vaquero of the Brush Country*, a book based largely on the personal recollections of John Young, a Texan of the older generation. The book is an accurate account of the life of the cowboys, of whom the author, J. Frank Dobie, writes: "The men of the Western saddle, however untutored in books some of them may have been, were not ignorant. Their profession was one that demanded skill, alertness, resourcefulness, close observation, will power, and fidelity." "Mustangs" has to do with those little fiery wild horses of the brush country. As you read it, you will get a glimpse of cowboy life in the old Southwest.

THE LONG, open divide between the Frio and Nueces rivers in McMullen and La Salle counties was one of the last ranges of southwest Texas for large herds of mustangs.[1] The mustangs would, of course, when closely pressed, take to the brush, and in the brush they made their final stand; but their favorite habitat was the mesquite-sprinkled prairies. Here on this divide of prairie and mesquite[2] I[3] saw the year after I went to Dog Town fully a thousand mustangs in one bunch; they had run together from many directions ahead of a big roundup of cattle. When they left the plain where they had gathered, they all left at once in one direction, passing not far from where I was riding. The rumble from their running was deafening, and they fairly shook the earth; a stampede of five times as many cattle could not have caused such disturbance.

Many people have wondered why at a time when horses were highly prized and sorely needed the ranch people did not domesticate more mustangs. Yet history shows that in the very years when mustangs were most numerous gentle horses were at peak prices and horse thieves and Comanche raiders were most active. The Comanches would ride, or walk, for days through vast numbers of mustangs in order to steal, at the risk of their lives, a few horses from the settlers. The wealth of the Plains Indians lay largely in horses, but they never went on the warpath over the extermination of the mustangs as they did over the extermination of the buffaloes. The lives and livelihood of the settlers were dependent upon horses, but most of them would have been glad if all the mustangs in the country had been run off.

Ranchmen in general regarded them as a great nuisance, good for nothing but to entice off gentle horses, to tramp up the range, to ruin water holes by their pawing, and — after barbed wire came — to tear down fences. The mustangs were continually running, and when they came to the newly strung fences they never veered. In tearing the fences down they cut themselves all to pieces. A wire cut at any time of the year except in the middle of winter meant screwworms,[4] and screwworms in horses are generally fatal. The toll of mustangs taken by the first fences was enormous. The remnants were cleared out of the pastures either by bullets or by men who drove them off as a joyful gift from the pasture owners.

While the country was still unfenced, captured mustangs had generally to be

[1] **mustangs:** small, hardy wild horses of the prairies. [2] **mesquite:** a small twisted tree native to the desert country of the Southwest. [3] **I:** John Young. The author writes Mr. Young's experiences in the first person.

[4] **screwworms:** the larvae of a fly which lays its eggs in sores or wounds. The larvae bore into the flesh, often with fatal results.

driven away from their native range before they could be released to graze in freedom. Otherwise, even after they were "broke," they were extremely likely to hear the call of the wild and rejoin what Will James[1] calls "the Wild Bunch." Among the native steeds of the prairies were fleet, hardy, and beautiful animals, some of which, like the Pacing White Stallion, Star Face, Black Devil, and the Blue Mare of the Washita, achieved legendary fame. As the frontiers advanced, the best mustangs were sought for with increasing eagerness and the proportion of inbred[2] and poorly shaped mustangs increased. There were many of this class. At a distance one of them with arched neck, distended nostrils, and flowing mane and tail looked graceful, even magnificent, but near at hand he was likely to appear gimlet-hammed and narrow-chested. The best horses among them were generally domesticated horses that had gone wild, and these were warier than the mustangs themselves. Occasionally a well-bred stallion escaped to them; then he and his offspring became marked prizes. By 1880 the wild bands of horses had been picked over by mustangers until good animals among them were not so common as they had formerly been.

As long as there were free mustangs to be caught, however, some men made a business of catching them. Many a cowboy killed a fifty-dollar horse trying to rope a twenty-dollar mustang. Sometimes in slack seasons the cowboys spent a good deal of time setting rope snares across trails in order to catch the wild horses, but they seldom caught anything that way. The mustang that was snared was usually a stallion leading his *manada*,[3] and he was likely to break either the rope or his own neck. On some of the horse ranches the men caught colts and raised them on cow's milk, but they were barely worth the trouble. The professional mustangers were the only men who caught mustangs in considerable numbers.

One summer I located, out on the divide between the Nueces and the Frio, a *manada* of mustangs that I decided to capture. The stallion was a beautiful sorrel and the mares and pony stock were above the average. The bunch numbered about thirty-five head, and with them was a mule. My plan was to "walk" them down and then drive them to a corral.

In order to walk mustangs down, two or more men relayed each other in riding after them until the bunch became too tired to run and grew so used to a man's following them that they would turn and drive as he directed. One man alone on one horse could walk a bunch of mustangs down if he hung onto them long enough. The time required for several men to walk a bunch down depended on how hard they rode, on whether or not they kept up the pursuit during the night, on the amount of water out, and on other conditions. There is a tradition that a party of forty-niners[4] lost their teams while crossing the plains and, in order to replace them, followed afoot after mustangs until they were able to catch some of them; hence, tradition adds, the technical use of the word *walking* among mustangers. Long before this, no doubt, Indians captured mustangs by going after them afoot; but it is doubtful if any cowboy or American mustanger ever footed it after wild horses.

To relay me in the walking game I took along a faithful Negro hand named Bill Nunn. We made camp near a water hole

[1] **Will James:** a well-known writer of books on the West, author of "On the Dodge" (see page 38). [2] **inbred:** When animals mate with other animals closely related to them, such as sisters and brothers, the stock weakens. The offspring of such mating are said to be inbred.

[3] **manada:** a Spanish word meaning herd or drove. [4] **forty-niners:** the men who went to California in 1849 in the rush for gold.

that was, I judged, about the center of the range over which the mustangs would run when we got them to going. Camp consisted of a few provisions, a blanket apiece, and plenty of extra horses. The horses could be hobbled [1]; or if one of us was around camp and not too sleepy, they might be loose-herded. All mustangs had a given range beyond the limits of which they seldom went; when they reached the boundary of this range, no matter how closely pursued, they would soon circle back. Thus a mustang hunter could count on keeping within the vicinity of a certain spot. The range was seldom more than twenty-five or thirty miles across and was often much less.

Although I did not propose to do much nightwork, I timed our hunt to begin in the full of the moon. The morning was still fresh when I struck the *manada,* having left Bill in camp with instructions to be on the watch to furnish me with a change of mounts. The mustangs ran a mile or two and then stopped. Their next run was for four or five miles — and they really ran. I loped and trotted along behind them all day, and they never went near camp. Over on Quintanilla Creek they got all the water they wanted while I was trailing far behind. At dark they appeared as fresh as they had been when I first flushed them. My horse was fresh also. I had not struck a gait faster than a gallop all day. I decided to keep on worrying the mustangs for two or three hours.

Despite the bright moonlight, I could see only a short distance ahead, and the solid turf of low mesquite grass made their tracks hard to see. As they frequently veered their course, I could not always guess in which direction I should follow in order to come up with them again. Now, some horses will trail other horses by smell almost as well as dogs can trail, provided the sign is fresh; however, a horse shows his trailing abilities, generally, only when he is eager to get with his own bunch. That night the horse I was riding seemed to know that I needed some help in following the mustangs — no friends of his. In many places he put his nose to the ground, and when he did this I let him take his course — invariably the right one. Several times the mule among the mustangs discovered their exact whereabouts by whistling. Between ten and eleven o'clock I staked my horse and bedded down on leggings, slicker, and saddle. In a morral attached to the horn [2] of my saddle I had some bread, dried beef, and coffee, with an empty tomato can for a coffeepot; so I did not go without breakfast. As soon as it was light enough to see I was after mustangs again. About ten o'clock old Bill, who had been watching from the top of a hill, saw us and took my place.

Our bunch of mustangs would, while running, frequently dash into other bunches, but the sorrel stallion never let one of his herd get away and the bunches always quickly separated. We knew the markings on our bunch so well that we could not confuse them with other mustangs even in the distance. After they had been followed for two or three days, they were noticeably slower than other mustangs in getting away. In another day or two they were so toned down that we could almost set our own pace in keeping up with them — a walk or a gallop. The mule, true to form, was the most alert and the most skittish animal among them.

We soon learned the habits and runs of the bunch so well that Bill or I could have relieved the other at almost any hour. Some days by means of short reliefs we

[1] **hobbled:** tied by the legs. Horses are hobbled so that they may move about without running away.

[2] **horn:** the high knoblike protuberance at the front and on top of a saddlebow.

pressed the mustangs pretty hard, but they generally got time at night to rest a little and to graze and sleep.

Finally the bunch was so tired that we could ride along close to them and turn them — all but the mule. He would snort, stiffen his tail, and trot on ahead; apparently he never dozed. However, I got close enough to read the brand on him and to note a collar mark on his shoulder. At the end of the tenth day I told Bill that the mustangs were walked down and that we would pen them on the morrow. I told him to take the saddle horses and camp outfit in, and with a couple of Mexican hands and a bunch of gentle stock horses to meet me somewhere about the old stagestand on the Guadalupe Creek next day. Before he left, I caught an extra-good horse that I had ridden but once on the entire hunt. He was unusually fat, but I did not contemplate any very hard running.

I had no trouble in pointing the *manada,* and for a while they went along fine, the mule playing in front as usual. Then he decided to turn back; so he just high-tailed himself around me, the mustangs following. I headed them right again, but again the mule led them back. He had his mind made up, and pretty soon I discovered that he, rather than the stallion, was going to manage the mustangs that day. When I undertook to force the mustangs to turn, they scattered and did not get together again until I allowed them to enter some brush. I followed them out of the brush, headed them right again, and again they turned and scattered. By now I was riding hard and fighting hard. I actually got close enough to some of the mustangs to whip them over the noses with my quirt.[1] I pulled my six-shooter and killed two of them that were particularly woodenheaded. The mule was causing all the trouble, however. He was the most valuable animal in the lot, but after a while I realized that I could do nothing with the bunch so long as he was around. I shot him dead. Immediately the mustangs were under control again.

We went trailing along slowly and quietly now. Then I noticed my horse quivering. At once I jumped down and took my saddle off. I knew what that quivering meant. I stuck my knife in the horse to bleed him — an old-time remedy that had virtue in it — but the blood that came out was thin and actually appeared to be mingled with melted tallow. In five minutes the horse was dead. I had ridden him to death, though I had not ridden him nearly so hard or so far as I have ridden many other horses. The day was fearfully hot.

There I was afoot twenty-five miles from the pens on the Guadalupe, and not a cow ranch or a cow camp anywhere in the country. One chance and one chance only I had for a mount. About two miles from where I was, a kind of range enemy by the name of Sullivan had a sheep ranch. I did not know him personally, though I had seen him and I knew him to be both a rough Irishman and a hard hater of all cowmen — but any port in a storm. When I walked with heels just about blistered up to his sheep-smelling shanty, the sun was two hours below the meridian. Mr. Sullivan was on the front gallery.[2] He did not say anything about a cup of coffee, and I immediately told him my troubles.

"Do you know," he said, "what I think of a man that will ride his horse to death? I think he is a brute."

I agreed with him all right and said that I had no excuse except that I did not realize how fat and soft my horse was. I told him that I had ridden many horses

[1] **quirt:** a riding whip with a short handle and a braided rawhide lash.

[2] **gallery:** a long, narrow balcony such as many ranch homes have.

twice as hard even in hot weather without hurting them.

"Well," said Sullivan, "what assurance have I that you won't kill my horse if I let you have one?"

"Nothing but my word," I replied.

It was plain that Mr. Sullivan did not care about lending me a horse. Then, after he had finished his lecture, he said that he did not have any horses up and that it would be night before any of his men came in with a horse. I merely replied that I would stay until I got something to ride.

"Now, young man," he bantered me, "can you *ride?*"

"Yes, sir," I answered, "I can ride, I have ridden, and I will ride anything that wears wool, hair, or feathers, I don't care what."

I saw old man Sullivan half grin. "There's a mule staked down there in the valley," he said, "that's been rode one or two saddles. If you think you can ride him, take him. Sorry I can't let you have a saddle, but I guess you can lead him out to where your saddle is."

I thanked Mr. Sullivan and went after his muleship. It still appeared to be mule day. The mule proved to be a long-legged four-year-old, as scary as it is possible for a mule to be. When I untied the rope from the tree he was staked to, he at once wheeled and dragged me for a hundred yards. I stopped him, but could not lead him. He did not know how to lead. I would drag him a while and then he would drag me; sometimes we were going in the right direction and sometimes in the opposite direction.

I hurried all I could, for I still had hopes of getting in behind the mustangs and taking them on to the corral. The leather leggings and six-shooter I had on did not make the weather seem any cooler. The mule and I were getting a little better acquainted and we were making fairly good time when I stepped almost on a rattlesnake that had been asleep in the shade of a little bush. At his rattle I jumped forward as far as I could; the mule snorted and jumped back, at the same time wheeling for a run. He pulled me square over the rattlesnake, which was a monster, and the rattlesnake struck. He must have got a square strike, for he hung his fangs in the edge of my leggings so that he held on. I jumped, kicked, ran, and wanted to fly. The mule was not moving a bit too fast to suit me — and he was moving.

Directly the snake's fangs broke off and I stopped the mule. I pulled out my six-shooter with murder in my heart, and the only reason I did not shoot was because I could not decide which to kill first, the mule or the rattlesnake. I delayed to examine the place where the snake had struck. One of his fangs was still in the leggings, and at once I cut a generous slice of leather off with it and threw it away. Then I reflected that the mule must have been actually scared — as much scared perhaps as I was — and that, therefore, he was not to blame for jumping and running. I decided further that the snake must have been considerably scared also. If I fired at the snake, I knew that the mule would get worse scared than ever. I seemed to have a sympathy for scared things; so I put the gun back in its holster, pulled the rope across my shoulder, and trudged on.

When we got well in sight of the dead horse, I realized that the worst was yet to come. My saddle was right at the dead horse, and there was not a tree or a bush anywhere about to which I could tie the mule. No amount of work could get him up close enough for me, while holding the end of the rope, to grab my blanket and saddle. I worked until I was exhausted. Then while I was wiping the sweat out of my eyes with a bandanna handkerchief that was wringing wet, I thought of a ruse that I should have thought of an hour before — a ruse that all cowboys know.

The idea seemed to freshen me, and I climbed down the rope until I got near enough to the mule to rub his nose and head. Finally I got hold of his ear, pulled it down until I got the tip of it between my teeth, and held it tight. That is the only way to hold a mule. It must be understood that I weighed at that time only a hundred and thirty-five pounds. After I got the mule well eared, it was comparatively easy to work the bandanna over his head, tie the ends of it to the hackamore (rope halter), and then slip the adjusted bandanna down over his eyes. He was blindfolded. I was now able to back him up to within reach of my rig, though backing him was no small job. At last, however, he was saddled and bridled and I was aboard.

When I leaned over and raised the bandanna blind so that the mule could see, his first glance was at the dead horse almost under his nose. He whirled, kicked at the fearful object, and began pitching. That mule seemed to take two jumps to one jump made by any pitching horse that I had ever ridden. At the same time he was kicking, and he actually kicked my feet out of the stirrups. He was absolutely crazy with fear. When he finally quit pitching, he stood stiff in his tracks and snorted — just snorted. I spurred him to make him go and he began pitching again. The only reason I was able to stay on him was that I had to stay on him. I have no idea how long we had it around and around. When he finally decided to travel, the sun was nearly down, the mustangs were nowhere in sight, and I felt mighty weak and lonesome.

With that mule there was no use trying to camp out in the hope of finding the mustangs next morning. I felt it in my bones that if I ever dismounted I should never be able to ride him again. I did not want to go back to Sullivan's ranch. I pulled out for the camp where good old Bill Nunn was no doubt anxiously awaiting me twenty-five miles away. Nobody nowadays knows how far twenty-five miles is; the only way to know is to ride a wild, stubborn, idiotic mule for twenty-five miles on a dark night without a trail to follow.

The night was cloudy, and, without a star or any other object to guide by, keeping the mule in a direct course proved to be no simple matter. He had his head set on going back to Sullivan's or somewhere else. Two strata of clouds were flying overhead, one going east and one going west. Once in a while a patch of stars shone. It was only by keeping watch on the clouds and the occasional stars that I kept any sense of direction. As long as I sat still in the saddle, the mule jogged along fairly well; but every time I shifted my weight, he shied and resumed his bucking. I don't think I have ever been quite so near exhaustion as I was that night. The east was lighting when I entered the stage road that ran from Dog Town to Fort Ewell. Then for the first time I struck a gallop, and by sunrise I was in camp. Bill and his Mexicans were all ready to start out on a hunt for me.

After I had drunk about a half gallon of black coffee and consumed bread pones and fried sowbelly in proportion, I felt really generous. I called Bill Nunn over to where I was squatted, still "playing the coffeepot," and told him that I would make him a present of my interest in all the mustangs left in Texas; in addition I offered to lend him saddle horses to ride while he caught them. I had never set myself up as a mustanger; I was through with mustangs forever. Bill took me up on part of the offer, for he got one of the Mexicans to help him and not long afterward brought in the *manada* we had learned to know so well. He sold them for a very fair price.

THINK BACK OVER WHAT YOU HAVE READ

Walking Down Mustangs with a Cowboy

1. What pictures will you hereafter associate with mustangs? In what kind of country did "the Wild Bunch," as Will James called them, roam?

2. What methods did the professional mustangers use to catch mustangs? Of what did "walking down" mustangs consist? What plans did this particular Texas cowboy make to corral the beautiful sorrel stallion and his *manada?*

3. How did the mule adopted by the mustangs upset the cowboy's plans for capturing the *manada?* How did the cowboy try to solve the problem which the mule created?

4. What incidents in the story seem to justify the sheep rancher's hatred for cowboys? To what extent did he reveal his distrust of cowboys to the mustang hunter? What irony lay in his offering him a mule to replace his dead horse? How was the first mule's death avenged?

5. What incidents explain the cowboy's decision that he was "through with mustangs forever"?

Increase Your Power over Words

6. The following words are associated with life on a Western ranch. If you are not already familiar with their specific meaning, look them up first in the essay you have just read and then, with the help of footnote, Glossary, or dictionary, verify their meaning within the context in which you find them.

mustang (page 252)	corral (page 253)
mesquite (page 252)	quirt (page 255)
manada (page 253)	horn (of a saddle, page 254)
hobble (page 254)	

For Ambitious Students

7. J. Frank Dobie is one of the best writers on the life and tradition of the Southwest. There will be some students in the class who will wish to read all of *A Vaquero of the Brush Country.* Other books by Mr. Dobie are *Coronado's Children* and *Apache Gold and Yaqui Silver.* These offer good material for parallel reading. Or you might try Andy Adams's *The Log of a Cowboy* or J. Evetts Haley's *Charles Goodnight.*

THE DRIVE

by Stewart Edward White (1873–   )

In Western "thrillers" you have seen the Western cowboy battling with Indians, rescuing helpless heroines, and shooting it out with cattle rustlers. According to popular repute, he lives a thrilling and dangerous life. The modern cowboy faces many dangers, but they are the dangers natural to his very useful and not always adventurous job. His task is to herd and care for thousands of cattle which will someday find their way to the food markets of the world.

The author of this selection from *Arizona Nights* knows the West. He has lived among the cowboys and has ridden the range. He will tell you about the life of the cow hand as it really is.

A CRY awakened me. It was still deep night. The moon sailed overhead, the stars shone unwavering like candles, and a chill breeze wandered in from the open spaces of the desert. I raised myself on my elbow, throwing aside the blankets and the canvas tarpaulin. Forty other indistinct, formless bundles on the ground all about me were sluggishly astir. Four figures passed and repassed between me and a red fire. I knew them for the two cooks and the horse wranglers.[1] One of the latter was grumbling.

"Didn't git in till moon-up last night," he growled. "Might as well trade my bed for a lantern and be done with it."

Even as I stretched my arms and shivered a little, the two wranglers threw down their tin plates with a clatter, mounted horses, and rode away in the direction of the thousand acres or so known as the pasture.

[1] **wranglers:** men in charge of the riding horses.

I pulled on my clothes hastily, buckled in my buckskin shirt, and dove for the fire. A dozen others were before me. It was bitterly cold. In the east the sky had paled the least bit in the world, but the moon and stars shone on bravely and undiminished. A band of coyotes [1] was shrieking desperate blasphemies against the new day, and the stray herd, awakening, was beginning to bawl and bellow.

Two craterlike Dutch ovens,[2] filled with pieces of fried beef, stood near the fire; two galvanized water buckets, brimming with soda biscuits, flanked them; two tremendous coffeepots stood guard at either end. We picked us each a tin cup and a tin plate from the box at the rear of the chuck wagon [3]; helped ourselves from a Dutch oven, a pail, and a coffeepot; and squatted on our heels as close to the fire as possible. Men who came too late borrowed the shovel, scooped up some coals, and so started little fires of their own about which new groups formed.

While we ate, the eastern sky lightened. The mountains under the dawn looked like silhouettes cut from slate-colored paper; those in the west showed faintly luminous. Objects about us became dimly visible. We could make out the windmill, and the adobe of the ranch houses, and the corrals. The cowboys arose one by one, dropped their plates into the dishpan, and began to hunt out their ropes. Everything was obscure and mysterious in the faint gray light. I watched Windy Bill near his tarpaulin. He stooped to throw over the canvas. When he bent, it was before daylight; when he straightened his back, daylight had come. It was just like that, as though someone had reached out his hand to turn on the illumination of the world.

The eastern mountains were fragile; the plain was ethereal, like a sea of liquid gases. From the pasture we heard the shoutings of the wranglers, and made out a cloud of dust. In a moment the first of the *remuda* [4] came into view, trotting forward with the free grace of the unburdened horse. Others followed in procession: those near sharp and well defined, those in the background more or less obscured by the dust, now appearing plainly, now fading like ghosts. The leader turned unhesitatingly into the corral. After him poured the stream of the *remuda* — two hundred and fifty saddle horses — with an unceasing thunder of hoofs.

Immediately the cook camp was deserted. The cowboys entered the corral. The horses began to circle around the edge of the inclosure as around the circumference of a circus ring. The men, grouped at the center, watched keenly, looking for the mounts they had already decided on. In no time each had recognized his choice, and, his loop [5] trailing, was walking toward that part of the revolving circumference where his pony dodged. Some few whirled the loop, but most cast it with a quick flip. It was really marvelous to observe the accuracy with which the noose would fly, past a dozen tossing heads, and over a dozen backs, to settle firmly about the neck of an animal perhaps in the very center of the group. But again, if the first throw failed, it was interesting to see how the selected pony would dodge, double back, twist, turn, and hide to escape a second cast. And it was equally interesting to observe how his companions would help him. They seemed to realize that they were not wanted, and would push themselves between the cowboy and his intended mount with the utmost boldness. In the thick

[1] **coyotes:** a species of animal resembling the wolf. [2] **Dutch ovens:** sheet-metal ovens for roasting or baking before an open fire. [3] **chuck wagon:** wagon carrying stove and provisions.

[4] **remuda:** a Spanish word (pronounced rā-mo͞o′thä) meaning the horses from which are chosen those to be used for the day. [5] **loop:** that is, the loop of the lariat.

dust that instantly arose, and with the bewildering thunder of galloping, the flashing change of grouping, the rush of the charging animals, recognition alone would seem almost impossible, yet in an incredibly short time each had his mount, and the others, under convoy of the wranglers, were meekly wending their way out over the plain. There, until time for a change of horses, they would graze in a loose and scattered band, requiring scarcely any supervision. Escape? Bless you, no, that thought was the last in their minds.

In the meantime the saddles and bridles were adjusted. Always in a cowboy's "string" of from six to ten animals the boss assigns him two or three broncos to break in to the cow business. Therefore, each morning we could observe a half dozen or so men gingerly leading wicked-looking little animals out to the sand "to take the pitch out of them." One small black, belonging to a cowboy called the Judge, used more than to fulfill expectations of a good time.

"Go to him, Judge!" someone would always remark.

"If he ain't goin' to pitch, I ain't goin' to make him," the Judge would grin as he swung aboard.

The black would trot off quite calmly and in a most matter-of-fact way, as though to shame all slanderers of his lamblike character. Then, as the bystanders would turn away, he would utter a squeal, throw down his head, and go at it. He was a very hard bucker and made some really spectacular jumps, but the trick on which he based his claims to originality consisted in standing on his hind legs at so perilous an approach to the perpendicular that his rider would conclude he was about to fall backward and then suddenly springing forward in a series of stiff-legged bucks. The first maneuver induced the rider to loosen his seat in order to be ready to jump from under, and the second threw him before he could regain his grip.

"And they say a horse don't think!" exclaimed an admirer.

But as these were broken horses — save the mark! — the show was all over after each had had his little fling. We mounted and rode away, just as the mountain peaks to the west caught the rays of a sun we should not enjoy for a good half-hour yet.

I had five horses in my string, and this morning rode "that C S horse, Brown Jug." Brown Jug was a powerful and well-built animal, about fourteen two in height, and possessed of a vast enthusiasm for cow work. As the morning was frosty, he felt good.

At the gate of the water corral we separated into two groups. The smaller, under the direction of Jed Parker, was to drive the mesquite in the wide flats; the rest of us, under the command of Homer, the roundup captain, were to sweep the country even as far as the base of the foothills near Mount Graham. Accordingly we put our horses to the full gallop.

Mile after mile we thundered along at a brisk rate of speed. Sometimes we dodged in and out among the mesquite bushes, alternately separating and coming together again; sometimes we swept over grassy plains apparently of illimitable extent; sometimes we skipped and hopped and buck-jumped through and over little gullies, barrancas,[1] and other sorts of malpais[2] — but always without drawing rein. The men rode easily, with no thought to the way nor care for the footing. The air came back sharp against our faces. The warm blood stirred by the rush flowed more rapidly. We experienced a delightful glow. Of the morning cold

[1] **barrancas:** ravines with steep sides. [2] **malpais:** (măl′pīs′) the rough surface of a congealed lava stream.

only the very tips of our fingers and the ends of our noses retained a remnant. Already the sun was shining low and level across the plains. The shadows of the canyons modeled the hitherto flat surfaces of the mountains.

After a time we came to some low hills helmeted with the outcrop of a rock escarpment. Hitherto they had seemed a termination of Mount Graham, but now, when we rode around them, we discovered them to be separated from the range by a good five miles of sloping plain. Later we looked back and would have sworn them part of the Dos Cabesas system, did we not know them to be at least eight miles distant from that rocky rampart. It is always that way in Arizona. Spaces develop of whose existence you had not the slightest intimation. Hidden in apparently plane surfaces are valleys and prairies. At one sweep of the eye you embrace the entire area of an eastern state, but, nevertheless, the reality as you explore it foot by foot proves to be infinitely more than the vision has promised.

Beyond the hill we stopped. Here our party divided again, half to the right and half to the left. We had ridden, up to this time, directly away from camp; now we rode a circumference of which headquarters was the center. The country was pleasantly rolling and covered with grass. Here and there were clumps of soapweed.[1] Far in a remote distance lay a slender dark line across the plain. This we knew to be mesquite; and, once entered, we knew it, too, would seem to spread out vastly. And then this grassy slope on which we now rode would show merely as an insignificant streak of yellow. It is also like that in Arizona. I have ridden in succession through grassland, brushland, flower land, desert. Each in turn seemed entirely to fill the space of the plains between the mountains.

From time to time Homer halted us and detached a man. The business of the latter was then to ride directly back to camp, driving all cattle before him. Each was in sight of his right- and left-hand neighbor. Thus was constructed a dragnet whose meshes contracted as home was neared.

I was detached, when of our party only the cattleman and Homer remained. They would take the outside. This was the post of honor and required the hardest riding; for as soon as the cattle should realize the fact of their pursuit, they would attempt to "break" past the end and up the valley. Brown Jug and I congratulated ourselves on an exciting morning in prospect.

Now, wild cattle know perfectly well what a drive means, and they do not intend to get into a roundup if they can help it. Were it not for the two facts that they are afraid of a mounted man and cannot run quite so fast as a horse, I do not know how the cattle business would be conducted. As soon as a band of them caught sight of any one of us, they curled their tails and away they went at a long, easy lope that a domestic cow would stare at in wonder. This was all very well; in fact, we yelled and shrieked and otherwise uttered cow calls to keep them going — to "get the cattle started," as they say. But pretty soon a little band of the many scurrying away before our thin line began to bear farther and farther to the east. When in their judgment they should have gained an opening, they would turn directly back and make a dash for liberty. Accordingly the nearest cowboy clapped spurs to his horse and pursued them.

It was a pretty race. The cattle ran easily enough, with long, springy jumps that carried them over the ground faster than appearances would lead one to believe. The cow pony, his nose stretched

[1] **soapweed:** a plant, part of which may be used as soap.

out, his ears slanted, his eyes snapping with joy of the chase, flew fairly "belly to earth." The rider sat slightly forward, with the cowboy's loose seat. A whirl of dust, strangely insignificant against the immensity of a desert morning, rose from the flying group. Now they disappeared in a ravine, only to scramble out again the next instant, pace undiminished. The rider merely rose slightly and threw up his elbows to relieve the jar of the rough gully. At first the cattle seemed to hold their own, but soon the horse began to gain. In a short time he had come abreast of the leading animal. The latter stopped short with a snort, dodged back, and set out at right angles to his former course. From a dead run the pony came to a stand in two fierce plunges, doubled like a shot, and was off on the other tack. An unaccustomed rider would here have lost his seat. The second dash was short. With a final shake of the head the steers turned to the proper course in the direction of the ranch. The pony dropped unconcernedly to the shuffling jog of habitual progression.

Far away stretched the arc of our cordon. The most distant rider was a speck, and the cattle ahead of him were like maggots endowed with a smooth, swift onward motion. As yet the herd had not taken form; it was still too widely scattered. Its units, in the shape of small bunches, momently grew in numbers. The distant plains were crawling and alive with minute creatures making toward a common tiny center.

Immediately in our front the cattle at first behaved very well. Then far down the long gentle slope I saw a break for the upper valley. The manikin [1] that represented Homer at once became even smaller as it departed in pursuit. The cattleman moved down to cover Homer's territory until he should return, and I in turn edged farther to the right. Then another break from another bunch. The cattleman rode at top speed to head it. Before long he disappeared in the distant mesquite. I found myself in sole charge of a front three miles long.

The nearest cattle were some distance ahead and trotting along at a good gait. As they had not yet discovered the chance left open by unforseen circumstance, I descended and took in on my cinch while yet there was time. Even as I mounted, an impatient movement on the part of experienced Brown Jug told me that the cattle had seen their opportunity.

I gathered the reins and spoke to the horse. He needed no further direction, but set off at a wide angle, nicely calculated, to intercept the truants.[2] Brown Jug was a powerful beast. The spring of his leap was as whalebone. The yellow earth began to stream past like water. Always the pace increased with a growing thunder of hoofs. It seemed that nothing could turn us from the straight line, nothing check the headlong momentum of our rush. My eyes filled with tears from the wind of our going. Saddle strings streamed behind. Brown Jug's mane whipped my bridle hand. Dimly I was conscious of soapweed, sacaton,[3] mesquite, as we passed them. They were abreast and gone before I could think of them or how they were to be dodged. Two antelope bounded away to the left; birds rose hastily from the grasses. A sudden *chirk, chirk, chirk* rose all about me. We were in the very center of a prairie-dog town; but before I could formulate in my mind the probabilities of holes and broken legs,[4] the *chirk, chirk, chirking* had fallen astern. Brown Jug had skipped and dodged successfully.

[1] **manikin:** At a distance Homer looked like a dwarf.

[2] **truants:** runaways. [3] **sacaton:** a coarse grass. [4] **broken legs:** Prairie dogs are burrowing animals. Therefore, there is danger that a horse may step in one of their holes and break a leg.

We were approaching the cattle. They ran stubbornly and well, evidently unwilling to be turned until the latest possible moment. A great rage at their obstinacy took possession of us both. A broad shallow wash crossed our way; but we plunged through its rocks and boulders recklessly, angered at even the slight delay they necessitated. The hard land on the other side we greeted with joy. Brown Jug extended himself with a snort.

Suddenly a jar seemed to shake my very head loose. I found myself staring over the horse's head directly down into a deep and precipitous gully, the edge of which was so cunningly concealed by the grasses as to have remained invisible to my blurred vision. Brown Jug, however, had caught sight of it at the last instant, and had executed one of the wonderful stops possible only to a cow pony.

But already the cattle had discovered a passage above, and were scrambling down and across. Brown Jug and I, at more sober pace, slid off the almost perpendicular bank and out the other side. A moment later we had headed them. They whirled; and without the necessity of any suggestion on my part Brown Jug turned after them, and so quickly that my stirrup actually brushed the ground. After that we were masters. We chased the cattle far enough to start them well in the proper direction, and then pulled down to a walk in order to get a breath of air.

But now we noticed another band, back on the ground over which we had just come, doubling through in the direction of Mount Graham. A hard run set them to rights. We turned. More had poured out from the hills. Bands were crossing everywhere, ahead and behind. Brown Jug and I set to work.

Being an indivisible unit, we could chase only one bunch at a time; and, while we were after one, a half dozen others would be taking advantage of our preoccupation. We could not hold our own. Each run after an escaping bunch had to be on a longer diagonal. Gradually we were forced back, and back, and back; but still we managed to hold the line unbroken. Never shall I forget the dash and clatter of that morning. Neither Brown Jug nor I thought for a moment of sparing horseflesh, nor of picking a route. We made the shortest line, and paid little attention to anything that stood in the way. A very fever of resistance possessed us. It was like beating against a head wind, or fighting fire, or combating in any other way any of the great forces of nature. We were quite alone. The cattleman and Homer had vanished. To our left the men were fully occupied in marshaling the compact brown herds that had gradually massed, for these antagonists of mine were merely the outlying remnants.

I suppose Brown Jug must have run nearly twenty miles with only one check. Then we chased a cow some distance and into the dry bed of a stream, where she whirled on us savagely. By luck her horn hit only the leather of my saddle skirts, so we left her; for when a cow has sense enough to "get on the peck,"[1] there is no driving her farther. We gained nothing and had to give ground; but we succeeded in holding a semblance of order, so that the cattle did not break and scatter far and wide. The sun had by now well risen and was beginning to shine hot. Brown Jug still ran gamely and displayed as much interest as ever, but he was evidently tiring. We were both glad to see Homer's gray showing in the fringe of mesquite.

Together we soon succeeded in throwing the cows into the main herd. And, strangely enough, as soon as they had joined a compact band of their fellows

[1] **"get on the peck"**: cowboy slang for turn rebellious.

their wildness left them and, convoyed by outsiders, they set themselves to plodding energetically toward the home ranch.

As my horse was somewhat winded, I joined the "drag" at the rear. Here by course of natural sifting soon accumulated all the lazy, gentle, and sickly cows, and the small calves. The difficulty now was to prevent them from lagging and dropping out. To that end we indulged in a great variety of the picturesque cow calls peculiar to the cowboy. One found an old tin can which by the aid of a few pebbles he converted into a very effective rattle.

The dust rose in clouds and eddied in the sun. We slouched easily in our saddles. The cowboys compared notes as to the brands they had seen. Our ponies shuffled along, resting, but always ready for a dash in chase of an occasional bull calf or yearling with independent ideas of its own.

Thus we passed over the country, down the long gentle slope to the "sink" of the valley, whence another long gentle slope ran to the base of the other ranges. At greater or lesser distances we caught the dust, and made out dimly the masses of the other herds collected by our companions and by the party under Jed Parker. They went forward toward the common center with a slow ruminative movement, and the dust they raised went with them.

Little by little they grew plainer to us, and the home ranch, hitherto merely a brown shimmer in the distance, began to take on definition as the group of buildings, windmills, and corrals we knew. Miniature horsemen could be seen galloping forward to the open white plain where the herd would be held. Then the mesquite enveloped us; and we knew little more, save the anxiety lest we overlook laggards in the brush, until we came out on the edge of that same white plain.

Here were more cattle, thousands of them, and billows of dust, and a great bellowing, and dim, mounted figures riding and shouting ahead of the herd. Soon they succeeded in turning the leaders back. These threw into confusion those that followed. In a few moments the cattle had stopped. A cordon of horsemen sat at equal distances holding them in.

"Pretty good haul," said the man next to me: "a good five thousand head."

THINK BACK OVER WHAT YOU HAVE READ

Participating in a Round-Up

1. With what pictures in his mind does the cowboy start his day? What details appealed to you? On page 259 the author says, "Everything was *obscure* and *mysterious* in the faint gray light." What things, in particular?

2. From your reading, what picture did you get of horse wrangling? of a *remuda?* What did you learn about the "thinking" of horses? the skill of cowboys and horse wranglers?

3. Of what did the day's "cow work" consist? How was the work divided and organized? What kind of generalship did Homer display? Of what did a cowboy's "string" consist? What was the "post of honor"? With what details can you illustrate how it deserves its name?

4. On what two facts in cow nature is a roundup of wild cattle based? On what kinds of skill of both cowboy and pony does its success depend? What thrilling successes of Brown Jug can you recount? Which one was most spectacular? What does the author mean when he speaks of man and horse being an "indivisible unit"? Of what importance is this fact in a roundup?

5. What is the final picture that you see when the roundup is complete? At what moment does tension begin to relax? What is a drag? What sounds are associated with the last stages of a cattle roundup?

Increase Your Power over Words

6. The prefixes *il, in, im,* mean not. Thus the word *inactive* means not active; *impure* means not pure; *illegal* means not legal. What, then, does *illimitable* (page 260) mean? *insignificant* (page 262)? *indivisible* (page 263)?

Composition Suggestion

7. The following titles are suggested for a composition based on your reading of *Arizona Nights* or other books dealing with ranch life:

The Cowboy's Lariat	Branding
The Ranch Country	Meat for the Tables of the World
The Cow Pony	
Life on the Range	Longhorn Cattle
The Cowboy's Equipment	Horsebreaking

KEEPER OF THE BULLS

by Courtney Riley Cooper (1886–1940)

You haven't forgotten Zenobia, whose "infidelity" to her keeper and new-found love for the doctor who had treated her wounds provide the basis for Henry Cuyler Bunner's amusing story on page 2. Such faithfulness — and occasional fickleness — is no fiction but a well-recognized trait in elephant nature, a trait to be dramatically illustrated in the essay which follows.

Animals learn much from their trainers; but their trainers also learn much from them, not only about animal nature, but about human nature as well. And in this thrilling account of circus adventures you will find human foibles reproduced in the escapades of elephants, as well as a whole social system illustrated in the behavior of an elephant herd.

The author of this selection, for many years associated with one of America's great circuses, knew elephants — not only as you know them, lumbering along, trunk to tail at the end of the circus parade, or performing clumsy tricks under the big top. From intimate contact he knew their whims, their prejudices, their loves, their hates, their intelligence, their stupidity. In this selection from *Lions 'n' Tigers 'n' Everything* he introduces you to the elephant trainer — the "keeper of the bulls" — and to the elephant leader, in whom all the other elephants in the herd place the same sort of trust as does the "queen" in her keeper. But let us be on our way to the circus lot to get acquainted with Old Mom, and Kas and Mo, and Leader Mary. Once you have made their acquaintance, the chances are that you will never again see an elephant in circus or zoo without wondering what kind of fellow he is.

PLEASE forgive a garrulity when the subject is elephants and the narrator a circus man. They are so many-sided, these pachyderms, so lovable, so exasperating, and so fearful that their complete story is a far greater one than that of all the other menagerie animals combined.

There are certain well-founded American traditions regarding the equally American circus which it seems almost sacrilege to disturb. For instance, it has been handed from generation to generation that when a big show goes into territory composed of many small towns the circus splits into several parts like the fabled joint snake and exhibits in three or four places at once. Again, it's a certainty that the fiercest beasts in captivity are the lions and the tigers and that if ever one of them should escape it at once would vent the pent-up rage of years of imprisonment by killing everyone in sight. By the same line of reasoning the bravest man on the whole blatant organization must be the lion trainer, who twice daily — rain or shine — goes into the dens with these beasts and by a narrow margin comes forth with skin and body still hanging together. A different existence, indeed, from that of the bull man [1] — who has nothing to do save to keep his placid, gigantic, ever-begging charges from eating too many peanuts, to bring them forth now and then that they may push a few wagons complacently around the lot, or trot them into the ring during the crowded hours of the performance to do the hootchy-kootchy [2] in their lumbering, comical fashion, to play a big mouth harp with their trunks until that laughing, easygoing trainer takes it away from them, to cavort at a pachydermic game of baseball or bear the million-dollar beauty around the arena at the head of the grand

[1] **bull man**: elephant keeper. [2] **hootchy-kootchy**: a kind of dance.

entree.[1] All in all, comparatively speaking, it would seem much easier than shooting a blank-cartridge revolver into the bellowing jaws of a roaring lion. Of course, he must be handy always to warn the uneducated that his big, clumsy charges hate tobacco and that they never forget an injury; but those are only little idiosyncrasies which bob up even with some human beings. No matter how placid a person or beast may be —

But to get back to the traditions. A show never splits and never exhibits in several places at once. The lion and tiger trainer has his troubles, it is true, but his is not the hardest job of the show. And the life of the elephant keeper isn't placid!

For, as it often happens with traditions, the usual reasoning is wrong. In the first place, the bulls are not placid, just as they are not clumsy, just as they do not remember an injury for years, and just as they do not promptly set upon the man who insults their taste with a juicy plug of tobacco. Perhaps long, long ago there may have been a solitary elephant that disliked nicotine, but times evidently have changed. Today a plug of tobacco is a titbit for any elephant, and more than once is a visitor's pocket ransacked by an inquiring trunk searching for a chew. Elephants eat tobacco just as they eat sugar cane or popcorn or peanuts or candy. To them it is a delicacy. Nor is the taste confined only to chewing tobacco; if you'll keep your eyes open the next time you go to a circus, you may even see elephants shooting snipes [2] where visitors have dropped their cigar butts along the picket line. Which ends that.

Their memories are no longer than those of any other intelligent animal, and their clumsiness and slowness are things that exist only in appearance. As for the relationship of ease between the lot of the keeper of the lions and the keeper of the bulls, the lion trainer leads a bored existence. All that is necessary for him to do is to keep a whip rein on a group of beasts and by a reasonable amount of care guard his own skin. The keeper of the bulls has an entirely different task.

Inconsistency is a thing which surrounds an elephant on every side in his life in the circus. Just as he is the best-liked beast of the menagerie, so is he the most feared. Just as he is the thing that must be counted upon literally to drag the show out of the mud when the mire of a wet circus lot has sunk every wagon to the wheel hubs and so entangled the heavy conveyances that horseflesh, even tractors, lose their efficiency, so on the very next day he may wreck everything he has worked so hard to save. He will swing forward confidently to the attack should a lion make a breakaway, but the proximity of a mouse or even a small, harmless snake on a country wayside is the signal for hysteria. He will carry a cannon on his back into a performance and stand immobile while the booming charge breaks in deafening fashion above him, and then, on the next Fourth of July, "go flighty" at the popping of a penny firecracker. He will remain at a picket line through confusion and turmoil while thousands of persons crowd about him, then pull up stakes and chase the daylights out of a candy vender who consistently offends him by selling dainties among the showgoers instead of distributing them free along the elephant line. He is the most sagacious animal in captivity, yet when he becomes frightened he doesn't know enough to turn out of the way of a brick building. His daily food consists of fully two hundred pounds of roughage, a few pounds of coal which he munches greedily if he can but get it, a

[1] **grand entree:** the opening parade in which all the performers, both human and animal, take part. [2] **shooting snipes:** a slang term for picking up cigar butts.

bushel or so of grain, ten or twenty pounds of pure dirt — chocolate loam or swamp muck preferred — and a tub or two of water, yet he will quit it all gladly for one lonely peanut or a piece of candy. In the circus world they've changed an old, old expression to fit their own needs:

"Inconsistency, thy name is elephant!"[1]

For, it seems, the paradox is a continual thing with the great pachyderms which form the backbone of practically every circus. There is never a time in which they are not depended upon to save the show in times of late arrivals, muddy or sandy lots, or on long hauls from the unloading runs to the exhibition grounds, when the two or three tons of flesh and bone and muscle which every elephant possesses are thrown into play to augment the efforts of the straining draft stock and chugging tractors. Yet, by the same token, upon one man and one alone depends the task of keeping them the placid, humorous clowns which they really should be — the keeper of the bulls.

In explanation, a herd of elephants — and in some of the big circuses a herd will number as high as twenty-five members — is built upon the monarchial system,[2] with a princess or two, a queen and a king in control. The princesses and queen are elephants; the only male ruler allowed is the superintendent of the herd, the man to whom the queen, or leader, vows allegiance. No matter what other men may do, what other men may command, if the keeper of the herd decides otherwise, then otherwise is the result. The leader obeys him above all others; the princesses obey her, and the male members tag along in a group of bulky camp followers, citizens, agitators, and revolutionists. The males make the trouble in an elephant monarchy; the females make the laws and enforce them.

As an example: Old Mom and her herd were in Canada several years ago, and one of its stands was Winnipeg. The performances were dated for Monday and, as is usual with a circus, the show had arrived in town a day ahead. The tents had been erected, the seats placed, the animals fed and exercised, the ring curbs fastened into position, the hippodrome track smoothed into readiness, the rigging for the various aerial acts set, and the circus had settled to rest.

In the menagerie the lions and tigers nodded sleepily, with nothing to disturb them from their Sunday slothfulness. The elephant picket line was calm and peaceful, the long trunks weaving lazily at the transference of a full portion of roughage from ground to mouth. Group by group the circus people departed from the lot, townward bound, for the usual Sunday stroll and the luxury of a night in a hotel instead of the cramped berths of the sleepers. Only the watchmen were left about the various tents, only the assistants in the menagerie.

Night came, starlit and peaceful. The torches began to gleam about the circus grounds, spots of limited brilliance barely sufficient to provide protection against the pitfalls of stakes and wagon tongues and tight-pulled guy ropes. Hours passed in torpid peace. Downtown the superintendent of the elephant herd, Fred Alispaw, seated himself at the table of a night restaurant and glanced across toward his wife, awaiting her decision on the menu of an after-theater supper. He called a waiter. He began the giving of an order. Then suddenly the café, the street, the city were in darkness, following a green blaze of lightning and its consequent crash of thunder. A moment more and the

[1] **"inconsistency, thy name is elephant":** a parody on a famous line in Shakespeare's *Hamlet* — "Frailty, thy name is woman."
[2] **monarchial system:** that is, an elephant herd is like a monarchy in that it has a king or queen to rule over it.

rain was pelting, borne at the fore of a forty-mile gale. Winnipeg all in a second had become a storm-stricken city, its lights extinguished by a lightning bolt which had struck one of the main feed wires, its streetcar service blocked, its streets running small rivers from the rain, its every activity for the moment halted. In the café diners laughed, struck matches, and waited for the lights to come on again, all but one man, stumbling through the darkness toward the doorway, Fred Alispaw, keeper of the bulls.

"Stay here until the lights come on!" he ordered hastily of his wife. "I've got to get to the lot!"

"But the cars are stopped."

"Can't help that. I'll find a taxi! I've got to get to the lot!"

Out into the sheetlike rain he went, to leap to the running board of the first passing automobile and literally commandeer it for a trip to the circus grounds several miles away. His experience with elephants and the instinctive knowledge of what the beasts might do under circumstances such as this demanded swift action, and plenty of it. More, intuition proved correct!

The storm had struck as suddenly at the circus grounds as in the city. With the first flash of lightning the wind had swept through the menagerie tent with galelike force, lifting the side walling and causing it to slap and bellow and snap in queer ghostly fashion. The elephant herd, peaceful and drowsing at its double row of stakes only a moment before, had heard and seen!

There was no keeper to reassure them; only assistants. To an elephant an assistant counts for little if the supreme voice is absent, and right at that moment Alispaw was miles away. In vain the menagerie men sank their bull hooks[1] into the ears of their plunging charges, then, bobbing about like so many plummets, strove in vain to hold the beasts in line. Even Old Mom, the head of the herd, had become panicky with the rest, not from fear of the storm but from the fright caused by the sight of that twisting, writhing side wall as it had shown for an instant in the glare of the lightning. To the elephants it represented some unknown bellowing monster about to attack; the unexplained thing always means trouble in an elephant herd. So the stampede had begun.

One by one the extra stakes were dragged from the ground. One by one the frantic animal attendants were thrown aside or knocked down by the flail-like blows of tossing trunks. The thunder now bore an obbligato of screaming, hissing cat animals, crouched in fear in their dens; of shouting men; of rending stakes, clanking chains, and squealing, trumpeting elephants. Then still another thunder, that of ton-heavy bodies plunging across the menagerie tent, the crashing of timbers as they knocked poles and cages from their path, and the stampede of the nine-elephant herd was on! A moment later the stages, the poles, the seats and grandstand of the main tent were splintering and snapping as some sixty thousand pounds of fear-maddened elephant flesh tore madly here and there in the big inclosure, rushing wildly, then wheeling as frantically in the other direction as a lightning flash showed that writhing, flapping thing of windblown canvas surrounding them on every side. Greater and greater the frenzy became; in the milling two of the males collided and began to fight with swift, smashing rushes and lashing trunks. Louder and louder became the squealing and trumpeting — suddenly to lull. A voice had come faintly from the darkness of the menagerie tent — every torch long had been extinguished — a

[1] **bull hooks:** rods with a hook at the end with which the keepers control the elephant.

voice which caused Old Mom to turn and to trumpet with a new note.

"Mom — Mom! Here I am!"

Again the call sounded and Old Mom answered, the queen obeying the command of her overlord. The fighting ceased. A new signal sounded from the throat of Old Mom. The elephants steadied. A moment later Alispaw, standing in the connection between the menagerie and the main tent, saw revealed in a flash of lightning a great hulking shadow coming slowly but steadily toward him, while in the rear there followed eight others, practically abreast! Old Mom had heard the voice she sought. That was enough!

But the fight had only begun. The storm now was taking on a new intensity, a new fury, and the trainer knew that he had but two allies, Mom and Frieda, her elephantine lady in waiting. As soon as possible he caught the two elephants by their ears and stood between them, talking to them, reassuring them, while they wrapped their trunks about him and squealed their delight; while the rest of the herd milled and trumpeted about them, each crowding its utmost to be near the thing which to them meant safety. For nearly an hour it continued, with the fate of the show in the hands of one man, literally buried in a bumping, jostling mass of thirty tons of frightened elephants — one man whom they trusted and whose presence alone could hold them against a new panic. Then slowly, with the aid of his assistants and a lone flickering torch, he began the task of working the mammals back to their picket line.

For Mom and for Frieda it was comparatively easy. For the rest it was a far more difficult task. Alispaw could not be in every place at once, and the moment the herd became strung out to the slightest degree there would be a concerted rush to be near the lead elephants and the keeper who guided them. In vain the assistants strove to drive them back, and at last one of the men, losing his head, struck violently at one of the beasts with an iron-tipped tent stake, only to miscalculate. The blow struck Alispaw, and he dropped unconscious, and the note of fright in Old Mom's bellow brought a new spasm of fear and a resumption of the milling to the rest of the herd.

Once more they circled and crowded — all but one. That one was Old Mom, half crouched over the prostrate trainer whimpering and touching him with her trunk, and through her frightened curiosity forming a bulwark against the rest of the surging herd. For a full five minutes this continued; then, dizzy and reeling, the keeper crawled to his feet and renewed his calls of assurance. The storm lessened. Slowly Old Mom wheeled into place at the picket line and submitted to her chains. Frieda came beside her; then, still trembling, still grunting and squealing and protesting, the rest followed. Daylight found the picket line again a thing of comparatively peaceful elephants, and all because of one man!

Nor is this at all unusual. Strictly otherwise. With the Barnum and Bailey Circus is a quiet, gentle-voiced man who has been the keeper of the show's big herd of elephants for more than a quarter of a century, while his aid at the head of the herd is an ancient lady of some eighty-five summers who can read his every intonation, his every command, and who forces her will upon the rest of the herd or knows the reason why! In elephantdom there appears to be a certain respect for superiority; the leader of the herd attacks with impunity any beast under her control, no matter how fierce it may be, how big or how favored in fighting proclivities. In the winter quarters of one of the Western circuses is a glaring patch of cement work which a few years ago stopped up a gaping hole of some ten feet in diameter where a leader elephant butted a recalcitrant member of her herd through an eighteen-inch brick wall! When the keeper of a herd has the allegiance of that herd's leader, he has fought half his battle. But that keeper may be forced to leave suddenly, and what then?

That's exactly the question every circus owner asks when there is a sudden shift in the superintendency of the elephant line, and in which there is no time to work in a new keeper gradually as the person in command. More than once it has meant trouble, not only to the circus but to the elephant. In view of this, enter Snyder.

They called him the biggest elephant in captivity. Whether he was or not, he was one of the best performers, one of the most intractable, and at the same time one of the most valuable. When Snyder departed this life it meant that a twenty-five thousand-dollar performing tusker, trained to walk on his hind hoofs about the whole circumference of the hippodrome track, at the same time carrying his trainer on his three-foot tusks, left the circus world forever. As a result his trainers were selected with care, and the slightest evidence of must,[1] or badness, in his eyes was the signal for instant and various activities to hold him from a stampede. Far better to keep a valuable elephant out of parades and performances — even to imprison him day after day in the bull cars — than to run the risk of a rampage which may end in the necessity of an execution.

Consequently Henry Boucher, a trainer, was eased into Snyder's life with all the care of the launching of a yacht when his old keeper resigned a few years ago. The elephant gradually accepted his new master, then came to love him. Two years passed, in which Boucher held the big performer safe from runaways, stampedes, and temperamental outbreaks. Then, a year ago, in Salina, Kansas, the trainer became violently ill and was forced to leave the circus on short notice.

The next day Snyder grunted and snorted and trumpeted in vain. His trainer was gone. That afternoon the beast was kept out of performance, and he weaved uneasily at his picket chain, slapping his trunk viciously at every passing candy seller — how every elephant hates them — even refusing food. His eyes began to cloud slightly, the first indication of must. The matinee performance ended, and an assistant, assigned to the position of substitute trainer, released the chain which held the betusked brute and led him into the empty big top, or main tent, for a first rehearsal under new management.

Snyder listened to just one command. Then with a rush he knocked the substitute from his path, splintered the quarter poles which crisscrossed before him, smashed a path through a tier of seats, broke through the side walling, lowered his head, then with a great butting lurch overturned the first wagon he saw, headed back through the side walling of the menagerie, seized the monkey cage at its tongue base with his trunk and threw it from him like a boy throwing a baseball. The cat animals began to roar and screech; he made for the dens, one by one, and overturned them. The hippopotamus grunted excitedly in his five-ton den, and Snyder rushed for it like the maddened thing he was; an impact followed like the crashing of runaway engines, and the den, with its bulky freight, catapulted through the side wall and ten feet clear of the tent.

They tried to surround him by peaceful elephants, to mingle him with the rest of the herd, and thus return him to captivity. It was useless. Snyder had turned renegade; he recognized no superior and he

[1] **must:** frenzy.

fought the leader of the herd with the same frenzy that he fought any inanimate object which blocked his path. So at last they sent for rifles; nor was it long before twenty-five thousand dollars in elephant flesh became only an object for a museum. Four steel bullets in his brain had ended the career of an elephant which had refused to recognize anyone but the master of his choice.

So you see there are grounds for that circus saying regarding inconsistency. Once an elephant becomes thoroughly angry, little can block his path. Yet in the regular course of events that same elephant actually can be afraid of his own shadow!

On one of the big shows are Kas and Mo, named respectively and respectfully for Kansas and Missouri. Both are what are known to the bull men as agitators, both flighty, unreasoning, and seemingly always anxious to find something that will serve as an excuse for trouble. Both also are punks, the circus name for anything not yet full-grown, and the lack of maturity in age may account for the equal absence of steadiness in character. In any event, their course has been a stormy one. Their first day on the show, when they arrived fresh from India in the care of a Singhalese,[1] ended with a general stampede of the entire herd when the two punks decided to run straight through it without an introduction; the panic, although it lasted only the length of a city block, resulted in nearly a thousand dollars in damages. The first windy day after their arrival brought a breakaway on their part, and the danger of a like action on the part of the adult members of the herd. The first parade was one of constant attempts at runaways and the smashing of a two-hundred-dollar plate-glass window. Finally there came the time when, at the slightest hint of any unusual happening, Kas and Mo were loaded hurriedly into the first available wagon and sent unceremoniously to the cars. This continued during the entire first season.

However, elephant trainers are persistent beings, and all that winter the keeper of the herd labored with Kas and Mo to bring them to a condition of dependability. To every possible noise, action, and circumstance that might cause fear on their part they were subjected, until the flighty brutes were considered proof against anything that might occur on a circus lot. Then they were turned over to Lucia Zora, wife of the menagerie superintendent, for a novelty in elephant training — the driving of the diminutive pachyderms in tandem style before a flower-bedecked two-wheel cart. It really seemed that Kas and Mo had reformed. They learned quickly; they obeyed every command.

Springtime came and the show went forth to its final exhibition stand, rehearsing, as is usual, for three days before the opening date. Everything was lovely. Kas and Mo, garlanded and festooned with strands of paper flowers, took their place in the grand entree like veterans. Zora was pleased. So was the keeper of the bulls. So was the owner of the show. So was everyone. The past was forgotten.

The opening day arrived. Kas and Mo went into parade with their woman trainer, their garlands of roses, and their high-wheeled cart, looking neither to the right nor to the left. At the afternoon performance they moved into their position in the elephant section of the grand entree in a manner both joyous and faithful. Night arrived, the chandeliers gleamed, the signal to prepare for entree sounded from the whistle of the equestrian director, and the punks took their place at the head of the section, awaiting the time when the rest of the entree should emerge

[1] **Singhalese:** a native of Ceylon, the large island south of India.

from the flags, or performers' entrance, that they, with the remainder of the menagerie exhibits, might enter at the other end of the tent, thus filling the hippodrome track simultaneously. At the head of the tandem was Kas, somewhat anxiously awaiting the signal to start. At the left was a low-hung chandelier which caught the beast's body and silhouetted it against the near-by side wall of the menagerie tent. Beyond was a main tent filled with gaping spectators, staring vapidly toward the empty rings and stages and hippodrome track, waiting for the show to begin. And just then Kas saw its shadow on the side wall.

The punk grunted and raised its trunk. Over at the side wall that mysterious thing raised its trunk also. Kas fidgeted. So did the shadow. The big ears of Kas distended in fright. Over there a pair of black ears moved in unison. Everything that Kas did was immediately aped by that thing on the wall. It was too much.

A squeal, a snort, then suddenly the crowded tent saw a tandem team of elephants pitch through the gay dividing curtain and swing into the hippodrome track at full speed, the rose-bedecked cart careening behind them on one wabbling wheel, and behind this the entire elephant herd, following excitedly and without a reason save the fact that Kas and Mo were leading the way. A moment later the cart hit a ring curb, while the bespangled Lucia Zora dived gracefully and far through the air to a dazed position on a pile of canvas, and the runaway elephant parade went on!

Around the hippodrome track they thundered, two squealing baby elephants in the lead, ten excited, bewildered adult beasts in the rear, and the whole shouting, panting menagerie force trailing vainly in their dust. The first curve came and the punks left their cart leaning in drunken, awry fashion where it had collided with a center pole. The second, and they tangled in their flower-decorated harness, but they went on! A third curve, a fourth, then straight through the dividing curtain they plunged again, the rest of the herd after them, and back to their places in the picket line! Meanwhile out there in the main tent an amused crowd stared again at an empty hippodrome track, not knowing whether the whole thing had been an accident or some new form of elephant race!

Naturally it is an impossibility for any man or set of men to maintain an unbroken record of halting panics. Their charges are too big, too possessed with temperament, too prone to become frightened at the most puerile things for a keeper always to outguess them and outmaneuver them. However, the number of panics on the part of the various elephant herds in which damage is caused or the big brutes actually succeed in getting away is so far overshadowed by the attempts at revolt which are broken up in their inception that there is not an opportunity for comparison. Hardly a day passes among the various circuses that at least one elephant does not decide to pit his will against that of the man in charge. But actual panics, with consequent damage, happen extremely seldom. In fact, strange as it may seem, the actual breakaways of any extent in circus history are so few that they number less than a score. When it is considered that there are fully fifty circuses in America which possess elephants, some idea may be gained of the efficacy of those men who manage the herds, who day after day outguess and outgeneral their charges — the keepers of the bulls. But one hears little of these clashes of will. In the life of the keeper of the bulls his failures become public property; his successes are reflected in his pay envelope only, and the crowd often goes home without even the thrill of knowing that an elephantine revolution was nipped in the making.

For instance, few persons in Berkeley, California, remember an elephant stampede in that city. The very persons who saw it probably would be willing to take oath that nothing of the kind ever happened.

Yet there was a stampede, and one that for at least five minutes threatened to be extremely serious.

Berkeley, in the circus dictionary, is a " rah-rah " town, a feared thing to a menagerie department. It means a college, and the traditional enmity that has grown up between tent shows and student bodies through long years of fights and troubles occasioned by the overexuberance of youth and the disturbances that almost invariably follow the attendance at a performance of a large body of students with their class yells, their chain steps, and snake dances. Circuses are composed of high-strung persons who risk their lives as a part of their daily work, and of equally high-strung horses and other animals. Disturbances during the performances are not to their liking.

But on this particular morning in Berkeley things apparently were going exceedingly well.

The parade had started on time from a lot, and now was traversing the longest and most crowded street of the whole route. The bands were blaring happily. The bull section, numbering some twelve animals, was shuffling along the asphalt in peace and contentment.

Suddenly from around a corner there swung into line with the parade a lockstep crew of some three hundred students, their feet stamping the pavement in unison, their lips chanting a monotonous college song, joining the procession directly behind the bull section. The elephant keepers spurred up their horses and attempted to stop the demonstration. The college men simply grinned at them and tramped steadily on. Time after time the bull men gave warning of what the result of the monotonous chant and still more monotonous tramp-tramp-tramp of hundreds of stamping feet might be. The parade marshal looked around wildly for police. They were somewhere else. He strove to block the marching line with his horse. They circled him and went on, still beside the shuffling bull line.

Now ears were distending. Piglike eyes were rolling in their too small sockets. Heavy skins were beginning to wrinkle.

At last there came a call from Shorty, the head keeper, and the elephant men gave up their task. " Don't try to break up that line. If they won't stop, let 'em go. These bulls'll break at the first roughhouse. Stand by to tail 'em down! "

Into position shot the assistants, each ready to dig his spurs into his horse at the first sign of a break. Far ahead went Shorty, taking his position just behind the gigantic trembling Mary, bearing the Ten Thousand Dollar Queen of the Harem at the head of the section, a harem beauty who, incidentally, just at that moment wished she was back in Coshocton[1]; in fact, anywhere except in that bobbing *howdah*.[2] Leader Mary was beginning to shimmy slightly with increased fright, and her shuffle on the hot asphalt carried a new wiggle of impending danger. Then the marching three hundred broke into a weird class yell, and the stampede began.

Straight forward went Leader Mary, to scrape a lion's cage, to swerve slightly to one side, then, with the Ten Thousand Dollar Queen of the Harem squawking aimlessly in the howdah, to lead off in a wild scramble straight down the street, with the rest of the herd smashing along in her rear. Then it was that the prepara-

[1] **Coshocton:** a town in Ohio. [2] **howdah:** a canopied seat on the elephant's back.

tions of Shorty, the keeper of the bulls, went into execution.

At the first move of the elephant section the horses of keepers moved also — in a furious pace, for the speed of an elephant is a deceptive thing, and it is a good horse that can keep abreast of him once he unlimbers into full steam ahead. The stamping college men were left behind now; even the front section of the parade with its suddenly hushed band and blank-faced clowns was passed almost in an instant. Out of them all only the Ten Thousand Dollar Queen of the Harem was left, still bouncing in her howdah, still squealing and squawking, while, spurs deep in their horses, the elephant men strove their best to keep abreast of the fast-traveling bull section, echoing and re-echoing the shout of Shorty at the head of the line:

"Hi there! Mule up! Mule up there, Mary! Freida — Frenchy — Sultan — tails! Tails there — tails!"

It was a double command, which traveled along the line and back again as fast as men could voice it, the order to run, and at the same time for each elephant to grasp the tail of the beast before him. Blocks passed while throats grew hoarse, and while the thick-packed throngs of the curbings stared vacuously, wondering why the circus should be in such a hurry to get its elephants out of the line of march.

But never a warning sounded, never a hint that a panic was in progress; only that repeated and re-repeated command:

"Tails there! Mule up, you! Tails — tails!" All of it meant an experiment in elephant psychology, and one that had been tried many times before. At last the command sank in. The second elephant of the line grasped the tail of Leader Mary and continued to run. The third elephant obeyed; the fourth, the fifth, and on through the whole section.

But the command continued:

"Mule up there — mule up! Tails!"

Another two blocks and the command changed; more, the elephant line obeyed. A block after that, and the whole section was peacefully shuffling along again, simply through the fact that the frightened beasts had been made to believe that their trainer really desired them to run and that in their breakaway they were merely carrying out orders. Nor could they know that in obeying the command of tails they handicapped themselves so that the speed of one could be no greater than that of another, and that as long as the leader kept to a straight line so must the rest.

Further, the occupation of their single-track minds in the execution of an order which coincided with their natural tendencies had wiped out in forgetfulness the fact that something had threatened them, and brought to them the belief that their trainer merely was running them away from an obnoxious thing. Therefore, when the command came to slow down they did so in confidence, and in the assurance that any danger was over. Many a person went that day from watching the parade, wondering perhaps why the elephant trainer should desire to put his beasts through their paces. But few of them realized that the little play of speed had saved not only the circus but the downtown section of Berkeley, with its thronged sidewalks, from disaster.

With it all, the life of a bull keeper is a thing of constant gambling. He has none of the assurances with which the performers of other beasts are blessed; the lion or tiger trainer has his cages and the knowledge that, even should a vicious cat escape, a bullet or two from a heavy-calibered revolver at close range can finish him. It takes a steel-jacket army bullet to make an elephant even realize he's being shot!

More, the beasts are too big to be caged. They are too strong for anything except a perfect network of drop-forged chains. Even then, nothing short of a pile driver can set wood deep enough into the ground to hold them when they really desire to run. It's wholly a matter of a good leader of the herd, good princesses working under her, the hope that there are few agitators or revolutionists in the rest of the monarchy, and a strong trust in fate and the breaks of circumstance. For even the elephant keeper never knows what may start his difficulties. An invasion of fleas in the sandy districts of the West can do it; an elephant's hide can turn a leaden revolver bullet, but it can't stand fleas! There's trouble even in mosquitoes.

For the flea and the mosquito evidently have more judgment regarding the points of vulnerability in an elephant's hide than does a bullet. They select the soft spots behind the ears, the eyelids and tender mouth and flanks for their work, and once they arrive in numbers trouble begins. It is not at all unusual to see elephants being dosed with flea preventives. The mosquito pest is far more rare, but at least one runaway is chargeable to this cause.

Incidentally, the instance gave another credit mark to the career of Old Mom, and another example of at least one elephant with common sense. The show was making a Sunday run in Canada, by which it bridged a long expanse of territory between money-making stands, heading far into the north of the Dominion, where few shows had exhibited and where the natives would be glad to part with a double admission price for the pleasure of seeing a bigger circus than usual. The run had been preceded by several days of moist, mosquito-breeding weather, with the result that when the show train made a feed stop at a small prairie settlement, and the elephants were unloaded for a trip of half a mile to the nearest water, the insects swarmed in such millions that they almost obliterated the lettering of the railroad cars. About the railroad tracks several hundred smudges were lighted, thus freeing that exact territory from the pests, but the elephants weren't fortunate. They were forced to travel out into the country for water, and the mosquitoes went with them.

By the time the watering process was finished every elephant was crusted with stinging, poisonous insects and squealing with discomfort. They pulled from their keepers; in vain Old Mom, obeying the commands of Alispaw, strove to hold them in line. She bellowed; she butted; she lashed with her trunk — but to no purpose. A moment more and an inveterate agitator made the break, followed by two others, and instantly the rest of the herd rushed after them. More, Old Mom broke from the bull-hooked grasp of her keeper, and with Frieda, her handmaiden, beside her, swung madly into flight also!

It seemed that at last the ability of Old Mom to command a situation was lost. Faster and faster she went, passing the slower members of the herd and at last forcing her way to the very front of the stampede, Frieda puffing along in her wake. For a full eighth of a mile she led the rush straight out into the prairie; then the pursuers, far in the rear, noticed that she was beginning to turn in her course. Soon she had made a semicircle and was leading the plunging herd straight back in the direction of the cars.

Thundering on they went, the workmen and clustered performers parting spasmodically as they approached the runs, Old Mom still in the lead, and heading, it seemed, on a straight path for the sleeping cars and the crash which seemed inevitable. Once an elephant loses its head it takes no cognizance of what may be before it; its mentality knows a beeline only, no matter if the obstruction be a stone quarry.

Nearer, nearer! Then it suddenly became evident that Old Mom evidently was in full possession of her faculties — and a bright idea. At the tracks she swerved; and while horses and workmen scurried for safety, she led the way straight to the elephant cars and climbed in!

The runs, or running board by which the beasts usually made their entrance and exit, had been removed in preparation for the switching of the cars. So the climbing operation was a literal one. With the rest of the bulls behind her, Old Mom, grunting and squealing, made the ascent, and Frieda followed.

Then in the semidarkness of the smudge-filled car she trumpeted happily, and the rest of the herd crowded in after her. A stampede of nearly a mile was over without a cent of damage.

In fact, Old Mom, with her faith and her levelheadedness, has meant salvation in many an instance. I once saw this sensible old elephant lead her herd across the cable bridge which connects Wheeling, West Virginia, with the Ohio side, with a storm in progress, the surroundings inky black, the rain pelting, the keepers almost as terrified as the brutes, with the beams of the bridge cracking from overweight, and the structure itself swinging fully eight feet from side to side! Below was a sheer drop to the Ohio River; two elephants had become panic-stricken and had broken from the bull man in attendance, rushing frantically forward to the protection of their leader. The rest of the herd had begun to mill, with only a thirty-foot width of bridge as their arena; bull men were befuddled and nearly blinded by the pelting rain. Yet Old Mom held true to the commands of her trainer and, with weird trumpetings which sounded sharp above even the rush of wind and crackling of thunder, someway, somehow, reassured her herd. Then with the ever-present Frieda at her side, she began to lead the way, slow step after slow step to the opposite side.

That very slowness was the salvation of the herd; instinctively they knew that she was testing the bridge, and by some sort of animal understanding, did likewise. The rocking lessened. A half-hour later Old Mom brought her charges safe out at the other side, every elephant walking in comical, gingerly fashion for a full block after leaving the structure, for all the world like overgrown fat boys trying to negotiate an area of eggshells.

Yet even Mom has her failings, her likes and dislikes; and once, at least, her discipline has ended in tragedy. Woeful is the life of the subject elephant that defies Old Mom, ancient though she may be. Well past the hundred-year mark in age, dependable when every other bull of the picket line is frantic, there is one failing; Old Mom is a disciplinarian to the point of being a martinet. More than that, she is as foolish in her likes as a person in second childhood, and her favorite is the worst troublemaker of the whole herd!

Long ago they named him Billy, a quarrelsome, snobby little runt of an elephant that spends half his time in winter quarters striving to slap the daylights out of the hoglike old hippopotamus that wallows in his permanent tank near the picket line, and the remainder of his existence in stealing feed from the rest of the elephants. Nor does one of that bull line dare to protest! Immediately there comes a squeal from Billy, and from farther down the line a bellow of anger from Old Mom, where, eyes glaring, trunk twisting, ears wide, she wheels forward toward her picket pin and prepares to free herself that she may punish the offender. For punishment is swift and sure to those who offend her by offending her pet. Billy, to Old Mom, is a little angel. He can do no wrong. To the rest of the herd he is an obnoxious, selfish, obtrusive little devil that can do no right. They hate him. But they submit, rather than feel the thump of Old Mom's trunk, or the pile-driver impact of her hard skull. Winter quarters or the road, it is all the same. Old Mom has taught her little angel her secrets of escape, with the result that he wanders the elephant line at will, in spite of stakes, bonds, or even keepers. Old Mom's protection of Billy extends to humans, and the runt does as he pleases.

For eight years had this continued when the tragedy came. For eight years, Floto, the stodgiest, most amiable male member of the herd, had submitted to every indignity one elephant can heap upon another. Billy had stolen his feed. Billy had edged forward when visitors arrived with peanuts, and literally taken them out of Floto's trunk. Floto had protested and been punished, and so Floto had endured. But during those eight years the hatred was being stored against a day of judgment. And near the end of the season, at Orange, Texas, it came.

The press services which carried the story of that day's event announced that someone had given Floto a chew of tobacco and that he had gone mad because of it. But that was only tradition and a guess. Floto was one of the best tobacco eaters of the picket line. And Floto had something more on his mind than a bad taste. The story of his death is one of rebellion and revenge.

Old Mom was out on the lot, busily pushing the wagons into position for the loading of the night. The matinee was over. The menagerie tent was drowsing in that calm which intervenes between the afternoon show and the gleaming chandeliers of night. Floto was at his picket pin, glorying in his portion of hay. Then came Billy.

He rooted in as usual and began to gobble Floto's feed share, even as he had done for eight years. But this time Old Mom was not there to protect him. Floto snorted and warned the runt out of his way. But the fat little Billy only grunted and reached for another trunkful. It was the final insult.

A weird trumpet blast, and the three-ton Floto rose high on his haunches. Then with a sudden thumping drop he came to all fours again and, seizing his piggish enemy in his trunk, raised him squealing over his head, only to throw him, breathless, to the ground, and then, breaking his stay chains, to leap upon his pudgy enemy before the smaller elephant could regain his feet. A moment of mauling followed, in which thundering hoofs knocked resistance from the fallen beast, and then, using his head for a combination roller and battering ram, the angered elephant scraped the body of the beleaguered animal along the hard sandy ground until the heavy flesh was torn from the runt's body in great patches and the blood flowed from fully a dozen wounds.

Animal men with bull hooks strove futilely to pull him away. He shook them off and began to pound the prostrate Billy with flail-like blows of his trunk, suddenly to halt and wheel, trembling, yet defiant. Old Mom, with Charles Churchill, her keeper, at her head, was swinging under the side wall to restore order. But the time for that was past.

Floto was in the position of a cornered criminal. He had disobeyed every law of the mistress of the herd, and now he defied her. He did not even wait for Old Mom to approach him. Head lowered, trunk tightly curled, he swung forward to the attack, butted her out of the way, and plunged through the side wall out into the sparsely peopled circus lot — an outlaw at last.

Wagons tumbled out of his way as he crashed into them. Ticket boxes turned to matchwood when he caught them and crushed them with swift stamping blows of his heavy forefeet. Ropes parted like strings before his plowing progress. A workman crossed his path; the elephant caught him in his trunk and threw him thirty feet into an irrigation ditch. Back to the menagerie he went, to butt every elephant that faced him, to overturn cages, to seize frightened, screaming ponies and break their backs. Then they called for the rifles.

Only thirty-thirties were in the ticket wagon, equipped with leaden bullets. But the animal men felt that enough shots from them might suffice; at least they might be able to hold the maddened beast at bay until a rushing automobile, already sent townward, could return with army rifles. Hurriedly the guns were distributed and the magazines filled. Then as fast as hands could work the levers thirty shots were fired at the head of the outlaw, every one striking its mark.

But the bullets did little more than pierce the heavy flesh; some of them dropped to the ground without even breaking the thick armor of hide that covered the elephant's skull.

He stood and took the shots, one after another, hardly seeming to notice their impact. Then suddenly, as though bewildered, as though seeking a reason for it all, he whirled for a moment in aimless circles, then headed straight for the empty big top. The bullets had not entered the animal's thick skull, but something akin to a thought had. The stinging of the speeding lead in some way seemed to convey an idea to the brute that the humans who had commanded him were now striving to force him to do a certain thing, and in a hazy moment of obedience he hurried to its execution as swiftly as possible — the only thing he knew!

Into the center ring he rushed, to halt, a single elephant in the middle of a deserted circus tent. There, alone, *sans* the music, *sans* the crowds, *sans* the brilliance and the brightness which usually accompanied the performance, Floto the outlaw, the blood streaming from thirty bullet holes, without guidance, without even a cue, went through every figure of his act, while at the connections the men of the circus stood and watched, unable to cope with him, unable to kill him, unable to conquer him; watched while he waltzed about the ring, while he knelt over an imaginary trainer, while he walked on his hind hoofs; and while, with a sudden change of thought, he crashed across the stages, tore down a section of seats, and then, bursting through the side wall, ran for the open country.

All that night they trailed him, a trail of broken fences, of smashed chicken yards, of wide swaths through growing crops! The next morning they found Floto a bare half mile from town, where he evidently was circling back to the circus. But he still was the outlaw, still the renegade. He sighted the armed men and trumpeted. Then with a swift movement he turned toward a telegraph pole and wrapped his trunk about it. There was a sharp crackle. Wires spit and sang as they popped. Floto had snapped the pole clean at its base and, swinging it even as an angered man would swing a club, had headed straight toward his hunters! There they killed him, with three swift volleys of steel-jacketed bullets, even as he charged them — Floto who had feared discipline enough to become a renegade!

THINK BACK OVER WHAT YOU HAVE READ

Making the Acquaintance of Elephants

1. What common misconceptions about elephants are you prepared to have corrected? What have been your own notions about elephant nature? Does the author contradict any of them?

2. With what concrete illustrations can you demonstrate the circus parody "Inconsistency, thy name is elephant" (page 267)?

3. What tactics are used to halt a panic in an elephant herd? How did Alispaw quiet the elephants the night of the thunderstorm? How did Shorty, in Berkeley, control the stampede the day the college boys decided to parade behind the elephants?

4. How do the elephant leaders control their herds? How, for example, did Old Mom quiet her frightened herd the night of the storm? How did she save the circus lot from destruction the night in Canada when her herd was attacked by mosquitoes?

5. What unrehearsed circus acts were really panics, unrecognized by all but the elephants' keepers?

6. What dangers occur when elephant trainers are changed? What does the tragedy of Snyder illustrate about elephant nature?

7. What is your idea of a renegade among elephants? What did Floto do to deserve the name?

Following Some of the Implications of the Essay

8. What is a "monarchial system" among elephants? On what elephant traits is it based? Under what circumstances does it work successfully? Under what circumstances is it likely to break down?

9. What is a monarchial system in human society? On what human traits is it based? Under what circumstances does it work successfully?

10. From such an analysis can you see why a democratic system of government would not work among elephants? On what assumptions about human behavior, then, does a democratic system of government rest?

11. What did you find to admire about the way elephants relied on their leaders? Can you derive any human lesson from their behavior? What dangers do you see in a blind trust in human leadership?

12. What parallel do you see between a renegade among elephants and a human outlaw?

13. Did you notice that the leaders among circus elephant herds were "queens" — not kings? Perhaps you can find the name for this particular kind of monarchial system. Ancient Egypt had such a system.

14. Suppose that the elephant herd — a much larger one — were to be reorganized into a feudal system. How would that change Old Mom's position in the herd? Would Frieda become more or less important? Under such a system, how would Alispaw have operated the night of the storm?

Increase Your Power over Words

15. In the word *immobile* the prefix *im* means not and *mobile* means movable. The word *automobile* springs from the same Latin root: *auto,* by itself, and *mobile,* movable; that is, movable under its own power or by itself. What, then, does *mobilize* mean?

16. *Animate* comes from another Latin word, *animare,* which means to fill with breath; hence, to live. *Animate,* therefore, means living. *Inanimate* means not living or lifeless. You will note that the same Latin root is found in the words *animal, animation.*

17. Look up in a dictionary the meaning of *drop-forged.* Then explain the term *drop-forged chains* (page 275).

For Ambitious Students

18. If you are interested in the life of the circus, you will find *Lions 'n' Tigers 'n' Everything,* the book from which "Keeper of the Bulls" is taken, well worth reading in its entirety. Other books by the same author are *Under the Big Top* and *Boss Elephant. Barnum,* by M. R. Werner, deals with the career of one of the greatest of American showmen, the famous P. T. Barnum.

OUR BACK-YARD CIRCUS

by Martin Johnson (1884–1937)

Now that your interest has been aroused in the elephant as a personality of the circus, you will find it interesting to follow him back to the native wilds from which he was captured, as you may do in the essay that follows. Here you will find in the wild elephant the same common sense, the same reckless courage during anger, that you found in the tame elephant.

Until his death a few years ago, Martin Johnson, with his wife Osa, was a photographer of wild life in the wilds of Africa. In such films as *Safari, Lion,* and *Congorilla,* which are also the titles of his books, he brought the jungle back with him to America and showed it to a fascinated public. The essay that follows is from *Safari.*

ONE DAY at Paradise[1] my Meru carpenter came running to the door of my laboratory very much excited and shouting in Swahili, " Elephants! Elephants! "

This wasn't exactly news, for the woods about us were full of the big animals. But I grabbed my big Akeley camera[2] and tripod and followed the man to the back of the shack, hoping as usual to get something out of the ordinary. There in the open scrub about two hundred yards away were fifteen elephants, several bulls, four or five cows, three half-grown animals, and two babies. They were all just feeding along as comfortably as could be.

Of course, I started to grind out film. When I had turned down about two hundred feet, what was my surprise to see Osa[3] duck up between me and the elephants and shout, " What are you doing? Have you gone crazy? " There she was, weeding her strawberries in the garden not a hundred yards from the herd of wild elephants and blissfully ignorant of its presence. Our calling back and forth and the movements of the boys about the camp finally caused the beasts to move on down toward the lake, but not before I had another good view filmed of elephant life.

Years ago in Kansas as a small boy, long before I ever dreamed I'd go to Africa to live, I watched the big grayish-black beasts waddle by on circus day with their curious, shuffling walk. They looked so slow and stupid, so indifferent to what went on about them, so grotesquely out of place amid the trumpery of civilization, that even as a small boy I wondered vaguely what they might be like in their own native haunts.

As I grew older I picked up the traditional beliefs about the elephant. I learned to think of him as a mixture of viciousness and sagacity when he was aroused, and as a profoundly dumb brute when left to his own devices. I knew he was trained at hauling teak in India and at doing meaningless tricks in America.

I heard many tales of the elephant's power of memory and desire for revenge. " Don't feed the elephant " was a sign we all knew was based on the fact that the beast might become violent if given red pepper instead of peanuts. An elephant killed a man in Brooklyn who burned his trunk with his lighted cigar. " Alice," one of the New York Zoo collection, vented her anger by rushing into the Reptile House and throwing to the concrete floor glass showcases filled with poisonous snakes. And so on.

To the lay eye[4] the African elephant seems the same animal as the Indian elephant, which is the species always seen in circuses. The reason for this choice is that the Hindu for centuries has domesticated elephants for purposes of labor and transportation. An African native shrinks from such intimacy with the huge quadrupeds. Hence the African elephant has long had cause to fear man, if only through constant threat of the ivory hunters.

We don't shoot elephants or anything else at Lake Paradise. Our chief work consists solely of filming wild game in its natural habitat. As a result, there has grown up among the elephant herds in our vicinity none of the terror and vindictiveness so often reported from India, where herds attack native villages en masse[5] and do terrible damage.

Two incidents, while somewhat extreme, illustrate what I mean. About twenty years ago a train on the railway

[1] **Paradise:** Lake Paradise, in British East Africa. The Johnsons made their home on the shores of this lake. [2] **Akeley camera:** a camera specially adapted to the photography of wild life, invented by Carl Akeley, the great naturalist who assembled the animals for Africa Hall of the American Museum of Natural History in New York. [3] **Osa:** Mrs. Johnson.

[4] **lay eye:** that is, to the eye of one not familiar with elephants. [5] **en masse:** originally a French phrase meaning all together.

in Burma[1] was attacked by an elephant. The engineer whistled as he took a grade. A big bull elephant feeding near by interpreted the blast as a challenge. He loudly trumpeted his acceptance of the invitation to do battle. He lowered his head and made for the oncoming train. Once on the tracks he met it almost exactly head-on. The engineer had no time to stop. Probably he was so dumfounded by the sight of the huge beast galloping toward him that he was powerless to act. Engine and elephant collided with a terrific crash. The latter's massive head was caved in and he was instantly killed. But the momentum of his enormous carcass weighing several tons did its work. The engine was derailed and its front end crushed to a shapeless mass.

Contrast the atmosphere around Lake Paradise where Osa rushed in one morning from her garden with flushed face and flashing eyes, exclaiming:

" Oh, I think it's mean of them! "

" Who? " I snapped, wondering angrily if the natives had been misbehaving.

" Those elephants. They've been at my vegetable garden again! "

Wild elephants, too — wild and free as the mammoth and mastodon were in their day, and nearly as big.

I think our guide Boculy knows more about elephants than any man living. He could study a single elephant track and usually in a few minutes tell me just how many there were in the herd, where they had gone, what they were doing, and what we should do to find and photograph them.

He was an absolutely tireless fellow. Indeed, he never could understand any of the rest of us getting tired. Time and again he walked us for three or four hours up and down hills and across rough, sun-scorched stones, until we would call a halt in sheer exhaustion.

[1] **Burma**: a country in Asia, east of India.

He was never at a loss for a reply if I tried to hurry him. When we halted in case we had not already found game, I would usually say, " Now let's go where the game has gone, Boculy."

To which he would invariably reply, " But, Master, they are not there."

He had a lot of queer maxims. If he failed for a considerable time to find elephants, he would say one of three things was the cause:

" Shauri ako " . . . Business caused by you (the white man).

" Shauri Muunga " . . . Business caused by God.

" Shauri mvua." . . . Business caused by rain.

When he made up his mind that we were not finding game for one of these reasons, he usually insisted on giving up the hunt for the day and would not look any further.

Early in our stay I explained to Boculy how I planned to do a lot of photographic work of animals from the protection of blinds. This, I told him, would give me a chance to observe them in an undisturbed state. But he only grinned and said something about my not knowing what I was saying. Sure enough he proved to be correct. For the finest films of elephants which I took were made right out in the open.

I had many a lesson in trailing elephants from Boculy without his knowing it. One day he walked along looking at some tracks which were at least twenty-four hours old. He was talking to himself most of the time. Now and then he would stop and look at the track and point in the direction he evidently thought the animal might have gone. He would then pick a twig or leaf up and name the hour it had been chewed on. Presently he was tracking over short grass where there wasn't a single sign visible to my untrained eye, not a smear of mud or dirt left by the animal's foot. Finally he would take scent like a bloodhound, go off like an arrow, and in a few minutes turn around with a grin — pointing to the elephant he had been following. It was uncanny.

Sometimes he had arguments with himself when he didn't come on the elephants as soon as he thought he ought to. He'd stop and look at the ground and say, "Yes, yes." Then shake his head and slowly say, "No, no." At last he would suddenly exclaim, "*Yes!*" with conviction and we would be off to find another herd of elephants before an hour passed.

When the time came for us seriously to take the trail, we didn't have to go far for a great deal of our best film. I simply talked things over with Boculy, decided on how and where we should operate, and organized my *safari*,[1] or field expedition, to suit.

There was one particular herd I had been wanting to get at for months. It wasn't large, but there were some young ones in it which I wanted to photograph. We finally set off after it fully equipped with plenty of porters for our gear and with food for about two weeks' travel.

We camped near the edge of the jungle after a march of nearly twenty miles. About five the next morning Boculy woke us. He whispered something about elephants in my ear. I hurried out of the tent and saw ten elephants walking quietly along about four hundred yards away. Two were so young that they looked like Christmas toys. They were toddling, bumping up against their mothers and stopping and turning around just like children on a street. Each mother would turn around every now and then and slap her offspring with her trunk. This would make the little fellow squeal and he would trot along obediently again.

[1] **safari:** native word for an expedition into the field.

Two more were about six months old. They were very solemn, even more so than the grown-up ones. But every now and then they would get bored with the march they were on and start to wander off. A severe grunt from one of the older ones would bring them back into line.

We hustled around and got our cameras ready. It was still too dark to photograph but I thought we could follow without the animals seeing us, especially as the wind was from them to us.

Just before the sun came up, the whole line walked along the top of a small hill. They came to a halt. Silhouetted against the sky, they made a wonderful picture — a picture of which I have often dreamed. I had seen films of camels silhouetted against the sky. At last I could make one of elephants. I lost no time in doing so.

We left camp after breakfast. About an hour later we were stopped suddenly by Boculy, who stepped softly back with his hand raised for silence. Ahead of us were seven elephants, just beside the trail. I ran back a few steps and motioned for the camera boys to hurry. We set up the cameras as quickly as we could; but the elephants walked into the brush, feeding as they went.

I had just about decided that they were going to have a sleep under cover when I heard a noise on the other side of the trail. More elephants had come up. I crept ahead and saw three. They, too, were settling down for a sleep in the dark forest, where it would be impossible to make pictures. Boculy was annoyed with me. He could never understand that I needed plenty of light for pictures. He thought my magic box ought to be able to see in the dark as well as in the light, certainly if it were magic enough to reproduce moving creatures months later.

We didn't dare disturb the elephants. Had they stampeded us, we never could have escaped them. There were no trees to climb and their anger at being waked up would have been uncontrollable. I had the cameras gathered up and hurried my party along the trail, hoping that we should meet some elephants which were not yet bound for bed. The heat probably was making them all sleepy. Hardly had we started when we ran into three more right ahead of us.

"You stay here," whispered Boculy, who wanted to reconnoiter.

I agreed but wanted him to take a gun-bearer with him. He shook his head. It was pretty brave of him. He never would have stopped a stampede. He would have been crushed to a pulp in two minutes if the animals had started his way.

Hardly had he gone ten feet when I saw him jump into the air with a smothered exclamation. I ran ahead a few steps. Right there beside him was the largest cobra[1] I had ever seen. It was at least ten feet long and as big around as my arm; it was lying flat, not coiled, as one would expect. Its head was about two feet from the ground and its neck was spread out larger than my hand in anger.

Boculy retreated, trembling all over. He could hardly speak, he was so terrified. He was not scared of elephants, but snakes always frightened him. Hoping to chase the reptile off the trail, he carefully selected a stick from some dead brush beside the trail and threw it at the creature. The snake struck viciously at the piece just as it fell. We could have shot it but did not want to disturb the elephants.

While this snake interlude was going on, we made so much noise that we waked up the herd. The first thing we knew twenty or thirty of the big animals were screaming and snorting around us, crashing over trees, banging into one another, and creating a general pandemonium. Luckily for us they decided to run away. Two minutes later they had disappeared. Once more the jungle silence had descended. Even the cobra vanished.

This is one of the thrills of our work. It is never possible to tell whether the death with which we are surrounded in many forms is going to descend upon us or going to evaporate. Whichever happens, it usually happens quickly and without much warning.

As time went on we had a chance to study individual elephants and their behavior. One of the most entertaining sights was always a female elephant with her baby. An elephant is weirdly proportioned in every direction, from its curling trunk to its silly little tail. When its features are reduced to miniature, as in the young animal, few more comical sights can be seen. True, there are young elephants in the zoo. But there the mothers need show little of the assiduous care we so often see in Africa.

I remember coming on a number of elephants one broiling hot summer day on the plains. One mother was accompanied by a baby that could have been but a few days old. The little one was suffering pitifully from the heat. It whined and wobbled and persistently refused to keep pace with the older animals. Finally the mother lost all patience with it. She knew just what to do. Pausing at a near-by water hole she proceeded to give her toto[2] regular jungle-heat treatment. First she butted the little fellow off his balance and held him down with her big forefoot while he lay squawking. Then she sucked up a trunkful of mud and squirted it all over the suffering infant's body. Despite his protests she repeated this performance again and again until her baby must have been greatly recovered.

Surely elephant parents are the most

[1] **cobra:** a large poisonous snake which, when angry, dilates its neck to resemble a hood.

[2] **toto:** baby elephant.

tolerant in the world. I have seen them submit to all kinds of inconvenience on the trail from skylarking youngsters. But when the adult's patience becomes exhausted, chastisement with trunk or butting head is always sure to follow.

A young elephant holds to its mother's tail with its trunk when passing through long grass just as a child holds its mother's hand. When she pauses in the shade of a tree, it goes to nursing just like any calf.

One day about noon, almost on the edge of the desert, we came upon three full-grown females, one half-grown male, and one little toto, the smallest elephant I have ever seen; it could not have been more than a week old. Osa nearly cried out, she wanted it so badly; but she controlled herself, though I could see that she was trembling with eagerness and delight in the way she has when anything strikes her as particularly beautiful or cunning.

They had not caught either sight or scent of us and I placed my cameras, grinding away, as they went through their maneuvers. First the four older ones would walk ahead; then pause to wait for the little toto, which would come running up like a clumsy little pup, back off, then charge under its mother for its dinner. Then it would lie down lazily and the others would considerately wait until it had had its nap out or they thought it had had enough. Then the three would start off, the mother nudging it gently until the little one would at last get up and join the others. All then journeyed slowly on until they reached a mud puddle. Here they lay down, rolled, and threw mud over each other, the baby having as good a time as any of them.

While they were playing, I had left my first station and crept up to a bush behind them. But the quick-witted mother, catching the move, turned to the baby, which had trotted off toward me, threw her trunk around it, and held it tight for a few seconds, at last giving it a little slap with her trunk, as much as to say, "Here, cut that out. Don't you go running away or you'll get into trouble!" This done, off they started again in little stages, always waiting for the baby, who was forever playing, to come up; and so they disappeared in the forest.

From time to time we had adventures with single elephants. In a way these were more interesting because they gave us a different angle on elephant character. With a big herd around, one had to keep so much on the outlook that detailed observation was difficult.

One morning we fell in with a big bull wandering about by himself. We sighted him some distance away feeding among some young trees. Through the glasses we could see him bending the thin trunks down and nibbling the tender leaves.

Skirting the spot widely, we put the wind right so it would blow from him to us and not reveal our presence. An elephant supposedly has poor eyesight, although I have a suspicion this theory may be due to his natural indifference to other living beings, acquired through centuries of practical immunity from attack. At any rate, it is sometimes possible to get right up to him if one watches the wind. The trouble is that on a hot, calm day little breezes whirl about so capriciously one is betrayed no matter how much trouble is taken. We hustled the camera boys and gunbearers along until we were within about fifty yards of the big fellow. Our *safari* column was well away and there seemed to be no other game present except the elephant. This was providential, because it meant that he would likely go on about his business long enough for us to make a good film and plenty of stills.

Luck played into our hands. Gradually

our jumbo[1] wandered closer and closer. Osa was bursting with excitement. The natives could scarcely restrain their exclamations of delight as well as of apprehension. The high point came when he was little more than twenty feet away, literally towering above us. He chose a tree that was too strong for him to break with his trunk, so he put his brains to work as well as his muscles. Pulling the sapling down as far as it would go with his trunk, he held it with his tusks while he reached up and got a new hold. He repeated this twice. Finally the tree snapped and he wrestled the whole upper part down to the ground. Slowly he went to work among the leafy branches, selecting the tender young shoots and buds. It was superb!

When he had eaten all he wanted, he walked around the tree and came directly toward us. As there was no use taking any more movies, I had Osa pick up her rifle while I used the still camera. About the third snap, the elephant suddenly saw us. He stopped so abruptly that his huge bulk swayed in our direction.

Now he did things an elephant does when he is startled. His great fan ears went out as if to catch the slightest whisper of sound. His long trunk projected forward, waving sinuously in the air like a black snake while he sniffed away for some telltale odor that would reveal the identity of the strange intruders on his meal.

We did not move. Osa stood braced and ready to shoot if the fellow charged. The boys bravely held their ground. I " shot " another still or two in order to record the fine picture of elephantine curiosity before me.

Now we witnessed a characteristic of the dignity of these animals. A rhino would at once have charged angrily or have galloped off in cowardly fashion. One of the cat family, a lion or a leopard, would have lashed itself into a fury. A giraffe or zebra would have changed its mind half a dozen times, advancing and retreating until it dashed off in a panic of fright. Not so the elephant.

After a long smell and the best look its little beady eyes could take, the elephant backed a pace or two, then slowly turned and walked deliberately away. He was not angry; neither was he afraid. He had probably never been shot at in his life. Had he decided we were enemies, he would have charged; we knew this by sad experience. We were very thankful that he didn't, as we were right out in the open with no cover or refuge.

Not long after this we fell in with another elephant that took our presence in a much more animated fashion. He was feeding like the first one. But the background was different, and he behaved as if he were really wide awake. So I determined to film him. I managed to get the cameras set up in a wide, open space before he saw us. As Osa was tired out after a hard morning, she stayed back on the top of a high rock from which she could watch the surrounding country. In a few minutes the elephant started coming in our direction. At a distance of about thirty yards he backed off to the tree from which he had been eating. But he was too nervous to continue his meal.

Once more he came to investigate us, walking in comical little goose steps as though ready to charge or to run at the slightest provocation. About fifty feet away he began circling to get our wind. His short black tail waved stiffly in the air and his trunk was out. Finally he got a sniff of us. He didn't like it. He began to lash his tail and stamp the ground. His trunk swung angrily to and fro. But he couldn't for the life of him make up his mind to charge. When about forty feet from us he ran back a few yards, then

[1] **jumbo**: a very large elephant.

whirled and came at us again. He had his head held high in the peculiar way elephants have when they are angry. He did this four times.

All the while I was getting priceless films. Finally the old warrior lost his nerve. I think it was the fact that we did not retreat which undermined his courage as much as anything. He just turned around all of a sudden and ran as fast as he could for the nearest cover.

Not all our encounters ended so tamely. One day, very early in our African experiences, Boculy came running into camp. I could tell he was excited because of the way his hands moved around. He kept lifting them and letting them fall and then gripping his fingers. He was saying things in short jerks.

" Big elephants ! " he exclaimed. " All together. Very quiet."

By that we knew the elephants were feeding and not looking for trouble.

I called to Osa to get her rifle. In five minutes our gunbearers were under way with pieces slung on their shoulders. The camera boys were swinging up their heavy loads.

In fifteen minutes we were up to the herd. The animals were out in the open. If we had posed them, they couldn't have been better placed for a picture. There were three big cows and two bulls. Two younger ones wandered around, bumping up against the legs of their elders and grunting funny little high-pitched grunts. One of the bulls was a fine tusker. His gleaming ivory showed milk-white in the sun.

This time Osa took the crank, while I went forward as " movie director " to start action among the animals. I was afraid for her to go forward. There was no cover in case the beasts charged.

She cranked away for all she was worth, while I walked gingerly toward the herd. The first thing I knew, the big bull saw me. He raised his trunk and spread out his ears, shifting his feet about angrily. He snorted. Then with a furious grunt he charged.

I ran. Sometimes we got our picture under such circumstances and then stopped the elephants by yelling and waving our hands. This time I was too close and the elephant gaining too fast. I swung about and tried to dodge. It was the only thing I could do to save my life. But my strategy was futile. The bull came right on for me. Like sheep, the other seven elephants tore after him. To my surprise there were about a dozen more behind these seven which we hadn't seen. Elephants seemed everywhere and they were all headed for us.

Osa was scared stiff but she kept turning the crank. She knew she was getting a superb picture and there was nothing she could do about me yet.

By the time I reached the camera, the elephants were only a few feet behind. Osa's gunbearer had been at her elbow every instant. Now with one quick motion she took her rifle from him and fired. It was an easy shot so far as a target went. Her target was as big as a barn. But it took a lot of nerve to stand there and shoot under the circumstances — shoot and hit a fatal spot.

Her shot didn't kill the elephant at once but it diverted him from his murderous course. He nearly knocked the camera down when he passed it. He fell a little further on. The herd hesitated for a moment. Then all turned and ran.

Osa had her own private experiences with the cameras and elephants. Without telling me, one day, she took what she thought was my best Graflex and walked over to the Old Lady Water Hole, two miles from our camp. The camera was carried in a black leather case swung over the shoulder of her black boy. A bull elephant, two females, and a little toto were having a great time here, throwing water all over themselves, shower-fashion, with their trunks; and the mother was giving a bath to her baby. After the infant was bathed and dried in the sun, he made for his mother and nursed away, both mother and child as happy as you please. The old bull walked bravely about, raising his trunk and stripping the buds from the trees. Now and then he uprooted a sapling, much as a boy leaps over a gate from sheer joy of living or to show his strength. It was altogether a happy family party.

Often on the plains the light is not favorable, for the heat waves, which amateurs mistake for light, prevent clarity. But here conditions were excellent. Osa, too, had taken pains to get to the windward of the elephants, not always an easy task where the breezes curl and eddy through the dongas.[1] Now she asked her boy to hand over the camera, her eye still on the happy group, determined to surprise me with an unusual picture. But when she looked down at the black leather case which she supposed to be a camera, she discovered to her horror that she had brought our medicine case along instead of the Graflex. She spent two hours that evening telling me what a beautiful picture she might have had.

One thing I often noticed about elephants was what seemed to be a sort of mental telepathy that went on between them. I have seen this sort of thing so many times that I have wondered if it were possible there could be some sort of wireless operation that goes on. The elephants have very stiff hairs in their ears and in their nostrils. These could readily be used as antennae to catch emanations that the human being is quite unconscious of.

On many occasions I have seen an elephant, separated by perhaps several hundred yards from the rest of the herd, seemingly warn his comrades of a danger he himself has discovered. It almost seemed that he sent some mental signal to the others, for they would suddenly become restless and alarmed, even though I am sure they could not see the lone elephant nor discover the danger for themselves.

One night Osa and I were in our blind down in the mimosa near the lake with the moon shining between the drifting clouds, waiting to see what would turn up. About 11:30 P.M. Osa nudged me. Four hundred yards to the left of us appeared a long file of elephants. They walked to a spot not far from our flashlight apparatus and stopped there for about five minutes with their long trunks, up in the air, waving about as if for a scent. Then one elephant left the crowd and walked very slowly down toward the water. He would go about fifteen feet, then stop and wave his trunk about; then go on a bit more. We could see him so plainly that he gave us the impression of being distinctly puzzled, feeling there was something wrong but not sure what it was.

Then this investigator walked back to the rest of the herd and for about fifteen minutes they all held a sort of conference. Not a sound, mind you — just a standing quietly around as if whispering together. I know they could not have seen the apparatus, for I had it perfectly concealed. It wasn't the wind either; our position was such that it would not have been possible for the wind to have blown from us to them. Nevertheless, some sense told this elephant that something was wrong; but what he wasn't sure. Moreover, he was not going to advise his friends to take a chance. Finally, they all quietly made their way to the water by a route that took them around the cameras. After a good drink they melted soundlessly into the forest and we got no picture.

[1] **dongas:** ravines.

As time went on the elephants got bolder whenever their food dried up in the forest. Every night we would see them and they would trumpet through the evening hours, as they crashed through the *boma,*[1] until they came alongside our house and caught the human scent.

One old lady developed the habit of breaking into our garden. The drought now had dried everything up but the sweet potatoes, which, like camels, can go a long time without water.

This elephant was particularly orderly and systematic, choosing a space of about ten feet square and eating ten feet square of sweet potatoes, then going away without disturbing any of the surrounding plants. In this case she differed from almost every wild animal I have known.

We noticed that she entered the *boma,* the thorns of which did not seem to make much impression on her leathern hide, at a hole she made alongside a great yellow-wood tree. There we set up our wires and cameras; and we had just gone to bed when we heard the boom and ran out, taking our rifles with us. In the woods near by we heard a terrific thrashing and found that the elephant had carted away about four square yards of our *boma,* from which she was trying to free herself.

So thrilled were we at the prospect of another good elephant picture that we took our plates to the laboratory as we were, in our pajamas, and there developed them. They came out wonderfully sharp and clear, showing two elephants apparently; in reality only one, for we had caught the sweet-potato thief going and coming.

This lady, we thought, would not visit us again, but next night we heard the boom and found that this crazy elephant had rushed away with four more square yards of our fence. Again we developed the films in our pajamas, getting a thrill out of it, I think, that no slaughtering hunter knows.

We felt sure that now we had seen the last of her. Still, elephants are of one-track minds; they keep on coming in spite of all obstacles. And again, this third evening, we heard a breaking of branches on the edge of the forest, and a general thrashing around, and found the same matriarch grazing contentedly, pulling down her branches and nipping off the shoots. No big booms of flashlights were going to disturb her; and to show that she was not afraid she walked through the hole in the *boma* which she had just made and went along the row of houses, where the boys slept, like a runaway elephant going up a town street, and quietly proceeded to strip off one of the thatchings as a final gesture of independence. It must have been startling for the boys to wake up and see the roofs being slowly lifted off above their heads, and in a moment we heard a succession of cries and the straw huts disgorged frightened black figures that ran, tripped, and tumbled on all fours all up and down the narrow path.

This, of course, was trying, even though it enabled us to study the ways of elephants. And, indeed, hers were not the usual ways of elephants. Every part of the garden was reeking with the scent of the boys, which would not have disturbed the elephants of Siam and India, who are trained in captivity to draw great trunks of teakwood trees and to plow, but almost always sends their wild brothers of Africa crashing through the trees. The boys solved the problem by saying simply that that "*tembo*"[2] was crazy.

We gradually became so accustomed to elephants that we felt far less fear of them than we should have. A curious experience sometime later showed that it is not safe in Africa ever to be off guard.

[1] **boma:** a defensive inclosure; a stockade, in this instance made of thornbushes.

[2] **"tembo":** the native name for elephant.

We started out one morning for a donga several miles away and on the trail noticed a grass fire a considerable distance from us. About 10:00 A.M. Osa spotted four elephants in the donga below us, one young bull and three females. I got to work with my camera and inside of thirty minutes had used every lens, from the shortest focus to the longest. By this time the elephants had decided to graze. They left the trees and came out into the opening, slowly gathering grass and throwing it over them, now and then pulling up a young tree.

Suddenly we were made aware of the unexpected approach of the fire by a sudden roar of flames. Apparently the conflagration had almost died out at a small donga beyond the elephants, but on crossing it had come to dry grass as high as our heads. Now it swept down on us with the speed of a train. We were standing on a small peninsula of land where the donga took a turn. Before we knew it, we found ourselves entirely cut off; in every direction the grass was on fire, already scorching us with its heat. There was but one thing to do, and that was to go over the little cliff near by and take our chances with the elephants.

I am still wondering how we escaped broken necks and cameras. We all went over the top together, falling and scrambling down the cliff toward the elephants. The latter whirled about and stood with trunks out and ears up. At this moment they, too, got the roar and scent of the fire. They stuck their tails into the air and dashed for the far side of the donga, while we followed at best speed. When we emerged, the elephants had disappeared.

I have often heard people boast about killing an elephant. We were both sorry we had to kill one. Our thrill came in a fine film.

Years of this sort of work have, of course, given me a pretty close insight into elephant character. My views have changed since as a boy I watched circus elephants on parade. In fact, they are still changing as I live more and more with the unspoiled animals.

I have come to look upon an elephant as the dignified old gentleman of the wilderness. Often he is of great age, and his size prevents his plunging about the way lighter animals do. Yet he is not sluggish the way other elderly beasts come to be; it is only fair to cite the rhino as an example of an undignified creature despite his size.

Certainly the elephant is no fool. He attends to his own business and lets other creatures severely alone. He leads a quiet family life. And he does not prey on the land or lives of other species.

That the Indian elephant is easily tamed is no reflection upon the elephant's character in general. He is not weak-willed. Rather does he possess a kind of native philosophy deeply planted in his heart. Quicker than the cats and more thoroughly than the cattle does he perceive the futility of resisting captivity imposed by man. So he goes about his tasks or his tricks calmly and efficiently, and probably enjoys life little less than when he was free.

I do not take any too seriously stories about an elephant's vindictiveness. I think most intelligent lower animals remember a human being who has wronged them. Dogs do. Also there are vicious members of the elephant family just as of most other kinds of animals. A vicious dog or horse is equally on the lookout for trouble, though their smaller size makes less impression on their keepers when trouble comes.

I like elephants and I admire them. And I believe the normal pachyderm elephant is a kind, conservative animal that knows his place in life and is wholly content to keep it.

THINK BACK OVER WHAT YOU HAVE READ

Increasing Your Knowledge of Elephants

1. What traditional beliefs about the elephant had Martin Johnson accepted ever since he was a boy? Would Courtney Riley Cooper have accepted them? Would the incident, related by Martin Johnson, of the elephant that charged a train in Burma be accepted by Cooper as typical elephant behavior?

2. Of what did Boculy's method of tracking elephants consist?

3. What pictures of baby elephants appealed to you? With what instances can you illustrate a mother elephant's tolerance? discipline?

4. What are the dangers of stampede among wild elephants? Do they arise from causes similar to those which produce panic in captivity?

5. What good pictures of the alarmed elephant was Martin Johnson able to take? What did Jumbo look like when he was startled?

6. By what means does the elephant detect danger? Why is it necessary for hunters to "watch the wind"?

7. With what pictures does Martin Johnson illustrate the natural dignity of the elephant? his "philosophic" outlook on life? his sheeplike quality during panic? Do these characteristics square with Cooper's observations?

8. What observations did Johnson make about "mental telepathy" among elephants?

9. In what poses do you visualize these elephants, photographed by Johnson: the old lady in Osa's garden, the jumbo, the old warrior shot by Osa?

Increase Your Power over Words

10. On page 284 occurs the word *capriciously*, referring to the manner in which the wind changed suddenly. *Caprice* (noun), *capricious* (adjective), and *capriciously* (adverb) come from the Italian word *capro* meaning goat. If you have ever watched goats, you may have noticed that they are given to quick starts and changes of mind. Hence *capricious*, which originally meant goatlike, has come to mean unsteady, changeable, moody, fickle.

Can you think of any other words derived from the names of animals and used to describe human characteristics? *Kittenish* is one. What others?

11. Many English words are based on the Latin stem *mater* meaning mother. *Maternal* means motherly; *maternity* is motherhood. *Matricide* (from *mater*, mother, and *caedere*, to kill) means the murder of one's mother, also the person who commits such a murder. The word *matriarch* (page 288) is derived from the Latin *mater* and the Greek *archos* meaning ruler. A *matriarch*, therefore, is a woman who is the ruler of her family. What does *patriarch* mean?

For Ambitious Students

12. If this selection has interested you in Africa, you may follow it by readings in other books, such as:

Akeley, C. E., *In Brightest Africa*
Akeley, M. L., *Carl Akeley's Africa*
Bradley, Mary, *On the Gorilla Trail*
Johnson, Martin, *Lion; Congorilla*
Roosevelt, Theodore, *African Game Trails*

On the Firing Line of Science

WITH HELMET AND HOSE

by William Beebe (1877–)

One of the most interesting recent contributions to the essay form has been made by science. Gaining rapidly in artistic merit as well as in popularity, the picturesque scientific observation seems already to have won a permanent place in literature. The writing of William Beebe, a distinguished zoologist, is a brilliant example of this happy alliance between art and science.

You should add the name of William Beebe to your growing list of literary acquaintances. He has followed the trail of scientific romance into remote parts of the globe, into distant jungle and tropical island and lonely desert. One of his conquests is described in *Arcturus Adventure*, from which the following essay is taken. This book, which tells of an expedition that he headed in 1925 to explore marine life in the Sargasso Sea, belongs to a long list of thrilling titles in which the secrets of nature are revealed to you with poetic insight.

This is a long essay which will test your

powers of sustained interest. If we cannot don a diving suit, we may at least offer ourselves the treat of vicarious experience. But the same call for patience applies to reading as to scientific observation; if we are to enjoy the adventure of exploration, we must give our senses a chance to respond to the wealth of strange detail that assails them.

I AM twenty feet under water with a huge copper helmet on my head, tilting with my trident against an olive-green grouper over a yard long, who is much too fearless and inquisitive for my liking. Not until I have pricked him sharply with the grains[1] does he leave off nosing my legs with his mean jaws and efficient teeth. It suddenly occurs to me how knightlike I am as far as the metal cask goes, and then, in spite of the strange world all about, my mind goes back to the long-ago Christmases when a new-published Henty[2] book was an invariable and almost the best gift. I instantly know that if ever I succeed in shackling these divings to mere awkward words it must be called "With Helmet and Hose"; and if any modern boy, grown-up, or gentle reader does not know why, explanations will do no good.

I wish I could credit my present passionate enthusiasm for diving beneath strange tropical waters to a lifelong suppressed desire — an *idée fixe*[3] which would not be gainsaid. But unfortunately, this is not so. My only excuse is that I suffer intermittently from what my artist once offered as a definition of a monkey, a desire to be somewhere else than I am.

Considering carefully this whirling ball of mud[4] upon which I found myself, I read in books and saw pictures of jungles and deserts, and my desire to see them was just a little stronger than the many obstacles between; I had breathed the air and watched birds fly for an unconscionable number of years before I began my first wobbly taxiing across a flying field. Since then I have left the earth under pleasant and unpleasant conditions over three hundred times and, except twice, returned safely.

Without shame I confess that I have lain awake nights and spent innumerable hours of my life in gazing at the moon and planets — nay, even at the Small Magellanic Cloud[5] — with desire and longing, for if one wishes to visit interstellar space,[6] one might as well hold the thought of a passage on Tomlinson's[7] route as on a mensurable moon trip. Up to the present, twenty-two thousand feet is as far as I have been able to rise above solid ground.

Another realm which has always seemed as remote as the moon is the depth of the ocean. My reading and wishing never took any concrete, definite direction until the trip I made to the Galápagos[8] on the *Noma*. Then I first realized the glories and desirability of the submarine world. This at once encouraged and then disheartened me — the encouragement coming from the ease of diving from a boat or a pier and watching for a brief moment the fish and sea things, simultaneously with the realization of the futility of such a brief, blurred glimpse.

I inspected a number of divers' outfits one day and found nothing tempting in the enormously cumbersome suits. Then, just before I sailed on the *Arcturus*, I bought my helmet. The paraphernalia accompanying it was so simple that I doubted its efficiency, but at least it was an effort in the right direction of investigation of a new world.

[1] **grains:** a short-pronged harpoon or trident. [2] **Henty:** once a popular writer of boys' books, the title of one of which is not unlike the title of this essay. [3] **idée fixe:** fixed notion (French). [4] **ball of mud:** the earth

[5] **Small Magellanic Cloud:** one of the cloudlike star clusters in the Milky Way near the Southern Cross. [6] **interstellar space:** the space between the stars. [7] **Tomlinson:** in his poem "Tomlinson" Kipling tells of a man who died and went through space to both heaven and hell. [8] **Galápagos:** an island group in the Pacific Ocean southwest of Panama.

During the first part of the *Arcturus* adventure the sea was too rough to think of using it, even a few feet below the gangway, but when we moored close under the cliffs of Darwin Bay at Tower Island[1] — our old Galápagos anchorage — I brought up the box from the hold and unlimbered the diving apparatus. The helmet was a big, conical affair of copper, made to rest on the shoulders, with a hose connection on the right side and two oblique windows in front. Around the bottom extended a flange on which four flattened pieces of lead were hung, each weighing ten pounds. This made a total of sixty pounds for the entire thing. The hose, which was of the ordinary common or garden variety, was attached at one end to the helmet and at the other to a double-action automobile pump, which screwed to a board and was operated by a long iron lever pushed back and forth. Almost at once we elaborated a method of operation which was so simple and satisfactory, even to the slightest details, that no change was necessary after weeks and months of use.

Our regular mode of diving is as follows. We start out from the *Arcturus* in a flat-bottomed boat which has a square, eighteen-inch glass set in the bottom amidships. To the stern is fastened a long metal Jacob's-ladder,[2] rolled up when not in use. We are towed or we row to the shore — preferably to the base of cliffs or steep rocks, as that affords considerable depth close inshore and rocky places are loved by hosts of fish. We anchor as close to the cliffs as is safe, and roll out the ladder so that it sways in midwater or rests upon the bottom. The pump is in the bow, the handle fixed, and the leather washer carefully screwed in. The hose is cleared of kinks and is looped, partly overboard. A hand line is tied to the top of the helmet, and the inside of the glass window is coated with a film of glycerine to prevent the breath of the diver from condensing and so clouding it. The four lead weights are slipped over the flange on the helmet base, and all is ready for the diver. A hand waterglass is near for constant lookout for danger, and one or two long-handled harpoons.

In bathing suit I climb down the ladder over the stern and dip to my neck, being careful not to wet my head. Then John lifts the helmet; I give a last, quick look around, draw a deep breath, duck into it, and as it settles firmly on my shoulders I climb slowly down. The sensation just above the water is of unbearable weight; but the instant I immerse this goes and the weight of the helmet with all the lead is only a gentle pressure, sufficient to give perfect stability. Meanwhile Ruth Rose[3] has started to pump.

From a blurred view of the water surface and the boat's stern, I sink instantly to clear vision under water. I descend three rungs and reach up for the short harpoon or grains which is put into my hand. At the fourth or fifth rung the air presses perceptibly on my ears and I relieve it by swallowing. I descend slowly, swallowing now and then, and when the last rung has been reached, I lower myself easily by one arm, and lightly rest on the bottom. If serious danger threatens or the pumping should go wrong for any reason, I have only to lift up the helmet, duck out from under it, and swim to the surface. The level of the water keeps constantly at the level of my neck or throat, and if I lean far forward it gradually rises to my mouth. But there is no splashing, no sense of oppression.

In most of the great changes or experiences which come to us humans, such as

[1] **Tower Island:** one of the Galápagos Islands.
[2] **Jacob's-ladder:** a flexible ladder suspended from the top.
[3] **Ruth Rose:** the staff historian of the expedition.

seeing our first palm tree or circus or volcano, the first reading of *Alice,*[1] diving, a battle, discovering the method of complete relaxation, or really being *in* the only Borneo in the world, it is not, as so many people think, the first few minutes which are the most wonderful. It is the subsequent gradual appreciation which develops that realization of the wonder and the beauty of the thing close at hand. It is so easy to miss this almost conscious appraisement; and after the trip or performance or experience is past, we long for just one moment of the actuality so that this or that could be seen again and remembered more clearly. Before I started on my trip around the world in my search for wild pheasants,[2] someone gave me one of the most valuable hints I have ever had. It seems a foolish little game when I come to write it down, but it is based on a very sound realization of a great human weakness — the contempt bred by myopic familiarity,[3] the absolute necessity for even an artificial perspective. It consists merely in shutting your eyes when you are in the midst of a great moment, or close to some marvel of time and space, and convincing yourself that you are at home again with the experience over and past. And what would you wish most to have examined or done if you could turn time and space back again? A hundred questions rush into this induced mental vacuum: What were the color and shape of the wild blossoms upon which that pheasant fed? What was the sound of the antiaircraft shells? At what speed did the lava flow? Et cetera.

And so, as I said, I swung myself lightly down from the ladder and stood on the bottom. I gazed out with interest on the rocks and fish about me, but felt a vague feeling of disappointment. I was breathing so easily; the water outside might have been correctly heated air as far as any bodily sensation went; I was looking through a pane of glass at fish swimming about — exactly what I have done and seen a hundred times in our aquarium in New York. I felt only as if I were in a very small, strange, but perfectly comfortable room looking upon a wonderful tank of living fish with a most excellently painted background. The shock of entrance into this long-anticipated world had not been as radical as my imagination had pictured, even though I cannot recall having visualized instant attacks by huge sharks or the feel of the snaky tentacle of an approaching great octopus. The fact of my bodily comfort and the vivid memory of aquariums all over the world had deadened the stupendous marvel of it all.

I sat down on a convenient rock, shut my eyes, and recited my lesson: *I am not at home, nor near any city or people; I am far out in the Pacific on a desert island, sitting on the bottom of the ocean; I am deep down under the water in a place where no human being has ever been before; it is one of the greatest moments of my whole life; thousands of people would pay large sums, would forego much, for five minutes of this!*

This was enough. I opened my eyes and saw, resting on a rock not more than three inches away from my face, the red bull of Kim.[4] It was the strangest little blenny[5] in the world, five inches long and mostly all head, with tail enough only to steady him in his place on the boulder. His long snout with nostrils flaring at the tip, his

[1] **Alice:** *Alice in Wonderland.* [2] **search for wild pheasants:** On one of his expeditions Beebe made a trip around the world in search of rare pheasants. The story of this trip is told in his book *Pheasant Jungles.* [3] **myopic familiarity:** that is, we are shortsighted and do not notice the common things immediately before our eyes.

[4] **Kim:** In Kipling's novel the boy Kim seeks for a red bull on a green field, which turns out to be the insignia on the flag of his father's old regiment. [5] **blenny:** a species of fish whose appearance Beebe is about to describe.

broad, flat crown surmounted by two curving horns, made him absurdly like a prize bull. He was dull scarlet with splashes of golden brown along his sides, which was well enough, but a bull does not have tatters and fringes of blue and yellow scattered all over him (unless we choose to consider the cruel *banderillas*[1] as ornamental). My blenny's eyes were silver with hieroglyphics of purple in them; and as I looked, he puffed a puff of water at my window and was gone.

I was quite reoriented now. The hardest thing was to realize that I was *wet.* It was the old story of the value of comparison. All of me was wet and I could not reach up into dry air, so I had no sensation of wetness. I looked at my fingers, however, and saw the beginning of washerwoman's wrinkles, so was convinced! I reached out and picked a starfish from the rock in front; and as it slowly crawled over my hand, I realized to the full that this was a wild starfish and not one brought from somewhere else and placed there for me to look at.

It was the morning of April the ninth when I went down for the first time, on a coral bank in Darwin Bay. I made five descents but recall very few details, because at the moment when I was ducking inside the helmet for the second time I saw, a few yards away, one of the greatest gray sharks I have ever seen, a giant of a generous eleven or twelve feet, cutting the water with his great dark fin. My companions did not fail to remind me of my notorious scorn of sharks,[2] so with a rather sickly grin I went down. The dominant impression of this first experience was of the disconcertingly narrow field of vision — the oblique panes of glass in the helmet permitting only about sixty degrees. What I had seen at the surface kept my imagination busy with the keenest desire to see what was transpiring in the remaining three hundred degrees of my visual circle. I am certain that from above I must have looked like some strange sort of owl, whose head continually revolved first in one and then in the opposite direction.

It is idle to say that I, and I think all of us who went down, did not feel at first exceedingly nervous. It was disconcerting, as I have said, not to be able to see directly behind by a quick turn of the head; and until I became accustomed to the nibbling touch of some little fish who was investigating this strange creature so new to its world, I would often leap up in expectation of seeing some monster of the deep about to attack me. This stage passed and I soon felt perfectly at home. On the very few occasions when some creature seemed tempted to make a tentative hostile approach, it appeared to be the snaky hose extending to the surface and the constant stream of bubbles which deterred it.

In the afternoon of the same April day I submerged near the foot of the great cliffs, and, as I have described, disciplined myself into a greater realization of the wonder of it. I think my first surprise was of the constant movement of everything, not so much individually as of the whole in relation to the rocks and bottom. I knew, of course, that the boat was rising and falling with every surge, which heaved and settled in turn, as each wave passed, to break against the cliffs. I found this same motion extended downward, with less and less force, until at thirty feet it all but died away. At present in about twenty feet of water I felt it strongly. I would be sitting quietly without the slightest tremor when, gently and without shock, every fish in sight, every

[1] **banderillas:** darts thrown by bullfighters into the sides of the bull. [2] **notorious scorn of sharks:** William Beebe elsewhere in his writing has ridiculed the idea that sharks are particularly dangerous.

bit of weed or hydroid,[1] the anchor rope, the shadow of the boat, the hose and myself swayed toward the land. One could resist it by clinging firmly to the rock, but the supreme joy, because of its impossibility in the air above, was to balance carefully and let oneself be wafted through space and deposited safely on the next rock. There followed a period of complete rest, and back again everything would come. It was so soothing, so rhythmical, that one yielded to it at times in a daze of sheer enjoyment. Where the water is not too deep and the bottom is sand or powdered shells, it is evident that the great surges are not a simple, compact movement; for here are made visible little, individual whirlwinds and casual, separate breezes which twist the shell dust about or send up clouds of sand about my body.

In days to come I was to find the surge sometimes a very real danger, as when at Cocos[2] I went down in a smashing, thrashing sea and was scraped and torn back and forth across lacerating knife points of coral and poisonous spines of urchins until flesh and blood could no longer stand it. Like getting one's sea legs it soon became second nature to anticipate the swell, to lean against it, to shift the balance, so that everything moved except myself and the eternal rocks.

Now, day by day, occurred the accidents by which I learned how to do things, little by little relinquishing the ideas which, on dry land, had seemed feasible and important. For a day or two I could not understand why during certain dives the fish were so much tamer than at other times. The clue came to me when a rather heavy swell was running and I found that, if I gave to the movement of the water, all the inhabitants, from gobies to groupers, from shrimps to sharks, accepted me as something new but harmless which the waves had washed in; but if I resisted the aquatic wind and maintained place and posture, I became an object of suspicion. This was the first of many radical differences which I was to find between the world of dry land and that of the underwater: on land, to move is to arouse fear among the wild creatures; here I did it by remaining still.

I walked, or half walked, half floated, toward the cliffs. The rocks were almost bare in this bay, like those between tides, and the multitudes of lesser aquatic creatures were concealed beneath them. The water was quiet, and between surges was often perfectly clear, so that I could see plainly the cliffs rising high in air above that narrow straight line which marked the division between the two kingdoms. I went as far as my hose tether would permit and reached a boulder on which, the day before, at low tide, I had sat comfortably in the clear, cool air of the upper world.

Turning back, I saw that I had become a Pied Piper[3] of sorts, leading a host of fish which followed in my train. The sun was out now in full strength and no fish, however strange and unknown to me, could hold my eyes from the marvel of distance. As I walked toward the cliffs I had also worked a little toward the east and the view I had, as I turned, was of another slope than that over which I had come. The bottom thus far was not wholly unlike the cliff above the water, but before me now the slope fell away in a manner which was beyond all experience — a breath-stopping fall, down which one could not topple headlong, but

[1] **hydroid:** a peculiar sea animal greatly resembling a plant. [2] **Cocos:** a Pacific island visited by Beebe. Read the chapter on Cocos in *Arcturus Adventure;* also to be found in *Exploring with Beebe.*

[3] **Pied Piper:** a reference to the old story of the piper whose playing lured all the rats from the town of Hamelin.

only roll and slide slowly, to be overcome, not by swift speed of descent or smashing blow, but by a far more terrible slow increase of pressure of the invisible medium, whose very surface film is death to us. To detect a faint, colorless shape now and then, through the azure curtain, and never to know whether it was rock or living creature — things such as this made every descent an ineradicable memory.

My range of vision was perhaps fifty feet in every direction, but for all I could tell it might have been fifty feet or fifty miles. The sun's rays filtered down as though through the most marvelous cathedral ever imagined — intangible, oblique rays which the eye could perceive but no lip describe. With distance, these became more and more luminous, more wondrously brilliant, until rocks died away in a veritable purple glory. No sunset, no mist on distant mountains that I have seen, could compare with this. One had to sit quietly and absorb these beauties before one could remember to be an ichthyologist.[1]

As I was reveling in pure sensuous delight at this color of colors, a small object appeared in mid-water close to my little glass window and was instantly obscured by half a dozen little fish which darted about it, some actually flicking my helmet with their tails. Just as I saw that the suspended object was a baited hook, a baby scarlet snapper snatched at it, darted downward, and was at once drawn up into the boat. As I looked after it, an idea came to me and I followed the snapper upward by way of the ladder. When the helmet was lifted off and I could speak, I expressed my wants, and descended again. Soon there fell slowly at my feet a small stone to which was tied a juicy and scarcely dead crab. I picked this up, waved it back and forth so as to scatter the impelling incense of its body, and as if by magic, from behind me, from crevices upon which I was seated, seemingly materializing from the clear water, came fish and fish and fish. It is far from my intention to give a detailed list of all of these. The effect upon the reader in this connection would be much the same as my own sensations at this time if, by chance, my friend working the pump in the boat above had suddenly dropped off to sleep. Their names, numbers, colors, and habits are all set down elsewhere in a more suitable place — *Zoologica*.[2]

Even if I wished to speak of them in a homely way I could not; for most of them have had visited upon them the names only of the official, scientific census taker, while the rest have no names at all. So, Adamlike, I had to give them all temporary names until I could identify them, or christen them with my own binomial terms. It was long before I could disentangle individual characteristics from the whirling mass. The first four fishes rushed for the bait —

And yet another four;
And thick and fast they came at last,
And more, and more, and more —

so that, until I could shut my mind to the abstract marvel of it and my eyes to the kaleidoscopic, hypnotic effect, ichthyology gained little of specific factual contribution. I waved my magic crab; I may have murmured Plop! Glub! and Bloob! — which is what the bubbles say when I first immerse — and the hosts came. Within three minutes from the time when the crab first fell into my hand, I had five hundred fish swirling around my crab and hand and head. Similes failed. I thought of the hosts of yellow butterflies I have seen fluttering at arm's length on Boomboom Point; I thought of the maze of

[1] **ichthyologist:** student of fish life.

[2] **Zoologica:** the official records of the New York Zoological Society.

wings of the pigeons of St. Mark's,[1] but no memory of the upper world was in place here — this was a wholly new thing.

Often there was a central nucleus a foot or more in diameter, of solid fish, so that the bait and my arm to the elbow were quite invisible. Twenty or twenty-five species were represented, and, like birds, they were graded with exquisite exactness as to correlation of fear and size. The great majority were small, from two to four inches in length, and these were wholly without fear, nibbling my hand — passing between my fingers but always just avoiding capture, no matter how quickly I shut my fist. Six- and eight-inch fish also came near, but were more ready to dart off at any sudden movement of mine. On the outskirts hung a fringe of still larger fish, hungry and rushing in now and then for a snap at the delicious morsel which they saw their lesser fellows enjoying, but always with less abandon to the temptation of the moment. The tameness of the little chaps, however, was so astounding that the relatively greater wariness of the larger fish scarcely deserved the name of suspicion, not to say fear. Another unexpected thing was the rapidity with which these fish lost even this slight suspicion and learned to connect my appearance with food. If I dived in the same spot several times a day and several days in succession, fish would approach in numbers and investigate my hands and trident [2] with much greater eagerness and, I presume, with expectancy, than they ever displayed on the occasion of the first dive, before I had repeatedly tempted them with freshly killed crabs. I could even recognize certain individuals, characterized by some peculiarity of color or form.

Before I go on to speak, even casually, of the fish themselves, I must tell of my second discovery. As with the crab baiting and so much else in my life, it was by sheer accident that I learned of the possibility of spearing fish twenty to thirty feet under water. The first few times I dived I carried a powerful harpoon with a long metal handle, thinking I could lay it down and pick it up more readily than if it had been buoyant. The big green grouper which I mentioned in my opening sentence was bothering me, shoving his big jaws close to my arms and legs, so I struck idly at him, missing of course, and to my astonishment he instantly attacked the prongs of the trident. Again I stabbed when he was broadside on and struck him so hard that he tore away with difficulty, whereupon he took himself off and sulked under a great mushroom coral.

I remembered this incident and the following day had a special grains made out of three large, straightened fishhooks fixed in the end of a yard-long wooden handle. This I took down with me and waited until my regular crab bait came sailing down. I caught the stone and wedged it in a crevice of the rock, where the crab was only partly exposed. The fact of the invisibility of the food made little difference in the swiftness and the numbers of the arrivals. Their keen powers of scent drew them like filings to a magnet; and although only three or four fish could find room for a simultaneous nibble, yet scores waited behind, or pushed and wedged themselves in, reminding me of the buffet at a supper dance.

At last I decided to try my new weapon. On several former descents I had noticed a very common fish which was new to me, and now there were twenty or thirty in sight, nibbling at the crab, swimming in and out of crevices, and doing all the things which are imperative for small fish to do on occasions such as this. They were

[1] **St. Mark's:** the great cathedral in Venice, in front of which hundreds of pigeons are ever present. [2] **trident:** suggestive of Neptune's three-pronged fork.

smug little fellows, high-backed like sunfish, brownish-black, with only two outstanding features — delicately beautiful bright orange tips to the pectoral fins and a white base to the tail. Twice I leveled my trident and stabbed, and twice I missed. Then I found a new point of balance along the handle, struck again, and had a fish caught fast — my first *Pomacentrus leucorus*.

And now my undersea sprang a new surprise on me. Although I am a scientist and a hunting scientist, I hate to take life. Under the provocation of extreme danger to me or mine, I have always valued human life at less than nothing; but shooting down a savage as he is rushing you is one thing and deliberately spearing a fish which you have been watching and which swims about close to your face and hands in perfect fearlessness is quite another. However, one can be tenderhearted without being sentimental, and if I need the facts for science, to complete the life history of a whole species, I will shoot a dove on her eggs without compunction. I sympathize, on the other hand, with the Hindoo fishermen of the Laccadives [1] who are not allowed by their faith to take life, and hence, when they have drawn their nets, they rush ashore and lay the still living fish gently upon leaves and moss. Later they return, and finding, to their surprise, a lot of fish which are quite dead, it is permitted that they gather them up to sell or to eat.

So it was not with the unmixed feelings of a triumphant Neptune or a successful ichthyologist that I clambered up the ladder and when near the surface held out my trident with the impaled fish. My pleasure in the feat was heightened when I finally ascended and found my fish swimming unconcernedly about in the well of the boat. As a matter of fact, a much greater percentage of my speared individuals recovered and survived, living and feeding contentedly for weeks in our aquariums, than of those we caught on hook and line. Almost invariably the tip of the grains would penetrate only the mass of back muscles, leaving quite untouched the head and the vital organs of the body.

I experimented with all sorts of methods, such as putting a bit of crab on the trident itself. This was a complete failure; for the fish would crowd around it head-on, and with all my efforts I never succeeded in even touching a fish when in this position. It can very naturally shoot forward and backward with infinitely greater speed and facility than move sideways against such a heavy medium. So my efforts were always directed at fish broadside on. This method of attack was so new to their experience that even when just missed they darted aside only far enough to escape the thrust, then returned at once and examined the trident with deep interest. Sometimes I would scrape off a few scales and then these most astounding creatures would rush back in great excitement and snap up, one by one, each floating scale, " getting a bit of their own back," as it were.

The smaller fish were as easy to reach with the prongs as if they were blackberries fastened to a stem, but they were so small and agile that they slipped between and around the barbs. The easiest of all to secure were the medium-sized herbivorous fish such as the yellow-tailed surgeons and the gorgeously colored angelfish. These came inspired only by curiosity and drifted about me aimlessly or nibbled at the rock by my elbow. The sign of Cancer [2] meant nothing to them,

[1] **Laccadives:** an island group in the Arabian Sea.

[2] **sign of Cancer:** one of the twelve divisions of the heavens through which the sun passes in a year. It is represented by a crab in the almanacs. Here it refers humorously to the crab used by Beebe to attract the fish.

and their efficient poisonous spines or defense of whatever kind wrought a self-confidence which carried them through life calmly and without fear. I had merely to wait until they approached and turned their broad profiles when a quick flick of the wrist meant their transference to life in one of our aquariums — where they continued to live placidly and undisturbed by any change which fate had brought to them. The number of the surgeons which I took was limited only by desire for specimens or the capacity of our aquariums, for my capture of one conveyed no alarm or sense of insecurity, and when I again climbed down the ladder the chances were that I would find the remainder of the school in the same spot, undisturbed.

The best sport was to be had with the brilliantly colored wrasse. They were among the most active and swift, slender and supple as eels, with an abundance of fins for doing everything that perfect control demands. Two species in particular were always about, although never more than a half dozen were in sight at once. Nature must have relegated the coloring of some of these fish to an amateur assistant, for it was crude, blatant, and, judged by human ideas of ornamentation, in execrably bad taste. Yet as I saw it — a living organism — winding in and out of dark crevices, or twisting almost on its back to get a nibble at crab meat, it seemed rather an exquisite mass of palette splashes.[1] The head was scarlet, the body, fins, and tail mostly bright grass green. The head was outlined in dark blue, and from the lips, which were solidly of the same color, five blue lines streamed backward, flowing in irregular bands through the eye and across the cheeks, saturating the pectoral fins. The whole green body was thickly banded with irregular vertical lines of an unnamable dull maroon — like thick heavy streaks of some awful rain or acid stains. The tail had a stiff, unnatural pattern, like a great scarlet H drawn crudely over the green. I was happy when at last I outwitted a six-inch green wrasse and put him aboard, where he lived for two months, allowing us to paint and study him at our leisure.

The other wrasse was simpler, but even more striking in pattern and coloration, and to the last defied my every effort. Twice I struck and marked them; and day after day the same individuals would come about as bold as ever, flaunting their scars and wounds in my face. One of these had two jagged holes well into his side; yet they apparently gave him no concern nor interfered at all with his speed and control, and he easily avoided every attack which I launched. These fish were about five inches in length, bright Tyrian purple over all, with a broad vertical band of sulphur yellow extending down from the neck around the body and including the pectoral fins. While I was exerting every muscle to get him, I called him many names in the quiet of my helmet; but these are neither here nor there. No written description fits him; and until I return and with greater skill succeed in overcoming his cleverness, he can be called only the Yellow-banded Purple Wrasse.

The little round, brownish-black *Pomacentrus* fish of two species were the most abundant of the four-inchers and were the most absolute home bodies, each living in his particular crack or crevice, from which he frequently rushed out and attacked ferociously any fish which approached too near, regardless of its size.

Another field of work of tremendous interest was suggested when I turned over the first stone and saw the mass of life covering the underside and filling the crevices. I arranged to have a pail lowered

[1] **palette splashes:** splashes of color on the mixing board of an artist.

on a rope and, squatting low on the floor of the bay, I filled the pail and gave the signal to draw it up. Five pailfuls provided a tub of rocks. This was left standing in the sun for a day, and at the end of that time there had crept out an amazing array of interesting beings — beautiful sea worms, starfishes, squillas, hermit crabs, and shrimps of every hue; a number of strange larval fish and an adult, formed, wonderfully patterned, quite fearless moray eel exactly one and one-half inches in length. This tapped a fertile and untouched field, providing organisms which cannot be dredged because of their shelter under and within coral and stones — and not to be gathered by wading alongshore at low tide, since twenty feet of water lay above them.

The obliquity of the two windows [1] in the helmet made it necessary to look out of either one or the other exclusively when engaged in observation or work which required accurate correlation of eye and hand. Seldom have I seen a funnier sight than the earnest efforts of any of our party before they learned of this optical effect. Through the waterglass a pale figure would be seen crouched on the bottom, industriously picking up stones and carefully dropping them about two feet from the bucket. After much hard labor the helmeted creature would raise the empty bucket and gaze at it in puzzled astonishment. In imagination we could see the large question mark poised in mid-water over his head. Another laborsaving individual decided to pick the specimens themselves off the rocks; and long streamers of algae [2] and clumps of hydroids were gathered and carefully placed in the bucket, only to float instantly out and up to us while he was looking for other equally buoyant specimens. Don Quixote's horse [3] was nothing compared to the worker's ultimate idea of the capacity of that pail.

From first to last I could never guess, from examining the bottom through a waterglass, what a submersion would yield, or even look like, except in the most general, superficial way. It was like judging a shore line from a ship with all the indentations flattened, all the coves and little bays concealed in the optical straightening, and the wicked, crashing breakers smoothed from behind into harmless-appearing ripples. In many lights the bottom, even only twenty feet down, appears merely undulating or paved with huge stones.

One of the last dives I made in Darwin Bay showed such an aspect from above. I went down rather deeply but very slowly, for I always came under the spell of the ever-wonderful blueness of distance. It seemed impossible, even after all the times I had studied it, that invisibility or opacity of whatever distance could result from such a luminous medium. When at last I rested on the bottom, I watched three white-striped angelfish chasing one another in sheer play. They drew my attention upward to where they were breaking the surface film, not far from the boat whose keel was bobbing absurdly up and down. The angelfish then curved downward, the long filaments streaming from the fins above and below and giving the appearance of even greater speed. They rose and fell, circled about, turned on their backs, and fell into nose dives as easily as I sat still. Finally, the emotion over, whatever it was, they all came to rest still high up in mid-water. It occurred to me that in comparison our own world is practically one of two planes, while this is really the one of three. It is fair to com-

[1] The two windows were set at an angle to each other; **obliquity** is related to the word *oblique*. [2] **algae:** kinds of seaweed.

[3] **Don Quixote's horse:** The horse of Don Quixote, in Cervantes' famous story, was very thin and always hungry.

pare fish only with birds, and even birds need two perching props and do not dare to develop wings or feather fins beneath the body, for, sooner or later, they must alight, while a fish can live, eat, and sleep poised in mid-water.

I turned my attention from the fish to the scene behind me, and the absurdity of my appraisement from the waterglass became apparent. I was standing a few yards away from a boulder as big as a cottage, and my heart gave a leap as I saw a curved flight of steps — giant steps like those up which I had once climbed Cheops.[1] They began on my side at the doorless entrance of the sinister cottage, slowly encircled it, and vanished behind it in a soul-stirring abyss of blueness, which, from a delicate shade near at hand, blued more and more clearly into infinite depth and space. I believe that Sime[2] would have loved this scene and Dunsany[3] would have deemed it not unfitting for the habitation of gnomes. Töten Insel treasured no more mystery in its perspective than did this. As I watched, a bit of greenish-black coral which projected eavelike began to move and crawl slowly downward, and with it went dangling things which I had taken for strands of dead seaweed but which on this edifice might well have been awful stalactites or icicles of sorts. The octopus climbed down, hesitated, felt about in different directions, and then descended the steps, flowing along the angles like some horrid viscid fluid in animal form. The most active imagination could not have set the scene better, or found a more appropriate actor.

But like the double miracle of the stars falling into the volcano the end was not yet. A mist of yellow-tailed surgeons drifted across the stairs and the dread boulder, and for a moment their calm matter-of-factness lessened the sinister feeling of the whole thing. A strong desire arose to look around the corner of the stair for myself. I was submerged so deeply that as I stood I could barely reach the lowest rung of the ladder; indeed, I was occasionally lifted a few inches from the ground as the boat rose to a greater swell. But I knew the hose was new and stout and even if I began to fall with that terrible slowness, as seemed easily possible to my imagination, I could surely climb back up my own string. One finger relaxed, and I was about to take the chance when a mote, very faint and pale, stirred the blueness as if some wondrous tapestry curtain were troubled by a breath of air.

The thing grew denser, took form, and became concrete, and a flat, round-fronted head, lazily undulating, wound through the water over the steps, a nine-foot shark weaving along where I would have been a minute later. My common-sense theory of the harmlessness of these beings still held good — in the last few days dozens of them had approached within a few yards of me — but the eerie character of this place had penetrated even my prison of copper and glass; and when I realized where my precious ladder would drift to when I relinquished my hold, looked down at my unprotected limbs and realized that I had not even a trident with me, I decided to go through life with the mystery of the stairway unsolved. The great, gray being, wafting along its hundreds of pounds of body by slow, gentle undulations, kept on and on until again hidden by the blue light. When I ascended to a world of greater reality, I took with me the memory of the beings to which legend and fact have brought the greatest notoriety of anything in the sea, and the setting in which I found them will never

[1] **Cheops:** the great pyramid in Egypt. [2] **Sime:** an artist who drew very fanciful subjects. [3] **Dunsany:** a modern Irish writer, much of whose work is exceedingly fanciful.

pass from mind — the Edge of the Edge of the World.

THINK BACK OVER WHAT YOU HAVE READ

Acquiring Interesting Information from the Essay

1. What new facts of interest about diving equipment did you gain from the essay? What details in the mode of diving interested you? With what scientific principles involved were you already familiar? Which ones awakened new curiosity?

2. What interesting facts did you learn about sensation under water? Which details suggest pleasure?

3. What lesson in psychology did you learn from Beebe's "foolish little game" of shutting his eyes when in the midst of a great moment? What did this little game accomplish for him undersea? What might it accomplish for you on dry land? With what illustrations of your own can you match his first "vague disappointment" under water? Have you been aware of similar initial disappointment in the air, for example?

4. With what possibilities for sport under water did Beebe acquaint you?

5. What interesting glimpses of fish nature did you catch from this essay? What new facts about instinct and habit?

6. What amusing optical delusions did you learn? For what effects is a person entirely unprepared in his first submersion?

Appreciating the Picturesque Style of the Essay

7. In what sea specimens did Beebe interest you by means of his picturesque description?

8. Of what interesting sensations of pressure and movement did he make you aware by the power of his description? What illustrations can you quote to the class?

9. What literary allusions did you notice in the essay? With which ones were you familiar? About which was your curiosity aroused? What is the effect of allusions in this kind of essay?

10. What impressions of unusual color did you gain from the essay?

11. What striking glimpses of fish in large numbers did you gain from the essay? With what comparisons did Beebe describe the effect they made upon him?

12. What picture does your imagination see of the giant stairway? What eerie drama was enacted on these stairs? What details made the scene fantastic?

Composition Suggestion

13. *Learning to observe.* What chances do you see in your school for patient observation? Does not the greenhouse, or the automotive department, or the art room, or the gymnasium suggest possibilities for a picturesque description written for someone not as accustomed to the scene as you are? Here is a good chance to try out William Beebe's "foolish little game" and see whether you can sharpen your senses so as to see the familiar with new vision.

For Ambitious Students

14. *On the trail of scientific adventure.* The following books are but a start toward a delightful reading hobby. Perhaps you will choose to read in this field for your outside reading project for a term.

Beebe, William, *Arcturus Adventure; Beneath Tropic Seas*

Hudson, W. H., *The Book of a Naturalist; Idle Days in Patagonia*

Fabre, J. H., *The Life of the Spider; The Life of the Caterpillar; Our Humble Helpers*

BRUCE: TRAIL OF THE TSETSE

by Paul de Kruif (1890–)

It is grim irony that those who have given themselves to destroying life should occupy a larger place in man's memory than those who have devoted themselves to the science of saving it. Since early childhood you have heard of the great deeds of Alexander the Great and Julius Caesar and Napoleon Bonaparte; the names of Grant and Sheridan and Stonewall Jackson and Foch and Hindenburg and Pershing are on the tip of every schoolboy's tongue. But what do you know about Ross and Grassi and Koch and Pasteur and Lister? Before you turned to this chapter had you ever heard of David Bruce? Yet these men have done more for humanity than all the soldiers of history put together. They, too, fought brave battles; however, they left in their wake not desolation and death but knowledge and hope. It is one thing to march forth to war with flags flying and bands playing and crowds cheering and with the assurance of medals and parades and glory when you return; it is quite a different story to spend lonely hours in stuffy laboratories, to be exposed constantly to mysterious infections from microbes more deadly than bullets, and with no more than a chance of being called anything but a fool for your pains.

You are about to read of the patient struggle of one of these unsung heroes, a brave soldier of science, David Bruce. In a thrilling book of scientific discovery, *Microbe Hunters,* Paul de Kruif tells of Bruce's fearless search for the cause of African sleeping sickness. In this brief biography you will witness quite a different kind of exploration from that of the last selection, and a brand-new kind of adventure. Notice, as you read, the particular qualities of heroism displayed. Notice, too, how exciting is the conquest of science.

"YOUNG MAN!" — the face of the Director General of the British Army Medical Service changed from an irritated red to an indignant mauve color — "young man, I will send you to India; I will send you to Zanzibar; I will send you to Timbuctoo — I will send you anywhere I please" (the majestic old gentleman was shouting now, and his face was a positively furious purple) — "but you may be sure I shall not send you to Natal!"[1] Reverberations.

What could David Bruce do but salute and withdraw from His Presence? He had schemed; he had begged and pulled wires; finally he had dared the anger of this Jupiter so that he might go hunt microbes in South Africa. It was in the early eighteen nineties; Theobald Smith, in America, had just made that revolutionary jump ahead in microbe hunting — he had just shown how death may be carried by a tick, and only by a tick, from one animal to another. And now this David Bruce, physically as adventurous as Theobald Smith was mildly professorial, wanted to turn that corner after Smith. Africa swarmed with mysterious viruses[2] that made the continent a hell to live in; in the olive-green mimosa thickets and the jungle, hummed and sizzled a hundred kinds of flies and ticks and gnats. What a place for discoveries, for swashbuckling microscopings and lone-wolf bug huntings Africa must be!

It was in the nature of David Bruce to do things his superiors and elders didn't want him to do. Just out of medical school in Edinburgh, he had joined the British Army Medical Service, not to fight, nor to save lives, nor (at that time) to get a chance to hunt microbes — nor for any such noble objects. He had joined it because he wanted to marry. They hadn't a shilling, neither Bruce nor his sweetheart; their folks called them thirteen kinds of romantic idiots. Why couldn't they wait until David had established himself in a nice practice?

So Bruce joined the army, and married on a salary of one thousand dollars a year.

In certain ways he was not a model soldier. He was disobedient and, what is much worse, tactless. Still a lieutenant, he one day disapproved of the conduct of his colonel and offered to knock him down. If you could see him now, past seventy, with shoulders of a longshoreman and a barrel chest sloping down to his burly equator,[3] if you could hear him swear through a mustache Hindenburg[4] would be proud to own, you would understand he could, had it been necessary, have put that colonel on his back and laughed at the court-martial that would have been sure to follow. He was ordered to the English garrison on the Island of Malta in the

[1] **Natal:** a province in South Africa.

[2] **viruses:** poisons produced by an infectious disease, by means of which the disease is communicated to another. [3] **equator:** humorous for waist. [4] **Hindenburg:** one of the great German generals in the World War, later president of Germany.

Mediterranean; with him went Mrs. Bruce — it was their honeymoon. Here again he showed himself to be things soldiers seldom are. He was energetic, as well as romantic. There was a mysterious disease in the island. It was called Malta fever. It was an ill that sent pains up and down the shinbones of soldiers and made them curse the day they took the Queen's shilling. Bruce saw it was silly to sit patting the heads of these sufferers and futile to prescribe pills for them — he must find the cause of Malta fever!

So he got himself into a mess. In an abandoned shack he set up a laboratory (little enough he knew about laboratories!) and here he spent weeks learning how to make a culture medium,[1] out of beef broth and agar-agar,[2] to grow the unknown germ of Malta fever in. It ought to be simple to discover it. His ignorance made him think that, and in his inexperience he got the sticky agar-agar over hands and face; it stained his uniform; the stuff set into obstinate jelly when he tried to filter it; he spent weeks doing a job a modern laboratory helper would accomplish in a couple of hours. He said unmentionable things; he called Mrs. Bruce from the tennis lawn and demanded (surely any woman knew better how to cook) that she help him. Out of his thousand dollars a year he bought monkeys — improvidently — at one dollar and seventy-five cents apiece. He tried to inject the blood of the tortured soldiers into these creatures, but they wriggled out of his hands and bit him and scratched him and were in general infernally lively nuisances. He called to his wife, "Will you hold this monkey for me?"

That was the way she became his assistant, and, as you will see, for thirty years she remained his right hand, going with him into the most pestilential dirty holes any microbe hunter has ever seen, sharing his poverty, beaming on his obscure glories; she was so important to his tremendous but not notorious conquests.

They were such muddlers at first, it is hard to believe it — but together these newly wed bacteriologists worked and discovered the microbe of Malta fever, and were ordered from Malta for their pains. "What was Bruce up to, anyway?" So asked the high medical officers of the garrison. "Why wasn't he *treating* the suffering soldiers — what for was he sticking himself away there in the hole he called his laboratory?" And they denounced him as an idiot, a visionary, a good-for-nothing monkey tamer and dabbler with test tubes. And just — he did do this twenty years later — as he might have discovered how the little bacillus of Malta fever sneaks from the udders of goats into the blood of British Tommies,[3] he was ordered away to Egypt.

Then he was ordered back to England, to the Army Medical School at Netley, to teach microbe hunting there — for hadn't he discovered the germ of an important disease? Here he met (at last God was good to him) His Excellency, the Honorable Sir Walter Hely-Hutchinson, Governor of Natal and Zululand, et cetera, et cetera. Together these two adventurers saw visions and made plans. His Excellency knew nothing about microbes and had perhaps never heard of Theobald Smith, but he had a colonial administrator's dream of Africa buzzing with prosperity under the Union Jack.[4] Bruce cared no fig for expansion of the Empire, but he knew there must be viruses sneaking from beast to beast and man to man on the stingers of bugs and

[1] **culture medium:** the substance in which germs are grown. [2] **agar-agar:** a jellylike substance derived from certain seaweeds, used as a culture in growing bacteria.

[3] **Tommies:** a name given British soldiers. [4] **Union Jack:** the British flag.

flies. He wanted (and so did Mrs. Bruce) to investigate strange diseases in impossible places.

It was then that he, only a brash captain, went to the majestic Director General, and I have just told how he was demolished. But even Directors General cannot remember the uppish wishes of all of their pawns and puppets; directors may propose, but adroit wirepulling sometimes disposes. And presently, in 1894, Surgeon Major David Bruce and Mrs. Bruce are in Natal, traveling by ox team ten miles a day toward Ubombo in Zululand. The temperature in the shade of their double tent often reached one hundred and six; swarms of tsetse flies escorted them, harassed them, flopped on them with the speed of express trains, and stung them like little adders; they were howled at by hyenas and growled at by lions. They spent part of every night scratching tick bites. But Bruce and his wife, the two of them, were the First British Nagana Commission to Zululand. So they were happy.

They were commanded to find out everything about the disease called nagana — the pretty native name for an unknown something that made great stretches of South Africa into a desolate place, impossible to farm in, dangerous to hunt big game in, suicidal to travel in. Nagana means "depressed and low in spirits." Nagana steals into fine horses and makes their coats stare[1] and their hair fall out; while the fat of these horses melts away, nagana grows watery pouches on their bellies and causes a thin rheum to drip from their noses; a milky film spreads over their eyes and they go blind; they droop and at last die — every last horse touched by the nagana dies. It was the same with cattle. Farmers tried to improve their herds by importing new stock; cows sent to them fat and in prime condition came miserably to their kraals — to die of nagana. Fat droves of cattle, sent away to far-off slaughterhouses, arrived there hairless, hidebound skeletons. There were strange belts of country through which it was death for animals to go. And the big game hunters! They would start into these innocent-seeming thickets with their horses and pack mules; one by one — in certain regions, mind you — their beasts wilted under them. When these hunters tried to hoof it back, sometimes they got home.

Bruce and Mrs. Bruce came at last to Ubombo — it was a settlement on a high hill, looking east toward the Indian Ocean across sixty miles of plain, and the olive-green of the mimosa thickets of this plain was slashed with the vivid green of glades of grass. On the hill they set up their laboratory; it consisted of a couple of microscopes, a few glass slides, some knives and syringes and perhaps a few dozen test tubes — smart young medical students of today would stick up their noses at such a kindergarten affair! Here they set to work, with sick horses and cattle brought up from the plain below — for Providence had so arranged it that beasts could live on the barren hill of Ubombo absolutely safe from nagana, but just let a farmer lead them down into the juicy grass of that fertile plain and the chances were ten to one they would die of nagana before they became fat on the grass. Bruce shaved the ears of the horses and jabbed them with a scalpel; a drop of blood welled out, and Mrs. Bruce, dodging their kicks, touched off the drops onto thin glass slides.

It was hot. Their sweat dimmed the lenses of their microscopes; they rejoiced in necks cramped from hours of looking; they joked about their red-rimmed eyes. They gave strange nicknames to their sick cows and horses; they learned to talk some Zulu. It was as if there were no

[1] **stare**: bristle.

Directors General or superior officers in existence, and Bruce felt himself for the first time a free searcher.

And very soon they made their first step ahead: in the blood of one of their horses, sick to death, Bruce spied a violent unwonted dancing among the faintly yellow, piled-up blood corpuscles; he slid his slide along the stage of his microscope till he came to an open space in the jungle of blood cells.

There, suddenly, popped into view the cause of the commotion — a curious little beast (much bigger than any ordinary microbe though), a creature with a blunt rear end and a long, slim, lashing whip with which he seemed to explore in front of him. A creature shaped like a panatella cigar; only it was flexible, almost tying itself in knots sometimes, and it had a transparent graceful fin running the length of its body. Another of the beasts swam into the open space under the lens, and another. What extraordinary creatures! They didn't go stupidly along like common microbes — they acted like intelligent little dragons. Each one of them darted from one round red blood cell to another: he would worry at it, try to get inside it, tug at it and pull it, push it along ahead of him — then suddenly off he would go in a straight line and bury himself under a mass of the blood cells lining the shore of the open space.

"Trypanosomes,[1] these are!" cried Bruce, and he hurried to show them to his wife. In all animals sick with nagana they found these finned beasts; in the blood they were, and in the fluid of their puffy eyelids, and in the strange yellowish jelly that replaced the fat under their skins. And never a one of them could Bruce find in healthy dogs and horses and cows. But as the sick cattle grew sicker, these vicious snakes swarmed more and more thickly in their blood until, when the animals lay gasping, next to death, the microbes writhed in them in quivering masses, so that you would swear their blood was made up of nothing else. It was horrible!

But how did these trypanosomes get from a sick beast to a healthy one? "Here on the hill we can keep healthy animals in the same stables with the sick ones, and never a one of the sound animals comes down. . . . Here on the hill no cow or horse has ever been known to get nagana!" muttered Bruce. "Why?"

He began to dream experiments, when the long arm of the authorities — maybe it was that dear old Director General remembering — found him again: Surgeon Major Bruce was to proceed to Pietermaritzburg for duty in the typhoid epidemic raging there.

Only five weeks they had been at this work when they started back to Pietermaritzburg, ten miles a day by ox team through the jungle. He started treating soldiers for typhoid fever, but as usual — thief that he was — he stole time to try to find out something about typhoid fever, in a laboratory set up, since there was no regular one, of all places — in the morgue. There in the sickening vapors of the deadhouse Bruce puttered in snatched moments, got typhoid fever himself, nearly died, and before he got thoroughly better was sent out as medical officer to a filibustering expedition got up to "protect" a few thousand square miles more of territory for the Queen. It looked like the end for him. Hely-Hutchinson's wires got tangled; there seemed no chance ever to work at nagana again. When the expedition had pierced a couple of hundred miles into the jungle, all of the horses and mules of this benevolent little army up and died, and what was left of the men

[1] **Trypanosomes:** minute parasites adapted to living in the blood of animals.

had to try to hoof it back. A few came out, and David Bruce was among the lustiest of those gaunt hikers.

Nearly a year had been wasted. But who can blame those natural enemies of David Bruce, the high authorities, for keeping him from research? They looked at him; they secretly trembled at his burliness and his mustaches and his air of the Berserker.[1] This fellow was born for a soldier! But they were so busy, or forgot, and presently Hely-Hutchinson did his dirty work again, and in September, 1895, Bruce and his wife got back to Ubombo to try to untangle the knot of how nagana gets from a sick animal to a healthy one. And here Bruce followed, for the first time, Theobald Smith around that corner. Like Theobald Smith, Bruce was a man to respect and to test folk hunches and superstitions. He respected the beliefs of folks; himself he had no fancy super-scientific thoughts and never talked big words — yes, he respected such hunches; but he must test them!

" It is the tsetse flies cause nagana," said some experienced Europeans. " Flies bite domestic animals and put some kind of poison in them."

" Nagana is caused by big game," said the wise Zulu chiefs and medicine men. " The discharges of the buffalo, the quagga, and waterbuck, the koodoo — these contaminate the grass and the watering places, so it is horses and cattle are hit by the nagana."

" But why do we always fail to get our horses safe through the fly country — why is nagana called the fly disease? " asked the Europeans.

" Why, it's easy to get animals through the fly belt so long as you don't let them eat or drink! " answered the Zulus.

Bruce listened and then proceeded to try out both ideas. He took good healthy horses and tied heavy canvas bags round their noses so they couldn't eat nor drink; he led them down the hill to the pleasant-looking midday hell in the mimosa thickets; here he kept them for hours. While he watched to see they didn't slip their nose bags, swarms of pretty brown and gold tsetses buzzed around them, flopped onto the kicking horses, and in twenty seconds swelled themselves up into bright balloons of blood. The world seemed made of tsetse flies, and Bruce waved his arms. " They were enough to drive one mad! " he told me, thirty years afterward. I can see him talking to those pests in the language of a dock-foreman, to the wonder of his Zulus. Day after day this procession of Bruce, the Zulus, and the experimental horses went down into the thorns, and each afternoon, as the sun went down behind Ubombo, Bruce and his migrating experiment grunted and sweated back up the hill.

Then, in a little more than fifteen days, to the delight of Bruce and his wife, the first of those horses who had served as a fly restaurant turned up seedy in the morning and hung his head. And in the blood of this horse appeared the vanguard of the microscopic army of finned wee devils that tussled so intelligently with the red blood cells.

So it was with every horse taken down into the mimosa, and not one of them had eaten a blade of grass nor had one swallow of water down there; one and all, they died of the nagana.

" Good, but it is not proved yet, one way or another," said Bruce. " Even if the horses didn't eat or drink, they may have *inhaled* those trypanosomes from the air — that's the way the greatest medical authorities think malaria is passed on from one man to the next, though it sounds like rot to me." But for Bruce nothing was rot until experiment proved it rot. " Here's the way to see! " he cried. " Instead of

[1] **Berserker:** a strong, fierce warrior of Norse legend.

taking the horses down, I'll bring the flies up."

So he bought more healthy horses, kept them safe on the hill thousands of feet above the dangerous plain; then once more he went down the hill — how that man loved to hunt, even for such idiotic game as flies! — and with him he took a decoy horse. The tsetses landed on the horse; Bruce and the Zulus picked them off gently, hundreds of them, and stuck them into an ingenious cage made of muslin. Then back up the hill, to clap the cage buzzing with flies onto the back of a healthy horse. Through a clever glass window in one of the cage sides they watched the greedy brutes make their meal by sticking their stingers through the muslin. And in less than a month it was the same with these horses, who had never eaten, nor drunk, nor even inhaled the air of the plain — every one died of the nagana.

How they worked, Bruce and his wife! They post-mortemed dead horses; they named a sick horse "The Unicorn" and tried to keep him alive with arsenic. To find out how long a tsetse fly can carry the trypanosomes on his stinger they put cages of flies on sick dogs and then at intervals of hours, and days, let them feed on healthy ones. They fed dying heifers hot pails of coffee; mercifully they shot dogs thinned by the nagana to sad bags of bones. Mrs. Bruce sterilized silk threads to dip in blood swarming with trypanosomes, then sewed these threads under the hides of healthy dogs to find out how long such blood might remain deadly. There was now no doubt the tsetse flies, and only the flies, could carry the nagana, and now Bruce asked:

"But where do the tsetses of the plain *get* the trypanosomes they stick into cows and horses? In those fly belts there are often no horses or cattle sick with nagana, for months. Surely the flies [he was wrong here] can't stay infected for months — it must be they get them from the wild animals, the big game!" That was a possibility after his heart. Here was a chance to do something else than sit at a microscope. He forgot instantly about the more patient, subtle jobs that demanded to be done — teasing jobs, for a little man, jobs like tracing the life of the trypanosomes in the flies. "The microbes must be in game!" and he buckled on his cartridge belt and loaded his guns. Into the thickets he went and shot Burchell's zebras; he brought down koodoos and slaughtered waterbucks. He slashed open the dead beasts and from their hot hearts sucked up syringes full of blood, and jogged back up the hill with them. He looked through his microscopes for trypanosomes in these bloods, but didn't find them. But there was a streak of the dreamer in him. "They may be there, too few to see," he muttered, and to prove they were there he shot great quantities of the blood from ten different animals into healthy dogs. So he discovered that the nagana microbes may lurk in game, waiting to be carried to gentler beasts by the tsetse. So it was Bruce made the first step toward the opening up of Africa.

And Hely-Hutchinson saw how right he had been about David Bruce. "'Ware the tsetse fly," he told his farmers. "Kill the tsetse fly; clear the thickets in which it likes to breed; drive out, exterminate the antelope from which it sucks the trypanosomes." So Bruce began ridding Africa of nagana.

Then came the Boer War. Bruce and Mrs. Bruce found themselves besieged in Ladysmith[1] with nine thousand other Englishmen. There were thirty medical officers in the garrison, but not one surgeon. With each whine and burst of the

[1] **Ladysmith:** a city in South Africa, besieged by the Boers during the Boer War.

shells from the Boers' "Long Tom" the rows of the wounded grew; there were moanings, and a horrid stench from legs that should be amputated. "Think of it! Not one of those medicos could handle a knife! Myself, I was only a laboratory man," said Bruce, "but I had cut up plenty of dogs and guinea pigs and monkeys — so why not soldiers? There was one chap with a bashed-up knee . . . well, they chloroformed him; and while they were at that, I sat in the next room reading Treve's *Surgery* on how to take out a knee joint. Then I went in and did it. We saved his leg." So Bruce became Chief Surgeon, and fought and starved, nearly to death, with the rest. What a boy that Bruce was! In 1924 in Toronto, in a hospital as he lay propped up, a battered bronchitic giant, telling me this story, his bright eye belied his skin wrinkled and the color of old parchment; and there was no doubt he was as proud of his slap-dash surgery and his sulky battles with the authorities as of any of his discoveries in microbe hunting. He chuckled through phlegm that gurgled deep in his ancient air tubes, "Those red-tape fellows — I always had to fight their red tape, until at last I got too str-r-rong for them!"

Presently, two years after Ladysmith, he became stronger than they. And they came asking him to hunt microbes.

For death was abroad on the shores of Lake Victoria Nyanza, in Central Africa, on the Equator. It crept; it jumped; it kept popping up in new villages; it was in a way a very merciful death — though slow — for it was without pain, turning from a fitful fever into an unconquerable laziness strange to see in the busy natives of the lake shore; it passed, this death, from lethargy into a ridiculous sleepiness that made the mouths of the Negroes fall open while they ate; it went at last from such a drowsiness into a delicious coma — no waking from this! — and into a horrible unnatural coldness that merged with the chill of the grave. Such was the African sleeping sickness. In a few years it had killed hundreds of thousands of the people of Uganda; it had sent brave missionaries to meet their God, and English colonial administrators home to their final slumber. It was turning the most generous soil on earth back into an unproductive preserve for giraffes and hyenas. The British Colonial Office was alarmed; shareholders began to fear for their dividends; natives — those who were left — began to leave their villages of shaggy, high-pitched, thatch-roofed huts. And the scientists and doctors?

Well, the scientists and doctors were working at it. Up till now the wisest ones were as completely ignorant of what was this sleeping death as the blackest trader in bananas was ignorant. No one could tell how it stole from a black father to his neighbor's dusky pickaninnies. But now the Royal Society sent out a commission made up of three searchers; they sailed for Uganda and began researches with the blood and spinal fluid of unhappy black men doomed with this drowsy death.

They groped; they sweat in the tropic heat; they formed different opinions: one was pretty sure a curious long worm that he found in the black men's blood was the cause of this death; a second had no definite opinion that I know of; the third, Castellani, thought at first that the wee villain back of the sleeping death was a streptococcus, like the microbe that causes sore throats.

That was way off the truth; but Castellani had the merit of working with his hands, trying this, trying that, devising ingenious ways of looking at the juices of those darkies. And so one day — by one of those unpredictable stumbles that lie at the bottom of so many discoveries — Castellani happened on one of those nasty little old friends of David Bruce, a trypanosome. From inside the backbone of a deadly, drowsy black man Castellani had got fluid — to look for streptococcus. He put that fluid into a centrifuge — that works like a cream separator — to try to whirl possible microbes down to the bottom of the tube in the hope to find streptococcus. Down the barrel of his microscope Castellani squinted at a drop of the gray stuff from the bottom of the fluid and saw —

A trypanosome, and this beast was very much the same type of wiggler David Bruce had fished out of the blood of horses dying of nagana. Castellani kept squinting; found more trypanosomes, in the spinal juices and even in the blood of half a dozen doomed darkies.

That was the beginning; for if Castellani had not seen them, told Bruce about them, they might never have been found.

Meanwhile the smolder of the sleeping death broke into a flare that threatened English power in Africa. And the Royal Society sent the veteran David Bruce down there, with the trained searcher Nabarro, with Staff Sergeant Gibbons, who could do anything from building roads to fixing a microscope. Then, of course, Mrs. Bruce was along; she had the title of assistant, but Bruce paid her fare.

They came down to Uganda, met Castellani. He told Bruce about the streptococcus and the trypanosomes. Back to the laboratory went these two. Microscopes were unpacked, set up; doomed darkies carried in. Heavy needles were jabbed into these sad people's spines. Castellani, the young Nabarro, and Mrs. Bruce bent over their microscopes to find the yes or no of the discovery of Castellani. There they sat, in this small room on the Equator, squinting down the barrels of their machines at a succession of gray nothingnesses.

A bellow from Bruce, "I've got one!" The rest crowd round, squint in turn, exclaim as they watch the writhing trypanosome poke his exploring whip about in the gray field of the lens. Then they go back to their places, to shout discovery in their turn. So it went, from breakfast till the swift dusk of evening. In every single sample of spinal fluid from each one of his more than forty sleeping-sickness patients, Bruce and his companions found those trypanosomes.

"But they may be in healthy people's spines, too!" said Bruce. Bruce knew that if he found them in healthy Negroes all this excitement would be only a wild-goose chase; he must prove they were to be found only in folks with sleeping sickness. But to get fluid out of healthy people's spines? Folks dopey from the sleeping death didn't mind it so much; but to jab one of those big needles into the back of healthy wide-awake colored people, who had no wish to be martyrs to science. . . . Can you blame them? It is no picnic having such a spear stuck into your spine. Then Bruce hit on a crafty scheme. He went to the hospital, where there was a fine array of patients with all kinds of diseases but no sleeping sickness; and then, flimflamming them into thinking the operation would do them good, this liar in the holy cause of microbe hunting jabbed his needles into the smalls of the backs of Negroes with broken legs and with headaches, and into their brothers or sisters who were suffering from yaws[1] or the itch. From all of them he got spinal fluid.

And it was a great success. Not one of these folks, who had no sleeping sickness, harbored a single trypanosome in the fluid of their spines. Maybe the operation did do them some good; but no matter, they had served their purpose. The trypano-

[1] **yaws:** a tropical skin disease.

some, Castellani and Bruce now knew, was the cause of sleeping sickness!

Now — and this is rare in the dreamers who find fundamental facts in science — Bruce was a fiend for practical applications, not poetically like Pasteur, for Bruce wasn't given to such lofty soarings nor was he practical in the dangerous manner of the strange genius Paul Ehrlich, a brilliant German scientist; but the moment he turned to the study of a new plague, Bruce's gray eyes would dart round, he would begin asking himself questions: What is the natural home of the virus of this disease? How does it get from sick to healthy? What is its fountain and origin? Is there anything *peculiar* in the way this sleeping sickness has spread?

That was the way he went at it now. He had discovered the trypanosome that was the cause. There were a thousand pretty little researches to tempt the scholar in him, but he brushed all these aside. Old crafty hand at searching that he was, he fished round in his memories, and came to nagana, and screwed up his eyes. "Is there anything peculiar about the way sleeping sickness is *located* in this country?" he pondered.

He sniffed around. With Mrs. Bruce he explored the high-treed shores of the lake, the islands, the rivers, the jungle. Then the common-sense eye which sees things a hundred searchers might stumble over and go by showed him the answer. It was strange — suspiciously strange — that sleeping sickness was only found in a very narrow strip of country along the water — only along the water, on the islands, up the river. Even by the Ripon Falls, where Victoria Nyanza gives herself up to the making of the Nile, there were cases of it, but never inland. That must mean some insect, a blood-sucking insect, which lives only near water must carry the disease. That was his guess; why, I cannot tell you. "Maybe it is a tsetse fly, a special one living only near lake shores and river-banks!"

So Bruce went around asking everybody about tsetse flies in Uganda. He inquired of local bug experts: no, they were sure tsetse flies could not live at an altitude above three thousand feet. He asked the native headmen, even the black Prime Minister of Uganda: sorry, we have a bloodsucking fly called Kivu; but there are no tsetse flies in Uganda.

But there must be!

And there were. One day as they walked through the Botanical Garden at Entebbe, Bruce pushing his bulky body between the rows of tropic plants ahead of his small wife, there was a glad shriek from her. "Why, David! There are two tsetses on your back!" That woman was a scientific Diana. She swooped on those two tsetses, and caught them, and gave them a practical pinch — just enough to kill them — and then showed them to her husband. They had been perched, ready to strike, within a few inches of his neck. Now they knew they were on the trail.

Hard work began in the laboratory; already Bruce had found an excellent experimental animal — the monkey — which he could put into a beautiful fatal sleep, just like that of a man, by injecting fluid from the spines of doomed Negroes. But now to catch tsetse flies. They armed themselves with butterfly nets and the glass-windowed cages they had invented in Zululand. Then these inseparable searchers climbed into canoes; lusty crews of black boys shot them across the lake. Along the banks they walked; it was charming in the shade there — but listen! Yes, there was the buzz of the tsetse. They tried to avoid being bitten. They were bitten, and stayed awake nights wondering what would happen; they went back to the laboratory and clapped the cages on the backs of monkeys. It was a good time for them.

That is the secret of those fine discoveries Bruce made. It was because he was a hunter, not only with his mind — but a bold, everlastingly curious, snouting hunter with his body too. If he had sat back and listened to those missionaries, or stayed listening to those bug experts, he would never have learned that Kivu was the Uganda name for the tsetse. He would never have found the tsetse. But he carried the fight to the enemy, and as for Mrs. Bruce — that woman was better than a third hand or two extra pairs of eyes for him.

Now they planned and did terrible experiments. Day after day they caused tsetse flies to feed on patients near to death (already too deep in sleep to be annoyed by the insects); they interrupted the flies in the midst of their meal and put the angry, half-satisfied cages of them on the backs of monkeys. With all the tenderness of high-priced nurses watching over Park Avenue babies they saw to it that only their experimental flies, and no chance flies from outside, got a meal off those beasts. Other searchers might have rolled their thumbs waiting to see what happened to the monkeys, but not Bruce.

He proceeded to call in a strange gang of coworkers to help him in one of the most amazing tests of all microbe hunting. Bruce asked for an audience from the high-plumed, gay-robed potentate Apolo Kagwa, Prime Minister of Uganda. He told Apolo he had discovered the microbe of the sleeping death which was killing so many thousands of his people. He informed him many thousands more already had the parasite in their blood and were doomed. " But there is a way to stop the ruin that faces your country, for I have reason to believe it is the tsetse fly — the insect you call Kivu — and *only* this insect that carries the poisonous germ from a sick man to a healthy one — "

The magnificent Apolo broke in. " But I cannot believe that is so. Kivu has been on the lake shore always, and my people have only begun to be taken by the sleeping sickness during the last few years."

Bruce didn't argue. He bluffed, as follows: " If you do not believe me, give me a chance to prove it to you. Go down, Apolo Kagwa, to the Crocodile Point on the lake shore, where Kivu swarms so. Sit on the shore there with your feet in the water for five minutes. Don't keep off the flies, and I'll promise you'll be a dead man in two years! "

The bluff was perfect. " What, then, is to be done, Colonel Bruce? " asked Apolo.

" Well, I must be dead sure I am right," Bruce told him. Then he showed Apolo a great map of Uganda. " If I'm right, where there is sleeping sickness there we will find tsetse flies too. Where there are no tsetse there should be no sleeping sickness."

So Bruce gave Apolo butterfly nets, and killing bottles, and envelopes; he gave directions about the exact way to set down all the facts, and he told how Apolo's darky minions might pinch the flies without getting stabbed themselves. " And then we will put our findings down on this map, and see if I'm right."

Apolo was nothing if not intelligent and efficient. He said he would see what could be done. There were bows and amiable formalities. In a jiffy the black Prime Minister had called for his head chief, the Sekibobo; and all the paraphernalia, with rigid directions, went from the Sekibobo to the lesser headmen, and from them down to the canoemen — the wheels of that perfect feudal system were set going.

Presently the envelopes began to pour in on Bruce and called him away from his monkey experiments. They cluttered the laboratory; they called him from his peerings into the intestines of tsetse flies, where he looked for trypanosomes. Rapidly, with perfectly recorded facts — most of them set down by intelligent blacks and some by missionaries — the envelopes came in. It was a kind of scientific coworking you would have a hard time finding among white folks, even white medical men. Each envelope had a grubby assorted mess of biting flies. They had a dirty time sorting them; but every time they found a tsetse, a redheaded pin went into that spot on the map — and if a report of "sleeping sickness present" came with that fly, a blackheaded pin joined it. From the impressive Sekibobo down to the lowest fly boy, Apolo's men had done their work with an automatic perfection. At last the red and black dots on the map showed that where there were tsetses there was the sleeping death, and where there were no tsetses there was no single case of sleeping sickness!

The job looked finished. The unhappy monkeys bitten by the flies which had sucked the blood of dying Negroes — these monkey's mouths fell open while they tried to eat their beloved bananas; they went to sleep and died. Other monkeys never bitten by flies — but kept in the same cages, eating out of the same dishes — those monkeys never showed a sign of the disease. Here were experiments as clean, as pretty as the best ones Theobald Smith had made.

But now for action! Whatever of the dreamer and laboratory experimenter there was in him — and there was much — those creative parts of David Bruce went to sleep, or evaporated out of him; he became the surgeon of Ladysmith once more, and the rampageous shooter of lions and killer of koodoos. To wipe out the sleeping sickness! That seemed the most brilliantly simple job now. Not that there weren't countless thousands of blacks with trypanosomes in their blood, and all these folks must die of course; not that there weren't buzzing billions of tsetses singing their hellish tune on the lake shore — but here was the point: *Those flies lived only on the lake shore!* And if they had no more sleeping-sickness blood to suck, then . . . And Apolo Kagwa was absolute Tsar of all Uganda. Apolo, Bruce knew, trusted him, adored him.

Now to wipe sleeping sickness from the earth!

To conference with Bruce once more came Apolo and the Sekibobo and the lesser chiefs. Bruce told them the simple logic of what was to be done.

"Of course, that can be done," said Apolo. He had seen the map. He was convinced. He made a dignified wave of the hand to his chiefs and gave a few words of explanation. So Bruce and Mrs. Bruce went back to England. Apolo gave his order, and then the pitiful population of black men and their families streamed inland out of the lake-shore villages, away — not to return for years, or ever — from those dear shady places where they and the long line of their forefathers had fished and played and bargained and begot their kind; canoes, loaded with mats and earthen pots and pickaninnies, set out (not to return) from the thickly peopled island, and the weird outlandish beating of the tom-toms no longer boomed across the water.

"Not one of you," commanded Apolo, "may live within fifteen miles of the lake shore; not one of you is to visit the lake again. Then the sleeping death will die out; for the fly Kivu lives only by the water, and when you are gone she will no longer have a single sick one from whom to suck the fatal poison. When all of our people who are now sick have died, you may go back — and it will be safe to live by the lake shore for always."

Without a word — it is incredible to us law-abiding folks — they obeyed their potentate.

The country around Lake Victoria Nyanza grew, in the frantic way tropical green things grow, back into the primordial jungle; crocodiles snoozed on the banks where big villages had been. Hippopotami waddled onto the shore and sniffed in the deserted huts. The tribes of the lake, inland, were happy, for no more of them came down with that fatal drowsiness. So Bruce began to rid Africa of sleeping sickness.

It was a triumph — in a time of great victories in the fight of men against death. The secret of the spread of malaria had been found in India and Italy. And as for yellow fever — it seemed as if the yellow jack was to be put to sleep for good. Great eminences of the medical profession pointed in speeches amid cheers to the deeds of medicine. The British Empire rang with hosannas for David Bruce. He was promoted colonel. He was dubbed Knight Commander of the Bath. Lady Bruce? Well, she was proud of him and stayed his assistant, obscurely. And Bruce still paid, out of his miserable colonel's salary, her fare on those expeditions they were always making.

Africa looked safe for the black men and open to the benevolent white men. But nature had other notions. She had cards up her sleeve. She almost never lets herself be conquered at a swoop, Napoleonically, as Bruce and Apolo (and who can blame them?) thought they had done. Nature was not going to let her vast specimen cabinet be robbed so easily of every last one of those pretty parasites, the trypanosomes of sleeping sickness. A couple of years passed; and suddenly the Kavirondo people, on the east shore of the lake, where sleeping death had never been — these folks began to go to sleep and not wake up. And there were disturbing reports of hunters coming down with sleeping sickness even in those places that should have been safe, in the country from which all human life had been moved away. The Royal Society sent out another commission (Bruce was busy with that affair of goat's milk giving Malta fever) and one of these new commissioners was a bright young microbe hunter, Tulloch. He went on a picnic one day to a nice part of the shore whose dark green was dotted with scarlet flowers. It must be safe there now, they thought; but a tsetse buzzed, and in less than a year Tulloch had drowsed into his last cold sleep. The commission went home.

Bruce — you would think he would be looking by this time for some swivel-chair, button-pressing job — packed his kit-bag and went back to Uganda to see what he had left out of those experiments that had looked so sure. He had gone off half-cocked, with that Napoleonic plan of moving a nation, but who can blame him? It had looked so simple, and how expect even the craftiest of the cheaters of nature to find out, in a year, every single nook where nature hides the living poisons to kill the presumptuous men who cheat her! Lady Bruce, as usual, went with him, and they found new epidemics of sleeping sickness flaring up in unwonted places. It was a miserable, discouraging business.

Bruce was a modest man who had no foolish vanity to tell him that his own theories were superior to brute facts. "My plan has been a washout," you can hear him grumbling. "Somewhere, aside from the human being, those tsetses must get the trypanosomes — maybe it's like the nagana; maybe they can live in wild beasts' blood, too."

Now if Bruce had theories that were a little too simple, he was, just the same, an exceedingly crafty experimenter; if he had a foolish faith in his experiments, he had the persistence to claw his way out of the bogs of disappointment that his simplicity and love of gorgeous deeds got him into. What a stubborn man he was! For, when you think of the menagerie of birds, beasts, fishes, and reptiles Uganda is, you wonder why he didn't pack his bags and start back for England. But no. Once more the canoeman paddled Bruce and his lady across to that tangled shore, and they caught flies in places where for three years no man had been. Strange experiments they made in a heat to embarrass a salamander; one laborious complicated record in his notes tells of two thousand eight hundred and seventy-six flies (which could never have bitten a human sleeping-sickness patient) fed on five monkeys, and two of these monkeys came down with the disease!

"The trypanosomes must be hiding in wild animals!" Bruce cries. So they go to the dangerous Crocodile Point and catch wild pigs and African gray and purple herons; they bleed sacred ibises and glossy ones; they stab and get blood from plovers and kingfishers and cormorants — and even crocodiles! Everywhere they look for those deadly, hiding, thousandth-of-an-inch-long wigglers.

They caught tsetse flies on Crocodile Point. See the fantastic picture of them there, gravely toiling at a job fit for a hundred searchers to take ten years at. Bruce sits with his wife on the sand in the middle of a ring of barebacked paddlers who squat round them. The tsetses buzz down onto the paddlers' backs. The fly boys pounce on them; hand them to Bruce, who snips off their heads, waves the buzzing devils away from his own neck, determines the sex of each fly caught, dissects out its intestine — and smears the blood in them on thin glass slides.

Washouts, most of these experiments; but one day, in the blood of a native cow from the Island of Kome, not hurting that cow at all but ready to be sucked up by the tsetse for stabbing under the skin of the first man it meets, Bruce found the trypanosome of sleeping sickness. He sent out word, and presently a lot of bulls and cows were driven up the hill to Mpumu by order of Apolo Kagwa. Bruce, himself in the thick of it, directed dusty fly bitings of these cattle — yes! there was no doubt the sleeping-sickness virus could live in them. Then there were scuffles in the hot pens with fresh-caught antelope. They were thrown; they were tied; Bruce held dying monkeys across their flanks and let harmless tsetses, bred in the laboratory, feed on the monkey and then on the buck.

"The fly country around the lake shore will have to be cleared of antelope too, as well as men, before the Kivu become harmless," Bruce said at last to Apolo.

And now the sleeping death really disappeared from the shores of Lake Victoria Nyanza.

The ten thousand smaller microbe hunters who work at lesser jobs today, as well as the dozen towering ones — all of them have to take some risk of death. But if the ten thousand smaller microbe hunters of today could by some chemistry be changed into death fighters like Bruce! There was something diabolical in the risks he took, and something yet more devilish in the way he could laugh — with a dry humor — and wish other microbe hunters might have died to prove some of his own theories. But he had a right to wish death for others.

"Can young tsetse flies, bred in the laboratory, inherit the sleeping-sickness trypanosome from their mothers?" Surely there was a chance of it (Theobald Smith's mother ticks bequeathed the Texas-fever microbe to their children). But analogies are for philosophers and lawyers. "*Are* artificially hatched young tsetses dangerous?" asks Bruce. "No!" he can answer. "For two members of the commission [modestly he does not say which two members] allowed hundreds of tsetse flies, bred in the laboratory, to bite them. And the result was negative."

But no man knew what the result would be before he tried. And the deaths from sleeping sickness (according to the best figures) are one hundred out of one hundred.

How he enjoyed hearing of other men trying to kill themselves to find out! His last African foray was in 1911 — he stayed until 1914. He was near sixty; his blacksmith's strength was beginning to crack from a nasty infection of his air tubes got from I know not what drenching rains or chills of high tropic nights. But a new form of sleeping sickness — terrible stuff that killed in a few months instead of years — had just broken out in Nyassaland and Rhodesia. There was a great scientific quarrel on. Was the trypanosome causing this disease some new beast just out of the womb of nature — or was it nothing else than Bruce's old parasite of nagana, tired of butchering only cows, dogs, and horses and now learning to kill men?

Bruce went to work at it. A German in Portuguese East Africa said, "This trypanosome is a new kind of bug!" Bruce retorted, "On the contrary, it is nothing but the nagana germ hopping from cows to men."

Then this German — his name was Taute — took the blood of an animal about to die of nagana and shot five cubic centimenters of it — it held millions of trypanosomes — under his own skin to prove the nagana parasite does not kill men. And he let scores of tsetse flies bite him — flies whose bellies and spit glands were crammed with the writhing microbes. He did these things to prove his point!

Was Bruce shocked at this? Listen to him, then. "It is a matter for some scientific regret that these experiments were not successful — though we can ill spare our bold and somewhat rash colleague — for then the question would have been answered. As it is, these negative experiments prove nothing. It may be that only one man in a thousand would become infected that way."

Merciless Bruce! Poor Taute! He tried conscientiously to kill himself, and Bruce says it is too bad he did not die. He made the ultimate gesture — surely the God of searchers will reward him — then Bruce (and he is right) criticizes the worth of Taute's lone desperate experiment!

Nyassaland was the last battlefield of Bruce against the sleeping sickness, and it was his most hopeless one. For here he found that the *Glossina morsitans* (that is the name of the tsetse carrier of the sickness) does not make its home only on the shores of lakes and rivers, but buzzes and bites from one end of Nyassaland to the other; there is no way of running away from it, no chance of moving nations out from under it here. Bruce stuck at it; he spent years at measurements of the lengths of trypanosomes — monotonous enough this work was to have driven a subway ticket chopper mad — he was trying to find out whether the nagana and this new disease were one and the same thing. He ended by not finding out, and he finished with this regret: that it was *at present* impossible to do the experiment to clinch the matter one way or the other.

That experiment was the injection of the nagana trypanosomes, not into one, or a hundred — but a thousand — human beings.

But there was grisly hope left in the old Viking. "*At present* it is impossible," he said, while he believed that somewhere, somewhen, men may be found, in the mass, who will be glad to die for truth.

But when great armies of men so offer themselves, to fight death, just as they now delight to fight each other, it will be because they are led on by captains such as David Bruce.

THINK BACK OVER WHAT YOU HAVE READ

Admiring the Spirit of Bruce

1. What examples can you cite of Bruce's indefatigable patience?

2. What attitude did he take toward his own mistakes?

3. How large a part of his success was due to his independence — not to say disobedience — of spirit? What examples of "taking the law in his own hands" can you cite? How do you justify each bold disregard of objections? To what extent was he willing to conform to rules and regulations? Did his independence excite antagonism? Why or why not?

4. What examples can you cite to show that Bruce was not only a scientist but a man of quick decision and of vigorous action as well?

5. What picture do you form of Bruce as a married man? What kind of husband was he? To what qualities does his congenial workaday partnership with his wife testify?

6. What instances show that Bruce was essentially an explorer? What qualities does he share with Byrd, in spite of the distance between their two fields?

Respecting the Sleuthing Methods of Science

7. What part does "muddling" play in scientific discovery? What part does it play in unraveling a murder mystery? What does this suggest?

8. What realization did this biography give you of the microbe hunter at work? What sense of microscopic observation did you get? With what brief passages can you illustrate your impression of Bruce's workday?

9. What part does asking questions of oneself play in scientific discovery? With what questions did Bruce set his mind to work? What does this suggest to you as a practical hint for thinking? In what particular questions did Bruce resemble Sherlock Holmes on the scent of a criminal?

10. To what fantastic limits did Bruce's labors go? What grim picture do you see in your imagination of Bruce and his wife catching the deadly tsetse flies? of Bruce infecting squirming monkeys and kicking horses, and so forth?

11. What ingenious devices did Bruce use to establish scientific proof? How, for example, did he prove that the trypanosomes of sleeping sickness did not live in the spinal fluid of healthy natives? that animals did not contract nagana from eating or drinking? What other facts did he establish? by what means?

Appreciating the Style of the Biographer

12. What is De Kruif's attitude toward Bruce? How can you tell? With what brief passages can you illustrate your points?

13. What method did De Kruif use to secure at least part of his material? What comment are you led to make about this method?

14. What tribute does De Kruif pay to Mrs. Bruce? By what kind of suggestions does he do it? What passages can you quote to show his obvious admiration for her? What passages indicate, however, that for all his admiration for her she must accept a subordinate place in the biography of her husband? To what quality in structure does this testify?

15. What examples of swift narrative can you cite from the biography: of De Kruif's ability to deal with the past without slowing up his narrative? of his ability to handle explanation without long, tedious digression?

16. What passages of effective description can you quote? What sentences gave you a sense of horror at the pitiful ravages of nagana? What glimpses of Africa did you receive from your reading? What sentences made the microbe loom large in your imagination? What possibilities for a story of horror would Poe find in this biography?

For Ambitious Students

17. *The lure of science.* If you are interested in the great work that science is doing for the good of mankind, you will find many thrilling stories in these books by Paul de Kruif: *Microbe Hunters, Men against Death, Hunger Fighters.*

18. *The fascination of the microscope.* Perhaps a group of students familiar with the operation of a microscope will borrow one from the science department of your school and permit the class to see for themselves a magnified germ. What are your impressions?

THE MYSTERY OF MIGRATION

by Alan Devoe (1909–)

The fascination of nature study arises from the fact that no matter how much you learn there is always more that you do not know and that lures you on to further discoveries. Thus life is never dull to scientists. You will find the following essay, written by a well-known naturalist, as interesting as a mystery story. After you have read it, you will never again see migrating birds without thinking of the marvelous instinct that controls their flight.

THEY ARE gone now. No robins carol from the fence posts; no medley of catbird tunes issues from the blackberry tangles; no woodcocks rise on whirring wings from our swamplands and marshes. The populace of birds is now meager and tuneless. Once again the annual mystery has come about. Once again the summer birds have vanished.

It is a phenomenon older than the memory of man. Ages ago Ojibways and Pequots [1] tilted bronze faces to the sun to watch the wild geese go honking southward, and tribal storytellers invented legends to explain the mystery. White men of science wrote solemn monographs asserting that in winter the birds retired to hollow trees, to hibernate until spring like woodchucks, and so erudite a man as Dr. Samuel Johnson [2] supposed that the English swallows spent the winter sleeping in the river mud of the Thames. The theories were innumerable and unconfirmed. They still are. We are not now quite so naïve, of course, as to fancy that the birds spend the winter asleep in caves or river bottoms, and we know quite well that they migrate to warmer climates. We have checked their routes, and clocked their arrivals and departures, and graphed their journeyings with great accuracy. And, having done this, we can still only stand awed and wondering. What impulse is abroad on autumn nights to tell these orioles and phoebes and sandpipers that the time for traveling is at hand? What secret inner knowledge guides these millions of wings on their long intricate courses? It is not known.

The preparations for migration begin long before the coming of the fall. They begin, in a real sense, with the molt, in latter summer when the care of the fledglings is over; for it is then that worn, frayed feathers are replaced by new ones and the bird's light-boned body acquires fresh buoyance. Like many another happening in fields and forests, the molting of the birds is so casual and unspectacular an event that hardly one man in a thousand even remarks its occurrence; but it deserves rank among the minor miracles. Two feathers, and two feathers only, are shed at one time, and they are shed with perfect symmetry. The middle feather of each wing is the first to go. When the new, replacement feathers for these gaps have achieved half their growth, another pair of quills loosens and is shed. With perfect precision the process continues until a whole new plumage has come into being. So gradual is the process, so nicely contrived, that at no time is more than a single pair of feathers missing; at no time is the bird's flight mechanism unbalanced or impaired. And in the case of certain of our species the miracle is of an even more arresting kind. There is the metamorphosis, for instance, which the male scarlet tanagers undergo. Before the moltingtime their flame-red plumage affords one of the gaudiest colors in our countryside. When the molt has ended, they are arrayed in dingy green. It will hide them, on their southward flight, from the sharp, preying eyes of hawks.

[1] **Ojibways and Pequots:** tribes of American Indians. [2] **Dr. Samuel Johnson:** a great literary man and scholar of the eighteenth century, author of the first English dictionary.

Photos, Margaret Bourke-White from Life Magazine

SCIENCE IS THE GREAT ENEMY OF SUPERSTITION. The routing of false belief by dependable knowledge is the thrilling story told by these pictures. Inch by inch the test tube and the telescope are triumphing over magic and superstition. You will meet this issue in "We Aren't Superstitious," and will come across it again in *Silas Marner*.

Can you imagine the man at the telescope (*right*) seriously "thanking his lucky stars" for good fortune? Can you imagine the trained observers of the sky who look out from the silver domes above regarding a meteor as an ill omen?

WITCHCRAFT, SORCERY,

Superstitious persons believe in cures by magic or blame sickness and pain on some witch and her imps (*left*) or the evil eye. In contrast, the young scientist (*below*) is determining in the laboratory whether a patient has received the right amount of a powerful new drug, sulfanilamide, for a cure.

British Museum *Ewing Galloway*

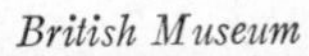

AND TEST TUBES

Man no longer merely *imagines* the cause and cure of disease; he submits his guesses to laboratory test. A technician (*right*) is studying a disease germ in a throat culture in order to determine suitable treatment. The crystal-gazer (*below*) pretends to find the answers to his client's problems in a globe of glass. Note the similar globular shape of the crystal and the technician's liter flask. How different, though, is the use made of them!

Photos, Ewing Galloway

Photos, Culver

SUPERSTITION WINS OVER TRUTH. In the picture above you see T. H. Mattison's painting of the trial of George Jacobs of Salem for witchcraft. In earlier times hysterical women were brought before a magistrate and sometimes sentenced to death as witches (*below*).

"The world is not yet free from superstition," says the author of "We Aren't Superstitious." What superstitions exist today?

There is a second preparation for the great autumn flight, and it consists of smaller flights in the nature of trials. Ever since July the adult male robins have been leading their fledglings to communal roosting places, usually deep-hidden in the leafy woods, and the grackles and swallows and starlings have similarly massed together in tremendous hordes. At every daybreak the great flocks issue forth; and all day they wheel and veer together through the autumn sky, returning at nightfall to the place of their communal sleep. This is the time when wings are trained and strengthened, when flight patterns [1] are established and co-ordinated, when there is perfected that deep and subtle mass harmony of motion which no scientist can pretend to understand. Uncountable thousands of gulls, of swifts, of cowbirds are learning one of the most ancient and most unfathomable techniques in nature.

There is a third and final preparation. It is the same preparation which skunks and bears and woodchucks make before their winter sleep. It is the taking on of surplus nourishment, the building of a reserve of fat. In obedience to a dim behest the flycatchers now enormously increase their consumption of tree hoppers and crickets, the tanagers hunt crane flies more voraciously than ever, and the dried weed seeds in man's pastures and gardens are stripped by flocks of finches and sparrows. The birds are insuring that they shall have a reservoir of strength on which to draw should there be a scarcity of food along their flight line. If the findings of dissectionists [2] are significant, the tiny brains in these small feathered skulls can hardly be capable of shrewd foresighted reasoning or, indeed, of any clear prevision of the journey ahead. The urge which moves them must have another source than mind. No man, yet, can give it any name.

[1] **flight patterns:** When birds fly in large numbers, they fly in well-established formations.
[2] **dissectionists:** those who dissect animals to discover scientific facts about them.

In late July the bobolinks vanish. They are among the first to go. The route of their travels has been fully mapped, and it is known that they are on the wing for nearly two months before they reach the small patch of river-watered jungle which for inscrutable reasons they deem the most suitable wintering place. They pass through South Carolina in the latter part of August; at the turn of the month, through Florida; in September they are in Cuba. Sometimes they cover four hundred miles in a single night, and always they press southward — down the Andes, across the Amazon, over the great Brazilian plains. When at last they halt, it is in the marshlands on the upper Paraguay River.

The departure of the bobolinks is followed presently, in latter August and throughout September, by the going of the flycatchers, the vireos, the warblers. Our autumn woods are thronged then with voyaging companies of birds. By October the last of them has passed and disappeared, and by November there have arrived to take their places such winter visitants as juncos and tree sparrows, crossbills and pine grosbeaks — a colorless and relatively songless little band, but hardily equipped for clinging to frozen sumac stalks in the whipping January wind and foraging in snow-drifted pastures for stray thistle seeds. They have nested and passed the summer to the north of us, some of them as far north as Hudson Bay and the Arctic coast, and they will return to those bleak regions before our first hepaticas bloom.

Prodigious as are the travels of the birds — the tiny blackpoll warblers voyaging five thousand miles, the scimitar-winged[1] nighthawks migrating from the Yukon to Argentina — the rate of speed is in most cases not extremely high. The average is usually some thirty or forty miles a day, and on the return flights in the spring may be hardly more than twenty. The trek is leisurely and often interrupted, with side excursions to feeding grounds en route and sometimes total rests for several days. But sometimes, too, there are flights of five hundred miles without a single pause, as when the ruby-throated hummingbirds cross the Gulf of Mexico to Yucatan, and it is known that the golden plovers which fly from Alaska to Hawaii cover the whole span of two thousand miles without a respite.

Men used to be puzzled by the fact that, although the migrating birds must number many millions, only occasional flocks are seen passing overhead. We know now why it is. We know that only the swiftest travelers — those species that need have no fear of hawks — undertake to fly by day. The rest fly only in the night. On a night in autumn when the moon is full it is possible to watch with field glasses the endless passing, high above the earth, of feathered legions. It is even possible, if the watcher be in a woods or other quiet place, to hear faintly the remote music of the flight — the soft whistle of thrushes, the thin fluting of woodcocks. It is not an experience that the listener readily forgets.

Why do the birds migrate at all? We shall have to be very much wiser than at present before we know. Perhaps it began in the glacial era, when the Arctic ice fields advanced southward; perhaps it is chiefly a physiological problem, subtly allied to periodic changes in the food supply. By what sense, or combination of senses, do thrushes and snipe and meadow larks find their way unerringly along complex thousand-mile routes which no man could possibly follow without directional instruments, and what inner bidding moves the individual members of the flocks to wheel and turn and dip in unbroken unison?

It has been supposed, in answer to the first question, that perhaps the great mountain ranges and watercourses are the guides; and on the second question some ornithologists[2] have theorized that perhaps the birds possess — as almost certainly the ant world does — some sense that is outside our human ken entirely.

This much only can we say with surety: that every fall and every spring the woods and sky present us, for the looking and the listening, with a magic pageantry of beating wings and with a reminder — not unwelcome in a time as bitterly confused as ours — that the ancient unknowable harmonies of the universe still endure.

THINK BACK OVER WHAT YOU HAVE READ

1. What explanation was given in olden times to account for the disappearance of birds in the winter season? What facts do we now know about that disappearance?

2. In what three ways do birds prepare for their autumn migration? In what ways are these preparations mysterious? Which one of these strikes you as most remarkable?

3. What examples of co-operation among birds do you find in this essay?

4. What does this essay tell you about the distances flown by migrating birds? about the rate of speed? Trace on a map the flights mentioned and estimate the distances.

5. How many of the birds mentioned in this essay do you know? Can you describe them?

6. Be prepared to tell the class about the habits of any birds that you have especially observed. Are any of those habits mysterious? Can you find any explanation for them?

7. Since the Southern Hemisphere has hot

[1] **scimitar-winged:** with wings shaped like scimitars, Oriental swords with curved blades.

[2] **ornithologists:** those who make a special study of birds.

and cold seasons, just as the Northern Hemisphere does, can you explain why many birds fly deep into South America as cold weather approaches?

8. What explanation can you give for the fact that, though millions of birds migrate, " only occasional flocks are seen passing overhead "?

9. What theories have been advanced to answer the question, Why do the birds migrate at all?

10. In what particular respect do birds prove more capable than human beings? What explanations have been given for this superiority?

For Ambitious Students

11. Compile a special annotated bibliography of magazine articles which deal with the mystery of migration to be used in a science class, perhaps, by a group of students especially interested in birds.

12. Read Constance Rourke's *Audubon* and report to the class on the personality of this great bird lover.

13. Give an oral report on " Bird Habits That I Have Observed."

THE POPOVER STARS

by E. E. Slosson (1865–1929)

We take stars overhead at night more or less for granted. To our senses — stirred by the poet — they are pinpricks of light. " Pinpricks, indeed! " exclaims the scientist. " They are blazing suns."

A sun? Did you know that there is more than one sun in the sky? What is a sun, anyway? Perhaps you had better find out. The following essay will help you.

E. E. Slosson was a notable writer on scientific subjects. Throughout his long career as scientist and author it was his practice to tell of science in simple language so that all who read could understand even the most difficult subject matter. " The Popover Stars " is an excellent example of his work.

IN THE Washington hotels they have a curious custom. A Negro boy wanders about the dining room with a curious tin box slung from his shoulders. When I saw him first passing from table to table and holding out the box to each diner in turn, I thought he was collecting contributions for the Armenians or Chinese or some other sufferers; and I felt in my pocket for the smallest coin that would rattle satisfactorily. But when he came to me he opened the tin contraption, and I saw that I was expected to take out something instead of to put in something. I stuck in my hand and pulled out a popover. A popover is a kind of hollowhearted muffin. It is very light, and one can eat a lot of them without getting enough calories to upset his trial balance; and, what's a wonder, they are not charged for on the bill, no matter how often the boy with the hatbox comes around or how many you take at a time. The popover is constructed on the model of a dirigible, a thin silky shell blown out from the inside by some hot gas.

While I was ruminating over the popover, I was struck by its resemblance to the giant stars that I had been reading about. These, like the popover, are not so substantial as they seem, for they, too, are puffed out by some internal expansive agency. But these stars have not any crust like the popovers and their dough is not sticky, so that the puzzle is to find out why they do not either fly to pieces or fall together.

For instance, consider the big red star that the astronomers know as Betelgeuse in Orion,[1] but which the vulgar call " Beetlejuice in O'Ryan." If you need an introduction to Betelgeuse, ask your grandmother to point him out to you. For in her day every respectable person was supposed to know the names of the constellations and the cabinet officers.[2] The

[1] **Orion:** a large constellation. [2] **cabinet officers:** members of the President's cabinet, who are the heads of the executive departments of the federal government.

younger generation does not seem to care about either. But however indifferent you may be to the heavenly bodies, you probably can recognize at sight two constellations — the Big Dipper and the three stars that form the Belt of Orion. Now, Betelgeuse is the Alpha or leading star in Orion and lies in the giant's shoulder, so that you can find it even though you may not have a grandmother handy to use as a star finder.

When Betelgeuse was measured on Mount Wilson[1] by means of Michelson's interferometer[2] in 1920, it was found to be about two hundred and fifty million miles in diameter, almost big enough to fill the orbit of Mars and allow the earth, Venus, and Mercury[3] to travel around their regular orbits inside. Perhaps our sun was about that size in its younger and stronger days before Mars had seceded and established its independence. But since then the sun has shrunk so that it would take about thirty million suns to fill up Betelgeuse.

And then there is a bright star in Scorpion[4] so red that the Greeks named it Antares,[5] the antagonist[6] of Mars; but they are not to be compared in bulk, for Antares is about four hundred million miles in diameter and, therefore, about seventy million times larger in volume than our sun.

But we must not allow ourselves to be overawed by the red giants. They are bigger than the mind of man may conceive, but they are not so substantial as the body of man. The density of the sun is only a quarter of the density of the earth, but these stars are more tenuous still. They are merely giant gasbags — minus the bag. They are lighter than air, in some cases a thousand times lighter, more like what we call a vacuum.

Our wise youngsters will not be content with the rimes of old Mother Goose but will demand a new version something like this:

> Twinkle, twinkle, giant star,
> I know exactly what you are,
> An incandescent ball of gas
> Condensing to a solid mass.
>
> Twinkle, twinkle, giant star,
> I need not wonder what you are,
> For seen by spectroscopic ken
> You're helium and hydrogen.[7]

For the stars reverse the rules of plants and animals. They grow smaller as they grow older. The red giants are the infants of the stellar world. As they settle down, they shrink.

On the start the stars are reduced to their elements; more than that, for the elements themselves are reduced to their electrical components, the protons and electrons, mere fragments of atoms. The attraction of gravitation acts upon these flying particles, keeping them together in great gaseous globes and drawing them together with smaller solid spheres.

Here the question naturally arises: Why do not the particles come together at once? Why do they stay up (that is, out) instead of falling down (that is, in)? Why do the giant stars remain so swollen for untold millions of years? Gravity is all the time pulling the particles to a common center. What force keeps them apart?

The answer that is now given to this question would have been thought ridiculous to a former generation. For the an-

[1] **Mount Wilson:** a mountain in California on top of which is one of the largest observatories in the world. [2] **Michelson's interferometer:** an attachment to a telescope, invented by the great physicist Albert A. Michelson, used to measure the diameters of stars. [3] **Mars, Venus, Mercury:** planets. [4] **Scorpion:** a southern constellation. [5] **Antares:** In Greek mythology the war god (called Mars by the Romans) was named Ares. The prefix *anti* in Greek means like; therefore, Antares means like Mars. So called because both are red in color. [6] **antagonist:** rival.

[7] **helium and hydrogen:** two gases.

swer is that the stars are kept swollen out by the pressure of the light inside of them.

Now, we did not use to think of light's exerting any pressure, for we could not conceive of light's having anything like weight, inertia, or momentum. For these were properties of matter, and light was classed with heat and electric radiations as energy. In those days — away back in the last century — a very strict line was drawn between matter and energy. But now we know that when a sunbeam strikes the earth it gives it a push just as dropping a stone on it does. The force of the impact of light rays is infinitesimal, but upon such minute particles as make up the giant stars it must have a perceptible effect. The radiant energy from the outer layers of the star streams off unrestricted into empty space. A beam of it may reach our earth after several centuries of travel. But the light and heat from the interior parts of the star, radiating straightaway in all directions, cannot get out so easily; for the ray strikes against the particles above and is driven back in a new direction, only to run up against another particle and be again deflected. In the course of time, hundreds of years perhaps, the imprisoned ray may find its way out of the maze, since there is plenty of space between the particles of the gaseous star, but only after many rebuffs. The rays at such high temperatures as the stars are of very high frequency vibration, more like the X rays, which will lose half their power in penetrating a distance of eight inches through the air. So if the star has the density of air, the rays would generally get tired out before they have gone many inches.

But every time a ray is turned back it gives a kick to the particle that checked it on its outward way. These accumulated kicks keep the particles from crowding in to the center as fast as they otherwise might. It is as if a strong hot wind were blowing outward from within the star. The heat comes from within, not from without as with the popovers in the oven. The source of the heat is surmised to be formation of heavier atoms than the primeval hydrogen.

It is only as the radiant light and heat escape into outer space that the particles, freed from its interference, can settle down comfortably together and cool off. But this takes a long time, for the radiation in attempting to escape has set the particles into more rapid motion; and as they draw nearer together they jostle one another more frequently, and this increases their agitation. So a gaseous star at first gets hotter as it contracts, its temperature rising from three thousand to ten thousand degrees centigrade and its color changing from red to blue. Then as it loses heat it shrinks and solidifies and runs back to red and finally becomes black and cold.

Our sun must be classed as a late yellow dwarf, though that sounds like a variety of pea. He is gradually becoming redder in the face; but it is the rubicund visage of old age, not the rosy flush of youth.

But let us not be ashamed of our little old sun. If we measure by mass instead of mere girth, he can stand comparison with any of the starry host. He is not so puffed up as the younger stars, but he has more solidity and amounts to about as much on the whole. Even the heaviest and hottest of the stars, the bluish-white helium giants, are none more than eighteen times the mass of the sun, and some of the stars we see have less than a tenth of the sun's weight. It is better for us to have a sun that is in the cooling-off than in the heating-up stage, and it will be many millions of years before we need order our furs for an Eskimo existence to the end of time.

THINK BACK OVER WHAT YOU HAVE READ

Acquiring Interesting Information

1. What is a popover? In what way does a star resemble a popover? What important fact about stars does this comparison help you to understand?

2. With only words at your command, how would you tell someone how to locate Orion and the Big Dipper in the sky at night? What other stars, planets, and constellations referred to in the essay can you locate?

3. In your own language tell about the composition of the stars. Does the parody on "Twinkle, twinkle, little star" help your understanding?

4. How does time affect the size and color of the stars? Why?

5. Discuss the effect of light on the structure of a star.

6. Is the sun a young or an old star? How do you know?

7. How hot are the stars? What happens when they cool? Do you know what we call a star that has cooled?

8. Speaking of Betelgeuse, the author says that "perhaps our sun was about that size in its younger and stronger days before Mars had seceded and established its independence." What does this statement tell you about the origin of Mars?

Increase Your Power over Words

9. To understand this essay you should understand the meaning of the scientific terms mentioned. When you have read this list of words and their definitions, look back to see how they were used in the selection. If they are still not clear to you, no doubt your science teacher will explain them to you.

vacuum (page 322), a space from which most of the air or gas has been eliminated.

proton (page 322), a particle, smaller than an atom, bearing a positive charge of electricity.

electron (page 322), a particle, smaller than an atom, bearing a negative charge of electricity.

atom (page 322), the smallest particle of an elementary substance that has all the chemical properties of the element.

inertia (page 323), tendency to remain in a state of rest; idleness.

momentum (page 323), a word describing how long a body will move against a given resistance before it stops.

density (page 322), the relation of the mass of a substance to its volume (bulk or size).

The Challenge of Today

AMERICA

by Dorothy Thompson (1894–   )

Are you old enough to be interested in your government or should you wait until you can vote? Even in countries where people have less freedom than we Americans, the youth are taught to take great pride in their government and its ways.

In the essay which follows, you will discover the reasons for one American's pride in her country and in its form of government — democracy. As you read, ask yourself whether or not democracy is worthy of the interest and loyalty of young Americans. If you believe that it is, perhaps you will agree with Dorothy Thompson, the author, that the success of America's experiment with democracy means hope and courage for the whole world.

IN THE preface to the 1855 edition of *Leaves of Grass*,[1] which is one of the greatest essays ever written in this country, on the poet and America, and the poet's relation to America, Walt Whitman wrote: "The largeness of Nature and of this nation were *monstrous* without a corresponding largeness and generosity of the spirit of the citizen." And without a

[1] **Leaves of Grass:** This book of poems by the American poet, Walt Whitman, remains today one of the greatest pieces of literature praising democracy.

breed of men full-sized, capable of universal sympathy, full of pride and affection and generosity, this country would indeed be monstrous. Here it lies in the center of the world, looking out on the two great oceans, looking out on the east to the old world, the cradle of white western civilization, looking out here on the west to a still older world, of still older races, out of which have come all the great religions and the deepest of human wisdoms. Here lives no race, but a race of races — a new kind of man bred out of many old kinds of men — in a climate more fierce, more radioactive, less temperate than that of Europe — in a climate that encompasses all climates. Here is no nation, but a nation of nations, a continent enclosing many different kinds of cultures and slowly making them into one culture.

When I think of America, I see it in a series of pictures — of moving pictures. I see the tight white and green farms of Vermont; the quick lush summers knee-deep in fern and field flowers; the narrow faces and the ironic grins of the Vermonters; the love of thrift and the strange inhibited hospitality of the people; the deep quiet lakes, the hills that are never too high for cattle to graze on them, the long, long bitter winters; small friendly communities where free, independent farmers still help build each other's barns and cut each other's wood; where the hired man calls the farmer by his first name; where the women from the farms and villages will come to cook for you, "to help out," but where you never can find anyone with the spirit or attitude of a servant.

I think of the incredible city of Manhattan — sometimes I think it too incredible to last — where the languages of a dozen nations are heard on the streets; where there are more Italians than in any Italian city except Rome; more Jews than there are in Jerusalem or in any other town on earth; where there are more Irish than there are in Dublin.

I think of the temperate and civilized — and uncivilized Carolinas; of Annapolis, the most beautiful eighteenth-century town in the whole English-speaking world; of the long quays of Savannah and the opulent laziness of the South, and the queer intellectual vigor that has always come up in the South whenever people thought that it was dead — from the South that has repeatedly given us our greatest statesmen.

I think of the great Southwest with a climate in which it is almost impossible to die. Texas, where you could settle a whole nation — yes, even now, when they say our frontiers are exhausted. And here, California, the earth's *Eldorado*,[1] bigger than all of Italy, with a population only one-seventh that of Italy; great glittery beaches out of which rise the towers of oil wells. The finest fruits on earth. The most enchanting American city: San Francisco.

Yes, this country would be monstrous without a corresponding largeness and generosity of the spirit of its citizens.

This country is only five generations old. In the days of our great-great-great-grandfathers it was still a howling wilderness, still unexplored. Today it is the most powerful single nation on the face of the earth.

This country has seven million farms valued at thirty-three billion dollars. It produces three and a half times as much corn as any other nation in the world. It produces more wheat than any other nation on earth except Soviet Russia. In the great industrial towns of the East and the Middle West — in twenty-six counties of this vast nation — it produces almost as much steel and four times as many auto-

[1] **Eldorado:** a rich region sought by the early Spanish conquerors of America.

mobiles as all the rest of the world combined.

It is so enormous and so powerful that gigantic public works are lost in it; they are done casually without any ballyhoo.[1] We have the greatest roads ever built since the Romans, and they were built without Fascism and without forced labor. In our lifetimes we have undertaken one of the greatest reclamation jobs ever done in the history of mankind. We have taken the Columbia and the Colorado Rivers and bent them, diverted them, stopped them, and pushed them around to create a whole new province in which men can settle and live, to create a lake so vast that it is an internal sea — and most people in the United States don't even know about it.

Here is the imagination which could conceive Wilson's dream of a world-state. Is it so fantastic? Is it more fantastic than what this country is? Here is the imagination which could conceive a frontier [2] on another nation, three thousand miles long and at all places vulnerable, and without a single fort. You think that is not something to have accomplished in history? Maybe it is the greatest thing that we have accomplished in history: the idea that two continental nations could live in permanent friendship.

And because of our geography, our position between two oceans, the largeness of the nation, the necessary wideness of sympathy and imagination, this country is of all countries in the world the most susceptible to what happens outside its own boundaries. Throughout our history, we have counseled isolation. Never in our history have we been isolationists. Upon this country beat all the ideas and all the conflicts of the whole world — for in this country are the peoples of the whole world, and in this country is a certain type of mind, which is impatient of boundaries; which is able to contemplate things near and very far — nothing too far.

For five generations people have been coming here with a dream. Sometimes the dream was grandiose.[3] The men who built New England came here with a dream of religious freedom. They came here as refugees, persecuted because they wouldn't bend their consciences. Acadians trekked [4] to Louisiana also to find a world in which they could be themselves. And some came here hoping to find gold in the streets. And some came because they were herded up in Hungarian and Slavic villages and brought over here like cattle under false pretentions, full of false hopes. But in all of their minds there was something common. For all of them there was a magnet. And the magnet was that they thought that here, in their own way, they could stand up, and look their neighbors in the face, and call themselves men, and not slaves.

And in five generations we have produced on this continent a race. You think there's not an American race? It's funny. Here we are made up of every stock in the world, and yet you can tell an American if you see him on the streets of Berlin, or Vienna, or Paris. What is an American? A typical American? An American is a fellow whose grandfather was a German forty-eighter who settled in Wisconsin and married a Swede, whose mother's father married an Englishwoman, whose son met a girl at college, whose mother was an Austrian and whose father was a Hungarian Jew and their son in the twentieth century right now is six feet tall — we are perhaps the tallest race on earth — goes to a state college, plays football, can't speak a word of any known lan-

[1] **ballyhoo:** can you guess the meaning of this slang term which supplied a need in our language and, for that reason, lived? [2] **frontier:** what frontier?

[3] **grandiose:** lavish — more than grand. [4] **trekked:** made a long journey.

guage except American, and is doubtful whether he ever had a grandfather.

This American has several characteristics. He doesn't like to take orders. If you speak to him in a friendly way, he will do almost anything you ask him — inside reason. If you once get him into a war, he is a very good fighter, but he has a very low opinion of war. He doesn't like to commit himself to stay forever in one place. He is restless, and an inveterate traveler in his own country or elsewhere if he can afford it. He is incredibly ingenious. He can devise more ways to save himself work than any other known race of human beings; that's probably why he has invented so many gadgets. He is enormously inventive. This is one of the greatest races of inventors ever produced. He was born free and he shows it by the way he moves. He is the best-nourished human being on the face of the earth. I know there are parts of this country where this is not true. It's got to be made better. But just the same the per capita consumption of food in the United States is higher than it is anywhere else, and the food that is consumed is more expensive and more various than it is anywhere else, taken for the country as a whole.

Now, what I am saying is this: we have got as far as we have, not only because we have a continent rich in resources — there are other continents rich in resources — we have got as far as we have because we produced a certain kind of human being and a certain type of mind. That human being is, first of all, a fellow with his eye on the future and not on the past. He is skeptical,[1] and yet he has eternal faith. He constantly tries to think why something doesn't work as well as it should and how you can make it better. He is the kind of human being who likes to go off on his own and start something. If anyone wants to come with him, that's all right, too. He's a born democrat — and democrats are born, not made. He hates a stuffed shirt [2] and he doesn't like to be high-hatted. He is suspicious of anybody who pretends to be better than he is. Nobody except the Scots and the Jews has such a passion for education as has the American.

I say all this because I hope that we are going to keep this kind of race alive. This race has emerged out of the concept of equality. Now don't misunderstand this word "equality." Equality does not mean that everybody is as good as everybody else. The American concept of equality is that every person has a right to a break. It is based on the belief in the immense value of every individual, and the right of every individual to make out of himself the very best human being that he can. The questions that Americans naturally ask concerning other human beings are: "What does he do?" and, "What sort of a guy is he?" and, "Does he know his stuff?"

The attitude of Americans toward themselves and toward all other human beings, the fact that we are a race of races, and a nation of nations, the fact of our outlook upon two oceans — and the miracle of the creation of this country out of stock that for such a large part represents the frustrations [3] of European dreams and the rejection of human material — all these combine to make us a messianic [4] people, with a feeling of mission not only for ourselves but for the world. This has been true from our very beginnings. Our whole political literature, which is one of the greatest possessed by any nation, reiterates the conception that the values that we cherish are of universal validity.

[1] **skeptical:** a *skeptic* questions; he doesn't accept ideas without examining them.

[2] **stuffed shirt:** can you guess how this slang term originated? [3] **frustrations:** disappointments. [4] **messianic people:** people with a message, a mission.

The Declaration of Independence contains these words:

"We hold these truths to be self-evident, that all *men* are created equal — [not all Americans] — and that they are endowed by their Creator with certain unalienable rights, among them life, liberty, and the pursuit of happiness."

And when we wrote the Constitution, we made one which is not confined to any geographic area, but is infinitely expandable.

In all the great speeches of Lincoln, there is the same sense of the American mission. In his farewell speech at Springfield, he spoke of the United States as "the last great hope of earth." And he closed the Gettysburg Address, that great apostrophe to popular government, with the words: "Shall not perish from the earth." He did not say "from this soil." He, like all great Americans, and above all the poets, conceived that there was some cosmic significance[1] about this country and about this great experiment. And that feeling is still in the American heart. It is expressed in our reaction, our spontaneous[2] reaction, to all assaults against human rights, to the degradation of personality, to all crimes against human freedom, to all persecutions and bigotries,[3] and, above all, to all tyranny wherever it raises it head, in the most remote quarters of the globe. And since we are a free people, and are not inhibited[4] in our expression, all such crimes have been protested by the American people as individuals long in advance of the protests of their government. Time and again in our history we have broken off diplomatic relations with countries because they have persecuted Jews or Armenians, or any other branch of the human race. We have been told that it is none of our business; but in some undefined way, we know it is some of our business; that the sense and meaning of our life is that we should be sensitive to such things.

[1] **cosmic significance:** importance for the whole world. [2] **spontaneous:** instinctive. [3] **bigotries:** intolerant viewpoints. [4] **inhibited:** held back, prevented from freedom.

THINK BACK OVER WHAT YOU HAVE READ

Getting at the Author's Meaning

1. What kind of people does the author believe America must have in order to match its great size?
2. What illustrations of America's vastness and greatness are cited in this essay?
3. America was built by many different people "who came here with a dream." What was that dream?
4. What does Miss Thompson believe to be the characteristics of an American? Do you agree? Would you add any other characteristics?

Applying the meaning of this essay to your own school and community

5. Describe to the class a man or woman whom you know and admire as a true American. What traits and ways of acting are typical of this person? Be sure to select a real man or woman whom you know, but don't use names.
6. How might life in your community change if democracy were to fail in America? If Dorothy Thompson had used your community as one of her moving pictures, what would she have said about it?
7. What sacrifices and troubles did the Pilgrims endure? Can you feel that they were real men and woman or do they seem only a story in a book? Did any of your parents or ancestors face hardships when they came to this country? What were they?
8. What problems do you face as an American? Are any of these problems school problems?

For Ambitious Students

9. A book on America which all Americans should read is *The Epic of America* by James Truslow Adams. The epilogue to this book has become very famous. The entire February issue of *Fortune Magazine* in 1940 was devoted to the topic of America, and in February, 1939,

the *Survey Graphic* published "Calling America," which has become one of the most widely discussed magazine issues in recent years.

THE JERSEY DEVIL CAME

by Ruth Crawford

One of the greatest problems confronting our nation today is that of unemployment. Not until recent years has the United States made any real progress in dealing with it. Though hard times have in the past thrown many people out of work, those hard times were not nationwide. Localities wrestled with the problem as best they could. Since the great business collapse of 1929, however, the unemployment question has been national in scope. Therefore, the national government has been forced to take a hand, and progressive steps have been taken to insure workers against the losses of unemployment.

The particular problem discussed in this essay is that which arose when the development of new and more efficient machinery threw thousands of workers out of employment. That problem is not solved, for every year more efficient machines are invented which can do work more and more quickly and economically. Here is a real problem for you to think about. Social-security laws may insure pay to unemployed laborers, but they do not give employment; and it is employment that makes men independent and self-respecting.

Ruth Crawford poses the issue in a way that will make it seem very real to you. She herself first met this problem as a child, listening to her father talk about machines which took men's jobs away from them. One of those machines was called the Jersey Devil. How it came into her life and how it cheated her and her family of their chance of security and happiness is dramatically described for you below.

MY MOTHER was thought to have done very well for herself when she married my father. Her people were coal miners; he was a glass blower. Glass blowers, some thirty years ago, made good money. They went places, even though it was only from one factory to another. They were notoriously good spenders — easy come, easy go. They could generally afford hired girls to assist their wives. If they could not afford a steady girl, they at least were able to pay some woman to do the washing and ironing.

Added to those advantages of my mother's marriage — as far as their children were concerned — were the interesting vacations which went with the trade. Every summer the fire went out. That meant the factory was shut down so that the furnaces might be put in order to handle next season's orders of beers, whiskies, sodies, ketchups, medicines — all names of bottles. So for two or three months the blowers had to live on the fruits of their winter's labors. At that time the industry was run on what might be called a paternalistic basis. As I remember, my father drew twenty dollars a week. We lived well on that. But he made twice that much or more, the rest being held in trust by the factory until the fire went out.

When that happened, the blowers could scab. That is, they, strong union men, could take employment as mill hands, go down into the mines, or get cheap work in other industries not so highly organized as the glass trade. This my father refused to do. Taking some other devil's bread out of his mouth, he used to say contemptuously of his fellow tradesmen who forgot the principles of unionism.

No, instead of getting another job when the fire was out, he used to pack himself and family in the day coach and go visiting. It was on one of these vacations that I first heard of the Jersey Devil. We had just arrived for the visit with my mother's people, in a little mining town near St. Louis.

How dark it was that night! Cuddled on the well seat by my father, I tormented myself with fascinating stories my cousins had told me the summer before about people who fell in wells. I was afraid to fall asleep. I might dream that my father had fallen in the well. Certain it was that if I really fell asleep and were caught at it I would be aroused and sent upstairs to bed alone. So I slept by snatches. In that half-awake stage I heard the words " Jersey Devil."

My father was telling about it.

" What's the Jersey Devil, Papa? "

" It's a great big mosquito that flies over Jersey and it'll get you if you ain't a good girl," one of the men answered.

That night it wasn't the well that kept me awake. It was a mosquito with the horns and tail of a devil, riding a pitchfork, witch fashion, and hunting me out. And my father couldn't save me from this horror which I knew to be the Jersey Devil.

He couldn't save me, for he couldn't save himself. The Jersey Devil came. It was the name of the first machine that made glass bottles — made them three, four, five times faster than my father could blow them, for all his skill. It was inevitable that the Jersey Devil should get his job. It was part of the worshiped progress, and it was well that it came. No more do men have to stand before blazing furnaces, nor have their young sons blister their hands carrying-in for them. But my youth was spent knowing the Jersey Devil to be a great evil, responsible for all our woes, for it had taken my father's job away from him. Other machines were taking other men's jobs away from them, too, away from men, artisans, skilled, proud tradesmen who in mid-life found themselves bereft of their trade. They are the unnecessary man power that stand in our bread lines because Jersey Devils can turn out more of this world's goods than the world at present knows how to use. What of them? What of their families? Was their story the same as ours?

There was no peace to be had. Summertime was no longer the set time for the fire to go out. The fire was always going out, as one manufacturer after another closed down his plant for a general readjustment. His competitors were getting in new-model machines before his workmen knew how to operate the old. So he must get a still newer model. There was the waste of experimentation, as each sought the machine which would make whiskies, sodies, beers, ketchups with the help of fewer and fewer men.

If the manufacturers were insecure, what of the workmen? Young as we children were — I was nine at the time — the horror of that insecurity was communicated to us. The Crawford boys were learning how to run the machines. But there were days when the machine's entire output would be lost. The new wonder-workers were not perfect; what machinists there were used the trial-and-error method [1] in repairing; and the glass blowers strove vainly, ruining dozen after dozen bottles trying to discover for themselves what was wrong, or else stood in the midst of the turmoil waiting their turn to have the machinists look in at their shop. Because no one was to blame, everyone was to blame.

About that time the factory closed down. My Uncle Will, whose patience had been exhausted weeks before, had gone on to East St. Louis, where the factory still had blowshops. He sent for my father.

That job was the last my father was ever to know of prosperity. Temporarily his plans for getting out of the glasshouse were silenced, but only because the troubles at hand challenged all his resources. He was breadwinner, nurse, housekeeper through a harrowing six months. The new baby, a girl, was born on the hottest of July days. Two weeks later my mother left her bed to hold the four-year-old boy

[1] **used the trial-and-error method:** that is, learned by experience.

in her arms while my father poured whisky down the child's throat, a desperate attempt to break diphtheria phlegm.

There was never a happier day than the one when the board of health had the place fumigated. But the next day I was in bed. The sign was on the door again. Two weeks later the other boy had scarlet fever. When the signs finally came off the house, our mother was an invalid.

Do economists ever hear of such stories? If so, how do they have the heart to send out pamphlets telling that if so and so is put in the bank for so many weeks at the age of fifty a man can retire? One such calamitous year as ours would have wiped away more than the average workingman could save in ten years. The wonder is that he saves at all, facing the futility of any so-called security he might hope to master.

Everything was gone, and the farm bought as an investment ten years ago was mortgaged. My father realized then what we were up against; my mother was thankful we were all alive. So when normalcy returned to our group, my father was off again on his imagined way of getting out of the glasshouse. Even under the most favorable of circumstances, his trade would never give him security. And faced with a trade which was soon to be no more, he was a fool not to take a chance on something else.

Meantime Uncle Will had married again. With his family — his children, his wife's and their own baby — he was living on a farm beyond the bluffs of the Mississippi, on the outskirts of Belleville, my mother's home. They were looking forward to the day when my uncle would leave the factory for good and make the farm pay. My uncle was going to make the adjustment gradually. Since he knew nothing of farming, he was going to earn a living in the glasshouse while the farm was put on a paying basis. The city man's old dream!

We spent our Sundays with them. Coming home on the interurban, the argument would start again. We ought to buy a place like that, my father would say. And send our children to school like the one there. Just when they were ready for high school? my mother would ask.

It was the one argument he could not answer. His own future was to count as nothing against getting an education for us, so that we wouldn't have to work for a living. No matter what had happened to him, he was going to save us. We would never have to depend on our hands. In the vague way the uneducated have of accounting for differences in prosperity, knowledge, to him, was the money-maker.

But school or no school, we did move to the country; but not to the farm. It was to a pleasant little cottage on a small plot of land near Uncle Will's place. The immediate cause was the shutting down of the factory to put in machines. A long, long struggle of job hunting was ahead for my father. We had to live where we could survive on next to nothing while he hunted work.

It is enough to be alone and unemployed, but how much more terrifying it is to be head of a family and jobless. Every morning before daylight my father would leave the house for the long interurban ride to the city to make the rounds of the stockyards, the steel mills, the enameling plants. He wanted something, anything that would tide him over until he could get hold of a glasshouse job. He, the proud union man of other days, asking for work as a laborer. Worse, being refused. No experience and nearing forty. Physical examinations had been introduced as factory requirements. Sometimes he couldn't pass these.

One night we waited supper for him so long that we all agreed he must be working somewhere. At last he came in, all dirty. So he really had been working. We were so relieved. But he was bitter and ashamed. He was working on the section [1] with a gang — and for only a dollar and fifty cents a day. Christmas was coming. He supposed we should be thankful. Now there would be something at least for the two little ones. There was enough for a toy for them and also for Uncle Will's little ones, who still believed in Santa Claus.

So had the section hand believed in a Santa Claus once. He had believed that all labor was honorable, that a man was to be respected who bemeaned himself to earn an honest living instead of stealing. There was one form of stealing, though, that was more honorable than earning an honest living, but the word "exploitation" [2] had not been publicized at the time my father dug the frozen earth with pick and shovel. A dollar and a half a day was the price the world paid him for his labor. Into the bargain he threw his self-confidence. A youth can work in a gang and be interested in it as an adventure. But at forty one is not so sure that someday, somewhere, there will be a wealth-giving opportunity.

"I'll be cleaning the streets next," my father said bitterly.

"Shame on you, Ed; you know this can't last forever," my mother said.

One night she sent us down the road to meet him, to tell him that a letter had come about a job he should write for in Indianapolis. An old friend, reminded by letter to keep watch for him, had remembered. Two days later there was a telegram from the boss telling him to come on. It was a machine job. That, even we children knew, meant trouble such as he had gone through before. But no word of foreboding was spoken as we bustled about packing his clothes into the suitcase while they were still hot from the irons. Bill and I were to help him carry his things the mile and a half to the interurban which would take him to East St. Louis, where he could catch the Indianapolis train. None of us cried.

"Not many kids got a Dad as good as we've got," Bill said when the streetcar had taken him away.

Every two weeks thereafter a registered letter would come from him containing a twenty-dollar bill. He kept the same amount for himself, out of it paying board and room, laundry, union dues, and carfare. There was no money being saved to bring us to him. It was not worth while trying to borrow the money, for, as he wrote, there was no telling how long his job would last. Something was always going wrong with the machines. The factory might close down anytime. He was writing to other places to see if he couldn't find something that would earn enough to have us with him. . . .

In the middle of July the fire went out. But in late September my father and Uncle Will went away again. They had landed jobs in a Terre Haute factory. They must have done better than in Indianapolis, for by Thanksgiving the belongings of the two families were packed in a freight car headed for Terre Haute.

I was left behind, to stay with my mother's relatives and finish the high-school term. Glowing letters came to me relating the miracle of a high school near where the others had located in Terre Haute. I spent the next two months building more and more fantastic pictures of the life I was soon to lead. I would have nice cloth dresses again. We would have a house with a bathroom and lights. Friends I would make would come there for parties.

[1] **section:** a portion of railroad track assigned to a gang of men for maintenance. [2] **"exploitation":** the selfish use of laborers for the private gain of the employer by the payment of low wages for long hours of work.

But when I arrived, it was to find the family lodged in the meanest quarters it had ever been in. All were there except Bill. He, I was told, had a job as carrying-in boy at one of the glass factories.

"Doesn't he go to school?"

"Not this term."

They were holding something back.

My father turned away from my questioning eyes. "Your Pop ain't much good any more, Ruthie," he said.

He had been laid off since Christmas. The little Bill made had been supporting them. Bill, or Shrimp as he had been nicknamed because of his size, was not yet sixteen and the breadwinner. Bill was working in a factory.

He came home that night too dirty to kiss me until he had washed. He did the talking as we gathered around the table. All the solicitude of the family was for him. The best piece of the round steak was his, for he had been working hard. Bill had become head of the family. It was he who had decided that I was to go to school even though there was no money. As for him, he'd work now. Later on he'd get a day job, not a job with three shifts, and he'd go to night school to catch up on what he had missed.

Bill never came to see that fine school. He had just turned eighteen when war was declared. He joined three days later. He thought his motive was pure patriotism. But was it not really a way out? An honorable way to have a try at success for himself? A way out without leaving us stranded, for regularly his entire check came home to us.

Taking a long chance on a job, while in high school I passed the state teachers' examination. All that was needed then was to survive through a term at the Normal. Then I might get a school.

The war made the plan work. It took men from the industries, so that a man in his forties was found to be good for something. My father found work in a machine shop in a glass factory. Thus the economic tension was lifted long enough for the term to be had at Normal. And because the war had drained the country of man power, and teachers were leaving their profession for more lucrative employment, an untrained seventeen-year-old girl was given a job teaching.

I sent such glowing accounts home that after a month I guess they thought I could bear up under the news. There was this prohibition amendment,[1] and the factory's orders for beers had been canceled. The factory had shut down. They hadn't wanted me to know, but now it was all right. The man who owned the dairy had given him a job driving one of the milk wagons. It wasn't very much, but it would do for a while.

And in the same mail there was a letter from my father, trying to make a joke. As if Jersey Devils weren't enough trouble, they had to stop making beer bottles. But I was not to worry. He had something to do, not much, but it was better than nothing. And when Bill came home from the war, we'd all find a way to get on Easy Street.[2]

THINK BACK OVER WHAT YOU HAVE READ

Understanding the Author's Message

1. What was the position of glass blowers thirty years ago? What difference would it make in the spirit of today if large numbers of workers occupied a similar position?

2. What principles of unionism did the author's father adhere to faithfully?

3. What incident in her childhood marked the author's first realization of the "horror" — as she calls it — of insecurity? In what simple terms does a child express such a horror?

[1] **prohibition amendment:** the Eighteenth Amendment to the Constitution of the United States, which prohibited the manufacture and sale of alcoholic liquor. This amendment has been repealed. [2] **Easy Street:** a slang term for prosperity.

4. What specifically was the Jersey Devil? How do you suppose it first got its name?

5. What insight into the human waste that accompanies machine efficiency does the author give you? What, for example, were the conditions that Uncle Will ran away from?

6. The words *social security* — or *insecurity* — sound like dull economic terms; this author, however, endows them with dramatic meaning. What kind of insecurity does the average industrial worker face? What was the insecurity which Mr. Crawford faced? Of what did " one such calamitous year " as his daughter tells you about consist?

7. How had Uncle Will attempted, on his own, to gain a measure of security for himself and family? What is the " city man's dream " which for a time tempted Mr. Crawford to get out of industry?

8. How does the insecurity of the breadwinner in a family communicate itself to children? How does it thwart and misdirect their lives? Does the author tell you? How, for example, was the life of the author herself affected by her father's unsteady employment? What did it do to her brother Bill's life? How might their lives have been different had the Jersey Devil never come?

9. To what kind of hope for the future did the father eventually turn? Did he ever completely give up?

10. Think back over the working years of Mr. Crawford, a skilled worker and an upright man, whose story is recounted for you by his daughter: He started as glass blower who " made good money." He ended as a driver of a milk wagon. What, in your own words, is the significance of that story? What does it mean? What does the author think that it means? She doesn't tell you in so many words; but she expects you to draw the same conclusion from the facts she presents as she does. What is it?

Increase Your Power over Words

11. The Latin word for father is *pater*. Many English words are derived from it. *Paternalistic* (page 329) means acting like a father toward a child; having a fatherly interest. *Paternity* means fatherhood. *Patricide* or *parricide* means the murder of one's father. A *patron* is a guardian or protector. *Patriot* is indirectly derived from the same stem. Can you trace its meaning back to its original source?

12. Another interesting word derived from Latin is *interurban* (page 331). *Inter* means between; *urban* (from *urbs,* city) means relating to a city. Therefore, *interurban* means between cities. Here it is used as a noun and refers to the electric cars that run from city to city.

What other words that begin with *inter* do you know?

Composition Suggestion

13. The essay which you have just read calls your attention to the human troubles which resulted from one particular laborsaving device. Of course this is only one phase of a very complicated problem. In one sense, as you have learned, the machine has been a bane to mankind; in others it has been a blessing. Does the solution to the problem posed by Miss Crawford lie in scrapping machines and returning to a more primitive way of life, or in learning how to control them? With this question in mind you are hereby enjoined to consider the following topic to be discussed on paper: Drawing chiefly upon your own observation for material, analyze the changes in life produced by the automobile, the airplane, or the electrified home — or any other important invention. What are the real benefits to man offered by these machines? What misuses require social or individual control?

For Ambitious Students

14. The following topics for special investigation should provide interesting material for class discussion:

a. Social-security laws. What laws are now in effect?
b. Workmen's compensation laws. What laws are now in effect?
c. Socialized medicine. What do its advocates propose?
d. The National Recovery Act. How has it aided unemployment?
e. The Works Progress Administration. How has it aided unemployment?
f. Trade unionism. How does Labor propose to meet the problem of machines displacing men?

WE AREN'T SUPERSTITIOUS

by Stephen Vincent Benét (1898–)

When we are actually in a forest we see only trees, towering above us. From the air, however, we see not separate trees but the forest as a whole — its shape, extent, and relation to the rest of the landscape. Sometimes we say of people who are *in* a situation and thus unable to get a clear view of its meaning as a whole, "They cannot see the forest for the trees." Here, then, is a reason, often overlooked by students, for studying history: because we are not a part of the past, we are more likely to understand it.

In the essay that follows, a somewhat shortened version, the author writes about the year 1692. He is thinking, however, about the year 1939, the year in which he wrote his essay. Although he deals with the past, he is really asking you to think about the present; to apply to the present a lesson which looks sharp and clear when we view it from a distance of two hundred and fifty years.

USUALLY, our little superstitious rituals and propitiations don't hurt our daily lives. Usually. And then, on occasion, a superstition — a belief — flares into crowd madness and kills and kills again before it has run its course. As it did in Salem Village in 1692.

That story is worth retelling, as a very typical example of what wild belief and crowd hysteria can do to an average community. For Salem Village in 1691 was no different in any way from any one of a dozen little New England hamlets. It didn't expect celebrity or notoriety, and its citizens were the average people of their day and age. There was the main road and the parsonage and the meeting-house, the blockhouse, the Ingersoll house where travelers put up for the night, the eight or nine other houses that made up the village. Beyond lay the outlying farms with their hard-working farmers; a few miles away lay Salem Town itself; fifteen miles away, the overgrown village that was Boston. King Philip's War [1] had been over for some fourteen years and the colony [2] was recovering from the shock of it; there were still individual slayings by Indians, but the real power of the Indian was very largely broken. Men might look forward, with hope, to peace and thriving for a time.

And as for the men and women of Salem Village — they were tough and knotty stock, if you like; not widely lettered; not particularly tolerant, especially in religion; but no different from their neighbors at Andover and Topsfield or in Boston itself. There were sensible men and stupid men among them, model housewives and slatterns, troublemakers and more peaceable folk.

And yet to this ordinary community in the early spring of 1692 came a madness that was to shake all Massachusetts before its fever was burned out. We are wiser now. We do not believe in witches. But if, say, three cases of Asiatic cholera were discovered in your own home town, and certified as such by the local board of health — and if your local newspaper promptly ran a boxed warning to all citizens on the front page — you would have some faint idea of how the average Salem Villager felt when the "afflicted children" denounced their first victims.

For witchcraft, to almost all the New Englanders of 1692, was as definite, diagnosable, and dangerous an evil as bubonic plague.[3] It had its symptoms, its prognosis, and its appalling results. Belief in it was as firmly fixed in most people's minds as belief in the germ theory of disease is in ours.

Three years before, Salem Village had got a new minister — the Reverend Samuel Parris, ex-merchant in the West Indies. The most important thing about Samuel Parris was the fact that he brought with him to Salem Village two West Indian servants — a man known as John Indian and a woman named Tituba. And when he bought those two or their

[1] **King Philip's War:** a serious Indian uprising in New England (1675–76) under the leadership of a chieftain named Philip. [2] **colony:** Massachusetts.

[3] **bubonic plague:** a fatal, contagious disease spread by rats.

services in the West Indies, he was buying a rope that was to hang nineteen men and women of New England — so odd are the links in the circumstantial chain.

Perhaps the nine-year-old Elizabeth Parris, the daughter of the parsonage, boasted to her new friends of the odd stories Tituba told and the queer things she could do. Perhaps Tituba herself let the report of her magic powers be spread about the village. She must have been as odd and imagination-stirring a figure as a parrot or a tame monkey in the small New England town. And the winters were long and white — and any diversion a godsend.

In any case, during the winter of 1691–92 a group of girls and women began to meet nightly at the parsonage, with Tituba and her fortunetelling as the chief attraction. Elizabeth Parris, at nine, was the youngest; then came Abigail Williams, eleven, and Ann Putnam, twelve. The rest were older — Mercy Lewis, Mary Wolcott, and Elizabeth Hubbard were seventeen; Elizabeth Booth and Susan Sheldon, eighteen; and Mary Warren and Sarah Churchill, twenty. Three were servants — Mercy Lewis had been employed by the Reverend George Burroughs, a previous minister of Salem Village, and now worked for the Putnams; Mary Warren was a maid at the John Procters'; Sarah Churchill, at the George Jacobs'. All, except for Elizabeth Parris, were adolescent or just leaving adolescence.

The elder women included a pair of gossipy, superstitious busybodies — Mrs. Pope and Mrs. Bibber; and young Ann Putnam's mother, Ann Putnam, Sr., who deserves a sentence to herself.

For the Putnams were a powerful family in the neighborhood and Ann Putnam, married at seventeen and now only thirty, is described as handsome, arrogant, temperamental, and high-strung. She was also one of those people who can cherish a grudge and revenge it.

The circle met — the circle continued to meet — no doubt with the usual giggling, whispering, and gossip. From mere fortunetelling it proceeded to other and more serious matters — table rapping,[1] perhaps, and a little West Indian voodoo [2] — weird stories told by Tituba and weird things shown, while the wind blew outside and the big shadows flickered on the wall. Adolescent girls, credulous servants, superstitious old women — and the two enigmatic figures of Tituba, the West Indian, and Ann Putnam, Sr.

But soon the members of the circle began to show hysterical symptoms. They crawled under tables and chairs; they made strange sounds; they shook and trembled with nightmare fears. The thing became a village celebrity — and more. Something strange and out of nature was happening — who had ever seen normal young girls behave like these young girls? And no one — certainly not the Reverend Samuel Parris — even suggested that a mixed diet of fortunetelling, ghost stories, and voodoo is hardly the thing for impressionable minds during a long New England winter. Hysteria was possession by an evil spirit; pathological lying, the devil putting words into one's mouth. The Reverend Samuel became very busy. Grave ministers were called in to look at the afflicted children. A Dr. Gregg gave his opinion. It was almost too terrible to believe, and yet what else could be believed? Witchcraft!

Meanwhile, one may suppose, the "afflicted children," like most hysterical subjects, enjoyed the awed stares, the horrified looks, the respectful questions that greeted them, with girlish zest. They

[1] **table rapping:** communication with spirits of the dead by means of raps on a table, supposedly given by those spirits in answer to questions.
[2] **voodoo:** a form of sorcery found among certain Negroes, especially in Haiti.

had been unimportant girls of a little hamlet; now they were, in every sense of the word, spot news. And any reporter knows what that does to certain kinds of people. They continued to writhe and demonstrate — and be the center of attention. There was only one catch about it. If they were really bewitched, somebody must be doing the bewitching.

On the twenty-ninth of February, 1692, in the midst of an appropriate storm of thunder and lightning, three women — Sarah Good, Sarah Osburn, and Tituba — were arrested on the deadly charge of bewitching the children.

The next day, March 1, two magistrates, Justice Hawthorne and Justice Corwin, arrived with appropriate pomp and ceremony. The first hearing was held in the crowded meetinghouse of the village; and all Salem swarmed to it, as crowds in our time have swarmed to other sleepy little villages suddenly notorious.

The children — or the children and Tituba — had picked their first victims well. Sarah Good and Sarah Osburn were old women of no particular standing in the community.

We can imagine that meetinghouse — and the country crowd within it — on that chill March day. At one end was the majesty of the law — and the "afflicted children," where all might see them and observe. Dressed in their best, very likely, and with solicitous relatives near at hand. Do you see Mercy Lewis? Do you see Ann Putnam? And then the whole crowd turned to one vast, horrified eye. For there was the accused — the old woman — the witch!

The justices — grim Justice Hawthorne in particular — had, evidently, arrived with their minds made up. For the first question addressed to Sarah Good was, bluntly:

"What evil spirit have you familiarity with?"

"None," said the piping old voice. But everybody in the village knew worthless Sarah Good. And the eye of the audience went from her to the deadly row of "afflicted children" and back again.

"Have you made no contracts with the devil?" proceeded the Justice.

"No."

The Justice went to the root of the matter at once.

"Why do you hurt these children?"

A rustle must have gone through the meetinghouse at that. Aye, that's it; the Justice speaks shrewdly; hark to the Justice! Aye, but look, too! Look at the children! Poor things, poor things!

"I do not hurt them. I scorn it," said Sarah Good defiantly. But the Justice had her now; he was not to be brushed aside.

"Who, then, do you employ to do it?"

"I employ nobody."

"What creature do you employ then?" For all witches had familiars.[1]

"No creature, but I am falsely accused." But the sweat must have been on the old woman's palms by now.

The Justice considered. There was another point, minor but illuminating.

"Why did you go away muttering from Mr. Parris, his house?"

"I did not mutter, but I thanked him for what he gave my child."

The Justice returned to the main charge, like any prosecuting attorney.

"Have you made no contract with the devil?"

"No."

It was time for Exhibit A. The Justice turned to the children. Was Sarah Good one of the persons who tormented them? Yes, yes! — and a horrified murmur running through the crowd. And then, before the awe-stricken eyes of all, they began to be tormented. They writhed; they grew stiff; they contorted; they were stricken

[1] **familiars:** spirits attending on a witch.

moaning or speechless. Yet, when they were brought to Sarah Good and allowed to touch her, they grew quite quiet and calm. For, as everyone knew, a witch's physical body was like an electric conductor — it reabsorbed, on touch, the malefic force discharged by witchcraft into the bodies of the tormented. Everybody could see what happened — and everybody saw. When the meetinghouse was quiet, the Justice spoke again.

" Sarah Good, do you not see now what you have done? Why do you not tell us the truth? Why do you torment these poor children? "

And with these words Sarah Good was already hanged. For all that she could say was, " I do not torment them." And yet everyone had seen her, with their own eyes.

Sarah Osburn's examination followed the same course, the same prosecutor's first question, the same useless denial, the same epileptic feats [1] of the " afflicted children," the same end.

Then Tituba was examined and gave them their fill of marvels, prodigies, and horrors.

The West Indian woman, a slave in a strange land, was fighting for her life, and she did it shrewdly and desperately. She admitted, repentantly, that she had tormented the children. But she had been forced to do so. By whom? By Goody Good and Goody Osburn and two other witches whom she hadn't yet been able to recognize. Her voodoo knowledge aided her — she filled the open ears of Justices and crowd with tales of hairy familiars and black dogs, red cats and black cats and yellow birds, the phantasm of a woman with legs and wings. And everybody could see that she spoke the truth. For, when she was first brought in, the children were tormented at her presence; but as soon as she had confessed and turned king's evidence,[2] she was tormented herself, and fearfully. To Boston Jail with her — but she had saved her neck.

The hearing was over; the men and women of Salem and its outlying farms went broodingly or excitedly back to their homes to discuss the fearful workings of God's providence. Here and there a common-sense voice murmured a doubt or two — Sarah Good and Sarah Osburn were no great loss to the community; but still, to convict two old women of heinous crime on the testimony of greensick girls and a West Indian slave! But, on the whole, the villagers of Salem felt relieved. The cause of the plague had been found; it would be stamped out and the afflicted children recover. The Justices, no doubt, congratulated themselves on their prompt and intelligent action. The " afflicted children " slept, after a tiring day — they were not quite so used to such performances as they were to become.

As for the accused women, they went to Boston Jail — to be chained there while waiting trial and gallows.

Meanwhile, on an outlying farm, Giles Corey, a turbulent, salty old fellow of eighty-one, began to argue the case with his wife, Martha. He believed, fanatically, in the " afflicted children." She did not, and said so — even going so far as to say that the magistrates were blinded and she could open their eyes. It was one of those marital disputes that occur between strong-willed people. And it was to bring Martha Corey to the gallows and Giles Corey to an even stranger doom.

[1] **epileptic feats:** The children feigned a kind of fit similar to that of a person afflicted with epilepsy.

[2] **turned king's evidence:** gave evidence for the government by confessing the crime and testifying against her accomplices. We now call it "state's evidence." Usually one who turns state's evidence is given lighter punishment than his accomplices.

Yet now there was a lull, through which people whispered.

As for what went on in the minds of the "afflicted children," during that lull, we may not say. But this much is evident. They had seen and felt their power. The hearing had been the greatest and most exciting event of their narrow lives. And it was so easy to do; they grew more and more ingenious with each rehearsal. You twisted your body and groaned — and grown people were afraid.

Add to this the three girl-servants, with the usual servants' grudges against present or former masters. Add to this that high-strung, dominant woman Ann Putnam, Sr., who could hold a grudge and remember it. Such a grudge as there might be against the Towne sisters, for instance — they were all married women of the highest standing, particularly Rebecca Nurse. So suppose — just suppose — that one of them were found out to be a witch? And hadn't Tituba deposed that there were other women, besides Good and Osburn, who made her torment the children?

On March 19 Martha Corey and Rebecca Nurse were arrested on the charge of witchcraft. On March 21 they were examined and committed. And with that the real reign of terror began.

Salem Village, as a community, was no longer sane.

Let us get it over quickly. The Salem witches ceased to be Salem's affair — they became a matter affecting the whole colony. Sir William Phips, the new governor, appointed a special court of oyer and terminer [1] to try the cases. And the hangings began.

On January 1, 1692, no one, except possibly the "circle children," had heard of Salem witches. On June 10 Bridget Bishop was hanged. She had not been one of the first accused, but she was the first to suffer. She had been married three times, kept a roadhouse on the road to Beverley where people drank rum and played shovelboard, and dressed, distinctively for the period, in a "black cap and black hat and red paragon bodice broidered and looped with diverse colors." But those seem to have been her chief offenses. When questioned, she said, "I never saw the devil in my life."

All through the summer the accusations, the arrests, the trials, came thick and fast till the jails were crowded. Nor were those now accused friendless old beldames like Sarah Good. They included Captain John Alden (son of Miles Standish's friend [2]), who saved himself by breaking jail, and the wealthy and prominent Englishes, who saved themselves by flight. The most disgraceful scenes occurred at the trial of the saintly Rebecca Nurse. Thirty-nine citizens of Salem were brave enough to sign a petition for her, and the jury brought in a verdict of "not guilty." The mob in the sweating courtroom immediately began to cry out, and the presiding judge as much as told the jury to reverse their verdict. They did so, to the mob's delight. Then the governor pardoned her. And "certain gentlemen of Salem" — and perhaps the mob — persuaded him into reversing his pardon. She was hanged on Gallows Hill on July 19 with Sarah Good, Sarah Wilds, Elizabeth How, and Susanna Martin.

Susanna Martin's only witchcraft seems to have been that she was an unusually tidy woman and had once walked a muddy road without getting her dress bedraggled. No, I am quoting from testimony, not inventing. As for Elizabeth How, a neighbor testified, "I have been

[1] **court of oyer and terminer:** a higher criminal court.

[2] **Miles Standish's friend:** a reference to the famous story, told in Longfellow's *The Courtship of Miles Standish,* of Miles Standish, captain of Plymouth, who engaged his friend John Alden to propose for him to Priscilla Mullins. As it turned out, Alden himself married Priscilla.

acquainted with Goodwife How as a naybor for nine or ten years and I never saw any harm in her but found her just in her dealings and faithful to her promises. . . . I never heard her revile any person but she always pitied them and said, 'I pray God forgive them now.' " But the children cried, "I am stuck with a pin. I am pinched," when they saw her — and she hanged.

It took a little more to hang the Reverend George Burroughs. He had been Salem Village's second minister — then gone on to a parish in Maine. And the cloth[1] had great sanctity. But Ann Putnam and Mercy Lewis managed to doom him between them, with the able assistance of the rest of the troupe. Mr. Burroughs was unfortunate enough to be a man of unusual physical strength — anyone who could lift a gun by putting four fingers in its barrel must do so by magic arts. Also he had been married three times. So when the ghosts of his first two wives, dressed in winding sheets, appeared in a sort of magic-lantern show to Ann Putnam and cried out that Mr. Burroughs had murdered them — the cloth could not save him then.

Here and there in the records gleams a flash of frantic common sense. Susanna Martin laughs when Ann Putnam and her daughter go into convulsions at her appearance. When asked why, she says, "Well I may, at such folly. I never hurt this woman or her child in my life." John Proctor, the prosperous farmer who employed Mary Warren, said sensibly, before his arrest, "If these girls are left alone, we will all be devils and witches. They ought all to be sent to the whipping post." He was right enough about it — but his servant helped hang him.

Judge, jury, and colony preferred to believe the writhings of the children; the stammerings of those whose sows had died inexplicably; the testimony of such as Bernard Peach, who swore that Susanna Martin had flown in through his window, bent his body into the shape of a "whoope," and sat upon him for an hour and a half.

One hanging on June 10, five on July 19, five on August 19, eight on September 22, including Mary Easty and Martha Corey. And of these the Reverend Noyes remarked, with unction, "What a sad thing it is to see eight firebrands of hell hanging there!" But for stubborn Giles Corey a different fate was reserved.

The old man had begun by believing in the whole hocus-pocus. He had quarreled with his wife about it. He had seen her arrested as a witch, insulted by the magistrates, condemned to die. Two of his sons-in-law had testified against her; he himself had been closely questioned as to her actions and had made the deposition of a badgered and simple man. Yes, she prayed a good deal; sometimes he couldn't hear what she said — that sort of thing. The memory must have risen to haunt him when she was condemned. Now he himself was in danger.

Well, he could die as his wife would. But there was the property — his goods, his prospering lands. By law, the goods and property of those convicted of witchcraft were confiscated by the state and the name attainted.[2] With a curious, grim heroism, Giles Corey drew up a will leaving that property to the two sons-in-law who had not joined in the prevailing madness. And then at his trial, he said, "I will not plead. If I deny, I am condemned already in courts where ghosts appear as witnesses and swear men's lives away."

A curious, grim heroism? It was so. For those who refused to plead either guilty or not guilty in such a suit were liable to the old English punishment called *peine*

[1] **the cloth:** the clergy.

[2] **attainted:** deprived of all civil rights.

forte et dure.[1] It consisted in heaping weights or stones upon the unhappy victim till he accepted a plea — or until his chest was crushed. And exactly that happened to old Giles Corey. They heaped the stones upon him until they killed him — and two days before his wife was hanged, he died. But his property went to the two loyal sons-in-law, without confiscation — and his name was not attainted. So died Giles Corey, New England to the bone.

And then, suddenly and fantastically as the madness had come, it was gone.

The "afflicted children," at long last, had gone too far. They had accused the governor's lady. They had accused Mrs. Hall, the wife of the minister at Beverley and a woman known throughout the colony for her virtues. And there comes a point when driven men and women revolt against blood and horror. It was that which ended Robespierre's terror[2] — it was that which ended the terror of the "afflicted children." The thing had become a *reductio ad absurdum.*[3] If it went on, logically, no one but the "afflicted children" and their protégées would be left alive.

In 1706 Ann Putnam made public confession that she had been deluded by the devil in testifying as she had. She had testified in every case but one. And in 1711 the colony of Massachusetts paid fifty pounds to the heirs of George Burroughs, twenty-one pounds to the heirs of Giles Corey — five hundred and seventy-eight pounds in all to the heirs of various victims. An expensive business for the colony, on the whole.

What happened to the survivors? Well, the Reverend Samuel Parris quit Salem Village to go into business in Boston and died at Sudbury in 1720. And Ann Putnam died in 1716 and from the stock of the Putnams sprang Israel Putnam, the Revolutionary hero. And from the stock of the "witches," the Nurses and the others, sprang excellent and distinguished people of service to state and nation. And hanging Judge Hawthorne's descendant was Nathaniel Hawthorne.[4]

We have no reason to hold Salem up to obloquy. It was a town, like another, and a strange madness took hold of it. But it is no stranger thing to hang a man for witchcraft than to hang him for the shape of his nose[5] or the color of his skin.[6] We are not superstitious, no. Well, let us be a little sure we are not. For persecution follows superstition and intolerance as fire follows the fuse. And once we light that fire we cannot foresee where it will end or what it will consume — any more than they could in Salem two hundred and forty-five years ago.

THINK BACK OVER WHAT YOU HAVE READ

Understanding the Nature of Crowd Hysteria

1. The author describes Salem in 1692 as an "average community." Does this fact seem to you important? Why?

2. To what incident is it possible to trace the start of the crowd hysteria in Salem? What factors in the situation seem to you responsible for the chain of events that followed? How might a wise person have checked the start of such crowd madness?

3. In fanning the flame of hysteria, what part was played by gossip? secret grudge? desire for revenge?

4. What are the symptoms of hysteria? How did the hysterical children act? How would a modern doctor explain such symptoms? How

[1] **peine forte et dure:** a French phrase meaning strong and hard punishment. [2] **Robespierre's terror:** the Reign of Terror in the French Revolution. Robespierre was one of those responsible for it. [3] **reductio ad absurdum:** a Latin expression meaning an absurdity; literally, a reducing to the absurd.

[4] **Nathaniel Hawthorne:** the great American novelist and short-story writer. [5] **shape of his nose:** a reference to the persecution of the Jews. [6] **color of his skin:** a reference to the lynching of Negroes.

were they explained in 1692? How much of the children's hysteria can you see through? What motives caused them to act as they did? What less harmful examples of the same thing have you yourself observed?

5. How do you explain the fact that the children accused two innocent people of bewitching them? What fears caused them to invent such a terrible falsehood? What did they gain by it? What would they have lost had they admitted the facts? Compare their first victims with their last. What is the horrible lesson which such a comparison drives home?

6. Notice the nature of the "proof" of guilt with which the judge was satisfied. Wherein lay the flaw in his reasoning? "And everybody could see that she [Tituba] spoke the truth" (page 338) — what had the judge and the spectators mistaken for truth?

7. To what degree do you hold Tituba responsible for what happened in 1692?

8. How do you account for the fact that the people of Salem accepted the witch trials? Why wasn't doubt more prevalent?

9. Note carefully the wholesale accusations that followed the first wave of hysteria. What forces were at work? Which accusation seemed to you most fantastic? How do you account for the fact that it was believed?

10. What flashes of "frantic common sense" shone through the crowd hysteria? Why were they not more effective?

11. Can you explain the fact that "judge, jury, and colony *preferred* to believe the writhings of the children"? What terrible lesson is implied in the word *preferred?*

12. In what lay the grim heroism of Giles Corey? What irony do you see in his fate?

13. Why did the madness cease — seemingly of its own accord? What parallels in history help to explain the same thing?

14. What was time's rebuke to Salem? its revenge on the witch-hunters? Can you tell? Note carefully what happened to the survivors and draw your own conclusion.

Applying This Essay to Modern Times

15. In the last paragraph of the essay which you have just read occur these words: "For persecution follows superstition and intolerance as fire follows the fuse." With what examples of modern persecution can you parallel those of Salem in 1692? From what false beliefs did they arise? What "fires of intolerance" have you seen lighted in your day? To what extent have they spread?

16. To what extent does modern youth "will to believe" in superstition? Which of *their* "little rituals" are innocent? Which ones are dangerous? How do you explain the fact that people might prefer to believe in magic? What unwelcome responsibilities does common sense put upon us?

17. Why is doubt important in learning to be reasonable? What part does doubt play in scientific investigation? Suppose that a modern scientist had appeared on the Salem scene two hundred and fifty years ago. What difference would it have made? How would he have gone about sifting evidence?

18. What examples of crowd hysteria have you ever read about in the newspaper? been a part of? any? in football season? Does school spirit sometimes develop into a "strange madness"?

19. It is common to speak of "witch-hunting" symbolically, to apply it to any attempt to hunt out the individual who stands apart from the crowd and to persecute him. What examples of witch-hunting can you cite which illustrate the tyranny of the crowd over the individual?

20. What part does propaganda play in working up "crowd hysteria"?

21. What irony do you see in the title of the essay?

Increase Your Power over Words

22. The essay which you have just read has introduced you to a group of words all relating in one way or another to the subject of witchcraft. Look up the meaning of the following words and use them in sentences of your own invention: ritual (page 335) propitiation (page 335) malefic (page 338) phantasm (page 338).

23. Can you guess from the context the meanings of the italicized words in these sentences?

a. "*Adolescent* girls, *credulous* servants, *superstitious* old women — and the two *enigmatic* figures of Tituba, the West Indian, and Ann Putnam, Sr." (page 336).

b. "We have no reason to hold Salem up to *obloquy*" (page 341).

Not Exactly Serious

THE NOBLEST INSTRUMENT

by Clarence Day (1874–1935)

Here is a humorous satire exposing the folly of parents who, out of vanity, try to force their children into molds unsuited to them. The ridicule in this essay is good-natured and restrained and for these reasons in good taste.

" The Noblest Instrument " is but one essay in the book entitled *Life with Father,* a book in which a parent is portrayed through the eyes of a child. It is not often that adults take occasion to look at themselves through the eyes of the young. Perhaps it would be better for parents — and teachers — if they did. Herein, then, lies the particular mission of humor, such as is to be found in this essay: it permits us to come at truth about life through a new door; or — to change the figure — to catch an unexpected glimpse of ourselves through a mirror. Dorothy Canfield, the novelist, describes *Life with Father* not only as " enchanting, delicious, and riotously comic " but also as " profoundly human, wise, and above all, true." It is to these last three adjectives that your attention is especially directed. The other three will take care of themselves.

FATHER had been away, reorganizing some old upstate railroad. He returned in an executive mood and proceeded to shake up our home. In spite of my failure as a singer, he was still bound to have us taught music. We boys were summoned before him and informed that we must at once learn to play on something. We might not appreciate it now, he said, but we should later on. " You, Clarence, will learn the violin. George, you the piano. Julian — well, Julian is too young yet. But you older boys must have lessons."

I was appalled at this order. At the age of ten it seemed a disaster to lose any more of my freedom. The days were already too short for our games after school; and now here was a chunk to come out of playtime three days every week. A chunk every day, we found afterward, because we had to practice.

George sat at the piano in the parlor and faithfully learned to pound out his exercises. He had all the luck. He was not an inspired player, but at least he had some ear for music. He also had the advantage of playing on a good robust instrument, which he didn't have to be careful not to drop and was in no danger of breaking. Furthermore, he did not have to tune it. A piano had some good points.

But I had to go through a blacker and more gruesome experience. It was bad enough to have to come in from the street and the sunlight and go down into our dark little basement where I took my lessons. But that was only the opening chill of the struggle that followed.

The whole thing was uncanny. The violin itself was a queer, fragile, cigar-boxy thing that had to be handled most gingerly. Nothing sturdy about it. Why, a fellow was liable to crack it putting it into its case. And then my teacher — he was queer too. He had a queer pickled smell.

I dare say he wasn't queer at all really; but he seemed so to me, because he was different from the people I generally met. He was probably worth a dozen of some of them, but I didn't know it. He was one of the violins [1] in the Philharmonic,[2] and an excellent player — a grave, middle-aged little man who was obliged to give lessons.

He wore a black, wrinkled frock coat and a discolored gold watch chain. He had small, black-rimmed glasses; not tortoise-shell, but thin rims of metal. His

[1] **one of the violins:** one of the musicians who played the violin in the orchestra. [2] **Philharmonic:** the celebrated Philharmonic Orchestra of New York.

violin was dark, rich, and polished, and would do anything for him.

Mine was balky and awkward, brand new, and of a light, common color.

The violin is intended for persons with a passion for music. I wasn't that kind of person. I liked to hear a band play a tune that we could march up and down to; but try as I would, I could seldom whistle such a tune afterward. My teacher didn't know this. He greeted me as a possible genius.

He taught me how to hold the contraption, tucked under my chin. I learned how to move my fingers here and there on its handle or stem. I learned how to draw the bow across the strings, and thus produce sounds.

Does a mother recall the first cry of her baby, I wonder? I still remember the strange cry at birth of that new violin.

My teacher, Herr[1] M., looked as though he had suddenly taken a large glass of vinegar. He sucked in his breath. His lips were drawn back from his teeth, and his eyes tightly shut. Of course, he hadn't expected my notes to be sweet at the start; but still, there was something unearthly about that first cry. He snatched the violin from me, examined it, readjusted its pegs, and comforted it gently by drawing his own bow across it. It was only a new and not especially fine violin, but the sounds it made for him were more natural — they were classifiable sounds. They were not richly musical, but at least they had been heard before on this earth.

He handed the instrument back to me with careful directions. I tucked it up under my chin again and grasped the end tight. I held my bow exactly as ordered. I looked up at him, waiting.

"Now," he said nervously.

I slowly raised the bow, drew it downward.

[1] **Herr**: a German title equivalent to Mr.

This time there were *two* dreadful cries in our little front basement. One came from my new violin and one from the heart of Herr M.

Herr M. presently came to, and smiled bravely at me, and said if I wanted to rest a moment he would permit it. He seemed to think I might wish to lie down a while and recover. I didn't feel any need of lying down. All I wanted was to get through the lesson. But Herr M. was shaken. He was by no means ready to let me proceed. He looked around desperately, saw the music book, and said he would now show me that. We sat down side by side on the window seat, with the book in his lap, while he pointed out the notes to me with his finger and told me their names.

After a bit, when he felt better, he took up his own violin and instructed me to watch him and note how he handled the strings. And then at last he nerved himself to let me take my violin up again. "Softly, my child, softly," he begged me, and stood facing the wall.

We got through the afternoon somehow, but it was a ghastly experience. Part of the time he was maddened by the mistakes I kept making, and part of the time he was plain wretched. He covered his eyes. He seemed ill. He looked often at his watch, even shook it as though it had stopped; but he stayed the full hour.

That was Wednesday. What struggles he had with himself before Friday, when my second lesson was due, I can only dimly imagine; and, of course, I never even gave them a thought at the time. He came back to recommence teaching me, but he had changed — he had hardened. Instead of being cross, he was stern; and instead of sad, bitter. He wasn't unkind to me but we were no longer companions. He talked to himself, under his breath; and sometimes he took bits of paper and

Courtesy of the artist and The New Yorker

FROM THE HEIGHTS OF THE RIDICULOUS TO THE LOWEST DEPTHS OF THE PUN

To most people "elephants is elephants." But to the circus trainer there's a difference and each elephant has more or less his own personality as you discovered in "The Keeper of the Bulls."

Similarly, to the thoughtless, humor is just humor: a story is funny or it isn't funny, and that's all there is about it.

But *is* that all? Stories and essays may be amusing in different ways and to different degrees, and your ability to recognize these differences determines, in large measure, the extent to which you will enjoy them. Likewise, humorous pictures reveal different degrees and kinds of humor.

"Zenobia's Infidelity" is an example of the height of the ridiculous, but the situation in this picture pushes that brand of humor to its limits.

Courtesy of the artist and The Saturday Review of Literature

"I just loved your autobiography — I hope you'll write another."

WHY DO WE LAUGH? Do you laugh at the foolish blunders of other people because it makes you feel superior to them? Investigate the causes of laughter, and you may learn something about human behavior. Does your amusement at the speeches of two people on this page depend partly upon your conviction that you could never say or do anything quite so stupid?

"Of course I'll still need him. He's the one who knows the stops."

Courtesy of the artist and Collier's Magazine

"A simple 'yes' or 'no' will be sufficient, Madame."

Courtesy of the artist and The New Yorker

THE HUMOR OF EMBARRASSMENT. Women's hats are always supposed to be funny. The very correct manners of the floorwalker (*above*) remind one of the "inimitable Jeeves" in the Wodehouse story, adding to the amusement we always seem to discover in hats.

We like to laugh at those who hold too high an opinion of themselves, especially if they consider themselves better than we are. The absurd impossibility of the picture below only adds to the humor of the dog's conceit.

"She's been like that ever since she was glorified in one of Albert Payson Terhune's stories."

Courtesy of the artist and The Saturday Review of Literature

"We feel that we owe you an explanation."

THE HUMOR OF UNDERSTATEMENT. One kind of humor that you hear and see very frequently depends for its effect upon *understatement*. From the example above, can you tell what is meant by this word? What examples of it have you heard the radio comedians use?

Perhaps the finest kind of humor is that which extracts a smile rather than a guffaw. Like the experiences of the two boys in "The Noblest Instrument" and "The Whipping," William Steig's drawings of Small Fry (*below*) have a human and familiar touch which lifts them above the level of broad, ordinary humor.

"*I* am *hurrying!*"

Courtesy of the artist and The New Yorker

did little sums on them gloomily, and then tore them up.

During my third lesson I saw the tears come to his eyes. He went up to Father and said he was sorry but he honestly felt sure I'd never be able to play.

Father didn't like this at all. He said he felt sure I would. He dismissed Herr M. briefly — the poor man came stumbling back down in two minutes. In that short space of time he had gallantly gone upstairs in a glow, resolved upon sacrificing his earnings for the sake of telling the truth. He returned with his earnings still running but with the look of a lost soul about him, as though he felt that his nerves and his sanity were doomed to destruction. He was low in his mind, and he talked to himself more than ever. Sometimes he spoke harshly of America, sometimes of fate.

But he no longer struggled. He accepted this thing as his destiny. He regarded me as an unfortunate something, outside the human species, whom he must simply try to labor with as well as he could. It was a grotesque, indeed a hellish experience, but he felt he must bear it.

He wasn't the only one — he was at least not alone in his sufferings. Mother, though expecting the worst, had tried to be hopeful about it, but at the end of a week or two I heard her and Margaret[1] talking it over. I was slaughtering a scale in the front basement when mother came down and stood outside the door in the kitchen hall and whispered, "Oh, Margaret!"

I watched them. Margaret was baking a cake. She screwed up her face, raised her arms, and brought them down with hands clenched.

"I don't know what we shall do, Margaret."

"The poor little feller," Margaret whispered. "He can't make the thing go."

This made me indignant. They were making me look like a lubber. I wished to feel always that I could make anything go.

I now began to feel a determination to master this thing. History shows us many examples of the misplaced determinations of men — they are one of the darkest aspects of human life; they spread so much needless pain — but I knew little history. And I viewed what little I did know romantically — I should have seen in such episodes their heroism, not their futility. Any role that seemed heroic attracted me, no matter how senseless.

Not that I saw any chance for heroism in our front basement, of course. You had to have a battlefield or something. I saw only that I was appearing ridiculous. But that stung my pride. I hadn't wanted to learn anything whatever about fiddles or music; but since I was in for it, I'd do it and show them I could. A boy will often put in enormous amounts of his time trying to prove he isn't as ridiculous as he thinks people think him.

Meanwhile Herr M. and I had discovered that I was nearsighted. On account of the violin's being an instrument that sticks out in front of one, I couldn't stand close enough to the music book to see the notes clearly. He didn't at first realize that I often made mistakes from that cause. When he and I finally comprehended that I had this defect, he had a sudden new hope that this might have been the whole trouble and that when it was corrected I might play like a human being at last.

Neither of us ventured to take up this matter with Father. We knew that it would have been hard to convince him that my eyes were not perfect, I being a son of his and presumably made in his image; and we knew that he immediately would have felt we were trying to make

[1] **Margaret:** the maid.

trouble for him and would have shown an amount of resentment which it was best to avoid. So Herr M., instead, lent me his glasses. These did fairly well. They turned the dim grayness of the notes into a queer bright distortion; but the main thing was they did make them brighter, so that I now saw more of them. How well I remember those little glasses. Poor, dingy old things. Herr M. was nervous about lending them to me; he feared that I'd drop them. It would have been safer if they had been spectacles: but no, they were pince-nez; and I had to learn to balance them across my nose as well as I could. I couldn't wear them up near my eyes because my nose was too thin there; I had to put them about halfway down, where there was enough flesh to hold them. I also had to tilt my head back, for the music stand was a little too tall for me. Herr M. sometimes mounted me on a stool, warning me not to step off. Then when I was all set, and when he without his glasses was blind, I would smash my way into the scales again.

All during the long winter months I worked away at this job. I gave no thought, of course, to the family. But they did to me. Our house was heated by a furnace, which had big warm-air pipes; these ran up through the walls with wide outlets into each room, and sound traveled easily and ringingly through their roomy tin passages. My violin could be heard in every part of the house. No one could settle down to anything while I was practicing. If visitors came, they soon left. Mother couldn't even sing to the baby. She would wait, watching the clock, until my long hour of scalework was over, and then come downstairs and shriek at me that my time was up. She would find me sawing away with my forehead wet, and my hair wet and stringy, and even my clothes slowly getting damp from my exertions. She would feel my collar, which was done for, and say I must change it. "Oh, mother! Please!" — for I was in a hurry now to run out and play. But she wasn't being fussy about my collar, I can see, looking back; she was using it merely as a barometer or gauge of my pores. She thought I had better dry myself before going out in the snow.

It was a hard winter for mother. I believe she also had fears for the baby. She sometimes pleaded with father, but no one could ever tell father anything. He continued to stand like a rock against stopping my lessons.

Schopenhauer,[1] in his rules for debating, shows how to win a weak case by insidiously transferring an argument from its right field and discussing it, instead, from some irrelevant but impregnable angle. Father knew nothing of Schopenhauer and was never insidious, but, nevertheless, he had certain natural gifts for debate. In the first place, his voice was powerful and stormy; and he let it out at full strength and kept on letting it out with a vigor that stunned his opponents. As a second gift, he was convinced at all times that his opponents were wrong. Hence, even if they did win a point or two it did them no good; for he dragged the issue to some other ground then, where he and Truth could prevail. When mother said it surely was plain enough that I had no ear, what was his reply? Why, he said that the violin was the noblest instrument invented by man. Having silenced her with this solid premise, he declared that it followed that any boy was lucky to be given the privilege of learning to play it. No boy should expect to learn it immediately. It required persistence. Everything, he had found, required persistence. The motto was, Never give up.

All his life, he declared, he had persevered in spite of discouragement, and he

[1] **Schopenhauer:** Arthur Schopenhauer (1788–1860), a German philosopher.

meant to keep on persevering; and he meant me to, too. He said that none of us realized what he had had to go through. If he had been the kind that gave up at the very first obstacle, where would he have been now — where would any of the family have been? The answer was, apparently, that we'd either have been in a very bad way, poking round for crusts in the gutter, or else nonexistent. We might have never even been born if father had not persevered.

Placed beside this record of father's vast trials overcome, the little difficulty of my learning to play the violin seemed a trifle. I faithfully spurred myself on again, to work at the puzzle. Even my teacher seemed impressed with these views on persistence. Though older than father, he had certainly not made as much money, and he bowed to the experience of a practical man who was a success. If he, Herr M., had been a success, he would not have had to teach boys; and sitting in this black pit in which his need of money had placed him, he saw more than ever that he must learn the ways of this world. He listened with all his heart, as to a god, when father shook his forefinger and told him how to climb to the heights where financial rewards were achieved. The idea he got was that perseverance was sure to lead to great wealth.

Consequently our front basement continued to be the home of lost causes.

Of course, I kept begging Herr M. to let me learn just one tune. Even though I seldom could whistle them, still I liked tunes; and I knew that, in my hours of practicing, a tune would be a comfort. That is, for myself. Here again I never gave a thought to the effect upon others.

Herr M., after many misgivings, to which I respectfully listened — though they were not spoken to me, they were muttered to himself pessimistically — hunted through a worn old book of selections and, after much doubtful fumbling, chose as simple a thing as he could find for me — for me and the neighbors.

It was spring now, and windows were open. That tune became famous.

What would the musician who had tenderly composed this air, years before, have felt if he had foreseen what an end it would have, on Madison Avenue, and how, before death, it would be execrated by that once peaceful neighborhood. I engraved it on their hearts, not in its true form but in my own eerie versions. It was the only tune I knew. Consequently I played and replayed it.

Even horrors when repeated grow old and lose part of their sting. But those I produced were, unluckily, never the same. To be sure, this tune kept its general structure the same, even in my sweating hands. There was always the place where I climbed unsteadily up to its peak, and that difficult spot where it wavered, or staggered, and stuck; and then a sudden jerk of resumption — I came out strong on that. Every afternoon when I got to that difficult spot, the neighbors dropped whatever they were doing to wait for that jerk, shrinking from the moment and yet feverishly impatient for it to come.

But what made the tune and their anguish so different each day? I'll explain. The strings of a violin are wound at the end around pegs, and each peg must be screwed in and tightened till the string sounds just right. Herr M. left my violin properly tuned when he went. But suppose a string broke or that somehow I jarred a peg loose. Its string then became slack and soundless. I had to retighten it. Not having an ear, I was highly uncertain about this.

Our neighbors never knew at what degree of tautness I'd put such a string. I didn't myself. I just screwed her up tight enough to make a strong reliable sound. Neither they nor I could tell which string would thus appear in a new role each day, nor foresee the profound transformations this would produce in that tune.

All that spring this unhappy and ill-destined melody floated out through my window and writhed in the air for one hour daily, in sunshine or storm. All that spring our neighbors and I daily toiled to its peak, and staggered over its hump, so to speak, and fell wailing through space.

Things now began to be said to mother which drove her to act. She explained to father that the end had come at last. Absolutely. "This awful nightmare cannot go on," she said.

Father pooh-poohed her.

She cried. She told him what it was doing to her. He said that she was excited and that her descriptions of the sounds I made were exaggerated and hysterical — must be. She was always too vehement, he shouted. She must learn to be calm.

"But you're downtown; *you* don't have to hear it!"

Father remained wholly skeptical.

She endeavored to shame him. She told him what awful things the neighbors were saying about him because of the noise I was making, for which he was responsible.

He couldn't be made to look at it that way. If there really were any unpleasantness, then I was responsible. He had provided me with a good teacher and a good violin — so he reasoned. In short, he had done his best; and no father could have done more. If I made hideous sounds after all that, the fault must be mine. He said that mother should be stricter with me, if necessary, and make me try harder.

This was the last straw. I couldn't try harder. When mother told me his verdict I said nothing, but my body rebelled. Self-discipline had its limits, and I wanted to be out: it was spring. I skimped my hours of practice when I heard the fellows playing outside. I came home late for lessons, even forgot them. Little by little they stopped.

Father was outraged. His final argument, I remember, was that my violin had cost twenty-five dollars; if I didn't learn it the money would be wasted, and he couldn't afford it. But it was put to him that my younger brother, Julian, could learn it, instead, later on. Then summer came, anyhow, and we went for three months to the seashore; and in the confusion of this father was defeated and I was set free.

In the autumn little Julian was led away one afternoon and imprisoned in the front basement in my place. I don't remember how long they kept him down there, but it was several years. He had an ear, however, and I believe he learned to play fairly well. This would have made a happy ending for Herr M. after all; but it was some other teacher, a younger man, who was engaged to teach Julian. Father said Herr M. was a failure.

THINK BACK OVER WHAT YOU HAVE READ

Confirming Dorothy Canfield's Judgment of the Essay

1. Father's "executive mood," described in the first paragraph, accounts for his initial folly — the folly which his son is about to expose. Notice *how* he goes about lining up his boys for music lessons, and *why*. If his way wasn't the right way or a good way, what is? Wherein lay his mistake? Wherein did he fail to understand boys? to understand Clarence in particular? Why was his choice of Herr M. as a music teacher for Clarence a poor one?

2. Why do you suppose Herr M. changed between the first and the second lesson from "cross" to "stern," from "sad" to "bitter"? Ponder the values of these words carefully. Can you find an explanation of his *bitterness?* Why had he "hardened"? Was he bitter against Clarence? against Clarence's father? He seemed very upset when he "went up to father" and said that Clarence would "never be able to play." What was upsetting him? Was it Clarence's playing? or something else? Why

does Clarence refer to him later as a "lost soul"?

3. On what basis do you rate "mother" and Margaret, the maid, more understanding of children than "father"?

4. At what moments did you feel sorry for Clarence? Was the situation at any time funny to him? Would you have felt like laughing at him had you been watching him practice? Did anyone in the whole family ever feel like laughing at him?

5. On page 346 Clarence says that "no one could ever tell father anything," and then he proceeds to tell you why his mother's pleadings that he be allowed to stop his lessons did not, for a whole winter, come to anything. He summarizes father's tactics under the term *Schopenhauer's rules for debating.* It might be well for you to study these tactics carefully. Of what did they consist? Why were they successful? Did you ever use similar tactics? or hear others use them? How could they have been combated? Why were mother's tactics powerless against them? Why were Herr M.'s tactics powerless against them? Clarence's? At what point in the story do you see father's resistance gradually being worn down? Did father admit his final defeat? In what ways did father *always* win?

Increase Your Power over Words

6. Without looking them up in a dictionary, what do you think is the meaning of each of the italicized words in the following sentences?

a. "He also had the advantage of playing on a good *robust* instrument" (page 343).

b. "But I had to go through a blacker and more *gruesome* experience" (page 343).

Composition Suggestion

7. Write a humorous satire, based on your own observation and in the vein of the last two essays, on any of the following topics or any similar ones approved by your teacher:

a. Sins committed against children

b. If dogs could only speak (or write about the sins committed against them)!

c. They call it education.

For Ambitious Students

8. *Life with Father* has been made into a play. Perhaps a group of students will volunteer to read aloud or dramatize one or two scenes from the book.

THE WHIPPING

by Hiram Percy Maxim (1869–1936)

In this essay you are to meet another father portrayed through the eyes of a boy. This time, however, it is the father who understands the boy and the mother who needs the lesson. The satire of the essay is directed against unwise punishment of children.

"The Whipping" is taken from *A Genius in the Family,* the author's reminiscences of his father, the celebrated engineer and inventor, Sir Hiram Stevens Maxim, who is best known for the invention of the Maxim gun, the first successful automatic gun.

AS I grew older it was natural that I should become more and more of a problem to my mother. My besetting sins were teasing my sisters and breaking things around the house. Finally a day came when I did a thing which my mother felt was beyond her.

She had a full-length pier glass in her room which extended from the floor to the ceiling. It had a white marble base with a flat place on the latter which extended out into the room about a foot. Little Florence discovered that a large glass marble would bounce beautifully off this base. One day she was bouncing her marble in front of the pier glass, and it occurred to me that it would surprise her very much were I to snatch the marble while it was in the air. I edged up, and when I was within reach I made a quick pass to snatch the marble. But I miscalculated. Instead of closing my hand upon it, I struck it with my hand and knocked it against the pier glass, which it broke.

I told my mother, and when she came upstairs and beheld her broken mirror she sank into a chair and wept. I was desolated. It hurt me inexpressibly that I should be the cause of my mother's weeping. She told me that I had got beyond her control and that she would have to turn me over to my father for a good whipping, that I paid no attention to her and, as things were going, there was no living with me.

Turning me over to my father for a good whipping was a brand-new idea to me. I could not remember that my father had ever laid a hand upon me, except possibly once, when I was very young indeed, when he tapped me gently with the tongue of his draftsman's T square.[1] This was very light and very thin and stung for a moment. It would not bruise. It is an admirable instrument for administering a little corporal punishment.

That evening after my father had come home he was led up to the broken pier glass and shown my latest and worst offense. It appeared to prostrate him utterly. He sank into a chair, held his head in his hands, rocked back and forth in exquisite agony, and gave several similar indications of being completely undone by the spectacle. He made it an extremely painful scene for me, and I certainly did feel low in my mind. My mother told him that I was getting entirely out of hand and that he must give me a good whipping or I would break everything in the house besides making them all thoroughly miserable. Father said he was too prostrated to undertake the whipping then but that he would attend to it after supper.

Supper was a doleful affair. I had never sat through such a nerve-wearing ordeal before. I was in the deepest disgrace, and everybody, including little Florence, was sunk in woe. I had never been so thoroughly unhappy.

After supper my father announced that he would read his paper first and when he had finished he would take up the whipping matter. I had never had a whipping. My mother had spanked me aplenty, but I did not regard that as a whipping. I wondered what it would be like to be whipped. I waited patiently until my father had finished his evening paper, sitting in a deep gloom meanwhile but with no fear or terror. My woe was born of having broken my mother's pier glass, which she treasured, and of throwing the whole family into gloom.

When my father had finished his paper he got up briskly, saying, "Well now. Come along, Percy. Let's attend to this whipping business." He led the way out into the back yard, where we visited my mother's shrubs and bushes — from which a suitable whip was to be cut. My father had his pocketknife open, ready to cut when he found a stalk that met the requirements. He explained to me that it was necessary to find one that had just the right length and thickness and straightness. If it were too short, it would not have enough spring. If it were too long, it would have too much spring and would break. If it were too thin, it would be weak; whereas if it were too thick, it would bruise — which, of course, would not do.

We searched and searched without finding anything that just suited. I became interested in the problem and pointed out several likely-looking sticks which appeared as though they might answer the exacting specifications. He discussed my selections with me, examining each one with care. After spending quite a time at it, he finally decided that the best thing to do would be to cut several and try them. He cut a long thin one, a long thick one, a middle-length one, and several other compromises. This made five whips. I was very much impressed with his technique. I could see that between all of the whips it was more than likely that one would be found which would suit much better than possibly could be the case were one only to be selected by guessing. I did not recognize it at the time, but I

[1] **T square**: a ruler with a crossbar at one end which serves as a guide; so called because it is shaped like a T.

had received my first lesson in engineering research.

After all had been prepared and whittled down smooth, he said, " Now come along up to my room and we will try them." He led the way to the third-floor front, which was his room. Arrived here, he took off his coat, his collar and necktie, and rolled up his sleeves. I was a bit concerned at this, for it suggested that a whipping must be something calling for considerable activity. He laid the five whips on the bed and, taking one at a time, he smote the coverlet. The savage whir and the succeeding whack sounded all over the house. He put real muscle into it. The long thin whip broke. He explained that he had expected this to happen, for the stick was too thin for its length. The thick one made a fearful whir and whack when it hit the coverlet. We rejected this one because it was evident that it would bruise. Later on I heard my mother say that she never suffered such horrible nervous strain in all her life, listening to the savage whir of the whip and the awful whack as it struck. She imagined my little body might be receiving these blows; but as I did not cry out and as she could hear me talking calmly afterward, she assumed that I could not be suffering very acutely. I firmly believe that most of this bed-whacking business was for my mother's benefit, as she sat downstairs trying to read.

When we had whacked the bed coverlet for a long time, testing the whips and breaking most of them, my father was far from being satisfied. He sat down on the edge of the bed and outlined in his clear way the problem as it confronted us. Said he, " What we need is something fairly long, very strong, and yet very light. It also must be very springy. Where can we find such a thing which we could use for a whip? "

We thought and thought. By this time I was as keenly interested in the solution of the problem as though someone else were to receive the whipping. I suggested a baseball bat; but in the same breath I pointed out that it was unsuitable, although I pointed out that it would hit awful hard.

" Oh, *much* too hard," he replied. " Why, you could break a man's back with a baseball bat, and kill him." He recoiled at the suggestion of a baseball bat.

" I suppose a broomstick would be too stiff, too," I ventured.

" Altogether too stiff and too heavy. It would break bones and be very dangerous."

There was a long pause here while we both thought. Then an idea occurred to me. " Gosh, Papa! I know the very thing. That thin cane of yours." Among his walking sticks was a very thin one which I used to admire.

" By Jove! " he exclaimed. " That's a good idea. Go and fetch it."

I remember hurrying downstairs to the clothes closet in the butler's pantry, where the canes and umbrellas were kept. As I ran through the reception room, being in my usual hurry, I had to pass my mother. She seemed much surprised to see me hurrying to the clothes closet. She asked me what I was after. I answered:

" We're trying to find a good whip. We're going to try the thin cane."

She asked something else, but I was much too busy to stop just then and explain. She afterward said that my being in such a hurry to find a cane with which to be whipped seemed one of the most extraordinary things she ever heard of.

When I returned with the thin cane, my father whacked the coverlet with it with all his might. It made a particularly savage noise. My mother must have winced when she heard it. After whacking the bed coverlet until my mother was ready to fly out of her skin, my father shook his head and handed the cane to me, asking me to try it and say what I thought. I had noticed him putting a lot of " beef " into his blows, so I decided to put in all I had. Getting the best grip I could, which was difficult on account of the curved handle, I whacked the bed coverlet for all that was in me. It only made a fair noise, and my father feared my mother might not hear it. He told me to put more " beef " into it. I wiped off my hands, took a fresh grip, took careful aim, and belabored the coverlet with all my might. When my father expressed disappointment over the weight of my blows, I explained that the curved handle got in my way and that no one could hit hard, with the handle where it was. My father was not satisfied, and we went into executive session again. It was quite apparent to me what was required, but we would have to do a lot of searching around to find just exactly the thing. It must have appeared this way to my father, too, for he finally said:

" Well, I guess we shall have to give up the whipping, Percy. We can't seem to find the right whip. But, anyway, you understand that you must be more careful around the house and that you must not make so much trouble for Mamma, don't you; and you will begin tomorrow morning and try to be a better boy, won't you, Percy? "

I was very deeply impressed by the way he said it. He was asking me as a favor to him and to Mamma to do something. I realized that it would be very mean indeed of me to fail to do as he asked. And it would be yet meaner not to try to make things more pleasant for Mamma. So I said, " Yes, Papa. I will." And then we went downstairs and explained to Mamma that the whipping matter had to be called off. I am glad to be able to say that I kept my promise in pretty fair shape, as time proved.

THINK BACK OVER WHAT YOU HAVE READ

Appreciating the Satire of the Essay

1. What did the boy's mother mean when she said that he " had got beyond her control "? Does this indictment of the boy seem to you extravagant? Did the mother in this case act as you think a wise mother should? Was turning the boy over to his father for a whipping a good idea?

2. The mother turned against her child in anger for breaking the mirror. What did the father do when he first saw what had been done? What was the boy's first reaction to his mother's threat? to his father's pretended grief over the mirror?

3. Notice what the father says to the boy as he takes him out to find a suitable whip. Does it give you any clue to what is to follow? Were the words designed to frighten the boy?

4. What reasons can you offer for the father's delay in selecting a whip? for his long-continued experimentation with the whips?

5. At what point in the story does the boy indicate that his father's first lesson in " engineering research " has been grasped? What irony do you see in his ready grasp of this lesson?

6. What lesson do you think " Mamma " learned? At what point did you realize that the whipping was for her rather than for Percy?

DID YOU NOTICE HOW THE ESSAYS WERE WRITTEN?

Style, like form, grows out of an author's relationship to his subject matter. How, for example, does E. E. Slosson *feel* about stars? or Antoine St. Exupéry about the elements? When you have answered this question, you are on the way toward solving the mystery of style. For style, it must be remembered, is not mere decoration; it is not something added to content, like frosting to a cake. Rather, it is like something that blooms — providing the seed has been planted in fertile soil. There are no rules for style. And there is no standard yardstick by which to measure *good* style. Style, like form, is good or bad depending on the purpose of the author. And just as there are many different forms in which a story may be told, so are there many different styles in which an essay or biography may be written.

The resources of an essayist or biographer, however, can be named. Here are some of the means by which the authors in this section of the text succeeded in winning your interest in their subject matter.

Descriptive power. Without the power to summon graphic pictures to the imagination of the reader, or to stir his senses by apt comparison, an essayist or biographer would be severely handicapped. Of what use to read about an airplane flight unless the writer can reproduce his sensations for us to feel with something of the same thrill that he did? Of what use to talk about being blind unless the author can make us realize her handicap?

Swift narrative and exposition. A skillful writer knows when to linger over detail and when to hurry on to the next picture. He knows, too, how to point up for his reader the meaning which is to be derived from those pictures. Perhaps you remember that in " The Jersey Devil Came " you were really following a story, although a story interrupted frequently by the author's comment and a story told in a straightforward manner without the dramatic suspense found in the " short story." Both of these narrative essays, as they might be called, *subordinated detail* to suit their particular purpose. Their pictures, in other words, were illustrations — illustrations of ideas.

Appeal to the imagination. An essayist or biographer — as well as a story writer or poet — has resource to the metaphor and simile[1] and to allusion.[2] William Beebe, for example, resorts to both.

Sentence rhythm. It is a mistake to regard rhythm as belonging exclusively to poetry. Prose has rhythm, too. Indeed, everyone has his own speech rhythm, as characteristic as his walk. So does each essay writer have his own more or less peculiar sentence rhythm. Read " The Popover Stars " aloud, for example and see if Slosson *sounds* like William Beebe.

These, then, are the language devices used by writers to engage the interest of their readers. These are the devices which combine mysteriously to produce style — a style that reveals sympathy, admiration, amusement, resentment, or some other strong reaction to life on the part of an author. In order that you may become more alert to such differences in style in your reading, the following questions, to be used in review of this section of the text, are suggested for class discussion:

1. How would you compare, or contrast, the descriptive powers of the following writers: Beebe, St. Exupéry, Slosson?
2. Suppose that Slosson had been moved to write on the mystery of migration. Would he have produced a different sort of article from that of Devoe? in what respects?
3. Do you see any difference between the attitudes of J. Frank Dobie and Stewart Edward White toward the subjects they are writing about? between Courtney Riley Cooper and Martin Johnson?
4. What kind of appeal is common to the essays by Etsu Inagaki Sugimoto and Helen Keller? Are their styles alike in any ways?
5. What is the special manner in which Ruth Crawford develops her main point that the displacement of men by machines plays havoc in people's lives? *How* does she get you to realize the importance of the issue? How does Stephen Vincent Benét get you to consider the question of superstition? in the usual way?
6. What is the method used in common by Clarence Day and Hiram Percy Maxim to call your attention to the sins committed against children?
7. Of all the styles introduced to you in this section, which ones strike you as being particularly picturesque? earnest? challenging? whimsical? moving? inspiring?

[1] For a fuller discussion of these devices turn to page 413. [2] If you have forgotten what an allusion is, refer again to page 148.

SUGGESTIONS FOR FURTHER READING

Abe Lincoln Grows Up by Carl Sandburg
The early years, told by a great writer. The reader follows Lincoln until he is nineteen.

An American Doctor's Odyssey by Victor Heiser
Although this is a long book, adventure follows the author from the first exciting chapter on the Johnstown flood until the last page.

A Child Went Forth by Helen M. Doyle
The autobiography of a girl whose determination to become a doctor dispelled obstacles that would have defeated many men.

Canoeing with the Cree by Arnold Sevareid
Two high-school boys make a canoe trip from their home to Hudson Bay, paddling 2,250 miles. This is a true account of a trip which required courage, stamina, and perseverance.

Far Away and Long Ago by W. H. Hudson
Hudson, a famous naturalist, describes his life as a boy on the South American pampas, the "wild West" of our neighbor continent.

Friends and Fiddlers by Catherine Bowen
This is a book not to be missed. Those who play some musical instrument will wish the book were longer, but anyone who plays a mouth organ or sings in his shower will like the book. Humor and music and biography are mixed in a delightful way.

Indian Boyhood by Charles Eastman
The autobiography of a Sioux Indian named Ohiyesa who takes the name of Charles Eastman when he accepts the white man's ways. The book tells of his Indian playmates, childhood games, hunting, forest adventures, dances, feasts, and campfires.

Jane Addams of Hull House by Winifred Wise
In spite of ill-health, Jane Addams determined to champion the cause of the poor. Her inspiring work in social service, a fair deal for workers, the making of Americans, the vote for women, and the cause of peace enter into this book.

Julia Newberry's Diary by Julia Newberry and *Maud* edited by Richard Lee Strout
Two diaries of real girls who lived in the 1800's. Anyone who thinks girls in those days didn't lead exciting lives should read these diaries immediately. Julia lived through the Chicago fire to become a belle in Europe, where she died suddenly and tragically. Maud is still living, but her troubles with boys are over. She is much more interested in her grandchildren now.

Madame Curie by Eve Curie
A daughter writes of her famous mother, whose devotion to science and the search for radium led her through many hardships.

Marbacka by Selma Lagerlöf
Childhood of a girl in Sweden who later became a world-famous writer and Nobel prize winner.

Mexican Interlude by Joseph H. Jackson
A picture of our neighbor to the south, telling of the old as well as the new.

Microbe Hunters by Paul de Kruif
Why is this book read from high school through college? Why do libraries need so many copies of it? Does it mark a new frontier in the advance of American civilization?

On the Bottom by Edward Ellsburg
The inspiring leadership of a commander and the almost superhuman nerve, skill, and determination of a rescue diving crew results in the raising of a wrecked submarine from 130 feet of water. Equally interesting is Ellsburg's latest book, *Men under the Sea,* which closes with an account of the *Squalus* disaster and the rescue of thirty-three men.

Sagittarius Rising by Cecil Lewis
Cecil Lewis was an English aviator during the World War. He has never lost the thrill of man's conquest of the air.

Sam Houston, Patriot by Flora Warren Seymour
Sam Houston's whole life was exciting. Founding the Texas Republic was his most memorable adventure, but this book recounts many others.

The Watcher in the Woods by Dallas Lore Sharp
If you like nature lore, if you enjoy the woods and wish to sharpen your powers of observation, this account of wild life will be next on your library card.

Victors of Peace by Arthur Quiller-Couch
These are the stories of three people whose service to humanity was unselfish — Father Damien, Louis Pasteur, and Florence Nightingale.

Your Wings by Assen Jordanoff
This is one of the most fascinating books on aviation ever published. The author, an aviator himself, speaks to the reader as if instructor and student were in a plane together. Many drawings and diagrams clarify points which are difficult to explain in words.

HOW GOOD IS YOUR TASTE IN MAGAZINES?

Here is a list of magazines which are commonly found on newsstands. Not all are of equal worth. Which ones do you read?

American
Atlantic Monthly
Better Homes and Gardens
Collier's
Cosmopolitan
Daring Detective
Etude
Fighting Wings of the Aces
Flying Aces
Good Housekeeping
Harper's
Liberty
Life
McCall's
Nation
National Geographic
New Republic
Newsweek
Open Road for Boys
Pathfinder
Popular Aviation
Popular Mechanics
Ranch Romances
Reader's Digest
Saturday Evening Post
Scholastic
Scientific American
Screen Romances
Time
Travel
True Confessions
True Story
Western Trails
Woman's Home Companion

Just below you will find three descriptions of magazines. Which titles above would you place with each of these descriptions?

LEVEL I. *Good Magazines:* those which contain valuable, well-written articles and original stories. These magazines do not stoop to meet the reader's ordinary level of understanding but credit him with intelligence and a willingness to think and learn. News and current events are reported fairly with a minimum of propaganda and sensationalism.

LEVEL II. *Average Magazines:* those which attempt to please the average reader by offering stories and articles which do not run contrary to his attitudes or his expectations. Often these are well edited and some very good material is included. News magazines on this level are fairly reliable, but inaccuracies and one-sided points of view occasionally appear.

LEVEL III. *Trash Magazines:* those which exist purely to make money and consequently appeal to the weaknesses of buyers. Stories are built upon the same formula, the reader need not worry that the slightest strain will be placed upon his intelligence, and the shoddy flimflam of hair-raising action or tearful love betrays a hack writer grinding out work at a penny a line.

BALLADS AND TALES

MOST POPULAR songs have their brief day of fame and, after a few weeks on the "hit parade," quietly breathe their last. Out of the many, however, a few remain: "St. Louis Blues" and "Alexander's Ragtime Band" because of their irresistible rhythms; "The Sidewalks of New York" and "Golden Slippers" because of their tunes, simple and easy to sing. Even more lasting, however, are those songs which spring up anonymously from the people themselves: cowboy songs like "Home on the Range" and Negro spirituals like "Deep River." These are the folk songs of America, the ballads which you know, made up not only by cowboy and Negro but by sailor, lumberjack, mountaineer, and railroad worker.

Not only songs, but tales and poems come from the people. Yarns about Paul Bunyan and Babe, the enormous blue ox, originated with the early lumberjacks. Perhaps at scout camps you have added your own "tall one" to the Paul Bunyan legend. Pecos Bill, the vaquero who once mounted a real cyclone and rode it off across the plains, was created by the cowpunchers of the Southwest, and the legends about Davy Crockett stretch from Tennessee to Texas. All these heroes were real men whose daring exploits stirred popular imagination. Paul was a Canadian who lived in the early 1800's, and Davy Crockett, a name with which you are already familiar, fought in the war for Texas independence.

Fundamental qualities of the ballad. Ballads and tales are the oldest form of literature. Their original purpose was to tell a story that would stir the emotions. In form they were not as polished as the modern imitations. With their simple earnestness and dramatic force, these old tales spoken in verse were, however, for all their artistic crudity, a powerful stimulant to primitive audiences. Woven out of the sorrows and hardships of life, the common lot of mankind in olden days, they are predominantly tragic and somber in tone.

The trick of luring the audience into choral response gave the ballad its popular refrain, a tag by which we now recognize its folk origin. Except for the four-lined stanza with its alternate lines of rhyme — a pattern easy to memorize — the ballad maker was permitted wide choice of form. He might repeat or skip a beat or vary his accent at pleasure. The urge to get on with his story left little inclination to smooth out the lines of his verse, so that stanzas were often roughhewn.

Modern literary ballads. The form and spirit of these old ballads have been carried on by poets of modern times. Masefield and Kipling — whom you are to meet in this section — not only have captured the forceful rhythms and the sturdy storytelling power of the old ballad, but to these have added skillful versifying and pictorial power; so that the literary ballad, as the more finished product is called, has become a popular poetic form.

You will find among the narrative poems in this section of the book a wide variety of tales ranging from the old folk ballad to the modern literary tale. But in all the stories you will hear echoes of the past: the sharp stab of intense feeling, the surge of vigorous rhythm, and the swift-moving dramatic narrative — all these are qualities of the old-fashioned ballad.

Old Ballads

IN EARLY Scottish and English ballads favorite themes occur over and over again, and, like the quilting patterns of our great-grandmother's day, endings such as the rose-and-briar ending of "The Douglas Tragedy" were handed down from one generation to another. Around such heroic names as Black Douglas and Robin Hood there grew up whole cycles of ballads. By all these signs you may recognize in the poems presented here the folk origin of ballads. Notice, as you read the first two poems, the theme of secret elopement, a favorite theme in all literature but here made more romantic by a medieval setting. You will feel the sullen tragedy of the first and the hushed suspense of the second. "By the Turret Stair," you will see, has the ease and grace which indicate a later authorship than "The Douglas Tragedy." The Robin Hood ballad, you will recognize, is set to the happy, carefree tune characteristic of all the legends of Sherwood Forest.

THE DOUGLAS TRAGEDY

Old Scottish Ballad

"Rise up, rise up, now, Lord Douglas," she says,
"And put on your armor so bright;
Let it never be said that a daughter of thine
Was married to a lord under night.

"Rise up, rise up, my seven bold sons, 5
And put on your armor so bright,
And take better care o' your youngest sister,
For your eldest's awa' the last night."

He's mounted her on a milk-white steed,
And himself on a dapple gray, 10
With a bugelet horn hung down by his side,
And lightly they rode away.

8. **awa'**: away. 9. **He**: Lord William, named in the next stanza, the lover who stole Lord Douglas's daughter.

Lord William lookit o'er his left shoulder,
To see what he could see,
And there he spy'd her seven brethren bold, 15
Come riding over the lee.

"Light down, light down, Lady Margaret," he said,
"And hold my steed in your hand,
Until that against your seven brethren bold,
And your father, I mak' a stand." 20

She held his steed in her milk-white hand,
And never shed one tear,
Until that she saw her seven brethren fa',
And her father hard-fighting, who lov'd her so dear.

"O hold your hand, Lord William!" she said, 25
"For your strokes they are wondrous sair;
True lovers I can get many a ane,
But a father I can never get mair."

O she's ta'en out her handkerchief,
It was o' the holland sae fine, 30
And aye she dighted her father's bloody wounds,
That were redder than the wine.

"O chuse, O chuse, Lady Margaret," he said,
"O whether will ye gang or bide?"
"I'll gang, I'll gang, Lord William," she said, 35
"For ye have left me no other guide."

He's lifted her on a milk-white steed;
And himself on a dapple gray,
With a bugelet horn hung down by his side,
And slowly they baith rade away. 40

O they rade on, and on they rade,
And a' by the light o' the moon,
Until they came to yon wan water,
And there they lighted down.

They lighted down to tak' a drink 45
O' the spring that ran sae clear,
And down the stream ran his gude heart's blood,
And sair she gan to fear.

"Hold up, hold up, Lord William," she says,
"For I fear that you are slain." 50
"'Tis naething but the shadow o' my scarlet cloak,
That shines in the water sae plain."

O they rade on, and on they rade,
And a' by the light o' the moon,
Until they cam' to his mother's ha' door,
And there they lighted down. 56

"Get up, get up, lady mother," he says,
"Get up and let me in!
Get up, get up, lady mother," he says,
"For this night my fair lady I've win. 60

"O mak my bed, lady mother," he says,
"O mak it braid and deep,
And lay Lady Margaret close at my back,
And the sounder I will sleep."

Lord William was dead lang ere midnight, 65
Lady Margaret lang ere day,
And all true lovers that go thegither,
May they have mair luck than they!

Lord William was buried in St. Mary's kirk,
Lady Margaret in Mary's quire; 70
Out o' the lady's grave grew a bonny red rose,
And out o' the knight's a brier.

23. **fa'**: fall. 26. **sair**: sore. 27. **ane**: one. 28. **mair**: more. 29. **ta'en**: taken. 34. **gang or bide**: go or stay. 40. **baith**: both.

55. **ha'**: hall. 65. **lang**: long. 69. **kirk**: church. 70. **quire**: choir.

And they twa met, and they twa plat,
  And fain they wad be near;
And a' the warld might ken right weel 75
  They were twa lovers dear.

But bye and rade the Black Douglas,
  And wow, but he was rough!
For he pull'd up the bonny brier,
  And flang 't in St. Mary's Loch. 80

73. **plat**: intertwined. 77. **Black Douglas**: probably a descendant of the Lord Douglas killed in stanza seven. 80. **Loch**: lake.

BY THE TURRET STAIR

Anonymous Literary Ballad of about the Year 1400

Run, run, little page, tell your lady fair
That her lover waits by the turret stair,
That the stars are out, and the night wind blows
Up the garden path from the crimson rose!
  Run, run, little page! 5

Haste, haste, little page, ere the round moon's rim
Peeps over the edge of the forest dim,
And the wolfhound bays from his kennel deep!
And the warder peers from the castle keep!
  Haste, haste, little page! 10

Soft, soft, little page, lest her sire may guess,
By her look of fear and of fond distress,
That he hides in the night by the turret stair
Who would steal from her bower the flower so fair!
  Soft, soft, little page! 15

List, list, little page! Did the nightjar cry,
Or was it the low wind murmuring by?
And was there the sound of a faint footfall
Far away in the depths of the vaulted hall?
  List, list, little page! 20

9. **keep**: the stronghold of a castle.

See, see, little page, who, clad in white,
Steals out of the door in the shadowy light!
Is't an angel? Aye, 'tis my lady fair,
And she speeds to her love down the turret stair!
  See, see, little page! 25

Farewell, little page, far away, away,
Through the gloom of night to the bloom of day,
My lady sweet and I must fare
Till we reach the foot of *my* turret stair!
  Farewell, little page! 30

HOW ROBIN HOOD RESCUED THE WIDOW'S SONS

Old English Ballad

There are twelve months in all the year,
  As I hear many say,
But the merriest month in all the year
  Is the merry month of May.

Now Robin Hood is to Nottingham gone,
  With a link a down, and a day, 6
And there he met a silly old woman,
  Was weeping on the way.

"What news? what news? thou silly old woman,
  What news hast thou for me?" 10
Said she, "There's my three sons in Nottingham town
  Today condemned to die."

"O, have they parishes burnt?" he said,
  "Or have they ministers slain?
Or have they robbed any virgin? 15
  Or other men's wives have ta'en?"

6. **With a link a down, and a day**: These are mere tra-la-la words without meaning. 9. **silly**: as used here, simple rather than foolish.

"They have no parishes burnt, good sir,
Nor yet have ministers slain,
Nor have they robbed any virgin,
Nor other men's wives have ta'en." 20

"O, what have they done?" said Robin Hood,
"I pray thee tell to me."
"It's for slaying of the king's fallow deer,
Bearing their long bows with thee."

"Dost thou not mind, old woman," he said, 25
"How thou mad'st me to sup and dine?
By the truth of my body," quoth bold Robin Hood,
"You could not tell it in better time."

Now Robin Hood is to Nottingham gone,
With a link a down, and a day, 30
And there he met with a silly old palmer,
Was walking along the highway.

"What news? what news? thou silly old man,
What news, I do thee pray?"
Said he, "Three squires in Nottingham town 35
Are condemned to die this day."

"Come change thy apparel with me, old man,
Come change thy apparel for mine;
Here is ten shillings in good silver,
Go drink it in beer or wine." 40

"O, thine apparel is good," he said,
"And mine is ragged and torn;
Wherever you go, wherever you ride,
Laugh not an old man to scorn."

"Come change thy apparel with me, old churl, 45
Come change thy apparel with mine;
Here is a piece of good broad gold,
Go feast thy brethren with wine."

Then he put on the old man's hat,
It stood full high on the crown: 50
"The first bold bargain that I come at,
It shall make thee come down!"

Then he put on the old man's cloak,
Was patched black, blue, and red;
He thought it no shame, all the day long,
To wear the bags of bread. 56

Then he put on the old man's breeks,
Was patched from leg to side:
"By the truth of my body," bold Robin can say,
"This man loved little pride!" 60

Then he put on the old man's hose,
Were patched from knee to wrist:
"By the truth of my body," said bold Robin Hood,
"I'd laugh if I had any list."

Then he put on the old man's shoes, 65
Were patched both beneath and aboon:
Then Robin Hood swore a solemn oath,
"It's good habit that makes a man."

Now Robin Hood is to Nottingham gone,
With a link a down, and a down, 70
And there he met with the proud sheriff,
Was walking along the town.

"Save you, save you, sheriff!" he said;
"Now heaven you save and see!
And what will you give to a silly old man
Today will your hangman be?" 76

"Some suits, some suits," the sheriff he said,
"Some suits I'll give to thee;
Some suits, some suits, and pence thirteen,
Today's a hangman's fee." 80

24. The widow's sons were apparently members of Robin Hood's band of outlaws. 31. **palmer:** pilgrim or beggar.

57. **breeks:** breeches. 62. **wrist:** ankle. 64. **list:** inclination. 68. **habit:** suit of clothes. 73. **Save you:** short for God save you!

Then Robin he turns him round about,
 And jumps from stock to stone:
"By the truth of my body," the sheriff he said,
 "That's well jumpt, thou nimble old man!"

"I was ne'er a hangman in all my life, 85
 Nor yet intends to trade:
But curst he be," said bold Robin,
 "That first was a hangman made!

"I've a bag for meal, and a bag for malt,
 And a bag for barley and corn; 90
A bag for bread, and a bag for beef,
 And a bag for my little small horn.

"I have a horn in my pocket,
 I got it from Robin Hood,
And still when I set it to my mouth, 95
 For thee it blows little good."

"O, wind thy horn, thou proud fellow!
 Of thee I have no doubt.
I wish that thou give such a blast,
 Till both thy eyes fall out." 100

The first loud blast that he did blow,
 He blew both loud and shrill;
A hundred and fifty of Robin Hood's men
 Came riding over the hill.

The next loud blast that he did give, 105
 He blew both loud and amain,
And quickly sixty of Robin Hood's men
 Came shining over the plain.

"O, who are those," the sheriff he said,
 "Come tripping over the lea?" 110
"They're my attendants," brave Robin did say;
 "They'll pay a visit to thee."

They took the gallows from the slack,
 They set it in the glen, 114
They hanged the proud sheriff on that,
 And released their own three men.

81. **him:** himself. 113. **slack:** square, or commons, where gallows was set up.

THINK BACK OVER WHAT YOU HAVE READ

Responding to the Theme of Romantic Elopement

1. What picturesque details, typical of the times, do you notice in the setting of medieval elopement?
2. What dramatic tableaux do you see in your imagination after reading the first two poems? Were you an artist, what colors would you use to paint them? What words and phrases from the poems give you suggestions?
3. What is the dramatic effect of dialogue in the first poem? To what end does the conversation between Lord William and his bride move with fateful certainty? At what point in the ballad were you first aware of its direction? What lines uttered by Lord William are full of dramatic interest?
4. What progress do the extra lines in each of the six stanzas of the monologue "By the Turret Stair" make? What pictures does each of these poetic injunctions summon to mind?
5. What symbolism do you see in the rose-and-briar ending of "The Douglas Tragedy"?
6. What lines in the first poem are clumsy in their rhythm? By what rhymes does the second poem suggest greater literary finish? Do you detect any clues of group authorship in the first poem; that is, stanzas suggesting that they were written by different persons?
7. What realization of life in the Middle Ages do you get from these two poems? What hints of dark romance? of grim tragedy? What epitaphs would you write, in the manner of a newspaper headline, for Lord William and his bride?

Recognizing the Earmarks of the Robin Hood Tradition

8. What elements in the third poem of this group are typical of the Robin Hood legends?
9. What lines recapture the happy, carefree nature of Robin?
10. What lines reveal his traditional virtues: generosity, gratitude, and good nature?
11. What spritely comedy do you see in the stanzas that describe his change of apparel with the palmer? What fun does Robin get out of the transaction? From his description, what picture do you see of him in his new togs? (Perhaps someone in the class will sketch him.)
12. What elements in the last two stanzas

make the ending of the tale a popular one? What other versions of the same theme can you cite from legendary lore?

Increase Your Power over Words

13. In "The Douglas Tragedy" you met the word *holland* (line 30). Your dictionary will tell you that it is fine, unbleached linen, first manufactured in Holland, from which country it takes its name. Probably it was first called *Holland linen;* then the word *linen* was dropped and *holland* alone was used. We have many words in our language similarly derived. *China* was originally *Chinaware* (still called *chinaware* at times) because the first porcelainware came from China. No doubt you have heard of *morocco,* a fine leather first made by the Moors, natives of the country Morocco. *Sèvres* is a fine porcelain made at Sèvres, a town in France.

Can you think of any other words that have the names of the places where they originated?

For Ambitious Students

14. *A study of folklore.* Have you a folklore society in your neighborhood? If so, perhaps you can find out some of the interesting things they are doing and report to the class.

What local songs or ballads do you know? Perhaps you live in a community where ballads flourish and have caught at firsthand the spirit of oral tradition.

The following bibliography will suggest possibilities for a study of American folklore:

Colcord, Joanna, *Roll and Go, Songs of American Sailormen*
Davis, A. K., Jr. (ed.), *The Traditional Ballads of Virginia*
Dobie, J. F., *Texas and Southwestern Lore*
Erickson, F. H., and Smith, M. W. (eds.), *Minstrelsy of Maine*
Korson, G. A., *Songs and Ballads of the Anthracite Miner*
Lomax, J. A., *Cowboy Songs and Other Frontier Ballads*
McGill, Josephine (ed.), *Folk Songs of Kentucky Mountains*
Sandburg, Carl, *The American Songbag*
Smith, L. A., *The Music of the Waters*
Sturges, E. B., and Hughes, Robert (eds.), *Songs of the Hills of Vermont*

15. *The theme of elopement in literature.* The following poems deal with the romantic theme of elopement:

Campbell, Thomas, "Lord Ullin's Daughter"
Keats, John, "The Eve of St. Agnes"
Scott, Walter, "Lochinvar"; "Jock of Hazeldean"

16. *Robin Hood in song and ballad.*

Child, F. J. (ed.), *Ballads,* Vol. V
Sargent, H. C., and Kittredge, G. L. (eds.), *English and Scottish Popular Ballads*
Perkins, L. F., *Robin Hood, His Deeds and Adventures as Recounted in Old English Ballads*
Dietrick, Laurabelle, and Franz-Walsh, Joseph, *The Merry Ballads of Robin Hood*

17. *Gathering ballad material from the newspaper.* What news stories clipped from the daily papers suggest to you a theme or an incident or characterization typical of the old ballads? Can you find a modern variation of the Robin Hood theme? or of Lord William's and Lady Margaret's elopement? Who are our popular heroes whose names should be extolled in song? What tragic incidents, typical of the times, stir the same response in every heart? After the class has discussed thoroughly the possibilities of putting modern news in ballad form, perhaps some members of the class will attempt an imitation of the ballad measure.

Modern Literary Ballads

VERY LIKELY you noticed in the old ballads you have just read the effective use of dialogue to carry forward the story. This device is frequently used in modern literary ballads in order to intensify the dramatic effect.

You have overheard bits of dramatic dialogue on the street corner, in the lobby, or over the counter; and you are, therefore, familiar with the need for guessing what it means from hints let fall by the speakers themselves. This is the feat demanded of you in reading dramatic poetry. In the poems that follow, you must paint in the background yourself from odds and ends only faintly suggested. But the task, for all its initial difficulty, is appealing to the imagination. Read slowly enough to reconstruct each of the stage settings in which the dialogues take place, so that you will " see " the poem as well as " hear " it.

REBECCA NIXON AND MARTHA WAUGH

by Wilfrid Wilson Gibson (1880–)

If your clock's going at all, it must be slow.
Surely, it's stopped?

It stopped a week ago.

A week ago — and you have let it stand?

I hadn't the heart to wind it up. No hand
But Ben's has turned the key since he, himself, 5
Put the clock there upon the mantelshelf
The day that we came home for the first time
To set up house together; and its chime
Had never failed to sound an hour since then,
Unless he had it down to clean; for Ben 10
Was handy and could always overhaul
A clock, though it was not his trade at all,
As well as any watchmaker. His heart
Doted on wheels: he'd handle every part
So daintily that you could never guess
His job was hewing coal. I must confess 16
Wheels always daunted me: but Ben's brain went
By clockwork; and his happiest hours were spent
Sorting old clocks and trying to make them go. 19
And that one's never been a second slow
In all these years or half a second fast,
Or failed to strike . . . until Ben breathed his last
On Monday morn before the stroke of three. . . .
Though all the town's clocks hammered presently
As if they struck my heart. . . . Ben always wound 25
That clock each Sunday; but when the last came round
He'd been in bed a week, and his poor mind
Was wandering — though his fingers tried to wind
Some ghostly clock that troubled him all night —
And when I stole downstairs and struck a light, 30
I missed the tick; and with a still white face
Ben's clock was standing silent in its place
With motionless hands just on the stroke of three.
Its heart had stopped when Ben's stopped. As for me
I'll never wind it up again: I know 35
Even if I cared, no touch could make it go
But Ben's; and those still hands will always keep
My heart in mind. . . .

Nay, Martha, you need sleep.
You mustn't brood like this. Try to forget.
Come, let me wind it up for you, and set 40
The old clock going. Only think how Ben
Would hate to have it standing.

Wind it then.
Ben hated a stopped clock: and now he's gone,
It seems I've got to keep things going on.

OLD CHRISTMAS MORNING

A Kentucky Mountain Ballad

by Roy Helton (1886–)

" Where you coming from, Lomey Carter,
So airly over the snow?
And what's them pretties you got in your hand,
And where you aiming to go?

" Step in, honey! Old Christmas morning
I ain't got nothing much; 6
Maybe a bite of sweetness and corn bread,
A little ham meat and such.

" But come in, honey! Sally Anne Barton's
Hungering after your face. 10
Wait till I light my candle up:
Set down! There's your old place.

" Now where you been so airly this morning? "
" Graveyard, Sally Anne.
Up by the trace in the salt-lick meadows
Where Taulbe kilt my man." 16

" Taulbe ain't to home this morning . . .
I can't scratch up a light:
Dampness gets on the heads of the matches; 19
But I'll blow up the embers bright."

" Needn't trouble. I won't be stopping:
Going a long ways still."
" You didn't see nothing, Lomey Carter,
Up on the graveyard hill? "

" What should I see there, Sally Anne Barton? " 25
" Well, sperits do walk last night."

" There were an elderbush a-blooming
While the moon still give some light."

" Yes, elderbushes, they bloom, Old Christmas,
And critters kneel down in their straw.
Anything else up in the graveyard? " 31

" One thing more I saw:
I saw my man with his head all bleeding
Where Taulbe's shot went through."

" What did he say? " 35
" He stooped and kissed me."
" What did he say to you? "

" Said, Lord Jesus forguv your Taulbe;
But he told me another word;
He said it soft when he stooped and kissed me. 40
That were the last I heard."

" Taulbe ain't to home this morning."

" I know that, Sally Anne,
For I kilt him, coming down through the meadow
Where Taulbe kilt my man. 45

" I met him upon the meadow trace
When the moon were fainting fast,
And I had my dead man's rifle gun
And kilt him as he come past."

" But I heard two shots."

" 'Twas his was second: 50
He shot me 'fore he died:
You'll find us at daybreak, Sally Anne Barton:
I'm laying there dead at his side."

THE CODE

by Robert Frost (1875–   )

There were three in the meadow by the brook
Gathering up windrows, piling cocks of hay,
With an eye always lifted toward the west
Where an irregular sun-bordered cloud
Darkly advanced with a perpetual dagger 5
Flickering across its bosom. Suddenly
One helper, thrusting pitchfork in the ground,
Marched himself off the field and home. One stayed.
The town-bred farmer failed to understand.

"What is there wrong?"

"Something you just now said." 10

"What did I say?"

"About our taking pains."

"To cock the hay? — because it's going to shower?
I said that more than half an hour ago.
I said it to myself as much as you."

"You didn't know. But James is one big fool. 15
He thought you meant to find fault with his work.
That's what the average farmer would have meant.
James would take time, of course, to chew it over
Before he acted: he's just got round to act."

"He is a fool if that's the way he takes me." 20

"Don't let it bother you. You've found out something.
The hand that knows his business won't be told
To do work better or faster — those two things.
I'm as particular as anyone:
Most likely I'd have served you just the same. 25
But I know you don't understand our ways.
You were just talking what was in your mind,
What was in all our minds, and you weren't hinting.

"Tell you a story of what happened once:
I was up here in Salem at a man's 30
Named Sanders with a gang of four or five
Doing the haying. No one liked the boss.
He was one of the kind sports call a spider,

All wiry arms and legs that spread out wavy
From a humped body nigh as big's a biscuit. 35
But work! that man could work, especially
If by so doing he could get more work
Out of his hired help. I'm not denying
He was hard on himself. I couldn't find
That he kept any hours — not for himself. 40
Daylight and lantern light were one to him:
I've heard him pounding in the barn all night.
But what he liked was someone to encourage.
Them that he couldn't lead he'd get behind
And drive, the way you can, you know, in mowing — 45
Keep at their heels and threaten to mow their legs off.
I'd seen about enough of his bulling tricks
(We call that bulling). I'd been watching him.
So when he paired off with me in the hayfield
To load the load, thinks I, Look out for trouble. 50
I built the load and topped it off; old Sanders
Combed it down with the rake and says, 'O. K.'
Everything went well till we reached the barn
With a big catch to empty in a bay.
You understand that meant the easy job 55
For the man up on top of throwing *down*
The hay and rolling it off wholesale,
Where on a mow it would have been slow lifting.
You wouldn't think a fellow'd need much urging
Under these circumstances, would you now? 60
But the old fool seizes his fork in both hands,
And looking up bewhiskered out of the pit,
Shouts like an army captain, 'Let her come!'
Thinks I, D'ye mean it? 'What was that you said?'
I asked out loud, so's there'd be no mistake, 65
'Did you say, Let her come?' 'Yes, let her come.'
He said it over, but he said it softer.
Never you say a thing like that to a man,
Not if he values what he is. God, I'd as soon
Murdered him as left out his middle name. 70
I'd built the load and knew right where to find
Two or three forksful I picked lightly round for
Like meditating, and then I just dug in
And dumped the rackful on him in ten lots.
I looked over the side once in the dust 75
And caught sight of him treading-water-like,
Keeping his head above. 'Damn ye,' I says
'That gets ye!' He squeaked like a squeezed rat.
That was the last I saw or heard of him.
I cleaned the rack and drove out to cool off. 80

As I sat mopping hayseed from my neck,
And sort of waiting to be asked about it,
One of the boys sings out, 'Where's the old man?'
'I left him in the barn under the hay.
If ye want him, ye can go and dig him out.' 85
They realized from the way I swabbed my neck
More than was needed something must be up.
They headed for the barn; I stayed where I was.
They told me afterward. First they forked the hay,
A lot of it, out into the barn floor. 90
Nothing! They listened for him. Not a rustle.
I guess they thought I spiked him in the temple
Before I buried him, or I couldn't have managed.
They excavated more. 'Go keep his wife
Out of the barn.' Someone looked in a window, 95
And curse me if he wasn't in the kitchen
Slumped way down in a chair, with both his feet
Stuck in the oven, the hottest day that summer.
He looked so clean disgusted from behind
There was no one that dared to stir him up, 100
Or let him know that he was being looked at.
Apparently I hadn't buried him
(I may have knocked him down); but my just trying
To bury him had hurt his dignity.
He had gone to the house so's not to meet me. 105
He kept away from us all afternoon.
We tended to his hay. We saw him out
After a while picking peas in the garden:
He couldn't keep away from doing something."

"Weren't you relieved to find he wasn't dead?" 110

"No! and yet I don't know — it's hard to say.
I went about to kill him fair enough."

"You took an awkward way. Did he discharge you?"

"Discharge me? No! He knew I did just right."

APPRECIATING THE DRAMATIC FORCE OF THE POEMS

"Rebecca Nixon and Martha Waugh"

1. How many different kinds of associations did the clock stir in Martha's mind? What part had the clock played in Ben's life? in Martha's and Ben's happy life together? in his illness? in his death? What part was it to play hereafter in Martha's new loneliness? By what signs can you tell?

2. What is the effect of this heavy emphasis on the clock? What does it suggest to you about the ways of grief? Why should a clock — or any other little thing — loom so large in sorrow?

3. What does the last line of the poem say to you? What does it tell you about life?

4. What is the tone of the dialogue between Martha and Rebecca in contrast to that of Sally Anne and Lomey in " Old Christmas Morning "? What impressions do you form of the two women in this scene? of the two women in the earlier poem?

" Old Christmas Morning "

5. What is the first shock your imagination gets from the poem? What lines deliver it? What are the elements in the grim contrast you have discovered? Notice Sally Anne's greeting to Lomey Carter and the latter's reply.

6. What is the effect of the fifth stanza upon you?

7. What contrast do you notice between the lines uttered by Sally Anne Barton and Lomey Carter? How does Sally Anne speak? Lomey Carter? What is the effect upon you of such a contrast?

8. What do you think were the last words which Lomey Carter heard from the lips of her dying man? How can you tell?

9. In the first half of the poem who does the most talking? In the second half? What does this signify?

10. With what emotion will you regard a feud hereafter? How has the poem altered or deepened your attitude?

" The Code "

11. By what dramatic incident did the " town-bred farmer " find " out something "? How important was the message which the " helper " who " stayed " gave him? By what dramatic means did the helper communicate his message?

12. What phrases characterized for you quickly the boss in the farm hand's story? What bitter conflict existed between him and his men?

13. By what dramatic incident did the farm hand teach his boss a lesson? What phrases communicated to you the horror of the boss's plight? What dark hint of tragedy lurked between the lines?

14. What is the effect upon you of the farm hand's answer to the question, " Weren't you relieved to find he wasn't dead "?

15. In what manner does Robert Frost tell his tale? How does this poem differ from the old ballads? Is it an appropriate manner? How can you tell?

Monologues

YOU HAVE seen how dialogue is used in the preceding group of poems as a means of telling a story. Ballad writers also make frequent use of monologue; that is, a story told not by two persons talking together but by one person talking to an implied audience. A story seems more convincing when it is told by the chief actor. That is why many a gripping tale is told in the first person. You will note the effectiveness of monologue in the poems which you will now read.

KIT CARSON'S RIDE

by Joaquin Miller (1841–1913)

" Run? Run? See this flank, sir, and I do love him so!
But he's blind, badger-blind. Whoa, 'Pache, boy, whoa.
No, you wouldn't believe it to look at his eyes,
But he's blind, badger-blind, and it happened this wise:

2. **'Pache:** The horse is named Apache.

"We lay in the grass and the sunburnt clover 5
That spread on the ground like a great brown cover
Northward and southward, and west and away
To the Brazos, where our lodges lay,
One broad and unbroken level of brown.
We were waiting the curtains of night to come down 10
To cover us trio and conceal our flight
With my brown bride, won from an Indian town
That lay in the rear the full ride of a night.

"We lounged in the grass — her eyes were in mine,
And her hands on my knee, and her hair was as wine 15
In its wealth and its flood, pouring on and all over
Her bosom wine-red, and pressed never by one.
Her touch was as warm as the tinge of the clover
Burnt brown as it reached to the kiss of the sun.
Her words they were low as the lute-throated dove, 20
And as laden with love as the heart when it beats
In its hot, eager answer to earliest love,
Or the bee hurried home by its burthen of sweets.

"We lay low in the grass on the broad plain levels,
Old Revels and I, and my stolen brown bride; 25
'Forty full miles if a foot, and the devils
Of red Comanches are hot on the track
When once they strike it. Let the sun go down
Soon, very soon,' muttered bearded old Revels
As he peer'd at the sun lying low on his back, 30
Holding fast to his lasso. Then he jerked at his steed
And he sprang to his feet, and glanced swiftly around,
And then dropped, as if shot, with an ear to the ground;
Then again to his feet, and to me, to my bride,
While his eyes were like flame, his face like a shroud, 35
His form like a king, and his beard like a cloud,
And his voice loud and shrill, as both trumpet and reed, —
'Pull, pull in your lassos, and bridle to steed,
And speed you if ever for life you would speed.
Ay, ride for your lives, for your lives you must ride! 40
For the plain is aflame, the prairie on fire,
And the feet of wild horses hard flying before
I heard like a sea breaking high on the shore,
While the buffalo come like a surge of the sea,
Driven far by the flame, driving fast on us three 45
As a hurricane comes, crushing palms in his ire.'

"We drew in the lassos, seized the saddle and rein,
Threw them on, cinched them on, cinched them over again,

And again drew the girth; and sprang we to horse,
With head to the Brazos, with a sound in the air 50
Like the surge of a sea, with a flash in the eye,
From that red wall of flame reaching up to the sky;
A red wall of flame and a black rolling sea
Rushing fast upon us, as the wind sweeping free
And afar from the desert blown hollow and hoarse. 55

"Not a word, not a wail from a lip was let fall,
We broke not a whisper, we breathed not a prayer,
There was work to be done, there was death in the air,
And the chance was as one to a thousand for all.

"Twenty miles! . . . thirty miles! 60
. . . a dim distant speck. . . .
Then a long reaching line, and the Brazos in sight!
And I rose in my seat with a shout of delight.
I stood in my stirrup, and looked to my right —
But Revels was gone; I glanced by my shoulder 65
And saw his horse stagger; I saw his head drooping
Hard down on his breast, and his naked breast stooping
Low down to the mane, as so swifter and bolder
Ran reaching out for us the red-footed fire.
He rode neck to neck with a buffalo bull, 70
That made the earth shake where he came in his course,
The monarch of millions, with shaggy mane full
Of smoke and of dust, and it shook with desire
Of battle, with rage and with bellowings hoarse.
His keen, crooked horns, through the storm of his mane, 75
Like black lances lifted and lifted again;
And I looked but this once, for the fire licked through,
And Revels was gone, as we rode two and two.

"I looked to my left then — and nose, neck, and shoulder
Sank slowly, sank surely, till back to my thighs, 80
And up through the black blowing veil of her hair
Did beam full in mine her two marvelous eyes,
With a longing and love yet a look of despair
And of pity for me, as she felt the smoke fold her,
And flames leaping far for her glorious hair. 85
Her sinking horse faltered, plunged, fell and was gone
As I reached through the flame and I bore her still on.
On! into the Brazos, she, 'Pache and I —
Poor, burnt, blinded 'Pache, I love him. . . .
That's why." 90

THE HORSE THIEF

by William Rose Benét (*1886–*)

There he moved, cropping the grass at the purple canyon's lip.
His mane was mixed with the moonlight that silvered his snow-white side,
For the moon sailed out of a cloud with the wake of a spectral ship.
I crouched and I crawled on my belly, my lariat coil looped wide.

Dimly and dark the mesas broke on the starry sky. 5
A pall covered every color of their gorgeous glory at noon.
I smelt the yucca and mesquite, and stifled my heart's quick cry,
And wormed and crawled on my belly to where he moved against the moon!

Some Moorish barb was that mustang's sire. His lines were beyond all wonder.
From the prick of his ears to the flow of his tail he ached in my throat and eyes. 10
Steel and velvet grace! As the prophet says, God had "clothed his neck with thunder."
Oh, marvelous with the drifting cloud he drifted across the skies!

And then I was near at hand — crouched, and balanced, and cast the coil;
And the moon was smothered in cloud, and the rope through my hands with a rip!
But somehow I gripped and clung, with the blood in my brain aboil, — 15
With a turn round the rugged tree stump there on the purple canyon's lip.

Right into the stars he reared aloft, his red eye rolling and raging.
He whirled and sunfished and lashed, and rocked the earth to thunder and flame.
He squealed like a regular devil horse. I was haggard and spent and aging —
Roped clean, but almost storming clear, his fury too fierce to tame. 20

And I cursed myself for a tenderfoot moon-dazzled to play the part,
But I was doubly desperate then, with the posse pulled out from town,
Or I'd never have tried it. I only knew I must get a mount and a start.
The filly had snapped her foreleg short. I had had to shoot her down.

So there he struggled and strangled, and I snubbed him around the tree. 25
Nearer, a little nearer — hoofs planted, and lolling tongue —
Till a sudden slack pitched me backward. He reared right on top of me.
Mother of God — that moment! He missed me . . . and up I swung.

Somehow, gone daft completely and clawing a bunch of his mane,
As he stumbled and tripped in the lariat, there I was — up and astride. 30
And cursing for seven counties! And the mustang? *Just insane!*
Crack-bang! went the rope; we cannoned off the tree — then — gods, that ride!

A rocket — that's all, a rocket! I dug with my teeth and nails.
Why, we never hit even the high spots (though I hardly remember things),

9. **barb**: a very fast horse, brought originally by the Moors to Spain.

But I heard a monstrous booming like a thunder of flapping sails 35
When he spread — well, *call* me a liar! — when he spread those wings, those wings!

So white that my eyes were blinded, thick-feathered and wide unfurled
They beat the air into billows. We sailed, and the earth was gone.
Canyon and desert and mesa withered below, with the world.
And then I knew that mustang; for I — was Bellerophon! 40

Yes, glad as the Greek, and mounted on a horse of the elder gods,
With never a magic bridle or a fountain-mirror nigh!
My chaps and spurs and holster must have looked it? What's the odds?
I'd a leg over lightning and thunder, careering across the sky!

And forever streaming before me, fanning my forehead cool, 45
Flowed a mane of molten silver; and just before my thighs
(As I gripped his velvet-muscled ribs, while I cursed myself for a fool),
The steady pulse of those pinions — their wonderful fall and rise!

The bandanna I bought in Bowie blew loose and whipped from my neck.
My shirt was stuck to my shoulders and ribboning out behind. 50
The stars were dancing, wheeling and glancing, dipping with smirk and beck.
The clouds were flowing, dusking and glowing. We rode a roaring wind.

We soared through the silver starlight to knock at the planets' gates.
New shimmering constellations came whirling into our ken.
Red stars and green and golden swung out of the void that waits 55
For man's great last adventure; the Signs took shape — and then

I knew the lines of that Centaur the moment I saw him come!
The musical-box of the heavens all around us rolled to a tune
That tinkled and chimed and trilled with silver sounds that struck you dumb,
As if some archangel were grinding out the music of the moon. 60

Melody-drunk on the Milky Way, as we swept and soared hilarious,
Full in our pathway, sudden he stood — the Centaur of the Stars,
Flashing from head and hoofs and breast! I knew him for Sagittarius.
He reared and bent and drew his bow. He crouched as a boxer spars.

Flung back on his haunches, weird he loomed — then leapt — and the dim void lightened. 65
Old White Wings shied and swerved aside, and fled from the splendor-shod.
Through a flashing welter of worlds we charged. I knew why my horse was frightened.
He *had* two faces — a dog's and a man's — that Babylonian god!

40. **Bellerophon:** a Grecian hero who rode the winged horse Pegasus. 49. **Bowie:** a town in Texas. 56. **Signs:** signs of the zodiac, a belt of twelve constellations in the heavens. 57. **Centaur:** Centaurus, a constellation depicted as a mythological centaur, a creature half man and half horse. 63. **Sagittarius:** a constellation depicted as a centaur shooting an arrow. You will find pictures of all these constellations in an encyclopedia, given under each name.

Also, he followed us real as fear. Ping! went an arrow past.
My broncho buck-jumped, humping high. We plunged . . . I guess that's all! 70

I lay on the purple canyon's lip, when I opened my eyes at last —
Stiff and sore and my head like a drum, but I broke no bones in the fall.

So you know — and now you may string me up. Such was the way you caught me.
Thank you for letting me tell it straight, though you never could greatly care.
For I took a horse that wasn't mine! . . . But there's one the heavens brought me, 75
And I'll hang right happy, because I know he is waiting for me up there.

From creamy muzzle to cannon bone, by God, he's a peerless wonder!
He is steel and velvet and furnace fire, and death's supreme prize;
And never again shall be roped on earth that neck that is "clothed with thunder." . . .
String me up, Dave! Go dig my grave! *I rode him across the skies!* 80

CERELLE

by Margaret Bell Houston

There was a score of likely girls
Around the prairie side,
But I went down to Galveston
And brought me home a bride.

A score or more of handsome girls, 5
Of proper age and size,
But the pale girls of Galveston
Have seashine in their eyes.

As pale as any orange flower,
Cerelle. The gold-white sands 10
Were like her hair, and drifting shells,
White fairy shells, her hands.

I think she liked my silver spurs
A-clinking in the sun.
She'd never seen a cowboy till 15
I rode to Galveston.

She'd never known the chaparral,
Nor smell of saddle leather,
Nor seen a roundup or a ranch,
Till we rode back — together. 20

3. **Galveston:** a seaport city in Texas.

Shall I forget my mother's eyes?
"Is this the wife you need?
Is this the way you bring me rest
From forty men to feed?"

Cerelle — I think she did her best 25
All year. She'd lots to learn.
Dishes would slip from out her hands
And break, the bread would burn,

And she would steal away at times
And wander off to me, 30
And when the wind was in the south
She'd say, "I smell the sea!"

She changed. The white and gold grew dull,
As when a soft flame dies,
And yet she kept until the last 35
The seashine in her eyes. . . .

There are (I make a husband's boast)
No stronger arms than Ann's.
She has a quip for all the boys,
And sings among the pans. 40

At last my mother takes her rest,
And that's how things should be.
But when the wind is in the south
There is no rest for me.

A BALLAD OF JOHN SILVER

by John Masefield (1878–)

We were schooner-rigged and rakish, with a long and lissome hull,
And we flew the pretty colors of the crossbones and the skull;
We'd a big black Jolly Roger flapping grimly at the fore,
And we sailed the Spanish Water in the happy days of yore.

We'd a long brass gun amidship, like a well-conducted ship, 5
We had each a brace of pistols and a cutlass at the hip;
It's a point which tells against us, and a fact to be deplored,
But we chased the goodly merchantmen and laid their ships aboard.

Then the dead men fouled the scuppers and the wounded filled the chains,
And the paintwork all was spatter-dashed with other people's brains. 10
She was boarded, she was looted, she was scuttled till she sank,
And the pale survivors left us by the medium of the plank.

O! then it was (while standing by the taffrail on the poop)
We could hear the drowning folk lament the absent chicken coop;
Then, having washed the blood away, we'd little else to do 15
Than to dance a quiet hornpipe as the old salts taught us to.

O! the fiddle on the fo'c'sle, and the slapping naked soles,
And the genial "Down the middle, Jake, and curtsy when she rolls!"
With the silver seas around us and the pale moon overhead,
And the lookout not a-looking and his pipe bowl glowing red. 20

Ah! the pig-tailed, quidding pirates and the pretty pranks we played,
All have since been put a stop to by the naughty Board of Trade;
The schooners and the merry crews are laid away to rest,
A little south the sunset in the Islands of the Blest.

12. **plank**: The favorite way for pirates to dispose of their captives was to blindfold them and have them walk a plank set over the side of the ship. When they reached the end of the plank, they fell into the sea and were drowned. 17. **fo'c'sle**: forecastle, the forward part of the vessel, where the sailors eat and sleep.

THINK BACK OVER WHAT YOU HAVE READ

Interpreting the Stories

"Kit Carson's Ride"

1. What lines set the scene for this poem? How would you describe the country? Find the Brazos River on a map.

2. What familiar theme, already noted in the old ballads, do you find in this tale? What circumstance shifts our interest from this theme?

3. What episodes are most dramatic? Tell what happens to each of the persons of the story; to the horse. How does the story end?

4. How does the rhythm of the poem suggest the mad ride? Tap off this rhythm on your desk with a pencil. What does it suggest?

"The Horse Thief"

5. At what point in the poem were you aware that the horse thief was talking to his captors?

6. What phrases gave you a sense of the horse thief's keen appreciation of horses?

7. What details of the horse thief's tale would have held you spellbound had you been listening as he told it? At what point in his story would you have become doubtful? What explanation of the wild ride would you have made to yourself? What lines give you the hint?

8. How many interruptions are suggested in the narrative? What remarks do you imagine were made to call forth the replies of the horse thief? How can you tell? What is the effect of these interruptions? What impression of the horse thief do they awaken in your imagination?

9. With what mixture of feelings would you regard the horse thief had you been one of his captors?

10. What is the effect of the last line of the poem? What comment are you led to make about the importance of last lines?

"Cerelle"

11. How well fitted was Cerelle to be the bride of a cowboy? How do you know? How did the cowboy's mother feel about her? What sort of woman did she want her son to marry?

12. What lines describe Cerelle? How does this description help you understand her character?

13. What line shows that Cerelle was not happy?

14. How did Ann differ from Cerelle? Was she a better or worse wife for the cowboy? What lines show you the cowboy's real feelings?

15. What is the pathos of the story? the romance?

"A Ballad of John Silver"

16. What pictures does your imagination see of the pirate ship in "the happy days of yore"? What details from the poem suggest the picture to you?

17. What picture does the poem give you of the pirates aboard a Spanish merchantman? What words of pictorial quality can you quote?

18. What picture do you see of the pirates celebrating their victory? What details are highly colored?

For Ambitious Students

19. Perhaps these poems have aroused within you an enthusiasm for romantic adventure in verse. Perhaps several members of the class will volunteer to search for other poems with a romantic flavor. Your librarian will help you find them. It may be best for you to concentrate on a theme, such as: Poems of the West, Poems of the Sea, Poems of War, Poems of Wandering.

Hero Tales

AS YOU might expect, heroism is a favorite theme of ballads, and one of the most popular heroes of all minstrelsy is the warrior who loses the fight but remains unbeaten. Over and over again this song has thrilled the heart of man. Poets of all ages have been inspired by the invincible spirit.

In the first two poems that follow, you will meet two gallant gentlemen in very different settings. The first author, Tennyson, was the brilliant popularizer of the Arthurian legend in the nineteenth century; this legend you will meet later on. Here again he has turned to the romantic past for his inspiration. The second poet, Stephen Vincent Benét — a brother of William Rose Benét, whom you met a few pages back as the author of "The Horse Thief" — is a modern poet, from whose long narrative *John Brown's Body* the portrait of Lee is taken. As you read these two poems, notice the thrilling qualities of each hero described and the stirring passages of description that set your mind on fire.

The third poem tells the story, not of a famous hero, but of a boy in the Confederate Army who came to the notice of the author and was taken into his home. The story, therefore, is a true one — just the kind that is suitable for a stirring ballad. Many people consider this poem one of the finest ballads in American literature.

This invincible spirit is treated in still another manner in the fourth poem of the group, "The Broncho That Would Not Be Broken." Vachel Lindsay is another modern American poet, whose experiments in the field of rhythm have made him a pioneer in poetry. In his poem introduced to you here, you will find that man has no monopoly on dauntless courage and proud rebellion. A colt is the hero of this poem, with no reflections cast upon the splendor of the heroes in the preceding tales.

THE REVENGE

by Alfred, Lord Tennyson (1809–1892)

At Florés in the Azorés, Sir Richard Grenville lay,
And a pinnace, like a fluttered bird, came flying from far away;
"Spanish ships of war at sea! we have sighted fifty-three!"
Then sware Lord Thomas Howard: "'Fore God I am no coward;
But I cannot meet them here, for my ships are out of gear, 5
And the half my men are sick. I must fly, but follow quick.
We are six ships of the line; can we fight with fifty-three?"

Then spake Sir Richard Grenville: "I know you are no coward;
You fly them for a moment to fight with them again.
But I've ninety men and more that are lying sick ashore. 10
I should count myself the coward if I left them, my Lord Howard,
To these Inquisition dogs and the devildoms of Spain."
So Lord Howard passed away with five ships of war that day,
Till he melted like a cloud in the silent summer heaven;
But Sir Richard bore in hand all his sick men from the land 15
Very carefully and slow,
Men of Bideford in Devon,
And we laid them on the ballast down below;
For we brought them all aboard,
And they blest him in their pain, that they were not left to Spain, 20
To the thumbscrew and the stake, for the glory of the Lord.

He had only a hundred seamen to work the ship and to fight,
And he sailed away from Florés till the Spaniard came in sight,
With his huge sea castles heaving upon the weather bow.
"Shall we fight or shall we fly? 25
Good Sir Richard, tell us now,

1. **Azorés:** islands in mid-Atlantic. 4. **Howard:** English admiral in command of the fleet. 12. **Inquisition:** Grenville feared that his men, if captured, would be subjected to the judgment of the Spanish Inquisition, an agency of the Roman Church which attempted to make Protestants renounce their heresies by the infliction of torture. 17. **Devon:** an English county. 21. **thumbscrew:** an instrument of torture by which a person's thumb was crushed by the gradual turning of a screw.

For to fight is but to die!
There'll be little of us left by the time this sun be set."
And Sir Richard said again: "We be all good Englishmen.
Let us bang these dogs of Seville, the children of the devil, 30
For I never turned my back upon Don or devil yet."

Sir Richard spoke and he laughed, and we roared a hurrah, and so
The little *Revenge* ran on sheer into the heart of the foe,
With her hundred fighters on deck, and her ninety sick below;
For half of their fleet to the right and half to the left were seen, 35
And the little *Revenge* ran on through the long sea lane between.

Thousands of their soldiers looked down from their decks and laughed,
Thousands of their seamen made mock at the mad little craft
Running on and on, till delayed
By their mountainlike *San Philip* that, of fifteen hundred tons, 40
And upshadowing high above us with her yawning tiers of guns,
Took the breath from our sails, and we stayed.

And while now the great *San Philip* hung above us like a cloud,
Whence the thunderbolt will fall
Long and loud, 45
Four galleons drew away
From the Spanish fleet that day,
And two upon the larboard and two upon the starboard lay,
And the battle thunder broke from them all.

But anon the great *San Philip,* she bethought herself and went, 50
Having that within her womb that had left her ill-content;
And the rest they came aboard us, and they fought us hand to hand,
For a dozen times they came with their pikes and musketeers,
And a dozen times we shook 'em off as a dog that shakes his ears,
When he leaps from the water to the land. 55

And the sun went down, and the stars came out far over the summer sea,
But never a moment ceased the fight of the one and the fifty-three.
Ship after ship, the whole night long, their high-built galleons came,
Ship after ship, the whole night long, with her battle thunder and flame;
Ship after ship, the whole night long, drew back with her dead and her shame, 60
For some were sunk and many were shattered, and so could fight us no more —
God of battles, was ever a battle like this in the world before?

For he said, "Fight on! fight on!"
Tho' his vessel was all but a wreck;
And it chanced that, when half of the summer night was gone, 65
With a grisly wound to be drest, he had left the deck,

30. **Seville**: a city in Spain. 31. **Don**: a Spanish title equivalent to the English Sir.

But a bullet struck him that was dressing it suddenly dead,
And himself, he was wounded again in the side and the head,
And he said, "Fight on! fight on!"

And the night went down, and the sun smiled out far over the summer sea, 70
And the Spanish fleet with broken sides lay round us all in a ring;
But they dared not touch us again, for they feared that we still could sting,
So they watched what the end would be.
And we had not fought them in vain,
But in perilous plight were we, 75
Seeing forty of our poor hundred were slain,
And half of the rest of us maimed for life
In the crash of the cannonades and the desperate strife;
And the sick men down in the hold were most of them stark and cold,
And the pikes were all broken or bent, and the powder was all of it spent; 80
And the masts and the rigging were lying over the side;
But Sir Richard cried in his English pride:
"We have fought such a fight, for a day and a night,
As may never be fought again!
We have won great glory, my men! 85
And a day less or more
At sea or ashore,
We die — does it matter when?
Sink me the ship, Master Gunner — sink her, split her in twain!
Fall into the hands of God, not into the hands of Spain!" 90

And the gunner said, "Ay, ay," but the seamen made reply:
"We have children, we have wives,
And the Lord hath spared our lives.
We will make the Spaniard promise, if we yield, to let us go;
We shall live to fight again and to strike another blow." 95
And the lion there lay dying, and they yielded to the foe.

And the stately Spanish men to their flagship bore him then,
Where they laid him by the mast, old Sir Richard caught at last,
And they praised him to his face with their courtly foreign grace;
But he rose upon their decks, and he cried: 100
"I have fought for Queen and Faith like a valiant man and true;
I have only done my duty as a man is bound to do:
With a joyful spirit I, Sir Richard Grenville, die!"
And he fell upon their decks, and he died.

And they stared at the dead that had been so valiant and true, 105
And had holden the power and glory of Spain so cheap
That he dared her with one little ship and his English few;
Was he devil or man? He was devil for aught they knew,
But they sank his body with honor down into the deep,
And they manned the *Revenge* with a swarthier, alien crew, 110

And away she sailed with her loss and longed for her own;
When a wind from the lands they had ruined awoke from sleep,
And the water began to heave and the weather to moan,
And or ever that evening ended, a great gale blew,
And a wave like the wave that is raised by an earthquake grew, 115
Till it smote on their hulls and their sails and their masts and their flags,
And the whole sea plunged and fell on the shot-shattered navy of Spain,
And the little *Revenge* herself went down by the island crags
To be lost evermore in the main.

LEE

by Stephen Vincent Benét (*1898–*)

The night had fallen on the narrow tent.
—Deep night of Virginia summer when the stars
Are burning wax in the near, languid sky
And the soft flowers hardly close all night
But bathe in darkness, as a woman bathes
In a warm, fragrant water, and distill 6
Their perfume still, without the fire of the sun.

The army was asleep as armies sleep.
War lying on a casual sheaf of peace
For a brief moment, and yet with armor on, 10
And yet in the child's deep sleep, and yet so still.
Even the sentries seemed to walk their posts
With a ghost footfall that could match that night.

The aide-de-camp knew certain lines of Greek
And other such unnecessary things 15
As birds and music, that are good for peace
But are not deemed so serviceable for war.
He was a youth with an inquisitive mind
And doubtless had a failing for romance,
But then he was not twenty, and such faults 20
May sometimes be excused in younger men
Even when such creatures die, as they have done
At one time or another, for some cause
Which we are careful to point out to them
Much later, was no cause worth dying for, 25
But cannot reach them with our arguments
Because they are uneconomic dust.

So, when the aide-de-camp came toward the tent,
He knew that he was sleepy as a dog,
And yet the starlight and the gathered scents 30
Moved in his heart—like the unnecessary
Themes of a music fallen from a cloud
In light, upon a dark water.
And though he had
Some bitterness of mind to chew upon,
As well as messages that he must give 35
Before he slept, he halted in his tracks.
He saw, imprinted on the yellow light,
That made the tent a hollow jack-o'-lantern,
The sharp, black shadow of a seated man,
The profile like the profile on a bust. 40
Lee in his tent, alone.
He had some shadow papers in his hand,
But you could see he was not reading them,
And, if he thought, you could not read his thoughts, 44
Even as shadows, by any light that shines.

"You'd know that face among a million faces,"
Thought the still watcher, "and yet, his hair and beard
Have quite turned white, white as the dogwood bloom
That blossomed on the way to Chancellorsville
When Jackson was alive and we were young 50
And we were winning and the end was near.
And now, I guess, the end is near enough
In spite of everything that we can do,
And he's alone tonight and Jackson's dead.
I saw him in the Wilderness that day 55
When he began to lead the charge himself
And the men wouldn't let him.
Gordon spoke
And then the men themselves began to yell
'Lee to the rear — General Lee to the rear!'
I'll hear that all my life. I'll see those paws 60
Grabbing at Traveler and the bridle rein
And forcing the calm image back from death.
Reckon that's what we think of you, Marse Robert,
Reckon that's what we think, what's left of us,
The poor old devils that are left of us. 65
I wonder what he thinks about it all.
He isn't staring, he's just sitting there.
I never knew a man could look so still
And yet look so alive in his repose.

It doesn't seem as if a cause could lose 70
When it's believed in by a man like that.
And yet we're losing.
And he knows it all.
No, he won't ever say it. But he knows.

I'd feel more comfortable if he'd move.

We had a chance at Spottsylvania, 75
We had some chances in the Wilderness.
We always hurt them more than we were hurt
And yet we're here — and they keep coming on.

What keeps us going on? I wish I knew.
Perhaps you see a man like that go on 80
And then you have to follow.
There can't be
So many men that men have followed so.

And yet, what is it for? What is it for?
What does he think?
His hands are lying there
Quiet as stones or shadows in his lap. 85
His beard is whiter than the dogwood bloom,
But there is nothing ruined in his face,
And nothing beaten in those steady eyes.
If he's grown old, it isn't like a man,
It's more the way a river might grow old. 90
My mother knew him at old dances once.
She said he liked to joke and he was dark then,
Dark and as straight as he can stand today.
If he would only move, I could go forward.

You see the faces of spear-handling kings
In the old books they taught us from at school; 96

49. **Chancellorsville:** The Battle of Chancellorsville, a Confederate victory, was fought May 1, 2, and 3, 1863. Chancellorsville is south of the Rappahannock River in Virginia. General Jackson was killed in the battle. 50. **Jackson:** Thomas J. Jackson, one of the greatest Confederate generals, generally known as "Stonewall" Jackson. 55. **Wilderness:** A furious battle, favorable to the Confederates, was fought May 5 and 6, 1864, in the Wilderness, a section south of the Rapidan River in Virginia. 57. **Gordon:** General John B. Gordon of the Confederate Army. 61. **Traveler:** the name of General Lee's horse. 63. **Marse Robert:** the name by which Lee was affectionately known to his men.

75. **Spottsylvania:** At Spottsylvania Court House in Virginia, May 10, 12, and 18, 1864, the Confederates foiled General Grant's effort to break through their lines.

Big Agamemnon with his curly beard,
Achilles in the cruelty of his youth,
And Oedipus before he tore his eyes.
I'd like to see him in that chariot rank,
With Traveler pulling at the leader pole.
I don't think when the winged claws come down 102
They'll get a groan from him.
So we go on.
Under the claws. And he goes on ahead."

The sharp-cut profile moved a fraction now, 105
The aide-de-camp went forward on his errand.

97. **Agamemnon:** commander-in-chief of the Greeks at the siege of Troy. 98. **Achilles:** greatest Greek hero of the Trojan War. 99. **Oedipus:** the Greek hero who solved the riddle of the Sphinx.

LITTLE GIFFEN

by Francis Orray Ticknor (1822–1874)

Out of the focal and foremost fire,
Out of the hospital walls as dire;
Smitten of grapeshot and gangrene,
(Eighteenth battle, and *he* sixteen!)
Specter! such as you seldom see, 5
Little Giffen, of Tennessee!

"Take him and welcome!" the surgeons said;
Little the doctor can help the dead!
So we took him; and brought him where
The balm was sweet in the summer air;
And we laid him down on a wholesome bed,— 11
Utter Lazarus, heel to head!

And we watched the war with bated breath,—
Skeleton boy against skeleton death.
Months of torture, how many such? 15
Weary weeks of the stick and crutch;
And still a glint of the steel-blue eye
Told of a spirit that wouldn't die,

And didn't. Nay, more! in death's despite
The crippled skeleton "learned to write."
"Dear mother," at first, of course; and then 21
"Dear captain," inquiring about the men.
Captain's answer: "Of eighty and five,
Giffen and I are left alive."

Word of gloom from the war, one day; 25
Johnston pressed at the front, they say.
Little Giffen was up and away;
A tear — his first — as he bade good-by,
Dimmed the glint of his steel-blue eye.
"I'll write, if spared!" There was news of the fight; 30
But none of Giffen. He did not write.

I sometimes fancy that, were I king
Of the princely Knights of the Golden Ring,
With the songs of the minstrel in mine ear,
And the tender legend that trembles here, 35
I'd give the best on his bended knee,
The whitest soul of my chivalry,
For "Little Giffen," of Tennessee.

THE BRONCHO THAT WOULD NOT BE BROKEN

by Vachel Lindsay (1879–1931)

A little colt — broncho, loaned to the farm
To be broken in time without fury or harm,
Yet black crows flew past you, shouting alarm,
Calling "Beware," with lugubrious singing. . . .

The butterflies there in the bush were romancing, 5
The smell of the grass caught your soul in a trance,
So why be a-fearing the spurs and the traces,
O broncho that would not be broken of dancing?

You were born with the pride of the lords great and olden
Who danced, through the ages, in corridors golden. 10
In all the wide farmplace the person most human.
You spoke out so plainly with squealing and capering,
With whinnying, snorting, contorting, and prancing,
As you dodged your pursuers, looking askance,
With Greek-footed figures, and Parthenon paces, 15
O broncho that would not be broken of dancing.

The grasshoppers cheered. "Keep whirling," they said.
The insolent sparrows called from the shed
"If men will not laugh, make them wish they were dead."
But arch were your thoughts, all malice displacing, 20
Though the horse killers came, with snake whips advancing.
You bantered and cantered away your last chance.
And they scourged you; with hell in their speech and their faces,
O broncho that would not be broken of dancing.

"Nobody cares for you," rattled the crows, 25
As you dragged the whole reaper next day down the rows.
The three mules held back, yet you danced on your toes.
You pulled like a racer, and kept the mules chasing.
You tangled the harness with bright eyes side-glancing,
While the drunk driver bled you — a pole for a lance — 30
And the giant mules bit at you — keeping their places.
O broncho that would not be broken of dancing.

In that last afternoon your boyish heart broke.
The hot wind came down like a sledge hammer stroke.
The blood-sucking flies to a rare feast awoke. 35
And they searched out your wounds, your death warrant tracing.
And the merciful men, their religion enhancing,
Stopped the red reaper to give you a chance.
Then you died on the prairie, and scorned all disgraces,
O broncho that would not be broken of dancing. 40

15. **Parthenon paces:** paces such as one sees pictured in the carvings on the Parthenon, the temple of Athena on the Acropolis at Athens.

THINK BACK OVER WHAT YOU HAVE READ

Appreciating the Gallant Heroism of Sir Richard Grenville

1. What qualities endeared Sir Richard to his men? With what brief passages from "The Revenge" can you illustrate?

2. What qualities in Sir Richard did the Spaniards respect? What qualities made him seem like a lion?

3. What details of overwhelming odds made his bravery loom the larger?

4. What picture of gallantry on the part of the Spaniards impressed you?

Appreciating the Impressive Portrait of Lee

5. What picture do you see of Lee framed by the opening of the tent? What qualities made the aide-de-camp say, "You'd know that face among a million faces"?

6. What illustrations can you cite from the poem to show that Lee, like Grenville, was beloved of his men?

7. What lines can you quote to show Lee's invincible spirit? What vivid comparisons bring this idea home to you?

Appreciating the Gallantry of Little Giffen

8. What lines show the apparent hopelessness of Little Giffen's condition? What lines tell of his response to medical treatment?

9. From what lines do you come to know the dauntless spirit of Little Giffen? How does it compare with that of Grenville? of Lee?

10. Explain the meaning of the last stanza. Do you agree with the poet's admiration? Why?

11. In your own words give a character sketch of Little Giffen.

12. How do you feel about Little Giffen? Was he foolhardy or brave? What is the difference? Is it possible to be both?

Appreciating the Proud Spirit of the Broncho

13. What phrases communicate to you the proud spirit of the broncho?

14. What phrases told you of the overwhelming odds against which the broncho was fighting? of the kind of fight he put up? of his defeat? of the fact that he was still unbeaten?

15. In what manner is this poem written? Where do you feel the poet's sympathy? his understanding? his restraint?

Responding to the Beauty of the Poems

16. What phrases of pictorial beauty can you find to quote in "The Revenge"? What passages can you quote to show how the rhythm brings out the meaning of the poem? What lines of thrilling challenge can you quote? of inspiring sentiment?

17. What descriptions of great beauty do you find in "Lee" which gave you a sense of the loveliness of a Southern night? of the hush of an army at rest? of the picture of Lee in repose? What phrases gave you an inspiring glimpse into the heart of the aide-de-camp? What adjectives can you think of to describe the music of the lines? Perhaps someone in the class will read the poem aloud and let you *hear* its beauty. Does it *sound* different from "The Revenge"? How? Where in particular does it suggest repose? Where, particularly, does "The Revenge" suggest action?

18. What lines in the poem bring the story of Little Giffen to a dramatic close? Why are these lines effective? What stanza is most beautiful to the ear? What lines reveal the boy's fighting spirit?

19. What lines in "The Broncho That Would Not Be Broken" gave you a clear picture of the colt? What poetic device kept the setting constantly in mind? What sounds did you hear — through the colt's ears? What associations did they bring to mind? What pictures will you remember? What did you notice about the rhythm of this poem? What is the rhyming scheme? How appropriate is the rhythm? What does it suggest to your imagination?

For Ambitious Students

20. *Invincible spirits.* Here is an inspiring theme — with accompanying bibliography — for a term's exploration into biography:

Benson, A. C., and Tatham, H. F. W., *Men of Might*

Carré, J. M., *Frail Warrior* (life of Robert Louis Stevenson)

De Kruif, P. H., *Men against Death*

Dutton, C. J., *Samaritans of Molokai* (life of Father Damien)

Meigs, C. L., *Invincible Louisa* (life of Louisa May Alcott)

Quiller-Couch, Sir Arthur, *Victors of Peace*

Wright, W. B., *Master of Men* (biography of Chinese Gordon)

Tales of Action

ONE OF the most successful modern ballad writers was Rudyard Kipling. In the course of a richly adventurous life he found many themes suited to the ballad form. His first important book of poems was *Barrack Room Ballads,* based largely on the life of the British soldier whom Kipling knew so well. These poems are written in the dialect of the British soldier, a detail which adds considerable zest and realism to the stories. *Barrack Room Ballads* was followed by other volumes of verse, the best known of which are *The Seven Seas* and *The Five Nations.* There is a masculine vigor in Kipling's poetry, but there is fine artistry as well.

DANNY DEEVER

by Rudyard Kipling (1865–1936)

" What are the bugles blowin' for? " said Files-on-Parade.
" To turn you out, to turn you out," the Color Sergeant said.
" What makes you look so white, so white? " said Files-on-Parade.
" I'm dreadin' what I've got to watch," the Color Sergeant said.
For they're hangin' Danny Deever, you can 'ear the dead march play, 5
The regiment's in 'ollow square — they're hangin' him today;
They've taken of his buttons off an' cut his stripes away,
An' they're hangin' Danny Deever in the mornin'.

" What makes the rear-rank breathe so 'ard? " said Files-on-Parade.
" It's bitter cold, it's bitter cold," the Color Sergeant said. 10
" What makes that front-rank man fall down? " says Files-on-Parade.
" A touch o' sun, a touch o' sun," the Color Sergeant said.
They are hangin' Danny Deever, they are marchin' of 'im round,
They 'ave 'alted Danny Deever by 'is coffin on the ground;
An' 'e'll swing in 'arf a minute for a sneakin', shootin' hound — 15
O they're hangin' Danny Deever in the mornin'!

" 'Is cot was right-'and cot to mine," said Files-on-Parade.
" 'E's sleepin' out an' far tonight," the Color Sergeant said.
" I've drunk 'is beer a score o' times," said Files-on-Parade.
" 'E's drinkin' bitter beer alone," the Color Sergeant said. 20
They are hangin' Danny Deever, you must mark 'im to 'is place,
For 'e shot a comrade sleepin' — you must look 'im in the face;
Nine 'undred of 'is county an' the regiment's disgrace,
While they're hangin' Danny Deever in the mornin'.

1. **Files-on-Parade:** a noncommissioned army officer who looks after various details of formation, closing the files of marching soldiers as they turn, etc. 2. **Color Sergeant:** the soldier who carries the flag.

"What's that so black agin the sun?" said Files-on-Parade. 25
"It's Danny fightin' 'ard for life," the Color Sergeant said.
"What's that that whimpers over'ead?" said Files-on-Parade.
"It's Danny's soul that's passin' now," the Color Sergeant said.
For they're done with Danny Deever, you can 'ear the quickstep play,
The regiment's in column, an' they're marchin' us away; 30
Ho! the young recruits are shakin', an' they'll want their beer today,
After hangin' Danny Deever in the mornin'.

FUZZY-WUZZY

Soudan Expeditionary Force

by Rudyard Kipling (1865–1936)

We've fought with many men acrost the seas,
An' some of 'em was brave an' some was not.
The Paythan an' the Zulu an' Burmese;
But the Fuzzy was the finest o' the lot.
We never got a ha'porth's change of 'im: 5
'E squatted in the scrub an' 'ocked our 'orses,
'E cut our sentries up at Sua*kim*,
An' 'e played the cat an' banjo with our forces.

So 'ere's *to* you, Fuzzy-Wuzzy, at your 'ome in the Sudan;
You're a pore benighted 'eathen but a first-class fightin' man; 10
We gives you your certificate, an' if you want it signed
We'll come an' 'ave a romp with you whenever you're inclined.

We took our chanst among the Kyber 'ills,
The Boers knocked us silly at a mile,
The Burman give us Irriwaddy chills, 15
An' a Zulu *impi* dished us up in style:
But all we ever got from such as they
Was pop to what the Fuzzy made us swaller;
We 'eld our bloomin' own, the papers say,
But man for man the Fuzzy knocked us 'oller. 20

Then 'ere's *to* you, Fuzzy-Wuzzy, an' the missis and the kid;
Our orders was to break you, an' of course we went an' did.
We sloshed you with Martinis, an' it wasn't 'ardly fair;
But for all the odds agin' you, Fuzzy-Wuz, you broke the square.

3. **Paythan:** race of people in India. 3. **Zulu:** native of Zululand in South Africa. 3. **Burmese:** people of Burma in Asia. 5. **ha'porth's:** half-pennyworth's. 6. **'ocked:** hocked; that is, lamed the horses by cutting their hamstrings. 7. **Suakim:** Suakin, a town in the Sudan. 9. **Fuzzy-Wuzzy:** the soldiers' nickname for the bushy-haired natives of the Sudan. 13. **Kyber 'ills:** the Khyber Hills in northern India between India and Afghanistan. 14. **Boers:** the Dutch residents of South Africa. 15. **Irriwaddy:** a river in Burma. 16. **impi:** a body of native armed men. 23. **Martinis:** a make of rifle. 24. **broke the square:** broke through the regiment which was drawn up in the form of a square to resist attack.

'E 'asn't got no papers of 'is own, 25
'E 'asn't got no medals nor rewards,
So we must certify the skill 'e's shown
In usin' of 'is long two-'anded swords:
When 'e's 'oppin' in an' out among the bush
With 'is coffin-'eaded shield an' shovel spear, 30
An 'appy day with Fuzzy on the rush
Will last an 'ealthy Tommy for a year.

So 'ere's *to* you, Fuzzy-Wuzzy, an' your friends which are no more,
If we 'adn't lost some messmates we would 'elp you to deplore;
But give an' take's the gospel, an' we'll call the bargain fair, 35
For if you 'ave lost more than us, you crumpled up the square!

'E rushes at the smoke when we let drive,
'An before we know, 'e's 'ackin' at our 'ead;
'E's all 'ot sand an' ginger when alive,
An' 'e's generally shammin' when 'e's dead. 40
'E's a daisy, 'e's a ducky, 'e's a lamb!
'E's a injia-rubber idiot on the spree,
'E's the on'y thing that doesn't give a damn
For a regiment o' British infantree!

So 'ere's *to* you, Fuzzy-Wuzzy, at your 'ome in the Sudan; 45
You're a pore benighted 'eathen but a first-class fightin' man;
An' 'ere's *to* you, Fuzzy-Wuzzy, with your 'ayrick 'ead of 'air —
You big black boundin' beggar — for you broke a British square!

47. **'ayrick:** looking like a hayrick.

THINK BACK OVER WHAT YOU HAVE READ

Recognizing the Dramatic Spirit

"Danny Deever"

1. What different parts do Files-on-Parade and the Color Sergeant play in this brief drama? What do the questions and answers indicate about the relationship between the two soldiers? about the personality of each? How do the questions of Files-on-Parade gain in intensity? Is the Color Sergeant more or less moved than Files-on-Parade? Does he offer any consolation to his comrade? to himself? How do you know?

2. What scene do you reconstruct in your imagination from the hints let fall in the dialogue?

3. With what feelings did you finish reading the poem? What adjectives would you apply to the scene you have just witnessed?

4. What elements of sadness do you find in the poem?

5. Have you ever had somewhat similar feelings about someone who was severely punished for a misdemeanor? Was your feeling one of indignation? of pity? of terror? or what?

"Fuzzy-Wuzzy"

6. What qualities did the British Tommy appreciate in Fuzzy-Wuzzy? What British qualities are indirectly revealed by the poem? What lines can you quote to illustrate?

7. What phrases give you a picturesque glimpse of the native of the Sudan? What was his final achievement that inspired Kipling to sing his praises? Do you share his enthusiasm? Why?

8. With what similar feelings of admiration

can you match Kipling's admiration for an "enemy"?

For Ambitious Students

9. If you would like to know Kipling's poetry better, you should read the volumes mentioned on page 385. Many of these poems, you will find, lend themselves admirably to recitation and song. Perhaps you can borrow phonograph records of Kipling's ballads and catch their bold dramatic spirit through music. Or some members of the class who have taken lessons in dramatic reading may wish to present a Kipling program. Possibly members of your school's Glee Club will sing "Danny Deever" to the class or assembly.

LYRIC POETRY

WHAT IS it that stirs a writer to express himself in verse? Precisely the same experiences which make your blood race faster and your eyes light up, which cause a lump in your throat or tears in your eyes — the joy, the sadness, the awe, the ecstasy that all people feel at one time or another.

Ballads and tales relate a story, but lyrics express the way a poet feels. Since an outburst of feeling is but momentary, lyrics are usually brief. Like all poetry, they must be read aloud; for their magic depends as much upon the music of words as upon the pictures and ideas they stir in your mind. Thus word music varies with the emotion behind the poem. Thus there is always a close harmony between thought and rhythm and choice of words. As you may observe for yourself in the poems of this section, there are as many different poetic patterns in lyric poetry as there are impressions to be revealed.

Earth's Lowly Creatures

THE BONDS between man and beast are many and close. Often some of the finest traits of both appear when the two are comrades. The sight of a sturdy boy playing with his dog will bring a smile to the face of a bitter man. No wonder! That comradeship is almost as old as man's world. It goes back to times when early man hunted with his dog for food, and slept with him for warmth and safety. And so the poets, who explore so many sides of life, have naturally written about dogs and cats and birds and the animals of the fields and forests.

DANIEL WEBSTER'S HORSES

by Elizabeth J. Coatsworth
(1893–   )

If when the wind blows
Rattling the trees
Clicking like skeletons'
Elbows and knees,

You hear along the road 5
Three horses pass —
Do not go near the dark
Cold window glass.

If when the first snow lies
Whiter than bones 10
You see the mark of hoofs
Cut to the stones,

Hoofs of three horses
Going abreast —
Turn about, turn about, 15
A closed door is best!

Upright in the earth
Under the sod
They buried three horses
Bridled and shod, 20

Daniel Webster's horses —
He said as he grew old,
" Flesh, I loved riding,
Shall I not love it, cold?

" Shall I not love to ride 25
Bone astride bone,
When the cold wind blows
And snow covers stone?

" Bury them on their feet
With bridle and bit. 30
They were fine horses —
See their shoes fit."

23–24. **Flesh . . . cold:** If the poet had written out the whole idea, what would she have said for these two lines?

THE CIRCUS-POSTERED BARN

by Elizabeth J. Coatsworth
(1893–)

When Dobbin and Robin, unharnessed from the plow,
Stamp smoking to their stalls,
They pass beneath white horses with long manes
Shining upon the walls,
White horses airily leaping through great hoops 5
Along applauding tracks
Or carrying princesses in rosy tights
Upon their backs.

And Daisy, Madge, and Buttercup
Raise their soft eyes, 10
Where through the darkness of the web-hung stable
Hippopotami arise,
Shaking the water from their enormous shoulders
Floundering in savage mud,
Showing those muzzles huge enough to ponder 15
An epic cud.

And Tom beside a rathole in the boarding
Meets the still stare
Of eyes fiercer than his eyes and a large lithe body
Above him there — 20
Despondent grow the inmates of the barnyard;
Not one achieves
The superpowers of those supermammals
Beneath the eaves!

12. **Hippopotami:** plural of hippopotamus. 16. An **epic** is usually a poem of enormous and imposing sweep. What kind of cud would an epic cud be?

THE MONKEY

by Nancy Campbell

I saw you hunched and shivering on the stones,
The bleak wind piercing to your fragile bones,
Your shabby scarlet all inadequate:
A little ape that had such human eyes
They seemed to hide behind their miseries — 5

Their dumb and hopeless bowing down
to fate —
Some puzzled wonder. Was your monkey
soul
Sickening with memories of gorgeous
days,
Of tropic playfellows and forest ways,
Where, agile, you could swing from bole
to bole 10
In an enchanted twilight with great flowers
For stars; or on a bough the long night
hours
Sit out in rows, and chatter at the moon?
Shuffling you went, your tiny chilly hand
Outstretched for what you did not understand; 15
Your puckered mournful face begging a
boon
That but enslaved you more. They who
passed by
Saw nothing sorrowful; gave laugh or
stare,
Unheeding that the little antic there
Played in the gutter such a tragedy. 20

FOUR LITTLE FOXES

by Lew Sarett (*1888–*)

Speak gently, Spring, and make no sudden sound;
For, in my windy valley, yesterday I found
New-born foxes squirming on the ground —
Speak gently.

Walk softly, March, forbear the bitter blow; 5
Her feet within a trap, her blood upon the snow,
The four little foxes saw their mother go —
Walk softly.

Go lightly, Spring, oh, give them no alarm;
When I covered them with boughs to shelter them from harm, 10
The thin blue foxes suckled at my arm —
Go lightly.

Step softly, March, with your rampant hurricane;
Nuzzling one another, and whimpering with pain,
The new little foxes are shivering in the rain — 15
Step softly.

A CHILD'S PET

by William Henry Davies (*1870–*)

When I sailed out of Baltimore,
With twice a thousand head of sheep,
They would not eat, they would not drink,
But bleated o'er the deep.

Inside the pens we crawled each day, 5
To sort the living from the dead;
And when we reached the Mersey's
mouth,
Had lost five hundred head.

7. **Mersey:** the river in England at the mouth of which Liverpool is situated.

Yet every night and day one sheep,
That had no fear of man or sea, 10
Stuck through the bars its pleading face,
And it was stroked by me.

And to the sheepmen standing near,
" You see," I said, " this one tame sheep?
It seems a child has lost her pet, 15
And cried herself to sleep."

So every time we passed it by,
Sailing to England's slaughterhouse,
Eight ragged sheepmen — tramps and thieves — 19
Would stroke that sheep's black nose.

"NOTATION ON IMMORTALITY"

by Nancy Byrd Turner (1880–)

We sat debating many things together,
Old Rover drowsy on the floor, and then,
Watching him hunt in dreams, we argued whether
A dog will live again.

Searching the Scriptures, " Perish as a beast " 5
We could recall, and in another place,
" Without are dogs " — in all the scroll no least
Promise for Rover's race.

Lean and unkempt beside his owner's chair
He sprawled. We could not clearly picture him 10
Ranging around with sheep burrs in his hair,
Among the seraphim.

The fire went out, the hall clock struck eleven.
Stretching, he sighed, and edged a little way
Nearer his master's foot — already in heaven 15
And asking but to stay.

12. **seraphim:** angels.

THINK BACK OVER WHAT YOU HAVE READ

Understanding the Poets' Meaning

1. In which of these poems does the writer say everything he wants you to know? Which poems stimulate you to use your imagination?

2. Why does the poet feel sorry for the monkey? What *miseries* stir her sympathies? In " A Child's Pet " what thought arouses the sympathies of the ragged sheepmen? In " Four Little Foxes " what lines pulled at your own heartstrings?

3. What fearful idea does Elizabeth Coatsworth imply in " Daniel Webster's Horses "? Can you suggest a reason why the lines of the poem are so short and jerky? Read the poem aloud, and then guess.

4. In " The Circus-Postered Barn " who are Dobbin, Robin, Daisy, Madge, Buttercup, and Tom? Be sure you know! What clues does the poet give you? In each stanza what circus animal is compared with what barnyard animal? What human feelings are imagined for the animals in the last four lines?

5. On what subject did the human beings debate in " Notation on Immortality "? What answers did the Bible furnish? What answer did old Rover furnish?

Increase Your Power over Words

6. *Boon* (page 391) is an old word which came to England in the early days with the fierce Norse invaders. It was their word for prayer. Today we use it to mean a favor asked. How is *boon* used in " The Monkey "?

7. *Lithe, agile, supple, nimble, limber, pliable,* and *flexible* all describe movement, yet each has a special shade of meaning. Try to place the best one of these adjectives before each of the following nouns. *Do not mark the book.*

acrobat	willow branch
python (snake)	sapling
leather	licorice stick
ballet dancer	bread dough
wits	diving board

Think of at least six opposites for these words.

Wanderlust and Wander Weariness

The little Road says Go
The little House says Stay.[1]

TWO contradictory impulses dwell in the human heart, the love of home and a longing for far places. The whistle of a train at night, in the distance; the breath of salt-sea air to one who has known the ocean — these can set the blood racing with an age-old longing which the poets understand. Perhaps they will " put a fire in *your* heels "; at least your heart will keep time to the rhythm of their verses. Beware of your desire to discover what is at the end of the lane or beyond the horizon. Other poets sing the weariness of the wanderer and the love of home. The note of sadness in the last two poems of this section may cool the fire in your heels — for a while.

[1] From "The House and the Road" by Josephine Preston Peabody.

TRADE WINDS

by John Masefield (1878–)

In the harbor, in the island, in the Spanish Seas,
Are the tiny white houses and the orange trees,
And day long, night long, the cool and pleasant breeze
Of the steady trade winds blowing.

There is the red wine, the nutty Spanish ale, 5
The shuffle of the dancers, the old salt's tale,
The squeaking fiddle, and the soughing in the sail
Of the steady trade winds blowing.

And o' nights there's fireflies and the yellow moon,
And in the ghostly palm trees the sleepy tune 10
Of the quiet voice calling me, the long low croon
Of the steady trade winds blowing.

6. **salt's:** sailor's.

A WANDERER'S SONG

by John Masefield (1878–)

A wind's in the heart of me, a fire's in my heels,
I am tired of brick and stone and rumbling wagon wheels;
I hunger for the sea's edge, the limits of the land,
Where the wild old Atlantic is shouting on the sand.

Oh, I'll be going, leaving the noises of the street, 5
To where a lifting foresail-foot is yanking at the sheet;

To a windy, tossing anchorage where yawls and ketches ride,
Oh, I'll be going, going, until I meet the tide.

And first I'll hear the sea wind, the mewing of the gulls,
The clucking, sucking of the sea about the rusty hulls, 10
The songs at the capstan in the hooker warping out,
And then the heart of me'll know I'm there or thereabout.

Oh, I am tired of brick and stone, the heart of me is sick,
For windy, green, unquiet sea, the realm of Moby Dick;
And I'll be going, going, from the roaring of the wheels, 15
For a wind's in the heart of me, a fire's in my heels.

7. **yawls and ketches:** small boats with sails. 10. **hulls:** sides of the ship. 11. **songs . . . out:** songs on deck as the ship sails. 14. **Moby Dick:** the great white whale in Herman Melville's novel of the sea, *Moby Dick*.

TEWKESBURY[1] ROAD

by John Masefield (*1878–*)

It is good to be out on the road, and going one knows not where,
Going through meadow and village, one knows not whither nor why;
Through the gray light drift of the dust, in the keen cool rush of the air,
Under the flying white clouds, and the broad blue lift of the sky;

And to halt at the chattering brook, in the tall green fern at the brink 5
Where the harebell grows, and the gorse, and the foxgloves purple and white;
Where the shy-eyed delicate deer troop down to the pools to drink,
When the stars are mellow and large at the coming on of the night.

O! to feel the warmth of the rain, and the homely smell of the earth,
Is a tune for the blood to jig to, a joy past power of words; 10
And the blessed green comely meadows seem all a-ripple with mirth
At the lilt of the shifting feet, and the dear wild cry of the birds.

[1] **Tewkesbury:** a city in England.

TRAVEL

by Edna St. Vincent Millay
(*1892–*)

The railroad track is miles away,
And the day is loud with voices speaking;
Yet there isn't a train goes by all day
But I hear its whistle shrieking.

All night there isn't a train goes by, 5
Though the night is still for sleep and dreaming,
But I see its cinders red on the sky,
And hear its engine steaming.

My heart is warm with the friends I make,
And better friends I'll not be knowing; 10
Yet there isn't a train I wouldn't take,
No matter where it's going.

THE TICKET AGENT

by Edmund Leamy (1889–)

Like any merchant in a store
Who sells things by the pound or score,

He deals with scarce perfunctory glance
Small passkeys to the world's romance.

He takes dull money, turns and hands 5
The roadways to far-distant lands.

Bright shining rail and fenceless sea
Are partners to his wizardry.

He calls off names as if they were
Just names to cause no heart to stir. 10

For listening you'll hear him say
". . . and then to Aden and Bombay." . . .
Or ". . . 'Frisco first and then to Nome,
Across the Rocky Mountains — home." . . .

And never catch of voice to tell 15
He knows the lure or feels the spell.

Like any salesman in a store,
He sells but tickets — nothing more.

And casual as any clerk 19
He deals in dreams, and calls it — work!

12. **Aden:** a port in southern Arabia. 12. **Bombay:** a city in India. 13. **'Frisco:** San Francisco. 13. **Nome:** a city in Alaska.

A WET SHEET AND A FLOWING SEA

by Allan Cunningham (1784–1842)

A wet sheet and a flowing sea,
  A wind that follows fast,
And fills the white and rustling sail,
  And bends the gallant mast;
And bends the gallant mast, my boys, 5
  While, like the eagle free,
Away the good ship flies, and leaves
  Old England on the lee.

O for a soft and gentle wind!
  I heard a fair one cry; 10
But give to me the snoring breeze
  And white waves heaving high;
And white waves heaving high, my boys,
  The good ship tight and free —
The world of waters is our home, 15
  And merry men are we.

There's tempest in yon hornèd moon,
  And lightning in yon cloud;
And hark the music, mariners!
  The wind is piping loud; 20
The wind is piping loud, my boys,
  The lightning flashes free —
While the hollow oak our palace is,
  Our heritage the sea.

23. **hollow oak:** the hull of a ship.

ROOFS

by Joyce Kilmer (1886–1918)

The road is wide and the stars are out and the breath of the night is sweet,
And this is the time when wanderlust should seize upon my feet.
But I'm glad to turn from the open road and the starlight on my face,
And to leave the splendor of out-of-doors for a human dwelling place.

I never have seen a vagabond who really liked to roam 5
All up and down the streets of the world and not to have a home:
The tramp who slept in your barn last night and left at break of day
Will wander only until he finds another place to stay.

2. **wanderlust:** a word appropriated from the German, meaning the desire for travel.

A gypsyman will sleep in his cart with canvas overhead;
Or else he'll go into his tent when it is time for bed. 10
He'll sit on the grass and take his ease so long as the sun is high,
But when it is dark he wants a roof to keep away the sky.

If you call a gypsy a vagabond, I think you do him wrong,
For he never goes a-traveling but he takes his home along.
And the only reason a road is good, as every wanderer knows, 15
Is just because of the homes, the homes, the homes to which it goes.

They say that life is a highway and its milestones are the years,
And now and then there's a tollgate where you buy your way with tears.
It's a rough road and a steep road and it stretches broad and far,
But at last it leads to a golden town where golden houses are. 20

AN OLD WOMAN OF THE ROADS

by Padraic Colum (1881–)

O, to have a little house!
To own the hearth and stool and all!
The heaped up sods upon the fire,
The pile of turf against the wall!

To have a clock with weights and chains
And pendulum swinging up and down! 6
A dresser filled with shining delph,
Speckled and white and blue and brown!

I could be busy all the day
Clearing and sweeping hearth and floor,
And fixing on their shelf again 11
My white and blue and speckled store!

I could be quiet there at night
Beside the fire and by myself,
Sure of a bed and loath to leave 15
The ticking clock and the shining delph!

Oh! but I'm weary of mist and dark,
And roads where there's never a house nor bush,
And tired I am of bog and road,
And the crying wind and the lonesome hush! 20

And I am praying to God on high,
And I am praying Him night and day,
For a little house — a house of my own —
Out of the wind's and the rain's way.

THINK BACK OVER WHAT YOU HAVE READ

Responding to the Vagabond Longing

1. What pictures does " Trade Winds " suggest to your imagination? What words of pleasant sound can you quote? What details of romantic association color the pictures?

2. By what sign, in " A Wanderer's Song," does the poet expect to know that he is at sea? What sights and sounds does he long for? Of what sights and sounds is he weary? On the basis of your own experience perhaps you can interpret this weariness.

3. Of what pleasures of the road were you made keenly aware in " Tewkesbury Road "? What phrases appealed to you?

4. Judging from his three poems introduced to you here, what is Masefield's idea of romance? How clearly does he touch upon your own secret longings? With what phrases can you illustrate?

5. What details in " Travel " suggest to you the romance associated with trains? What line or lines reveal most strikingly the poet's longing?

6. How would you expect the ticket agent to react to Tewkesbury Road? or to " the harbor, in the island, in the Spanish Seas "? What details would he be likely merely to take for

granted? What romantic associations would he miss? On the contrary, what would Edna St. Vincent Millay's response most likely be to the "bright shining rail" which the ticket agent disregarded? What is "the spell" which he missed?

7. In "A Wet Sheet and a Flowing Sea" the poet prefers the sea in which of its moods? With what words would you describe the rhythm of this poem?

8. Into which of these poems could you read your own personal experience? What details have you, too, noticed? What moods did you appreciate most? Why?

9. Be prepared to tell the class of similar experiences in your own life.

10. What reply does Joyce Kilmer make in "Roofs" to Masefield's refrain "a fire's in my heels"? What details in "An Old Woman of the Roads" give vivid testimony to Joyce Kilmer's suggestion that vagabonds grow weary of the open road?

Appreciating the Sentiment of the Poems

11. What details of romantic association in "An Old Woman of the Roads" cling to the idea of home? What details of contrasting appeal would you set beside those of romantic association in "Trade Winds"? "A Wanderer's Song"? "Tewkesbury Road"? "Travel"?

Composition Suggestion

12. If you had the choice, what part of the world would you like to visit? Write your answer in detail, giving reasons for your choice.

For Ambitious Students

13. If you should like to follow up the theme of Wanderlust in lyric poetry, you will enjoy the following poems:

Akins, Zoe, "The Wanderer"
Byrne, Don, "To the World's Edge"
Carman, Bliss, "A Vagabond Song"
Gould, Gerald, "Wander-Thirst"
Hovey, Richard, "The Sea Gypsy"
Kipling, Rudyard, "Mandalay"
Masefield, John, "Sea Fever"

14. These poems may be read if you desire to follow up the theme of home life:

Burns, Robert, "The Cotter's Saturday Night"
Johns, Orrick, "Little Things"
Ledwidge, Francis, "Behind the Closed Eye"
Morley, Christopher, "To the Little House"
Whittier, J. G., "Snowbound"

Imaginative Insight

CARL SANDBURG, one of the poets represented in this section, says that poetry is "the opening and closing of a door." If you will think about what he means by this saying, you may decide that the poet "opens the door" to a thought which otherwise you might have missed. Then if you read so well that you truly make the poet's thought your own, the "closing of the door" means that this thought will hereafter be secure in your memory.

Notice as you read this group of poems that the poet's door does not necessarily lead to strange rooms and unusual scenes. Here it leads to an old house, a skyscraper, and an aquarium — all of them familiar to you. In other words, the poet's door leads to a new way of seeing, which makes the old, new; the dull, bright; and the empty, full of meaning.

AT THE AQUARIUM

by Max Eastman (1883–   )

Serene the silver fishes glide,
Stern-lipped, and pale, and wonder-eyed!
As through the aged deeps of ocean,
They glide with wan and wavy motion!
They have no pathway where they go. 5
They flow like water to and fro.
They watch with never-winking eyes,
They watch with staring, cold surprise,
The level people in the air,

The people peering, peering there: 10
Who wander also to and fro,
And know not why or where they go,
Yet have a wonder in their eyes,
Sometimes a pale and cold surprise.

And neigh like Boanerges;
Then, punctual as a star,
Stop — docile and omnipotent — 15
At its own stable door.

13. **Boanerges:** "sons of Thunder." See Mark 3:17.

A RAILROAD TRAIN

by Emily Dickinson (1830–1886)

I like to see it lap the miles,
And lick the valleys up,
And stop to feed itself at tanks;
And then, prodigious, step

Around a pile of mountains, 5
And, supercilious, peer
In shanties by the sides of roads;
And then a quarry pare

To fit its sides, and crawl between,
Complaining all the while 10
In horrid, hooting stanza;
Then chase itself downhill

DESERTED

by Madison Cawein (1865–1914)

The old house leans upon a tree
Like some old man upon a staff:
The night wind in its ancient porch
Sounds like a hollow laugh.

The heaven is wrapped in flying clouds 5
As grandeur cloaks itself in gray:
The starlight flitting in and out,
Glints like a lantern ray.

The dark is full of whispers. Now 9
A foxhound howls: and through the night,
Like some old ghost from out its grave,
The moon comes misty-white.

BLUEBERRIES

by Robert Frost (1875–)

Robert Frost, whose poems rank among the finest of our time, will please you with his quiet, conversational tone and tender humor. Notice, as you read "Blueberries," how clear and simple the language is, yet how musical. If you will *listen* carefully, perhaps some of the lines which you hear will linger in your memory.

"You ought to have seen what I saw on my way
To the village, through Patterson's pasture today:
Blueberries as big as the end of your thumb,
Real sky-blue, and heavy, and ready to drum
In the cavernous pail of the first one to come! 5
And all ripe together, not some of them green
And some of them ripe! You ought to have seen!"

"I don't know what part of the pasture you mean."

"You know where they cut off the woods — let me see —
It was two years ago — or no! — can it be 10
No longer than that? — and the following fall
The fire ran and burned it all up but the wall."

"Why, there hasn't been time for the bushes to grow.
That's always the way with the blueberries, though:
There may not have been the ghost of a sign 15
Of them anywhere under the shade of the pine,
But get the pine out of the way, you may burn
The pasture all over until not a fern
Or grass-blade is left, not to mention a stick,
And presto, they're up all around you as thick 20
And hard to explain as a conjuror's trick."

"It must be on charcoal they fatten their fruit.
I taste in them sometimes the flavor of soot.
And after all really they're ebony-skinned:
The blue's but a mist from the breath of the wind, 25
A tarnish that goes at a touch of the hand,
And less than the tan with which pickers are tanned."

"Does Patterson know what he has, do you think?"

"He may and not care and so leave the chewink
To gather them for him — you know what he is. 30
He won't make the fact that they're rightfully his
An excuse for keeping us other folk out."

"I wonder you didn't see Loren about."

"The best of it was that I did. Do you know,
I was just getting through what the field had to show 35
And over the wall and into the road,
When who should come by, with a democrat-load
Of all the young chattering Lorens alive,
But Loren, the fatherly, out for a drive."

"He saw you, then? What did he do? Did he frown?" 40

"He just kept nodding his head up and down.
You know how politely he always goes by.
But he thought a big thought — I could tell by his eye —
Which being expressed, might be this in effect:
'I have left those there berries, I shrewdly suspect, 45
To ripen too long. I am greatly to blame.'"

"He's a thriftier person than some I could name."

"He seems to be thrifty; and hasn't he need,
With the mouths of all those young Lorens to feed?
He has brought them all up on wild berries, they say, 50

24. **ebony:** really a black, shiny wood from a jungle tree. To most people, it means very black. 29. **chewink:** a bird of the finch family.

Like birds. They store a great many away.
They eat them the year round, and those they don't eat
They sell in the store and buy shoes for their feet."

"Who cares what they say? It's a nice way to live,
Just taking what nature is willing to give, 55
Not forcing her hand with harrow and plow."

"I wish you had seen his perpetual bow —
And the air of the youngsters! Not one of them turned,
And they looked so solemn — absurdly concerned."

"I wish I knew half what the flock of them know 60
Of where all the berries and other things grow,
Cranberries in bogs and raspberries on top
Of the boulder-strewn mountain, and when they will crop.
I met them one day and each had a flower
Stuck into his berries as fresh as a shower; 65
Some strange kind — they told me it hadn't a name."

"I've told you how once not long after we came,
I almost provoked poor Loren to mirth
By going to him of all people on earth
To ask if he knew any fruit to be had 70
For the picking. The rascal, he said he'd be glad
To tell if he knew. But the year had been bad.
There had been some berries — but those were all gone.
He didn't say where they had been. He went on:
'I'm sure — I'm sure' — as polite as could be. 75
He spoke to his wife in the door, 'Let me see,
Mame, we don't know any good berrying place?'
It was all he could do to keep a straight face."

"If he thinks all the fruit that grows wild is for him,
He'll find he's mistaken. See here, for a whim, 80
We'll pick in the Pattersons' pasture this year.
We'll go in the morning, that is, if it's clear,
And the sun shines out warm: the vines must be wet.
It's so long since I picked I almost forget
How we used to pick berries; we took one look round, 85
Then sank out of sight like trolls underground,
And saw nothing more of each other, or heard,
Unless when you said I was keeping a bird
Away from its nest, and I said it was you.
'Well, one of us is.' For complaining it flew 90
Around and around us. And then for a while

58–59. Why didn't the children turn to look back? Can you guess why they looked so "solemn — absurdly concerned"? 86. **trolls**: dwarfs who live in caves; in appearance, like the famous dwarfs who befriended Snow White.

We picked, till I feared you had wandered a mile,
And I thought I had lost you. I lifted a shout
Too loud for the distance you were, it turned out,
For when you made answer, your voice was as low 95
As talking — you stood up beside me, you know."

" We shan't have the place to ourselves to enjoy —
Not likely, when all the young Lorens deploy.
They'll be there tomorrow, or even tonight.
They won't be too friendly — they may be polite — 100
To people they look on as having no right
To pick where they're picking. But we won't complain.
You ought to have seen how it looked in the rain,
The fruit mixed with water in layers of leaves,
Like two kinds of jewels, a vision for thieves." 105

98. **deploy:** This is an example of the perfect word for the idea expressed. Are you sure you know precisely what it means?

TEXAS

by Amy Lowell (1874–1925)

In all her poetry Amy Lowell avoided vague, misty ideas. She tried, always, to use words accurately, to present a clear, hard image which the reader could see, hear, or feel. Because of this hard brilliance, readers have described her poems as " bits of bright enamel." Notice, as you read " Texas," how many *pictures* you see.

I went a-riding, a-riding,
Over a great long plain.
And the plain went a-sliding, a-sliding
Away from my bridle rein.
Fields of cotton, and fields of wheat, 5
Thunder-blue gentians by a wire fence,
Standing cypress, red and tense,
Holding its flower rigid like a gun,
Dressed for parade by the running wheat,
By the little bouncing cotton. Terribly sweet 10
The cardinals sing in the live-oak trees,
And the long plain breeze,
The prairie breeze,
Blows across from swell to swell
With a ginger smell. 15
Just ahead, where the road curves round,
A long-eared rabbit makes a bound
Into a wheat field, into a cotton field,
His track glitters after him, and goes still again
Over to the left of my bridle rein. 20

But over to the right is a glare — glare — glare —
Of sharp glass windows.
A narrow square of brick jerks thickly up above the cotton plants,
A raucous mercantile thing flaring the sun from thirty-six windows,
Brazenly declaring itself to the lovely fields. 25
Tramcars run like worms about the feet of this thing,
The coffins of cotton bales feed it,
The threshed wheat is its golden blood.
But here it has no feet,
It has only the steep ironic grin of its thirty-six windows, 30
Only its basilisk eyes counting the fields,
Doing sums of how many buildings to a city, all day and all night.

11. **cardinals:** birds with brilliant red plumage, among the most beautiful of American birds.

31. **basilisk:** a dragonlike creature of mythical origin. The breath, even the *look*, of a basilisk was said to be fatal.

Once they went a-riding, a-riding,
Over the great long plain.
Cowboys singing to their dogie steers, 35
Cowboys perched on forty-dollar saddles,
Riding to the North, six months to get there,
Six months to reach Wyoming.
"Hold up, paint horse, herd the little dogies,
Over the lone prairie." 40
Bones of dead steers,
Bones of dead cowboys,
Under the wheat, maybe.
The skyscraper sings another way,
A tune of steel, of wheels, of gold. 45
The ginger breeze blows, blows all day
Tanged with flowers and mold.
And the Texas sky whirls down, whirls down,
Taking long looks at the fussy town.
An old sky and a long plain 50
Beyond, beyond, my bridle rein.

SKYSCRAPER

by Carl Sandburg (1878–)

Many high-school students today have heard Carl Sandburg read his own poetry, for he has lectured extensively in recent years. They remember his white hair, the deep lines in his face, and the husky, musical quality of his voice. Others who haven't seen him have read his poems and know him as the poet of modern industrial America and of the common people.

If you have always thought poetry needed to rhyme and bounce along in a set rhythm, "Skyscraper" will be even more of a surprise to you than "Blueberries" or "Texas"; and if you haven't closed your mind to new ideas, "Skyscraper" will be merely the beginning of your acquaintance with a great poet.

By day the skyscraper looms in the smoke and sun and has a soul.
Prairie and valley, streets of the city, pour people into it and they mingle, among its twenty floors, and are poured out again back to the streets, prairies and valleys.
It is the men and women, boys and girls so poured in and out all day that give the building a soul of dreams and thoughts and memories.
(Dumped in the sea or fixed in a desert, who would care for the building or speak its name or ask a policeman the way to it?)

Elevators slide on their cables and tubes catch letters and parcels and iron pipes carry gas and water in and sewage out. 5
Wires climb with secrets, carry light and carry words, and tell terrors and profits and loves — curses of men grappling plans of business and questions of women in plots of love.

Hour by hour the caissons reach down to the rock of the earth and hold the building to a turning planet.
Hour by hour the girders play as ribs and reach out and hold together the stone walls and floors.
Hour by hour the hand of the mason and the stuff of the mortar clinch the pieces and parts to the shape an architect voted.
Hour by hour the sun and the rain, the air and the rust, and the press of time running into centuries, play on the building inside and out and use it. 10

7. **caissons:** supports for the foundation of a building.

Men who sunk the pilings and mixed the mortar are laid in graves where the wind whistles a wild song without words

And so are men who strung the wires and fixed the pipes and tubes and those who saw it rise floor by floor.

Souls of them all are here, even the hod carrier begging at back doors hundreds of miles away and the bricklayer who went to state's prison for shooting another man while drunk.

(One man fell from a girder and broke his neck at the end of a straight plunge — he is here — his soul has gone into the stones of the building.)

On the office doors from tier to tier — hundreds of names and each name standing for a face written across with a dead child, a passionate lover, a driving ambition for a million-dollar business or a lobster's ease of life. 15

Behind the signs on the doors they work and the walls tell nothing from room to room.

Ten-dollar-a-week stenographers take letters from corporation officers, lawyers, efficiency engineers, and tons of letters go bundled from the building to all ends of the earth.

Smiles and tears of each office girl go into the soul of the building just the same as the master-men who rule the building.

Hands of clocks turn to noon hours and each floor empties its men and women who go away and eat and come back to work.

Toward the end of the afternoon all work slackens and all jobs go slower as the people feel day closing on them. 20

One by one the floors are emptied. . . . The uniformed elevator men are gone. Pails clang. . . . Scrubbers work, talking in foreign tongues. Broom and water and mop clean from the floors human dust and spit, and machine grime of the day.

Spelled in electric fire on the roof are words telling miles of houses and people where to buy a thing for money. The sign speaks till midnight.

Darkness on the hallways. Voices echo. Silence holds. . . . Watchmen walk slow from floor to floor and try the doors. Revolvers bulge from their hip pockets. . . . Steel safes stand in corners. Money is stacked in them.

A young watchman leans at a window and sees the lights of barges butting their way across a harbor, nets of red and white lanterns in a railroad yard, and a span of glooms splashed with lines of white and blurs of crosses and clusters over the sleeping city.

By night the skyscraper looms in the smoke and the stars and has a soul. 25

THINK BACK OVER WHAT YOU HAVE READ

Sharing the Poets' Vision

1. What did the poet see with his eyes "At the Aquarium"? What with his imagination? What comment does he make about life? What feeling does the poet arouse in you?

2. What verbs make you see "A Railroad Train" with new vision? With what is the railroad train compared?

3. Every word, every appeal to your senses mounts up to one single impression in "De-

serted." What is that impression? What does the poet see and hear that an unimaginative person would miss?

4. Read aloud the passages describing the blueberries in Robert Frost's poem. Which lines reveal his keen observation of the commonplace things in nature? Which lines reveal his understanding of people?

5. What contrasting pictures do you see in "Texas"? What is the poet's purpose in making these contrasts?

6. What effective comparisons do you find in "Texas"?

7. What part of the poem refers to the Texas of today? of yesterday? What are the poet's impressions of Texas? What phrases in "Texas" are most vividly descriptive? What adverbs are especially descriptive?

8. What details in "Skyscraper" give you a sense of the crowds which go in and out of skyscrapers? What lines suggest the ghosts which haunt them? What pictures did your imagination catch of the daily pageant behind their walls? What sense of the ceaseless activity going on within them? of the silence at night after the workday is over?

9. What words and phrases made you regard a skyscraper in a different manner from what you had before? What new beauty did the poem make you realize?

10. What is the poet's idea of the "soul" of a skyscraper? In what lines does he tell you his idea?

Increase Your Power over Words

11. A submissive, gentle, obedient animal or person who is easy to manage is said to be *docile* (page 398). On a scale like this

docile	easy to control	controllable	difficult to control	ungovernable

where would you place the following animals?

cow	kitten
dog	house cat
Indian pony	collie
Shetland pony	bulldog
Ferdinand the Bull	colt
most bulls	calf

12. The prefix *omni* means all. A bus which carries all passengers who will pay is called an *omnibus* in England; sometimes we use the word in America, too. An *omnivorous* animal eats all kinds of food, whereas a *carnivorous* animal eats mainly meat, or flesh. Very frequently we stretch the word *omnivorous* to a new use and speak of people who read a great deal — and almost everything — as *omnivorous* readers. Can you see why? Sometimes a collection in one book of a number of murder-mystery stories is entitled *An Omnibus of Crime;* or if the stories are all by Terhune, who writes about dogs, the book may be called *A Dog Omnibus* or *The Terhune Omnibus.* Can you explain the implications of such book titles? Now take *omnipotent* apart. What kind of king would be *omnipotent?* Why is God said to be *omniscient* and *omnipresent?*

Now that you really know *docile* and *omnipotent,* look back at the last line of "A Railroad Train." Do you understand now the imagination with which Emily Dickinson sees a train?

For Ambitious Students

13. You have noticed, in poems like "Blueberries" and "Texas," the poets' ability to see sharp, clear details. To develop such powers of observation, you must awaken your five senses. Keep in your notebook, for entries of accurate sensory description, a page like this:

SIGHT	SOUND	SMELL	TASTE	TOUCH
(blueberries) "The blue's but a mist from the breath of the wind."	saxophones' gibbering and slithering sound	pungent orange peel	the crisp, salt-sweetness of bacon	my dog's cold, wet nose mud oozing between my toes

Make certain that most of the entries derive from your own experience, your own direct observation. However, you may begin your project by entering some of the best examples from the poems you have just read.

The Troubled Heart

SINCE POETS are imaginative, they look understandingly into the hearts of their fellow men. They share the weight of injustice with the oppressed and the burden of sorrow with the grieving. As you read the poems in this group, you will see how modern poets can tell movingly of the lives of common people.

NANCY HANKS

1784–1818

by Rosemary and Stephen Vincent Benét

If Nancy Hanks
Came back as a ghost,
Seeking news
Of what she loved most,
She'd ask first 5
" Where's my son?
What's happened to Abe?
What's he done?

" Poor little Abe,
Left all alone 10
Except for Tom,
Who's a rolling stone;
He was only nine
The year I died.
I remember still 15
How hard he cried.

" Scraping along
In a little shack,
With hardly a shirt
To cover his back, 20
And a prairie wind
To blow him down,
Or pinching times
If he went to town.

1. **Nancy Hanks:** the mother of Abraham Lincoln. 7. **Abe:** Lincoln. 11. **Tom:** brother of Abraham Lincoln.

" You wouldn't know 25
About my son?
Did he grow tall?
Did he have fun?
Did he learn to read?
Did he get to town? 30
Do you know his name?
Did he get on? "

NEGRO SPIRITUALS[1]

by Rosemary and Stephen Vincent Benét

We do not know who made them.
The lips that gave them birth
Are dust in the slaves' burying ground,
Anonymous as earth.

The poets, the musicians, 5
Were bondsmen bred and born.
They picked the master's cotton,
They hoed the master's corn.

The load was heavy on their backs,
The way was long and cold, 10
— But out of stolen Africa,
The singing river rolled,
And David's hands were dusky hands,
But David's harp was gold.

[1] **Spirituals:** primitive religious songs of the American Negroes, composed during the years of slavery.

CALIBAN[1] IN THE COAL MINES

by Louis Untermeyer (*1885–*)

God, we don't like to complain
We know that the mine is no lark —
But — there's the pools from the rain;
But — there's the cold and the dark.

[1] **Caliban:** a character in Shakespeares' *The Tempest* who becomes a slave on his own island.

God, You don't know what it is — 5
You, in Your well-lighted sky —
Watching the meteors whiz;
Warm, with the sun always by.

God, if You had but the moon
Stuck in Your cap for a lamp, 10
Even You'd tire of it soon,
Down in the dark and the damp.

Nothing but blackness above
And nothing that moves but the cars. . . .
God, if You wish for our love, 15
Fling us a handful of stars!

from *THE PEOPLE, YES*

by Carl Sandburg (1878–)

From the four corners of the earth,
from corners lashed in wind
and bitten with rain and fire,
from places where the winds begin
and fogs are born with mist children, 5
tall men from tall rocky slopes come
and sleepy men from sleepy valleys,
their women tall, their women sleepy,
with bundles and belongings
with little ones babbling, "Where to now? what next?" 10

. . . .

In the darkness with a great bundle of grief the people march.
In the night, and overhead a shovel of stars for keeps, the people march:
"Where to? what next?"

THINK BACK OVER WHAT YOU HAVE READ

Interpreting the Poems

1. In which of these poems do you detect resentment? indignation? Can you present evidence from any of them to show that the poet is expressing sympathy? admiration? despair? hope? Which poem reveals tenderness?

2. By what picture does Untermeyer in "Caliban in the Coal Mines" suggest to you the pitiful lack in the coal miner's lot? What details drive home the point? What evidence of revolt do you find? of loss of faith?

3. Who are "the people" in Carl Sandburg's poem? Toward what goals are they marching? From the time of kings and Pharaohs until the present day, what advances have the people made in their march? What setbacks have come to them? Is the march finished? What is in the "bundle of grief" which the people carry?

Increase Your Power over Words

4. One of the Latin words for horse is *caballus*. From this word *cavalcade* (page 412) is derived indirectly. It means a procession of persons, usually on horseback. Closely allied to this word are *cavalier* and *cavalry*. Look up the meanings of these words and discover how they are related to their Latin stem.

Composition Suggestion

5. About what injustices have *you* been troubled? Have you *seen* intolerance or prejudice at work? Have you felt or seen the humiliation of poverty? Your first consideration in this composition should be sincerity and intensity of feeling.

For Ambitious Students

6. The following poems are further examples of the interest poets have taken in the problems and troubles of their fellow men:

Browning, E. B., "The Cry of the Children"
Burns, Robert, "On Seeing a Wounded Hare Limp by Me"; "Address to the Unco Guid"
Evans, F. W., "The Flower Factory"
Hood, Thomas, "The Song of the Shirt"
Markham, Edwin, "The Man with the Hoe"
Sandburg, Carl, "To a Contemporary Bunk-Shooter"
Schauffler, R. H., "Scum o' the Earth"

7. Some students will wish to read more poems by Rosemary and Stephen Vincent Benét. They will find them in the volume from which the poems in this collection are taken, *A Book of Americans*. The whole book *The People, Yes* by Carl Sandburg makes exciting reading.

"Life Has Loveliness to Sell"[1]

POETS, of course, are not the only people who are uplifted by beauty. On the contrary, everyone remembers scenes such as a calm lake under moonlight; a ski jumper swooping downward against a winter sky; a bend in a country road where grainfields run to the horizon; wet city streets, black and silver in the electric lights — such pictures have sent a wordless thrill through all of us. But a poet brings words and thrills together. He is not mute before beauty as most of us are. If he is a good poet, he not only can *tell* how he sees beauty in the world about him but can *give* part of his secret to us.

STARS

by Sara Teasdale (1884–1932)

Alone in the night
  On a dark hill
With pines around me
  Spicy and still,

And a heaven full of stars 5
  Over my head,
White and topaz
  And misty-red;

Myriads with beating
  Hearts of fire 10
That aeons
  Cannot vex or tire;

Up the dome of heaven
  Like a great hill,
I watch them marching 15
  Stately and still,

And I know that I
  Am honored to be
Witness
  Of so much majesty. 20

[1] Sara Teasdale.

GOD'S WORLD

by Edna St. Vincent Millay (1892–)

O world, I cannot hold thee close enough!
  Thy winds, thy wide gray skies!
  Thy mists that roll and rise!
Thy woods, this autumn day, that ache and sag
And all but cry with color! That gaunt crag 5
To crush! To lift the lean of that black bluff!
World, World, I cannot get thee close enough!

Long have I known a glory in it all,
  But never knew I this;
  Here such a passion is 10
As stretcheth me apart. Lord, I do fear
Thou'st made the world too beautiful this year.
My soul is all but out of me, — let fall
No burning leaf; prithee, let no bird call.

NOCTURNE IN A DESERTED BRICKYARD

by Carl Sandburg (1878–)

Stuff of the moon
Runs on the lapping sand
Out of the longest shadows.
Under the curving willows,
And round the creep of the wave line, 5
Fluxions of yellow and dusk on the waters
Make a wide dreaming pansy of an old pond in the night.

DAYS

by Karle Wilson Baker (1878–)

Some days my thoughts are just cocoons — all cold, and dull, and blind,
They hang from dripping branches in the gray woods of my mind;
And other days they drift and shine — such free and flying things!
I find the gold dust in my hair, left by their brushing wings.

A BALLADE[1]—CATALOGUE OF LOVELY THINGS

by Richard le Gallienne (1876–)

I would make a list against the evil days
Of lovely things to hold in memory:
First, I would set down my lady's lovely face,
For earth has no such lovely thing as she;
And next I add, to bear her company,
The great-eyed virgin star that morning brings; 6
Then the wild rose upon its little tree —
So runs my catalogue of lovely things.

The enchanted dogwood, with its ivory trays,
The water lily in its sanctuary 10
Of reeded pools, and dew-drenched lilac sprays,
For thee, of all fair flowers, the fairest be;
Next write I down the great name of the sea,
Lonely in greatness as the names of kings;
Then the young moon that hath us all in fee — 15
So runs my catalogue of lovely things.

[1] **Ballade:** an Old French poetic form consisting usually of three eight-line stanzas and a four-line *envoi* (see note on p. 408). The same rhyme sounds are used in all stanzas; therefore, only three rhyme sounds are found in the entire poem. The last line of the first stanza is repeated at the end of the other stanzas.

Imperial sunsets that in crimson blaze
Along the hills, and, fairer still to me,
The fireflies dancing in a netted maze
Woven of twilight and tranquillity;
Shakespeare and Virgil, their high poesy; 21
Then a great ship, splendid with snowy wings,
Voyaging on into eternity —
So runs my catalogue of lovely things.

ENVOI[1]

Prince, not the gold bars of thy treasury,
Not all thy jeweled scepters, crowns, and rings, 26
Are worth the honeycomb of the wild bee —
So runs my catalogue of lovely things.

[1] **Envoi:** The ballade was always addressed to a particular person who is named in the last stanza, called an *envoi* (French for *messenger*) because it sums up the message of the poem.

THINK BACK OVER WHAT YOU HAVE READ

Sharing the Poet's Vision of Beauty

1. Have you ever looked at the stars on a clear summer's night? How does the word *alone* intensify the mood of "Stars"? Why does the poet say the stars were "marching up the dome of heaven"? What does this tell you about the length of time she watched the heavens?
2. What words and phrases in "God's World" revealed to you the poet's pleasure in beholding nature's loveliness? What details appealed to her senses?
3. A brickyard in the sunshine is a very ugly thing. Under what conditions does Sandburg find it beautiful? By what details does he make you see the picture?
4. Describe to the class some ugly object which you have seen transformed by moonlight.
5. Bring to class a copy of Walter de la Mare's poem "Silver." Contrast it with "Nocturne in a Deserted Brickyard." How are the two poems similar?
6. How does Richard Le Gallienne express

rom Rockwellkentiana, copyright, 1933, Harcourt, Brace and Company

THE ARTIST, WHETHER POET OR PAINTER, IS INTERESTED IN *HOW* AND *WHAT*. In the discussion which concludes the poetry section in this book, you see that a poet realizes that *how an idea is expressed* — not only what he is saying — deserves keenest attention. A painter must also pay attention to the *how*. How he paints is of the utmost importance in achieving the effect he wants to create in his picture.

In the painting above notice how Rockwell Kent has emphasized the coldness of the scene and the sense of human life surrounded by a bleak, forbidding country. What part of the painting is the point of greatest interest? Do the heavy black lines of the mountain purposely direct your eyes towards this focal point, or did Rockwell Kent just accidentally happen to paint them that way? How does the color of the sky and the sharp contrast of black and white make you feel? Warm or cold? This oil painting, called "Sledging," was painted in Greenland in 1932.

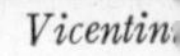

Vicentin

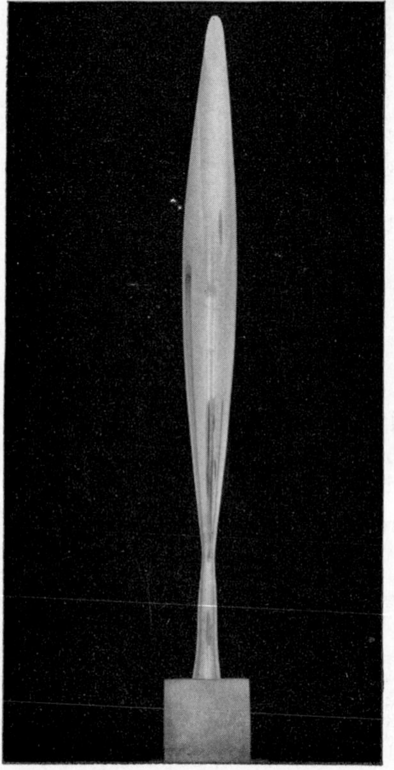

ARTISTS USE RHYTHM, TOO. In poetry and music rhythm delights our ears; whereas in art, rhythm must appeal to our eyes. Notice how skilfully Leonard Butler, a modern American painter, uses rhythm in his picture, "Calm of Evening." The sweeping diagonal lines of the hills move in the same direction, and the flowing bank of white clouds repeats the soft line of the horizon. The artist's problem is like that of the composer and poet in another way. Rhythm that is too regular in poetry or music becomes monotonous or "jingly." How does Mr. Butler break the soft monotony, the regularity of the flowing, rhythmic lines in this picture?

Notice how the sculptor Brancusi has expressed an idea in his "Bird in Space" (*left*).

Museum of Modern Art

Vicentini

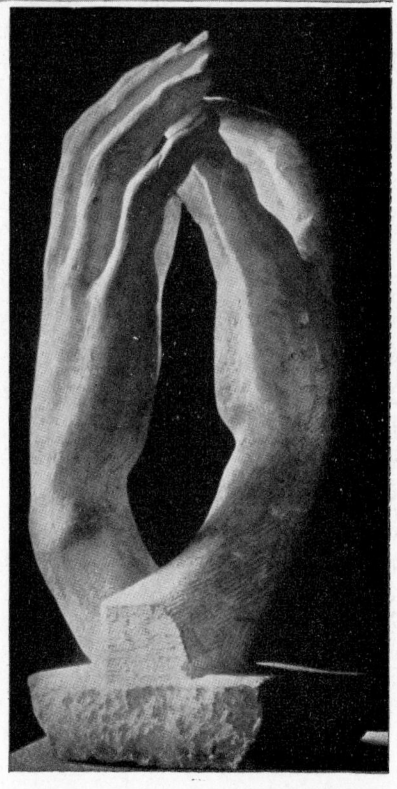

THE ARTIST AND THE POET USE VARIETY. To increase interest, a poet will introduce variety. Sometimes he will vary the length of the lines or use different rhythms. Sometimes he will introduce conversation as Robert Frost does in "Blueberries," page 398. Can you call to mind anything musicians do to prevent their pieces from becoming tiresome to listeners or dancers? In his portrait of a student (*above*), Sarkisian achieves variety by his use of light and shadow. Expert photographers use lighting in their work for the same reason.

The simplest and most common things became subjects for the great sculptor Rodin. Notice how he used the shape of hands to suggest the arches of a cathedral and to express the idea of worship. ("The Cathedral," *right*)

Rodin Museum

Photo, Giraudon

WHAT DO YOU SEE IN A PICTURE? If the French painter Daumier had not called his picture "The Street-Singers," how would you have decided what figures he wished to emphasize? Why is the arch placed just where it is? How does he use light and shade? In poems like "The Horse Thief" page 372 or "Daniel Webster's Horses" page 389, do you notice the dominant effect the poet wishes you to feel? How does he accomplish his purpose?

the rewards of recognizing beauty? What "lovely things" in his catalogue do you, too, "hold in memory"? What others can you add?

For Ambitious Students

7. In the manner of Richard Le Gallienne, in "A Ballade — Catalogue of Lovely Things," or of Rupert Brooke, in "These I Have Loved" from *The Great Lover,* list your own catalogue of lovely things.

8. Find these poems in the library:

Brooke, Rupert, "The Great Lover"
Carman, Bliss, "Daisies"
Lanier, Sidney, "Song of the Chattahoochee"
Wordsworth, William, "I Wandered Lonely as a Cloud"

From the enjoyment which each of these poets finds in nature, which poet would you be disposed to like best? Find more of his poems and read them.

Of Heroic Mold

HEROES OF all ages have been made out of the same stuff — the stuff it takes to stand up against life. Courage, daring, persistence, and fairness — these are the qualities which we all wish to possess and with which we endow ourselves in our daydreams. These are the qualities it takes, furthermore, to realize our dreams. They are the qualities, too, possessed by the pioneer, the explorer, and the conqueror. These are the qualities which the poets in this group sing about.

TOMORROW

by John Masefield (1878–)

Oh, yesterday the cutting edge drank thirstily and deep,
The upland outlaws ringed us in and herded us as sheep,
They drove us from the stricken field and bayed us into keep;
But tomorrow,
By the living God, we'll try the game again! 5

Oh, yesterday our little troop was ridden through and through,
Our swaying, tattered pennons fled, a broken, beaten few,
And all a summer afternoon they hunted us and slew;
But tomorrow,
By the living God, we'll try the game again! 10

And here upon the turret top the balefire glowers red,
The wake lights burn and drip about our hacked, disfigured dead,
And many a broken heart is here and many a broken head;
But tomorrow,
By the living God, we'll try the game again! 15

PLAY THE GAME

Vitaï Lampada

by Sir Henry John Newbolt
(*1862–*)

There's a breathless hush in the close to-night —
  Ten to make and the match to win —
A bumping pitch and a blinding light,
  An hour to play and the last man in.
And it's not for the sake of a ribboned coat, 5
  Or the selfish hope of a season's fame,
But his captain's hand on his shoulder smote —
  "Play up! Play up! and play the game!"

The sand of the desert is sodden red —
  Red with the wreck of a square that broke; 10
The Gatling's jammed and the colonel dead,
  And the regiment blind with dust and smoke.
The river of death has brimmed his banks,
  And England's far, and honor a name,
But the voice of a schoolboy rallies the ranks: 15
  "Play up! Play up! and play the game!"

This is the word that year by year,
  While in her place the school is set,
Every one of her sons must hear,
  And none that hears it dare forget. 20
This they all with a joyful mind
  Bear through life like a torch in flame,
And, falling, fling to the host behind —
  "Play up! Play up! and play the game!"

1. **close:** athletic field. 3. **bumping pitch:** a term in the English game of cricket. 5. **ribboned coat:** given to members of the team as lettered sweaters are given in America. 11. **Gatling:** a kind of machine gun.

SAM HOUSTON

1793–1863

by Rosemary and Stephen Vincent Benét

Whenever Sam Houston felt ill at ease
He'd go and live with the Cherokees,
For he liked their ways and he liked their dress
And the free, proud life of the wilderness.

This buckskin hero from Tennessee 5
Had a life as checkered as lives can be.
There was speech and duel and love and ire,
And all of it lived like a prairie fire.

He was up and down, he was hissed and cheered,
But there never was anything Houston feared. 10

His dreams were huge and his costumes showy
And his private honor bright as a bowie.

He's the pride and boast of the Lone Star State
For he fought her battles and made her great, 14
And, on either side of the wide Atlantic,
You won't find anyone more romantic.

1. **Sam Houston:** one of the leaders of the secession of Texas from Mexico. He became president of the Republic of Texas. 12. **bowie:** kind of hunting knife. 13. **Lone Star State:** Texas.

THE OREGON TRAIL

by Arthur Guiterman (*1871–*)

Two hundred wagons, rolling out to Oregon
  Breaking through the gopher holes, lurching wide and free,
Crawling up the mountain pass, jolting, grumbling, rumbling on,
  Two hundred wagons, rolling to the sea.

From East and South and North they flock, to muster, row on row, 5
A fleet of ten-score prairie ships beside Missouri's flow.
The bullwhips crack, the oxen strain, the canvas-hooded files
Are off upon the long, long trail of sixteen hundred miles.
The women hold the guiding lines; beside the rocking steers
With goad and ready rifle walk the bearded pioneers 10
Through clouds of dust beneath the sun, through floods of sweeping rain
Across the Kansas prairie land, across Nebraska's plain.

Two hundred wagons, rolling out to Oregon,
  Curved around the campfire flame at halt when day is done,
Rest a while beneath the stars, yoke again and lumber on, 15
  Two hundred wagons, rolling with the sun.

Among the barren buttes they wind beneath the jealous view
Of Blackfoot, Pawnee, Omaha, Arapahoe, and Sioux.
No savage threat may check their course, no river deep and wide;
They swim the Platte, they ford the Snake, they cross the Great Divide. 20
They march as once from India's vales through Asia's mountain door
With shield and spear on Europe's plain their fathers marched before.
They march where leap the antelope and storm the buffalo
Still westward as their fathers marched ten thousand years ago.

Two hundred wagons, rolling out to Oregon 25
  Creeping down the dark defile below the mountain crest,
Surging through the brawling stream, lunging, plunging, forging on,
  Two hundred wagons, rolling toward the West.

Now toils the dusty caravan with swinging wagon poles
Where Walla Walla pours along, where broad Columbia rolls. 30
The long-haired trapper's face grows dark and scowls the painted brave;
Where now the beaver builds his dam the wheat and rye shall wave.
The British trader shakes his head and weighs his nation's loss,
For where those hardy settlers come the Stars and Stripes will toss.
Then block the wheels, unyoke the steers; the prize is his who dares; 35
The cabins rise, the fields are sown, and Oregon is theirs!
        They will take, they will hold,
        By the spade in the mold,
        By the seed in the soil,
        By the sweat and the toil, 40
        By the plow in the loam,
        By the school and the home!

Two hundred wagons, rolling out to Oregon,
  Two hundred wagons, ranging free and far,
Two hundred wagons, rumbling, grumbling, rolling on, 45
  Two hundred wagons, following a star!

THINK BACK OVER WHAT YOU HAVE READ

Understanding and Applying the Ideas Gained

1. Notice the part which the word *tomorrow* plays in Masefield's poem. How many times does he repeat it? Where? How? Does this help to express more effectively the main idea of the poem? Can you tell how? What qualities of character are admired in this poem? Are they suitable only to a battlefield, or could they be applied in everyday life? in school? on the athletic field?
2. What story is suggested in " Tomorrow "?
3. What is meant by " play the game " in *Vitaï Lampada?* According to the poem what relationship exists between school life and later life?
4. What value do you see in school spirit? Is winning the most important thing in school athletics? What good may come from losing? Are you sure of your answer, or are you only repeating something you have always heard? How do you know?
5. How did the pioneers of " The Oregon Trail " develop their traits when they had no English or American school sports to teach them to " play the game "? What is meant by " a star " at the end of the poem? Could a star of this sort be as effective as athletics in developing heroes?

WHAT DOES AN IDEA GAIN FROM BEING PUT INTO VERSE FORM?

Why don't poets present whatever they wish to say in ordinary sentences? Perhaps we can best answer this question by comparing two different versions of the same story. Here it is told in prose:

MOONLIGHT

On nights when the moon was out, my father used to go about the house pulling down the shades. Because he had been a frontiersman in his youth, he remembered the raids which the Comanche Indians made on the settlers during moonlight nights. For that reason he came to prefer darkness.

Now read it in verse, and see whether you gain anything:

MOONLIGHT

by Berta Hart Nance (1883-   )

My father hated moonlight,
And pulled the curtains down
Each time the snows of moonlight
Came drifting on the town.

He was an old frontiersman,
And on their deadly raids,
Comanches rode by moonlight
In stealthy cavalcades;

And took the settlers' horses,
Or left a trail of red, —
He came to love the darkness,
And hate the moon, he said.

Poetry stirs emotions. If you have been at all sensitive to the rhythm, the length of the lines, and the choice of words, the poetic form should have stirred in you a feeling about the facts related in the story. With a sudden, sharp twist, you cease to be merely *reading about* something and find yourself *experiencing* something — a feeling of fear, a dread of moonlight. Thus we see once again that not only *what* is said but also *how* it is said is of the utmost importance in its effect upon the reader.

Like music, words appropriately arranged can create a mood in the listener; they can lure him to far-off southern islands, as in " Trade Winds," or sadden him with the picture of four little foxes whimpering in the rain. In another form the same idea might disturb the listener little more than facts recited in an almanac. Just what is this magic by which a poet stirs the imagination and touches the emotions of sensitive, appreciative readers? Three resources are his if he be skillful; rhythm, word music, and imagery.

Rhythm. Rhythm, the most important of these, links poetry to many other enjoyable activities — swimming, skating, dancing, music, and swinging, to mention only a few. There is, in all of us, a love of rhythmic regularity; we like to have a musical note or an accent in a word come at the expected interval, just as we like to keep in step.

By rhythm in poetry we mean that the stressed syllables of our words are arranged according to some pattern. If you repeat the following lines aloud, you will notice that your own voice stresses the syllables indicated by bold-faced type:

In the **har**bor, in the **is**land, in the **Span**ish **Seas,**
Are the **ti**ny white **hous**es and the **or**ange **trees.**

When these stresses become unpleasantly pronounced in poor reading, we label such effort "singsong." In order to avoid such monotony, the poets frequently upset their rhythm patterns long enough to break the stiff regularity.

Some patterns are better suited to certain ideas than they are to others. The short, breathless rhythm of "Daniel Webster's Horses" fits a ghostly legend, while the easy, natural rhythm of "Blueberries" suggests the characteristic speech of everyday life.

Word music. If you have an alert ear, you will have noticed another resource of poetry. The sounds of words may be used to further the poet's purpose. Very often he rhymes words, usually at the ends of lines; occasionally he varies this by rhyming within the line (called *internal rhyme*). Perhaps you noticed this in "The Revenge"?

Another familiar use of sound is *alliteration,* a repetition of the same initial letter sound in a group of successive words. This is the oldest musical device of English poetry. Notice its use in these lines:

Serene the **s**ilver fishes glide,
Stern-lipped, and pale, and wonder-eyed!

You will find many other examples if you will search for them.

Somewhat like alliteration is *assonance,* the repetition of the same vowel sound in a group of words. For instance:

I could be **quiet** there at **night**
Beside the **fire** and **by myself.**

Still another device which poets use is *onomatopoeia,* the suggestion of meaning by means of sound. Our language is full of words which originated through an effort to describe sound. Thus *boom, clash, bang, whisper, murmur* are onomatopoetic words. Poe's "The Bells" is a familiar example: you remember the *tinkling* sleigh bells, the firebells that *clang* and *clash,* and the iron funeral bells resounding in a *muffled monotone.* The drone of flies is unmistakable in Keats's line, "The murmurous haunt of flies on summer eves." Such sound effects make poetry much more meaningful.

Imagery. Besides its musical character, poetry is also distinguished by the poet's rich use of imaginative suggestion. Much that he sees reminds him of something else. Notice, for example, in "The Horse Thief," the comparisons suggested by the italicized words:

There he moved, cropping the grass at the purple *canyon's lip.*
His mane was mixed with the moonlight that silvered his snow-white side,
For the moon sailed out of a cloud *with the wake of a spectral ship.*

Such resemblances are called *similes,* if *like* or *as* are used, and *metaphors* if the comparison is assumed or implied as are those just quoted. This is but a partial answer to the question put to you, on page 412.

Review of Poetry. It is time now for you to apply what you have learned to the poems you have just read:

1. Notice which of your five senses receive these impressions:

Thunder-blue gentians by a wire fence

The clucking, sucking of the sea about the rusty hulls

The prairie breeze,
Blows across from swell to swell
With a ginger smell.

2. Find further examples in the poems of an appeal to all five senses.

3. In this book you will find three poems in which the rhythm contributes to the impression of riding horseback: "Kit Carson's Ride," "Texas," and "The Horse Thief." How has rhythm been varied in each to match the different rides?

4. Which poems in this book have used an irregular pattern of rhythm and rhyme? Can you suggest any reasons why these departures from the ordinary are appropriate to the purposes of the poems?

5. Find two or three poems like "Stars" which express seriously the poets' deepest feelings. Compare these with several light poems such as "A Ballad of John Silver." What differences in rhythm do you notice immediately? upon closer examination?

6. What effect do the consonants have in the words used in the poem "At the Aquarium"? How do the vowels aid the poem's mood in "Stars"? Can you find any other poems in which word music plays a hidden part?

Choral Speaking

UNTIL RECENTLY, perhaps, the only instance of groups speaking rhythmically and in unison has appeared in American sport. School yells at football and basket ball games arouse a feeling of unity and group strength among the spectators that often inspires the players to make greater efforts. These group yells are distantly related to the chanting of primitive American Indian tribes as they beat their tom-toms in preparation for war.

Speaking in unison may serve purposes other than winning games or wars, however. Within the last ten years many of us have been discovering choral reading, rhythmic speaking in unison, used for artistic purposes. The rapid increase in the number of verse-speaking choirs, both in America and Europe, indicates that modern man has rediscovered a lost art.

Two thousand years ago the Greeks spoke sections of their plays in chorus. Later the minstrels and troubadours of the Middle Ages recited for the groups of people who gathered before the vast fireplaces of feudal castles or about tables in the inns. The tales they recited became so familiar that the audience would join in, frequently clapping to accent the rhythm. Although for many years choral speaking disappeared, people have once more discovered how enjoyable it is to speak rhythmically together and to use different groups of voices to produce the varied qualities of tone, pitch, and volume that are possible to the human voice.

Why not try it yourself if you haven't already done so? Then you can best judge how natural and pleasant verse speaking is. The following suggestions will guide you in handling the poems in this section.

SUGGESTIONS FOR CHORAL SPEAKING

1. Each member of the class should read aloud a brief passage from some story or poem while the rest of the class listens intently to the quality and pitch of each successive voice. Listening with eyes closed as each speaker reads will help you to concentrate on voice alone. Most classes find it easier to compare voices if the same brief passage is used.

2. Your teacher, with help from the class, will group the voices according to their similarity. You may have to experiment with this; furthermore the sound effects you want in a certain poem may lead you to modify your

voice groupings occasionally. Perhaps you will not wish to use the voices of the whole class in every poem. Sometimes a poem may seem to call for only boys' voices or for a small group of girls' voices, perfectly matched. *Don't be afraid to experiment.*

3. As a group, you should next discuss the meaning of the first poem you plan to use. Everyone should make suggestions; an interpretation that will best reveal the mood and feeling of the poem should be your aim.

4. By the time you have agreed upon the meaning and interpretation, you will already know fairly well the lines of the poem and the way it divides into parts. Now you will want to plan how to use your voice groupings. Suggestions are given for the poems in this section, but don't hesitate to adapt these suggestions to your own class and your own ideas.

5. Here are three *Don'ts* [1]

a. Don't speak every poem in exactly the same way and give every stanza the same pitch.

b. Don't sing or chant your poems. Think primarily of the meaning and speak naturally in familiar speech rhythms. Don't let sound become more important to you than meaning.

c. Don't speak constantly in a heavy, labored manner. Develop a light, flexible tone and speech. People singing hymns in church tend to drag. So will your verse choir if you aren't careful.

Your teacher may wish to supplement these suggestions with exercises to develop good breathing methods and good resonance, as well as with practice on vowels and consonants for good articulation and flexibility. Any of the better textbooks in speech will offer help on all these problems. Remember, however, that the most important objective is for you to feel the mood of the poem and to understand it. Without this, the exercises will be of little value.

SEA CHANTEYS

In the days of the sailing vessel, song accompanied work. Sea chanteys were work songs, sung not so much to entertain as to lighten some heavy task or to encourage flagging energies. A good chantey, it was said, was worth an extra man. But woe betide the sailor who "roused a chantey when there worn't no need." Forecastle ditties might be sung after supper over a pipe as the spirit moved; but a chantey was for mocking wind and wave, when all hands bent to the task of lowering sail while shrouds boomed and sea birds screamed.

Every duty on shipboard had its own song: hoisting anchor, hauling sail, manning the capstan bars, loading cargo — all were performed to a tune especially timed so as to meet the particular pull or to guide the grip of the hands. You will recognize such a rhythm in the song "So Handy." Of all the ship's gear, the capstan bars are the most symbolic of seafaring labor. Round and round in a circle the men shambled, pushing the oaken bars to wind the heavy cables, singing lustily in the rhythm of their movements. "Heave Away" is a capstan chantey.

Choose a boy with a good voice to read the solo lines. In addition to a strong, vigorous voice, he should have an ease and confidence of manner. However, acting of any kind should be incidental rather than pronounced. The class as a whole — or perhaps a group of boys' voices only — should read the alternating refrains and the stanzas printed in italics. This should be done with a rousing, rhythmic swing.

Instead of a solo voice, you may wish to use two boys with very similar voices.

SO HANDY

Oh, up aloft this yard must go,
So handy, my boys, so handy!
Oh, up aloft from down below,
So handy, my boys, so handy!

We'll hoist it high before we go, 5
So handy, my boys, so handy!
And when it's up we'll leave it so,
So handy, my boys, so handy!

Oh, sing and haul and haul and sing,
So handy, my boys, so handy! 10
Right up aloft this yard we'll bring,
So handy, my boys, so handy!

Stretch her leech and show her clew,
So handy, my boys, so handy!

[1] Adapted from *Choral Speaking* by Marjorie Gullan, Expression Company, Boston, Mass.

1. **yard:** the spar that extends sails. 13. **leech:** the after edge of a sail. 13. **clew:** the after lower corner of a sail.

A few more pulls to bring her through,
So handy, my boys, so handy! 16

I thought I heard the first mate say,
So handy, my boys, so handy!
" Give one more pull and then belay."
So handy, my boys, so handy! 20

19. **belay:** make fast by winding a rope around a cleat.

HEAVE AWAY

Sometimes we're bound for Liverpool, more times we're bound for France.

CHORUS

Heave away . . . my Johnny, heave away away!
Sometimes we're bound for Liverpool, more times we're bound for France,
And away, my Johnny boy, we're all bound to go!

Oh, Johnny, you're a rover, and today you sail away. 5
Heave away . . . my Johnny, heave away away!
It's I will be your own sweetheart if you will only stay.
And away, my Johnny boy, we're all bound to go!

CHORUS

Heave away . . . my Johnny, heave away away!
Sometimes we're bound for Liverpool, more times we're bound for France,
And away, my Johnny boy, we're all bound to go! 11

Oh, Johnny, you're a rover, and today you sail away.
Heave away . . . my Johnny, heave, away away!
It's I will be your own sweetheart if you will only stay.
And away, my Johnny, we're all bound to go! 15

CHORUS

THE DUKE OF PLAZA-TORO

by W. S. Gilbert (1836–1911)

The long lines at the beginning of each stanza may be recited as the class wishes, but surely you will want four different students to speak alone when you arrive at

" That celebrated,
Cultivated,
Underrated
Nobleman,"

with the whole group ending:

" The Duke of Plaza-Toro! "

The solo voices should reveal the mock seriousness as they build to a minor climax at the end of each stanza. This is an excellent poem for experimentation. Let the class make suggestions, try various plans, and choose the idea which best reveals the poem's humor and rhythm.

In enterprise of martial kind,
When there was any fighting,
He led his regiment from behind
(He found it less exciting).
But when away his regiment ran, 5
His place was at the fore, O!
That celebrated,
Cultivated,
Underrated
Nobleman, 10
The Duke of Plaza-Toro!
In the first and foremost flight, ha, ha!
You always found that knight, ha, ha!
That celebrated,
Cultivated, 15
Underrated
Nobleman,
The Duke of Plaza-Toro!

When, to evade destruction's hand,
To hide they all proceeded, 20
No soldier in that gallant band
Hid half as well as he did.
He lay concealed throughout the war,
And so preserved his gore, O!
That unaffected, 25
Undetected,
Well-connected
Warrior,
The Duke of Plaza-Toro!

In every doughty deed, ha, ha! 30
He always took the lead, ha, ha!
That unaffected,
Undetected,
Well-connected
Warrior, 35
The Duke of Plaza-Toro!

When told that they would all be shot
Unless they left the service,
That hero hesitated not,
So marvelous his nerve is. 40
He sent his resignation in,
The first of all his corps, O!
That very knowing,
Overflowing,
Easygoing 45
Paladin,
The Duke of Plaza-Toro!
To men of grosser clay, ha, ha!
He always showed the way, ha, ha!
That very knowing, 50
Overflowing,
Easygoing
Paladin,
The Duke of Plaza-Toro!

BUFFALO DUSK

by Carl Sandburg (*1878–*)

Although this is free verse, its rhythm will not be difficult for verse speaking. The first two lines and the last two may be spoken by the same people. In the middle passage the voices of those who have the opening lines should be augmented by several more in order to emphasize the striking images and the rich tonal values of words like *sod, dust,* and *pageant of dusk*. The final lines must close the poem with dignity. Throughout the whole poem the speakers must sense the poet's feeling for the vast primitive West of America before the intrusion of highways, gas stations, and hot-dog stands. The splendor of a past glory can be suggested in these lines.

No more than fifteen or eighteen persons should speak this poem, but their voices should blend together perfectly. No voice should stand out from the others, and the poem should be carefully practiced. After the final word the group should hold its pose for a moment, retaining the mood in a silence which extends beyond the last word of the poem.

The buffaloes are gone.
And those who saw the buffaloes are gone.
Those who saw the buffaloes by thousands and how they pawed the prairie sod into dust with their hoofs, their great heads down, pawing on in a great pageant of dust,
Those who saw the buffaloes are gone.
And the buffaloes are gone.

THE SONG MY PADDLE SINGS

by E. Pauline Johnson (*1861–1913*)

This is an exceptionally interesting poem for a verse choir to speak. From a quiet beginning, as the canoe idles on a windless evening, the movement of the poem mounts to a splendid climax when the canoe plunges through the rapids. The poem finishes once again in tranquillity. The voices may be increased, in both number and intensity, for the middle passages.

A single voice — or several blending voices — might speak the first two lines of each stanza, with a chorus reciting the last three of each. Note, however, in stanzas one and two that the solo voice has four lines and the chorus five.

West wind, blow from your prairie nest,
Blow from the mountains, blow from the west.
The sail is idle, the sailor too;
O! wind of the west, we wait for you.
Blow, blow! 5
I have wooed you so,
But never a favor you bestow.
You rock your cradle the hills between,
But scorn to notice my white lateen.

I stow the sail, unship the mast: 10
I wooed you long but my wooing's past;
My paddle will lull you into rest.
O! drowsy wind of the drowsy west,

Sleep, sleep,
By your mountain steep, 15
Or down where the prairie grasses sweep.
Now fold in slumber your laggard wings,
For soft is the song my paddle sings.

August is laughing across the sky,
Laughing while paddle, canoe, and I, 20
Drift, drift,
Where the hills uplift
On either side of the current swift.

The river rolls in its rocky bed;
My paddle is plying its way ahead; 25
Dip, dip,
While the waters flip
In foam as over their breast we slip.

And oh, the river runs swifter now;
The eddies circle about my bow. 30
Swirl, swirl!
How the ripples curl
In many a dangerous pool awhirl!

And forward far the rapids roar,
Fretting their margin for evermore. 35
Dash, dash,
With a mighty crash,
They seethe, and boil, and bound, and splash.

Be strong, O paddle! be brave, canoe!
The reckless waves you must plunge into.
Reel, reel, 41
On your trembling keel,
But never a fear my craft will feel.

We've raced the rapid, we're far ahead!
The river slips through its silent bed. 45
Sway, sway,
As the bubbles spray
And fall in tinkling tunes away.

And up on the hills against the sky,
A fir tree rocking its lullaby, 50
Swings, swings,
Its emerald wings,
Swelling the song that my paddle sings.

THE GOLDEN CITY OF ST. MARY

by John Masefield (*1876–*)

The words and images in this poem suggest the soft Southern winds and quiet rhythm of waves against a beach. Among the consonants notice how the *m*'s and *n*'s are used like a countermelody for the *s*'s. What vowels are emphasized?

For the first and last stanzas in which the word *I* is used, you may wish to imagine a sailor is speaking and use a solo voice. In that case the chorus would speak the descriptions of the Golden City of St. Mary, stanzas two and three. These two stanzas must be spoken softly and musically, yet very distinctly. They will require a great deal of practice, and the speakers must not allow repetition to dull either the vividness of their mental pictures or the feeling of peacefulness which the lines evoke.

If your choir is to be small — and for this poem that is preferable — you may wish to have the whole choir speak all four stanzas.

Out beyond the sunset, could I but find the way,
Is a sleepy blue laguna which widens to a bay,
And there's the Blessed City — so the sailors say —
The Golden City of St. Mary.

It's built of fair marble — white — without a stain, 5
And in the cool twilight when the sea winds wane
The bells chime faintly, like a soft, warm rain,
In the Golden City of St. Mary.

Among the green palm trees where the fireflies shine,
Are the white tavern tables where the gallants dine, 10
Singing slow Spanish songs like old mulled wine,
In the Golden City of St. Mary.

Oh, I'll be shipping sunsetwards and westward-ho
Through the green toppling combers a-shattering into snow,
Till I come to quiet moorings and a watch below, 15
In the Golden City of St. Mary.

THE PALATINE

by Willa Cather (1876–)

This poem seems best suited to a small group, with the lighter voices taking the lines of the little brother and the darker or huskier voices answering. If you have already read *Julius Caesar,* this poem with its comment on the fall of the great Roman empire will be easier for you to interpret.

" Have you been with the king to Rome,
Brother, big brother ? "
" I've been there and I've come home.
Back to your play, little brother."

" Oh, how high is Caesar's house, 5
Brother, big brother ? "
" Goats about the doorways browse ;
Nighthawks nest in the burnt rooftree.
Home of the wild bird and home of the bee,
A thousand chambers of marble lie 10
Wide to the sun and wind and the sky.
Poppies we find amongst our wheat
Grow on Caesar's banquet seat.
Cattle crop and neatherds drowse
On the floors of Caesar's house." 15

" But what has become of Caesar's gold,
Brother, big brother ? "
" The times are bad and the world is old —
Who knows the where of the Caesar's gold ? 19
Night comes black o'er the Caesar's hill ;
The wells are deep and the tales are ill ;
Fireflies gleam in the damp and mold —
All that is left of the Caesar's gold.
Back to your play, little brother."

" What has become of the Caesar's men,
Brother, big brother ? " 26
" Dogs in the kennel and wolf in the den
Howl for the fate of the Caesar's men,
Slain in Asia, slain in Gaul,
By Dacian border and Persian wall. 30
Rhineland orchard and Danube fen
Fatten their roots on Caesar's men."

" Why is the world so sad and wide,
Brother, big brother ? "
" Saxon boys by their fields that bide 35
Need not know if the world is wide.
Climb no mountain but Shere-end Hill,
Cross no water but goes to mill.
Ox in the stable and cow in the byre,
Smell of the wood smoke and sleep by the fire ; 40
Sunup in seedtime — a likely lad
Hurts not his head that the world is sad.
Back to your play, little brother."

A SELECTED LIST OF BOOKS AND ARTICLES ON CHORAL READING

Choral Speaking by Georgia M. Corp. University Extension Division, University of Wisconsin. Madison, Wisconsin, 1937.
An inexpensive pamphlet which every verse choir should own.

Choral Speaking by Marjorie Gullan. Expression Company, Boston, Mass., 1932.

A thorough and detailed discussion. It contains one of the best simple explanations of meter and rhythm in print.

" Choral Speaking and Its Values " by Emma G. Meader, *The Quarterly Journal of Speech,* April, 1936 (Vol. XXII, pp. 235–45).

Conducting Experiences in English by Angela Broening and Others. National Council of Teachers of English, 1939.

Chapter XII, on choral speaking, has many suggestions and directions by those who have tried choral reading.

Speech by W. G. Hedde and W. N. Brigance. J. B. Lippincott Co., 1937.

The chapter on " Choral Reading " is a valuable help.

The Speech Choir by Marjorie Gullan. Harper and Brothers, 1937.

Practical and clear discussion of choral-reading problems with suggestions and help for more than one hundred poems which are printed in the book.

Other poems in this book which are suitable for choral reading are " Four Little Foxes," " A Wet Sheet and a Flowing Sea," and " By the Turret Stair."

THE DRAMA

NOT SO long ago an occasional traveling company and home talent represented the only sources of theatrical enjoyment for Americans who lived any distance from large cities. Nevertheless, stories brought to life by real men and women have such a fascination that even in the late 1870's, at the time when Sitting Bull and his Indians massacred Custer's army, a stock company was playing Shakespeare in the near-by town of Deadwood.

Today all that is changed. No longer must we wait for the curtain to rise a few times each year at the Grand Opera House. Within walking distance in every town and city are one, if not two, neighborhood theaters, and the automobile makes attendance possible for families from farms and ranches. Even closer at hand is the radio; a mere turn of the dial can transport to our homes a radio play with Helen Hayes or Lionel Barrymore. Good stage plays are given more frequently, too, and are more accessible.

Unfortunately quantity doesn't include quality. Many of the plays on the stage, screen, and radio waste our time with pointless, trivial nonsense which we quickly forget. Since most of us spend some time with these modern forms of the drama, we need to pick and choose wisely if we are to find a proper balance between drama for light enjoyment and drama which enriches our experience or moves us to honest reflection.

Encouraging future predicted for American drama. In spite of the silliness of a great section of modern drama, we need not be overly alarmed. Stupid plays and uncritical audiences to view them existed in Shakespeare's day. Much that is fine and splendid exists for those who want it, and some serious students of the drama find signs of an approaching "golden age" for the American theater. If their predictions are sound, those of you who are using this text and acting in high-school dramatics may be privileged to become the audience and players in another great period of the theater similar to that which glorified England in the days of Queen Elizabeth and James I.

The drama neglects no corner of life. One reason for the belief in an American golden age may be the astounding variety of stories which are coming from the pens of modern writers of plays. We, the American people, are a rich source for great drama. The deep, merging ideals of our immigrant ancestors, their dream of a world in which all men should enjoy the fullness of life and the opportunity to develop their abilities regardness of class lines, and our present serious problems — every corner of life on this continent offers material for significant plays.

High-school students must surely be aware that their corner has not been overlooked. In *What a Life!* the entire plot develops in the office of a principal in one of our large city high schools. The president of the junior class, school dances, and study-hall misbehavior are molded into a drama so exciting and popular that a series of radio plays has been built around the hero, Henry Aldrich. *Dead End*, both on the stage and in the movies, presented realistically the influence of slums on boys and girls. On the screen talented Deanna Durbin has captured for enormously large audiences a freshness of quality which characterizes the finest type of American schoolgirl; and Mickey Rooney is representing the boys. More and more frequently the theater, whether stage, movie, or radio, is discovering interesting dramatic material in the lives of American youth.

The drama has a long, colorful history. Just as there are great excitement and rivalry during tryouts for every high-school play today, so has there been for long centuries a similar interest in acting. The drama is among the oldest of arts, perhaps the very oldest. With the flickering light and shadow of his fire for a setting, the cave man must have acted the stories of his hunting triumphs before his tribe. The courts of ancient Egypt and Persia produced lavish pageants, and the Greeks developed dramatists whose plays are still among the greatest known to the world. From their ritual of worship for the gods, these Greek dramatists developed a lofty form of tragedy and a clever, witty drama which they called comedy.

The plays of the Middle Ages, like those of Greece, originated in religious worship. At first, incidents from the life of Jesus were presented in the churches by priests who wanted to help their ignorant congregations to understand the Bible. Even though the people didn't understand Latin, the power of dramatic presentation was so tremendous that eventually the priests decided to present their plays outdoors in order to have room for the action and the audiences and in order to relinquish gradually any responsibility for an activity which was becoming more popular than the Mass. Ordinary men soon began to act these "mystery plays," as they were called, and before long enterprising players had rigged up stages on wagons and were traveling from town to town.

From these beginnings — and they are the barest hint of a long, colorful story — the English drama reached its first great peak under Queen Elizabeth. No introduction to plays would be complete without a bow to the great Shakespeare, whose plays are still the most popular ever acted on any stage past or present.

Science and the modern world change the theater. The plays of Queen Elizabeth's day were written for the particular stage of the time, a crude affair judged by modern standards, modeled after the old courtyard, surrounded by balconies, of the typical inn. Just as it took the automobile a long time to escape completely from the old horse-and-buggy design from which it descended, so has it taken plays a long time to escape the bondage of the historic theater. The moving picture and the radio play are still hampered by their indebtedness to the legitimate stage and are not yet fully aware of the artistic possibilities which lie within their own field. They are like birds which have not yet been away from their parents, reluctant to take flight and soar on their own wings. As yet they tend to use stories and characters from successful novels and stage plays. Mickey Mouse is one of the outstanding new creations to the credit of these expanding forms of the drama. He is a curious little symbol of the future when imagination and skill may use the movies and radio — or perhaps television — to create a wonderful new drama, perhaps greater than the world has yet known.

How to enjoy reading a play. Except for a few brief stage directions the action of a play is left entirely to the imagination of the reader. He must follow the story entirely by inference, figuring out what happens chiefly from what the characters say. He must set the stage in his own mind and determine what kind of people are talking almost entirely from what they say. All this is a difficult feat to perform and requires practice. Whether we see a play on the screen or stage, or listen to it over the radio, or read it from a book, if we are to enjoy it fully we must learn to cope with its special form.

Short Plays

YOU MAY think of the one-act play as a dramatic version of a short story. Here you will find the same sharp focus of attention, the same impressive unity, to which your attention was drawn in your study of the short story. Plays are stories told by actors on a stage. Because they are more difficult to read than short stories or novels, they remain to many readers a closed door of reading interest. It is for this reason that your reading of drama in this book may well begin with the reading of one-act plays, which will make no such demands on your reading skill as will the full-length Shakespearean play which is to follow.

ONE SPECIAL FOR DOC[1]

A Radio Play

by Milton Geiger (1907–)

At first, when radios were still objects of amazement and wonder, almost all broadcast programs were musical. Now that the novelty has vanished, the art of drama is penetrating this new medium. In particular the short play has become popular, for the radio listener, unlike a theater audience, does not usually have two hours to spend on one program.

With sound the only means of communica-

[1] This play is protected by copyright and is not to be presented or to be reproduced in any manner without the written consent of the author and owner, Milton E. M. Geiger, 470 Public Square Bldg., Cleveland, Ohio.

tion, and under firm pressure to hold as large an audience as possible for the sponsor's advertising, the successful radio writer must submit plays which are both brief and varied.

The play which follows was written expressly for radio and was first produced on the Rudy Vallee hour, November 12, 1936, with Henry Hull speaking the leading role of Doc Harshaw. In 1938 Don Ameche, in *One Special for Doc,* pleased the radio listeners to such an extent that the Columbia Broadcasting System made this drama the nucleus of a popular series of programs which ran for forty-two weeks. *One Special for Doc* has also been broadcast several times in Europe.

As you read this radio script, try to " hear " the voices and sounds. Unless you can read imaginatively, the characters will be merely names without personalities. You must *hear* the voice of " Doc " if you are to appreciate his keen understanding of the boy in this story.

CHARACTERS

YOUNG MAN (ALLEN)

DOC HARSHAW, a shrewd, middle-aged druggist, kindly, helpful, cleverly humane

JULIE, Allen's sweetheart

HANK, owner of Hank's Barbecue; a Greek

SOUND PROPS. *Rumble of thunder; rushing wind. Door of drugstore — open and close — door has latch, not knob. Rattling of bottles in drawer; cash register; silver coins; dishes being slammed on lunch counter; drive and patter of rain; footsteps in wet gravel; ticking of large clock.*

SETTING. *There are a rush of wind and a loud beat of thunder as the* YOUNG MAN *enters* DOC HARSAW'S *drugstore. Door slams shut. There is a pause. Then* HARSHAW *clears his throat tentatively and speaks. His voice betrays the curiosity in his mind. It is peculiar that this boy should be out in such weather.*

Harshaw. Er . . . good evening.

Young Man (*after short pause*). Huh? Oh . . . oh . . . yes. Good evening. (*Then after seeming to reflect a moment*) Not much! (*There is an unexpected bitterness in his words. Clearly he is much upset about something.*)

Harshaw. H'm. . . . Well, it *is* a bit spongy out. But I like it. Keeps the world at bay for a while.

Young Man (*with short, nervous laugh*). Oh . . . if I'm intruding . . .

Harshaw. Oh . . . no, no, no, no, no, no, no, no. Nice to have you, I'm sure.

Young Man (*briskly*). Well . . . I originally intended this to be a business call of sorts. So here goes. . . . Fact of the matter is, I've cut myself. See . . . I attempted to bandage it up. Nasty cut!

Harshaw (*with a note of gentle mockery*). Oh, now that's too-o-o-o-o bad!

Young Man (*deaf to irony*). Oh, not that bad! But . . . well . . . those things can develop into something serious, I've been told. Infection, you know.

Harshaw. By all means. Infection.

Young Man. Er . . . so I'd like a bottle of those — what-do-you-call-'ems. . . . They're blue tablets. You know? In a crinkly blue bottle?

Harshaw. Oh, yes. One moment, please.

[SOUND. *Clatters in drawer full of bottles. Clears throat.*]

Er . . . er . . . these?

Young Man (*with greatly increased agitation*). Yes . . . yes . . . that . . . that's what I mean. Er . . . how much are they, please?

Harshaw. Enough, I assure you. But first I'll have to register this sale. Have to register all sales of . . . (*He pauses and places added emphasis on his last words.*) . . . of . . . deadly poisons.

Young Man (*as though to himself*). Deadly . . . poisons! (*Then sharply*) Why must you register it? I'm not going to murder my aunt, you know!

Harshaw (*brusquely*). Matter of fact, young feller, I don't know anything of the sort. That's quite beside the point. It's the law that I register the sale of a dangerous poison, and the law is operating strictly in your interest. It's for your own protection. Now . . . name, please?

Young Man (*hesitates*). Well . . . all right. Er . . . Peter Jones.

Harshaw (*dubiously*). Jones, eh? Very well. (*Spells slowly as he writes.*) P-e-t-e-r J-o-n-e-s. Address?

Young Man. That too? 2236 Forest Grove.

Harshaw. 2-2-3-6 F-o-r-e-s-t G-r-o-v-e. Purpose of deadly poison?

Young Man. Antiseptic for wound.

Harshaw. Uh-huh. Twenty-five seven-and-a-half-grain tablets. And then I sign my own proud name and fill in the date and hour of purchase, and that's that! That didn't hurt one bit now, did it? You'll be mighty careful with this stuff, won't you? Ever use it before?

Young Man. Certainly. I . . . I've just gone through the last of one bottle and so I had to run out for more. I was sharpening my pencil with a rusty blade and it slipped.

Harshaw (*amiably informative, chatty*). It isn't the rust that does the damage. It's the germs under the rust scales. Uh . . . that's a mighty pretty gold and onyx ring you're wearing under that bandage. Class ring?

Young Man (*irritably*). Yes. High school. Can't get it off. I guess I've sort of grown into it. My — my girl gave it to me. Wouldn't let me buy my own. (*Suddenly impatient*) I'm in a hurry, Doc. How much will that come to?

[SOUND. *A rumble of thunder and a greater burst of rain against the windows.*]

Harshaw. Won't you be wanting some bandage and adhesive tape? What's the rush? It's raining the Amazon River out there. Stick around a little. (*His voice suddenly confidential, inviting confidences*) Stick around, boy. We ought to talk.

Young Man. Wha . . . what do you mean?

Harshaw (*chatty again*). You know, sometimes people get sore because I ask all these questions when they buy poisons for their own good and legitimate reasons. "Do you think I'm going to murder my aunt?" they ask me. Or . . .

Young Man (*apologetic, sheepish*). Oh . . . I didn't mean to . . .

Harshaw. Or they want to know do I think they're considering suicide. It's no affair of mine if they *are*. They can if they like. They can dissolve the lining right out of their stomachs if it suits them. I've the law to comply with. Look . . . suppose your wife . . .

Young Man (*savagely*). I'm not married!

Harshaw (*taken aback*). All right, all right. Mere manner of speaking. Suppose then the . . . er . . . police should find you moaning in your bathroom. They'd come to me as one of the town's druggists. They'd say, "Mr. Harshaw, did a young feller with a gray slouch hat and a tan topcoat and worried brown eyes and a gold and onyx class ring buy any poison here lately?" And I'd tell them, "Why, yes. He got some blue antiseptic tablets. Why?" And they'd say, "Okay, Doc. That's all we want to know. Thanks." By that time, though, there wouldn't be much they could do for you.

Young Man (*unguardedly*). Wouldn't there?

Harshaw (*gravely*). No. The stuff's purgatory! It . . . it's the worst thing a fellow can take. Horrible! (*Intensely, with a climactic rising of his voice as he proceeds*) It's like white-hot coals burning and eating and searing your innards. Your stomach's afire! The membranes burn and wither away and you scream and squirm and pray you'll die. I . . . I can't describe the agony of it! Weeks . . . months, maybe, of torture . . . eating . . . tearing you apart . . . burning! The narcotics the doctors give you don't help much. It's corrosive — like acid, you know.

Young Man (*shaken*). No. I . . . I didn't know that.

Harshaw. Yes, if you die, so much the better for you. Because the nervous shock will wreck you for life. And your stomach's so badly burned that you spend the rest of your days on a diet of gruel and buttered toast and warm milk. Buttered toast and warm milk! When all the time your starving body cries out for a thick, juicy steak and strong bread!

Young Man. You . . . you're hurting my shoulder!

Harshaw (*laughs shortly*). Oh, I didn't know. Sorry. (*Slaps boy's shoulder in camaraderie.*)

Young Man. That . . . that was some lecture! I guess you know though. It's your business.

Harshaw (*significantly*). Sure. It's my business. Other things are my business, too.

Young Man. What do you mean . . . other things, too?

Harshaw (*gently*). Listen, boy . . . you didn't cut yourself. Now *did* you?

[*Long moment of silence. We hear the* YOUNG MAN'S *labored breathing.*]

[SOUND. *Roll of thunder*]

Young Man (*defiantly*). Well . . . all right! So I didn't cut myself! What about it? Here . . . I'll take off the bandage. There! Not a scratch! Feel better now, Sherlock Holmes?

Harshaw (*without triumph*). I knew it. Don't you know you can't dip a gold ring into a solution of this stuff without the gold's turning to silver? Forms an amalgam. Where's your high-school chemistry, boy?

Young Man (*in distraction*). I don't know . . . I don't know! I wanted to . . . Oh . . . I don't know anything, now! Please don't ask me any more questions. Maybe I'd better go.

Harshaw. No. Tell you what. I'm closing up now, and it's not raining too heavily. We'll walk it off and talk it over. And maybe we'll stop at Hank's Barbecue for a snack. Talk it over, see? What do you say, kid?

Young Man. All right. All right, I guess.

Harshaw. Good boy! You read a magazine or something and I'll start counting up. . . .

[SOUND. *Cash register rings. Clink and jingle of coins. Fade down and out. Fade-in footsteps of* HARSHAW *and* YOUNG MAN *walking on wet gravel. Rain and remote thunder*]

Minute you came in I knew something was wrong. It's bad stuff lettin' yourself go that way. You have a lot to live for.

Young Man. I must have been crazy, Doc.

Harshaw. You looked fairly prosperous for a youngster. And you looked healthy. So I figured it couldn't be that. That leaves one other thing — especially when the principal . . . or principals . . . are young and foolish. (*Pause*) Is she pretty?

Young Man (*choking up*). She's . . . beautiful!

Harshaw. Well . . . if you'd like to talk . . . go ahead. Maybe you'll feel better about it all.

Young Man. I *want* to talk. And I'm glad it's you I have to talk to. (*Pause*) It seems so . . . so trivial, now. But I can't go back to her! I can't!

Harshaw. It's not that bad.

Young Man. I don't know. Julie and I have been sweethearts ever since we were kids in school. In high school we were inseparable. We always said we . . . we'd get married. We meant everything to each other. It's been a long time, Doc . . . waiting. But I couldn't ever seem to make enough money at any of my jobs. . . .

Harshaw. You're young. . . .

Young Man. Tonight . . . tonight I came down to see her. I . . . I never saw her looking so lovely. Something in silver and black that made her look whiter and more beautiful than I'd ever seen her. She was waiting for someone . . . and I knew she wasn't expecting *me*. . . .

[SOUND. *Fade* YOUNG MAN'S *voice. Silence. Then* YOUNG MAN'S *voice speaking a little tensely, resentfully*]

You're beautiful tonight, Julie. I've never seen you so . . . so . . . radiant and . . . all.

Julie (*subdued and tense*). Thank you, Allen.

Allen. That's . . . a . . . a mighty sweet dress you're wearing. I never saw it, Julie.

Julie (*trying to be gay*). Yes . . . yes . . . I just had it made. Isn't it a terrible night!

[*Pause in which we feel* ALLEN'S *slow, burning resentment and suspicion*]

Allen. Yes . . . Julie. Terrible.

Julie. Allen! Don't look at me so . . . strangely. As though I'd done something terribly wrong.

Allen. Nothing wrong. Unless it's just a little bit wrong to throw over the fellow that's been crazy about you ever since he was a kid in velvet pants.

Julie. Oh, Allen! Don't think wrong of me. I've fought with myself. I don't want to lose you. But Pearson has been such a good friend to us. Mother and me. We were going to the theater.

Allen. The theater. Harmless enough. The theater. But there'll be another in a week and another after that, and another. And a string of them makes a courtship. And an expensive one that I can't afford yet — or maybe ever. I'm only an engineer. All right. Take Pearson! He's platinum-plated enough. Take him! (*Laughs.*) And I thought I was tops! Sweet little school romance blossoming into cactus!

Julie. Allen! What are you saying? . . .

Allen. You've said it yourself. "Allen, not yet. We've got to save. We want to start right, Allen. We mustn't start the voyage with a light sail and an empty hold." Very prettily put! But a mockery. The run-around, if you please! Well, I'm through waiting for Pearson to take you from under my nose. I'm through, I tell you! I'm through!

[SOUND. *Voice fades out hysterically. Fade-in* ALLEN'S *voice again, talking to* HARSHAW *in the rain.*]

So that was that. And here we are.

Harshaw. You're young. I was young, too.

[SOUND. *Moment of silence. Thunder rolls distantly.*]

Well, here's Hank's place.

[SOUND. *Door opens and closes.*]

Hey, Hank, I've brought customers. Do I get ten percent? Five? I'll settle for doughnuts.

Hank. Hi, Doc. You shure beeg kidder. Ho, ho! (*Businesslike*) What'll gonna be? Bum night, hah? What'll gonna be?

Harshaw. What'll gonna be, kid? Unquote.

Allen. I don't know. That hamburger with grilled onion on rye sounds pretty good. And coffee.

Hank. Shure. What'll gonna be for you, boss?

Harshaw. Er . . . I'll have my special. The regular thing.

Hank (*puzzled*). Hah?

Harshaw. My special. Would you mind bending a little closer, Hank?

Hank. Sure, Hukkay. (*Unintelligible whispering*) Oh, shure, boss! (*Shouts.*) Wan Hambur-r-r-r-k wit' greeled hunnion hon rye! Wan spashul for Doc! Make queek!

Voice (*distant*). Commink hupp!

Hank. I be right out, boss.

Harshaw. All right, Hank. No rush. (*Slight pause.* HARSHAW *whistles softly.*) Well, kid, this isn't much, but it's a lot better than St. Luke's or emergency clinic, eh?

Allen. Stop it, Doc. I've been a fool.

Harshaw. I was coming around to that. But I was going to call it something else. Extreme youth, or something like that. It's a condition we all go through between the ages of, say, eighteen and thirty-five. Roughly, that.

Allen (*laughing a little*). Roughly is right.

[SOUND. *Ticking of large clock grows louder as silence continues. . . . Ticking monotonously*]

Maybe I ought to go back. I wonder, should I go back?

Harshaw. I don't know. Some get over the disease quickly, and seldom have relapses. Up to the individual.

Hank. Here komm! Hamburk wit' greeled hunnion!

[SOUND. *Dishes slam down on counter.*]

Anda wan spashul for Doc! Haw, haw, haw, haw. . . .

[SOUND. *Slide of dishes and fade-out on* HANK *laughing*]

Harshaw (*with strange melancholy, slowly*). One special for Doc. Days without end. One special for Doc.

Allen (*with dawning amazement and comprehension*). One . . . special . . for . . . Doc! You! Warm milk . . . and buttered toast. Warm milk . . .

Harshaw (*in same sad voice*). You see? Do you understand now?

Allen (*dazed*). I . . . I see! For life. Warm milk and buttered toast.

Harshaw. And gruel. Don't forget the gruel.

Allen (*agitated*). I . . . I don't think . . . I want my sandwich. I'm going, Doc. I've got to go. Sorry . . . Doc. . . .

Harshaw. Yes, boy. Go. Go back to her . . . to Julie. . . . She needs you and wants you as badly as you need and want her. Wait for her if you must. She'll wait, too. But go back.

Allen. I'm going. You bet I am! So long. I'll be seeing you.

Harshaw (*softly*). Good night.

Allen (*hesitating*). Thanks. And . . . I'm sorry about . . . you know. Awful sorry.

Harshaw. It's all right, kid. Good night.

Allen. Good night. And thanks.

Harshaw (*calling after him*). And give her my love!

[SOUND. *Door slams hard.* HARSHAW *sighs.*]

Hmmmmmmmmmmm. Crazy kid. Lucky he came to me. I guess I handled *that* prescription all right! (*Chuckles softly, then shouts.*) Hey, Hank!

Hank (*off mike*). Commink, boss!

Harshaw (*shouting*). Hank! Let's see some food. I'll have a steak an inch thick, with mushrooms and fried potatoes. And a gallon of tough coffee. And, for heaven's sake, take this awful-looking stuff out of my sight, will ya!

[CURTAIN]

THINK BACK OVER WHAT YOU HAVE READ

Understanding the Characters

1. Do you remember the druggist and his wife in the short story "That's What Happened to Me"? How might this play have

ended if Allen had gone to their drugstore? Can you remember a time when someone's thoughtfulness or kindliness helped you through an unhappy day?

2. Why does Doc Harshaw impress you as a man whom you would like? Locate speeches in the script which give you this impression and read them aloud. What characters in recent American books or movies are like Doc Harshaw? When you have read *Silas Marner* (page 582), consider whether or not Dolly Winthrop shares any of their qualities.

3. If you were quick to understand the clues the author provided, you knew almost immediately that the boy wasn't a dangerous gangster. What were those clues? When did you first suspect his real intention? Up until that time what possibilities did you consider? (Surely you didn't just read passively without realizing that the author was leading to *something?*) Why do playwrights bring in only characters who have some purpose?

4. What is your reaction to the episode in which Allen and Julie quarrel? What is its purpose in this script, or could it be omitted just as well? Are you convinced that the quarrel is serious enough to drive a young man to such desperate action? What might you say about his common sense or emotional stability?

Increase Your Power over Words

5. We hear much these days about *soil erosion.* Natural elements like wind, rain, and floods have worn away the topsoil over whole areas of land in the United States. In two documentary films, *The River* and *The Plow That Broke the Plains,* our government has called the attention of the American people to the reasons for erosion and the wasteland which results. With the help of scientists we are reclaiming land which nature has taken away from us.

Thus the soil is said to *erode* or wear away. *Erode* sounds and looks very much like *corrode,* which also means to wear away but by chemical processes rather than by natural processes. Perhaps you have worn a cheap ring or wristband which has *corroded.* On page 426 Doc Harshaw refers to the blue antiseptic tablets as *corrosive.* Have you noticed that both these words look like *rodent,* the family name for rats, mice, squirrels, and beavers? Could you do some sleuthing in the dictionary to discover the connection?

For Ambitious Students

6. So very simple it is! You need no high-priced equipment, no microphone, no amplifier. But you do need students with pep, clear voices, and good enunciation. Just turn around and face the back of the room. Then the students you have chosen to play the parts will find it absolutely necessary to rely on voice and sound alone to convey their meaning. The better their expression, the better their play. If your desk won't move, sit still and let the players go to the back of the room. Shutting your eyes during the "program" will add to the illusion.

If you produce *One Special for Doc,* you should first be able to answer these questions. Remember, this is a radio play.

a. Why are all four voices in this play so different? Why was it a good idea to have Hank speak broken English?

b. Explain the reason for the small number of characters.

c. Do you suppose the author purposely wrote his speeches so short and his words so simple?

d. How must the surprise ending be spoken?

7. Perhaps you feel that *One Special for Doc* is too mature for your talents. Why not try a comedy of your own writing or adapt a story like "The Monkey's Paw" or "The Milk Pitcher"? Remember that the announcer can splice your scenes together and narrate the most difficult episodes.

IN THE ZONE

by Eugene O'Neill (1888–)

Surely you have puzzled over the behavior of the people who make up your world. Perhaps a friend has suddenly dropped you, or some boy in class seems unable to control his temper in spite of the fact that everyone is beginning to avoid him. Have you ever had a grouchy neighbor or known a sarcastic person whose tongue literally dripped acid? How does it feel to be popular? These and a host of other questions keep us wondering about our friends and acquaintances. Still more bewildering is the behavior of people whom we read about in the newspapers or view in the newsreels. Many of them govern countries, manage large corporations, or lead labor unions, and what they think and do profoundly affects our lives.

Even when you ask someone to explain his actions, you don't always get the real reason. To be perfectly honest, you can't always explain *your own behavior,* can you? It is because of these limitations, and because of our great need to understand better than we do, that good books mean so much to us. Good literature can help us to interpret human experience, to know more about the people whom we meet every day.

A man whose experiences have sharpened his insight into the mystery of life records his thoughts for other people. If he sees clearly and writes with honesty and beauty, we call his work literature. Of course, to profit from his insight, you must read carefully so you will not misunderstand. In the play that follows, do your share. Eight sailors are the only characters. Nevertheless, when you have finished reading about them, your understanding of all men and women should be increased. Remember that the stage directions are important; note the season and the year; imagine a face and personality for each man; and in your mind paint a clear picture of the ship's forecastle, noting especially that the portholes are covered with black cloth. Make certain, at the very beginning of the drama, that you understand what each man says and what he means. Every word and deed must count in a play as short as *In the Zone.*

The author of this play is acknowledged to be America's greatest dramatist. He is known throughout the world, and you may have seen the movie versions of three plays he has written, *Strange Interlude, Anna Christie,* and *Ah, Wilderness!* As a boy he toured America with his actor father, whose enormous success in *The Count of Monte Cristo* is a story your grandmother may know. Expelled from Princeton, young Eugene became a sailor, knocking about for two years in the ports of South America and Europe. Later he tried acting, reporting, and writing, and at last found his life's work. Three different times he has been awarded the Pulitzer Prize for the best play of the year.

CHARACTERS

SMITTY, THE "DUKE," twenty-five — slender — his face is refined, and handsome in a weak way

DAVIS, middle-aged — thin face with a black mustache

SWANSON, middle-aged — short, stocky Swede with a bushy blond mustache

SCOTTY, just past twenty — thin and wiry — sandy hair

IVAN, in the thirties — hulking and awkward, with a broad, stupid, swarthy face

JACK, twenty-eight — tall, well-built, dark, and rather good-looking in a tough sort of way

DRISCOLL, thirty — a powerfully built Irishman with a battered, good-natured face

COCKY, fifty — a wizened runt of a man with a straggling wisp of gray mustache

PAUL, a Norwegian

SCENE. *The seamen's forecastle of the British tramp steamer* Glencairn. *Sleeping bunks are built against the sides. On the right, above the bunks, three or four portholes covered with black cloth can be seen. In the left foreground, a doorway. On the floor near it, a pail with a tin dipper. Oilskins are hanging from hooks near the doorway.*

A lantern in the middle of the floor, turned down very low, throws a dim light around the place. Five men — SCOTTY, IVAN, SWANSON, SMITTY, *and the Norwegian,* PAUL — *are in their bunks, apparently asleep. There is no sound but the deep breathing of the sleepers and the rustling of the oilskins against each other as the ship rolls. It is about ten minutes of twelve in the night. The time is the spring of 1915.*

SMITTY *turns slowly in his bunk and, leaning out over the side, looks from one to another of the men as if he were assuring himself they are asleep. Then he climbs carefully out of his bunk and stands in the middle of the forecastle, fully dressed but in his stocking feet, glancing around him suspiciously. Reassured, he leans down and cautiously pulls out a suitcase from under the bunks in front of him.*

Just at that moment DAVIS *appears in the doorway, carrying a large steaming coffeepot in his hand. He stops short when he sees* SMITTY. *A puzzled expression comes over his face, followed by one of suspicion, and he retreats farther back in the alleyway, where he can watch* SMITTY *without being seen.*

All of the latter's movements indicate a fear of discovery. He takes out a small bunch of keys and unlocks the suitcase, making a slight noise as he does so. SCOTTY *wakes up and peers at him over the side of his bunk.* SMITTY *opens the suitcase and takes out a small black tin box.* SCOTTY'S *eyes nearly pop out of his head with fright when he sees this; but he shuts them tight as* SMITTY *turns around, and opens them again in time to see him place the black box carefully under his mattress.* SMITTY *then climbs back into his bunk, taking great care to make no noise, closes his eyes, and commences to snore loudly.*

DAVIS *enters the forecastle, places the coffeepot beside the lantern, and goes from one to the other of the sleepers — with the exception of* PAUL, *who is dayman — and shakes them vigorously, saying to each in a low voice, "Near eight bells,* SCOTTY. *Arise and shine,* OLLIE. *Eight bells,* IVAN." *He stops before* SMITTY'S *bunk and looks at him with a keen glance of mistrust which is both curious and timid. He reaches out his hand to grab* SMITTY'S *shoulder, hesitates, and finally ends up by saying gruffly, "Eight bells,* SMITTY." *Upon which he sits down on a bench as far away from* SMITTY *as the narrow forecastle will permit, glancing at him every moment out of the corner of his eye.*

SMITTY *yawns loudly with a great pretense of having been dead asleep. All the rest of the men tumble out of their bunks, stretching and gaping, and commence to pull on their shoes. Except for these, they are fully dressed.* SCOTTY *betrays great inward uneasiness, staring suspiciously at* SMITTY *whenever the latter's back is turned. The coffeepot is passed around and placed back again beside the lantern. They munch their biscuits and sip their coffee in a dull silence.*

Davis (*suddenly jumping to his feet — nervously*). Where's that air comin' from?

[*All are startled and look at him wonderingly.*]

Swanson (*grumpily*). What air? I don't feel nothing.

Davis (*excitedly*). I kin feel it — a draft. (*He stands on the bench and looks around — suddenly exploding*). Fool of a squarehead! (*He leans over the upper bunk in which* PAUL *is sleeping and slams the porthole shut.*) I got a good notion to report him. Serve him bloody [1] well right! What's the use o' blindin' the ports when that thickhead goes an' leaves 'em open?

Swanson (*yawning — too sleepy to be aroused by anything — carelessly*). Dey don't see what little light go out yust one port.

Scotty (*protestingly*). Dinna be a loon,[2] Swanson! D'ye no ken [3] the dangerr o' showin' a licht [4] wi' a pack o' submarines lyin' aboot?

Ivan (*shaking his shaggy oxlike head in an emphatic affirmative*). Dot's right, Scotty. I don' li-ike blow up, no, by devil!

Smitty (*his manner slightly contemptuous*). I don't think there's much danger of meeting any of their submarines, not until we get into the war zone, at any rate.

Davis (*he and* SCOTTY *look at* SMITTY *suspiciously — harshly*). You don't, eh? (*He lowers his voice and speaks slowly.*)

[1] **bloody:** this is considered a vulgar term of profanity in England. [2] **loon:** fool. [3] **ken:** know. [4] **licht:** light.

Well, we're in the war zone right this minit if you wants to know.

[*The effect of this speech is instantaneous. All sit bolt upright on their benches and stare at* DAVIS.]

Smitty. How do you know, Davis?

Davis (*angrily*). 'Cos Drisc heard the First[1] send the Third[2] below to wake the skipper when we fetched the zone — about five bells, it was. Now whata y' got to say?

Smitty (*conciliatingly*). Oh, I wasn't doubting your word, Davis; but you know they're not pasting up bulletins to let the crew know when the zone is reached — especially on ammunition ships like this.

Ivan (*decidedly*). I don't li-ike dees voyage. Next time I ship on a windjammer Boston to River Plate,[3] load with wood only so it float, by golly!

Swanson (*fretfully*). I hope British navy blow 'em up, those submarines!

Scotty (*looking at* SMITTY, *who is staring at the doorway in a dream, his chin on his hands. Meaningly*). It is no the submarrines only we've to fear, I'm thinkin'.

Davis (*assenting eagerly*). That's no lie, Scotty.

Swanson. You mean the mines?

Scotty. I wasna thinkin' o' mines eitherr.

Davis. There's many a good ship blown up and at the bottom of the sea, what never hit no mine or torpedo.

Scotty. Did ye neverr read of the German spies and the dirrty work they're doin' all the war?

[*He and* DAVIS *both glance at* SMITTY, *who is deep in thought and is not listening to the conversation*.]

Davis. An' the clever way they fool you!

[1] **First:** first mate. [2] **Third:** third mate. [3] **River Plate:** Rio de la Plata, in South America.

Swanson. Sure; I read it in paper many time.

Davis. Well . . . (*He is about to speak but hesitates and finishes lamely.*) You got to watch out, that's all I says.

Ivan (*drinking the last of his coffee and slamming his fist on the bench explosively*). I tell you dis rotten coffee give me bellyache, yes!

[*They all look at him in amused disgust.*]

Scotty (*sardonically*). Dinna fret about it, Ivan. If we blow up ye'll no be mindin' the pain in your middle.

[JACK *enters. He is a young American with a tough, good-natured face. He wears dungarees and a heavy jersey.*]

Jack. Eight bells, fellers.

Ivan (*stupidly*). I don' hear bell ring.

Jack. No, and yuh won't hear any ring, yuh boob (*lowering his voice unconsciously*), now we're in the war zone.

Swanson (*anxiously*). Is the boats all ready?

Jack. Sure; we can lower 'em in a second.

Davis. A lot o' good the boats'll do, with us loaded deep with all kinds o' dynamite and stuff the like o' that! If a torpedo hits this hooker[4] we'll all be dead b'fore you could wink your eye.

Jack. They ain't goin' to hit us, see? That's my dope. Whose wheel[5] is it?

Ivan (*sullenly*). My wheel. (*He lumbers out.*)

Jack. And whose lookout?

Swanson. Mine, I tink. (*He follows* IVAN.)

Jack (*scornfully*). A lot of use keepin' a lookout! We couldn't run away or fight if we wanted to. (*To* SCOTTY *and* SMITTY) Better look up the bo'sun or the Fourth, you two, and let 'em see you're awake.

[4] **hooker:** ship. [5] **Whose wheel:** Whose turn to steer.

[SCOTTY *goes to the doorway and turns to wait for* SMITTY, *who is still in the same position, head on hands, seemingly unconscious of everything.* JACK *slaps him roughly on the shoulder and he comes to with a start.*]

Aft and report, Duke! [1] What's the matter with yuh — in a dope dream?

[SMITTY *goes out after* SCOTTY *without answering.* JACK *looks after him with a frown.*]

He's a queer guy. I can't figger him out.

Davis. Nor no one else. (*Lowering his voice — meaningly*) An' he's liable to turn out queerer than any of us think if we ain't careful.

Jack (*suspiciously*). What d'yuh mean?

[*They are interrupted by the entrance of* DRISCOLL *and* COCKY.]

Cocky (*protestingly*). Blimey if I don't fink [2] I'll put in this 'ere watch ahtside on deck. (*He and* DRISCOLL *go over and get their cups.*) I down't want to be caught in this 'ole if they 'its us. (*He pours out coffee.*)

Driscoll (*pouring his*). Divil a bit ut wud matther where we arre. Ye'd be blown to smithereens b'fore ye cud say your name. (*He sits down, overturning, as he does so, the untouched cup of coffee which* SMITTY *had forgotten and left on the bench. They all jump nervously as the tin cup hits the floor with a bang.* DRISCOLL *flies into an unreasoning rage.*) Who's the dirty scut left this cup where a man 'ud sit on ut?

Davis. It's Smitty's.

Driscoll (*kicking the cup across the forecastle*). Does he think he's too much av a bloody gentleman to put his own away loike the rist av us? If he does, I'm the bye'll beat that noshun out av his head.

[1] **Duke:** The men call him Duke because they think he is putting on airs. [2] **fink:** think. Cocky is a cockney.

Cocky. Be the airs 'e puts on you'd think 'e was the Prince of Wales. Wot's 'e doin' on a ship, I arsks yer? 'E ain't now good as a sailor, is 'e? Dawdlin' abaht on deck like a chicken wiv 'is 'ead cut orf!

Jack (*good-naturedly*). Aw, the Duke's all right. S'posin' he did ferget his cup — what's the dif? (*He picks up the cup and puts it away — with a grin.*) This war zone stuff's got yer goat, Drisc — and yours too, Cocky — and I ain't cheerin' much fur it myself, neither.

Cocky (*with a sigh*). Blimey, it ain't no bleedin' joke, yer first trip, to know as there's a ship full of shells li'ble to go orf in under your bloomin' feet, as you might say, if we gets 'it be a torpedo or mine. (*With sudden savagery*) Calls theyselves 'uman bein's, too! Blarsted 'Uns!

Driscoll (*gloomily*). 'Tis me last trip in the bloody zone, God help me. The divil take their twenty-foive per cent bonus — and be drowned like a rat in a trap in the bargain, maybe.

Davis. Wouldn't be so bad if she wasn't carryin' ammunition. Them's the kind the subs is layin' for.

Driscoll (*irritably*). Fur the love av hivin, don't be talkin' about ut. I'm sick wid thinkin' and jumpin' at iviry bit av a noise.

[*There is a pause during which they all stare gloomily at the floor.*]

Jack. Hey, Davis, what was you sayin' about Smitty when they come in?

Davis (*with a great air of mystery*). I'll tell you in a minit. I want to wait an' see if he's comin' back. (*Impressively*) You won't be callin' him all right when you hears what I seen with my own eyes. (*He adds with an air of satisfaction*) An' you won't be feelin' no safer, neither.

[*They all look at him with puzzled glances full of a vague apprehension.*]

Driscoll. Blarst ut.

[*He fills his pipe and lights it. The others, with an air of remembering something they had forgotten, do the same.* SCOTTY *enters.*]

Scotty (*in awed tones*). Mon, but it's clear outside the nicht! Like day.

Davis (*in low tones*). Where's Smitty, Scotty?

Scotty. Out on the hatch starin' at the moon like a mon half daft.

Davis. Kin you see him from the doorway?

Scotty (*goes to doorway and carefully peeks out*). Aye; he's still there.

Davis. Keep your eyes on him for a moment. I've got something I wants to tell the boys and I don't want him walkin' in in the middle of it. Give a shout if he starts this way.

Scotty (*with suppressed excitement*). Aye, I'll watch him. And I've somethin' myself to tell aboot his Lordship.

Driscoll (*impatiently*). Out wid ut! You're talkin' more than a pair av auld women wud be standin' in the road, and gittin' no further along.

Davis. Listen! You 'member when I went to git the coffee, Jack?

Jack. Sure, I do.

Davis. Well, I brings it down here same as usual and got as far as the door there when I sees him.

Jack. Smitty?

Davis. Yes, Smitty! He was standin' in the middle of the fo'c'sle there (*pointing*) lookin' around sneakin'like at Ivan and Swanson and the rest 's if he wants to make certain they're asleep.

[*He pauses significantly, looking from one to the other of his listeners.* SCOTTY *is nervously dividing his attention between* SMITTY *on the hatch outside and* DAVIS'S *story, fairly bursting to break in with his own revelations.*]

Jack (*impatiently*). What of it?

Davis. Listen! He was standin' right there (*pointing again*) in his stockin' feet — no shoes on, mind, so he wouldn't make no noise!

Jack (*spitting disgustedly*). Aw!

Davis (*not heeding the interruption*). I seen right away somethin' on the queer was up so I slides back into the alleyway where I kin see him but he can't see me. After he makes sure they're all asleep, he goes in under the bunks there — bein' careful not to raise a noise, mind! — an' takes out his bag there. (*By this time everyone,* JACK *included, is listening breathlessly to his story.*) Then he fishes in his pocket an' takes out a bunch o' keys an' kneels down beside the bag an' opens it.

Scotty (*unable to keep silent longer*). Mon,[1] didn't I see him do that same thing wi' these two eyes. 'Twas just that moment I woke and spied him.

Davis (*surprised, and a bit nettled to have to share his story with anyone*). Oh, you seen him, too, eh? (*To the others*) Then Scotty kin tell you if I'm lyin' or not.

Driscoll. An' what did he do whin he'd the bag opened?

Davis. He bends down and reaches out his hand sort o' scared-like — like it was somethin' dang'rous he was after — an' feels round in under his duds [2] — hidden in under his duds an' wrapped up in 'em it was — an' he brings out a black iron box!

Cocky (*looking around him with a frightened glance*). Blimey!

[*The others likewise betray their uneasiness, shuffling their feet nervously.*]

Davis. Ain't that right, Scotty?

Scotty. Right as rain, I'm tellin' ye!

Davis (*to the others with an air of satisfaction*). There you are! (*Lowering his voice*) An' then what d'you suppose he

[1] **Mon:** man. [2] **duds:** clothes.

did? Sneaks to his bunk an' slips the black box in under his mattress — in under his mattress, mind!

Jack. And it's there now?

Davis. Course it is!

[JACK *starts toward* SMITTY'S *bunk*. DRISCOLL *grabs him by the arm.*]

Driscoll. Don't be touchin' ut, Jack!

Jack. Yuh needn't worry. I ain't goin' to touch it. (*He pulls up* SMITTY'S *mattress and looks down. The others stare at him, holding their breaths. He turns to them, trying hard to assume a careless tone.*) It's there, aw right.

Cocky (*miserably upset*). I'm gointer 'op it aht on deck. (*He gets up, but* DRISCOLL *pulls him down again.* COCKY *protests.*) It fair guvs me the trembles sittin' still in 'ere.

Driscoll (*scornfully*). Are ye frightened, ye toad? 'Tis a shameful thing fur grown men to be shiverin' loike childer at a bit av a black box. (*Scratching his head in uneasy perplexity*) Still, ut's queer, the looks av ut.

Davis (*sarcastically*). A bit of a black box, eh? How big d'you think them (*hesitating*) things has to be — big as this fo'c'sle?

Jack (*in a voice meant to be reassuring*). Aw, I'll bet it ain't nothin' but some coin he's saved he's got locked up in there.

Davis (*scornfully*). That's likely, ain't it? Then why does he act so s'picious? He's been on ship near two year, ain't he? He knows there ain't no thiefs in this fo'c'sle, don't he? An' you know 's well 's I do he didn't have no money when he came on board an' he ain't saved none since. Don't you? (JACK *doesn't answer.*) Listen! D'you know what he done after he put that thing in under his mattress? An' Scotty'll tell you if I ain't speakin' truth. He looks round to see if anyone's woke up —

Scotty. I clapped my eyes shut when he turned round.

Davis. An' then he crawls into his bunk an' shuts his eyes, an' starts in *snorin'*, *pretendin'* he was asleep; mind!

Scotty. Aye, I could hear him.

Davis. An' when I goes to call him I don't even shake him. I just says, "Eight bells, Smitty," in a'most a whisperlike, an' up he gets yawnin' an' stretchin' fit to kill hisself 's if he'd been dead asleep.

Cocky. Blimey!

Driscoll (*shaking his head*). Ut looks bad, divil a doubt av ut.

Davis (*excitedly*). An' now I come to think of it, there's the porthole. How'd it come to git open, tell me that? I know'd well Paul never opened it. Ain't he grumblin' about bein' cold all the time?

Scotty. The mon that opened it meant no good to this ship, whoever he was.

Jack (*sourly*). What porthole? What're yuh talkin' about?

Davis (*pointing over* PAUL'S *bunk*). There. It was open when I come in. I felt the cold air on my neck an' shut it. It woulda been clear's a lighthouse to any sub that was watchin' — an' we s'posed to have all the ports blinded! Who'd do a dirty trick like that? It wasn't none of us, nor Scotty here, nor Swanson, nor Ivan. Who would it be, then?

Cocky (*angrily*). Musta been 'is bloody Lordship.

Davis. For all 's we know he mighta been signalin' with it. They does it like that by winkin' a light. Ain't you read how they gets caught doin' it in London an' on the coast?

Cocky (*firmly convinced now*). An' wots 'e doin' aht alone on the 'atch[1] — keepin' 'isself clear of us like 'e was afraid?

Driscoll. Kape your eye on him, Scotty.

Scotty. There's no a move oot o' him.

[1] **'atch:** hatch; cover over opening into hold.

Jack (*in irritated perplexity*). But ain't he an Englishman? What'd he wanta —

Davis. English? How d'we know he's English? Cos he talks it? That ain't no proof. Ain't you read in the papers how all them German spies they been catchin' in England has been livin' there for ten, often as not twenty, years, an' talks English as good's anyone? An' look here, ain't you noticed he don't talk natural? He talks it too good, that's what I mean. He don't talk exactly like a toff, does he, Cocky?

Cocky. Not like any toff as I ever met up wiv.

Davis. No; an' he don't talk it like us, that's certain. An' he don't look English. An' what d'we know about him when you come to look at it? Nothin'! He ain't ever said where he comes from or why. All we knows is he ships on here in London 'bout a year b'fore the war starts, as an A.B.[1] — stole his papers most lik'ly — when he don't know how to box the compass, hardly. Ain't that queer in itself? An' was he ever open with us like a good shipmate? No; he's always had that sly air about him 's if he was hidin' somethin'.

Driscoll (*slapping his thigh — angrily*). Divil take me if I don't think ye have the truth av ut, Davis.

Cocky (*scornfully*). Lettin' on be 'is silly airs, and all, 'e's the son of a blarsted earl or somethink!

Davis. An' the name he calls hisself — Smith! I'd risk a quid [2] of my next pay day that his real name is Schmidt, if the truth was known.

Jack (*evidently fighting against his own conviction*). Aw, say, you guys give me a pain! What'd they want puttin' a spy on this old tub for?

Davis (*shaking his head sagely*). They're deep ones, an' there's a lot o' things a sailor'll see in the ports he puts in ought to be useful to 'em. An' if he kin signal to 'em an' they blows us up it's one ship less, ain't it? (*Lowering his voice and indicating* SMITTY's *bunk*) Or if he blows us up hisself.

Scotty (*in alarmed tones*). Hush, mon! Here he comes!

[SCOTTY *hurries over to a bench and sits down. A thick silence settles over the forecastle. The men look from one to another with uneasy glances.* SMITTY *enters and sits down beside his bunk. He is seemingly unaware of the dark glances of suspicion directed at him from all sides. He slides his hand back stealthily over his mattress and his fingers move, evidently feeling to make sure the box is still there. The others follow this movement carefully with quick looks out of the corners of their eyes. Their attitudes grow tense as if they were about to spring at him. Satisfied the box is safe,* SMITTY *draws his hand away slowly and utters a sigh of relief.*]

Smitty (*in a casual tone which to them sounds sinister*). It's a good light night for the subs if there's any about.

[*For a moment he sits staring in front of him. Finally he seems to sense the hostile atmosphere of the forecastle and looks from one to the other of the men in surprise. All of them avoid his eyes. He sighs with a puzzled expression and gets up and walks out of the doorway. There is silence for a moment after his departure, and then a storm of excited talk breaks loose.*]

Davis. Did you see him feelin' if it was there?

Cocky. 'E ain't arf a sly one wiv 'is talk of submarines, blind 'im!

Scotty. Did ye see the sneakin' looks he gave us?

Driscoll. If ivir I saw black shame on

[1] **A.B.**: able-bodied seaman. [2] **quid**: slang for pound.

a man's face 'twas on his whin he sat there!

Jack (*thoroughly convinced at last*). He looked bad to me. He's a crook, aw right.

Davis (*excitedly*). What'll we do? We gotter do somethin' quick or —

[*He is interrupted by the sound of something hitting against the port side of the forecastle with a dull, heavy thud. The men start to their feet in wild-eyed terror and turn as if they were going to rush for the deck. They stand that way for a strained moment, scarcely breathing and listening intently.*]

Jack (*with a sickly smile*). Aw! It's on'y a piece of driftwood or a floatin' log. (*He sits down again.*)

Davis (*sarcastically*). Or a mine that didn't go off — that time — or a piece o' wreckage from some ship they've sent to Davy Jones.[1]

Cocky (*mopping his brow with a trembling hand*). Blimey! (*He sinks back weakly on a bench.*)

Driscoll (*furiously*). Blarst ut! No man at all cud be puttin' up wid the loike av this — an' I'm not wan to be fearin' anything or any man in the worrld'll stand up to me face to face; but this divil's trickery in the darrk — (*He starts for* SMITTY'S *bunk.*) I'll throw ut out wan av the portholes an' be done wid ut. (*He reaches toward the mattress.*)

Scotty (*grabbing his arm — wildly*). Arre ye daft, mon?

Davis. Don't monkey with it, Drisc. I knows what to do. Bring the bucket o' water here, Jack, will you?

[JACK *gets it and brings it over to* DAVIS.]

An' you, Scotty, see if he's back on the hatch.

Scotty (*cautiously peering out*). Aye, he's sittin' there the noo.

[1] **Davy Jones:** a nautical expression meaning bottom of the sea.

Davis. Sing out if he makes a move. Lift up the mattress, Drisc — careful now!

[DRISCOLL *does so with infinite caution.*]

Take it out, Jack — careful — don't shake it now! Here — put it in the water — easy! There, that's fixed it!

[*They all sit down with great sighs of relief.*]

The water'll git in and spoil it.

Driscoll (*slapping* DAVIS *on the back*). Good wurrk for ye, Davis, ye scut! (*He spits on his hands aggressively.*) An' now what's to be done wid that blackhearted thraitor?

Cocky (*belligerently*). Guv 'im a shove in the marf and 'eave 'im over the side!

Davis. An' serve him right!

Jack. Aw, say, give him a chance. Yuh can't prove nothin' till yuh find out what's in there.

Driscoll (*heatedly*). Is ut more proof ye'd be needin' afther what we've seen an' heard? Then listen to me — and ut's Driscoll talkin' — if there's divilment in that box an' we see plain 'twas his plan to murrdher his own shipmates that have served him fair (*He raises his fist.*) I'll choke his rotten hearrt out wid me own hands, an' over the side wid him, and one man missin' in the mornin'.

Davis. An' no one the wiser. He's the balmy kind what commits suicide.

Cocky. They 'angs spies ashore.

Jack (*resentfully*). If he's done what yuh think I'll croak him myself. Is that good enough for yuh?

Driscoll (*looking down at the box*). How'll we be openin' this, I wonder?

Scotty (*from the doorway — warningly*). He's standin' up.

Davis. We'll take his keys away from him when he comes in. Quick, Drisc! You an' Jack get beside the door and grab him.

[*They get on either side of the door.* DAVIS *snatches a small coil of rope from one of the upper bunks.*]

This'll do for me an' Scotty to tie him.

Scotty. He's turrnin' this way — he's comin'! (*He moves away from door.*)

Davis. Stand by to lend a hand, Cocky.

Cocky. Righto.

[*As* SMITTY *enters the forecastle he is seized roughly from both sides and his arms pinned behind him. At first he struggles fiercely; but seeing the uselessness of this, he finally stands calmly and allows* DAVIS *and* SCOTTY *to tie up his arms.*]

Smitty (*when they have finished — with cold contempt*). If this is your idea of a joke I'll have to confess it's a bit too thick for me to enjoy.

Cocky (*angrily*). Shut yer marf, 'ear!

Driscoll (*roughly*). Ye'll find ut's no joke, me bucko, b'fore we're done wid you. (*To* SCOTTY) Kape your eye peeled, Scotty, and sing out if anyone's comin'.

[SCOTTY *resumes his post at the door.*]

Smitty (*with the same icy contempt*). If you'd be good enough to explain —

Driscoll (*furiously*). Explain, is ut? 'Tis you'll do the explainin' — an' quick, or we'll know the reason why. (*To* JACK *and* DAVIS) Bring him here, now.

[*They push* SMITTY *over to the bucket.*]

Look here, ye murrdherin' swab. D'you see ut?

[SMITTY *looks down with an expression of amazement, which rapidly changes to one of anguish.*]

Davis (*with a sneer*). Look at him! S'prised, ain't you? If you wants to try your dirty spyin' tricks on us, you've gotter git up earlier in the mornin'.

Cocky. Thought yer weren't 'arf a fox, didn't yer?

Smitty (*trying to restrain his growing rage*). What — what do you mean? That's only — How dare — What are you doing with my private belongings?

Cocky (*sarcastically*). Ho yus! Private b'longings!

Driscoll (*shouting*). What is ut, ye swine? Will you tell us to our faces? What's in ut?

Smitty (*biting his lips — holding himself in check with a great effort*). Nothing but — That's my business. You'll please attend to your own.

Driscoll. Oho, ut is, is ut? (*Shaking his fist in* SMITTY'S *face*) Talk aisy now if ye know what's best for you. Your business, indade! Then we'll be makin' ut ours, I'm thinkin'. (*To* JACK *and* DAVIS) Take his keys away from him an' we'll see if there's one'll open ut, maybe.

[*They start in searching* SMITTY, *who tries to resist and kicks out at the bucket.* DRISCOLL *leaps forward and helps them push him away.*]

Try to kick ut over, wud ye? Did ye see him then? Tryin' to murrdher us all, the scut! Take that pail out av his way, Cocky.

[SMITTY *struggles with all his strength and keeps them busy for a few seconds. As* COCKY *grabs the pail,* SMITTY *makes a final effort and, lunging forward, kicks again at the bucket but only succeeds in hitting* COCKY *on the shin.* COCKY *immediately sets down the pail with a bang and, clutching his knee in both hands, starts hopping around the forecastle, groaning and swearing.*]

Cocky. Ooow! Strike me pink! Kicked me, 'e did! Bloody, bleedin', rotten Dutch[1] 'og! (*Approaching* SMITTY, *who has given up the fight and is pushed back against the wall near the doorway with* JACK *and* DAVIS *holding him on either side*

[1] **Dutch:** German.

—*wrathfully, at the top of his lungs*) Kick me, will yer? I'll show yer what for, yer bleedin' sneak!

[*He draws back his fist.* DRISCOLL *pushes him to one side.*]

Driscoll. Shut your mouth! D'you want to wake the whole ship?

[COCKY *grumbles and retires to a bench, nursing his sore shin.*]

Jack (*taking a small bunch of keys from* SMITTY'S *pocket*). Here yuh are, Drisc.

Driscoll (*taking them*). We'll soon be knowin'.

[*He takes the pail and sits down, placing it on the floor between his feet.* SMITTY *again tries to break loose, but he is too tired and is easily held back against the wall.*]

Smitty (*breathing heavily and very pale*). Cowards!

Jack (*with a growl*). Nix on the rough talk, see! That don't git yuh nothin'.

Driscoll (*looking at the lock on the box in the water and then scrutinizing the keys in his hand*). This'll be ut, I'm thinkin'. (*He selects one and gingerly reaches his hand in the water.*)

Smitty (*his face grown livid—chokingly*). Don't you open that box, Driscoll. If you do, so help me, I'll kill you if I have to hang for it.

Driscoll (*pausing—his hand in the water*). Whin I open this box I'll not be the wan to be kilt, me sonny bye! I'm no dirty spy.

Smitty (*his voice trembling with rage. His eyes are fixed on* DRISCOLL'S *hand*). Spy? What are you talking about? I only put that box there so I could get it quick in case we were torpedoed. Are you all mad? Do you think I'm— (*Chokingly*) You stupid curs! You cowardly dolts!

[DAVIS *claps his hand over* SMITTY'S *mouth.*]

Davis. That'll be enough from you!

[DRISCOLL *takes the dripping box from the water and starts to fit in the key.* SMITTY *springs forward furiously, almost escaping from their grasp, and drags them after him halfway across the forecastle.*]

Driscoll. Hold him, ye divils!

[*He puts the box back in the water and jumps to their aid.* COCKY *hovers on the outskirts of the battle, mindful of the kick he received.*]

Smitty (*raging*). Cowards! Rotten curs! (*He is thrown to the floor and held there.*) Cowards! Cowards!

Driscoll. I'll shut your dirty mouth for you. (*He goes to his bunk and pulls out a big wad of waste and comes back to* SMITTY.)

Smitty. Cowards! Cowards!

Driscoll (*with no gentle hand slaps the waste over* SMITTY'S *mouth*). That'll teach you to be misnamin' a man, ye sneak. Have ye a handkerchief, Jack? (JACK *hands him one and he ties it tightly around* SMITTY'S *head over the waste.*) That'll fix your gab. Stand him up now, and tie his feet, too, so he'll not be movin'.

[*They do so and leave him with his back against the wall near* SCOTTY. *Then they all sit down beside* DRISCOLL, *who again lifts the box out of the water and sets it carefully on his knees. He picks out the key, then hesitates, looking from one to the other uncertainly.*]

We'd best be takin' this to the skipper, d'you think, maybe?

Jack (*irritably*). Drat the old man. This is our game and we c'n play it without no help.

Cocky. Now bleedin' horficers,[1] I says!

[1] **horficers:** officers.

Davis. They'd only be takin' all the credit and makin' heroes of theyselves.

Driscoll (*boldly*). Here goes, thin!

[*He slowly turns the key in the lock. The others instinctively turn away. He carefully pushes the cover back on its hinges and looks at what he sees inside with an expression of puzzled astonishment. The others crowd up close. Even* SCOTTY *leaves his post to take a look.*]

What is ut, Davis?

Davis (*mystified*). Looks funny, don't it? Somethin' square tide up in a rubber bag. Maybe it's dynamite — or somethin' — you can't never tell.

Jack. Aw, it ain't got no works. So it ain't no bomb, I'll bet.

Davis (*dubiously*). They makes them all kinds, they do.

Jack. Open it up, Drisc.

Davis. Careful now.

[DRISCOLL *takes a black rubber bag resembling a large tobacco pouch from the box and unties the string which is wound tightly around the top. He opens it and takes out a small packet of letters also tied up with string. He turns these over in his hands and looks at the others questioningly.*]

Jack (*with a broad grin*). On'y letters! (*Slapping* DAVIS *on the back*) Yuh're a fine Sherlock Holmes, ain't yuh? Letters from his best girl too, I'll bet. Let's turn the Duke loose, what d'yuh say? (*He starts to get up.*)

Davis (*fixing him with a withering look*). Don't be so smart, Jack. Letters, you says, 's if there never was no harm in 'em. How d'you s'pose spies gets their orders and sends back what they finds out if it ain't by letters and such things? There's many a letter is worser'n any bomb.

Cocky. Righto! They ain't as innercent as they looks, I'll take me oath, when you read 'em. (*Pointing at* SMITTY) Not 'is Lordship's letters; not be no means!

Jack (*sitting down again*). Well, read 'em and find out.

[DRISCOLL *commences untying the packet. There is a muffled groan of rage and protest from* SMITTY.]

Davis (*triumphantly*). There! Listen to him! Look at him tryin' to git loose! Ain't that proof enough? He knows well we're findin' him out. Listen to me! Love letters, you says, Jack, 's if they couldn't harm nothin'. Listen! I was readin' in some magazine in New York on'y two weeks back how some German spy in Paris was writin' love letters to some woman spy in Switzerland who sent 'em on to Berlin, Germany. To read 'em you wouldn't s'pect nothin' — just mush and all. (*Impressively*) But they had a way o' doin' it — a sneakin' way. They had a piece o' plain paper with pieces cut out of it an' when they puts it on top o' the letter they sees on'y the words what tells them what they wants to know. An' the Frenchies gets beat in a fight all on account o' that letter.

Cocky (*awed*). Blimey! They ain't 'arf smart bleeders!

Davis (*seeing his audience is again all with him*). An' even if these letters of his do sound all right, they may have what they calls a code. You can't never tell. (*To* DRISCOLL, *who has finished untying the packet*) Read one of 'em, Drisc. My eyes is weak.

Driscoll (*takes the first one out of its envelope and bends down to the lantern with it. He turns up the wick to give him a better light*). I'm no hand to be readin' but I'll try ut.

[*Again there is a muffled groan from* SMITTY *as he strains at his bonds.*]

Davis (*gloatingly*). Listen to him! He knows. Go ahead, Drisc!

Driscoll (*his brow furrowed with concentration*). Ut begins, " Dearest Man " — (*His eyes travel down the page.*) An' thin there's a lot av blarney tellin' him how much she misses him now she's gone away to singin' school — an' how she hopes he'll settle down to rale woork an' not be skylarkin' around now that she's away loike he used to before she met up wid him — and ut ends: " I love you betther than anythin' in the worrld. You know that, don't you, dear? But b'fore I can agree to live out my life wid you, you must prove to me that the black shadow — I won't menshun ut's hateful name but you know what I mean — which might wreck both our lives, does not exist for you. You can do that, can't you, dear? Don't you see you must for my sake? " (*He pauses for a moment — then adds gruffly*) Ut's signed, " Edith."

[*At the sound of the name* SMITTY, *who has stood tensely with his eyes shut as if he were undergoing torture during the reading, makes a muffled sound like a sob and half turns his face to the wall.*]

Jack (*sympathetically*). What's the use of readin' that stuff even if —

Davis (*interrupting him sharply*). Wait! Where's that letter from, Drisc?

Driscoll. There's no address on the top av ut.

Davis (*meaningly*). What'd I tell you? Look at the postmark, Drisc — on the envelope.

Driscoll. The name that's written is Sidney Davidson, wan hunderd an' —

Davis. Never mind that. O' course it's a false name. Look at the postmark.

Driscoll. There's a furrin stamp on ut by the looks av ut. The mark's blurred so it's hard to read. (*He spells it out laboriously.*) *B-e-r* — the nixt is an *l*, I think — *i* — an' an *n*.

Davis (*excitedly*). Berlin! What did I tell you? I knew them letters was from Germany.

Cocky (*shaking his fist in* SMITTY'S *direction*). Rotten 'ound!

[*The others look at* SMITTY *as if this last fact had utterly condemned him in their eyes.*]

Davis. Give me the letter, Drisc. Maybe I kin make somethin' out of it. (DRISCOLL *hands the letter to him.*) You go through the others, Drisc, and sing out if you sees anythin' queer.

[*He bends over the first letter as if he were determined to figure out its secret meaning.* JACK, COCKY, *and* SCOTTY *look over his shoulder with eager curiosity.* DRISCOLL *takes out some of the other letters, running his eyes quickly down the pages. He looks curiously over at* SMITTY *from time to time, and sighs frequently with a puzzled frown.*]

Davis (*disappointedly*). I gotter give it up. It's too deep for me, but we'll turn 'em over to the perlice when we docks at Liverpool to look through. This one I got was written a year before the war started, anyway. Find anythin' in yours, Drisc?

Driscoll. They're all the same as the first — lovin' blarney, an' how her singin' is doin', and the great things the Dutch teacher says about her voice, an' how glad she is that her Sidney bye is worrkin' harrd an' makin' a man av himself for her sake.

[SMITTY *turns his face completely to the wall.*]

Davis (*disgustedly*). If we on'y had the code!

Driscoll (*taking up the bottom letter*). Hullo! Here's wan addressed to this ship — S.S. *Glencairn*, ut says — whin we was in Cape Town sivin months ago — (*Looking at the postmark*) Ut's from London.

Davis (*eagerly*). Read it!

[*There is another choking groan from* SMITTY.]

Driscoll (*reads slowly — his voice becomes lower and lower as he goes on*). Ut begins wid simply the name Sidney Davidson — no dearest or sweetheart to this wan. "Ut is only from your chance meetin' wid Harry — whin you were drunk — that I happen to know where to reach you. So you have run away to sea loike the coward you are because you knew I had found out the truth — the truth you have covered over with your mean little lies all the time I was away in Berlin and blindly trusted you. Very well, you have chosen. You have shown that your drunkenness means more to you than any love or faith av mine. I am sorry — for I loved you, Sidney Davidson — but this is the end. I lave you — the mem'ries; an' if ut is any satisfaction to you I lave you the real-i-zation that you have wrecked my loife as you have wrecked your own. My one remainin' hope is that nivir in God's worrld will I ivir see your face again. Good-by. Edith."

[*As he finishes there is a deep silence, broken only by* SMITTY'S *muffled sobbing. The men cannot look at each other.* DRISCOLL *holds the rubber bag limply in his hand and some small white object falls out of it and drops noiselessly on the floor. Mechanically* DRISCOLL *leans over and picks it up, and looks at it wonderingly.*]

Davis (*in a dull voice*). What's that?

Driscoll (*slowly*). A bit av a dried-up flower — a rose, maybe.

[*He drops it into the bag and gathers up the letters and puts them back. He replaces the bag in the box, and locks it and puts it back under* SMITTY'S *mattress. The others follow him with their eyes. He steps softly over to* SMITTY *and cuts the ropes about his arms and ankles with his sheath knife, and unties the handkerchief over the gag.* SMITTY *does not turn around but covers his face with his hands and leans his head against the wall. His shoulders continue to heave spasmodically but he makes no further sound.*]

Driscoll (*stalks back to the others — there is a moment of silence, in which each man is in agony with the hopelessness of finding a word he can say — then* DRISCOLL *explodes*). Are we never goin' to turn in fur a wink av sleep?

[*They all start as if awakening from a bad dream and gratefully crawl into their bunks, shoes and all, turning their faces to the wall and pulling their blankets up over their shoulders.* SCOTTY *tiptoes past* SMITTY *out into the darkness. . . .* DRISCOLL *turns down the light and crawls into his bunk as the curtain falls.*]

THINK BACK OVER WHAT YOU HAVE READ

Using the Play to Broaden Your Understanding of All Human Behavior

1. How do you act when you are tense, nervous, or tired? Do you lose your temper more easily? If a man in a large, busy office wants to ask his boss for a raise, should he do so early in the morning or late in the afternoon? Why were the sailors in this story so short-tempered and so suspicious? Why is Driscoll so upset when he overturns Smitty's cup of coffee? On days when everything seems to go wrong, is your own frame of mind ever the root of the trouble? Would recognizing that help at all?

2. Do people ever derive any pleasure from making things worse than they are? Why do some people exaggerate an unpleasant happening when they tell about it? Did you notice that Davis enjoyed telling the others about Smitty? Why is he nettled when Scotty breaks

in to share the telling of Smitty's queer actions?

3. If you can account for the behavior of Davis and Scotty, perhaps you have located the factor which underlies all gossip. Does it account for the fact that gossip is more frequent in small towns than, say, among the members of the President's cabinet?

4. How does suspicion twist everything into evidence against Smitty? Have you seen any movies or known of any court trials in which circumstantial evidence was used to convict an innocent person? Have you ever been misunderstood or unjustly accused because of such unfair evidence? Is it fair to say that snap judgment and jumping to unwarranted conclusions are the marks of a half-educated man?

5. Explain why Smitty had gained the resentment of the *Glencairn* sailors, even before the play begins. What application does this have to our own relations with others?

6. Do you accept this play as a truthful comment on life? If so, what have you learned about sailors and men in general? What facts in the author's life and in the play lead you to believe this is an honest interpretation of human behavior? (If you disagree and protest that men do *not* act like this, your class should certainly have a valuable discussion. The experience of every student can be focused on the problem of how men would really act in a situation such as this.)

7. Why was Smitty hiding the letters? Should we feel sorry for Smitty or should we condemn him as a weakling?

8. Did the men have a right to open the box if Smitty wouldn't tell them what he had in it?

Appreciating Dramatic Structure

9. Why doesn't O'Neill let the audience know, at the outset, what the black box contains?

10. Why is it absolutely necessary for the dramatist to have the letters in a rubber bag with a string wound tightly around the top? In real life, would this seem as plausible as it does on the stage?

11. Can you discover any places in which O'Neill builds up your suspense by delaying the opening of the box?

12. Why do the men leave their shoes on at the end of the play? How does this one gesture testify to O'Neill's skill as a playwright who knows how to economize on time by weighting a single word or action with real significance?

Increase Your Power over Words

13. The word *sardonic* has come down to us from the superstitions of the past. Originally it was the Greek name for the island of Sardinia, which is just south of Corsica, Napoleon's birthplace, and now belongs to Italy. The Greeks had heard that a certain Sardinian weed could cause one to laugh without any real feeling of mirth and the laughter would be so violent that death would result. Because Sardinia was so far away, no one was able to disprove the story and soon everyone believed it. We no longer believe the tale, but the word still means forced, bitter, or heartless. *Sardonic laughter* or a *sardonic expression* means, therefore, a mocking or sneering laugh or statement, one without sincere mirth behind it. Why does Scotty speak *sardonically* on page 432?

14. Although you will not find a whole story written out for you, any fairly large dictionary will give you a clue concerning the origin of *sinister.* If you are a good Sherlock Holmes, you can trace *sinister,* like *sardonic,* back to the superstitions of the past. Why does Smitty's casual tone of voice (page 436) seem *sinister* to the sailors? What does he say?

For Ambitious Students

15. Although Eugene O'Neill wrote *In the Zone* during the World War, about seven years before radios came into wide use, the play has excellent possibilities for broadcasting purposes. As you read, did you notice that the excitement in the play was created almost entirely by what was said? The play's only swift action is a fight, yet the suspense mounts to a point which is remarkable in a one-act play. Over the radio or in a theater, *In the Zone* could not fail to grip the attention of an audience. Inasmuch as you have already read one play written expressly for radio, you should be able to see the possibilities that other plots offer for radio production. Reread *In the Zone,* assuming that you are planning programs for a large broadcasting system and someone has suggested this play to you as a possibility for next week's "Theater Hour." Notice whether or not the voices of the men could be easily differentiated by the radio listeners. What changes would need to be made and what sound effects would be needed? How could you present the action which occurs before anyone speaks in this play? Rewrite the play and present it to the class in its new form.

I WAS TALKING ACROSS THE FENCE THIS MORNING

by Charles S. Brooks (1878–1934)

Very likely you read *Gulliver's Travels* when you were young, or perhaps you saw the technicolor movie version of Jonathan Swift's famous story of the sailor who discovered the land of Lilliput. In this strange country, you will remember, midgets only five and six inches high had set up a government very much like that of England, and, like the English, they were constantly at war.

It is possible, however, that you did not know *Gulliver's Travels* had a double meaning, that it ridiculed some of the leading English statesmen of Swift's time and exposed the faults of mankind in general. You can imagine what a furor it created. Lords who had been insulted, and angry readers too, never forgave Swift for this satire. No one enjoys having his faults held up to ridicule, and that is exactly what satire does.

Like *Gulliver's Travels,* the play which you are about to read is a satire, for it ridicules something the author dislikes. However, this modern writer chooses only one weakness, which all of us share to some extent; and although he pokes sly fun at us, we cannot feel that he is unkind. Since you cannot truly appreciate this play unless you take it to heart just a bit yourself, watch for the common fault or weakness which is satirized. You won't have much difficulty. The title, the stage properties, even the names of the characters, will give you clues.

CHARACTERS

MR. BARREL	MR. QUART
MRS. BARREL	TOM PINT
MR. GALLON	NANCY PINT

The SCENE *is the platform of a country railway station. We see the "down" track parallel to and behind the footlights, with the station house across the back. This track is purely ornamental, as we cannot expect that even the most ambitious of producers will find a way of pushing a full-size train of Pullmans so near the footlights. We must suppose that the "up" track is behind the station house, where, now and then, it emits a clang and a rumble. We have no idea how these effects are accomplished, but we suggest a half dozen grass rollers borrowed from the neighbors and shoved along a concrete floor.*

In the center of the stage is the door to the ticket office, and on each side of it a bench. There is a blackboard with its announcements — as, for instance, "No. 7 is 5 min. late." A curious person may learn the number of miles to Chicago and New York. A luggage truck stands at the right of the platform. We suggest a semaphore with an arm that drops as a train comes near.

It is a summer afternoon.

As the curtain rises, a man enters from the left along the platform, deposits a shabby bag on the bench, and goes to buy his ticket. We see him at the wicket, through the open door. His bag carries a sticker, "Niagara Falls."

He comes again to the platform, sits down beside his bag at one end of the bench, and reads a cheap magazine. He is MR. QUART, *about thirty years old, a man who might be a bookkeeper in a department store. We have in mind a friend who resembles* MR. QUART *and who has these last ten years been shooting at flies at noonday with a rubber band from his pen tray.*

And now another man, MR. GALLON, *enters. He is about forty years of age. His bag is better than* MR. QUART'S, *and its sticker is marked "Yellowstone Park."* MR. GALLON *is a merchant, the head of a small hardware store, a prominent member of the Boosters' Club. If* MR. QUART *gets a salary of less than four thousand dollars a year,* MR. GALLON'S *salary and dividends amount to rather more than ten thousand dollars.* MR. GALLON *sits at the extreme end of* MR. QUART'S *bench. He draws out the* Saturday Evening Post *and reads it.*

Presently TOM PINT, *the station's baggageman, enters from the ticket office. He is a jolly little fellow, now in a flannel shirt, who scratches along without too much grumbling on a wage of a hundred dollars a month.* PINT *goes to the blackboard and chalks up the news that Number Seven is now ten minutes late. He retires, whistling, to the ticket office.*

MR. GALLON *rises, looks at the board, at his watch, at the track, as if it were the culprit for the delay, and sits down again.*

Gallon. She's late.

Quart. So she is. Ten minutes.

Gallon. She's always late.

Quart. Do you go up this way very often, Mr. Gallon?

Gallon. Not by train. Usually by motor. Your name is —

Quart. Quart. Q-u-a-r-t. I met you, Mr. Gallon, at the Boosters'. Heard your speech, "The Wheels of Business and How to Oil Them."

Gallon. Did you, now? Glad to meet a Booster. I thought you looked familiar. It's buying keeps 'em greased.

Quart. There's no fear they'll go dry as long as women spend their time shopping. My wife —

Gallon. Just so. If they stayed at home for just a week, everyone's business would go flop.

Quart. Do you tell your wife that?

Gallon. It doesn't pay to be entirely literal. She needs no encouragement.

Quart. What are you driving, Mr. Gallon?

Gallon. Packard.

Quart. She's a nice little buggy. I wish I could afford one.

Gallon. What's yours?

Quart. A Shevvy.

Gallon. That's what I used to own.

Quart. Got it secondhand. If you don't mind a bent mudguard, she's as good as you need.

Gallon. And you've got to have a car — these days you do — to save the dogs.

Quart. I can't say, however, that Mrs. Quart likes her. The Liters [1] bought a this year's model.

Gallon. Who are they?

Quart. They live next door. My wife talks across the fence with her. Old man Liter drove home his new Shevvy last Saturday. It made my old bus look pretty shabby. The wife's nose has been out of joint all week.

Gallon. You can get a new car yourself, on the installment plan.

Quart. Don't I know? That's the way I got the Victorina, the radio, and the kitchen stove. I'll be paying on the baby cart — that's what I tell the wife — the best little woman in the world — I'll be paying on the baby cart, I tell her, long after the twins are married. This greasing the wheels of business is all right for a rich fellow like you who don't know what it is to get along on a salary like mine.

[TOM PINT *enters from the ticket office and chalks up the added information that Number Seven is now fifteen minutes late.*]

A fellow like you, Mr. Gallon, don't realize what it is to go on month after month, hoping you'll get a raise and wondering what you'll do if the boss don't come across. Ever snap flies with a rubber band?

Gallon. No.

Quart. That's what I do at the lunch hour — fidgeting and worrying.

Pint. Are you speaking of wages?

Quart. Yes.

Pint. If it ain't impertinence, what does a feller in your line get?

Quart. I don't get four thousand, not

[1] A *liter* is a French measurement just slightly larger than the American *quart*. Do you suppose the author is choosing the name **Liter** purposely?

by several hundred berries. That's what I ought to get.

Pint. Golly! You should worry. If I had that much, I'd say I was rich.

Quart. You don't own a car. That's the difference.

Pint. I don't need one. See that little white house down the track? That's where I live. It's just easy walking.

Quart. And I suppose you don't own a Victorina.

Pint. I don't want one of 'em.

Quart. There you are. You don't grease the wheels of business a little bit. I've got to own one.

Pint. What for?

Quart. Because it's done. That's the reason.

Pint. What do you mean — it's done?

Quart. Anybody that's what on our street has 'em. Radios, for instance. The Liters own a super-hyper-quadruplidyne. Mine's just a superdyne; so the old lady don't like it. And I don't like it much myself. The Liters can get Memphis and New Orleans. I've got to listen to Syracuse and Buffalo. What's yours, Mr. Gallon?

Gallon. It's a super-hyper-octodyne. Mahogany case, all carved Louis Quince [1] — some kind of fruit. I can get Frisco — when I ought to be in bed.

Quart. There you are, Pint. Mr. Gallon can get Frisco. I'm glad Mrs. Quart don't hear you say that.

Gallon. It's a bit staticky, of course. You can't tell tunes. But it's worth sitting up just to know you're the only fellow on the station.

Quart. We're saving up now to make a first payment on just a double superquad.

Pint. We've got an old piano. And it's paid for. My wife, Nancy, plays it, and she sings. When you're getting a hundred a month and you've three kids shoving their toes right through their shoes, it's all you want. The last train goes through at eight o'clock — the last train that stops — the others go snooting by at sixty miles an hour. I go home and put my feet on the radiator. And it's pretty swell, sitting there, listening to my wife. Some literary feller is always leaving a magazine around the station — *Beauty Hints,* mostwise — so I read 'em nights. It makes it worth while to have winter coming on, it's so jolly snug in slippers.

Quart. I've only two kids, but that's enough.

Pint. Beg your pardon, Mr. Gallon, but how many have you?

Gallon. One.

Pint. It's much better than none at all. I wouldn't exchange any of mine — not for a whole carload of your double-hyper-what-you-call-'ems, not if they reached Brazil. Going up on Number Eleven, Mr. Quart?

Quart. Yes.

Pint. She's on time. I'll come for your bag in a couple of minutes. Nancy — she's my wife — and she loves to sing. Wouldn't want a Victorina in the house. (*Exit* PINT.)

Quart. He seems like a contented party. Of course, he ain't had advantages like you and me, and ain't cultured.

Gallon. There's probably a vacant lot both sides of him, and his wife don't get ideas across the fence. Twelve hundred a year and three children!

Quart. I don't see how he does it. I was getting double that four years ago. And I said then that if I ever got three thousand I'd have everything I wanted. But now I need four thousand. With that I'd be able to lay up a bit for a rainy day.

Gallon. It would be the same if you had ten thousand.

[1] Louis the Fifteenth would be Louis *Quinze* in French. Gallon's mispronunciation sounds like **quince,** the name we use for a small yellow fruit which makes excellent preserves.

Quart. Oh, come now, Mr. Gallon. That's rolling in wealth.

Gallon. It's what I make. And do you think it is enough?

Quart. I'd like to have it for just one year.

Gallon. What I need is twenty-five. If I had that amount salted down sure, I'd sell the shop. Quick jiffy, I would. But you've got to have twenty-five on our street. The women have nothing to do but shop.

Quart. Greasing the wheels of business.

Gallon. Getting the wheels all smudged, I tell the wife. You'd think they owned Windsor Castle on our street. I'm hardly used to a carpet before it's ripped up and another down. Do you happen to know the Brown-Johnses?

Quart. Slightly. A rich fellow.

Gallon. They live next door. My wife runs in for tea.

Quart. And gets ideas.

Gallon. The Brown-Johnses have joined the country club. So we've got to, or we can't entertain.

Quart. What's the matter with a restaurant?

Gallon. Not classy enough.

Quart. So the missis says.

Gallon. I'm not blaming Mrs. Gallon — as fine a little woman as ever breathed. I don't want, myself, to take a back seat behind the Brown-Johnses. I won't have my wife driving around in a car that hasn't four-wheel brakes. You can't be really happy, not on our street, unless you've got an automatic clutch.

Quart. That's what my next is going to be.

Gallon. On that bag of yours, Quart, there's a sticker of Niagara Falls — just two hours up the line.

Quart. That's where we go for the Fourth.

Gallon. That's where the Gallon family used to spend their vacations. The kid used to have a fine time throwing sticks in the river to see 'em swirl. It used to be fun taking a streetcar down to the rapids.

Quart. We went down the rapids last year, but I didn't see you.

Gallon. We don't go there any more. You see, two years ago the Brown-Johnses broke off from the Falls and went to Yellowstone Park. Look at that sticker on the bag, Quart. We're going to the Yellowstone now, ourselves.

Quart. The missis and I are getting tired of the Falls. This summer we're thinking of taking the buggy into Canada.

Gallon. I suppose the Liters are there now.

Quart. How did you guess it? We got a card yesterday saying, "Having a fine time. Wish you were here."

[PINT *enters.*]

Pint. Number Eleven is in sight. There's no hurry, Mr. Quart.

Gallon. Where do you go, Pint, for your vacation?

Pint. Which ain't often, of course. It's this way, I don't get up for the six-two. Sweetest thing in the world — just to lie in bed and let her whistle. Then 'long about seven I go off my back stoop due south for exactly fifty feet. That's where the vegetables are — the slickest golden-bantam corn you ever tasted. It's just fifteen minutes from pickin' to eatin'.

Gallon. I can't afford a garden. I kept books on my tomatoes and found they cost me a dollar each.

Pint. Not when you mind 'em yourself. There she is. Number Eleven is comin' in. Let me take your bag, Mr. Quart.

Quart. So long, Mr. Gallon. I suppose you're taking Number Seven the other way.

Gallon. Right!

[QUART *and* PINT *leave.* GALLON *retires behind his* Saturday Evening Post.

There is a grinding of wheels offstage, if our producer can manage it. Number Eleven has stopped. Another grinding, and Number Eleven is on her way. Presently PINT *enters, carrying* MR. BARREL's *bag. It is expensively made of leather, and on it is a sticker marked "Hotel Splendiferous, Biarritz."* MR. BARREL *follows — the pink of fashion: spats, a flower in his lapel; what you will, to denote a box of coupons.*[1]]

Barrel. Is my man here, Pint?

Pint. Sorry, Mr. Barrel, but I ain't seen him yet. It's your chauffeur, Tony, you mean, I suppose.

Barrel. It's awkward to have him late.

Pint. Very annoying, sir. I'll just put your bag here, Mr. Barrel, until he comes. (*He puts the bag on the bench and is tipped.*) Thank you, sir. (*It is a bill.*) Thank you, sir! Hope you're well, sir.

Barrel. Quite.

Gallon. Good morning, Mr. Barrel.

Barrel. Oh, Gallon, is that you?

Gallon. I'm waiting for Number Seven.

Barrel. Are you? Mrs. Barrel is coming in on Number Seven from Chicago.

Gallon. And I suppose you'll be motoring out to Stony Meadows.

Barrel. If Tony doesn't forget to bring the Rolls.

Gallon. You can't beat a Rolls.

Barrel. Nice little car.

Gallon. That's a grand place you have, Mr. Barrel.

Barrel. It's a big care and a big expense. I've a dozen men on the grounds alone. And they're all lazy. I don't dare look at the pay roll.

Gallon. Just paying for one of your stables would wreck me.

Barrel. Hard times, Gallon. I fret a bit, myself. It isn't as if I were one of these rich men. Mrs. Barrel — a lovely woman, Gallon — she likes Stony Meadows. I keep it for her. I'm really too busy to enjoy it — must be in the city five days a week. I suppose I would like it if I had time.

Pint. It's like my vegetables, Mr. Barrel. The more I dig, the better I like my golden bantam. I wish they would run these trains different — bunch 'em, so I could get home. I don't get off until Number Seventeen has gone through. And it's dark, then, even in June, when there's a lot of weedin' to do.

Barrel. Well, I don't do any weeding, Pint. I wish I might. I need the exercise. I don't even get time to see my horses — fifteen of them, eating their heads off.

Pint. But I suppose the missis and the kids enjoy 'em.

Barrel. I have no children.

Pint. Think of that!

Gallon. I was noticing your new stable, Mr. Barrel, as I was driving by in my Packard.

Barrel. I had to build it. The old stable was out of date. Old Tun[2] — Do you know him, Gallon?

Gallon. He's the one that owns the big house next to yours.

Barrel. Yes. Mrs. Tun and my wife are very thick. Well, old Tun was drawing plans for a stable. I couldn't have him getting ahead of me. Not that I cared, but Mrs. Barrel — you know what women are.

Pint. There comes Number Seven. Let me take your bag, Mr. Gallon.

Gallon. Glad to see you, Mr. Barrel.

Barrel. You, too, Gallon. You might take a look, Pint, for Mrs. Barrel, and help her with her bag. She's on Number Seven.

[1] **box of coupons:** wealthy people invest their money in bonds and spend only the interest or coupons which their money makes for them. The coupons are little sections of paper attached to the bonds. At certain intervals they may be clipped off and exchanged for money.

[2] **Tun:** Don't confuse this word with *ton.* Is a *tun* larger or smaller than a *barrel?* Guess from the play.

Pint. Yes, sir.

[PINT *picks up* GALLON's *bag. He and* GALLON *enter the station house, leaving* MR. BARREL. MR. BARREL *sits and pulls from his pocket a copy of the* Wall Street Journal. . . . *And now* PINT *re-enters, carrying* MRS. BARREL's *leather dressing case. It is without stickers. We must suppose that she moves among city and country houses, without demeaning herself to public accommodation.* MRS. BARREL *follows. Mink!*]

Barrel (rising languidly). Glad to see you, Millie. Tony hasn't come.

Mrs. Barrel. How annoying!

Pint. I'll be on the lookout, Mr. Barrel.

[PINT *leaves the platform.* BARREL *resumes his* Wall Street Journal. MRS. BARREL *turns the pages of* Country Life. *There is a pause. Presently* MRS. BARREL *looks up from her pages.*]

Mrs. Barrel. You remember the Bruhouses, whom we met last year in Biarritz?

Barrel. Yes. Big man — Bruhouse.

Mrs. Barrel. And how kind they were to us — our week end on their yacht.

Barrel. What was their boat called — the *Spendthrift?*

Mrs. Barrel. The Spindrift.[1] Well, here's an article about them. It seems just like meeting old friends.

Barrel. What's the article say?

Mrs. Barrel. It's three whole pages, with the prettiest kind of pictures. Fancy that — in *Country Life.* Right next to a house party for the Prince of Wales. I saved the magazine. I thought you might like to read the article.

Barrel. Big man — Bruhouse. What's it about?

[1] **Spindrift:** foam or spray blown from a stormy sea. A good name for a boat?

Mrs. Barrel. It says that they have bought Ruby Castle in Devonshire. And here are the pictures. The hall, drawing room, the sun parlor, the armory, the great dining room paneled in thirteenth-century oak.

Barrel. Bruhouse is the president of the International Gadget Company. I suppose he has an income of a cool million a year.

Mrs. Barrel. And wasn't it nice that kind of person was nice to us?

Barrel. Well, what about it?

Mrs. Barrel. That's what I'm coming to. In this same magazine that tells about Ruby Castle there are a lot of advertisements. And there is one about another castle — Norman Towers, it's called. It's for sale. Listen, Herbert! View of the Channel! A wooded park of a thousand acres! A tennis court! Eighteen master bedrooms! Two baths!

Barrel. We've got nine at Stony Meadows.

Mrs. Barrel. Don't be absurd, darling.

Barrel. Well, what of it?

Mrs. Barrel. It says that Norman Towers is the "grandest building of the twelfth century that is still under roof."

Barrel. What is that to me?

Mrs. Barrel. I thought you might be interested. You know how much you liked the Bruhouses.

Barrel. Why interested? You could buy Windsor Castle if you wanted to pay the price.

Mrs. Barrel. That's the point. Norman Towers is offered at a sacrifice. And it's only five miles from Ruby Castle.

Barrel. How much?

Mrs. Barrel. Only three hundred thousand — funny little things that look like *L*'s.[2] I don't know how much that is in our money.

[2] **L's:** £ is the English sign for a pound sterling, worth about five dollars in United States money when this play was written.

Barrel. I hope you are not suggesting that I buy it.

Mrs. Barrel. I don't know why not. You never liked Stony Meadows; and it's getting to bore me, frankly. You know how we like the Bruhouses, and it's only five miles from them. *Country Life* would be sure to write us up.

[PINT *enters and interrupts.*]

Pint. Your car is here, Mr. Barrel.

[*He takes the two bags and goes off with them along the platform.* MR. *and* MRS. BARREL *follow, talking as they go.*]

Barrel. Can't afford it in these hard times.

Mrs. Barrel. We could economize in other ways. I'd buy my dresses in Paris, where they're cheap. You know, Herbert, how I've always wanted to live in England — two months every summer. Eighteen master bedrooms! A thousand acres! "The grandest building of the twelfth century that is still under roof." Only five miles from Ruby Castle.

[*They have passed from sight.* PINT *re-enters. He erases the chalk marks on his board. Presently he looks down the tracks and waves his hand. He straightens his tie and rolls down his sleeves. . . . And now his wife enters* — NANCY PINT. *She is a pretty young woman in gingham, from the kitchen. She carries a lunchbox.*]

Pint. Well, I'm glad to see you, Nancy. How are the kids?

Nancy. They're all right.

Pint. Did Tommy get off to school?

Nancy. Yes. Are you hungry?

Pint. Like a couple of roarin' lions.

[NANCY *unties the lunchbox.* PINT *looks into it.*]

Ham sandwiches and milk — and apples. What's that thing in the napkin?

Nancy. Fresh cake. Right out of the oven.

Pint. Yum!

[*They divide the lunch and sit on the bench to eat. Both have finished their sandwich and are ready for the cake before a word is spoken.*]

Nancy. Tom!

Pint. What is it, Nancy?

Nancy. You know that old piano of ours?

Pint. Do I? It's fine to hear you play and sing, after Number Seventeen has gone through. I was telling some passengers of mine about your singing. Me with my feet in slippers on the radiator.

Nancy. I was talking across the fence this morning to that lady who lives next door.

Pint. The one that runs the wireless talkin' machine.

Nancy. Yes. It's a single-dyne.

Pint. One of them things.

Nancy. And I was thinking, Tom, as the old piano was wearing out, we might —

Pint. Might what?

Nancy. Might buy one of those single-dynes on installment.

[PINT *puts down his hunk of cake. He puts down his apple. He regards his wife intently. A look comes on him as on Caesar's face when Brutus stabbed. There is a pause.*]

Pint. Well, I'll be . . .

[THE CURTAIN FALLS SO RAPIDLY THAT WE DO NOT QUITE CATCH THE LAST WORD.]

THINK BACK OVER WHAT YOU HAVE READ

Recognizing the Humor and Satire of the Play

1. Does the author seem to be poking sly fun at the characters in this play? Can you find any lines which seem to be invitations for you

to smile with the author over some human weakness or self-centered giveaway?

2. What thought occurs to you as each man blames his wife for "greasing the wheels of business" too much? Are the wives entirely to blame? Judging from the very last scene, what does the author think? Even so, can you be sure when this author is serious or when he has his tongue in his cheek?

3. What does the play seem to teach about the relation between money and happiness? Do you agree, or is this play reflecting the wishful thinking of most people who don't have money?

4. Locate Quart's reason for owning a car. Is it a good reason? What reasons do you give your parents when you want to drive the car, buy a new dress, or borrow money for another movie?

5. Besides a frank mention of salaries, what other ways are used to indicate the characters' financial station in life.

6. From evidence within the play and from your own observations of the world, venture a guess on the following: Does Mr. Barrel buy Norman Towers with its eighteen master bedrooms? Does Nancy Pint get a single-dyne radio?

7. How seriously do you think this author meant us to take this play? Just what do you think his purpose was in writing it? To judge with any fairness you must take the whole play into account — its length, the dialogue, the attitude the author seems to take, and most certainly the ending.

8. Did you catch the author's pun on *Spindrift* when Barrel and his wife are talking?

9. Why do you like to see your own name in the paper — or, better yet, your picture? Or don't you? Bring to class a page from the society section of a newspaper, and see whether or not you can learn anything about your fellow man (or fellow woman!) from studying it. What is Mrs. Barrel's *real* reason for wanting Norman Towers?

10. You have often heard that love and hate, laughter and tears, joy and sorrow are closely related. Could this little play be turned into a tragedy by a dramatist with a different attitude toward his material? Indicate what would need to be done — what changes and additions, what shifts in emphasis.

Composition Suggestion

11. Certainly no one wishes to be queer, but we can bend too far in the direction of being "like everyone else." Keeping up with the Joneses can be carried to a ridiculous extreme. With what concrete instances from school life can you illustrate this theme? Try telling or writing an anecdote that has this point to it.

For Ambitious Students

12. Read the first two or three chapters of *Walden* by Henry Thoreau, the noted American author who believed that the more things a man owned the poorer he became. Look up, also, the life of Gandhi, the Hindu lawyer and leader whose ideas about living resulted from his study of Thoreau.

13. Relate the ideas which lie back of *I Was Talking across the Fence This Morning* to the ideas of Thoreau. Possibly you will wish to read all of *Walden;* for if you once start it, you will find yourself reluctant to put it down.

14. Read *The Bluebird* by Maurice Maeterlinck. What identical theme does *I Was Talking across the Fence This Morning* have in common with this book?

A Full-Length Play

IN 1938 *Julius Caesar* was a hit of the season. Not only the usual theater crowd but bulging carloads and busloads of high-school students converged on New York City's Mercury Theater. Here Orson Welles was acting Brutus every night to capacity crowds of every age and fortune. The story had spread. *Julius Caesar* was tremendous! As a special reward at the end of a successful football season, one coach brought his entire football team to see the play. High-school students began to urge their teachers to arrange theater parties in order to take advantage of the special rates for English classes.

This production of Shakespeare's great play flaunted no lavish scenery or costumes. Three steps, a barren brick wall at the back, clever use of lights, and modern clothing — nothing more, not even a curtain to pull between acts; and still the crowds came, filling every seat in the theater.

"Julius Caesar" has modern implications. The cause of this unusual interest lay in *Julius Caesar's* timeliness. Mark Antony may have orated to the Roman mob two thousand years ago; Shakespeare may have written the play three hundred years ago; but the problem of liberty and freedom is still important to people. An audience who had seen the European dictators in newsreels recognized Caesar's jutting chin, his striding gait, his cross-belted uniform. Caesar's exalted opinion of himself, Mark Antony's rabble-rousing speech, "Friends, Romans, countrymen," and the cheering mob with outstretched hands — all were familiar.

Every age adapts Shakespeare to its own taste, and ours is an age of radio orators, dictators, and shouting crowds. The audience who watched this version of *Julius Caesar* in modern dress learned that propaganda was not a new method of controlling people's minds. They wondered how our country might keep the freedom our immigrant ancestors won for us on this continent and how we might gain more of it for all our people. They pondered, too, how in these times of depression and change we will be able to allow organizations like the Nazi Bund the freedom to meet without losing to their ranks all our unemployed youth. Dictators find their strength in masses of dissatisfied, unhappy young people who are prevented from contributing their energy or ability to the world in which they live. Perhaps the tense audiences at the Mercury Theater remembered the high-school seniors in a Western state who chose as their class motto "Unemployment, here *we* come."

Some people who saw the play protested that this was no longer Shakespeare's *Julius Caesar.* In their opinion this parallel of Rome's dying republic and Europe's disappearing democracy placed too much emphasis on a single strand of a richly woven drama. Yet if Will Shakespeare could have seen this modern performance of his play surely he would have approved. Many were the times he had changed an older play or story to fit the interests of *his* day. This New York audience, leaning forward and gripping their neighbors' coat sleeves, would have pleased him.

A popular play three hundred years ago. Anyway, *Julius Caesar* was a hit. But this was not the first time crowds had shoved at the ticket window of this eternal drama. On the twenty-first of September, 1599 — twenty-one years before the Pilgrims landed in New England — a German traveler, returning from a visit to London, wrote in his *Record of Travel:*

> I with my companions after dinner somewhere about two o'clock were rowed across the river to see in the straw-thatched house there the tragedy of the first emperor, *Julius Caesar,* acted extremely well with scarcely more than fifteen persons.

You may imagine that there were many other boats besides that of the German traveler crossing the "silver-sliding" Thames, making it seem like a Venetian Grand Canal. Probably most of the gay crowd was bound, as he was, for the Bankside, a suburb of London across the river, devoted to Maypole dances, archery contests, bullbaiting, and stage plays. If he set out very early after dinner, perhaps he had time, before the trumpet blasts which announced that the play was to start, to inspect the Bear

Garden, where immense bears, tied to stakes, fought fiercely with great mastiffs set to worry and torment them. At the theater it is hardly possible that he joined the "penny knaves" in the "pit" — as the unroofed yard surrounded by three tiers of galleries was called — who passed the time before the play began by eating and drinking, smoking, and playing cards. It is more likely that he paid a shilling to occupy one of the sections of the first or second gallery, from which he could look down upon the stage projecting into the yard as a person in a box in our modern theater looks down upon the audience. For half a crown he would have been allowed to sit on the stage itself, along with the gallants who shouted ribald jokes to the actors during the play. If he were a guest of a nobleman, he would have sat in one of the "lords' boxes."

The play which the German traveler saw that September day was the same *Julius Caesar* which the Mercury Theater audiences saw in 1938. As today, historical plays were popular in London. William Shakespeare was at the height of his success as an interpreter of picturesque moments in history. Most of the persons who paid their pennies to see Shakespeare's plays could not read. There were no newspapers, magazines, or radios. Books were few. A writer of plays, therefore, had a clear field. Already Shakespeare had scored successes with his plays about Richard II and III, and about Henry IV and V. Now he had turned from English history to the days of ancient Rome. *Julius Caesar* had taken London by storm as it did New York in 1938. The jostling crowds in the "pit" liked the spirited lines of Cassius and Brutus, and the moving oratory of Mark Antony. Above all, they too, like our modern audiences, enjoyed the excitement of the play — its interwoven plots, assassinations, and battles.

Will Shakespeare, genius and human being. Of the fifteen actors mentioned by the German traveler, Shakespeare himself was probably one. Very likely he took a fairly important, though not a leading, part, for as a playwright whose business it was to keep the Lord Chamberlain's company in plays his hands were more than full. Although there is no exact proof, Dick Burbage probably took the part of Brutus or Mark Antony. Burbage was the first great Shakespearean actor. Already this young genius had packed the yard and galleries with applauding audiences that had come to see him in the part of Richard III. And later he was to be the first great Hamlet, a part in which many of the great actors of modern times have earned their title of "star."

Some years before the day on which the German traveler told in his record of seeing *Julius Caesar* played, Shakespeare had come to London from his home town to throw in his lot as actor and playwright with the new profession of the theater, which was then gaining prominence much the same as the motion-picture industry has expanded in this country within a few years. Now he was one of the leading theatrical men of his times.

The "straw-thatched house" of which the German traveler wrote was the new Globe Theater. It was built out of the timbers of the old "theater" on the other side of London, the first permanent playhouse to take the place of the innyard where formerly strolling players set up a makeshift stage and entertained the people who gathered there. Now it was one of several theaters on the Bankside to draw the crowds on Sundays and holidays across London Bridge, that most fascinating of promenades lined with **shops.** Even lords and ladies came to the theaters; for although at first the magistrates of the town frowned upon all theatrical performances as a cause of riot and the spread of the plague, and forced them outside the city gates, Her Majesty Queen Elizabeth set her seal of approval upon plays and secretly encouraged the growth of the theater.

Perhaps at the very moment that the German traveler " went in wonder " from the Globe after the performance, the auburn-haired, lithe young Shakespeare — now a man of thirty-five — was on his way to Stratford. Often, we may believe, this popular playwright grew homesick for the quiet, peaceful little village where he was born and to which he had but recently moved his family from London. Its pointed spire in the distance; the tiled roof of New Place; the picturesque old Elizabethan house he had just bought in his prosperity; the slow-moving Avon River with its gently sloping banks, daisy-starred in summer, with " willows aslant " the stream; the walled-in garden with the fruit trees silvered by the moon — these drew him home for frequent visits.

Democracy and freedom not new problems in the world. Echoing and re-echoing down the centuries — faintly at first, but with gradually increasing vigor — has been the voice of the common man crying out against the tyranny of his leaders. In our own time the ordinary people of all the world have no desire to kill one another, and yet wars continue. To what extent the leaders are responsible, history will reveal to future generations. Many times in the history of ancient Rome the voice of revolt against false leaders was silenced by bloody massacre, only to rise again and recall to ears that had forgotten its sound the traditional right of the common people to take part in shaping their destiny.

From earliest days in ancient Rome, after the descendants of Romulus and Remus had done away with their kings, the common people, called plebeians, were entitled to two elected " tribunes," who might stop any act of the two " consuls " or a decree of the senate (which was hostile to their traditional rights). The aristocrats of ancient Rome, descendants of the three Latin tribes who had first formed the city, were called patricians. Only patricians could be senators. For centuries the rights of the two classes, the plebeians and the patricians, clashed in bloody conflict.

As the city of Rome grew rich from foreign conquests, the patricians became giddy with power and wrung heavier and heavier taxes from the poor. Senators confiscated land of the plebeians to build up their estates, which were worked by foreign slaves captured in war. In 133 B.C. the plebeians, led by their tribunes, the Gracchi brothers, revolted. There followed a succession of army generals who appealed first to the masses for support and then to the senators. At one extreme was the tyrant Sulla, who massacred in cold blood all the leaders of the people's party. Such " purges " have occurred since the World War; they are not confined to ancient history. Then came the popular hero Pompey, who repealed the unjust laws of Sulla and sought the support of the common people. His career was marked by a succession of brilliant foreign conquests; and he returned to Rome the idol of the people, to celebrate his victories in a splendid triumph while the thronged streets cheered.

Caesar began his career as a popular hero. When Pompey was at the height of his popularity, there appeared on the Roman scene another leader destined to incite the social upheaval about which you are to read in the play that follows. Julius Caesar was a soldier distinguished for brave deeds. He had won popular acclaim, furthermore, as the director of public games who provided spectacular gladiatorial shows in the Circus Maximus.

While Pompey was in the Far East, subjecting foreign kings to the will of Rome, Caesar was in Spain. Both conquerors returned to Rome flushed with victory, to join their power with that of a rich senator, Crassus, into the First Triumvirate — an agreement of "three men working together," as the term literally means. Yet neither Pompey nor Caesar was satisfied. Both wished to gain more power, and each hoped finally to conquer the other. In order to strengthen his own position with the people, Caesar set out to conquer Gaul — the territory that lay to the north of Italy. Pompey became, meanwhile, the Governor of Spain.

At home the Roman senators began to feel uneasy at the growing power of their military leaders. In a sudden act of fear they summoned Caesar home, ordering him to abandon his army and to return as a private citizen. As Caesar approached the Rubicon River, the boundary line between his northern province and Rome, he hesitated. To cross the Rubicon with his army in disobedience of the decree of the senate was an act of war; to disband his army was to yield before he had a chance to test his strength. It was a bold decision that he made. He crossed the river. Alarmed by his daring, the senators recalled Pompey to help subdue Caesar. The armies of Pompey and Caesar met on the plains of Thessaly. Pompey was defeated and fled to Egypt, pursued by Caesar. One day an Egyptian, thinking to gain Caesar's favor, presented him with Pompey's head.

Caesar rose to great power in Rome. Caesar then returned to Rome in triumph. For days the celebration lasted, one day dedicated to his victories in Gaul, another to his conquests in Greece, and still another to his victory in Africa. Crowds of Egyptian slaves, carrying sacks of wheat, paraded in the streets of Rome. Floats drawn by horses showed the Egyptian Pyramids and the Sphinx. An Egyptian princess marched in the parade, her arms bound with golden chains.

After his "triumph" Caesar set about reorganizing the government. By the time of this play he had diminished the senate's powers, forcing it to pass decrees that gave him the right to decide upon war, to conduct elections, and to make appointments without consulting the people. Meekly and obediently the senate declared Caesar to be "perpetual dictator" with unlimited powers. Ultimately, it was thought, he meant to make himself Emperor.

Now you are ready for the play itself.

JULIUS CAESAR

by William Shakespeare (1564–1616)

In this play the Roman mob is to act an exceedingly important part. From what you have read or know about large crowds of people, would you be willing to trust to their wisdom when they become highly excited? In many European countries today the leaders of the people encourage them to mass together for great demonstrations, at which skillful speakers agitate them to a frenzy of excitement. Playing upon primitive forces like fear and hate, or the more complicated *patriotism,* these orators arouse emotions rather than intelligence. The most famous scene in this play is just such a mass meeting, and Shakespeare begins to build toward it at the very opening of his play. Notice that the hero Pompey is scarcely dead before the commoners have transferred their shouts to his conqueror, Caesar. Notice, too, how easily the throng is dispersed by Marullus who is not afraid to tell them, "Be gone!"

This is only one example of Shakespeare's

superb craftsmanship. The first act prepares us in many other ways for the events to come. Don't fail to observe the soothsayer's weird warning to Caesar. First-class dramatists never write such events into their first acts without a reason.

DRAMATIS PERSONAE

JULIUS CAESAR

OCTAVIUS CAESAR, MARCUS ANTONIUS, M. AEMILIUS LEPIDUS — triumvirs after the death of Julius Caesar

PUBLIUS, POPILIUS LENA — senators

MARCUS BRUTUS, CASSIUS, CASCA, TREBONIUS, LIGARIUS, DECIUS BRUTUS, METELLUS CIMBER, CINNA — conspirators

FLAVIUS, MARULLUS — tribunes

ARTEMIDORUS, a Sophist of Cnidos

A SOOTHSAYER

LUCILIUS, TITINIUS, MESSALA, YOUNG CATO, VOLUMNIUS — friends to Brutus and Cassius

VARRO, CLITUS, CLAUDIUS, STRATO, LUCIUS, DARDANIUS — servants to Brutus

PINDARUS, servant to Cassius

CALPURNIA, wife to Caesar

PORTIA, wife to Brutus

SENATORS, CITIZENS, GUARDS, ET CETERA

SCENE. *During a great part of the play, at Rome; afterward at Sardis and near Philippi*

ACT I

SCENE I. *Rome. A street*

[Can you bring to mind from your reading about ancient Rome a narrow street lined with arched doorways and overhanging balconies, open booths and bright-colored awnings? Can you imagine men in togas — one, perhaps, in a litter carried by dark-skinned slaves?

Here, on such a street, a crowd of common people have gathered to watch a Roman "triumph," a grand military procession celebrating, in this case, Caesar's victory over Pompey's sons at Munda, Spain. It is early afternoon, and beneath the clear Italian sky the lemon-colored buildings glint in the warm sunshine. The chattering crowd is expectant — you have seen them, in modern dress, at the Pasadena Rose Parade or at home on circus day or Memorial Day. Off stage, you feel, is all the rest of Rome, massed along similar streets; you can almost hear a band playing somewhere.]

[Suddenly, dramatically, the two tribunes enter — MARULLUS *and* FLAVIUS.[1] *They scowl and their appearance sobers the crowd.]*

FLAVIUS. Hence! Home, you idle creatures! get you home!
Is this a holiday? What! know you not,
Being mechanical, you ought not walk
Upon a laboring day without the sign
Of your profession? Speak, what trade art thou? 5

CARPENTER. Why, sir, a carpenter.

MARULLUS. Where is thy leather apron and thy rule?
What dost thou with thy best apparel on?
You, sir, what trade are you?

COBBLER. Truly, sir, in respect of a fine workman, I am but, as you would say, 10
a cobbler.

MARULLUS. But what trade art thou? answer me directly.

COBBLER. A trade, sir, that, I hope, I may use with a safe conscience; which is, indeed, sir, a mender of bad soles.

MARULLUS. What trade, thou knave? thou naughty knave, what trade? 15

COBBLER. Nay, I beseech you, sir, be not out with me: yet if you be out, sir, I can mend you.

MARULLUS. What mean'st thou by that? mend me, thou saucy fellow!

COBBLER. Why, sir, cobble you.

FLAVIUS. Thou art a cobbler, art thou? 20

COBBLER. Truly, sir, all that I live by is with the awl: I meddle with no tradesman's matters, nor women's matters, but with awl. I am, indeed, sir, a surgeon to old shoes; when they are in great danger, I recover them. As proper men as ever trod upon neat's leather have gone upon my handiwork.

FLAVIUS. But wherefore art not in thy shop today? 25
Why dost thou lead these men about the streets?

[1] Before starting in to read, pronounce the characters' names to yourself: **Marullus** (mȧ-rŭl'ŭs) and **Flavius** (flā'vĭ-ŭs). 4–5. Notice this custom of the times. Can you guess a good reason for it? 11. **cobbler** has a double meaning here. Besides referring to a mender of shoes it refers to a bungling workman. The Cobbler is deliberately punning; that is, using a word in a double sense. Such plays on words were very popular in Shakespeare's day. 14. Do you see the double meaning of **soles?** 16. What is the double meaning of **out with me?** 21. The Cobbler is still punning. Do you follow him?

COBBLER. Truly, sir, to wear out their shoes, to get myself into more work. But, indeed, sir, we make holiday, to see Caesar and to rejoice in his triumph.

MARULLUS. Wherefore rejoice? What conquest brings he home?
What tributaries follow him to Rome, 30
To grace in captive bonds his chariot wheels?
You blocks, you stones, you worse than senseless things!
O you hard hearts, you cruel men of Rome,
Knew you not Pompey? Many a time and oft
Have you climb'd up to walls and battlements, 35
To towers and windows, yea, to chimney tops,
Your infants in your arms, and there have sat
The livelong day, with patient expectation,
To see great Pompey pass the streets of Rome:
And when you saw his chariot but appear, 40
Have you not made an universal shout,
That Tiber trembled underneath her banks?
And do you now put on your best attire?
And do you now cull out a holiday?
And do you now strew flowers in his way 45
That comes in triumph over Pompey's blood?
Be gone!
Run to your houses, fall upon your knees,
Pray to the gods to intermit the plague
That needs must light on this ingratitude. 50

[*Exeunt all the* COMMONERS.]

FLAVIUS. See, whether their basest metal be not mov'd;
They vanish tongue-tied in their guiltiness.
Go you down that way toward the Capitol;
This way will I: disrobe the images,
If you do find them deck'd with ceremonies. 55

MARULLUS. May we do so?
You know it is the feast of Lupercal.

FLAVIUS. It is no matter; let no images
Be hung with Caesar's trophies. I'll about,
And drive away the vulgar from the streets: 60
So do you too, where you perceive them thick.
These growing feathers pluck'd from Caesar's wing
Will make him fly an ordinary pitch,
Who else would soar above the view of men
And keep us all in servile fearfulness. 65

[*Exeunt.*]

54. Why do you think the tribunes were about to **disrobe the images;** that is, the statues of Caesar? 57. For the **feast of Lupercal** see the explanation at the beginning of the next scene. 62–64. Make sure that you understand this comparison before you proceed further: What did the tribunes do that might be compared with plucking feathers? **Pitch** is a word used in falconry to mean height. In what way could Caesar be said to **soar?**

SCENE II. *A public place*

[A large public square. Pillared buildings, statues of heroes wreathed in garlands, and a fountain in the center present a scene of splendor and dignity.

It is February 15, the day of the Lupercalia, a feast of purification in honor of Lupercus, an old god of shepherds, celebrated on the Palatine Hill. On this day young men of the nobility, anointed with oil of olives, run up and down the city striking certain women with a whip of goat's hide, as a good omen. Such women, it was thought, would "shake off their curse" of childlessness. Antony is ready for this custom.]

[*Flourish.*[1] *Enter* CAESAR; ANTONY, *for the course;* CALPURNIA, PORTIA, DECIUS, BRUTUS, CASSIUS,[2] *and* CASCA; *a great crowd following, among them a* SOOTHSAYER.]

CAESAR. Calpurnia!
CASCA. Peace, ho! Caesar speaks.
CAESAR. Calpurnia!
CALPURNIA. Here, my lord.
CAESAR. Stand you directly in Antonius' way, 5
When he doth run his course. Antonius!
ANTONY. Caesar, my lord?
CAESAR. Forget not, in your speed, Antonius,
To touch Calpurnia; for our elders say,
The barren, touched in this holy chase, 10
Shake off their sterile curse.
ANTONY. I shall remember:
When Caesar says "do this," it is perform'd.
CAESAR. Set on; and leave no ceremony out.

[*Flourish. They start out, with music playing.*]

SOOTHSAYER. Caesar! 15
CAESAR (*halting*). Ha! who calls?
CASCA. Bid every noise be still: peace yet again!

[*Music ceases.*]

CAESAR. Who is it in the press that calls on me?
I hear a tongue, shriller than all the music.
Cry "Caesar!" Speak; Caesar is turn'd to hear. 20
SOOTHSAYER. Beware the ides of March.
CAESAR. What man is that?
BRUTUS. A soothsayer bids you beware the ides of March.
CAESAR. Set him before me; let me see his face.
CASSIUS. Fellow, come from the throng;

[SOOTHSAYER *advances;* CASCA *sets him before* CAESAR.]

look upon Caesar. 25

[1] A **flourish** was a blare of music, Shakespeare's way of announcing the entrance of royalty or of a person of very high rank. [2] Pronounce these characters' names before you start to read: **Calpurnia** (kăl-pŭr′nĭ-ȧ), **Decius** (dĕ′shŭs), **Cassius** (kăsh′ĭŭs). 9–11. You can well imagine that such a great man as Caesar would wish for heirs to carry on his name. So far his wife had remained childless. 12–13. Does Antony's reply remind you of anything Flavius said in the preceding scene? What? 18. What do you think Caesar means by **in the press?** What word would you substitute for *press?* 21. The **ides of March:** March 15.

CAESAR. What say'st thou to me now? speak once again.
SOOTHSAYER. Beware the ides of March.
CAESAR. He is a dreamer; let us leave him: pass.

[*Caesar may cover his momentary uneasiness by brusquely turning away. The hush which has swept over the crowd is broken as the music starts up again. The last stragglers depart down the street, and we see Brutus, standing alone, serious and thoughtful. Cassius, who has purposely waited for such an opportunity, approaches him.*]

CASSIUS. Will you go see the order of the course?
BRUTUS. Not I. 30
CASSIUS. I pray you, do.
BRUTUS. I am not gamesome. I do lack some part
Of that quick spirit that is in Antony.
Let me not hinder, Cassius, your desires;
I'll leave you. 35
CASSIUS. Brutus, I do observe you now of late:
I have not from your eyes that gentleness
And show of love as I was wont to have:
You bear too stubborn and too strange a hand
Over your friend that loves you. 40
BRUTUS. Cassius,
Be not deceiv'd: if I have veil'd my look,
I turn the trouble of my countenance
Merely upon myself. Vexed I am
Of late with passions of some difference. 45
Conceptions only proper to myself,
Which give some soil perhaps to my behaviors;
But let not therefore my good friends be griev'd —
Among which number, Cassius, be you one —
Nor construe any further my neglect, 50
Than that poor Brutus, with himself at war,
Forgets the shows of love to other men.
CASSIUS. Then, Brutus, I have much mistook your passion;
By means whereof this breast of mine hath buried
Thoughts of great value, worthy cogitations. 55
Tell me, good Brutus, can you see your face?
BRUTUS. No, Cassius; for the eye sees not itself
But by reflection, by some other things.
CASSIUS. 'T is just:
And it is very much lamented, Brutus, 60
That you have no such mirrors as will turn
Your hidden worthiness into your eye,

29. How would you ask this question of Brutus? Remember what you yourself have so far "seen" of the festival. 32. **gamesome:** fond of sports. 51. Keep in mind that Brutus is **with himself at war.** Before you have finished the scene, you will find out why. 53–54. In what way had Cassius mistaken Brutus's manner? And with what result? Can you tell in your own words the meaning of these lines?

That you might see your shadow. I have heard,
Where many of the best respect in Rome —
Except immortal Caesar — speaking of Brutus 65
And groaning underneath this age's yoke,
Have wish'd that noble Brutus had his eyes.

BRUTUS. Into what dangers would you lead me, Cassius,
That you would have me seek into myself
For that which is not in me? 70

CASSIUS. Therefore, good Brutus, be prepar'd to hear:
And since you know you cannot see yourself
So well as by reflection, I, your glass,
Will modestly discover to yourself
That of yourself which you yet know not of. 75
And be not jealous on me, gentle Brutus:
Were I a common laugher, or did use
To stale with ordinary oaths my love
To every new protester; if you know
That I do fawn on men and hug them hard 80
And after scandal them, or if you know
That I profess myself in banqueting
To all the rout, then hold me dangerous.

[*Flourish and shout*]

BRUTUS. What means this shouting? I do fear, the people
Choose Caesar for their king. 85

CASSIUS. Ay, do you fear it?
Then must I think you would not have it so.

BRUTUS. I would not, Cassius; yet I love him well.
But wherefore do you hold me here so long?
What is it that you would impart to me? 90
If it be aught toward the general good,
Set honor in one eye and death i' th' other,
And I will look on both indifferently;
For let the gods so speed me as I love
The name of honor more than I fear death. 95

CASSIUS. I know that virtue to be in you, Brutus,
As well as I do know your outward favor.
Well, honor is the subject of my story.
I cannot tell what you and other men
Think of this life; but, for my single self, 100
I had as lief not be as live to be
In awe of such a thing as I myself.

65. Does Cassius mean to praise Caesar when he calls him **immortal?** 76. **jealous on me**: suspicious of me. 77. What modern word can you substitute for **laugher?** 80–81. What words of your own can you substitute for these lines? 86. Notice how Cassius has caught Brutus up on his use of the word **fear!** Do you see how it gives him the opening he has been seeking? What do you suspect he is trying to do with Brutus? 101–02. Cassius means by these lines that Caesar is no different from himself; he will not stand **in awe** of a person no better than himself. You will see in his speech that follows why he thinks that Caesar is unworthy of awe.

I was born free as Caesar; so were you:
We both have fed as well, and we can both
Endure the winter's cold as well as he: 105
For once, upon a raw and gusty day,
The troubled Tiber chafing with her shores,
Caesar said to me "Dar'st thou, Cassius, now
Leap in with me into this angry flood,
And swim to yonder point?" Upon the word, 110
Accoutered as I was, I plunged in
And bade him follow; so indeed he did.
The torrent roar'd, and we did buffet it
With lusty sinews, throwing it aside
And stemming it with hearts of controversy. 115
But ere we could arrive the point propos'd,
Caesar cried "Help me, Cassius, or I sink!"
I, as Aeneas, our great ancestor,
Did from the flames of Troy upon his shoulder
The old Anchises bear, so from the waves of Tiber 120
Did I the tired Caesar. And this man
Is now become a god, and Cassius is
A wretched creature and must bend his body,
If Caesar carelessly but nod on him.
He had a fever when he was in Spain, 125
And when the fit was on him, I did mark
How he did shake: 't is true, this god did shake:
His coward lips did from their color fly,
And that same eye whose bend doth awe the world
Did lose his luster: I did hear him groan: 130
Ay, and that tongue of his that bade the Romans
Mark him and write his speeches in their books,
Alas, it cried, "Give me some drink, Titinius,"
As a sick girl. Ye gods, it doth amaze me
A man of such a feeble temper should 135
So get the start of the majestic world
And bear the palm alone.

[*Shout. Flourish*]

BRUTUS. Another general shout!
I do believe that these applauses are
For some new honors that are heap'd on Caesar. 140
CASSIUS. Why, man, he doth bestride the narrow world
Like a Colossus, and we petty men
Walk under his huge legs and peep about

115. You are familiar with the word **controversy** in the sense of an argument. Here it means rivalry. 137. The **palm** is a symbol of victory. It was given by Romans as a prize in athletic contests. 142. The **Colossus** was an immense bronze statue supposed to have stood astride the entrance to the harbor at Rhodes, and was regarded as one of the seven wonders of the world. It was broken by an earthquake.

To find ourselves dishonorable graves.
Men at some time are masters of their fates: 145
The fault, dear Brutus, is not in our stars,
But in ourselves, that we are underlings.
" Brutus " and " Caesar ": what should be in that " Caesar "?
Why should that name be sounded more than yours?
Write them together, yours is as fair a name; 150
Sound them, it doth become the mouth as well;
Weigh them, it is as heavy; conjure with 'em,
" Brutus " will start a spirit as soon as " Caesar."
Now, in the names of all the gods at once,
Upon what meat doth this our Caesar feed, 155
That he is grown so great? Age, thou are sham'd!
Rome, thou has lost the breed of noble bloods!
When went there by an age, since the great flood,
But it was fam'd with more than with one man?
When could they say till now, that talk'd of Rome, 160
That her wide walls encompass'd but one man?
Now is it Rome indeed and room enough,
When there is in it but one only man.
O, you and I have heard our fathers say,
There was a Brutus, once, that would have brook'd 165
The eternal devil to keep his state in Rome
As easily as a king.

BRUTUS. That you do love me, I am nothing jealous;
What you would work me to, I have some aim:
How I have thought of this and of these times, 170
I shall recount hereafter; for this present,
I would not, so with love I might entreat you,
Be any further mov'd. What you have said
I will consider; what you have to say
I will with patience hear, and find a time 175
Both meet to hear and answer such high things.
Till then, my noble friend, chew upon this:
Brutus had rather be a villager
Than to repute himself a son of Rome
Under these hard conditions as this time 180
Is like to lay upon us.

CASSIUS. I am glad that my weak words
Have struck but thus much show of fire from Brutus.

BRUTUS. The games are done and Caesar is returning.

153. Cassius is referring to the old black art of magic in which conjurers used big and important names to raise evil spirits from the lower world. 162. Cassius is punning here on the sound of **Rome** and **room.** In Shakespeare's day the two words were pronounced very nearly alike. 165. Brutus believed himself a descendant of an ancient Roman patriot who led the revolt that expelled the last of the Tarquin kings, and established the Roman Republic. 168. **nothing jealous:** not doubtful. 169. What word would you use for **aim** in this sentence? 178–79. Brutus is saying in effect that being a Roman citizen in these days is worse than not being a citizen at all.

CASSIUS. As they pass by, pluck Casca by the sleeve; 185
And he will, after his sour fashion, tell you
What hath proceeded worthy note today.

[*A march playing. Re-enter* CAESAR *and his train.*]

BRUTUS. I will do so. But, look you, Cassius,
The angry spot doth glow on Caesar's brow,
And all the rest look like a chidden train: 190
Calpurnia's cheek is pale; and Cicero
Looks with such ferret and such fiery eyes
As we have seen him in the Capitol,
Being cross'd in conference by some senators.

CASSIUS. Casca will tell us what the matter is. 195

CAESAR. Antonius!

ANTONY. Caesar?

CAESAR. Let me have men about me that are fat:
Sleek-headed men and such as sleep o' nights:
Yond Cassius has a lean and hungry look; 200
He thinks too much: such men are dangerous.

ANTONY. Fear him not, Caesar; he's not dangerous;
He is a noble Roman and well given.

CAESAR. Would he were fatter! But I fear him not.
Yet, if my name were liable to fear, 205
I do not know the man I should avoid
So soon as that spare Cassius. He reads much;
He is a great observer, and he looks
Quite through the deeds of men; he loves no plays,
As thou dost, Antony; he hears no music; 210
Seldom he smiles, and smiles in such a sort
As if he mock'd himself and scorn'd his spirit
That could be mov'd to smile at anything.
Such men as he be never at heart's ease
Whiles they behold a greater than themselves, 215
And therefore are they very dangerous.
I rather tell thee what is to be fear'd
Than what I fear; for always I am Caesar.
Come on my right hand, for this ear is deaf,
And tell me truly what thou think'st of him. 220

[*A march. Exeunt* CAESAR *and all his train but* CASCA.]

CASCA. You pull'd me by the cloak; would you speak with me?

190. **chidden** comes from the word *chide*, which means rebuke. What phrase can you substitute for **chidden train?** 191. Cicero was a friend of Caesar, and a famous and powerful orator. 201. Does Caesar's comment remind you of anything in the conversation between Cassius and Brutus that you have just read? What? 215. Does this remark of Caesar's square with what you have already learned of Cassius? In what way? 217. What do you think is on Caesar's mind?

BRUTUS. Ay, Casca; tell us what hath chanc'd today,
That Caesar looks so sad.

CASCA. Why, you were with him, were you not?

BRUTUS. I should not then ask Casca what had chanc'd. 225

CASCA. Why, there was a crown offer'd him: and being offer'd him, he put it by with the back of his hand, thus; and then the people fell a-shouting.

BRUTUS. What was the second noise for?

CASCA. Why, for that too.

CASSIUS. They shouted thrice: what was the last cry for? 230

CASCA. Why, for that too.

BRUTUS. Was the crown offer'd him thrice?

CASCA. Ay, marry, was 't, and he put it by thrice, every time gentler than other; and at every putting-by mine honest neighbors shouted.

CASSIUS. Who offer'd him the crown? 235

CASCA. Why, Antony.

BRUTUS. Tell us the manner of it, gentle Casca.

CASCA. I can as well be hang'd as tell the manner of it: it was mere foolery; I did not mark it. I saw Mark Antony offer him a crown — yet 't was not a crown neither, 't was one of these coronets — and, as I told you, he put it by 240 once: but, for all that, to my thinking, he would fain have had it. Then he offer'd it to him again; then he put it by again: but, to my thinking, he was very loath to lay fingers off it. And then he offer'd it the third time; he put it the third time by: and still as he refus'd it, the rabblement shouted and clapp'd their chapp'd hands and threw up their sweaty nightcaps and 245 utter'd such a deal of stinking breath because Caesar refus'd the crown that it had almost chok'd Caesar; for he swounded and fell down at it: and for mine own part, I durst not laugh, for fear of opening my lips and receiving the bad air.

CASSIUS. But, soft, I pray you: what! did Caesar swound? 250

CASCA. He fell down in the market place, and foam'd at mouth, and was speechless.

BRUTUS. 'Tis very like: he hath the falling sickness.

CASSIUS. No, Caesar hath it not; but you and I
And honest Casca, we have the falling sickness.

CASCA. I know not what you mean by that; but I am sure Caesar fell down. If 255 the tag-rag people did not clap him and hiss him, according as he pleas'd and displeas'd them, as they use to do the players in the theater, I am no true man.

BRUTUS. What said he when he came unto himself?

CASCA. Marry, before he fell down, when he perceiv'd the common herd was 260 glad he refus'd the crown, he plucked me ope his doublet and offer'd them his throat to cut. An I had been a man of any occupation, if I would not have taken him at a word, I would I might go to hell among the rogues. And so he fell. When he came to himself again, he said if he had done or said any-

227. With what gesture do you imagine Casca accompanied his words? 252. According to history, Caesar was subject to epilepsy. 254. What double meaning do you see in the use of **falling sickness** here? Does Cassius mean what Casca refers to? 260–62. What, in your own words, is the grim fact that Casca reports? 261–62. Was this a mere gesture on Caesar's part? Why do you suppose he offered the crowd his throat to cut?

thing amiss, he desir'd their worships to think it was his infirmity. 265
Three or four wenches, where I stood, cried "Alas, good soul!" and forgave him with all their hearts: but there's no heed to be taken of them; if Caesar had stabb'd their mothers, they would have done no less.

BRUTUS. And after that, he came, thus sad, away?

CASCA. Ay. 270

CASSIUS. Did Cicero say anything?

CASCA. Ay, he spoke Greek.

CASSIUS. To what effect?

CASCA. Nay, an I tell you that, I'll ne'er look you i' th' face again: but those that understood him smil'd at one another and shook their heads; but, for 275 mine own part, it was Greek to me. I could tell you more news too: Marullus and Flavius, for pulling scarfs off Caesar's images, are put to silence. Fare you well. There was more foolery yet, if I could remember it.

CASSIUS. Will you sup with me tonight, Casca?

CASCA. No, I am promis'd forth. 280

CASSIUS. Will you dine with me tomorrow?

CASCA. Ay, if I be alive and your mind hold and your dinner worth the eating.

CASSIUS. Good: I will expect you.

CASCA. Do so. Farewell, both. (*Exit.*)

BRUTUS. What a blunt fellow is this grown to be! 285
He was quick mettle when he went to school.

CASSIUS. So is he now in execution
Of any bold or noble enterprise,
However he puts on this tardy form.
This rudeness is a sauce to his good wit, 290
Which gives men stomach to digest his words
With better appetite.

BRUTUS. And so it is. For this time I will leave you:
Tomorrow, if you please to speak with me,
I will come home to you; or, if you will, 295
Come home to me, and I will wait for you.

CASSIUS. I will do so. Till then, think of the world.

[*Exit* BRUTUS.]

Well, Brutus, thou art noble; yet, I see,
Thy honorable metal may be wrought
From that it is disposed: therefore it is meet 300
That noble minds keep ever with their likes;
For who so firm that cannot be seduc'd?
Caesar doth bear me hard; but he loves Brutus:
If I were Brutus now and he were Cassius,
He should not humor me. I will this night, 305

276. Think back to scene i. Do you remember the two tribunes, Flavius and Marullus? What has happened to them? Does this remind you of anything in modern dictator-controlled countries?
304–05. Cassius seems to mean that he would not let Caesar influence him as Caesar does Brutus.

In several hands, in at his windows throw,
As if they came from several citizens,
Writings all tending to the great opinion
That Rome holds of his name; wherein obscurely
Caesar's ambition shall be glanced at: 310
And after this let Caesar seat him sure;
For we will shake him, or worse days endure.

310. What more common phrase can you substitute for **glanced at?** 311. What words of your own can you substitute for **seat him sure?**

SCENE III. *The same. A street*

[*Notice that it is thundering and lightning and the street is seen only in intermittent flashes. The earth "shakes like a thing unfirm," and those men who are about "go through a tempest-dropping fire." Such "strife in heaven" was regarded as an ill omen.*]

[*Thunder and lightning. Enter, from opposite sides,* CASCA *and* CASSIUS.]

CASSIUS. Who's there?
CASCA. A Roman.
CASSIUS. Casca, by your voice.
CASCA. Your ear is good. Cassius, what night is this!
CASSIUS. A very pleasing night to honest men. 5
CASCA. Who ever knew the heavens menace so?
CASSIUS. Those that have known the earth so full of faults.
Now could I, Casca, name to thee a man
Most like this dreadful night,
A man no mightier than thyself or me 10
In personal action, yet prodigious grown
And fearful, as these strange eruptions are.
CASCA. 'Tis Caesar that you mean; is it not, Cassius?
CASSIUS. Let it be who it is: for Romans now
Have thews and limbs like to their ancestors; 15
But, woe the while! our fathers' minds are dead,
And we are govern'd with our mothers' spirits;
Our yoke and sufferance show us womanish.
CASCA. Indeed, they say the senators tomorrow
Mean to establish Caesar as a king; 20
And he shall wear his crown by sea and land,
In every place, save here in Italy.
CASSIUS. I know where I will wear this dagger then;
Cassius from bondage will deliver Cassius.
If I know this, know all the world besides, 25

7. Notice how quickly Cassius brings up the subject that is on his mind. What is the chief of the **faults** of which he complains? 18. What phrase can you substitute for **sufferance?** Do not the first two syllables give you a clue? 24. What is Cassius suggesting that he will do?

That part of tyranny that I do bear
I can shake off at pleasure.

[*Thunder still*]

CASCA. So can I:
So every bondman in his own hand bears
The power to cancel his captivity. 30
CASSIUS. And why should Caesar be a tyrant then?
Poor man! I know he would not be a wolf,
But that he sees the Romans are but sheep:
He were no lion, were not Romans hinds.
Where hast thou led me? I perhaps speak this 35
Before a willing bondman; then I know
My answer must be made. But I am arm'd,
And dangers are to me indifferent.
CASCA. You speak to Casca, and to such a man
That is no fleering telltale. Hold, my hand: 40
Be factious for redress of all these griefs,
And I will set this foot of mine as far
As who goes farthest.
CASSIUS. There's a bargain made.
Now know you, Casca, I have mov'd already 45
Some certain of the noblest-minded Romans
To undergo with me an enterprise
Of honorable-dangerous consequence;
And I do know, by this, they stay for me
In Pompey's porch: for now, this fearful night, 50
There is no stir or walking in the streets;
And the complexion of the element
In favor's like the work we have in hand,
Most bloody, fiery, and most terrible.
CASCA. Stand close awhile, for here comes one in haste. 55
CASSIUS. 'T is Cinna; I do know him by his gait;
He is a friend.

[*Enter* CINNA.]

Cinna, where haste you so?
CINNA. To find out you. Who's that? Metellus Cimber?
CASSIUS. No, it is Casca; one incorporate 60
To our attempts. Am I not stay'd for, Cinna?
CINNA. I am glad on't. What a fearful night is this!
CASSIUS. Am I not stay'd for? tell me.

36–37. Supposing Casca *had* been a **willing bondman.** What **answer** would Cassius have had to make to him? in what way? Why? 40. **fleering:** mocking. 41. **Be factious:** form a party. 50. **Pompey's porch:** the portico of Pompey's theater. 53. **in favor:** in appearance. 60–61. How would you say what Cassius means by **one incorporate to our attempts?** Perhaps what has gone before will give you the hint.

CINNA. Yes, you are.
O Cassius, if you could 65
But win the noble Brutus to our party —
CASSIUS. Be you content. Good Cinna, take this paper,
And look you lay it in the praetor's chair,
Where Brutus may but find it; and throw this
In at his window; set this up with wax 70
Upon old Brutus's statue: all this done,
Repair to Pompey's porch, where you shall find us.
Is Decius Brutus and Trebonius there?
CINNA. All but Metellus Cimber; and he's gone
To seek you at your house. Well, I will hie, 75
And so bestow these papers as you bade me.
CASSIUS. That done, repair to Pompey's theater.

[*Exit* CINNA.]

Come, Casca, you and I will yet ere day
See Brutus at his house: three parts of him
Is ours already, and the man entire 80
Upon the next encounter yields him ours.
CASCA. O, he sits high in all the people's hearts:
And that which would appear offense in us,
His countenance, like richest alchemy,
Will change to virtue and to worthiness. 85
CASSIUS. Him and his worth and our great need of him
You have right well conceited. Let us go,
For it is after midnight; and ere day
We will awake him and be sure of him.

[*Exeunt.*]

67–71. Do you remember what Cassius told himself he was going to do at the end of the last scene to wake Brutus up? He is now putting his plans into action. 83. What **offense** has Casca probably in mind? 87. **conceited**: thought out or grasped.

ACT II

[*Your impression of Caesar is not very much to his credit, is it? Do you know why? Stop to discover whether or not you have let Cassius' opinion color yours, or does Caesar himself act and speak to his own discredit? In this next act you will learn more about Caesar's character, especially in the scene with one of the conspirators, a smooth, wily fellow named Decius Brutus.*

Act II is Shakespeare's big chance to increase the suspense. The plot against Caesar gathers force; everything is in readiness, and at any moment the storm will break. Can you picture the audience of Shakespeare's day? In the " pit " the people forget to crack nuts, and stand tiptoe with mouths hanging wide open. The hush spreads over the whole audience, and children clutch their parents' hands while masked ladies in the galleries move closer to their escorts. Then just at the end of the act something happens which heightens the strain to the breaking point. Just at that moment the act comes to an end!]

SCENE I. *Rome.* BRUTUS'S *orchard*[1]

[*You may imagine a garden with fountains and flowers. Below tall dark cypress trees are small statues exquisitely carved from white marble. At the opening of the scene Brutus is wandering out into the night, restless and wakeful, during a lull in the storm referred to in the last scene. The lightning still flashes, and the stars are hidden from view so that Brutus cannot guess " how near to day " it is.*]

[*Enter* BRUTUS.]

BRUTUS. What, Lucius, ho!
I cannot by the progress of the stars,
Give guess how near to day. Lucius, I say!
I would it were my fault to sleep so soundly.
When, Lucius, when! Awake, I say! What! Lucius! 5

[*Enter* LUCIUS.]

LUCIUS. Call'd you, my lord?
BRUTUS. Get me a taper in my study, Lucius:
When it is lighted, come and call me here.
LUCIUS. I will, my lord. (*Exit.*)
BRUTUS. It must be by his death: and for my part, 10
I know no personal cause to spurn at him,
But for the general. He would be crown'd:
How that might change his nature, there's the question.
It is the bright day that brings forth the adder;
And that craves wary walking. Crown him? — that! — 15
And then, I grant, we put a sting in him,
That at his will he may do danger with.
The abuse of greatness is, when it disjoins
Remorse from power: and, to speak truth of Caesar,
I have not known when his affections swayed 20
More than his reason. But 'tis a common proof,
That lowliness is young ambition's ladder,
Whereto the climber upward turns his face;
But when he once attains the upmost round,
He then unto the ladder turns his back, 25
Looks in the clouds, scorning the base degrees
By which he did ascend. So Caesar may.
Then, lest he may, prevent. And, since the quarrel
Will bear no color for the thing he is,
Fashion it thus; that what he is, augmented, 30
Would run to these and these extremities:
And therefore think him as a serpent's egg
Which, hatch'd, would, as his kind, grow mischievous,
And kill him in the shell.

[*Re-enter* LUCIUS.]

[1] **orchard:** here used in the sense of garden. 1. Pronounce **Lucius** (lu'sh*us*) before you start to read. 4. What has kept Brutus from going to sleep? 10. Whose **death?** Why **must** it be? And what is the **It** that death is expected to accomplish?

LUCIUS. The taper burneth in your closet, sir. 35
Searching the window for a flint, I found
This paper, thus seal'd up; and I am sure
It did not lie there when I went to bed.

[*Gives him the letter.*]

BRUTUS. Get you to bed again; it is not day.
Is not tomorrow, boy, the ides of March? 40
LUCIUS. I know not, sir.
BRUTUS. Look in the calendar, and bring me word.
LUCIUS. I will, sir. (*Exit.*)
BRUTUS. The exhalations whizzing in the air
Give so much light that I may read by them. 45

[*Opens the letter and reads.*]

Brutus, thou sleep'st: awake! and see thyself.
Shall Rome, etc. Speak! strike! redress!

" Brutus, thou sleep'st: awake! "
Such instigations have been often dropp'd
Where I have took them up. 50
" Shall Rome, etc." Thus must I piece it out:
Shall Rome stand under one man's awe? What, Rome?
My ancestors did from the streets of Rome
The Tarquin drive, when he was call'd a king.
" Speak! strike! redress! " Am I entreated 55
To speak and strike? O Rome, I make thee promise;
If the redress will follow, thou receivest
Thy full petition at the hand of Brutus!

[*Re-enter* LUCIUS.]

LUCIUS. Sir, March is wasted fifteen days.

[*Knocking within*]

BRUTUS. 'Tis good. Go to the gate; somebody knocks. 60

[*Exit* LUCIUS.]

Since Cassius first did whet me against Caesar,
I have not slept.
Between the acting of a dreadful thing
And the first motion, all the interim is
Like a phantasma, or a hideous dream: 65
The Genius and the mortal instruments
Are then in council; and the state of man,

37. Who put the **paper** there? 44. **exhalations whizzing:** After the storm in which Cassius and Casca meet on the street, extraordinary displays resembling meteors continued to flash. 48. As you read from this point on, notice carefully the quotation marks, so that you will be able to distinguish Brutus's comments from those in the note.

Like to a little kingdom, suffers then
The nature of an insurrection.

[*Re-enter* LUCIUS.]

LUCIUS. Sir, 't is your brother Cassius at the door, 70
Who doth desire to see you.

BRUTUS. Is he alone?

LUCIUS. No, sir, there are more with him.

BRUTUS. Do you know them?

LUCIUS. No, sir; their hats are pluck'd about their ears, 75
And half their faces buried in their cloaks,
That by no means I may discover them
By any mark of favor.

BRUTUS. Let 'em enter.

[*Exit* LUCIUS.]

They are the faction. O conspiracy! 80
Sham'st thou to show thy dang'rous brow by night,
When evils are most free? O, then by day
Where wilt thou find a cavern dark enough
To mask thy monstrous visage? Seek none, conspiracy;
Hide it in smiles and affability: 85
For if thou path, thy native semblance on,
Not Erebus itself were dim enough
To hide thee from prevention.

[*Enter the conspirators* CASSIUS, CASCA, DECIUS, CINNA, METELLUS CIMBER, *and* TREBONIUS.]

CASSIUS. I think we are too bold upon your rest:
Good morrow, Brutus; do we trouble you? 90

BRUTUS. I have been up this hour — awake all night.
Know I these men that come along with you?

CASSIUS. Yes, every man of them; and no man here
But honors you; and every one doth wish
You had but that opinion of yourself 95
Which every noble Roman bears of you.
This is Trebonius.

BRUTUS. He is welcome hither.

CASSIUS. This, Decius Brutus.

BRUTUS. He is welcome too. 100

CASSIUS. This, Casca; this, Cinna; and this, Metellus Cimber.

BRUTUS. They are all welcome.
What watchful cares do interpose themselves
Betwixt your eyes and night?

CASSIUS. Shall I entreat a word? 105

86. **path:** walk about or show thyself. 88. **prevention:** discovery. Brutus means by the sentence you have just read that the safe way to hide a conspiracy is behind smiles and pleasant manners. If the conspirators show themselves abroad undisguised, in their true colors (**thy native semblance on**), nothing, not even darkness itself (**Erebus**), can keep their purpose concealed.

SHAKESPEARE IN MODERN DRESS. When Orson Welles produced *Julius Caesar*, he used modern dress to emphasize the play's application to our own times. Caesar and his soldiers (*above*) are shown in military uniform. (*Below*) Brutus is almost ready to join Cassius's plot. (*Right*) Portia pleads with Brutus.

Photos, Culver

Ewing Galloway

"CAESARS" AND SOCIAL DISTRESS. No modern Caesar reaches a place of power unless conditions like unemployment, hunger, ignorance, or terror exist in his country. Jobless youth, unhappy and dissatisfied, contributed to the rise of Hitler and Mussolini.

Can you relate the pictures on this page to your study of *Julius Caesar?*

Warner F. Clapp *Hansel Mieth from Life Magazine*

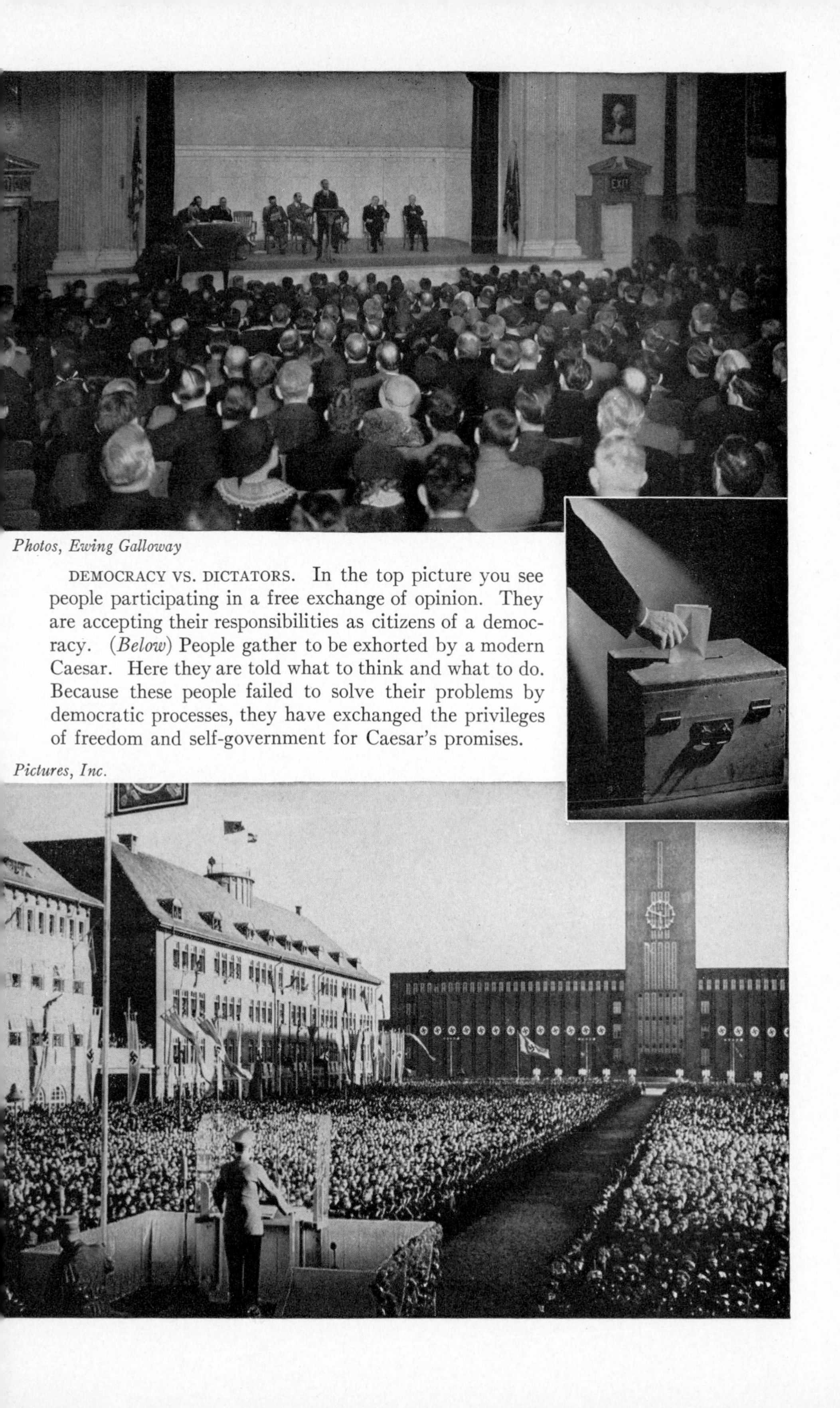

Photos, Ewing Galloway

DEMOCRACY VS. DICTATORS. In the top picture you see people participating in a free exchange of opinion. They are accepting their responsibilities as citizens of a democracy. (*Below*) People gather to be exhorted by a modern Caesar. Here they are told what to think and what to do. Because these people failed to solve their problems by democratic processes, they have exchanged the privileges of freedom and self-government for Caesar's promises.

Pictures, Inc.

University of Minnesota Laboratory

You will recognize these two scenes. In the student production (*above*) Antony is playing upon the emotions of the mob as he speaks Caesar's funeral oration. (*Below*) This scene, where Caesar is about to be stabbed, is from a professional production of 1912. Brutus (the kneeling figure on the left) was played by Tyrone Power, the father of the popular movie star.

Culver

[BRUTUS *and* CASSIUS *whisper.*]

DECIUS. Here lies the east: doth not the day break here?

CASCA. No.

CINNA. O, pardon, sir, it doth; and yon gray lines
That fret the clouds are messengers of day.

CASCA. You shall confess that you are both deceiv'd. 110
Here, as I point my sword, the sun arises,
Which is a great way growing on the south,
Weighing the youthful season of the year.
Some two months hence up higher toward the north
He first presents his fire; and the high east 115
Stands, as the Capitol, directly here.

BRUTUS. Give me your hands all over, one by one.

CASSIUS. And let us swear our resolution.

BRUTUS. No, not an oath: if not the face of men,
The sufferance of our souls, the time's abuse, — 120
If these be motives weak, break off betimes,
And every man hence to his idle bed;
So let high-sighted tyranny range on,
Till each man drop by lottery. But if these,
As I am sure they do, bear fire enough 125
To kindle cowards and to steel with valor
The melting spirits of women, then, countrymen,
What need we any spur but our own cause,
To prick us to redress? what other bond
Than secret Romans, that have spoke the word, 130
And will not palter? and what other oath
Than honesty to honesty engag'd,
That this shall be, or we will fall for it?

CASSIUS. But what of Cicero? shall we sound him?
I think he will stand very strong with us. 135

CASCA. Let us not leave him out!

CINNA. No, by no means!

METELLUS. O, let us have him! for his silver hairs
Will purchase us a good opinion
And buy men's voices to commend our deeds: 140
It shall be said, his judgment rul'd our hands;
Our youths and wildness shall no whit appear,
But all be buried in his gravity.

BRUTUS. O, name him not: let us not break with him;
For he will never follow anything 145
That other men begin.

CASSIUS. Then leave him out.

CASCA. Indeed he is not fit.

117. Guess what Cassius has just said to Brutus that leads him now to shake hands all over again with the conspirators.

DECIUS. Shall no man else be touch'd but only Caesar?
CASSIUS. Decius, well urg'd. I think it is not meet 150
Mark Antony, so well belov'd of Caesar,
Should outlive Caesar: we shall find of him
A shrewd contriver; and, you know, his means,
If he improve them, may well stretch so far
As to annoy us all: which to prevent, 155
Let Antony and Caesar fall together.
BRUTUS. Our course will seem too bloody, Caius Cassius,
To cut the head off and then hack the limbs,
Like wrath in death and envy afterward;
For Antony is but a limb of Caesar. 160
Let us be sacrificers, but not butchers, Caius.
We all stand up against the spirit of Caesar;
And in the spirit of men there is no blood:
O, that we then could come by Caesar's spirit,
And not dismember Caesar! But, alas, 165
Caesar must bleed for it! And, gentle friends,
Let's kill him boldly, but not wrathfully;
Let's carve him as a dish fit for the gods,
Not hew him as a carcass fit for hounds:
And let our hearts, as subtle masters do, 170
Stir up their servants to an act of rage,
And after seem to chide 'em. This shall make
Our purpose necessary and not envious:
Which so appearing to the common eyes,
We shall be call'd purgers, not murderers. 175
And for Mark Antony, think not of him;
For he can do no more than Caesar's arm
When Caesar's head is off.
CASSIUS. Yet I fear him;
For in the ingrafted love he bears to Caesar — 180
BRUTUS. Alas, good Cassius, do not think of him.
If he love Caesar, all that he can do
Is to himself, take thought and die for Caesar:
And that were much he should; for he is given
To sports, to wildness and much company. 185
TREBONIUS. There is no fear in him; let him not die;
For he will live, and laugh at this hereafter.
'T is time to part.
CASSIUS. But it is doubtful yet,
Whether Caesar will come forth today, or no; 190
For he is superstitious grown of late,

183–84. By **take thought** Brutus means to be despondent. He suggests, further, that there is some chance that Antony might die from the shock of Caesar's death, because he is a man given to fast living and is therefore not in the best of condition. In other words, he does not rate Mark Antony as a person who counts for very much as an enemy. Keep this remark of Brutus in mind as you read on.

Quite from the main opinion he held once
Of fantasy, of dreams and ceremonies.
It may be, these apparent prodigies,
The unaccustom'd terror of this night, 195
And the persuasion of his augurers,
May hold him from the Capitol today.

DECIUS. Never fear that: if he be so resolv'd,
I can o'ersway him; for he loves to hear
That unicorns may be betray'd with trees, 200
And bears with glasses, elephants with holes,
Lions with toils, and men with flatterers;
But when I tell him he hates flatterers,
He says he does, being then most flattered.
Let me work; 205
For I can give his humor the true bent,
And I will bring him to the Capitol.

CASSIUS. Nay, we will all of us be there to fetch him.

BRUTUS. By the eighth hour; is that the uttermost?

CINNA. Be that the uttermost, and fail not then. 210

METELLUS. Caius Ligarius doth bear Caesar hard,
Who rated him for speaking well of Pompey:
I wonder none of you have thought of him.

BRUTUS. Now, good Metellus, go along by him:
He loves me well, and I have given him reasons; 215
Send him but hither, and I'll fashion him.

CASSIUS. The morning comes upon 's: we'll leave you, Brutus.
And, friends, disperse yourselves; but all remember
What you have said, and show yourselves true Romans.

BRUTUS. Good gentlemen, look fresh and merrily; 220
Let not our looks put on our purposes,
But bear it as our Roman actors do,
With untir'd spirits and formal constancy:
And so good morrow to you every one.

[*Exeunt all but* BRUTUS.]

Boy! Lucius! Fast asleep? It is no matter; 225
Enjoy the honey-heavy dew of slumber:
Thou hast no figures nor no fantasies,
Which busy care draws in the brains of men:
Therefore thou sleep'st so sound.

[*Enter* PORTIA.]

PORTIA. Brutus, my lord! 230

BRUTUS. Portia, what mean you? wherefore rise you now?

196. **augurers:** religious officials whose duty it was to foretell the future by interpreting omens. 211. How would *you* say **doth bear Caesar hard?** 216. Guess how Brutus intends to **fashion him.** Whom?

It is not for your health thus to commit
Your weak condition to the raw cold morning.

PORTIA. Nor for yours neither. You've ungently, Brutus,
Stole from my bed: and yesternight, at supper, 235
You suddenly arose, and walk'd about,
Musing and sighing, with your arms across,
And when I ask'd you what the matter was,
You star'd upon me with ungentle looks;
I urg'd you further; then you scratched your head, 240
And too impatiently stamp'd with your foot;
Yet I insisted; yet you answer'd not,
But, with an angry wafture of your hand,
Gave sign for me to leave you.
Dear my lord, 245
Make me acquainted with your cause of grief.

BRUTUS. I am not well in health, and that is all.

PORTIA. Brutus is wise, and, were he not in health,
He would embrace the means to come by it.

BRUTUS. Why, so I do. Good Portia, go to bed. 250

PORTIA. Is Brutus sick? and is it physical
To walk unbraced and suck up the humors
Of the dank morning? What, is Brutus sick,
And will he steal out of his wholesome bed,
To dare the vile contagion of the night 255
And tempt the rheumy and unpurged air
To add unto his sickness? No, my Brutus;
You have some sick offense within your mind,
Which, by the right and virtue of my place,
I ought to know of: and, upon my knees, 260
I charm you, by my once commended beauty,
By all your vows of love and that great vow
Which did incorporate and make us one,
That you unfold to me, yourself, your half,
Why you are heavy, and what men tonight 265
Have had resort to you: for here have been
Some six or seven, who did hide their faces
Even from darkness.

BRUTUS. Kneel not, gentle Portia.

PORTIA. I should not need, if you were gentle Brutus. 270
Within the bond of marriage, tell me, Brutus,
Is it excepted I should know no secrets
That appertain to you?

BRUTUS. O ye gods!
Render me worthy of this noble wife! 275

[*Knocking within*]

Hark, hark! one knocks: Portia, go in awhile;

And by and by thy bosom shall partake
The secrets of my heart.
All my engagements I will construe to thee,
All the charactery of my sad brows: 280
Leave me with haste.

[*Exit* PORTIA.]

Lucius, who's that knocks?

[*Re-enter* LUCIUS *with* LIGARIUS, *who has a handkerchief tied about his head.*]

LUCIUS. Here is a sick man that would speak with you.
BRUTUS. Caius Ligarius, that Metellus spake of.
Boy, stand aside. Caius Ligarius! how? 285
LIGARIUS. Vouchsafe good morrow from a feeble tongue.
BRUTUS. O, what a time have you chose out, brave Caius,
To wear a kerchief! Would you were not sick!
LIGARIUS. I am not sick, if Brutus have in hand
Any exploit worthy the name of honor. 290
BRUTUS. Such an exploit have I in hand, Ligarius,
Had you a healthful ear to hear of it.
LIGARIUS. By all the gods that Romans bow before,
I here discard my sickness!
What's to do? 295
BRUTUS. A piece of work that will make sick men whole.
LIGARIUS. But are not some whole that we must make sick?
BRUTUS. That must we also. What it is, my Caius,
I shall unfold to thee, as we are going
To whom it must be done. 300
LIGARIUS. Set on your foot,
And with a heart new-fir'd I follow you,
To do I know not what: but it sufficeth
That Brutus leads me on.
BRUTUS. Follow me, then.

[*Exeunt.*]

288. It was the custom in Shakespeare's day for a sick person to tie a **kerchief** on his head in the hope that it would "mend him." An old English custom is thus attributed to the Romans.

SCENE II. CAESAR'S *house*

[*It is early morning after the stormy night on which the conspirators met at Brutus's house. The heavens are still troubled, and Caesar's night, like Brutus's, has been robbed of its rest.*

Caesar's house was on the Palatine Hill overlooking the Forum. Heavy draperies, patterned floors of marble, statues on pedestals, and draped couches convey an atmosphere of magnificence. Tall candelabra shed a soft light.]

[*Thunder and lightning. Enter* CAESAR.]

CAESAR. Nor heaven nor earth have been at peace tonight.
Thrice hath Calpurnia in her sleep cried out,
"Help! ho! they murder Caesar!" Who's within?

[*Enter a* SERVANT.]

SERVANT. My lord?
CAESAR. Go bid the priests do present sacrifice, 5
And bring me their opinions of success.
SERVANT. I will, my lord. (*Exit.*)

[*Enter* CALPURNIA.]

CALPURNIA. What mean you, Caesar? think you to walk forth?
You shall not stir out of your house today!
CAESAR. Caesar shall forth. The things that threaten'd me 10
Ne'er look'd but on my back; when they shall see
The face of Caesar, they are vanished.
CALPURNIA. Caesar, I never stood on ceremonies,
Yet now they fright me. There is one within
Recounts most horrid sights seen by the watch. 15
Fierce fiery warriors fight upon the clouds,
In ranks and squadrons and right form of war,
Which drizzled blood upon the Capitol.
O Caesar! these things are beyond all use,
And I do fear them. 20
CAESAR. What can be avoided
Whose end is purposed by the mighty gods?
Yet Caesar shall go forth; for these predictions
Are to the world in general as to Caesar.
CALPURNIA. When beggars die, there are no comets seen; 25
The heavens themselves blaze forth the death of princes.
CAESAR. Cowards die many times before their deaths;
The valiant never taste of death but once.
Of all the wonders that I yet have heard,
It seems to me most strange that men should fear, 30
Seeing that death, a necessary end,
Will come when it will come.

[*Re-enter* SERVANT.]

What say the augurers?
SERVANT. They would not have you stir forth today.
Plucking the entrails of an offering forth, 35
They could not find a heart within the beast.
CAESAR. The gods do this in shame of cowardice:
Caesar should be a beast without a heart

13. Calpurnia means that she has never before believed much in auguries, but now they frighten her. 23–24. Caesar means that there is nothing about the signs just mentioned by his wife that shows them aimed particularly at him. Rather, they seem to apply **to the world in general.** 27. Do you see how **Cowards die many times before their deaths?** How? 36–38. Notice the words **a beast without a heart.** What does Caesar mean by his use of the phrase?

If he should stay at home today for fear.
Caesar shall go forth. 40

CALPURNIA. Alas, my lord,
Your wisdom is consum'd in confidence.
Do not go forth today: call it my fear
That keeps you in the house, and not your own.
We'll send Mark Antony to the senate house; 45
And he shall say you are not well today. (*She kneels.*)
Let me, upon my knee, prevail in this.

CAESAR. Mark Antony shall say I am not well;
And, for thy humor, I will stay at home.

[*Enter* DECIUS.]

Here's Decius Brutus, he shall tell them so. 50

DECIUS. Caesar, all hail! Good morrow, worthy Caesar:
I come to fetch you to the senate house.

CAESAR. And you are come in very happy time
To bear my greetings to the senators
And tell them that I will not come today: 55
Cannot, is false, and that I dare not, falser:
I will not come today: tell them so, Decius.

CALPURNIA. Say he is sick.

CAESAR. Shall Caesar send a lie?
Have I in conquest stretch'd mine arm so far 60
To be afeard to tell graybeards the truth?
Decius, go tell them Caesar will not come.

DECIUS. Most mighty Caesar, let me know some cause,
Lest I be laugh'd at when I tell them so.

CAESAR. The cause is in my will: I will not come. 65
That is enough to satisfy the senate,
But for your private satisfaction,
Because I love you, I will let you know,
Calpurnia here, my wife, stays me at home.
She dreamt tonight she saw my statue, 70
Which, like a fountain with a hundred spouts,
Did run pure blood; and many lusty Romans
Came smiling, and did bathe their hands in it:
And these does she apply for warnings, and portents,
And evils imminent; and on her knee 75
Hath begg'd that I will stay at home today.

DECIUS. This dream is all amiss interpreted!
It was a vision fair and fortunate!
Your statue spouting blood in many pipes,
In which so many smiling Romans bath'd, 80

75. **imminent:** threatening to occur immediately. 77–84. Do you remember how in the last scene Decius promised the conspirators that he could "o'ersway" Caesar if "the persuasion of his augurers" should "hold him from the Capitol"? Notice how skillfully he is doing it.

Signifies that from you great Rome shall suck
Reviving blood, and that great men shall press
For tinctures, stains, relics, and cognizance.
This by Calpurnia's dream is signified.

CAESAR. And this way have you well expounded it. 85

DECIUS. I have, when you have heard what I can say.
And know it now: the senate have concluded
To give this day a crown to mighty Caesar.
If you shall send them word you will not come,
Their minds may change. Besides, it were a mock 90
Apt to be render'd, for someone to say,
"Break up the senate till another time,
When Caesar's wife shall meet with better dreams!"
If Caesar hide himself, shall they not whisper,
"Lo, Caesar is afraid"? 95

CAESAR. How foolish do your fears seem now, Calpurnia!
I am ashamed I did yield to them.
Give me my robe, for I will go.

[*Enter* PUBLIUS, BRUTUS, LIGARIUS, METELLUS, CASCA, TREBONIUS, *and* CINNA.]

And look where Publius is come to fetch me.

PUBLIUS. Good morrow, Caesar. 100

CAESAR. Welcome, Publius.
What, Brutus, are you stirr'd so early too?
Good morrow, Casca. Caius Ligarius,
Caesar was ne'er so much your enemy
As that same ague which hath made you lean. 105

[*Enter* ANTONY.]

See! Antony, that revels long o' nights,
Is notwithstanding up. Good morrow, Antony.

ANTONY. So to most noble Caesar.

CAESAR. Bid them prepare within:
I am to blame to be thus waited for. 110
Now, Cinna: now, Metellus. What, Trebonius!
I have an hour's talk in store for you;
Remember that you call on me today:
Be near me, that I may remember you.

TREBONIUS. Caesar, I will: (*Aside*) and so near will I be, 115
That your best friends shall wish I had been further.

CAESAR. Good friends, go in, and taste some wine with me;
And we, like friends, will straightway go together.

BRUTUS (*aside.*) That every like is not the same, O Caesar,
The heart of Brutus yearns to think upon! 120

[*Exeunt.*]

111. Caesar was interrupted in his greetings to these men by the entrance of Antony. He is now resuming his greetings. 118. Notice that Brutus winces at the phrase **like friends.** Do you blame him?

SCENE III. *A street near the Capitol*

[*The Capitol was on the southern summit of the Capitoline Hill. One hundred steps led up to it from the Forum. For this scene you may imagine its white columns visible in the distance.*

It is still early morning of the day on which Caesar expects to go to the senate. Soon the crowds will gather to watch him pass by with his train. Artemidorus, a doctor of rhetoric, who was familiar with some of Brutus's confederates and knew something of the plot against Caesar, is astir while yet the streets are empty. He has an important "schedule" — or document — to present to Caesar.]

[*Enter* ARTEMIDORUS, *with a paper.*]

ARTEMIDORUS (*reads*). Caesar, beware of Brutus; take heed of Cassius; come not near Casca; have an eye to Cinna; trust not Trebonius; mark well Metellus Cimber; Decius Brutus loves thee not: thou hast wronged Caius Ligarius. There is but one mind in all these men, and it is bent against Caesar. If thou beest not immortal, look about you: security gives way to conspiracy. 5
The mighty gods defend thee! Thy lover, Artemidorus.
Here will I stand till Caesar pass along,
And as a suitor will I give him this.
My heart laments that virtue cannot live
Out of the teeth of emulation. 10
If thou read this, O Caesar, thou mayest live;
If not, the Fates with traitors do contrive. (*Exit.*)

ACT III

SCENE I. *Rome. Before the Capitol*

[*"The ides of March are come!" With these very words the third act begins. Everything in the play so far has pointed toward this moment. The soothsayer has shrilled his eerie warning; the conspirators, after winning Brutus to their cause, have set this day for Caesar's death; flashing comets during a night of thunder and storm have created an atmosphere tense with expectation. Will Artemidorus upset the conspirators' plans? If all goes well, how will Antony act? Should Cassius have yielded to Brutus on the matter of assassinating Antony too? Whatever is to happen, one thing is certain. We must watch for the mob. Shakespeare did not write that very first scene without some dramatic purpose, and in this act, surely, the multitude will play its part.*]

[*Caesar and his followers have paused just outside the Capitol. Several people advance and present him with petitions as he ascends the stairs. Artemidorus is one. Imagine, as in your mind you follow the crowd inside, an arc of stiff-backed, uncomfortable-looking wooden seats for the senators, set in tiers, facing the great statue of Pompey. On a raised platform in a chair of state sits Caesar, while around him press his petitioners, some on bended knees, all eager for his attention. Beside him on a bench are many scrolls, petitions set aside temporarily. Before him is the unwound scroll of Cimber's suit. Casca stands to one side and behind Caesar. The other conspirators are close by.*]

[*A crowd of people; among them* ARTEMIDORUS *and the* SOOTHSAYER. *Flourish. Enter* CAESAR, BRUTUS, CASSIUS, CASCA, DECIUS, METELLUS, TREBONIUS, CINNA, ANTONY, LEPIDUS, POPILIUS, PUBLIUS, *and others.*]

CAESAR (*to the* SOOTHSAYER). The ides of March are come.
SOOTHSAYER. Ay, Caesar; but not gone.
ARTEMIDORUS. Hail, Caesar! (*Gives him a paper.*) Read this schedule.
DECIUS (*giving him a paper.*) Trebonius doth desire you to o'erread,
At your best leisure, this his humble suit. 5
ARTEMIDORUS. O Caesar, read mine first; for mine's a suit
That touches Caesar nearer. Read it, great Caesar!
CAESAR. What touches us ourself shall be last served.
ARTEMIDORUS. Delay not, Caesar! read it instantly!
CAESAR. What, is the fellow mad? 10
PUBLIUS (*thrusting him back*). Sirrah, give place.
CASSIUS. What, urge you your petitions in the street?
Come to the Capitol.

[CAESAR *goes up to the senate house, the rest following.*]

POPILIUS. I wish your enterprise today may thrive.
CASSIUS. What enterprise, Popilius? 15
POPILIUS. Fare you well.

[*Advances to* CAESAR.]

BRUTUS. What said Popilius Lena?
CASSIUS. He wished today our enterprise might thrive.
I fear our purpose is discovered.
BRUTUS. Look, how he makes to Caesar. Mark him. 20
CASSIUS. Casca, be sudden, for we fear prevention.
Brutus, what shall be done? If this be known,
Cassius or Caesar never shall turn back,
For I will slay myself.
BRUTUS. Cassius, be constant: 25
Popilius Lena speaks not of our purposes,
For, look, he smiles, and Caesar doth not change.
CASSIUS. Trebonius knows his time; for, look you, Brutus,
He draws Mark Antony out of the way.

[*Exeunt* ANTONY *and* TREBONIUS.]

DECIUS. Where is Metellus Cimber? Let him go, 30
And presently prefer his suit to Caesar.
BRUTUS. He is addressed: press near and second him.
CINNA. Casca, you are the first that rears your hand.
CAESAR. Are we all ready? What is now amiss
That Caesar and his senate must redress? 35
METELLUS. Most high, most mighty, and most puissant Caesar,
Metellus Cimber throws before thy seat
A humble heart, — (*Kneeling*)
CAESAR. Thy brother by decree is banished:

18–24. Notice how suspicious Cassius is. How do you account for the fact that Brutus is less nervous than Cassius? 28. From this line what do you guess Trebonius' part in the plot to be?

If thou dost bend and pray and fawn for him, 40
I spurn thee like a cur out of my way.
Know, Caesar doth not wrong; nor without cause
Will he be satisfied.

METELLUS. Is there no voice more worthy than my own,
To sound more sweetly in great Caesar's ear 45
For the repealing of my banish'd brother?

BRUTUS. I kiss thy hand, but not in flattery, Caesar,
Desiring thee that Publius Cimber may
Have an immediate freedom of repeal.

CAESAR. What, Brutus! 50

CASSIUS. Pardon, Caesar; Caesar, pardon:
As low as to thy foot doth Cassius fall,
To beg enfranchisement for Publius Cimber.

CAESAR. I could be well mov'd, if I were as you:
If I could pray to move, prayers would move me: 55
But I am constant as the northern star,
Of whose true-fix'd and resting quality
There is no fellow in the firmament.
The skies are painted with unnumber'd sparks,
They are all fire and every one doth shine; 60
But there's but one in all doth hold his place:
So in the world: 't is furnish'd well with men,
And men are flesh and blood, and apprehensive;
Yet in the number I do know but one
That unassailable holds on his rank, 65
Unshak'd of motion: and that I am he,
Let me a little show it, even in this;
That I was constant Cimber should be banish'd,
And constant do remain to keep him so.

CINNA. O Caesar, — 70

CAESAR. Hence! wilt thou lift up Olympus?

DECIUS. Great Caesar, —

CAESAR. Doth not Brutus bootless kneel?

CASCA. Speak, hands, for me!

[CASCA *first, then the other conspirators and* MARCUS BRUTUS *stab* CAESAR.]

CAESAR. *Et tu, Brute!* Then fall, Caesar! (*Dies.*) 75

CINNA. Liberty! Freedom! Tyranny is dead!
Run hence, proclaim, cry it about the streets!

CASSIUS. Some to the common pulpits, and cry out
"Liberty, freedom, and enfranchisement!"

54–55. People who plead for others are likely to be themselves moved by pleading. Caesar does not plead, nor is he moved by pleading. Cassius, on the contrary, is not so constant. What do you suppose Cassius was thinking to himself as Caesar made this reply to him? 73. Caesar means that it is useless for Decius to plead when Brutus, Caesar's best friend, has failed in his pleading.

BRUTUS. People and senators, be not affrighted; 80
Fly not; stand still: ambition's debt is paid.
CASCA. Go to the pulpit, Brutus.
DECIUS. And Cassius too.
BRUTUS. Where's Publius?
CINNA. Here, quite confounded with this mutiny. 85
METELLUS. Stand fast together, lest some friend of Caesar's
Should chance —
BRUTUS. Talk not of standing. Publius, good cheer;
There is no harm intended to your person,
Nor to no Roman else: so tell them, Publius. 90
CASSIUS. And leave us, Publius, lest that the people,
Rushing on us, should do your age some mischief.
BRUTUS. Do so: and let no man abide this deed,
But we the doers.

[*Re-enter* TREBONIUS.]

CASSIUS. Where is Antony? 95
TREBONIUS. Fled to his house amaz'd.
Men, wives, and children stare, cry out, and run
As it were doomsday.
BRUTUS. Fates, we will know your pleasures!
That we shall die, we know, 't is but the time 100
And drawing days out, that men stand upon.
CASSIUS. Why, he that cuts off twenty years of life
Cuts off so many years of fearing death.
BRUTUS. Grant that, and then is death a benefit:
So are we Caesar's friends, that have abridg'd 105
His time of fearing death. Stoop, Romans, stoop,
And let us bathe our hands in Caesar's blood
Up to the elbows, and besmear our swords:
Then walk we forth, even to the market place,
And, waving our red weapons o'er our heads, 110
Let's all cry "Peace, freedom, and liberty!"
CASSIUS. Stoop, then, and wash. How many ages hence
Shall this our lofty scene be acted over
In states unborn and accents yet unknown!
BRUTUS. How many times shall Caesar bleed in sport, 115
That now on Pompey's basis lies along
No worthier than the dust!
CASSIUS. So oft as that shall be,
So often shall the knot of us be call'd
The men that gave their country liberty. 120
DECIUS. What, shall we forth?
CASSIUS. Ay, every man away:

95. Do you remember what Trebonius had been assigned to do?

Brutus shall lead; and we will grace his heels
With the most boldest and best hearts of Rome.

[*Enter a* SERVANT.]

BRUTUS. Soft! who comes here? A friend of Antony's. 125
SERVANT. Thus, Brutus, did my master bid me kneel;
Thus did Mark Antony bid me fall down;
And, being prostrate, thus he bade me say:
Brutus is noble, wise, valiant, and honest;
Caesar was mighty, bold, royal, and loving; 130
Say I love Brutus, and I honor him;
Say I fear'd Caesar, honor'd him, and lov'd him.
If Brutus will vouchsafe that Antony
May safely come to him and be resolv'd
How Caesar hath deserv'd to lie in death, 135
Mark Antony shall not love Caesar dead
So well as Brutus living, but will follow
The fortunes and affairs of noble Brutus
Thorough the hazards of this untrod state
With all true faith. So says my master Antony. 140
BRUTUS. Thy master is a wise and valiant Roman;
I never thought him worse.
Tell him, so please him come unto this place,
He shall be satisfied, and, by my honor,
Depart untouch'd. 145
SERVANT. I'll fetch him presently. (*Exit.*)
BRUTUS. I know that we shall have him well to friend.
CASSIUS. I wish we may: but yet have I a mind
That fears him much; and my misgiving still
Falls shrewdly to the purpose. 150
BRUTUS. But here comes Antony.

[*Re-enter* ANTONY.]

Welcome, Mark Antony.
ANTONY (*looking at the body of* CAESAR). O mighty Caesar! dost thou lie so low?
Are all thy conquests, glories, triumphs, spoils,
Shrunk to this little measure? Fare thee well. 155
I know not, gentlemen, what you intend,
Who else must be let blood, who else is rank:
If I myself, there is no hour so fit
As Caesar's death hour, nor no instrument
Of half that worth as those your swords, made rich 160
With the most noble blood of all this world.
I do beseech ye, if you bear me hard,

156. What sudden change of voice and manner do you imagine accompanies the saying of this line?

Now, whilst your purpled hands do reek and smoke,
Fulfill your pleasure. Live a thousand years,
I shall not find myself so apt to die: 165
No place will please me so, no mean of death,
As here by Caesar, and by you cut off,
The choice and master spirits of this age.

BRUTUS. O Antony, beg not your death of us!
Though now we must appear bloody and cruel, 170
As, by our hands and this our present act,
You see we do, yet see you but our hands
And this the bleeding business they have done:
Our hearts you see not; they are pitiful;
And pity to the general wrong of Rome — 175

CASSIUS. Your voice shall be as strong as any man's
In the disposing of new dignities.

BRUTUS. Only be patient till we have appeas'd
The multitude, beside themselves with fear,
And then we will deliver you the cause, 180
Why I, that did love Caesar when I struck him,
Have thus proceeded.

ANTONY. I doubt not of your wisdom.
Let each man render me his bloody hand:
First, Marcus Brutus, will I shake with you; 185
Next, Caius Cassius, do I take your hand;
Now, Decius Brutus, yours; now yours, Metellus;
Yours, Cinna; and, my valiant Casca, yours;
Though last, not least in love, yours, good Trebonius.
Gentlemen all, — alas, what shall I say? 190
My credit now stands on such slippery ground,
That one of two bad ways you must conceit me,
Either a coward or a flatterer. (*Looks down at* CAESAR'S *body.*)
That I did love thee, Caesar, O, 't is true:
If then thy spirit look upon us now, 195
Shall it not grieve thee dearer than thy death
To see thy Antony making his peace,
Shaking the bloody fingers of thy foes,
Most noble! in the presence of thy corse?
Had I as many eyes as thou hast wounds, 200
Weeping as fast as they stream forth thy blood,
It would become me better than to close
In terms of friendship with thine enemies.

CASSIUS. Mark Antony, —

ANTONY. Pardon me, Caius Cassius: 205
The enemies of Caesar shall say this;
Then, in a friend, it is cold modesty.

192. You have met the word **conceit** earlier in the play. Can you follow its meaning from the sense of the sentence?

CASSIUS. I blame you not for praising Caesar so;
But what compact mean you to have with us?
Will you be prick'd in number of our friends; 210
Or shall we on, and not depend on you?

ANTONY. Therefore I took your hands, but was, indeed,
Sway'd from the point, by looking down on Caesar.
Friends am I with you all and love you all,
Upon this hope, that you shall give me reasons 215
Why and wherein Caesar was dangerous.

BRUTUS. Or else were this a savage spectacle.
Our reasons are so full of good regard
That were you, Antony, the son of Caesar,
You should be satisfied. 220

ANTONY. That's all I seek:
And am moreover suitor that I may
Produce his body to the market place,
And in the pulpit, as becomes a friend,
Speak in the order of his funeral. 225

BRUTUS. You shall, Mark Antony.

CASSIUS. Brutus, a word with you.
(*Aside to* BRUTUS) You know not what you do. Do not consent
That Antony speak in his funeral!
Know you how much the people may be mov'd 230
By that which he will utter?

BRUTUS. By your pardon:
I will myself into the pulpit first,
And show the reason of our Caesar's death:
What Antony shall speak, I will protest 235
He speaks by leave and by permission,
And that we are contented Caesar shall
Have all true rites and lawful ceremonies.
It shall advantage more than do us wrong.

CASSIUS. I know not what may fall. I like it not. 240

BRUTUS. Mark Antony, here take you Caesar's body.
You shall not in your funeral speech blame us,
But speak all good you can devise of Caesar,
And say you do 't by our permission;
Else shall you not have any hand at all 245
About his funeral. And you shall speak
In the same pulpit whereto I am going,
After my speech is ended.

ANTONY. Be it so;
I do desire no more. 250

BRUTUS. Prepare the body then, and follow us.

[*Exeunt all but* ANTONY.]

238. What are the advantages that Brutus sees in according Caesar **all true rites?**

ANTONY. O, pardon me, thou bleeding piece of earth,
That I am meek and gentle with these butchers!
Thou art the ruins of the noblest man
That ever lived in the tide of times. 255
Woe to the hand that shed this costly blood!
Over thy wounds now do I prophesy, —
Which, like dumb mouths, do ope their ruby lips
To beg the voice and utterance of my tongue —
A curse shall light upon the limbs of men; 260
Domestic fury and fierce civil strife
Shall cumber all the parts of Italy;
Blood and destruction shall be so in use
And dreadful objects so familiar
That mothers shall but smile when they behold 265
Their infants quarter'd with the hands of war;
All pity chok'd with custom of fell deeds:
And Caesar's spirit, ranging for revenge,
With Ate by his side come hot from hell,
Shall in these confines with a monarch's voice 270
Cry "Havoc," and let slip the dogs of war,
That this foul deed shall smell above the earth
With carrion men, groaning for burial.

[*Enter a* SERVANT.]

You serve Octavius Caesar, do you not?
SERVANT. I do, Mark Antony. 275
ANTONY. Caesar did write for him to come to Rome.
SERVANT. He did receive his letters, and is coming;
And bid me say to you by word of mouth —
O Caesar! — (*Seeing the body*)
ANTONY. Thy heart is big; get thee apart and weep. 280
Passion, I see, is catching; for mine eyes,
Seeing those beads of sorrow stand in thine,
Began to water. Is thy master coming?
SERVANT. He lies tonight within seven leagues of Rome.
ANTONY. Post back with speed and tell him what hath chanc'd. 285
Here is a mourning Rome, a dangerous Rome,
No Rome of safety for Octavius yet;
Hie hence, and tell him so. Yet, stay awhile;
Thou shalt not back till I have borne this corse
Into the market place: there shall I try, 290
In my oration, how the people take
The cruel issue of these bloody men;
According to the which, thou shalt discourse

254. Notice the change in Antony's manner now that he is alone. What explanation do you give yourself for his pretense before the conspirators? 269. **Ate** (ā'tē): a goddess of revenge. 287. Octavius was a nephew of Caesar. Why might it be unsafe for him to come to Rome? 290–92. What plan do you see forming itself in Antony's mind?

To young Octavius of the state of things.
Lend me your hand. 295

[*Exeunt with* CAESAR'S *body*.]

SCENE II. *The Forum*

[*Several days have passed since Caesar was killed. A few hours after his murder his body was carried to his mansion overlooking the Forum, where Calpurnia received it. During the night she transferred all her treasures and Caesar's private papers to the house of Antony. The conspirators, meanwhile, had taken possession of the Capitol with a force of gladiators.*

The scene opens on the day of Caesar's funeral, a public ceremony decreed by the senate. Processions usually entered the Forum, Rome's great public square and center of communal life, by the Sacred Way, proceeding on through the great triumphal arch of Titus past the magnificent temples that were set in the hills. On one side of the Forum rose the Palatine Hill, crowned by the splendid palaces of great Romans. Between the temples a road lined with shops dipped down to the river Tiber, to the great wharves where river barges brought merchandise from the port of Ostia. Another road led to the Circus Maximus, where the great chariot races were held. Between the temples stood the speakers' stands, the "common pulpits" referred to in the last scene, from which the eloquent voices of Roman orators moved the people. It is to one of these pulpits that Brutus and Cassius are proceeding, followed by the noisy plebeians. At some distance back you may imagine Mark Antony following slowly and solemnly the body of Caesar carried on a bier.]

[*Enter* BRUTUS *and* CASSIUS, *and a throng of* CITIZENS.]

CITIZENS. We will be satisfied! let us be satisfied!
BRUTUS. Then follow me and give me audience, friends.
Cassius, go you into the other street,
And part the numbers.
Those that will hear me speak, let 'em stay here; 5
Those that will follow Cassius, go with him;
And public reasons shall be rendered
Of Caesar's death.
FIRST CITIZEN. I will hear Brutus speak.
SECOND CITIZEN. I will hear Cassius; and compare their reasons, 10
When severally we hear them rendered.

[*Exit* CASSIUS, *with some of the* CITIZENS. BRUTUS *goes into the pulpit*.]

THIRD CITIZEN. The noble Brutus is ascended: silence!
BRUTUS. Be patient till the last.
Romans, countrymen, and lovers! hear me for my cause, and be silent, that you may hear: believe me for mine honor, and have respect to mine 15 honor, that you may believe: censure me in your wisdom, and awake your senses, that you may the better judge. If there be any in this assembly, any dear friend of Caesar's, to him I say, that Brutus's love to Caesar was no less than his. If then that friend demand why Brutus rose against Caesar, this is my answer: — Not that I lov'd Caesar less, but that I lov'd Rome 20

19–20. In these lines you have Brutus's famous justification for his faithlessness to a friend. Repeat the lines to yourself so that you will remember them.

more. Had you rather Caesar were living and die all slaves, than that Caesar were dead, to live all free men? As Caesar lov'd me, I weep for him; as he was fortunate, I rejoice at it; as he was valiant, I honor him: but, as he was ambitious, I slew him. There is tears for his love; joy for his fortune; honor for his valor; and death for his ambition. Who is here so base that would 25 be a bondman? If any, speak; for him have I offended. Who is here so rude that would not be a Roman? If any, speak; for him have I offended. Who is here so vile that will not love his country? If any, speak; for him have I offended. I pause for a reply.

ALL. None, Brutus, none! 30

BRUTUS. Then none have I offended. I have done no more to Caesar than you shall do to Brutus. The question of his death is enroll'd in the Capitol; his glory not extenuated, wherein he was worthy, nor his offenses enforced, for which he suffered death.

[*Enter* ANTONY *and others, with* CAESAR'S *body*.]

Here comes his body, mourn'd by Mark Antony: who, though he had 35 no hand in his death, shall receive the benefit of his dying, a place in the commonwealth; as which of you shall not? With this I depart, — that, as I slew my best lover for the good of Rome, I have the same dagger for myself, when it shall please my country to need my death.

ALL. Live, Brutus! live! live! 40

FIRST CITIZEN. Bring him with triumph home unto his house!

SECOND CITIZEN. Give him a statue with his ancestors!

THIRD CITIZEN. Let him be Caesar!

FOURTH CITIZEN. Caesar's better parts
Shall be crown'd in Brutus! 45

FIRST CITIZEN. We'll bring him to his house
With shouts and clamors!

BRUTUS. My countrymen, —

SECOND CITIZEN. Peace! silence! Brutus speaks.

FIRST CITIZEN. Peace, ho! 50

BRUTUS. Good countrymen, let me depart alone,
And, for my sake, stay here with Antony:
Do grace to Caesar's corpse, and grace his speech
Tending to Caesar's glories; which Mark Antony,
By our permission, is allow'd to make. 55
I do entreat you, not a man depart
Save I alone, till Antony have spoke.

[*Descends from the pulpit, and goes out*.]

FIRST CITIZEN. Stay, ho! and let us hear Mark Antony.

THIRD CITIZEN. Let him go up into the public chair;
We'll hear him. Noble Antony, go up. 60

ANTONY. For Brutus's sake, I am beholding to you.

[*Goes into the pulpit*.]

32. **question**: reason.

FOURTH CITIZEN. What does he say of Brutus?
THIRD CITIZEN. He says, for Brutus's sake,
He finds himself beholding to us all.
FOURTH CITIZEN. 'T were best he speak no harm of Brutus here! 65
FIRST CITIZEN. This Caesar was a tyrant!
Nay, that's certain:
We are blest that Rome is rid of him.
SECOND CITIZEN. Peace! let us hear what Antony can say.
ANTONY. You gentle Romans, — 70
CITIZENS. Peace, ho! let us hear him.
ANTONY. Friends, Romans, countrymen, lend me your ears;
I come to bury Caesar, not to praise him.
The evil that men do lives after them,
The good is oft interred with their bones; 75
So let it be with Caesar. The noble Brutus
Hath told you Caesar was ambitious:
If it were so, it was a grievous fault;
And grievously hath Caesar answer'd it.
Here, under leave of Brutus and the rest — 80
For Brutus is an honorable man;
So are they all, all honorable men —
Come I to speak in Caesar's funeral.
He was my friend, faithful and just to me.
But Brutus says he was ambitious; 85
And Brutus is an honorable man.
He hath brought many captives home to Rome,
Whose ransoms did the general coffers fill:
Did this in Caesar seem ambitious?
When that the poor have cried, Caesar hath wept: 90
Ambition should be made of sterner stuff.
Yet Brutus says he was ambitious;
And Brutus is an honorable man.
You all did see that on the Lupercal
I thrice presented him a kingly crown, 95
Which he did thrice refuse: was this ambition?
Yet Brutus says he was ambitious;
And, sure, he is an honorable man.
I speak not to disprove what Brutus spoke,
But here I am to speak what I do know. 100
You all did love him once, not without cause;
What cause withholds you, then, to mourn for him?
O judgment! thou art fled to brutish beasts,

81. From this point on in his speech, notice how often and in what manner Antony uses the word **honorable.** In what tone do you guess he says it here? To express what attitude? Does he mean what he says? 86. Does Antony change his tone as he says **honorable** in this sentence? How? 93. What force is the word **honorable** gaining as Antony continues to repeat it? Do you see? What change is taking place in the minds of the people? 99. Is Antony speaking the truth here?

And men have lost their reason! Bear with me;
My heart is in the coffin there with Caesar, 105
And I must pause till it come back to me.

FIRST CITIZEN. Methinks there is much reason in his sayings.

SECOND CITIZEN. If thou consider rightly of the matter,
Caesar has had great wrong.

THIRD CITIZEN. Has he, masters! 110
I fear there will a worse come in his place.

FOURTH CITIZEN. Mark'd ye his words? He would not take the crown
Therefore 't is certain he was not ambitious.

FIRST CITIZEN. If it be found so, some will dear abide it!

SECOND CITIZEN. Poor soul! his eyes are red as fire with weeping. 115

THIRD CITIZEN. There's not a nobler man in Rome than Antony.

FOURTH CITIZEN. Now mark him, he begins again to speak.

ANTONY. But yesterday the word of Caesar might
Have stood against the world; now lies he there,
And none so poor to do him reverence. 120
O masters, if I were dispos'd to stir
Your hearts and minds to mutiny and rage,
I should do Brutus wrong, and Cassius wrong,
Who, you all know, are honorable men.
I will not do them wrong; I rather choose 125
To wrong the dead, to wrong myself and you,
Than I will wrong such honorable men.
But here's a parchment with the seal of Caesar;
I found it in his closet; 't is his will:
Let but the commons hear this testament — 130
Which, pardon me, I do not mean to read —
And they would go and kiss dead Caesar's wounds
And dip their napkins in his sacred blood,
Yea, beg a hair of him for memory,
And, dying, mention it within their wills, 135
Bequeathing it as a rich legacy
Unto their issue.

FOURTH CITIZEN. We'll hear the will! Read it, Mark Antony.

ALL. The will! the will! we will hear Caesar's will!

ANTONY. Have patience, gentle friends, I must not read it; 140
It is not meet you know how Caesar lov'd you.
You are not wood, you are not stones, but men;
And, being men, hearing the will of Caesar,
It will inflame you, it will make you mad:
'T is good you know not that you are his heirs; 145
For, if you should, O, what would come of it!

104–06. In what attitude do you picture Antony as he utters the sentence beginning **Bear with me?** What is he expecting to accomplish by this attitude? 121–22. What idea has Antony carefully planted in the minds of the crowd at the same time that he denies doing so? 124. Has the word **honorable** gained additional force? Pronounce it to yourself as you think Antony would say it here. 133. **napkins:** handkerchiefs.

FOURTH CITIZEN. Read the will! we'll hear it, Antony!
You shall read us the will! Caesar's will!
ANTONY. Will you be patient? will you stay awhile?
I have o'ershot myself to tell you of it:
I fear I wrong the honorable men 150
Whose daggers have stabb'd Caesar; I do fear it.
FOURTH CITIZEN. They were traitors! Honorable men!
ALL. The will! the testament!
SECOND CITIZEN. They were villians, murderers: the will! read the will! 155
ANTONY. You will compel me, then, to read the will?
Then make a ring about the corpse of Caesar,
And let me show you him that made the will.
Shall I descend? and will you give me leave?
SEVERAL CITIZENS. Come down. 160
SECOND CITIZEN. Descend.
THIRD CITIZEN. You shall have leave.

[ANTONY *comes down from the pulpit.*]

FOURTH CITIZEN. A ring; stand round.
FIRST CITIZEN. Stand from the hearse; stand from the body.
SECOND CITIZEN. Room for Antony, most noble Antony! 165
ANTONY. Nay, press not so upon me; stand far off.
SEVERAL CITIZENS. Stand back! room! bear back!
ANTONY. If you have tears, prepare to shed them now.
You all do know this mantle. I remember
The first time ever Caesar put it on; 170
'T was on a summer's evening, in his tent,
That day he overcame the Nervii.
Look, in this place ran Cassius' dagger through.
See what a rent the envious Casca made!
Through this the well-beloved Brutus stabb'd; 175
And as he pluck'd his cursed steel away,
Mark how the blood of Caesar follow'd it,
As rushing out of doors, to be resolved
If Brutus so unkindly knock'd, or no;
For Brutus, as you know, was Caesar's angel. 180
Judge, O you gods, how dearly Caesar lov'd him!
This was the most unkindest cut of all;
For when the noble Caesar saw him stab,
Ingratitude, more strong than traitors' arms,
Quite vanquish'd him: then burst his mighty heart; 185
And, in his mantle muffling up his face,
Even at the base of Pompey's statue,
Which all the while ran blood, great Caesar fell.
O, what a fall was there, my countrymen!
Then I, and you, and all of us fell down, 190
Whilst bloody treason flourish'd over us.

O, now you weep; and, I perceive, you feel
The dint of pity: these are gracious drops.
Kind souls, what! weep you when you but behold
Our Caesar's vesture wounded? Look at you here, 195

[*Lifting the mantle from* CAESAR'S *face*]

Here is himself, marr'd, as you see, with traitors.

FIRST CITIZEN. O piteous spectacle!
SECOND CITIZEN. O noble Caesar!
THIRD CITIZEN. O woeful day!
FOURTH CITIZEN. O traitors, villains! 200
FIRST CITIZEN. O most bloody sight!
SECOND CITIZEN. We will be reveng'd.
ALL. Revenge! About! Seek! Burn! Fire! Kill! Slay!
Let not a traitor live!
ANTONY. Stay, countrymen. 205
FIRST CITIZEN. Peace there! hear the noble Antony.
SECOND CITIZEN. We'll hear him, we'll follow him, we'll die with him!
ANTONY. Good friends, sweet friends, let me not stir you up
To such a sudden flood of mutiny.
They that have done this deed are honorable: 210
What private griefs they have, alas, I know not,
That made them do it: they are wise and honorable,
And will, no doubt, with reasons answer you.
I come not, friends, to steal away your hearts:
I am no orator, as Brutus is; 215
But, as you know me all, a plain blunt man,
That love my friend; and that they know full well
That gave me public leave to speak of him:
For I have neither wit, nor words, nor worth,
Action, nor utterance, nor the power of speech, 220
To stir men's blood: I only speak right on.
I tell you that which you yourselves do know;
Show you sweet Caesar's wounds — poor, poor, dumb mouths! —
And bid them speak for me: but were I Brutus,
And Brutus Antony, there were an Antony 225
Would ruffle up your spirits and put a tongue
In every wound of Caesar that should move
The stones of Rome to rise and mutiny!
ALL. We'll mutiny!
FIRST CITIZEN. We'll burn the house of Brutus. 230
THIRD CITIZEN. Away, then! Come, seek the conspirators!
ANTONY. Yet hear me, countrymen. Yet hear me speak.
ALL. Peace, ho! Hear Antony. Most noble Antony!
ANTONY. Why, friends, you go to do you know not what:
Wherein hath Caesar thus deserv'd your loves? 235

Alas, you know not. I must tell you, then:
You have forgot the will I told you of.

ALL. Most true. The will! Let's stay and hear the will.

ANTONY. Here is the will, and under Caesar's seal.
To every Roman citizen he gives, 240
To every several man, seventy-five drachmas.

SECOND CITIZEN. Most noble Caesar! We'll revenge his death!

THIRD CITIZEN. O royal Caesar!

ANTONY. Hear me with patience.

ALL. Peace, ho! 245

ANTONY. Moreover, he hath left you all his walks,
His private arbors and new-planted orchards,
On this side Tiber; he hath left them you,
And to your heirs forever, common pleasures,
To walk abroad, and recreate yourselves. 250
Here was a Caesar! when comes such another?

FIRST CITIZEN. Never, never! Come, away, away!
We'll burn his body in the holy place,
And with the brands fire the traitors' houses
Take up the body. 255

SECOND CITIZEN. Go fetch fire.

THIRD CITIZEN. Pluck down benches.

FOURTH CITIZEN. Pluck down forms, windows, anything!

[*Exeunt* CITIZENS *with the body.*]

ANTONY. Now let it work. Mischief, thou art afoot,
Take thou what course thou wilt! 260

[*Enter a* SERVANT.]

How now, fellow!

SERVANT. Sir, Octavius is already come to Rome.

ANTONY. Where is he?

SERVANT. He and Lepidus are at Caesar's house.

ANTONY. And thither will I straight to visit him: 265
He comes upon a wish. Fortune is merry,
And in this mood will give us anything.

SERVANT. I heard him say, Brutus and Cassius
Are rid like madmen through the gates of Rome.

ANTONY. Belike they had some notice of the people, 270
How I had mov'd them. Bring me to Octavius.

[*Exeunt.*]

237. Had Antony forgotten to read **the will?** Or did he deliberately postpone reading it? Why? 259. What has Antony finally accomplished? 268–69. What is the first result of Antony's speech? Do not these lines tell you? What has happened? 270–71. Can you imagine what Cassius might have said to Brutus as they fled from the city?

ACT IV

SCENE I. *A house in Rome*

[*More than nineteen months have elapsed since the assassination of Julius Caesar. A " triumvirate " composed of Antony, Octavius, and Lepidus has been proclaimed, and the conspirators have fled from Rome to gather an army in Asia Minor and Greece.*

Sitting around a table with a list of the chief citizens before them, Antony, Octavius, and Lepidus are picking out the names of those whom they suspect to be unfriendly to their cause. Before leaving Rome to combat the forces of Brutus and Cassius in Asia Minor, the triumvirs decide to leave no enemies in their rear. They do not hesitate to add to the list of those who must die the names of their own kinsmen. Today we call such ruthless tactics a " purge."]

[ANTONY, OCTAVIUS, *and* LEPIDUS, *seated at a table*]

ANTONY. These many, then, shall die; their names are prick'd.
OCTAVIUS. Your brother too must die; consent you, Lepidus?
LEPIDUS. I do consent, —
OCTAVIUS. Prick him down, Antony.
LEPIDUS. Upon condition Publius shall not live, 5
Who is your sister's son, Mark Antony.
ANTONY. He shall not live; look, with a spot I damn him.
But, Lepidus, go you to Caesar's house;
Fetch the will hither, and we shall determine
How to cut off some charge in legacies. 10
LEPIDUS. What, shall I find you here?
OCTAVIUS. Or here, or at the Capitol.

[*Exit* LEPIDUS.]

ANTONY. This is a slight unmeritable man,
Meet to be sent on errands: is it fit,
The threefold world divided, he should stand 15
One of the three to share it?
OCTAVIUS. So you thought him;
And took his voice who should be prick'd to die
In our black sentence and proscription.
ANTONY. Octavius, I have seen more days than you: 20
And though we lay these honors on this man
To ease ourselves of divers sland'rous loads,
He shall but bear them as the ass bears gold,
To groan and sweat under the business,
Either led or driven, as we point the way; 25
And having brought our treasure where we will,
Then take we down his load, and turn him off,
Like to the empty ass, to shake his ears,
And graze in commons.

1. Notice how Antony has already changed. The man who mourned the death of Caesar at the hands of the conspirators is now condemning to death those who oppose his will. 9. Do you remember how Antony made use of Caesar's **will** to inflame the mob? Notice what he is doing now.

OCTAVIUS. You may do your will; 30
But he's a tried and valiant soldier.
ANTONY. So is my horse, Octavius; and for that
I do appoint him store of provender:
It is a creature that I teach to fight,
To wind, to stop, to run directly on, 35
His corporal motion govern'd by my spirit.
And, in some taste, is Lepidus but so;
He must be taught and train'd and bid go forth;
A barren-spirited fellow; one that feeds
On abjects, orts and imitations, 40
Which, out of use and staled by other men,
Begin his fashion: do not talk of him,
But as a property. And now, Octavius,
Listen great things: — Brutus and Cassius
Are levying powers: we must straight make head: 45
Therefore let our alliance be combin'd,
Our best friends made, our means stretch'd;
And let us presently go sit in council
How covert matters may be best disclos'd,
And open perils surest answered. 50
OCTAVIUS. Let us do so: for we are at the stake,
And bay'd about with many enemies;
And some that smile have in their hearts, I fear,
Millions of mischiefs.

[*Exeunt.*]

40. **abjects:** things thrown away. 40. **orts:** fragments. 51. **at the stake:** a comparison that comes from the sport of bearbaiting popular in Shakespeare's time, in which a bear was tied to a stake and tormented by dogs.

SCENE II. *Camp near Sardis. Before* BRUTUS'S *tent*

[*About a year has elapsed since the last scene. Brutus and Cassius are encamped near Sardis, an ancient city in Asia Minor, famous once as the western terminal of the old royal road of Cyrus the Great and again as a city in flames that started the war between the Greeks and the Persians. Since their flight from Rome, after Mark Antony had turned the people against them, the conspirators have been raising a large army in Macedonia, Greece, and Asia Minor.*

For this scene you may imagine a military encampment with a spotlight turned on Brutus's tent, and Brutus dressed in armor.]

[*Drum. Enter* BRUTUS, LUCILIUS, LUCIUS, *and* SOLDIERS; TITINIUS *and* PINDARUS *meeting them.*]

BRUTUS. Stand, ho!
LUCILIUS. Give the word, ho! and stand.
BRUTUS. What now, Lucilius! is Cassius near?
LUCILIUS. He is at hand; and Pindarus is come
To do you salutation from his master. 5

BRUTUS. He greets me well. Your master, Pindarus,
In his own change, or by ill officers,
Hath given me some worthy cause to wish
Things done, undone: but, if he be at hand,
I shall be satisfied. 10

PINDARUS. I do not doubt
But that my noble master will appear
Such as he is, full of regard and honor.

BRUTUS. He is not doubted. A word, Lucilius.
How he received you, let me be resolved. 15

LUCILIUS. With courtesy and with respect enough;
But not with such familiar instances,
Nor with such free and friendly conference,
As he hath used of old.

BRUTUS. Thou hast described 20
A hot friend cooling: ever note, Lucilius,
When love begins to sicken and decay,
It useth an enforced ceremony.
There are no tricks in plain and simple faith;
But hollow men, like horses hot at hand, 25
Make gallant show and promise of their mettle:
But when they should endure the bloody spur,
They fall their crests, and, like deceitful jades,
Sink in the trial. Comes his army on?

LUCILIUS. They mean this night in Sardis to be quarter'd; 30
The greater part, the horse in general,
Are come with Cassius.

BRUTUS. Hark! he is arriv'd.

[*Low march within*]

March gently on to meet him.

[*Enter* CASSIUS *and his powers.*]

CASSIUS. Stand, ho! 35

BRUTUS. Stand, ho! Speak the word along.

FIRST SOLDIER. Stand!

SECOND SOLDIER. Stand!

THIRD SOLDIER. Stand!

CASSIUS. Most noble brother, you have done me wrong. 40

BRUTUS. Judge me, you gods! wrong I mine enemies?
And, if not so, how should I wrong a brother?

CASSIUS. Brutus, this sober form of yours hides wrongs;
And when you do them —

BRUTUS. Cassius, be content; 45
Speak your griefs softly: I do know you well.
Before the eyes of both our armies here,
Which should perceive nothing but love from us,

Let us not wrangle: bid them move away;
Then in my tent, Cassius, enlarge your griefs, 50
And I will give you audience.

CASSIUS. Pindarus,
Bid our commanders lead their charges off
A little from this ground.

BRUTUS. Lucilius, do you the like; and let no man 55
Come to our tent till we have done our conference.
Let Lucius and Titinius guard our door.

[*Exeunt.*]

SCENE III. BRUTUS'S *tent*

[*Imagine the interior of Brutus's tent. In this scene, considered by some critics the greatest single scene in the play, the two generals take up their quarrel in private, with Titinius, a friend, and Lucius, a trusted servant, on guard at the door.*]

[*Enter* BRUTUS *and* CASSIUS.]

CASSIUS. That you have wrong'd me doth appear in this:
You have condemn'd and noted Lucius Pella
For taking bribes here of the Sardians;
Wherein my letters, praying on his side
Because I knew the man, were slighted off. 5

BRUTUS. You wrong'd yourself to write in such a case.

CASSIUS. In such a time as this it is not meet
That every nice offense should bear his comment.

BRUTUS. Let me tell you, Cassius, you yourself
Are much condemn'd to have an itching palm; 10
To sell and mart your offices for gold
To undeservers.

CASSIUS. I an itching palm!
You know that you are Brutus that speaks this,
Or, by the gods, this speech were else your last! 15

BRUTUS. The name of Cassius honors this corruption,
And chastisement doth therefore hide his head.

CASSIUS. Chastisement!

BRUTUS. Remember March, the ides of March remember:
Did not great Julius bleed for justice's sake? 20
What villain touch'd his body, that did stab,
And not for justice? What, shall one of us,
That struck the foremost man of all this world
But for supporting robbers, shall we now
Contaminate our fingers with base bribes, 25
And sell the mighty space of our large honors

2. **noted:** marked for disgrace. Guess what it was the Sardians bribed Lucius Pella to give them? 8. **nice:** trivial. Cassius is saying that Brutus should not comment upon every trivial offense. 16. Brutus is saying in effect that when a person as great as Cassius is corrupt he goes unpunished. 24. **but for supporting robbers:** One of the reasons for killing Caesar, which Brutus cites, is that Caesar himself protected those who robbed and "spoiled" under his authority.

For so much trash as may be grasped thus?
I had rather be a dog, and bay the moon,
Than such a Roman.

CASSIUS.. Brutus, bait not me! 30
I'll not endure it. You forget yourself,
To hedge me in; I am a soldier, I,
Older in practice, abler than yourself
To make conditions.

BRUTUS. Go to; you are not, Cassius. 35

CASSIUS. I am.

BRUTUS. I say you are not.

CASSIUS. Urge me no more, I shall forget myself.
Have mind upon your health! tempt me no further.

BRUTUS. Away, slight man! 40

CASSIUS. Is 't possible?

BRUTUS. Hear me, for I will speak.
Must I give way and room to your rash choler?
Shall I be frightened when a madman stares?

CASSIUS. O ye gods, ye gods! must I endure all this? 45

BRUTUS. All this! ay, more: fret till your proud heart break;
Go show your slaves how choleric you are,
And make your bondmen tremble. Must I budge?
Must I observe you? must I stand and crouch
Under your testy humor? By the gods, 50
You shall digest the venom of your spleen,
Though it do split you! for, from this day forth,
I'll use you for my mirth, yea, for my laughter,
When you are waspish.

CASSIUS. Is it come to this? 55

BRUTUS. You say you are a better soldier:
Let it appear so; make your vaunting true,
And it shall please me well: for mine own part,
I shall be glad to learn of noble men.

CASSIUS. You wrong me every way; you wrong me, Brutus; 60
I said, an elder soldier, not a better:
Did I say "better"?

BRUTUS. If you did, I care not.

CASSIUS. When Caesar liv'd, he durst not thus have mov'd me.

BRUTUS. Peace, peace! you durst not so have tempted him. 65

CASSIUS. I durst not!

BRUTUS. No.

CASSIUS. What! durst not tempt him!

BRUTUS. For your life you durst not.

CASSIUS. Do not presume too much upon my love; 70
I may do that I shall be sorry for.

51. The **spleen** was considered the seat of the passions. 69. Here Brutus looks straight at Cassius and says each word very slowly.

BRUTUS. You have done that you should be sorry for.
There is no terror, Cassius, in your threats,
For I am arm'd so strong in honesty
That they pass by me as the idle wind, 75
Which I respect not. I did send to you
For certain sums of gold, which you denied me:
For I can raise no money by vile means.
By heaven, I had rather coin my heart,
And drop my blood for drachmas, than to wring 80
From the hard hands of peasants their vile trash
By any indirection. I did send
To you for gold to pay my legions,
Which you denied me: was that done like Cassius?
Should I have answer'd Caius Cassius so? 85
When Marcus Brutus grows so covetous,
To lock such rascal counters from his friends,
Be ready, gods, with all your thunderbolts;
Dash him to pieces!

CASSIUS. I denied you not. 90

BRUTUS. You did.

CASSIUS. I did not: he was but a fool that brought
My answer back. Brutus hath riv'd my heart:
A friend should bear his friend's infirmities,
But Brutus makes mine greater than they are. 95

BRUTUS. I do not, till you practice them on me.

CASSIUS. You love me not.

BRUTUS. I do not like your faults.

CASSIUS. A friendly eye could never see such faults.

BRUTUS. A flatterer's would not, though they do appear 100
As huge as high Olympus.

CASSIUS. Come, Antony, and young Octavius, come!
Revenge yourselves alone on Cassius,
For Cassius is aweary of the world;
Hated by one he loves; brav'd by his brother; 105
Check'd like a bondman; all his faults observ'd,
Set in a notebook, learn'd, and conn'd by rote,
To cast into my teeth. O, I could weep
My spirit from mine eyes! There is my dagger,
And here my naked breast; within, a heart 110
Dearer than Plutus's mine, richer than gold:
If that thou be be'st a Roman, take it forth;
I, that denied thee gold, will give my heart.
Strike, as thou didst at Caesar; for, I know,
When thou didst hate him worst, thou lovedst him better 115
Than ever thou lovedst Cassius!

93–94. Notice that Cassius is changing his attitude. He half admits, now, that he has been guilty. Why do you suppose he changes his tactics?

BRUTUS. Sheathe your dagger:
Be angry when you will, it shall have scope;
Do what you will, dishonor shall be humor.
O Cassius, you are yoked with a lamb 120
That carries anger as the flint bears fire;
Who, much enforced, shows a hasty spark,
And straight is cold again.

CASSIUS. Hath Cassius liv'd
To be but mirth and laughter to his Brutus, 125
When grief and blood ill-temper'd, vexeth him?

BRUTUS. When I spoke that, I was ill-temper'd too.

CASSIUS. Do you confess so much? Give me your hand.

BRUTUS. And my heart too.

CASSIUS. O Brutus! 130

BRUTUS. What's the matter?

CASSIUS. Have not you love enough to bear with me,
When that rash humor which my mother gave me
Makes me forgetful?

BRUTUS. Yes, Cassius; and, from henceforth, 135
When you are overearnest with your Brutus,
He'll think your mother chides, and leave you so.
(*He calls loudly.*) Lucius, a bowl of wine.

CASSIUS. I did not think you could have been so angry.

BRUTUS. O Cassius, I am sick of many griefs. 140
Portia is dead.

CASSIUS. Ha! Portia!

BRUTUS. She is dead.

CASSIUS. How 'scaped I killing when I cross'd you so?
O insupportable and touching loss! 145
Upon what sickness?

BRUTUS. Impatient of my absence,
And grief that young Octavius with Mark Antony
Have made themselves so strong: — for with her death
That tidings came; — with this she fell distract, 150
And, her attendants absent, swallow'd fire.

CASSIUS. And died so?

BRUTUS. Even so.

CASSIUS. O ye immortal gods!

[*Enter* LUCIUS *with wine and taper.*]

BRUTUS. Speak no more of her. Give me a bowl of wine. 155
In this I bury all unkindness, Cassius. (*Drinks.*)
Come in, Titinius!

[*Exit* LUCIUS. *Enter* TITINIUS, *with* MESSALA.]

Welcome, good Messala.

Now sit we close about this taper here,
And call in question our necessities. 160

CASSIUS. Portia, art thou gone?

BRUTUS. No more, I pray you.
Messala, I have here received letters,
That young Octavius and Mark Antony
Come down upon us with a mighty power, 165
Bending their expedition toward Philippi.

MESSALA. Myself have letters of the selfsame tenor.

BRUTUS. With what addition?

MESSALA. That by proscription and bills of outlawry,
Octavius, Antony, and Lepidus 170
Have put to death an hundred senators.

BRUTUS. Therein our letters do not well agree;
Mine speak of seventy senators that died
By their proscriptions, Cicero being one.

CASSIUS. Cicero one! 175

BRUTUS. Well, to our work alive. What do you think
Of marching to Philippi presently?

CASSIUS. I do not think it good.

BRUTUS. Your reason?

CASSIUS. This it is: 180
'Tis better that the enemy seek us:
So shall he waste his means, weary his soldiers,
Doing himself offense; whilst we, lying still,
Are full of rest, defense, and nimbleness.

BRUTUS. Good reasons must, of force, give place to better, 185
The people 'twixt Philippi and this ground
Do stand but in a forc'd affection;
For they have grudg'd us contribution:
The enemy, marching along by them,
By them shall make a fuller number up, 190
Come on refresh'd, new-added, and encourag'd;
From which advantage shall we cut him off,
If at Philippi we do face him there,
These people at our back.

CASSIUS. Hear me, good brother. 195

BRUTUS. Under your pardon. You must note beside,
That we have tried the utmost of our friends,
Our legions are brimful, our cause is ripe:
The enemy increaseth every day;
We, at the height, are ready to decline. 200
There is a tide in the affairs of men,
Which, taken at the flood, leads on to fortune:
Omitted, all the voyage of their life

181. Brutus fears that Antony's forces might be able to win over the people between Philippi and Sardis to his own cause, and thus swell his numbers.

Is bound in shallows and in miseries.
On such a full sea are we now afloat; 205
And we must take the current when it serves,
Or lose our ventures.

CASSIUS. Then, with your will, go on;
We'll along ourselves, and meet them at Philippi.

BRUTUS. The deep of night is crept upon our talk, 210
And nature must obey necessity;
Which we will niggard with a little rest.
There is no more to say?

CASSIUS. No more. Good night:
Early tomorrow will we rise, and hence. 215

BRUTUS. Lucius!

[*Enter* LUCIUS.]

My gown.

[*Exit* LUCIUS.]

Farewell, good Messala.
Good night, Titinius. Noble, noble Cassius,
Good night, and good repose. 220

CASSIUS. O my dear brother!
This was an ill beginning of the night:
Never come such division 'tween our souls!
Let it not, Brutus.

BRUTUS. Everything is well. 225

CASSIUS. Good night, my lord.

BRUTUS. Good night, good brother.

TITINIUS. MESSALA. Good night, Lord Brutus.

BRUTUS. Farewell, everyone.

[*Exeunt all but* BRUTUS. *Re-enter* LUCIUS, *with the gown.*]

Give me the gown. Where is thy instrument? 230

LUCIUS. Here in the tent.

BRUTUS. What, thou speak'st drowsily?
Poor knave, I blame thee not; thou art o'erwatched.
Call Claudius and some other of my men;
I'll have them sleep on cushions in my tent. 235

LUCIUS. Varro and Claudius!

[*Enter* VARRO *and* CLAUDIUS.]

VARRO. Calls my lord?

BRUTUS. I pray you, sirs, lie in my tent and sleep;
It may be I shall raise you by and by
On business to my brother Cassius. 240

206–07. Twice before Brutus's opinion has prevailed. Do you remember when, and with what results? 230. The **instrument** referred to was a kind of stringed instrument.

VARRO. So please you, we will stand and watch your pleasure.
BRUTUS. I will not have it so: lie down, good sirs;
It may be I shall otherwise bethink me.
Look, Lucius, here's the book I sought for so;
I put it in the pocket of my gown. 245

[VARRO *and* CLAUDIUS *lie down.*]

LUCIUS. I was sure your lordship did not give it me.
BRUTUS. Bear with me, good boy, I am much forgetful.
Canst thou hold up thy heavy eyes awhile,
And touch thy instrument a strain or two?
LUCIUS. Ay, my lord, an 't please you. 250
BRUTUS. It does, my boy:
I trouble thee too much, but thou art willing.
LUCIUS. It is my duty, sir.
BRUTUS. I should not urge thy duty past thy might,
I know young bloods look for a time of rest. 255
LUCIUS. I have slept, my lord, already.
BRUTUS. It was well done; and thou shalt sleep again;
I will not hold thee long. If I do live,
I will be good to thee.

[*Music, and a song*]

This is a sleepy tune. O murd'rous slumber, 260
Lay'st thou thy leaden mace upon my boy,
That plays the music? Gentle knave, good night;
I will not do thee so much wrong to wake thee.
If thou dost nod, thou break'st thy instrument;
I'll take it from thee. And, good boy, good night. 265
Let me see, let me see; is not the leaf turn'd down
Where I left reading? Here it is, I think.

[*Enter the Ghost of* CAESAR.]

How ill this taper burns! Ha! who comes here?
I think it is the weakness of mine eyes
That shapes this monstrous apparition. 270
It comes upon me. Art thou anything?
Art thou some god, some angel, or some devil,
That mak'st my blood cold and my hair to stare?
Speak to me what thou art.
GHOST. Thy evil spirit, Brutus. 275
BRUTUS. Why com'st thou?
GHOST. To tell thee thou shalt see me at Philippi.
BRUTUS. Well; then I shall see thee again?
GHOST. Ay, at Philippi.

258. Notice that Brutus seems to have some doubt about the outcome of tomorrow. Have you?
268. The presence of a ghost was supposed to cause the lights to burn blue.

BRUTUS. Why, I will see thee at Philippi, then. 280

[*Exit Ghost.*]

Now I have taken heart thou vanishest:
Ill spirit, I would hold more talk with thee.
Boy, Lucius! Varro! Claudius! Sirs, awake!
Claudius!

LUCIUS. The strings, my lord, are false. 285
BRUTUS. He thinks he still is at his instrument.
Lucius, awake!
LUCIUS. My lord?
BRUTUS. Didst thou dream, Lucius, that thou so criedst out?
LUCIUS. My lord, I do not know that I did cry. 290
BRUTUS. Yes, that thou didst: didst thou see anything?
LUCIUS. Nothing, my lord.
BRUTUS. Sleep again, Lucius. Sirrah Claudius! (*To* VARRO)
Fellow thou, awake!
VARRO. My lord? 295
CLAUDIUS. My lord?
BRUTUS. Why did you so cry out, sirs, in your sleep?
VARRO. CLAUDIUS. Did we, my lord?
BRUTUS. Ay: saw you anything?
VARRO. No, my lord, I saw nothing. 300
CLAUDIUS. Nor I, my lord.
BRUTUS. Go and commend me to my brother Cassius:
Bid him set on his powers betimes before,
And we will follow.
VARRO. CLAUDIUS. It shall be done, my lord. 305

[*Exeunt.*]

ACT V

SCENE I. *The plains of Philippi*

[*Philippi was a city founded by Philip of Macedon, the father of Alexander the Great. Cassius' and Brutus's armies are here to meet the armies of Antony and Octavius coming from Rome. The scene is a desolate plain edged with low hills and jutting rocks.*]

[*March. Drum. Enter* BRUTUS, CASSIUS, *and their* ARMY; LUCILIUS, TITINIUS, MESSALA, *and others.*]

CASSIUS. Now, most noble Brutus,
The gods today stand friendly, that we may,
Lovers in peace, lead on our days to age!
But since the affairs of men rest still incertain,
Let's reason with the worst that may befall. 5
If we do lose this battle, then is this

The very last time we shall speak together:
What are you then determined to do?
You are contented to be led in triumph
Through the streets of Rome? 10

BRUTUS. No, Cassius, no: think not, thou noble Roman,
That ever Brutus will go bound to Rome;
He bears too great a mind. But this same day
Must end that work the ides of March begun;
And whether we shall meet again I know not. 15
Therefore our everlasting farewell take:
For ever, and for ever, farewell, Cassius!
If we do meet again, why, we shall smile;
If not, why then, this parting was well made.

CASSIUS. For ever, and for ever, farewell, Brutus! 20
If we do meet again, we'll smile indeed;
If not, 't is true this parting was well made.

BRUTUS. Why, then, lead on. O, that a man might know
The end of this day's business ere it come!
But it sufficeth that the day will end, 25
And then the end is known. Come, ho! away!

[*Exeunt.*]

SCENE II. *The field of battle*

[*Alarums. Enter* CASSIUS *and* TITINIUS.]

CASSIUS. O, look, Titinius, look, the villains fly!
Myself have to mine own turn'd enemy:
This ensign here of mine was turning back;
I slew the coward, and did take it from him.

TITINIUS. O Cassius, Brutus gave the word too early; 5
Who, having some advantage on Octavius,
Took it too eagerly: his soldiers fell to spoil,
Whilst we by Antony are all inclos'd.

[*Enter* PINDARUS.]

PINDARUS. Fly further off, my lord, fly further off!
Mark Antony is in your tents, my lord: 10
Fly, therefore, noble Cassius, fly far off!

CASSIUS. This hill is far enough. Look, look, Titinius;
Are those my tents where I perceive the fire?

TITINIUS. They are, my lord.

CASSIUS. Titinius, if thou lovest me, 15
Mount thou my horse, and hide thy spurs in him

1–2. Cassius' soldiers, obeying Brutus's orders to attack Octavius' wing, failed to watch the enemy's other wing and were soon surrounded by the troops of Mark Antony. Whereupon some of Cassius' horsemen and footmen broke rank and fled for their lives toward the sea. 3–4. Perceiving his soldiers losing ground, Cassius did his best to keep them from fleeing. He took an **ensign** (flag) from one of the ensign-bearers and stuck it fast at his feet, but he failed to check the retreat.

Till he have brought thee up to yonder troops,
And here again; that I may rest assured
Whether yond troops are friend or enemy.

TITINIUS. I will be here again, even with a thought. (*Exit.*) 20

CASSIUS. Go, Pindarus, get higher on that hill;
My sight was ever thick; regard Titinius,
And tell me what thou not'st about the field.

[PINDARUS *ascends the hill.*]

This day I breathed first: time is come round,
And where I did begin, there shall I end; 25
My life is run his compass. Sirrah, what news?

PINDARUS (*above*). O my lord!

CASSIUS. What news?

PINDARUS (*above*). Titinius is inclosed round about
With horsemen, that make to him on the spur! 30
Yet he spurs on! Now they are almost on him!
Now, Titinius! Now some light. O, he lights too.
He's ta'en! (*Shout*) And, hark, they shout for joy.

CASSIUS. Come down; behold no more.
O, coward that I am, to live so long 35
To see my best friend ta'en before my face!

[PINDARUS *descends.*]

Come hither, sirrah:
In Parthia did I take thee prisoner;
And then I swore thee, saving of thy life,
That whatsoever I did bid thee do, 40
Thou shouldst attempt it. Come now, keep thine oath;
Now be a freeman: and with this good sword,
That ran through Caesar's bowels, search this bosom.
Stand not to answer: here, take thou the hilts;
And, when my face is cover'd, as 't is now, 45
Guide thou the sword.

[PINDARUS *guides the blade while* CASSIUS *falls upon it.*]

Caesar, thou art reveng'd,
Even with the sword that kill'd thee. (*Dies.*)

PINDARUS. So, I am free; yet would not so have been,
Durst I have done my will. O Cassius, 50
Far from this country Pindarus shall run,
Where never Roman shall take note of him. (*Exit.*)

[*Exit.*]

19. These are troops that Brutus has sent to aid Cassius. They are **friend.** 29–33. Pindarus does not interpret the scene correctly. Titinius is **inclosed** by friends who shout for joy at Brutus's victory over Octavius.

[*The stage has been darkening slowly. After Pindarus' disappearance, all is still; but in the distance the noise of battle continues. Messala hastens across the stage, discovers Cassius, turns, and rushes back in the direction from which he came.*]

[*Re-enter* MESSALA *with* BRUTUS, *young* CATO, STRATO, VOLUMNIUS, *and* LUCILIUS.]

BRUTUS. Where, where, Messala, doth his body lie?
MESSALA. Lo, yonder.
CATO. He is slain. 55
BRUTUS. O Julius Caesar, thou art mighty yet!
Thy spirit walks abroad, and turns our swords
In our own proper entrails.

[*Low alarums*]

The last of all the Romans, fare thee well!
It is impossible that ever Rome 60
Should breed thy fellow. Friends, I owe more tears
To this dead man than you shall see me pay.
I shall find time, Cassius, I shall find time.
Come, therefore, and to Thasos send his body:
His funerals shall not be in our camp, 65
Lest it discomfort us. Lucilius, come;
And come, young Cato; let us to the field.
'T is three o'clock; and, Romans, yet ere night
We shall try fortune in a second fight.

[*Exeunt.*]

SCENE III. *Another part of the field*

[*The most important detail in this scene is mentioned in the first line: a large rock on which Brutus and his friends sit down to take counsel, after fleeing from capture since the last scene. Night is upon them, and it is difficult to recognize their faces.*]

[*Enter* BRUTUS, DARDANIUS, CLITUS, STRATO, *and* VOLUMNIUS.]

BRUTUS. Come, poor remains of friends, rest on this rock.
CLITUS. Statilius show'd the torchlight, but, my lord,
He came not back: he is or ta'en or slain.
BRUTUS. Sit thee down, Clitus: slaying is the word;
It is a deed in fashion. Hark thee, Clitus. (*Whispering*) 5
CLITUS. What, I, my lord? No, not for all the world.
BRUTUS. Peace then! no words.
CLITUS. I'll rather kill myself.
BRUTUS. Hark thee, Dardanius. (*Whispering*)
DARDANIUS. Shall I do such a deed? 10
CLITUS. O Dardanius!
DARDANIUS. O Clitus!

2. Statilius is a scout sent out by Brutus to check up on the results of the battle. If all went well with him, he was to signal with a **torchlight** once. After he had shown his torch once, he was captured and slain.

CLITUS. What ill request did Brutus make to thee?
DARDANIUS. To kill him, Clitus. Look, he meditates.
CLITUS. Now is that noble vessel full of grief, 15
That it runs over even at his eyes.
BRUTUS. Come hither, good Volumnius; list a word.
VOLUMINIUS. What says my lord?
BRUTUS. Why, this, Volumnius:
The ghost of Caesar hath appear'd to me 20
Two several times by night; at Sardis once,
And, this last night, here in Philippi fields:
I know my hour is come.
VOLUMNIUS. Not so, my lord.
BRUTUS. Nay, I am sure it is, Volumnius. 25
Thou seest the world, Volumnius, how it goes;
Our enemies have beat us to the pit:

[*Low alarums*]

It is more worthy to leap in ourselves,
Than to tarry till they push us. Good Volumnius,
Thou know'st that we two went to school together: 30
Even for that our love of old, I prithee,
Hold thou my sword hilts, whilst I run on it.
VOLUMNIUS. That's not an office for a friend, my lord.

[*Alarum still*]

CLITUS. Fly, fly, my lord; there is no tarrying here.
BRUTUS. Farewell to you; and you; and you, Volumnius. 35
Strato, thou has been all this while asleep;
Farewell to thee too, Strato. Countrymen,
My heart doth joy that yet in all my life
I found no man but he was true to me.
I shall have glory by this losing day 40
More than Octavius and Mark Antony
By this vile conquest shall attain unto.
So fare you well at once; for Brutus's tongue
Hath almost ended his life's history:
Night hangs upon mine eyes; my bones would rest, 45
That have but labor'd to attain this hour.

[*Alarum. Cry within,* "Fly, fly, fly!"]

CLITUS. Fly, my lord, fly.
BRUTUS. Hence! I will follow.

[*Exeunt* CLITUS, DARDANIUS, *and* VOLUMNIUS.]

I prithee, Strato, stay thou by thy lord:
Thou art a fellow of a good respect; 50

36. Notice that Strato has not been influenced by the refusal of the others to kill Brutus. Watch to see whether this makes any difference.

Thy life hath had some snatch of honor in it:
Hold then my sword, and turn away thy face,
While I do run upon it. Wilt thou, Strato?

STRATO. Give me your hand first. Fare you well, my lord.

BRUTUS. Farewell, good Strato. (*Runs on his sword.*) 55
Caesar, now be still:
I kill'd not thee with half so good a will. (*Dies.*)

[*Alarum. Retreat. Enter* OCTAVIUS, ANTONY, *and the* ARMY.]

[*Standing sadly near the body of his dead friend, Strato averts his face and pays no attention to the entering troops. Octavius halts the men while Antony walks forward and kneels. He regards the face of Brutus intently; then looking toward the distant plain, he speaks slowly and as if to himself.*]

ANTONY. This was the noblest Roman of them all:
All the conspirators, save only he,
Did that they did in envy of great Caesar;
He only, in a general honest thought 60
And common good to all, made one of them.
His life was gentle, and the elements
So mix'd in him that Nature might stand up
And say to all the world "This was a man!"

[*Exeunt.*]

THINK BACK OVER WHAT YOU HAVE READ

Understanding the Pattern of the Play

Act I

1. Developments in the story (or plot) must happen more quickly in a play than in a novel. For what reason? What is accomplished by the very first scene in this play? What purpose did Shakespeare have in mind when he wrote this scene? Could you think of another beginning just as effective?

2. In almost every drama there is a struggle between opposing forces. How soon do you know, in this play, what the opposing forces are to be? What characters will surely be drawn into the struggle?

3. What effect does Shakespeare want Cassius to have on the audience? How does he talk and act? Does he use gestures? Is he nervous or calm? Why would the whole play be ruined if Cassius should strike the audience as an amusing character?

4. Pay close attention to the difference between the characters of Brutus and Cassius. Which one is a thinker? Which one a doer? Which one is idealistic and gentle? Is it Brutus or Cassius who is practical and shrewd? The contrast between the two is one of Shakespeare's master strokes. In your school which type gets elected to class offices? Which type succeeds best in the politics of your state? Perhaps you can name a statesman who combines both qualities.

5. Caesar's speeches in scene II are not at all useful in furthering the actual plot of this drama. What purpose, then, did Shakespeare have in mind when he wrote Caesar's speeches?

6. What motive lies behind the following words of Cassius to Casca?
"Where hast thou led me? I perhaps speak this
Before a willing bondman."
Has Cassius really forgotten himself? Or were these words spoken with deliberate intent?

Act II

7. Does it disturb you to have Brutus talk out loud to himself at the beginning of this act? Before you condemn this old stage convention, which Shakespeare's audience never questioned, discuss with your classmates some

of the silent movies, scarcely fifteen years old, which have recently been revived. What made audiences laugh at them? Will high-school students of the future laugh at any of our plays and movies? Will they be surprised to learn that we considered blindness pathetic but used deaf people as comic characters? Imagine yourself in the year 3000 viewing a historic relic from twentieth-century Hollywood. What, do you think, would seem odd or strange to you? By the way, why *does* Shakespeare have Brutus talk out loud? How do modern dramatists meet this problem, or do they have trouble too?

8. How should Ligarius deliver his speech at the end of scene 1? What reaction did Shakespeare expect from the audience?

9. Are Brutus's motives becoming an important consideration in the plot of this drama? With what reasons did Brutus convince himself that for the good of Rome Caesar must die? In what two particulars did Brutus influence the conspirators' plans? What indication did Brutus give that he did not relish the thought of joining in a plot to kill his friend?

10. Is there someone in your class who will act out the scene between Caesar, Calpurnia, and Decius Brutus? How should Decius and Caesar speak in order to reveal their characters? How do Shakespeare's lines help to characterize the two men? Why is this a scene of great suspense whenever *Julius Caesar* is acted before an audience?

11. Caesar's courtesy toward the conspirators is meant to have what effect on the audience?

12. How do Brutus and Caesar differ in their attitude toward their wives? What purpose might Shakespeare have had in mind?

Act III

13. The French have long believed that every good drama should have one scene that must be played, that cannot possibly be omitted — a scene that is obligatory. Which scene, Caesar's death or Antony's speech, would a producer be *obliged* to retain if he were eliminating one of them? In the movies you have seen lately have there been any obligatory scenes?

14. What moment did Casca choose for rearing the first hand? Was it a dramatic moment? Why?

15. Contrast the speeches of Brutus and Antony.

16. Did you notice that Shakespeare almost gets "caught" at one place in this act? How does he manage, just before Antony's funeral speech, to get Brutus off the stage without permitting the rattlebrained crowd to follow him?

17. Why did Cassius fear to have Antony speak at Caesar's funeral? How did Brutus convince him that it would be to the advantage of the conspirators? How did Antony convince the conspirators that he was loyal to their cause in spite of his friendship for Caesar? What indication did you find that Antony was to remain loyal to Caesar?

Act IV

18. Antony, Octavius, and Lepidus are the "triumvirate" in power. What do you think of the three? Which one is weakest? most dishonest? Which one reveals neither strength or weakness, remaining an unknown factor in the future?

19. What is the unimportant incident which Cassius and Brutus quarrel over? What do you think is the real reason for their harsh words to each other? Are you disappointed in them or sorry for them?

20. In your opinion does the scene in which Lucius falls asleep over his harp have any purpose in this play? Why not omit it?

Act V

21. Did Cassius and Brutus part for the last time as friends or enemies? Would the play be more or less tragic if their parting had been otherwise? Don't answer hastily but consider the problem thoughtfully.

22. Who dies first, Cassius or Brutus? Does this seem appropriate?

23. A drama as stirring as *Julius Caesar* needs to end conclusively and suitably. Has the conflict which started *Julius Caesar* come to an end? Is the final speech effective when spoken by Antony, or would you prefer to have Strato speak it? Why?

Relating Julius Caesar *to the World of Today*

24. Have you ever considered very carefully the meaning of democracy? Just what are the basic differences between a republic and a dictatorship? Is it important for ordinary people to think or discuss politics in a totalitarian country? in a democracy?

25. Why do dictators have to dispose of their opponents as Caesar does with Marillus

and Flavius? How does a president or a governor in a democracy treat his opponents?

26. How important is propaganda in the modern world? What is your reaction to the following statements from *Mein Kampf* by Adolf Hitler? The first one is from Chapter X; the second, from Chapter VI.

a. "By and large, readers may be divided into three groups:
Those who believe everything they read;
Those who no longer believe anything;
Those minds which critically examine what they read, and judge accordingly.

"The first group is numerically far the largest. This constitutes the great masses of the people, and accordingly represents the most simple-minded part of the nation. . . . Today, when the ballots of the masses are final, the decisive factor is with the most numerous group, and this is the first class: the crowd of the simple-minded or credulous."

b. "All propaganda must be popular in tone, and must keep its intellectual level to the capacity of the least intelligent among those at whom it is directed. . . . And if it is necessary, as in the case of propaganda for the sustaining of a war, to affect a whole people, there can never be enough caution about avoiding excessive intellectual demands."

What is Hitler's impression of most people? How does it conflict with the American ideal? Judging from Hitler's statements, what courses in your school would he eliminate?

27. Was Mark Antony's opinion of the common people of Rome similar to Hitler's opinion of the great masses of the people? Does Antony burden the people with any difficult ideas?

28. What accounts for Antony's actions after Caesar's assassination? Is he really interested in avenging his friend's death, or does he stir up a civil war for some other reason? What are some of the reasons which cause wars? Were the reasons the same in Caesar's time as they are today?

29. At one time Antony says, "I am no orator, as Brutus is; but, as you know me all, a plain blunt man." Does this remind you of anything which is frequently done by office seekers who want votes?

30. Are there indications that any Brutuses exist in the dictator countries today? In world history what attempts, successful or unsuccessful, have been made to assassinate dictators or tyrants?

31. How can America avoid dictatorship? What kind of citizens will we need? Is there anything you yourself can do to help while you are still in school?

32. In your own life what decisions have been difficult to make because, as in Brutus's case, no one solution seemed entirely right? Perhaps you have noticed classmates cheating in an examination. Should you lose their regard by reporting them or have your own examination score lowered by remaining silent?

33. Does power increase a man's desire for more and more power? From your study of history what men do you recall who have attained positions of great power?

34. How do you explain Cassius' motives? Do you find it easy to make a decision about Cassius, or is he so human that his character has both good and bad elements?

35. Perhaps there is something more in what Cassius said about Caesar than mere envy. Do you think so? Is it good for people to worship leaders blindly? Is it good for the leader to be thus worshiped? Or is Cassius like some fellow students you know, always happiest when talking against someone who is popular or successful?

36. Think back over the play. Of the various men who talked of acting for the good of Rome, how many had selfish motives? Was there a single one who remained true to an ideal? Was Brutus wholly unselfish, or can you discover some falseness in him?

Visualizing Julius Caesar *on the Elizabethan Stage*

One of the difficulties of producing *Julius Caesar,* or any other Shakespearean play, on a modern stage is the difficulty of shifting the setting for so many scenes. The long waits between acts while the properties of a street scene, for example, are whisked away to make room for those of the interior of the Roman Capitol make the witnessing of the play on a modern stage for some people something of an endurance contest. This was not true in Shakespeare's day. Acted upon the stage for which the play was intended, the short scenes of *Julius Caesar* created no problem of staging at all. On the contrary, by alternating between the "inner stage" and the "outer stage," the play progressed from one scene to another with only the briefest interruptions.

The outer stage of the Elizabethan theater,

as you may see from the drawing on page 514,[1] was a raised platform projecting out into the "pit," or yard. It was without scenery and for the most part without properties. Such stage directions in *Julius Caesar* as "A public place" or "A street near the Capitol" or "The field of battle" indicate that the scene was designed for the outer stage.

stage was thus revealed as the interior of the senate house. Or, in similar fashion, scene III of Act IV, within "Brutus's tent," followed close upon scene II, "Before Brutus's tent," with no more effort than that required to draw the curtains.

Windows over each of the two doors on either side of the stage were used whenever the

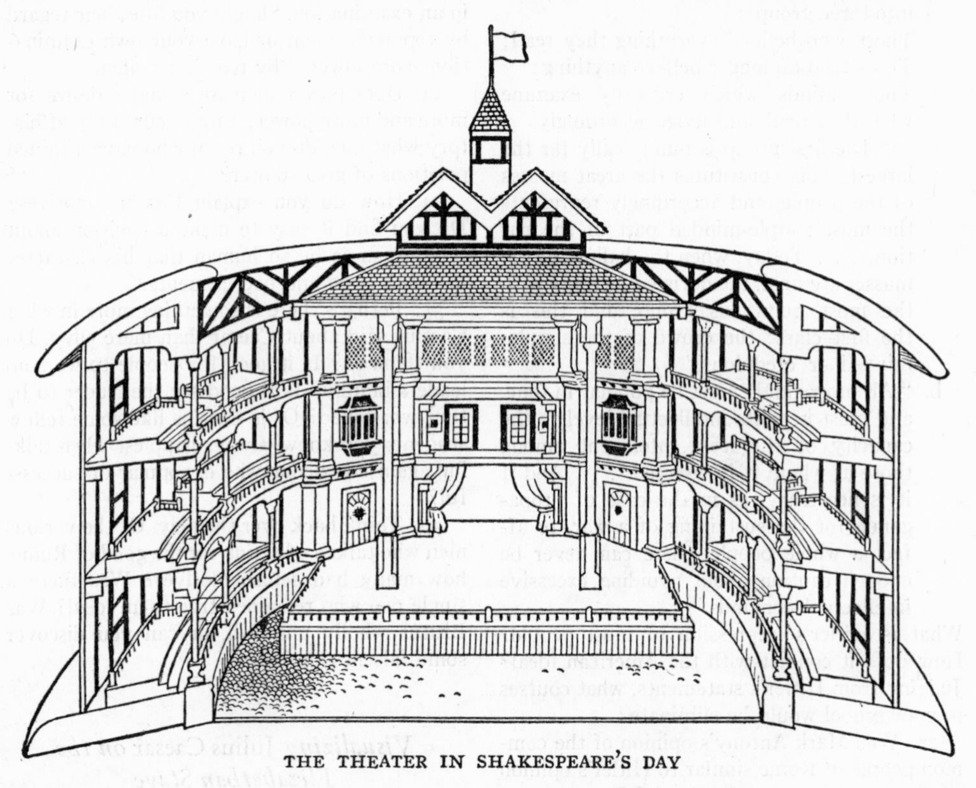

THE THEATER IN SHAKESPEARE'S DAY

One of the inner stages, as you will see from the picture, was placed at the rear and separated from the outer stage by a curtain. It was reserved for places of such definite location as "Brutus's orchard" or a room in "Caesar's house." Thus it was possible to set the inner stage during the progress of a scene that took place on the outer stage.

The advantage of this arrangement is well illustrated by the continuous action made possible in Act III, scene I, in spite of the shift of location. The street scene "Before the Capitol" took place on the outer stage, while the entrance into the Capitol was accomplished by merely drawing the curtains aside. The inner

play called for a balcony or tower scene. Costumes seldom aimed at historical accuracy; thus *Julius Caesar* was originally acted for the most part in the garb of Elizabeth's day.

37. How is a play influenced by the audience? by the kind of stage used? by the people who act it? What effect, do you suppose, did such items have on the following elements of *Julius Caesar?*

a. the number of women in the play
b. the appearance of Caesar's ghost
c. the rather large number of deaths in the play
d. the play's opening scene — the impudent cobbler and his puns
e. the use of omens and superstitions
f. the speeches of Brutus and Antony to the Roman plebeians

[1] The drawing is based on the scale model of Shakespeare's Playhouse by H. Ernest Conklin, copyright 1934.

Increase Your Power over Words

Great poets always extend the meanings of old and familiar words by their new and varied use of them. Ordinarily the growth of language is by inches until some master phrasemaker like Shakespeare gives it a tremendous shove forward. Ever since his day the English language has been richer because of the vocabulary he willed to us.

It would be a mistake, therefore, to leave your study of a Shakespearean play without a glance back at the words with which you are gradually becoming more familiar as you read. See whether you can catch something of their rare, old flavor; listen to their sounds; look for their picturesque beauty; and feel, if you can, the quiet pull on your thoughts. Perhaps the strange idiom presently will ring with pleasant familiarity in your ears and you will find yourself reaching out for one of Shakespeare's phrases to use in a conversational emergency. Such a miracle has happened before. Maybe it will happen to you.

The search for interesting and significant words in the play can be greatly simplified by dividing the class into five groups, each one assuming the responsibility of combing a single act for the types of words called for below.

38. *Quaint, Idiomatic Expressions.* Examples of such expressions are " Peace, ho! " or " I pray you, do." Every age and every locality has its set of commonly used expressions employed in the everyday situations of life. What would we say today instead of " Peace, ho! " if we wished to gain attention for someone as Casca did for Caesar in Act I, scene II, line 2? For each expression of this type found, students should include also a comment explaining the situation that calls for such an expression, our modern equivalent, and the frequency with which the idiom occurs in the act in question.

39. *Familiar Words Used in an Unfamiliar Sense.* The word *scandal,* for example, is a familiar noun; but Shakespeare uses it as a verb: ". . . if you know that I do fawn on men and hug them hard and after *scandal* them " (Act I, scene II, lines 79–81). In that same sentence *after* is used in the sense of " afterward." It will be interesting for a group of students to see how many such expressions they can find in a single act. Beside each Shakespearean usage set down the modern usage.

40. *New Words.* This list contains words whose meaning has become clear from the context. " And do you now *cull* out a holiday " (Act I, scene I, line 48)? It isn't difficult to guess the meaning of *cull* from the way it is used in the sentence. And *cull* is a new word to add to one's vocabulary — providing that it has happened to strike your fancy. The best way to learn new words is within their phrases: What else could one " *cull* out " besides a " holiday "? Such a question addressed to oneself, and answered, is a good way of fixing new words in the memory.

41. *Picturesque Comparisons.*

" These growing feathers pluck'd from Caesar's wing
Will make him fly an ordinary pitch."
(Act I, scene I, lines 62–63)

What do you see as you read these lines? The force of this comparison will all depend upon how vividly your imagination sees a picture. In order to make sure that the comparison has force for you, try representing the picture by a drawing or a colored print cut out from the advertising section of a magazine.

42. *Words Met Over and Over Again.* Do certain words seem to you essentially Shakespearean? That is, does Shakespeare use them often enough so that in your mind they will always be associated with him? The words *honor, honorable, dishonorable,* and so on, are such words: " Yet I see thy *honorable* metal may be wrought "; " find ourselves *dishonorable* graves "; " Say I love Brutus, and I *honor* him "; " Believe me for mine *honor* "; " So are they all, all *honorable* men." It is quite possible that students have felt the force of certain words as they read the play. Is there a certain type of word that seems to you typically Shakespearean? It is such words you are looking for in this brief study of his vocabulary.

Drawing Shakespeare into the Conversation

43. *Mimicking Shakespeare.* In order to catch the flavor of Shakespeare's idiom, it will prove amusing for several groups in the class to mimic the quaint expressions to be found in the play of *Julius Caesar*. What difference in effect can be created by substituting for common expressions in ordinary situations those compiled in list I? Perhaps a group of students will volunteer to write a little skit featuring Shakespearean idiom. Here are some scenes that might be used:

a. An exasperated parent listening to the "petitions" of a group of youngsters
b. Two boys quarreling over the way the affairs of a club have been managed

44. *Quoting Shakespeare.* When you know Shakespeare well, it is natural to quote from his plays. Certain words and phrases that have attracted your attention naturally spring to your lips. Look back over the play and see whether there are not words and phrases that you would like to remember. It might be such a brief passage as this:

". . . ever note, Lucilius,
When love begins to sicken and decay,
It useth an enforced ceremony."
(Act IV, scene II, lines 21–23)

For Ambitious Students

Surely you must have noticed that the man Julius Caesar in this play is not like the man whom your history books consider one of the outstanding leaders and statesmen of all time. Many critics believe that Shakespeare did a great wrong to Caesar in his picture of him. Did Shakespeare have any evidence on which to base the qualities of conceit and weakness he attributes to Caesar in this play? Did he have to change the character to write a better drama?

45. This curious inconsistency offers an opportunity to do some interesting research. An alert student wishing to do a thorough job will gather information from reliable histories, from original sources like Plutarch's *Lives,* and from opinions of such famous Shakespearean critics as Hazlitt, Rolfe, Brandes, and Hudson. The following books will be especially useful to students who become interested in the real Julius Caesar. These books will make splendid reading, and as oral reports will be very valuable to the class. A star means that the book has been particularly interesting to other high-school students.

Caesar, A Sketch by J. A. Froude
For good readers interested in Roman history. A full description of the political, military, and social activities of Julius Caesar and of the men and characteristics of his time.

* *Freedom, Farewell!* by Phyllis Bentley
This recent novel, based on the life of Julius Caesar from his youth to his death, will allow you to know Caesar as a living man. The battles, riots, and assassinations make for fast reading, and the story of a republic which traded freedom for security will set you to thinking of our own world today.

A Friend of Caesar by W. S. Davis
During Caesar's campaigns against Pompey two courageous young Roman lovers, Drusus and Cornelia, are separated when Drusus, for the sake of his country, decides to take the side of Caesar. Any sophomore who likes exciting, yet complicated, stories will like this book.

Julius Caesar by John Buchan
A clear, energetic account of how a powerful, yet cultured, man who took his first army from the pavements of Rome achieved everlasting fame. A short, well-organized book.

The Julius Caesar Murder Case by Wallace Irwin
This purports to be the *true* story of the murder of Julius Caesar, dug up by a Roman reporter and retold by Mr. Irwin. The book is great fun, and you don't have to believe it.

* *Three Children and Shakespeare* by A. T. White
Although this book is easy to read, the story of *Julius Caesar* is told so well in Chapters XIII to XVIII that many students will find them helpful. Chapter XVIII, particularly, is outstanding, for it makes Shakespeare live again as a human being.

46. Read the chapter called "The Peacemaker" in *The Autobiography of Lincoln Steffens.* Prepare a newspaper editorial on the role of the idealist in history. Did President Wilson fail, like Brutus, because the Antonys of Europe took advantage of his trust in other people's honesty? Is it possible to be practical and yet retain one's idealism? Older people are interested today in what youth is thinking about such problems. A letter for the public-opinion column of your local newspaper might be printed if it were written with force, sincerity, and clarity. If that fails, your school paper, or at least the classroom bulletin board, might be an avenue to publication.

47. List quickly and briefly all the superstitions you can find in this play. Use your list as the springboard of a talk to be delivered to your classmates. Just when they are most amused at these sixteenth-century absurdities, jolt them into the twentieth century with all the speed and vigor at your command. An American high-school student with his eyes open knows enough about superstition to start

a Senate investigation. Begin with the unwashed socks a certain basketball player insists on wearing at every game, and don't stop till you've sobered your audience! A good ending might be one such as you find at the close of " We Aren't Superstitious " in the " Chronicles of Experience " section.

SUGGESTIONS FOR FURTHER READING

Books about Words and Language

A Dictionary of American Slang by Maurice Weseen

Students usually enjoy a discussion of slang. This book, along with the slang version of the Declaration of Independence in the earlier edition of *The American Language* by H. L. Mencken, gives point and value to the discussion.

English, Past and Present by R. C. Trench

Words, English Roots and How They Grow by Margaret Ernst

Very useful. Inexpensive. Easy style.

English Synonyms Explained by George Crabbe

General Language by Lilly Lindquist and *General Language* by Bugbee, L. M., Clark, Parsons, and Swett

Excellent resources for a study of the history and relationships of languages.

In a Word by Margaret Ernst

You will be surprised to discover how far words have traveled from their original meanings. Thurber's absurd illustrations keep you chuckling.

Phrase Origins by Alfred Holt

You will find these explanations both entertaining and instructive.

Picturesque Word Origins. G. and C. Merriam Co., Springfield, Mass.

Contains a picture and an explanation for each word included.

Thesaurus Dictionary of the English Language by F. A. March

Why Do You Talk Like That? by Richard Burton

Words and Their Ways in English Speech by G. L. Kittredge and B. L. Greenough

You Don't Say by A. H. Holt

Use this book if you want to be sure of the correct pronunciation (or pronunciations) of a word

Your Everyday Vocabulary: How to Enlarge It by J. T. Baker

Bibliography on Shakespeare

Boas, Mrs. Frederick, *Shakespeare's England*

Compton's Encyclopedia, Vol. XIII

Mabie, H. W., *William Shakespeare, Poet, Dramatist, Man*

MacCracken, H. N., Pierce, F. E., and Durham, W. H., *An Introduction to Shakespeare*

Masson, David, *Shakespeare Personally*

Neilson, W. A., and Thorndike, A. H., *The Facts about Shakespeare*

Ordish, T. F., *Shakespeare's London*

Rhodes, R. C., *The Staging of Shakespeare*

Rolfe, W. J., *A Life of William Shakespeare; Shakespeare the Boy*

Spencer, Hazelton, *The Art and Life of William Shakespeare*

Thorndike, A. H., *Shakespeare's Theater*

Historical Fiction Based on Elizabethan Times

Bennett, John, *Master Skylark*

Black, William, *Judith Shakespeare*

Clark, Imogen, *Will Shakespeare's Little Lad*

Mickelson, Miriam, *Petticoat King*

Sabatini, Raphael, *Hounds of God*

Scott, Walter, *Kenilworth*

Roman History Made Readable

Church, A. J., *Roman Life in the Days of Cicero*

Fowler, W. W., *Social Life at Rome in the Age of Cicero*

Giles, A. F., *The Roman Civilization*

Harding, C. H. and S. B., *The City of the Seven Hills*

Johnston, H. W., *The Private Life of the Romans*

King, G. C., *The Rise of Rome*

Haaren, J. H., and Poland, A. B., *Famous Men of Rome*

Tappan, E. M., *The Story of the Roman People*

Victrola Records from Julius Caesar

Act II, scene 1, " Brutus and Portia " by E. H. Sothern and Julia Marlowe, No. 6296

" Antony's Oration " by E. H. Sothern, No. 6295

The Orson Welles edition of *Julius Caesar,* an album of eleven double-faced, twelve-inch recordings, produced by Columbia, available to schools through Harper & Brothers, Publishers, New York. Orson Welles plays the two parts of Antony and Cassius; George Coulouris is Brutus.

Suggestions for Producing Julius Caesar

In a little book entitled *Forty-Minute Plays from Shakespeare* by Fred G. Barker you will find the shortened play of *Julius Caesar,* under the title of *Brutus and Cassius,* with simple directions for acting and costuming. If the play as presented in this text seems too long and difficult to produce, Barker's shorter version will serve admirably. Simple tryouts for the different parts may be arranged, with the class as a whole acting as judge. Students who have discovered in their reading a preference for this or that part should memorize a brief passage and recite it before the class. Perhaps the best advice for youthful actors is that given by Ellen Terry to a little girl who had come to recite a piece to her in the hope of learning from the lips of the great Shakespearean actress that she had in her the true signs of genius. Said Miss Terry to the little girl — or so it has been told — "My dear, forget your lips, forget your voice, forget your gestures — just think what the *words mean.* The rest will take care of itself."

Books about the Elizabethan Stage

Barker, F. G., *Forty-Minute Plays from Shakespeare* (pp. 357–60)
Rhodes, R. C., *The Stagery of Shakespeare*
Thorndike, A. H., *Shakespeare's Theater*

Great Actors Who Have Played Brutus and Antony

Alexander, R. C. (ed.), *Diary of David Garrick*
Goodale, K. M., *Behind the Scenes with Edwin Booth*
Lockridge, Richard, *Darling of Misfortune: Edwin Booth*
Sothern, E. H., *The Melancholy Tale of Me*

Famous Shakespearean Actors

Craig, Gordon, *Ellen Terry and Her Secret Self; Henry Irving*
Jones, H. A., *The Shadow of Henry Irving*
Reade, Charles, *Peg Woffington*
Russell, C. E., *Julia Marlowe, Her Life and Art*
Terry, Ellen, *Memoirs*

HOW INTERESTED HAVE YOU BECOME IN DRAMATIC FORM?

Drama is a form of literature which depends not on words alone but on actors as well. Because real people speak and move about in drama, the illusion is concentrated, sharp, and immediate. Of course, in this book you have read the plays; but you have brought to your reading your past experiences with plays — you have pictured them as they would appear to you if they were acted. It is this power of seeming real which gives the drama form its special appeal.

Plot. The complete chain of events that makes up the story of a drama is called the *plot.* Usually, after these events have occurred, a change has taken place in the lives of the main characters in the play. In *Julius Caesar* the lives of Brutus, Antony, and Cassius are changed forever by the events which lead up to the assassination of Caesar.

Usually the plot arises from a *conflict* of some kind which creates a feeling of *suspense.* You notice this in *In the Zone,* which dramatizes a struggle between men — a struggle so fierce that it reaches a climax of physical force. Do you begin to see how the drama form, with its conflict happening right before our eyes, can make us catch our breath and lean forward, anxious to learn the outcome? The excitement of a prize fight or a football game and the suspense of a drama are basically the same. A drama, however, is much more complex and exciting, for the lives of the characters are involved. Not every play must have a conflict, but plays which lack a clash of personalities or a collision of purposes are rare.

Character. On the stage each character must make himself felt by what he does. There is no chance for the author to interrupt and say, " See here, I meant the villain to be smooth." He must appear so. On the stage or the screen we depend upon the actors to interpret the lines for us, to show us what kind of person would say this or that; but in reading a play we must depend upon our own powers of character analysis. We must appreciate each line for what it suggests as well as for what it means.

Setting. Each scene of a play is a picture as well as a story. How keenly are you aware of color? of artistic arrangement? Does your mood quickly respond to the grotesque shadows of a room? or to the sound of rain in *One Special for Doc?* Do you feel the swaying of the ship in O'Neill's play *In the Zone?* How much detail do you notice? Do you visualize the accuracy of the costumes? the furniture? These are the more subtle imaginative values of play reading which you should not overlook. To ignore them in your eagerness to get on with the story is to deny yourself the pleasure of complete response.

Timing. Because plays are performed in a theater, by actors, for an audience, time becomes an important consideration. Audiences are human and they grow weary. It is impossible for them to forget about the play for a while and do something else as they could if they were reading a novel. Consequently, dramas seldom last longer than two or three hours. Shakespeare's plays, for instance, need to be cut for modern audiences.

Time enters into the dramatist's problem in another way. What impression of time is the audience to receive from a play? Shall the events of the drama seem to happen rapidly or slowly? Did you realize that all the action of *Julius Caesar* really covered a period of over two years? Yet Shakespeare's play impresses us with the rush of events and mounting tension; everything seems to be happening in quick succession.

Getting started. The first impression we receive of a drama must be a good impression; the play must get under way as soon as possible if it is to seize the attention of the audience. In *Julius Caesar* we realize from the very first scene that trouble is about to break in Rome. We know that the conflict will be between Caesar and those who are not loyal to him; and before the second scene is over, we know the plot, if not in detail, at least in direction. Note, too, the masterful and immediate opening of the action in O'Neill's play. The curtain is barely up when Davis and Scotty discovered Smitty's suspicious actions.

If you are aware of such factors as those just discussed, you will enjoy the reading of drama as a form much more than before. To test your awareness, see how well you can answer these questions:

1. How do you decide what kind of characters you are reading about in *One Special for Doc?* What are your clews? In *Julius Caesar* and *In the Zone* you learn a great deal about Brutus and Smitty by hearing what others say about them. Can you find these places?

2. What effect does the silent action at the beginning of *In the Zone* have on you? Why is this effect more compelling in a drama than it would be in a short story or a novel?

3. The conflict in *I Was Talking across the Fence This Morning* is not between people but between false and real values. What are these values? Which set seems to win in the Pint family? Is such a conflict between values as suit-

able for the drama form as a conflict between individuals? Compare *In the Zone* and *I Was Talking across the Fence This Morning.*

4. Which of the short stories in this book would make the best dramas? "Now There Is Peace"? "Sleet Storm"? "The Revolt of Mother"? others? Justify your answer in terms of what you have learned about the drama form.

SUGGESTIONS FOR FURTHER READING

Long Plays

As You Like It by William Shakespeare
Adventure, disguise, and troubles are the ingredients of this ever-popular and amusing play.

Berkeley Square by John Balderston
A modern American finds himself in London two hundred years ago. More disconcerting than that, he falls in love with a girl whom he can't bring back to the present with him.

Cavalcade by Noel Coward
Two English families from different classes face a changing world during the years from 1900 until today.

Elizabeth the Queen by Maxwell Anderson
The queen sacrifices personal plans for the power she holds as a ruler.

The Green Goddess by William Archer
When three English people are forced to land their plane in a central Asiatic country, the ruler holds them for revenge. An exciting melodrama.

The Lost Colony by Paul Green
Every year this play is acted on Roanoke Island in North Carolina. This is the very spot from which Sir Walter Raleigh's English colonists disappeared. One of the true unsolved mysteries of all time.

The Melting Pot by Israel Zangwill
A talented foreign boy, destined for a great musical career, struggles to find a place in America, the melting pot of the world.

The Power and the Glory by Karel Čapek
All people over forty-five are dying of a mysterious disease. A young doctor discovers a cure but refuses to use it to save anyone who will not renounce war. What chances of success do you think he would have in stopping war?

Prologue to Glory by E. P. Conkle
A two-act play about Lincoln's early years. We see him as a lanky rail splitter who can hold his own in a fight, as a storekeeper, and in tragic manhood after the death of Anne Rutledge.

The Rivals by R. B. Sheridan
When more than one man wants a lady for his bride, complications arise — as always.

R. U. R. by Karel Čapek
Mechanical men become intelligent and revolt against their makers.

What a Life! by Clifford Goldsmith
Henry Aldrich, other high-school students, and their teachers carry on their daily lives — largely in the principal's office. The play has both comedy and a serious meaning. (In *The Best Plays of 1938–39*)

Yellow Jack by Sidney Howard and Paul De Kruif
A dramatization of adventure in medicine. The struggle of Walter Reed and his colleagues against the unknown germ of yellow fever becomes a very moving drama.

LONG NARRATIVE POEMS

YOU PROBABLY remember how in the story of the *Odyssey* the shipwrecked Ulysses is entertained at a feast by the greathearted Alcinoüs; and how, as the minstrel sings of the Trojan War, Ulysses weeps; and Alcinoüs bids him tell *his* story: why he has wandered so far, and what strange cities he has seen, and the great deeds he has done. And so the godlike stranger tells his long tale of adventure, of his exciting escape from the Cyclops, and of the wicked enchantment of Circe, and of the dangerous maneuver between Scylla and Charybdis. And when the tale was finished, the great hall was silent, for the princes were overcome with fear and awe and wonder.

Epic poetry one of earliest forms of literature. Ulysses' method of telling a story, his slow and serious unfolding of a tale, with its picturesque digressions, was the popular mode of expression in ancient times. You have already discovered in your study of the short story how the brief, concise forms of literature, the neatly timed and sharply focused incidents, belong to a later period of man's development. The epic poem, or folk epic, as the long narrative in verse is called, was one of the earliest forms of literature to take definite shape. You may think of it as the proud forebear of the modern short story and novel. It was sung by minstrels as a continued ballad, or it was told by a chieftain to inspire his warriors. In primitive times there was no speed limit to set the pace of a story, no modern theater with its precise demands on time and space, no twentieth-century hurry and rush with chinks of time to be filled in by brief résumés and synopses. Life was simple and unified. There was only one story to be told — the story of heroism. It had infinite variations, to be sure, but it celebrated always the same theme. All the virtues of an age, moreover, could be summed up in one man. With life more complex, it is no longer possible to imagine a single national hero to be worshiped. Countless varieties of heroes fill the pages of modern tales.

" Idylls of the King," a literary epic. But civilized man, for all his progress, periodically hankers after the primitive. The desire to face life in the raw, or in single combat, still stirs in the heart of man, even though he has invented machines and organized vast armies to fight his battles for him. So it is that the hero tales of long ago keep their freshness of appeal. They lie close to the heart of man, alongside his instincts, and as such they have been the source of inspiration for many a writer of modern times. The simplicity of style, the grandeur of purpose, and the slow-moving force of the story, bearing its listeners out upon a great tide of feeling, have been imitated over and over again in literature. These later imitations of the old epic, to be introduced to you in the poems that follow, are called literary epics. Tennyson's *Idylls of the King* is often referred to as the Arthurian epic and in basic organization and loftiness of theme resembles the old hero tales. But its highly ornamented style is more recent. From it you will catch something of the high seriousness and the picturesque grandeur of those first long narrative poems which occupy such a venerable place in literary tradition.

IDYLLS OF THE KING

by Lord Alfred Tennyson (1809–1892)

The name of King Arthur, like that of Robin Hood or William Tell, belongs to the story lore of mankind. Around these names cluster so many legends that it is impossible to separate fact from fancy. That there was such a Celtic hero as Arthur, in the early days of Britain, when the original inhabitants were being pushed back farther and farther into the fastnesses of the Welsh mountains by Saxon invaders, is highly probable. His bravery and wisdom and goodness were extolled far and wide in song and story, until his name came to stand in the early centuries for the ideal of chivalry itself. In the middle of the fifteenth century these romantic legends were collected by Sir Thomas Malory, an English knight, and were included in the first books to be published by William Caxton, the man who introduced printing into England. For generations these tales were the favorite reading of English gentlemen. Then suddenly, after 1634 — the date of the last edition until 1816 — they were forgotten. They were rediscovered, however, in the nineteenth century by a more sophisticated generation which had learned finally to treasure its past.

Most famous among those to feel the glamour of these old tales was the poet Alfred Tennyson. Early in his boyhood he had first responded to their subtle magic and in his first poems used them as a favorite theme. He worked intermittently for thirty years on the complete retelling of these stories in the long epiclike poem introduced to you here.

The *Idylls of the King* is a series of twelve parables revolving around the impressive figure of King Arthur. Each *Idyll* is a highly wrought picture, designed to show by allegory the persistent conflict between man's higher and his lower self. Running through the elaborate tapestry is a thread of high moral purpose. Only two of the *Idylls* are reproduced for you here in their complete form; the first and the seventh. But in order that you may catch something of the allegorical significance of the poem as a whole, the intervening *Idylls* are briefly summarized.

Tennyson was regarded during the reign of Queen Victoria as the foremost poet in the English language. Reared carefully in a clergyman's household, in a highly intellectual atmosphere, the young Tennyson showed little inclination to wander from the straight and narrow path to success. His life for the most part was serene and uneventful and in interest is eclipsed by his poetry. In 1850, the year in which he published " In Memoriam," the celebrated poem honoring the name of his college friend Arthur Hallam, he was made poet laureate, succeeding William Wordsworth, the nature poet. The *Idylls of the King* is his greatest single achievement.

THE COMING OF ARTHUR

Have you ever noticed after riding in a train or automobile all day how the rhythm of the movement lingers in your memory? If you close your eyes, you can feel the swaying and the jolting still beating in your pulses.

Readers of poetry often experience a similar sensation upon finishing a long poem; the swing of the lines gets into their minds and makes it easy to think in time with the rhythm. Although the poem stops, the tune goes on.

All this is testimony of the fact that our muscles, once they become used to a movement, are reluctant to give it up; or that our minds, once accustomed to a particular rhythm, find it a help and not a hindrance to reading.

One of your first considerations in setting out to read the first *Idyll,* therefore, is to adjust your mind to the form of the story. At first it will seem strange. A new rhythm frequently gives difficulty to all but experienced readers. You will overcome some of the difficulty if you get into the habit of pronouncing all proper names aloud so as to *hear* the words as well as see them. Does your pronunciation fit in with the movement of the line? Say this line over to yourself, stressing the syllables indicated:

Le-od′-o-gran, the King of Cam′-e-liard

Now read this version of the same line:

Le-od′-o-gran, the King of Ca-mel′-i-ard

Do you see how the movement of the line is spoiled by the changed pronunciation of the last word? Once you feel the rhythm of the lines, you will have an aid to pronunciation close at hand.

You should direct some of your energy, also, in your reading of the first *Idyll,* toward getting your bearings. Try to catch something of the spirit of the times — to feel the high moral purpose of King Arthur's court. You should begin, also, to sense the personality of the great king, for he is the sun around which all the other knights revolve. Take time to notice the various mystic symbols which give the story its legendary character. The events in the story are important only as a thread to follow; they should not hold your exclusive attention.

Leodogran, the king of Cameliard,
Had one fair daughter, and none other child;
And she was fairest of all flesh on earth,
Guinevere, and in her his one delight.

For many a petty king ere Arthur came — 5
Ruled in this isle and, ever waging war
Each upon other, wasted all the land;
And still from time to time the heathen host
Swarmed overseas, and harried what was left.
And so there grew great tracts of wilderness, — 10
Wherein the beast was ever more and more,
But man was less and less, till Arthur came.
For first Aurelius lived and fought and died,
And after him King Uther fought and died,
But either failed to make the kingdom one. — 15
And after these King Arthur for a space,
And through the puissance of his Table Round,
Drew all their petty princedoms under him,
Their king and head, and made a realm and reigned.

And thus the land of Cameliard was waste, — 20
Thick with wet woods, and many a beast therein,
And none or few to scare or chase the beast;
So that wild dog and wolf and boar and bear
Came night and day, and rooted in the fields,
And wallowed in the gardens of the king. — 25
And ever and anon the wolf would steal

The children and devour, but now and then,
Her own brood lost or dead, lent her fierce teat
To human sucklings; and the children, housed
In her foul den, there at their meat would growl, 30
And mock their foster mother on four feet,
Till, straightened, they grew up to wolflike men,
Worse than the wolves. And King Leodogran
Groaned for the Roman legions here again
And Caesar's eagle; then his brother king, 35
Urien, assailed him; last a heathen horde,
Reddening the sun with smoke and earth with blood,
And on the spike that split the mother's heart
Spitting the child, brake on him, till, amazed,
He knew not whither he should turn for aid. 40

But — for he heard of Arthur newly crowned,
Though not without an uproar made by those
Who cried: " He is not Uther's son " — the king
Sent to him, saying, " Arise, and help us thou!
For here between the man and beast we die." 45

And Arthur yet had done no deed of arms,
But heard the call and came; and Guinevere
Stood by the castle walls to watch him pass;
But since he neither wore on helm or shield
The golden symbol of his kinglihood, 50
But rode a simple knight among his knights,
And many of these in richer arms than he,
She saw him not, or marked not, if she saw,
One among many, though his face was bare.
But Arthur, looking downward as he past, 55
Felt the light of her eyes into his life
Smite on the sudden, yet rode on, and pitched
His tents beside the forest. Then he drave
The heathen; after, slew the beast, and felled
The forest, letting in the sun, and made 60
Broad pathways for the hunter and the knight,
And so returned.

For while he lingered there,
A doubt that ever smoldered in the hearts

34. **the Roman legions** first occupied Britain in 55 B.C. 35. **Caesar's eagle:** the emblem of the Roman Caesars. 36. **heathen horde:** the Anglo-Saxons, invaders from the north coast of Europe, who conquered the Celts — the original inhabitants of Britain. The first forty lines sum up briefly the history of Britain up to the year 450. 39. **spitting the child:** piercing with spears. Putting meat on a pointed rod for roasting is called *spitting*. Notice the grim comparison implied. 43. The significance of this line will become clear as you read on. Enemies of Arthur denied his royal birth, and therefore his right to the crown. 62. **there:** in Leodogran's kingdom.

Of those great lords and barons of his realm
Flashed forth and into war; for most of these 65
Colleaguing with a score of petty kings,
Made head against him, crying: "Who is he
That he should rule us? who hath proven him
King Uther's son? for lo! we look at him,
And find nor face nor bearing, limbs nor voice, 70
Are like to those of Uther whom we knew.
This is the son of Gorloïs, not the king;
This is the son of Anton, not the king."

And Arthur, passing thence to battle, felt
Travail, and throes and agonies of the life, 75
Desiring to be joined with Guinevere,
And thinking as he rode: "Her father said
That there between the man and beast they die.
Shall I not lift her from this land of beasts
Up to my throne and side by side with me? 80
What happiness to reign a lonely king,
Vext — O ye stars that shudder over me,
O earth that soundest hollow under me,
Vext with waste dreams? for saving I be joined
To her that is the fairest under heaven, 85
I seem as nothing in the mighty world,
And cannot will my will nor work my work
Wholly, nor make myself in mine own realm
Victor and lord. But were I joined with her,
Then might we live together as one life, 90
And reigning with one will in everything
Have power on this dark land to lighten it,
And power on this dead world to make it live."

Thereafter — as he speaks who tells the tale —
When Arthur reached a field of battle bright 95
With pitched pavilions of his foe, the world
Was all so clear about him that he saw
The smallest rock far on the faintest hill,
And even in high day the morning star.
So when the king had set his banner broad, 100
At once from either side, with trumpet blast,
And shouts, and clarions shrilling unto blood,
The long-lanced battle let their horses run.

72–73. The reason for the confusion as to Arthur's father — whether Gorloïs or Uther or Anton — is to be made clear later on. The point to be kept in mind here is merely that Arthur's royal birth is disputed by those who do not wish to see him crowned king. 94. **he:** Sir Thomas Malory, already mentioned in the introduction on page 522. 96–97. Compare these lines with lines 127–28. What part do you think Arthur's love for Guinevere played in changing his outlook on the world? Note also lines 56–57. With these clews, how do you explain his might on the field of battle?

And now the barons and the kings prevailed,
And now the king, as here and there that war 105
Went swaying; but the powers who walk the world
Made lightnings and great thunders over him,
And dazed all eyes, till Arthur by main might,
And mightier of his hands with every blow,
And leading all his knighthood threw the kings 110
Carádos, Urien, Cradlemont of Wales,
Claudius, and Clariance of Northumberland,
The King Brandagoras of Latangor,
With Anguisant of Erin, Morganore,
And Lot of Orkney. Then, before a voice 115
As dreadful as the shout of one who sees
To one who sins, and deems himself alone
And all the world asleep, they swerved and brake
Flying, and Arthur called to stay the brands
That hacked among the flyers: "Ho! they yield!" 120
So like a painted battle the war stood
Silenced, the living quiet as the dead,
And in the heart of Arthur joy was lord.
He laughed upon his warrior whom he loved
And honored most. "Thou dost not doubt me king 125
So well thine arm hath wrought for me today."
"Sir and my liege," he cried, "the fire of God
Descends upon thee in the battlefield:
I know thee for my king!" Whereat the two,
For each had warded either in the fight, 130
Sware on the field of death a deathless love.
And Arthur said, "Man's word is God in man:
Let chance what will, I trust thee to the death."

Then quickly from the foughten field he sent
Ulfius, and Brastias, and Bedivere, 135
His new-made knights, to King Leodogran,
Saying, "If I in aught have served thee well,
Give me thy daughter Guinivere to wife."

Whom when he heard, Leodogran in heart
Debating — "How should I that am a king, 140
However much he holp me at my need,
Give my one daughter saving to a king,
And a king's son?" — lifted his voice, and called
A hoary man, his chamberlain, to whom

111–14. It will be good practice to try the pronunciation of these names in accordance with the suggestions made on page 523. 124. **his warrior whom he loved**: Lancelot, a very important character in the *Idylls*. Notice the pledge of friendship that follows (line 131). You will have occasion to think back to this pledge later on in the story. 127–29. Notice how Lancelot is convinced of Arthur's kingship.

He trusted all things, and of him required 145
His counsel: "Knowest thou aught of Arthur's birth?"

Then spake the hoary chamberlain and said:
"Sir King, there be but two old men that know;
And each is twice as old as I, and one
Is Merlin, the wise man that ever served 150
King Uther through his magic art; and one
Is Merlin's master — so they call him — Bleys,
Who taught him magic; but the scholar ran
Before the master, and so far that Bleys
Laid magic by, and sat him down, and wrote 155
All things and whatsoever Merlin did
In one great annal book, where afteryears
Will learn the secret of our Arthur's birth."

To whom the King Leodogran replied:
"O friend, had I been holpen half as well 160
By this King Arthur as by thee today,
Then beast and man had had their share of me;
But summon here before us yet once more
Ulfias, and Brastias, and Bedivere."

Then, when they came before him, the king said: 165
"I have seen the cuckoo chased by lesser fowl,
And reason in the chase; but wherefore now
Do these your lords stir up the heat of war,
Some calling Arthur born of Gorloïs,
Others of Anton? Tell me, ye yourselves, 170
Hold ye this Arthur for King Uther's son?"

And Ulfias and Brastias answered, "Ay."
Then Bedivere, the first of all his knights
Knighted by Arthur at his crowning, spake —
For bold in heart and act and word was he, 175
Whenever slander breathed against the king —

"Sir, there be many rumors on his head:
For there be those who hate him in their hearts,
Call him baseborn, and since his ways are sweet,
And theirs are bestial, hold him less than man; 180
And there be those who deem him more than man,
And dream he dropt from heaven; but my belief
In all this matter — so ye care to learn —
Sir, for ye know that in King Uther's time
The prince and warrior Gorloïs, he that held 185

153–4. **the scholar ran before the master**: the scholar surpassed the master.

Tintagil castle by the Cornish sea,
Was wedded with a winsome wife, Ygerne;
And daughters had she borne him — one whereof,
Lot's wife, the Queen of Orkney, Bellicent,
Hath ever like a loyal sister cleaved 190
To Arthur — but a son she had not borne.
And Uther cast upon her eyes of love;
But she, a stainless wife of Gorloïs,
So loathed the bright dishonor of his love
That Gorloïs and King Uther went to war, 195
And overthrown was Gorloïs and slain.
Then Uther in his wrath and heat besieged
Ygerne within Tintagil, where her men,
Seeing the mighty swarm about their walls,
Left her and fled, and Uther entered in, 200
And there was none to call to but himself.
So, compassed by the power of the king,
Enforced she was to wed him in her tears,
And with a shameful swiftness; afterward,
Not many moons, King Uther died himself, 205
Moaning and wailing for an heir to rule
After him, lest the realm should go to wrack.
And that same night, the night of the new year,
By reason of the bitterness and grief
That vext his mother, all before his time 210
Was Arthur born, and all as soon as born
Delivered at a secret postern gate
To Merlin, to be holden far apart
Until his hour should come; because the lords
Of that fierce day were as the lords of this, 215
Wild beasts, and surely would have torn the child
Piecemeal among them, had they known; for each
But sought to rule for his own self and hand,
And many hated Uther for the sake
Of Gorloïs. Wherefore Merlin took the child, 220
And gave him to Sir Anton, an old knight
And ancient friend of Uther; and his wife
Nursed the young prince, and reared him with her own;
And no man knew. And ever since the lords
Have foughten like wild beasts among themselves, 225
So that the realm has gone to wrack; but now,
This year, when Merlin — for his hour had come —
Brought Arthur forth, and set him in the hall,
Proclaiming, 'Here is Uther's heir, your king,'
A hundred voices cried: 'Away with him! 230

191. **she:** Ygerne. See line 187. 214. **Until his hour should come:** until Arthur should be declared king.

No king of ours! a son of Gorloïs he;
Or else the child of Anton, and no king,
Or else baseborn.' Yet Merlin through his craft,
And while the people clamored for a king,
Had Arthur crowned; but after, the great lords 235
Banded, and so brake out in open war."

Then while the king debated with himself
If Arthur were the child of shamefulness,
Or born the son of Gorloïs after death,
Or Uther's son and born before his time, 240
Or whether there were truth in anything
Said by these three, there came to Cameliard,
With Gawain and young Modred, her two sons,
Lot's wife, the Queen of Orkney, Bellicent;
Whom as he could, not as he would, the king 245
Made feast for, saying, as they sat at meat:
"A doubtful throne is ice on summer seas.
Ye come from Arthur's court. Victor his men
Report him! Yea, but ye — think ye this king —
So many those that hate him, and so strong, 250
So few his knights, however brave they be —
Hath body enow to hold his foemen down?"

"O king," she cried, "and I will tell thee: few,
Few, but all brave, all of one mind with him;
For I was near him when the savage yells 255
Of Uther's peerage died, and Arthur sat
Crowned on the dais, and his warriors cried:
'Be thou the king, and we will work thy will
Who love thee.' Then the king in low deep tones,
And simple words of great authority, 260
Bound them by so strait vows to his own self
That when they rose, knighted from kneeling, some
Were pale as at the passing of a ghost,
Some flushed, and others dazed, as one who wakes
Half-blinded at the coming of a light. 265

"But when he spake, and cheered his Table Round
With large, divine, and comfortable words,
Beyond my tongue to tell thee — I beheld
From eye to eye through all their order flash
A momentary likeness of the king; 270
And ere it left their faces, through the cross
And those around it and the Crucified,
Down from the casement over Arthur, smote

268–70. Notice the mystic unity of the Round Table suggested in these lines.

Flame color, vert, and azure, in three rays,
One falling upon each of three fair queens 275
Who stood in silence near his throne, the friends
Of Arthur, gazing on him, tall, with bright
Sweet faces, who will help him at his need.

"And there I saw mage Merlin, whose vast wit
And hundred winters are but as the hands 280
Of loyal vassals toiling for their liege.

"And near him stood the Lady of the Lake,
Who knows a subtler magic than his own —
Clothed in white samite, mystic, wonderful.
She gave the king his huge cross-hilted sword, 285
Whereby to drive the heathen out; a mist
Of incense curled about her, and her face
Well-nigh was hidden in the minster gloom;
But there was heard among the holy hymns
A voice as of the waters, for she dwells 290
Down in a deep — calm, whatsoever storms
May shake the world — and when the surface rolls,
Hath power to walk the waters like our Lord.

"There likewise I beheld Excalibur
Before him at his crowning borne, the sword 295
That rose from out the bosom of the lake,
And Arthur rowed across and took it — rich
With jewels, elfin Urim, on the hilt,
Bewildering heart and eye — the blade so bright
That men are blinded by it — on one side, 300
Graven in the oldest tongue of all this world,
'Take me,' but turn the blade and ye shall see,
And written in the speech ye speak yourself,
'Cast me away!' And sad was Arthur's face
Taking it, but old Merlin counseled him: 305
'Take thou and strike! the time to cast away
Is yet far off.' So this great brand the king
Took, and by this will beat his foemen down."

Thereat Leodogran rejoiced, but thought
To sift his doubtings to the last, and asked, 310
Fixing full eyes of question on her face:
"The swallow and the swift are near akin,
But thou are closer to this noble prince,

275. **three fair queens:** symbolic of the three Christian virtues, Faith, Hope, and Charity. 282. **Lady of the Lake:** symbolic of religion or the church. 294. **Excalibur:** Arthur's magic sword, about which you will hear more as you read on. 295–96. The picture shifts here to an earlier one of which Bellicent was reminded by the vision of the sword. 298. **Urim:** mystic Jewish ornaments.

Being his own dear sister"; and she said:
"Daughter of Gorloïs and Ygerne am I." 315
"And therefore Arthur's sister?" asked the king.
She answered, "These be secret things," and signed
To those two sons to pass, and let them be.
And Gawain went, and breaking into song
Sprang out, and followed by his flying hair 320
Ran like a colt, and leapt at all he saw;
But Modred laid his ear beside the doors,
And there half heard — the same that afterward
Struck for the throne, and striking found his doom.

And then the queen made answer: "What know I? 325
For dark my mother was in eyes and hair,
And dark in hair and eyes am I; and dark
Was Gorloïs; yea, and dark was Uther too,
Well-nigh to blackness; but this king is fair
Beyond the race of Britons and of men. 330
Moreover, always in my mind I hear
A cry from out the dawning of my life,
A mother weeping, and I hear her say:
'O that ye had some brother, pretty one,
To guard thee on the rough ways of the world.'" 335

"Ay," said the king, "and hear ye such a cry?
But when did Arthur chance upon thee first?"

"O king!" she cried, "and I will tell thee true:
He found me first when yet a little maid.
Beaten I had been for a little fault 340
Whereof I was not guilty; and out I ran
And flung myself down on a bank of heath,
And hated this fair world and all therein,
And wept, and wished that I were dead; and he —
I know not whether of himself he came, 345
Or brought by Merlin, who, they say, can walk
Unseen at pleasure — he was at my side,
And spake sweet words, and comforted my heart,
And dried my tears, being a child with me.
And many a time he came, and evermore 350
As I grew greater grew with me; and sad
At times he seemed, and sad with him was I,
Stern, too, at times, and then I loved him not,
But sweet again, and then I loved him well.

315. Bellicent is thus Arthur's half sister. 318. Bellicent did not wish her two sons to hear the secret she is about to tell. 322–24. Notice that Modred listens at the door. And notice the prophecy of his doom. What trait would you guess is to be his undoing?

And now of late I see him less and less, 355
But those first days had golden hours for me,
For then I surely thought he would be king.

"But let me tell thee now another tale:
For Bleys, our Merlin's master, as they say,
Died but of late, and sent his cry to me, 360
To hear him speak before he left his life.
Shrunk like a fairy changeling lay the mage;
And when I entered told me that himself
And Merlin ever served about the king,
Uther, before he died; and on the night 365
When Uther in Tintagil past away
Moaning and wailing for an heir, the two
Left the still king, and passing forth to breathe,
Then from the castle gateway by the chasm
Descending through the dismal night — a night 370
In which the bounds of heaven and earth were lost —
Beheld, so high upon the dreary deeps
It seemed in heaven, a ship, the shape thereof
A dragon winged, and all from stem to stern
Bright with a shining people on the decks, 375
And gone as soon as seen. And then the two
Dropt to the cove, and watched the great sea fall,
Wave after wave, each mightier than the last,
Till last, a ninth one, gathering half the deep
And full of voices, slowly rose and plunged 380
Roaring, and all the wave was in a flame;
And down the wave and in the flame was borne
A naked babe, and rode to Merlin's feet,
Who stoopt and caught the babe, and cried: 'The king!
Here is an heir for Uther!' And the fringe 385
Of that great breaker, sweeping up the strand,
Lashed at the wizard as he spake the word,
And all at once all round him rose in fire,
So that the child and he were clothed in fire.
And presently thereafter followed calm, 390
Free sky and stars. 'And this same child,' he said,
'Is he who reigns; nor could I part in peace
Till this were told. And saying this the seer
Went through the strait and dreadful pass of death,
Not ever to be questioned any more 395
Save on the further side; but when I met
Merlin, and asked him if these things were truth —
The shining dragon and the naked child

358. In primitive times it was very common for legends of miraculous birth to grow up around a hero's name. It is such a legend that you are to hear from Bellicent's lips.

Descending in the glory of the seas —
He laughed as is his wont, and answered me 400
In riddling triplets of old time, and said:

"'Rain, rain, and sun! a rainbow in the sky!
A young man will be wiser by and by;
An old man's wit may wander ere he die.

"'Rain, rain, and sun! a rainbow on the lea! 405
And truth is this to me, and that to thee;
And truth or clothed or naked let it be.

"'Rain, sun, and rain! and the free blossom blows:
Sun, rain, and sun! and where is he who knows?
From the great deep to the great deep he goes.' 410

"So Merlin riddling angered me; but thou
Fear not to give this king thine only child,
Guinevere, so great bards of him will sing
Hereafter; and dark sayings from of old
Ranging and ringing through the minds of men, 415
And echoed by old folk beside their fires
For comfort after their wage work is done,
Speak of the king; and Merlin in our time
Hath spoken also, not in jest, and sworn
Though men may wound him that he will not die, 420
But pass, again to come, and then or now
Utterly smite the heathen underfoot;
Till these and all men hail him for their king."

She spake and King Leodogran rejoiced,
But musing, "Shall I answer yea or nay?" 425
Doubted, and drowsed, nodded and slept, and saw,
Dreaming, a slope of land that ever grew,
Field after field, up to a height, the peak
Haze-hidden, and thereon a phantom king,
Now looming, and now lost; and on the slope 430
The sword rose, the hind fell, the herd was driven,
Fire glimpsed; and all the land from roof and rick,
In drifts of smoke before a rolling wind,
Streamed to the peak, and mingled with the haze
And made it thicker; while the phantom king 435
Sent out at times a voice; and here or there

401. **riddling triplets:** riddles in three rhyming lines, as composed by the Welsh bards, such as follow. 404. Does Merlin seem to believe in the tale told by Bleys? Does Bellicent believe it? Notice line 412. Does this give you a clew? 429–35. Compare these lines with lines 58–61 and 104–28. What resemblance do you see? Out of what stuff had Leodogran's dreams been woven? Refer again to the lines above.

Stood one who pointed toward the voice, the rest
Slew on and burnt, crying: "No king of ours,
No son of Uther, and no king of ours";
Till with a wink his dream was changed, the haze 440
Descended, and the solid earth became
As nothing, but the king stood out in heaven,
Crowned. And Leodogran awoke, and sent
Ulfius, and Brastias, and Bedivere,
Back to the court of Arthur answering yea. 445

Then Arthur charged his warrior whom he loved
And honored most, Sir Lancelot, to ride forth
And bring the queen, and watched him from the gates;
And Lancelot past away among the flowers —
For then was latter April — and returned 450
Among the flowers, in May, with Guinevere.
To whom arrived, by Dubric the high saint,
Chief of the church in Britain, and before
The stateliest of her altar shrines, the king
That morn was married, while in stainless white, 455
The fair beginners of a nobler time,
And glorying in their vows and him, his knights
Stood round him, and rejoicing in his joy.
Far shone the fields of May through open door,
The sacred altar blossomed white with May, 460
The sun of May descended on their king,
They gazed on all earth's beauty in their queen,
Rolled incense, and there past along the hymns
A voice as of the waters, while the two
Sware at the shrine of Christ a deathless love; 465
And Arthur said, "Behold, thy doom is mine.
Let chance what will, I love thee to the death!"
To whom the queen replied with drooping eyes:
"King and my lord, I love thee to the death!"
And holy Dubric spread his hands and spake: 470
"Reign ye, and live and love, and make the world
Other, and may thy queen be one with thee,
And all this order of thy Table Round
Fulfill the boundless purpose of their king!"

So Dubric said; but when they left the shrine 475
Great lords from Rome before the portal stood,
In scornful stillness gazing as they past;
Then while they paced a city all on fire

443. What was his impression on waking? Can you see why this led him to send immediately for Arthur? 447–48. Keep it in mind that it was Lancelot whom Arthur sent for Guinevere. You will have occasion later on in the story to think back to this incident.

With sun and cloth of gold, the trumpets blew,
And Arthur's knighthood sang before the king: 480

"Blow trumpet, for the world is white with May!
Blow trumpet, the long night hath rolled away!
Blow through the living world — 'Let the king reign!'

"Shall Rome or heathen rule in Arthur's realm?
Flash brand and lance, fall battle-ax upon helm, 485
Fall battle-ax, and flash brand! Let the king reign!

"Strike for the king and live! his knights have heard
That God hath told the king a secret word.
Fall battle-ax, and flash brand! Let the king reign!

"Blow trumpet! he will lift us from the dust. 490
Blow trumpet! live the strength, and die the lust!
Clang battle-ax, and clash brand! Let the king reign!

"Strike for the king and die! and if thou diest,
The king is king, and ever wills the highest.
Clang battle-ax, and clash brand! Let the king reign! 495

"Blow, for our sun is mighty in his May!
Blow, for our sun is mightier day by day!
Clang battle-ax, and clash brand! Let the king reign!

"The king will follow Christ, and we the king,
In whom high God hath breathed a secret thing. 500
Fall battle-ax, and clash brand! Let the king reign!"

So sang the knighthood, moving to their hall.
There at the banquet those great lords from Rome,
The slowly fading mistress of the world,
Strode in and claimed their tribute as of yore. 505
But Arthur spake: "Behold, for these have sworn
To wage my wars, and worship me their king;
The old order changeth, yielding place to new;
And we that fight for our fair father Christ,
Seeing that ye be grown too weak and old 510
To drive the heathen from your Roman wall,
No tribute will we pay." So those great lords
Drew back in wrath, and Arthur strove with Rome.

And Arthur and his knighthood for a space
Were all one will, and through that strength the king 515
Drew in the petty princedoms under him,
Fought, and in twelve great battles overcame
The heathen hordes, and made a realm and reigned.

484. Arthur was champion of the Celts, the original inhabitants of Britain, against the invaders; that is, the Romans and the Anglo-Saxons (**heathen**).

THINK BACK OVER WHAT YOU HAVE READ

Recognizing the Legendary Quality of the Story

1. Judging from "The Coming of Arthur," in what kind of an emergency did legendary heroes flourish? What was the great need which called forth Arthur's heroic qualities? What modern parallel can you think of which would similarly give rise to national heroes? Do we have any national emergencies today which were not known in Arthur's day grave enough to call forth a hero?

2. What rumors grew up concerning Arthur's birth? Why do you suppose the birth of legendary heroes is frequently shrouded in mystery? Can you think of any reason why mankind should prefer to believe in the miraculous origin of its heroes? What added appeal would it have? Why would it tend to preserve greater unity among his followers? From your knowledge of legends, what other stories of miraculous birth can you compare with that of Arthur? Is there any common element in all the stories?

3. How do you account for the special importance usually given in legends to pure royal descent? Suppose that Arthur *had* been "basely" born? From the point of view of his followers, what difference would it have made? What lesson can you draw from the fact that his enemies questioned his birth rather than his power? Can you think of a modern parallel instance in which this kind of attack is made upon "heroes"? What does this tendency reveal about human nature?

4. From what mystic source did Arthur draw his power? From your knowledge of other legends, what other mystic symbols can you place side by side with Excalibur? Out of what human needs were such symbols created? What passages can you quote to show Arthur's mystic power? to suggest the mystic authority of the Round Table?

Catching the Spirit of Chivalry

5. What lines can you quote to show that, according to the ideals of chivalry,

a. a high value was placed upon friendship?
b. service was considered a privilege as well as a duty?
c. strength in arms and physical courage were applauded?
d. loyalty to an oath was maintained with religious fervor?
e. modesty was a coveted virtue?
f. tenderness was considered compatible with strength?
g. a high unity of purpose was the basis of knightly fellowship?
h. divine guidance was trusted?

Responding to Tennyson's Style

6. What pictures did your imagination see as you read the story?

7. Suppose that you were to plan a specially illustrated edition of "The Coming of Arthur." What passages would you mark for graphic representation? What pictures suggest color to your mind? What title would you give each picture?

8. What comparisons can you find which appeal especially to your imagination?

9. What lines appealed to you for their sound or movement? Did some lines linger in your memory? Did you enjoy saying aloud some particular passage? Which one?

10. With what adjectives would you describe the flow of the lines? Quote a brief passage to illustrate the force of the descriptive words that you choose to describe Tennyson's style.

11. Which of Tennyson's descriptive words and phrases seem to you particularly vivid?

SUMMARIES OF THE INTERVENING IDYLLS

In the first *Idyll* you have seen how Arthur's court has been established in spite of discord and suspicion. In the second *Idyll* the great Round Table is gloriously at work redressing human wrongs. In the story of "Gareth and Lynette," briefly summarized for you below, lofty ambition triumphs over false pride and rumor has not yet started to undermine faith in the ideals of knighthood. But in the next three *Idylls* jealousy and treachery raise their heads and man's baser self seems to reassert itself. The doom of Arthur's kingdom which was prophesied in "The Coming of Arthur"[1] is slowly approaching. The patient faithfulness of Enid in the second summary and the fidelity of the two brothers in the third suggest but a temporary truce between the high and the low; the seeds of evil have been planted and the grim harvest is not far away. This, you remem-

[1] See lines 304–07, 322–24, and 418–22.

ber, is the underlying theme of the *Idylls of the King*. As you read the four summaries that follow, notice how this theme — " Sense at war with soul," as Tennyson expressed it in his dedication " To the Queen " — gains power.

The *Idylls* therefore, as you will see for yourself, have a double interest: the stories and the themes behind them. In your reading of fairy tales you have already met faithful wives and loyal brothers and wicked sorcerers. Enid is like the patient Griselda; Vivien is cut to the very same pattern as Circe, who beguiled the wandering Ulysses. Over and over again we meet these same types of characters in the legends of the past. Do you see how these stock characters stand for the growing ideals of man? These are the stories man told to himself as he dreamed and aspired. The ideals which they represent — somewhat too obviously, it is true, according to modern standards — were the ideals of a great epoch in human development, and they are the steppingstones by which man has attained his present standards. Tennyson expressed the ideals of knighthood in his dedication " To the Queen ":

" Who [1] reverenced his conscience as his king;
Whose glory was, redressing human wrong;
Who spake no slander, no, nor listened to it;
Who loved one only and who clave to her."

How difficult it was to live up to this ideal of knighthood is illustrated in the stories that follow.

GARETH AND LYNETTE

It is now the happy prime of Arthur's reign, when the kingdom has been united and the Round Table has been established. Camelot is the home of justice and righteousness, and chivalry is in full bloom. Gareth, the last tall son of Lot and Bellicent, Arthur's half sister, brooded over his fate. Although he could tilt with a proven knight, his mother counted him still a child and sought to keep him home with her in pity for her loneliness; she would not let him go to Arthur's court and wield his sword for justice — not, at least, until he walked through fire. " Thou shalt go disguised to Arthur's hall," she said, thinking to discourage him, " and hire thyself among the scullions and the kitchen knaves, and thou shalt serve a twelvemonth and a day." And Gareth yielded to her will and set off on foot for Camelot, where he came upon the king, seated at the Table Round, surrounded by his shining knights. And after listening to the cries " A boon, Sir King " by those oppressed, and seeing many a knight ride away to right a wrong, at last he, too, approached the king and, in a voice made weak by hunger, asked to be allowed to serve a twelvemonth and a day, nameless, among the kitchen knaves. And Arthur, seeing him " a goodly youth and worth a goodlier boon," granted his wish.

[1] **who**: ideal knight.

And so for a month Gareth, all for glory, underwent the sooty yoke of kitchen vassalage. And as he went about among the kitchen knaves, he heard exciting tales about the jousts and tournaments and about the brave Sir Lancelot, Arthur's favorite knight. And then his mother, repenting of the vow she made him swear, sent word to Arthur and told him who he was, and Gareth asked to be given the first quest that he might make his name.

On this same day there came to Arthur's hall a lovely damsel of high lineage in distress, Lynette by name, asking for Sir Lancelot to do battle for her sister, imprisoned by a wicked knight. Then up spoke Gareth, asking for the quest, and Arthur gave it to him. A blush of shame and wrath spread over the maiden's face as she left the hall, with Gareth following after. Thereupon, as he rode beside her, she reviled him and called him kitchen knave and scullion. But Gareth followed until they came at last to the river that looped around the Castle Perilous, where the Lady Lyonors was besieged until she should give her consent to wed the wicked knight. And as Gareth fought and overthrew the three that called themselves, in fantasy, Day, Morning Star, Noon Sun, and Evening Star and guarded the entrance to the castle, the maiden's scorn grew less and less. At length there came behind the two a strange knight to avenge those whom Gareth had overthrown. At one touch from the skilled spear Gareth himself fell to the ground, overthrown by Lancelot, in disguise, who at Arthur's bidding had come to see that no real harm came to his erstwhile kitchen knave.

As the three drew near the castle, the knight called Death approached them, and Gareth, having exchanged shields with Lancelot and received from him a fresh charger, in one fierce stroke hurled Death to the ground. From out the black armor issued a blooming boy, who cried for mercy. " Slay me not," he said; " my three brethren bade me do it, to make a horror all about the house, and stay the world from

Lady Lyonors. They never dreamed the passes would be past."

And so the Lady Lyonors was rescued and Gareth won his quest. And some say that Sir Gareth wedded Lyonors, but those that told the tale still later said he married the maiden Lynette.

THE MARRIAGE OF GERAINT *and* GERAINT AND ENID

One Whitsuntide,[1] while Arthur was holding court at old Caerleon on Usk in Wales,[2] Guinevere, with Geraint, Prince of Devon and a Knight of the Round Table, was watching the progress of a hunt. A strange knight rode by. He refused to tell his name when the queen sent a lady in waiting to ask him. Geraint received the same treatment, and he resolved to follow the knight and avenge this insult to Guinevere. All day he followed the stranger until he saw him enter a fortress at the end of a straggling village. Geraint went into the town to secure lodgings but found all the inns filled. There was so much tumult and bustle, besides, that Geraint asked what it all meant; but the only answer he got was, "The sparrow hawk." Finally in an armorer's shop he was told of a tournament to be held next day; hence the confusion in the town. The armorer told Geraint that he might possibly secure harborage with the old Earl Yniol in the tumble-down castle over the bridge.

Geraint went there, met the earl in the courtyard, and was courteously invited to share such humble entertainment as could be provided. While still in the court he heard a voice singing and at once said to himself, "Here, by God's grace, is the one voice for me." On entering the castle there was every sign of faded magnificence; but when he saw Enid, he thought, "Here, by God's rood,[3] is the one maid for me."

After supper Geraint told Yniol who he was and what had brought him there. When he described the strange knight, the earl said that he recognized him as his wicked nephew who, when Enid refused to marry him, had despoiled the earl of his possessions. As further insult he held a tournament each year, with a general challenge to anyone who wanted to dispute with him that his lady was the fairest in the land. That tournament was to be held next day. Here was Geraint's opportunity; all he wanted was fighting equipment. This, the earl said, he could furnish, but more was necessary — a lady for whom to fight. At once Geraint proposed Enid; if he won, he would make her his wife.

The next day there was a great crowd on the field of tourney. The challenger stepped forward to offer his lady the annual prize of beauty, a golden sparrow hawk; but he was stopped with "Forbear; there is a worthier." Surprised to see a knight in Yniol's rusty armor, he cried, "Do battle for it then." Twice they clashed, with honors about even; but when Geraint heard Yniol cry, "Remember the great insult done to the queen," his strength was increased and he brought the nephew down. "Thy name?" he demanded, and the knight, his pride broken because men had seen him fall, replied, "Edyrn, son of Nudd." On pain of death Geraint made him promise to go to the queen and abide her judgment, and to restore Yniol to his rights.

On the morning of the third day Geraint insisted that he had to return to court and asked that Enid prepare for the journey. To Enid all this was rather sudden, all the more because she lacked proper raiment for her first appearance at court; but by good fortune a dress which had been pillaged from their belongings at their downfall was returned that morning, and Enid's mother was arraying her in it. When Geraint heard from Yniol what was going on, he asked that the girl be dressed in the faded silk in which he had first seen her. Seeing the disappointment of the two women, Geraint explained to the mother how the queen had made a promise that whatever bride he brought "herself would clothe her like the sun in heaven."

When Geraint and Enid arrived at court, the queen welcomed them; and the wedding festivities lasted a week. Enid, because of her great beauty and her modesty, became a general favorite, and especially so of the queen, at which Geraint was pleased.

After a time, however, there were such persistent rumors of the love between Lancelot and Guinevere that Geraint, fearful that the honor of Enid might become smirched because

[1] **Whitsuntide:** the week that begins the seventh Sunday after Easter, a church festival week commemorating the descent of the Holy Ghost upon the apostles. [2] Usk is now in Monmouthshire, England. [3] **rood:** crucifix.

of her intimacy with the queen, asked permission from Arthur to return to his own home. Once there, Geraint determined that nothing that a husband could do should be left undone to keep his wife true. He gave up all his regular activities as a knight and a prince to stay at home with Enid. After a while his own people began to say nasty things about their once valiant prince who now loafed all day at home to be with his beautiful wife. Enid heard these reports and was sad, but dared not tell Geraint because of her " bashful delicacy " and her husband's jealous temper. Geraint, noticing a change in Enid, jumped to the conclusion that she was sighing for some lover at court. One morning while Geraint still lay asleep Enid went over the situation in her mind, bemoaning half aloud her lack of will power to tell her husband the truth, and concluded, " O me, I fear that I am no true wife! " Geraint awoke just in time to hear that last remark and became terribly angry — the anger of jealousy — for now he was convinced that his suspicions had been well founded. He " hurled his huge limbs out of bed " and ordered his horse and her palfrey to be prepared for a journey into the wilderness. " Put on thy worst and meanest dress," he told Enid; and when she asked for some explanation, he only said, " I charge thee, ask not, but obey." Sadly she put on the dress of faded silk in which Geraint had first seen her, in the vain hope that he would come to his senses when he saw and recognized it.

Geraint ordered Enid to ride on ahead and not to speak to him; but when she saw three bandits hiding behind a rock and overheard them planning to kill the laggard knight and take his armor and damsel, she warned him. All the thanks she got was a scolding for her disobedience. Geraint easily disposed of the three, took their horses and armor, and ordered Enid to drive the horses before her. When Geraint saw what difficulty she had in obeying him, he felt some pity; but presently he became angrier than ever. Three more scoundrels were given treatment similar to that of the first three. They went on until noon, and Geraint gave a farmer's boy a horse and armor for the food he was carrying to mowers in a field. The boy obtained lodgings for the night for them. It happened that they were in the territory of the Earl Limours, who had once courted Enid but who was such a drunkard that, according to the tale that Yniol had told Geraint, he was drunk even when he came to woo. This precious knight, hearing there was a stranger in his town, came to make a courtesy call. Geraint furnished liberal refreshments, and Limours, before he left, seeing that all was not well between Enid and her husband, offered Enid his assistance in getting rid of Geraint if she would join him. In order to gain time Enid told him to come in the morning, hoping in the meanwhile to warn Geraint. This she accomplished rather awkwardly; but they left before the arrival of Limours, Geraint giving the remaining horses and armor to his host of the night.

They went on as before until Limours and his followers caught up with them. In the fight Geraint was wounded but victorious. As they once more proceeded, Geraint fell off his horse in a faint; and Enid sat by the side of the road in the hope that someone might come along to give her assistance. They were now in the domain of the lawless and turbulent Earl Doorm. At noon the earl himself came along, and, because Enid was fair, he ordered her taken to his castle with the unconscious Geraint. There all afternoon Geraint lay, with Enid softly weeping by his side trying to revive him. He finally came out of his swoon; but when he saw Enid crying, he feigned sleep in order to make sure that she was weeping for him.

That evening there was a loud feast in Doorm's hall. When the red-headed earl had eaten and drunk copiously, he noticed Enid at the end of the hall drooping by the side of Geraint. He ordered her to eat and drink, but she said she would do so only if her lord arose and bade her do it. Doorm assured her that Geraint would never rise again, and then mocked at a knight who would clothe such beauty in such rags. He offered her rich garments, but Enid told the story of the faded dress. The angry and baffled earl slapped Enid on the cheek, at which she gave a sharp cry. This brought Geraint to his feet at last. He grasped his sword and with one blow " the russet-bearded head rolled on the floor." The followers of Doorm rushed away in fear.

Geraint, convinced that his wife was true, apologized and promised that he " will henceforth rather die than doubt." As they rode away, they were challenged by a knight in armor — no other than Edyrn, son of Nudd, now a reformed and honored knight of the Round Table, who had been sent to warn Doorm to quit his lawless habits. Edyrn acted as their guide to Arthur, who was not far away, and Geraint and Enid lived happily ever after.

BALIN AND BALAN

Balin, called "the Savage" because of his quick and violent temper, had been banished from the court of Arthur for striking a servant. After three years he returned with his twin brother Balan, and Arthur took them both into favor. Balin worshiped Lancelot and, thinking that one of the reasons why Lancelot had achieved such fame was the favor of the queen, asked whether he might not wear some slight token of her good will. She allowed him to wear her crown on his shield; and now he felt secure against his savage temper, even after his brother had gone on his first quest — to rid the forest of a demon.

But one day he saw the queen and Lancelot walking in the garden and overheard their conversation. He became exceedingly angry because he thought it too intimate, and rushed from the court without asking the king's permission. He rode madly all day until he came to the court of Garlon, nephew of King Pellam, neither of whom was friendly toward Arthur. They had to extend hospitality to Balin; but at the table they made insulting insinuations about Lancelot and the queen — confirming his own thoughts, although he tried not to believe them. Next morning he was again insulted by Garlon, whom he fought. In the duel Balin broke his sword and, as he had broken his lance the day before, he rushed into a chapel and seized a long lance that lay on the altar. He managed to get to his horse and once more galloped madly away. At last, his horse tired out, Balin dismounted, hung his shield on a branch, vowing never again to wear it, and lay down.

While Balin lay there, it chanced that Vivien, a damsel from the wicked court of King Mark of Cornwall, passed by with a squire on their way to Arthur's court. She saw the shield on the tree and a powerful knight lying apparently dead; but when he awoke, she, pretending to be a damsel in distress, appealed to Balin to be her knight and guide her to the court. Balin once more became angry at himself for having, as he thought, defiled the monogram on his shield. Vivien, thinking to win his favor, told a lying tale of Lancelot and the queen; but this story, added to his own observation and the taunts of Garlon, at last confirmed Balin's worst suspicions. He tore the shield from the tree, stamped on the crown with his heel, and uttered a weird shriek of anger.

Balan, his quest unfulfilled, heard that shriek and thought that now he was surely upon the demon. Not recognizing his brother nor the strange shield, he set upon Balin, who had seized the shield of Vivien's squire and mounted his horse. Balan, pierced by Balin's lance, fell from his horse; Balin was crushed by his weary horse falling on him. Both knights lay unconscious. Vivien asked her squire to unloose their helmets so that she could see what the knights were like. They appeared dead and she and her squire rode on.

The cool breeze revived the brothers for a moment, and they recognized each other. Balin took upon himself the full blame after telling Balan what had happened. Balin was convinced that his fate would be dark in the hereafter, but Balan said simply, "Good night, true brother, here! Good morrow there!" They died in each other's arms.

MERLIN AND VIVIEN

King Mark of Cornwall, never taken into the favor of Arthur, readily fell in with Vivien's idea of going to the court to test its virtues, so constantly extolled by wandering minstrels. On her arrival she won tolerance from the queen by her story of the wrongs suffered from Mark. Being worldly-wise, she took note of conditions at Arthur's court — at this time filled with knights because there was no war. She was early convinced of the love between Lancelot and Guinevere and Arthur's ignorance of it. Her mission was to stir up trouble, but she proceeded craftily. She tried to spread gossip and once threw out hints to the king himself, but he simply stared at her blankly. She was determined to fasten herself on somebody and finally picked Merlin. He was old and world-weary after having for so many years been the king's builder and chief adviser in all the practical details of statecraft other than war. The attentions of the pretty young woman flattered him, and at times he half believed that she loved him.

In the course of time there fell on Merlin "a great melancholy," because he saw that the great work of his life was about to crash and that he was powerless to stop it. Rather than see the ruin of everything he loved he decided to leave. Vivien followed him, although uninvited, as he stepped into a boat. They crossed the channel into Brittany and wandered into the forest, Vivien having set her mind on getting from Merlin the charm of "woven paces and of waving arms "[1] of which Merlin in an unguarded moment had once told her.

From this point on, the story is nothing more than Vivien's attempt to gain this charm. She used every trick that a wily, beautiful woman could possibly work on an old man who was equally wily. She made constant protestations of her love; he put her off, through either silence or laughter, or by telling her riddling tales. Once in a while he almost seemed to yield, but recovered in time; then she wept, but even this last resort of a clever woman did not work. She tried the subterfuge of hurt feelings, declaring that she could stand thwarted love no longer, and threatened to leave him. Merlin weakened but again caught himself in time. It happened that a storm was coming on, and Merlin sought shelter. Vivien, the wily, let the storm beat on her until the old man out of pity drew her to shelter. The storm was raging, and Vivien resorted to one final trick. "Before I leave," she said, "may the lightning make my scheming brain to a cinder, if I lie." Just then there was a terrific flash, lightning struck a tree near by, and Vivien in genuine fright clung to Merlin for protection, but never forgetting her main purpose. While tempest roared and lightning flashed, she clung to him; and at last "Merlin, overtalked and overworn," told her the charm and fell asleep. Immediately she worked the charm on him and he lay in the hollow of an oak as if dead, while Vivien cried, "I have made his glory mine," and rushed through the forest shouting, "Fool!" The forest echoed, "Fool!"

THINK BACK OVER WHAT YOU HAVE READ

Recognizing the Allegorical Significance of the Stories

The simple mind sees only extreme differences: for example, the difference between black and white or the difference between hot and cold. It does not recognize subtle variations of degree which lie between these two limits. Thus, in his early groping after ideas, primitive man was inclined to oversimplify the problems of good and evil. Right was right, and wrong was wrong; a villain was all bad, and a hero was all good. He did not make fine distinctions between *somewhat good* and *sometimes bad,* for his mind had not yet sharpened and refined its perceptions.

This mental trait, you have already discovered, is revealed in the legends of the past. As you consider, hereafter, the value of the stories which you read, or the pictures which you see on the screen, keep this idea in mind. Barring superficial differences in costume and setting, how far do they progress beyond the primitive pattern? The following questions for discussion will help you appreciate the pattern as it is expressed in the preceding summaries:

1. What incidents in the stories you have just read remind you of other well-known fairy tales? Is there anything to suggest Cinderella? What elements of plot are typical of the fairy-tale pattern?

2. What facts of life — such as the common enmity of brothers or the mysterious behavior of the insane — can you think of which might explain how each story originated? What secret hopes of mankind do you think the following story incidents stand for? How does the story itself seem to solve, imaginatively, the problem raised?

   a. the lovely Enid, discovered in faded silk rags and taken to court without proper raiment
   b. the courteous earl, despoiled of his possessions by his wicked nephew
   c. the impulsive Balin, wearing the queen's token as a charm against his savage temper
   d. Balin, tearing the shield from the tree and stamping on the crown of the false queen with his heel
   e. Merlin, locked in his own charm, lying as if dead in the hollow of the oak

3. According to the fairy-tale pattern, what virtues are always rewarded? What virtues are especially reverenced in women? in men?

4. What practical lesson in faith do the stories seem to preach? Which of the stories is a parable illustrating the evil of shattered faith? Can you think of a reason why faith was considered so important in the early history of mankind?

[1] **woven paces:** intricate magic steps. **waving arms:** gestures of sorcery.

"The man so wrought on, even seem'd to lie,
Closed in the four walls of a hollow tower,
From which was no escape forever more;
And none could find that man forever more,
Nor could he see but him who wrought the charm
Coming and going, and he lay as dead
And lost to life and use and name and fame."
(from "Merlin and Vivien")

LANCELOT AND ELAINE

Dramatic interest centers in conflict. The most simple form of drama is an athletic contest in which two opposing sides try to defeat each other. In life, however, dramatic conflict is more subtle. The lines of battle are not sharply drawn, and the contending forces are not easily recognized. Sometimes the real issue of combat is disguised; sometimes the villain masquerades as the hero. Sometimes, too, the conflict is mental rather than physical and the weapons used are emotional rather than material. Human motives are seldom simple and direct and clear; and human relationships, therefore, are often a tangle of interacting aims and desires. For these reasons life itself teems with dramatic interest.

In your reading of the *Idylls* so far you have already encountered hints of dramatic conflict. In "The Coming of Arthur," you remember, the doom of Arthur's kingdom was prophesied; and in the later *Idylls* the wicked buzz of gossip threatened to poison faith in the ideals of the Round Table. In the tragic story that follows, this sense of dramatic foreboding is partially fulfilled. You will feel, as you read of Elaine's ill-fated love and of Lancelot's secret betrayal of Arthur's trust, the keen edge of dramatic irony. The ever-faithful king, although standing always on the brink of discovery, remains unaware of the canker that eats at the heart of his kingdom. Thus irony is added to irony.

As you read the story, you will wish to pay special attention to the dramatic conflicts. Notice the subtle enmity between Lancelot and the queen which flourishes in spite of their great love. Do you see how each is at war with himself? Notice the impassable barrier between Lancelot and Elaine and how Arthur's goodness, his inability to suspect another, makes him an easy victim of intrigue. You will find all these dramatic conflicts told in language of rare beauty and power. In no other *Idyll* will you find more finely wrought comparisons. In no other *Idyll* are the pictures of chivalry more glamorous.

Elaine the fair, Elaine the lovable,
Elaine, the lily maid of Astolat,
High in her chamber up a tower to the east
Guarded the sacred shield of Lancelot;
Which first she placed where morning's earliest ray 5
Might strike it, and awake her with the gleam;
Then fearing rust or soilure fashioned for it
A case of silk, and braided thereupon
All the devices blazoned on the shield
In their own tinct, and added, of her wit, 10
A border fantasy of branch and flower,
And yellow-throated nestling in the nest.
Nor rested thus content, but day by day,
Leaving her household and good father, climbed
That eastern tower, and entering barred her door, 15
Stript off the case, and read the naked shield,
Now guessed a hidden meaning in his arms,
Now made a pretty history to herself
Of every dint a sword had beaten in it,
And every scratch a lance had made upon it, 20
Conjecturing when and where: this cut is fresh;
That ten years back; this dealt him at Caerlyle;
That at Caerleon; this at Camelot;
And ah, God's mercy, what a stroke was there!
And here a thrust that might have killed, but God 25

22–23. These places were famous because of Arthur's victories.

Broke the strong lance, and rolled his enemy down,
And saved him; so she lived in fantasy.

How came the lily maid by that good shield
Of Lancelot, she that knew not even his name?
He left it with her, when he rode to tilt 30
For the great diamond in the diamond jousts,
Which Arthur had ordained, and by that name
Had named them, since a diamond was the prize.

For Arthur, long before they crowned him king,
Roving the trackless realms of Lyonesse, 35
Had found a glen, gray boulder, and black tarn.
A horror lived about the tarn, and clave
Like its own mists to all the mountainside;
For here two brothers, one a king, had met
And fought together; but their names were lost; 40
And each had slain his brother at a blow;
And down they fell and made the glen abhorred,
And there they lay till all their bones were bleached,
And lichened into color with the crags
And he that once was king had on a crown 45
Of diamonds, one in front and four aside.
And Arthur came, and laboring up the pass,
All in a misty moonshine, unawares
Had trodden that crowned skeleton, and the skull
Brake from the nape, and from the skull the crown 50
Rolled into light, and turning on its rims
Fled like a glittering rivulet to the tarn.
And down the shingly scaur he plunged, and caught,
And set it on his head, and in his heart
Heard murmurs, "Lo, thou likewise shalt be king." 55

Thereafter, when a king, he had the gems
Plucked from the crown, and showed them to his knights
Saying, " These jewels, whereupon I chanced
Divinely, are the kingdom's, not the king's —
For public use; henceforward let there be, 60
Once every year, a joust for one of these,
For so by nine years' proof we needs must learn
Which is our mightiest, and ourselves shall grow
In use of arms and manhood, till we drive
The heathen, who, some say, shall rule the land 65

35. **Lyonesse:** frequently mentioned in Arthurian legend and supposed to have been a land between Cornwall and the Scilly Islands, which are now submerged. 55. Notice the suggestion that Arthur's kingship was of miraculous origin. In "The Coming of Arthur," you remember, such references were frequent. 65. Notice the prophecy of the downfall of Arthur's kingdom.

Hereafter, which God hinder! " Thus he spoke,
And eight years past, eight jousts had been, and still
Had Lancelot won the diamond of the year,
With purpose to present them to the queen
When all were won; but, meaning all at once 70
To snare her royal fancy with a boon
Worth half her realm, had never spoken word.

Now for the central diamond and the last
And largest, Arthur, holding then his court
Hard on the river nigh the place which now 75
Is this world's hugest, let proclaim a joust
At Camelot, and when the time drew nigh
Spake — for she had been sick — to Guinevere:
" Are you so sick, my queen, you cannot move
To these fair jousts? " " Yea, lord," she said, " ye know it." 80
" Then will ye miss," he answered, " the great deeds
Of Lancelot, and his prowess in the lists,
A sight ye love to look on." And the queen
Lifted her eyes, and they dwelt languidly
On Lancelot, where he stood beside the king. 85
He, thinking that he read her meaning there,
" Stay with me, I am sick; my love is more
Than many diamonds," yielded; and a heart
Love-loyal to the least wish of the queen —
However much he yearned to make complete 90
The tale of diamonds for his destined boon —
Urged him to speak against the truth, and say:
" Sir king, mine ancient wound is hardly whole,
And lets me from the saddle "; and the king
Glanced first at him, then her, and went his way. 95
No sooner gone than suddenly she began:

" To blame, my lord Sir Lancelot, much to blame!
Why go ye not to these fair jousts? the knights
Are half of them our enemies, and the crowd
Will murmur, ' Lo the shameless ones, who take 100
Their pastime now the trustful king is gone! ' "
Then Lancelot, vext at having lied in vain:
" Are ye so wise? ye were not once so wise,
My queen, that summer when ye loved me first.
Then of the crowd ye took no more account 105
Than of the myriad cricket of the mead,
When its own voice clings to each blade of grass,
And every voice is nothing. As to knights,

70–72. In other words, Lancelot kept secret his intention to present the diamonds to the queen. 76. **world's hugest:** London.

Them surely can I silence with all ease.
But now my loyal worship is allowed 110
Of all men; many a bard, without offense,
Has linked our names together in his lay,
Lancelot, the flower of bravery, Guinevere,
The pearl of beauty; and our knights at feast
Have pledged us in this union, while the king 115
Would listen smiling. How then? is there more?
Has Arthur spoken aught? or would yourself,
Now weary of my service and devoir,
Henceforth be truer to your faultless lord?"

She broke into a little scornful laugh: 120
"Arthur, my lord, Arthur, the faultless king,
That passionate perfection, my good lord —
But who can gaze upon the sun in heaven?
He never spake a word of reproach to me,
He never had a glimpse of mine untruth, 125
He cares not for me; only here today
There gleamed a vague suspicion in his eyes;
Some meddling rogue has tampered with him — else
Rapt in this fancy of his Table Round,
And swearing men to vows impossible, 130
To make them like himself; but, friend, to me
He is all fault who hath no fault at all,
For who loves me must have a touch of earth;
The low sun makes the color; I am yours,
Not Arthur's, as ye know, save by the bond. 135
And therefore hear my words: go to the jousts;
The tiny-trumpeting gnat can break our dream
When sweetest; and the vermin voices here
May buzz so loud — we scorn them, but they sting."

Then answered Lancelot, the chief of knights: 140
"And with what face, after my pretext made,
Shall I appear, O queen, at Camelot, I
Before a king who honors his own word
As if it were his God's?"

"Yea," said the queen,
"A moral child without the craft to rule, 145
Else had he not lost me; but listen to me,
If I must find you wit: we hear it said
That men go down before your spear at a touch,
But knowing you are Lancelot; your great name,
This conquers; hide it therefore; go unknown. 150

126–27. Compare these lines with lines 92–96. 135. **bond:** that is, of marriage. 141–44. Refer again to lines 93–94.

Win! by this kiss you will, and our true king
Will then allow your pretext, O my knight,
As all for glory; for to speak him true,
Ye know right well, how meek soe'er he seem,
No keener hunter after glory breaths. 155
He loves it in his knights more than himself;
They prove to him his work; win and return."

Then got Sir Lancelot suddenly to horse,
Wroth at himself. Not willing to be known,
He left the barren-beaten thoroughfare, 160
Chose the green path that showed the rarer foot,
And there among the solitary downs,
Full often lost in fancy, lost his way;
Till as he traced a faintly shadowed track,
That all in loops and links among the dales 165
Ran to the Castle of Astolat, he saw
Fired from the west, far on a hill, the towers.
Thither he made, and blew the gateway horn.
Then came an old, dumb, myriad-wrinkled man,
Who let him into lodging and disarmed. 170
And Lancelot marveled at the wordless man;
And issuing found the Lord of Astolat
With two strong sons, Sir Torre and Sir Lavaine,
Moving to meet him in the castle court;
And close behind them stept the lily maid 175
Elaine, his daughter; mother of the house
There was not. Some light jest among them rose
With laughter dying down as the great knight
Approached them; then the Lord of Astolat:
"Whence comest thou, my guest, and by what name 180
Livest between the lips? for by thy state
And presence I might guess thee chief of those,
After the king, who eat in Arthur's halls.
Him have I seen; the rest, his Table Round,
Known as they are, to me they are unknown." 185

Then answered Lancelot, the chief of knights:
"Known am I, and of Arthur's hall, and known,
What I by mere mischance have brought, my shield.
But since I go to joust as one unknown
At Camelot for the diamond, ask me not; 190
Hereafter ye shall know me — and the shield —
I pray you lend me one, if such you have,
Blank, or at least with some device not mine."

187–88. Read the lines **"Known am I . . . and known . . . my shield"** and the meaning will become clear.

Then said the Lord of Astolat, "Here is Torre's;
Hurt in his first tilt was my son, Sir Torre; 195
And so, God wot, his shield is blank enough.
His ye can have." Then added plain Sir Torre:
"Yea, since I cannot use it, ye may have it."
Here laughed the father saying, "Fie, sir churl,
Is that an answer for a noble knight? 200
Allow him! but Lavaine, my younger here,
He is so full of lustihood, he will ride,
Joust for it, and win, and bring it in an hour,
And set it in this damsel's golden hair,
To make her thrice as willful as before." 205

"Nay, father, nay, good father, shame me not
Before this noble knight," said young Lavaine,
"For nothing. Surely I but played on Torre;
He seemed so sullen, vext he could not go.
A jest, no more! for, knight, the maiden dreamt 210
That someone put this diamond in her hand,
And that it was too slippery to be held,
And slipt and fell into some pool or stream,
The castle well, belike; and then I said
That *if* I went and *if* I fought and won it — 215
But all was jest and joke among ourselves —
Then must she keep it safelier. All was jest.
But, father, give me leave, and if he will,
To ride to Camelot with this noble knight;
Win shall I not, but do my best to win; 220
Young as I am, yet would I do my best."

"So ye will grace me," answered Lancelot,
Smiling a moment, "with your fellowship
O'er these waste downs whereon I lost myself,
Then were I glad of you as guide and friend; 225
And you shall win this diamond — as I hear,
It is a fair large diamond — if ye may,
And yield it to this maiden, if ye will."
"A fair large diamond," added plain Sir Torre,
"Such be for queens, and not for simple maids." 230
Then she, who held her eyes upon the ground,
Elaine, and heard her name so tost about,
Flushed slightly at the slight disparagement
Before the stranger knight, who, looking at her,
Full courtly, yet not falsely, thus returned: 235
"If what is fair be but for what is fair,
And only queens are to be counted so,

201. **Allow him** is said in sarcasm. 203. **it**: the diamond.

Rash were my judgment then, who deem this maid
Might wear as fair a jewel as is on earth,
Not violating the bond of like to like." 240

He spoke and ceased; the lily maid Elaine,
Won by the mellow voice before she looked,
Lifted her eyes and read his lineaments.
The great and guilty love he bare the queen,
In battle with the love he bare his lord, 245
Had marred his face, and marked it ere his time.
Another sinning on such heights with one,
The flower of all the west and all the world,
Had been the sleeker for it; but in him
His mood was often like a fiend, and rose 250
And drove him into wastes and solitudes
For agony, who was yet a living soul.
Marred as he was, he seemed the goodliest man
That ever among ladies ate in hall,
And noblest, when she lifted up her eyes. 255
However marred, of more than twice her years,
Seamed with an ancient sword cut on the cheek,
And bruised and bronzed, she lifted up her eyes
And loved him, with that love which was her doom.

Then the great knight, the darling of the court, 260
Loved of the loveliest, into that rude hall
Stept with all grace, and not with half disdain
Hid under grace, as in a smaller time,
But kindly man moving among his kind;
Whom they with meats and vintage of their best 265
And talk and minstrel melody entertained.
And much they asked of court and Table Round,
And ever well and readily answered he;
But Lancelot, when they glanced at Guinevere,
Suddenly speaking of the wordless man, 270
Heard from the baron that, ten years before,
The heathen caught and reft him of his tongue.
"He learnt and warned me of their fierce design
Against my house, and him they caught and maimed;
But I, my sons, and little daughter fled 275
From bonds or death, and dwelt among the woods
By the great river in a boatman's hut.
Dull days were those, till our good Arthur broke
The pagan yet once more on Badon hill."

248–49. Queen Guinevere (**The flower of all the west**) did not show in her face the sign of a tormented conscience, as did Lancelot. 269–70. **when they glanced at** (that is, referred to) **Guinevere,** Lancelot changed the subject and asked about the old man who answered the gateway horn at Astolat. See line 169. 272–79. The baron is talking, explaining how the wordless man had lost his tongue. 279. **Badon hill:** the last of Arthur's great battles.

"O there, great lord, doubtless," Lavaine said, rapt 280
By all the sweet and sudden passion of youth
Toward greatness in its elder, "you have fought.
O, tell us — for we live apart — you know
Of Arthur's glorious wars." And Lancelot spoke
And answered him at full, as having been 285
With Arthur in the fight which all day long
Rang by the white mouth of the violent Glem;
And in the four loud battles by the shore
Of Duglas; that on Bassa; then the war
That thundered in and out the gloomy skirts 290
Of Celidon the forest; and again
By Castle Gurnion, where the glorious king
Had on his cuirass worn our Lady's head,
Carved of one emerald centered in a sun
Of silver rays that lightened as he breathed; 295
And at Caerleon had he helped his lord,
When the strong neighings of the wild white horse
Set every gilded parapet shuddering;
And up in Agned-Cathregonion too,
And down the waste sand shores of Trath Treroit, 300
Where many a heathen fell; "and on the mount
Of Badon I myself beheld the king
Charge at the head of all his Table Round,
And all his legions crying Christ and him,
And break them; and I saw him, after, stand 305
High on a heap of slain, from spur to plume
Red as the rising sun with heathen blood,
And seeing me, with a great voice he said:
'They are broken, they are broken!' for the king,
However mild he seems at home, nor cares 310
For triumph in our mimic wars, the jousts —
For if his own knight casts him down, he laughs,
Saying his knights are better men than he —
Yet in this heathen war the fire of God
Fills him; I never saw his like; there lives 315
No greater leader."

While he uttered this,
Low to her own heart said the lily maid:
"Save your great self, fair lord"; and when he fell
From talk of war to traits of pleasantry —
Being mirthful he, but in a stately kind — 320
She still took note that, when the living smile
Died from his lips, across him came a cloud
Of melancholy severe, from which again,

297. **white horse**: emblem of the invading Saxons.

Whenever in her hovering to and fro
The lily maid had striven to make him cheer, 325
There brake a sudden-beaming tenderness
Of manners and of nature; and she thought
That all was nature, all, perchance, for her.
And all night long his face before her lived,
As when a painter, poring on a face, 330
Divinely through all hindrance finds the man
Behind it, and so paints him that his face,
The shape and color of a mind and life,
Lives for his children, ever at its best
And fullest; so the face before her lived, 335
Dark-splendid, speaking in the silence, full
Of noble things, and held her from her sleep,
Till rathe she rose, half-cheated in the thought
She needs must bid farewell to sweet Lavaine.
First as in fear, step after step, she stole 340
Down the long tower stairs, hesitating;
Anon, she heard Sir Lancelot cry in the court:
"This shield, my friend, where is it?" and Lavaine
Past inward, as she came from out the tower.
There to his proud horse Lancelot turned, and smoothed 345
The glossy shoulder, humming to himself.
Half-envious of the flattering hand, she drew
Nearer and stood. He looked, and, more amazed
Than if seven men had set upon him, saw
The maiden standing in the dewy light. 350
He had not dreamed she was so beautiful.
Then came on him a sort of sacred fear,
For silent, though he greeted her, she stood
Rapt on his face as if it were a god's.
Suddenly flashed on her a wild desire 355
That he should wear her favor at the tilt.
She braved a riotous heart in asking for it.
"Fair lord, whose name I know not — noble it is,
I well believe, the noblest — will you wear
My favor at this tourney?" "Nay," said he, 360
"Fair lady, since I never yet have worn
Favor of any lady in the lists.
Such is my wont, as those who know me know."
"Yea, so," she answered; "then in wearing mine
Needs must be lesser likelihood, noble lord, 365
That those who know should know you." And he turned
Her counsel up and down within his mind,
And found it true, and answered, "True my child.
Well, I will wear it; fetch it out to me;
What is it?" and she told him, "A red sleeve 370

Broidered with pearls," and brought it; then he bound
Her token on his helmet, with a smile
Saying, "I never yet have done so much
For any maiden living," and the blood
Sprang to her face and filled her with delight; 375
But left her all the paler when Lavaine
Returning brought the yet-unblazoned shield,
His brother's; which he gave to Lancelot,
Who parted with his own to fair Elaine;
"Do me this grace, my child, to have my shield 380
In keeping till I come." "A grace to me,"
She answered, "twice today. I am your squire!"
Whereat Lavaine said laughing, "Lily maid,
For fear our people call you lily maid
In earnest, let me bring your color back; 385
Once, twice, and thrice: now get you hence to bed."
So kissed her, and Sir Lancelot his own hand,
And thus they moved away; she stayed a minute,
Then made a sudden step to the gate, and there —
Her bright hair blown about her serious face 390
Yet rosy-kindled with her brother's kiss —
Paused by the gateway, standing near the shield
In silence, while she watched their arms far off
Sparkle, until they dipt below the downs.
Then to her tower she climbed, and took the shield, 395
There kept it, and so lived in fantasy.

Meanwhile the new companions past away
Far o'er the long backs of the bushless downs,
To where Sir Lancelot knew there lived a knight
Not far from Camelot, now for forty years 400
A hermit, who had prayed, labored and prayed,
And ever laboring had scooped himself
In the white rock a chapel and a hall
On massive columns, like a shore-cliff cave,
And cells and chambers; all were fair and dry; 405
The green light from the meadows underneath
Struck up and lived along the milky roofs;
And in the meadows tremulous aspen trees
And poplars made a noise of falling showers.
And thither wending there that night they bode. 410

But when the next day broke from underground,
And shot red fire and shadows through the cave,
They rose, heard mass, broke fast, and rode away.
Then Lancelot saying, "Hear, but hold my name
Hidden, you ride with Lancelot of the Lake," 415

Abashed Lavaine, whose instant reverence,
Dearer to true young hearts than their own praise,
But left him leave to stammer, "Is it indeed?"
And after muttering, "The great Lancelot,"
At last he got his breath and answered, "One, 420
One have I seen — that other, our liege lord,
The dread Pendragon, Britain's king of kings,
Of whom the people talk mysteriously,
He will be there — then were I stricken blind
That minute, I might say that I had seen." 425

So spake Lavaine, and when they reached the lists
By Camelot in the meadow, let his eyes
Run through the peopled gallery which half round
Lay like a rainbow fallen upon the grass,
Until they found the clear-faced king, who sat 430
Robed in red samite, easily to be known,
Since to his crown the golden dragon clung,
And down his robe the dragon writhed in gold,
And from the carven work behind him crept
Two dragons gilded, sloping down to make 435
Arms for his chair, while all the rest of them
Through knots and loops and folds innumerable
Fled ever through the woodwork, till they found
The new design wherein they lost themselves,
Yet with all ease, so tender was the work; 440
And, in the costly canopy o'er him set,
Blazed the last diamond of the nameless king.

Then Lancelot answered young Lavaine and said:
"Me you call great; mine is the firmer seat,
The truer lance; but there is many a youth 445
Now crescent, who will come to all I am
And overcome it; and in me there dwells
No greatness, save it be some far-off touch
Of greatness to know well I am not great.
There is the man." And Lavaine gaped upon him 450
As on a thing miraculous, and anon
The trumpets blew; and then did either side,
They that assailed, and they that held the lists,
Set lance in rest, strike spur, suddenly move,
Meet in the midst, and there so furiously 455
Shock that a man far off might well perceive,
If any man that day were left afield,

420–25. Lavaine means that to have seen Arthur was so great a privilege that it would compensate for blindness. 450. **There is the man:** Lancelot probably points to Arthur as he says this.

The hard earth shake, and a low thunder of arms.
And Lancelot bode a little, till he saw
Which were the weaker; then he hurled into it 460
Against the stronger; little need to speak
Of Lancelot in his glory! King, duke, earl,
Count, baron — whom he smote, he overthrew.

But in the field were Lancelot's kith and kin,
Ranged with the Table Round that held the lists, 465
Strong men, and wrathful that a stranger knight
Should do and almost overdo the deeds
Of Lancelot; and one said to the other, "Lo!
What is he? I do not mean the force alone —
The grace and versatility of the man! 470
Is it not Lancelot?" "When has Lancelot worn
Favor of any lady in the lists?
Not such his wont, as we that know him know."
"How then? who then?" a fury seized them all,
A fiery family passion for the name 475
Of Lancelot, and a glory one with theirs.
They couched their spears and pricked their steeds, and thus,
Their plumes driven backward by the wind they made
In moving, all together down upon him
Bare, as a wild wave in the wide North Sea, 480
Green-glimmering toward the summit, bears, with all
Its stormy crests that smoke against the skies,
Down on a bark, and overbears the bark
And him that helms it; so they overbore
Sir Lancelot and his charger, and a spear 485
Down-glancing lamed the charger, and a spear
Pricked sharply his own cuirass, and the head
Pierced through his side, and there snapt and remained.

Then Sir Lavaine did well and worshipfully;
He bore a knight of old repute to the earth, 490
And brought his horse to Lancelot where he lay.
He up the side, sweating with agony, got,
But thought to do while he might yet endure,
And being lustily holpen by the rest,
His party — though it seemed half miracle 495
To those he fought with — drave his kith and kin,
And all the Table Round that held the lists,
Back to the barrier; then the trumpets blew
Proclaiming his the prize who wore the sleeve
Of scarlet and the pearls; and all the knights, 500
His party, cried: "Advance and take thy prize
The diamond"; but he answered, "Diamond me

No diamonds! for God's love, a little air!
Prize me no prizes, for my prize is death!
Hence will I, and I charge you, follow me not." 505

He spoke, and vanished suddenly from the field
With young Lavaine into the poplar grove.
There from his charger down he slid, and sat,
Gasping to Sir Lavaine, " Draw the lance head."
" Ah, my sweet lord Sir Lancelot," said Lavaine, 510
" I dread me, if I draw it, you will die."
But he: " I die already with it; draw —
Draw " — and Lavaine drew, and Sir Lancelot gave
A marvelous great shriek and ghastly groan,
And half his blood burst forth, and down he sank 515
For the pure pain, and wholly swooned away.
Then came the hermit out and bare him in;
There stanched his wound; and there, in daily doubt
Whether to live or die, for many a week
Hid from the wild world's rumor by the grove 520
Of poplars with their noise of falling showers,
And ever-tremulous aspen trees, he lay.

But on that day when Lancelot fled the lists,
His party, knights of utmost North and West,
Lords of waste marshes, kings of desolate isles, 525
Came round their great Pendragon, saying to him:
" Lo, sire, our knight, through whom we won the day
Hath gone sore wounded, and hath left his prize
Untaken, crying that his prize is death."
" Heaven hinder," said the king, " that such an one, 530
So great a knight as we have seen today —
He seemed to me another Lancelot —
Yea, twenty times I thought him Lancelot —
He must not pass uncared for. Wherefore rise,
O Gawain, and ride forth and find the knight. 535
Wounded and wearied, needs must he be near.
I charge you that you get at once to horse.
And, knights and kings, there breathes not one of you
Will deem this prize of ours is rashly given;
His prowess was too wondrous. We will do him 540
No customary honor; since the knight
Came not to us, of us to claim the prize,
Ourselves will send it after. Rise and take
This diamond, and deliver it, and return,
And bring us where he is, and how he fares, 545
And cease not from your quest until ye find."

So saying, from the carven flower above,
To which it made a restless heart, he took
And gave the diamond; then from where he sat
At Arthur's right, with smiling face arose, 550
With smiling face and frowning heart, a prince
In the midnight and flourish of his May,
Gawain, surnamed the Courteous, fair and strong,
And after Lancelot, Tristram, and Geraint,
And Gareth, a good knight, but therewithal 555
Sir Modred's brother, and the child of Lot,
Nor often loyal to his word, and now
Wroth that the king's command to sally forth
In quest of whom he knew not, made him leave
The banquet and concourse of knights and kings. 560

So all in wrath he got to horse and went;
While Arthur to the banquet, dark in mood,
Past, thinking: "Is it Lancelot who hath come
Despite the wound he spake of, all for gain
Of glory, and hath added wound to wound, 565
And ridden away to die?" So feared the king,
And, after two days' tarriance there, returned.
Then when he saw the queen, embracing asked:
"Love, are you yet so sick?" "Nay, lord," she said.
"And where is Lancelot?" Then the queen amazed: 570
"Was he not with you? won he not your prize?"
"Nay, but one like him." "Why, that like was he."
And when the king demanded how she knew,
Said, "Lord, no sooner had ye parted from us
Than Lancelot told me of a common talk 575
That men went down before his spear at a touch,
But knowing he was Lancelot; his great name
Conquered; and therefore would he hide his name
From all men, even the king, and to this end
Had made the pretext of a hindering wound, 580
That he might joust unknown of all, and learn
If his old prowess were in aught decayed;
And added, 'Our true Arthur, when he learns,
Will well allow my pretext, as for gain
Of purer glory.'"

Then replied the king: 585
"Far lovelier in our Lancelot had it been,
In lieu of idly dallying with the truth,
To have trusted me as he hath trusted thee.
Surely his king and most familiar friend
Might well have kept his secret. True, indeed, 590

Albeit I know my knights fantastical,
So fine a fear in our large Lancelot
Must needs have moved my laughter; now remains
But little cause for laughter; his own kin —
Ill news, my queen, for all who love him, this! — 595
His kith and kin, not knowing, set upon him;
So that he went sore wounded from the field.
Yet good news too; for goodly hopes are mine
That Lancelot is no more a lonely heart.
He wore, against his wont, upon his helm 600
A sleeve of scarlet, broidered with great pearls,
Some gentle maiden's gift."

"Yea, lord," she said,
"Thy hopes are mine," and saying that, she choked,
And sharply turned about to hide her face,
Past to her chamber, and there flung herself 605
Down on the great king's couch, and writhed upon it,
And clenched her fingers till they bit the palm,
And shrieked out "Traitor!" to the unhearing wall,
Then flashed into wild tears, and rose again,
And moved about her palace, proud and pale. 610

Gawain the while through all the region round
Rode with his diamond, wearied of the quest,
Touched at all points except the poplar grove,
And came at last, though late, to Astolat;
Whom glittering in enameled arms the maid 615
Glanced at, and cried: "What news from Camelot, lord?
What of the knight with the red sleeve?" "He won."
"I knew it," she said. "But parted from the jousts
Hurt in the side"; whereat she caught her breath;
Through her own side she felt the sharp lance go; 620
Thereon she smote her hand; well-nigh she swooned;
And, while he gazed wonderingly at her, came
The Lord of Astolat out, to whom the prince
Reported who he was, and on what quest
Sent, that he bore the prize and could not find 625
The victor, but had ridden a random round
To seek him, and had wearied of the search.
To whom the Lord of Astolat: "Bide with us,
And ride no more at random, noble prince!
Here was the knight, and here he left a shield; 630
This will he send or come for; furthermore
Our son is with him; we shall hear anon,
Needs must we hear." To this the courteous prince
Accorded with his wonted courtesy,

Courtesy with a touch of traitor in it, 635
And stayed; and cast his eyes on fair Elaine;
Where could be found face daintier? then her shape
From forehead down to foot, perfect — again
From foot to forehead exquisitely turned:
"Well — if I bide, lo! this wild flower for me!" 640
And oft they met among the garden yews,
And there he set himself to play upon her
With sallying wit, free flashes from a height
Above her, graces of the court, and songs,
Sighs, and low smiles, and golden eloquence, 645
And amorous adulation, till the maid
Rebeled against it, saying to him, "Prince,
O loyal nephew of our noble king,
Why ask you not to see the shield he left,
Whence you might learn his name? Why slight your king, 650
And lose the quest he sent you on, and prove
No surer than our falcon yesterday,
Who lost the hern we slipt her at, and went
To all the winds?" "Nay, by mine head," said he,
"I lose it, as we lose the lark in heaven, 655
O damsel, in the light of your blue eyes;
But an ye will it let me see the shield."
And when the shield was brought, and Gawain saw
Sir Lancelot's azure lions, crowned with gold,
Ramp in the field, he smote his thigh, and mocked: 660
"Right was the king! our Lancelot! that true man!"
"And right was I," she answered merrily, "I,
Who dreamed my knight the greatest knight of all."
"And if I dreamed," said Gawain, "that you love
This greatest knight, your pardon! lo, ye know it! 665
Speak therefore; shall I waste myself in vain?"
Full simple was her answer: "What know I?
My brethren have been all my fellowship;
And I, when often they have talked of love,
Wished it had been my mother, for they talked, 670
Meseemed, of what they knew not; so myself —
I know not if I know what true love is,
But if I know, then, if I love not him,
I know there is none other I can love."
"Yea, by God's death," said he, "ye love him well, 675
But would not, knew ye what all others know,
And whom he loves." "So be it," cried Elaine,
And lifted her fair face and moved away;
But he pursued her, calling: "Stay a little!
One golden minute's grace! he wore your sleeve; 680
Would he break faith with one I may not name?

Must our true man change like a leaf at last?
Nay — like enow: why then, far be it from me
To cross our mighty Lancelot in his loves!
And, damsel, for I deem you know full well 685
Where your great knight is hidden, let me leave
My quest with you; the diamond also; here!
For if you love, it will be sweet to give it;
And if he love, it will be sweet to have it
From your own hand; and whether he love or not, 690
A diamond is a diamond. Fare you well
A thousand times! — a thousand times farewell!
Yet, if he loves, and his love hold, we two
May meet at court hereafter; there, I think,
So ye will learn the courtesies of the court, 695
We two shall know each other."

Then he gave,
And slightly kissed the hand to which he gave,
The diamond, and all wearied of the quest
Leapt on his horse, and caroling as he went
A true-love ballad, lightly rode away. 700

Thence to the court he past; there told the king
What the king knew, "Sir Lancelot is the knight."
And added, "Sire, my liege, so much I learnt;
But failed to find him, though I rode all round
The region; but I lighted on the maid 705
Whose sleeve he wore; she loves him; and to her,
Deeming our courtesy is the truest law,
I gave the diamond; she will render it;
For by mine head she knows his hiding place."

The seldom-frowning king frowned, and replied: 710
"Too courteous truly! ye shall go no more
On quest of mine, seeing that ye forget
Obedience is the courtesy due to kings."

He spake and parted. Wroth, but all in awe,
For twenty strokes of the blood, without a word, 715
Lingered that other, staring after him;
Then shook his hair, strode off, and buzzed abroad
About the maid of Astolat, and her love.
All ears were pricked at once, all tongues were loosed:
"The maid of Astolat loves Sir Lancelot, 720
Sir Lancelot loves the maid of Astolat."
Some read the king's face, some the queen's, and all

693. Compare this line with line 599. 715. **twenty strokes of the blood:** a few seconds. 716. **that other:** Gawain.

Had marvel what the maid might be, but most
Predoomed her as unworthy. One old dame
Came suddenly on the queen with the sharp news. 725
She, that had heard the noise of it before,
But sorrowing Lancelot should have stooped so low,
Marred her friend's aim with pale tranquillity.
So ran the tale like fire about the court,
Fire in dry stubble a nine days' wonder flared, 730
Till even the knights at banquet twice or thrice
Forgot to drink to Lancelot and the queen,
And pledging Lancelot and the lily maid
Smiled at each other, while the queen, who sat
With lips severely placid, felt the knot 735
Climb in her throat, and with her feet unseen
Crushed the wild passion out against the floor
Beneath the banquet, where the meats became
As wormwood and she hated all who pledged.

But far away the maid in Astolat, 740
Her guiltless rival, she that ever kept
The one-day-seen Sir Lancelot in her heart,
Crept to her father, while he mused alone,
Sat on his knee, stroked his gray face, and said:
"Father, you call me willful, and the fault 745
Is yours who let me have my will, and now,
Sweet father, will you let me lose my wits?"
"Nay," said he, "surely." "Wherefore, let me hence,"
She answered, "and find out our dear Lavaine."
"Ye will not lose your wits for dear Lavaine; 750
Bide," answered he, "we needs must hear anon
Of him, and of that other." "Ay," she said,
"And of that other, for I needs must hence
And find that other, wheresoe'er he be,
And with mine own hand give his diamond to him, 755
Lest I be found as faithless in the quest
As yon proud prince who left the quest to me.
Sweet father, I behold him in my dreams
Gaunt as it were the skeleton of himself,
Death-pale, for the lack of gentle maiden's aid. 760
The gentler born the maiden, the more bound,
My father, to be sweet and serviceable
To noble knights in sickness, as ye know,
When these have worn their tokens; let me hence,
I pray you." Then her father nodding said: 765
"Ay, ay, the diamond; wit ye well, my child,

728. **Marred her friend's aim**: gave no sign of being affected by the gossip, thus spoiling whatever satisfaction the "old dame" might have felt in reporting it.

Right fain were I to learn this knight were whole,
Being our greatest; yea, and you must give it —
And sure I think this fruit is hung too high
For any mouth to gape for save a queen's — 770
Nay, I mean nothing; so then, get you gone,
Being so very willful you must go."

Lightly, her suit allowed, she slipt away,
And while she made her ready for her ride
Her father's latest word hummed in her ear: 775
"Being so very willful you must go,"
And changed itself and echoed in her heart:
"Being so very willful you must die."
But she was happy enough and shook it off,
As we shake off the bee that buzzes at us; 780
And in her heart she answered it and said:
"What matter, so I help him back to life?"
Then far away with good Sir Torre for guide
Rode o'er the long backs of the bushless downs
To Camelot, and before the city gates 785
Came on her brother with a happy face
Making a roan horse caper and curvet
For pleasure all about a field of flowers;
Whom when she saw: "Lavaine," she cried, "Lavaine,
How fares my lord Sir Lancelot?" He amazed: 790
"Torre and Elaine! why here? Sir Lancelot!
How know ye my lord's name is Lancelot?"
But when the maid had told him all her tale,
Then turned Sir Torre, and being in his moods
Left them, and under the strange-statued gate, 795
Where Arthur's wars were rendered mystically,
Past up the still rich city to his kin,
His own far blood, which dwelt at Camelot;
And her, Lavaine across the poplar grove
Led to the caves; there first she saw the casque 800
Of Lancelot on the wall; her scarlet sleeve,
Though carved and cut, and half the pearls away,
Streamed from it still; and in her heart she laughed,
Because he had not loosed it from his helm,
But meant once more perchance to tourney in it. 805
And when they gained the cell wherein he slept,
His battle-writhen arms and mighty hands
Lay naked on the wolfskin, and a dream
Of dragging down his enemy made them move.
Then she that saw him lying unsleek, unshorn, 810
Gaunt as it were the skeleton of himself,

778. What do you think put this thought into Elaine's mind?

Uttered a little tender dolorous cry.
The sound not wonted in a place so still
Woke the sick knight, and while he rolled his eyes
Yet blank from sleep, she started to him, saying: 815
" Your prize the diamond sent you by the king."
His eyes glistened; she fancied, " Is it for me?"
And when the maid had told him all the tale
Of king and prince, the diamond sent, the quest
Assigned to her not worthy of it, she knelt 820
Full lowly by the corners of his bed,
And laid the diamond in his open hand;
Her face was near, and as we kiss the child
That does the task assigned, he kissed her face.
At once she slipt like water to the floor. 825
" Alas," he said, " your ride hath wearied you.
Rest must you have." " No rest for me," she said;
" Nay, for near you, fair lord, I am at rest."
What might she mean by that? his large black eyes,
Yet larger through his leanness, dwelt upon her 830
Till all her heart's sad secret blazed itself
In the heart's colors on her simple face;
And Lancelot looked and was perplext in mind;
And being weak in body said no more,
But did not love the color; woman's love, 835
Save one, he not regarded, and so turned
Sighing, and feigned a sleep until he slept.

Then rose Elaine and glided through the fields,
And past beneath the weirdly sculptured gates
Far up the dim rich city to her kin; 840
There bode the night; but woke with dawn, and past
Down through the dim rich city to the fields,
Thence to the cave. So day by day she past
In either twilight ghostlike to and fro
Gliding, and every day she tended him, 845
And likewise many a night; and Lancelot
Would, though he called his wound a little hurt
Whereof he should be quickly whole, at times
Brain-feverous in his heat and agony, seem
Uncourteous, even he; but the meek maid 850
Sweetly forebore him ever, being to him
Meeker than any child to a rough nurse,
Milder than any mother to a sick child,
And never woman yet, since man's first fall,
Did kindlier unto man, but her deep love 855
Upbore her; till the hermit, skilled in all

835. **color:** reread lines 831–32 if this reference is not clear.

The simples and the science of that time,
Told him that her fine care had saved his life.
And the sick man forgot her simple blush,
Would call her friend and sister, sweet Elaine, 860
Would listen for her coming and regret
Her parting step, and held her tenderly,
And loved her with all love except the love
Of man and woman when they love their best,
Closest and sweetest, and had died the death 865
In any knightly fashion for her sake.
And peradventure had he seen her first
She might have made this and that other world
Another world for the sick man; but now
The shackles of an old love straitened him, 870
His honor rooted in dishonor stood,
And faith unfaithful kept him falsely true.

Yet the great knight in his mid-sickness made
Full many a holy vow and pure resolve.
These, as but born of sickness, could not live; 875
For when the blood ran lustier in him again,
Full often the bright image of one face,
Making a treacherous quiet in his heart,
Dispersed his resolution like a cloud.
Then if the maiden, while that ghostly grace 880
Beamed on his fancy, spoke, he answered not,
Or short and coldly, and she knew right well
What the rough sickness meant, but what this meant
She knew not, and the sorrow dimmed her sight,
And drave her ere her time across the fields 885
Far into the rich city, where alone
She murmured, "Vain, in vain; it cannot be
He will not love me; how then? must I die?"
Then as a little helpless innocent bird,
That has but one plain passage of few notes, 890
Will sing the simple passage o'er and o'er
For all an April morning, till the ear
Wearies to hear it, so the simple maid
Went half the night repeating, "Must I die?"
And now to right she turned, and now to left, 895
And found no ease in turning or in rest;
And "Him or death," she muttered, "death or him,"
Again and like a burthen, "Him or death."

But when Sir Lancelot's deadly hurt was whole,
To Astolat returning rode the three. 900
There morn by morn, arraying her sweet self

In that wherein she deemed she looked her best,
She came before Sir Lancelot, for she thought:
" If I be loved, these are my festal robes,
If not, the victim's flowers before he fall." 905
And Lancelot ever prest upon the maid
That she should ask some goodly gift of him
For her own self or hers: " And do not shun
To speak the wish most near to your true heart;
Such service have ye done me that I make 910
My will of yours, and prince and lord am I
In mine own land, and what I will I can."
Then like a ghost she lifted up her face,
But like a ghost without the power to speak.
And Lancelot saw that she withheld her wish, 915
And bode among them let a little space
Till he should learn it; and one morn it chanced
He found her in among the garden yews,
And said, " Delay no longer, speak your wish,
Seeing I go today"; then out she brake: 920
" Going? and we shall never see you more.
And I must die for want of one bold word."
" Speak; that I live to hear," he said, " is yours."
Then suddenly and passionately she spoke:
" I have gone mad. I love you; let me die." 925
" Ah, sister," answered Lancelot, " what is this?"
And innocently extending her white arms,
" Your love," she said, " your love — to be your wife."
And Lancelot answered, " Had I chosen to wed,
I had been wedded earlier, sweet Elaine; 930
But now there never will be wife of mine."
" No, no," she cried, " I care not to be wife,
But to be with you still, to see your face,
To serve you, and to follow you through the world."
And Lancelot answered, " Nay, the world, the world, 935
All ear and eye, with such a stupid heart
To interpret ear and eye, and such a tongue
To blare its own interpretation — nay,
Full ill then should I quit your brother's love,
And your good father's kindness." And she said: 940
" Not to be with you, not to see your face —
Alas, for me then, my good days are done!"
" Nay, noble maid!" he answered, " ten times nay!
This is not love, but love's first flash in youth,
Most common; yea, I know it of mine own self; 945
And you yourself will smile at your own self
Hereafter, when you yield your flower of life
To one more fitly yours, not thrice your age.

And then will I, for true you are and sweet
Beyond mine old belief in womanhood, 950
More specially should your good knight be poor,
Endow you with broad land and territory
Even to the half my realm beyond the seas,
So that would make you happy; furthermore,
Even to the death, as though ye were my blood, 955
In all your quarrels will I be your knight.
This will I do, dear damsel, for your sake,
And more than this I cannot."

While he spoke
She neither blushed nor shook, but deathly pale
Stood grasping what was nearest, then replied: 960
" Of all this will I nothing"; and so fell,
And thus they bore her swooning to her tower.

Then spake, to whom through those black walls of yew
Their talk had pierced, her father: " Ay, a flash,
I fear me, that will strike my blossom dead. 965
Too courteous are ye, fair Lord Lancelot.
I pray you, use some rough discourtesy
To blunt or break her passion."

Lancelot said:
" That were against me; what I can I will";
And there that day remained, and toward even 970
Sent for his shield; full meekly rose the maid,
Stript off the case, and gave the naked shield;
Then, when she heard his horse upon the stones,
Unclasping flung the casement back, and looked
Down on his helm, from which her sleeve had gone. 975
And Lancelot knew the little clinking sound;
And she by tact of love was well aware
That Lancelot knew that she was looking at him.
And yet he glanced not up, nor waved his hand,
Nor bade farewell, but sadly rode away. 980
This was the one discourtesy that he used.

So in her tower alone the maiden sat.
His very shield was gone; only the case,
Her own poor work, her empty labor, left.
But still she heard him, still his picture formed 985
And grew between her and the pictured wall.
Then came her father, saying in low tones:
" Have comfort," whom she greeted quietly.
Then came her brethren saying, " Peace to thee,
Sweet sister," whom she answered with all calm. 990

But when they left her to herself again,
Death, like a friend's voice from a distant field
Approaching through the darkness, called; the owls
Wailing had power upon her, and she mixt
Her fancies with the sallow-rifted glooms 995
Of evening and the moanings of the wind.

And in those days she made a little song,
And called her song "The Song of Love and Death,"
And sang it; sweetly could she make and sing.

"Sweet is true love though given in vain, in vain; 1000
And sweet is death who puts an end to pain:
I know not which is sweeter, no, not I.

"Love, art thou sweet? then bitter death must be;
Love, thou art bitter; sweet is death to me.
O Love, if death be sweeter, let me die. 1005

"Sweet love, that seems not made to fade away;
Sweet death, that seems to make us loveless clay;
I know not which is sweeter, no, not I.

"I fain would follow love, if that could be;
I needs must follow death, who calls for me; 1010
Call and I follow, I follow! let me die."

High with the last line scaled her voice, and this,
All in a fiery dawning wild with wind
That shook her tower, the brothers heard, and thought
With shuddering: "Hark the phantom of the house 1015
That ever shrieks before a death," and called
The father, and all three in hurry and fear
Ran to her, and lo! the blood-red light of dawn
Flared on her face, she shrilling, "Let me die!"

As when we dwell upon a word we know, 1020
Repeating, till the word we know so well
Becomes a wonder, and we know not why,
So dwelt the father on her face, and thought:
"Is this Elaine?" till back the maiden fell,
Then gave a languid hand to each, and lay, 1025
Speaking a still good morrow with her eyes.
At last she said, "Sweet brothers, yesternight
I seemed a curious little maid again,
And happy as when we dwelt among the woods,
And when ye used to take me with the flood 1030
Up the great river in the boatman's boat.

Only ye would not pass beyond the cape
That has the poplar on it; there ye fixt
Your limit, oft returning with the tide.
And yet I cried because ye would not pass 1035
Beyond it, and far up the shining flood
Until we found the palace of the king.
And yet ye would not; but this night I dreamed
That I was all alone upon the flood,
And then I said, 'Now shall I have my will.' 1040
And there I woke, but still the wish remained.
So let me hence that I may pass at last
Beyond the poplar and far up the flood,
Until I find the palace of the king.
There will I enter in among them all, 1045
And no man there will dare to mock at me;
But there the fine Gawain will wonder at me,
And there the great Sir Lancelot muse at me;
Gawain, who bade a thousand farewells to me,
Lancelot, who coldly went, nor bade me one. 1050
And there the king will know me and my love,
And there the queen herself will pity me,
And all the gentle court will welcome me,
And after my long voyage I shall rest!"

"Peace," said her father, "O my child, ye seem 1055
Lightheaded, for what force is yours to go
So far, being sick? and wherefore would ye look
On this proud fellow again, who scorns us all?"

Then the rough Torre began to heave and move,
And bluster into stormy sobs and say: 1060
"I never loved him; an I meet with him,
I care not howsoever great he be,
Then will I strike at him and strike him down;
Give me good fortune, I will strike him dead,
For this discomfort he hath done the house." 1065

To whom the gentle sister made reply:
"Fret not yourself, dear brother, nor be wroth,
Seeing it is no more Sir Lancelot's fault
Not to love me than it is mine to love
Him of all men who seems to me the highest." 1070

"Highest?" the father answered, echoing "highest?"—
He meant to break the passion in her—"nay,
Daughter, I know not what you call the highest;
But this I know, for all the people know it,
He loves the queen, and in an open shame; 1075

And she returns his love in open shame;
If this be high, what is it to be low?"

Then spake the lily maid of Astolat:
"Sweet father, all too faint and sick am I
For anger; these are slanders; never yet 1080
Was noble man but made ignoble talk.
He makes no friend who never made a foe.
But now it is my glory to have loved
One peerless, without stain; so let me pass,
My father, howsoe'er I seem to you, 1085
Not all unhappy, having loved God's best
And greatest, though my love had no return;
Yet, seeing you desire your child to live,
Thanks, but you work against your own desire;
For if I could believe the things you say 1090
I should but die the sooner; wherefore cease,
Sweet father, and bid call the ghostly man
Hither, and let me shrive me clean and die."

So when the ghostly man had come and gone,
She, with a face bright as for sin forgiven, 1095
Besought Lavaine to write as she devised
A letter, word for word; and when he asked:
"Is it for Lancelot, is it for my dear lord?
Then will I bear it gladly," she replied,
"For Lancelot and the queen and all the world, 1100
But I myself must bear it." Then he wrote
The letter she devised; which being writ
And folded: "O sweet father, tender and true,
Deny me not," she said — "ye never yet
Denied my fancies — this, however strange, 1105
My latest: lay the letter in my hand
A little ere I die, and close the hand
Upon it; I shall guard it even in death.
And when the heat has gone from out my heart,
Then take the little bed on which I died 1110
For Lancelot's love, and deck it like the queen's
For richness, and me also like the queen
In all I have of rich, and lay me on it.
And let there be prepared a chariot bier
To take me to the river, and a barge 1115
Be ready on the river, clothed in black.
I go in state to court, to meet the queen.
There surely I shall speak for mine own self,
And none of you can speak for me so well.
And therefore let our dumb old man alone 1120

Go with me; he can steer and row, and he
Will guide me to that palace, to the doors."

She ceased; her father promised; whereupon
She grew so cheerful that they deemed her death
Was rather in the fantasy than the blood. 1125
But ten slow mornings past, and on the eleventh
Her father laid the letter in her hand,
And closed the hand upon it, and she died.
So that day there was dole in Astolat.

But when the next sun brake from underground, 1130
Then, those two brethren slowly with bent brows
Accompanying, the sad chariot bier
Past like a shadow through the field, that shone
Full summer, to that stream whereon the barge,
Palled all its length in blackest samite, lay. 1135
There sat the lifelong creature of the house,
Loyal, the dumb old servitor, on deck,
Winking his eyes, and twisted all his face.
So those two brethren from the chariot took
And on the black decks laid her in her bed, 1140
Set in her hand a lily, o'er her hung
The silken case with braided blazonings,
And kissed her quiet brows, and saying to her:
"Sister, farewell forever," and again:
"Farewell, sweet sister," parted all in tears. 1145
Then rose the dumb old servitor, and the dead,
Oared by the dumb, went upward with the flood —
In her right hand the lily, in her left
The letter — all her bright hair streaming down —
And all the coverlid was cloth of gold 1150
Drawn to her waist, and she herself in white
All but her face, and that clear-featured face
Was lovely, for she did not seem as dead,
But fast asleep, and lay as though she smiled.

That day Sir Lancelot at the palace craved 1155
Audience of Guinevere, to give at last
The price of half a realm, his costly gift,
Hard-won and hardly won with bruise and blow,
With deaths of others, and almost his own,
The nine-years-fought-for diamonds; for he saw 1160
One of her house, and sent him to the queen
Bearing his wish, whereto the queen agreed

1162–69. In other words, Lancelot's messenger could see by the queen's shadow on the wall that she was not as unmoved by his proposal as her statuelike manner indicated. And so he parted from her happy.

With such and so unmoved a majesty
She might have seemed her statue, but that he,
Low-drooping till he well-nigh kissed her feet 1165
For loyal awe, saw with a sidelong eye
The shadow of some piece of pointed lace,
In the queen's shadow, vibrate on the walls,
And parted, laughing in his courtly heart.

All in an oriel on the summer side, 1170
Vine-clad, of Arthur's palace toward the stream,
They met, and Lancelot kneeling uttered: "Queen,
Lady, my liege, in whom I have my joy,
Take, what I had not won except for you,
These jewels, and make me happy, making them 1175
An armlet for the roundest arm on earth,
Or necklace for a neck to which the swan's
Is tawnier than her cygnet's; these are words;
Your beauty is your beauty, and I sin
In speaking, yet O, grant my worship of it 1180
Words, as we grant grief tears. Such sin in words
Perchance, we both can pardon; but, my queen,
I hear of rumors flying through your court.
Our bond, as not the bond of man and wife,
Should have in it an absoluter trust 1185
To make up that defect: let rumors be;
When did not rumors fly? these, as I trust
That you trust me in your own nobleness,
I may not well believe that you believe."

While thus he spoke, half turned away, the queen 1190
Brake from the vast oriel-embowering vine
Leaf after leaf, and tore, and cast them off,
Till all the place whereon she stood was green;
Then, when he ceased, in one cold passive hand
Received at once and laid aside the gems 1195
There on a table near her, and replied:

"It may be I am quicker of belief
Than you believe me, Lancelot of the Lake.
Our bond is not the bond of man and wife.
This good is in it, whatsoe'er of ill, 1200
It can be broken easier. I for you
This many a year have done despite and wrong
To one whom ever in my heart of hearts
I did acknowledge nobler. What are these?
Diamonds for me! they had been thrice their worth 1205
Being your gift, had you not lost your own.

1206. **own**: own worth.

To loyal hearts the value of all gifts
Must vary as the giver's. Not for me!
For her! for your new fancy. Only this
Grant me, I pray you; have your joys apart. 1210
I doubt not that, however changed, you keep
So much of what is graceful; and myself
Would shun to break those bounds of courtesy
In which as Arthur's queen I move and rule;
So cannot speak my mind. An end to this! 1215
A strange one! yet I take it with amen.
So pray you, add my diamonds to her pearls;
Deck her with these; tell her, she shines me down:
An armlet for an arm to which the queen's
Is haggard, or a necklace for a neck 1220
O, as much fairer — as a faith once fair
Was richer than these diamonds — hers not mine —
Nay, by the mother of our Lord himself,
Or hers or mine, mine now to work my will —
She shall not have them."

Saying which she seized, 1225
And, through the casement standing wide for heat,
Flung them, and down they flashed, and smote the stream.
Then from the smitten surface flashed, as it were,
Diamonds to meet them, and they past away.
Then while Sir Lancelot leant, in half disdain 1230
At love, life, all things, on the window ledge,
Close underneath his eyes, and right across
Where these had fallen, slowly passed the barge
Whereon the lily maid of Astolat
Lay smiling, like a star in blackest night. 1235

But the wild queen, who saw not, burst away
To weep and wail in secret; and the barge,
On to the palace doorway sliding, paused.
There two stood armed, and kept the door; to whom,
All up the marble stair, tier over tier, 1240
Were added mouths that gaped, and eyes that asked:
"What is it?" but that oarsman's haggard face,
As hard and still as is the face that men
Shape to their fancy's eye from broken rocks
On some cliffside, appalled them, and they said: 1245
"He is enchanted, cannot speak — and she,

1211–14. Guinevere is saying in effect that, even though Lancelot loves her no more (as she fears), he would still perform the outward graces of love, as would she; but even so, she is not deceived by these courtesies. 1216. **A strange one:** *one* refers to *end:* a strange end to their affair. She is referring to the fact that both of them would "shun to break those bounds of courtesy"; therefore, they can't be frank with each other.

Look how she sleeps — the fairy queen, so fair!
Yea, but how pale! what are they? flesh and blood?
Or come to take the king to fairyland?
For some do hold our Arthur cannot die, 1250
But that he passes into fairyland."

While thus they babbled of the king, the king
Came girt with knights; then turned the tongueless man
From the half face to the full eye, and rose
And pointed to the damsel and the doors. 1255
So Arthur bade the meek Sir Percivale
And pure Sir Galahad to uplift the maid;
And reverently they bore her into hall.
Then came the fine Gawain and wondered at her,
And Lancelot later came and mused at her, 1260
And last the queen herself, and pitied her;
But Arthur spied the letter in her hand,
Stoopt, took, brake seal, and read it; this was all:

"Most noble lord, Sir Lancelot of the Lake,
I, sometime called the maid of Astolat, 1265
Come, for you left me taking no farewell,
Hither, to take my last farewell of you.
I loved you, and my love had no return,
And therefore my true love has been my death.
And therefore to our Lady Guinevere, 1270
And to all other ladies, I make moan:
Pray for my soul, and yield me burial.
Pray for my soul thou too, Sir Lancelot,
As thou art a knight peerless."

Thus he read;
And ever in the reading lords and dames 1275
Wept, looking often from his face who read
To hers which lay so silent, and at times,
So touched were they, half-thinking that her lips
Who had devised the letter moved again.

Then freely spoke Sir Lancelot to them all: 1280
"My lord liege Arthur, and all ye that hear,
Know that for this most gentle maiden's death
Right heavy am I; for good she was and true,
But loved me with a love beyond all love
In women, whomsoever I have known. 1285
Yet to be loved makes not to love again;
Not at my years, however it hold in youth.
I swear by truth and knighthood that I gave

No cause, not willingly, for such a love.
To this I call my friends in testimony. 1290
Her brethren, and her father, who himself
Besought me to be plain and blunt, and use,
To break her passion, some discourtesy
Against my nature; what I could, I did.
I left her and I bade her no farewell; 1295
Though, had I dreamt the damsel would have died,
I might have put my wits to some rough use,
And helped her from herself."

Then said the queen —
Sea was her wrath, yet working after storm:
" Ye might at least have done her so much grace, 1300
Fair lord, as would have helped her from her death."
He raised his head, their eyes met and hers fell,
He adding, " Queen, she would not be content
Save that I wedded her, which could not be.
Then might she follow me through the world, she asked; 1305
It could not be. I told her that her love
Was but the flash of youth, would darken down,
To rise hereafter in a stiller flame
Toward one more worthy of her — then would I,
More specially were he she wedded poor, 1310
Estate them with large land and territory
In mine own realm beyond the narrow seas,
To keep them in all joyance; more than this
I could not; this she would not, and she died."

He pausing, Arthur answered, " O my knight, 1315
It will be to thy worship, as my knight,
And mine, as head of all our Table Round,
To see that she be buried worshipfully."

So toward that shrine which then in all the realm
Was richest, Arthur leading, slowly went 1320
The marshaled order of their Table Round,
And Lancelot sad beyond his wont, to see
The maiden buried, not as one unknown,
Nor meanly, but with gorgeous obsequies,
And mass, and rolling music, like a queen. 1325
And when the knights had laid her comely head
Low in the dust of half-forgotten kings,
Then Arthur spake among them: " Let her tomb
Be costly, and her image thereupon,
And let the shield of Lancelot at her feet 1330
Be carven, and her lily in her hand.

And let the story of her dolorous voyage
For all true hearts be blazoned on her tomb
In letters gold and azure! " which was wrought
Thereafter; but when now the lords and dames 1335
And people, from the high door streaming, brake
Disorderly, as homeward each, the queen,
Who marked Sir Lancelot where he moved apart,
Drew near, and sighed in passing, " Lancelot,
Forgive me; mine was jealousy in love." 1340
He answered with his eyes upon the ground,
" That is love's curse; pass on, my queen, forgiven."
But Arthur, who beheld his cloudy brows,
Approached him, and with full affection said:

" Lancelot, my Lancelot, thou in whom I have 1345
Most joy and most affiance, for I know
What thou hast been in battle by my side,
And many a time have watched thee at the tilt
Strike down the lusty and long-practiced knight
And let the younger and unskilled go by 1350
To win his honor and to make his name,
And loved thy courtesies and thee, a man
Made to be loved; but now I would to God,
Seeing the homeless trouble in thine eyes,
Thou couldst have loved this maiden, shaped, it seems, 1355
By God for thee alone, and from her face,
If one may judge the living by the dead,
Delicately pure and marvelously fair,
Who might have brought thee, now a lonely man
Wifeless and heirless, noble issue, sons 1360
Born to the glory of thy name and fame,
My knight, the great Sir Lancelot of the Lake."

Then answered Lancelot, " Fair she was, my king,
Pure, as you ever wish your knights to be.
To doubt her fairness were to want an eye, 1365
To doubt her pureness were to want a heart —
Yea, to be loved, if what is worthy love
Could bind him, but free love will not be bound."

" Free love, so bound, were freest," said the king.
" Let love be free; free love is for the best; 1370
And, after heaven, on our dull side of death,
What should be best, if not so pure a love
Clothed in so pure a loveliness? yet thee
She failed to bind, though being, as I think,
Unbound as yet, and gentle, as I know." 1375

And Lancelot answered nothing, but he went,
And at the inrunning of a little brook
Sat by the river in a cove, and watched
The high reed wave, and lifted up his eyes
And saw the barge that brought her moving down, 1380
Far off, a blot upon the stream, and said
Low in himself, "Ah, simple heart and sweet,
Ye loved me, damsel, surely with a love
Far tenderer than my queen's. Pray for thy soul?
Ay, that will I. Farewell too — now at last — 1385
Farewell, fair lily. 'Jealousy in love?'
Not rather dead love's harsh heir, jealous pride?
Queen, if I grant the jealousy as of love,
May not your crescent fear for name and fame
Speak, as it waxes, of a love that wanes? 1390
Why did the king dwell on my name to me?
Mine own name shames me, seeming a reproach,
Lancelot, whom the Lady of the Lake
Caught from his mother's arms — the wondrous one
Who passes through the vision of the night — 1395
She chanted snatches of mysterious hymns
Heard on the winding waters, eve and morn
She kissed me saying, 'Thou art fair, my child,
As a king's son,' and often in her arms
She bare me, pacing on the dusky mere. 1400
Would she had drowned me in it, where'er it be!
For what am I? what profits me my name
Of greatest knight? I fought for it, and have it;
Pleasure to have it, none; to lose it, pain:
Now grown a part of me: but what use in it? 1405
To make men worse by making my sin known?
Or sin seem less, the sinner seeming great?
Alas for Arthur's greatest knight, a man
Not after Arthur's heart! I needs must break
These bonds that so defame me; not without 1410
She wills it; would I, if she willed it? nay,
Who knows? but if I would not, then may God,
I pray him, send a sudden angel down
To seize me by the hair and bear me far,
And fling me deep in that forgotten mere, 1415
Among the tumbled fragments of the hills."

So groaned Sir Lancelot in remorseful pain,
Not knowing he should die a holy man.

THINK BACK OVER WHAT YOU HAVE READ

Noticing the Dramatic Conflict in the Story

1. Does Elaine deserve to be called *willful?* In what dramatic ways does this quality express itself?

2. What are the elements of tragedy in Elaine's love for Lancelot? What is the invisible barrier between them? What utterances of Lancelot can you quote to show the pathetic hopelessness of Elaine's attachment?

3. Why must Elaine's love have seemed to Lancelot particularly ironic? Irony, you will remember, is the quality which makes a particular coincidence seem to have been planned by a mischievous fate. Do you see anything in the story of "Lancelot and Elaine" to remind you how perverse time can be? Suppose that each event in the story had been differently *timed.* What difference would it have made?

4. What lines can you quote to show the irony of Arthur's trust in Lancelot? At what moments does he come close to discovering the bitter secret?

5. What moments in Elaine's brief love life seem to you particularly pathetic? Why?

6. What secret conflicts smolder in Guinevere's heart? What are her objections to Arthur? Review especially lines 121–57.

7. What secret conflicts tear at Lancelot's heart? Why is there no relief from his suffering? Suppose that he were to make his sin known: would it help matters? Would it relieve his mind, or add to his woe? Why? Review especially lines 1376–1416.

Catching the Spirit of Chivalry as Revealed in the Idyll

8. What lines can you quote to show the knightly qualities of Lancelot: his fine courtesy? his sportsmanship?

9. In what way does Gawain illustrate an unchivalrous nature?

10. What lines can you quote to show how women were reverenced in the age of chivalry?

Recognizing the Beauty of Comparisons in the Poem

11. Look up the following lines and note the beauty of the comparisons. What picture does your imagination see? What details would you emphasize were you to paint or draw the picture? How apt is the comparison? To what quality does it picturesquely draw your attention?

lines 50–2	lines 477–85	lines 889–96
lines 131–4	lines 650–4	lines 1020–5
lines 137–9	lines 729–34	lines 1227–9
lines 330–7	lines 768–70	lines 1242–5

12. What other comparisons can you find that appeal to your imagination? Perhaps those members of the class who can draw or paint will convert the more suggestive comparisons into pictures for the bulletin board in your room.

Finding Poetic Epigrams

13. Much of the poetic interest in the *Idylls of the King* lies in the beauty of single lines that hold in their brief compass a great, fundamental truth. Notice, for example, the following:

> "Never yet
> Was noble man but made ignoble talk."

Do you see how this line can be lifted completely out of its context and yet still say something of importance? The truth of the statement is not dependent upon any particular setting; it applies to modern times as well as to the Middle Ages. Its brevity, moreover, tempts the reader to quote. We call such meaningful lines *epigrams,* and they are one of the marks of great poetry. It will pay the class to look back over the *Idyll* just read and to note the single or double lines worth remembering. With what illustrations of your own can you expand each epigram? Which ones give you a keener insight into human nature? Which ones would you like to remember? For what occasion would they serve as an appropriate motto?

SUMMARIES OF THE REMAINING IDYLLS

The five summaries which follow recount briefly the tragic story of the breaking up of the Round Table after the disillusioned knights set off in quest of the Holy Grail, a miraculous cup supposed to have been used by Jesus Christ at the Last Supper and brought to England by Joseph of Arimathea. For many years it was treasured as a sacred relic, and many miracles were credited to its power. Then it suddenly disappeared, and various stories grew up concerning its whereabouts. It became, finally, the symbol of purity and was said to appear in visions to those whose lives were holy. In the confusion which followed their loss of faith in the ideals of chivalry, the knights of the Round Table began to look for a miracle to reunite them; and so one by one they set out in search of the Holy Grail, and Arthur's kingdom received a blow from which it could not recover. Tragedy and disillusionment followed, and King Arthur died. In the summaries of the last five *Idylls* you will be interested chiefly in the fortunes of the characters you have already met and in the fate of the Round Table.

THE HOLY GRAIL

The story is told in the form of a conversation between Sir Percivale and a recluse monk named Ambrosius. According to this story, there came a time in the kingdom of Arthur when there was spiritual reaction against the worldliness of the court. With the medieval belief in the supernatural, the vision of the Holy Grail, as reported by Percivale's sister, a mystic nun, was given ready credence. The pure Sir Galahad was her first convert and Percivale followed. One day, at a banquet held when Arthur was away on a quest, there was a tremendous storm which filled everyone with fear. They thought that the Grail was in their presence, and Percivale, who declared that he had not seen it, made a vow that he was going in search of the holy cup; and many followed, including Lancelot, Gawain, and others prominent in the Round Table. When Arthur returned and saw what had happened, he was sad because, strangely enough, he felt that all those going on this quest were following " wandering fires " and not doing that which his order stood for. To him this quest seemed as the first step in the breaking up of the Round Table. " Many of you, yea most, will return no more," was his dark prophecy; but since they had sworn to go, he told them they must go.

The rest of the story concerns the adventures of Sir Percivale himself and those of the knights he met on his journey. These adventures were of a wildly mystic and miraculous type and must be interpreted allegorically as experiences of the soul. When the hunters of the Grail returned, scarcely a tenth of those who went, they told their experiences to Arthur. Sir Bors and Sir Percivale declared they had seen the Grail, Lancelot thought that he had seen it, but Gawain only mocked at it. Percivale was still sufficiently wrought up to declare that he would devote himself for the rest of his life to seclusion and prayer. Galahad never returned. To Arthur the whole adventure merely proved that his prophecy was fulfilled. He pointed to the empty chairs, and he once more declared his idea of what his duty was as king. A king must guard that which he rules, not run away from it before his work is done.

PELLEAS AND ETTARRE

Sir Pelleas of the Isles was one of the new young knights created by Arthur to fill the gap left by the quest of the Holy Grail. Like Gareth, Balin, and Lavaine in earlier stories, this young knight lived off from the beaten tracks of the more civilized world of his day and, consequently, knew of Arthur and his court mostly by hearsay. To his young heart the ideals of chivalry were all that mattered if he could but be one of those carrying them out. In order to give his young knights an opportunity to show their skill on the field of tourney, Arthur proclaimed a tournament at Caerleon on Usk. He quietly asked all the older and more experienced knights to stay off the field; in fact, his instructions practically made victory certain for Pelleas.

Pelleas, on his way to Caerleon, lay down at noon to avoid the summer midday sun. As he half dozed, lost in a romantic dream of the new life of chivalry, especially the part which concerned love, he suddenly heard voices close at hand — soft feminine voices — and as he looked he beheld a vision: a group of wondrously beautiful damsels with three knights. Pelleas, used to the coarse women of his own wind-swept isles, was struck dumb by so much beauty. When one who seemed the chief of the party asked him the way to Caerleon, Pelleas barely stammered a reply. The lady turned to her friends with a slow smile, and the others smiled with her. To Pelleas she seemed the most beautiful creature in the world. " Is Guinevere herself so beautiful? " he thought. Slender was her hand and small her shape, but mature in womanhood. Her large violet eyes were the haunts of scorn. Such was Ettarre, a great lady in her land.

Pelleas offered to guide them to Caerleon. On the way Ettarre, while thoroughly bored with the country knight and his crude manners, nevertheless noted his great strength and thought that perhaps, after all, she might achieve her greatest social ambition — that of hearing herself proclaimed Queen of Beauty by the knight winning the tournament. So she flattered Pelleas by promising to be his lady-love if he won the prize for her. " O happy world," thought Pelleas, and, " I the happiest of all." He won; and as she in her joyous pride crowned herself before the great crowd at the tournament, she " for the last time was gracious " to Pelleas.

When Ettarre and her friends left for their home, Pelleas followed although uninvited. Scorned, slighted, insulted, Pelleas thought that lovely ladies tested the true love of their knights in that manner. Even when they arrived at Ettarre's castle and the drawbridge was pulled up before Pelleas could follow the others to her door, he still did not lose heart. He camped on the field before the castle, certain that he would be summoned when his probation period was up. But Ettarre ordered her three knights to drive Pelleas away. They were overthrown by Pelleas. A week later she once more ordered him driven away, with the same result except that Pelleas heard her order him bound and brought before her. So he let himself be bound, just to be in her presence. He still thought " these be the ways of ladies." He was thrust out, and then Ettarre ordered her men to attack all at once and kill him. This they tried to do. As the three attacked, it chanced that Sir Gawain came along and, seeing the unequal combat, was about to go to help Pelleas; but that gallant said, " He needs no help who doth his lady's will." Once more he is victor over the three and lets himself be bound as before; but this time Ettarre has him thrown out at once, with a hint of death if he be brought in again. But Pelleas, disillusioned at last, replied that she would see him no more.

Gawain the Courteous, justly angry at the treatment given a fellow knight, unloosed Pelleas and threw the bonds over the walls. Having also recognized Pelleas as the victor of the recent tournament, he was all the angrier at Ettarre and offered to help by taking the armor of Pelleas; then, going to her door, he would say that he had slain him. She would invite him in and then he would so laud Pelleas that she would be sorry at his death and at having lost so faithful a lover. Pelleas, a bit skeptical, said to Gawain, " Art thou not he whom men call light-of-love? " But there was nothing better to do; so Gawain went, promising to be back in three days. When he did not return in that time, Pelleas at night went up to the castle gate, which was open, and what he saw at last convinced him of the hollowness of the ideals of chivalry which he had taken so literally. His first impulse was to kill; but he merely left his sword to let them know that he had been there, and then he mounted his horse and dashed madly away. Near court he met Lancelot, whom he attacked, but he was overthrown. Together they entered the hall. There his remarks, veiled but ominous, cast a pall over all, especially Guinevere and Lancelot, who thought of the " dolorous day to be " and were silent. The story ends with the thought of Modred, " The time is hard at hand."

THE LAST TOURNAMENT

At the suggestion of Guinevere a tournament was announced at which the prize was to be a ruby necklace which Arthur had found long before on a child that had been carried to an eagle's nest. Before the tournament a churl, maimed and mauled, arrived at court with the story that the Red Knight had injured him and sent him to Arthur to say that he spurned Arthur's ideals, that his court was a sham anyhow, and all the knights frauds and liars. Furthermore, the Red Knight declared that he had set up a court of his own whose ideals were exactly the opposite of Arthur's. The situation was one that Arthur thought sufficiently important for his own individual attention, so he asked Lancelot to preside at the tournament.

The day of the tournament was gloomy. As the jousts began, there was " one low roll of autumn thunder," and there was a " wet wind blowing." Lancelot himself was plunged into gloomy thoughts and failed to take note of the many violations of the field rules. To make matters worse, the tournament was won by Sir Tristram, who had made a late entrance. Lancelot did not like Tristram and made a sarcastic comment to him as he handed him the prize; but Tristram countered by a reference to Lancelot's relations with the queen, and then, taking the ruby necklace, he rode along the gallery where the ladies sat and, instead of awarding the prize as the custom was, he said that he was sorry but his Queen of Beauty was not there. Then he rode away. " All courtesy is dead," was murmured among the ladies, and the day ended wet and gloomy.

The next day it chanced that Tristram met Sir Dagonet, the king's fool, and from their conversation it becomes plain that conditions at Arthur's court were at the breaking point. Strangely enough, it is the fool who best realizes this, and the reader is fully prepared for what follows. Meanwhile Arthur has wiped out the wicked nest of the Red Knight and is on his way home.

The story of "The Last Tournament" is broken by the introduction of part of the Tristram story. After the tournament Tristram returned to Queen Isolt, wife of King Mark of Cornwall, to give her the ruby necklace. There are the barest hints of how Tristram had brought Isolt from Ireland to be his uncle's wife, how they had fallen in love, how Tristram had been banished, and how he had gone to France and there fallen in love with another Isolt and married her. He abandoned her, however, and it is on the way back to Cornwall that he decides to enter the tournament. As he presents the necklace to Isolt, he is slain by Mark, who has stealthily crept up behind him.

That same night Arthur returned "all in a death-dumb autumn-dripping gloom" to find the queen's bower dark and the voice of Dagonet sobbing, "I shall never make thee laugh again." What had happened is told in the next *Idyll.*

GUINEVERE

Into this story Tennyson has condensed that part of the Arthur story which tells of the breaking up of the kingdom and the Round Table, for which the reader was prepared in the two preceding *Idylls.* He goes back to tell how Lancelot had once caught Modred, the evil spirit of Tennyson's story, spying upon him and Guinevere. He knocked Modred off the garden wall and kicked him around in the dust but, recognizing him as Arthur's nephew, did not kill him because he reverenced "king's blood in a bad man." Modred had allied himself with the invading Saxons and all the evil spirits of Arthur's court, and he was biding his time to revolt and seize the kingdom.

The queen, realizing that the end was at hand, asked Lancelot to return to his own land; but he refused unless she accompany him. They left secretly after Modred and his followers had once more found them together, and it was for that reason that the queen's bower was dark in the story of "The Last Tournament." When they came to a parting of the road, the queen refused to go farther with Lancelot and went to a convent at Almesbury, where the rest of this story takes place. Guinevere asked the nuns to give shelter to one in distress without question for the time being. For many a week she lived here unknown, with no companion but a young girl novice. From the innocent talk of this girl Guinevere learned what was going on in the outside world: that the wicked queen had fled with Lancelot, who sheltered her in his castle; that the king was making war on Lancelot; that Modred had openly revolted at last and had a large following. Guinevere was greatly stirred by all she heard, especially because she recognized that what the girl had said about the sinful queen was all too true. She determined never to see Lancelot again; but even as she thought, her mind went back to those golden days when as ambassador for Arthur he had come to conduct her to court. As she was dreaming of the past, there was the loud sound of a warrior riding to the door and a cry, "The king!" She heard armed feet coming toward her and fell prone before Arthur.

Arthur made a long speech in which he summed up all he had hoped to accomplish when he married her. The speech goes on for some hundreds of lines, telling of his love and forgiveness but adding that he can never take her back nor ever see her again. The king left, and Guinevere had not been able to say a word. After he had gone, she burst out in a passion of self-blame and tried to convince herself that she really loved Arthur better than she had loved Lancelot. The nuns, knowing at last who their mysterious refugee was, treated her kindly; and long after, when their abbess died, Guinevere became the head of the convent, dying three years later.

Arthur in his speech had referred to the war he was waging against the rebel barons, under Modred, and this prepares the reader for the powerful story of "The Passing of Arthur."

THE PASSING OF ARTHUR

The last of the twelve *Idylls* recounts the mystic ritual of Arthur's death. After the last weird battle of the West, after Arthur himself had slain Modred but himself lay wounded on the field of battle, he was carried to a near-by chapel by Sir Bedivere, the last left of all the knights of the Round Table. His end was near, and so he called Sir Bedivere to his side and bade him take the magic sword Excalibur and throw it far out into the lake near by. Twice Sir Bedivere took the sword from Arthur but failed to do his bidding, and twice Arthur upbraided him. The third time he took the precious brand, with its jeweled hilt, and threw it far out into the lake, and saw a hand appear, clothed in white samite, and take the sword and draw it under. Thus did the symbol of Arthur's authority vanish from the earth.

And now peace came to Arthur. He asked Sir Bedivere to help him to the margin of the lake, where a black barge hove in sight and three black queens placed Arthur on his bier. Slowly the barge moved away, and Sir Bedivere was left alone to ponder over Arthur's words spoken as he lay dying: "The old order changeth, yielding place to new; and God fulfills himself in many ways."

Thus Arthur passed but did not die. In spite of his downfall, his life was not in vain. His memory still lives in the hearts of men.

THINK BACK OVER WHAT YOU HAVE READ

Seeing the Relation of the Summaries to the Story as a Whole

1. What evidence can you cite to show that Arthur remained the perfect king until the last?

2. Of what did Pelleas' disillusionment consist? How did Tristram betray the ideals of chivalry?

3. What parallel to the story of Lancelot's winning the diamond for Guinevere did you find in the summaries?

4. How does Modred live up to the prophecy about him you met earlier in the *Idylls?*

5. What typical elements of reaction did you notice in the breakup of the Round Table? Think of the way some club you once belonged to began to dissolve. What were the first signs of discontent? What difficulties? How was the final rupture accomplished? With such a pattern in mind think back to the downfall of Arthur's kingdom.

Increase Your Power over Words

6. Although these words are associated with the age of chivalry, they are often used figuratively in modern writing. If, therefore, you are to read with full enjoyment, you should know the historical background of such words as these. To what fact in history do they refer?

mage (page 530)	liege (pages 526, 530)
boon (page 537)	quest (page 537)
joust (pages 537, 543)	squire (page 551)
	tilt (pages 537, 543)
lay (page 545)	tourney (page 538)

For Ambitious Students

7. *Filling in the gaps in the story.* Before leaving the study of the *Idylls of the King,* you will wish to have in your mind the complete stories of each of the great heroes of Arthurian legend. From the following books you may learn more about Lancelot and Galahad and Guinevere and any other of the characters about whom your curiosity has been aroused. Perhaps different groups in the class will agree to fill in the gaps left in the story by the briefer versions of this text.

Lanier, Sidney, *The Boys' King Arthur* (a simplified Malory)
Newell, W. W., *King Arthur and the Table Round*
Pyle, Howard, *The Story of the Champions of the Round Table; The Story of King Arthur and His Knights; The Story of Sir Lancelot and His Companions*
Sterling, M. B., *The Story of Sir Galahad*

8. *The allegorical significance of the* Idylls. The following books will help you interpret the underlying meaning of the *Idylls of the King.*

Alden, R. M., "Arthurian Epic" (in *Alfred Tennyson*)
Gurteen, S. H. V., *The Arthurian Epic*
Littledale, Harold, *Essays on Tennyson's Idylls of the King*
Patten, C. B., *The Meaning of the Idylls of the King*

9. *The age of chivalry.* The age of chivalry is one of the great epochs in the history of mankind. Its influence on the thought of the world has been great. Many of our present-day ideas about service and loyalty and sportsmanship are rooted in this medieval conception. To understand it, therefore, as a force in the world, is a step toward understanding life itself. But to appreciate it fully you must do more than memorize a few facts about it; you must *feel* it as though you yourself had been a part of it. The following historical novels will help you catch the spirit of this great age through your imagination. These books may

serve perhaps as your outside reading list during the period that the class is studying the *Idylls of the King.*

Alden, R. M., *Knights of the Silver Shield*
Bulwer-Lytton, E. R., *Harold*
Daniel, Hawthorne, *The Honor of Dunmore; The Shadow of the Sword*
Douglas, Donald, *Falcon's Flight*
Hyde, M. P., *Singing Sword*
Kingsley, Charles, *Hereward the Wake*
Meyer, C. F., *The Saint*
Prior, Loveday, *Law unto Themselves*
Scott, Walter, *Ivanhoe; The Talisman*

10. *The Arthurian theme in literature.* Now that you have seen how Tennyson has dealt with the King Arthur stories, it will interest you to read other adaptations of the same theme.

Arnold, Matthew, *Tristram and Iseult*
Erskine, John, *Galahad*
Field, Eugene, *Proper Trewe Idyll of Camelot*
Robinson, E. A., *Tristram*
Twain, Mark, *A Connecticut Yankee in King Arthur's Court*
Wagner, Richard, *Parsifal* (opera)

11. *Celtic background of Arthurian stories.* The richness of Celtic imagination has long been recognized, and stories of early Welsh and Irish heroes offer a specially fertile field for legend hunters. The following books will acquaint you with this picturesque background of folklore in which the Arthurian stories are rooted.

Brooks, Edward, *Wonder Stories from the Mabinogion*
Chambers, E. K., *Arthur of Britain*
Colum, Padraic, *The Island of the Mighty*
Jones, W. L., *King Arthur in History and Legend*
Lanier, Sidney (ed.), *Knightly Legends of Wales*
Loomis, R. S., *Celtic Myth and Arthurian Romance*
Wilmot-Buxton, E. M., *Stories of Early England*

WHAT WORDS DENOTING LITERARY FORM SHALL YOU REMEMBER?

The following questions are designed to help you fix in mind certain words, already introduced to you, which are important to an appreciation of literary form:

1. How does a folk epic differ from a literary epic? Which is *Idylls of the King?*

2. In your own words define an epic. How does it differ from a ballad? What are its essentials — those qualities without which it would no longer be an epic?

3. About what other legendary heroes besides King Arthur have epics been written? Do you know? If not, can you find out?

4. Look up in an encyclopedia or dictionary the following words and illustrate their meaning by reference to the *Idylls of the King:* allegory, parable, cycle, saga.

5. Where have you ever heard the word *epic* used outside an English class? Do sports writers ever use the word? Suppose that a radio feature were announced as "The Epic of America." What would you be led to expect?

THE NOVEL

THE FORMS of literature to which you have been introduced in this text — the epic, the ballad, the lyric, the play, the short story, the essay, and now the novel — are in part outgrowths of the daily habits of mankind at a particular age. Thus in his early days man listened to long, rambling tales recited or sung by wandering minstrels; out of such experience grew the epic. Or he sang at his work to relieve tedium or loneliness, and thus originated the ballad. Or, to come down to modern times, he twirled a dial and let voices into his room; hence the radio skit and the radio play.

These literary types may be explained in still another way: each form that you have met is the outgrowth, also, of man's way of thinking at a particular stage in his development. Like you, the race grows up; childish habits of mind give way to mature thinking. Early man, like you, once looked out upon the world with childish wonder and gave imagined reasons for the mysteries he could not explain: why the sun rose, why people died, or why ships were lost at sea. Like you, too, he dreamed of the self he would like to be — a self strong and brave and able to cope with all the problems of life with magnificent ease. Like you, he daydreamed and told himself fairy stories — stories of heroic adventure in which it was pleasant to believe, stories in which all mysteries were solved and all difficulties overcome. Such stories make up the myths and the legends of the past.

There came a time, however, when fairy tales no longer sufficed. Mankind had grown up. Life wasn't a matter of luck after all. Behind each disaster lay a reason to be discovered and combated. The mythical world of dragons to be overcome, of angry gods to be appeased, became but an amusing or beautiful memory. In its place was a stern world of cause and effect, a world of facts that must be faced. It was in this stage of development that the novel was born.

Such a time came after mankind had learned to read, when books could be printed cheaply enough for the mass of people to buy them, and as the struggle for existence relaxed enough to permit the common man to think about any other life than his own. Such a time we place roughly in the middle of the eighteenth century. One hundred years later, the period to which George Eliot belongs, the novel came to full flower and has remained a popular literary form ever since.

In George Eliot's time it became the fashion to tell stories of everyday life; to describe characters not as they ought to be or might have been, but as they really were; to let them speak for themselves, moreover, in natural dialogue instead of literary language; to tell homely truths about life; and to picture accurately a definite locality rather than to imagine for a setting a golden paradise. This is the spirit of realism, a mood of writing which you have already met in your reading of the short story. It is the mood of the novel which follows.

Silas Marner is an intimate study of a man's personality changing under the force of circumstances. It is the kind of novel in which you will find yourself less interested in *what* happens than in *why* it happens. To develop adequately such an interest, you can see, calls for a full-length story.

SILAS MARNER

by George Eliot (Mary Ann Evans, 1819–1880)

George Eliot knew intimately the scenes she describes in *Silas Marner*. The best of her novels are those based on her early impressions of rural England. As a child she knew and loved the rolling countryside around Griff. It was the day of the picturesque manor house and the quaint tenant's cottage, of fox hunting, and of fast mail coaches. To read *Adam Bede* and *Middlemarch* and *Felix Holt* is to be set down in the midst of the twenties and thirties of the last century and to feel thoroughly at home in the English Midlands.

Mary Ann Evans was a very serious child. As she grew up, she never lost that intensity of nature which expresses itself in the high moral tone of her writing. After her father gave up his position of business agent at the Arbury estate, she became at twenty-one the busy mistress of a farmhouse near Coventry. She made butter and cheese, and preserved fruit; she gave German lessons and studied Italian from a traveling master; she read philosophy and played favorite tunes to her father. As a child she had been a voracious reader and an able student. Fortunate in her teachers, she made the most of the meager education offered to girls in those days by the village boarding schools. After her father's death she traveled for a while in Europe. Her literary career did not begin until she was well into middle life.

Up until the time she met G. H. Lewes, with whom she afterward lived very happily for the greater part of her life, she had not given serious thought to the writing of novels. As a member of the staff of the *Westminster Review,* one of the leading literary magazines of the day, her writing consisted chiefly of scholarly criticism. Recognizing in her diary, which she kept during one of their trips abroad, a keen power of observation, Mr. Lewes suggested on their return that she try fiction. Her first novel, *Scenes from Clerical Life,* was submitted to *Blackwood's Magazine* in installments under the pen name of George Eliot. Even the publishers did not know that the author was a woman. The world was still a little dubious about the propriety of a woman's using her mind. Charles Dickens was among the first to guess that the author of *Adam Bede,* which followed close upon the heels of *Scenes from Clerical Life,* was not a man.

PART I

You have seen the slow, heavy start of a long railroad train just pulling out of the station. You do not expect a Twentieth Century Limited to take off with the ease of an automobile. Before the powerful locomotive can gain speed and momentum, it must overcome the great drag of resistance.

In similar fashion it takes time for a long, complicated story to get under way. The plot does not begin to move at once. A good reader, therefore, is patient and waits for the story to unfold.

As you read the two chapters that follow, preferably at a single sitting, try to give your imagination a chance to feel keenly a different time and place. Try actually to see in your mind's eye the stone cottage at Raveloe, and to hear with your mind's ear the humming of the loom. Linger long enough over the details of description to make them summon a vivid picture to mind.

Along with finding your bearings in rural England of a century ago, you will start your acquaintance in these chapters with the character of the lonely weaver, Silas Marner, for whom the story is named. Notice, as you read, how cruel injustice changes the course of his life and what a strange turn his resentment takes against a false accusation.

CHAPTER I

IN THE days when the spinning wheels hummed busily in the farmhouses — and even great ladies, clothed in silk and thread lace, had their toy spinning wheels of polished oak — there might be seen, in districts far away among the lanes, or deep in the bosom of the hills, certain pallid undersized men, who, by the side of the brawny countryfolk, looked like the remnants of a disinherited race. The shepherd's dog barked fiercely when one of these alien-looking men appeared on the upland, dark against the early winter sunset; for what dog likes a figure bent under a heavy bag? — and these pale men rarely stirred abroad without that mysterious burden. The shepherd himself, though he had good reason to believe that the bag held nothing but flaxen thread, or else the long rolls of strong linen spun from that thread, was not quite sure that this trade of weaving, indispensable though it was, could be carried on entirely without the help of the Evil One. In that far-off time superstition clung easily round every person or thing that was at all unwonted, or even intermittent and occasional merely, like the visits of the peddler or the knife grinder. No one knew where wandering men had their homes or their origin; and how was a man to be explained unless you at least knew somebody who knew his father and mother? To the peasants of old times, the world outside their own direct experience was a region of vagueness and mystery; to their untraveled thought a state of wandering was a conception as dim as the winter life of the swallows that came back with the spring; and even a settler, if he came from distant parts, hardly ever ceased to be viewed with a remnant of distrust, which would have prevented any surprise if a long course of inoffensive conduct on his part had ended in the commission of a crime; especially if he had any reputation for knowledge, or showed any skill in handicraft. All cleverness, whether in the rapid use of that difficult instrument the tongue, or in some other art unfamiliar to villagers, was in itself suspicious; honest folk, born and bred in a visible manner, were mostly not overwise or clever — at least, not beyond such a matter as knowing the signs of the weather; and the process by which rapidity and dexterity of any kind were acquired was so wholly hidden that they partook of the nature of conjuring. In this way it came to pass that those scattered linen weavers — emigrants from the town into the country — were to the last regarded as aliens by their rustic neighbors, and usually contracted the eccentric habits which belong to a state of loneliness.

In the early years of this century, such a linen weaver, named Silas Marner, worked at his vocation in a stone cottage that stood among the nutty hedgerows near the village of Raveloe, and not far from the edge of a deserted stone pit. The questionable sound of Silas's loom, so unlike the natural cheerful trotting of the winnowing machine, or the simpler rhythm of the flail, had a half-fearful fascination for the Raveloe boys, who would often leave off their nutting or birds'-nesting to peep in at the window of the stone cottage, counterbalancing a certain awe at the mysterious action of the loom by a pleasant sense of scornful superiority, drawn from the mockery of its alternating noises, along with the bent, treadmill attitude of the weaver. But sometimes it happened that Marner, pausing to adjust an irregularity in his thread, became aware of the small scoundrels, and, though chary of his time, he liked their intrusion so ill that he would descend from his loom, and, opening the door, would fix on them a gaze that was always enough to make them take to their legs in terror. For how was it possible to believe that those large brown protuberant eyes in Silas Marner's pale face really saw nothing very distinctly that was not close to them, and not rather that their dreadful stare could dart cramp, or rickets, or a wry mouth at any boy who happened to be in the rear? They had, perhaps, heard their fathers and mothers hint that Silas Marner could cure folks' rheumatism if he had a mind, and add, still more darkly, that if you could only speak the devil fair enough he might save you the cost of the doctor. Such strange lingering echoes of the old demon worship might perhaps even now be caught by the diligent listener among the gray-haired peasantry; for the rude mind with difficulty associates the ideas of power and benignity. A shadowy conception of power that by much persuasion can be induced to refrain from inflicting harm is the shape most easily taken by the sense of the Invisible in the minds of men who have always been pressed close by primitive wants, and to whom a life of hard toil has never been illuminated by any enthusiastic religious faith. To them pain and mishap present a far wider range of possibilities than gladness and enjoyment: their imagination is almost barren of the images that feed desire and hope, but is all overgrown by recollections that are a perpetual pasture to fear. "Is there anything you can fancy that you would like to eat?" I once said to an old laboring man, who was in his last illness, and who had refused all the food his wife had offered him. "No," he answered, "I've never been used to nothing but common victual, and I can't eat that." Experience had bred no fancies in him that could raise the phantasm of appetite.

And Raveloe was a village where many of the old echoes lingered, undrowned by new voices. Not that it was one of those barren parishes lying on the outskirts of civilization — inhabited by meager sheep and thinly scattered shepherds; on the contrary, it lay in the rich central plain of what we are pleased to call Merry England, and held farms which, speaking from a spiritual point of view, paid highly desirable tithes. But it was nestled in a snug well-wooded hollow, quite an hour's journey on horseback from any turnpike, where it was never reached by the vibrations of the coach horn or of public opinion. It was an important-looking village, with a fine old church and large churchyard in the heart of it, and two or three large brick-and-stone homesteads, with well-walled orchards and ornamental weathercocks, standing close upon the road, and lifting more imposing fronts than the rectory, which peeped from among the trees on the other side of the churchyard — a village which showed at once the summits of its social life, and told the practiced eye that there was no great park and manor house in the vicinity, but that there were several chiefs in Raveloe who could farm badly quite at their ease, drawing enough money from their bad farming, in those wartimes,[1] to live in a rollicking fashion, and keep a jolly Christmas, Whitsun,[2] and Easter tide.

It was fifteen years since Silas Marner had first come to Raveloe; he was then simply a pallid young man, with prominent, shortsighted brown eyes whose appearance would have had nothing strange for people of average culture and experience, but for the villagers near whom he had come to settle it had mysterious peculiarities which corresponded with the exceptional nature of his occupation and his advent from an unknown region called "North'ard." So had his way of life; he invited no comer to step across his doorsill, and he never strolled into the village to drink a pint at the Rainbow, or to gossip at the wheelwright's; he sought no man or woman, save for the purposes of his calling, or in order to supply himself with necessaries; and it was soon clear to the Raveloe lasses that he would never urge one of them to accept him against her will — quite as if he had heard them declare that they would never marry a dead man come to life again. This view of Marner's personality was not without another ground than his pale face and unexampled eyes; for Jem Rodney, the mole catcher, averred that, one evening as he was returning homeward, he saw Silas Marner leaning against a stile with a heavy bag on his back, instead of resting the bag on the stile as a man in his senses would have done; and that, on coming up to him, he saw that Marner's eyes were set like a dead man's, and he spoke to him, and shook him, and his limbs were stiff, and his hands clutched the bag as if they'd been made of iron; but just as he had made up his mind that the weaver was dead, he came all right again, like, as you might say, in the winking of an eye, and said "Good night," and walked off. All this Jem swore he had seen, more by token that it was the very day he had been mole catching on Squire Cass's land, down by the old saw pit. Some said Marner must have been in a "fit," a word which seemed to explain things otherwise incredible; but the argumentative Mr. Macey, clerk of the parish, shook his head, and asked if anybody was ever known to go off in a fit and not fall down. A fit was a stroke, wasn't it? and it was in the nature of a stroke to partly take away the use of a man's limbs and throw him on the parish, if he'd got no children to look to. No, no; it was no stroke that would let a man stand on his legs, like a horse between the shafts, and then walk off as soon as you can say "Gee!" But there might be such a thing as a man's soul being loose from his body, and going out and in, like a bird out of its nest and back; and that was how folks got overwise, for they went to school in this shell-less state to those who could teach them more than their neighbors could learn with their five senses and the parson. And where did Master Marner get his knowledge of herbs from — and charms, too, if he liked to give them away? Jem Rodney's story was no more than what might have been expected by anybody who had seen how Marner had cured Sally Oates, and made her sleep like a baby, when her heart had been beating enough to burst her body for two months and more, while she had been under the doctor's care. He might cure more folks if he would; but he was worth speaking fair, if it was only to keep him from doing you a mischief.

[1] **in those wartimes:** Between the years 1789 and 1815 England was at war with France. After the French Revolution of 1789 France was surrounded by enemies who sided with the deposed nobility. In 1793 France declared war on England. In 1796 Napoleon Bonaparte began his campaign to conquer Europe. He was defeated at Waterloo in 1815 by the English general, the Duke of Wellington. [2] **Whitsun:** an old church festival day which came the seventh Sunday after Easter.

It was partly to this vague fear that Marner was indebted for protecting him from the persecution that his singularities might have drawn upon him, but still more to the fact that, the old linen weaver in the neighboring parish of Tarley being dead, his handicraft made him a highly welcome settler to the richer housewives of the district, and even to the more provident cottagers, who had their little stock of yarn at the year's end. Their sense of his usefulness would have counteracted any repugnance or suspicion which was not confirmed by a deficiency in the quality or the tale[1] of the cloth he wove for them. And the years had rolled on without producing any change in the impressions of the neighbors concerning Marner, except the change from novelty to habit. At the end of fifteen years the Raveloe men said just the same things about Silas Marner as at the beginning; they did not say them quite so often, but they believed them much more strongly when they did say them. There was only one important addition which the years had brought; it was, that Master Marner had laid by a fine sight of money somewhere, and that he could buy up "bigger men" than himself.

But while opinion concerning him had remained nearly stationary, and his daily habits had presented scarcely any visible change, Marner's inward life had been a history and a metamorphosis, as that of every fervid nature must be when it has fled, or been condemned, to solitude. His life, before he came to Raveloe, had been filled with the movement, the mental activity, and the close fellowship, which, in that day as in this, marked the life of an artisan early incorporated in a narrow religious sect, where the poorest layman has the chance of distinguishing himself by gifts of speech, and has, at the very least, the weight of a silent voter in the government of his community. Marner was highly thought of in that little hidden world, known to itself as the church assembling in Lantern Yard: he was believed to be a young man of exemplary life and ardent faith; and a peculiar interest had been centered in him ever since he had fallen, at a prayer meeting, into a mysterious rigidity and suspension of consciousness, which, lasting for an hour or more, had been mistaken for death. To have sought a medical explanation for this phenomenon would have been held by Silas himself, as well as by his minister and fellow members, a willful self-exclusion from the spiritual significance that might lie therein. Silas was evidently a brother selected for a peculiar discipline; and though the effort to interpret this discipline was discouraged by the absence, on his part, of any spiritual vision during his outward trance, yet it was believed by himself and others that its effect was seen in an accession of light and fervor. A less truthful man than he might have been tempted into the subsequent creation of a vision in the form of resurgent memory; a less sane man might have believed in such a creation; but Silas was both sane and honest, though, as with many honest and fervent men, culture had not defined any channels for his sense of mystery, and so it spread itself over the proper pathway of inquiry and knowledge. He had inherited from his mother some acquaintance with medicinal herbs and their preparation — a little store of wisdom which she had imparted to him as a solemn bequest — but of late years he had had doubts about the lawfulness of applying this knowledge, believing that herbs could have no efficacy without prayer, and that prayer might suffice without herbs; so that his inherited delight to wander through the fields in search of foxglove and dande-

[1] **tale**: an uncommon word for amount.

lion and coltsfoot began to wear to him the character of a temptation.

Among the members of his church there was one young man, a little older than himself, with whom he had long lived in such close friendship that it was the custom of their Lantern Yard brethren to call them David and Jonathan.[1] The real name of the friend was William Dane, and he, too, was regarded as a shining instance of youthful piety, though somewhat given to overseverity toward weaker brethren, and to be so dazzled by his own light as to hold himself wiser than his teachers. But whatever blemishes others might discern in William, to his friend's mind he was faultless; for Marner had one of those impressible self-doubting natures which, at an inexperienced age, admire imperativeness and lean on contradiction. The expression of trusting simplicity in Marner's face, heightened by that absence of special observation, that defenseless, deerlike gaze which belongs to large prominent eyes, was strongly contrasted by the self-complacent suppression of inward triumph that lurked in the narrow slanting eyes and compressed lips of William Dane. One of the most frequent topics of conversation between the two friends was assurance of salvation; Silas confessed that he could never arrive at anything higher than hope mingled with fear, and listened with longing wonder when William declared that he had possessed unshaken assurance ever since, in the period of his conversion, he had dreamed that he saw the words "calling and election sure" standing by themselves on a white page in the open Bible. Such colloquies have occupied many a pair of pale-faced weavers, whose unnurtured souls have been like young winged things, fluttering forsaken in the twilight.

[1] **David and Jonathan:** two friends of the Bible who loved each other dearly.

It had seemed to the unsuspecting Silas that the friendship had suffered no chill even from his formation of another attachment of a closer kind. For some months he had been engaged to a young servant woman, waiting only for a little increase to their mutual savings in order to their marriage; and it was a great delight to him that Sarah did not object to William's occasional presence in their Sunday interviews. It was at this point in their history that Silas's cataleptic fit occurred during the prayer meeting; and amidst the various queries and expressions of interest addressed to him by his fellow members, William's suggestion alone jarred with the general sympathy toward a brother thus singled out for special dealings. He observed that, to him, this trance looked more like a visitation of Satan than a proof of divine favor, and exhorted his friend to see that he hid no accursed thing within his soul. Silas, feeling bound to accept rebuke and admonition as a brotherly office, felt no resentment, but only pain, at his friend's doubts concerning him; and to this was soon added some anxiety at the perception that Sarah's manner toward him began to exhibit a strange fluctuation between an effort at an increased manifestation of regard and involuntary signs of shrinking and dislike. He asked her if she wished to break off their engagement; but she denied this: their engagement was known to the church, and had been recognized in the prayer meetings; it could not be broken off without strict investigation, and Sarah could render no reason that would be sanctioned by the feeling of the community. At this time the senior deacon was taken dangerously ill, and, being a childless widower, he was tended night and day by some of the younger brethren or sisters. Silas frequently took his turn in the night watching with William, the one relieving the other at two in the morning. The old man, contrary to expectation, seemed to be on the way to recovery, when one night Silas, sitting up by his bedside, observed that his usual audible breathing had ceased. The candle was burning low, and he had to lift it to see the patient's face distinctly. Examination convinced him that the deacon was dead — had been dead some time, for the limbs were rigid. Silas asked himself if he had been asleep, and looked at the clock: it was already four in the morning. How was it that William had not come? In much anxiety he went to seek for help, and soon there were several friends assembled in the house, the minister among them, while Silas went away to his work, wishing he could have met William to know the reason of his nonappearance. But at six o'clock, as he was thinking of going to seek his friend, William came, and with him the minister. They came to summon him to Lantern Yard, to meet the church members there; and to his inquiry concerning the cause of the summons the only reply was, " You will hear." Nothing further was said until Silas was seated in the vestry, in front of the minister, with the eyes of those who to him represented God's people fixed solemnly upon him. Then the minister, taking out a pocket knife, showed it to Silas, and asked him if he knew where he had left that knife? Silas said he did not know that he had left it anywhere out of his own pocket — but he was trembling at this strange interrogation. He was then exhorted not to hide his sin, but to confess and repent. The knife had been found in the bureau by the departed deacon's bedside — found in the place where the little bag of church money had lain, which the minister himself had seen the day before. Some hand had removed that bag; and whose hand could it be, if not that of the man to whom the knife belonged? For some time Silas was mute with astonishment; then he said, " God will clear me; I know nothing about the knife being there, or the money being gone. Search me and my dwelling; you will find nothing but three pounds five of my own savings, which William Dane knows I have had these six months." At this William groaned, but the minister said, " The proof is heavy against you, brother Marner. The money was taken in the night last past, and no man was with our departed brother but you, for William Dane declares to us that he was hindered by sudden sickness from going to take his place as usual, and you yourself said that he had not come; and, moreover, you neglected the dead body."

" I must have slept," said Silas. Then, after a pause, he added, " Or I must have had another visitation like that which you have all seen me under, so that the thief must have come and gone while I was not in the body, but out of the body. But, I say again, search me and my dwelling, for I have been nowhere else."

The search was made, and it ended — in William Dane's finding the well-known bag, empty, tucked behind the chest of drawers in Silas's chamber! On this William exhorted his friend to confess, and not to hide his sin any longer. Silas turned a look of keen reproach on him, and said, " William, for nine years that we have gone in and out together, have you ever known me to tell a lie? But God will clear me."

" Brother," said William, " how do I know what you may have done in the secret chambers of your heart, to give Satan an advantage over you? "

Silas was still looking at his friend. Suddenly a deep flush came over his face, and he was about to speak impetuously, when he seemed checked again by some inward shock that sent the flush back and made him tremble. But at last he spoke feebly, looking at William.

"I remember now — the knife wasn't in my pocket."

William said, "I know nothing of what you mean." The other persons present, however, began to inquire where Silas meant to say that the knife was, but he would give no further explanation; he only said, "I am sore stricken; I can say nothing. God will clear me."

On their return to the vestry there was further deliberation. Any resort to legal measures for ascertaining the culprit was contrary to the principles of the church in Lantern Yard, according to which prosecution was forbidden to Christians, even had the case held less scandal to the community. But the members were bound to take other measures for finding out the truth, and they resolved on praying and drawing lots.[1] This resolution can be a ground of surprise only to those who are unacquainted with that obscure religious life which has gone on in the alleys of our towns. Silas knelt with his brethren, relying on his own innocence being certified by immediate divine interference, but feeling that there was sorrow and mourning behind for him even then — that his trust in man had been cruelly bruised. *The lots declared that Silas Marner was guilty.* He was solemnly suspended from church membership, and called upon to render up the stolen money; only on confession, as the sign of repentance, could he be received once more within the folds of the church. Marner listened in silence. At last, when everyone rose to depart, he went toward William Dane, and said, in a voice shaken by agitation —

"The last time I remembered using my knife was when I took it out to cut a strap for you. I don't remember putting it in my pocket again. *You* stole the money, and you have woven the plot to lay the sin at my door. But you may prosper, for all that; there is no just God that governs the earth righteously, but a God of lies, that bears witness against the innocent."

There was a general shudder at this blasphemy.

William said meekly, "I leave our brethren to judge whether this is the voice of Satan or not. I can do nothing but pray for you, Silas."

Poor Marner went out with that despair in his soul, that shaken trust in God and man, which is little short of madness to a loving nature. In the bitterness of his wounded spirit, he said to himself, "*She* will cast me off, too." And he reflected that, if she did not believe the testimony against him, her whole faith must be upset, as his was. To people accustomed to reason about the forms in which their religious feeling has incorporated itself, it is difficult to enter into that simple, untaught state of mind in which the form and the feeling have never been severed by an act of reflection. We are apt to think it inevitable that a man in Marner's position should have begun to question the validity of an appeal to the divine judgment by drawing lots; but to him this would have been an effort of independent thought such as he had never known; and he must have made the effort at a moment when all his energies were turned to the anguish of disappointed faith. If there is an angel who records the sorrows of men as well as their sins, he knows how many and deep are the sorrows that spring from false ideas for which no man is culpable.

Marner went home, and for a whole day sat alone, stunned by despair, without any impulse to go to Sarah and attempt to win her belief in his innocence. The second day he took refuge from benumbing unbelief by getting into his loom

[1] **drawing lots:** an old method of determining guilt. It was thought that the person who drew the unlucky symbol was accused by fate.

and working away as usual; and before many hours were past, the minister and one of the deacons came to him with the message from Sarah, that she held her engagement to him at an end. Silas received the message mutely, and then turned away from the messengers to work at his loom again. In little more than a month from that time, Sarah was married to William Dane; and not long afterward it was known to the brethren in Lantern Yard that Silas Marner had departed from the town.

CHAPTER II

Even people whose lives have been made various by learning sometimes find it hard to keep a fast hold on their habitual views of life, on their faith in the invisible — nay, on the sense that their past joys and sorrows are a real experience, when they are suddenly transported to a new land, where the beings around them know nothing of their history, and share none of their ideas — where their mother earth shows another lap, and human life has other forms than those on which their souls have been nourished. Minds that have been unhinged from their old faith and love have perhaps sought this Lethean [1] influence of exile, in which the past becomes dreamy because its symbols have all vanished, and the present, too, is dreamy because it is linked with no memories. But even *their* experience may hardly enable them thoroughly to imagine what was the effect on a simple weaver like Silas Marner, when he left his own country and people and came to settle in Raveloe. Nothing could be more unlike his native town, set within sight of the widespread hillsides, than this low, wooded region, where he felt hidden even from the heavens by the screening trees and hedgerows. There was nothing here, when he rose in the deep morning quiet and looked out on the dewy brambles and rank tufted grass, that seemed to have any relation with that life centering in Lantern Yard, which had once been to him the altar place of high dispensations. The whitewashed walls; the little pews where well-known figures entered with a subdued rustling, and where first one well-known voice and then another, pitched in a peculiar key of petition, uttered phrases at once occult and familiar, like the amulet worn on the heart; the pulpit where the minister delivered unquestioned doctrine, and swayed to and fro, and handled the book in a long-accustomed manner; the very pauses between the couplets of the hymn, as it was given out, and the recurrent swell of voices in song; these things had been the channel of divine influences to Marner — they were the fostering home of his religious emotions — they were Christianity and God's kingdom upon earth. A weaver who finds hard words in his hymnbook knows nothing of abstractions; as the little child knows nothing of parental love, but only knows one face and one lap toward which it stretches its arms for refuge and nurture.

And what could be more unlike that Lantern Yard world than the world in Raveloe? — orchards looking lazy with neglected plenty; the large church in the wide churchyard, which men gazed at lounging at their own doors in service-time; the purple-faced farmers jogging along the lanes or turning in at the Rainbow; homesteads, where men supped heavily and slept in the light of the evening hearth, and where women seemed to be laying up a stock of linen for the life to come. There were no lips in Raveloe from which a word could fall that would stir Silas Marner's benumbed faith to a sense of pain. In the early ages of the

[1] **Lethean:** from Lethe, the river in Hades the waters of which caused forgetfulness.

world, we know, it was believed that each territory was inhabited and ruled by its own divinities, so that a man could cross the bordering heights and be out of the reach of his native gods, whose presence was confined to the streams and the groves and the hills among which he had lived from his birth. And poor Silas was vaguely conscious of something not unlike the feeling of primitive men, when they fled thus, in fear or in sullenness, from the face of an unpropitious deity. It seemed to him that the Power he had vainly trusted in among the streets and at the prayer meetings was very far away from this land in which he had taken refuge, where men lived in careless abundance, knowing and needing nothing of that trust which, for him, had been turned to bitterness. The little light he possessed spread its beams so narrowly that frustrated belief was a curtain broad enough to create for him the blackness of night.

His first movement after the shock had been to work in his loom; and he went on with this unremittingly, never asking himself why, now he was come to Raveloe, he worked far on into the night to finish the tale of Mrs. Osgood's table linen sooner than she expected — without contemplating beforehand the money she would put into his hand for the work. He seemed to weave, like the spider, from pure impulse, without reflection. Every man's work, pursued steadily, tends in this way to become an end in itself, and so to bridge over the loveless chasms of his life. Silas's hand satisfied itself with throwing the shuttle, and his eye with seeing the little squares in the cloth complete themselves under his effort. Then there were the calls of hunger; and Silas, in his solitude, had to provide his own breakfast, dinner, and supper, to fetch his own water from the well, and put his own kettle on the fire; and all these immediate promptings helped, along with the weaving, to reduce his life to the unquestioning activity of a spinning insect. He hated the thought of the past; there was nothing that called out his love and fellowship toward the strangers he had come amongst; and the future was all dark, for there was no Unseen Love that cared for him. Thought was arrested by utter bewilderment, now its old narrow pathway was closed and affection seemed to have died under the bruise that had fallen on its keenest nerves.

But at last Mrs. Osgood's table linen was finished, and Silas was paid in gold. His earnings in his native town, where he worked for a wholesale dealer, had been after a lower rate; he had been paid weekly, and of his weekly earnings a large proportion had gone to objects of piety and charity. Now, for the first time in his life, he had five bright guineas put into his hand; no man expected a share of them, and he loved no man that he should offer him a share. But what were the guineas to him who saw no vista beyond countless days of weaving? It was needless for him to ask that, for it was pleasant to him to feel them in his palm, and look at their bright faces, which were all his own; it was another element of life, like the weaving and the satisfaction of hunger, subsisting quite aloof from the life of belief and love from which he had been cut off. The weaver's hand had known the touch of hard-won money even before the palm had grown to its full breadth; for twenty years, mysterious money had stood to him as the symbol of earthly good, and the immediate object of toil. He had seemed to love it little in the years when every penny had its purpose for him; for he loved the *purpose* then. But now, when all purpose was gone, that habit of looking toward the money and grasping it with a sense of fulfilled effort made a loam that was deep enough for the seeds of desire; and as

Silas walked homeward across the fields in the twilight, he drew out the money, and thought it was brighter in the gathering gloom.

About this time an incident happened which seemed to open a possibility of some fellowship with his neighbors. One day, taking a pair of shoes to be mended, he saw the cobbler's wife seated by the fire, suffering from the terrible symptoms of heart disease and dropsy, which he had witnessed as the precursors of his mother's death. He felt a rush of pity at the mingled sight and remembrance, and, recalling the relief his mother had found from a simple preparation of foxglove, he promised Sally Oates to bring her something that would ease her, since the doctor did her no good. In this office of charity, Silas felt, for the first time since he had come to Raveloe, a sense of unity between his past and present life, which might have been the beginning of his rescue from the insectlike existence into which his nature had shrunk. But Sally Oates's disease had raised her into a personage of much interest and importance among the neighbors, and the fact of her having found relief from drinking Silas Marner's "stuff" became a matter of general discourse. When Doctor Kimble gave physic, it was natural that it should have an effect; but when a weaver, who came from nobody knew where, worked wonders with a bottle of brown waters, the occult character of the process was evident. Such a sort of thing had not been known since the Wise Woman[1] at Tarley died; and she had charms as well as "stuff"; everybody went to her when their children had fits. Silas Marner must be a person of the same sort, for how did he know what would bring back Sally Oates's breath, if he didn't know a fine sight more than that? The Wise Woman had words that she muttered to herself, so that you couldn't hear what they were, and if she tied a bit of red thread round the child's toe the while, it would keep off the water in the head. There were women in Raveloe, at that present time, who had worn one of the Wise Woman's little bags round their necks, and, in consequence, had never had an idiot child, as Ann Coulter had. Silas Marner could very likely do as much, and more; and now it was all clear how he should have come from unknown parts, and be so "comical-looking." But Sally Oates must mind and not tell the doctor, for he would be sure to set his face against Marner; he was always angry about the Wise Woman, and used to threaten those who went to her that they should have none of his help any more.

Silas now found himself and his cottage suddenly beset by mothers who wanted him to charm away the whooping cough, or bring back the milk, and by men who wanted stuff against the rheumatics or the knots in the hands; and, to secure themselves against a refusal, the applicants brought silver in their palms. Silas might have driven a profitable trade in charms as well as in his small list of drugs; but money on this condition was no temptation to him; he had never known an impulse toward falsity, and he drove one after another away with growing irritation, for the news of him as a wise man had spread even to Tarley, and it was long before people ceased to take long walks for the sake of asking his aid. But the hope in his wisdom was at length changed into dread, for no one believed him when he said he knew no charms and could work no cures, and every man and woman who had an accident or a new attack after applying to him set the misfortune down to Master Marner's ill will and irritated glances. Thus it came to pass that his movement of pity toward Sally Oates, which had given him a tran-

[1] **Wise Woman:** sorceress.

sient sense of brotherhood, heightened the repulsion between him and his neighbors, and made his isolation more complete.

Gradually the guineas, the crowns, and the half crowns grew to a heap, and Marner drew less and less for his own wants, trying to solve the problem of keeping himself strong enough to work sixteen hours a day on as small an outlay as possible. Have not men, shut up in solitary imprisonment, found an interest in marking the moments by straight strokes of a certain length on the wall, until the growth of the sum of straight strokes, arranged in triangles, has become a mastering purpose? Do we not wile away moments of inanity or fatigued waiting by repeating some trivial movement or sound, until the repetition has bred a want, which is incipient habit? That will help us to understand how the love of accumulating money grows an absorbing passion in men whose imaginations, even in the very beginning of their hoard, showed them no purpose beyond it. Marner wanted the heaps of ten to grow into a square, and then into a larger square; and every added guinea, while it was itself a satisfaction, bred a new desire. In this strange world, made a hopeless riddle to him, he might, if he had had a less intense nature, have sat weaving, weaving — looking toward the end of his pattern, or toward the end of his web, till he forgot the riddle, and everything else but his immediate sensations; but the money had come to mark off his weaving into periods, and the money not only grew, but it remained with him. He began to think it was conscious of him, as his loom was, and he would on no account have exchanged those coins, which had become his familiars, for other coins with unknown faces. He handled them, he counted them, till their form and color were like the satisfaction of a thirst to him; but it was only in the night, when his work was done, that he drew them out to enjoy their companionship. He had taken up some bricks in his floor underneath his loom, and here he had made a hole in which he set the iron pot that contained his guineas and silver coins, covering the bricks with sand whenever he replaced them. Not that the idea of being robbed presented itself often or strongly to his mind; hoarding was common in country districts in those days; there were old laborers in the parish of Raveloe who were known to have their savings by them, probably inside their flock beds[1]; but their rustic neighbors, though not all of them as honest as their ancestors in the days of King Alfred,[2] had not imaginations bold enough to lay a plan of burglary. How could they have spent the money in their own village without betraying themselves? They would be obliged to "run away" — a course as dark and dubious as a balloon journey.

So, year after year, Silas Marner had lived in this solitude, his guineas rising in the iron pot, and his life narrowing and hardening itself more and more into a mere pulsation of desire and satisfaction that had no relation to any other being. His life had reduced itself to the functions of weaving and hoarding, without any contemplation of an end toward which the functions tended. The same sort of process has perhaps been undergone by wiser men, when they have been cut off from faith and love — only, instead of a loom and a heap of guineas, they have had some erudite research, some ingenious project, or some well-knit theory. Strangely Marner's face and figure shrank and bent themselves into a constant mechanical relation to the objects of his life, so that he

[1] **flock beds:** beds filled with small pieces of wool. [2] **in the days of King Alfred:** Back in the ninth century it was said that a purse of gold lying in the road was safe from thieves.

produced the same sort of impression as a handle or a crooked tube, which has no meaning standing apart. The prominent eyes that used to look trusting and dreamy now looked as if they had been made to see only one kind of thing that was very small, like tiny grain, for which they hunted everywhere; and he was so withered and yellow that, though he was not yet forty, the children always called him "Old Master Marner."

Yet even in this stage of withering a little incident happened which showed that the sap of affection was not all gone. It was one of his daily tasks to fetch his water from a well a couple of fields off, and for this purpose, ever since he came to Raveloe, he had had a brown earthenware pot, which he held as his most precious utensil, among the very few conveniences he had granted himself. It had been his companion for twelve years, always standing on the same spot, always lending its handle to him in the early morning, so that its form had an expression for him of willing helpfulness, and the impress of its handle on his palm gave a satisfaction mingled with that of having the fresh clear water. One day as he was returning from the well he stumbled against the step of the stile, and his brown pot, falling with force against the stones that overarched the ditch below him, was broken in three pieces. Silas picked up the pieces and carried them home with grief in his heart. The brown pot could never be of use to him any more, but he stuck the bits together and propped the ruin in its old place for a memorial.

This is the history of Silas Marner until the fifteenth year after he came to Raveloe. The livelong day he sat in his loom, his ear filled with its monotony, his eyes bent close down on the slow growth of sameness in the brownish web, his muscles moving with such even repetition that their pause seemed almost as much a constraint as the holding of his breath. But at night came his revelry; at night he closed his shutters, and made fast his doors, and drew forth his gold. Long ago the heap of coins had become too large for the iron pot to hold them, and he had made for them two thick leather bags, which wasted no room in their resting place, but lent themselves flexibly to every corner. How the guineas shone as they came pouring out of the dark leather mouths! The silver bore no large proportion in amount to the gold, because the long pieces of linen which formed his chief work were always partly paid for in gold, and out of the silver he supplied his own bodily wants, choosing always the shillings and sixpences to spend in this way. He loved the guineas best, but he would not change the silver — the crowns and half crowns that were his own earnings, begotten by his labor; he loved them all. He spread them out in heaps and bathed his hands in them; then he counted them and set them up in regular piles, and felt their rounded outline between his thumb and fingers, and thought fondly of the guineas that were only half-earned by the work in his loom, as if they had been unborn children — thought of the guineas that were coming slowly through the coming years, through all his life, which spread far away before him, the end quite hidden by countless days of weaving. No wonder his thoughts were still with his loom and his money when he made his journeys through the fields and the lanes to fetch and carry home his work, so that his steps never wandered to the hedge banks and the laneside in search of the once familiar herbs; these, too, belonged to the past, from which his life had shrunk away, like a rivulet that has sunk far down from the grassy fringe of its old breadth into a little shivering thread, that cuts a groove for itself in the barren sand.

But about the Christmas of that fifteenth year a second great change came over Marner's life, and his history became blent in a singular manner with the life of his neighbors.

CHAPTER III

Not infrequently when brothers fall out they become bitter enemies. It is so with the Cass brothers, whom you are to meet in this chapter. Their quarrel at the Red House sows the first seeds of dramatic interest in the story. Read slowly enough to appreciate fully the contrast in their characters. What differences do you notice? What hints of future difficulty does their hostility give?

The greatest man in Raveloe was Squire Cass, who lived in the large red house, with the handsome flight of stone steps in front and the high stables behind it, nearly opposite the church. He was only one among several landed parishioners, but he alone was honored with the title of Squire; for though Mr. Osgood's family was also understood to be of timeless origin — the Raveloe imagination having never ventured back to that fearful blank when there were no Osgoods — still he merely owned the farm he occupied; whereas Squire Cass had a tenant or two, who complained of the game to him quite as if he had been a lord.

It was still that glorious wartime which was felt to be a peculiar favor of Providence toward the landed interest,[1] and the fall of prices had not yet come to carry the race of small squires and yeomen down that road to ruin for which extravagant habits and bad husbandry were plentifully annointing their wheels. I am speaking now in relation to Raveloe and the parishes that resembled it; for our old-fashioned country life had many different aspects, as all life must have when it is spread over a various surface, and breathed on variously by multitudinous currents, from the winds of heaven to the thoughts of men, which are forever moving and crossing each other, with incalculable results. Raveloe lay low among the bushy trees and the rutted lanes, aloof from the currents of industrial energy and Puritan earnestness; the rich ate and drank freely, accepting gout and apoplexy as things that ran mysteriously in respectable families, and the poor thought that the rich were entirely in the right of it to lead a jolly life; besides, their feasting caused a multiplication of orts, which were the heirlooms of the poor. Betty Jay scented the boiling of Squire Cass's hams, but her longing was arrested by the unctuous liquor in which they were boiled; and when the seasons brought round the great merrymakings, they were regarded on all hands as a fine thing for the poor. For the Raveloe feasts were like the rounds of beef and the barrels of ale — they were on a large scale, and lasted a good while, especially in the wintertime. After ladies had packed up their best gowns and topknots in bandboxes, and had incurred the risk of fording streams on pillions with the precious burden in rainy or snowy weather, when there was no knowing how high the water would rise, it was not to be supposed that they looked forward to a brief pleasure. On this ground it was always contrived in the dark seasons, when there was little work to be done, and the hours were long, that several neighbors should keep open house in succession. So soon as Squire Cass's standing dishes diminished in plenty and freshness, his guests had nothing to do but to walk a little higher up the village to Mr. Osgood's, at the Orchards, and they found hams and chines uncut, pork pies with the scent of the fire in them, spun butter in all its freshness — everything, in fact, that appetites at leisure could desire, in perhaps

[1] In time of war food prices go up. Therefore, land becomes more valuable.

greater perfection, though not in greater abundance, than at Squire Cass's.

For the Squire's wife had died long ago, and the Red House was without that presence of the wife and mother which is the fountain of wholesome love and fear in parlor and kitchen; and this helped to account not only for there being more profusion than finished excellence in the holiday provisions, but also for the frequency with which the proud Squire condescended to preside in the parlor of the Rainbow rather than under the shadow of his own dark wainscot; perhaps, also, for the fact that his sons had turned out rather ill. Raveloe was not a place where moral censure was severe, but it was thought a weakness in the Squire that he had kept all his sons at home in idleness; and though some license was to be allowed to young men whose fathers could afford it, people shook their heads at the courses of the second son, Dunstan, commonly called Dunsey Cass, whose taste for swopping and betting might turn out to be a sowing of something worse than wild oats. To be sure, the neighbors said, it was no matter what became of Dunsey — a spiteful, jeering fellow, who seemed to enjoy his drink the more when other people went dry — always provided that his doings did not bring trouble on a family like Squire Cass's, with a monument in the church, and tankards older than King George. But it would be a thousand pities if Mr. Godfrey, the eldest, a fine, open-faced, good-natured young man, who was to come into the land someday, should take to going along the same road with his brother, as he had seemed to do of late. If he went on in that way, he would lose Miss Nancy Lammeter; for it was well known that she had looked very shyly on him ever since last Whitsuntide twelvemonth, when there was so much talk about his being away from home days and days together. There was something wrong, more than common — that was quite clear; for Mr. Godfrey didn't look half so fresh-colored and open as he used to do. At one time everybody was saying, What a handsome couple he and Miss Nancy Lammeter would make! and if she could come to be mistress at the Red House there would be a fine change, for the Lammeters had been brought up in that way, that they never suffered a pinch of salt to be wasted, and yet everybody in their household had of the best, according to his place. Such a daughter-in-law would be a saving to the old Squire, if she never brought a penny to her fortune; for it was to be feared that, notwithstanding his incomings, there were more holes in his pocket than the one where he put his own hand in. But if Mr. Godfrey didn't turn over a new leaf, he might say "Good-by" to Miss Nancy Lammeter.

It was the once hopeful Godfrey who was standing, with his hands in his side pockets and his back to the fire, in the dark wainscoted parlor, one late November afternoon, in that fifteenth year of Silas Marner's life at Raveloe. The fading gray light fell dimly on the walls decorated with guns, whips, and foxes' brushes, on coats and hats flung on the chairs, on tankards sending forth a scent of flat ale, and on a half-choked fire, with pipes propped up in the chimney corners, signs of a domestic life destitute of any hallowing charm, with which the look of gloomy vexation on Godfrey's blond face was in sad accordance. He seemed to be waiting and listening for someone's approach, and presently the sound of a heavy step, with an accompanying whistle, was heard across the large empty entrance hall.

The door opened, and a thickset, heavy-looking young man entered, with the flushed face and the gratuitously elated bearing which mark the first stage of intoxication. It was Dunsey, and at the sight of him Godfrey's face parted with some of its gloom to take on the more active expression of hatred. The handsome brown spaniel that lay on the hearth retreated under the chair in the chimney corner.

"Well, Master Godfrey, what do you want with me?" said Dunsey, in a mocking tone. "You're my elders and betters, you know; I was obliged to come when you sent for me."

"Why, this is what I want — and just shake yourself sober and listen, will you?" said Godfrey savagely. He had himself been drinking more than was good for him, trying to turn his gloom into uncalculating anger. "I want to tell you, I must hand over that rent of Fowler's to the Squire, or else tell him I gave it you; for he's threatening to distrain[1] for it, and it'll all be out soon, whether I tell him or not. He said, just now, before he went out, he should send word to Cox to distrain, if Fowler didn't come and pay up his arrears this week. The Squire's short o' cash, and in no humor to stand any nonsense; and you know what he threatened, if ever he found you making away with his money again. So, see and get the money, and pretty quickly, will you?"

"Oh!" said Dunsey sneeringly, coming nearer to his brother and looking in his face. "Suppose, now, you get the money yourself, and save me the trouble, eh? Since you was so kind as to hand it over to me, you'll not refuse me the kindness to pay it back for me; it was your brotherly love made you do it, you know."

Godfrey bit his lips and clenched his fist. "Don't come near me with that look, else I'll knock you down."

"Oh, no, you won't," said Dunsey, turning away on his heel, however. "Because I'm such a good-natured brother, you know. I might get you turned out of house and home, and cut off with a shilling any day. I might tell the Squire how his handsome son was married to that nice young woman, Molly Farren, and was very unhappy because he couldn't live with his drunken wife, and I should slip into your place as comfortable as could be. But, you see, I don't do it — I'm so easy and good-natured. You'll take any trouble for me. You'll get the hundred pounds for me — I know you will."

"How can I get the money?" said Godfrey, quivering. "I haven't a shilling to bless myself with. And it's a lie that you'd slip into my place; you'd get yourself turned out, too, that's all. For if you begin telling tales, I'll follow. Bob's my father's favorite — you know that very well. He'd only think himself well rid of you."

"Never mind," said Dunsey, nodding his head sideways as he looked out of the window. "It 'ud be very pleasant to me to go in your company — you're such a handsome brother, and we've always been so fond of quarreling with one another I shouldn't know what to do without you. But you'd like better for us both to stay at home together; I know you would. So you'll manage to get that little sum o' money, and I'll bid you good-by, though I'm sorry to part."

Dunstan was moving off, but Godfrey rushed after him and seized him by the arm, saying, with an oath —

"I tell you, I have no money; I can get no money."

"Borrow of old Kimble."

"I tell you, he won't lend me any more, and I shan't ask him."

"Well then, sell Wildfire."

"Yes, that's easy talking. I must have the money directly."

"Well, you've only got to ride him to the hunt tomorrow. There'll be Bryce and

[1] distrain: a legal word meaning to seize property in payment of debt.

Keating there, for sure. You'll get more bids than one."

"I dare say, and get back home at eight o'clock, splashed up to the chin. I'm going to Mrs. Osgood's birthday dance."

"Oho!" said Dunsey, turning his head on one side, and trying to speak in a small mincing treble. "And there's sweet Miss Nancy coming; and we shall dance with her, and promise never to be naughty again, and be taken into favor, and" —

"Hold your tongue about Miss Nancy, you fool," said Godfrey, turning red, "else I'll throttle you."

"What for?" said Dunsey, still in an artificial tone, but taking a whip from the table and beating the butt end of it on his palm. "You've a very good chance. I'd advise you to creep up her sleeve again; it 'ud be saving time if Molly should happen to take a drop too much laudanum someday, and make a widower of you. Miss Nancy wouldn't mind being a second, if she didn't know it. And you've got a good-natured brother, who'll keep your secret well, because you'll be so very obliging to him."

"I'll tell you what it is," said Godfrey, quivering, and pale again, "my patience is pretty near at an end. If you'd a little more sharpness in you, you might know that you may urge a man a bit too far, and make one leap as easy as another. I don't know but what it is so now; I may as well tell the Squire everything myself — I should get you off my back, if I got nothing else. And, after all, he'll know sometime. She's been threatening to come herself and tell him. So, don't flatter yourself that your secrecy's worth any price you choose to ask. You drain me of money till I have got nothing to pacify *her* with, and she'll do as she threatens someday. It's all one. I'll tell my father everything myself, and you may go to the devil."

Dunsey perceived that he had overshot his mark, and that there was a point at which even the hesitating Godfrey might be driven into decision. But he said, with an air of unconcern —

"As you please; but I'll have a draught of ale first." And ringing the bell, he threw himself across two chairs, and began to rap the window seat with the handle of his whip.

Godfrey stood, still with his back to the fire, uneasily moving his fingers among the contents of his side pockets, and looking at the floor. That big muscular frame of his held plenty of animal courage, but helped him to no decision when the dangers to be braved were such as could neither be knocked down nor throttled. His natural irresolution and moral cowardice were exaggerated by a position in which dreaded consequences seemed to press equally on all sides, and his irritation had no sooner provoked him to defy Dunstan and anticipate all possible betrayals, than the miseries he must bring on himself by such a step seemed more unendurable to him than the present evil. The results of confession were not contingent, they were certain; whereas betrayal was not certain. From the near vision of that certainty he fell back on suspense and vacillation with a sense of repose. The disinherited son of a small squire, equally disinclined to dig and to beg, was almost as helpless as an uprooted tree, which, by the favor of earth and sky, had grown to a handsome bulk on the spot where it first shot upward. Perhaps it would have been possible to think of digging with some cheerfulness if Nancy Lammeter were to be won on those terms; but, since he must irrevocably lose *her* as well as the inheritance, and must break every tie but the one that degraded him and left him without motive for trying to recover his better self, he could imagine no future for himself on the other side of confession but that of "'listing for a soldier" — the most desperate step, short of suicide, in the eyes of respectable families. No! he would rather trust to casualties than to his own resolve — rather go on sitting at the feast and sipping the wine he loved, though with the sword hanging over him and terror in his heart, than rush away into the cold darkness where there was no pleasure left. The utmost concession to Dunstan about the horse began to seem easy, compared with the fulfillment of his own threat. But his pride would not let him recommence the conversation otherwise than by continuing the quarrel. Dunstan was waiting for this, and took his ale in shorter draughts than usual.

"It's just like you," Godfrey burst out, in a bitter tone, "to talk about my selling Wildfire in that cool way — the last thing I've got to call my own, and the best bit of horseflesh I ever had in my life. And if you'd got a spark of pride in you, you'd be ashamed to see the stables emptied, and everybody's sneering about it. But it's my belief you'd sell yourself, if it was only for the pleasure of making somebody feel he'd got a bad bargain."

"Ay, ay," said Dunstan, very placably, "you do me justice, I see. You know I'm a jewel for 'ticing people into bargains. For which reason I advise you to let *me* sell Wildfire. I'd ride him to the hunt tomorrow for you with pleasure. I shouldn't look so handsome as you in the saddle, but it's the horse they'll bid for, and not the rider."

"Yes, I dare say — trust my horse to you!"

"As you please," said Dunstan, rapping the window seat again with an air of great unconcern. "It's *you* have got to pay Fowler's money; it's none of my business. You received the money from him when you went to Bramcote, and *you* told the Squire it wasn't paid. I'd nothing to do with that; you chose to be so obliging as to give it me, that was all. If you don't want to pay the money, let it alone; it's all one to me. But I was willing to accommodate you by undertaking to sell the horse, seeing it's not convenient to you to go so far tomorrow."

Godfrey was silent for some moments. He would have liked to spring on Dunstan, wrench the whip from his hand, and flog him to within an inch of his life; and no bodily fear could have deterred him; but he was mastered by another sort of fear, which was fed by feelings stronger even than his resentment. When he spoke again, it was in a half-conciliatory tone.

"Well, you mean no nonsense about the horse, eh? You'll sell him all fair, and hand over the money? If you don't, you know, everything 'ull go to smash, for I've got nothing else to trust to. And you'll have less pleasure in pulling the house over my head, when your own skull's to be broken, too."

"Ay, ay," said Dunstan, rising; "all right. I thought you'd come round. I'm the fellow to bring old Bryce up to the scratch. I'll get you a hundred and twenty for him, if I get you a penny."

"But it'll perhaps rain cats and dogs tomorrow, as it did yesterday, and then you can't go," said Godfrey, hardly knowing whether he wished for that obstacle or not.

"Not *it*," said Dunstan. "I'm always lucky in my weather. It might rain if you wanted to go yourself. You never hold trumps, you know — I always do. You've got the beauty, you see, and I've got the luck, so you must keep me by you for your crooked sixpence [1]; you'll *ne*-ver get along without me."

"Confound you, hold your tongue!" said Godfrey impetuously. "And take care to keep sober tomorrow, else you'll

[1] To carry a **crooked sixpence** was supposed to bring good luck.

get pitched on your head coming home, and Wildfire might be the worse for it."

"Make your tender heart easy," said Dunstan, opening the door. "You never knew me see double when I'd got a bargain to make; it 'ud spoil the fun. Besides, whenever I fall, I'm warranted to fall on my legs."

With that, Dunstan slammed the door behind him, and left Godfrey to that bitter rumination on his personal circumstances which was now unbroken from day to day save by the excitement of sporting, drinking, card playing, or the rarer and less oblivious pleasure of seeing Miss Nancy Lammeter. The subtle and varied pains springing from the higher sensibility that accompanies higher culture are perhaps less pitiable than that dreary absence of impersonal enjoyment and consolation which leaves ruder minds to the perpetual urgent companionship of their own griefs and discontents. The lives of those rural forefathers whom we are apt to think very prosaic figures — men whose only work was to ride round their land, getting heavier and heavier in their saddles, and who passed the rest of their days in the half-listless gratification of senses dulled by monotony — had a certain pathos in them nevertheless. Calamities came to *them,* too, and their early errors carried hard consequences; perhaps the love of some sweet maiden, the image of purity, order, and calm, had opened their eyes to the vision of a life in which the days would not seem too long, even without rioting; but the maiden was lost, and the vision passed away, and then what was left to them, especially when they had become too heavy for the hunt, or for carrying a gun over the furrows, but to drink and get merry, or to drink and get angry, so that they might be independent of variety, and say over again with eager emphasis the things they had said already any time that twelvemonth? Assuredly, among these flushed and dull-eyed men there were some whom — thanks to their native human kindness — even riot could never drive into brutality; men who, when their cheeks were fresh, had felt the keen point of sorrow or remorse, had been pierced by the reeds they leaned on, or had lightly put their limbs in fetters from which no struggle could loose them; and under these sad circumstances, common to us all, their thoughts could find no resting place outside the ever-trodden round of their own petty history.

That, at least, was the condition of Godfrey Cass in this six and twentieth year of his life. A movement of compunction, helped by those small indefinable influences which every personal relation exerts on a pliant nature, had urged him into a secret marriage, which was a blight on his life. It was an ugly story of low passion, delusion, and waking from delusion, which needs not to be dragged from the privacy of Godfrey's bitter memory. He had long known that the delusion was partly due to a trap laid for him by Dunstan, who saw in his brother's degrading marriage the means of gratifying at once his jealous hate and his cupidity. And if Godfrey could have felt himself simply a victim, the iron bit that destiny had put into his mouth would have chafed him less intolerably. If the curses he muttered half aloud when he was alone had had no other object than Dunstan's diabolical cunning, he might have shrunk less from the consequences of avowal. But he had something else to curse — his own vicious folly, which now seemed as mad and unaccountable to him as almost all our follies and vices do when their promptings have long passed away. For four years he had thought of Nancy Lammeter, and wooed her with tacit patient worship, as the woman who made him think of the future with joy; she would be his wife,

WEAVING, YESTERDAY AND TODAY. Today the loom is almost as much a mystery to us as it was to the boys of Raveloe who peeped in at the window of Silas Marner's stone cottage. In the twentieth century, swift machinery in factories has replaced the individual weaver in his home.

Perhaps you have woven something by hand? The simple principle of all weaving, from ancient Egypt to our own times, is illustrated in these pictures. The long threads stretching ahead of the man and woman are called the warp. The short crosswise threads which are pulled through the warp are called the woof or weft.

Photos, Culver

Taunt

Culver

THE SETTING OF SILAS MARNER. (*Above*) The Rainbow Inn may not seem especially lively to you when you read about it, but to the men of Raveloe it took the place of radio, newspaper, club, and movie. No wonder the inns became such familiar landmarks in every old English village.

(*Left*) An English village like Raveloe, where Silas Marner sold much of the linen he wove, was a quiet place a hundred years ago. Can you stretch your imagination backwards to a life without the inventions of our day?

DIVERSIONS IN RAVELOE

In Raveloe, those who sang in the village choir (*left*) felt a sense of importance. Not all of them sang in tune, evidently, for Ben Winthrop, who is convinced that Mr. Tookey's inside isn't made right for music, urges Tookey to stick to "amens."

Parties meant much in the lives of such isolated villagers. Young and old enjoyed them together. At Squire Cass's party, as in the picture (*right*), dancing, cards, gossip, and matchmaking were the chief diversions.

Photos, Culver

Culver

A SADDLE BUILT FOR TWO. Almost no one today knows what a pillion is, yet everyone in Silas Marner's time had ridden on one of these pillow-like pads which were strapped behind the saddle. Nancy Lammeter used one when she rode behind her father to the party at the Red House.

and would make home lovely to him, as his father's home had never been; and it would be easy, when she was always near, to shake off those foolish habits that were no pleasures, but only a feverish way of annulling vacancy. Godfrey's was an essentially domestic nature, bred up in a home where the hearth had no smiles, and where the daily habits were not chastised by the presence of household order. His easy disposition made him fall in unresistingly with the family courses, but the need of some tender permanent affection, the longing for some influence that would make the good he preferred easy to pursue, caused the neatness, purity, and liberal orderliness of the Lammeter household, sunned by the smile of Nancy, to seem like those fresh bright hours of the morning, when temptations go to sleep, and leave the ear open to the voice of the good angel, inviting to industry, sobriety, and peace. And yet the hope of this paradise had not been enough to save him from a course which shut him out of it forever. Instead of keeping fast hold of the strong silken rope by which Nancy would have drawn him safe to the green banks, where it was easy to step firmly, he had let himself be dragged back into mud and slime, in which it was useless to struggle. He had made ties for himself which robbed him of all wholesome motive, and were a constant exasperation.

Still, there was one position worse than the present; it was the position he would be in when the ugly secret was disclosed; and the desire that continually triumphed over every other was that of warding off the evil day, when he would have to bear the consequences of his father's violent resentment for the wound inflicted on his family pride — would have, perhaps, to turn his back on that hereditary ease and dignity which, after all, was a sort of reason for living, and would carry with him the certainty that he was banished forever from the sight and esteem of Nancy Lammeter. The longer the interval, the more chance there was of deliverance from some, at least, of the hateful consequences to which he had sold himself; the more opportunities remained for him to snatch the strange gratification of seeing Nancy, and gathering some faint indications of her lingering regard. Toward this gratification he was impelled, fitfully, every now and then, after having passed weeks in which he had avoided her as the far-off, bright-winged prize, that only made him spring forward, and find his chain all the more galling. One of those fits of yearning was on him now, and it would have been strong enough to have persuaded him to trust Wildfire to Dunstan rather than disappoint the yearning, even if he had not had another reason for his disinclination toward the morrow's hunt. That other reason was the fact that the morning's meet was near Batherley, the market town where the unhappy woman lived, whose image became more odious to him every day; and to his thought the whole vicinage was haunted by her. The yoke a man creates for himself by wrongdoing will breed hate in the kindliest nature; and the good-humored, affectionate-hearted Godfrey Cass was fast becoming a bitter man, visited by cruel wishes, that seemed to enter, and depart, and enter again, like demons who had found in him a ready-garnished home.

What was he to do this evening to pass the time? He might as well go to the Rainbow, and hear the talk about the cockfighting; everybody was there, and what else was there to be done? Though, for his own part, he did not care a button for cockfighting. Snuff, the brown spaniel, who had placed herself in front of him, and had been watching him for some time, now jumped up in impatience for the expected caress. But Godfrey thrust her away without looking at her, and left the room, followed humbly by the unresenting Snuff — perhaps because she saw no other career open to her.

CHAPTER IV

If you are to appreciate fully this chapter and the next, you must let your senses run away with you. You must actually feel the atmosphere of the cottage near the stone pit on the night when the fate of Dunsey Cass crosses that of Silas Marner. What details of weather accentuate the loneliness of the scene? At first you must share Dunsey's mood as he pushes open the door and looks in on the deserted room. What does he see? What does he smell? Does he hear anything? What is the effect of the room upon him? Next you must share Silas Marner's feeling for the room. It will look different through his eyes. How? What shock to his senses does the night bring?

Dunstan Cass, setting off in the raw morning, at the judiciously quiet pace of a man who is obliged to ride to cover on his hunter, had to take his way along the lane which, at its farther extremity, passed by the piece of unenclosed ground called the stonepit, where stood the cottage, once a stonecutter's shed, now for fifteen years inhabited by Silas Marner. The spot looked very dreary at this season, with the moist trodden clay about it, and the red, muddy water high up in the deserted quarry. That was Dunstan's first thought as he approached it; the second was, that the old fool of a weaver, whose loom he heard rattling already, had a great deal of money hidden somewhere. How was it that he, Dunstan Cass, who had often heard talk of Marner's miserliness, had never thought of suggesting to Godfrey that he should frighten or persuade the old fellow into lending the money on the excellent security of the young Squire's prospects? The resource occurred to him now as so easy and agreeable, especially as Marner's hoard was likely to be large enough to leave Godfrey a handsome surplus beyond his immediate needs, and enable him to accommodate his faithful brother, that he had almost turned the horse's head toward home again. Godfrey would be ready enough to accept the suggestion; he would snatch eagerly at a plan that might save him from parting with Wildfire. But when Dunstan's meditation reached this point, the inclination to go on grew strong and prevailed. He didn't want to give Godfrey that pleasure; he preferred that Master Godfrey should be vexed. Moreover, Dunstan enjoyed the self-important consciousness of having a horse to sell, and the opportunity of driving a bargain, swaggering, and, possibly, taking somebody in. He might have all the satisfaction attendant on selling his brother's horse, and not the less have the further satisfaction of setting Godfrey to borrow Marner's money. So he rode on to cover.

Bryce and Keating were there, as Dunstan was quite sure they would be — he was such a lucky fellow.

"Heyday," said Bryce, who had long had his eye on Wildfire, "you're on your brother's horse today; how's that?"

"Oh, I've swapped with him," said Dunstan, whose delight in lying, grandly independent of utility, was not to be diminished by the likelihood that his hearer would not believe him. "Wildfire's mine now."

"What! has he swapped with you for that big-boned hack of yours?" said Bryce, quite aware that he should get another lie in answer.

"Oh, there was a little account between us," said Dunsey carelessly, "and Wildfire made it even. I accommodated him by taking the horse, though it was against my will, for I'd got an itch for a mare o' Jortin's — as rare a bit o' blood as ever you threw your leg across. But I shall keep Wildfire, now I've got him, though I'd a bid of a hundred and fifty for him the other day, from a man over at Flitton — he's buying for Lord Cromleck — a fellow with a cast in his eye, and a green waistcoat. But I mean to stick to Wildfire; I shan't get a better at a fence in a hurry. The mare's got more blood, but she's a bit too weak in the hindquarters."

Bryce, of course, divined that Dunstan wanted to sell the horse, and Dunstan knew that he divined it (horsedealing is only one of many human transactions carried on in this ingenious manner); and they both considered that the bargain was in its first stage, where Bryce replied ironically —

"I wonder at that now; I wonder you mean to keep him; for I never heard of a man who didn't want to sell his horse, getting a bid of half as much again as the horse was worth. You'll be lucky if you get a hundred."

Keating rode up now, and the transaction became more complicated. It ended in the purchase of the horse by Bryce for a hundred and twenty, to be paid on the delivery of Wildfire, safe and sound, at the Batherley stables. It did occur to Dunsey that it might be wise for him to give up the day's hunting, proceed at once to Batherley, and, having waited for Bryce's return, hire a horse to carry him home with the money in his pocket. But the inclination for a run, encouraged by confidence in his luck, and by a draught of brandy from his pocket pistol at the conclusion of the bargain, was not easy to overcome, especially with a horse under him that would take the fences to the admiration of the field. Dunstan, however, took one fence too many, and got his horse pierced with a hedge stake. His own ill-favored person, which was quite unmarketable, escaped without injury; but poor Wildfire, unconscious of his price, turned on his flank, and painfully panted his last. It happened that Dunstan, a short time before, having had to get down to arrange his stirrup, had muttered a good many curses at this interruption, which had thrown him in the rear of the hunt near the moment of glory, and under this exasperation had taken the fences more blindly. He would soon have been up with the hounds again, when the fatal accident happened; and hence he was between eager riders in advance, not troubling themselves about what happened behind them, and far-off stragglers, who were as likely as not to pass quite aloof from the line of road in which Wildfire had fallen. Dunstan, whose nature it was to care more for immediate annoyances than for remote consequences, no sooner recovered his legs, and saw that it was all over with Wildfire, than he felt a satisfaction at the absence of witnesses to a position which no swaggering could make enviable. Reinforcing himself, after his shake, with a little brandy and much swearing, he walked as fast as he could to a coppice on his right hand, through which it occurred to him that he could make his way to Batherley without danger of encountering any member of the hunt. His first intention was to hire a horse there and ride home forthwith, for to walk many miles without a gun in his hand, and along an ordinary road, was as much out of the question to him as to other spirited young men of his kind. He did not much mind about taking the bad news to Godfrey, for he had to offer him at the same time the resource of Marner's money; and if Godfrey kicked, as he always did, at the notion of making a fresh debt, from which he himself got the smallest share of advantage, why, he wouldn't kick long; Dunstan felt sure he could worry Godfrey into anything. The idea of Marner's money kept growing in vividness, now the want of it had become immediate; the prospect of having to make his appearance with the muddy boots of a pedestrian at Batherley, and to encounter the grinning queries of stablemen, stood unpleasantly in the way of his impatience to be back at Raveloe and carry out his felicitous plan; and a casual visitation of his waistcoat pocket, as he was ruminating, awakened his memory to the fact that the two or three small coins his forefinger encountered there were of too pale a color to cover that small debt, without payment of which the stablekeeper had declared he would never do any more business with Dunsey Cass. After all, according to the direction in which the run had brought him, he was not so very much farther from home than he was from Batherley; but Dunsey, not being remarkable for clearness of head, was only led to this conclusion by the gradual perception that there were other reasons for choosing the unprecedented course of walking home. It was now nearly four o'clock, and a mist was gathering; the sooner he got into the road the better. He remembered having crossed the road and seen the fingerpost only a little while before Wildfire broke down; so, buttoning his coat, twisting the lash of his hunting whip compactly round the handle, and rapping the tops of his boots with a self-possessed air, as if to assure himself that he was not at all taken by surprise, he set off with the sense that he was undertaking a remarkable feat of bodily exertion, which somehow, and at some time, he should be able to dress up and magnify to the admiration of a select circle at the Rainbow. When a young gentleman like Dunsey is reduced to so exceptional a mode of locomotion as walking, a whip in his hand is a desirable corrective to a too bewildering dreamy sense of unwontedness in his position; and Dunstan, as he went along through the gathering mist, was always rapping his whip somewhere. It was Godfrey's whip, which he had chosen to take without leave because it had a gold handle; of course no one could see, when Dunstan held it, that the name *Godfrey Cass* was cut in deep letters on that gold handle — they could only see that it was a very handsome whip. Dunsey was not without fear that he might meet some acquaintance in whose eyes he would cut a pitiable figure, for mist is no screen when people get close to each other; but when he at last found himself in the well-known Raveloe lanes without having met a soul, he silently remarked that that was part of his usual good luck. But now the mist, helped by the evening darkness, was more of a screen than he desired, for it hid the ruts into which his feet were liable to slip — hid everything, so that he had to guide his steps by dragging his whip along the low bushes in advance of the hedgerow. He must soon, he thought, be getting near the opening at the stone pit; he should find it out by the break in the hedgerow. He found it out, however, by another circumstance which he had not expected — namely, by certain gleams of light, which he presently guessed to proceed from Silas Marner's cottage. That cottage and the money hidden within it had been in his mind continually during his walk, and he had been imagining ways of cajoling and tempting the weaver to part with the immediate possession of his money for the sake of receiving interest. Dunstan felt as if there must be a little frightening added to the cajolery, for his own arithmetical convictions were not clear enough to afford him any forcible demonstration as to the advantages of interest; and as for security, he regarded it vaguely as a means of cheating a man by making him believe that he would be paid. Altogether, the operation on the miser's mind was a task that Godfrey would be sure to hand over to his more daring and cunning brother; Dunstan had made up his mind to that; and by the time he saw the light gleaming through the chinks of Marner's shutters, the idea of a dialogue with the weaver had become so familiar to him that it occurred to him as quite a natural thing to make the acquaintance forthwith. There might be several conveniences attending this course; the weaver had possibly got a lantern, and Dunstan was tired of feeling his way. He was still nearly three-quarters of a mile from home, and the lane was becoming unpleasantly slippery, for the mist was passing into rain. He turned up the bank, not without some fear lest he might miss the right way, since he was not certain whether the light were in front or on the side of the cottage. But he felt the ground before him cautiously with his whip handle, and at last arrived safely at the door. He knocked loudly, rather enjoying the idea that the old fellow would be frightened at the sudden noise. He heard no movement in reply; all was silence in the cottage. Was the weaver gone to bed, then? If so, why had he left a light? That was a strange forgetfulness in a miser. Dunstan knocked still more loudly, and, without pausing for a reply, pushed his fingers through the latch hole, intending to shake the door and pull the latchstring up and down, not doubting that the door was fastened. But, to his surprise, at this double motion the door opened, and he found himself in front of a bright fire, which lit up every corner of the cottage — the bed, the loom, the three chairs, and the table — and showed him that Marner was not there.

Nothing at that moment could be much more inviting to Dunsey than the bright fire on the brick hearth; he walked in and seated himself by it at once. There was something in front of the fire, too, that would have been inviting to a hungry man, if it had been in a different stage of cooking. It was a small bit of pork suspended from the kettle hanger by a string passed through a large door key, in a way known to primitive housekeepers unpossessed of jacks.[1] But the pork had been hung at the farthest extremity of the hanger, apparently to prevent the roasting from proceeding too rapidly during the owner's absence. The old staring simpleton had hot meat for his supper, then? thought Dunstan. People had always said he lived on moldy bread, on purpose to check his appetite. But where could he be at this time, and on such an evening, leaving his supper in this stage of preparation, and his door unfastened? Dunstan's own recent difficulty in making his way suggested to him that the weaver had perhaps gone outside his cottage to fetch in fuel, or for some such brief purpose, and had slipped into the stone pit. That was an interesting idea to Dunstan, carrying consequences of entire novelty. If the weaver was dead, who had a right to his money? Who would know where his money was hidden? *Who would know that anybody had come to take it away?* He went no farther into the subtleties of evidence; the pressing question, "Where *is* the money?" now took such entire possession of him as to make him quite forget that the weaver's death was not a certainty. A dull mind, once arriving at an inference that flatters a desire, is rarely able to retain the impression that the notion from which the inference started was purely problematic. And Dunstan's mind was as dull as the mind of a possible felon usually is. There were only three hiding places where he had ever heard of cottagers' hoards being found: the thatch, the bed, and a hole in the floor. Marner's cottage had no thatch; and Dunstan's first act, after a train of thought made rapid by the stimulus of cupidity, was to go up to the bed; but

[1] **jacks:** an instrument for turning the rod which held roasting meat.

while he did so, his eyes traveled eagerly over the floor, where the bricks, distinct in the firelight, were discernible under the sprinkling of sand. But not everywhere; for there was one spot, and one only, which was quite covered with sand, and sand showing the marks of fingers which had apparently been careful to spread it over a given space. It was near the treadles of the loom. In an instant Dunstan darted to that spot, swept away the sand with his whip, and, inserting the thin end of the hook between the bricks, found that they were loose. In haste he lifted up two bricks, and saw what he had no doubt was the object of his search; for what could there be but money in those two leathern bags? And, from their weight, they must be filled with guineas. Dunstan felt round the hole, to be certain that it held no more; then hastily replaced the bricks, and spread the sand over them. Hardly more than five minutes had passed since he entered the cottage, but it seemed to Dunstan like a long while; and though he was without any distinct recognition of the possibility that Marner might be alive, and might re-enter the cottage at any moment, he felt an undefinable dread laying hold on him as he rose to his feet with the bags in his hand. He would hasten out into the darkness, and then consider what he should do with the bags. He closed the door behind him immediately, that he might shut in the stream of light; a few steps would be enough to carry him beyond betrayal by the gleams from the shutter chinks and the latch hole. The rain and darkness had got thicker, and he was glad of it; though it was awkward walking with both hands filled, so that it was as much as he could do to grasp his whip along with one of the bags. But when he had gone a yard or two, he might take his time. So he stepped forward into the darkness.

CHAPTER V

When Dunstan Cass turned his back on the cottage, Silas Marner was not more than a hundred yards away from it, plodding along from the village with a sack thrown round his shoulders as an overcoat, and with a horn lantern[1] in his hand. His legs were weary, but his mind was at ease, free from the presentiment of change. The sense of security more frequently springs from habit than from conviction, and for this reason it often subsists after such a change in the conditions as might have been expected to suggest alarm. The lapse of time during which a given event has not happened is, in this logic of habit, constantly alleged as a reason why the event should never happen, even when the lapse of time is precisely the added condition which makes the event imminent. A man will tell you that he has worked in a mine for forty years unhurt by an accident, as a reason why he should apprehend no danger, though the roof is beginning to sink; and it is often observable that the older a man gets the more difficult it is to him to retain a believing conception of his own death. This influence of habit was necessarily strong in a man whose life was so monotonous as Marner's — who saw no new people and heard of no new events to keep alive in him the idea of the unexpected and the changeful; and it explains, simply enough, why his mind could be at ease, though he had left his house and his treasure more defenseless than usual. Silas was thinking with double complacency of his supper, first, because it would be hot and savory; and, secondly, because it would cost him nothing. For the little bit of pork was a present from that excellent housewife, Miss Priscilla Lammeter, to whom he had this day

[1] **horn lantern:** one made from horn, scraped thin enough for the light to shine through.

carried home a handsome piece of linen; and it was only on occasion of a present like this that Silas indulged himself with roast meat. Supper was his favorite meal, because it came at his time of revelry, when his heart warmed over his gold; whenever he had roast meat, he always chose to have it for supper. But this evening, he had no sooner ingeniously knotted his string fast round his bit of pork, twisted the string according to rule over his door key, passed it through the handle, and made it fast on the hanger, than he remembered that a piece of very fine twine was indispensable to his "setting up" a new piece of work in his loom early in the morning. It had slipped his memory, because, in coming from Mr. Lammeter's, he had not had to pass through the village; but to lose time by going on errands in the morning was out of the question. It was a nasty fog to turn out into, but there were things Silas loved better than his own comfort; so, drawing his pork to the extremity of the hanger, and arming himself with his lantern and his old sack, he set out on what, in ordinary weather, would have been a twenty minutes' errand. He could not have locked his door without undoing his well-knotted string and retarding his supper; it was not worth his while to make that sacrifice. What thief would find his way to the stone pits on such a night as this? and why should he come on this particular night, when he had never come through all the fifteen years before? These questions were not distinctly present in Silas's mind; they merely serve to represent the vaguely felt foundation of his freedom from anxiety.

He reached his door in much satisfaction that his errand was done; he opened it, and to his shortsighted eyes everything remained as he had left it, except that the fire sent out a welcome increase of heat. He trod about the floor while putting by his lantern and throwing aside his hat and sack, so as to merge the marks of Dunstan's feet on the sand in the marks of his own nailed boots. Then he moved his pork nearer to the fire, and sat down to the agreeable business of tending the meat and warming himself at the same time.

Anyone who had looked at him as the red light shone upon his pale face, strange straining eyes, and meager form, would perhaps have understood the mixture of contemptuous pity, dread, and suspicion with which he was regarded by his neighbors in Raveloe. Yet few men could be more harmless than poor Marner. In his truthful simple soul, not even the growing greed and worship of gold could beget any vice directly injurious to others. The light of his faith quite put out, and his affections made desolate, he had clung with all the force of his nature to his work and his money; and like all objects to which a man devotes himself, they had fashioned him into correspondence with themselves. His loom, as he wrought in it without ceasing, had in its turn wrought on him, and confirmed more and more the monotonous craving for its monotonous response. His gold, as he hung over it and saw it grow, gathered his power of loving together into a hard isolation like its own.

As soon as he was warm he began to think it would be a long while to wait till after supper before he drew out his guineas, and it would be pleasant to see them on the table before him as he ate his unwonted feast, for joy is the best wine, and Silas's guineas were the golden wine of that sort.

He rose and placed his candle unsuspectingly on the floor near his loom, swept away the sand without noticing any change, and removed the bricks. The sight of the empty hole made his heart leap violently, but the belief that his gold was gone could not come at once — only terror, and the eager effort to put an end to the terror. He passed his trembling hand all about the hole trying to think it possible that his eyes had deceived him; then he held the candle in the hole and examined it curiously, trembling more and more. At last he shook so violently that he let fall the candle, and lifted his hands to his head, trying to steady himself, that he might think. Had he put his gold somewhere else, by a sudden resolution last night, and then forgotten it? A man falling into dark water seeks a momentary footing even on sliding stones; and Silas, by acting as if he believed in false hopes, warded off the moment of despair. He searched in every corner, he turned his bed over, and shook it, and kneaded it; he looked in his brick oven where he laid his sticks. When there was no other place to be searched, he kneeled down again, and felt once more all round the hole. There was no untried refuge left for a moment's shelter from the terrible truth.

Yes, there was a sort of refuge which always comes with the prostration of thought under an overpowering passion; it was that expectation of impossibilities, that belief in contradictory images, which is still distinct from madness, because it is capable of being dissipated by the external fact. Silas got up from his knees trembling, and looked round at the table; didn't the gold lie there after all? The table was bare. Then he turned and looked behind him — looked all round his dwelling, seeming to strain his brown eyes after some possible appearance of the bags, where he had already sought them in vain. He could see every object in his cottage — and his gold was not there.

Again he put his trembling hands to his head, and gave a wild ringing scream, the cry of desolation. For a few moments after, he stood motionless; but the cry had relieved him from the first maddening pressure of the truth. He turned, and tottered toward his loom, and got into the seat where he worked, instinctively seeking this as the strongest assurance of reality.

And now that all the false hopes had vanished, and the first shock of certainty was past, the idea of a thief began to present itself, and he entertained it eagerly, because a thief might be caught and made to restore the gold. The thought brought some new strength with it, and he started from his loom to the door. As he opened it, the rain beat in upon him, for it was falling more and more heavily. There were no footsteps to be tracked on such a night — footsteps? When had the thief come? During Silas's absence in the daytime the door had been locked, and there had been no marks of any inroad on his return by daylight. And in the evening, too, he said to himself, everything was the same as when he had left it. The sand and bricks looked as if they had not been moved. *Was* it a thief who had taken the bags? or was it a cruel power that no hands could reach, which had delighted in making him a second time desolate? He shrank from this vaguer dread, and fixed his mind with struggling effort on the robber with hands, who could be reached by hands. His thoughts glanced at all the neighbors who had made any remarks, or asked any questions which he might now regard as a ground of suspicion. There was Jem Rodney, a known poacher,[1] and otherwise disreputable; he had often met Marner in his journeys across the fields, and had said something jestingly about the weaver's money; nay, he had once irritated Marner, by lingering at the fire when he called to light his pipe, instead of going about his business. Jem Rodney was the man — there was ease in the thought. Jem could be found

[1] **poacher:** one who steals game or fish from private preserves.

and made to restore the money. Marner did not want to punish him, but only to get back his gold which had gone from him, and left his soul like a forlorn traveler on an unknown desert. The robber must be laid hold of. Marner's ideas of legal authority were confused, but he felt that he must go and proclaim his loss; and the great people in the village — the clergyman, the constable, and Squire Cass — would make Jem Rodney, or somebody else, deliver up the stolen money. He rushed out in the rain, under the stimulus of this hope, forgetting to cover his head, not caring to fasten his door; for he felt as if he had nothing left to lose. He ran swiftly till want of breath compelled him to slacken his pace as he was entering the village at the turning close to the Rainbow.

The Rainbow, in Marner's view, was a place of luxurious resort for rich and stout husbands, whose wives had superfluous stores of linen; it was the place where he was likely to find the powers and dignities of Raveloe, and where he could most speedily make his loss public. He lifted the latch, and turned into the bright bar or kitchen on the right hand, where the less lofty customers of the house were in the habit of assembling, the parlor on the left being reserved for the more select society in which Squire Cass frequently enjoyed the double pleasure of conviviality and condescension. But the parlor was dark tonight, the chief personages who ornamented its circle being all at Mrs. Osgood's birthday dance, as Godfrey Cass was. And in consequence of this, the party on the high-screened seats in the kitchen was more numerous than usual; several personages, who would otherwise have been admitted into the parlor and enlarged the opportunity of hectoring and condescension for their betters, being content this evening to vary their enjoyment by taking their spirits-and-water where they could themselves hector and condescend in company that called for beer.

CHAPTER VI

Critics have rated the scene at the Rainbow, which is described in this chapter and the one following, as the most realistic scene in *Silas Marner*. Here you will find a faithful picture of village life as it was lived in the early nineteenth century. The characters you will meet are true to life, as the author herself knew them during her young, impressionable years when she was unconsciously accumulating story material for her later novels.

As you "listen in" on the conversation in Mr. Snell's kitchen, what impression do you form of Raveloe folks? What village gossip can you pick up? What village "characters" do you recognize? What is the effect of Silas Marner's announcement upon the little group?

The conversation, which was at a high pitch of animation when Silas approached the door of the Rainbow, had, as usual, been slow and intermittent when the company first assembled. The pipes began to be puffed in a silence which had an air of severity; the more important customers, who drank spirits and sat nearest the fire, staring at each other as if a bet were depending on the first man who winked; while the beer drinkers, chiefly men in fustian jackets and smock frocks, kept their eyelids down and rubbed their hands across their mouths, as if their draughts of beer were a funereal duty attended with embarrassing sadness. At last, Mr. Snell, the landlord, a man of a neutral disposition, accustomed to stand aloof from human differences as those of beings who were all alike in need of liquor, broke silence by saying in a doubtful tone to his cousin the butcher —

"Some folks 'ud say that was a fine beast you druv in yesterday, Bob?"

The butcher, a jolly, smiling, red-haired man, was not disposed to answer rashly. He gave a few puffs before he spat and replied, " And they wouldn't be fur wrong, John."

After this feeble delusive thaw, a silence set in as severely as before.

" Was it a red Durham ? " said the farrier,[1] taking up the thread of discourse after the lapse of a few minutes.

The farrier looked at the landlord, and the landlord looked at the butcher, as the person who must take the responsibility of answering.

" Red it was," said the butcher, in his good-humored husky treble, " and a Durham it was."

" Then you needn't tell *me* who you bought it of," said the farrier, looking round with some triumph ; "I know who it is has got the red Durhams o' this countryside. And she'd a white star on her brow, I'll bet a penny ? " The farrier leaned forward with his hands on his knees as he put this question, and his eyes twinkled knowingly.

" Well ; yes — she might," said the butcher slowly, considering that he was giving a decided affirmative. " I don't say contrairy."

" I knew that very well," said the farrier, throwing himself backward again, and speaking defiantly ; " if *I* don't know Mr. Lammeter's cows, I should like to know who does — that's all. And as for the cow you've bought, bargain or no bargain, I've been at the drenching [2] of her — contradick me who will."

The farrier looked fierce, and the mild butcher's conversational spirit was roused a little.

" I'm not for contradicking no man," he said ; " I'm for peace and quietness. Some are for cutting long ribs — I'm for cutting 'em short, myself ; but *I* don't quarrel with 'em. All I say is, it's a lovely carkiss — and anybody as was reasonable, it 'ud bring tears into their eyes to look at it."

" Well, it's the cow as I drenched, whatever it is," pursued the farrier angrily ; " and it was Mr. Lammeter's cow, else you told a lie when you said it was a red Durham."

" I tell no lies," said the butcher, with the same mild huskiness as before, " and I contradick none — not if a man was to swear himself black ; he's no meat o' mine, nor none o' my bargains. All I say is, it's a lovely carkiss. And what I say, I'll stick to ; but I'll quarrel wi' no man."

" No," said the farrier, with bitter sarcasm, looking at the company generally ; " and p'rhaps you aren't pigheaded ; and p'rhaps you didn't say the cow was a red Durham ; and p'rhaps you didn't say she'd got a star on her brow — stick to that, now you're at it."

" Come, come," said the landlord ; " let the cow alone. The truth lies atween you ; you're both right and both wrong, as I allays say. And as for the cow's being Mr. Lammeter's, I say nothing to that ; but this I say, as the Rainbow's the Rainbow. And for the matter o' that, if the talk is to be o' the Lammeters, *you* know the most upo' that head, eh, Mr. Macey ? You remember when first Mr. Lammeter's father come into these parts, and took the Warrens ? "

Mr. Macey, tailor and parish clerk, the latter of which functions rheumatism had of late obliged him to share with a small-featured young man who sat opposite him, held his white head on one side, and twirled his thumbs with an air of complacency, slightly seasoned with criticism. He smiled pityingly, in answer to the landlord's appeal, and said —

" Ay, ay ; I know, I know ; but I let other folks talk. I've laid by now, and gev up to the young uns. Ask them as have been to school at Tarley ; they've

[1] **farrier:** horseshoer and doctor of animals.
[2] **drenching:** giving her medicine.

learnt pernouncing; that's come up since my day."

" If you're pointing at me, Mr. Macey," said the deputy clerk, with an air of anxious propriety, " I'm nowise a man to speak out of my place. As the psalm says —

' I know what's right, nor only so,
But also practice what I know.' "

" Well, then, I wish you'd keep hold o' the tune when it's set for you; if you're for prac*tic*ing, I wish you'd prac*tice* that," said a large, jocose-looking man, an excellent wheelwright in his weekday capacity, but on Sundays leader of the choir. He winked, as he spoke, at two of the company, who were known officially as the " bassoon " and the " key bugle," in the confidence that he was expressing the sense of the musical profession in Raveloe.

Mr. Tookey, the deputy clerk, who shared the unpopularity common to deputies, turned very red, but replied, with careful moderation, " Mr. Winthrop, if you'll bring me any proof as I'm in the wrong, I'm not the man to say I won't alter. But there's people set up their own ears for a standard, and expect the whole choir to follow 'em. There may be two opinions, I hope."

" Ay, ay," said Mr. Macey, who felt very well satisfied with this attack on youthful presumption; " you're right there, Tookey. There's allays two 'pinions; there's the 'pinion a man has of himsen, and there's the 'pinion other folks have on him. There'd be two 'pinions about a cracked bell, if the bell could hear itself."

" Well, Mr. Macey," said poor Tookey, serious amidst the general laughter, " I undertook to partially fill up the office of parish clerk by Mr. Crackenthorp's desire, whenever your infirmities should make you unfitting; and it's one of the rights thereof to sing in the choir — else why have you done the same yourself? "

" Ah! but the old gentleman and you are two folks," said Ben Winthrop. " The old gentleman's got a gift. Why, the Squire used to invite him to take a glass, only to hear him sing the ' Red Rovier '; didn't he, Mr. Macey? It's a nat'ral gift. There's my little lad Aaron, he's got a gift — he can sing a tune off straight, like a throstle. But as for you, Master Tookey, you'd better stick to your ' Amens '; your voice is well enough when you keep it up in your nose. It's your inside as isn't right made for music; it's no better nor a hollow stalk."

This kind of unflinching frankness was the most piquant form of joke to the company at the Rainbow, and Ben Winthrop's insult was felt by everybody to have capped Mr. Macey's epigram.

" I see what it is plain enough," said Mr. Tookey, unable to keep cool any longer. " There's a consperacy to turn me out o' the choir, as I shouldn't share the Christmas money — that's where it is. But I shall speak to Mr. Crackenthorp; I'll not be put upon by no man."

" Nay, nay, Tookey," said Ben Winthrop. " We'll pay you your share to keep out of it — that's what we'll do. There's things folks 'ud pay to be rid on, besides varmin."

" Come, come," said the landlord, who felt that paying people for their absence was a principle dangerous to society; " a joke's a joke. We're all good friends here, I hope. We must give and take. You're both right and you're both wrong, as I say. I agree wi' Mr. Macey here, as there's two opinions; and if mine was asked, I should say they're both right. Tookey's right and Winthrop's right, and they've only got to split the difference and make themselves even."

The farrier was puffing his pipe rather fiercely, in some contempt at this trivial discussion. He had no ear for music himself, and never went to church, as being of the medical profession, and likely to be in requisition for delicate cows. But the butcher, having music in his soul, had listened with a divided desire for Tookey's defeat, and for the preservation of the peace.

"To be sure," he said, following up the landlord's conciliatory view, "we're fond of our old clerk; it's nat'ral, and him used to be such a singer, and got a brother as is known for the first fiddler in this countryside. Eh, it's a pity but what Solomon lived in our village, and could give us a tune when we liked; eh, Mr. Macey? I'd keep him in liver and lights for nothing — that I would."

"Ay, ay," said Mr. Macey, in the height of complacency; "our family's been known for musicianers as far back as anybody can tell. But them things are dying out, as I tell Solomon every time he comes round; there's no voices like what there used to be, and there's nobody remembers what we remember, if it isn't the old crows."

"Ay, you remember when first Mr. Lammeter's father come into these parts, don't you, Mr. Macey?" said the landlord.

"I should think I did," said the old man, who had now gone through that complimentary process necessary to bring him up to the point of narration; "and a fine old gentleman he was — as fine, and finer nor the Mr. Lammeter as now is. He came from a bit north'ard, so far as I could ever make out. But there's nobody rightly knows about those parts; only it couldn't be far north'ard, nor much different from this country, for he brought a fine breed o' sheep with him, so there must be pastures there, and everything reasonable. We heared tell as he'd sold his own land to come and take the Warrens, and that seemed odd for a man as had land of his own, to come and rent a farm in a strange place. But they said it was along of his wife's dying; though there's reasons in things as nobody knows on — that's pretty much what I've made out; yet some folks are so wise, they'll find you fifty reasons straight off, and all the while the real reason's winking at 'em in the corner, and they niver see't. Howsomever, it was soon seen as we'd got a new parish'ner as know'd the rights and customs o' things, and kep' a good house, and was well looked on by everybody. And the young man — that's the Mr. Lammeter as now is, for he'd niver a sister — soon begun to court Miss Osgood, that's the sister o' the Mr. Osgood as now is, and a fine handsome lass she was — eh, you can't think — they pretend this young lass is like her, but that's the way wi' people as don't know what come before 'em. *I* should know, for I helped the old rector, Mr. Drumlow as was — I helped him marry 'em."

Here Mr. Macey paused; he always gave his narrative in installments, expecting to be questioned according to precedent.

"Ay, and a partic'lar thing happened, didn't it, Mr. Macey, so as you were likely to remember that marriage?" said the landlord, in a congratulatory tone.

"I should think there did — a *very* partic'lar thing," said Mr. Macey, nodding sideways. "For Mr. Drumlow — poor old gentleman, I was fond on him, though he'd got a bit confused in his head, what wi' age and wi' taking a drop o' sommat warm when the service come of a cold morning. And young Mr. Lammeter, he'd have no way but he must be married in Janiwary, which, to be sure, 's a unreasonable time to be married in, for it isn't like a christening or a burying, as you can't help; and so Mr. Drumlow — poor old gentleman, I was fond on him

— but when he come to put the questions, he put 'em by the rule o' contrairy, like, and he says, 'Wilt thou have this man to thy wedded wife?' says he, and then he says, 'Wilt thou have this woman to thy wedded husband?' says he. But the partic'larest thing of all is, as nobody took any notice on it but me, and they answered straight off 'Yes,' like as if it had been me saying 'Amen' i' the right place, without listening to what went before."

"But *you* knew what was going on well enough, didn't you, Mr. Macey? You were live enough, eh?" said the butcher.

"Lor' bless you!" said Mr. Macey, pausing, and smiling in pity at the impotence of his hearer's imagination; "why, I was all of a tremble; it was as if I'd been a coat pulled by the two tails, like; for I couldn't stop the parson, I couldn't take upon me to do that; and yet I said to myself, I says, 'Suppose they shouldn't be fast married, 'cause the words are contrairy?' and my head went working like a mill, for I was allays uncommon for turning things over and seeing all round 'em; and I says to myself, 'Is't the meanin' or the words as makes folks fast i' wedlock?' For the parson meant right, and the bride and bridegroom meant right. But then, when I come to think on it, meanin' goes but a little way i' most things, for you may mean to stick things together and your glue may be bad, and then where are you? And so I says to mysen, 'It isn't the meanin', it's the glue.' And I was worreted as if I'd got three bells to pull at once, when we went into the vestry, and they begun to sign their names. But where's the use o' talking? — you can't think what goes on in a 'cute man's inside."

"But you held in for all that, didn't you, Mr. Macey?" said the landlord.

"Ay, I held in tight till I was by mysen wi' Mr. Drumlow, and then I out wi' everything, but respectful, as I allays did. And he made light on it, and he says, 'Pooh, pooh, Macey, make yourself easy,' he says; 'it's neither the meaning nor the words — it's the re*ges*ter does it — that's the glue.' So you see he settled it easy; for parsons and doctors know everything by heart, like, so as they aren't worreted wi' thinking what's the rights and wrongs o' things, as I'n been many and many's the time. And sure enough the wedding turned out all right, on'y poor Mrs. Lammeter — that's Miss Osgood as was — died afore the lasses was growed up; but for prosperity and everything respectable, there's no family more looked on."

Every one of Mr. Macey's audience had heard this story many times, but it was listened to as if it had been a favorite tune, and at certain points the puffing of the pipes was momentarily suspended, that the listeners might give their whole minds to the expected words. But there was more to come; and Mr. Snell, the landlord, duly put the leading question.

"Why, old Mr. Lammeter had a pretty fortin, didn't they say, when he come into these parts?"

"Well, yes," said Mr. Macey; "but I dare say it's as much as this Mr. Lammeter's done to keep it whole. For there was allays a talk as nobody could get rich on the Warrens, though he holds it cheap, for it's what they call Charity Land."

"Ay, and there's few folks know so well as you how it come to be Charity Land, eh, Mr. Macey?" said the butcher.

"How should they?" said the old clerk, with some contempt. "Why, my grandfather made the grooms' livery for that Mr. Cliff as came and built the big stables at the Warrens. Why, they're stables four times as big as Squire Cass's, for he thought o' nothing but hosses and hunting, Cliff didn't — a Lunnon tailor, some folks said, as had gone mad wi' cheating. For he couldn't ride; lor' bless you! they said he'd got no more grip o' the hoss than if his legs had been cross sticks; my grandfather heared old Squire Cass say so many and many a time. But ride he would, as if Old Harry had been a-driving him; and he'd a son, a lad o' sixteen; and nothing would his father have him do, but he must ride and ride — though the lad was frighted, they said. And it was a common saying as the father wanted to ride the tailor out o' the lad, and make a gentleman on him — not but what I'm a tailor myself, but in respect as God made me such, I'm proud on it, for 'Macey, Taylor,' 's been wrote up over our door since afore the queen's heads went out on the shillings.[1] But Cliff, he was ashamed o' being called a tailor, and he was sore vexed as his riding was laughed at, and nobody o' the gentlefolks hereabout could abide him. Howsomever, the poor lad got sickly and died and the father didn't live long after him, for he got queerer nor ever, and they said he used to go out i' the dead o' the night, wi' a lantern in his hand, to the stables, and set a lot o' lights burning, for he got as he couldn't sleep; and there he'd stand, cracking his whip and looking at his hosses; and they said it was a mercy as the stables didn't get burnt down wi' the poor dumb creatures in 'em. But at last he died raving, and they found as he'd left all his property, Warrens and all, to a Lunnon Charity, and that's how the Warrens come to be Charity Land; though, as for the stables, Mr. Lammeter never uses 'em — they're out o' all charicter — lor' bless you! if you was to set the doors a-banging in 'em, it 'ud sound like thunder half o'er the parish."

"Ay, but there's more going on in the stables than what folks see by daylight, eh, Mr. Macey?" said the landlord.

[1] In Queen Anne's time several issues of **shillings** bearing her likeness were made.

"Ay, ay; go that way of a dark night, that's all," said Mr. Macey, winking mysteriously, "and then make believe, if you like, as you didn't see lights i' the stables, nor hear the stamping o' the hosses, nor the cracking o' the whips, and howling, too, if it's tow'rt daybreak. 'Cliff's Holiday' has been the name of it ever sin' I were a boy; that's to say, some said as it was the holiday Old Harry[2] gev him from roasting, like. That's what my father told me, and he was a reasonable man, though there's folks nowadays know what happened afore they were born better nor they know their own business."

"What do you say to that, eh, Dowlas?" said the landlord, turning to the farrier, who was swelling with impatience for his cue. "There's a nut for *you* to crack."

Mr. Dowlas was the negative spirit in the company, and was proud of his position.

"Say? I say what a man *should* say as doesn't shut his eyes to look at a finger post. I say, as I'm ready to wager any man ten pound, if he'll stand out wi' me any dry night in the pasture before the Warren stables, as we shall neither see lights nor hear noises, if it isn't the blowing of our own noses. That's what I say, and I've said it many a time; but there's nobody 'ull ventur a ten pun' note on their ghos'es as they make so sure of."

"Why, Dowlas, that's easy betting, that is," said Ben Winthrop. "You might as well bet a man as he wouldn't catch the rheumatise if he stood up to 's neck in the pool of a frosty night. It 'ud be fine fun for a man to win his bet as he'd catch the rheumatise. Folks as believe in Cliff's Holiday aren't a-going to ventur near it for a matter o' ten pound."

"If Master Dowlas wants to know the truth on it," said Mr. Macey, with a sarcastic smile, tapping his thumbs together,

[2] **Old Harry:** provincial name for the devil.

"he's no call to lay any bet — let him go and stan' by himself — there's nobody 'ull hinder him; and then he can let the parish'ners know if they're wrong."

"Thank you! I'm obliged to you," said the farrier, with a snort of scorn. "If folk are fools, it's no business o' mine. *I* don't want to make out the truth about ghos'es; I know it a'ready. But I'm not against a bet — everything fair and open. Let any man bet me ten pound as I shall see Cliff's Holiday, and I'll go and stand by myself. I want no company. I'd as lief do it as I'd fill this pipe."

"Ah, but who's to watch you, Dowlas, and see you do it? That's no fair bet," said the butcher.

"No fair bet?" replied Mr. Dowlas angrily. "I should like to hear any man stand up and say I want to bet unfair. Come now, Master Lundy, I should like to hear you say it."

"Very like you would," said the butcher. "But it's no business o' mine. You're none o' my bargains, and I aren't a-going to try and 'bate your price. If anybody'll bid for you at your own vallying, let him. I'm for peace and quietness, I am."

"Yes, that's what every yapping cur is, when you hold a stick up at him," said the farrier. "But I'm afraid o' neither man nor ghost, and I'm ready to lay a fair bet. *I* aren't a turntail cur."

"Ay, but there's this in it, Dowlas," said the landlord, speaking in a tone of much candor and tolerance. "There's folks, i' my opinion, they can't see ghos'es, not if they stood as plain as a pikestaff before 'em. And there's reason i' that. For there's my wife, now, can't smell, not if she'd the strongest o' cheese under her nose. I never see'd a ghost myself, but then I says to myself, 'Very like I haven't got the smell for 'em.' I mean, putting a ghost for a smell, or else contrairiways. And so, I'm for holding with both sides; for, as I say, the truth lies between 'em. And if Dowlas was to go and stand, and say he'd never seen a wink o' Cliff's Holiday all the night through, I'd back him; and if anybody said as Cliff's Holiday was certain sure, for all that, I'd back *him* too. For the smell's what I go by."

The landlord's analogical argument was not well received by the farrier — a man intensely opposed to compromise.

"Tut, tut," he said, setting down his glass with refreshed irritation; "what's the smell got to do with it? Did ever a ghost give a man a black eye? That's what I should like to know. If ghos'es want me to believe in 'em, let 'em leave off skulking i' the dark and i' lone places — let 'em come where there's company and candles."

"As if ghos'es 'ud want to be believed in by anybody so ignirant!" said Mr. Macey, in deep disgust at the farrier's crass incompetence to apprehend the conditions of ghostly phenomena.

CHAPTER VII

Yet the next moment there seemed to be some evidence that ghosts had a more condescending disposition than Mr. Macey attributed to them, for the pale thin figure of Silas Marner was suddenly seen standing in the warm light, uttering no word, but looking round at the company with his strange unearthly eyes. The long pipes gave a simultaneous movement, like the antennae of startled insects, and every man present, not excepting even the skeptical farrier, had an impression that he saw, not Silas Marner in the flesh, but an apparition; for the door by which Silas had entered was hidden by the high-screened seats, and no one had noticed his approach. Mr. Macey, sitting a long way off the ghost, might be supposed to have felt an argumentative triumph, which would tend to neutralize his share of the general alarm. Had he not always said that when Silas Marner was in that strange trance of his, his soul went loose from his body? Here was the demonstration; nevertheless, on the whole, he would have been as well contented without it. For a few moments there was a dead silence, Marner's want of breath and agitation not allowing him to speak. The landlord, under the habitual sense that he was bound to keep his house open to all company, and confident in the protection of his unbroken neutrality, at last took on himself the task of adjuring the ghost.

"Master Marner," he said, in a conciliatory tone, "what's lacking to you? What's your business here?"

"Robbed!" said Silas gaspingly. "I've been robbed! I want the constable — and the Justice — and Squire Cass — and Mr. Crackenthorp."

"Lay hold on him, Jem Rodney," said the landlord, the idea of a ghost subsiding; "he's off his head, I doubt. He's wet through."

Jem Rodney was the outermost man, and sat conveniently near Marner's standingplace; but he declined to give his services.

"Come and lay hold on him yourself, Mr. Snell, if you've a mind," said Jem rather sullenly. "He's been robbed, and murdered, too, for what I know," he added, in a muttering tone.

"Jem Rodney!" said Silas, turning and fixing his strange eyes on the suspected man.

"Ay, Master Marner, what do ye want wi' me?" said Jem, trembling a little, and seizing his drinking can as a defensive weapon.

"If it was you stole my money," said Silas, clasping his hands entreatingly, and raising his voice to a cry, "give it me back — and I won't meddle with you. I won't set the constable on you. Give it me back, and I'll let you — I'll let you have a guinea."

"Me stole your money!" said Jem angrily. "I'll pitch this can at your eye if you talk o' *my* stealing your money."

"Come, come, Master Marner," said the landlord, now rising resolutely, and seizing Marner by the shoulder, "if you've got any information to lay, speak it out sensible, and show as you're in your right mind, if you expect anybody to listen to you. You're as wet as a drownded rat. Sit down and dry yourself, and speak straightforrard."

"Ah, to be sure, man," said the farrier, who began to feel that he had not been quite on a par with himself and the occasion. "Let's have no more staring and screaming, else we'll have you strapped for a madman. That was why I didn't speak at the first — thinks I, the man's run mad."

"Ay, ay, make him sit down," said several voices at once, well pleased that the reality of ghosts remained still an open question.

The landlord forced Marner to take off his coat, and then to sit down on a chair aloof from everyone else, in the center of the circle, and in the direct rays of the fire. The weaver, too feeble to have any distinct purpose beyond that of getting help to recover his money, submitted unresistingly. The transient fears of the company were now forgotten in their strong curiosity, and all faces were turned toward Silas, when the landlord, having seated himself again, said —

"Now, then, Master Marner, what's this you've got to say — as you've been robbed? Speak out."

"He'd better not say again as it was me robbed him," cried Jem Rodney hastily. "What could I ha' done with his money? I could as easy steal the parson's surplice, and wear it."

"Hold your tongue, Jem, and let's hear

what he's got to say," said the landlord. "Now, then, Master Marner."

Silas now told his story under frequent questioning, as the mysterious character of the robbery became evident.

This strangely novel situation of opening his trouble to his Raveloe neighbors, of sitting in the warmth of a hearth not his own, and feeling the presence of faces and voices which were his nearest promise of help, had doubtless its influence on Marner, in spite of his passionate preoccupation and his loss. Our consciousness rarely registers the beginning of a growth within us any more than without us; there have been many circulations of the sap before we detect the smallest sign of the bud.

The slight suspicion with which his hearers at first listened to him gradually melted away before the convincing simplicity of his distress; it was impossible for the neighbors to doubt that Marner was telling the truth, not because they were capable of arguing at once from the nature of his statements to the absence of any motive for making them falsely, but because, as Mr. Macey observed, "Folks as had the devil to back 'em were not likely to be so mushed" as poor Silas was. Rather, from the strange fact that the robber had left no traces, and had happened to know the nick of time, utterly incalculable by mortal agents, when Silas would go away from home without locking his door, the more probable conclusion seemed to be, that his disreputable intimacy in that quarter, if it ever existed, had been broken up, and that, in consequence, this ill turn had been done to Marner by somebody it was quite in vain to set the constable after. Why this preternatural felon should be obliged to wait till the door was left unlocked was a question which did not present itself.

"It isn't Jem Rodney as has done this work, Master Marner," said the landlord. "You mustn't be a-casting your eye at poor Jem. There may be a bit of a reckoning against Jem for the matter of a hare or so, if anybody was bound to keep their eyes staring open, and niver to wink; but Jem's been a-sitting here drinking his can, like the decentest man i' the parish, since before you left your house, Master Marner, by your own account."

"Ay, ay," said Mr. Macey, "let's have no accusing o' the innicent. That isn't the law. There must be folks to swear again' a man before he can be ta'en up. Let's have no accusing o' the innicent, Master Marner."

Memory was not so utterly torpid in Silas that it could not be wakened by these words. With a movement of compunction, as new and strange to him as everything else within the last hour, he started from his chair and went close up to Jem, looking at him as if he wanted to assure himself of the expression in his face.

"I was wrong," he said; "yes, yes — I ought to have thought. There's nothing to witness against you, Jem. Only you'd been into my house oftener than anybody else, and so you came into my head. I don't accuse you — I won't accuse anybody — only," he added, lifting up his hands to his head, and turning away with bewildered misery, "I try — I try to think where my guineas can be."

"Ay, ay, they're gone where it's hot enough to melt 'em, I doubt," said Mr. Macey.

"Tchuh!" said the farrier. And then he asked, with a cross-examining air, "How much money might there be in the bags, Master Marner."

"Two hundred and seventy-two pounds, twelve and sixpence, last night when I counted it," said Silas, seating himself again, with a groan.

"Pooh! why, they'd be none so heavy to carry. Some tramp's been in, that's all;

and as for the no footmarks, and the bricks and the sand being all right — why — your eyes are pretty much like a insect's, Master Marner; they're obliged to look so close, you can't see much at a time. It's my opinion as, if I'd been you, or you'd been me — for it comes to the same thing — you wouldn't have thought you'd found everything as you left it. But what I vote is, as two of the sensiblest o' the company should go with you to Master Kench, the constable's — he's ill i' bed, I know that much — and get him to appoint one of us his deppity; for that's the law, and I don't think anybody 'ull take upon him to contradick me there. It isn't much of a walk to Kench's; and then, if it's me as is deppity, I'll go back with you, Master Marner, and examine your premises; and if anybody's got any fault to find with that, I'll thank him to stand up and say it out like a man."

By this pregnant speech the farrier had re-established his self-complacency, and waited with confidence to hear himself named as one of the superlatively sensible men.

"Let us see how the night is, though," said the landlord, who also considered himself personally concerned in this proposition. "Why, it rains heavy still," he said, returning from the door.

"Well, I'm not the man to be afraid o' the rain," said the farrier. "For it'll look bad when Justice Malam hears as respectable men like us had a information laid before 'em and took no steps."

The landlord agreed with this view, and after taking the sense of the company, and duly rehearsing a small ceremony known in high ecclesiastical life as the *nolo episcopari*,[1] he consented to take on himself the chill dignity of going to Kench's. But to the farrier's strong disgust, Mr. Macey now started an objection to his proposing himself as a deputy constable; for that oracular old gentleman, claiming to know the law, stated, as a fact delivered to him by his father, that no doctor could be a constable.

"And you're a doctor, I reckon, though you're only a cow doctor — for a fly's a fly, though it may be a hossfly," concluded Mr. Macey, wondering a little at his own "'cuteness."

There was a hot debate upon this, the farrier being of course indisposed to renounce the quality of doctor, but contending that a doctor could be a constable if he liked — the law meant, he needn't be one if he didn't like. Mr. Macey thought this was nonsense, since the law was not likely to be fonder of doctors than of other folks. Moreover, if it was in the nature of doctors more than of other men not to like being constables, how came Mr. Dowlas to be so eager to act in that capacity?

"*I* don't want to act the constable," said the farrier, driven into a corner by this merciless reasoning; "and there's no man can say it of me, if he'd tell the truth. But if there's to be any jealousy and envying about going to Kench's in the rain, let them go as like it — you won't get me to go, I can tell you."

By the landlord's intervention, however, the dispute was accommodated. Mr. Dowlas consented to go as a second person disinclined to act officially; and so poor Silas, furnished with some old coverings, turned out with his two companions into the rain again, thinking of the long night hours before him, not as those do who long to rest, but as those who expect to "watch for the morning."

[1] **nolo episcopari:** Latin for "I do not wish to be made a bishop."

CHAPTER VIII

False beliefs interfere with human happiness. You may be thankful, for example, that the world no longer believes that guilt can be established by the drawing of lots, as in the days of Silas Marner. That idea has been discarded by civilized man for a long time. But in spite of great advances made in understanding the causes of things, a great deal of wrong thinking still hampers progress. If only we could change the ideas of man, a great many evils would disappear.

How *does* the world change its mind for the better? And how *does* mankind gradually see the light? One way of answering these questions for ourselves is to look back at the past and profit from the experience of our forefathers, as does Stephen Vincent Benét in his essay "We Aren't Superstitious," which you read on page 334. When we can see clearly the effect of wrong thinking on the lives of people in the past, we are less likely to be enslaved by present-day opinions.

You will appreciate this chapter and the two following more keenly if you will notice especially the thoughts of the times. Notice, for example, how large a part superstition plays in the lives of the simple village folks. Has the world changed its ideas about parental authority? about arrangements for marriage? What simple ideas ruled the lives of Mr. Macey and Dolly Winthrop? These are the kinds of questions which the story should stir in your mind as you read on.

When Godfrey Cass returned from Mrs. Osgood's party at midnight, he was not much surprised to learn that Dunsey had not come home. Perhaps he had not sold Wildfire, and was waiting for another chance — perhaps, on that foggy afternoon, he had preferred housing himself at the Red Lion at Batherley for the night, if the run had kept him in that neighborhood; for he was not likely to feel much concern about leaving his brother in suspense. Godfrey's mind was too full of Nancy Lammeter's looks and behavior, too full of the exasperation against himself and his lot, which the sight of her always produced in him, for him to give much thought to Wildfire or to the probabilities of Dunstan's conduct.

The next morning the whole village was excited by the story of the robbery, and Godfrey, like everyone else, was occupied in gathering and discussing news about it, and in visiting the stone pits. The rain had washed away all possibility of distinguishing footmarks, but a close investigation of the spot had disclosed, in the direction opposite to the village, a tinderbox, with a flint and steel, half sunk in the mud. It was not Silas's tinderbox, for the only one he had ever had was still standing on his shelf; and the inference generally accepted was that the tinderbox in the ditch was somehow connected with the robbery. A small minority shook their heads, and intimated their opinion that it was not a robbery to have much light thrown on it by tinderboxes, that Master Marner's tale had a queer look with it, and that such things had been known as a man's doing himself a mischief, and then setting the justice to look for the doer. But when questioned closely as to their grounds for this opinion, and what Master Marner had to gain by such false pretenses, they only shook their heads as before, and observed that there was no knowing what some folks counted gain; moreover, that everybody had a right to their own opinions, grounds or no grounds, and that the weaver, as everybody knew, was partly crazy. Mr. Macey, though he joined in the defence of Marner against all suspicions of deceit, also pooh-poohed the tinderbox; indeed, repudiated it as a rather impious suggestion, tending to imply that everything must be done by human hands, and that there was no power which could make away with the guineas without moving the bricks. Nevertheless, he turned round rather sharply on Mr. Tookey, when the zealous deputy, feeling that this was a view of the case peculiarly suited to a parish clerk, carried it still further, and doubted whether it was right to inquire into a robbery at all when the circumstances were so mysterious.

"As if," concluded Mr. Tookey — "as

if there was nothing but what could be made out by justices and constables."

"Now, don't you be for overshooting the mark, Tookey," said Mr. Macey, nodding his head aside admonishingly. "That's what you're allays at; if I throw a stone and hit, you think there's summat better than hitting, and you try to throw a stone beyond. What I said was against the tinderbox; I said nothing against justices and constables, for they're o' King George's[1] making, and it 'ud be ill-becoming a man in a parish office to fly out again' King George."

While these discussions were going on amongst the group outside the Rainbow a higher consultation was being carried on within, under the presidency of Mr. Crackenthorp, the rector, assisted by Squire Cass and other substantial parishioners. It had just occurred to Mr. Snell, the landlord — he being, as he observed, a man accustomed to put two and two together — to connect with the tinderbox which, as deputy constable, he himself had had the honorable distinction of finding, certain recollections of a peddler who had called to drink at the house about a month before, and had actually stated that he carried a tinderbox about with him to light his pipe. Here, surely, was a clue to be followed out. And as memory, when duly impregnated with ascertained facts, is sometimes surprisingly fertile, Mr. Snell gradually recovered a vivid impression of the effect produced on him by the peddler's countenance and conversation. He had a "look with his eye" which fell unpleasantly on Mr. Snell's sensitive organism. To be sure, he didn't say anything particular — no, except that about the tinderbox — but it isn't what a man says, it's the way he says it. Moreover, he had a swarthy foreignness of complexion which boded little honesty.

[1] **King George**: the third, who was reigning at the time.

"Did he wear earrings?" Mr. Crackenthorp wished to know, having some acquaintance with foreign customs.

"Well — stay — let me see," said Mr. Snell, like a docile clairvoyant, who would really not make a mistake if she could help it. After stretching the corners of his mouth and contracting his eyes, as if he were trying to see the earrings, he appeared to give up the effort, and said, "Well, he'd got earrings in his box to sell, so it's nat'ral to suppose he might wear 'em. But he called at every house, a'most, in the village; there's somebody else, mayhap, saw 'em in his ears, though I can't take upon me rightly to say."

Mr. Snell was correct in his surmise that somebody else would remember the peddler's earrings. For, on the spread of inquiry among the villagers, it was stated with gathering emphasis that the parson had wanted to know whether the peddler wore earrings in his ears, and an impression was created that a great deal depended on the eliciting of this fact. Of course everyone who heard the question, not having any distinct image of the peddler as *without* earrings, immediately had an image of him *with* earrings, larger or smaller, as the case might be; and the image was presently taken for a vivid recollection, so that the glazier's wife, a well-intentioned woman, not given to lying, and whose house was among the cleanest in the village, was ready to declare, as sure as ever she meant to take the sacrament the very next Christmas that was ever coming, that she had seen big earrings, in the shape of the young moon, in the peddler's two ears; while Jinny Oates, the cobbler's daughter, being a more imaginative person, stated not only that she had seen them, too, but that they had made her blood creep, as it did at that very moment while there she stood.

Also, by way of throwing further light

on this clue of the tinderbox, a collection was made of all the articles purchased from the peddler at various houses, and carried to the Rainbow to be exhibited there. In fact, there was a general feeling in the village that for the clearing-up of this robbery there must be a great deal done at the Rainbow, and that no man need offer his wife an excuse for going there while it was the scene of severe public duties.

Some disappointment was felt, and perhaps a little indignation also, when it became known that Silas Marner, on being questioned by the Squire and the parson, had retained no other recollection of the peddler than that he had called at his door, but had not entered his house, having turned away at once when Silas, holding the door ajar, had said that he wanted nothing. This had been Silas's testimony, though he clutched strongly at the idea of the peddler's being the culprit, if only because it gave him a definite image of a whereabout for his gold, after it had been taken away from its hiding place; he could see it now in the peddler's box. But it was observed with some irritation in the village that anybody but a "blind creatur" like Marner would have seen the man prowling about, for how came he to leave his tinderbox in the ditch close by if he hadn't been lingering there? Doubtless, he had made his observations when he saw Marner at the door. Anybody might know — and only look at him — that the weaver was a half-crazy miser. It was a wonder the peddler hadn't murdered him; men of that sort, with rings in their ears, had been known for murderers often and often; there had been one tried at the 'sizes, not so long ago but what there were people living who remembered it.

Godfrey Cass, indeed, entering the Rainbow during one of Mr. Snell's frequently repeated recitals of his testimony, had treated it lightly, stating that he himself had bought a penknife of the peddler, and thought him a merry grinning fellow enough; it was all nonsense, he said, about the man's evil looks. But this was spoken of in the village as the random talk of youth, "as if it was only Mr. Snell who had seen something odd about the peddler!" On the contrary, there were at least half a dozen who were ready to go before Justice Malam, and give in much more striking testimony than any the landlord could furnish. It was to be hoped Mr. Godfrey would not go to Tarley and throw cold water on what Mr. Snell said there, and so prevent the justice from drawing up a warrant. He was suspected of intending this, when, after midday, he was seen setting off on horseback in the direction of Tarley.

But by this time Godfrey's interest in the robbery had faded before his growing anxiety about Dunstan and Wildfire, and he was going, not to Tarley, but to Batherley, unable to rest in uncertainty about them any longer. The possibility that Dunstan had played him the ugly trick of riding away with Wildfire, to return at the end of a month, when he had gambled away or otherwise squandered the price of the horse, was a fear that urged itself upon him more, even, than the thought of an accidental injury; and now that the dance at Mrs. Osgood's was past, he was irritated with himself that he had trusted his horse to Dunstan. Instead of trying to still his fears he encouraged them, with that superstitious impression which clings to us all, that if we expect evil very strongly it is the less likely to come; and when he heard a horse approaching at a trot, and saw a hat rising above a hedge beyond an angle of the lane, he felt as if his conjuration had succeeded. But no sooner did the horse come within sight than his heart sank again. It was not Wildfire; and in a few moments more he discerned that the rider was not Dunstan, but Bryce, who pulled up to speak, with a face that implied something disagreeable.

"Well, Mr. Godfrey, that's a lucky brother of yours, that Master Dunsey, isn't he?"

"What do you mean?" said Godfrey hastily.

"Why, hasn't he been home yet?" said Bryce.

"Home? — no. What has happened? Be quick. What has he done with my horse?"

"Ah, I thought it was yours, though he pretended you had parted with it to him."

"Has he thrown him down and broken his knees?" said Godfrey, flushed with exasperation.

"Worse than that," said Bryce. "You see, I'd made a bargain with him to buy the horse for a hundred and twenty — a swinging price, but I always liked the horse. And what does he do but go and stake him — fly at a hedge with stakes in it, atop of a bank with a ditch before it. The horse had been dead a pretty good while when he was found. So he hasn't been home since, has he?"

"Home? — no," said Godfrey, "and he'd better keep away. Confound me for a fool! I might have known this would be the end of it."

"Well, to tell you the truth," said Bryce, "after I'd bargained for the horse, it did come into my head that he might be riding and selling the horse without your knowledge, for I didn't believe it was his own. I knew Master Dunsey was up to his tricks sometimes. But where can he be gone? He's never been seen at Batherley. He couldn't have been hurt, for he must have walked off."

"Hurt?" said Godfrey bitterly. "He'll never be hurt — he's made to hurt other people."

"And so you *did* give him leave to sell the horse, eh?" said Bryce.

"Yes; I wanted to part with the horse — he was always a little too hard in the mouth for me," said Godfrey, his pride making him wince under the idea that Bryce guessed the sale to be a matter of necessity. "I was going to see after him — I thought some mischief had happened. I'll go back now," he added, turning the horse's head, and wishing he could get rid of Bryce; for he felt that the long-dreaded crisis in his life was close upon him. "You're coming on to Raveloe, aren't you?"

"Well, no, not now," said Bryce. "I *was* coming round there, for I had to go to Flitton, and I thought I might as well take you in my way, and just let you know all I knew myself about the horse. I suppose Master Dunsey didn't like to show himself till the ill news had blown over a bit. He's perhaps gone to pay a visit at the Three Crowns, by Whitbridge — I know he's fond of the house."

"Perhaps he is," said Godfrey, rather absently. Then rousing himself, he said, with an effort at carelessness, "We shall hear of him soon enough, I'll be bound."

"Well, here's my turning," said Bryce, not surprised to perceive that Godfrey was rather "down"; "so I'll bid you good day, and wish I may bring you better news another time."

Godfrey rode along slowly, representing to himself the scene of confession to his father from which he felt that there was now no longer any escape. The revelation about the money must be made the very next morning; and if he withheld the rest, Dunstan would be sure to come back shortly, and, finding that he must bear the brunt of his father's anger, would tell the whole story out of spite, even though he had nothing to gain by it. There was one step, perhaps, by which he might still win Dunstan's silence and put off the evil day; he might tell his father that he had himself spent the money paid to him by Fowler; and as he had never been guilty of such an offense before, the affair would blow over after a little storming. But Godfrey could not bend himself to this. He felt that in letting Dunstan have the money he had already been guilty of a breach of trust hardly less culpable than that of spending the money directly for his own behoof; and yet there was a distinction between the two acts which made him feel that the one was so much more blackening than the other as to be intolerable to him.

"I don't pretend to be a good fellow," he said to himself: "but I'm not a scoundrel — at least, I'll stop short somewhere. I'll bear the consequences of what I *have* done sooner than make believe I've done what I never would have done. I'd never have spent the money for my own pleasure — I was tortured into it."

Through the remainder of this day Godfrey, with only occasional fluctuations, kept his will bent in the direction of a complete avowal to his father, and he withheld the story of Wildfire's loss till the next morning, that it might serve him as an introduction to heavier matter. The old Squire was accustomed to his son's frequent absence from home, and thought neither Dunstan's nor Wildfire's nonappearance a matter calling for remark. Godfrey said to himself again and again that if he let slip this one opportunity of confession he might never have another; the revelation might be made even in a more odious way than by Dunstan's malignity — *she* might come, as she had threatened to do. And then he tried to make the scene easier to himself by rehearsal; he made up his mind how he would pass from the admission of his weakness in letting Dunstan have the money to the fact that Dunstan had a hold on him which he had been unable to shake off, and how he would work up his father to expect something very bad before he told him the fact. The old Squire was an implacable man; he made resolutions in violent anger, and he was not to be moved from them after his anger had subsided — as fiery volcanic matters cool and harden into rock. Like many violent and implacable men, he allowed evils to grow under favor of his own heedlessness, till they pressed upon him with exasperating force, and then he turned round with fierce severity and became unrelentingly hard. This was his system with his tenants; he allowed them to get into arrears, neglect their fences, reduce their stock, sell their straw, and otherwise go the wrong way — and then, when he became short of money in consequence of this indulgence, he took the hardest measures and would listen to no appeal. Godfrey knew all this, and felt it with the greater force because he had constantly suffered annoyance from witnessing his father's sudden fits of unrelentingness, for which his own habitual irresolution deprived him of all sympathy. (He was not critical on the faulty indulgence which preceded these fits; *that* seemed to him natural enough.) Still there was just the chance, Godfrey thought, that his father's pride might see this marriage in a light that would induce him to hush it up, rather than turn his son out and make the family the talk of the country for ten miles round.

This was the view of the case that Godfrey managed to keep before him pretty closely till midnight, and he went to sleep thinking that he had done with inward debating. But when he awoke in the still morning darkness he found it impossible to reawaken his evening thoughts; it was as if they had been tired out and were not to be roused for further work. Instead of arguments for confession, he could now feel the presence of nothing but its evil consequences; the old dread of disgrace came back — the old shrinking from the thought of raising a hopeless barrier between himself and Nancy — the old disposition to rely on chances which might be favorable to him, and save him from betrayal. Why, after all, should he cut off the hope of them by his own act? He had seen the matter in a wrong light yesterday. He had been in a rage with Dunstan, and had thought of nothing but a thorough breakup of their mutual understanding; but what it would be really wisest for him to do was to try and soften his father's anger against Dunsey, and keep things as nearly as possible in their old condition. If Dunsey did not come back for a few days (and Godfrey did not know but that the rascal had enough money in his pocket to enable him to keep away still longer), everything might blow over.

CHAPTER IX

Godfrey rose and took his own breakfast earlier than usual, but lingered in the wainscoted parlor till his younger brothers had finished their meal and gone out, awaiting his father, who always took a walk with his managing man before breakfast. Everyone breakfasted at a different hour in the Red House, and the Squire was always the latest, giving a long chance to a rather feeble morning appetite before he tried it. The table had been spread with substantial eatables nearly two hours before he presented himself — a tall, stout man of sixty, with a face in which the knit brow and rather hard glance seemed contradicted by the slack and feeble mouth. His person showed marks of habitual neglect; his dress was slovenly; and yet there was something in the presence of the old Squire distinguishable from that of the ordinary farmers in the parish, who were perhaps every whit as refined as he, but, having slouched their way through life with a consciousness of being in the vicinity of their "betters," wanted that self-possession and authoritativeness of voice and carriage which belonged to a man who thought of superiors as remote existences, with whom he had personally little more to do than with America or the stars. The Squire had been used to parish homage all his life, used to the presupposition that his family, his tankards, and everything that was his were the oldest and best; and as he never associated with any gentry higher than himself, his opinion was not disturbed by comparison.

He glanced at his son as he entered the room, and said, "What, sir! haven't *you* had your breakfast yet?" but there was no pleasant morning greeting between them; not because of any unfriendliness, but because the sweet flower of courtesy is not a growth of such homes as the Red House.

"Yes, sir," said Godfrey, "I've had my breakfast, but I was waiting to speak to you."

"Ah! well," said the Squire, throwing himself indifferently into his chair, and speaking in a ponderous coughing fashion, which was felt in Raveloe to be a sort of privilege of his rank, while he cut a piece of beef, and held it up before the deerhound that had come in with him. "Ring the bell for my ale, will you? You youngsters' business is your own pleasure mostly. There's no hurry about it for anybody but yourselves."

The Squire's life was quite as idle as his sons', but it was a fiction kept up by himself and his contemporaries in Raveloe that youth was exclusively the period of folly, and that their aged wisdom was constantly in a state of endurance mitigated by sarcasm. Godfrey waited, before he spoke again, until the ale had been brought and the door closed — an interval during which Fleet, the deerhound, had consumed enough bits of beef to make a poor man's holiday dinner.

"There's been a cursed piece of ill luck with Wildfire," he began; "happened the day before yesterday."

"What! broke his knees?" said the Squire, after taking a draught of ale. "I thought you knew how to ride better than that, sir. I never threw a horse down in my life. If I had, I might ha' whistled for another, for *my* father wasn't quite so ready to unstring as some other fathers I know of. But they must turn over a new leaf — *they* must. What with mortgages and arrears I'm as short o' cash as a roadside pauper. And that fool Kimble says the newspaper's talking about peace. Why, the country wouldn't have a leg to stand on. Prices 'ud run down like a jack, and I should never get my arrears, not if I sold all the fellows up. And there's that damned Fowler, I won't put up with him any longer; I've told Winthrop to go to Cox this very day. The lying scoundrel told me he'd be sure to pay me a hundred last month. He takes advantage because he's on that outlying farm and thinks I shall forget him."

The Squire had delivered this speech in a coughing and interrupted manner, but with no pause long enough for Godfrey to make it a pretext for taking up the word again. He felt that his father meant to ward off any request for money on the ground of the misfortune with Wildfire, and that the emphasis he had thus been led to lay on his shortness of cash and his arrears was likely to produce an attitude of mind the utmost unfavorable for his own disclosure. But he must go on now he had begun.

"It's worse than breaking the horse's knees — he's been staked and killed," he said, as soon as his father was silent, and had begun to cut his meat. "But I wasn't thinking of asking you to buy me another horse; I was only thinking I'd lost the means of paying you with the price of Wildfire as I'd meant to do. Dunsey took him to the hunt to sell him for me the other day, and after he'd made a bargain for a hundred and twenty with Bryce he went after the hounds, and took some fool's leap or other that did for the horse at once. If it hadn't been for that, I should have paid you a hundred pounds this morning."

The Squire had laid down his knife and fork and was staring at his son in amazement, not being sufficiently quick of brain to form a probable guess as to what could have caused so strange an inversion of the paternal and filial relations as this proposition of his son to pay him a hundred pounds.

"The truth is, sir — I'm very sorry — I was quite to blame," said Godfrey. "Fowler did pay that hundred pounds. He paid it to me when I was over there one day last month. And Dunsey bothered me for the money, and I let him have it, because I hoped I should be able to pay it you before this."

The Squire was purple with anger before his son had done speaking, and found utterance difficult. "You let Dunsey have it, sir? And how long have you been so thick with Dunsey that you must collogue with him to embezzle my money? Are you turning out a scamp? I tell you I won't have it. I'll turn the whole pack of you out of the house together, and marry again. I'd have you to remember, sir, my property's got no entail on it; since my grandfather's time the Casses can do as they like with their land. Remember that, sir. Let Dunsey have the money! Why should you let Dunsey have the money? There's some lie at the bottom of it."

"There's no lie, sir," said Godfrey. "I wouldn't have spent the money myself, but Dunsey bothered me, and I was a fool and let him have it. But I meant to pay it whether he did or not. That's the whole story. I never meant to embezzle money, and I'm not the man to do it. You never knew me do a dishonest trick, sir."

"Where's Dunsey, then? What do you stand talking there for? Go and fetch Dunsey, as I tell you, and let him give account of what he wanted the money for, and what he's done with it. He shall repent it. I'll turn him out. I said I would, and I'll do it. He shan't brave me. Go and fetch him."

"Dunsey isn't come back, sir."

"What! did he break his own neck, then?" said the Squire with some disgust at the idea that, in that case, he could not fulfill his threat.

"No, he wasn't hurt, I believe, for the horse was found dead, and Dunsey must have walked off. I dare say we shall see him again by and by. I don't know where he is."

"And what must you be letting him have my money for? Answer me that," said the Squire, attacking Godfrey again, since Dunsey was not within reach.

"Well, sir, I don't know," said Godfrey hesitatingly. That was a feeble evasion, but Godfrey was not fond of lying, and, not being sufficiently aware that no sort of duplicity can long flourish without the help of vocal falsehoods, he was quite unprepared with invented motives.

"You don't know? I tell you what it is, sir. You've been up to some trick, and you've been bribing him not to tell," said the Squire with a sudden acuteness which startled Godfrey, who felt his heart beat violently at the nearness of his father's guess. The sudden alarm pushed him on to take the next step — a very slight impulse suffices for that on a downward road.

"Why, sir," he said, trying to speak with careless ease, "it was a little affair between me and Dunsey; it's no matter to anybody else. It's hardly worth while to pry into young men's fooleries; it wouldn't have made any difference to you, sir, if I'd not had the bad luck to lose Wildfire. I should have paid you the money."

"Fooleries! Pshaw! it's time you'd done with fooleries. And I'd have you know, sir, you *must* ha' done with 'em," said the Squire, frowning and casting an angry glance at his son. "Your goings on are not what I shall find money for any longer. There's my grandfather had his stables full o' horses, and kept a good house, too, and in worse times, by what I can make out; and so might I, if I hadn't four good-for-nothing fellows to hang on me like horse leeches. I've been too good a father to you all — that's what it is. But I shall pull up, sir."

Godfrey was silent. He was not likely to be very penetrating in his judgments, but he had always had a sense that his father's indulgence had not been kindness, and had had a vague longing for some discipline that would have checked his own errant weakness and helped his better will. The Squire ate his bread and meat hastily, took a deep draught of ale, then turned his chair from the table, and began to speak again.

"It'll be all the worse for you, you know — you'd need try and help me keep things together."

"Well, sir, I've often offered to take the management of things, but you know you've taken it ill always, and seemed to think I wanted to push you out of your place."

"I know nothing o' your offering or o' my taking it ill," said the Squire, whose memory consisted in certain strong impressions unmodified by detail; "but I know one while you seemed to be thinking o' marrying, and I didn't offer to put any obstacles in your way, as some fathers would. I'd as lieve you married

Lammeter's daughter as anybody. I suppose if I'd said you nay, you'd ha' kept on with it; but for want o' contradiction you've changed your mind. You're a shilly-shally fellow; you take after your poor mother. She never had a will of her own; a woman has no call for one, if she's got a proper man for her husband. But *your* wife had need have one, for you hardly know your own mind enough to make both your legs walk one way. The lass hasn't said downright she won't have you, has she?"

"No," said Godfrey, feeling very hot and uncomfortable; "but I don't think she will."

"Think! why haven't you the courage to ask her? Do you stick to it, you want to have *her* — that's the thing?"

"There's no other woman I want to marry," said Godfrey evasively.

"Well, then, let me make the offer for you, that's all, if you haven't the pluck to do it yourself. Lammeter isn't likely to be loath for his daughter to marry into *my* family, I should think. And as for the pretty lass, she wouldn't have her cousin — and there's nobody else, as I see, could ha' stood in your way."

"I'd rather let it be, please, sir, at present," said Godfrey, in alarm. "I think she's a little offended with me just now, and I should like to speak for myself. A man must manage these things for himself."

"Well, speak then and manage it, and see if you can't turn over a new leaf. That's what a man must do when he thinks o' marrying."

"I don't see how I can think of it at present, sir. You wouldn't like to settle me on one of the farms, I suppose, and I don't think she'd come to live in this house with all my brothers. It's a different sort of life to what she's been used to."

"Not come to live in this house? Don't tell me. You ask her, that's all," said the Squire, with a short, scornful laugh.

"I'd rather let the thing be at present, sir," said Godfrey. "I hope you won't try to hurry it on by saying anything."

"I shall do what I choose," said the Squire, "and I shall let you know I'm master; else you may turn out and find an estate to drop into somewhere else. Go out and tell Winthrop not to go to Cox's, but wait for me. And tell 'em to get my horse saddled. And, stop; look out and get that hack o' Dunsey's sold, and hand me the money, will you? He'll keep no more hacks at my expense. And if you know where he's sneaking — I dare say you do — you may tell him to spare himself the journey o' coming back home. Let him turn ostler and keep himself. He shan't hang on me any more."

"I don't know where he is; and if I did, it isn't my place to tell him to keep away," said Godfrey, moving toward the door.

"Confound it, sir, don't stay arguing, but go and order my horse," said the Squire, taking up a pipe.

Godfrey left the room, hardly knowing whether he were more relieved by the sense that the interview was ended without having made any change in his position, or more uneasy that he had entangled himself still further in prevarication and deceit. What had passed about his proposing to Nancy had raised a new alarm, lest by some after-dinner words of his father's to Mr. Lammeter he should be thrown into the embarrassment of being obliged absolutely to decline her when she seemed to be within his reach. He fled to his usual refuge, that of hoping for some unforeseen turn of fortune, some favorable chance which would save him from unpleasant consequences — perhaps even justify his insincerity by manifesting its prudence.

In this point of trusting to some throw

of fortune's dice Godfrey can hardly be called old-fashioned. Favorable chance is the god of all men who follow their own devices instead of obeying a law they believe in. Let even a polished man of these days get into a position he is ashamed to avow, and his mind will be bent on all the possible issues that may deliver him from the calculable results of that position. Let him live outside his income, or shirk the resolute honest work that brings wages, and he will presently find himself dreaming of a possible benefactor, a possible simpleton who may be cajoled into using his interest, a possible state of mind in some possible person not yet forthcoming. Let him neglect the responsibilities of his office, and he will inevitably anchor himself on the chance that the thing left undone may turn out not to be of the supposed importance. Let him betray his friend's confidence, and he will adore that same cunning complexity called chance, which gives him the hope that his friend will never know. Let him forsake a decent craft that he may pursue the gentilities of a profession to which nature never called him, and his religion will infallibly be the worship of blessed chance, which he will believe in as the mighty creator of success. The evil principle deprecated in that religion is the orderly sequence by which the seed brings forth a crop after its kind.

CHAPTER X

Justice Malam was naturally regarded in Tarley and Raveloe as a man of capacious mind, seeing that he could draw much wider conclusions without evidence than could be expected of his neighbors who were not on the commission of the peace. Such a man was not likely to neglect the clue of the tinderbox, and an inquiry was set on foot concerning a peddler, name unknown, with curly black hair and a foreign complexion, carrying a box of cutlery and jewelry, and wearing large rings in his ears. But either because inquiry was too slow-footed to overtake him, or because the description applied to so many peddlers that inquiry did not know how to choose among them, weeks passed away, and there was no other result concerning the robbery than a gradual cessation of the excitement it had caused in Raveloe. Dunstan Cass's absence was hardly a subject of remark; he had once before had a quarrel with his father, and had gone off, nobody knew whither, to return at the end of six weeks, take up his old quarters unforbidden, and swagger as usual. His own family, who equally expected this issue, with the sole difference that the Squire was determined this time to forbid him the old quarters, never mentioned his absence, and when his uncle Kimble or Mr. Osgood noticed it, the story of his having killed Wildfire, and committed some offense against his father, was enough to prevent surprise. To connect the fact of Dunsey's disappearance with that of the robbery occurring on the same day, lay quite away from the track of everyone's thought — even Godfrey's, who had better reason than anyone else to know what his brother was capable of. He remembered no mention of the weaver between them since the time, twelve years ago, when it was their boyish sport to deride him; and, besides, his imagination constantly created an alibi for Dunstan; he saw him continually in some congenial haunt, to which he had walked off on leaving Wildfire — saw him sponging on chance acquaintances, and meditating a return home to the old amusement of tormenting his elder brother. Even if any brain in Raveloe had put the said two facts together, I doubt whether a combination so injurious to the prescriptive respectability of a family with a mural monument[1] and venerable tankards would not have been suppressed as of unsound tendency. But Christmas puddings, brawn,[2] and abundance of spirituous liquors, throwing the mental originality into the channel of nightmare, are great preservatives against a dangerous spontaneity of waking thought.

When the robbery was talked of at the Rainbow and elsewhere, in good company, the balance continued to waver between the rational explanation founded on the tinderbox and the theory of an impenetrable mystery that mocked investigation. The advocates of the tinderbox-and-peddler view considered the other side a muddleheaded and credulous set, who, because they themselves were walleyed, supposed everybody else to have the same blank outlook; and the adherents of the inexplicable more than hinted that their antagonists were animals inclined to crow before they had found any corn — mere skimming dishes in point of depth — whose clear-sightedness consisted in supposing there was nothing behind a barn door because they couldn't see through it; so that, though their controversy did not serve to elicit the fact concerning the robbery, it elicited some true opinions of collateral importance.

But while poor Silas's loss served thus to brush the slow current of Raveloe conversation, Silas himself was feeling the withering desolation of that bereavement about which his neighbors were arguing at their ease. To anyone who had observed him before he lost his gold it might have seemed that so withered and shrunken a life as his could hardly be susceptible of a bruise, could hardly endure any subtraction but such as would put an end to it altogether. But in reality it had been an eager life, filled with immediate purpose, which fenced him in from the wide, cheerless unknown. It had been a clinging life; and though the object round which its fibers had clung was a dead, disrupted thing, it satisfied the need for clinging. But now the fence was broken down — the support was snatched away. Marner's thoughts could no longer move in their old round, and were baffled by a blank like that which meets a plodding ant when the earth has broken away on its homeward path. The loom was there, and the weaving, and the growing pattern in the cloth; but the bright treasure in the hole under his feet was gone; the prospect of handling and counting it was gone; the evening had no phantasm of delight to still the poor soul's craving. The thought of the money he would get by his actual work could bring no joy, for its meager image was only a fresh reminder of his loss; and hope was too heavily crushed by the sudden blow for his imagination to dwell on the growth of a new hoard from that small beginning.

He filled up the blank with grief. As he sat weaving, he every now and then moaned low, like one in pain; it was the sign that his thoughts had come round again to the sudden chasm — to the empty evening time. And all the evening, as he sat in his loneliness by his dull fire, he leaned his elbows on his knees, and clasped his head with his hands, and moaned very low — not as one who seeks to be heard.

And yet he was not utterly forsaken in his trouble. The repulsion Marner had always created in his neighbors was partly dissipated by the new light in which this misfortune had shown him. Instead of a man who had more cunning than honest folks could come by, and, what was worse, had not the inclination to use that cunning in a neighborly way, it was now apparent that Silas had not cunning enough to keep his own. He was generally spoken of as

[1] **mural monument:** Having a special monument built within a church wall was a sign of special respectability. [2] **brawn:** as used here, the flesh of a boar.

a "poor mushed creatur"; and that avoidance of his neighbors, which had before been referred to his ill will, and to a probable addiction to worse company, was now considered mere craziness.

This change to a kindlier feeling was shown in various ways. The odor of Christmas cooking being on the wind, it was the season when superfluous pork and black puddings are suggestive of charity in well-to-do families; and Silas's misfortune had brought him uppermost in the memory of housekeepers like Mrs. Osgood. Mr. Crackenthorp, too, while he admonished Silas that his money had probably been taken from him because he thought too much of it and never came to church, enforced the doctrine by a present of pigs' pettitoes, well calculated to dissipate unfounded prejudices against the clerical character. Neighbors, who had nothing but verbal consolation to give, showed a disposition not only to greet Silas, and discuss his misfortune at some length when they encountered him in the village, but also to take the trouble of calling at his cottage, and getting him to repeat all the details on the very spot; and then they would try to cheer him by saying, "Well, Master Marner, you're no worse off nor other poor folks, after all; and if you was to be crippled, the parish 'ud give you a 'lowance."

I suppose one reason why we are seldom able to comfort our neighbors with our words is that our good will gets adulterated, in spite of ourselves, before it can pass our lips. We can send black puddings and pettitoes without giving them a flavor of our own egoism; but language is a stream that is almost sure to smack of a mingled soil. There was a fair proportion of kindness in Raveloe; but it was often of a beery and bungling sort, and took the shape least allied to the complimentary and hypocritical.

Mr. Macey, for example, coming one evening expressly to let Silas know that recent events had given him the advantage of standing more favorably in the opinion of a man whose judgment was not formed lightly, opened the conversation by saying, as soon as he had seated himself and adjusted his thumbs —

"Come, Master Marner, why, you've no call to sit a-moaning. You're a deal better off to ha' lost your money, nor to ha' kep' it by foul means. I used to think, when you first come into these parts, as you were no better nor you should be; you were younger a deal than what you are now; but you were allays a staring, white-faced creatur, partly like a bald-faced calf, as I may say. But there's no knowing; it isn't every queer-looksed thing as Old Harry's had the making of — I mean, speaking o' toads and such; for they're often harmless, and useful against varmin. And it's pretty much the same wi' you, as fur as I can see. Though as to the yarbs and stuff to cure the breathing, if you brought that sort o' knowledge from distant parts, you might ha' been a bit freer of it. And if the knowledge wasn't well come by, why, you might ha' made up for it by coming to church reg'lar; for, as for the children as the Wise Woman charmed, I've been at the christening of 'em again and again, and they took the water just as well. And that's reasonable; for if Old Harry's a mind to do a bit o' kindness for a holiday, like, who's got anything against it? That's my thinking; and I've been clerk o' this parish forty year, and I know, when the parson and me does the cussing [1] of a Ash Wednesday, there's no cussing o' folks as have a mind to be cured without a doctor, let Kimble say what he will. And so, Master Marner, as I was saying — for there's windings i' things as they may

[1] **cussing:** Mr. Macey is referring to that part of the service required on Ash Wednesday in the Church of England which begins "Cursed is he."

carry you to the fur end o' the prayer book afore you get back to 'em — my advice is, as you keep up your sperrits; for as for thinking you're a deep un, and ha' got more inside you nor 'ull bear daylight, I'm not o' that opinion at all, and so I tell the neighbors. For, says I, you talk o' Master Marner making out a tale — why, it's nonsense, that is; it 'ud take a 'cute man to make a tale like that; and, says I, he looked as scared as a rabbit."

During his discursive address Silas had continued motionless in his previous attitude, leaning his elbows on his knees, and pressing his hands against his head. Mr. Macey, not doubting that he had been listened to, paused, in the expectation of some appreciatory reply, but Marner remained silent. He had a sense that the old man meant to be good-natured and neighborly; but the kindness fell on him as sunshine falls on the wretched — he had no heart to taste it, and felt that it was very far off him.

"Come, Master Marner, have you got nothing to say to that?" said Mr. Macey at last, with a slight accent of impatience.

"Oh," said Marner, slowly, shaking his head between his hands, "I thank you — thank you — kindly."

"Ay, ay, to be sure; I thought you would," said Mr. Macey; "and my advice is — have you got a Sunday suit?"

"No," said Marner.

"I doubted it was so," said Mr. Macey. "Now, let me advise you to get a Sunday suit; there's Tookey, he's a poor creatur, but he's got my tailoring business, and some o' my money in it, and he shall make a suit at a low price, and give you trust, and then you can come to church, and be a bit neighborly. Why, you've never heard me say 'Amen' since you come into these parts, and I recommend you to lose no time, for it'll be poor work when Tookey has it all to himself, for I mayn't be equil to stand i' the desk at all come another winter." Here Mr. Macey paused, perhaps expecting some sign of emotion in his hearer, but not observing any, he went on. "And as for the money for the suit o' clothes, why, you get a matter of a pound a week at your weaving, Master Marner, and you're a young man, eh, for all you look so mushed. Why, you couldn't ha' been five and twenty when you come into these parts, eh?"

Silas started a little at the change to a questioning tone, and answered mildly, "I don't know; I can't rightly say — it's a long while since."

After receiving such an answer as this it is not surprising that Mr. Macey observed, later on in the evening at the Rainbow, that Marner's head was "all of a muddle," and that it was to be doubted if he ever knew when Sunday came round, which showed him a worse heathen than many a dog.

Another of Silas's comforters, besides Mr. Macey, came to him with a mind highly charged on the same topic. This was Mrs. Winthrop, the wheelwright's wife. The inhabitants of Raveloe were not severely regular in their churchgoing, and perhaps there was hardly a person in the parish who would not have held that to go to church every Sunday in the calendar would have shown a greedy desire to stand well with Heaven, and get an undue advantage over their neighbors — a wish to be better than the "common run," that would have implied a reflection on those who had had godfathers and godmothers as well as themselves, and had an equal right to the burying service. At the same time it was understood to be requisite for all who were not household servants, or young men, to take the sacrament at one of the great festivals; Squire Cass himself took it on Christmas Day; while those who were held to be "good livers" went to church with greater, though still with moderate, frequency.

Mrs. Winthrop was one of these. She was in all respects a woman of scrupulous conscience, so eager for duties that life seemed to offer them too scantily unless she rose at half-past four, though this threw a scarcity of work over the more advanced hours of the morning, which it was a constant problem with her to remove. Yet she had not the vixenish temper which is sometimes supposed to be a necessary condition of such habits; she was a very mild, patient woman, whose nature it was to seek out all the sadder and more serious elements of life, and pasture her mind upon them. She was the person always first thought of in Raveloe when there was illness or death in a family, when leeches were to be applied, or there was a sudden disappointment in a monthly nurse. She was a " comfortable woman " — good-looking, fresh-complexioned, having her lips always slightly screwed, as if she felt herself in a sick-room with the doctor or the clergyman present. But she was never whimpering; no one had seen her shed tears; she was simply grave and inclined to shake her head and sigh, almost imperceptibly, like a funereal mourner who is not a relation. It seemed surprising that Ben Winthrop, who loved his quart pot and his joke, got along so well with Dolly; but she took her husband's jokes and joviality as patiently as everything else, considering that " men *would* be so," and viewing the stronger sex in the light of animals whom it had pleased Heaven to make naturally troublesome, like bulls and turkey cocks.

This good wholesome woman could hardly fail to have her mind drawn strongly toward Silas Marner now that he appeared in the light of a sufferer, and one Sunday afternoon she took her little boy Aaron with her, and went to call on Silas, carrying in her hand some small lard cakes, flat pastelike articles, much esteemed in Raveloe. Aaron, an apple-cheeked youngster of seven, with a clean starched frill, which looked like a plate for the apples, needed all his adventurous curiosity to embolden him against the possibility that the big-eyed weaver might do him some bodily injury; and his dubiety was much increased when, on arriving at the stone pits, they heard the mysterious sound of the loom.

" Ah, it is as I thought," said Mrs. Winthrop sadly.

They had to knock loudly before Silas heard them, but when he did come to the door he showed no impatience, as he would once have done, at a visit that had been unasked for and unexpected. Formerly, his heart had been as a locked casket with its treasure inside; but now the casket was empty, and the lock was broken. Left groping in darkness, with his prop utterly gone, Silas had inevitably a sense, though a dull and half-despairing one, that if any help came to him it must come from without; and there was a slight stirring of expectation at the sight of his fellow men, a faint consciousness of dependence on their good will. He opened the door wide to admit Dolly, but without otherwise returning her greeting than by moving the armchair a few inches as a sign that she was to sit down in it. Dolly, as soon as she was seated, removed the white cloth that covered her lard cakes, and said in her gravest way:

" I'd a baking yisterday, Master Marner, and the lard cakes turned out better nor common, and I'd ha' asked you to accept some if you'd thought well. I don't eat such things myself, for a bit o' bread's what I like from one year's end to the other, but men's stomichs are made so comical they want a change — they do, I know, God help 'em."

Dolly sighed gently as she held out the cakes to Silas, who thanked her kindly, and looked very close at them, absently, being accustomed to look so at everything he took into his hand — eyed all the while by the wondering bright orbs of the small Aaron, who had made an outwork of his mother's chair, and was peeping round from behind it.

"There's letters pricked on 'em," said Dolly. "I can't read 'em myself, and there's nobody, not Mr. Macey himself, rightly knows what they mean; but they've a good meaning, for they're the same as is on the pulpit cloth at church. What are they, Aaron, my dear?"

Aaron retreated completely behind his outwork.

"Oh, go, that's naughty," said his mother mildly. "Well, whativer the letters are, they've a good meaning; and it's a stamp as has been in our house, Ben says, ever since he was a little un, and his mother used to put it on the cakes, and I've allays put it on, too; for if there's any good, we've need of it i' this world."

"It's I.H.S.,"[1] said Silas, at which proof of learning Aaron peeped round the chair again.

"Well, to be sure, you can read 'em off," said Dolly. "Ben's read 'em to me many and many a time, but they slip out o' my mind again; the more's the pity, for they're good letters, else they wouldn't be in the church; and so I prick 'em on all the loaves and all the cakes, though sometimes they won't hold because o' the rising — for, as I said, if there's any good to be got we've need of it i' this world — that we have; and I hope they'll bring good to you, Master Marner, for it's wi' that will I brought you the cakes, and you see the letters have held better nor common."

Silas was as unable to interpret the letters as Dolly, but there was no possibility of misunderstanding the desire to give comfort that made itself heard in her quiet tones. He said, with more feeling than before, "Thank you — thank you kindly." But he laid down the cakes and seated himself absently — drearily unconscious of any distinct benefit toward which the cakes and the letters, or even Dolly's kindness, could tend for him.

"Ah, if there's good anywhere, we've need of it," repeated Dolly, who did not lightly forsake a servicable phrase. She looked at Silas pityingly as she went on. "But you didn't hear the church bells this morning, Master Marner? I doubt you didn't know it was Sunday. Living so lone here, you lose your count, I dare-say; and then, when your loom makes a noise, you can't hear the bells, more partic'lar now the frost kills the sound."

"Yes, I did; I heard 'em," said Silas, to whom Sunday bells were a mere accident of the day, and not part of its sacredness. There had been no bells in Lantern Yard.

"Dear heart!" said Dolly, pausing before she spoke again. "But what a pity it is you should work of a Sunday, and not clean yourself — if you *didn't* go to church; for if you'd a roasting bit, it might be as you couldn't leave it, being a lone man. But there's the bakehus, if you could make up your mind to spend a twopence on the oven now and then — not every week, in course — I shouldn't like to do that myself — you might carry your bit o' dinner there, for it's nothing but right to have a bit o' summat hot of a Sunday, and not to make it as you can't know your dinner from Saturday. But now, upo' Christmas Day, this blessed Christmas as is ever coming, if you was to take your dinner to the bakehus, and go to church, and see the holly and the yew, and hear the anthim, and then take the sacramen', you'd be a deal the better, and you'd know which end you stood on, and you could put your trust i' Them as knows better nor we do,

[1] **I.H.S.:** an ancient symbol of Christianity.

seein' you'd ha' done what it lies on us all to do."

Dolly's exhortation, which was an unusually long effort of speech for her, was uttered in the soothing persuasive tone with which she would have tried to prevail on a sick man to take his medicine or a basin of gruel for which he had no appetite. Silas had never before been closely urged on the point of his absence from church, which had only been thought of as a part of his general queerness; and he was too direct and simple to evade Dolly's appeal.

"Nay, nay," he said, "I know nothing o' church. I've never been to church."

"No!" said Dolly in a low tone of wonderment. Then bethinking herself of Silas's advent from an unknown country, she said, "Could it ha' been as they'd no church where you was born?"

"Oh, yes," said Silas meditatively, sitting in his usual posture of leaning on his knees and supporting his head. "There was churches — a many — it was a big town. But I knew nothing of 'em — I went to chapel."[1]

Dolly was much puzzled at this new word, but she was rather afraid of inquiring further, lest "chapel" might mean some haunt of wickedness. After a little thought she said —

"Well, Master Marner, it's niver too late to turn over a new leaf, and if you've niver had no church, there's no telling the good it'll do you. For I feel so set up and comfortable as niver was when I've been and heard the prayers, and the singing to the praise and glory o' God, as Mr. Macey gives out — and Mr. Crackenthorp saying good words, and more partic'lar on Sacramen' Day; and if a bit o' trouble comes, I feel as I can put up wi' it, for I've looked for help i' the right quarter, and gev myself up to Them as we must all give ourselves up to at the last; and if we'n done our part, it isn't to be believed as Them as are above us 'ull be worse nor we are, and come short o' Their'n."

Poor Dolly's exposition of her simple Raveloe theology fell rather unmeaningly on Silas's ears, for there was no word in it that could rouse a memory of what he had known as religion, and his comprehension was quite baffled by the plural pronoun, which was no heresy of Dolly's, but only her way of avoiding a presumptuous familiarity. He remained silent, not feeling inclined to assent to the part of Dolly's speech which he fully understood — her recommendation that he should go to church. Indeed, Silas was so unaccustomed to talk beyond the brief questions and answers necessary for the transaction of his simple business that words did not easily come to him without the urgency of a distinct purpose.

But now, little Aaron, having become used to the weaver's awful presence, had advanced to his mother's side, and Silas, seeming to notice him for the first time, tried to return Dolly's signs of goodwill by offering the lad a bit of lard cake. Aaron shrank back a little, and rubbed his head against his mother's shoulder, but still thought the piece of cake worth the risk of putting his hand out for it.

"Oh, for shame, Aaron," said his mother, taking him on her lap, however; "why, you don't want cake again yet awhile. He's wonderful hearty," she went on, with a little sigh; "that he is, God knows. He's my youngest, and we spoil him sadly, for either me or the father must allays hev him in our sight — that we must."

She stroked Aaron's brown head, and thought it must do Master Marner good to see such a "pictur of a child." But

[1] Silas Marner was formerly a religious dissenter; that is, he belonged to a sect which had broken away from the Church of England. Dissenters worshiped in **chapels** rather than in churches.

Marner, on the other side of the hearth, saw the neat-featured rosy face as a mere dim round, with two dark spots in it.

"And he's got a voice like a bird — you wouldn't think," Dolly went on; "he can sing a Christmas carril as his father's taught him; and I take it for a token as he'll come to good, as he can learn the good tunes so quick. Come, Aaron, stan' up and sing the carril to Master Marner, come."

Aaron replied by rubbing his forehead against his mother's shoulder.

"Oh, that's naughty," said Dolly gently. "Stan' up, when mother tells you, and let me hold the cake till you've done."

Aaron was not indisposed to display his talents, even to an ogre, under protecting circumstances, and after a few more signs of coyness, consisting chiefly in rubbing the backs of his hands over his eyes, and then peeping between them at Master Marner to see if he looked anxious for the "carril," he at length allowed his head to be duly adjusted, and standing behind the table which let him appear above it only as far as his broad frill, so that he looked like a cherubic head untroubled with a body, he began with a clear chirp and in a melody that had the rhythm of an industrious hammer —

> "God rest you merry gentlemen,
> Let nothing you dismay,
> For Jesus Christ our Savior
> Was born on Christmas Day."

Dolly listened with a devout look, glancing at Marner in some confidence that this strain would help to allure him to church.

"That's Christmas music," she said, when Aaron had ended and had secured his piece of cake again. "There's no other music equil to the Christmas music — 'Hark, the erol angels sing.' And you may judge what it is at church, Master Marner, with the bassoon and the voices, as you can't help thinking you're got to a better place a'ready — for I wouldn't speak ill o' this world, seeing as Them put us in it as knows best; but what wi' the drink, and the quarreling and the bad illnesses, and the hard dying, as I've seen times and times, one's thankful to hear of a better. The boy sings pretty, don't he, Master Marner?"

"Yes," said Silas absently, "very pretty."

The Christmas carol, with its hammer-like rhythm, had fallen on his ears as strange music, quite unlike a hymn, and could have none of the effect Dolly contemplated. But he wanted to show her that he was grateful, and the only mode that occurred to him was to offer Aaron a bit more cake.

"Oh, no, thank you, Master Marner," said Dolly, holding down Aaron's willing hands. "We must be going home now. And so I wish you good-by, Master Marner; and if you ever feel anyways bad in your inside, as you can't fend for yourself, I'll come and clean up for you, and get you a bit o' victual, and willing. But I beg and pray of you to leave off weaving of a Sunday, for it's bad for soul and body — and the money as comes i' that way 'ull be a bad bed to lie down on at the last, if it doesn't fly away, nobody knows where, like the white frost. And you'll excuse me being that free with you, Master Marner, for I wish you well — I do. Make your bow, Aaron."

Silas said "Good-by, and thank you kindly," as he opened the door for Dolly, but he couldn't help feeling relieved when she was gone — relieved that he might weave again and moan at his ease. Her simple view of life and its comforts, by which she had tried to cheer him, was only like a report of unknown objects, which his imagination could not fashion.

The fountains of human love and of faith in a divine love had not yet been unlocked, and his soul was still the shrunken rivulet, with only this difference, that its little groove of sand was blocked up, and it wandered confusedly against dark obstruction.

And so, notwithstanding the honest persuasions of Mr. Macey and Dolly Winthrop, Silas spent his Christmas Day in loneliness, eating his meat in sadness of heart, though the meat had come to him as a neighborly present. In the morning he looked out on the black frost that seemed to press cruelly on every blade of grass, while the half-icy red pool shivered under the bitter wind; but toward evening the snow began to fall, and curtained from him even that dreary outlook, shutting him close up with his narrow grief. And he sat in his robbed home through the livelong evening, not caring to close his shutters or lock his door, pressing his head between his hands and moaning, till the cold grasped him and told him that his fire was gray.

Nobody in this world but himself knew that he was the same Silas Marner who had once loved his fellow with tender love, and trusted in an unseen goodness. Even to himself that past experience had become dim.

But in Raveloe village the bells rang merrily, and the church was fuller than all through the rest of the year, with red faces among the abundant dark green boughs — faces prepared for a longer service than usual by an odorous breakfast of toast and ale. Those green boughs, the hymn and anthem never heard but at Christmas — even the Athanasian Creed, which was discriminated from the others only as being longer and of exceptional virtue, since it was only read on rare occasions — brought a vague exulting sense, for which the grown men could as little have found words as the children, that something great and mysterious had been done for them in heaven above, and in earth below, which they were appropriating by their presence. And then the red faces made their way through the black biting frost to their own homes, feeling themselves free for the rest of the day to eat, drink, and be merry, and using that Christian freedom without diffidence.

At Squire Cass's family party that day nobody mentioned Dunstan — nobody was sorry for his absence, or feared it would be too long. The doctor and his wife, Uncle and Aunt Kimble, were there, and the annual Christmas talk was carried through without any omissions, rising to the climax of Mr. Kimble's experience when he walked the London hospitals thirty years back, together with striking professional anecdotes then gathered. Whereupon cards followed, with Aunt Kimble's annual failure to follow suit and Uncle Kimble's irascibility concerning the odd trick which was rarely explicable to him, when it was not on his side, without a general visitation of tricks to see that they were formed on sound principles; the whole being accompanied by a strong steaming odor of spirits-and-water.

But the party on Christmas Day, being a strictly family party, was not the preeminently brilliant celebration of the season at the Red House. It was the great dance on New Year's Eve that made the glory of Squire Cass's hospitality, as of his forefathers', time out of mind. This was the occasion when all the society of Raveloe and Tarley, whether old acquaintances separated by long rutty distances, or cooled acquaintances separated by misunderstandings concerning runaway calves, or acquaintances founded on intermittent condescension, counted on meeting and on comporting themselves with mutual appropriateness. This was the occasion on which fair dames who came on pillions sent their bandboxes before them, supplied with more than their evening costume; for the feast was not to end with a single evening, like a paltry town entertainment, where the whole supply of eatables is put on the table at once and bedding is scanty. The Red House was provisioned as if for a siege; and as for the spare feather beds ready to be laid on floors, they were as plentiful as might naturally be expected in a family that had killed its own geese for many generations.

Godfrey Cass was looking forward to this New Year's Eve with a foolish, reckless longing that made him half deaf to his importunate companion, Anxiety.

"Dunsey will be coming home soon; there will be a great blowup, and how will you bribe his spite to silence?" said Anxiety.

"Oh, he won't come home before New Year's Eve, perhaps," said Godfrey; "and I shall sit by Nancy then and dance with her, and get a kind look from her in spite of herself."

"But money is wanted in another quarter," said Anxiety, in a louder voice, "and how will you get it without selling your mother's diamond pin? And if you don't get it . . ."

"Well, but something may happen to make things easier. At any rate, there's one pleasure for me close at hand — Nancy is coming."

"Yes, and suppose your father should bring matters to a pass that will oblige you to decline marrying her — and to give your reasons?"

"Hold your tongue, and don't worry me. I can see Nancy's eyes, just as they will look at me, and feel her hand in mine already."

But Anxiety went on, though in noisy Christmas company, refusing to be utterly quieted even by much drinking.

CHAPTER XI

You have felt earlier in the story the force of George Eliot's realistic description. In this chapter you are to catch another typical glimpse of the times. The scene at the Red House, you will see for yourself, is in marked contrast to the scene at the Rainbow which was described so vividly in Chapters VI and VII. Notice especially, as you read this chapter, all the little details of difference which make everyday life of the early nineteenth century seem so strangely unlike that of today. Notice, too, the words new to you which stand for things of long ago and give a quaint, old-fashioned touch to the picture.

Some women, I grant, would not appear to advantage seated on a pillion, attired in a drab joseph [1] and a drab beaver bonnet, with a crown resembling a small stewpan; for a garment suggesting a coachman's greatcoat, cut out under an exiguity of cloth that would only allow of miniature capes, is not well adapted to conceal deficiencies of contour, nor is drab a color that will throw sallow cheeks into lively contrast. It was all the greater triumph to Miss Nancy Lammeter's beauty that she looked thoroughly bewitching in that costume, as, seated on the pillion behind her tall, erect father, she held one arm round him, and looked down, with open-eyed anxiety, at the treacherous snow-covered pools and puddles, which sent up formidable splashings of mud under the stamp of Dobbin's foot. A painter would, perhaps, have preferred her in those moments when she was free from self-consciousness; but certainly the bloom on her cheeks was at its highest point of contrast with the surrounding drab when she arrived at the door of the Red House, and saw Mr. Godfrey Cass ready to lift her from the pillion. She wished her sister Priscilla had come up at the same time behind the servant, for then she would have contrived that Mr. Godfrey should have lifted off Priscilla

[1] **joseph**: riding cloak.

first, and, in the meantime, she would have persuaded her father to go round to the horse block instead of alighting at the doorsteps. It was very painful when you had made it quite clear to a young man that you were determined not to marry him, however much he might wish it, that he would still continue to pay you marked attentions; besides, why didn't he always show the same attentions if he meant them sincerely, instead of being so strange as Mr. Godfrey Cass was, sometimes behaving as if he didn't want to speak to her, and taking no notice of her for weeks and weeks, and then, all of a sudden, almost making love again? Moreover, it was quite plain he had no real love for her, else he would not let people have *that* to say of him which they did say. Did he suppose that Miss Nancy Lammeter was to be won by any man, squire or no squire, who led a bad life? That was not what she had been used to see in her own father, who was the soberest and best man in that countryside, only a little hot and hasty now and then if things were not done to the minute.

All these thoughts rushed through Miss Nancy's mind, in their habitual succession, in the moments between her first sight of Mr. Godfrey Cass standing at the door and her own arrival there. Happily, the Squire came out, too, and gave a loud greeting to her father, so that, somehow, under cover of this noise, she seemed to find concealment of her confusion and neglect of any suitably formal behavior while she was being lifted from the pillion by strong arms which seemed to find her ridiculously small and light. And there was the best reason for hastening into the house at once, since the snow was beginning to fall again, threatening an unpleasant journey for such guests as were still on the road. These were a small minority; for already the afternoon was beginning to decline, and there would not be too much time for the ladies who came from a distance to attire themselves in readiness for the early tea which was to inspirit them for the dance.

There was a buzz of voices through the house as Miss Nancy entered, mingled with the scrape of a fiddle preluding in the kitchen; but the Lammeters were guests whose arrival had evidently been thought of so much that it had been watched for from the windows, for Mrs. Kimble, who did the honors at the Red House on these great occasions, came forward to meet Miss Nancy in the hall, and conduct her upstairs. Mrs. Kimble was the Squire's sister, as well as the doctor's wife — a double dignity, with which her diameter was in direct proportion; so that a journey upstairs being rather fatiguing to her, she did not oppose Miss Nancy's request to be allowed to find her way alone to the Blue Room, where the Miss Lammeters' bandboxes had been deposited on their arrival in the morning.

There was hardly a bedroom in the house where feminine compliments were not passing and feminine toilettes going forward, in various stages, in space made scanty by extra beds spread upon the floor; and Miss Nancy, as she entered the Blue Room, had to make her little formal curtsy to a group of six. On the one hand, there were ladies no less important than the two Miss Gunns, the wine merchant's daughters from Lytherly, dressed in the height of fashion, with the tightest skirts and the shortest waists, and gazed at by Miss Ladbrook (of the Old Pastures) with a shyness not unsustained by inward criticism. Partly, Miss Ladbrook felt that her own skirt must be regarded as unduly lax by the Miss Gunns, and, partly, that it was a pity the Miss Gunns did not show that judgment which she herself would show if she were in their place, by stopping a little on this side of the fashion. On the other hand, Mrs. Ladbrook was standing in skullcap and front, with her turban in her hand, curtsying and smiling blandly and saying, "After you, ma'am," to another lady in similar circumstances, who had politely offered the precedence at the looking glass.

But Miss Nancy had no sooner made her curtsy than an elderly lady came forward, whose full white muslin kerchief and mobcap round her curls of smooth gray hair were in daring contrast with the puffed yellow satins and topknotted caps of her neighbors. She approached Miss Nancy with much primness, and said, with a slow, treble suavity —

"Niece, I hope I see you well in health." Miss Nancy kissed her aunt's cheek dutifully, and answered, with the same sort of amiable primness, "Quite well, I thank you, aunt, and I hope I see you the same."

"Thank you, niece, I keep my health for the present. And how is my brother-in-law?"

These dutiful questions and answers were continued until it was ascertained in detail that the Lammeters were all as well as usual, and the Osgoods likewise; also that Niece Priscilla must certainly arrive shortly, and that traveling on pillions in snowy weather was unpleasant, though a joseph was a great protection. Then Nancy was formally introduced to her aunt's visitors, the Miss Gunns, as being the daughters of a mother known to *their* mother, though now for the first time induced to make a journey into these parts; and these ladies were so taken by surprise at finding such a lovely face and figure in an out-of-the-way country place that they began to feel some curiosity about the dress she would put on when she took off her joseph. Miss Nancy, whose thoughts were always conducted with the propriety and moderation conspicuous in her manners, remarked to herself that the Miss Gunns were rather hard-featured than otherwise, and that such very low dresses as they wore might have been attributed to vanity if their shoulders had been pretty, but that, being as they were, it was not reasonable to suppose that they showed their necks from a love of display, but rather from some obligation not inconsistent with sense and modesty. She felt convinced, as she opened her box, that this must be her Aunt Osgood's opinion, for Miss Nancy's mind resembled her aunt's to a degree that everybody said was surprising, considering the kinship was on Mr. Osgood's side; and though you might not have supposed it from the formality of their greeting, there was a devoted attachment and mutual admiration between aunt and niece. Even Miss Nancy's refusal of her cousin Gilbert Osgood (on the ground solely that he was her cousin), though it had grieved her aunt greatly, had not in the least cooled the preference which had determined her to leave Nancy several of her hereditary ornaments, let Gilbert's future wife be whom she might.

Three of the ladies quickly retired, but the Miss Gunns were quite content that Mrs. Osgood's inclination to remain with her niece gave them also a reason for staying to see the rustic beauty's toilette. And it was really a pleasure — from the first opening of the bandbox, where everything smelt of lavender and rose leaves, to the clasping of a small coral necklace that fitted closely round her little white neck. Everything belonging to Miss Nancy was of delicate purity and nattiness; not a crease was where it had no business to be, not a bit of her linen professed whiteness without fulfilling its profession; the very pins on her pincushion were stuck in after a pattern from which she was careful to allow no aberration; and as for her own person, it gave the same idea of perfect unvarying neatness as the body of a little bird. It is true that her light brown hair was cropped behind like a boy's, and was dressed in front in a number of flat rings, that lay quite away from her face; but there was no sort of coiffure that could make Miss Nancy's cheek and neck look otherwise than pretty; and when at last she stood complete in her silvery twilled silk, her lace tucker, her coral necklace, and coral eardrops, the Miss Gunns could see nothing to criticize except her hands, which bore the traces of buttermaking, cheese crushing, and even still coarser work. But Miss Nancy was not ashamed of that, for while she was dressing she narrated to her aunt how she and Priscilla had packed their boxes yesterday, because this morning was baking morning, and since they were leaving home, it was desirable to make a good supply of meat pies for the kitchen; and as she concluded this judicious remark, she turned to the Miss Gunns that she might not commit the rudeness of not including them in the conversation. The Miss Gunns smiled stiffly, and thought what a pity it was that these rich country people, who could afford to buy such good clothes (really Miss Nancy's lace and silk were very costly), should be brought up in utter ignorance and vulgarity. She actually said "mate" for "meat," "'appen" for "perhaps," and "'oss" for "horse," which, to young ladies living in good Lytherly society, who habitually said 'orse, even in domestic privacy, and only said 'appen on the right occasions, was necessarily shocking. Miss Nancy, indeed, had never been to any school higher than Dame Tedman's; her acquaintance with profane[1] literature hardly went beyond the rhymes she had worked in her large sampler under the lamb and the shepherdess; and, in order to balance an account, she was obliged to effect her subtraction by removing visible metallic shillings and sixpences from a visible metallic total. There is hardly a servant maid in these days who is not better informed than Miss Nancy; yet she had the essential attributes of a lady — high veracity, delicate honor in her dealings, deference to others, and refined personal habits — and lest these should not suffice to convince grammatical fair ones that her feelings can at all resemble theirs, I will add that she was slightly proud and exacting, and as constant in her affection toward a baseless opinion as toward an erring lover.

The anxiety about sister Priscilla, which had grown rather active by the time the coral necklace was clasped, was happily ended by the entrance of that cheerful-looking lady herself, with a face made blowsy by cold and damp. After the first questions and greetings, she turned to Nancy and surveyed her from head to foot — then wheeled her round to ascertain that the back view was equally faultless.

"What do you think o' *these* gowns, Aunt Osgood?" said Priscilla, while Nancy helped her to unrobe.

"Very handsome indeed, niece," said Mrs. Osgood, with a slight increase of formality. She always thought Niece Priscilla too rough.

"I'm obliged to have the same as Nancy, you know, for all I'm five years older, and it makes me look yallow; for she never *will* have anything without I have mine just like it, because she wants us to look like sisters. And I tell her folks 'ull think it's my weakness makes me fancy as I shall look pretty in what she looks pretty in. For I *am* ugly — there's no denying that; I feature my father's family. But, law! I don't mind, do you?" Priscilla here turned to the

[1] **profane:** as used here, nonreligious.

Miss Gunns, rattling on in too much preoccupation with the delight of talking to notice that her candor was not appreciated. "The pretty uns do for flycatchers — they keep the men off us. I've no opinion o' the men, Miss Gunn — I don't know what *you* have. And as for fretting and stewing about what *they*'ll think of you from morning till night, and making your life uneasy about what they're doing when they're out o' your sight — as I tell Nancy, it's a folly no woman need be guilty of, if she's got a good father and a good home; let her leave it to them as have got no fortin, and can't help themselves. As I say, Mr. Have-your-own-way is the best husband, and the only one I'd ever promise to obey. I know it isn't pleasant, when you've been used to living in a big way, and managing hogsheads and all that, to go and put your nose in by somebody else's fireside, or to sit down by yourself to a scrag or a knuckle; but, thank God! my father's a sober man and likely to live; and if you've got a man by the chimney corner, it doesn't matter if he's childish — the business needn't be broke up."

The delicate process of getting her narrow gown over her head without injury to her smooth curls obliged Miss Priscilla to pause in this rapid survey of life, and Mrs. Osgood seized the opportunity of rising and saying —

"Well, niece, you'll follow us. The Miss Gunns will like to go down."

"Sister," said Nancy, when they were alone, "you've offended the Miss Gunns, I'm sure."

"What have I done, child?" said Priscilla, in some alarm.

"Why, you asked them if they minded about being ugly — you're so very blunt."

"Law, did I? Well, it popped out; it's a mercy I said no more, for I'm a bad un to live with folks when they don't like the truth. But as for being ugly, look at me, child, in this silver-colored silk — I told you how it 'ud be — I look as yallow as a daffadil. Anybody 'ud say you wanted to make a mawkin [1] of me."

"No, Priscy, don't say so. I begged and prayed of you not to let us have this silk if you'd like another better. I was willing to have *your* choice, you know I was," said Nancy, in anxious self-vindication.

"Nonsense, child! you know you'd set your heart on this; and reason good, for you're the color o' cream. It 'ud be fine doings for you to dress yourself to suit *my* skin. What I find fault with is that notion o' yours as I must dress myself just like you. But you do as you like with me — you always did from when first you begun to walk. If you wanted to go the field's length, the field's length you'd go; and there was no whipping you, for you looked as prim and innicent as a daisy all the while."

"Priscy," said Nancy gently, as she fastened a coral necklace, exactly like her own, round Priscilla's neck, which was very far from being like her own, "I'm sure I'm willing to give way as far as is right, but who shouldn't dress alike if it isn't sisters? Would you have us go about looking as if we were no kin to one another — us that have got no mother and not another sister in the world? I'd do what was right, if I dressed in a gown dyed with cheese coloring; and I'd rather you'd choose, and let me wear what pleases you."

"There you go again! You'd come round to the same thing if one talked to you from Saturday night till Saturday morning. It'll be fine fun to see how you'll master your husband and never raise your voice above the singing o' the kettle all the while. I like to see the men mastered!"

"Don't talk *so*, Priscy," said Nancy.

[1] **mawkin**: scarecrow.

blushing. "You know I don't mean ever to be married."

"Oh, you never mean a fiddlestick's end!" said Priscilla, as she arranged her discarded dress, and closed her bandbox. "Who shall *I* have to work for when father's gone, if you are to go and take notions in your head and be an old maid, because some folks are no better than they should be? I haven't a bit o' patience with you — sitting on an addled egg forever, as if there was never a fresh un in the world. One old maid's enough out o' two sisters; and I shall do credit to a single life, for God A'mighty meant me for it. Come, we can go down now. I'm as ready as a mawkin *can* be — there's nothing a-wanting to frighten the crows, now I've got my eardroppers in."

As the two Miss Lammeters walked into the large parlor together, anyone who did not know the character of both might certainly have supposed that the reason why the square-shouldered, clumsy, high-featured Priscilla wore a dress the facsimile of her pretty sister's was either the mistaken vanity of the one, or the malicious contrivance of the other in order to set off her own great beauty. But the good-natured, self-forgetful cheeriness and common sense of Priscilla would soon have dissipated the one suspicion; and the modest calm of Nancy's speech and manners told clearly of a mind free from all disavowed devices.

Places of honor had been kept for the Miss Lammeters near the head of the principal tea table in the wainscoted parlor, now looking fresh and pleasant with handsome branches of holly, yew, and laurel, from the abundant growths of the old garden; and Nancy felt an inward flutter, that no firmness of purpose could prevent, when she saw Mr. Godfrey Cass advancing to lead her to a seat between himself and Mr. Crackenthorp, while Priscilla was called to the opposite side between her father and the Squire. It certainly did make some difference to Nancy that the lover she had given up was the young man of quite the highest consequence in the parish — at home in a venerable and unique parlor, which was the extremity of grandeur in her experience, a parlor where *she* might one day have been mistress, with the consciousness that she was spoken of as "Madame Cass," the Squire's wife. These circumstances exalted her inward drama in her own eyes, and deepened the emphasis with which she declared to herself that not the most dazzling rank should induce her to marry a man whose conduct showed him careless of his character, but that, "love once, love always," was the motto of a true and pure woman, and no man should ever have any right over her which would be a call on her to destroy the dried flowers that she treasured, and always would treasure, for Godfrey Cass's sake. And Nancy was capable of keeping her word to herself under very trying conditions. Nothing but a becoming blush betrayed the moving thoughts that urged themselves upon her as she accepted the seat next to Mr. Crackenthorp; for she was so instinctively neat and adroit in all her actions, and her pretty lips met each other with such quiet firmness, that it would have been difficult for her to appear agitated.

It was not the rector's practice to let a charming blush pass without an appropriate compliment. He was not in the least lofty or aristocratic, but simply a merry-eyed, small-featured, gray-haired man, with his chin propped by an ample, many-creased white neckcloth, which seemed to predominate over every other point in his person, and somehow to impress its peculiar character on his remarks; so that to have considered his amenities apart from his cravat would have been a severe, and perhaps a dangerous, effort of abstraction.

"Ha, Miss Nancy," he said, turning his head within his cravat, and smiling down pleasantly upon her, "when anybody pretends this has been a severe winter, I shall tell them I saw the roses blooming on New Year's Eve — eh, Godfrey, what do *you* say?"

Godfrey made no reply, and avoided looking at Nancy very markedly; for though these complimentary personalities were held to be in excellent taste in old-fashioned Raveloe society, reverent love has a politeness of its own which it teaches to men otherwise of small schooling. But the Squire was rather impatient at Godfrey's showing himself a dull spark in this way. By this advanced hour of the day, the Squire was always in higher spirits than we have seen him in at the breakfast table, and felt it quite pleasant to fulfill the hereditary duty of being noisily jovial and patronizing; the large silver snuffbox was in active service, and was offered without fail to all neighbors from time to time, however often they might have declined the favor. At present, the Squire had only given an express welcome to the heads of families as they appeared; but always as the evening deepened, his hospitality rayed out more widely, till he had tapped the youngest guests on the back and shown a peculiar fondness for their presence, in the full belief that they must feel their lives more happy by their belonging to a parish where there was such a hearty man as Squire Cass to invite them and wish them well. Even in this early stage of his jovial mood, it was natural that he should wish to supply his son's deficiencies by looking and speaking for him.

"Ay, ay," he began, offering his snuffbox to Mr. Lammeter, who for the second time bowed his head and waved his hand in stiff rejection of the offer, "us old fellows may wish ourselves young tonight, when we see the mistletoe bough in the White Parlor. It's true, most things are gone back'ard in these last thirty years — the country's going down since the old king[1] fell ill. But when I look at Miss Nancy here, I begin to think the lasses keep up their quality; ding me if I remember a sample to match her, not when I was a fine young fellow, and thought a deal about my pigtail. No offense to you, madam," he added, bending to Mrs. Crackenthorp, who sat by him, "I didn't know *you* when you were as young as Miss Nancy here."

Mrs. Crackenthorp — a small, blinking woman, who fidgeted incessantly with her lace, ribbons, and gold chain, turning her head about and making subdued noises, very much like a guinea pig that twitches its nose and soliloquizes in all company indiscriminately — now blinked and fidgeted toward the Squire, and said, "Oh, no — no offense."

This emphatic compliment of the Squire's to Nancy was felt by others besides Godfrey to have a diplomatic significance; and her father gave a slight additional erectness to his back as he looked across the table at her with complacent gravity. That grave and orderly senior was not going to bate a jot of his dignity by seeming elated at the notion of a match between his family and the Squire's; he was gratified by any honor paid to his daughter; but he must see an alteration in several ways before his consent would be vouchsafed. His spare but healthy person, and high-featured firm face, that looked as if it had never been flushed by excess, was in strong contrast, not only with the Squire's, but with the appearance of the Raveloe farmers generally — in accordance with a favorite saying of his own, that "breed was stronger than pasture."

[1] **old king:** George III, who fell ill in 1810.

"Miss Nancy's wonderful like what her mother was, though; isn't she, Kimble?" said the stout lady of that name, looking round for her husband.

But Doctor Kimble (country apothecaries in old days enjoyed that title without authority of diploma), being a thin and agile man, was flitting about the room with his hands in his pockets, making himself agreeable to his feminine patients, with medical impartiality, and being welcomed everywhere as a doctor by hereditary right — not one of those miserable apothecaries who canvass for practice in strange neighborhoods, and spend all their income in starving their one horse, but a man of substance, able to keep an extravagant table like the best of his patients. Time out of mind the Raveloe doctor had been a Kimble; Kimble was inherently a doctor's name; and it was difficult to contemplate firmly the melancholy fact that the actual Kimble had no son, so that his practice might one day be handed over to a successor, with the incongruous name of Taylor or Johnson. But in that case the wiser people in Raveloe would employ Dr. Blick, of Flitton — as less unnatural.

"Did you speak to me, my dear?" said the authentic doctor, coming quickly to his wife's side; but, as if foreseeing that she would be too much out of breath to repeat her remark, he went on immediately — "Ha, Miss Priscilla, the sight of you revives the taste of that superexcellent pork pie. I hope the batch isn't near an end."

"Yes, indeed, it is, doctor," said Priscilla; "but I'll answer for it the next shall be as good. My pork pies don't turn out well by chance."

"Not as your doctoring does, eh, Kimble? — because folks forget to take your physic, eh?" said the Squire who regarded physic and doctors as many loyal churchmen regard the church and the clergy — tasting a joke against them when he was in health, but impatiently eager for their aid when anything was the matter with him. He tapped his box, and looked round with a triumphant laugh.

"Ah, she has a quick wit, my friend Priscilla has," said the doctor, choosing to attribute the epigram to a lady rather than allow a brother-in-law that advantage over him. "She saves a little pepper to sprinkle over her talk — that's the reason why she never puts too much into her pies. There's my wife now, she never has an answer at her tongue's end; but if I offend her, she's sure to scarify my throat with black pepper the next day, or else give me the colic with watery greens. That's an awful tit-for-tat." Here the vivacious doctor made a pathetic grimace.

"Did you ever hear the like?" said Mrs. Kimble, laughing above her double chin with much good humor, aside to Mrs. Crackenthorp, who blinked and nodded, and amiably intended to smile, but the intention lost itself in small twitchings and noises.

"I suppose that's the sort of tit-for-tat adopted in your profession, Kimble, if you've a grudge against a patient," said the rector.

"Never do have a grudge against our patients," said Mr. Kimble, "except when they leave us; and then, you see, we haven't the chance of prescribing for 'em. Ha, Miss Nancy," he continued, suddenly skipping to Nancy's side, "you won't forget your promise? You're to save a dance for me, you know."

"Come, come, Kimble, don't you be too for'ard," said the Squire. "Give the young uns fair play. There's my son Godfrey'll be wanting to have a round with you if you run off with Miss Nancy. He's bespoke her for the first dance, I'll be bound. Eh, sir! what do you say?" he continued, throwing himself backward, and looking at Godfrey. "Haven't you asked Miss Nancy to open the dance with you?"

Godfrey, sorely uncomfortable under this significant insistence about Nancy, and afraid to think where it would end by the time his father had set his usual hospitable example of drinking before and after supper, saw no course open but to turn to Nancy and say, with as little awkwardness as possible —

"No, I've not asked her yet, but I hope she'll consent — if somebody else hasn't been before me."

"No, I've not engaged myself," said Nancy quietly, though blushingly. (If Mr. Godfrey founded any hopes on her consenting to dance with him he would soon be undeceived, but there was no need for her to be uncivil.)

"Then I hope you've no objections to dancing with me," said Godfrey, beginning to lose the sense that there was anything uncomfortable in this arrangement.

"No, no objections," said Nancy, in a cold tone.

"Ah, well, you're a lucky fellow, Godfrey," said Uncle Kimble; "but you're my godson, so I won't stand in your way. Else I'm not so very old, eh, my dear?" he went on, skipping to his wife's side again. "You wouldn't mind my having a second after you were gone — not if I cried a good deal first?"

"Come, come, take a cup o' tea and stop your tongue, do," said good-humored Mrs. Kimble, feeling some pride in a husband who must be regarded as so clever and amusing by the company generally. If he had only not been irritable at cards!

While safe, well-tested personalities were enlivening the tea in this way, the sound of the fiddle approaching within a distance at which it could be heard distinctly made the young people look at each other with sympathetic impatience for the end of the meal.

"Why, there's Solomon in the hall," said the Squire, "and playing my fav'rite tune, *I* believe — 'The Flaxen-headed Plowboy' — he's for giving us a hint as we aren't enough in a hurry to hear him play. Bob," he called out to his third long-legged son, who was at the other end of the room, "open the door, and tell Solomon to come in. He shall give us a tune here."

Bob obeyed, and Solomon walked in, fiddling as he walked, for he would on no account break off in the middle of a tune.

"Here, Solomon," said the Squire, with loud patronage. "Round here, my man. Ah, I knew it was 'The Flaxen-headed Plowboy'; there's no finer tune."

Solomon Macey, a small, hale old man with an abundant crop of long white hair reaching nearly to his shoulders, advanced to the indicated spot, bowing reverently while he fiddled, as much as to say that he respected the company, though he respected the keynote more. As soon as he had repeated the tune and lowered his fiddle, he bowed again to the Squire and the rector, and said, "I hope I see your honor and your reverence well, and wishing you health and long life and a happy New Year. And wishing the same to you, Mr. Lammeter, sir; and to the other gentlemen, and the madams, and the young lasses."

As Solomon uttered the last words, he bowed in all directions solicitously, lest he should be wanting in due respect. But thereupon he immediately began to prelude, and fell into the tune which he knew would be taken as a special compliment by Mr. Lammeter.

"Thank ye, Solomon, thank ye," said Mr. Lammeter, when the fiddle paused again. "That's 'Over the Hills and Far Away,' that is. My father used to say to me whenever we heard that tune, 'Ah, lad, *I* come from over the hills and far away.' There's a many tunes I don't make head or tail of; but that speaks to me like the blackbird's whistle. I suppose it's the name; there's a deal in the name of a tune."

But Solomon was already impatient to prelude again, and presently broke with much spirit into "Sir Roger de Coverley," at which there was a sound of chairs pushed back, and laughing voices.

"Ay, ay, Solomon, we know what that means," said the Squire, rising. "It's time to begin the dance, eh? Lead the way, then, and we'll all follow you."

So Solomon, holding his white head on one side and playing vigorously, marched forward at the head of the gay procession into the White Parlor, where the mistletoe bough was hung, and multitudinous tallow candles made rather a brilliant effect, gleaming from among the berried holly boughs, and reflected in the old-fashioned oval mirrors fastened in the panels of the white wainscot. A quaint procession! Old Solomon, in his seedy clothes and long white locks, seemed to be luring that decent company by the magic scream of his fiddle — luring discreet matrons in turban-shaped caps, nay, Mrs. Crackenthorp herself, the summit of whose perpendicular feather was on a level with the Squire's shoulder — luring fair lassies complacently conscious of very short waists and skirts blameless of front folds — luring burly fathers, in large variegated waistcoats, and ruddy sons, for the most part shy and sheepish, in short nether garments and very long coattails.

Already, Mr. Macey and a few other privileged villagers, who were allowed to be spectators on these great occasions, were seated on benches placed for them near the door; and great was the admiration and satisfaction in that quarter when the couples had formed themselves for the dance, and the Squire led off with Mrs. Crackenthorp, joining hands with the rector and Mrs. Osgood. That was as it should be — that was what everybody had been used to — and the charter of Raveloe seemed to be renewed by the ceremony. It was not thought of as an unbecoming levity for the old and middle-aged people to dance a little before sitting down to cards, but rather as part of their social duties. For what were these if not to be merry at appropriate times, interchanging visits and poultry with due frequency, paying each other old-established compliments in sound traditional phrases, passing well-tried personal jokes, urging your guests to eat and drink too much out of hospitality, and eating and drinking too much in your neighbor's house to show that you liked your cheer? And the parson naturally set an example in these social duties. For it would not have been possible for the Raveloe mind, without a peculiar revelation, to know that a clergyman should be a pale-faced memento of solemnities, instead of a reasonably faulty man, whose exclusive authority to read prayers and preach, to christen, marry, and bury you, necessarily coexisted with the right to sell you the ground to be buried in, and to take tithe[1] in kind; on which last point, of course, there was a little grumbling, but not to the extent of irreligion — not of deeper significance than the grumbling at the rain, which was by no means accompanied with a spirit of impious defiance, but with a desire that the prayer for fine weather might be read forthwith.

There was no reason, then, why the rector's dancing should not be received as part of the fitness of things quite as much as the Squire's, or why, on the other hand, Mr. Macey's official respect should restrain him from subjecting the parson's performance to that criticism with which minds of extraordinary acuteness must

[1] **tithe**: a tenth part of the produce and stock which in olden days was given to the church.

necessarily contemplate the doings of their fallible fellow men.

"The Squire's pretty springy, considering his weight," said Mr. Macey, "and he stamps uncommon well. But Mr. Lammeter beats 'em all for shapes; you see, he holds his head like a sodger, and he isn't so cushiony as most o' the oldish gentlefolks — they run fat in general; and he's got a fine leg. The parson's nimble enough, but he hasn't got much of a leg; it's a bit too thick down'ard, and his knees might be a bit nearer wi'out damage; but he might do worse, he might do worse. Though he hasn't that grand way o' waving his hand as the Squire has."

"Talk o' nimbleness, look at Mrs. Osgood," said Ben Winthrop, who was holding his son Aaron between his knees. "She trips along with her little steps, so as nobody can see how she goes — it's like as if she had little wheels to her feet. She doesn't look a day older nor last year; she's the finest-made woman as is, let the next be where she will."

"I don't heed how the women are made," said Mr. Macey, with some contempt. "They wear nayther coat nor breeches; you can't make much out o' their shapes."

"Fayder," said Aaron, whose feet were busy beating out the tune, "how does that big cock's-feather stick in Mrs. Crackenthorp's yead? Is there a little hole for it, like in my shuttlecock?"

"Hush, lad, hush; that's the way the ladies dress theirselves, that is," said the father; adding, however, in an undertone to Mr. Macey, "It does make her look funny, though — partly like a short-necked bottle wi' a long quill in it. Hey, by jingo, there's the young Squire leading off now, wi' Miss Nancy for partners. There's a lass for you! — like a pink-and-white posy — there's nobody 'ud think as anybody could be so pritty. I shouldn't wonder if she's Madame Cass someday, arter all — and nobody more rightfuller, for they'd make a fine match. You can find nothing against Master Godfrey's shapes, Macey, *I'll* bet a penny."

Mr. Macey screwed up his mouth, leaned his head further on one side, and twirled his thumbs with a presto movement as his eyes followed Godfrey up the dance. At last he summed up his opinion.

"Pretty well down'ard, but a bit too round i' the shoulder blades. And as for them coats as he gets from the Flitton tailor, they're a poor cut to pay double money for."

"Ah, Mr. Macey, you and me are two folks," said Ben, slightly indignant at this carping. "When I've got a pot o' good ale, I like to swaller it, and do my inside good, i'stead o' smelling and staring at it to see if I can't find faut wi' the brewing. I should like you to pick me out a finer-limbed young fellow nor Master Godfrey — one as 'ud knock you down easier, or's more pleasanter-looksed when he's piert and merry."

"Tchuh!" said Mr. Macey, provoked to increased severity, "he isn't come to his right color yet; he's partly like a slack-baked pie. And I doubt he's got a soft place in his head, else why should he be turned round the finger by that offal Dunsey as nobody's seen o' late, and let him kill that fine hunting hoss as was the talk o' the country? And one while he was allays after Miss Nancy, and then it all went off again, like a smell o' hot porridge, as I may say. That wasn't my way when *I* went a-coorting."

"Ah, but mayhap Miss Nancy hung off, like, and your lass didn't," said Ben.

"I should say she didn't," said Mr. Macey, significantly. "Before I said 'sniff,' I took care to know as she'd say 'snaff,' and pretty quick, too. I wasn't a-going to open *my* mouth, like a dog at a fly, and snap it to again, wi' nothing to swaller."

"Well, I think Miss Nancy's a-coming round again," said Ben, "for Master Godfrey doesn't look so downhearted tonight. And I see he's for taking her away to sit down, now they're at the end o' the dance: that looks like sweethearting, that does."

The reason why Godfrey and Nancy had left the dance was not so tender as Ben imagined. In the close press of couples a slight accident had happened to Nancy's dress, which, while it was short enough to show her neat ankle in front, was long enough behind to be caught under the stately stamp of the Squire's foot, so as to rend certain stitches at the waist, and cause much sisterly agitation in Priscilla's mind, as well as serious concern in Nancy's. One's thoughts may be much occupied with love struggles, but hardly so as to be insensible to a disorder in the general framework of things. Nancy had no sooner completed her duty in the figure they were dancing than she said to Godfrey, with a deep blush, that she must go and sit down till Priscilla could come to her; for the sisters had already exchanged a short whisper and an open-eyed glance full of meaning. No reason less urgent than this could have prevailed on Nancy to give Godfrey this opportunity of sitting apart with her. As for Godfrey, he was feeling so happy and oblivious under the long charm of the country-dance with Nancy, that he got rather bold on the strength of her confusion, and was capable of leading her straight away, without leave asked, into the adjoining small parlor, where the card tables were set.

"Oh, no, thank you," said Nancy coldly, as soon as she perceived where he was going, "not in there. I'll wait here till Priscilla's ready to come to me. I'm sorry to bring you out of the dance and make myself troublesome."

"Why, you'll be more comfortable here by yourself," said the artful Godfrey; "I'll leave you here till your sister can come." He spoke in an indifferent tone.

That was an agreeable proposition, and just what Nancy desired; why, then, was she a little hurt that Mr. Godfrey should make it? They entered, and she seated herself on a chair against one of the card tables, as the stiffest and most unapproachable position she could choose.

"Thank you, sir," she said immediately. "I needn't give you any more trouble. I'm sorry you've had such an unlucky partner."

"That's very ill-natured of you," said Godfrey, standing by her without any sign of intended departure, "to be sorry you've danced with me."

"Oh, no, sir, I don't mean to say what's ill-natured at all," said Nancy, looking distractingly prim and pretty. "When gentlemen have so many pleasures, one dance can matter but very little."

"You know that isn't true. You know one dance with you matters more to me than all the other pleasures in the world."

It was a long, long while since Godfrey had said anything so direct as that, and Nancy was startled. But her instinctive dignity and repugnance to any show of emotion made her sit perfectly still, and only throw a little more decision into her voice as she said —

"No, indeed, Mr. Godfrey, that's not known to me, and I have very good reasons for thinking different. But if it's true, I don't wish to hear it."

"Would you never forgive me, then, Nancy — never think well of me, let what would happen — would you never think the present made amends for the past? Not if I turned a good fellow, and gave up everything you didn't like?"

Godfrey was half conscious that this sudden opportunity of speaking to Nancy alone had driven him beside himself; but blind feeling had got the mastery of his tongue. Nancy really felt much agitated by the possibility Godfrey's words suggested, but this very pressure of emotion that she was in danger of finding too strong for her roused all her power of self-command.

"I should be glad to see a good change in anybody, Mr. Godfrey," she answered, with the slightest discernible difference of tone, "but it 'ud be better if no change was wanted."

"You're very hardhearted, Nancy," said Godfrey pettishly. "You might encourage me to be a better fellow. I'm very miserable — but you've no feeling."

"I think those have the least feeling that act wrong to begin with," said Nancy, sending out a flash in spite of herself. Godfrey was delighted with that little flash, and would have liked to go on and make her quarrel with him; Nancy was so exasperatingly quiet and firm. But she was not indifferent to him *yet*.

The entrance of Priscilla, bustling forward and saying, "Dear heart alive, child, let us look at this gown," cut off Godfrey's hopes of a quarrel.

"I suppose I must go now," he said to Priscilla.

"It's no matter to me whether you go or stay," said that frank lady, searching for something in her pocket, with a preoccupied brow.

"Do *you* want me to go?" said Godfrey, looking at Nancy, who was now standing up by Priscilla's order.

"As you like," said Nancy, trying to recover all her former coldness, and looking down carefully at the hem of her gown.

"Then I like to stay," said Godfrey, with a reckless determination to get as much of this joy as he could tonight, and think nothing of the morrow.

CHAPTER XII

In this chapter you will begin to discover that the quiet story of *Silas Marner* gains suddenly in dramatic intensity. Notice as you read on through the next three chapters how fitting and well timed the events seem, as though a mischievous fate had deliberately planned that this and that should happen at the same time, and thus interweave the destinies of people far apart. Notice, too, what the events foretell. Unless you are alert to all such delicate suggestions implied by the events in the story, you will not appreciate the story to the full.

While Godfrey Cass was taking draughts of forgetfulness from the sweet presence of Nancy, willingly losing all sense of that hidden bond which at other moments galled and fretted him so as to mingle irritation with the very sunshine, Godfrey's wife was walking with slow uncertain steps through the snow-covered Raveloe lanes, carrying her child in her arms.

This journey on New Year's Eve was a premeditated act of vengeance which she had kept in her heart ever since Godfrey, in a fit of passion, had told her he would sooner die than acknowledge her as his wife. There would be a great party at the Red House on New Year's Eve, she knew; her husband would be smiling and smiled upon, hiding *her* existence in the darkest corner of his heart. But she would mar his pleasure; she would go in her dingy rags, with her faded face, once as handsome as the best, with her little child that had its father's hair and eyes, and disclose herself to the Squire as his eldest son's wife. It is seldom that the miserable can help regarding their misery as a wrong inflicted by those who are less miserable. Molly knew that the cause of her dingy rags was not her husband's neglect, but the demon Opium to whom she was enslaved, body and soul, except in the lingering mother's tenderness that refused to give him her hungry child. She knew this well; and yet, in the moments of wretched unbenumbed consciousness, the sense of her want and degradation transformed itself continually into bitterness toward Godfrey. *He* was well off; and if she had her rights she would be well off, too. The belief that he repented his marriage, and suffered from it, only aggravated her vindictiveness. Just and self-reproving thoughts do not come to us too thickly, even in the purest air, and with the best lessons of heaven and earth; how should those white-winged delicate messengers make their way to Molly's poisoned chamber, inhabited by no higher memories than those of a barmaid's paradise of pink ribbons and gentlemen's jokes?

She had set out at an early hour, but had lingered on the road, inclined by her indolence to believe that if she waited under a warm shed the snow would cease to fall. She had waited longer than she knew, and now that she found herself belated in the snow-hidden ruggedness of the long lanes, even the animation of a vindictive purpose could not keep her spirit from failing. It was seven o'clock, and by this time she was not very far from Raveloe, but she was not familiar enough with those monotonous lanes to know how near she was to her journey's end. She needed comfort, and she knew but one comforter — the familiar demon in her bosom; but she hesitated a moment, after drawing out the black remnant, before she raised it to her lips. In that moment the mother's love pleaded for painful consciousness rather than oblivion — pleaded to be left in aching weariness, rather than to have the encircling arms benumbed so that they could not feel the dear burden. In another moment Molly had flung something away, but it was not the black remnant — it was an empty phial. And she walked on again under the breaking cloud, from which there came now and then the light of a quickly veiled star, for a freezing wind had sprung up since the snowing had ceased. But she walked always more and more drowsily, and clutched more and more automatically the sleeping child at her bosom.

Slowly the demon was working his will, and cold and weariness were his helpers. Soon she felt nothing but a supreme immediate longing that curtained off all futurity — the longing to lie down and sleep. She had arrived at a spot where her footsteps were no longer checked by a hedgerow, and she had wandered vaguely, unable to distinguish any objects, notwithstanding the wide whiteness around her, and the growing starlight. She sank down against a straggling furze bush, an easy pillow enough; and the bed of snow, too, was soft. She did not feel that the bed was cold, and did not heed whether the child would wake and cry for her. But her arms had not yet relaxed their instinctive clutch; and the little one slumbered on as gently as if it had been rocked in a lace-trimmed cradle.

But the complete torpor came at last: the fingers lost their tension, the arms unbent; then the little head fell away from the bosom, and the blue eyes opened wide on the cold starlight. At first there was a little peevish cry of "mammy," and an effort to regain the pillowing arm and bosom; but mammy's ear was deaf, and the pillow seemed to be slipping away backward. Suddenly, as the child rolled downward on its mother's knees, all wet with snow, its eyes were caught by a bright glancing light on the white ground, and, with the ready transition of infancy, it was immediately absorbed in watching the bright living thing running toward it, yet never arriving. That bright living thing must be caught; and in an instant the child had slipped on all fours, and held out one little hand to catch the gleam. But the gleam would not be caught in that way, and now the head was held up to see where the cunning gleam came from. It came from a very bright place; and the little one, rising on its legs, toddled through the snow, the old grimy shawl in which it was wrapped trailing behind it, and the queer little bonnet dangling at its back — toddled on to the open door of Silas Marner's cottage, and right up to the warm hearth, where there was a bright fire of logs and sticks, which had thoroughly warmed the old sack (Silas's greatcoat) spread out on the bricks to dry. The little one, accustomed to be left to itself for long hours without notice from its mother, squatted down on the sack, and spread its tiny hands toward the blaze, in perfect contentment, gurgling and making many inarticulate communications to the cheerful fire, like a new-hatched gosling beginning to find itself comfortable. But presently the warmth had a lulling effect, and the little golden head sank down on the old sack, and the blue eyes were veiled by their delicate, half-transparent lids.

But where was Silas Marner while this strange visitor had come to his hearth? He was in the cottage, but he did not see the child. During the last few weeks, since he had lost his money, he had contracted the habit of opening his door and looking out from time to time, as if he thought that his money might be somehow coming back to him, or that some trace, some news of it, might be mysteriously on the road, and be caught by the listening ear or the straining eye. It was chiefly at night, when he was not occupied in his loom, that he fell into this repetition of an act for which he could have assigned no definite purpose, and which can hardly be understood except by those who have undergone a bewildering separation from a supremely lovely object. In the evening twilight, and later whenever the night was not dark, Silas looked out on that narrow prospect round the stone pits, listening and gazing, not with hope, but with mere yearning and unrest.

This morning he had been told by some of his neighbors that it was New Year's Eve, and that he must sit up and hear the old year rung out and the new rung in, because that was good luck, and might bring his money back again. This was only a friendly Raveloe way of jesting with the half-crazy oddities of a miser, but it had perhaps helped to throw Silas into a more than usually excited state. Since the oncoming of twilight he had opened his door again and again, though only to shut it immediately at seeing all distance veiled by the falling snow. But the last time he opened it the snow had ceased, and the clouds were parting here and there. He stood and listened, and gazed for a long while — there was really something on the road coming toward him then, but he caught no sign of it; and the stillness and the wide trackless snow seemed to narrow his solitude, and touched his yearning with the chill of despair. He went in again, and put his right hand on the latch of the door to close it — but he did not close it; he was arrested, as he had been already since his loss, by the invisible wand of catalepsy,[1] and stood like a graven image, with wide but sightless eyes, holding open his door, powerless to resist either the good or evil that might enter there.

When Marner's sensibility returned, he continued the action which had been arrested, and closed his door, unaware of the chasm in his consciousness, unaware of any intermediate change, except that the light had grown dim, and that he was chilled and faint. He thought he had been too long standing at the door and looking out. Turning toward the hearth where the two logs had fallen apart, and sent forth only a red uncertain glimmer, he seated himself on his fireside chair, and was stooping to push his logs together, when, to his blurred vision, it seemed as if there

[1] **catalepsy:** the trancelike state to which Silas Marner was subject.

were gold on the floor in front of the hearth. Gold! — his own gold — brought back to him as mysteriously as it had been taken away! He felt his heart begin to beat violently, and for a few moments he was unable to stretch out his hand and grasp the restored treasure. The heap of gold seemed to glow and get larger beneath his agitated gaze. He leaned forward at last, and stretched forth his hand; but instead of the hard coin with the familiar resisting outline, his fingers encountered soft warm curls. In utter amazement, Silas fell on his knees and bent his head low to examine the marvel; it was a sleeping child — a round, fair thing, with soft yellow rings all over its head. Could this be his little sister come back to him in a dream — his little sister whom he had carried about in his arms for a year before she died, when he was a small boy without shoes or stockings? That was the first thought that darted across Silas's blank wonderment. *Was* it a dream? He rose to his feet again, pushed his logs together, and, throwing on some dried leaves and sticks, raised a flame; but the flame did not disperse the vision — it only lit up more distinctly the little round form of the child and its shabby clothing. It was very much like his little sister. Silas sank into his chair powerless, under the double presence of an inexplicable surprise and a hurrying influx of memories. How and when had the child come in without his knowledge? He had never been beyond the door. But along with that question, and almost thrusting it away, there was a vision of the old home and the old streets leading to Lantern Yard — and within that vision another, of the thoughts which had been present with him in those far-off scenes. The thoughts were strange to him now, like old friendships impossible to revive; and yet he had a dreamy feeling that this child was somehow a message come to him from that far-off life; it stirred fibers that had never been moved in Raveloe — old quiverings of tenderness — old impressions of awe at the presentiment of some Power presiding over his life; for his imagination had not yet extricated itself from the sense of mystery in the child's sudden presence, and had formed no conjectures of ordinary natural means by which the event could have been brought about.

But there was a cry on the hearth; the child had awaked, and Marner stooped to lift it on his knee. It clung round his neck, and burst louder and louder into that mingling of inarticulate cries with "mammy" by which little children express the bewilderment of waking. Silas pressed it to him, and almost unconsciously uttered sounds of hushing tenderness, while he bethought himself that some of his porridge, which had got cold by the dying fire, would do to feed the child with if it were only warmed up a little.

He had plenty to do through the next hour. The porridge, sweetened with some dry brown sugar from an old store which he had refrained from using for himself, stopped the cries of the little one, and made her lift her blue eyes with a wide quiet gaze at Silas, as he put the spoon into her mouth. Presently she slipped from his knee and began to toddle about, but with a pretty stagger that made Silas jump up and follow her lest she should fall against anything that would hurt her. But she only fell in a sitting posture on the ground, and began to pull at her boots, looking up at him with a crying face as if the boots hurt her. He took her on his knee again, but it was some time before it occurred to Silas's dull bachelor mind that the wet boots were the grievance, pressing on her warm ankles. He got them off with difficulty, and baby was at once happily occupied with the primary mystery of her own toes, inviting Silas, with much chuckling, to consider the mystery, too. But the wet boots had at last suggested to Silas that the child had been walking on the snow, and this roused him from his entire oblivion of any ordinary means by which it could have entered or been brought into his house. Under the prompting of this new idea, and without waiting to form conjectures, he raised the child in his arms, and went to the door. As soon as he had opened it, there was the cry of "mammy" again, which Silas had not heard since the child's first hungry waking. Bending forward, he could just discern the marks made by the little feet on the virgin snow, and he followed their track to the furze bushes. "Mammy!" the little one cried again and again, stretching itself forward so as almost to escape from Silas's arms, before he himself was aware that there was something more than the bush before him — that there was a human body, with the head sunk low in the furze, and half-covered with the shaken snow.

CHAPTER XIII

It was after the early suppertime at the Red House, and the entertainment was in that stage when bashfulness itself had passed into easy jollity, when gentlemen, conscious of unusual accomplishments, could at length be prevailed on to dance a hornpipe, and when the Squire preferred talking loudly, scattering snuff, and patting his visitors' backs, to sitting longer at the whist table — a choice exasperating to Uncle Kimble, who, being always volatile in sober business hours, became intense and bitter over cards and brandy, shuffled before his adversary's deal with a glare of suspicion, and turned up a mean trump card with an air of inexpressible disgust, as if in a world where such things could happen one might as well enter on a course of reckless profligacy. When the evening had advanced to this pitch of freedom and enjoyment, it was usual for the servants, the heavy duties of supper being well over, to get their share of amusement by coming to look on at the dancing; so that the back regions of the house were left in solitude.

There were two doors by which the White Parlor was entered from the hall, and they were both standing open for the sake of air; but the lower one was crowded with the servants and villagers, and only the upper doorway was left free. Bob Cass was figuring in a hornpipe, and his father, very proud of his lithe son, whom he repeatedly declared to be just like himself in his young days, in a tone that implied this to be the very highest stamp of juvenile merit, was the center of a group who had placed themselves opposite the performer, not far from the upper door. Godfrey was standing a little way off, not to admire his brother's dancing, but to keep sight of Nancy, who was seated in the group, near her father. He stood aloof, because he wished to avoid suggesting himself as a subject for the Squire's fatherly jokes in connection with matrimony and Miss Nancy Lammeter's beauty, which were likely to become more and more explicit. But he had the prospect of dancing with her again when the hornpipe was concluded, and in the meanwhile it was very pleasant to get long glances at her quite unobserved.

But when Godfrey was lifting his eyes from one of those long glances they encountered an object as startling to him at that moment as if it had been an apparition from the dead. It *was* an apparition from that hidden life which lies, like a dark by-street, behind the goodly ornamented façade that meets the sunlight and the gaze of respectable admirers. It was his own child, carried in Silas Marner's arms. That was his instantaneous impression, unaccompanied by doubt, though he had not seen the child for months past; and when the hope was rising that he might possibly be mistaken, Mr. Crackenthorp and Mr. Lammeter had already advanced to Silas in astonishment at this strange advent. Godfrey joined them immediately, unable to rest without hearing every word — trying to control himself, but conscious that if anyone noticed him they must see that he was white-lipped and trembling.

But now all eyes at that end of the room were bent on Silas Marner; the Squire himself had risen, and asked angrily, "How's this? — what's this? — what do you do coming in here in this way?"

"I'm come for the doctor — I want the doctor," Silas had said, in the first moment, to Mr. Crackenthorp.

"Why, what's the matter, Marner?" said the rector. "The doctor's here; but say quietly what you want him for."

"It's a woman," said Silas, speaking low, and half breathlessly, just as Godfrey came up. "She's dead, I think — dead in the snow at the stone pits — not far from my door."

Godfrey felt a great throb; there was one terror in his mind at that moment; it was, that the woman might *not* be dead. That was an evil terror — an ugly inmate to have found a nestling place in Godfrey's kindly disposition; but no disposition is a security from evil wishes to a man whose happiness hangs on duplicity.

"Hush, hush!" said Mr. Crackenthorp. "Go out into the hall there. I'll fetch the doctor to you. Found a woman in the snow — and thinks she's dead," he added, speaking low to the Squire. "Better say as little about it as possible; it will shock the ladies. Just tell them a poor woman is ill from cold and hunger. I'll go and fetch Kimble."

By this time, however, the ladies had pressed forward, curious to know what could have brought the solitary linen weaver there under such strange circumstances, and interested in the pretty child, who, half alarmed and half attracted by the brightness and the numerous company, now frowned and hid her face, now lifted up her head again and looked round placably, until a touch or a coaxing word brought back the frown, and made her bury her face with new determination.

"What child is it?" said several ladies at once, and, among the rest, Nancy Lammeter, addressing Godfrey.

"I don't know — some poor woman's who has been found in the snow, I believe," was the answer Godfrey wrung from himself with a terrible effort. ("After all, *am* I certain?" he hastened to add, in anticipation of his own conscience.)

"Why, you'd better leave the child here, then, Master Marner," said good-natured Mrs. Kimble, hesitating, however, to take those dingy clothes into contact with her own ornamented satin bodice. "I'll tell one o' the girls to fetch it."

"No — no — I can't part with it, I can't let it go," said Silas abruptly. "It's come to me — I've a right to keep it."

The proposition to take the child from him had come to Silas quite unexpectedly, and his speech, uttered under a strong sudden impulse, was almost like a revelation to himself; a minute before he had no distinct intention about the child.

"Did you ever hear the like?" said Mrs. Kimble, in mild surprise, to her neighbor.

"Now, ladies, I must trouble you to stand aside," said Mr. Kimble, coming from the cardroom, in some bitterness at the interruption, but drilled by the long habit of his profession into obedience to unpleasant calls, even when he was hardly sober.

"It's a nasty business turning out now, eh, Kimble?" said the Squire. "He might ha' gone for your young fellow — the 'prentice, there — what's his name?"

"Might? ay — what's the use of talking about might?" growled Uncle Kimble, hastening out with Marner, and followed by Mr. Crackenthorp and Godfrey. "Get me a pair of thick boots, Godfrey, will you? And stay, let somebody run to Winthrop's and fetch Dolly — she's the best woman to get. Ben was here himself before supper; is he gone?"

"Yes, sir, I met him," said Marner; "but I couldn't stop to tell him anything, only I said I was going for the doctor, and he said the doctor was at the Squire's. And I made haste and ran, and there was nobody to be seen at the back o' the house, and so I went in to where the company was."

The child, no longer distracted by the bright light and the smiling women's faces, began to cry and call for "mammy," though always clinging to Marner, who had apparently won her thorough confidence. Godfrey had come back with the boots, and felt the cry as if some fiber were drawn tight within him.

"I'll go," he said hastily, eager for some movement; "I'll go and fetch the woman — Mrs. Winthrop."

"Oh, pooh, — send somebody else," said Uncle Kimble, hurrying away with Marner.

"You'll let me know if I can be of any use, Kimble," said Mr. Crackenthorp. But the doctor was out of hearing.

Godfrey, too, had disappeared; he was gone to snatch his hat and coat, having just reflection enough to remember that he must not look like a madman; but he rushed out of the house into the snow without heeding his thin shoes.

In a few minutes he was on his rapid way to the stone pits by the side of Dolly, who, though feeling that she was entirely in her place in encountering cold and snow on an errand of mercy, was much concerned at a young gentleman's getting his feet wet under a like impulse.

"You'd a deal better go back, sir," said Dolly, with respectful compassion. "You've no call to catch cold; and I'd ask you if you'd be so good as tell my husband to come, on your way back — he's at the Rainbow, I doubt — if you found him any way sober enough to be o' use. Or else, there's Mrs. Snell 'ud happen send the boy up to fetch and carry, for there may be things wanted from the doctor's."

"No, I'll stay, now I'm once out — I'll stay outside here," said Godfrey, when they came opposite Marner's cottage. "You can come and tell me if I can do anything."

"Well, sir, you're very good; you've a tender heart," said Dolly, going to the door.

Godfrey was too painfully preoccupied to feel a twinge of self-reproach at this undeserved praise. He walked up and down, unconscious that he was plunging ankle-deep in snow, unconscious of everything but trembling suspense about what was going on in the cottage, and the effect of each alternative on his future lot. No, not quite unconscious of everything else. Deeper down, and half smothered by passionate desire and dread, there was the sense that he ought not to be waiting on these alternatives; that he ought to accept the consequences of his deeds, own the miserable wife, and fulfill the claims of the helpless child. But he had not moral courage enough to contemplate that active renunciation of Nancy as possible for him; he had only conscience and heart enough to make him forever uneasy under the weakness that forbade the renunciation. And at this moment his mind leaped away from all restraint toward the sudden prospect of deliverance from his long bondage.

"Is she dead?" said the voice that predominated over every other within him. "If she is, I may marry Nancy; and then I shall be a good fellow in future, and have no secrets, and the child — shall be taken care of somehow." But across that vision came the other possibility — "She may live, and then it's all up with me."

Godfrey never knew how long it was before the door of the cottage opened and Mr. Kimble came out. He went forward to meet his uncle, prepared to suppress the agitation he must feel, whatever news he was to hear.

"I waited for you, as I'd come so far," he said, speaking first.

"Pooh, it was nonsense for you to come out. Why didn't you send one of the men? There's nothing to be done. She's dead — has been dead for hours, I should say."

"What sort of woman is she?" said Godfrey, feeling the blood rush to his face.

"A young woman, but emaciated, with long black hair. Some vagrant — quite in rags. She's got a wedding ring on, however. They must fetch her away to the workhouse tomorrow. Come, come along."

"I want to look at her," said Godfrey. "I think I saw such a woman yesterday. I'll overtake you in a minute or two."

Mr. Kimble went on, and Godfrey turned back to the cottage. He cast only one glance at the dead face on the pillow, which Dolly had smoothed with decent care; but he remembered that last look at his unhappy hated wife so well that at the end of sixteen years every line in the worn face was present to him when he told the full story of this night.

He turned immediately toward the hearth where Silas Marner sat lulling the child. She was perfectly quiet now, but not asleep — only soothed by sweet porridge and warmth into that wide-gazing calm which makes us older human beings, with our inward turmoil, feel a certain awe in the presence of a little child, such as we feel before some quiet majesty or beauty in the earth or sky — before a steady-glowing planet, or a full-flowered eglantine, or the bending trees over a silent pathway. The wide-open blue eyes looked up at Godfrey's without any uneasiness or sign of recognition; the child could make no visible audible claim on its father; and the father felt a strange mixture of feelings, a conflict of regret and joy, that the pulse of that little heart had no response for the half-jealous yearning in his own, when the blue eyes turned away from him slowly, and fixed themselves on the weaver's queer face, which was bent low down to look at them, while the small hand began to pull Marner's withered cheek with loving disfiguration.

"You'll take the child to the parish tomorrow?" asked Godfrey, speaking as indifferently as he could.

"Who says so?" said Marner sharply. "Will they make me take her?"

"Why, you wouldn't like to keep her, should you — an old bachelor like you?"

"Till anybody shows they've a right to take her away from me," said Marner. "The mother's dead, and I reckon it's got no father; it's a lone thing — and I'm a lone thing. My money's gone, I don't know where — and this is come from I don't know where. I know nothing — I'm partly mazed."

"Poor little thing!" said Godfrey. "Let me give something toward finding it clothes."

He had put his hand in his pocket and found half a guinea, and, thrusting it into Silas's hand, he hurried out of the cottage to overtake Mr. Kimble.

"Ah, I see it's not the same woman I saw," he said, as he came up. "It's a pretty little child; the old fellow seems to want to keep it; that's strange for a miser like him. But I gave him a trifle to help him out; the parish isn't likely to quarrel with him for the right to keep the child."

"No; but I've seen the time when I might have quarreled with him for it myself. It's too late now, though. If the child ran into the fire, your aunt's too fat to overtake it; she could only sit and grunt like an alarmed sow. But what a fool you are, Godfrey, to come out in your dancing shoes and stockings in this way — and you one of the beaux of the evening, and at your own house! What do you mean by such freaks, young fellow? Has Miss Nancy been cruel, and do you want to spite her by spoiling your pumps?"

"Oh, everything has been disagreeable tonight. I was tired to death of jigging and gallanting, and that bother about the hornpipes. And I'd got to dance with the other Miss Gunn," said Godfrey, glad of the subterfuge his uncle had suggested to him.

The prevarication and white lies which a mind that keeps itself ambitiously pure is as uneasy under as a great artist under the false touches that no eye detects but his own, are worn as lightly as mere trimmings when once the actions have become a lie.

Godfrey reappeared in the White Parlor with dry feet, and, since the truth must be told, with a sense of relief and gladness that was too strong for painful thoughts to struggle with. For could he not venture now, whenever opportunity offered, to say the tenderest things to Nancy Lammeter — to promise her and himself that he would always be just what she would desire to see him? There was no danger that his dead wife would be recognized; those were not days of active inquiry and wide report; and as for the registry of their marriage, that was a long way off, buried in unturned pages, away from everyone's interest but his own. Dunsey might betray him if he came back; but Dunsey might be won to silence.

And when events turn out so much better for a man than he has had reason to dread, is it not a proof that his conduct has been less foolish and blameworthy than it might otherwise have appeared? When we are treated well, we naturally begin to think that we are not altogether unmeritorious, and that it is only just we should treat ourselves well, and not mar our own good fortune. Where, after all, would be the use of his confessing the past to Nancy Lammeter, and throwing away his happiness? — nay, hers? for he felt some confidence that she loved him. As for the child, he would see that it was cared for; he would never forsake it; he would do everything but own it. Perhaps it would be just as happy in life without being owned by its father, seeing that nobody could tell how things would turn out, and that — is there any other reason wanted? — well, then, that the father would be much happier without owning the child.

CHAPTER XIV

There was a pauper's burial that week in Raveloe, and up Kench Yard at Batherley it was known that the dark-haired woman with the fair child, who had lately come to lodge there, was gone away again. That was all the express note taken that Molly had disappeared from the eyes of men. But the unwept death, which, to the general lot, seemed as trivial as the summer-shed leaf, was charged with the force of destiny to certain human lives that we know of, shaping their joys and sorrows even to the end.

Silas Marner's determination to keep the "tramp's child" was matter of hardly less surprise and iterated talk in the village than the robbery of his money. That softening of feeling toward him which dated from his misfortune, that merging of suspicion and dislike in a rather contemptuous pity for him as lone and crazy, was now accompanied with a more active sympathy, especially amongst the women. Notable mothers, who knew what it was to keep children "whole and sweet"; lazy mothers, who knew what it was to be interrupted in folding their arms and scratching their elbows by the mischievous propensities of children just firm on their legs, were equally interested in conjecturing how a lone man would manage with a two-year-old child on his hands, and were equally ready with their suggestions; the notable chiefly telling him what he had better do, and the lazy ones being emphatic in telling him what he would never be able to do.

Among the notable mothers, Dolly Winthrop was the one whose neighborly offices were the most acceptable to Marner, for they were rendered without any show of bustling instruction. Silas had shown her the half guinea given to him by Godfrey, and had asked her what he should do about getting some clothes for the child.

"Eh, Master Marner," said Dolly, "there's no call to buy, no more nor a pair o' shoes; for I've got the little petticoats as Aaron wore five years ago, and it's ill spending the money on them baby clothes, for the child 'ull grow like grass i' May, bless it — that it will."

And the same day Dolly brought her bundle, and displayed to Marner, one by one, the tiny garments in their due order of succession, most of them patched and darned, but clean and neat as fresh-sprung herbs. This was the introduction to a great ceremony with soap and water, from which Baby came out in new beauty, and sat on Dolly's knee, handling her toes and chuckling and patting her palms together with an air of having made several discoveries about herself, which she communicated by alternate sounds of "gug-gug-gug," and "mammy." The "mammy" was not a cry of need or uneasiness; Baby had been used to utter it without expecting either tender sound or touch to follow.

"Anybody 'ud think the angils in heaven couldn't be prettier," said Dolly, rubbing the golden curls and kissing them. "And to think of its being covered wi' them dirty rags — and the poor mother — froze to death; but there's Them as took care of it, and brought it to your door, Master Marner. The door was open, and it walked in over the snow, like as if it had been a little starved robin. Didn't you say the door was open?"

"Yes," said Silas meditatively. "Yes — the door was open. The money's gone I don't know where, and this is come from I don't know where."

He had not mentioned to anyone his unconsciousness of the child's entrance, shrinking from questions which might lead to the fact he himself suspected — namely, that he had been in one of his trances.

"Ah," said Dolly, with soothing gravity, "it's like the night and the morning, and the sleeping and the waking, and the rain and the harvest — one goes and the other comes, and we know nothing how nor where. We may strive and scrat and fend, but it's little we can do arter all — the big things come and go wi' no striving o' our'n — they do, that they do; and I think you're in the right on it to keep the little un, Master Marner, seeing as it's been sent to you, though there's folks as thinks different. You'll happen be a bit moithered with it while it's so little; but I'll come, and welcome, and see to it for you; I've a bit o' time to spare most days, for when one gets up betimes i' the morning, the clock seems to stan' still tow'rt ten, afore it's time to go about the victual. So, as I say, I'll come and see to the child for you, and welcome."

"Thank you . . . kindly," said Silas, hesitating a little. "I'll be glad if you'll tell me things. But," he added uneasily, leaning forward to look at Baby with some jealousy, as she was resting her head backward against Dolly's arm, and eyeing him contentedly from a distance, "but I want to do things for it myself, else it may get fond o' somebody else, and not fond o' me. I've been used to fending for myself in the house — I can learn, I can learn."

"Eh, to be sure," said Dolly gently. "I've seen men as are wonderful handy wi' children. The men are awk'ard and contrary mostly, God held 'em — but when the drink's out of 'em, they aren't unsensible, though they're bad for leeching and bandaging — so fiery and unpatient. You see this goes first, next the skin," proceeded Dolly, taking up the little shirt and putting it on.

"Yes," said Marner docilely, bringing his eyes very close, that they might be initiated in the mysteries; whereupon Baby seized his head with both her small arms, and put her lips against his face with purring noises.

"See there," said Dolly, with a woman's tender tact, "she's fondest o' you. She want's to go o' your lap, I'll be bound. Go, then; take her, Master Marner; you can put the things on, and then you can say as you've done for her from the first of her coming to you."

Marner took her on his lap, trembling, with an emotion mysterious to himself, at something unknown dawning on his life. Thought and feeling were so confused within him that if he had tried to give them utterance he could only have said that the child was come instead of the gold — that the gold had turned into the child. He took the garments from Dolly, and put them on under her teaching, interrupted, of course, by Baby's gymnastics.

"There, then! why, you take to it quite easy, Master Marner," said Dolly; "but what shall you do when you're forced to sit in your loom? For she'll get busier and mischievouser every day — she will, bless her. It's lucky as you've got that high hearth i'stead of a grate, for that keeps the fire more out of her reach; but if you've got anything as can be spilt or broke, or as is fit to cut her fingers off, she'll be at it — and it is but right you should know."

Silas meditated a little while in some perplexity. "I'll tie her to the leg o' the loom," he said at last — "tie her with a good long strip o' something.

"Well, mayhap that'll do, as it's a little gell, for they're easier persuaded to sit i' one place nor the lads. I know what the lads are, for I've had four — four I've had, God knows — and if you was to take and tie 'em up, they'd make a fighting and a crying as if you was ringing the pigs.[1] But I'll bring you my little chair, and some bits o' red rag and things for her to play wi'; an' she'll sit and chatter to 'em as if they was alive. Eh, if it wasn't a sin to the lads to wish 'em made different, bless 'em, I should ha' been glad for one of 'em to be a little gell; and to think as I could ha' taught her to scour, and mend, and the knitting, and everything. But I can teach 'em this little un, Master Marner, when she gets old enough."

"But she'll be *my* little un," said Marner, rather hastily. "She'll be nobody else's."

"No, to be sure; you'll have a right to her if you're a father to her, and bring her up according. But," added Dolly, coming to a point which she had determined beforehand to touch upon, "you must bring her up like christened folk's children, and take her to church, and let her learn her catechise, as my little Aaron can say off — the 'I believe,' and everything, and 'hurt nobody by word or deed' — as well as if he was the clerk. That's what you must do, Master Marner, if you'd do the right thing by the orphin child."

[1] **ringing the pigs:** putting rings in their noses.

Marner's pale face flushed suddenly under a new anxiety. His mind was too busy trying to give some definite bearing to Dolly's words for him to think of answering her.

"And it's my belief," she went on, "as the poor little creature has never been christened, and it's nothing but right as the parson should be spoke to; and if you was noways unwilling, I'd talk to Mr. Macey about it this very day. For if the child ever went anyways wrong, and you hadn't done your part by it, Master Marner — 'noculation, and everything to save it from harm — it 'ud be a thorn i' your bed forever o' this side the grave; and I can't think as it 'ud be easy lying down for anybody when they'd got to another world, if they hadn't done their part by the helpless children as come wi'out their own asking."

Dolly herself was disposed to be silent for some time now, for she had spoken from the depths of her own simple belief, and was much concerned to know whether her words would produce the desired effect on Silas. He was puzzled and anxious, for Dolly's word "christened" conveyed no distinct meaning to him. He had only heard of baptism, and had only seen the baptism of grown-up men and women.

"What is it as you mean by 'christened'?" he said at last timidly. "Won't folks be good to her without it?"

"Dear, dear! Master Marner," said Dolly, with gentle distress and compassion. "Had you never no father nor mother as taught you to say your prayers, and as there's good words and good things to keep us from harm?"

"Yes," said Silas, in a low voice; "I know a deal about that — used to, used to. But your ways are different; my country was a good way off." He paused a few moments, and then added, more decidedly, "But I want to do everything as can be done for the child. And whatever's right for it i' this country, and you think 'ull do it good, I'll act according, if you'll tell me."

"Well, then, Master Marner," said Dolly, inwardly rejoiced, "I'll ask Mr. Macey to speak to the parson about it; and you must fix on a name for it, because it must have a name giv' it when it's christened."

"My mother's name was Hephzibah," said Silas, "and my little sister was named after her."

"Eh, that's a hard name," said Dolly. "I partly think it isn't a christened name."

"It's a Bible name," said Silas, old ideas recurring.

"Then I've no call to speak again' it," said Dolly, rather startled by Silas's knowledge on this head; "but you see I'm no scholard, and I'm slow in catching the words. My husband says I'm allays like as if I was putting the haft for the handle — that's what he says — for he's very sharp, God help him. But it was awk'ard calling your little sister by such a hard name, when you'd got nothing big to say, like — wasn't it, Master Marner?"

"We called her Eppie," said Silas.

"Well, if it was noways wrong to shorten the name, it 'ud be a deal handier. And so I'll go now, Master Marner, and I'll speak about the christening afore dark; and I wish you the best o' luck, and it's my belief as it'll come to you, if you do what's right by the orphin child; — and there's the 'noculation to be seen to; and as to washing its bits o' things, you need look to nobody but me, for I can do 'em wi' one hand when I've got my suds about. Eh, the blessed angil! you'll let me bring my Aaron one o' these days, and he'll show her his little cart as his father's made for him, and the black-and-white pup as he's got a-rearing."

Baby *was* christened, the rector deciding that a double baptism was the lesser risk to incur; and on this occasion Silas, making himself as clean and tidy as he could, appeared for the first time within the church, and shared in the observances held sacred by his neighbors. He was quite unable, by means of anything he heard or saw, to identify the Raveloe religion with his old faith; if he could at any time in his previous life have done so, it must have been by the aid of a strong feeling ready to vibrate with sympathy rather than by a comparison of phrases and ideas; and now for long years that feeling had been dormant. He had no distinct idea about the baptism and the church-going, except that Dolly had said it was for the good of the child; and in this way, as the weeks grew to months, the child created fresh and fresh links between his life and the lives from which he had hitherto shrunk continually into narrower isolation. Unlike the gold which needed nothing, and must be worshiped in close-locked solitude — which was hidden away from the daylight, was deaf to the song of birds, and started to no human tones — Eppie was a creature of endless claims and ever-growing desires, seeking and loving sunshine, and living sounds, and living movements; making trial of everything, with trust in new joy, and stirring the human kindness in all eyes that looked on her. The gold had kept his thoughts in an ever-repeated circle, leading to nothing beyond itself; but Eppie was an object compacted of changes and hopes that forced his thoughts onward, and carried them far away from their old eager pacing toward the same blank limit — carried them away to the new things that would come with the coming years, when Eppie would have learned to understand how her Father Silas cared for her; and made him look for images of that time in the ties and charities that bound together the families of his neighbors. The gold had asked that he should sit weaving longer and longer, deafened and blinded more and more to all things except the monotony of his loom and the repetition of his web; but Eppie called him away from his weaving, and made him think all its pauses a holiday, reawakening his senses with her fresh life, even to the old winter flies that came crawling forth in the early spring sunshine, and warming him into joy because *she* had joy.

And when the sunshine grew strong and lasting, so that the buttercups were thick in the meadows, Silas might be seen in the sunny midday, or in the late afternoon when the shadows were lengthening under the hedgerows, strolling out with uncovered head to carry Eppie beyond the stone pits to where the flowers grew, till they reached some favorite bank where he could sit down, while Eppie toddled to pluck the flowers, and make remarks to the winged things that murmured happily above the bright petals, calling "Dad-dad's" attention continually by bringing him the flowers. Then she would turn her ear to some sudden bird note, and Silas learned to please her by making signs of hushed stillness, that they might listen for the note to come again; so that when it came she set up her small back and laughed with gurgling triumph. Sitting on the banks in this way, Silas began to look for the once familiar herbs again; and as the leaves, with their unchanged outline and markings, lay on his palm, there was a sense of crowding remembrances from which he turned away timidly, taking refuge in Eppie's little world, that lay lightly on his enfeebled spirit.

As the child's mind was growing into knowledge, his mind was growing into memory; as her life unfolded, his soul, long stupefied in a cold, narrow prison, was unfolding too, and trembling gradually into full consciousness.

It was an influence which must gather

force with every new year; the tones that stirred Silas's heart grew articulate, and called for more distinct answers; shapes and sounds grew clearer for Eppie's eyes and ears, and there was more that " Dad-dad " was imperatively required to notice and account for. Also, by the time Eppie was three years old, she developed a fine capacity for mischief, and for devising ingenious ways of being troublesome, which found much exercise, not only for Silas's patience, but for his watchfulness and penetration. Sorely was poor Silas puzzled on such occasions by the incompatible demands of love. Dolly Winthrop told him that punishment was good for Eppie, and that as for rearing a child, without making it tingle a little in soft and safe places now and then, it was not to be done.

" To be sure, there's another thing you might do, Master Marner," added Dolly meditatively; " you might shut her up once i' the coalhole. That was what I did wi' Aaron; for I was that silly wi' the youngest lad as I could never bear to smack him. Not as I could find i' my heart to let him stay i' the coalhole more nor a minute, but it was enough to colly him all over, so as he must be new washed and dressed, and it was as good as a rod to him — that was. But I put it upo' your conscience, Master Marner, as there's one of 'em you must choose — ayther smacking or the coalhole — else she'll get so masterful, there'll be no holding her."

Silas was impressed with the melancholy truth of this last remark; but his force of mind failed before the only two penal methods open to him, not only because it was painful to him to hurt Eppie, but because he trembled at a moment's contention with her, lest she should love him the less for it. Let even an affectionate Goliath [1] get himself tied to a small tender thing, dreading to hurt it by pulling, and dreading still more to snap the cord, and which of the two, pray, will be master? It was clear that Eppie, with her short toddling steps, must lead Father Silas a pretty dance on any fine morning when circumstances favored mischief.

For example. He had wisely chosen a broad strip of linen as a means of fastening her to his loom when he was busy; it made a broad belt round her waist, and was long enough to allow of her reaching the truckle bed and sitting down on it, but not long enough for her to attempt any dangerous climbing. One bright summer's morning Silas had been more engrossed than usual in " setting up " a new piece of work, an occasion on which his scissors were in requisition. These scissors, owing to an especial warning of Dolly's, had been kept carefully out of Eppie's reach; but the click of them had had a peculiar attraction for her ear, and, watching the results of that click, she had derived the philosophic lesson that the same cause would produce the same effect. Silas had seated himself in his loom, and the noise of weaving had begun; but he had left his scissors on a ledge which Eppie's arm was long enough to reach; and now, like a small mouse, watching her opportunity, she stole quietly from her corner, secured the scissors, and toddled to the bed again, setting up her back as a mode of concealing the fact. She had a distinct intention as to the use of the scissors; and having cut the linen strip in a jagged but effectual manner, in two moments she had run out at the open door where the sunshine was inviting her, while poor Silas believed her to be a better child than usual. It was not until he happened to need his scissors that the terrible fact burst upon him; Eppie had run out by herself — had perhaps fallen into the stone pit. Silas, shaken by the worst fear that could have befallen him,

[1] **Goliath:** the giant in the Bible story whom David killed with a stone from a slingshot.

rushed out, calling "Eppie!" and ran eagerly about the unenclosed space, exploring the dry cavities into which she might have fallen, and then gazing with questioning dread at the smooth red surface of the water. The cold drops stood on his brow. How long had she been out? There was one hope — that she had crept through the stile and got into the fields where he habitually took her to stroll. But the grass was high in the meadow, and there was no descrying her, if she were there, except by a close search that would be a trespass on Mr. Osgood's crop. Still, that misdemeanor must be committed; and poor Silas, after peering all round the hedgerows, traversed the grass, beginning with perturbed vision to see Eppie behind every group of red sorrel, and to see her moving always farther off as he approached. The meadow was searched in vain; and he got over the stile into the next field, looking with dying hope toward a small pond which was now reduced to its summer shallowness, so as to leave a wide margin of good adhesive mud. Here, however, sat Eppie, discoursing cheerfully to her own small boot, which she was using as a bucket to convey the water into a deep hoofmark, while her little naked foot was planted comfortably on a cushion of olive-green mud. A red-headed calf was observing her with alarmed doubt through the opposite hedge.

Here was clearly a case of aberration in a christened child which demanded severe treatment; but Silas, overcome with convulsive joy at finding his treasure again, could do nothing but snatch her up, and cover her with half-sobbing kisses. It was not until he had carried her home, and had begun to think of the necessary washing, that he recollected the need that he should punish Eppie, and "make her remember." The idea that she might run away again and come to harm gave him unusual resolution, and for the first time he determined to try the coalhole — a small closet near the hearth.

"Naughty, naughty Eppie," he suddenly began, holding her on his knee, and pointing to her muddy feet and clothes; "naughty to cut with the scissors, and run away. Eppie must go into the coalhole for being naughty. Daddy must put her in the coalhole."

He half expected that this would be shock enough, and that Eppie would begin to cry. But instead of that, she began to shake herself on his knee, as if the proposition opened a pleasing novelty. Seeing that he must proceed to extremities, he put her into the coalhole, and held the door closed, with a trembling sense that he was using a strong measure. For a moment there was silence, but then came a little cry, "Opy, opy!" and Silas let her out again, saying, "Now Eppie 'ull never be naughty again, else she must go in the coalhole — a black, naughty place."

The weaving must stand still a long while this morning, for now Eppie must be washed and have clean clothes on; but it was to be hoped that this punishment would have a lasting effect, and save time in future; though, perhaps, it would have been better if Eppie had cried more.

In half an hour she was clean again, and Silas, having turned his back to see what he could do with the linen band, threw it down again, with the reflection that Eppie would be good without fastening for the rest of the morning. He turned round again, and was going to place her in her little chair near the loom, when she peeped out at him with black face and hands again, and said, "Eppie in de toalhole!"

This total failure of the coalhole discipline shook Silas's belief in the efficacy of punishment. "She'd take it all for fun," he observed to Dolly, "if I didn't hurt her, and that I can't do, Mrs. Winthrop. If she makes me a bit o' trouble I can bear it. And she's got no tricks but what she'll grow out of."

"Well, that's partly true, Master Marner," said Dolly sympathetically; "and if you can't bring your mind to frighten her off touching things, you must do what you can to keep 'em out of her way. That's what I do wi' the pups as the lads are allays a-rearing. They *will* worry and gnaw — worry and gnaw they will, if it was one's Sunday cap as hung anywhere so as they could drag it. They know no difference, God help 'em; it's the pushing o' the teeth as sets 'em on, that's what it is."

So Eppie was reared without punishment, the burden of her misdeeds being borne vicariously by Father Silas. The stone hut was made a soft nest for her, lined with downy patience; and also in the world that lay beyond the stone hut she knew nothing of frowns and denials.

Notwithstanding the difficulty of carrying her and his yarn or linen at the same time, Silas took her with him in most of his journeys to the farmhouses, unwilling to leave her behind at Dolly Winthrop's, who was always ready to take care of her; and little curly-headed Eppie, the weaver's child, became an object of interest at several outlying homesteads, as well as in the village. Hitherto he had been treated very much as if he had been a useful gnome or brownie — a queer and unaccountable creature, who must necessarily be looked at with wondering curiosity and repulsion, and with whom one would be glad to make all greetings and bargains as brief as possible, but who must be dealt with in a propitiatory way, and occasionally have a present of pork or garden stuff to carry home with him, seeing that without him there was no getting the yarn woven. But now Silas was met with open, smiling faces and cheerful questioning, as a person whose satisfactions and difficulties could be understood. Everywhere he must sit a little and talk about the child, and words of interest were always ready for him: "Ah, Master Marner, you'll be lucky if she takes the measles soon and easy!" — or, "Why, there isn't many lone men 'ud ha' been wishing to take up with a little un like that; but I reckon the weaving makes you handier than men as do outdoor work; you're partly as handy as a woman, for weaving comes next to spinning." Elderly masters and mistresses, seated observantly in large kitchen armchairs, shook their heads over the difficulties attendant on rearing children, felt Eppie's round arms and legs, and pronounced them remarkably firm, and told Silas that, if she turned out well (which, however, there was no telling), it would be a fine thing for him to have a steady lass to do for him when he got helpless. Servant maidens were fond of carrying her out to look at the hens and chickens, or to see if any cherries could be shaken down in the orchard; and the small boys and girls approached her slowly, with cautious movement and steady gaze, like little dogs face to face with one of their own kind, till attraction had reached the point at which the soft lips were put out for a kiss. No child was afraid of approaching Silas when Eppie was near him; there was no repulsion around him now, either for young or old; for the little child had come to link him once more with the whole world. There was love between him and the child that blent them into one, and there was love between the child and the world — from men and women with parental looks and tones to the red ladybirds and the round pebbles.

Silas began now to think of Raveloe life entirely in relation to Eppie; she must have everything that was good in Raveloe; and he listened docilely, that he might come to understand better what this life was, from which, for fifteen years, he had stood aloof as from a strange thing, wherewith he could have no communion; as some man who has a precious plant to which he would give a nurturing home in a new soil thinks of the rain, and the sunshine, and all influences, in relation to his nursling, and asks industriously for all knowledge that will help him to satisfy the wants of the searching roots, or to guard leaf and bud from invading harm. The disposition to hoard had been utterly crushed at the very first by the loss of his long-stored gold; the coins he earned afterward seemed as irrelevant as stones brought to complete a house suddenly buried by an earthquake; the sense of bereavement was too heavy upon him for the old thrill of satisfaction to arise again at the touch of the newly earned coin. And now something had come to replace his hoard which gave a growing purpose to the earnings, drawing his hope and joy continually onward beyond the money.

In old days there were angels who came and took men by the hand and led them away from the city of destruction. We see no white-winged angels now. But yet men are led away from threatening destruction; a hand is put into theirs which leads them forth gently toward a calm and bright land, so that they look no more backward; and the hand may be a little child's.

CHAPTER XV

There was one person, as you will believe, who watched, with keener though more hidden interest than any other, the prosperous growth of Eppie under the weaver's care. He dared not do anything that would imply a stronger interest in a poor man's adopted child than could be expected from the kindliness of the young Squire, when a chance meeting suggested a little present to a simple old fellow whom others noticed with good will; but he told himself that the time would come when he might do something toward furthering the welfare of his daughter without incurring suspicion. Was he very uneasy in the meantime at his inability to give his daughter her birthright? I cannot say that he was. The child was being taken care of, and would very likely be happy, as people in humble stations often were — happier, perhaps, than those brought up in luxury.

That famous ring that pricked its owner when he forgot duty and followed desire — I wonder if it pricked very hard when he set out on the chase, or whether it pricked but lightly then, and only pierced to the quick when the chase had long been ended, and hope, folding her wings, looked backward and became regret?

Godfrey Cass's cheek and eye were brighter than ever now. He was so undivided in his aims that he seemed like a man of firmness. No Dunsey had come back; people had made up their minds that he was gone for a soldier, or gone "out of the country," and no one cared to be specific in their inquiries on a subject delicate to a respectable family. Godfrey had ceased to see the shadow of Dunsey across his path; and the path now lay straight forward to the accomplishment of his best, longest-cherished wishes. Everybody said Mr. Godfrey had taken the right turn; and it was pretty clear what would be the end of things, for there were not many days in the week that he was not seen riding to the Warrens. Godfrey himself, when he was asked jocosely if the day had been fixed, smiled with the pleasant consciousness of a lover who could say "yes," if he liked. He felt a reformed man, delivered from temptation; and the vision of his future life seemed to him as a promised land for which he had no cause to fight. He saw himself with all his happiness centered on his own hearth, while Nancy would smile on him as he played with the children.

And that other child — not on the hearth — he would not forget it; he would see that it was well provided for. That was a father's duty.

PART II

CHAPTER XVI

Why do people act the way they do? Why, for example, was Silas Marner a hermit and a miser? Was it because he was bewitched, as some of the simple folk in Raveloe thought? Or was there some natural explanation for his strange behavior?

George Eliot thought that there was. Although she lived in an age of superstition, she herself was not superstitious. She believed that people were what they were largely because the conditions under which they lived made them so. In this point of view she was ahead of her time, and her novels are a forerunner of the modern psychological novels which attempt to give a natural explanation to human conduct.

During the period in which she was at work on *Silas Marner* she wrote to her publisher, "It is intended to set in a strong light the remedial influences of pure, natural relations." This is the underlying idea of the story, and it is illustrated particularly in this chapter and the one following. Notice first, as you read, the changes that have taken place in the character of Silas Marner in the sixteen years that elapse between Parts I and II. Can you recognize the "remedial influences" which have been at work? If you can, you will have appreciated the *theme* of the story as its author intended you should.

What changes have come over Godfrey and Nancy Cass? Can you account for these changes by your knowledge of what has happened earlier in the story?

It was a bright autumn Sunday, sixteen years after Silas Marner had found his new treasure on the hearth. The bells of the old Raveloe church were ringing the cheerful peal which told that the morning service was ended; and out of the arched doorway in the tower came slowly, retarded by friendly greetings and questions, the richer parishioners who had chosen this bright Sunday morning as eligible for churchgoing. It was the rural fashion of that time for the more important members of the congregation to depart first, while their humbler neighbors waited and looked on, stroking their bent heads or dropping their curtsies to any large ratepayer who turned to notice them.

Foremost among these advancing groups of well-clad people there are some whom we shall recognize, in spite of Time, who has laid his hand on them all. The tall blond man of forty is not much changed in feature from the Godfrey Cass of six and twenty; he is only fuller in flesh, and has only lost the indefinable look of youth — a loss which is marked even when the eye is undulled and the wrinkles are not yet come. Perhaps the pretty woman, not much younger than he, who is leaning on his arm, is more changed than her husband; the lovely bloom that used to be always on her cheek now comes but fitfully, with the fresh morning air or with some strong surprise; yet to all who love human faces best for what they tell of human experience, Nancy's beauty has a heightened interest. Often the soul is ripened into fuller goodness while age has spread an ugly film, so that mere glances can never divine the preciousness of the fruit. But the years have not been so cruel to Nancy. The firm yet placid mouth, the clear veracious glance of the brown eyes, speak now of a nature that has been tested and has kept its highest qualities; and even the costume, with its dainty neatness and purity, has more significance now the coquetries of youth can have nothing to do with it.

Mr. and Mrs. Godfrey Cass (any higher title has died away from Raveloe lips since the old Squire was gathered to his fathers and his inheritance was divided) have turned round to look for the tall aged man and the plainly dressed woman who are a little behind — Nancy having observed that they must wait for "father and Priscilla" — and now they all turn into a narrower path leading across the churchyard to a small gate opposite the Red House. We will not follow them now; for may there not be some others in this departing congregation whom we should like to see again — some of those who are not likely to be handsomely clad, and whom we may not recognize so easily as the master and mistress of the Red House?

But it is impossible to mistake Silas Marner. His large brown eyes seem to have gathered a longer vision, as is the way with eyes that have been shortsighted in early life, and they have a less vague, a more answering gaze; but in everything else one sees signs of a frame much enfeebled by the lapse of the sixteen years. The weaver's bent shoulders and white hair give him almost the look of advanced age, though he is not more than five and fifty; but there is the freshest blossom of youth close by his side — a blonde, dimpled girl of eighteen, who has vainly tried to chastise her curly auburn hair into smoothness under her brown bonnet. The hair ripples as obstinately as a brooklet under the March breeze, and the little ringlets burst away from the restraining comb behind and show themselves below the bonnet crown. Eppie cannot help being rather vexed about her hair, for there is no other girl in Raveloe who has hair at all like it, and she thinks hair ought to be smooth. She does not like to be blameworthy even in small things; you see how neatly her prayer book is folded in her spotted handkerchief.

That good-looking young fellow, in a new fustian suit, who walks behind her is not quite sure upon the question of hair in the abstract when Eppie puts it to him, and thinks that perhaps straight hair is the best in general, but he doesn't want Eppie's hair to be different. She surely divines that there is someone behind her who is thinking about her very particularly, and mustering courage to come to her side as soon as they are out in the lane, else why should she look rather shy, and take care not to turn away her head from her Father Silas, to whom she keeps murmuring little sentences as to who was at church, and who was not at church, and how pretty the red mountain ash is over the rectory wall!

"I wish *we* had a little garden, father, with double daisies in, like Mrs. Winthrop's," said Eppie, when they were out in the lane; "only they say it 'ud take a deal of digging and bringing fresh soil — and you couldn't do that, could you, father? Anyhow, I shouldn't like you to do it, for it 'ud be too hard work for you."

"Yes, I could do it, child, if you want a bit o' garden; these long evenings I could work at taking in a little bit o' the waste, just enough for a root or two o' flowers for you; and again, i' the morning, I could have a turn wi' the spade before I sat down to the loom. Why didn't you tell me before as you wanted a bit o' garden?"

"*I* can dig it for you, Master Marner," said the young man in fustian, who was now by Eppie's side, entering into the conversation without the trouble of formalities. "It'll be play to me after I've done my day's work, or any odd bits o' time when the work's slack. And I'll bring you some soil from Mr. Cass's garden — he'll let me, and willing."

"Eh, Aaron, my lad, are you there?" said Silas. "I wasn't aware of you; for when Eppie's talking o' things, I see nothing but what she's a-saying. Well, if you could help me with the digging, we might get her a bit o' garden all the sooner."

"Then, if you think well and good," said Aaron, "I'll come to the stone pits this afternoon, and we'll settle what land's to be taken in, and I'll get up an hour earlier i' the morning, and begin on it."

"But not if you don't promise me not to work at the hard digging, father," said Eppie. "For I shouldn't ha' said anything about it," she added, half bashfully, half roguishly, "only Mrs. Winthrop said as Aaron 'ud be so good, and — "

"And you might ha' known it without mother telling you," said Aaron. "And Master Marner knows too, I hope, as I'm able and willing to do a turn o' work for him, and he won't do me the unkindness to anyways take it out o' my hands."

"There, now, father, you won't work in it till it's all easy," said Eppie; "and you and me can mark out the beds and make holes and plant the roots. It'll be a deal livelier at the stone pits when we've got some flowers, for I always think the flowers can see us and know what we're talking about. And I'll have a bit o' rosemary, and bergamot, and thyme, because they're so sweet-smelling; but there's no lavender only in the gentlefolks' gardens, I think."

"That's no reason why you shouldn't have some," said Aaron, "for I can bring you slips of anything; I'm forced to cut no end of 'em when I'm gardening, and throw 'em away mostly. There's a big bed o' lavender at the Red House; the missis is very fond of it."

"Well," said Silas gravely, "so as you don't make free for us, or ask for anything as is worth much at the Red House; for Mr. Cass's been so good to us, and built us up the new end o' the cottage, and given us beds and things, as I couldn't abide to be imposin' for garden stuff or anything else."

"No, no, there's no imposin'," said Aaron; "there's never a garden in all the parish but what there's endless waste in it for want o' somebody as could use everything up. It's what I think to myself sometimes, as there need nobody run short o' victuals if the land was made the most on, and there was never a morsel but what could find its way to a mouth. It sets one thinking o' that — gardening does. But I must go back now, else mother 'ull be in trouble as I aren't there."

"Bring her with you this afternoon, Aaron," said Eppie; "I shouldn't like to fix about the garden, and her not know everything from the first — should *you*, father?"

"Ay, bring her if you can, Aaron," said Silas; "she's sure to have a word to say as 'll help us to set things on their right end."

Aaron turned back up the village, while Silas and Eppie went on up the lonely sheltered lane.

"O Daddy!" she began, when they were in privacy, clasping and squeezing Silas's arm, and skipping round to give him an energetic kiss. "My little old Daddy! I'm so glad. I don't think I shall want anything else when we've got a little garden; and I knew Aaron would dig it for us," she went on with roguish triumph; "I knew that very well."

"You're a deep little puss, you are," said Silas, with the mild, passive happiness of love-crowned age in his face; "but you'll make yourself fine and beholden to Aaron."

"Oh, no, I shan't," said Eppie, laughing and frisking; "he likes it."

"Come, come, let me carry your prayer book, else you'll be dropping it, jumping i' that way."

Eppie was now aware that her behavior was under observation, but it was only the observation of a friendly donkey, browsing with a log fastened to his foot — a meek donkey, not scornfully critical of human trivialities, but thankful to share in them, if possible, by getting his nose scratched; and Eppie did not fail to gratify him with her usual notice, though it was attended with the inconvenience of his following them, painfully, up to the very door of their home.

But the sound of a sharp bark inside, as Eppie put the key in the door, modified the donkey's views, and he limped away again without bidding. The sharp bark was the sign of an excited welcome that was awaiting them from a knowing brown terrier, who, after dancing at their legs in a hysterical manner, rushed with a worrying noise at a tortoise-shell kitten under the loom, and then rushed back with a sharp bark again, as much as to say, "I have done my duty by this feeble creature, you perceive"; while the lady mother of the kitten sat sunning her white bosom in the window, and looked round with a sleepy air of expecting caresses, though she was not going to take any trouble for them.

The presence of this happy animal life was not the only change which had come over the interior of the stone cottage. There was no bed now in the living room, and the small space was well filled with decent furniture, all bright and clean enough to satisfy Dolly Winthrop's eye. The oaken table and three-cornered oaken chair were hardly what was likely to be seen in so poor a cottage; they had come, with the beds and other things, from the Red House; for Mr. Godfrey Cass, as everyone said in the village, did very kindly by the weaver; and it was nothing but right a man should be looked on and helped by those who could afford it, when he had brought up an orphan child, and been father and mother to her — and had lost his money, too, so as he had nothing but what he worked for week by week, and when the weaving was going down, too — for there was less and less flax spun — and Master Marner was none so young. Nobody was jealous of the weaver, for he was regarded as an exceptional person, whose claims on neighborly help were not to be matched in Raveloe. Any superstition that remained concerning him had taken an entirely new color; and Mr. Macey, now a very feeble old man of fourscore and six, never seen except in his chimney corner or sitting in the sunshine at his doorsill, was of opinion that when a man had done what Silas had done by an orphan child it was a sign that his money would come to light again, or leastwise that the robber would be made to answer for it; for, as Mr. Macey observed of himself, his faculties were as strong as ever.

Silas sat down now and watched Eppie with a satisfied gaze as she spread the clean cloth, and set on it the potato pie, warmed up slowly in a safe Sunday fashion, by being put into a dry pot over a slowly dying fire, as the best substitute for an oven. For Silas would not consent to have a grate and oven added to his conveniences; he loved the old brick hearth as he had loved his brown pot — and was it not there when he had found Eppie? The gods of the hearth exist for us still; and let all new faith be tolerant of that fetishism, lest it bruise its own roots.

Silas ate his dinner more silently than usual, soon laying down his knife and fork, and watching half abstractedly Eppie's play with Snap and the cat, by which her own dining was made rather a lengthy business. Yet it was a sight that might well arrest wandering thoughts; Eppie, with the rippling radiance of her hair and the whiteness of her rounded chin and throat set off by the dark blue cotton gown, laughing merrily as the kitten held on with her four claws to one shoulder, like a design for a jug handle, while Snap on the right hand and Puss on the other put up their paws toward a morsel which she held out of the reach of both — Snap occasionally desisting in order to remonstrate with the cat by a cogent worrying growl on the greediness and futility of her conduct; till Eppie relented, caressed them both, and divided the morsel between them.

But at last Eppie, glancing at the clock, checked the play and said, "O Daddy, you're wanting to go into the sunshine to smoke your pipe. But I must clear away first, so as the house may be tidy when godmother comes. I'll make haste — I won't be long."

Silas had taken to smoking a pipe daily during the last two years, having been strongly urged to it by the sages of Raveloe, as a practice "good for the fits"; and this advice was sanctioned by Dr. Kimble, on the ground that it was as well to try what could do no harm — a principle which was made to answer for a great deal of work in that gentleman's medical practice. Silas did not highly enjoy smoking, and often wondered how his neighbors could be so fond of it; but a humble sort of acquiescence in what was held to be good had become a strong habit of that new self which had been developed in him since he had found Eppie on his hearth; it had been the only clue his bewildered mind could hold by in cherishing this young life that had been sent to him out of the darkness into which his gold had departed. By seeking what was needful for Eppie, by sharing the effect that everything produced on her, he had himself come to appropriate the forms of custom and belief which were the mold of Raveloe life; and as, with reawakening sensibilities, memory also reawakened, he had begun to ponder over the elements of his old faith, and blend them with his new impressions, till he recovered a consciousness of unity between his past and present. The sense of presiding goodness and the human trust which come with all pure peace and joy had given him a dim impression that there had been some error, some mistake, which had thrown that dark shadow over the days of his best years; and as it grew more and more easy to him to open his mind to Dolly Winthrop, he gradually communicated to her all he could describe of his early life. The communication was necessarily a slow and difficult process, for Silas's meager power of explanation was not aided by any readiness of interpretation in Dolly, whose narrow outward experience gave her no key to strange customs, and made every novelty a source of wonder that arrested them at every step of the narrative. It was only by fragments, and at intervals which left Dolly time to revolve what she had heard till it acquired some familiarity for her, that Silas at last arrived at the climax of the sad story — the drawing of lots, and its false testimony concerning him; and this had to be repeated in several interviews, under new questions on her part as to the nature of this plan for detecting the guilty and clearing the innocent.

"And yourn's the same Bible, you're sure o' that, Master Marner — the Bible as you brought wi' you from that country — it's the same as what they've got at church, and what Eppie's a-learning to read in?"

"Yes," said Silas, "every bit the same; and there's drawing o' lots in the Bible, mind you," he added in a lower tone.

"Oh, dear, dear," said Dolly, in a grieved voice, as if she were hearing an unfavorable report of a sick man's case. She was silent for some minutes; at last she said —

"There's wise folks, happen, as know

how it all is; the parson knows, I'll be bound; but it takes big words to tell them things, and such as poor folks can't make much out on. I can never rightly know the meaning o' what I hear at church, only a bit here and there, but I know it's good words — I do. But what lies upo' your mind — it's this, Master Marner: as, if Them above had done the right thing by you, They'd never ha' let you be turned out for a wicked thief when you was innicent."

"Ah!" said Silas, who had now come to understand Dolly's phraseology, "that was what fell on me like as if it had been red-hot iron; because, you see, there was nobody as cared for me or clave to me above nor below. And him as I'd gone out and in wi' for ten year and more, since when we was lads and went halves — mine own familiar friend, in whom I trusted, had lifted up his heel again' me, and worked to ruin me."

"Eh, but he was a bad un — I can't think as there's another such," said Dolly. "But I'm o'ercome, Master Marner; I'm like as if I'd waked and didn't know whether it was night or morning. I feel somehow as sure as I do when I've laid something up though I can't justly put my hand on it, as there was a rights in what happened to you, if one could but make it out; and you'd no call to lose heart as you did. But we'll talk on it again; for sometimes things come into my head when I'm leeching or poulticing, or such, as I could never think on when I was sitting still."

Dolly was too useful a woman not to have many opportunities of illumination of the kind she alluded to, and she was not long before she recurred to the subject.

"Master Marner," she said, one day that she came to bring home Eppie's washing, "I've been sore puzzled for a good bit wi' that trouble o' yourn and the drawing o' lots; and it got twisted back'ards and for'ards, as I didn't know which end to lay hold on. But it come to me all clear like, that night when I was sitting up wi' poor Bessy Fawkes, as is dead and left her children behind, God help 'em — it come to me as clear as daylight; but whether I've got hold on it now, or can anyways bring it to my tongue's end, that I don't know. For I've often a deal inside me as 'll never come out; and for what you talk o' your folks in your old country niver saying prayers by heart nor saying 'em out of a book, they must be wonderful cliver; for if I didn't know 'Our Father,' and little bits o' good words as I can carry out o' church wi' me, I might down o' my knees every night, but nothing could I say."

"But you can mostly say something as I can make sense on, Mrs. Winthrop," said Silas.

"Well, then, Master Marner, it come to me summat like this: I can make nothing o' the drawing o' lots and the answer coming wrong; it 'ud mayhap take the parson to tell that, and he could only tell us i' big words. But what come to me as clear as the daylight, it was when I was troubling over poor Bessy Fawkes, and it allays comes into my head when I'm sorry for folks, and feel as I can't do a power to help 'em, not if I was to get up i' the middle o' the night — it comes into my head as Them above has got a deal tenderer heart nor what I've got — for I can't be anyways better nor Them as made me; and if anything looks hard to me, it's because there's things I don't know on; and for the matter o' that, there may be plenty o' things I don't know on, for it's little as I know — that it is. And so, while I was thinking o' that, you come into my mind, Master Marner, and it all come pouring in; if *I* felt i' my inside what was the right and just thing by you, and them as prayed and drawed the lots, all but that wicked un, if *they*'d ha' done the right thing by you if they could, isn't there Them as was at the making on us, and knows better and has a better will? And that's all as ever I can be sure on, and everything else is a big puzzle to me when I think on it. For there was the fever come and took off them as were full-growed, and left the helpless children; and there's the breaking o' limbs; and them as 'ud do right and be sober have to suffer by them as are contrairy — eh, there's trouble i' this world, and there's things as we can niver make out the rights on. And all as we've got to do is to trusten, Master Marner — to do the right thing as fur as we know, and to trusten. For if us as knows so little can see a bit o' good and rights, we may be sure as there's a good and a rights bigger nor what we can know — I feel it i' my own inside as it must be so. And if you could but ha' gone on trustening, Master Marner, you wouldn't ha' run away from your fellow creaturs and been so lone."

"Ah, but that 'ud ha' been hard," said Silas, in an undertone; "it 'ud ha' been hard to trusten then."

"And so it would," said Dolly, almost with compunction; "them things are easier said nor done; and I'm partly ashamed o' talking."

"Nay, nay," said Silas, "you're i' the right, Mrs. Winthrop — you're i' the right. There's good i' this world — I've a feeling o' that now; and it makes a man feel as there's a good more nor he can see, i' spite o' the trouble and the wickedness. That drawing o' the lots is dark; but the child was sent to me; there's dealings with us — there's dealings."

This dialogue took place in Eppie's earlier years, when Silas had to part with her for two hours every day, that she might learn to read at the dame school, after he had vainly tried himself to guide her in that first step to learning. Now that she was grown up, Silas had often been led, in those moments of quiet outpouring which come to people who live together in perfect love, to talk with *her*, too, of the past, and how and why he had lived a lonely man until she had been sent to him. For it would have been impossible for him to hide from Eppie that she was not his own child: even if the most delicate reticence on the point could have been expected from Raveloe gossips in her presence, her own questions about her mother could not have been parried, as she grew up, without that complete shrouding of the past which would have made a painful barrier between their minds. So Eppie had long known how her mother had died on the snowy ground, and how she herself had been found on the hearth by Father Silas, who had taken her golden curls for his lost guineas brought back to him. The tender and peculiar love with which Silas had reared her in almost inseparable companionship with himself, aided by the seclusion of their dwelling, had preserved her from the lowering influences of the village talk and habits, and had kept her mind in that freshness which is sometimes falsely supposed to be an invariable attribute of rusticity. Perfect love has a breath of poetry which can exalt the relations of the least instructed human beings; and this breath of poetry had surrounded Eppie from the time when she had followed the bright gleam that beckoned her to Silas's hearth; so that it is not surprising if, in other things besides her delicate prettiness, she was not quite a common village maiden, but had a touch of refinement and fervor which came from no other teaching than that of tenderly nurtured unvitiated feeling. She was too childish and simple for her imagination to rove into questions about her unknown father; for a long while it did not even occur to her that she must have had a father; and the first time that the idea of her mother having had a husband presented itself to her was when Silas showed her the wedding ring which had been taken from the wasted finger, and had been carefully preserved by him in a little lacquered box shaped like a shoe. He delivered this box into Eppie's charge when she had grown up, and she often opened it to look at the ring; but still she thought hardly at all about the father of whom it was the symbol. Had she not a father very close to her, who loved her better than any real fathers in the village seemed to love their daughters? On the contrary, who her mother was and how she came to die in that forlornness were questions that often pressed on Eppie's mind. Her knowledge of Mrs. Winthrop, who was her nearest friend next to Silas, made her feel that a mother must be very precious: and she had again and again asked Silas to tell her how her mother looked, whom she was like, and how he had found her against the furze bush, led toward it by the little footsteps and the outstretched arms. The furze bush was there still; and this afternoon, when Eppie came out with Silas into the sunshine, it was the first object that arrested her eyes and thoughts.

"Father," she said, in a tone of gentle gravity, which sometimes came like a sadder, slower cadence across her playfulness, "we shall take the furze bush into the garden; it 'll come into the corner, and just against it I'll put snowdrops and crocuses, 'cause Aaron says they won't die out, but 'll always get more and more."

"Ah, child," said Silas, always ready to talk when he had his pipe in his hand, apparently enjoying the pauses more than the puffs, "it wouldn't do to leave out the furze bush; and there's nothing prettier, to my thinking, when it's yallow with flowers. But it's just come into my head what we're to do for a fence — mayhap Aaron can help us to a thought; but a fence we must have, else the donkeys and things 'ull come and trample everything down. And fencing's hard to be got at, by what I can make out."

"Oh, I'll tell you, Daddy," said Eppie, clasping her hands suddenly, after a minute's thought. "There's lots o' loose stones about, some of 'em not big, and we might lay 'em atop of one another, and make a wall. You and me could carry the smallest, and Aaron 'ud carry the rest — I know he would."

"Eh, my precious un," said Silas, "there isn't enough stones to go all round; and as for you carrying, why, wi' your little arms you couldn't carry a stone no bigger than a turnip. You're dillicate made, my dear," he added, with a tender intonation — "that's what Mrs. Winthrop says."

"Oh, I'm stronger than you think, Daddy," said Eppie; "and if there wasn't stones enough to go all round, why they'll go part o' the way, and then it'll be easier to get sticks and things for the rest. See here, round the big pit, what a many stones!"

She skipped forward to the pit, meaning to lift one of the stones and exhibit her strength, but she started back in surprise.

"Oh, father, just come and look here," she exclaimed — "come and see how the water's gone down since yesterday! Why, yesterday the pit was ever so full!"

"Well, to be sure," said Silas, coming to her side. "Why, that's the draining they're begun on, since harvest, i' Mr. Osgood's fields, I reckon. The foreman said to me the other day, when I passed by 'em, 'Master Marner,' he said, 'I shouldn't wonder if we lay your bit o' waste as dry as a bone.' It was Mr. Godfrey Cass, he said, had gone into the draining; he'd been taking these fields o' Mr. Osgood."

"How odd it 'll seem to have the old

pit dried up! " said Eppie, turning away, and stooping to lift rather a large stone. " See, Daddy, I can carry this quite well," she said, going along with much energy for a few steps, but presently letting it fall.

" Ah, you're fine and strong, aren't you? " said Silas, while Eppie shook her aching arms and laughed. " Come, come, let us go and sit down on the bank against the stile there, and have no more lifting. You might hurt yourself, child. You'd need have somebody to work for you — and my arm isn't overstrong."

Silas uttered the last sentence slowly, as if it implied more than met the ear; and Eppie, when they sat down on the bank, nestled close to his side, and, taking hold caressingly of the arm that was not overstrong, held it on her lap, while Silas puffed again dutifully at the pipe, which occupied his other arm. An ash in the hedgerow behind made a fretted screen from the sun, and threw happy playful shadows all about them.

" Father," said Eppie, very gently, after they had been sitting in silence a little while, " if I was to be married, ought I to be married with my mother's ring? "

Silas gave an almost imperceptible start, though the question fell in with the undercurrent of thought in his own mind, and then said, in a subdued tone, " Why Eppie, have you been a-thinking on it? "

" Only this last week, father," said Eppie, ingenuously, " since Aaron talked to me about it."

" And what did he say? " said Silas, still in the same subdued way, as if he were anxious lest he should fall into the slightest tone that was not for Eppie's good.

" He said he should like to be married, because he was a-going in four and twenty, and had got a deal of gardening work, now Mr. Mott's given up; and he goes twice a week regular to Mr. Cass's and once to Mr. Osgood's, and they're going to take him on at the Rectory."

" And who is it as he's wanting to marry? " said Silas, with rather a sad smile.

" Why, me, to be sure, Daddy," said Eppie, with dimpling laughter, kissing her father's cheek; " as if he'd want to marry anybody else! "

" And you mean to have him, do you? " said Silas.

" Yes, sometime," said Eppie, " I don't know when. Everybody's married sometime, Aaron says. But I told him that wasn't true; for, I said, look at father — he's never been married."

" No, child," said Silas, " your father was a lone man till you was sent to him."

" But you'll never be lone again, father," said Eppie tenderly. " That was what Aaron said — ' I could never think o' taking you away from Master Marner, Eppie.' And I said, ' It 'ud be no use if you did, Aaron.' And he wants us all to live together, so as you needn't work a bit, father, only what's for your own pleasure; and he'd be as good as a son to you — that was what he said."

" And should you like that, Eppie? " said Silas, looking at her.

" I shouldn't mind it, father," said Eppie, quite simply. " And I should like things to be so as you needn't work much. But if it wasn't for that, I'd sooner things didn't change. I'm very happy. I like Aaron to be fond of me, and come and see us often, and behave pretty to you — he always *does* behave pretty to you, doesn't he, father? "

" Yes, child, nobody could behave better," said Silas emphatically. " He's his mother's lad."

" But I don't want any change," said Eppie. " I should like to go on a long, long while, just as we are. Only Aaron does want a change; and he made me cry a bit — only a bit — because he said I didn't care for him, for if I cared for him I should want us to be married, as he did."

"Eh, my blessed child," said Silas, laying down his pipe as if it were useless to pretend to smoke any longer, "you're o'er-young to be married. We'll ask Mrs. Winthrop — we'll ask Aaron's mother what *she* thinks; if there's a right thing to do, she'll come at it. But there's this to be thought on, Eppie: things *will* change, whether we like it or not; things won't go on for a long while just as they are and no difference. I shall get older and helplesser, and be a burden on you, belike, if I don't go away from you altogether. Not as I mean you'd think me a burden — I know you wouldn't — but it 'ud be hard upon you; and when I look for'ard to that, I like to think as you'd have somebody else besides me — somebody young and strong, as 'll outlast your own life, and take care on you to the end." Silas paused, and, resting his wrists on his knees, lifted his hands up and down meditatively as he looked on the ground.

"Then, would you like me to be married, father?" said Eppie, with a little trembling in her voice.

"I'll not be the man to say no, Eppie," said Silas emphatically; "but we'll ask your godmother. She'll wish the right thing by you and her son, too."

"There they come then," said Eppie. "Let us go and meet 'em. Oh, the pipe! won't you have it lit again, father?" said Eppie, lifting that medicinal appliance from the ground.

"Nay, child," said Silas, "I've done enough for today. I think, mayhap, a little of it does me more good than so much at once."

CHAPTER XVII

While Silas and Eppie were seated on the bank discoursing in the fleckered shade of the ash tree, Miss Priscilla Lammeter was resisting her sister's arguments, that it would be better to take tea at the Red House, and let her father have a long nap, than drive home to the Warrens so soon after dinner. The family party (of four only) were seated round the table in the dark wainscoted parlor, with the Sunday dessert before them, of fresh filberts, apples, and pears, duly ornamented with leaves by Nancy's own hand before the bells had rung for church.

A great change has come over the dark wainscoted parlor since we saw it in Godfrey's bachelor days, and under the wifeless reign of the old Squire. Now all is polish, on which no yesterday's dust is ever allowed to rest, from the yard's width of oaken boards round the carpet to the old Squire's gun and whips and walking sticks, ranged on the stag's antlers above the mantelpiece. All other signs of sporting and outdoor occupation Nancy has removed to another room; but she has brought into the Red House the habit of filial reverence, and preserves sacredly in a place of honor these relics of her husband's departed father. The tankards are on the side table still, but the bossed silver is undimmed by handling, and there are no dregs to send forth unpleasant suggestions; the only prevailing scent is of the lavender and rose leaves that fill the vases of Derbyshire spar. All is purity and order in this once dreary room, for, fifteen years ago, it was entered by a new presiding spirit.

"Now, father," said Nancy, "*is* there any call for you to go home to tea? Mayn't you just as well stay with us? — such a beautiful evening as it's likely to be."

The old gentleman had been talking with Godfrey about the increasing poor rate [1] and the ruinous times, and had not heard the dialogue between his daughters.

[1] **poor rate:** a tax levied by the church wardens in a parish for the relief of the poor.

" My dear, you must ask Priscilla," he said, in the once firm voice, now become rather broken. " She manages me and the farm, too."

" And reason good as I should manage you, father," said Priscilla, " else you'd be giving yourself your death with rheumatism. And as for the farm, if anything turns out wrong, as it can't but do in these times, there's nothing kills a man so soon as having nobody to find fault with but himself. It's a deal the best way o' being master, to let somebody else do the ordering, and keep the blaming in your own hands. It 'ud save many a man a stroke, *I* believe."

" Well, well, my dear," said her father, with a quiet laugh, " I didn't say you don't manage for everybody's good."

" Then manage so as you may stay tea, Priscilla," said Nancy, putting her hand on her sister's arm affectionately. " Come now; and we'll go round the garden while father has his nap."

" My dear child, he'll have a beautiful nap in the gig, for I shall drive. And as for staying tea, I can't hear of it; for there's this dairymaid, now she knows she's to be married, turned Michaelmas, she'd as lief pour the new milk in the pig trough as into the pans. That's the way with 'em all; it's as if they thought the world 'ud be new-made because they're to be married. So come and let me put my bonnet on, and there'll be time for us to walk round the garden while the horse is being put in."

When the sisters were treading the neatly swept garden walks, between the bright turf that contrasted pleasantly with the dark cones and arches and wall-like hedges of yew, Priscilla said —

" I'm as glad as anything at your husband's making that exchange o' land with Cousin Osgood, and beginning the dairying. It's a thousand pities you didn't do it before; for it'll give you something to fill your mind. There's nothing like a dairy if folks want a bit o' worrit to make the days pass. For as for rubbing furniture, when you can once see your face in a table there's nothing else to look for; but there's always something fresh with the dairy; for even in the depths o' winter there's some pleasure in conquering the butter, and making it come whether or no. My dear," added Priscilla, pressing her sister's hand affectionately as they walked side by side, " you'll never be low when you've got a dairy."

" Ah, Priscilla," said Nancy, returning the pressure with a grateful glance of her clear eyes, " but it won't make up to Godfrey; a dairy's not so much to a man. And it's only what he cares for that ever makes me low. I'm contented with the blessings we have, if he could be contented."

" It drives me past patience," said Priscilla impetuously, " that way o' the men — always wanting and wanting, and never easy with what they've got; they can't sit comfortable in their chairs when they've neither ache nor pain, but either they must stick a pipe in their mouths, to make 'em better than well, or else they must be swallowing something strong, though they're forced to make haste before the next meal comes in. But joyful be it spoken, our father was never that sort o' man. And if it had pleased God to make you ugly, like me, so as the men wouldn't ha' run after you, we might have kept to our own family, and had nothing to do with folks as have got uneasy blood in their veins."

" Oh, don't say so, Priscilla," said Nancy, repenting that she had called forth this outburst; " nobody has any occasion to find fault with Godfrey. It's natural he should be disappointed at not having any children; every man likes to have somebody to work for and lay by for, and he always counted so on making a fuss with 'em when they were little. There's many another man 'ud hanker more than he does. He's the best of husbands."

"Oh, I know," said Priscilla, smiling sarcastically, "I know the way o' wives; they set one on to abuse their husbands, and then they turn round on one and praise 'em as if they wanted to sell 'em. But father 'll be waiting for me; we must turn now."

The large gig with the steady old gray was at the front door, and Mr. Lammeter was already on the stone steps, passing the time in recalling to Godfrey what very fine points Speckle had when his master used to ride him.

"I always *would* have a good horse, you know," said the old gentleman, not liking that spirited time to be quite effaced from the memory of his juniors.

"Mind you bring Nancy to the Warrens before the week's out, Mr. Cass," was Priscilla's parting injunction, as she took the reins, and shook them gently, by way of friendly incitement to Speckle.

"I shall just take a turn to the fields against the stone pits, Nancy, and look at the draining," said Godfrey.

"You'll be in again by teatime, dear?"

"Oh, yes, I shall be back in an hour."

It was Godfrey's custom on a Sunday afternoon to do a little contemplative farming in a leisurely walk. Nancy seldom accompanied him; for the women of her generation — unless, like Priscilla, they took to outdoor management — were not given to much walking beyond their own house and garden, finding sufficient exercise in domestic duties. So, when Priscilla was not with her, she usually sat with Mant's Bible [1] before her, and, after following the text with her eyes for a little while, she would gradually permit them to wander as her thoughts had already insisted on wandering.

But Nancy's Sunday thoughts were rarely quite out of keeping with the devout and reverential intention implied by the book spread open before her. She was not theologically instructed enough to discern very clearly the relation between the sacred documents of the past which she opened without method, and her own obscure, simple life; but the spirit of rectitude, and the sense of responsibility for the effect of her conduct on others, which were strong elements in Nancy's character, had made it a habit with her to scrutinize her past feelings and actions with self-questioning solicitude. Her mind not being courted by a great variety of subjects, she filled the vacant moments by living inwardly, again and again, through all her remembered experience, especially through the fifteen years of her married time, in which her life and its significance had been doubled. She recalled the small details, the words, tones, and looks, in the critical scenes which had opened a new epoch for her by giving her a deeper insight into the relations and trials of life, or which had called on her for some little effort of forbearance, or of painful adherence to an imagined or real duty — asking herself continually whether she had been in any respect blamable. This excessive rumination and self-questioning is perhaps a morbid habit inevitable to a mind of much moral sensibility when shut out from its due share of outward activity and of practical claims on its affections — inevitable to a noblehearted, childless woman, when her lot is narrow. "I can do so little — have I done it all well?" is the perpetually recurring thought; and there are no voices calling her away from that soliloquy, no peremptory demands to divert energy from vain regret or superfluous scruple.

There was one main thread of painful experience in Nancy's married life, and on it hung certain deeply felt scenes, which were the oftenest revived in retro-

[1] **Mant's Bible:** published by Richard Mant in 1817.

spect. The short dialogue with Priscilla in the garden had determined the current of retrospect in that frequent direction this particular Sunday afternoon. The first wandering of her thought from the text, which she still attempted dutifully to follow with her eyes and silent lips, was into an imaginary enlargement of the defense she had set up for her husband against Priscilla's implied blame. The vindication of the loved object is the best balm affection can find for its wounds. "A man must have so much on his mind," is the belief by which a wife often supports a cheerful face under rough answers and unfeeling words. And Nancy's deepest wounds had all come from the perception that the absence of children from their hearth was dwelt on in her husband's mind as a privation to which he could not reconcile himself.

Yet sweet Nancy might have been expected to feel still more keenly the denial of a blessing to which she had looked forward with all the varied expectations and preparations, solemn and prettily trivial, which fill the mind of a loving woman when she expects to become a mother. Was there not a drawer filled with the neat work of her hands, all unworn and untouched, just as she had arranged it there fourteen years ago — just, but for one little dress, which had been made the burial dress? But under this immediate personal trial Nancy was so firmly unmurmuring that years ago she had suddenly renounced the habit of visiting this drawer, lest she should in this way be cherishing a longing for what was not given.

Perhaps it was this very severity toward any indulgence of what she held to be sinful regret in herself that made her shrink from applying her own standard to her husband. "It is very different — it is much worse for a man to be disappointed in that way; a woman can always be satisfied with devoting herself to her husband, but a man wants something that will make him look forward more — and sitting by the fire is so much duller to him than to a woman." And always, when Nancy reached this point in her meditations — trying, with predetermined sympathy, to see everything as Godfrey saw it — there came a renewal of self-questioning. *Had* she done everything in her power to lighten Godfrey's privation? Had she really been right in the resistance which had cost her so much pain six years ago, and again four years ago — the resistance to her husband's wish that they should adopt a child? Adoption was more remote from the ideas and habits of that time than of our own; still Nancy had her opinion on it. It was as necessary to her mind to have an opinion on all topics, not exclusively masculine, that had come under her notice, as for her to have a precisely marked place for every article of her personal property; and her opinions were always principles to be unwaveringly acted on. They were firm, not because of their basis, but because she held them with a tenacity inseparable from her mental action. On all the duties and proprieties of life, from filial behavior to the arrangements of the evening toilette, pretty Nancy Lammeter, by the time she was three and twenty, had her unalterable little code, and had formed every one of her habits in strict accordance with that code. She carried these decided judgments within her in the most unobtrusive way; they rooted themselves in her mind, and grew there as quietly as grass. Years ago, we know, she insisted on dressing like Priscilla, because "it was right for sisters to dress alike," and because, "she would do what was right if she wore a gown dyed with cheese coloring." That was a trivial but typical instance of the mode in which Nancy's life was regulated.

It was one of those rigid principles, and

no petty egoistic feeling, which had been the ground of Nancy's difficult resistance to her husband's wish. To adopt a child, because children of your own had been denied you, was to try and choose your lot in spite of Providence; the adopted child, she was convinced, would never turn out well, and would be a curse to those who had willfully and rebelliously sought what it was clear that, for some high reason, they were better without. When you saw a thing was not meant to be, said Nancy, it was a bounden duty to leave off so much as wishing for it. And so far, perhaps, the wisest of men could scarcely make more than a verbal improvement in her principle. But the conditions under which she held it apparent that a thing was not meant to be depended on a more peculiar mode of thinking. She would have given up making a purchase at a particular place if, on three successive times, rain, or some other cause of Heaven's sending, had formed an obstacle; and she would have anticipated a broken limb or other heavy misfortune to anyone who persisted in spite of such indications.

"But why should you think the child would turn out ill?" said Godfrey, in his remonstrances. "She has thriven as well as child can do with the weaver; and *he* adopted her. There isn't such a pretty little girl anywhere else in the parish, or one fitter for the station we could give her. Where can be the likelihood of her being a curse to anybody?"

"Yes, my dear Godfrey," said Nancy, who was sitting with her hands tightly clasped together, and with yearning, regretful affection in her eyes. "The child may not turn out ill with the weaver. But, then, he didn't go to seek her, as we should be doing. It will be wrong; I feel sure it will. Don't you remember what that lady we met at the Royston Baths told us about the child her sister adopted? That was the only adopting I ever heard of; and the child was transported[1] when it was twenty-three. Dear Godfrey, don't ask me to do what I know is wrong; I should never be happy again. I know it's very hard for *you* — it's easier for me — but it's the will of Providence."

It might seem singular that Nancy — with her religious theory pieced together out of narrow social traditions, fragments of church doctrine imperfectly understood, and girlish reasonings on her small experience — should have arrived by herself at a way of thinking so nearly akin to that of many devout people, whose beliefs are held in the shape of a system quite remote from her knowledge — singular, if we did not know that human beliefs, like all other natural growths, elude the barriers of system.

Godfrey had from the first specified Eppie, then about twelve years old, as a child suitable for them to adopt. It had never occurred to him that Silas would rather part with his life than with Eppie. Surely the weaver would wish the best to the child he had taken so much trouble with, and would be glad that such good fortune should happen to her; she would always be very grateful to him, and he would be well provided for to the end of his life — provided for as the excellent part he had done by the child deserved. Was it not an appropriate thing for people in a higher station to take a charge off the hands of a man in a lower? It seemed an eminently appropriate thing to Godfrey, for reasons that were known only to himself; and by a common fallacy, he imagined the measure would be easy because he had private motives for desiring it. This was rather a coarse mode of estimating Silas's relation to Eppie; but we must remember that many of the impressions which Godfrey was likely to

[1] **transported:** as used here, sent to a penal colony in Australia.

gather concerning the laboring people around him would favor the idea that deep affections can hardly go along with callous palms and scant means; and he had not had the opportunity, even if he had had the power, of entering intimately into all that was exceptional in the weaver's experience. It was only the want of adequate knowledge that could have made it possible for Godfrey deliberately to entertain an unfeeling project; his natural kindness had outlived that blighting time of cruel wishes, and Nancy's praise of him as a husband was not founded entirely on a willful illusion.

"I was right," she said to herself, when she had recalled all their scenes of discussion — "I feel I was right to say him nay, though it hurt me more than anything; but how good Godfrey has been about it! Many men would have been very angry with me for standing out against their wishes; and they might have thrown out that they'd had ill luck in marrying me; but Godfrey has never been the man to say me an unkind word. It's only what he can't hide; everything seems so blank to him, I know; and the land — what a difference it 'ud make to him, when he goes to see after things, if he'd children growing up that he was doing it all for! But I won't murmur; and perhaps if he'd married a woman who'd have had children, she'd have vexed him in other ways."

This possibility was Nancy's chief comfort; and to give it greater strength, she labored to make it impossible that any other wife should have had more perfect tenderness. She had been *forced* to vex him by that one denial. Godfrey was not insensible to her loving effort, and did Nancy no injustice as to the motives of her obstinacy. It was impossible to have lived with her fifteen years and not be aware that an unselfish clinging to the right and a sincerity clear as the flower-born dew were her main characteristics; indeed, Godfrey felt this so strongly that his own more wavering nature, too averse to facing difficulty to be unvaryingly simple and truthful, was kept in a certain awe of this gentle wife who watched his looks with a yearning to obey them. It seemed to him impossible that he should ever confess to her the truth about Eppie; she would never recover from the repulsion the story of his earlier marriage would create, told to her now, after that long concealment. And the child, too, he thought, must become an object of repulsion; the very sight of her would be painful. The shock to Nancy's mingled pride and ignorance of the world's evil might even be too much for her delicate frame. Since he had married her with that secret on his heart he must keep it there to the last. Whatever else he did, he could not make an irreparable breach between himself and this long-loved wife.

Meanwhile, why could he not make up his mind to the absence of children from a hearth brightened by such a wife? Why did his mind fly uneasily to that void, as if it were the sole reason why life was not thoroughly joyous to him? I suppose it is the way with all men and women who reach middle age without the clear perception that life never *can* be thoroughly joyous; under the vague dullness of the gray hours, dissatisfaction seeks a definite object, and finds it in the privation of an untried good. Dissatisfaction, seated musingly on a childless hearth, thinks with envy of the father whose return is greeted by young voices — seated at the meal where the little heads rise one above another like nursery plants, it sees a black care hovering behind every one of them, and thinks the impulses by which men abandon freedom, and seek for ties, are surely nothing but a brief madness. In Godfrey's case there were further reasons why his thoughts should be continually solicited by this one point in his lot; his conscience, never thoroughly easy about Eppie, now gave his childless home the aspect of a retribution; and as the time passed on, under Nancy's refusal to adopt her, any retrieval of his error became more and more difficult.

On this Sunday afternoon it was already four years since there had been any allusion to the subject between them, and Nancy supposed that it was forever buried.

"I wonder if he'll mind it less or more as he gets older," she thought; "I'm afraid more. Aged people feel the miss of children; what would father do without Priscilla? And if I die, Godfrey will be very lonely — not holding together with his brothers much. But I won't be over-anxious, and trying to make things out beforehand; I must do my best for the present."

With that last thought Nancy roused herself from her reverie, and turned her eyes again toward the forsaken page. It had been forsaken longer than she imagined, for she was presently surprised by the appearance of the servant with the tea things. It was, in fact, a little before the usual time for tea; but Jane had her reasons.

"Is your master come into the yard, Jane?"

"No'm, he isn't," said Jane, with a slight emphasis, of which, however, her mistress took no notice.

"I don't know whether you've seen 'em, 'm," continued Jane, after a pause, "but there's folks making haste all one way, afore the front window. I doubt something's happened. There's niver a man to be seen i' the yard, else I'd send and see. I've been up into the top attic, but there's no seeing anything for trees. I hope nobody's hurt, that's all."

"Oh, no, I daresay there's nothing much the matter," said Nancy. "It's perhaps Mr. Snell's bull got out again, as he did before."

"I wish he mayn't gore anybody, then, that's all," said Jane, not altogether despising a hypothesis which covered a few imaginary calamities.

"The girl is always terrifying me," thought Nancy; "I wish Godfrey would come in."

She went to the front window and looked as far as she could see along the road, with an uneasiness which she felt to be childish, for there were now no such signs of excitement as Jane had spoken of, and Godfrey would not be likely to return by the village road, but by the fields. She continued to stand, however, looking at the placid churchyard with the long shadows of the gravestones across the bright green hillocks, and at the glowing autumn colors of the Rectory trees beyond. Before such calm external beauty the presence of a vague fear is more distinctly felt — like a raven flapping its slow wing across the sunny air. Nancy wished more and more that Godfrey would come in.

CHAPTER XVIII

It was a favorite theme of George Eliot's that wrongdoing carried with it the germ of its own punishment, and that somehow or other righteous living would be ultimately rewarded. As you read on notice how *justly* the problems of the story are solved in the next three chapters: notice how Godfrey Cass is forced by circumstances to accept the consequences of his early misdeeds, and how the wrong done originally to Silas Marner is balanced by the accidental good which came to him.

Someone opened the door at the other end of the room, and Nancy felt that it was her husband. She turned from the window with gladness in her eyes, for the wife's chief dread was stilled.

"Dear, I'm so thankful you're come," she said, going toward him. "I began to get" —

She paused abruptly, for Godfrey was laying down his hat with trembling hands, and turned toward her with a pale face and a strange unanswering glance, as if he saw her indeed, but saw her as part of a scene invisible to herself. She laid her hand on his arm, not daring to speak again; but he left the touch unnoticed, and threw himself into his chair.

Jane was already at the door with the hissing urn. "Tell her to keep away, will you?" said Godfrey; and when the door was closed again he exerted himself to speak more distinctly.

"Sit down, Nancy — there," he said, pointing to a chair opposite him. "I came back as soon as I could, to hinder anybody's telling you but me. I've had a great shock — but I care most about the shock it'll be to you."

"It isn't father and Priscilla?" said Nancy, with quivering lips, clasping her hands together tightly on her lap.

"No, it's nobody living," said Godfrey, unequal to the considerate skill with which he would have wished to make his revelation. "It's Dunstan — my brother Dunstan, that we lost sight of sixteen years ago. We've found him — found his body — his skeleton."

The deep dread Godfrey's look had created in Nancy made her feel these words a relief. She sat in comparative calmness to hear what else he had to tell. He went on —

"The stone pit has gone dry suddenly — from the draining, I suppose; and there he lies — has lain for sixteen years, wedged between two great stones. There's his watch and seals, and there's my gold-handled hunting whip, with my name on; he took it away, without my knowing, the day he went hunting on Wildfire, the last time he was seen."

Godfrey paused; it was not so easy to say what came next. "Do you think he drowned himself?" said Nancy, almost wondering that her husband should be so deeply shaken by what had happened all those years ago to an unloved brother, of whom worse things had been augured.

"No, he fell in," said Godfrey, in a low but distinct voice, as if he felt some deep meaning in the fact. Presently he added, "Dunstan was the man that robbed Silas Marner."

The blood rushed to Nancy's face and neck at this surprise and shame, for she had been bred up to regard even a distant kinship with crime as a dishonor.

"O Godfrey!" she said, with compassion in her tone, for she had immediately reflected that the dishonor must be felt still more keenly by her husband.

"There was the money in the pit," he continued — "all the weaver's money. Everything's been gathered up, and they're taking the skeleton to the Rainbow. But I came back to tell you; there was no hindering it; you must know."

He was silent, looking on the ground for two long minutes. Nancy would have said some words of comfort under this disgrace, but she refrained, from an instinctive sense that there was something behind — that Godfrey had something else to tell her. Presently he lifted his eyes to her face, and kept them fixed on her, as he said —

"Everything comes to light, Nancy, sooner or later. When God Almighty wills it, our secrets are found out. I've lived with a secret on my mind, but I'll keep it from you no longer. I wouldn't have you know it by somebody else, and not by me — I wouldn't have you find it out after I'm dead. I'll tell you now. It's been 'I will' and 'I won't' with me all my life — I'll make sure of myself now."

Nancy's utmost dread had returned. The eyes of the husband and wife met with awe in them, as at a crisis which suspended affection.

"Nancy," said Godfrey slowly, "when

I married you, I hid something from you — something I ought to have told you. That woman Marner found dead in the snow — Eppie's mother — that wretched woman — was my wife; Eppie is my child."

He paused, dreading the effect of his confession. But Nancy sat quite still, only that her eyes dropped and ceased to meet his. She was pale and quiet as a meditative statue, clasping her hands on her lap.

"You'll never think the same of me again," said Godfrey, after a little while, with some tremor in his voice.

She was silent.

"I oughtn't to have left the child unowned; I oughtn't to have kept it from you. But I couldn't bear to give you up, Nancy. I was led away into marrying her — I suffered for it."

Still Nancy was silent, looking down; and he almost expected that she would presently get up and say she would go to her father's. How could she have any mercy for faults that must seem so black to her, with her simple, severe notions?

But at last she lifted up her eyes to his again and spoke. There was no indignation in her voice — only deep regret.

"Godfrey, if you had but told me this six years ago, we could have done some of our duty by the child. Do you think I'd have refused to take her in, if I'd known she was yours?"

At that moment Godfrey felt all the bitterness of an error that was not simply futile, but had defeated its own end. He had not measured this wife with whom he had lived so long. But she spoke again, with more agitation.

"And — O Godfrey — if we'd had her from the first, if you'd taken to her as you ought, she'd have loved me for her mother — and you'd have been happier with me; I could better have bore my little baby dying, and our life might have been more like what we used to think it 'ud be."

The tears fell, and Nancy ceased to speak.

"But you wouldn't have married me then, Nancy, if I'd told you," said Godfrey, urged, in the bitterness of his self-reproach, to prove to himself that his conduct had not been utter folly. "You may think you would now, but you wouldn't then. With your pride and your father's, you'd have hated having anything to do with me after the talk there'd have been."

"I can't say what I should have done about that, Godfrey. I should never have married anybody else. But I wasn't worth doing wrong for — nothing is in this world. Nothing is so good as it seems beforehand — not even our marrying wasn't, you see." There was a faint sad smile on Nancy's face as she said the last words.

"I'm a worse man than you thought I was, Nancy," said Godfrey, rather tremulously. "Can you forgive me ever?"

"The wrong to me is but little, Godfrey; you've made it up to me — you've been good to me for fifteen years. It's another you did the wrong to; and I doubt it can never be all made up for."

"But we can take Eppie now," said Godfrey. "I won't mind the world knowing at last. I'll be plain and open for the rest o' my life."

"It'll be different coming to us, now she's grown up," said Nancy, shaking her head sadly. "But it's your duty to acknowledge her and provide for her; and I'll do my part by her, and pray to God Almighty to make her love me."

"Then we'll go together to Silas Marner's this very night, as soon as everything's quiet at the stone pits."

CHAPTER XIX

Between eight and nine o'clock that evening Eppie and Silas were seated alone in the cottage. After the great excitement the weaver had undergone from the events of the afternoon, he had felt a longing for this quietude, and had even begged Mrs. Winthrop and Aaron, who had naturally lingered behind everyone else, to leave him alone with his child. The excitement had not passed away; it had only reached that stage when the keenness of the susceptibility makes external stimulus intolerable — when there is no sense of weariness, but rather an intensity of inward life, under which sleep is an impossibility. Anyone who has watched such moments in other men remembers the brightness of the eyes and the strange definiteness that comes over coarse features from the transient influence. It is as if a new fineness of ear for all spiritual voices had sent wonder-working vibrations through the heavy mortal frame — as if "beauty born of murmuring sound"[1] had passed into the face of the listener.

Silas's face showed that sort of transfiguration, as he sat in his armchair and looked at Eppie. She had drawn her own chair toward his knees, and leaned forward, holding both his hands, while she looked up at him. On the table near them, lit by a candle, lay the recovered gold — the old long-loved gold, ranged in orderly heaps, as Silas used to range it in the days when it was his only joy. He had been telling her how he used to count it every night, and how his soul was utterly desolate till she was sent to him.

"At first, I'd a sort o' feeling come across me now and then," he was saying in a subdued tone, "as if you might be changed into the gold again; for sometimes, turn my head which way I would, I seemed to see the gold; and I thought I should be glad if I could feel it, and find it was come back. But that didn't last long. After a bit, I should have thought it was a curse come again if it had drove you from me, for I'd got to feel the need o' your looks and your voice and the touch o' your little fingers. You didn't know then, Eppie, when you were such a little un — you didn't know what your old Father Silas felt for you."

"But I know now, father," said Eppie. "If it hadn't been for you, they'd have taken me to the workhouse, and there'd have been nobody to love me."

"Eh, my precious child, the blessing was mine. If you hadn't been sent to save me, I should ha' gone to the grave in my misery. The money was taken away from me in time; and you see it's been kept — kept till it was wanted for you. It's wonderful — our life is wonderful."

Silas sat in silence a few minutes, looking at the money. "It takes no hold of me now," he said, ponderingly — "the money doesn't. I wonder if it ever could again — I doubt it might if I lost you, Eppie. I might come to think I was forsaken again, and lose the feeling that God was good to me."

At that moment there was a knocking at the door, and Eppie was obliged to rise without answering Silas. Beautiful she looked, with the tenderness of gathering tears in her eyes and a slight flush on her cheeks, as she stepped to open the door. The flush deepened when she saw Mr. and Mrs. Godfrey Cass. She made her little rustic curtsy, and held the door wide for them to enter.

"We're disturbing you very late, my dear," said Mrs. Cass, taking Eppie's hand, and looking in her face with an expression of anxious interest and admiration. Nancy herself was pale and tremulous.

Eppie, after placing chairs for Mr. and Mrs. Cass, went to stand against Silas, opposite to them.

"Well, Marner," said Godfrey, trying

[1] **"beauty born of murmuring sound":** quoted from Wordsworth's poem, "Three Years She Grew in Sun and Shower." Wordsworth was one of George Eliot's favorite poets.

to speak with perfect firmness, " it's a great comfort to me to see you with your money again, that you've been deprived of so many years. It was one of my family did you the wrong — the more grief to me — and I feel bound to make up to you for it in every way. Whatever I can do for you will be nothing but paying a debt, even if I looked no further than the robbery. But there are other things I'm beholden — shall be beholden to you for, Marner."

Godfrey checked himself. It had been agreed between him and his wife that the subject of his fatherhood should be approached very carefully, and that, if possible, the disclosure should be reserved for the future, so that it might be made to Eppie gradually. Nancy had urged this, because she felt strongly the painful light in which Eppie must inevitably see the relation between her father and mother.

Silas, always ill at ease when he was being spoken to by " betters," such as Mr. Cass — tall, powerful, florid men, seen chiefly on horseback — answered with some constraint —

" Sir, I've a deal to thank you for a'ready. As for the robbery, I count it no loss to me. And if I did, you couldn't help it; you aren't answerable for it."

" You may look at it in that way, Marner, but I never can; and I hope you'll let me act according to my own feeling of what's just. I know you're easily contented; you've been a hard-working man all your life."

" Yes, sir, yes," said Marner meditatively. " I should ha' been bad off without my work; it was what I held by when everything else was gone from me."

" Ah," said Godfrey, applying Marner's words simply to his bodily wants, " it was a good trade for you in this country, because there's been a great deal of linen weaving to be done. But you're getting rather past such close work, Marner; it's time you laid by and had some rest. You look a good deal pulled down, though you're not an old man, *are* you? "

" Fifty-five, as near as I can say, sir," said Silas.

" Oh, why, you may live thirty years longer — look at old Macey! And that money on the table, after all, is but little. It won't go far either way — whether it's put out to interest, or you were to live on it as long as it would last; it wouldn't go far if you'd nobody to keep but yourself, and you've had two to keep for a good many years now."

" Eh, sir," said Silas, unaffected by anything Godfrey was saying, " I'm in no fear o' want. We shall do very well — Eppie and me 'ull do well enough. There's few workingfolks have got so much laid by as that. I don't know what it is to gentlefolks, but I look upon it as a deal — almost too much. And as for us, it's little we want."

" Only the garden, father," said Eppie, blushing up to the ears the moment after.

" You love a garden, do you, my dear? " said Nancy, thinking that this turn in the point of view might help her husband. " We should agree in that; I give a deal of time to the garden."

" Ah, there's plenty of gardening at the Red House," said Godfrey, surprised at the difficulty he found in approaching a proposition which had seemed so easy to him in the distance. " You've done a good part by Eppie, Marner, for sixteen years. It 'ud be a great comfort to you to see her well provided for, wouldn't it? She looks blooming and healthy, but not fit for any hardships; she doesn't look like a strapping girl come of working parents. You'd like to see her taken care of by those who can leave her well off, and made a lady of her; she's more fit for it than for a rough life, such as she might come to have in a few years' time."

A slight flush came over Marner's face,

and disappeared, like a passing gleam. Eppie was simply wondering Mr. Cass should talk so about things that seemed to have nothing to do with reality; but Silas was hurt and uneasy.

"I don't take your meaning, sir," he answered, not having words at command to express the mingled feelings with which he had heard Mr. Cass's words.

"Well, my meaning is this, Marner," said Godfrey, determined to come to the point. "Mrs. Cass and I, you know, have no children — nobody to be the better for our good home and everything else we have — more than enough for ourselves. And we should like to have somebody in the place of a daughter to us — we should like to have Eppie, and treat her in every way as our own child. It 'ud be a great comfort to you in your old age, I hope, to see her fortune made in that way, after you've been at the trouble of bringing her up so well. And it's right you should have every reward for that. And Eppie, I'm sure, will always love you and be grateful to you; she'd come and see you very often, and we should all be on the lookout to do everything we could toward making you comfortable."

A plain man like Godfrey Cass, speaking under some embarrassment, necessarily blunders on words that are coarser than his intentions, and that are likely to fall gratingly on susceptible feelings. While he had been speaking, Eppie had quietly passed her arm behind Silas's head, and let her hand rest against it caressingly; she felt him trembling violently. He was silent for some moments when Mr. Cass had ended — powerless under the conflict of emotions, all alike painful. Eppie's heart was swelling at the sense that her father was in distress; and she was just going to lean down and speak to him, when one struggling dread at last gained the mastery over every other in Silas, and he said faintly —

"Eppie, my child, speak. I won't stand in your way. Thank Mr. and Mrs. Cass."

Eppie took her hand from her father's head, and came forward a step. Her cheeks were flushed, but not with shyness this time: the sense that her father was in doubt and suffering banished that sort of self-consciousness. She dropped a low curtsy, first to Mrs. Cass and then to Mr. Cass, and said —

"Thank you, ma'am — thank you, sir. But I can't leave my father, nor own anybody nearer than him. And I don't want to be a lady — thank you all the same" (here Eppie dropped another curtsy). "I couldn't give up the folks I've been used to."

Eppie's lip began to tremble a little at the last words. She retreated to her father's chair again, and held him round the neck; while Silas, with a subdued sob, put up his hand to grasp hers.

The tears were in Nancy's eyes, but her sympathy with Eppie was, naturally, divided with distress on her husband's account. She dared not speak, wondering what was going on in her husband's mind.

Godfrey felt an irritation inevitable to almost all of us when we encounter an unexpected obstacle. He had been full of his own penitence and resolution to retrieve his error as far as the time was left to him; he was possessed with all-important feelings, that were to lead to a predetermined course of action which he had fixed on as the right, and he was not prepared to enter with lively appreciation into other people's feelings counteracting his virtuous resolves. The agitation with which he spoke again was not quite unmixed with anger.

"But I've a claim on you, Eppie — the strongest of all claims. It's my duty, Marner, to own Eppie as my child, and provide for her. She's my own child; her mother was my wife. I've a natural claim on her that must stand before every other."

Eppie had given a violent start, and turned quite pale. Silas, on the contrary, who had been relieved, by Eppie's answer, from the dread lest his mind should be in opposition to hers, felt the spirit of resistance in him set free, not without a touch of parental fierceness. "Then, sir," he answered, with an accent of bitterness that had been silent in him since the memorable day when his youthful hope had perished — "then, sir, why didn't you say so sixteen year ago, and claim her before I'd come to love her, i'stead o' coming to take her from me now, when you might as well take the heart out o' my body? God gave her to me because you turned your back upon her, and He looks upon her as mine; you've no right to her! When a man turns a blessing from his door, it falls to them as take it in."

"I know that, Marner. I was wrong. I've repented of my conduct in that matter," said Godfrey, who could not help feeling the edge of Silas's words.

"I'm glad to hear it, sir," said Marner, with gathering excitement; "but repentance doesn't alter what's been going on for sixteen year. Your coming now and saying 'I'm her father,' doesn't alter the feelings inside us. It's me she's been calling her father ever since she could say the word."

"But I think you might look at the thing more reasonably, Marner," said Godfrey, unexpectedly awed by the weaver's direct truth-speaking. "It isn't as if she was to be taken quite away from you, so that you'd never see her again. She'll be very near you, and come to see you very often. She'll feel just the same toward you."

"Just the same?" said Marner, more bitterly than ever. "How'll she feel just the same for me as she does now, when we eat o' the same bit, and drink o' the same cup, and think o' the same things from one day's end to another? Just the same? That's idle talk. You'd cut us i' two."

Godfrey, unqualified by experience to discern the pregnancy of Marner's simple words, felt rather angry again. It seemed to him that the weaver was very selfish (a judgment readily passed by those who have never tested their own power of sacrifice) to oppose what was undoubtedly for Eppie's welfare; and he felt himself called upon, for her sake, to assert his authority.

"I should have thought, Marner," he said severely, "I should have thought your affection for Eppie would make you rejoice in what was for her good, even if it did call upon you to give up something. You ought to remember your own life's uncertain, and she's at an age now when her lot may soon be fixed in a way very different from what it would be in her father's home; she may marry some low workingman, and then, whatever I might do for her, I couldn't make her well off. You're putting yourself in the way of her welfare; and though I'm sorry to hurt you after what you've done, and what I've left undone, I feel now it's my duty to insist on taking care of my own daughter. I want to do my duty."

It would be difficult to say whether it were Silas or Eppie that was most deeply stirred by this last speech of Godfrey's. Thought had been very busy in Eppie as she listened to the contest between her old long-loved father and this new unfamiliar father who had suddenly come to fill the place of that black featureless shadow which had held the ring and placed it on her mother's finger. Her imagination had darted backward in conjectures, and forward in previsions, of what this revealed fatherhood implied; and there were words in Godfrey's last speech which helped to make the previsions especially definite. Not that these thoughts, either of past or future, determined her resolution — *that* was determined by the feelings which vibrated to every word Silas had uttered; but they raised, even apart from these feelings, a repulsion toward the offered lot and the newly revealed father.

Silas, on the other hand, was again stricken in conscience, and alarmed lest Godfrey's accusation should be true — lest he should be raising his own will as an obstacle to Eppie's good. For many moments he was mute, struggling for the self-conquest necessary to the uttering of the difficult words. They came out tremulously.

"I'll say no more. Let it be as you will. Speak to the child. I'll hinder nothing."

Even Nancy, with all the acute sensibility of her own affections, shared her husband's view, that Marner was not justifiable in his wish to retain Eppie, after her real father had avowed himself. She felt that it was a very hard trial for the poor weaver, but her code allowed no question that a father by blood must have a claim above that of any foster father. Besides, Nancy, used all her life to plenteous circumstances and the privileges of "respectability," could not enter into the pleasures which early nurture and habit connect with all the little aims and efforts of the poor who are born poor; to her mind, Eppie, in being restored to her birthright, was entering on a too-long-withheld but unquestionable good. Hence she heard Silas's last words with relief, and thought, as Godfrey did, that their wish was achieved.

"Eppie, my dear," said Godfrey, looking at his daughter, not without some embarrassment, under the sense that she was old enough to judge him, "it'll always be our wish that you should show your love and gratitude to one who's been a father to you so many years, and we shall want to help you to make him comfortable in every way. But we hope you'll come to love us as well; and though I haven't been what a father should ha' been to you all these years, I wish to do the utmost in my power for you for the rest of my life, and provide for you as my only child. And you'll have the best of mothers in my wife — that'll be a blessing you haven't known since you were old enough to know it."

"My dear, you'll be a treasure to me," said Nancy, in her gentle voice. "We shall want for nothing when we have our daughter."

Eppie did not come forward and curtsy, as she had done before. She held Silas's hand in hers, and grasped it firmly — it was a weaver's hand, with a palm and finger tips that were sensitive to such pressure — while she spoke with colder decision than before.

"Thank you, ma'am — thank you, sir, for your offers — they're very great, and far above my wish. For I should have no delight i' life any more if I was forced to go away from my father, and knew he was sitting at home a-thinking of me and feeling lone. We've been used to be happy together every day, and I can't think o' no happiness without him. And he says he'd nobody i' the world till I was sent to him, and he'd have nothing when I was gone. And he's took care of me and loved me from the first, and I'll cleave to him as long as he lives, and nobody shall ever come between him and me."

"But you must make sure, Eppie," said Silas, in a low voice — "you must make sure as you won't ever be sorry, because you've made your choice to stay among poor folks, and with poor clothes and things, when you might ha' had everything o' the best."

His sensitiveness on this point had increased as he listened to Eppie's words of faithful affection.

"I can never be sorry, father," said Eppie. "I shouldn't know what to think on or to wish for with fine things about me, as I haven't been used to. And it 'ud be poor work for me to put on things, and ride in a gig, and sit in a place at church, as 'ud make them as I'm fond of think me unfitting company for 'em. What could *I* care for then?"

Nancy looked at Godfrey with a pained, questioning glance. But his eyes were fixed on the floor, where he was moving the end of his stick, as if he were pondering on something absently. She thought there was a word which might perhaps come better from her lips than from his.

"What you say is natural, my dear child — it's natural you should cling to those who've brought you up," she said mildly; "but there's a duty you owe to your lawful father. There's perhaps something to be given up on more sides than one. When your father opens his home to you, I think it's right you shouldn't turn your back on it."

"I can't feel as I've got any father but one," said Eppie impetuously, while the tears gathered. "I've always thought of a little home where he'd sit i' the corner and I should fend and do everything for him; I can't think o' no other home. I wasn't brought up to be a lady, and I can't turn my mind to it. I like the workingfolks, and their victuals, and their ways. And," she ended passionately, while the tears fell, "I'm promised to marry a workingman, as'll live with father, and help me to take care of him."

Godfrey looked up at Nancy with a flushed face and smarting, dilated eyes. This frustration of a purpose toward which he had set out under the exalted consciousness that he was about to compensate in some degree for the greatest demerit of his life, made him feel the air of the room stifling.

"Let us go," he said, in an undertone.

"We won't talk of this any longer now," said Nancy, rising. "We're your well-wishers, my dear — and yours too, Marner. We shall come and see you again. It's getting late now."

In this way she covered her husband's abrupt departure, for Godfrey had gone straight to the door, unable to say more.

CHAPTER XX

Nancy and Godfrey walked home under the starlight in silence. When they entered the oaken parlor, Godfrey threw himself into his chair, while Nancy laid down her bonnet and shawl, and stood on the hearth near her husband, unwilling to leave him even for a few minutes, and yet fearing to utter any word lest it might jar on his feeling. At last Godfrey turned his head toward her, and their eyes met, dwelling in that meeting without any movement on either side. That quiet mutual gaze of a trusting husband and wife is like the first moment of rest or refuge from a great weariness or a great danger — not to be interfered with by speech or action which would distract the sensations from the fresh enjoyment of repose.

But presently he put out his hand, and as Nancy placed hers within it, he drew her toward him, and said —

"That's ended!"

She bent to kiss him, and then said, as she stood by his side, "Yes, I'm afraid we must give up the hope of having her for a daughter. It wouldn't be right to want to force her to come to us against her will. We can't alter her bringing up and what's come of it."

"No," said Godfrey, with a keen decisiveness of tone, in contrast with his usually careless and unemphatic speech — "there's debts we can't pay like money debts, by paying extra for the years that have slipped by. While I've been putting off and putting off, the trees have been growing — it's too late now. Marner was in the right in what he said about a man's turning away a blessing from his door; it falls to somebody else. I wanted to pass for childless once, Nancy — I shall pass for childless now against my wish."

Nancy did not speak immediately, but after a little while she asked, " You won't make it known, then, about Eppie's being your daughter? "

" No — where would be the good to anybody? — only harm. I must do what I can for her in the state of life she chooses. I must see who it is she's thinking of marrying."

" If it won't do any good to make the thing known," said Nancy, who thought she might now allow herself the relief of entertaining a feeling which she had tried to silence before, " I should be very thankful for father and Priscilla never to be troubled with knowing what was done in the past, more than about Dunsey; it can't be helped, their knowing that."

" I shall put it in my will — I think I shall put it in my will. I shouldn't like to leave anything to be found out, like this about Dunsey," said Godfrey meditatively. " But I can't see anything but difficulties that 'ud come from telling it now. I must do what I can to make her happy in her own way. I've a notion," he added, after a moment's pause, " it's Aaron Winthrop she meant she was engaged to. I remember seeing him with her and Marner going away from church."

" Well, he's very sober and industrious," said Nancy, trying to view the matter as cheerfully as possible.

Godfrey fell into thoughtfulness again. Presently he looked up at Nancy sorrowfully, and said —

" She's a very pretty, nice girl, isn't she, Nancy? "

" Yes, dear; and with just your hair and eyes. I wonder it had never struck me before."

" I think she took a dislike to me at the thought of my being her father. I could see a change in her manner after that."

" She couldn't bear to think of not looking on Marner as her father," said Nancy, not wishing to confirm her husband's painful impression.

" She thinks I did wrong by her mother as well as by her. She thinks me worse than I am. But she *must* think it; she can never know all. It's part of my punishment, Nancy, for my daughter to dislike me. I should never have got into that trouble if I'd been true to you — if I hadn't been a fool. I'd no right to expect anything but evil could come of that marriage — and when I shirked doing a father's part too."

Nancy was silent; her spirit of rectitude would not let her try to soften the edge of what she felt to be a just compunction. He spoke again after a little while, but the tone was rather changed; there was tenderness mingled with the previous self-reproach.

" And I got *you*, Nancy, in spite of all; and yet I've been grumbling and uneasy because I hadn't something else — as if I deserved it."

" You've never been wanting to me, Godfrey," said Nancy, with quiet sincerity. " My only trouble would be gone if you resigned yourself to the lot that's been given us."

" Well, perhaps it isn't too late to mend a bit there. Though it *is* too late to mend some things, say what they will."

CHAPTER XXI

A skillfully told story, like an airplane under the control of an expert pilot, makes a neat landing. It sets the reader's mind down as smoothly as it takes off on a flight of fancy.

For many years, you remember, Silas Marner had brooded over the grave wrong done him by his old friend William Dane, and he had confided to Dolly Winthrop his secret misgivings about the drawing of lots. At the opening of this chapter he has an old score to erase before he can be completely happy. Would it do any good for him to go back to Lantern Yard, do you think, and after all these years confront his accusers? Would that satisfy him, or you? Would such an interview make a "good" ending to the story?

As you read on notice how skillfully the author sets the old man's heart to rest — and the reader's mind — without starting up again the story that has already been told. On what note does the story end? Is it in harmony with the note on which it began? Has the wheel of Silas Marner's destiny made its complete turn? If it has, then it is time to bring his story to a close.

The next morning, when Silas and Eppie were seated at their breakfast, he said to her —

"Eppie, there's a thing I've had on my mind to do this two year, and now the money's been brought back to us, we can do it. I've been turning it over and over in the night, and I think we'll set out tomorrow, while the fine days last. We'll leave the house and everything for your godmother to take care on, and we'll make a little bundle o' things and set out."

"Where to go, Daddy?" said Eppie, in much surprise.

"To my old country — to the town where I was born — up Lantern Yard. I want to see Mr. Paston, the minister; something may ha' come out to make 'em know I was innicent o' the robbery. And Mr. Paston was a man with a deal o' light — I want to speak to him about the drawing o' the lots. And I should like to talk to him about the religion o' this countryside, for I partly think he doesn't know on it."

Eppie was very joyful, for there was the prospect not only of wonder and delight at seeing a strange country, but also of coming back to tell Aaron all about it. Aaron was so much wiser than she was about most things — it would be rather pleasant to have this little advantage over him. Mrs. Winthrop, though possessed with a dim fear of dangers attendant on so long a journey, and requiring many assurances that it would not take them out of the region of carriers' carts and slow wagons, was nevertheless well pleased that Silas should revisit his own country, and find out if he had been cleared from that false accusation.

"You'd be easier in your mind for the rest o' your life, Master Marner," said Dolly — "that you would. And if there's any light to be got up the Yard as you talk on, we've need of it i' this world, and I'd be glad on it myself, if you could bring it back."

So, on the fourth day from that time, Silas and Eppie, in their Sunday clothes, with a small bundle tied in a blue linen handkerchief, were making their way through the streets of a great manufacturing town. Silas, bewildered by the changes thirty years had brought over his native place, had stopped several persons in succession to ask them the name of this town, that he might be sure he was not under a mistake about it.

"Ask for Lantern Yard, father — ask this gentleman with the tassels on his shoulders a-standing at the shop door; he isn't in a hurry like the rest," said Eppie, in some distress at her father's bewilderment, and ill at ease, besides, amidst the noise, the movement, and the multitude of strange indifferent faces.

"Eh, my child, he won't know anything about it," said Silas; "gentlefolks didn't ever go up the Yard. But happen somebody can tell me which is the way to Prison Street, where the jail is. I know the way out o' that as if I'd seen it yesterday."

With some difficulty, after many turnings and new inquiries, they reached Prison Street; and the grim walls of the jail, the first object that answered to any image in Silas's memory, cheered him with the certitude, which no assurance of the town's name had hitherto given him, that he was in his native place.

"Ah," he said, drawing a long breath, "there's the jail, Eppie; that's just the same; I aren't afraid now. It's the third turning on the left hand from the jail doors — that's the way we must go."

"Oh, what a dark ugly place!" said Eppie. "How it hides the sky! It's worse than the workhouse. I'm glad you don't live in this town now, father. Is Lantern Yard like this street?"

"My precious child," said Silas, smiling, "it isn't a big street like this. I never was easy i' this street myself, but I was fond o' Lantern Yard. The shops here are all altered, I think — I can't make 'em out; but I shall know the turning, because it's the third."

"Here it is," he said, in a tone of satisfaction, as they came to a narrow alley. "And then we must go to the left again, and then straight for'ard for a bit, up Shoe Lane; and then we shall be at the entry next to the o'erhanging window, where there's the nick in the road for the water to run. Eh, I can see it all."

"O father, I'm like as if I was stifled," said Eppie. "I couldn't ha' thought as any folks lived i' this way, so close together. How pretty the stone pits 'ull look when we get back!"

"It looks comical to *me,* child, now — and smells bad. I can't think as it usened to smell so."

Here and there a sallow, begrimed face looked out from a gloomy doorway at the strangers, and increased Eppie's uneasiness, so that it was a longed-for relief when they issued from the alleys into Shoe Lane, where there was a broader strip of sky.

"Dear heart!" said Silas; "why, there's people coming out o' the Yard as if they'd been to chapel at this time o' day — a weekday noon!"

Suddenly he started and stood still, with a look of distressed amazement that alarmed Eppie. They were before an opening in front of a large factory, from which men and women were streaming for their midday meal.

"Father," said Eppie, clasping his arm, "what's the matter?"

But she had to speak again and again before Silas could answer her.

"It's gone, child," he said, at last, in strong agitation — "Lantern Yard's gone. It must ha' been here, because here's the house with the o'erhanging window — I know that — it's just the same; but they've made this new opening; and see that big factory! It's all gone — chapel and all."

"Come into that little brushshop and sit down, father — they'll let you sit down," said Eppie, always on the watch lest one of her father's strange attacks should come on. "Perhaps the people can tell you all about it."

But neither from the brushmaker, who had come to Shoe Lane only ten years ago, when the factory was already built, nor from any other source within his reach, could Silas learn anything of the old Lantern Yard friends, or of Mr. Paston, the minister.

"The old place is all swep' away," Silas said to Dolly Winthrop on the night of his return — "the little graveyard and everything. The old home's gone; I've no home but this now. I shall never know whether they got at the truth o' the robbery, nor whether Mr. Paston could ha' given me any light about the drawing o' the lots. It's dark to me, Mrs. Winthrop, that is; I doubt it'll be dark to the last."

"Well, yes, Master Marner," said Dolly, who sat with a placid listening face, now bordered by gray hairs; "I doubt it may. It's the will o' Them above as a many things should be dark to us; but there's some things as I've never felt i' the dark about, and they're mostly what comes i' the day's work. You were hard done by that once, Master Marner, and it seems as you'll never know the rights of it; but that doesn't hinder there *being* a rights, Master Marner, for all it's dark to you and me."

"No," said Silas, "no; that doesn't hinder. Since the time the child was sent to me and I've come to love her as myself, I've had light enough to trusten by; and, now she says she'll never leave me, I think I shall trusten till I die."

CONCLUSION

There was one time of the year which was held in Raveloe to be especially suitable for a wedding. It was when the great lilacs and laburnums in the old-fashioned gardens showed their golden and purple wealth above the lichen-tinted walls, and when there were calves still young enough to want bucketfuls of fragrant milk. People were not so busy then as they must become when the full cheese making and the mowing had set in; and, besides, it was a time when a light bridal dress could be worn with comfort and seen to advantage.

Happily the sunshine fell more warmly than usual on the lilac tufts the morning that Eppie was married, for her dress was a very light one. She had often thought, though with a feeling of renunciation, that the perfection of a wedding dress would be a white cotton, with the tiniest pink sprig at wide intervals; so that when Mrs. Godfrey Cass begged to provide one, and asked Eppie to choose what it should be, previous meditation had enabled her to give a decided answer at once.

Seen at a little distance as she walked across the churchyard and down the village, she seemed to be attired in pure white, and her hair looked like a dash of gold on a lily. One hand was on her husband's arm, and with the other she clasped the hand of her Father Silas.

"You won't be giving me away, father," she had said before they went to church; "you'll only be taking Aaron to be a son to you."

Dolly Winthrop walked behind with her husband; and there ended the little bridal procession.

There were many eyes to look at it, and Miss Priscilla Lammeter was glad that she and her father had happened to drive up to the door of the Red House just in time to see this pretty sight. They had come to keep Nancy company today, because Mr. Cass had to go away to Lytherly, for special reasons. That seemed to be a pity, for otherwise he might have gone, as Mr. Crackenthorp and Mr. Osgood certainly would, to look on at the wedding feast which he had ordered at the Rainbow, naturally feeling a great interest in the weaver who had been wronged by one of his own family.

"I could ha' wished Nancy had had the luck to find a child like that and bring her up," said Priscilla to her father, as they sat in the gig; "I should ha' had something young to think of then, besides the lambs and the calves."

"Yes, my dear, yes," said Mr. Lammeter; "one feels that as one gets older. Things look dim to old folks; they'd need have some young eyes about 'em, to let 'em know the world's the same as it used to be."

Nancy came out now to welcome her father and sister; and the wedding group had passed on beyond the Red House to the humbler part of the village.

Dolly Winthrop was the first to divine that old Mr. Macey, who had been set in his armchair outside his own door, would expect some special notice as they passed, since he was too old to be at the wedding feast.

"Mr. Macey's looking for a word from us," said Dolly; "he'll be hurt if we pass him and say nothing — and him so racked with rheumatiz."

So they turned aside to shake hands with the old man. He had looked forward to the occasion, and had his premeditated speech.

"Well, Master Marner," he said, in a voice that quavered a good deal, "I've lived to see my words come true. I was the first to say there was no harm in you, though your looks might be again' you; and I was the first to say you'd get your money back. And it's nothing but rightful as you should. And I'd ha' said the 'Amens,' and willing, at the holy matrimony; but Tookey's done it a good while now, and I hope you'll have none the worse luck."

In the open yard before the Rainbow the party of guests were already assembled, though it was still nearly an hour before the appointed feasttime. But by this means they could not only enjoy the slow advent of their pleasure; they had also ample leisure to talk of Silas Marner's strange history, and arrive by due degrees at the conclusion that he had brought a blessing on himself by acting like a father to a lone, motherless child. Even the farrier did not negative this sentiment; on the contrary, he took it up as peculiarly his own, and invited any hardy person present to contradict him. But he met with no contradiction, and all differences among the company were merged in a general agreement with Mr. Snell's sentiment, that when a man had deserved his good luck it was the part of his neighbors to wish him joy.

As the bridal group approached, a hearty cheer was raised in the Rainbow yard; and Ben Winthrop, whose jokes had retained their acceptable flavor, found it agreeable to turn in there and receive congratulations, not requiring the proposed interval of quiet at the stone pits before joining the company.

Eppie had a larger garden than she had ever expected there now; and in other ways there had been alterations at the expense of Mr. Cass, the landlord, to suit Silas's larger family. For he and Eppie had declared that they would rather stay at the stone pits than go to any new home. The garden was fenced with stones on two sides, but in front there was an open fence, through which the flowers shone with answering gladness, as the four united people came within sight of them.

"O father," said Eppie, "what a pretty home ours is! I think nobody could be happier than we are."

APPRECIATION THROUGH CLASS DISCUSSION

Informal discussion turns up furrows of thought. It sets us to thinking about new ideas or draws attention to a new point of view. Or it suddenly illuminates an old idea so that hereafter it lives in our minds. For these reasons discussion is a valuable aid to appreciation.

But profitable discussion is frequently difficult to arouse. Each student, like the customers at the Rainbow, waits for someone else to make the first comment. Or, if easy natural talk does for the moment flare up, it dies down again, with no one feeling any particular responsibility for fanning it into flame. Or sometimes a discussion degenerates into a mere bout of argument, an aimless batting of questions and answers back and forth to see who will miss first. These are the common disasters likely to overtake an informal discussion hour unless some provision is made to give each member of the class a definite responsibility. In order that discussion may be profitable, therefore, the following brief formula is offered for each student to follow in class recitation:

Open the discussion with a concrete illustration of the topic being considered. For example, if the class is about to discuss superstition as it is revealed in *Silas Marner,* the drawing of lots to determine guilt is a telling example to call to the attention of the class.

Find a significant quotation from the story itself which illuminates your illustration. On what page, for example, do you find the best description of the drawing of lots? What brief passage can you mark for reading aloud to the class?

Ask yourself what you think of the special instance you report. How do you *feel,* for example, toward the drawing of lots? Are you surprised that men put their faith in such a device? Can you imagine how men came to believe in its power? Are there any traces of such a belief in present-day thinking? Plan to tell the class your reactions to each illustration that you find.

THINK BACK OVER WHAT YOU HAVE READ

Appreciating the Historical Setting

1. What picturesque glimpse do you get of the itinerant weaver in Chapter I? What details impressed you? What feeling is aroused by the picture?

2. How vividly can you imagine the quaint little village of Raveloe from the descriptions in Chapters I and II? What phrases help you to erect the picture in your mind?

3. What clothes were in fashion in the early nineteenth century? What quaint customs are revealed in Chapter XI? What contrasts or comparisons with life today occur to you as you " watch " the festivities at the Red House on New Year's Eve? What pictures would you " take " were it possible to smuggle a camera onto the scene? What tableaux attract your attention for the typical glimpse they reveal?

4. How important was the horse in those days? What pictures of the horse age caught your eye in Chapters III and IV?

5. What were the amusements of the day? Review Chapters VI and XI in particular and see how many details of play you can find.

6. What did you notice in Chapter XI about the hospitality of the rich? What kind of host did Squire Cass make? How far did his hospitality extend? Is there anything to suggest that his annual entertainment was a typical custom of squires? What does it suggest about social life in the early nineteenth century?

7. What occupations are referred to in Chapter VI? To what kind of life could the ordinary village boy look forward? To what occupations would he turn? As the son of a squire what were Godfrey Cass's prospects, as suggested in Chapters III, VIII, and IX? What differences in social station are suggested in Chapter XI?

8. What did you notice about the way of a man with a maid in Chapter XI? In what respects was Nancy Lammeter a typical product of her times? What conventions governed the behavior of women in love?

Understanding the Characters

9. What details can you cite from Chapters I and II which show Silas Marner the victim of injustice? What was the effect on him of William Dane's treachery? of Sarah's belief in his guilt? Did he act as you would expect a person to act under such circumstances? Why?

10. What details can you quote from Chapters I and II to show the impression which Marner made upon the people of Raveloe? What had loneliness done to change his personality? How had habit wrought its effect? Why had he succumbed to both?

11. What kind of satisfaction did gold bring him? Why had the counting of his money become such an obsession with him? How had habit contributed to its strange effect upon him? What was the immediate effect of discovering that his gold was gone? Reread especially, in this connection, Chapters VII and X.

12. What details can you cite from Chapters VII and XII which show Silas roused into action? How has misfortune changed him? What are the benefits to be expected from such a drastic upset in his routine? What is the first impression of the new Silas on the villagers at the Rainbow?

13. What passage can you quote from Chapter XII to show the mystic connection between the child and the lost gold? What had gold stood for in Silas Marner's warped life? What satisfaction had it brought? How does the child represent for him a return of his gold? What elements in his new-found treasure make Silas Marner richer than he was before he lost his gold?

14. What are the changes wrought in Silas Marner by his love for Eppie? What details in Chapters XIV and XVI describe her influence? What were the first signs of change to be noticed in Chapter XIV? How was the dull routine of Silas Marner's day first upset? How was his loneliness banished? How did the child draw him into the community? What change came

over the Raveloe folks in regard to him? How do you account for the change?

15. What kind of old man was Silas in Chapters XVI to XXI? What qualities endeared him to Eppie? To what qualities were Godfrey and Nancy Cass blind? What native traits blossomed under happiness? What unnatural traits disappeared? What kind of restoration to his personality did Eppie make? How had she revived his faith? in what?

16. What details can you quote from Chapter III to show that Dunsey Cass is a thorn in Godfrey's flesh? What kind of hold does he have over Godfrey? Suggesting what about each one's character? Which one of the brothers, if either, do you respect?

17. How shrewd at bargaining is Dunsey? Find an illustration of his business methods from Chapter IV.

18. What factors in his home life do you think turned him into a reckless, dissipated idler?

19. What instances can you cite from Chapters VIII, XIII, and XV to show Godfrey Cass at the mercy of his conscience? How sincere a penitent do you regard the Squire's eldest son? Is he at any time really sorry for his misdeeds? or just regretful of the consequences? How can you tell?

20. How does Godfrey appear in your estimation as the victim of his father's wrath in Chapter IX? Do you feel sorry for him? Do you respect him? Would you like to tell the Squire "a thing or two" about his rearing of children?

21. Does Godfrey appear in a better light as the gallant wooer of Nancy in Chapter XI? What qualities does Nancy see in him? Is her love for him a tribute to his character or to hers? How can you tell?

22. What are your feelings about Godfrey in Chapter XIX? Do you think he deserves to have his way? Are Eppie's feelings toward her father sound? Does Godfrey get what he deserves? How does he take this last disappointment? Has he gained in manliness since his younger days? Do you like him better? What do you consider to be the fundamental flaw in his character?

23. What role does Squire Cass play in Chapter IX? With whom do your sympathies lie, Godfrey or his father? Why? What is wrong with the Squire as a father, judging from a modern point of view? What excuses can you make for him?

24. What details can you quote from Chapter XI to show him in a more attractive light? How does he appear in your eyes as the hearty host? What do you think his guests think of him? Does your respect for him increase? Do you like him any better? Why?

25. What impression does he make upon you as he accepts parish homage in this same chapter? Does he win your approval of squires?

26. What details can you cite from Chapter XI to show that Nancy Lammeter was the apple of her sister's eye? To what qualities does this testify in Nancy? in Priscilla?

27. What do you think of her as the coy maiden resisting Godfrey's advances?

28. What illustrations can you cite from Chapter XVII to show her as the faithful wife?

29. What amusing pictures does your imagination see of the lesser lights of Raveloe? What details can you quote from Chapter VI to show the tendency of the farrier to argue? the compromising traits of Mr. Snell? the talkativeness of Mr. Macey? the frankness of Ben Winthrop? What picture do you get in Chapter XI of the merry-eyed rector? the jesting doctor? old Solomon, the fiddler? Priscilla Lammeter, the self-appointed spinster?

Responding to the Atmosphere

30. What details suggest to you the loneliness of the stone pit in Chapter IV? What phrases communicate to you the dreariness of the fog?

31. What is the effect on your imagination of the chinks of light gleaming through Silas Marner's shutters as Dunsey Cass approaches the cottage in Chapter IV? Perhaps someone in the class will be able to sketch the picture which comes to mind. What title would you suggest for the picture? What was the effect of the beams of light upon Dunsey?

32. What sounds contribute to the atmosphere in the last part of Chapter IV?

33. What picture do you see through Dunsey's eyes in that first glimpse through the door? What details did he notice? What phrases can you quote to show the warm hospitality of the deserted room? What objects caught his attention? What was the total impression of the room upon him?

34. Supposing that you had seen Dunsey Cass through the window in Chapter IV as his eye caught sight of the loose brick in the

hearth. What details of manner and appearance would have impressed you?

35. What details of Dunsey's disappearance into the night appealed to your imagination? Of Silas's lantern lighting up the gloom? What mood is aroused by these two glimpses?

36. What irony is suggested to you in Chapter V by the picture of Silas, snug and cozy before the fire tending his meat?

37. What words or phrases made Silas's frenzied search for the missing gold appeal to your senses?

38. What details suggest the quiet sociability of the Rainbow kitchen in Chapters VI and VII?

39. What picture do you see among the bandboxes in the Blue Room of the Red House in Chapter XI? What details attracted your attention? What was the spirit of the room on New Year's Eve?

40. What glimpse of tea in the wainscoted parlor do you get from Chapter XI? What adjectives would you use to describe the quality of the picture?

41. Perhaps someone in the class will be able to reproduce in color his impression of old fiddling Solomon leading the gay procession into the White Parlor. What title would the class choose for the picture?

42. What picture do you get of the dance at the Red House through the eyes of the village spectators? What details attract their attention?

Exploring the Ideas of Silas Marner's World

43. What are your impressions of Mr. Snell as a detective in Chapter VIII? What did you learn from this chapter about the reliability of witnesses in the solution of a mystery?

44. What incidents can you quote from Chapter IX to show the rights of a father over his son in Silas Marner's day? What deference did sons show to a father's judgment? In what respects have times changed in this regard?

45. What was the relation of landlords and tenants in Silas Marner's day? What illustrations can you find in Chapter IX of the idleness of the landed gentry?

46. What part did "family" play in the contracting of a marriage? What was the basis of respectability in these times? Review especially in this connection Chapters IX, XI, and XIX.

47. What illustrations of the superstitions of the times can you glean from Chapters I, II, and VIII?

48. How important was duty in Silas Marner's day? What illustrations can you find in Chapters XI, XVII, and XIX of its hold over people?

49. What facts did you notice in Chapter X about keeping the Sabbath? about "accepting the will of the Lord"?

50. How does the whole story of *Silas Marner* illustrate the fact that in simple communities people who are different are regarded with suspicion?

Recognizing Dramatic Incidents

51. What elements in Molly's plans for revenge in Chapter XII seem to you dramatic? What is ironic about the time that she chooses for her revenge? Supposing that her plan had succeeded, what excitement would her disclosure have caused? Why do you think Molly preferred this particular kind of revenge? What secret bitterness tore at her heart? What satisfaction did she think she would gain by her plan?

52. What details impressed you with the grim pathos of her death in Chapter XII?

53. What effect would the scene of the baby following a beam of light have upon you, were you to see the story of *Silas Marner* pictured on the screen? Do you think that a moving-picture director would feature this scene? or omit it? On what facts in the story do you base your decision?

54. How convincing to your imagination is the scene in Chapter XII where Silas Marner sees his "gold" come back to him again? What details make the scene tense and dramatic? What purpose does the scene serve in the story?

55. What pictures do you get from this same chapter of the excited stir at the party following Silas Marner's announcement? What glimpse do you catch of Godfrey?

56. What details can you quote from Chapter XIII which show Silas Marner's dramatic insistence upon keeping the baby? Godfrey's labored control of his fears?

57. What form does the reader's excitement take in Chapter XIX? What are his fears for old Silas? What hope does he place on Eppie? Does she betray that hope or fulfill it? How? How much sympathy from the reader does Godfrey have a right to claim? Nancy?

58. How fitting is the ending of the story? How does Silas set his mind to rest in Chapter XXI? What passages can you quote to show that time has washed away an old scar?

Appreciating the Theme of the Story

59. What was the transformation wrought in Silas Marner's heart by a little child? What had happened to his heart before he found the baby? Think back to the time when Silas Marner was a young man. What traits did he show? Was he kind and sympathetic? What bitter thoughts must have coursed through his mind as he reflected upon the treachery of his friend and the faithlessness of his sweetheart? What kind of comfort did he find in withdrawing from people? from following a fixed routine? What had he missed all these years that the baby suddenly reminded him of?

60. What kind of faith did Eppie restore in him? Judging from Silas Marner's experience, how severe is the shock to people of discovering that those whom they have trusted turn out to be false? What kind of person would have withstood the blow better than Silas Marner? Would Dunsey have cared so much? Godfrey? Nancy? the Squire?

61. Supposing that Eppie had accepted Godfrey's and Nancy's proposal to come and live with them as Godfrey's daughter. To what lack in her character would such a decision testify? What would have been the effect on Silas Marner of another disappointment? How seriously did Eppie's refusal upset Godfrey? Do you expect that he was permanently affected by it? Would Eppie's coming to live with him have turned him into a happy man? Or was there something else that ate at Godfrey's vitals? What? On what faulty foundation had he tried to build happiness? On what truer basis did Silas build his more humble life? What must have been Eppie's feelings toward her father? Was she just in her decision? heartless? Should she have acted any differently? What comments are you led to make about the old proverb that "blood is thicker than water"? Does George Eliot suggest that something else is stronger than blood relation? What?

62. What incidents in the story suggest that wrongdoing is ultimately paid for? How did Dunsey pay his debt of dishonor? How does Godfrey's life testify to the truth that you can't run away from your misdeeds? At what point in the story should he have faced them courageously? What difference would it have made in his life? Was he right in thinking that in doing so he would have lost Nancy? On what do you base your opinion?

Increase Your Power over Words

Silas Marner introduced you to many new and interesting words and might well be reviewed, therefore, from the point of view of word interest. Dividing the class into groups, each group to comb the chapters for special kinds of word samples, will make quick work of a tedious task and permit the class as a whole to observe and comment upon a variety of aspects of vocabulary.

63. *Typical idiom of the times.* How did people say the simple, everyday things in Silas Marner's time? Here is a start for your list:

"Hold your tongue" (page 598).
"Ay, Ay" (page 599).
"Make your tender heart easy" (page 600).

64. *Words that name old-fashioned things.* What quaint words, like *joseph, pillion, stile, tankard, fusion,* and *shuttle,* can you collect?

65. *Guessing the meaning of words from the context.* What difficult words can you find to be used in a class exercise of figuring out the meaning of words from the way they are used in the sentences? For example, you hardly need a dictionary for such words as the following:

queries (page 587)
vista (page 591)
contingent (page 598)
vacillation (page 598)
surmise (page 620)
facsimile (page 642)
colloquies (page 587)

The sense of the sentence in which you find them almost gives their meaning away.

66. *Finding interest in the derivation of words.* In previous word studies you have begun to trace the origin of words and to recognize word families. This is an important way to fasten the meaning and spelling of new words in the mind. Notice the literal meaning of the following words; then find the word in the story and figure out its derived meaning from the context:

Intermittent (pages 583, 636) is built out of *inter* (between) and *mitto* (to send). What other words that you know are built out of *mitto?* Here is a start for your list: *remit, admit, commit.* In this connection notice *unremittingly* on page 591.

dexterity (page 583). *Dexter* and *sinister* (see page 443, no. 14) are Latin words meaning right and left. Can you figure out how dexterity came to mean skill?

eccentric (page 583) means literally off (*ec*) center.

aver (page 585) is related to *veracity* and *veritable,* for they all stem from the Latin word *verus* meaning true.

repugnance (pages 586, 648) stems from the Latin word *pugnus* meaning fist, and is related to *pugilist* and *pugnacious.* If *re* means back, what is the literal meaning of repugnant?

audible (page 588) comes from the Latin word *audio* meaning to hear. What other words belong to the same family?

frustrate (page 591) is related to the word *fraud.* Both come from the Latin word *frustra* which means in vain.

transient (pages 592, 616) is a member of another large word family. Literally the word means one who goes (*eo*) across (*trans*). Other words belonging to the same family are *transit, transitive, transition,* and *transitory.* Can you distinguish the difference in meaning between each of these words?

gratuitously (page 596) is related to *grateful* and *gratitude.* All come from the Latin word *gratus* meaning kind. A *gratuity* is a gift. Can you see *why?* What, then, does *gratuitously* mean?

placably (page 654) and *implacable* (page 623) come from the common root *placo* which means to appease. What does each word mean, then, in its context?

For Ambitious Students

67. *The life and personality of George Eliot.* The following books will acquaint you with the character of George Eliot. Perhaps different groups in the class will volunteer to read the books on the list and review them orally for the benefit of the other members of the class. Another group of students might attempt to dramatize some of the more interesting scenes from the life of George Eliot in the manner illustrated in such a book as *Scenes from the Great Novelists,* adapted and arranged for amateur performance by Elsie Fogerty.

Bolton, S. K., *Lives of Girls Who Became Famous* (a brief biographical summary)

Buckrose, J. E., *Silhouette of Mary Ann* (a fictionized biography)

Eliot, George, *The Mill on the Floss* (an autobiographical novel)

Gilbert, Ariadne, *Over Famous Thresholds* (a sketch of home surroundings)

Haldane, E. S., *George Eliot and Her Times* (a Victorian study)

Stephen, Leslie, *Hours in the Library,* Vol. III (a complete biography)

68. *Other realistic novels by George Eliot.* The following novels might well be considered an outside-of-class reading project for the semester by different groups in the class. Having read *Silas Marner* and *The Mill on the Floss,* some students are likely to add George Eliot to their list of favorite authors.

Adam Bede *Middlemarch*
Felix Holt *Scenes from Clerical Life*

69. *Dramatizing* Silas Marner. *Silas Marner* has been put into play form by F. S. Owen under the title *Silas Marner: A Drama in Four Acts.* This could well serve as a model from which the class might devise its own scenes either for amateur performance or as the basis from which to choose scenes for acting. A special committee from the class might well investigate the possibilities for producing *Silas Marner* either in whole or in part. In case the class wishes to adapt its own scenes, *Literature Dramatized for Classroom Use* by Mildred Allen Butler should prove a useful reference book.

70. *The growth of realism.* The following novels, arranged in their historical order, represent roughly the milestones in the growth of realistic literature. Different groups in the class might choose several consecutive books on the list for extra reading for the term and share their impressions of life through the ages, as it has been revealed by fiction, with the rest of the class in oral reports.

Burney, Fanny, *Evelina*
Goldsmith, Oliver, *The Vicar of Wakefield*
Austen, Jane, *Pride and Prejudice*
Dickens, Charles, *Oliver Twist*
Thackeray, W. M., *Vanity Fair*
Hardy, Thomas, *Far from the Madding Crowd*
Galsworthy, John, *The Forsyte Saga*
West, Rebecca, *The Judge*

ARE YOU INTERESTED IN HOW A NOVEL IS BUILT?

A novel is a long prose story with a more or less complicated plot. That is about all that can be said about its form to distinguish it from other forms. It follows no fixed pattern; indeed, each novel is more or less a law unto itself. Perhaps it is this very flexibility which accounts for the popularity of the novel.

Like a short story and a play it has *setting* and *characters* and perhaps a *theme*. And it has movement, or *development*. Like all stories it goes somewhere, that somewhere being determined by the *author's purpose* in laying bare a particular *situation* that has challenged his attention. In the novel that you have just read, that purpose was to show how the love of a child healed the wounds in an old man's heart. When that purpose was accomplished, the story had been told; and the *conflict* between the two elements in Silas Marner's nature — his bitterness over an injustice and his faith in his fellow man — was at length resolved. Thus the novel you have just read moves *from* William Dane's betrayal of Silas Marner, with its warping of Marner's nature, *to* Eppie's acknowledgment of Silas Marner as her "real" father, with its restoration of Marner's faith. What falls between — the difficulties along the way — makes up the *plot* of the story and determines its *climax*. You are already familiar with those difficulties: Dunsey's theft of Marner's money, the coming of Eppie and Silas's acceptance of a golden-haired baby in place of his beloved guineas, and the strange turn of fate when Silas stands to lose again all that he held dear in life. At the moment Godfrey Cass reveals himself as Eppie's natural father and Eppie is confronted with the choice of living on with her foster father or going to the Red House to live as a squire's daughter, you know that you have reached the high point of interest in the story. This is the *climax*. Will Eppie renounce Silas's claims of affection and cast him again into darkness? Or will she preserve his faith and let him live out his years in peace? Once that decision is made, the story has come to its end, or *denouement*. The test of Eppie's love has come; she meets it, and Silas Marner's redemption is complete. The problem raised has been solved. The story is over.

Roughly this is a map of the route you have taken in reading *Silas Marner*. In order that you may fix the technical terms (those in italics) in mind, however, the following questions may be used in review:

1. What is the opening situation from which the plot of the story springs? What seeds of conflict are there which must ultimately complicate the life of Silas Marner?
2. What factors in Marner's new life in Raveloe helped turn him into a miser? At what point in the story do you consider his transformation complete?
3. Suppose that Dunsey Cass had never stolen Marner's money. What bearing would this fact have had upon Silas's desire to keep and rear the baby that he found on his hearth? Any? Would he have acted differently? Of how much importance to the plot, then, was the disappearance of Marner's money? Of what use to the author's theme was this incident? Can you see?
4. How did Eppie change the course of Marner's life? For what development in his character was she responsible? At what point in the story is this second change in Marner complete?
5. Suppose that the stone pit had never been drained and that Godfrey had never been moved to confess his past and claim Eppie as his daughter. What difference would it have made in the story? Any? What bearing does this episode have upon the story of Silas Marner's being reclaimed by love? Does the episode alter the relationship between him and Eppie? Does it offer only a temporary obstacle in his path, one designed merely to continue the suspense? Or do you see a purpose which it serves?
6. In your own words state the theme of the story. Can you find a passage in the story where George Eliot more or less directly expresses it?
7. Is there a secondary plot in the story? Around what conflict does it center?

8. What other changes besides those in Marner's character can you trace? What circumstances wrought these changes?

FOR FURTHER READING OF NOVELS

The Altar of the Legion by Farnham Bishop and A. G. Brodeur
Historical adventure in England at the time of the Roman conquest. The lost land of Lyonesse figures in the story.

Black Majesty by J. W. Vandercook
Christophe, born a Negro slave, built for himself in Haiti a kingdom that during his reign ranked in the eyes of Europe as one of the New World powers.

The Blazed Trail by S. E. White
A young lumberman battles an unscrupulous corporation and wins.

A Girl Who Would Be Queen by E. P. Kelly and Clara Hoffmanowa
Based on the diary of a real Polish countess, this novel recaptures the glamour of Poland's glorious past.

Jim Davis by John Masefield
Jim Davis was an English boy whose curiosity led him straight to a smugglers' cave. Fearing discovery, the smugglers kidnap him.

Lost Horizon by James Hilton
A hidden land where the troubles of the world have been solved is discovered in Central Asia. A strange story with a curious ending.

Master Skylark by John Bennett
Visits to a prison, singing for Queen Elizabeth, and the friendship of Will Shakespeare enliven the story of a boy actor during an interesting era.

The Shadow of the Sword by Hawthorne Daniel
A French fisher lad, in the days of Joan of Arc, discovers a traitor to France, a man so important that to accuse him would mean death to the boy.

Swords on the Sea by A. D. Hewes
Stirring events at a time when Venice was mistress of the seas. Both boys and girls will find characters to admire in this exciting historical tale.

The Three Musketeers by Alexandre Dumas
D'Artagnan and his two companions find enemies in high places when they become involved in a court intrigue.

The Trumpeter of Krakow by E. P. Kelly
Adventures of a boy in Poland during the Middle Ages. He is involved in a mysterious struggle over a great crystal. Girls will like the story, too, for it has a heroine.

The Yearling by M. K. Rawlings
This story of a boy in the Florida hammock country has appealed to high-school students as well as to older readers.

OTHER NOVELS WHICH HAVE BEEN POPULAR WITH HIGH-SCHOOL STUDENTS

Brontë, Charlotte, *Jane Eyre*
Carroll, G. H., *As the Earth Turns*
Cather, Willa, *My Antonia*
Dickens, Charles, *A Tale of Two Cities*
Doneghy, Dagmar, *The Border*
Hawes, C. B., *Dark Frigate; Mutineers*
James, Will, *Smoky*
Lane, R. W., *Let the Hurricane Roar*
Lincoln, J. C., *Cap'n Erie*
London, Jack, *White Fang*
Morley, Christopher, *Haunted Bookshop; Parnassus on Wheels*
Nordhoff, C. B., and Hall, J. N., *Mutiny on the Bounty*
Orczy, Baroness, *The Scarlet Pimpernel*
Remarque, E. M., *All Quiet on the Western Front*
Stevenson, R. L., *Doctor Jekyl and Mr. Hyde*
Stockton, F. R., *The Casting away of Mrs. Lecks and Mrs. Aleshine*
Tarkington, Booth, *Alice Adams*
Wren, Percival, *Beau Geste*

Thinking It Over

How Much Did You Make of Your Reading Experience?

A GENERAL REVIEW

EXPERIENCE is of two kinds: direct and vicarious. Going by plane from Chicago to New York is direct experience; listening to someone tell about his flight, and imagining yourself in his place is vicarious experience. Vicarious experience is living *through others*. Thus reading is the great supplement to direct experience by which we extend the boundaries of our lives.

How much have you made of the vicarious experience offered you in this text? How much did it mean to you to take part (vicariously) in a round-up, fly across the North Pole, witness a witch-hunt, or follow the uncertain path of a revolution? What difference does it make that for a time you felt (through others) lonely, slighted, bullied, or cheated? What, in the way of a better understanding of life, has such experience netted you? Do you now comprehend human behavior somewhat better than you did before? Do you begin to see what social forces shape our lives?

The following plan for a general review will help you answer just such questions as these.

CENTERS OF INTEREST

1. INCREASING MY UNDERSTANDING OF ANIMAL NATURE

What have you learned from the following selections about the way animals feel? Do their actions remind you of people? Under what systems have they learned to live together? What, through the ages, has been the relationship between man and beast? Does it stand altogether to the credit of man? What are you led to reflect about the training of wild animals, the "breaking" of animals into "beasts of burden," the trapping of animals, the captivity of animals? In what other ways have these selections contributed to a better understanding of animals?

Readings

Short Story: Zenobia's Infidelity (p. 2)

Essays: Keeper of the Bulls (265), Our Back-Yard Circus (279), Mustangs (252)

Poems: The Broncho that Would Not Be Broken (382), The Monkey (390), The Circus-Postered Barn (390), Kit Carson's Ride (369), Four Little Foxes (391), Notation on Immortality (392), A Child's Pet (391)

2. OBSERVING LIFE UNDER VARIED CONDITIONS

Suppose that you had been born in a different place, at a different time, of a different race: What difference would it make? Suppose you had been set apart from your fellows by a special physical handicap, or by some special ability: How differently would you look out upon the world? Suppose you'd been born on the prairie instead of by the sea. Suppose you'd been brought up in the cattle country, or lived in a day when hardy men pushed westward to seek their fortune. How might an unusual talent have changed your life? What are the drawbacks of being set on a pedestal? Are the differences between races as great as you thought? In short, what have you learned from this group of selections about the part which environment plays in shaping personality? What illustrations from your reading can you cite? To what extent do you see yourself a product of the conditions under which you were born?

Readings

Stories: The Wind Fighters (118), Tonight in Person (77)

Essay: The Drive (258)

Biography: Cradled in a Snapping Turtle's Shell (173), Along the Rivers (177), Into the Shakes (184), The Education of Helen Keller (226), Strange Customs (219)

3. RESPONDING WITH APPROPRIATE FEELING TO DRAMATIC SITUATIONS

In each of the following selections your feelings were stirred and you read with a quickened heart beat. Something moved you. What was it? Can you put your finger on it? You were concerned about something; something arrested and held your attention. This is the dramatic element in the selection. You can best locate it, perhaps, by asking yourself how you *felt* during the reading of the selection: you were worried, perplexed, horrified, amused, or awed by — what? *Should* you have been? Does the situation warrant your feelings? Suppose you had felt like laughing after reading "Danny Deever"; suppose you felt nothing at all after reading "Now There is Peace"; then something has gone wrong; for you, the selection has missed fire, and it would be well to discuss with your classmates how they felt after reading these selections.

Readings

Stories: R. M. S. Titanic (159), The Man Who Won the War (149), The Monkey's Paw (59), Now There Is Peace (94), The Princess and the Puma (24), Twenty Cigarettes (136)

Narrative Poems: Rebecca Nixon and Martha Waugh (364), Old Christmas Morning (365), Danny Deever (385), The Douglas Tragedy (358), The Revenge (377), The Horse Thief (372), By the Turret Stair (360), Lancelot and Elaine (542)

Plays: Julius Caesar (455), One Special for Doc (423)

Biography: The Alamo (209), The Elements (244)

4. RECOGNIZING THE STUFF THAT HEROES ARE MADE OF

Heroes of all times, both great and small, arise out of life's needs. Looking back over this group of selections, what needs for heroic action can you recognize? What qualities do the heroes represented here have in common?

Readings

Stories: The White Tiger (50), On the Dodge (38), The Unfamiliar (85), The Wind Fighters (118), The Milk Pitcher (29)

Narrative Poems: The Revenge (377), Lee (380), How Robin Hood Rescued the Widow's Sons (360), Sam Houston (410), Little Giffen (382), Fuzzy-Wuzzy (386), The Coming of Arthur (522)

Essays: Byrd Flies to the North Pole (230)

5. APPRECIATING INDIVIDUALITY IN CHARACTER PORTRAYAL

Each one of the characters featured in this group of selections stands out sharply as an individual. By what characteristics shall you remember them? Has acquaintance with them taught you to respect difference among people? Some of the characters listed here are included, also, among the heroes in the preceding group. Are all heroes individualists? Are all individualists heroes? What, in your mind, is the difference? Where does each stand in relation to the crowd? What relationship should exist between the individual and the crowd? With what illustrations from your reading or your own first-hand experience can you illuminate your point?

Readings

Short Stories: Mr. K*a*p*l*a*n the Magnificent (11), The Milk Pitcher (29), The Revolt of Mother (125), Jeeves and the Yuletide Spirit (16)

Poems: Little Giffen (382), Nancy Hanks (405), Cerelle (374)

Biography: The Story of Five Strange Companions (198)

6. UNDERSTANDING OTHER PEOPLE'S FEELINGS

We can't get very far in the understanding of other people until we learn to forget ourselves and imagine how another feels. With what characters in this group of selections did you sympathize? What points of view did you understand? Which ones do you share?

Readings

Stories: Wind Fighters (118), Tonight in Person (177), Twenty Cigarettes (136), Under the Lion's Paw (108)

Play: One Special for Doc (423)

Poems: Four Little Foxes (391), A Child's Pet (391), Notation on Immortality (392), Cerelle (374), Trade Winds (393), A Wanderer's Song (393), Tewkesbury Road (394), Travel (394), A Wet Sheet and a Flowing Sea (395), Roofs (395), The Ticket Agent (395), Deserted (398), Texas (401), Skyscraper (402), Blueberries (398), At the Aquarium (397), Negro Spirituals (405), Days (408), A Railroad Train (398), Tomorrow (409), Play the Game (410)

7. PROBING FOR MOTIVES IN HUMAN BEHAVIOR

In this group of selections you discovered some of the hidden reasons why people act as they do. What light did your reading throw upon the self-centered impulses of people? In what ways did the people you met attempt to win approval, attain power, redeem their own failures, sidestep responsibility, blame others, or make up for disappointment? What makes people dodge the truth or withdraw from their fellows? What motives lie behind the actions of the characters in these selections?

Readings

Short Stories: That's What Happened to Me (72), Now There Is Peace (94)

Essays: We Aren't Superstitious (334), The Noblest Instrument (343), The Whipping (349)

Poems: The Code (366)

Plays: In the Zone (429), Julius Caesar (455), I Was Talking Across the Fence This Morning (444)

Novel: Silas Marner (582)

8. NOTICING HOW CHARACTER CHANGES UNDER THE FORCE OF CIRCUMSTANCES

In each of these selections, at least one of the characters grows. They are not quite the same at the end of the story as they were at the beginning. Something important happens to a bus driver, a soldier's father, a boy actor, a mother on a farm, a lonely weaver, a patriot, and a discouraged young man: what? What accounts for the change? What lesson is to be derived from the change?

Readings

Stories: Sleet Storm (98), Twenty Cigarettes (136), Tonight in Person (77), Revolt of Mother (125)
Novel: Silas Marner (582)
Plays: Julius Caesar (455), One Special for Doc (423)

9. GAINING AN INCREASED UNDERSTANDING OF THE SOCIAL FORCES WHICH INFLUENCE PEOPLE

Man does not live to himself alone. He lives among his fellows within a complicated social system, and oftentimes his interests run counter to those of the group. In each of the selections listed below an important social issue is raised, either directly or indirectly. What is it? What have you learned from your reading about social injustice? about the difficulties of achieving a real democracy? What light do these selections throw upon the problems of peace on earth and good will among men?

Readings

Story: Under the Lion's Paw (108)
Play: Julius Caesar (455)
Essays: America (324), The Jersey Devil Came (329)
Short Poems: The People, Yes (406), Caliban in the Coal Mines (405)
Narrative Poem: The Coming of Arthur (522)
Novel: Silas Marner (582)

10. FINDING INTEREST IN NATURE

In this group of selections you witnessed something of the beauty and the power and the mystery of nature. What pictures shall you remember? What sensations were communicated to you vividly?

Readings

Stories: Sleet Storm (98), The Wind Fighters (118), White Tiger (50)
Poems: Stars (407), God's World (407), A Ballade — Catalogue of Lovely Things (408), Nocturne in a Deserted Brickyard (407)
Essays: The Mystery of Migration (318), The Elements (244), With Helmet and Hose (290)

11. BECOMING IMBUED WITH THE SPIRIT OF SCIENCE

What *is* the spirit of science? How is it opposed to superstition? In what different ways does each selection listed below illustrate the spirit of the scientist?

Readings

Essays: With Helmet and Hose (290), Bruce: Trail of the Tsetse (302), The Mystery of Migration (318), Byrd Flies to the North Pole (230), We Aren't Superstitious (334)

12. EXPLORING THE REALM OF FANCY

Can you find the grain of truth that lies behind each of these fantasies? What might really have happened to give rise to such imaginings? In each what is the author trying to tell you? Merely a fantastic yarn? Or something else, in addition?

Readings

Short Stories: The Masque of the Red Death (66), The Monkey's Paw (59)
Short Poems: Daniel Webster's Horses (389), The Horse Thief (372)
Narrative Poem: The Coming of Arthur (522)

13. GARNERING SIGNIFICANT PICTURES OF THE PAST

Here is a group of selections which should bring to mind a series of significant pictures from the past: pictures of Roman senators and gallant knights, pirates, frontiersmen, and English squires. What comparisons can you make between your own age and those represented here?

Readings

Narrative Poems: The Coming of Arthur (522), Lancelot and Elaine (542)
Short Poems: A Ballad of John Silver (375), The Palatine (419), Buffalo Dusk (417), The Oregon Trail (410), By the Turret Stair (360)
Biography: Davy Crockett (173)
Play: Julius Caesar (455)
Novel: Silas Marner (582)

14. RESPONDING TO THE MUSIC OF WORDS

What progress have you made toward an honest enjoyment in the sound and movement of words? At what point in the longer poems did you begin to feel at home with blank verse? What passages ring in your ears? In which of the shorter poems did you feel that the rhythm was particularly appropriate to the thought expressed?

Readings

Short Poems: So Handy (415), Heave Away (416), The Song My Paddle Sings (417), The Golden City of St. Mary (418), The Duke of Plaza-Toro (416)
Narrative Poems: Idylls of the King (522), The Horse Thief (372)
Play: Julius Caesar (455)

Acknowledgments

THE editors of *Adventures in Appreciation,* a second revision, originally revised from *Adventures in Prose and Poetry,* are indebted to the following authors, periodicals, and publishers for permission to use the selections indicated, all rights in which are in all cases reserved by the owner of the copyright.

Keene Abbott: "The Wind Fighters" from *The Outlook,* copyright, 1916.

D. Appleton-Century Company: "The Popover Stars" from *Chats on Science* by Edwin Slosson; "The Unfamiliar" by Richard Connell, copyright, 1923, by D. Appleton-Century Company.

Hanson W. Baldwin: "R. M. S. Titanic," copyright, 1934, by Hanson W. Baldwin.

Stephen Vincent Benét: "We Aren't Superstitious," copyright, 1937, by Esquire, Inc. Reprinted by permission of the author.

Howard Brubaker: "The Milk Pitcher," copyright, 1929, by Howard Brubaker.

Robert Buckner: "The Man Who Won the War."

Jonathan Cape Limited: "A Child's Pet" by William H. Davies, from *Collected Poems of W. H. Davies.*

The Condé Nast Publications, Inc.: "Now There Is Peace" by Richard Sherman from *Vanity Fair,* copyright, 1933, by The Condé Nast Publications, Inc.

Coward-McCann, Inc.: "Daniel Webster's Horses" and "The Circus-Postered Barn" from *Compass Rose* by Elizabeth Coatsworth, copyright, 1929, by Coward-McCann, Inc.; "The Mystery of Migration," reprinted by special arrangement with Coward-McCann, Inc., publishers, from *Down to Earth* by Alan Devoe.

J. Frank Dobie: "Mustangs" from *A Vaquero of the Brush Country.*

Dodd, Mead & Company, Inc.: "The Horse Thief" by William Rose Benét. Used by permission of the publishers, Dodd, Mead & Company, Inc.; "The White Tiger" from *Man and Beast* by Samuel Scoville, Jr.; "The Monkey's Paw" by W. W. Jacobs. Used by permission of Dodd, Mead & Company, Inc.

Doubleday, Doran & Company, Inc.: "Jeeves and the Yuletide Spirit" from *Very Good Jeeves* by P. G. Wodehouse, copyright, 1926, 1927, 1929, 1930, reprinted by permission of Doubleday, Doran & Company, Inc.; "Strange Customs" from *A Daughter of the Samurai* by Etsu Inagaki Sugimoto, copyright, 1925, by Doubleday, Doran & Company, Inc.; "The Education of Helen Keller" from *The Story of My Life* by Helen Keller, copyright, 1903, 1931, reprinted by permission of Doubleday, Doran & Company, Inc.; "The Princess and the Puma" from *Heart of the West* by O. Henry, copyright, 1904, 1932, by Doubleday, Doran & Company, Inc.; "Robert E. Lee" from *John Brown's Body* by Stephen Vincent Benét, copyright, 1928; "A Ballade — Catalogue of Lovely Things" by Richard Le Gallienne from *The Junkman and Other Poems,* copyright, 1920, by Doubleday, Doran & Company, Inc.; "Roofs" from *Main Street and Other Poems* by Joyce Kilmer, copyright, 1917, by Doubleday, Doran & Company, Inc.; "Fuzzy-Wuzzy" from *Departmental Ditties and Barrack-Room Ballads,* copyright, 1892, 1899, by Rudyard Kipling, reprinted by permission of Doubleday, Doran & Company, Inc.

E. P. Dutton & Company, Inc.: "The Oregon Trail" from *I Sing the Pioneer* by Arthur Guiterman, published and copyrighted by E. P. Dutton & Company, Inc., New York; "Deserted" from *The Vale of Tempe* by Madison Cawein, published by E. P. Dutton & Company, Inc., New York.

Farrar & Rinehart, Inc.: "Sam Houston," "Negro Spirituals," and "Nancy Hanks" from *A Book of Americans,* published by Farrar & Rinehart, Inc., copyright, 1933, by Rosemary and Stephen Vincent Benét.

Corey Ford: "Tonight in Person," copyright, 1934, by The Crowell Publishing Company.

Hamlin Garland: "Under the Lion's Paw."

Milton E. M. Geiger: "One Special for Doc."

Harcourt, Brace and Company, Inc.: " Caliban in the Coal Mines " from *Challenge* by Louis Untermeyer, reprinted by permission of Harcourt, Brace and Company, Inc., holders of the copyright; " David Bruce " from *Microbe Hunters* by Paul de Kruif, copyright, 1926, by Harcourt, Brace and Company, Inc.; " Mr. Kaplan the Magnificent " from *The Education of Hyman Kaplan* by Leonard Q. Ross, copyright, 1937, by Harcourt, Brace and Company, Inc.; " Davy Crockett " from *Davy Crockett* by Constance Rourke, copyright, 1934, by Harcourt, Brace and Company, Inc.; " I Was Talking Across the Fence This Morning " from *The Tragedy of Josephine Maria and Other One-Act Plays* by Charles S. Brooks, copyright, 1931, by Harcourt, Brace and Company, Inc.; " Buffalo Dusk " from *Smoke and Steel* by Carl Sandburg, copyright, 1920, by Harcourt, Brace and Company, Inc.; " From the Four Corners of the Earth " and " In the Darkness with a Great Bundle of Grief the People March " from *The People, Yes* by Carl Sandburg, copyright, 1936, by Harcourt, Brace and Company, Inc.

Harper & Brothers: " The Whipping " from *A Genius in the Family* by Hiram Percy Maxim; " The Revolt of Mother " from *A New England Nun* by Mary W. Freeman.

Harper & Brothers, The Bookman Publishing Company, and Roy Helton: " Old Christmas Morning " from *Lonesome Water*.

Henry Holt and Company: " Blueberries " and " The Code " from *North of Boston* by Robert Frost; " Four Little Foxes " from *Slow Smoke* by Lew Sarett; " Skyscraper " and " Nocturne in a Deserted Brickyard " from *Chicago Poems* by Carl Sandburg.

Houghton Mifflin Company: " America " from *Let the Record Speak* by Dorothy Thompson, Houghton Mifflin Company, copyright, 1939, by Dorothy Thompson, reprinted by permission of the author and Houghton Mifflin Company; " Texas " from *What's O'Clock* by Amy Lowell, used by permission of, and arrangement with the publishers, Houghton Mifflin Company.

Margaret Bell Houston: " Cerelle."

The Kaleidograph Press: " Moonlight " from *Flute in the Distance* by Berta Hart Nance.

Alfred A. Knopf, Inc.: " The Noblest Instrument " from *Life With Father* by Clarence Day, " The Palatine " by Willa Cather, and " At the Aquarium " from *Colours of Life* by Max Eastman are reprinted by permission of, and special arrangement with, Alfred A. Knopf, Inc., authorized publishers.

Louise Lambertson: " Sleet Storm," *The Country Gentleman,* January, 1932; copyright, by Louise Lambertson, 1933.

Edmund Leamy: " The Ticket Agent."

Little, Brown & Company: " A Railroad Train " from *The Poems of Emily Dickinson,* Centenary Edition, edited by Martha Dickinson Bianchi and Alfred Leete Hampson, reprinted by permission of Little, Brown & Company; " Keeper of the Bulls " from *Lions 'n' Tigers 'n' Everything* by Courtney Ryley Cooper, reprinted and abridged by permission of Little, Brown & Company.

J. B. Lippincott Company: " Little Giffen " by Francis Orray Ticknor.

The Macmillan Company: " The Duke of Plaza-Toro " from W. S. Gilbert's *Bab Ballads, Songs of a Savoyard;* " The Golden City of St. Mary " from *Salt Water Poems and Ballads* by John Masefield; " A Wanderer's Song," " Tewkesbury Road," " A Ballad of John Silver," " Trade Winds," and " Tomorrow " from *Poems* by John Masefield; " The Broncho That Would Not Be Broken " from *Collected Poems* by Vachel Lindsay; " Rebecca Nixon and Martha Waugh " from *Collected Poems* by Wilfrid Wilson Gibson; " An Old Woman of the Roads " from *Poems* by Padraic Colum; " Stars " from *Flame and Shadow* by Sara Teasdale. All reprinted by permission of The Macmillan Company, publishers.

Edna St. Vincent Millay: " Travel " from *Second April,* published by Harper & Brothers, copyright, 1921, by Edna St. Vincent Millay; " God's World " from *Renascence,* published by Harper & Brothers, copyright, 1917, by Edna St. Vincent Millay.

Juanita Miller: " Kit Carson's Ride " by Joaquin Miller, reprinted by permission of Juanita Miller.

The Musson Book Company, Ltd.: " The Song My Paddle Sings " from *Flint and Feather,* the Complete Poems of E. Pauline Johnson, printed and copyrighted by The Musson Book Company, Ltd., Toronto, Canada.

Francis Newbolt: " Vitaï Lampada " from *Poems New and Old* by Sir Henry John Newbolt, as published by Messrs. John Murray.

Poetry, A Magazine of Verse and Miss Nancy Campbell: " The Monkey " by Nancy Campbell.

G. P. Putnam's Sons: " With Helmet and Hose " from *The Arcturus Adventure* by William Beebe; "Our Back Yard Circus" from *Safari* by Martin Johnson.

Random House, Inc.: "In the Zone" from *Moon of the Caribbees and Six Other Plays of the Sea* by Eugene O'Neill, reprinted by permission of Random House, Inc., New York, copyright, 1923, by Eugene O'Neill.

Reynal and Hitchcock, Inc.: "The Elements" reprinted by permission from *Wind, Sand, and Stars* by Antoine de Saint Exupéry, published by Reynal and Hitchcock, Inc.

Charles Scribner's Sons: "On the Dodge" from *Sun Up* by Will James; "The Jersey Devil Came" by Ruth Crawford from *Life in the United States;* "Zenobia's Infidelity" by H. C. Bunner.

Frederick A. Stokes Company: "Byrd Flies to the North Pole," reprinted by permission from *Struggle: Life and Exploits of Commander Byrd* by Charles J. V. Murphy, copyright, 1928, by Frederick A. Stokes Company.

Story and The Story Press: "That's What Happened to Me" by Michael Fessier.

Nancy Byrd Turner: "Notation on Immortality."

Stewart Edward White: "The Drive" from *Arizona Nights,* reprinted by permission of the author.

Philip Wylie: "Twenty Cigarettes," copyright, 1931, by Philip Wylie, reprinted by permission of the author.

Yale University Press: "Days" from *Blue Smoke* by Karle Wilson Baker.

The editors wish to thank Miss Decie Merwin for the attractive silhouettes preceding each major section of the volume.

They wish also to say a special word of appreciation to Miss Mary Rives Bowman of East Texas State Teachers College, Commerce, Texas, for her wise and practical suggestions, spiced with delightful humor.

Dictionary of Words, Names, and Phrases

This glossary contains pronunciations and definitions for the more important of the harder and comparatively unusual terms used in this book. For each word the definition is limited to the use of that word in this volume. For a word already explained in a word study, *Increase Your Power over Words*, only the pronunciation is given here, and reference is made to the page where the explanation may be found. For words with more than one accepted pronunciation, the most usual pronunciation is given.

The diacritical markings used are very simple: āce, senȧte, râre, băt, fäther, sofȧ, ėvent, ēven, ĕnd, mothẽr, fĭnd, sĭt, rōpe, ŏmit, côrd, hŏt, ūnit, ûnite, bûrn, cŭt, bōōt, fŏŏt, then. Both main accent (ʹ) and secondary accent (ʹ) are given.

In a few foreign words the exact pronunciation is not quite achieved.

A

Aachen (äʹkĕn). P. 151
abashed (ȧ-băshtʹ). Filled with awe
aberration (ăbʹẽr-āʹshŭn). A turning aside from the normal
abyss (ȧ-bĭsʹ). Anything bottomless or unbounded
accelerated (ăk-sĕlʹẽr-ātʹĕd). Hastened
acclimated (ă-klīʹmȧ-tĕd). P. 108
accolade (ăkʹō-lādʹ). P. 15
accouterment (ă-kōōʹtẽr-mĕnt). Dress; equipment
Achilles (ȧ-kĭlʹēz). P. 382
acquiesced (ăkʹwĭ-ĕstʹ). Agreed in silence
acrid (ăkʹrĭd). Bitter; sharp-tasting
acrobatic (ăkʹrō-bătʹĭk). Like one who performs daring gymnastic feats
addled (ădʹʹld). Spoiled
admonished (ăd-mŏnʹĭsht). Reproved gently
adobe (ȧ-dōʹbĭ). Unburnt brick dried in the sun
adolescent (ădʹō-lĕsʹĕnt). P. 342
adroit (ȧ-droitʹ). Skillful
adulation (ădʹū-lāʹshŭn). Excessive praise
adulterated (ȧ-dŭlʹtẽr-ātʹĕd). Made impure
aeon (ēʹŏn). A period of time too long to measure
aesthetic (ĕs-thĕtʹĭk). Appreciative of the beautiful
affiance (ă-fīʹăns). Trust
Agamemnon (ăgʹȧ-mĕmʹnŏn). P. 382
aggravated (ăgʹrȧ-vātʹĕd). Increased; made worse
aggrieved (ă-grēvdʹ). Distressed
aghast (ȧ-gȧstʹ). Struck with sudden horror
agile (ăjʹĭl). P. 392
agitation (ăjʹĭ-tāʹshŭn). Disturbance
aide-de-camp (ādʹdē-kămpʹ). An officer who assists a general
Alamo (äʹlä-mō). P. 209
albino (ăl-bīʹnō). P. 58
alleged (ă-lĕjdʹ). Declared; asserted
allegiance (ă-lēʹjăns). Loyalty to a sovereign
alleviate (ă-lēʹvĭ-āt). To lighten; to render more tolerable
allusion (ă-lūʹzhŭn). P. 148
amalgam (ȧ-mălʹgăm). An alloy of one or more metals with mercury
amenities (ȧ-mĕnʹĭ-tĭz). Manners
amorous (ămʹō-rŭs). Inclined to love
amorphous (ȧ-môrʹfŭs). Formless; shapeless
amulet (ămʹū-lĕt). A charm
Amundsen (äʹmŭn-sĕn). P. 233
analogous (ȧ-nălʹō-gŭs). Similar
analogy (ȧ-nălʹō-jĭ). Partial resemblance
Andrée (änʹdrȧ). P. 237
angular (ăngʹgū-lẽr). Rawboned; ungainly
animate (ănʹĭ-māt). P. 279
animation (ănʹĭ-māʹshŭn). P. 279
annulling (ă-nŭlʹlĭng). Doing away with
anon (ȧ-nŏnʹ). P. 72
anonymous (ȧ-nŏnʹĭ-mŭs). Nameless
Antares (ăn-tāʹrēz). P. 321
antecedent (ănʹtē-sēdʹĕnt). P. 230
antedate (ănʹtē-dāt). P. 230
antediluvian (ănʹtē-dĭ-lūʹvĭ-ăn). P. 230
antennae (ăn-tĕnʹē). The feelers which grow on the heads of insects
anteroom (ănʹtē-rōōmʹ). P. 230
anticlimax (ănʹtĭ-klīʹmăks). Descent from the sublime to the ridiculous
antimacassar (ănʹtĭ-mȧ-kăsʹẽr). A cover for the back or arms of a chair, sofa, etc.
antipathy (ăn-tĭpʹȧ-thĭ). An instinctive dislike
anti-slavery (ănʹtĭ-slāvʹẽr-ĭ). P. 230
aped (āpt). Imitated
apothecaries (ȧ-pŏthʹē-kȧʹrĭz). Those who sell and prepare medicines
apotheosis (ȧ-pŏthʹē-ōʹsĭs). Raising a man to the rank of a god
appall (ă-pôlʹ). To dismay
apprehend (ăpʹrē-hĕndʹ). Interpret the meaning of
apprehension (ăpʹrē-hĕnʹshŭn). Dread as to what may happen
apprehensive (ăpʹrē-hĕnʹsĭv). Fearful, as of trouble
aquatic (ȧ-kwătʹĭk). Growing in or frequenting water

arabesque (ăr′ȧ-bĕsk′). A decoration in low relief or color
Arapahoe (ȧ-răp′ȧ-hō). P. 411
Arimathea (ăr′ĭ-mȧ-thē′ȧ). P. 575
arrested (ȧ-rĕst′ĕd). Checked; held; attracted
artisan (är′tĭ-zăn). A man trained to work with his hands
asafetida (ăs′ȧ-fĕt′ĭ-dȧ). P. 10
ascertain (ăs′ēr-tān′). To find out definitely
aspiration (ăs′pĭ-rā′shŭn). The strong desire to attain a high or noble goal
assiduous (ă-sĭd′ū-ŭs). Persistent
assiduously (ă-sĭd′ū-ŭs-lĭ). Diligently; studiously
astrology (ăs-trŏl′ō-jĭ). The practice which claims to predict events by the position and mysterious influence on human affairs of the sun, moon, and planets
atom (ăt′ŭm). P. 324
attrition (ă-trĭsh′ŭn). Act of rubbing together; friction
audacious (ô-dā′shŭs). Bold; impudent
audibility (ô′dĭ-bĭl′ĭ-tĭ). Quality of being heard
audible (ô′dĭ-b′l). P. 699
august (ô-gŭst′). Having grandeur and dignity
authentic (ô-thĕn′tĭk). Duly authorized; genuine
avaricious (ăv′ȧ-rĭsh′ŭs). Greedy of gain
aver (ȧ-vûr′). P. 699
avowal (ȧ-vou′ăl). A frank acknowledgment
azure (ăzh′ūr). Sky-blue

B

bacteriologist (băk-tē′rĭ-ŏl′ō-jĭst). A student of the science which deals with bacteria
bakehus (bāk′hŭs). Bakehouse
Balan (bā′lăn). P. 540
balefire (bāl′fīr′). Funeral pyre
Balin (bā′lĭn). P. 540
ballast (băl′ăst). Any heavy substance put into the hold of a vessel to give stability
baptistry (băp′tĭs-trĭ). Separate building used for baptismal services
bard (bärd).
barometer (bȧ-rŏm′ē-tēr). An instrument for predicting changes of weather
barong (bä-rŏng′). P. 58
barracks (băr′ăks). A large structure for lodging soldiers
barrage (bȧ′räzh′). P. 15
bas-relief (bä′rē-lēf′). A form of sculpture in which the figures stand out very slightly from the background
bay (bā). To compel a hunted creature to face his difficulties when escape is impossible
beatific (bē′ȧ-tĭf′ĭk). Blissfully happy
Beatty (bē′tĭ). P. 152
befuddle (bē-fŭd′′l). To confuse
behest (bē-hĕst′). Command
Bellerophon (bĕ-lĕr′ō-fŏn). P. 373
benediction (bĕn′ē-dĭk′shŭn). P. 16
Benét (bĕ-nā′). P. 334
benignity (bē-nĭg′nĭ-tĭ). Kindness
bestial (bĕst′yăl). Brutish
Betelgeuse (bĕt′ĕl-gûz′). P. 321
Bexar (bā′är). P. 201
bibulous (bĭb′ū-lŭs). Inclined to drinking
bizarre (bĭ-zär′). P. 72
blackguard (blăg′ärd). A scoundrel
blasphemy (blȧs′fē-mĭ). Irreverent or mocking language about God or sacred things
blatant (blā′tănt). Noisy
bolus (bō′lŭs). A large pill, as for a horse
bondsman (bŏndz′măn). A male slave
boon (bo͞on). P. 392, p. 579
boor (bo͞or). A clumsy, ill-mannered person
booty (bo͞o′tĭ). Plunder of thieves and robbers
botany (bŏt′ȧ-nĭ). The science which deals with plants
Boulogne (bo͞o′lōn′y′). P. 152
Bowie (bo͞o′ĭ). P. 210
brash (brăsh). Hasty in temper; impetuous
brassard (brăs′ȧrd). Badge worn on the arm
bravado (brȧ-vä′dō). Boastful defiance
brazenly (brā′z′n-lĭ). Impudently; shamelessly
Brazos (brä′zōs). P. 210
bridge (brĭj). An observation platform above the deck of a ship
bridled (brī′d′ld). Checked
brocade (brō-kā′d). A silken fabric
bromide (brō′mīd). A compound of bromine with another element
buffeting (bŭf′ĕt-ĭng). Knocking about; struggling
buffoon (bŭ-fo͞on′). P. 108
buoyance (bo͞o′yăns). Variant of buoyancy (bo͞o′yăn-sĭ). Property of floating

C

Caerleon (kär-lē′ŏn). P. 542
cajole (kȧ-jōl′). Entice by soft words
calabash (kăl′ȧ-băsh). Gourdlike fruit from a tropical American tree
Calais (kăl′ā; kăl′ĭs; kȧ′lĕ′). P. 152
calamitous (kȧ-lăm′ĭ-tŭs). Causing misery; disastrous
calculable (kăl′kū-lȧ-b′l). Capable of being measured
caldron (kôl′drŭn). A large kettle or boiler
calorie (kăl′ō-rĭ). Unit of heat
camion (kȧ′myôn′). A motor truck used to carry cannon
candelabrum (kăn′dĕ-lä′brŭm). P. 72
candor (kăn′dēr). Openness; frankness
cannon bone (kăn′ŭn bōn). The bone from the hock joint to the fetlock
capacious (kȧ-pā′shŭs). Able to contain much
capricious (kȧ-prĭsh′ŭs). P. 290
carbine (kär′bīn). A short, light rifle
carnivorous (kär-nĭv′ō-rŭs). Flesh-eating
casement (kās′mĕnt). P. 72
casque (kȧsk). Helmet
caste (kȧst). P. 94
Castellani (kȧs′tĕ-län′ē). P. 309

castellated (kăs′tĕ-lāt′ĕd). Built with battlements, like a castle
casualty (kăzh′ū̇-ăl-tĭ). An accident; a disaster
cataleptic (kăt′ȧ-lĕp′tĭk). Subject to trancelike states
catapult (kăt′ȧ-pŭlt). Hurl
cavalcade (kăv′ăl-kād′). P. 406
cavalier (kăv′ȧ-lēr′). P. 406
cavalry (kăv′ăl-rĭ). P. 406
cavort (kȧ-vôrt′). To prance or caper about
censure (sĕn′shẽr). Faultfinding; reproof
Centaur (sĕn′tôr). P. 373
chamber (chām′bẽr). P. 72
changeling (chānj′lĭng). Child substituted by fairies
chaos (kā′ŏs). Utter disorder
chaps (chăps). Short for *chaparajos* (chä′pä-rä′hōs). Overalls of sheepskin or leather, usually open at the back
chary (châr′ĭ). Guarding with care
chastisement (chăs′tĭz-mĕnt). Punishment
checkered (chĕk′ẽrd). Marked by constant alternation, as of bad and good fortune
Cheops (kē′ŏps). P. 301
Cherbourg (shĕr′bo͝or′). P. 160
chevron (shĕv′rŭn). Badge consisting of two or more stripes meeting at an angle on the coat sleeve
chimerical (kī-mē′rĭ-kăl). Merely imaginary
chinaware (chī′nȧ-wâr′). P. 363
chine (chīn). The backbone of an animal with adjoining parts
chortle (chôr′t'l). To laugh in a chuckling, snorting fashion
chronic (krŏn′ĭk). P. 244
chronicle (krŏn′ĭ-kăl). P. 244
chronological (krŏn′ō̇-lŏj′ĭ-kăl). P. 244
chronometer (krō̇-nŏm′ē̇-tẽr). P. 244
cinch (sĭnch). To tighten the girth of a saddle. A saddle girth firmly fastened in place by loops and knots
circumspect (sûr′kŭm-spĕkt). P. 148
clairvoyant (klâr-voi′ănt). A person with ability to perceive things not visible
clambered (klăm′bẽrd). P. 108
Cocos (kō′kōs). P. 295
collateral (kŏ-lăt′ẽr-ăl). Descended from the same ancestor
collogue (kŏ-lōg′). Confer secretly
colloquies (kŏl′ō̇-kwĭz). P. 698
Cologne (kō̇-lōn′). P. 149
colossal (kō̇-lŏs′ăl). Huge; vast
coma (kō′mȧ). State of deep insensibility
Comanche (kō̇-măn′chē̇). P. 205
commandeer (kŏm′ăn-dēr′). To take forcibly for personal use
communal (kŏm′ū̇-năl). Living together
community (kŏ-mū′nĭ-tĭ). P. 108
compacted (kŏm-păk′tĕd). Composed or joined firmly
complacency (kŏm-plā′sĕn-sĭ). Self-satisfaction
component (kŏm-pō′nĕnt). Constituent part; ingredient
composure (kŏm-pō′zhẽr). Calmness
compunction (kŏm-pŭngk′shŭn). Remorse
conclave (kŏn′klāv). A secret meeting
concussion (kŏn-kŭsh′ŭn). Shock of collision
confiscation (kŏn′fĭs-kā′shŭn). Being taken over by authority
conjecture (kŏn-jĕk′tū̇r). Guess; forming opinions without definite proof
conjuring (kŭn′jẽr-ĭng). Practicing magic
constellation (kŏn-stĕ-lā′shŭn). Various groups of fixed stars in the sky
contemplate (kŏn′tĕm-plāt). To meditate on
contingent (kŏn-tĭn′jĕnt). P. 698
contour (kôn′to͞or). Shape
contraption (kŏn-trăp′shŭn). A contrivance; a newfangled device
contretemps (kôn′trē-tän′). An unfortunate accident; a hitch
contrivance (kŏn-trīv′ăns). Plan; invention
convoy (kŏn′voi). An escort
convulsive (kŏn-vŭl′sĭv). Violent; causing a great commotion emotionally
co-ordinate (kō̇-ôr′dĭ-nȧt). Harmoniously adjusted
coppice (kôp′ĭs). Thicket
cordon (kôr′dŏn). A line of men forming an extended chain
coroner (kŏr′ō̇-nẽr). An officer whose chief duty is to find out the cause of any violent or mysterious death
corral (kŏ-răl′). P. 258
correlation (kŏr′ē̇-lā′shŭn). Relation of part to part or of a part to a whole
corridor (kŏr′ĭ-dôr). P. 72
corroborated (kŏ-rŏb′ō̇-rāt-ĕd). Confirmed
corrode (kŏ-rōd′). P. 429
corrosive (kŏ-rō′sĭv). P. 429
corrugation (kŏr′o͝o-gā′shŭn). Wrinkle; furrow
countenance (koun′tē̇-năns). P. 72
counterbalancing (koun′tẽr-băl′ăns-ĭng). Opposing with an equal weight
courser (kōr′sẽr). A swift or spirited horse
covenant (kŭv′ē̇-nănt). Compact; agreement
credulity (krē̇-dū′lĭ-tĭ). Readiness to believe what one is told without asking for proof
credulous (krĕd′ū̇-lŭs). P. 342
crenelated (krĕn′ĕl-āt′ĕd). Furnished with battlements
crescent (krĕs′ĕnt). Increasing in power
crown (kroun). An English coin worth five shillings
cuirass (kwē̇-răs′). Armor covering upper trunk; breastplate
culpable (kŭl′pȧ-b'l). Guilty; blameworthy
cupidity (kū̇-pĭd′ĭ-tĭ). Greed
curvet (kûr′vĕt). Prance, as a horse
cutlass (kŭt′lȧs). A short, heavy sword with a wide, curved blade
cygnet (sĭg′nĕt). Young swan

D

dais (dā′ĭs). A raised platform
Danae (dăn′ā-ē). P. 25
dearth (dûrth). Want; scarcity
deferentially (dĕf′ēr-ĕn′shăl-lĭ). Showing respect
defile (dē-fīl′). A long, narrow pass, as between mountains
deft (dĕft). Neat and skillful in action
delf, delft, delph (dĕlf; dĕlft; dĕlf). A colored glazed earthenware
deluge (dĕl′ūj). P. 230
delusion (dē-lū′zhŭn). P. 148
demurred (dē-mûrd′). Hesitated
density (dĕn′sĭ-tĭ). P. 324
depended (dē-pĕnd′ĕd). P. 72
deprecate (dĕp′rē-kāt). To express disapproval of
deprecating (dĕp′rē-kāt′ĭng). P. 118
deprivation (dĕp′rĭ-vā′shŭn). State of having something taken away
deputation (dĕp′ū-tā′shŭn). Delegation
derisive (dē-rī′sĭv). P. 108
detractor (dē-trăk′tēr). One who takes credit from
deviation (dē′vĭ-ā′shŭn). A turning aside or away from
devious (dē′vĭ-ŭs). Indirect; rambling
dexterity (dĕks-tĕr′ĭ-tĭ). P. 698
diabolical (dī′ȧ-bŏl′ĭ-kăl). Devilish
diagnosable (dī′ăg-nōs′ȧ-b'l). Distinguishable by its characteristic phenomena
diffidently (dĭf′ĭ-dĕnt-lĭ). Without self-reliance
diminutive (dĭ-mĭn′ū-tĭv). Small or little
dirigible (dĭr′ĭ-jĭ-b'l). A balloon
disapprobation (dĭs-ăp′rō-bā′shŭn). Disapproval
disarmament (dĭs-är′mȧ-mĕnt). The reduction of military and naval forces
discoursing (dĭs-kôrs′ĭng). Conversing; discussing
discretion (dĭs-krĕsh′ŭn). Good judgment
discursive (dĭs-kûr′sĭv). Passing from one subject to another
disfiguration (dĭs-fĭg′ū-rā′shŭn). A marring in shape or beauty
disparagement (dĭs-păr′ĭj-mĕnt). Lowering in esteem
dispensation (dĭs′pĕn-sā′shŭn). Distribution of good and evil by God to man
dissipated (dĭs′ĭ-pāt′ĕd). Driven away; dispelled
dissolution (dĭs′ō-lū′shŭn). P. 72
distorted (dĭs-tôrt′ĕd). P. 108
dividers (dĭ-vīd′ērz). An instrument used in mechanical drawing for checking distances
docile (dŏs′ĭl). P. 404
dogie (dō′gĭ). A motherless calf
dolorous (dō′lēr-ŭs). Painful
doughty (dou′tĭ). Brave
down (doun). Treeless chalk uplands
drop-forge (drŏp′-fōrj′). P. 279
dubiety (dū-bī′ē-tĭ). Doubtfulness
dubiously (dū′bĭ-ŭs-lĭ). Doubtfully; questioningly
dungarees (dŭng′gȧ-rēz′). Cotton working trousers
durian (dōō′rĭ-ăn). An East Indian fruit which has a hard, prickly rind and an unpleasant odor
dusky (dŭs′kĭ). Somewhat dark
dynamos (dī′nȧ-mōz). Machines which convert mechanical energy into electric current

E

ebony (ĕb′ŭn-ĭ). P. 72
eccentric (ĕk-sĕn′trĭk). P. 699
economic (ē′kō-nŏm′ĭk). Relating to the production and use of wealth
ecstasy (ĕk′stȧ-sĭ). P. 10
edifice (ĕd′ĭ-fĭs). A building, especially one that is large and imposing
eerie (ē′rĭ). Creepy; uneasy; weird
efficacy (ĕf′ĭ-kȧ-sĭ). The power to produce desired results
egress (ē′grĕs). P. 72
Ehrlich (âr′lĭk). P. 311
electrified (ē-lĕk′trĭ-fīd). Thrilled; startled
Einstein (īn′stīn). P. 241
Eldorado (ĕl-dō-rä′dō). P. 325
electron (ē-lĕk′trŏn). P. 324
elephantine (ĕl′ē-făn′tĭn). P. 10
elicit (ē-lĭs′ĭt). Call forth
elocution (ĕl′ō-kū′shŭn). The art which teaches the proper use of voice and gesture in public speaking or reading
emaciated (ē-mā′shĭ-āt′ĕd). Wasted away by hunger or fatigue
emanating (ĕm′ȧ-nāt′ĭng). P. 72
emanation (ĕm′ȧ-nā′shŭn). Something that flows forth from a source
embellish (ĕm-bĕl′ĭsh). To make beautiful or elegant
embezzle (ĕm-bĕz′'l). To steal funds entrusted to one's care
eminently (ĕm′ĭ-nĕnt-lĭ). Clearly standing out
enhance (ĕn-hȧns′). To increase in attractiveness or value
enigmatic (ĕn′ĭg-măt′ĭk). P. 342
entail (ĕn-tāl′). Restrictions imposed by inheritance laws
Entebbe (ĕn-tĕb′ĕ). P. 311
enthrall (ĕn-thrôl′). P. 66
epic (ĕp′ĭk). P. 390
epicure (ĕp′ĭ-kūr). P. 218
epigram (ĕp′ĭ-grăm). Concise, meaningful expression
epithet (ĕp′ĭ-thĕt). P. 24
equestrian (ē-kwĕs′trĭ-ăn). Performing with horses
erode (ē-rōd). P. 429
erosion (ē-rō′zhŭn). P. 429
erudite (ĕr′ōō-dīt). Learned; scholarly
eruption (ē-rŭp′shŭn). A bursting out

escarpment (ĕs-kärp′mĕnt). A steep slope to a height; a cliff
etched (ĕcht). P. 108
eternity (ē-tûr′nĭ-tĭ). P. 108
ethereal (ē-thē′rē-ăl). Airy and delicate
etiquette (ĕt′ĭ-kĕt). Rules of conduct
evolution (ĕv′ō-lū′shŭn). A movement that is one of a series of movements
exasperating (ĕg-zăs′pēr-āt-ĭng). Annoying; provoking
execrable (ĕk′sē-krȧ-b'l). Bad; wretched
execrated (ĕk′sē-krāt′ĕd). Cursed; detested utterly
executive (ĕg-zĕk′ū-tĭv). Skillful in carrying into effect
exemplary (ĕg-zĕm′plȧ-rĭ). Serving as a model
exhilarate (ĕg-zĭl′ȧ-rāt). To enliven
exhort (ĕg-zôrt′). To urge strongly
exhortation (ĕk′sŏr-tā′shŭn). Incitement by words
exiguity (ĕk′sĭ-gū′ĭ-tĭ). Scantiness
exotic (ĕks-ŏt′ĭk). Belonging to another part of the world
expansive (ĕks-păn′sĭv). Having tendency to extend, spread
expiated (ĕks′pĭ-āt′ĕd). Atoned for; made amends for
exploit (ĕks-ploit′). To make use of for one's own profit
exultant (ĕg-zŭl′tănt). Rejoicing exceedingly

F

facetious (fȧ-sē′shŭs). Humorous; harmlessly teasing
facsimile (făk-sĭm′ĭlē). P. 698
fakir (fȧ-kēr′). In India, a religious beggar
fallible (făl′ĭ-b'l). Liable to be wrong
fanfare (făn′fâr). Display; a noisy parade
fantasy (făn′tȧ-sĭ). A product of the imagination
feasibility (fē′zĭ-bĭl′ĭ-tĭ). Practicability; condition of being practical
feign (fān). To pretend
felicitous (fē-lĭs′ĭ-tŭs). Happy; delightful
fervid (fûr′vĭd). Eager
festal (fĕs′tăl). Relating to a feast or holiday
fiasco (fē-ȧs′kō). P. 29
filament (fĭl′ȧ-mĕnt). Threadlike appendage
filial (fĭl′yăl). Becoming to a child
fissure (fĭsh′ēr). A narrow opening; a cleft
fixation (fĭks-ā′shŭn). A fixed or stable thing
flagrant (flā′grănt). Flaming or glaring
flange (flănj). A rim for attachment to another object
flaying (flā′ĭng). Stripping the skin from
fledgling (flĕj′lĭng). A bird that has just acquired the feathers necessary for flight
flexible (flĕk′sĭ-b'l). P. 392
Flores (flō′rĕs). P. 377
fluctuation (flŭk′tū-ā′shŭn). Frequent irregular change
fluxion (flŭk′shŭn). A flowing

focal (fō′kăl). Placed at a central point
Fokker (fŏk′ēr). P. 232
folklore (fōk′lôr′). P. 225
foreboding (fôr-bōd′ĭng). Portent; a feeling that misfortune is coming
formidable (fôr′mĭ-dȧ-b'l). Hard to deal with
fossil (fŏs′ĭl). A petrified animal or plant
fragile (frăj′ĭl). Easily broken; delicate
fraud (frôd). P. 699
frustrate (frŭs′trāt). P. 699
fumigate (fū′mĭ-gāt). To free of disease germs with fumes
furtively (fûr′tĭv-lĭ). Slyly; stealthily
fuselage (fū′zĕ-lĭj). The body of an airplane
fusillade (fū′zĭl-lād′). Rapidly repeated discharges of firearms
fusion (fū′zhŭn). P. 698
fustian (fŭs′chăn). Coarse twilled cotton cloth
futility (fū-tĭl′ĭ-tĭ). Uselessness; vanity

G

Galápagos (gä-lä′pä-gōs). P. 292
gallant (găl′ănt). Stately; grand
galled (gôld). Vexed; wearied
galleon (găl′ē-ŭn). A large sailing vessel with a high stern and three or four decks
Gallipoli (gȧ-lĭp′ō-lē). P. 155
gangrene (găng′grēn). The decay of some part of the body
garrulity (gă-rōō′lĭ-tĭ). Talkativeness
gauge (gāj). An instrument for finding the exact measurement
gaunt (gônt). Barren; grim; thin
Gawain (gô′wȧn). P. 529
genre (zhän′r'). Kind; sort
gentry (jĕn′trĭ). People in England ranking next to nobility
Geraint (gĕ-rānt′). P. 538
ghoulish (gōōl′ĭsh). P. 58
Goliad (gō′lĭ-ăd′). P. 210
gout (gout). A disease marked by painful inflammation of the joints
graph (grȧf). To trace
gratitude (grăt′ĭ-tūd). P. 699
gratuitously (grȧ-tū′ĭ-tŭs-lĭ). P. 699
gratuity (grȧ-tū′ĭ-tĭ). P. 699
grimace (grĭ-mās′). P. 108
grisly (grĭz′lĭ). Horrible; ghastly
grotesque (grō-tĕsk′). Characterized by fantastic combination of human and animal figures
growler (groul′ēr). The main part of an iceberg, that part which is submerged beneath the water
gruesome (grōō′sŭm). P. 349
guinea (gĭn′ĭ). An English coin worth twenty-one shillings

H

habiliment (hȧ-bĭl′ĭ-mĕnt). Clothing; attire
habitat (hăb′ĭ-tăt). Dwelling place

Haig (hāg). P. 152
harry (hăr'ĭ). To lay waste
hazardous (hăz'ēr-dŭs). Risky; dangerous
headright (hĕd'rīt'). A grant of land made to each citizen by the Constitution of Texas in 1836
hectoring (hĕk'tēr-ĭng). Bullying
heifer (hĕf'ēr). A young cow
heinous (hā'nŭs). Hateful; extremely wicked
herbivorous (hēr-bĭv'ō-rŭs). Eating plants
heritage (hĕr'ĭ-tĭj). The lot into which one is born
Hernani (ĕr-nä'nē). P. 69
hieroglyphic (hī'ēr-ō-glĭf'ĭk). Picture writing, like that of the Egyptians
hippodrome (hĭp'ō-drōm). A modern arena with seats for spectators
hoary (hôr'ĭ). White or gray with age; old; venerable
hobble (hŏb''l). P. 258
holland (hŏl'ănd). P. 363
horde (hōrd). Group; crowd
horizontal (hŏr'ĭ-zŏn'tăl). P. 251
horn (hôrn). P. 258
hornpipe (hôrn'pīp'). A lively dance, especially popular with sailors
Houston (hūs'tŭn). P. 210
Huguenot (hū'gĕ-nŏt). P. 217
humiliate (hū-mĭl'ĭ-āt). To humble
husbandry (hŭz'bănd-rĭ). Practice of agriculture
husking (hŭsk'ĭng). P. 117
hysteria (hĭs-tē'rĭ-ȧ). Morbid or convulsive excitement

I

idiosyncrasies (ĭd'ĭ-ō-sĭng'krȧ-sĭz). Peculiarities of thinking, acting, feeling
ignoble (ĭg-nō'b'l). Of mean quality
ignominiously (ĭg'nō-mĭn'ĭ-ŭs-lĭ). P. 29. Degradingly; shamefully
ill-assorted (ĭl-ă-sôrt'ĕd). P. 108
illegal (ĭ-lē'găl). P. 264
illimitable (ĭ-lĭm'ĭt-ȧ-b'l). P. 264
illuminate (ĭ-lū'mĭ-nāt). P. 230
illumined (ĭ-lū'mĭnd). P. 72
illusion (ĭ-lū'zhŭn). P. 148
imbecile (ĭm'bē-sĭl). A feeble-minded person
immerse (ĭ-mûrs'). Dip
imminent (ĭm'ĭ-nĕnt). Threatening to occur immediately
immobile (ĭ-mō'bĭl). P. 279
immortality (ĭm'ôr-tăl'ĭ-tĭ). Life that never ends
immunity (ĭ-mū'nĭ-tĭ). Freedom from
impact (ĭm'păkt). Striking together
impaired (ĭm-pârd'). Weakened; marred
impassive (ĭm-păs'ĭv). Unmoved
impeded (ĭm-pēd'ĕd). P. 72
imperativeness (ĭm-pĕr'ȧ-tĭv-nĕs). Necessity
imperial (ĭm-pē'rĭ-ăl). P. 72
imperturbable (ĭm'pēr-tûr'bȧ-b'l). Calm
impetuously (ĭm-pĕt'ū-ŭs-lĭ). Passionately; eagerly
implacable (ĭm-plā'kȧ-b'l). Unyielding
impostor (ĭm-pŏs'tēr). One who attempts to deceive others by adopting a false name or character
impotence (ĭm'pō-tĕns). Weakness; feebleness
impregnable (ĭm-prĕg'nȧ-b'l). Unconquerable
impregnated (ĭm-prĕg'nāt-ĕd). Fertilized; saturated
impressionable (ĭm-prĕsh'ŭn-ȧ-b'l). Easily influenced
impromptu (ĭm-prŏmp'tū). Without preparation
improvidently (ĭm-prŏv'ĭ-dĕnt-lĭ). Thriftlessly; wastefully
improvvisatori (ēm'prōv-vē'zä-tō'rē). Those who compose and sing short poems extempore
impugn (ĭm-pūn'). To assail by words
impure (ĭm-pūr'). P. 264
inactive (ĭn-ăk'tĭv). P. 264
inanimate (ĭn-ăn'ĭ-māt). Without life
inanity (ĭn-ăn'ĭ-tĭ). Emptiness
inarticulate (ĭn'är-tĭk'ū-lāt). Indistinctly pronounced; speechless
incalculable (ĭn-kăl'kū-lȧ-b'l). Not capable of being measured
incandescent (ĭn-kăn-dĕs'ĕnt). Glowing with intense heat; brilliant; shining
incipient (ĭn-sĭp'ĭ-ĕnt). Beginning
incongruous (ĭn-kŏng'grōō-ŭs). Unsuitable; inappropriate
inconsequential (ĭn-kŏn'sē-kwĕn'shăl). Unimportant
inconsistency (ĭn-kŏn-sĭs'tĕn-sĭ). Contradiction
incredible (ĭn-krĕd'ĭ-b'l). Hard to believe
incredulous (ĭn-krĕd'ū-lŭs). Indicating disbelief
indefatigable (ĭn'dē-făt'ĭ-gȧ-b'l). Untiring
indiscriminately (ĭn'dĭs-krĭm'ĭ-nȧt-lĭ). Without making a difference
indivisible (ĭn'dĭ-vĭz'ĭ-b'l). P. 264
indolence (ĭn'dō-lĕns). Laziness
ineradicable (ĭn'ē-răd'ĭ-kȧ-b'l). Incapable of being rooted out
inertia (ĭn-ûr'shĭ-ȧ). P. 324
inevitable (ĭn-ĕv'ĭ-tȧ-b'l). Unavoidable
inexplicable (ĭn-ĕks'plĭ-kȧ-b'l). Incapable of being explained
inferentially (ĭn'fēr-ĕn'shăl-lĭ). By a truth derived by reasoning or implication
infinitesimal (ĭn'fĭn-ĭ-tĕs'ĭ-măl). Immeasurably small
ingratiating (ĭn-grā'shĭ-āt'ĭng). Seeking favor
ingress (ĭn'grĕs). P. 72
inharmonious (ĭn'här-mō'nĭ-ŭs). Clashing
inhibition (ĭn'hĭ-bĭsh'ŭn). Restraint
innate (ĭn'nāt). Inborn; natural
inscrutable (ĭn-skrōō'tȧ-b'l). Incapable of being understood
insidious (ĭn-sĭd'ĭ-ŭs). Intended to entrap; crafty
insidiously (ĭn-sĭd'ĭ-ŭs-lĭ). Slyly; deceitfully
insignificant (ĭn'sĭg-nĭf'ĭ-kănt). P. 264

inspect (ĭn-spĕkt′). P. 148
interlude (ĭn′tẽr-lūd). P. 108
intermittent (ĭn′tẽr-mĭt′ĕnt). P. 698
interrogation (ĭn-tĕr′ō-gā′shŭn). Question; inquiry
interurban (ĭn′tẽr-ûr′băn). P. 334
intimacy (ĭn′tĭ-mȧ-sĭ). P. 108
intonation (ĭn′tō-nā′shŭn). The rise and fall of the speaking voice
intractable (ĭn-trăk′tȧ-b′l). Unmanageable
intrepidity (ĭn′trē-pĭd′ĭ-tĭ). Fearlessness
intricacies (ĭn′trĭ-kȧ-sĭz). Complexities
intuition (ĭn′tū-ĭsh′ŭn). Knowledge that comes to one without conscious thought
inveterate (ĭn-vĕt′ẽr-ĭt). Long standing
invisible (ĭn-vĭz′ĭ-b′l). P. 215
iridescent (ĭr′ĭ-dĕs′ĕnt). P. 10
ironic (ī-rŏn′ĭk). Expressing the opposite of what is meant
irrelevant (ĭ-rĕl′ē-vănt). Not pertaining to
irreparable (ĭ-rĕp′ȧ-rȧ-b′l). Not to be restored
irrevocable (ĭ-rĕv′ō-kȧ-b′l). Incapable of being recalled
Isolt (ĭ-sōlt′). P. 578
iterated (ĭt′ẽr-āt′ĕd). Said a second time

J

jade (jād). P. 58
jockeying (jŏk′ĭ-ĭng). Trying to obtain an advantage by skillful maneuvering
jocose (jō-kōs′). Droll; playful; humorous
Jolliet (zhō′lyā′). P. 174
joseph (jō′zĕf). P. 637
joust (jŭst; jo͞ost). P. 579
jovial (jō′vĭ-ăl). P. 118
judicious (jū-dĭsh′ŭs). Governed by sound judgment; wise
juniper (jo͞o′nĭ-pẽr). An evergreen tree with blue berrylike fruit

K

kaleidoscopic (kȧ-lī′dō-skŏp′ĭk). Variegated in colors
Kavirondo (kä′vē-rŏn′dō). P. 314
ken (kĕn). Reach of sight or knowledge
kilometer (kĭl′ō-mē′tẽr). P. 244
kreese (krēs). P. 58

L

labyrinth (lăb′ĭ-rĭnth). A confusing network of passages
labyrinthine (lăb′ĭ-rĭn′thĭn). Intricate; perplexing
lacerate (lăs′ẽr-āt). To tear
laconic (lȧ-kŏn′ĭk). Expressing much in few words; sparing in words
laggard (lăg′ẽrd). One who acts slowly
lair (lâr). The den of a wild animal
Lancelot (lȧn′sē-lŏt). P. 534
languid (lăn′gwĭd). Sluggish; listless
larboard (lär′bôrd). The left side of a ship as one faces the bow; now called port
latigo (lăt′ĭ-gō). A strap attached to a saddle for tightening the cinch
laudanum (lô′dȧ-nŭm). A poisonous narcotic drug
lavishing (lăv′ĭsh-ĭng). P. 10
lay (lā). P. 579
leech (lēch). A medicinal bloodsucker
leer (lēr). A sly, sidelong look of evil desire
lewd (lūd). Vulgar; indecent
liana (lē-ä′nȧ). P. 58
liege (lēj). P. 579
lieu (lū). Stead
limber (lĭm′bẽr). P. 392
lineaments (lĭn′ē-ȧ-mĕnts). Features
lingo (lĭng′gō). Any queer speech; jargon
lissome (lĭs′ŭm). Swift and light in motion
list (lĭst). Roll or register
litany (lĭt′ȧ-nĭ). Certain form of prayer
lithe (līth). P. 392
locomotion (lō′kō-mō′shŭn). Moving; travel
longshoremen (lông′shôr′mĕn). Those who work about wharves
lope (lōp). An easy, swinging gait
lubber (lŭb′ẽr). A big, clumsy, awkward fellow
lucrative (lū′krȧ-tĭv). Profitable; money-making
lugubrious (lū-gū′brĭ-ŭs). Mournful; sad
luminary (lū′mĭ-nā-rĭ). P. 230
luminous (lū′mĭ-nŭs). P. 230
luscious (lŭsh′ŭs). Delicious
lustihood (lŭs′tĭ-ho͝od). Robustness; vigor
lustrous (lŭs′trŭs). Gleaming; brilliant
Lynette (lĭ-nĕt′). P. 537
Lyonors (lī′ō-nŏrz′). P. 537

M

macadamize (măk-ăd′ăm-īz). To build or finish a road with broken stone pressed and rolled to a smooth, hard surface
mage (māj). Wizard; magician
Magellanic (măj′ĕ-lăn′ĭk; măg′ĕ-lăn′ĭk). P. 291
magenta (mȧ-jĕn′tȧ). A purplish red color
magnanimity (măg′nȧ-nĭm′ĭ-tĭ). P. 29
magnate (măg′nāt). P. 29
magnificent (măg-nĭf′ĭ-sĕnt). P. 29
magnify (măg′nĭ-fī). P. 29
magnitude (măg′nĭ-tūd). P. 29
maladjustment (măl′ă-jŭst′mĕnt). Bad regulation
malefic (mȧ-lĕf′ĭk). P. 342
malevolence (mȧ-lĕv′ō-lĕns). Quality of wishing evil or injury to others
malice (măl′ĭs). Evil desire to injure others
malign (mȧ-līn′). P. 66
malignant (mȧ-lĭg′nănt). Spiteful; resentful
mammal (măm′ăl). Member of that group of animals which feed their young by means of milk glands
mammoth (măm′ŭth). An enormous prehistoric elephant

manada (mä-nä'thä). P. 258
mandarin (măn'dȧ-rĭn). A Chinese high official
manifestation (măn'ĭ-fĕs-tā'shŭn). Proof of the existence; display
manipulate (mȧ-nĭp'ū-lāt). Control the action by skillful management
Marconi (mär-kō'nē). P. 160
martinet (mär'tĭ-nĕt'). Stickler for trivial details
mastodon (măs'tô-dŏn). A huge, elephantlike animal that no longer exists
Matadi (mȧ-tä'dē). P. 156
maternal (mȧ-tûr'năl). P. 290
matin (măt'ĭn). Pertaining to the morning
matriarch (mā'trĭ-ärk). P. 290
mauve (mōv). Soft lilac color
maxim (măk'sĭm). A general truth expressed briefly
mead (mēd). A meadow
medley (mĕd'lĭ). A composition made up of passages selected from different songs
megalomaniac (mĕg'ȧ-lô-mā'nĭ-ăk). An insane person who has a mania for believing himself great or exalted
memento (mē-mĕn'tō). Reminder
menagerie (mē-năj'ēr-ĭ). A collection of wild animals
mensurable (mĕn'sho͝o-rȧ-b'l). Capable of being measured
meridian (mē-rĭd'ĭ-ăn). Midday; highest apparent point of the sun
mesquite (mĕs-kēt'). P. 258
metamorphosis (mĕt'ȧ-môr'fō-sĭs). Transformation
meteorologist (mē'tē-ēr-ŏl'ô-jĭst). A person skilled in meteorology, the science which treats of the atmosphere and its phenomena
Michelson (mī'kĕl-sŭn). P. 322
midriff (mĭd'rĭf). The diaphragm
mince (mĭns). An affected walk
mincing (mĭns'ĭng). Affected; with assumed elegance
mine (mīn). A case containing high explosive, moored where it will destroy enemy ships
miniature (mĭn'ĭ-ȧ-tūr). Represented on a small scale
minster (mĭn'stēr). A monastery church
mitigated (mĭt'ĭ-gāt'ĕd). Made less painful
modicum (mŏd'ĭ-kŭm). A small quantity
Modred (mō'drĕd). P. 529
mollusk (mŏl'ŭsk). Any of numerous soft-bodied, hard-shelled animals
momentum (mô-mĕn'tŭm). P. 108, p. 324
monograph (mŏn'ô-grȧf). A scholarly paper on one particular subject
monopolize (mô-nŏp'ô-līz). To gain exclusive possession of
monotone (mŏn'ô-tōn). Utterance of one syllable after another without change of pitch or key
monotonous (mô-nŏt'ô-nŭs). Lacking variety
morocco (mô-rŏk'ō). P. 363
mortgaged (môr'gĭjd). Made over as security to one to whom a debt is owed
multiped (mŭl'tĭ-pĕd). P. 72
multitude (mŭl'tĭ-tūd). P. 72
mummer (mŭm'ēr). One who takes part in masked revels
mustang (mŭs'tăng). P. 258
myriad (mĭr'ĭ-ăd). P. 108
mystic (mĭs'tĭk). Partaking of mystery
mythology (mĭ-thŏl'ô-jĭ). A body of traditional stories in which are recorded a people's beliefs concerning origin, gods, heroes

N

Nacogdoches (năk'ô-dō'chĕz). P. 201
Nagaoka (nä'gȧ-ō'kȧ). P. 223
naïve (nä-ēv'). Unaffectedly simple; unsophisticated
Nansen (nän'sĕn). P. 238
Natal (nȧ-täl'). P. 303
Natchitoches (năk'ĭ-tŏsh'). P. 209
nattiness (năt'ĭ-nĕs). Neatness; spruceness
nausea (nô'shē-ȧ). Sickness of the stomach
nave (nāv). P. 218
neuralgia (nū-răl'jȧ). A sharp pain along the course of a nerve
neutralize (nū'trăl-īz). To counteract
nicotine (nĭk'ô-tēn). The pungent, colorless poison contained in tobacco
Nieuport (nē'o͞o-pōrt). P. 152
nimble (nĭm'b'l). P. 392
Nobile (nō'bĭ-lā). P. 242
nonexistent (nŏn'ĕg-zĭs'tĕnt). Not having actual being
normalcy (nôr'măl-sĭ). The usual or ordinary condition of things
Nueces (nū-ā'sȧs). P. 25
Nyassaland (nyä'sä-lănd'; nī-ăs'ȧ-lănd'). P. 316

O

oasis (ô-ā'sĭs). A fertile place in a desert
obbligato (ŏb'blē-gä'tō). A more or less independent accompanying part, played by a single instrument
Obion (ô-bī'ŏn). P. 185
oblique (ŏb-lēk'). P. 251
obliterated (ŏb-lĭt'ēr-āt'ĕd). Erased; blotted out
oblivious (ŏb-lĭv'ĭ-ŭs). Forgetful
obloquy (ŏb'lô-kwĭ). P. 342
obnoxious (ŏb-nŏk'shŭs). Hateful; offensive
obsequies (ŏb'sē-kwĭz). Funeral ceremonies
obtrusive (ŏb-tro͞o'sĭv). Unduly inclined to push forward
occult (ŏ-kŭlt'). Secret; mysterious
octave (ŏk'tāv). An interval of eight steps
Oedipus (ĕd'ĭ-pŭs; ē'dĭ-pŭs). P. 382
ominous (ŏm'ĭ-nŭs). Foreboding evil
omnibus (ŏm'nĭ-bŭs). P. 404
omnipotent (ŏm-nĭp'ô-tĕnt). P. 404
omnipresent (ŏm'nĭ-prĕz'ĕnt). P. 404
omniscient (ŏm-nĭsh'ĕnt). P. 404
omnivorous (ŏm-nĭv'ô-rŭs). P. 404
onslaught (ŏn'slôt'). P. 15

onyx (ŏn′ĭks). A black quartz
optimistic (ŏp′tĭ-mĭs′tĭk). P. 244
opulent (ŏp′ū-lĕnt). Rich
oracular (ō-răk′ū-lẽr). Very wise
orchestration (ŏr′kĕs-trā′shŭn). The arrangement of music
Orion (ō-rī′ŏn). P. 322
ort (ôrt). Scrap
ostler (ŏs′lẽr). Man who takes care of horses
overexuberance (ō′vẽr-ĕgz-ū′bẽr-ăns). More than superabundance
overtone (ō′vẽr-tōn′). P. 108

P

pachyderm (păk′ĭ-dûrm). One of a group of thick-skinned animals, such as the elephant, rhinoceros, etc.
pandemonium (păn′dē-mō′nĭ-ŭm). Wild uproar
panorama (păn′ō-rä′mȧ). An unobstructed view
paradox (păr′ȧ-dŏks). Something which seems absurd yet may be true
paraphernalia (păr′ȧ-fẽr-nā′lĭ-ȧ). Articles of equipment
pariah (pä′rĭ-ȧ). P. 94
parricide (păr′ĭ-sīd). P. 334
partook (pär-to͝ok′). Took something of
Pasteur (päs′tûr′). P. 311
paternity (pă-tûr′nĭ-tĭ). P. 334
pathological (păth′ō-lŏj′ĭ-kăl). Due to disease
patriarch (pā′trĭ-ärk). P. 290
patricide (păt′rĭ-sīd). P. 334
patriot (pā′trĭ-ŏt). P. 334
patron (pā′trŭn). P. 334
pavilion (pă-vĭl′yŭn). A large tent
Peary (pē′rĭ). P. 238
pectoral (pĕk′tō-răl). Pertaining to the breast
pedometer (pē-dŏm′ē-tẽr). P. 244
pemmican (pĕm′ĭ-kăn). Dried meat
penitence (pĕn′ĭ-tĕns). Sorrow for a wrongdoing
pennon (pĕn′ŭn). A flag or banner
penthouse (pĕnt′hous′). A house on a roof
peradventure (pûr′ăd-vĕn′tûr). Perhaps
perceptible (pẽr-sĕp′tĭ-b'l). Capable of being noticed
peremptory (pẽr-ĕmp′tō-rĭ). Not admitting of debate
perfunctory (pẽr-fŭngk′tō-rĭ). Done merely to discharge a duty; half-hearted; indifferent
perplexity (pẽr-plĕk′sĭ-tĭ). Bewilderment
perquisite (pûr′kwĭ-zĭt). Profit or gain
perspective (pẽr-spĕk′tĭv). P. 251
pessimistic (pĕs′ĭ-mĭs′tĭk). P. 244
pestilential (pĕs′tĭ-lĕn′shăl). Producing violent diseases
phantasm (făn′tăz'm). P. 342
pheal (fē′ăl). P. 58
phenomenon (fē-nŏm′ē-nŏn). Any natural fact or event which can be seen; occurrence
phial (fī′ăl). A small glass bottle
Philippi (fĭ-lĭp′ī). P. 503
physiological (fĭz′ĭ-ō-lŏj′ĭ-kăl). Relating to the functions of the organs and parts during life
pillion (pĭl′yŭn). P. 698
pinafore (pĭn′ȧ-fôr′). A loose sleeveless apron
pinang (pĭ-năng′). P. 58
pince-nez (păns′nā′). Eyeglasses attached to a string
pinions (pĭn′yŭns). Flight feathers
pinnace (pĭn′ĭs). A small, light, schooner-rigged vessel with oars
piñon (pē-nyōn′). A low-growing pine of western North America
piquancy (pē′kăn-sĭ). Stimulating to the taste
piquant (pē′kănt). Lively; sparkling
placable (plā′kȧ-b'l). P. 699
placid (plăs′ĭd). Calm; gentle; tranquil
plaza (plä′zȧ). An open square surrounded by buildings
pliable (plī′ȧ-b'l). P. 392
pliant (plī′ănt). P. 10
poignantly (poin′yănt-lĭ). Acutely; keenly
poop (po͞op). The raised deck in the stern of a vessel
posse (pŏs′ē). A number of men summoned by a sheriff to assist in carrying out the law
posterity (pŏs-tĕr′ĭ-tĭ). Future generations
postern gate (pōs′tẽrn gāt′). Rear or small gate
potentate (pō′tĕn-tāt). One who has great power
preachment (prēch′mĕnt). Moral lecture
precautionary (prē-kô′shŭn-ĕr′ĭ). Intended to prevent harm
precedence (prē-cēd′ĕns). Right of preceding in rank
precipitous (prē-sĭp′ĭ-tŭs). Very steep
precision (prē-sĭzh′ŭn). Accuracy; exactness
precursor (prē-kûr′sẽr). Forerunner
predicament (prē-dĭk′ȧ-mĕnt). A dangerous situation
predoom (prē-do͞om′). To doom or condemn beforehand
pregnancy (prĕg′năn-sĭ). Great weight or significance
prehensile (prē-hĕn′sĭl). Adapted for grasping
premier (prē′mĭ-ẽr). Prime minister
premise (prĕm′ĭs). A statement assumed as leading to a conclusion
premonitory (prē-mŏn′ĭ-tō-rĭ). Giving previous warning
preoccupation (prē-ŏk′ū-pā′shŭn). A state of being wrapped up in one's own affairs
prescriptive (prē-scrĭp′tĭv). Acquired by direction
presentiment (prē-zĕn′tĭ-mĕnt). Foreboding
presumptuous (prē-zŭmp′tū-ŭs). Bold; overconfident
preternatural (prē′tẽr-năt′ū-răl). Extraordinary; strange
pretext (prē′tĕkst). A false motive put forward to conceal the real one
prevarication (prē-văr′ĭ-kā′shŭn). Deception
prevision (prē-vĭzh′ŭn). Foresight
primeval (prī-mē′văl). Pertaining to the earliest age

prithee (prĭth'ē). Please
proclivities (prō-klĭv'ĭ-tĭz). Inclinations
procured (prō-kūrd').
prodigious (prō-dĭj'ŭs). Unusually great in quantity or size
profligacy (prŏf'lĭ-gȧ-sĭ). Corruption
profusion (prō-fū'zhŭn). P. 72
prognosis (prŏg-nō'sĭs). Forecast of the course and termination of a disease
prolongation (prō'lŏn-gā'shŭn). P. 251
propensity (prō-pĕn'sĭ-tĭ). Tendency
propitiation (prō-pĭsh'ĭ-ā'shŭn). P. 342
prosaic (prō-zā'ĭc). Commonplace; unimaginative; dull
proscenium (prō-sē'nĭ-ŭm). Stage
prospected (prŏs'pĕkt-ĕd). Searched or explored, especially for gold or oil
proton (prō'tŏn). P. 324
protuberant (prō-tū'bĕr-ănt). Bulging
provocation (prŏv'ō-kā'shŭn). That which excites to anger
proximity (prŏk-sĭm'ĭ-tĭ). Nearness
psychological (sī'kō-lŏj'ĭ-kăl). Pertaining to the science of the mind
pugilist (pū'jĭ-lĭst). P. 699
pugnacious (pŭg-nā'shŭs). P. 699
puissance (pū'ĭ-săns). Power; prowess
pulsation (pŭl-sā'shŭn). A single throb
pummeling, pommeling (pŭm'ĕl-ĭng). P. 251
purgatory (pûr'gȧ-tôr'ĭ). Any place of misery

Q

quarry (kwŏr'ĭ). Game, or the object of the hunt or chase
queries (kwē'rĭz). P. 698
quest (kwĕst). P. 579
quirky (kwûr'kĭ). Tricky
quirt (kwûrt). P. 258
quorum (kwôr'ŭm). The number of members of an assembly that the rules require to be present in order that business may legally be transacted

R

rajah bird (rä'jȧ bûrd). P. 58
rakish (rāk'ĭsh). P. 10
rampant (răm'pănt). Reared on the hind legs
rapport (ră-pōrt'). P. 16
rapt (răpt). Absorbed; entranced
rathe (rāth). Early
raucous (rô'kŭs). Harsh; rough; hoarse
recalcitrant (rē-kăl'sĭ-trănt). Unruly
reconciliation (rĕk'ŏn-sĭl'ĭ-ā'shŭn). A renewing of friendship after disagreement
rectilinear (rĕk-tĭ-lĭn'ē-ȧr). Moving in a straight line
rectitude (rĕk'tĭ-tūd). Uprightness
recurrent (rē-kûr'ĕnt). Repeated
referent (rĕf'ĕr-ĕnt). P. 225
reluctant (rē-lŭk'tănt). Unwilling; disinclined
render (rĕn'dĕr). To interpret
renegade (rĕn'ē-gād). A deserter
renunciation (rē-nŭn'sĭ-ā'shŭn). Giving up
reorient (rē-ō'rĭ-ĕnt). To determine the bearings of again; readjust
repartee (rĕp'ĕr-tē'). Conversation full of quick-witted, clever replies
repression (rē-prĕsh'ŭn). That which checks, curbs
repugnance (rē-pŭg'năns). P. 699
resinous (rĕz'ĭ-nŭs). Of resin, a substance obtained from certain trees, such as the pine and the fir
respect (rē-spĕkt'). P. 148
resumption (rē-zŭmp'shŭn). Act of beginning again
resurgent (rē-sûr'jĕnt). Sweeping back
reticence (rĕt'ĭ-sĕns). Reserve
retina (rĕt'ĭ-nȧ). Inner sensitive coating of the eyeball
retrospect (rĕt'rō-spĕkt). P. 148
revel (rĕv'ĕl). P. 72
reverential (rĕv'ĕr-ĕn'shăl). Expressing reverence
revery (rĕv'ĕr-ĭ). P. 72
ricocheted (rĭk'ō-shād'). P. 108
rigidity (rĭ-jĭd'ĭ-tĭ). Stiffness
ritual (rĭt'ū-ăl). P. 342
Robespierre (rō'bĕs-pyâr'; rō'bĕs-pĕr'). P. 341
robust (rō-bŭst'). P. 349
rodent (rō'dĕnt). P. 429
rotund (rō-tŭnd'). Round from plumpness
rowel (rou el). The small, sharp-pointed wheel of a spur
rubicund (ro͞o'bĭ-kŭnd). Ruddy
rudimentary (ro͞o'dĭ-mĕn'tȧ-rĭ). Elementary
Ruhr (ro͞or). P. 149
ruminating (ro͞o'mĭ-nāt'ĭng). Reflecting placidly on the same recurring themes
rusticity (rŭs-tĭs'ĭ-tĭ). Countrylike manners

S

saccharine (săk'ȧ-rĭn). Very sweet
sacrilege (săk'rĭ-lĕj). Crime of violating sacred things
sagacious (sȧ-gā'shŭs). P. 72
sagely (sāj'lĭ). Wisely
Sagittarius (săj'ĭ-tā'rĭ-ŭs). P. 373
Salamanca (săl'ȧ-măn'kȧ). P. 247
sallying (săl'lĭ-ĭng). Rushing out suddenly
samite (să'mīt). A kind of heavy silk stuff, generally interwoven with gold
Samurai (sä'mo͝o-rī). P. 219
sanctuary (săngk'tū-ĕr'ĭ). A place of shelter and contentment
sardonic (sär-dŏn'ĭk). Bitter; mocking
sardonically (sär-dŏn'ĭ-căl-lĭ). P. 443
sarong (sȧ-rŏng'). P. 58
scaur (skär). A steep, rocky eminence
scrutinize (skro͞o'tĭ-nīz). Examine carefully
scupper (skŭp'ĕr). A hole in the side of a ship to carry off water from the deck

scuttle (skŭt′'l). To cut a hole through the bottom of a vessel in order to sink her
sedate (sē-dāt′). P. 72
sedulous (sĕd′ū-lŭs). Diligent
seer (sē′ẽr). One who claims to foresee the future; a prophet
Semarang (sĕ-mä′räng). P. 50
sententiously (sĕn-tĕn′shŭs-lĭ). With much meaning
sepia (sē′pĭ-ȧ). A dark-brown color
serpentine (sûr′pĕn-tēn). P. 10
sèvres (sâ′vr′). P. 363
sextant (sĕks′tănt). A nautical instrument to determine latitude and longitude
shelling (shĕl′ĭng). P. 117
shocking (shŏk′ĭng). P. 117
shroud (shroud). P. 72
shuttle (shŭt′'l). P. 698
sibilance (sĭb′ĭ-lăns). Hissing sound
silhouetted (sĭl′o͝o-ĕt′ĕd). A figure outlined and filled in with black
simile (sĭm′ĭ-lē). A figure of speech which likens two different things
simulated (sĭm′ū-lāt′ĕd). Assumed the false appearance of
simultaneous (sī′mŭl-tā′nē-ŭs). Happening at the same time
Singhalese (sĭn′gȧ-lēz′). P. 271
singularities (sĭng′gū-lăr′ĭ-tĭz). Peculiarities; eccentricities
sinister (sĭn′ĭs-tẽr). P. 443
sinuous (sĭn′ū-ŭs). A curving in and out
Sioux (so͞o). P. 411
Siva (sē′vȧ; shē′vȧ). P. 53
sixpence (sĭks′pĕns). A British coin worth six English pence
skeptical (skĕp′tĭ-kăl). Doubtful; disbelieving
slattern (slăt′ẽrn). A slovenly woman
slice (slīs). To clear by means of a slice bar, as a fire
slithering (slĭth′ẽr-ĭng). Slipping or sliding
sloth (slōth). A tree-dwelling animal which clings upside down to the branches
slough (slo͞o). A marsh; swamp
snubbed (snŭb′d). Checked the motion of
sodden (sŏd′'n). Spiritless; dull
solicited (sō-lĭs′ĭt-ĕd). Requested; sought
solicitude (sō-lĭs′ĭ-tūd). Anxiety; worry
soliloquize (sō-lĭl′ō-kwīz). Talk to oneself
sophisticated (sō-fĭs′tĭ-kāt′ĕd). Wise in the ways of the world
soporific (sō′pō-rĭf′ĭk). Causing sleep
sorrel (sŏr′ĕl). Reddish brown
sough (sŭf). P. 230
spasmodically (spăz-mŏd′ĭ-căl-lĭ). P. 108
specter (spĕk′tẽr). A ghost
spectral (spĕk′trăl). Ghostly
spectroscopic (spĕk′trō-skŏp′ĭk). Produced by an optical instrument (spectroscope) for examining the spectra (light images)
speedometer (spēd-ŏm′ē-tẽr). P. 244
squire (skwīr). P. 579
stability (stȧ-bĭl′ĭ-tĭ). Steadiness
stance (stăns). Mode or manner of standing
starboard (stär′bôrd). The right side of the ship as one faces the bow
stellar (stĕl′ăr). Like a star
stevedore (stē′vĕ-dôr′). One who loads the cargoes of ships
stile (stīl). P. 698
stimulus (stĭm′ū-lŭs). Anything that arouses
stint (stĭnt). A task assigned
stockade (stŏk-ād′). A fence of upright posts used as a defensive barrier
stodgy (stŏj′ĭ). Thick; heavy
strait (strāt). Strict
stratagem (străt′ȧ-jĕm). A trick in war for deceiving the enemy
stratified (străt′ĭ-fīd). Arranged in layers
strut (strŭt). A bar to receive weight
stubble (stŭb′'l). P. 117
suavity (swăv′ĭ-tĭ). Smoothness of manner
submission (sŭb-mĭsh′ŭn). Yielding to power
subsequently (sŭb′sē-kwĕnt′lĭ). Following; coming afterward
subtleties (sŭt′'l-tĭz). Niceties of distinction
suite (swēt). P. 72
supercilious (sū′pẽr-sĭl′ĭ-ŭs). Contemptuously haughty
superlative (sū-pûr′lȧ-tĭv). Highest; best
superstitious (sū′pẽr-stĭsh′ŭs). P. 342
supple (sŭp′'l). P. 392
surmise (sûr-mīz′). P. 698
surplice (sûr′plĭs). Loose vestment worn by the clergy
susceptible (sŭ-sĕp′tĭ-b'l). Easily influenced
suspect (sŭs-pĕkt′). P. 148
swaggering (swăg′ẽr-ĭng). Walking with a conceited swing or strut
Swahili (swä-hē′lē). P. 280
swarthy (swôr′thĭ). Dark-skinned
swashbuckler (swŏsh′bŭk′lẽr). A blustering bully
symbolical (sĭm-bŏl′ĭ-kăl). Expressed in signs
symbolism (sĭm′bŭl-ĭzm). P. 225
symmetry (sĭm′ē-trĭ). Harmonious relation of several parts of the body to each other
synchronize (sĭn′krō-nīz). To agree in time

T

tacit (tăs′ĭt). Silent
taffrail (tăf′rāl). The rail around the stern of a ship
tale (tāl). A count; a summing
talisman (tăl′ĭs-măn). A figure engraved on a stone or ring, supposed to possess magical powers
tankard (tănk′ärd). P. 698
tarn (tärn). A mountain lake or pool
tarpaulin (tär-pô′lĭn). A heavy waterproof canvas
taut (tôt). Tight
tautness (tôt′nĕs). Tightness

teak (tēk). Timber of a tall East Indian tree
teetered (tē′tĕrd). P. 108
temperamental (tĕm′pĕr-ȧ-mĕn′tăl). Liable to sudden changes of mood
tenacious (tē-nā′shŭs). P. 118
tenant (tĕn′ănt). P. 118
tentacle (tĕn′tȧ-k'l). A feeler
tentatively (tĕn′tȧ-tĭv-lĭ). As an experiment
Thasos (thä′sŏs). P. 509
theological (thē′ō-lŏj′ĭ-kăl). In the laws, nature, and power of God
throttle (thrŏt′'l). A valve to control the supply of fuel to an engine
tilt (tĭlt). P. 579
tinderbox (tĭn′dĕr-bŏks′). A box designed to hold tinder, formerly used in kindling fire
Tintagel (tĭn-tăj′ĕl). P. 528
titanic (tī-tăn′ĭk). P. 10
titbit (tĭt′bĭt). A choice bit
tithe (tīth). A tenth part of some specific thing paid as a voluntary contribution
toff (tŏf). English slang for a fop or beau
toll (tōl). Entice; allure
tollgate (tōl′gāt′). A gate where toll is taken
topaz (tō′păz). A yellowish color
topography (tō-pŏg′rȧ-fĭ). The surface features of a particular region
torpid (tôr′pĭd). Lifeless; drowsy; inactive; dull
tourney (to͝or′nĭ). P. 579
tradition (trȧ-dĭsh′ŭn). P. 225
tranquillity (trăn-kwĭl′ĭ-tĭ). Calmness; composure
transfiguration (trăns-fĭg′ū-rā′shŭn). Change in appearance
transient (trăn′shĕnt). P. 699
transit (trăn′sĭt). P. 699
transition (trăn-zĭsh′ŭn). P. 699
transparent (trăns-pâr′ĕnt). So thin that one can see through it
transversal (trăns-vûr′săl). P. 251
traverse (trăv′ĕrs). Barrier
treadle (trĕd′'l). A flat piece attached to a crank and worked by the foot
trident (trī′dĕnt). A three-pronged fish spear
tripod (trī′pŏd). A three-legged support
truckle (trŭk′'l). A trundle bed, a kind of low bed on casters
trumpery (trŭm′pĕr-ĭ). Worthless finery
tucker (tŭk′ĕr). A piece of lace across the front of a dress
tumbrel (tŭm′brĕl). A two-wheeled dump cart
tumultuous (tū-mŭl′tū-ŭs). Violently confused
turbulent (tûr′bū-lĕnt). Not easily controlled
turnpike (tûrn′pīk′). A tollgate

U

unbenumbed (ŭn-bē-nŭmd′). Not deadened or stupefied
uncanny (ŭn-kăn′ĭ). Mysterious
unconscionable (ŭn-kŏn′shŭn-ȧ-b'l). Unreasonable
unction (ŭngk′shŭn). Excessive courtesy
unctuous (ŭngk′tū-ŭs). Greasy
undulate (ŭn′dū-lāt). To move up and down, or to and fro, in waves
unerringly (ŭn-ûr′ĭng-lĭ). Unfailingly
unkempt (ŭn-kĕmpt′). Not combed
unmeritorious (ŭn-mĕr′ĭ-tō′rĭ-ŭs). Not deserving reward or praise
unmitigated (ŭn-mĭt′ĭ-gāt′ĕd). Very bad
unnurtured (ŭn-nûr′tūrd). Untaught
unprecedented (ŭn-prĕs′ē-dĕn-tĕd). Unusual; new
unpremeditated (ŭn′prē-mĕd′ĭ-tāt′ĕd). Not planned beforehand
unpropitious (ŭn-prō-pĭsh′ŭs). Hostile
unremittingly (ŭn-rē-mĭt′ĭng-lĭ). Without interruption
unsophisticated (ŭn′sō-fĭs′tĭ-kāt′ĕd). Inexperienced
unsustain (ŭn-sŭs-tān′). Disprove
unwonted (ŭn-wŭn′tĕd). Unaccustomed
urgency (ûr′jĕn-sĭ). Necessity
usurer (ū′zho͞o-rĕr). A person who lends money and demands an unlawfully high rate of interest

V

vacillation (văs′ĭ-lā′shŭn). P. 698
vacuously (văk′ū-ŭs-lĭ). Vacantly; blankly
vacuum (văk′ū-ŭm). P. 324
vagrant (vā′grănt). Idle wanderer
validity (vȧ-lĭd′ĭ-tĭ). Rightness, founded on truth
vampire (văm′pīr). P. 58
variegated (vā′rĭ-ē-gāt′ĕd). Streaked with different colors
veer (vēr). To change in direction
vehement (vē′hē-mĕnt). Acting with violent feeling
veracious (vē-rā′shŭs). Truthful
veracity (vē-răs′ĭ-tĭ). P. 699
Verdun (vĕr′dŭn′). P. 155
veritable (vĕr′ĭ-tȧ-b'l). P. 699
versatility (vûr′sȧ-tĭl′ĭ-tĭ). Skill in many different lines of activity
vert (vûrt). Green
vertical (vûr′tĭ-kăl). P. 251
viand (vī′ănd). An article of food, especially meat
vicariously (vī-kā′rĭ-ŭs-lĭ). By substitution
vicinage (vĭs′ĭ-nȧj). Vicinity
Victoria Nyanza (nyän′zä). P. 309
vindication (vĭn-dĭ-kā′shŭn). The act of clearing a person from blame or accusation
vindictiveness (vĭn-dĭk′tĭv-nĕs). Revengefulness
vintage (vĭn′tĭj). Wine
visage (vĭz′ĭj). P. 72
vista (vĭs′tȧ). P. 72, p. 698
vixenish (vĭk′s'n-ĭsh). Shrewish
vociferous (vō-sĭf′ĕr-ŭs). Noisy
volatile (vŏl′ȧ-tĭl). Lively; changeable
voluptuous (vō-lŭp′tū-ŭs). P. 72
Von Hindenburg (fōn hĭn′dĕn-bo͝ork). P. 152

vortex (vôr′tĕks). Whirlpool
Vosges (vōzh). P. 152

W

wainscot (wān′skŏt). Lining for inner walls
wake lights (wāk līts). The lights which burn over the body of a dead person all night just before the burial
wane (wān). To grow smaller
wanton (wôn′tŭn). Unrestrained; wild
warren (wŏr′ĕn). A place where rabbits have their passages
wax (wăks). Grow
weretiger (wēr-tī′gēr). A person who becomes voluntarily or involuntarily a tiger
werewolf (wēr′wo͞olf′). P. 58
wheelright (hwēl′rīt′). Repairer of wheels, wagons, etc.
Willebroeck (vĭl′ĕ-bro͝ok). P. 157
windjammer (wĭnd′jăm′ēr). A sailing vessel
windrow (wĭnd′rō). A row of hay raked up to dry before being heaped into cocks
wizardry (wĭz′ärd-rĭ). Magic
wonted (wŭn′tĕd). Accustomed
wraith (rāth). Specter; apparition

Y

yearling (yēr′lĭng). An animal between one and two years old
Ygerne (ē-gĕrn′). P. 528
Yser (ē′zâr′). P. 152
Yucatan (yo͞o′kä-tän′). P. 320

Z

zoology (zō-ŏl′ō-jĭ). The branch of biology dealing with animal life

Index of Authors

Index of Titles